W9-ATA-277

IDW Publishing *presents*

BBC

DOCTOR WHO

Omnibus

Cover by Ben Templesmith
Collection Edits by Justin Eisinger and Alonzo Simon
Collection Design by Shawn Lee

Special thanks to Kate Bush, Georgie Britton, Caroline Skinner, Denise Paul, and Ed Casey at BBC Worldwide for their invaluable assistance.

IDW founded by Ted Adams, Alex Garner, Kris Oprisko, and Robbie Robbins |

ISBN: 978-1-61377-348-2

16 15 14 13   2 3 4 5

IDW®

Ted Adams, CEO & Publisher
Greg Goldstein, President & COO
Robbie Robbins, EVP/Sr. Graphic Artist
Chris Ryall, Chief Creative Officer/Editor-in-Chief
Matthew Ruzicka, CPA, Chief Financial Officer
Alan Payne, VP of Sales
Dirk Wood, VP of Marketing
Lorelei Bunjes, VP of Digital Services

Become our fan on Facebook **facebook.com/idwpublishing**
Follow us on Twitter **@idwpublishing**
Check us out on YouTube **youtube.com/idwpublishing**
www.IDWPUBLISHING.com

DOCTOR WHO OMNIBUS, VOLUME 1. MAY 2013. SECOND PRINTING. BBC, DOCTOR WHO (word marks, logos and devices), and TARDIS are trade marks of the British Broadcasting Corporation and are used under license. BBC logo © BBC 1996. Doctor Who logo © BBC 2009. TARDIS image © BBC 1963. © 2013 Idea and Design Works, LLC. All Rights Reserved. The IDW logo is registered in the U.S. Patent and Trademark Office. IDW Publishing, a division of Idea and Design Works, LLC. Editorial offices: 5080 Santa Fe St., San Diego, CA 92109. Any similarities to persons living or dead are purely coincidental. With the exception of artwork used for review purposes, none of the contents of this publication may be reprinted without the permission of Idea and Design Works, LLC. Printed in Korea. IDW Publishing does not read or accept unsolicited submissions of ideas, stories, or artwork.

Originally published as DOCTOR WHO Issues #1–6, DOCTOR WHO: THE WHISPERING GALLERY, DOCTOR WHO: THE TIME MACHINATION, DOCTOR WHO: AUTOPIA, DOCTOR WHO: COLD-BLOODED WAR, DOCTOR WHO: ROOM WITH A DEJA VIEW, DOCTOR WHO: BLACK DEATH WHITE LIFE, and DOCTOR WHO: THE FORGOTTEN Issues #1–6.

Contents

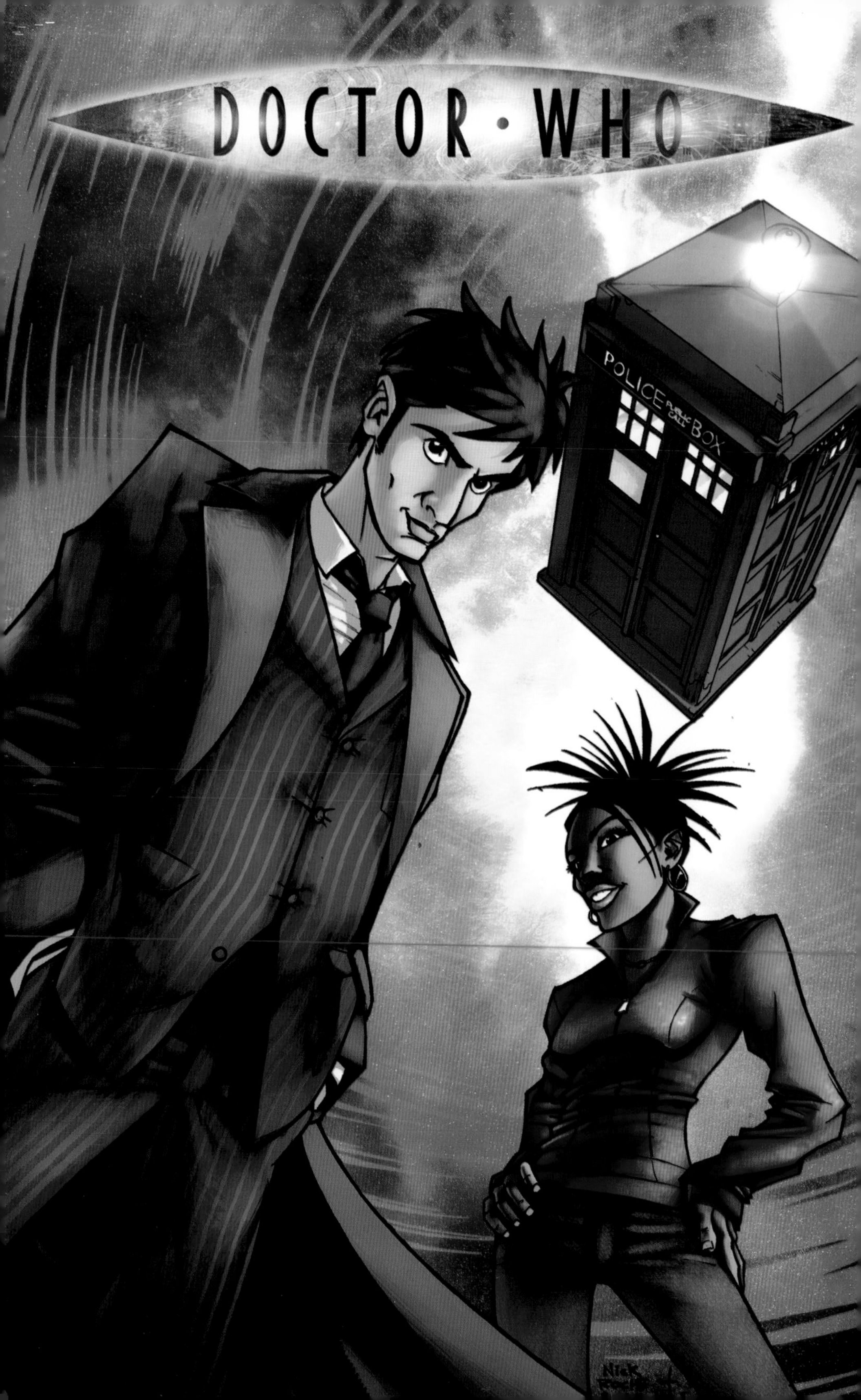
DOCTOR · WHO
POLICE PUBLIC CALL BOX

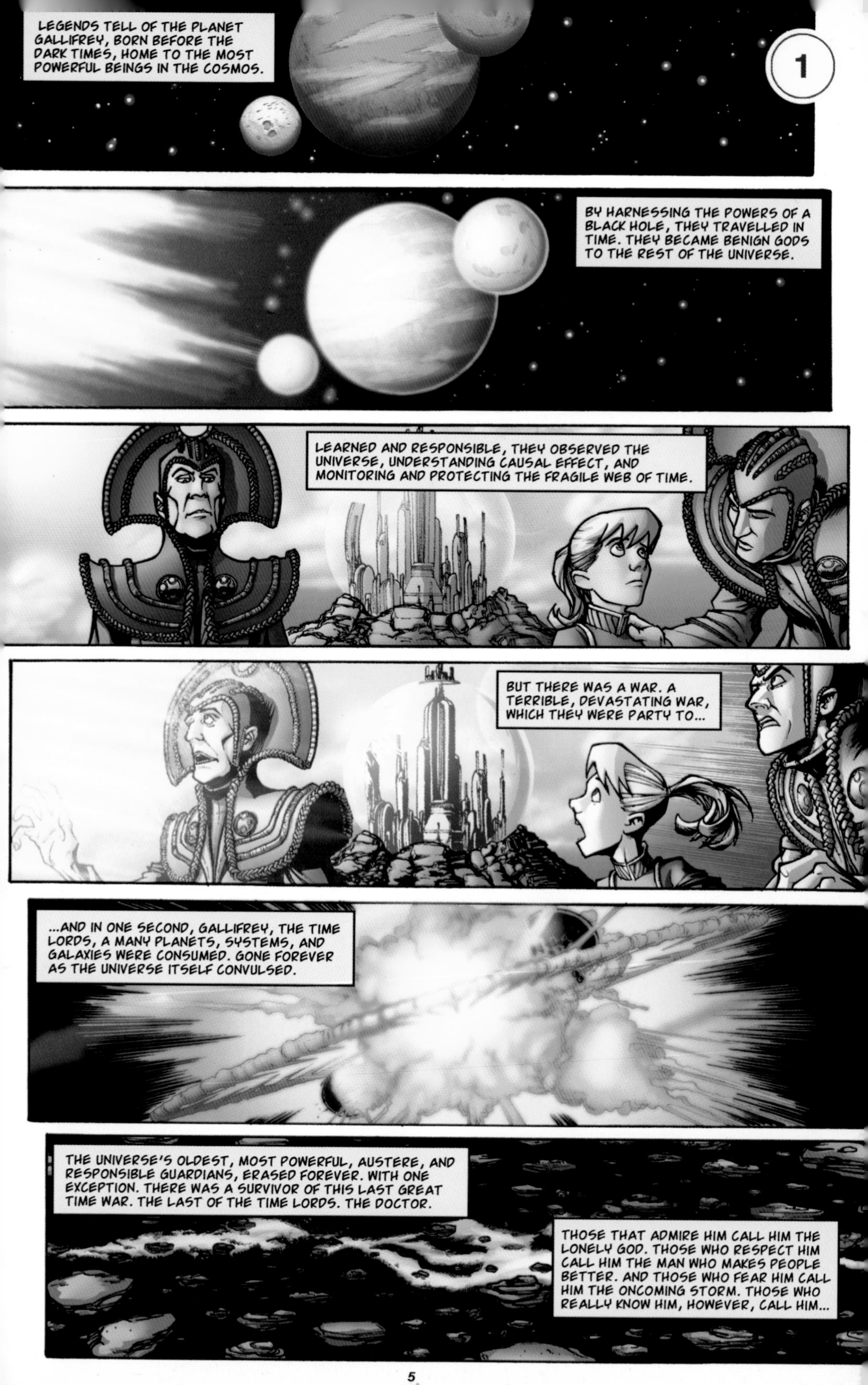
1
LEGENDS TELL OF THE PLANET GALLIFREY, BORN BEFORE THE DARK TIMES, HOME TO THE MOST POWERFUL BEINGS IN THE COSMOS.
BY HARNESSING THE POWERS OF A BLACK HOLE, THEY TRAVELLED IN TIME. THEY BECAME BENIGN GODS TO THE REST OF THE UNIVERSE.
LEARNED AND RESPONSIBLE, THEY OBSERVED THE UNIVERSE, UNDERSTANDING CAUSAL EFFECT, AND MONITORING AND PROTECTING THE FRAGILE WEB OF TIME.
BUT THERE WAS A WAR. A TERRIBLE, DEVASTATING WAR, WHICH THEY WERE PARTY TO...
...AND IN ONE SECOND, GALLIFREY, THE TIME LORDS, A MANY PLANETS, SYSTEMS, AND GALAXIES WERE CONSUMED. GONE FOREVER AS THE UNIVERSE ITSELF CONVULSED.
THE UNIVERSE'S OLDEST, MOST POWERFUL, AUSTERE, AND RESPONSIBLE GUARDIANS, ERASED FOREVER. WITH ONE EXCEPTION. THERE WAS A SURVIVOR OF THIS LAST GREAT TIME WAR. THE LAST OF THE TIME LORDS. THE DOCTOR.
THOSE THAT ADMIRE HIM CALL HIM THE LONELY GOD. THOSE WHO RESPECT HIM CALL HIM THE MAN WHO MAKES PEOPLE BETTER. AND THOSE WHO FEAR HIM CALL HIM THE ONCOMING STORM. THOSE WHO REALLY KNOW HIM, HOWEVER, CALL HIM...

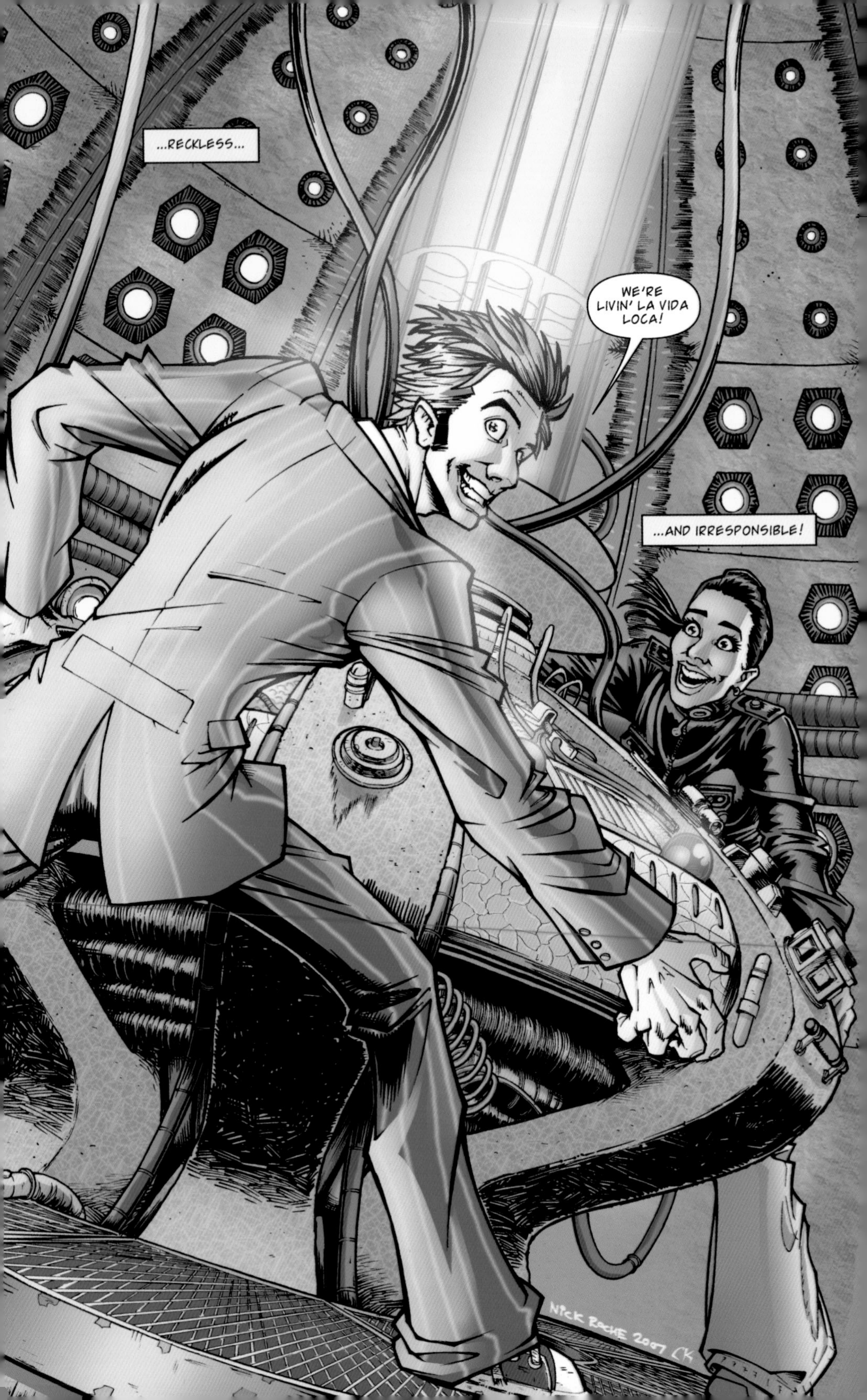
...RECKLESS...
WE'RE LIVIN' LA VIDA LOCA!
...AND IRRESPONSIBLE!
NICK ROCHE 2007 CK

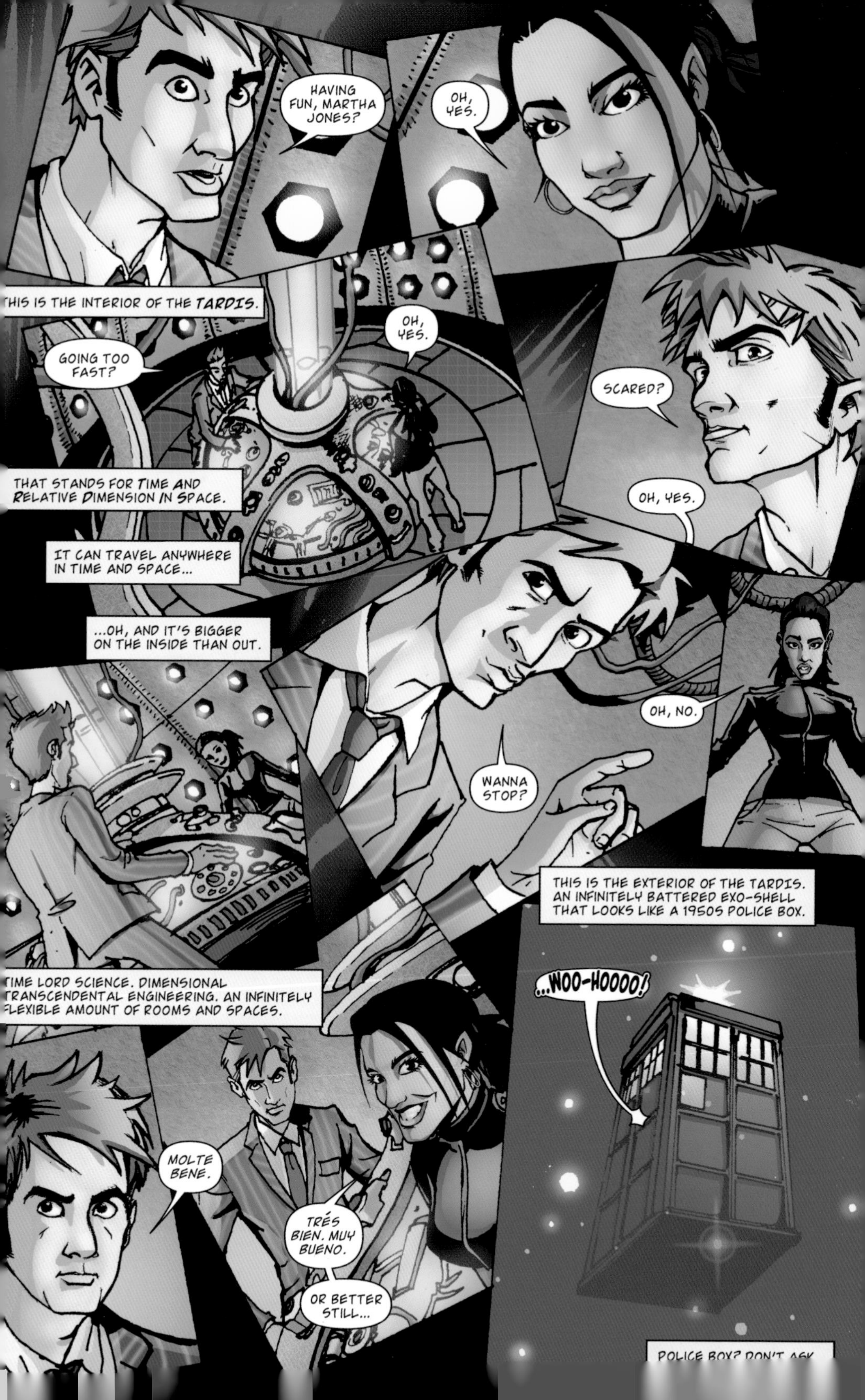
HAVING FUN, MARTHA JONES?
OH, YES.
THIS IS THE INTERIOR OF THE TARDIS.
GOING TOO FAST?
OH, YES.
THAT STANDS FOR TIME AND RELATIVE DIMENSION IN SPACE.
IT CAN TRAVEL ANYWHERE IN TIME AND SPACE...
SCARED?
OH, YES.
...OH, AND IT'S BIGGER ON THE INSIDE THAN OUT.
WANNA STOP?
OH, NO.
TIME LORD SCIENCE. DIMENSIONAL TRANSCENDENTAL ENGINEERING. AN INFINITELY FLEXIBLE AMOUNT OF ROOMS AND SPACES.
MOLTE BENE.
TRÉS BIEN. MUY BUENO.
OR BETTER STILL...
THIS IS THE EXTERIOR OF THE TARDIS. AN INFINITELY BATTERED EXO-SHELL THAT LOOKS LIKE A 1950S POLICE BOX.
...WOO-HOOOO!
POLICE BOX? DON'T ASK

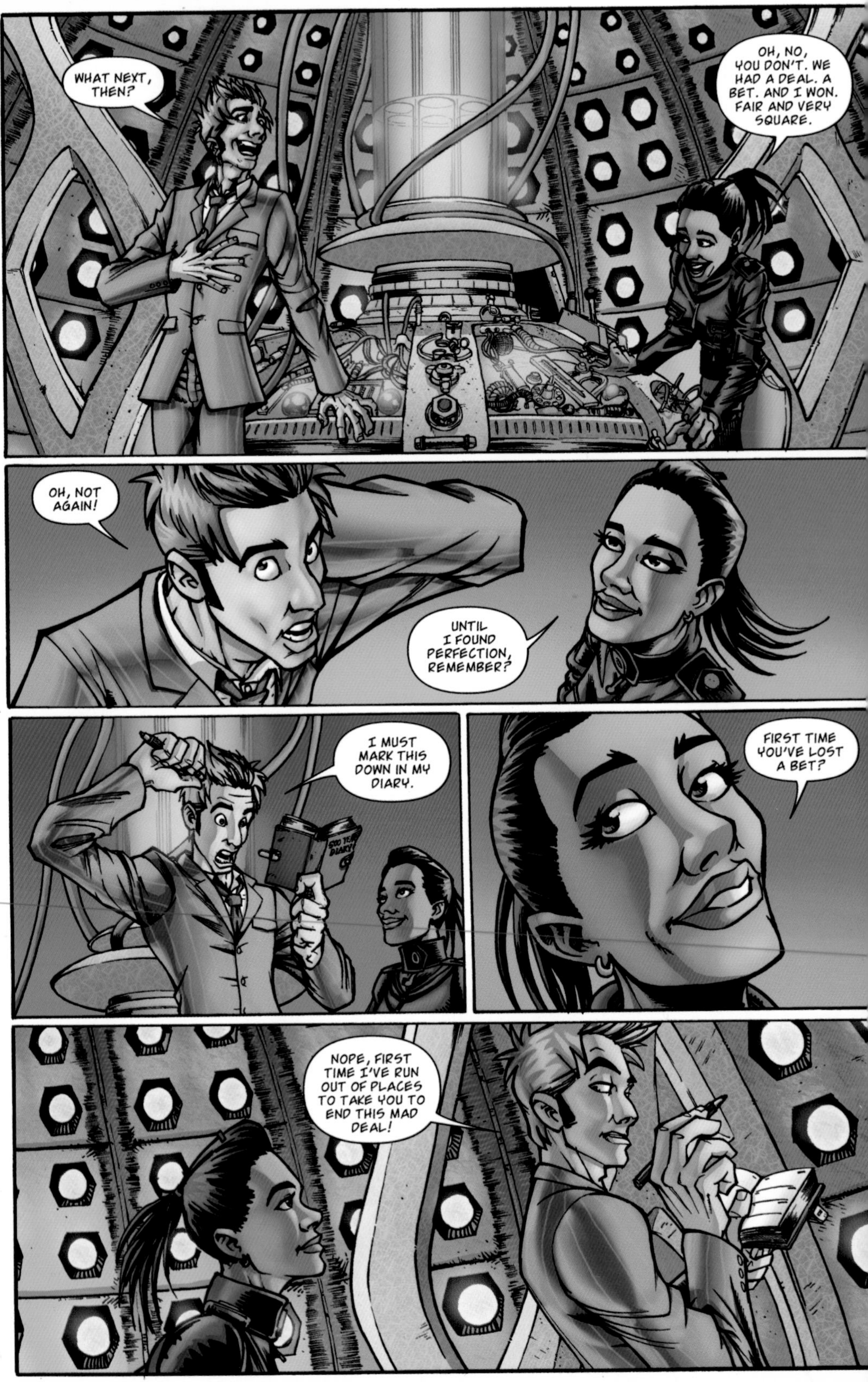
WHAT NEXT, THEN?
OH, NO, YOU DON'T. WE HAD A DEAL. A BET. AND I WON. FAIR AND VERY SQUARE.
OH, NOT AGAIN!
UNTIL I FOUND PERFECTION, REMEMBER?
I MUST MARK THIS DOWN IN MY DIARY.
500 YEAR DIARY
FIRST TIME YOU'VE LOST A BET?
NOPE, FIRST TIME I'VE RUN OUT OF PLACES TO TAKE YOU TO END THIS MAD DEAL!

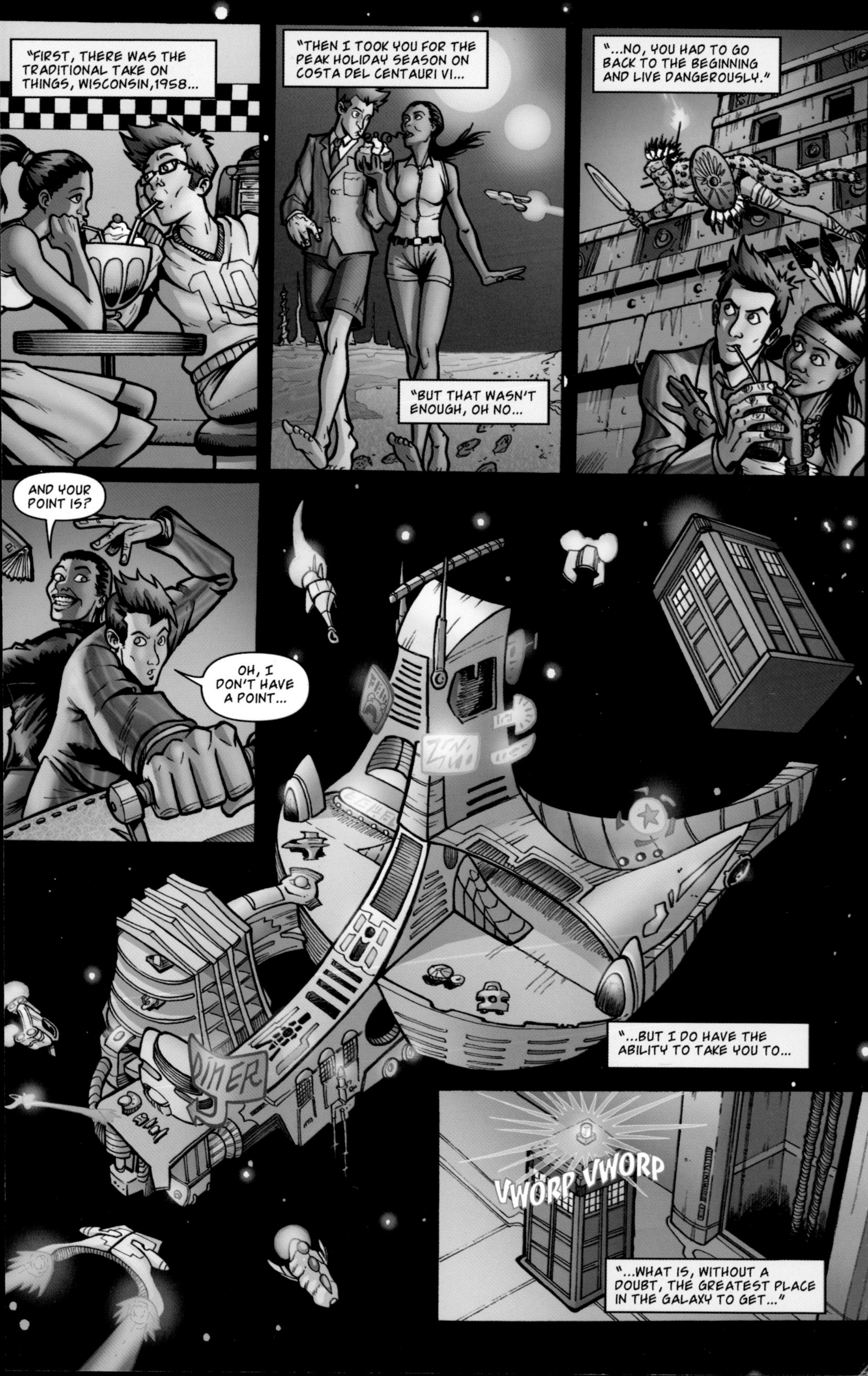
"FIRST, THERE WAS THE TRADITIONAL TAKE ON THINGS, WISCONSIN, 1958...
"THEN I TOOK YOU FOR THE PEAK HOLIDAY SEASON ON COSTA DEL CENTAURI VI...
"BUT THAT WASN'T ENOUGH, OH NO...
"...NO, YOU HAD TO GO BACK TO THE BEGINNING AND LIVE DANGEROUSLY."
AND YOUR POINT IS?
OH, I DON'T HAVE A POINT...
DINER
"...BUT I DO HAVE THE ABILITY TO TAKE YOU TO...
VWORP VWORP
"...WHAT IS, WITHOUT A DOUBT, THE GREATEST PLACE IN THE GALAXY TO GET..."

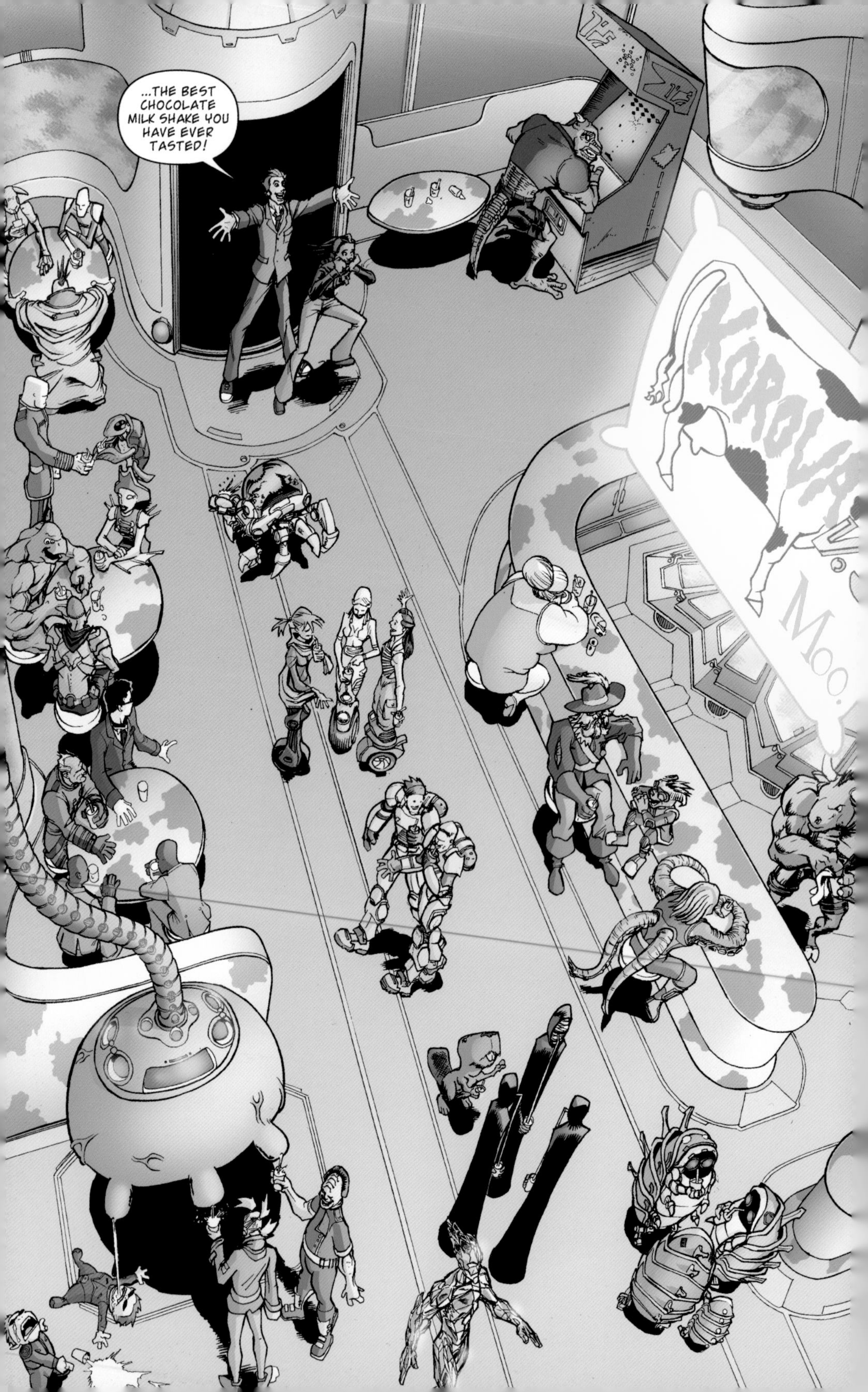
...THE BEST CHOCOLATE MILK SHAKE YOU HAVE EVER TASTED!
KOROVA
Moo.

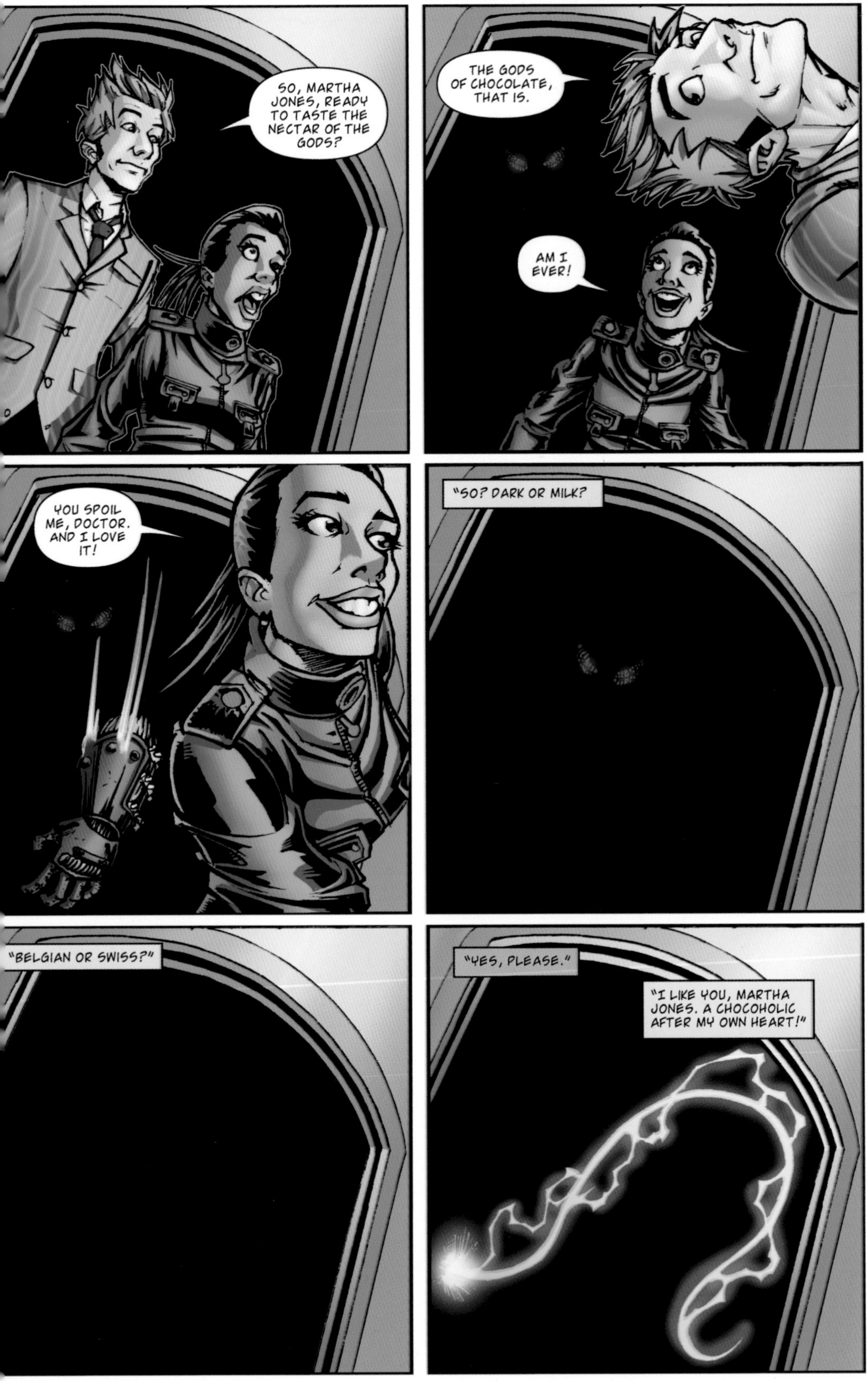
SO, MARTHA JONES, READY TO TASTE THE NECTAR OF THE GODS?
THE GODS OF CHOCOLATE, THAT IS.
AM I EVER!
YOU SPOIL ME, DOCTOR. AND I LOVE IT!
"SO? DARK OR MILK?
"BELGIAN OR SWISS?"
"YES, PLEASE."
"I LIKE YOU, MARTHA JONES. A CHOCOHOLIC AFTER MY OWN HEART!"

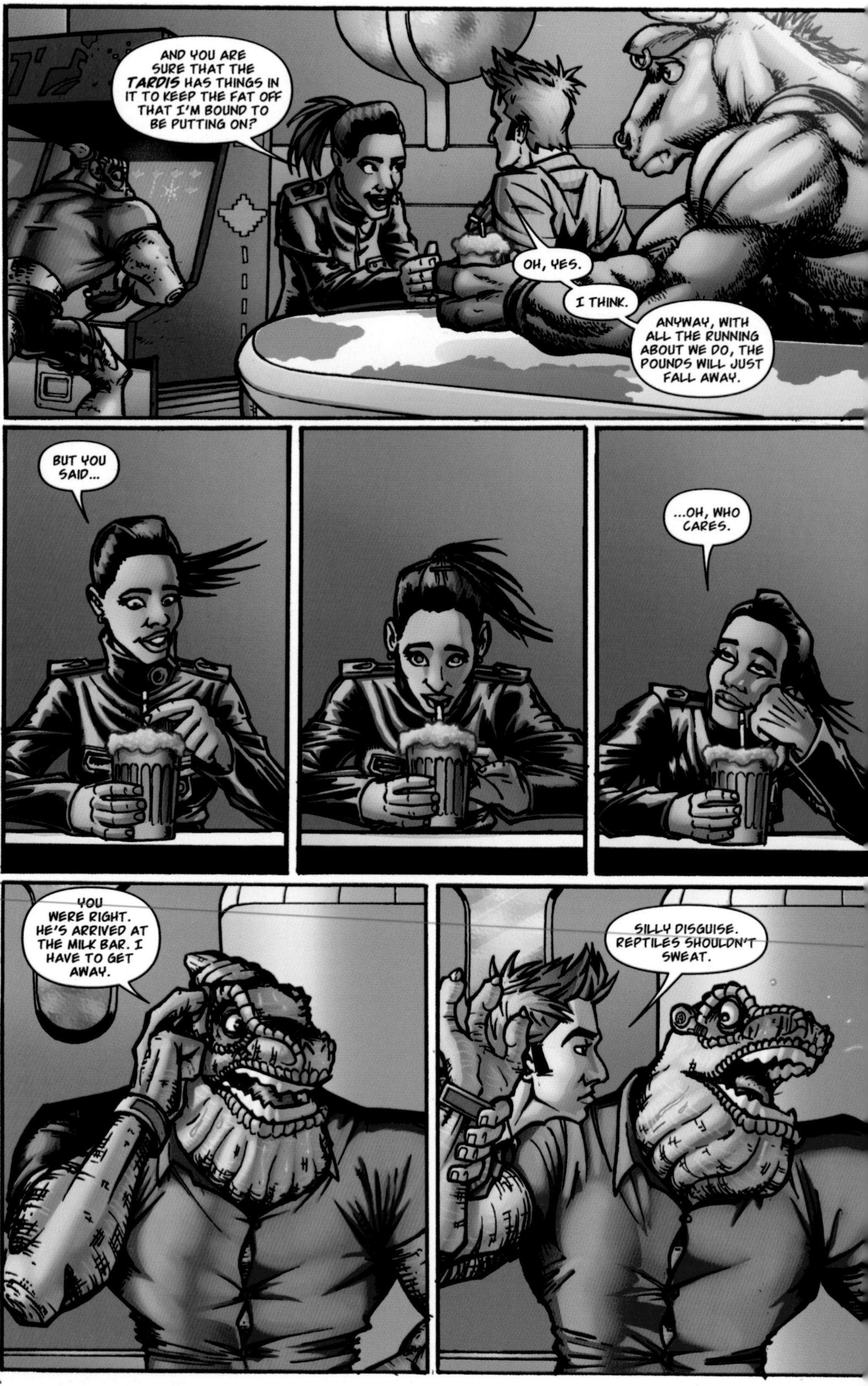

AND YOU ARE SURE THAT THE TARDIS HAS THINGS IN IT TO KEEP THE FAT OFF THAT I'M BOUND TO BE PUTTING ON?
OH, YES.
I THINK.
ANYWAY, WITH ALL THE RUNNING ABOUT WE DO, THE POUNDS WILL JUST FALL AWAY.
BUT YOU SAID...
...OH, WHO CARES.
YOU WERE RIGHT. HE'S ARRIVED AT THE MILK BAR. I HAVE TO GET AWAY.
SILLY DISGUISE. REPTILES SHOULDN'T SWEAT.

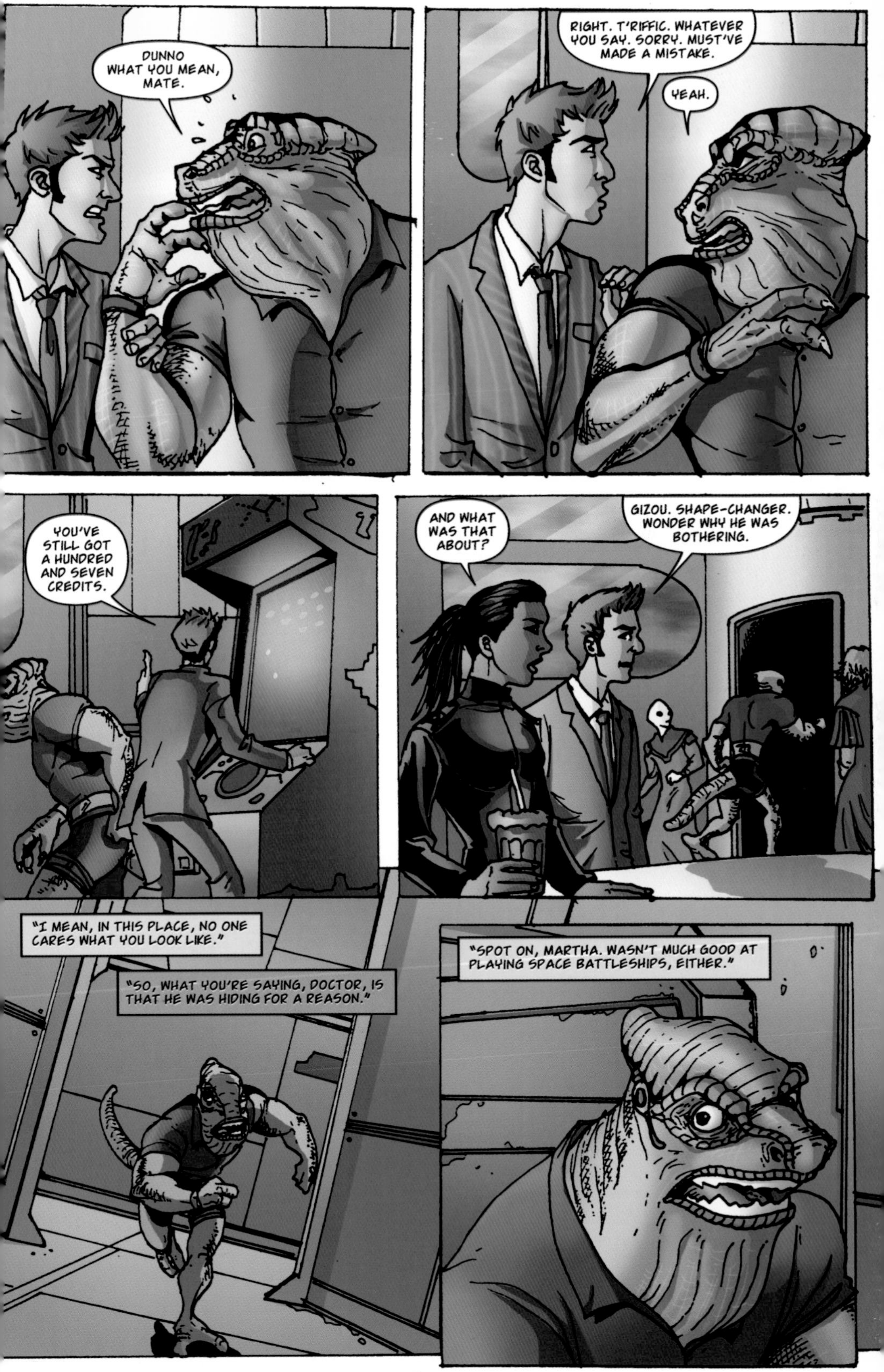
DUNNO WHAT YOU MEAN, MATE.
RIGHT. T'RIFFIC. WHATEVER YOU SAY. SORRY. MUST'VE MADE A MISTAKE.
YEAH.
YOU'VE STILL GOT A HUNDRED AND SEVEN CREDITS.
AND WHAT WAS THAT ABOUT?
GIZOU. SHAPE-CHANGER. WONDER WHY HE WAS BOTHERING.
"I MEAN, IN THIS PLACE, NO ONE CARES WHAT YOU LOOK LIKE."
"SO, WHAT YOU'RE SAYING, DOCTOR, IS THAT HE WAS HIDING FOR A REASON."
"SPOT ON, MARTHA. WASN'T MUCH GOOD AT PLAYING SPACE BATTLESHIPS, EITHER."

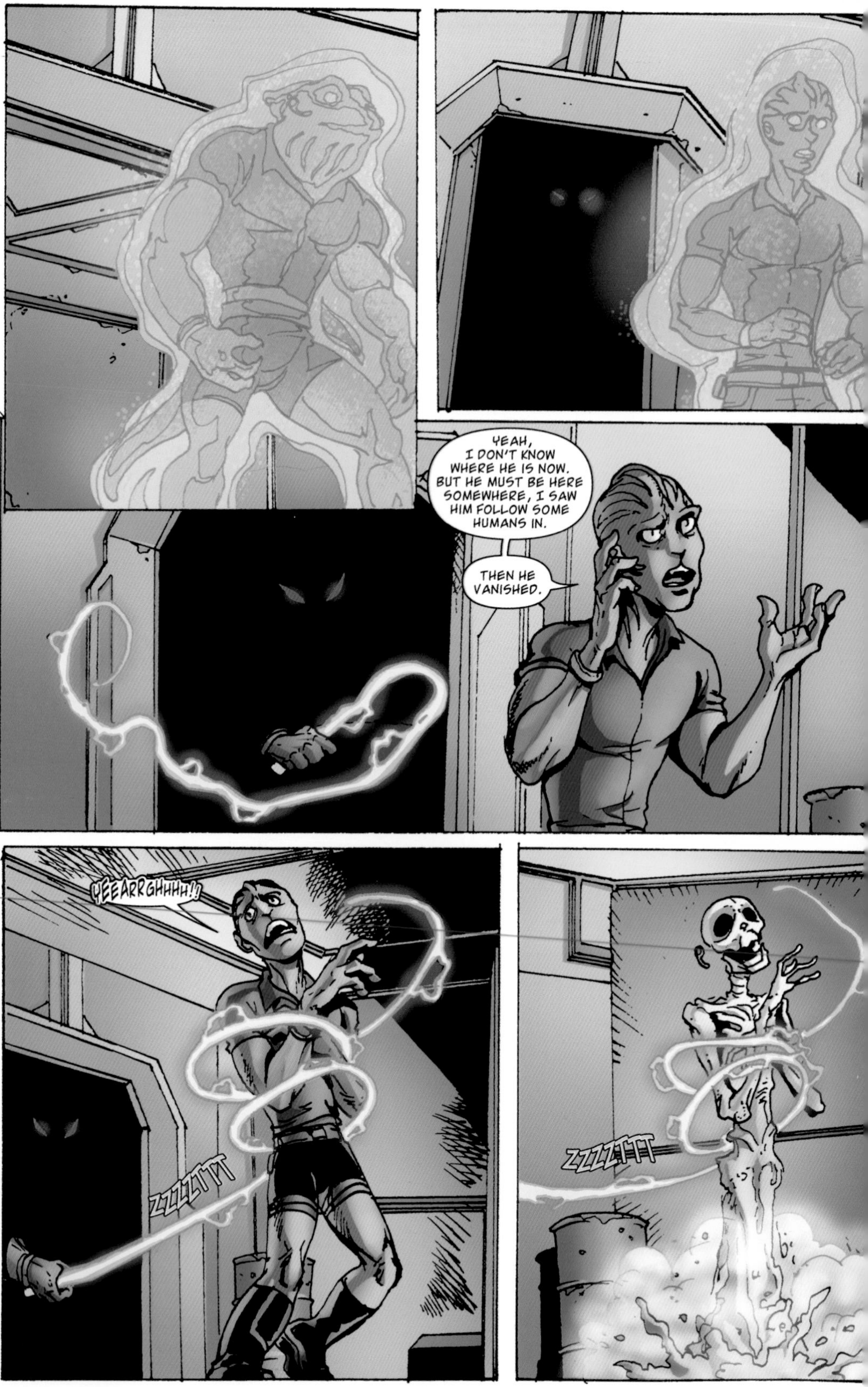
YEAH, I DON'T KNOW WHERE HE IS NOW. BUT HE MUST BE HERE SOMEWHERE, I SAW HIM FOLLOW SOME HUMANS IN.
THEN HE VANISHED.
YEEARRGHHHH!!
ZZZZTTTT
ZZZZTTTT

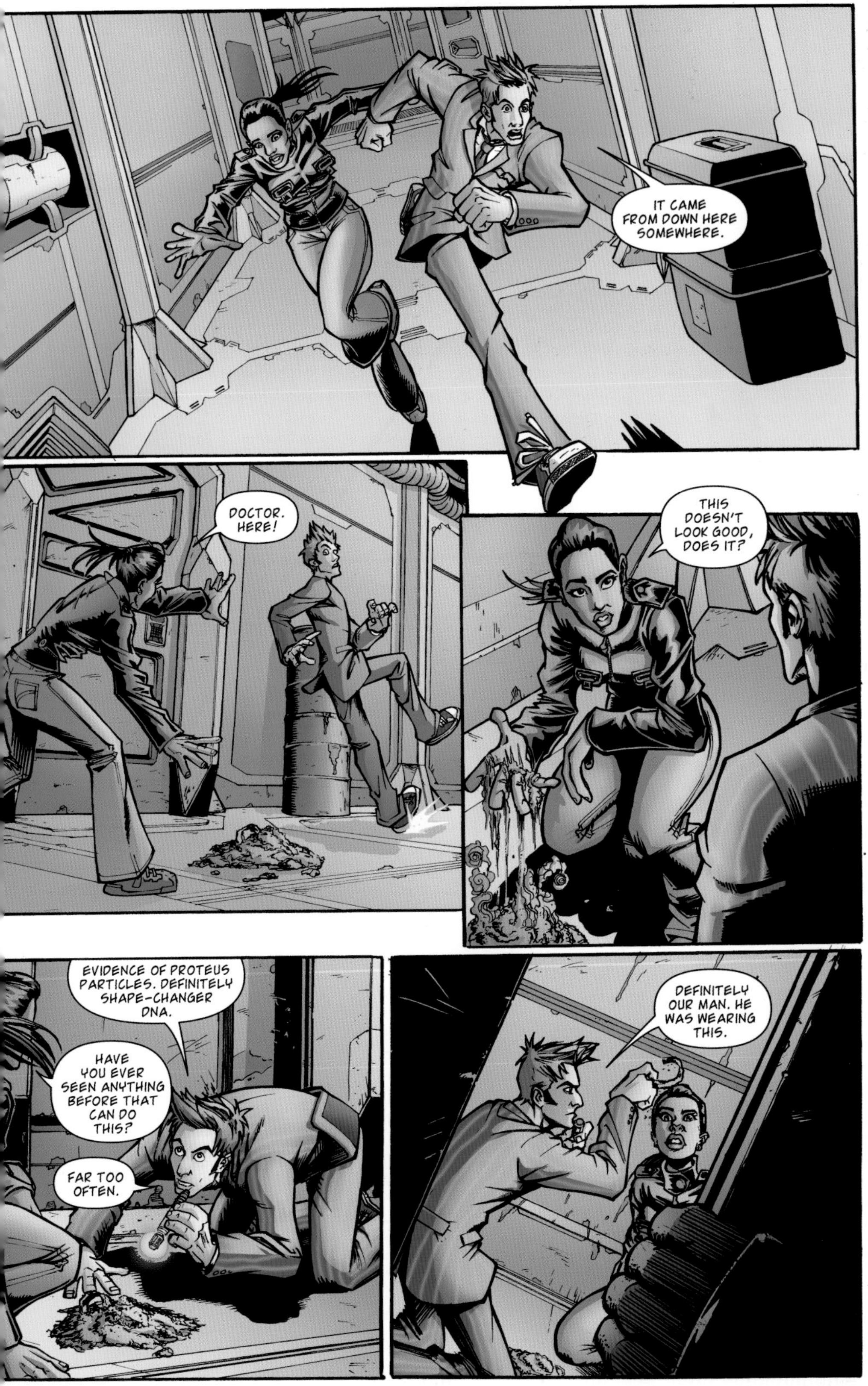
IT CAME FROM DOWN HERE SOMEWHERE.
DOCTOR. HERE!
THIS DOESN'T LOOK GOOD, DOES IT?
EVIDENCE OF PROTEUS PARTICLES. DEFINITELY SHAPE-CHANGER DNA.
HAVE YOU EVER SEEN ANYTHING BEFORE THAT CAN DO THIS?
FAR TOO OFTEN.
DEFINITELY OUR MAN. HE WAS WEARING THIS.

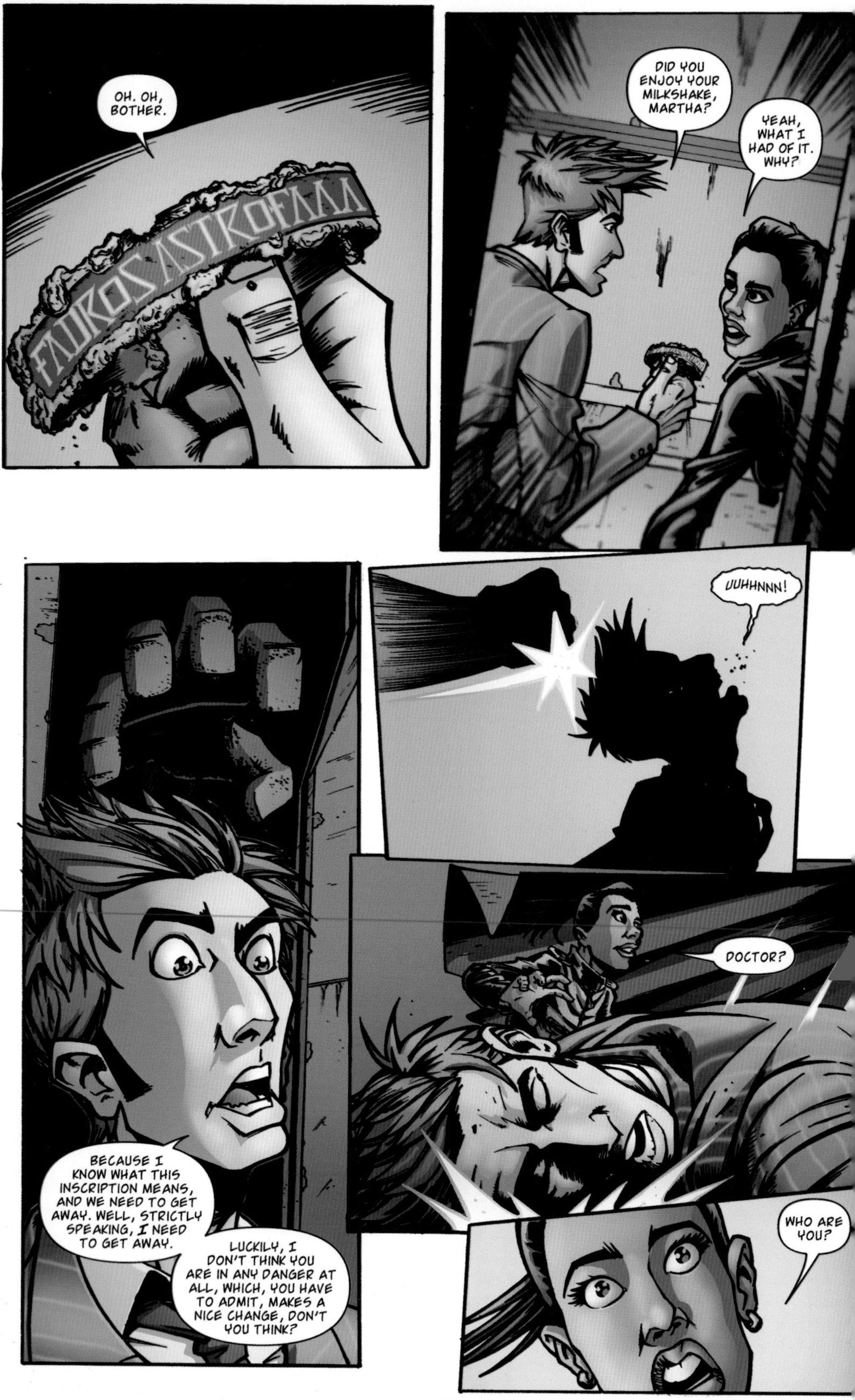
OH. OH, BOTHER.
FAUKOS ASTROFAAA
DID YOU ENJOY YOUR MILKSHAKE, MARTHA?
YEAH, WHAT I HAD OF IT. WHY?
BECAUSE I KNOW WHAT THIS INSCRIPTION MEANS, AND WE NEED TO GET AWAY. WELL, STRICTLY SPEAKING, I NEED TO GET AWAY.
LUCKILY, I DON'T THINK YOU ARE IN ANY DANGER AT ALL, WHICH, YOU HAVE TO ADMIT, MAKES A NICE CHANGE, DON'T YOU THINK?
UUHHNNN!
DOCTOR?
WHO ARE YOU?

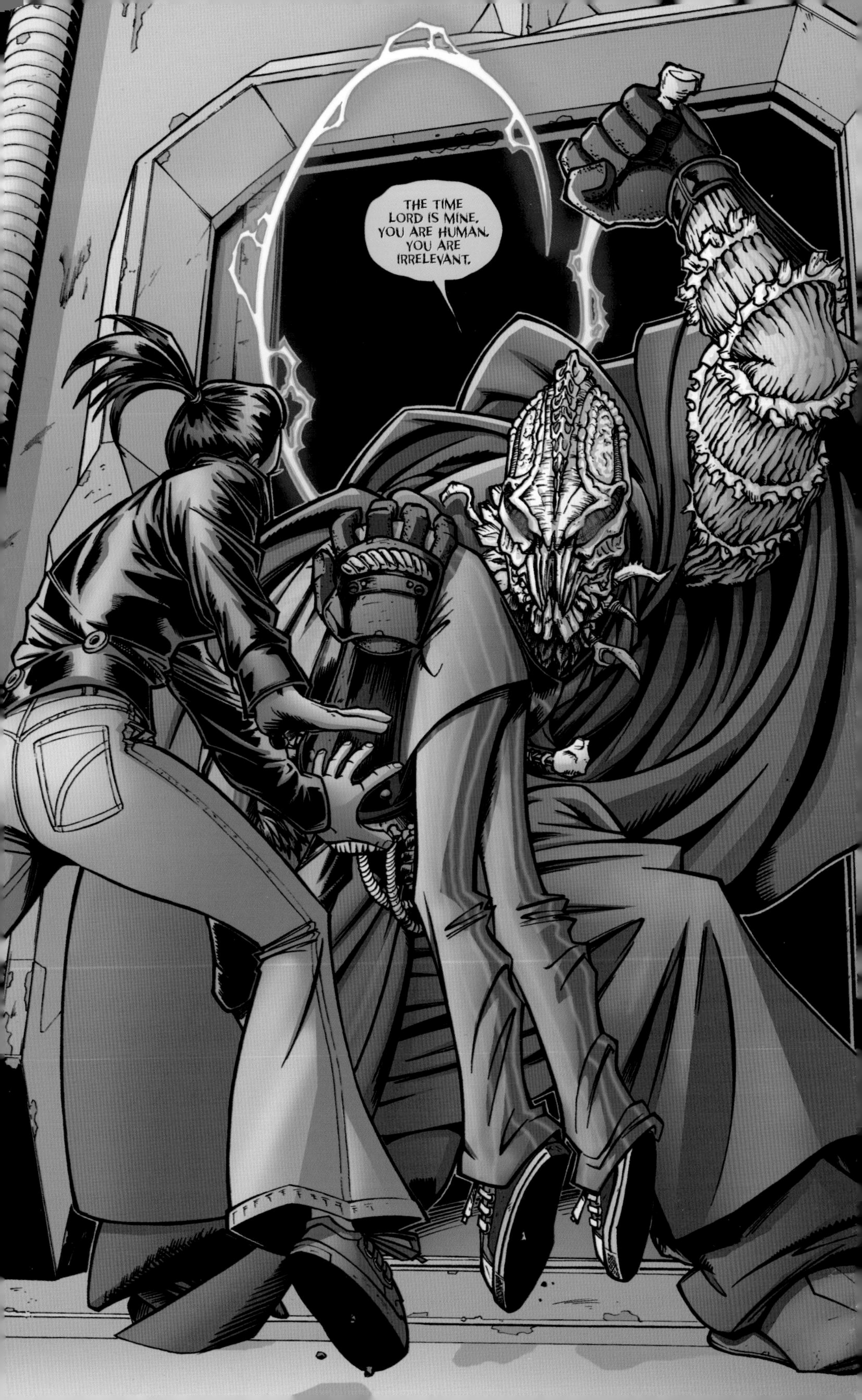
THE TIME LORD IS MINE. YOU ARE HUMAN. YOU ARE IRRELEVANT.

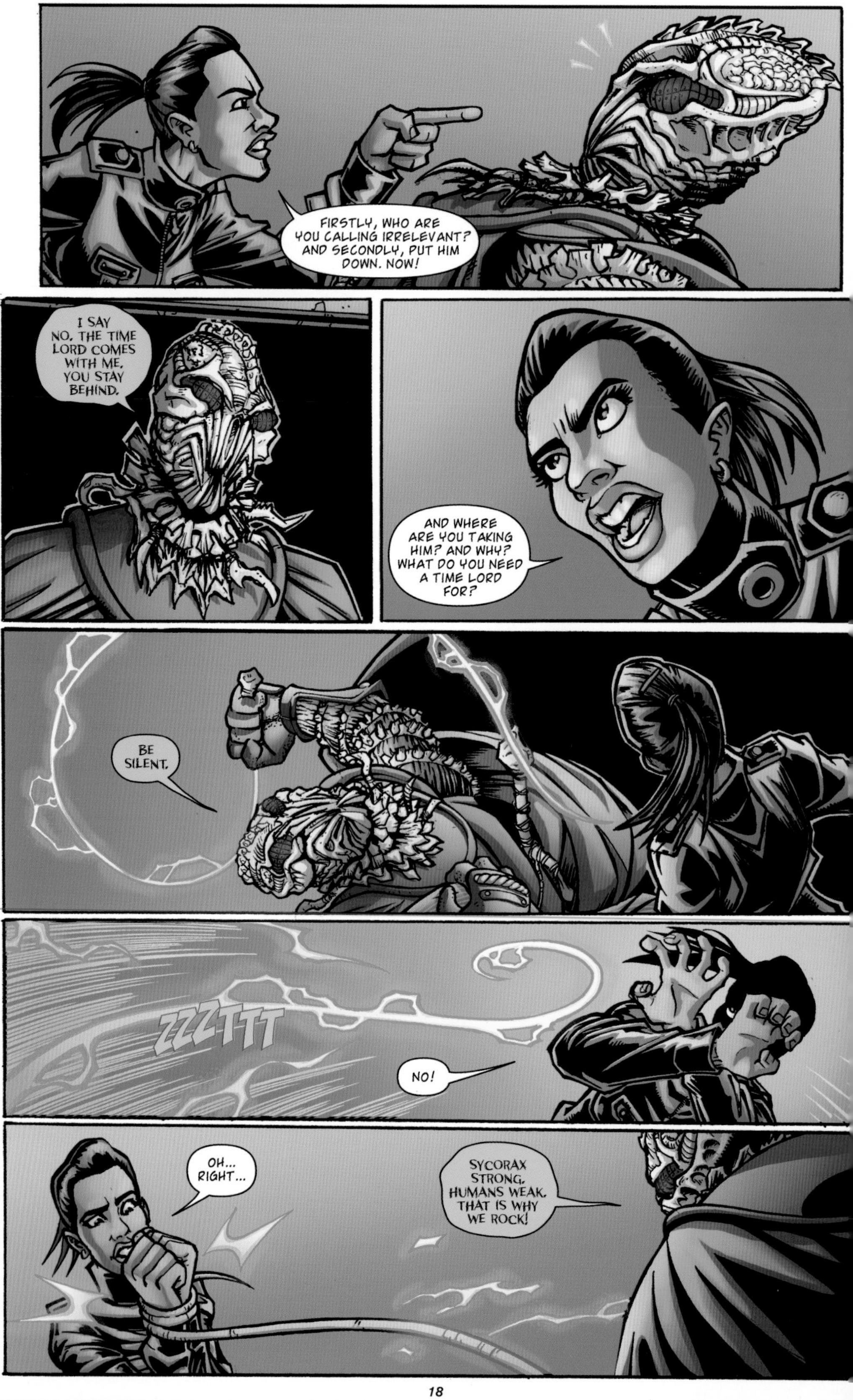
FIRSTLY, WHO ARE YOU CALLING IRRELEVANT? AND SECONDLY, PUT HIM DOWN. NOW!
I SAY NO. THE TIME LORD COMES WITH ME. YOU STAY BEHIND.
AND WHERE ARE YOU TAKING HIM? AND WHY? WHAT DO YOU NEED A TIME LORD FOR?
BE SILENT.
ZZZTTT
NO!
OH... RIGHT...
SYCORAX STRONG. HUMANS WEAK. THAT IS WHY WE ROCK!

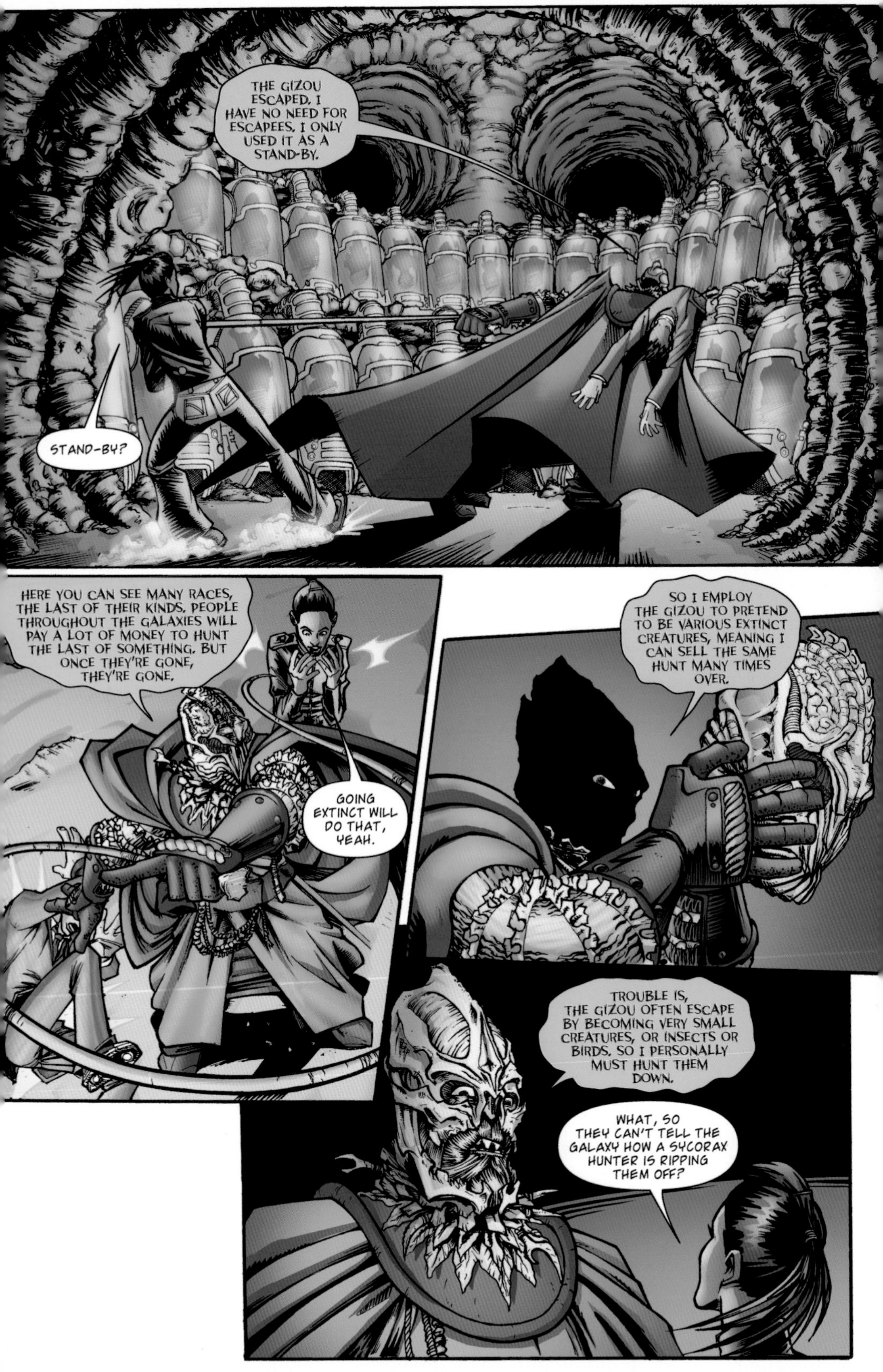
THE GIZOU ESCAPED. I HAVE NO NEED FOR ESCAPEES. I ONLY USED IT AS A STAND-BY.
STAND-BY?
HERE YOU CAN SEE MANY RACES, THE LAST OF THEIR KINDS. PEOPLE THROUGHOUT THE GALAXIES WILL PAY A LOT OF MONEY TO HUNT THE LAST OF SOMETHING. BUT ONCE THEY'RE GONE, THEY'RE GONE.
GOING EXTINCT WILL DO THAT, YEAH.
SO I EMPLOY THE GIZOU TO PRETEND TO BE VARIOUS EXTINCT CREATURES, MEANING I CAN SELL THE SAME HUNT MANY TIMES OVER.
TROUBLE IS, THE GIZOU OFTEN ESCAPE BY BECOMING VERY SMALL CREATURES, OR INSECTS OR BIRDS, SO I PERSONALLY MUST HUNT THEM DOWN.
WHAT, SO THEY CAN'T TELL THE GALAXY HOW A SYCORAX HUNTER IS RIPPING THEM OFF?

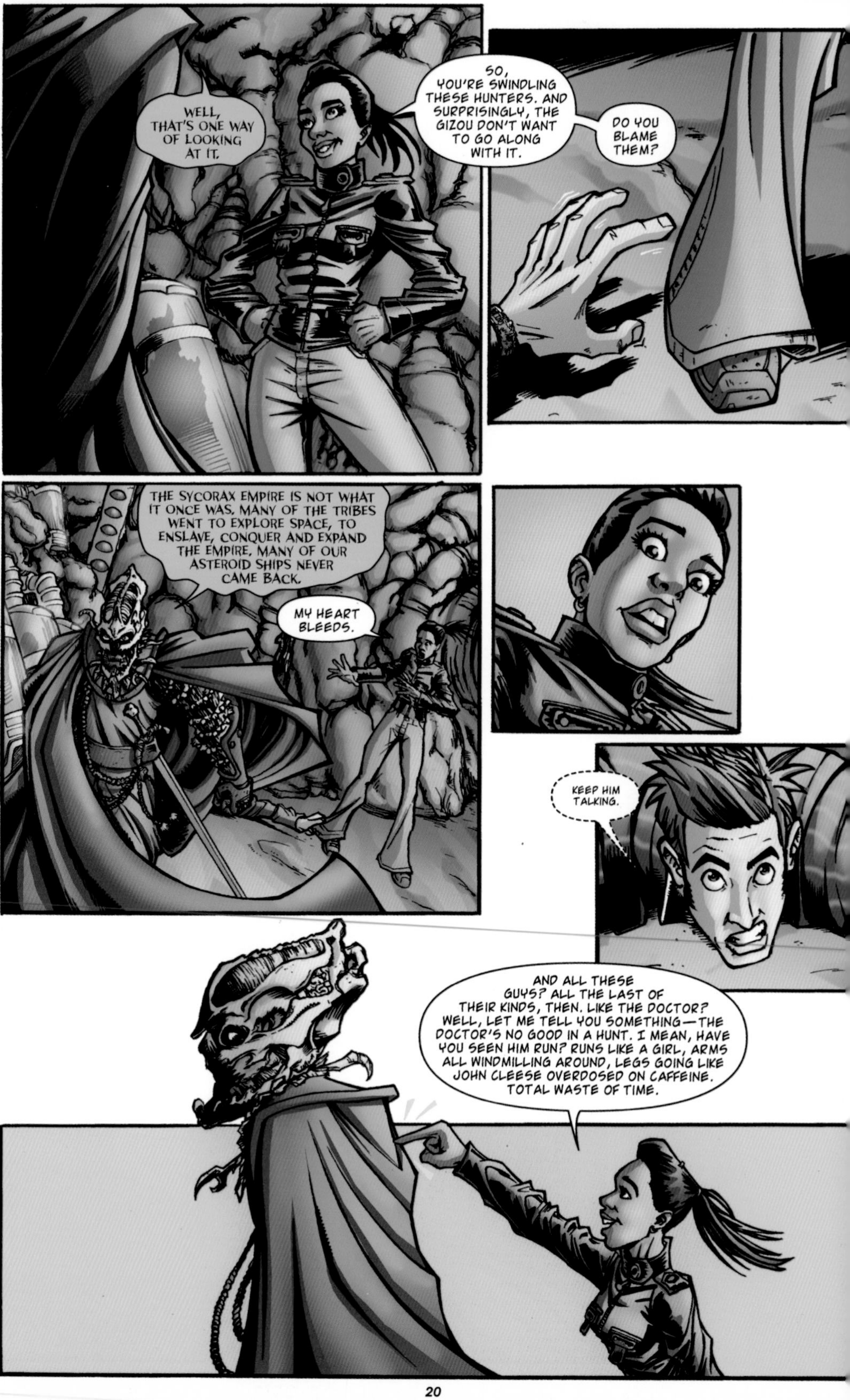

WELL, THAT'S ONE WAY OF LOOKING AT IT.
SO, YOU'RE SWINDLING THESE HUNTERS. AND SURPRISINGLY, THE GIZOU DON'T WANT TO GO ALONG WITH IT.
DO YOU BLAME THEM?
THE SYCORAX EMPIRE IS NOT WHAT IT ONCE WAS. MANY OF THE TRIBES WENT TO EXPLORE SPACE, TO ENSLAVE, CONQUER AND EXPAND THE EMPIRE. MANY OF OUR ASTEROID SHIPS NEVER CAME BACK.
MY HEART BLEEDS.
KEEP HIM TALKING.
AND ALL THESE GUYS? ALL THE LAST OF THEIR KINDS, THEN. LIKE THE DOCTOR? WELL, LET ME TELL YOU SOMETHING—THE DOCTOR'S NO GOOD IN A HUNT. I MEAN, HAVE YOU SEEN HIM RUN? RUNS LIKE A GIRL, ARMS ALL WINDMILLING AROUND, LEGS GOING LIKE JOHN CLEESE OVERDOSED ON CAFFEINE. TOTAL WASTE OF TIME.

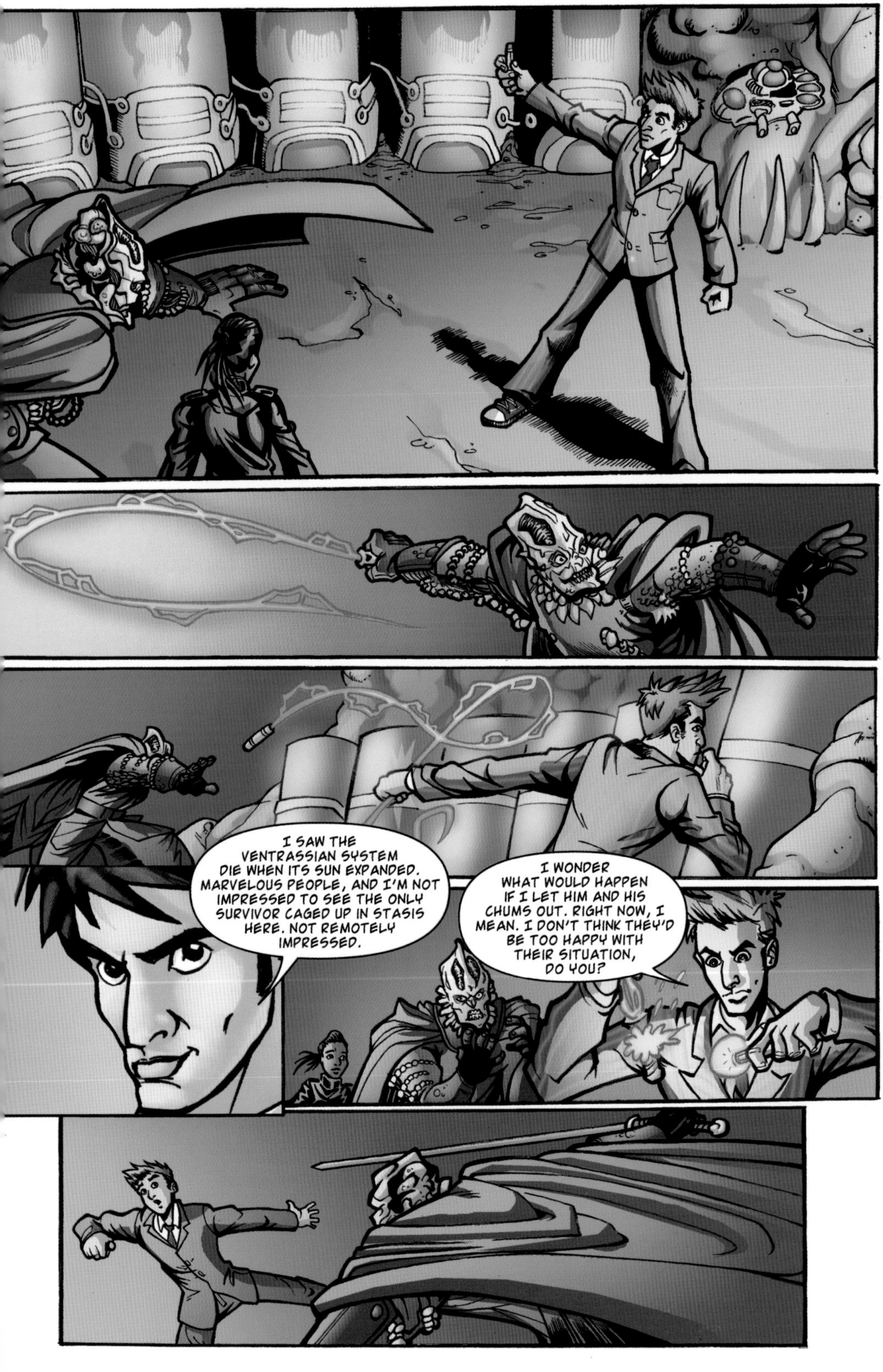
I SAW THE VENTRASSIAN SYSTEM DIE WHEN ITS SUN EXPANDED. MARVELOUS PEOPLE, AND I'M NOT IMPRESSED TO SEE THE ONLY SURVIVOR CAGED UP IN STASIS HERE. NOT REMOTELY IMPRESSED.
I WONDER WHAT WOULD HAPPEN IF I LET HIM AND HIS CHUMS OUT. RIGHT NOW, I MEAN. I DON'T THINK THEY'D BE TOO HAPPY WITH THEIR SITUATION, DO YOU?

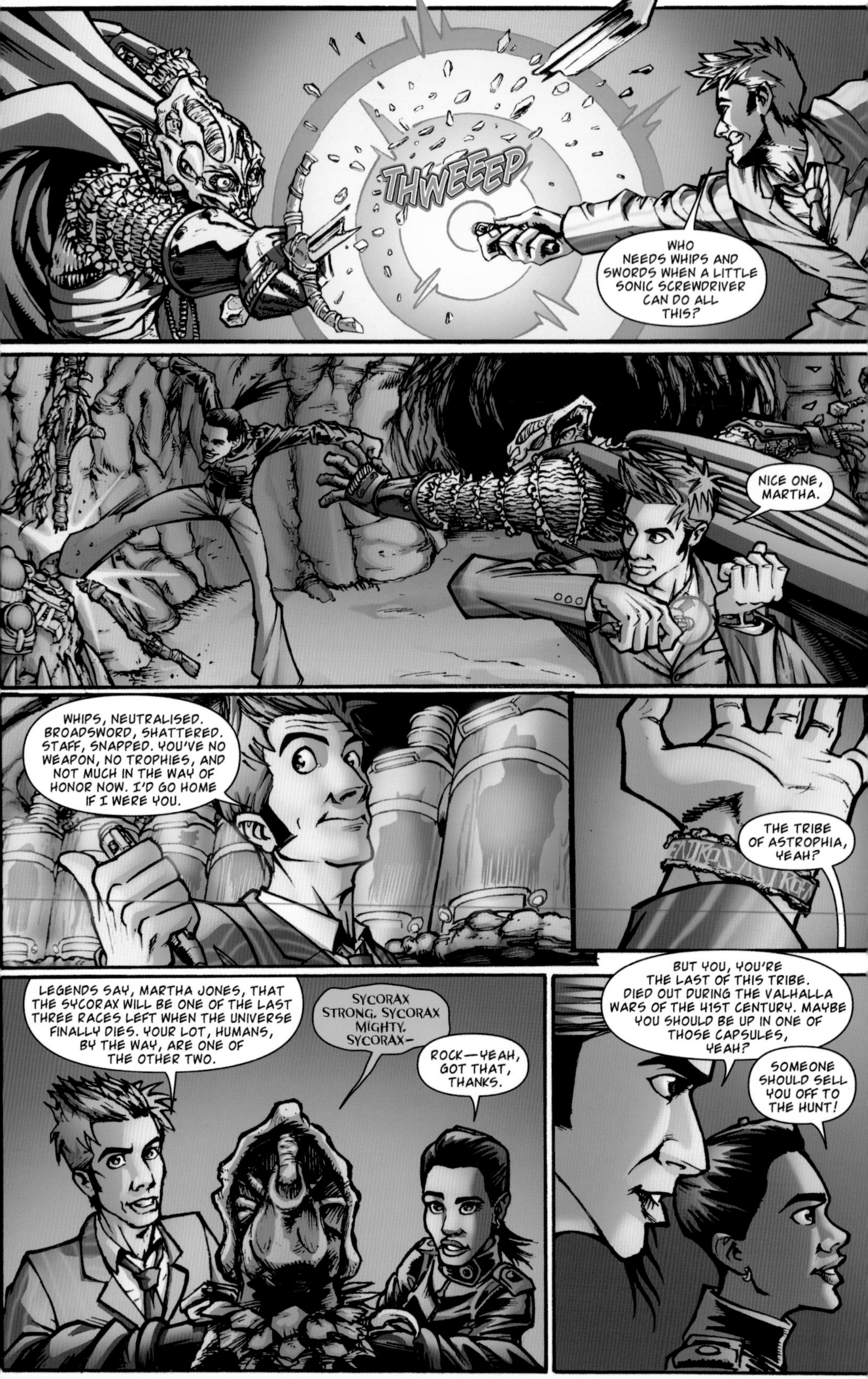
THWEEEP
WHO NEEDS WHIPS AND SWORDS WHEN A LITTLE SONIC SCREWDRIVER CAN DO ALL THIS?
NICE ONE, MARTHA.
WHIPS, NEUTRALISED. BROADSWORD, SHATTERED. STAFF, SNAPPED. YOU'VE NO WEAPON, NO TROPHIES, AND NOT MUCH IN THE WAY OF HONOR NOW. I'D GO HOME IF I WERE YOU.
THE TRIBE OF ASTROPHIA, YEAH?
LEGENDS SAY, MARTHA JONES, THAT THE SYCORAX WILL BE ONE OF THE LAST THREE RACES LEFT WHEN THE UNIVERSE FINALLY DIES. YOUR LOT, HUMANS, BY THE WAY, ARE ONE OF THE OTHER TWO.
SYCORAX STRONG. SYCORAX MIGHTY. SYCORAX—
ROCK—YEAH, GOT THAT, THANKS.
BUT YOU, YOU'RE THE LAST OF THIS TRIBE. DIED OUT DURING THE VALHALLA WARS OF THE 41ST CENTURY. MAYBE YOU SHOULD BE UP IN ONE OF THOSE CAPSULES, YEAH?
SOMEONE SHOULD SELL YOU OFF TO THE HUNT!

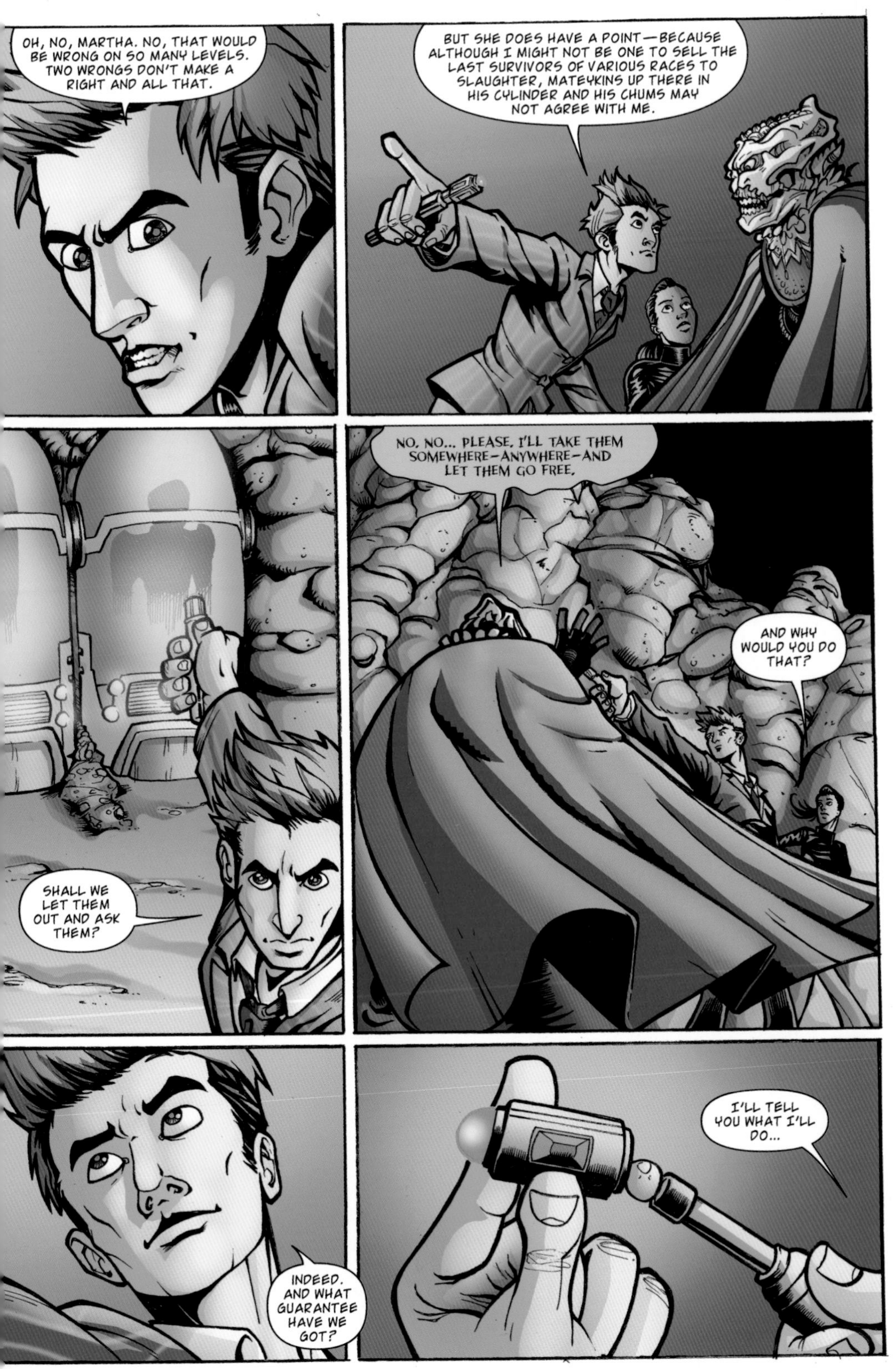
OH, NO, MARTHA. NO, THAT WOULD BE WRONG ON SO MANY LEVELS. TWO WRONGS DON'T MAKE A RIGHT AND ALL THAT.
BUT SHE DOES HAVE A POINT—BECAUSE ALTHOUGH I MIGHT NOT BE ONE TO SELL THE LAST SURVIVORS OF VARIOUS RACES TO SLAUGHTER, MATEYKINS UP THERE IN HIS CYLINDER AND HIS CHUMS MAY NOT AGREE WITH ME.
SHALL WE LET THEM OUT AND ASK THEM?
NO, NO... PLEASE. I'LL TAKE THEM SOMEWHERE—ANYWHERE—AND LET THEM GO FREE.
AND WHY WOULD YOU DO THAT?
INDEED. AND WHAT GUARANTEE HAVE WE GOT?
I'LL TELL YOU WHAT I'LL DO...

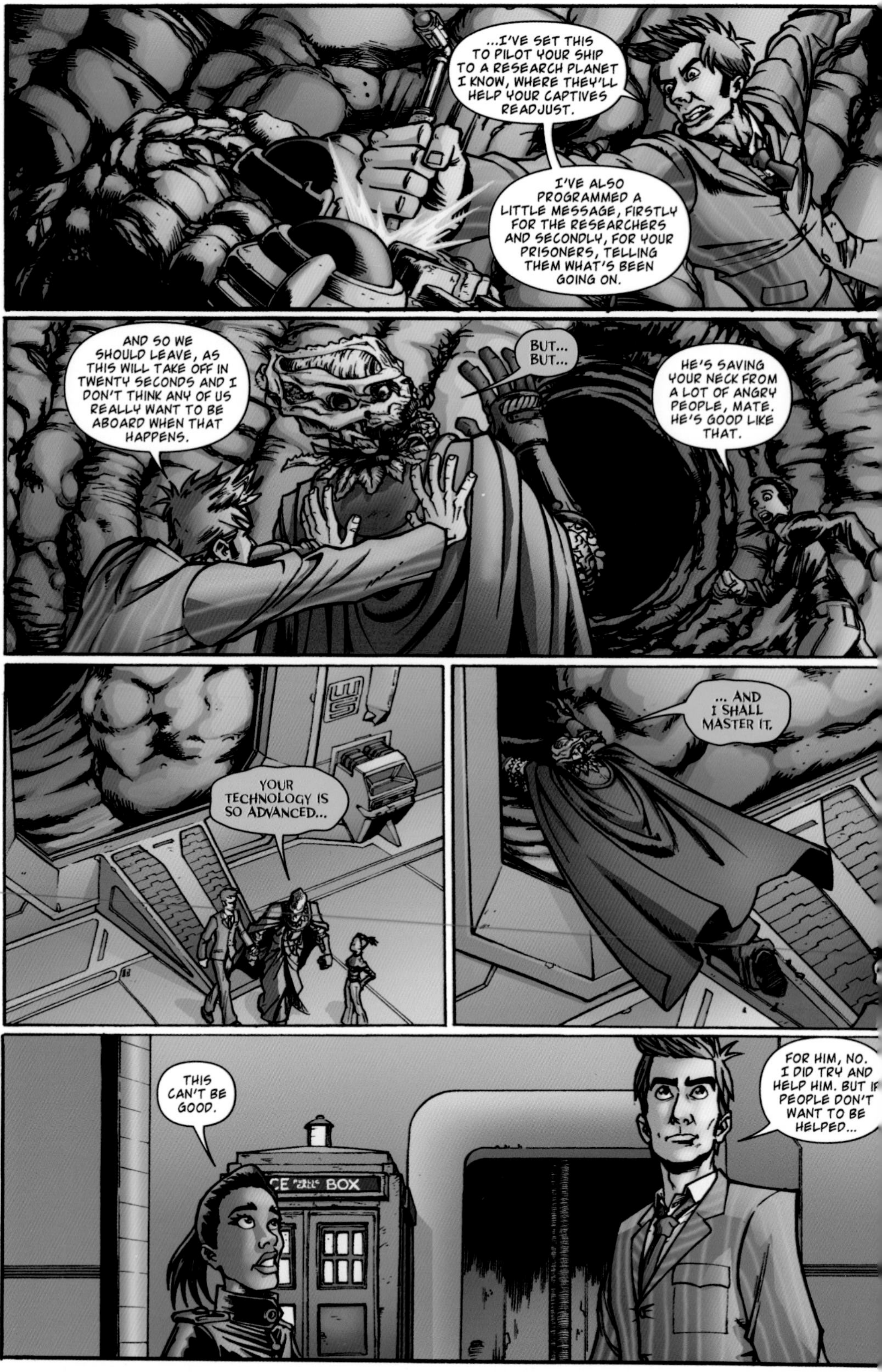
...I'VE SET THIS TO PILOT YOUR SHIP TO A RESEARCH PLANET I KNOW, WHERE THEY'LL HELP YOUR CAPTIVES READJUST.
I'VE ALSO PROGRAMMED A LITTLE MESSAGE, FIRSTLY FOR THE RESEARCHERS AND SECONDLY, FOR YOUR PRISONERS, TELLING THEM WHAT'S BEEN GOING ON.
AND SO WE SHOULD LEAVE, AS THIS WILL TAKE OFF IN TWENTY SECONDS AND I DON'T THINK ANY OF US REALLY WANT TO BE ABOARD WHEN THAT HAPPENS.
BUT... BUT...
HE'S SAVING YOUR NECK FROM A LOT OF ANGRY PEOPLE, MATE. HE'S GOOD LIKE THAT.
YOUR TECHNOLOGY IS SO ADVANCED...
... AND I SHALL MASTER IT.
THIS CAN'T BE GOOD.
FOR HIM, NO. I DID TRY AND HELP HIM. BUT IF PEOPLE DON'T WANT TO BE HELPED...
BOX

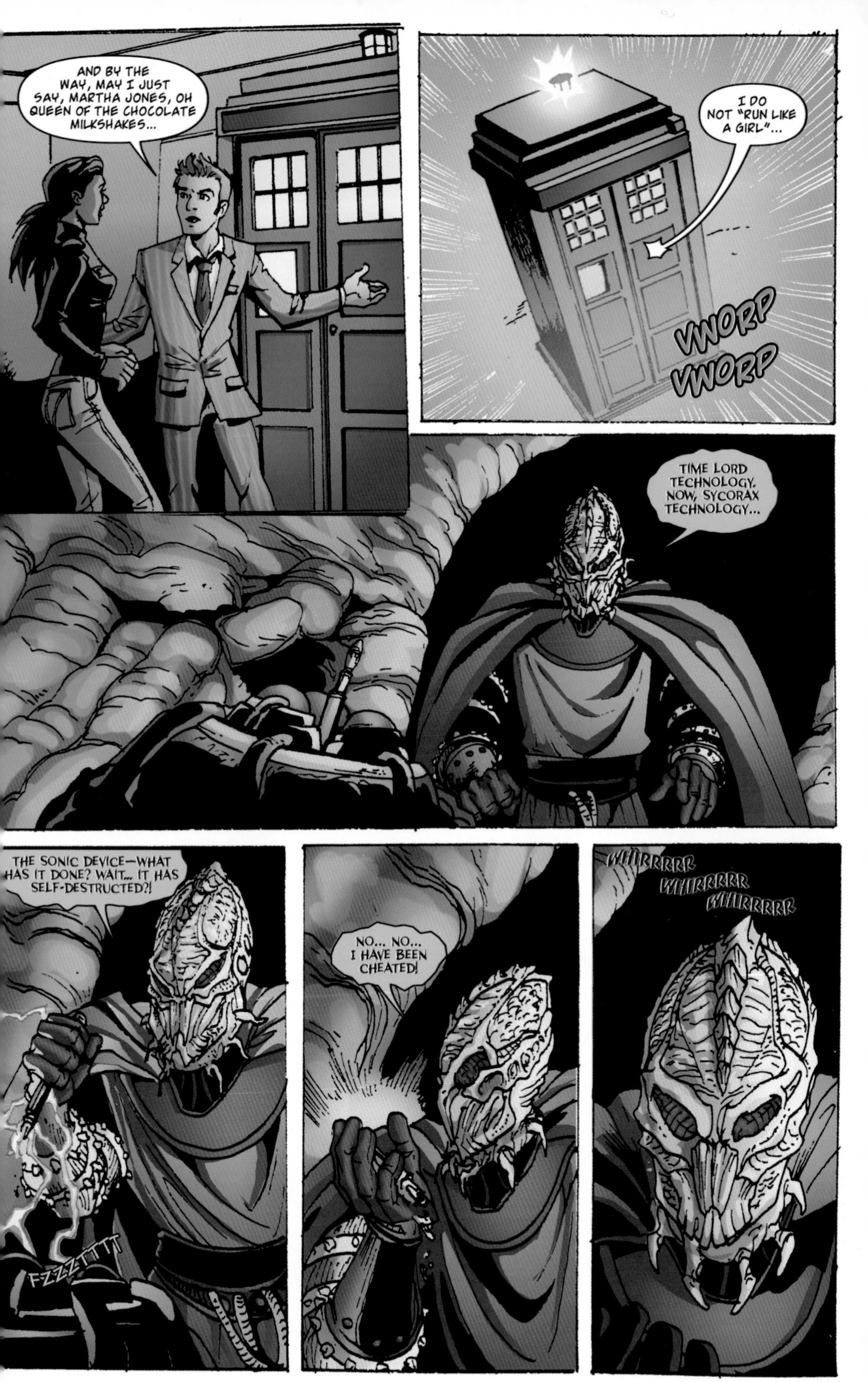
AND BY THE WAY, MAY I JUST SAY, MARTHA JONES, OH QUEEN OF THE CHOCOLATE MILKSHAKES...
I DO NOT "RUN LIKE A GIRL"...
VWORP
VWORP
TIME LORD TECHNOLOGY. NOW, SYCORAX TECHNOLOGY...
THE SONIC DEVICE—WHAT HAS IT DONE? WAIT... IT HAS SELF-DESTRUCTED?!
FZZZTTTT
NO... NO... I HAVE BEEN CHEATED!
WHIRRRRR
WHIRRRRR
WHIRRRRR

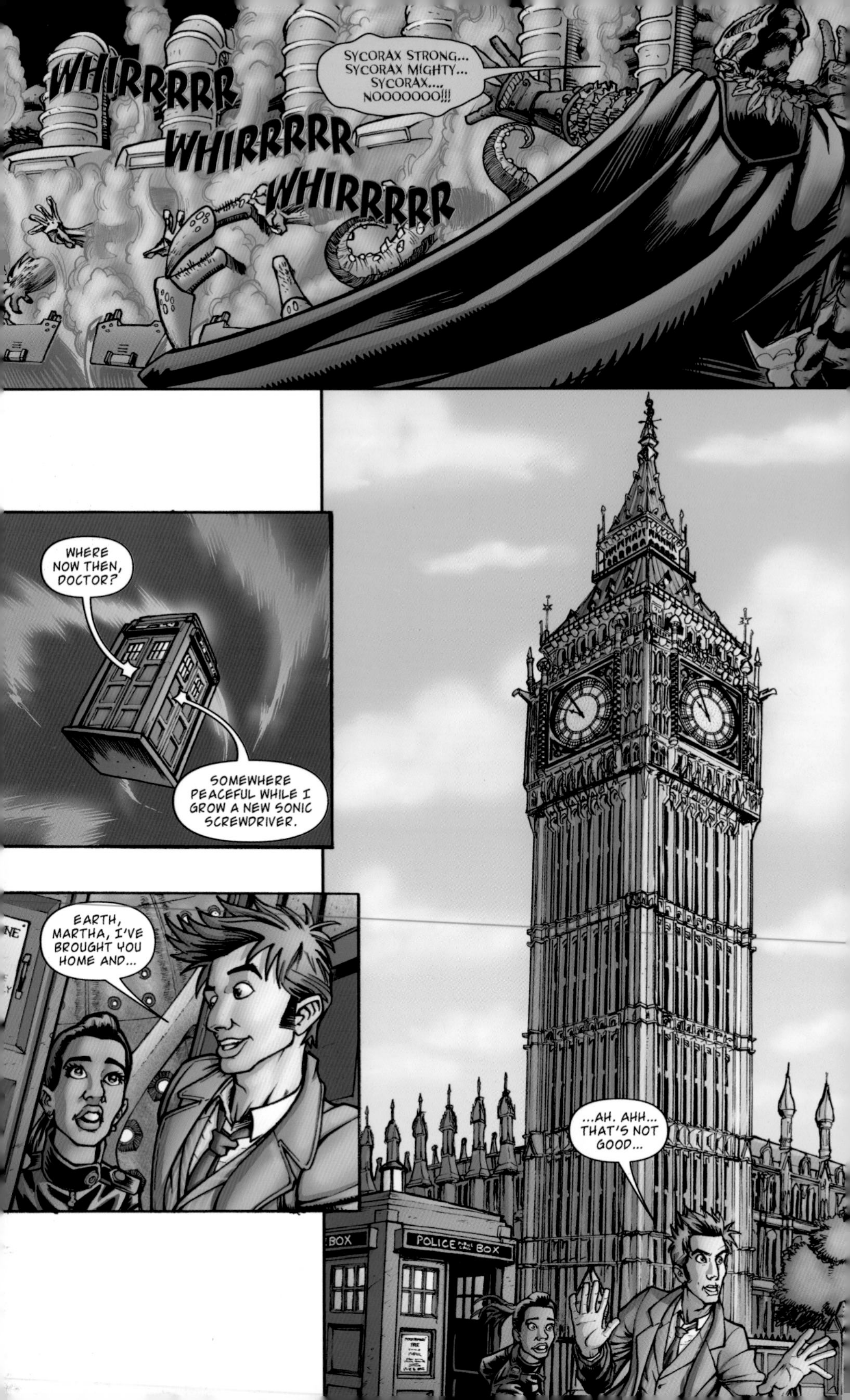
WHIRRRRR
SYCORAX STRONG... SYCORAX MIGHTY... SYCORAX..., NOOOOOOO!!!
WHIRRRRRR
WHIRRRRRR
WHERE NOW THEN, DOCTOR?
SOMEWHERE PEACEFUL WHILE I GROW A NEW SONIC SCREWDRIVER.
EARTH, MARTHA, I'VE BROUGHT YOU HOME AND...
...AH. AHH... THAT'S NOT GOOD...
POLICE BOX
BOX

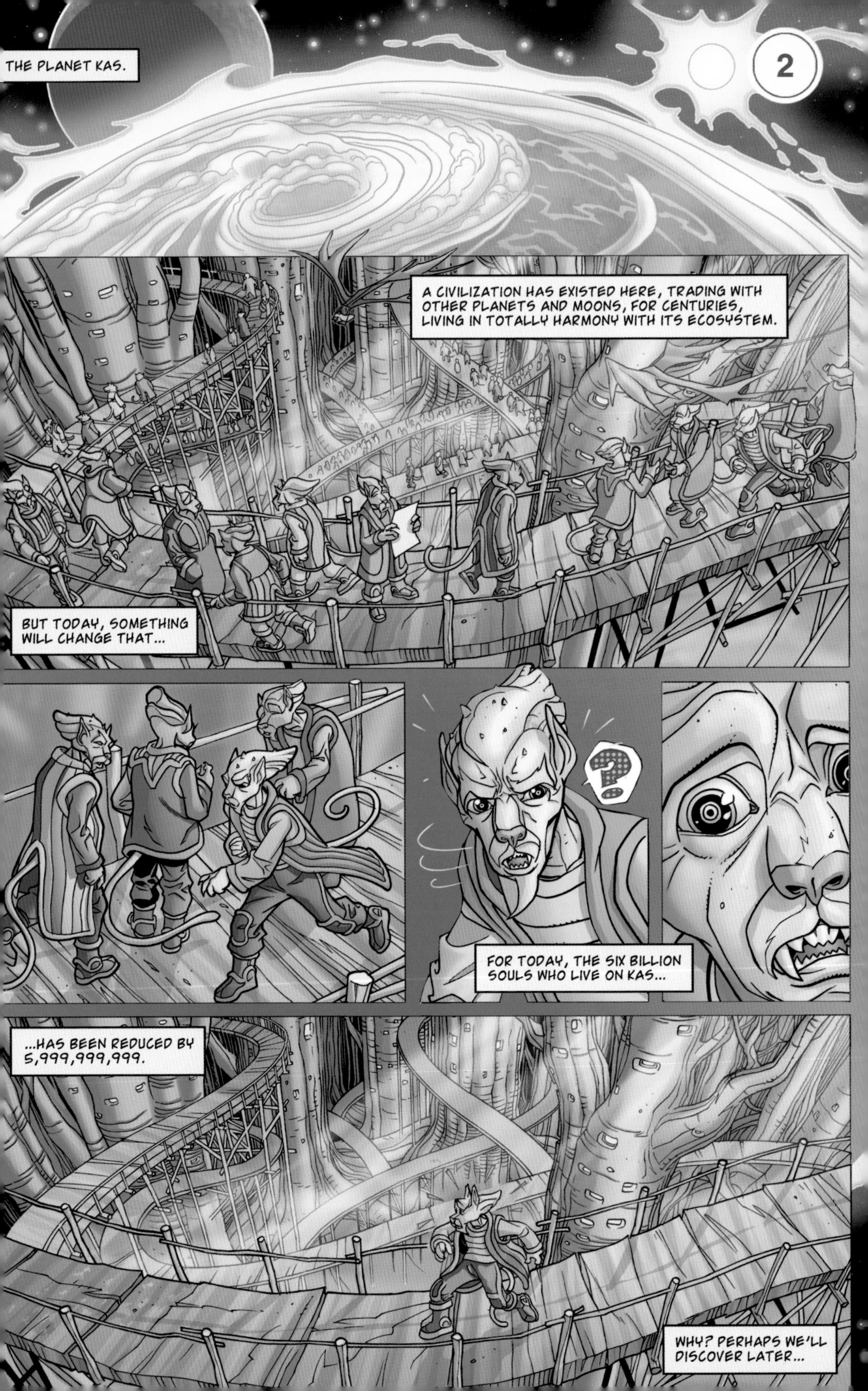
THE PLANET KAS.
2
A CIVILIZATION HAS EXISTED HERE, TRADING WITH OTHER PLANETS AND MOONS, FOR CENTURIES, LIVING IN TOTALLY HARMONY WITH ITS ECOSYSTEM.
BUT TODAY, SOMETHING WILL CHANGE THAT...
?
FOR TODAY, THE SIX BILLION SOULS WHO LIVE ON KAS...
...HAS BEEN REDUCED BY 5,999,999,999.
WHY? PERHAPS WE'LL DISCOVER LATER...

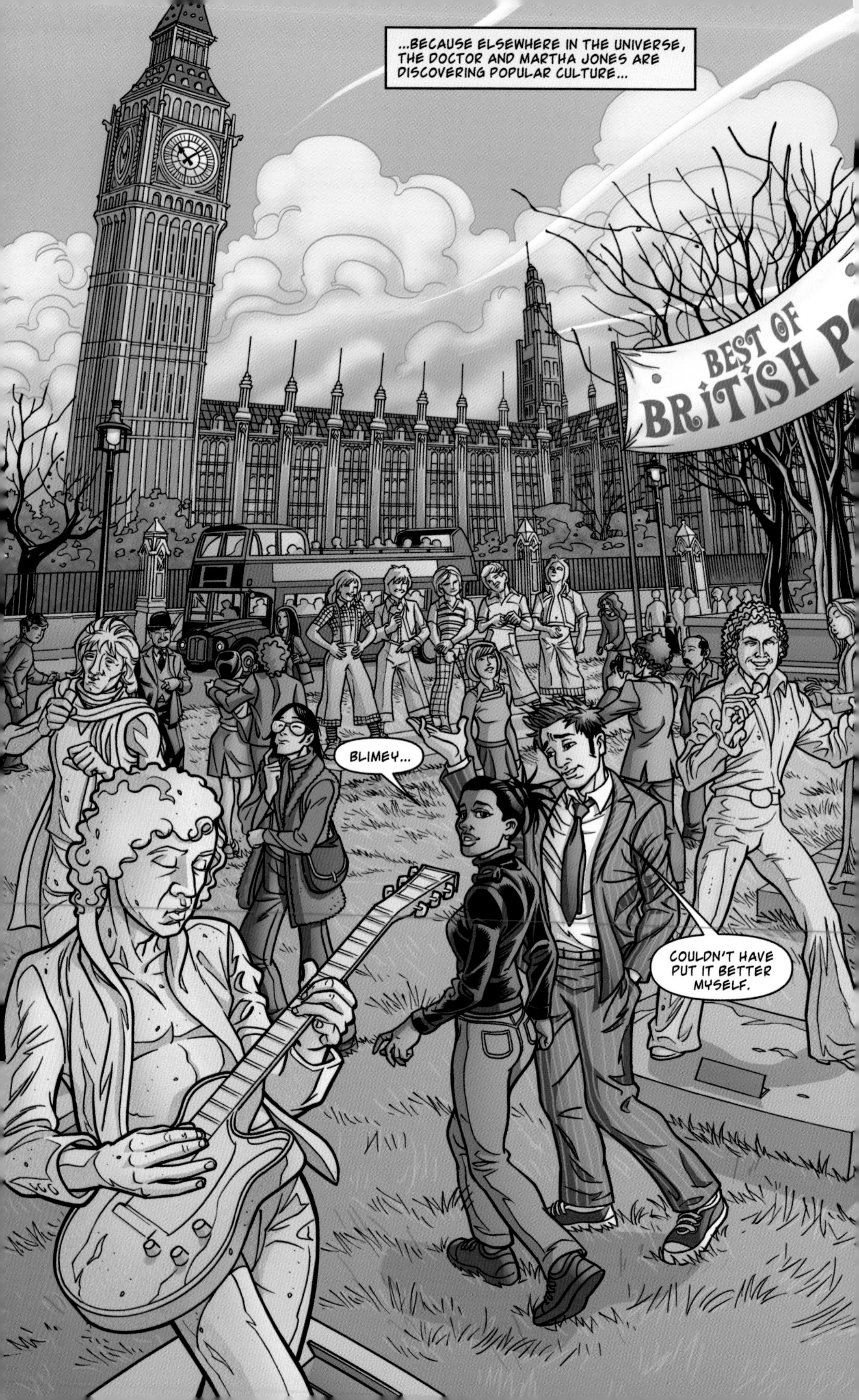
...BECAUSE ELSEWHERE IN THE UNIVERSE, THE DOCTOR AND MARTHA JONES ARE DISCOVERING POPULAR CULTURE...
BEST OF BRITISH PO
BLIMEY...
COULDN'T HAVE PUT IT BETTER MYSELF.

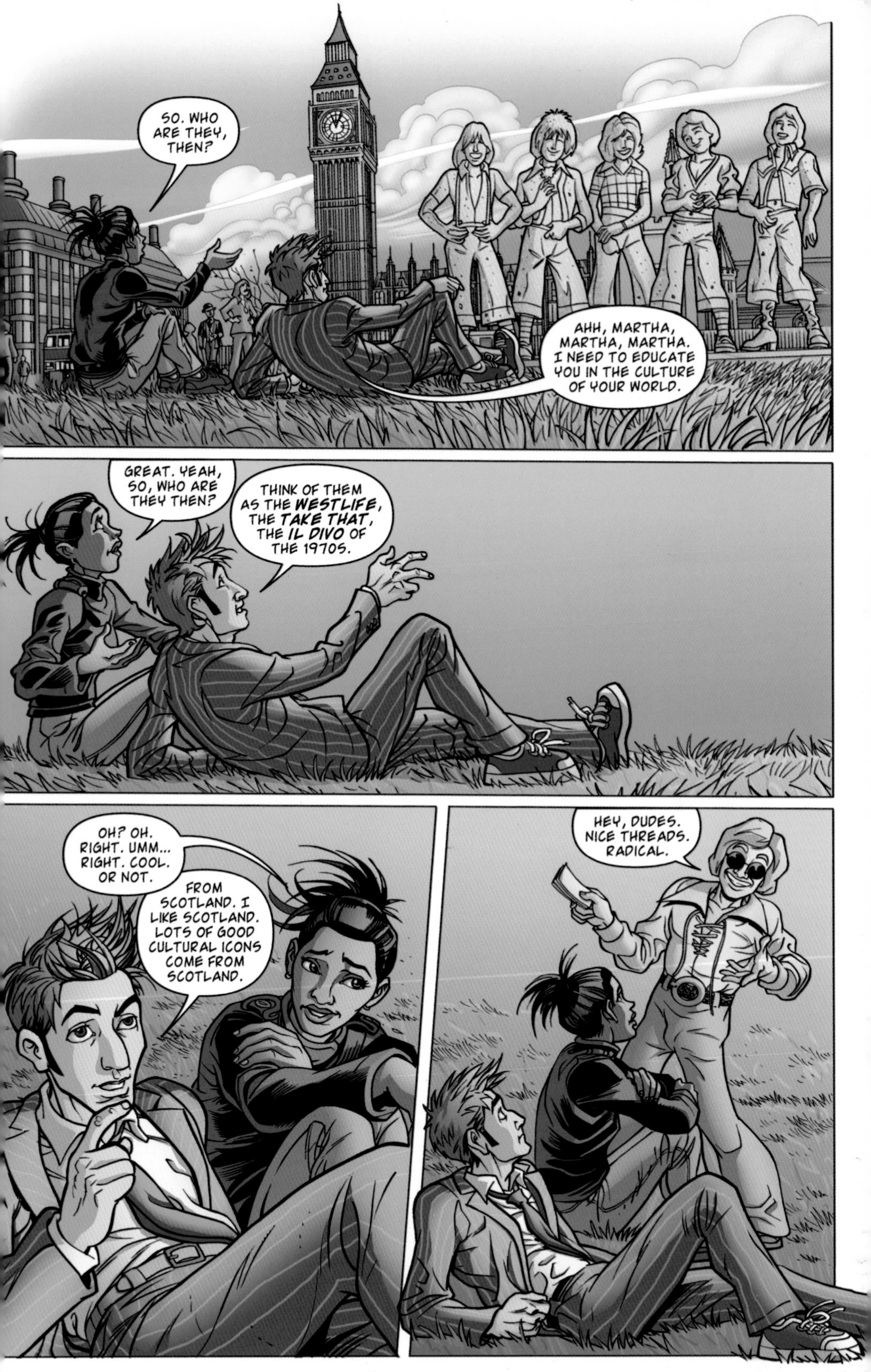
SO. WHO ARE THEY, THEN?
AHH, MARTHA, MARTHA, MARTHA. I NEED TO EDUCATE YOU IN THE CULTURE OF YOUR WORLD.
GREAT. YEAH, SO, WHO ARE THEY THEN?
THINK OF THEM AS THE WESTLIFE, THE TAKE THAT, THE IL DIVO OF THE 1970S.
FROM SCOTLAND. I LIKE SCOTLAND. LOTS OF GOOD CULTURAL ICONS COME FROM SCOTLAND.
OH? OH. RIGHT. UMM... RIGHT. COOL. OR NOT.
HEY, DUDES. NICE THREADS. RADICAL.

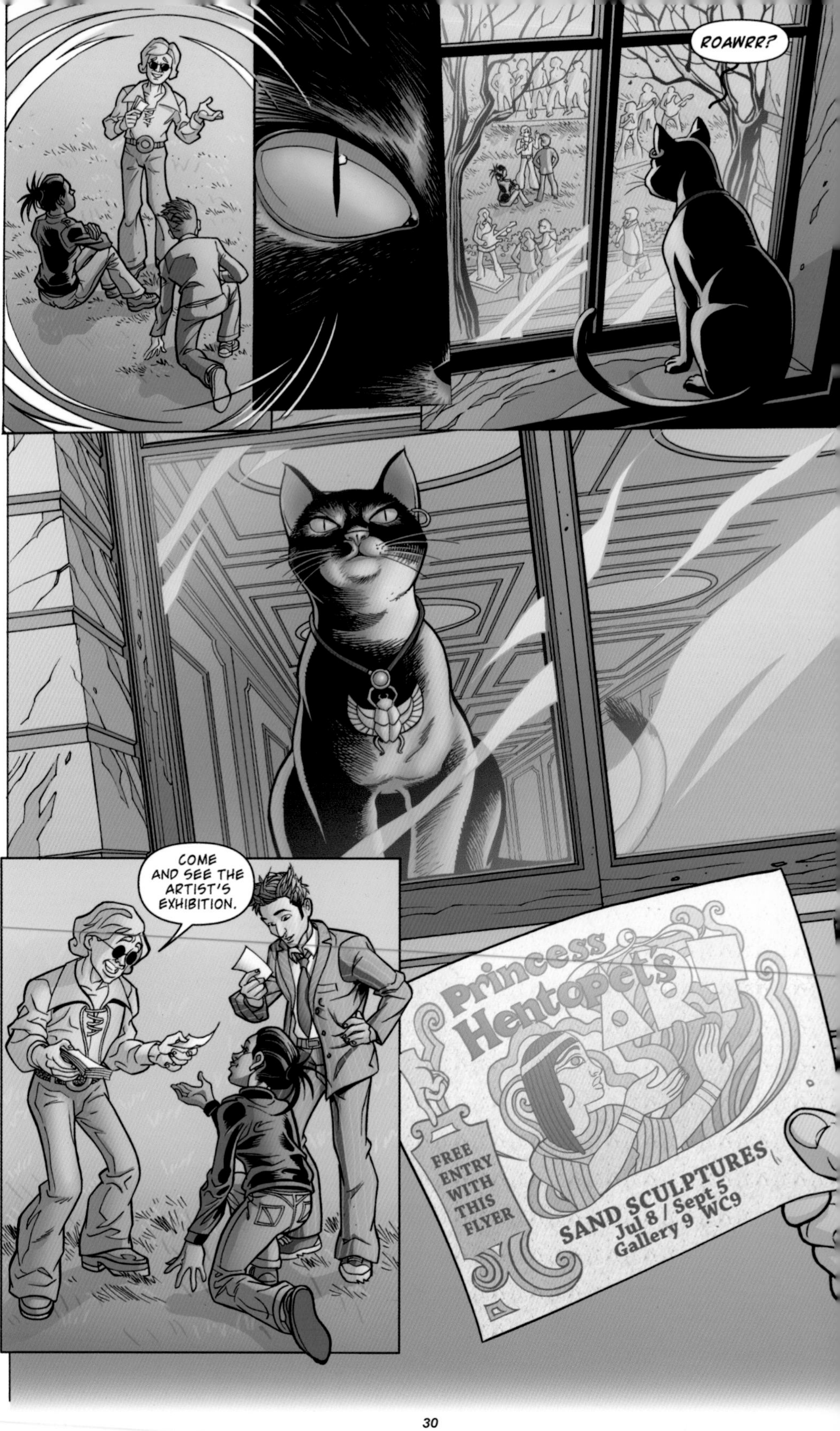
ROAWRR?
COME AND SEE THE ARTIST'S EXHIBITION.
Princess Hentopet's ART
FREE ENTRY WITH THIS FLYER
SAND SCULPTURES
Jul 8 / Sept 5
Gallery 9 WC9

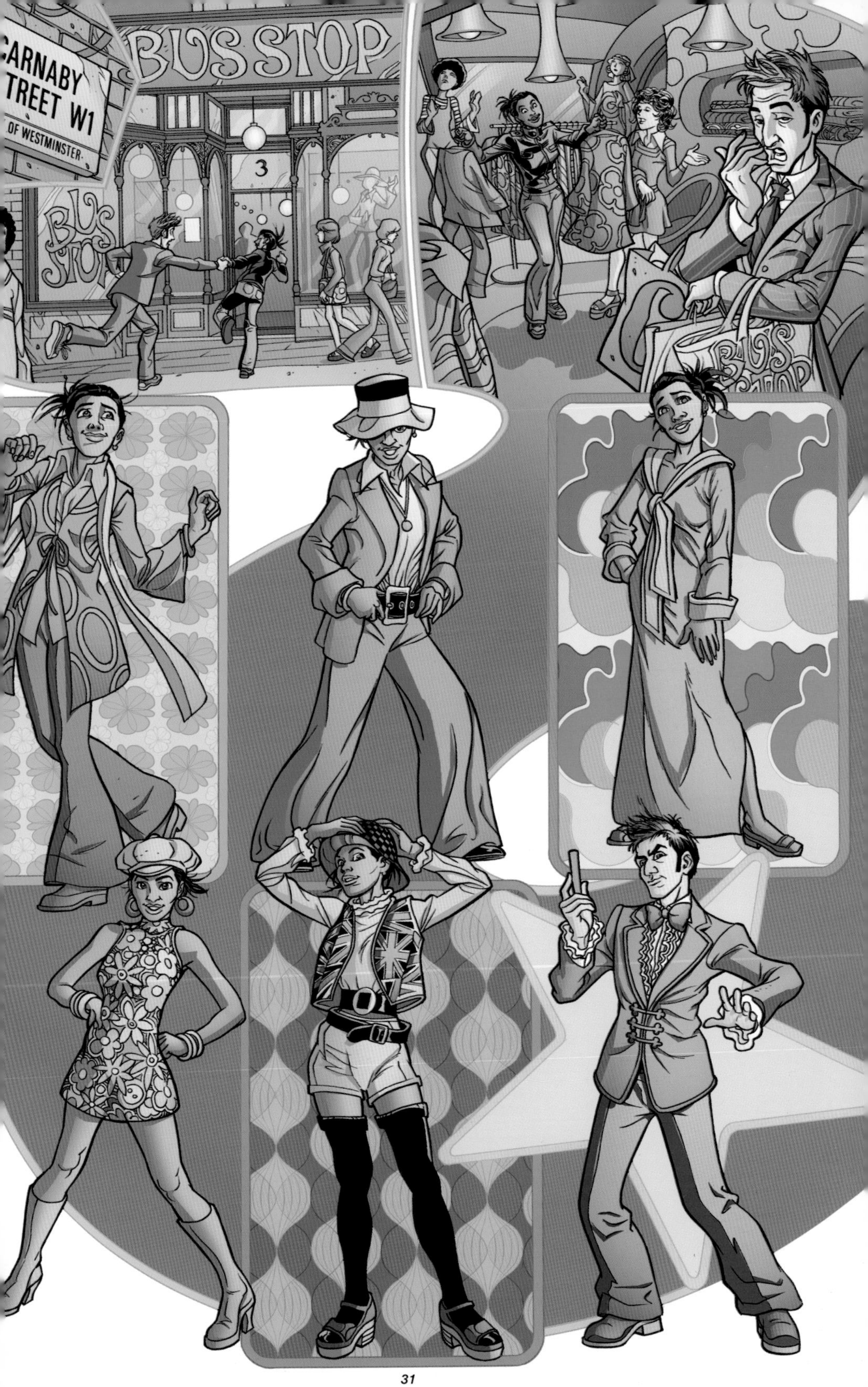

BUS STOP
CARNABY
TREET W1
OF WESTMINSTER
3
BUS STOP
BUS STOP

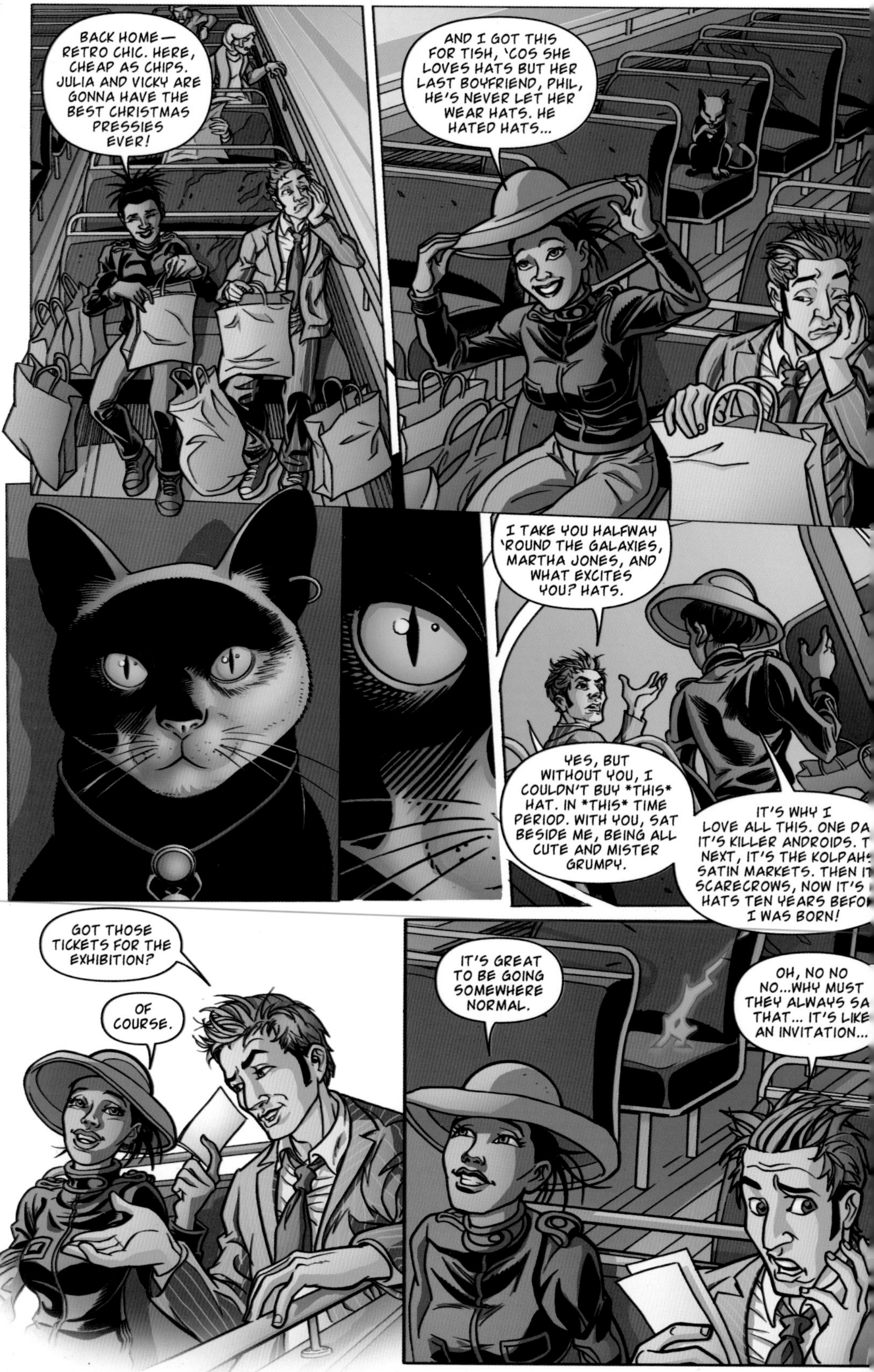
BACK HOME— RETRO CHIC. HERE, CHEAP AS CHIPS. JULIA AND VICKY ARE GONNA HAVE THE BEST CHRISTMAS PRESSIES EVER!
AND I GOT THIS FOR TISH, 'COS SHE LOVES HATS BUT HER LAST BOYFRIEND, PHIL, HE'S NEVER LET HER WEAR HATS. HE HATED HATS...
I TAKE YOU HALFWAY 'ROUND THE GALAXIES, MARTHA JONES, AND WHAT EXCITES YOU? HATS.
YES, BUT WITHOUT YOU, I COULDN'T BUY *THIS* HAT. IN *THIS* TIME PERIOD. WITH YOU, SAT BESIDE ME, BEING ALL CUTE AND MISTER GRUMPY.
IT'S WHY I LOVE ALL THIS. ONE DA IT'S KILLER ANDROIDS. T NEXT, IT'S THE KOLPAH SATIN MARKETS. THEN IT SCARECROWS, NOW IT'S HATS TEN YEARS BEFO I WAS BORN!
GOT THOSE TICKETS FOR THE EXHIBITION?
OF COURSE.
IT'S GREAT TO BE GOING SOMEWHERE NORMAL.
OH, NO NO NO...WHY MUST THEY ALWAYS SA THAT... IT'S LIKE AN INVITATION...

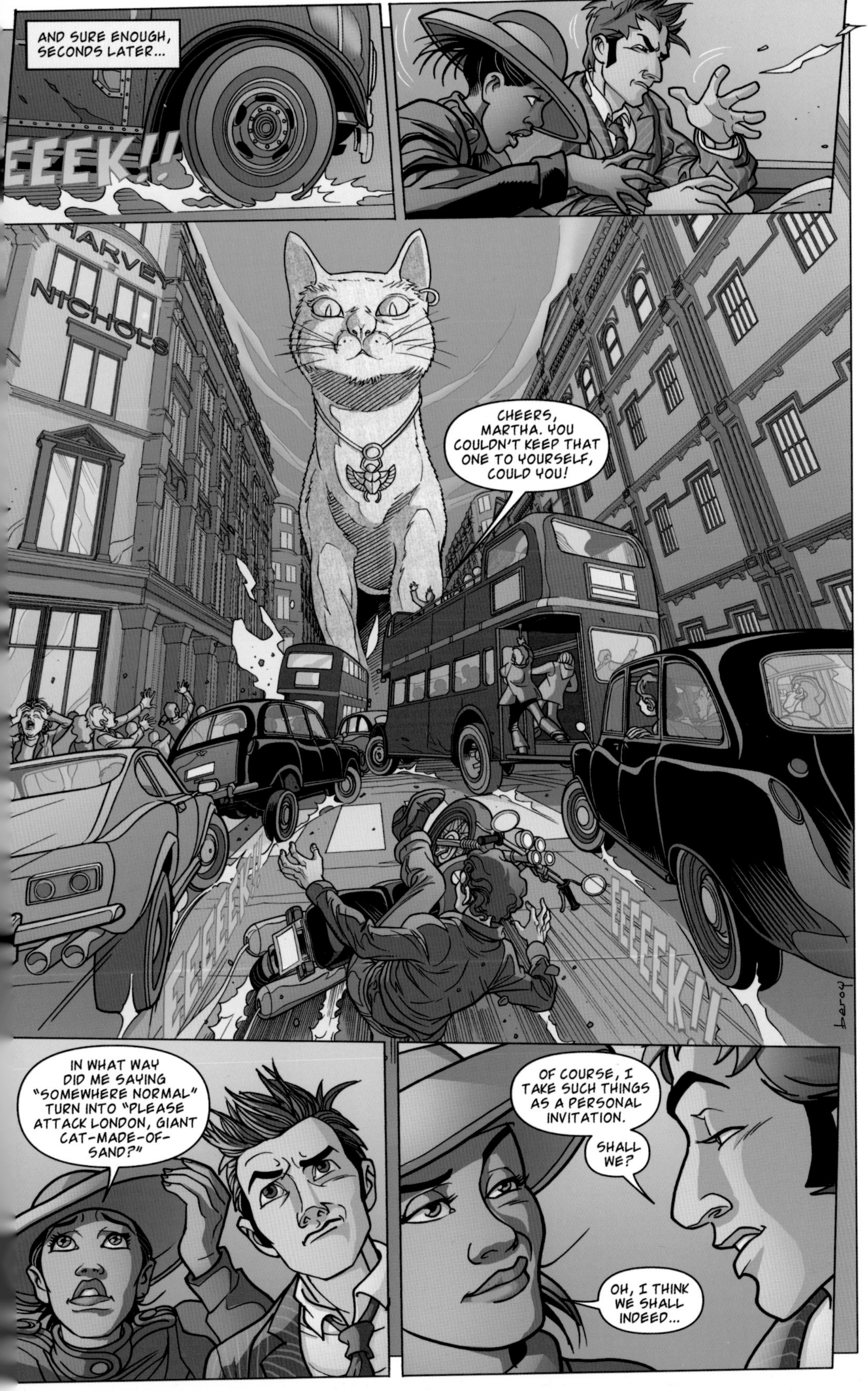
AND SURE ENOUGH, SECONDS LATER...
EEEK!!
HARVEY NICHOLS
CHEERS, MARTHA. YOU COULDN'T KEEP THAT ONE TO YOURSELF, COULD YOU!
EEEEK!!
beroy
IN WHAT WAY DID ME SAYING "SOMEWHERE NORMAL" TURN INTO "PLEASE ATTACK LONDON, GIANT CAT-MADE-OF-SAND?"
OF COURSE, I TAKE SUCH THINGS AS A PERSONAL INVITATION.
SHALL WE?
OH, I THINK WE SHALL INDEED...

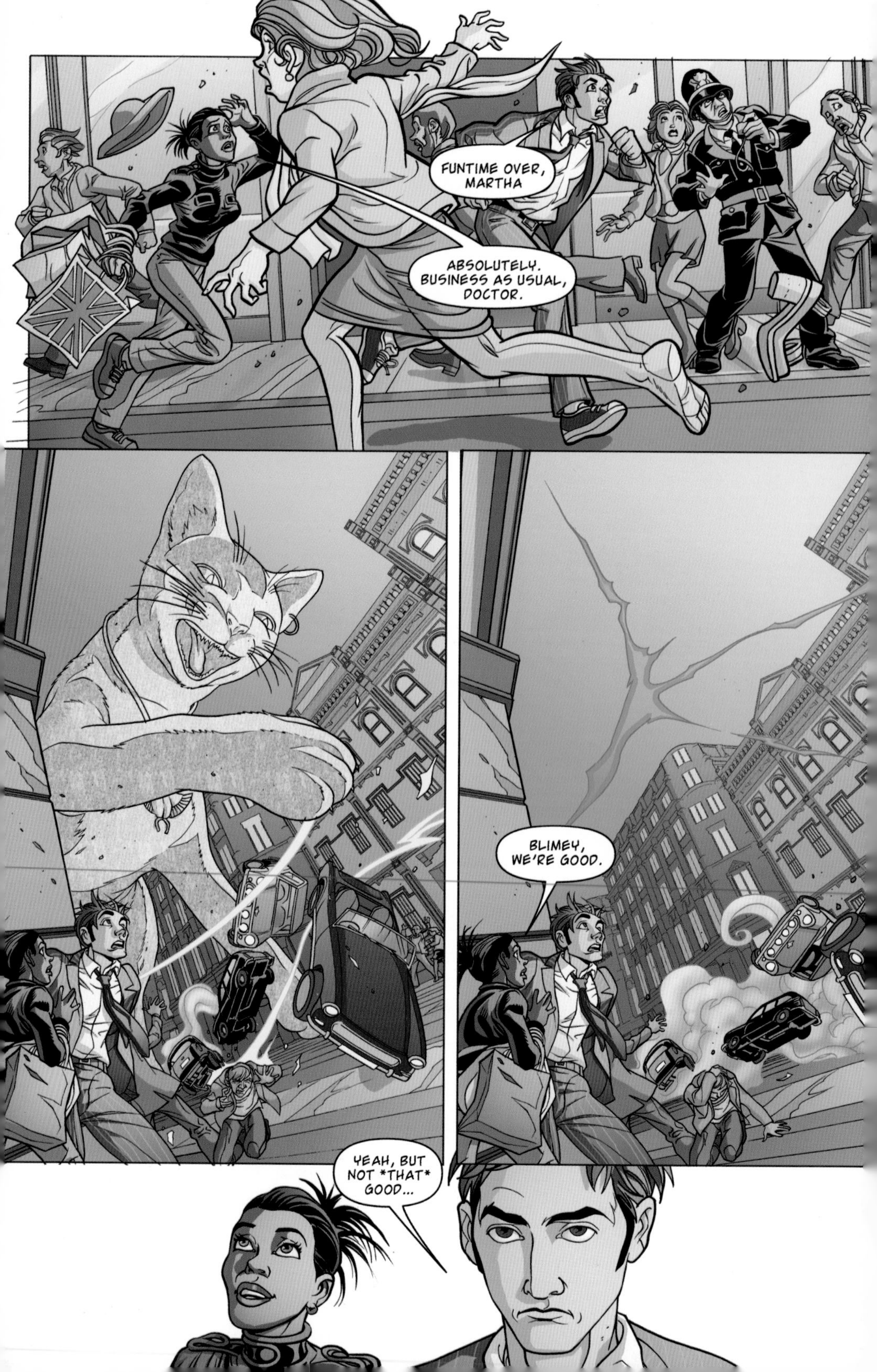
FUNTIME OVER, MARTHA
ABSOLUTELY. BUSINESS AS USUAL, DOCTOR.
BLIMEY, WE'RE GOOD.
YEAH, BUT NOT *THAT* GOOD...

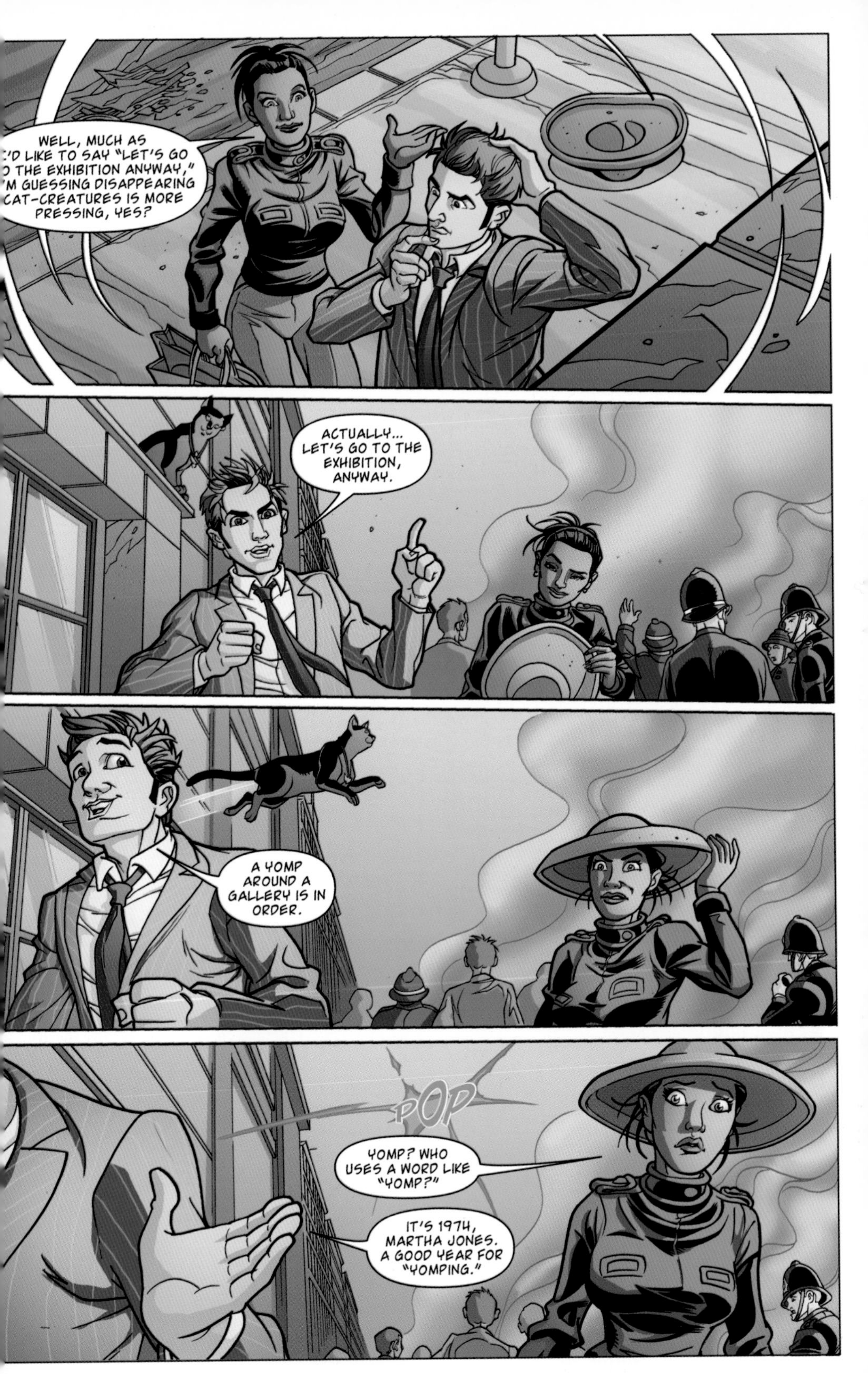
WELL, MUCH AS I'D LIKE TO SAY "LET'S GO TO THE EXHIBITION ANYWAY," I'M GUESSING DISAPPEARING CAT-CREATURES IS MORE PRESSING, YES?
ACTUALLY... LET'S GO TO THE EXHIBITION, ANYWAY.
A YOMP AROUND A GALLERY IS IN ORDER.
POP
YOMP? WHO USES A WORD LIKE "YOMP?"
IT'S 1974, MARTHA JONES. A GOOD YEAR FOR "YOMPING."

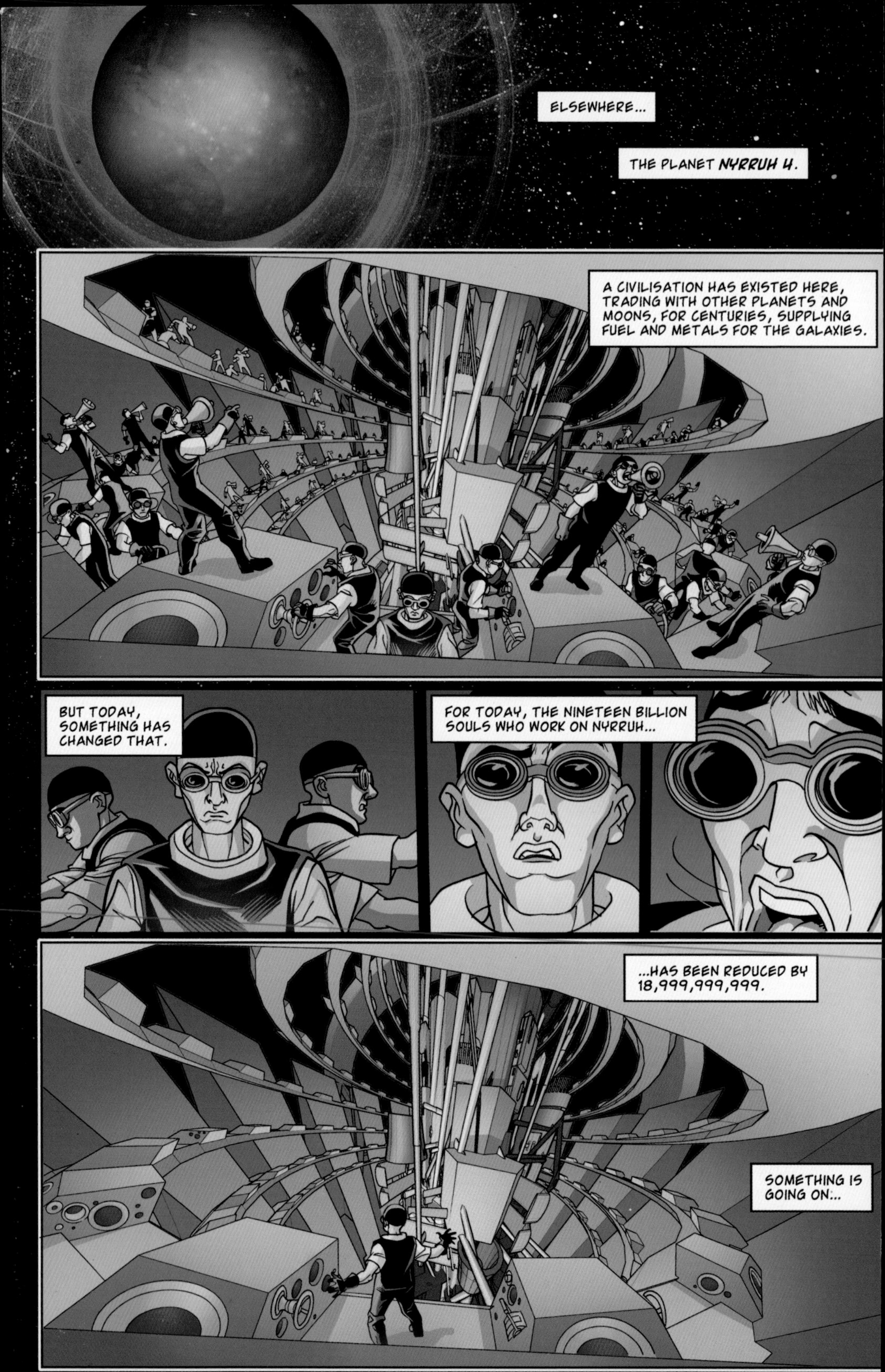
ELSEWHERE...
THE PLANET NYRRUH 4.
A CIVILISATION HAS EXISTED HERE, TRADING WITH OTHER PLANETS AND MOONS, FOR CENTURIES, SUPPLYING FUEL AND METALS FOR THE GALAXIES.
BUT TODAY, SOMETHING HAS CHANGED THAT.
FOR TODAY, THE NINETEEN BILLION SOULS WHO WORK ON NYRRUH...
...HAS BEEN REDUCED BY 18,999,999,999.
SOMETHING IS GOING ON:..

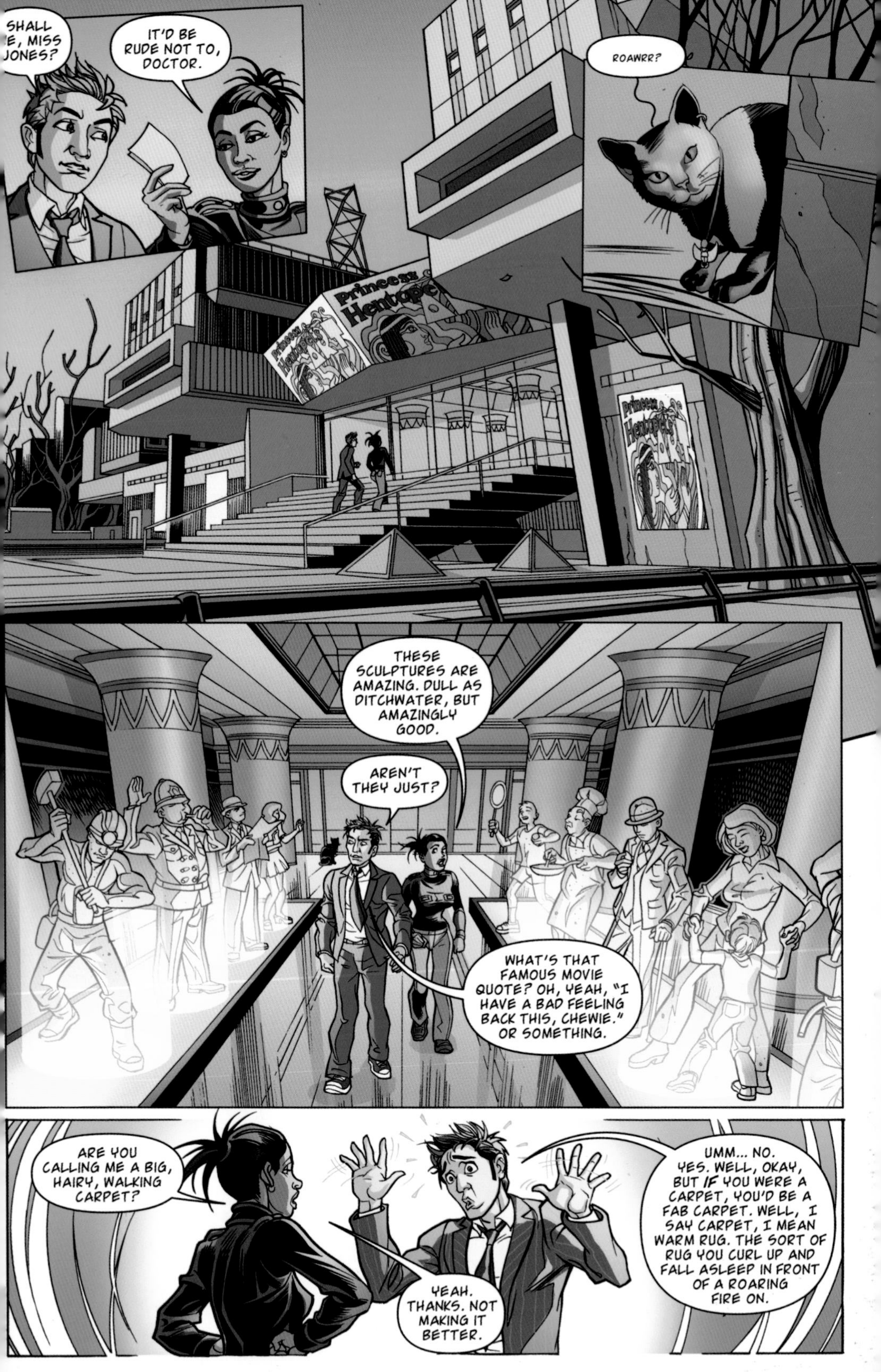
SHALL E, MISS JONES?
IT'D BE RUDE NOT TO, DOCTOR.
ROAWRR?
THESE SCULPTURES ARE AMAZING. DULL AS DITCHWATER, BUT AMAZINGLY GOOD.
AREN'T THEY JUST?
WHAT'S THAT FAMOUS MOVIE QUOTE? OH, YEAH, "I HAVE A BAD FEELING BACK THIS, CHEWIE." OR SOMETHING.
ARE YOU CALLING ME A BIG, HAIRY, WALKING CARPET?
UMM... NO. YES. WELL, OKAY, BUT IF YOU WERE A CARPET, YOU'D BE A FAB CARPET. WELL, I SAY CARPET, I MEAN WARM RUG. THE SORT OF RUG YOU CURL UP AND FALL ASLEEP IN FRONT OF A ROARING FIRE ON.
YEAH. THANKS. NOT MAKING IT BETTER.

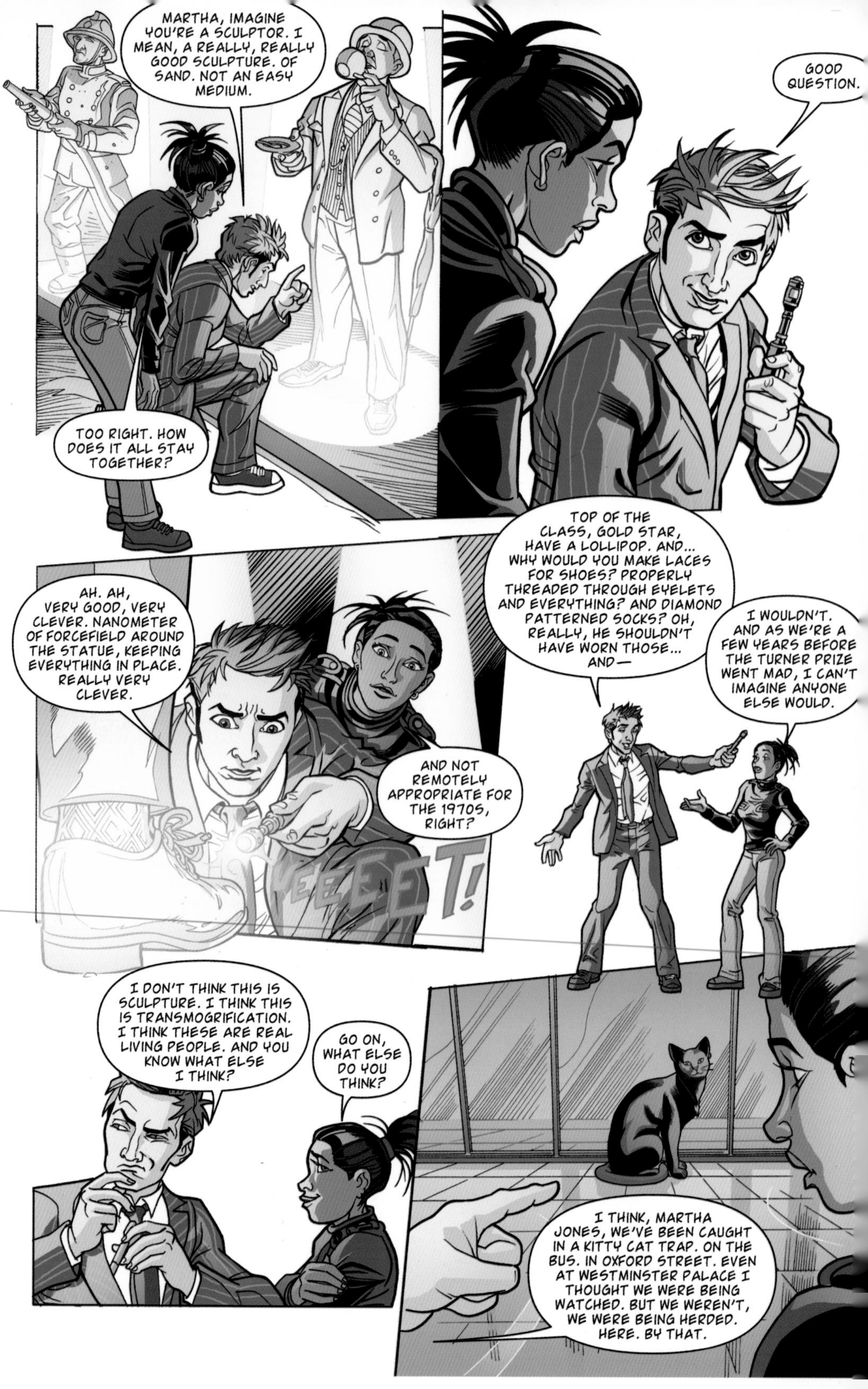
MARTHA, IMAGINE YOU'RE A SCULPTOR. I MEAN, A REALLY, REALLY GOOD SCULPTURE. OF SAND. NOT AN EASY MEDIUM.
TOO RIGHT. HOW DOES IT ALL STAY TOGETHER?
GOOD QUESTION.
AH. AH, VERY GOOD, VERY CLEVER. NANOMETER OF FORCEFIELD AROUND THE STATUE, KEEPING EVERYTHING IN PLACE. REALLY VERY CLEVER.
AND NOT REMOTELY APPROPRIATE FOR THE 1970S, RIGHT?
VEEEET!
TOP OF THE CLASS, GOLD STAR, HAVE A LOLLIPOP. AND... WHY WOULD YOU MAKE LACES FOR SHOES? PROPERLY THREADED THROUGH EYELETS AND EVERYTHING? AND DIAMOND PATTERNED SOCKS? OH, REALLY, HE SHOULDN'T HAVE WORN THOSE... AND—
I WOULDN'T. AND AS WE'RE A FEW YEARS BEFORE THE TURNER PRIZE WENT MAD, I CAN'T IMAGINE ANYONE ELSE WOULD.
I DON'T THINK THIS IS SCULPTURE. I THINK THIS IS TRANSMOGRIFICATION. I THINK THESE ARE REAL LIVING PEOPLE. AND YOU KNOW WHAT ELSE I THINK?
GO ON, WHAT ELSE DO YOU THINK?
I THINK, MARTHA JONES, WE'VE BEEN CAUGHT IN A KITTY CAT TRAP. ON THE BUS. IN OXFORD STREET. EVEN AT WESTMINSTER PALACE I THOUGHT WE WERE BEING WATCHED. BUT WE WEREN'T, WE WERE BEING HERDED. HERE. BY THAT.

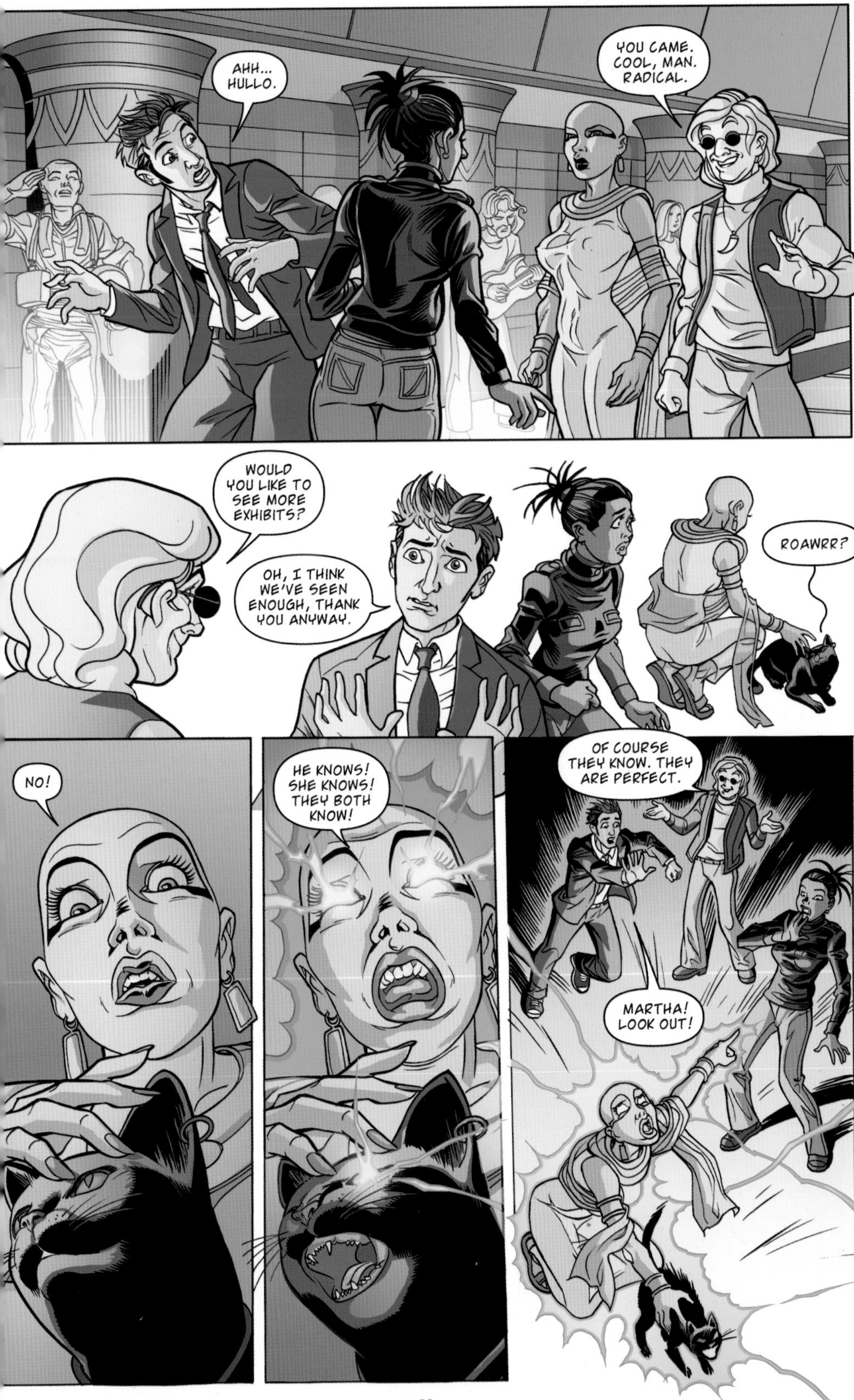
AHH... HULLO.
YOU CAME. COOL, MAN. RADICAL.
WOULD YOU LIKE TO SEE MORE EXHIBITS?
OH, I THINK WE'VE SEEN ENOUGH, THANK YOU ANYWAY.
ROAWRR?
NO!
HE KNOWS! SHE KNOWS! THEY BOTH KNOW!
OF COURSE THEY KNOW. THEY ARE PERFECT.
MARTHA! LOOK OUT!

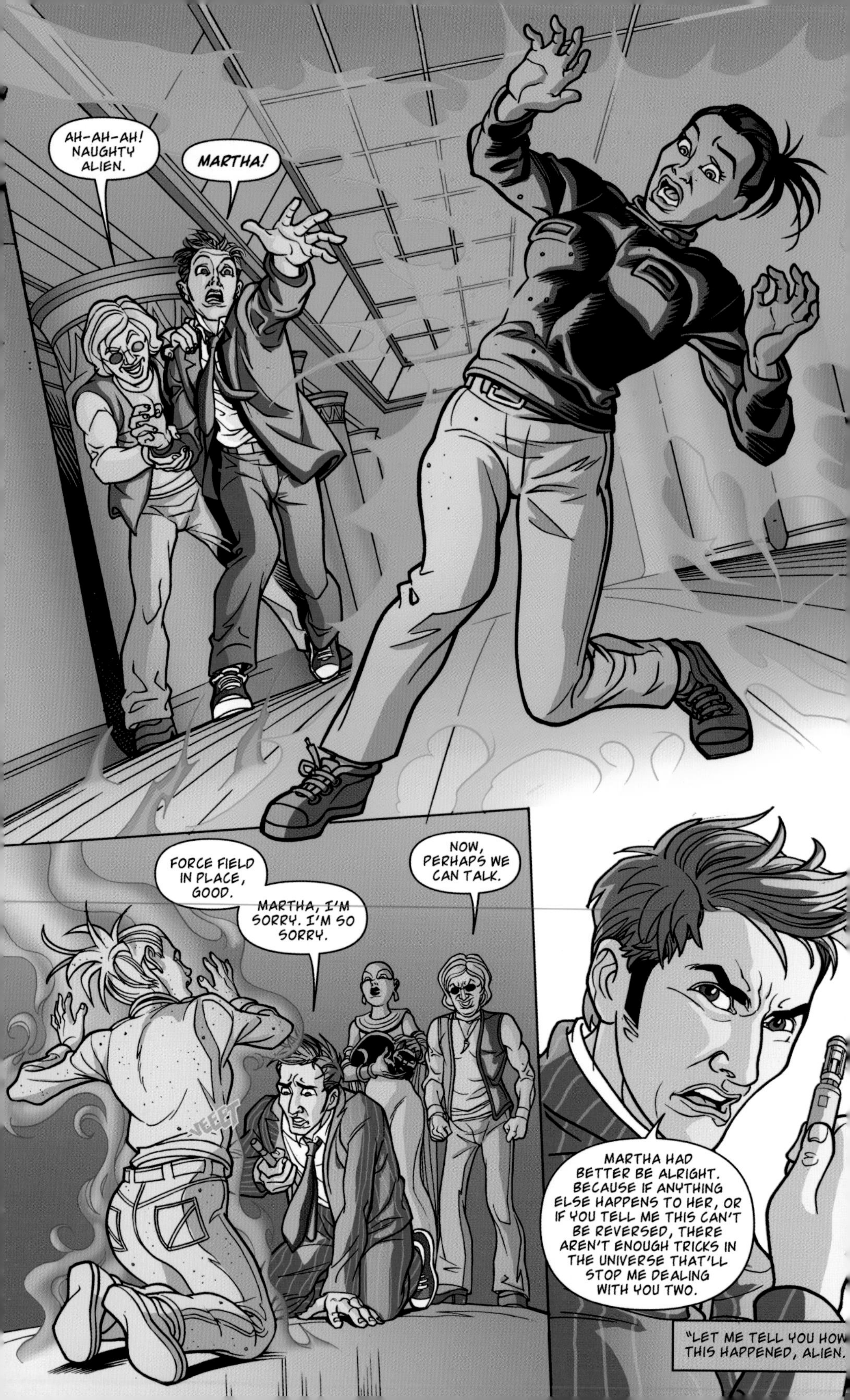
AH-AH-AH! NAUGHTY ALIEN.
MARTHA!
FORCE FIELD IN PLACE, GOOD.
MARTHA, I'M SORRY. I'M SO SORRY.
NOW, PERHAPS WE CAN TALK.
VEEET
MARTHA HAD BETTER BE ALRIGHT. BECAUSE IF ANYTHING ELSE HAPPENS TO HER, OR IF YOU TELL ME THIS CAN'T BE REVERSED, THERE AREN'T ENOUGH TRICKS IN THE UNIVERSE THAT'LL STOP ME DEALING WITH YOU TWO.
"LET ME TELL YOU HOW THIS HAPPENED, ALIEN.

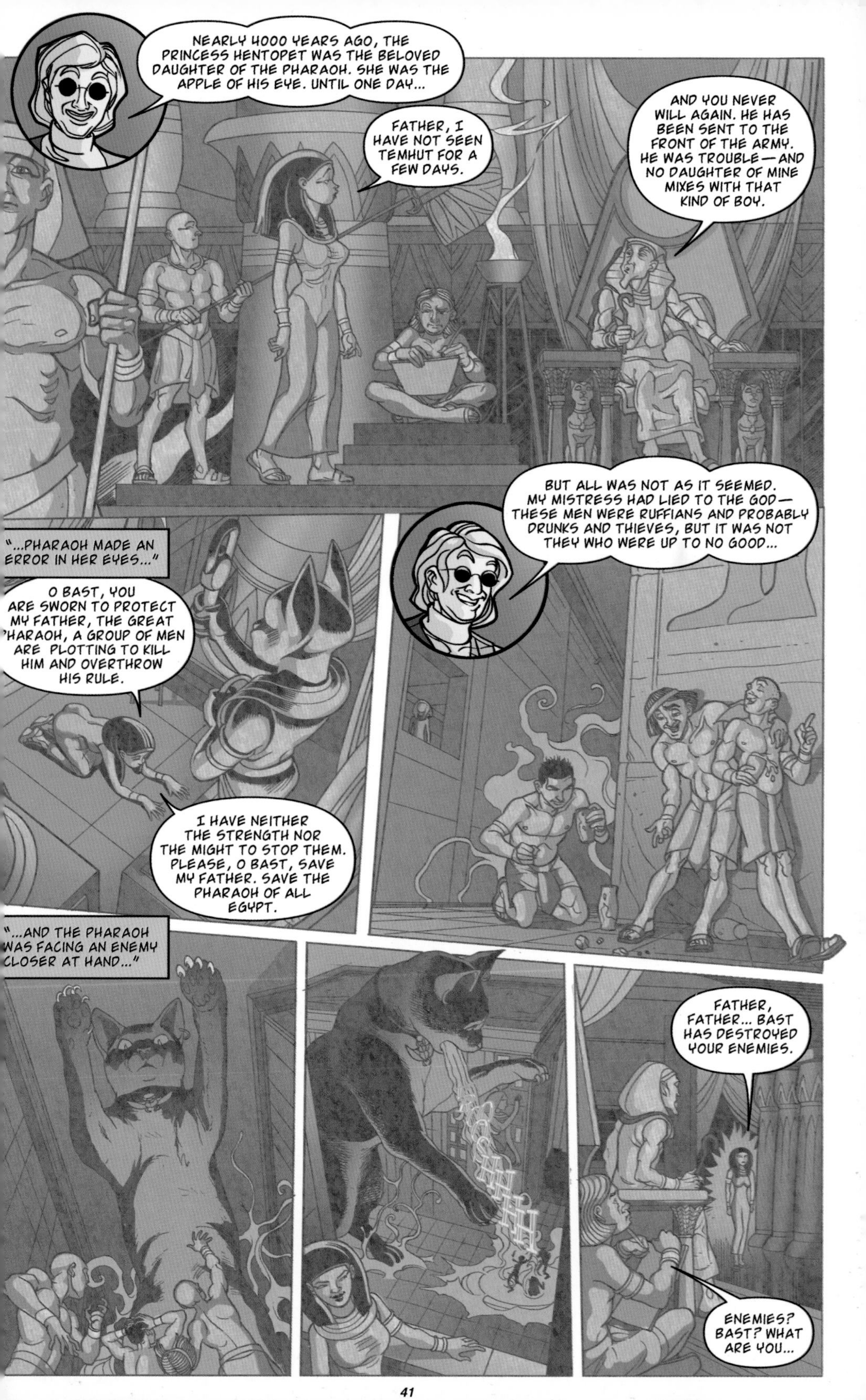
NEARLY 4000 YEARS AGO, THE PRINCESS HENTOPET WAS THE BELOVED DAUGHTER OF THE PHARAOH. SHE WAS THE APPLE OF HIS EYE. UNTIL ONE DAY...
FATHER, I HAVE NOT SEEN TEMHUT FOR A FEW DAYS.
AND YOU NEVER WILL AGAIN. HE HAS BEEN SENT TO THE FRONT OF THE ARMY. HE WAS TROUBLE—AND NO DAUGHTER OF MINE MIXES WITH THAT KIND OF BOY.
"...PHARAOH MADE AN ERROR IN HER EYES..."
O BAST, YOU ARE SWORN TO PROTECT MY FATHER, THE GREAT PHARAOH, A GROUP OF MEN ARE PLOTTING TO KILL HIM AND OVERTHROW HIS RULE.
I HAVE NEITHER THE STRENGTH NOR THE MIGHT TO STOP THEM. PLEASE, O BAST, SAVE MY FATHER. SAVE THE PHARAOH OF ALL EGYPT.
BUT ALL WAS NOT AS IT SEEMED. MY MISTRESS HAD LIED TO THE GOD—THESE MEN WERE RUFFIANS AND PROBABLY DRUNKS AND THIEVES, BUT IT WAS NOT THEY WHO WERE UP TO NO GOOD...
"...AND THE PHARAOH WAS FACING AN ENEMY CLOSER AT HAND..."
FATHER, FATHER... BAST HAS DESTROYED YOUR ENEMIES.
ENEMIES? BAST? WHAT ARE YOU...

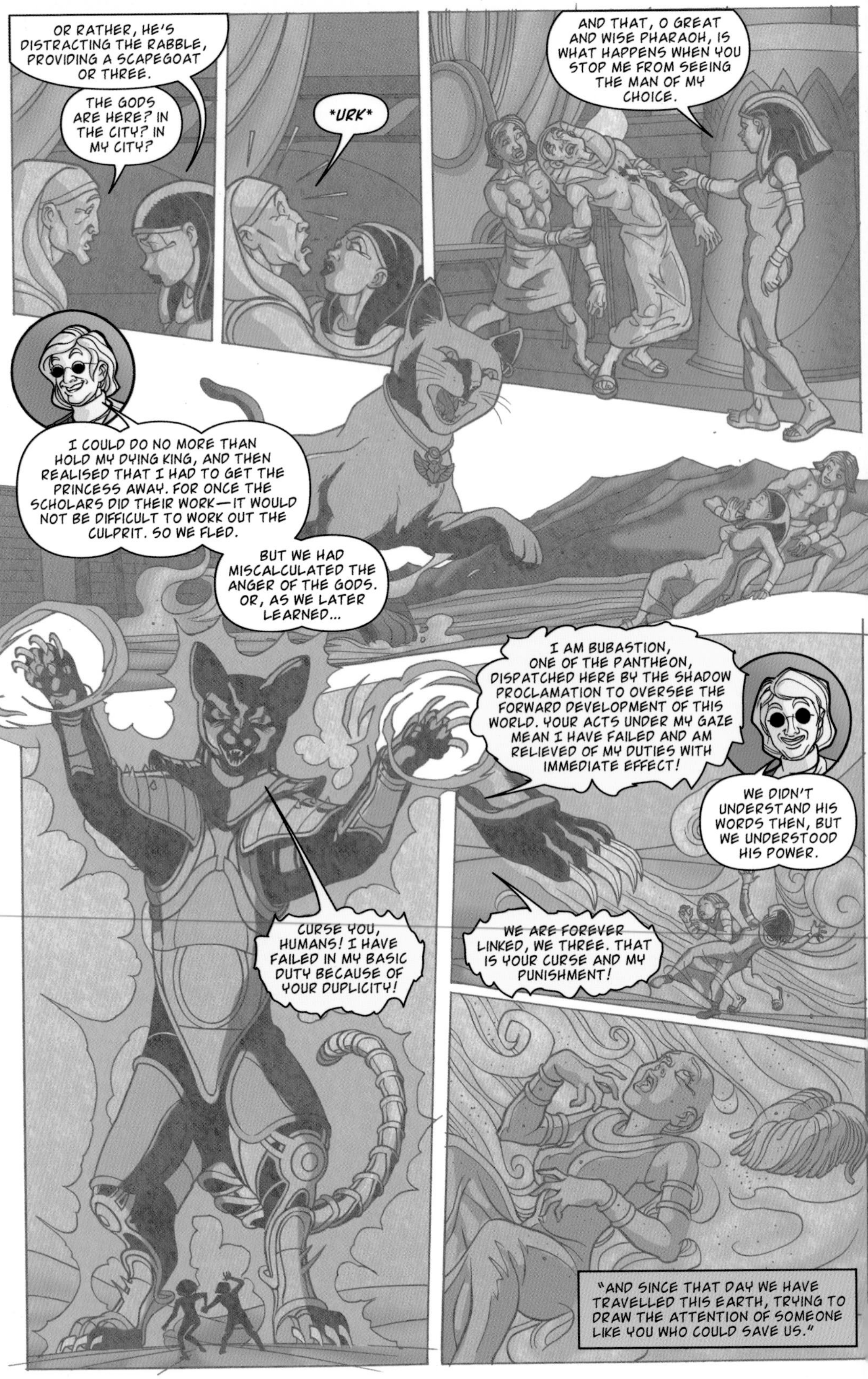
OR RATHER, HE'S DISTRACTING THE RABBLE, PROVIDING A SCAPEGOAT OR THREE.
THE GODS ARE HERE? IN THE CITY? IN MY CITY?
URK
AND THAT, O GREAT AND WISE PHARAOH, IS WHAT HAPPENS WHEN YOU STOP ME FROM SEEING THE MAN OF MY CHOICE.
I COULD DO NO MORE THAN HOLD MY DYING KING, AND THEN REALISED THAT I HAD TO GET THE PRINCESS AWAY. FOR ONCE THE SCHOLARS DID THEIR WORK—IT WOULD NOT BE DIFFICULT TO WORK OUT THE CULPRIT. SO WE FLED.
BUT WE HAD MISCALCULATED THE ANGER OF THE GODS. OR, AS WE LATER LEARNED...
I AM BUBASTION, ONE OF THE PANTHEON, DISPATCHED HERE BY THE SHADOW PROCLAMATION TO OVERSEE THE FORWARD DEVELOPMENT OF THIS WORLD. YOUR ACTS UNDER MY GAZE MEAN I HAVE FAILED AND AM RELIEVED OF MY DUTIES WITH IMMEDIATE EFFECT!
WE DIDN'T UNDERSTAND HIS WORDS THEN, BUT WE UNDERSTOOD HIS POWER.
CURSE YOU, HUMANS! I HAVE FAILED IN MY BASIC DUTY BECAUSE OF YOUR DUPLICITY!
WE ARE FOREVER LINKED, WE THREE. THAT IS YOUR CURSE AND MY PUNISHMENT!
"AND SINCE THAT DAY WE HAVE TRAVELLED THIS EARTH, TRYING TO DRAW THE ATTENTION OF SOMEONE LIKE YOU WHO COULD SAVE US."

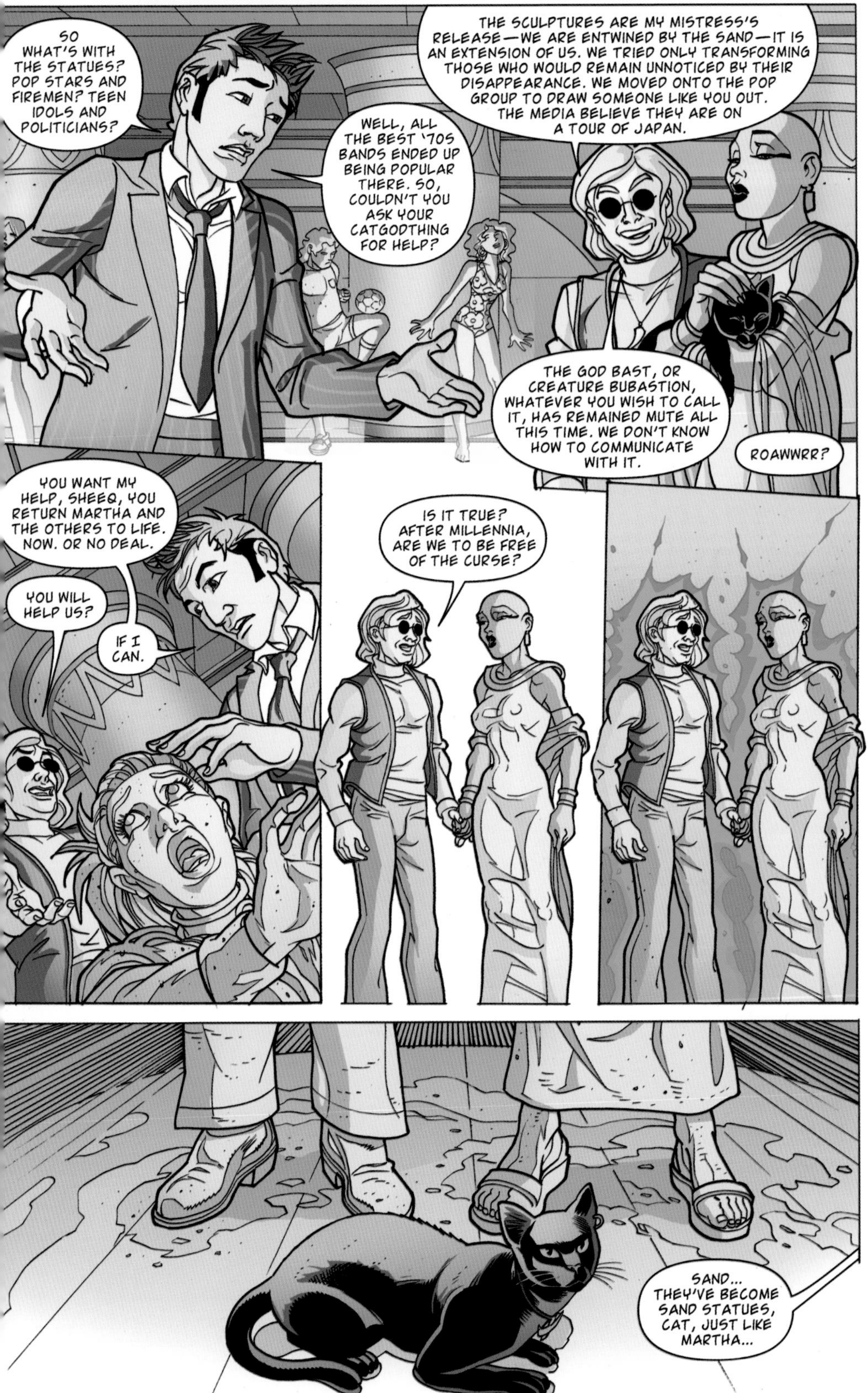

SO WHAT'S WITH THE STATUES? POP STARS AND FIREMEN? TEEN IDOLS AND POLITICIANS?
THE SCULPTURES ARE MY MISTRESS'S RELEASE—WE ARE ENTWINED BY THE SAND—IT IS AN EXTENSION OF US. WE TRIED ONLY TRANSFORMING THOSE WHO WOULD REMAIN UNNOTICED BY THEIR DISAPPEARANCE. WE MOVED ONTO THE POP GROUP TO DRAW SOMEONE LIKE YOU OUT. THE MEDIA BELIEVE THEY ARE ON A TOUR OF JAPAN.
WELL, ALL THE BEST '70S BANDS ENDED UP BEING POPULAR THERE. SO, COULDN'T YOU ASK YOUR CATGODTHING FOR HELP?
THE GOD BAST, OR CREATURE BUBASTION, WHATEVER YOU WISH TO CALL IT, HAS REMAINED MUTE ALL THIS TIME. WE DON'T KNOW HOW TO COMMUNICATE WITH IT.
ROAWWRR?
YOU WANT MY HELP, SHEEQ, YOU RETURN MARTHA AND THE OTHERS TO LIFE. NOW. OR NO DEAL.
YOU WILL HELP US?
IF I CAN.
IS IT TRUE? AFTER MILLENNIA, ARE WE TO BE FREE OF THE CURSE?
SAND... THEY'VE BECOME SAND STATUES, CAT, JUST LIKE MARTHA...

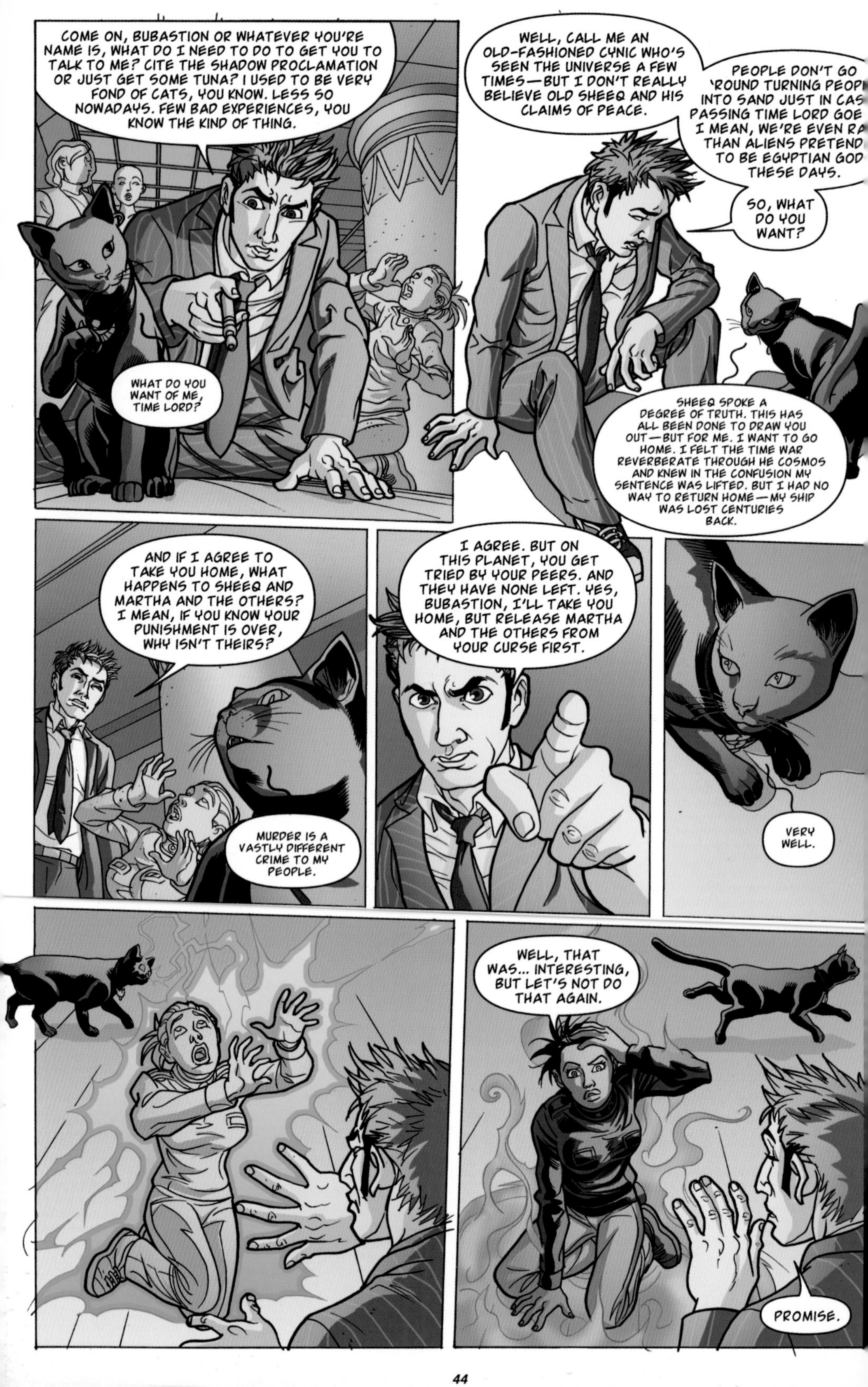

COME ON, BUBASTION OR WHATEVER YOU'RE NAME IS, WHAT DO I NEED TO DO TO GET YOU TO TALK TO ME? CITE THE SHADOW PROCLAMATION OR JUST GET SOME TUNA? I USED TO BE VERY FOND OF CATS, YOU KNOW. LESS SO NOWADAYS. FEW BAD EXPERIENCES, YOU KNOW THE KIND OF THING.
WHAT DO YOU WANT OF ME, TIME LORD?
WELL, CALL ME AN OLD-FASHIONED CYNIC WHO'S SEEN THE UNIVERSE A FEW TIMES—BUT I DON'T REALLY BELIEVE OLD SHEEQ AND HIS CLAIMS OF PEACE.
PEOPLE DON'T GO 'ROUND TURNING PEOP INTO SAND JUST IN CAS PASSING TIME LORD GOE I MEAN, WE'RE EVEN RA THAN ALIENS PRETEND TO BE EGYPTIAN GOD THESE DAYS.
SO, WHAT DO YOU WANT?
SHEEQ SPOKE A DEGREE OF TRUTH. THIS HAS ALL BEEN DONE TO DRAW YOU OUT—BUT FOR ME. I WANT TO GO HOME. I FELT THE TIME WAR REVERBERATE THROUGH HE COSMOS AND KNEW IN THE CONFUSION MY SENTENCE WAS LIFTED. BUT I HAD NO WAY TO RETURN HOME—MY SHIP WAS LOST CENTURIES BACK.
AND IF I AGREE TO TAKE YOU HOME, WHAT HAPPENS TO SHEEQ AND MARTHA AND THE OTHERS? I MEAN, IF YOU KNOW YOUR PUNISHMENT IS OVER, WHY ISN'T THEIRS?
MURDER IS A VASTLY DIFFERENT CRIME TO MY PEOPLE.
I AGREE. BUT ON THIS PLANET, YOU GET TRIED BY YOUR PEERS. AND THEY HAVE NONE LEFT. YES, BUBASTION, I'LL TAKE YOU HOME, BUT RELEASE MARTHA AND THE OTHERS FROM YOUR CURSE FIRST.
VERY WELL.
WELL, THAT WAS... INTERESTING, BUT LET'S NOT DO THAT AGAIN.
PROMISE.

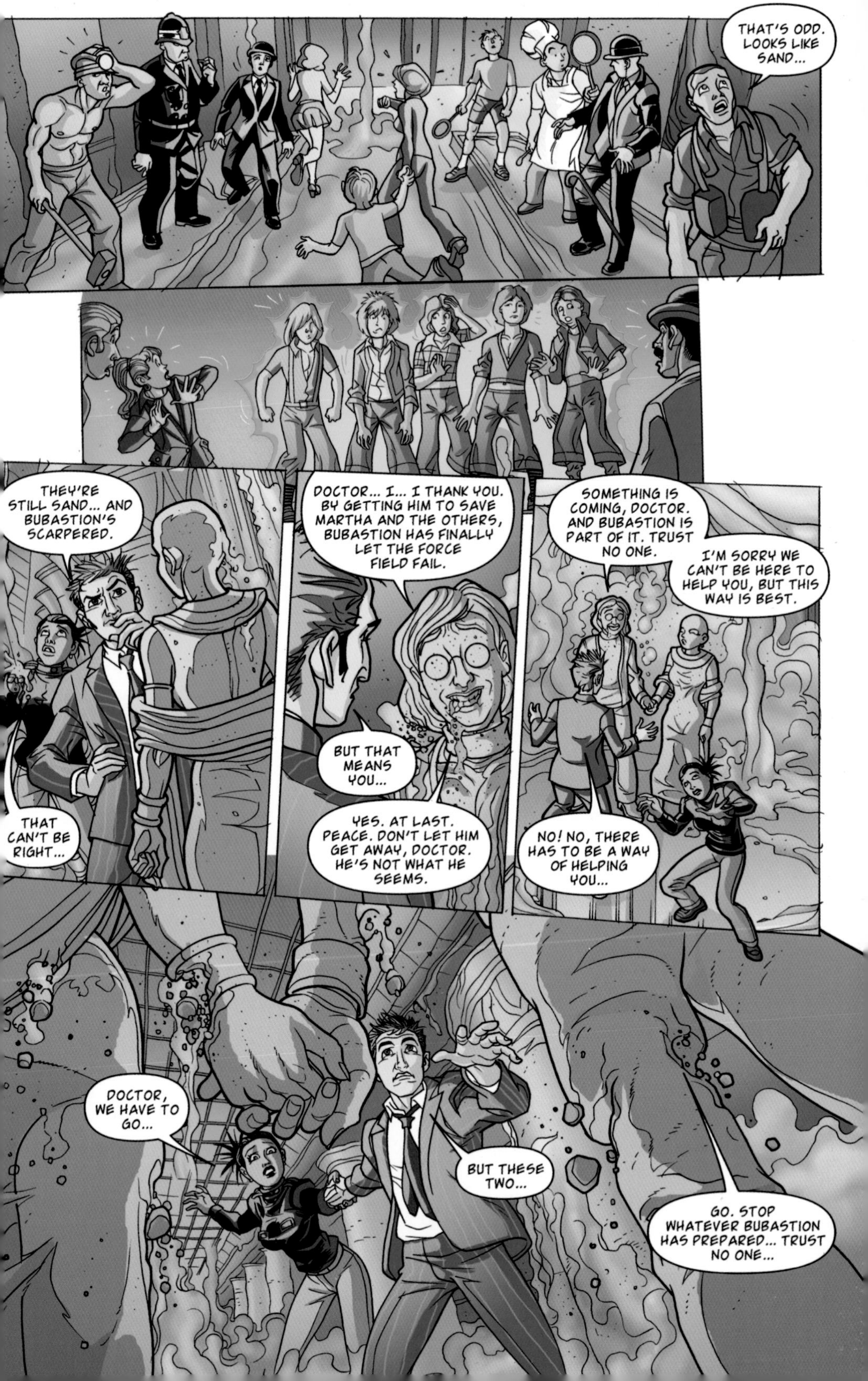
THAT'S ODD. LOOKS LIKE SAND...
THEY'RE STILL SAND... AND BUBASTION'S SCARPERED.
THAT CAN'T BE RIGHT...
DOCTOR... I... I THANK YOU. BY GETTING HIM TO SAVE MARTHA AND THE OTHERS, BUBASTION HAS FINALLY LET THE FORCE FIELD FAIL.
BUT THAT MEANS YOU...
YES. AT LAST. PEACE. DON'T LET HIM GET AWAY, DOCTOR. HE'S NOT WHAT HE SEEMS.
SOMETHING IS COMING, DOCTOR. AND BUBASTION IS PART OF IT. TRUST NO ONE.
I'M SORRY WE CAN'T BE HERE TO HELP YOU, BUT THIS WAY IS BEST.
NO! NO, THERE HAS TO BE A WAY OF HELPING YOU...
DOCTOR, WE HAVE TO GO...
BUT THESE TWO...
GO. STOP WHATEVER BUBASTION HAS PREPARED... TRUST NO ONE...

RUUUUUNNNN!

YOU THINK?

THAT CAT HAS ONE LARGE LITTER TRAY TO ITSELF—IF IT'S STILL THERE. BUT SOMEHOW I DOUBT IT.

I RECORDED THE WAVELENGTHS OF THE FORCE FIELD THAT SURROUNDED YOUR SANDY SELF. PLUG THAT INTO THE *TARDIS* AND IT SHOULD HOME IN ON ITS ORIGIN.

GREAT.

I'M SORRY, MARTHA. ARE YOU ALL RIGHT?

I'M FINE. BIT OF SAND BETWEEN MY TOES BUT MUM ALWAYS SAID I COULD LOSE A COUPLE OF INCHES. BUT CAN WE NOT DO THAT AGAIN?

"PROMISE YOU, MARTHA, WE'LL STAY WELL AWAY FROM SAND, BEACHES AND ANCIENT EGYPT FOR... OH, AT LEAST A MONTH. WELL, A WEEK. WELL, TILL THURSDAY, ANYWAY."

"THANKS, DOCTOR. REMIND ME, I TRAVEL WITH YOU BECAUSE?"

"'COS YOU LOVE IT."

"YOU KNOW, DOCTOR, I THINK YOU'RE RIGHT. I DO."

"SO, HAS THE SONIC SCREWDRIVER TOLD YOU WHERE WE'RE OFF TO?"

BUBASTION REPORTING IN. I'M COMING HOME.

"YEAH. YOU NOT GONNA IT, MARTHA SORRY."

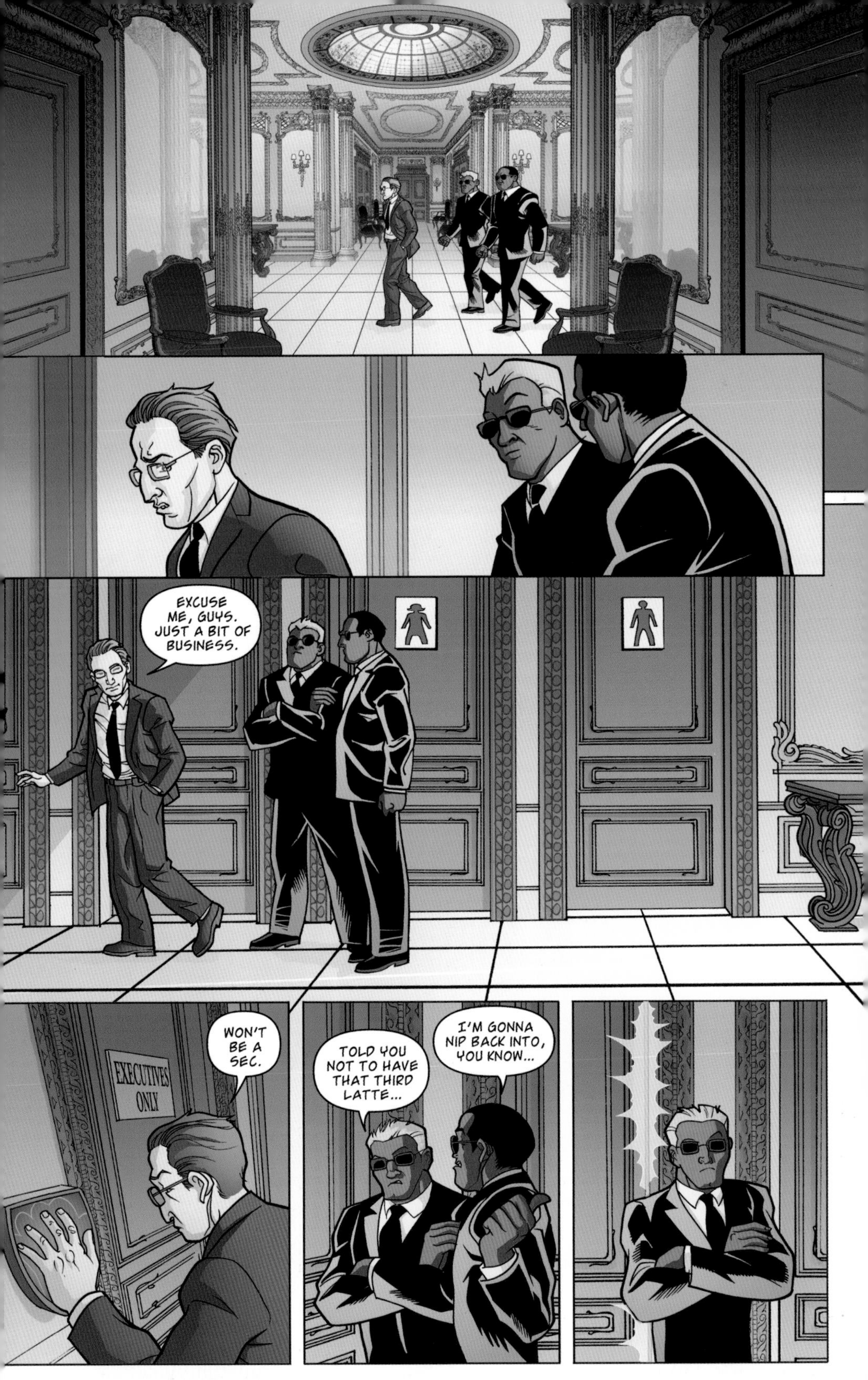
EXCUSE ME, GUYS. JUST A BIT OF BUSINESS.
EXECUTIVES ONLY
WON'T BE A SEC.
TOLD YOU NOT TO HAVE THAT THIRD LATTE...
I'M GONNA NIP BACK INTO, YOU KNOW...

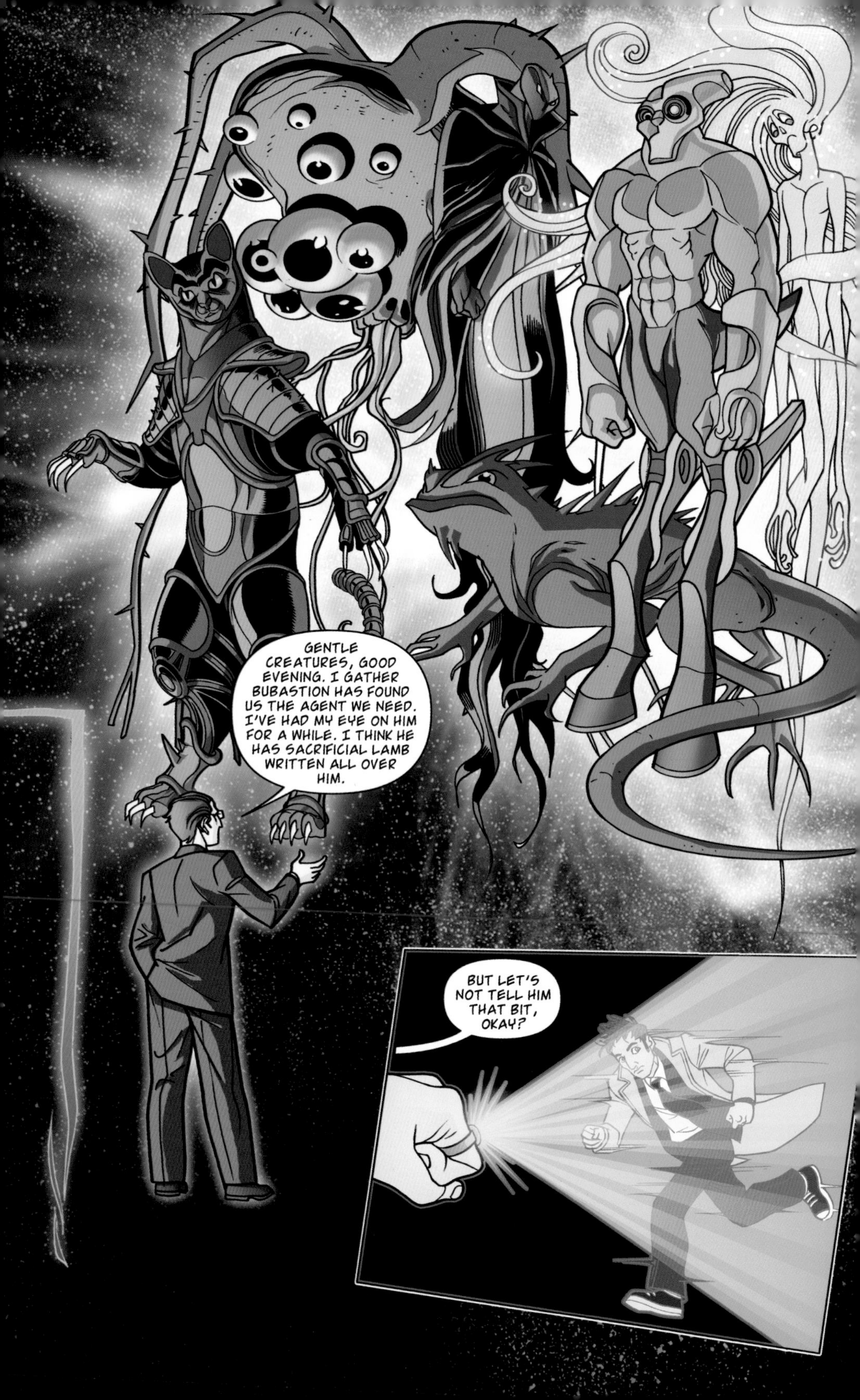
GENTLE CREATURES, GOOD EVENING. I GATHER BUBASTION HAS FOUND US THE AGENT WE NEED. I'VE HAD MY EYE ON HIM FOR A WHILE. I THINK HE HAS SACRIFICIAL LAMB WRITTEN ALL OVER HIM.
BUT LET'S NOT TELL HIM THAT BIT, OKAY?

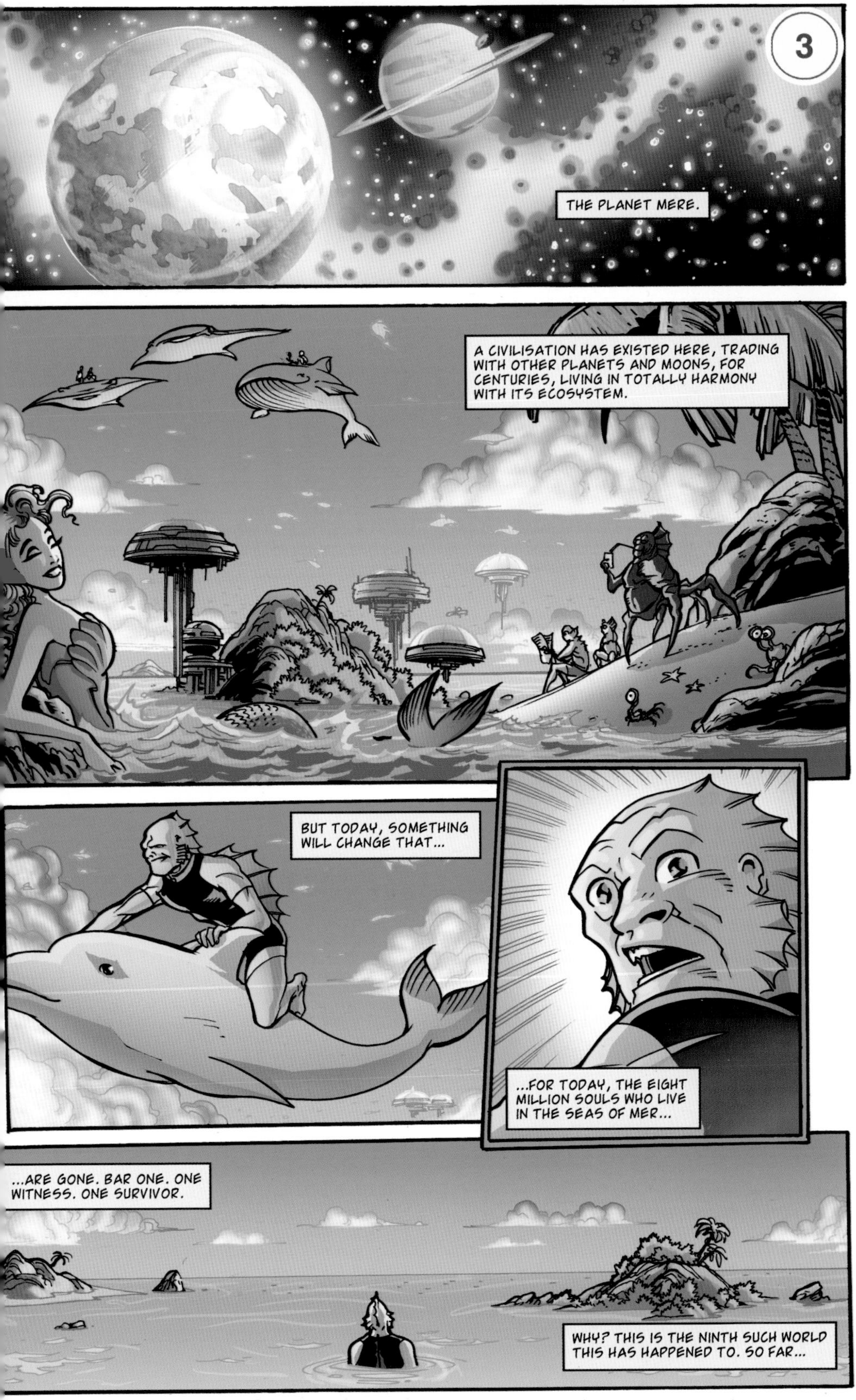
3
THE PLANET MERE.
A CIVILISATION HAS EXISTED HERE, TRADING WITH OTHER PLANETS AND MOONS, FOR CENTURIES, LIVING IN TOTALLY HARMONY WITH ITS ECOSYSTEM.
BUT TODAY, SOMETHING WILL CHANGE THAT...
...FOR TODAY, THE EIGHT MILLION SOULS WHO LIVE IN THE SEAS OF MER...
...ARE GONE. BAR ONE. ONE WITNESS. ONE SURVIVOR.
WHY? THIS IS THE NINTH SUCH WORLD THIS HAS HAPPENED TO. SO FAR...

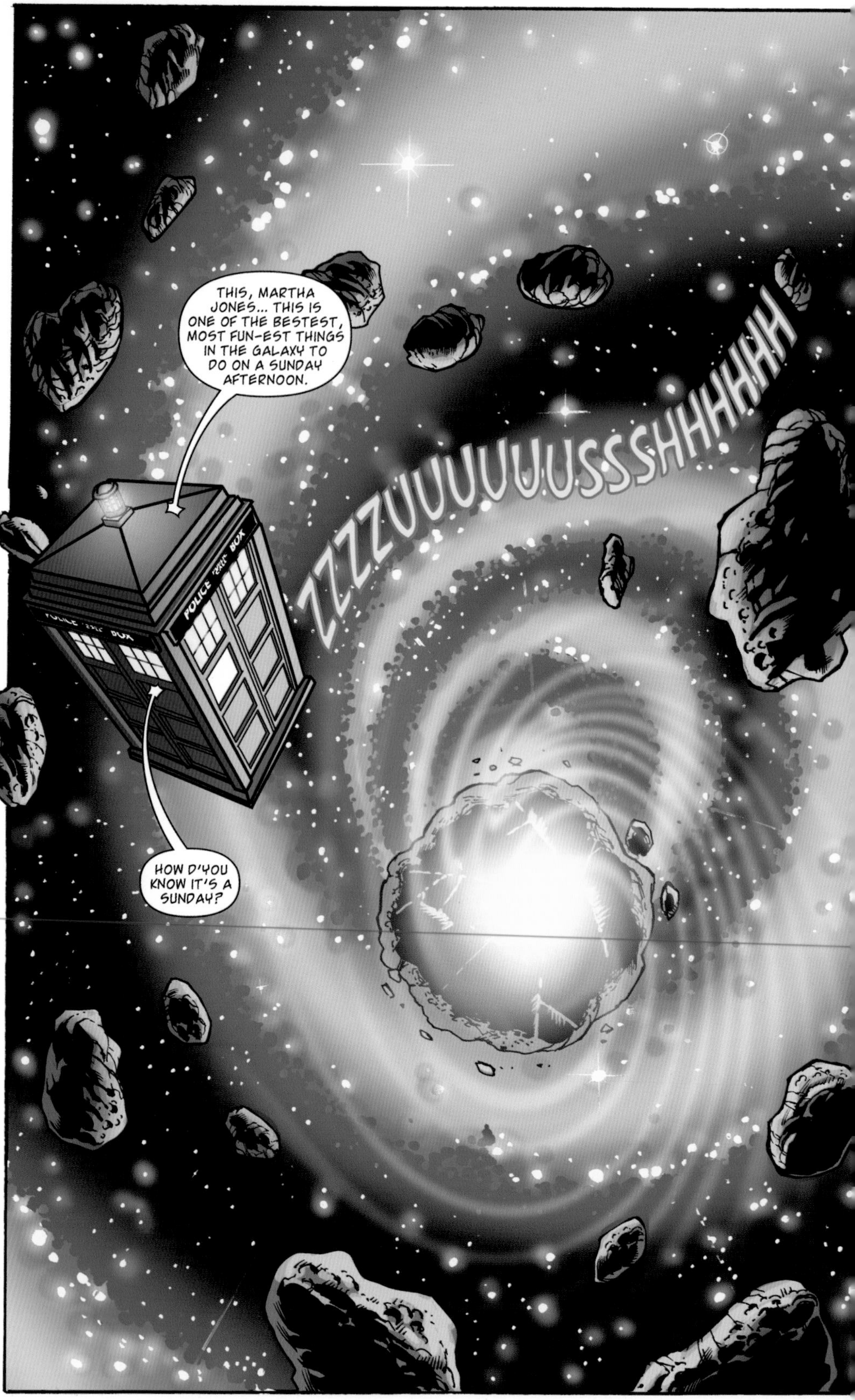
THIS, MARTHA JONES... THIS IS ONE OF THE BESTEST, MOST FUN-EST THINGS IN THE GALAXY TO DO ON A SUNDAY AFTERNOON.
HOW D'YOU KNOW IT'S A SUNDAY?
ZZZZUUUUUUUSSSHHHHHH
POLICE PUBLIC CALL BOX

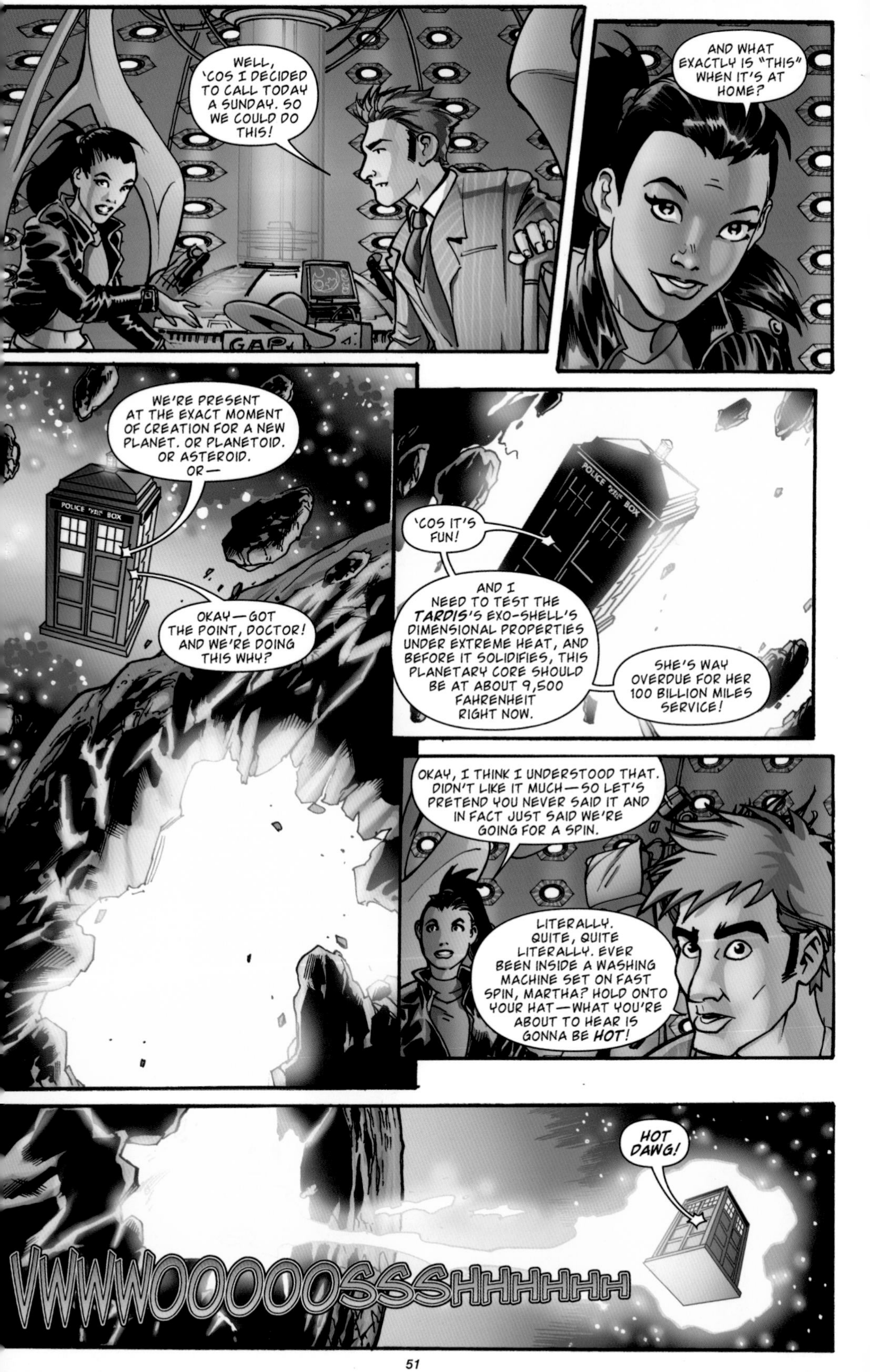
WELL, 'COS I DECIDED TO CALL TODAY A SUNDAY. SO WE COULD DO THIS!
AND WHAT EXACTLY IS "THIS" WHEN IT'S AT HOME?
WE'RE PRESENT AT THE EXACT MOMENT OF CREATION FOR A NEW PLANET. OR PLANETOID. OR ASTEROID. OR—
OKAY—GOT THE POINT, DOCTOR! AND WE'RE DOING THIS WHY?
'COS IT'S FUN!
AND I NEED TO TEST THE TARDIS'S EXO-SHELL'S DIMENSIONAL PROPERTIES UNDER EXTREME HEAT, AND BEFORE IT SOLIDIFIES, THIS PLANETARY CORE SHOULD BE AT ABOUT 9,500 FAHRENHEIT RIGHT NOW.
SHE'S WAY OVERDUE FOR HER 100 BILLION MILES SERVICE!
OKAY, I THINK I UNDERSTOOD THAT. DIDN'T LIKE IT MUCH—SO LET'S PRETEND YOU NEVER SAID IT AND IN FACT JUST SAID WE'RE GOING FOR A SPIN.
LITERALLY. QUITE, QUITE LITERALLY. EVER BEEN INSIDE A WASHING MACHINE SET ON FAST SPIN, MARTHA? HOLD ONTO YOUR HAT—WHAT YOU'RE ABOUT TO HEAR IS GONNA BE HOT!
HOT DAWG!
VWWWOOOOOOSSSSHHHHHH

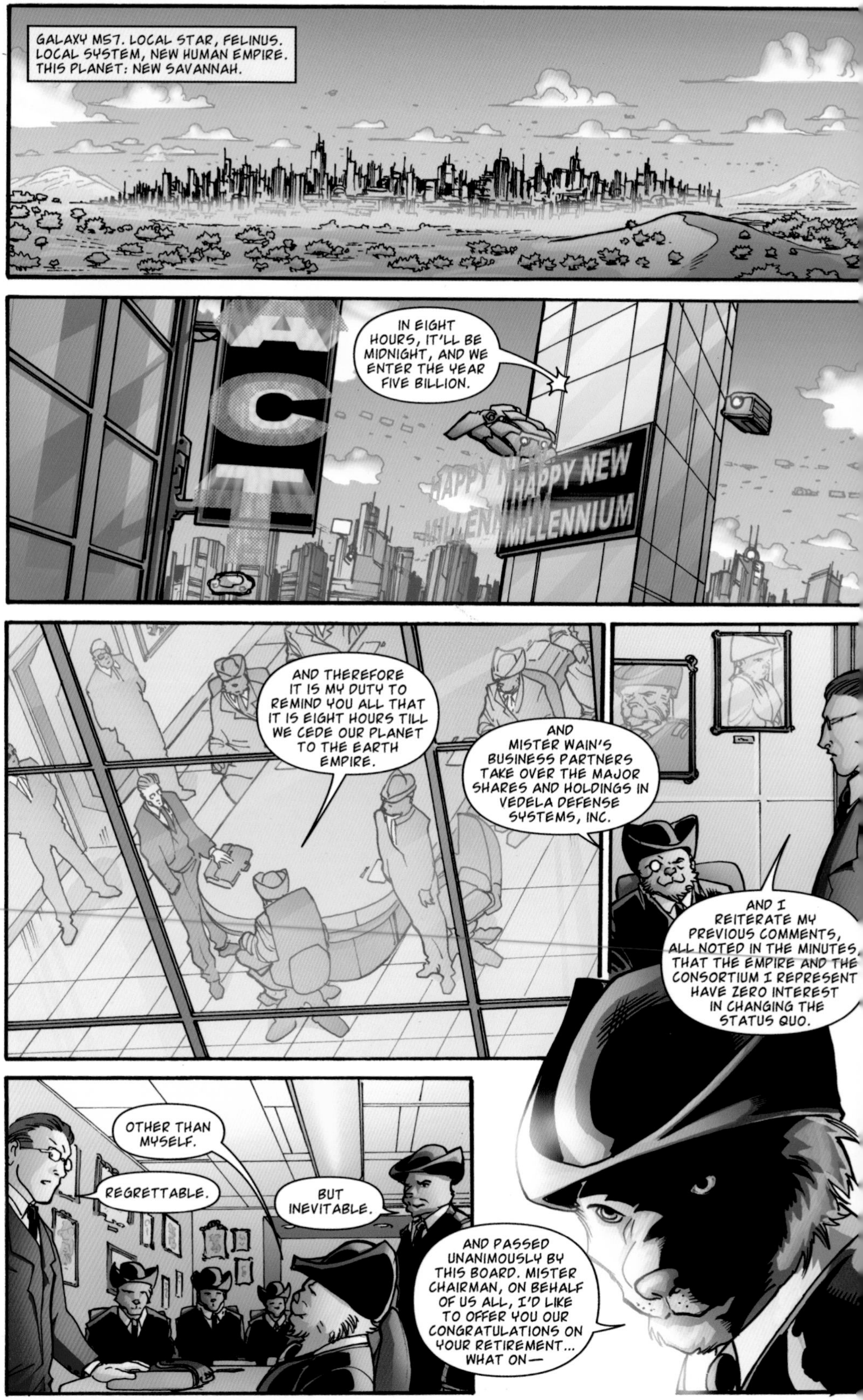
GALAXY M57. LOCAL STAR, FELINUS. LOCAL SYSTEM, NEW HUMAN EMPIRE. THIS PLANET: NEW SAVANNAH.
IN EIGHT HOURS, IT'LL BE MIDNIGHT, AND WE ENTER THE YEAR FIVE BILLION.
HAPPY NEW MILLENNIUM
AND THEREFORE IT IS MY DUTY TO REMIND YOU ALL THAT IT IS EIGHT HOURS TILL WE CEDE OUR PLANET TO THE EARTH EMPIRE.
AND MISTER WAIN'S BUSINESS PARTNERS TAKE OVER THE MAJOR SHARES AND HOLDINGS IN VEDELA DEFENSE SYSTEMS, INC.
AND I REITERATE MY PREVIOUS COMMENTS, ALL NOTED IN THE MINUTES, THAT THE EMPIRE AND THE CONSORTIUM I REPRESENT HAVE ZERO INTEREST IN CHANGING THE STATUS QUO.
OTHER THAN MYSELF.
REGRETTABLE.
BUT INEVITABLE.
AND PASSED UNANIMOUSLY BY THIS BOARD. MISTER CHAIRMAN, ON BEHALF OF US ALL, I'D LIKE TO OFFER YOU OUR CONGRATULATIONS ON YOUR RETIREMENT... WHAT ON—

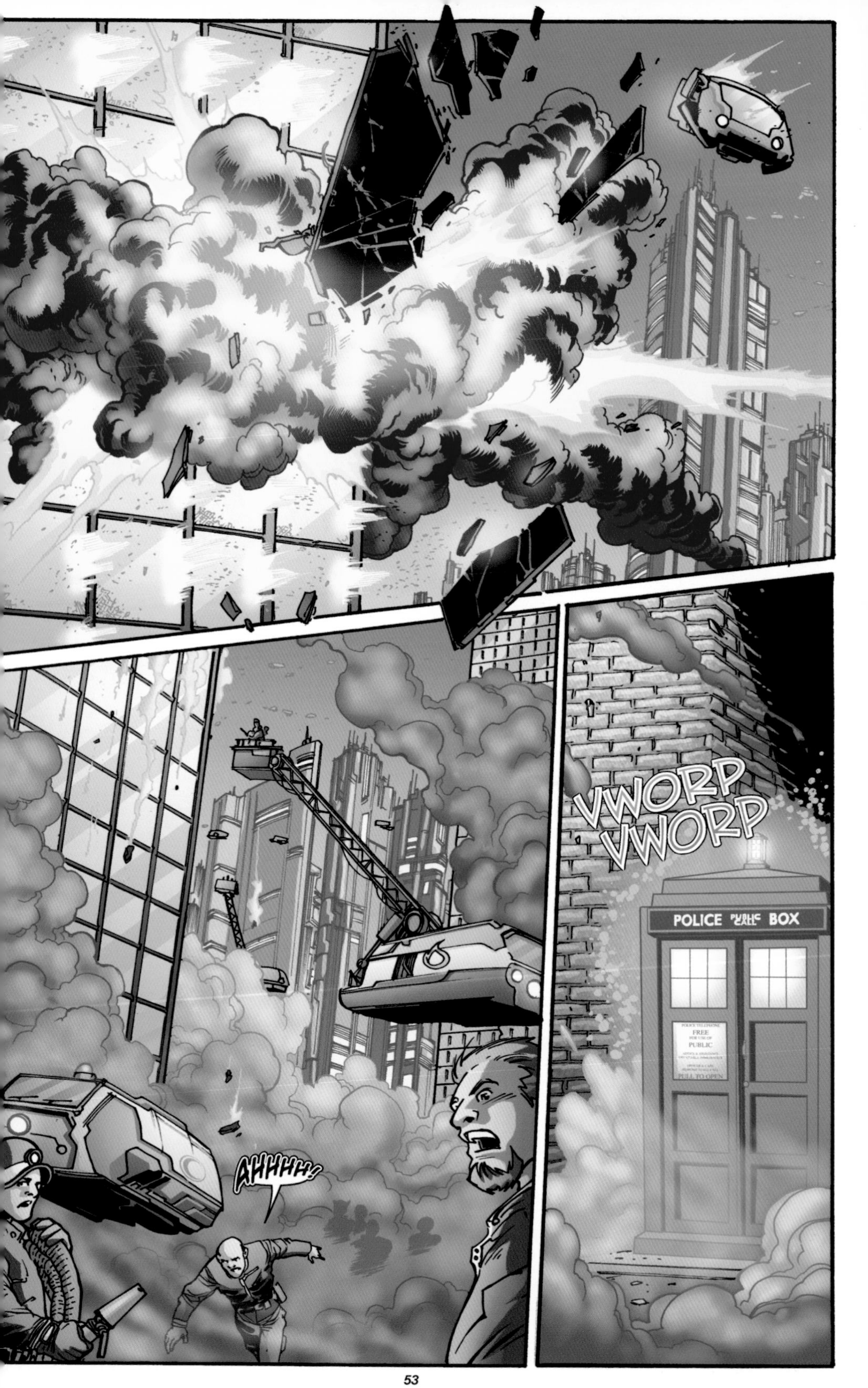
AHHHH!
VWORP VWORP
POLICE PUBLIC CALL BOX
POLICE TELEPHONE
FREE
FOR USE OF
PUBLIC
PULL TO OPEN

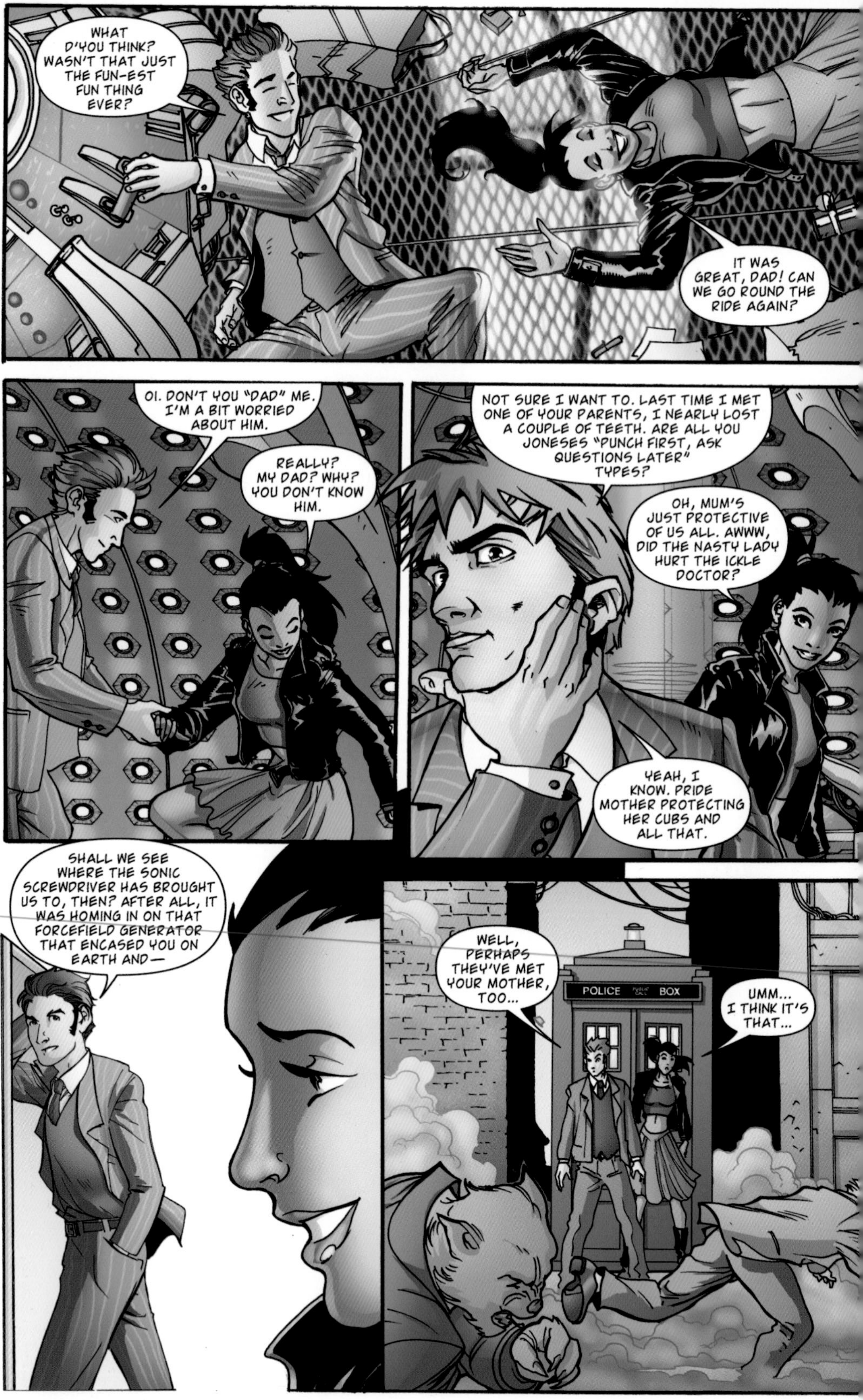
WHAT D'YOU THINK? WASN'T THAT JUST THE FUN-EST FUN THING EVER?
IT WAS GREAT, DAD! CAN WE GO ROUND THE RIDE AGAIN?
OI. DON'T YOU "DAD" ME. I'M A BIT WORRIED ABOUT HIM.
REALLY? MY DAD? WHY? YOU DON'T KNOW HIM.
NOT SURE I WANT TO. LAST TIME I MET ONE OF YOUR PARENTS, I NEARLY LOST A COUPLE OF TEETH. ARE ALL YOU JONESES "PUNCH FIRST, ASK QUESTIONS LATER" TYPES?
OH, MUM'S JUST PROTECTIVE OF US ALL. AWWW, DID THE NASTY LADY HURT THE ICKLE DOCTOR?
YEAH, I KNOW. PRIDE MOTHER PROTECTING HER CUBS AND ALL THAT.
SHALL WE SEE WHERE THE SONIC SCREWDRIVER HAS BROUGHT US TO, THEN? AFTER ALL, IT WAS HOMING IN ON THAT FORCEFIELD GENERATOR THAT ENCASED YOU ON EARTH AND—
WELL, PERHAPS THEY'VE MET YOUR MOTHER, TOO...
POLICE BOX
UMM... I THINK IT'S THAT...

WE SHOULD HELP.

I'LL HEAD TO THE BASE OF THE BUILDING. IF ALL THE AMBULANCES ARE UP AT THE TOP, PEOPLE HURT BY DEBRIS MIGHT NEED SOME MEDICAL ATTENTION.

GOOD CALL, DOCTOR JONES.

ZZZZKKKKKTTTT

RIGHT YOU ARE, BOYS...

... JOB WELL DONE, I THINK. TIME TO REPORT IN AND THEN GET OFF THIS PLANET BEFORE MIDNIGHT.

WON'T THEY HAVE CLOSED OFF THE SHUTTLEPORTS?

YEAH, WE DON'T WANT TO BE STUCK HERE.

ALL CONTINGENCES PREPARED FOR, BOYS. NOW, SHIFT!

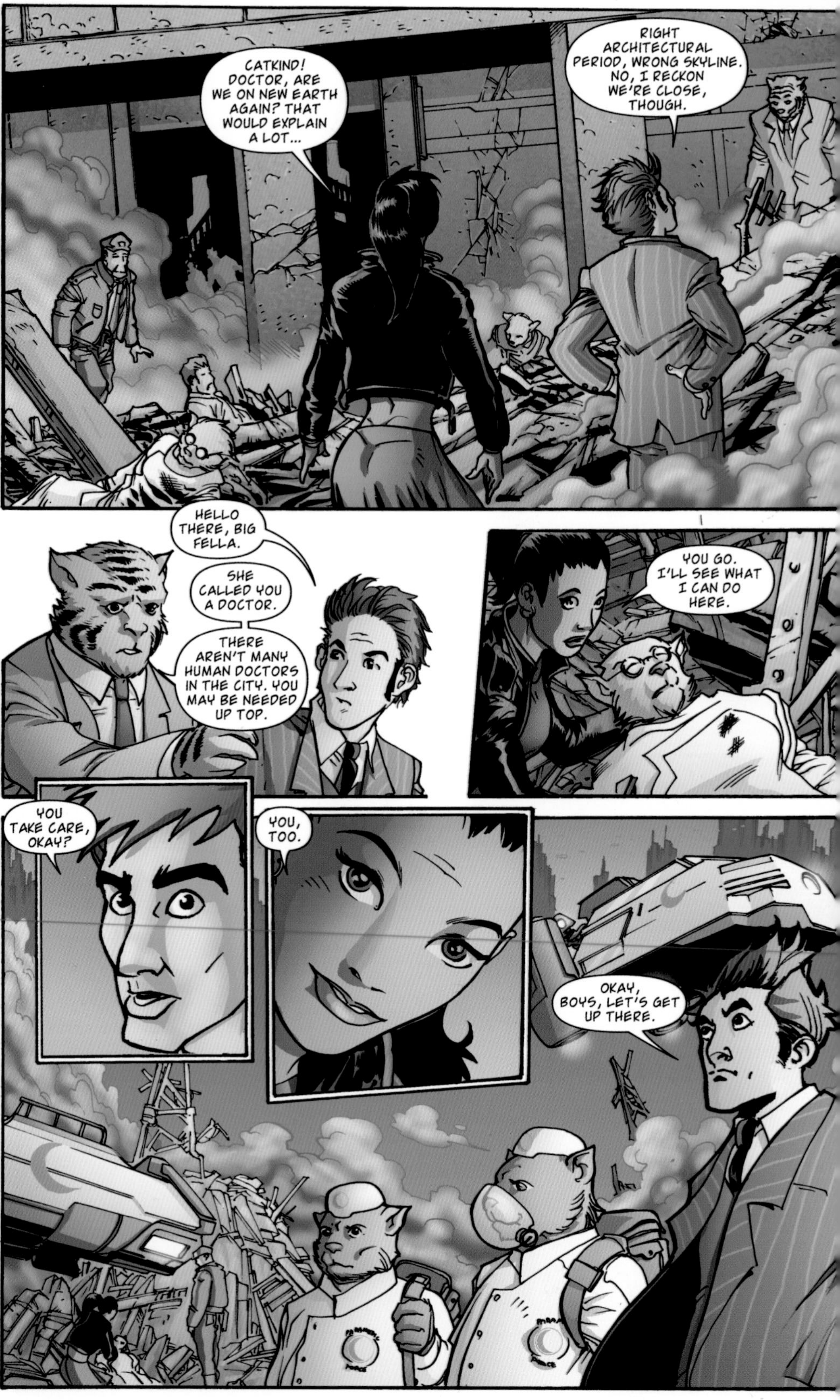
CATKIND! DOCTOR, ARE WE ON NEW EARTH AGAIN? THAT WOULD EXPLAIN A LOT...
RIGHT ARCHITECTURAL PERIOD, WRONG SKYLINE. NO, I RECKON WE'RE CLOSE, THOUGH.
HELLO THERE, BIG FELLA.
SHE CALLED YOU A DOCTOR.
THERE AREN'T MANY HUMAN DOCTORS IN THE CITY. YOU MAY BE NEEDED UP TOP.
YOU GO. I'LL SEE WHAT I CAN DO HERE.
YOU TAKE CARE, OKAY?
YOU, TOO.
OKAY, BOYS, LET'S GET UP THERE.

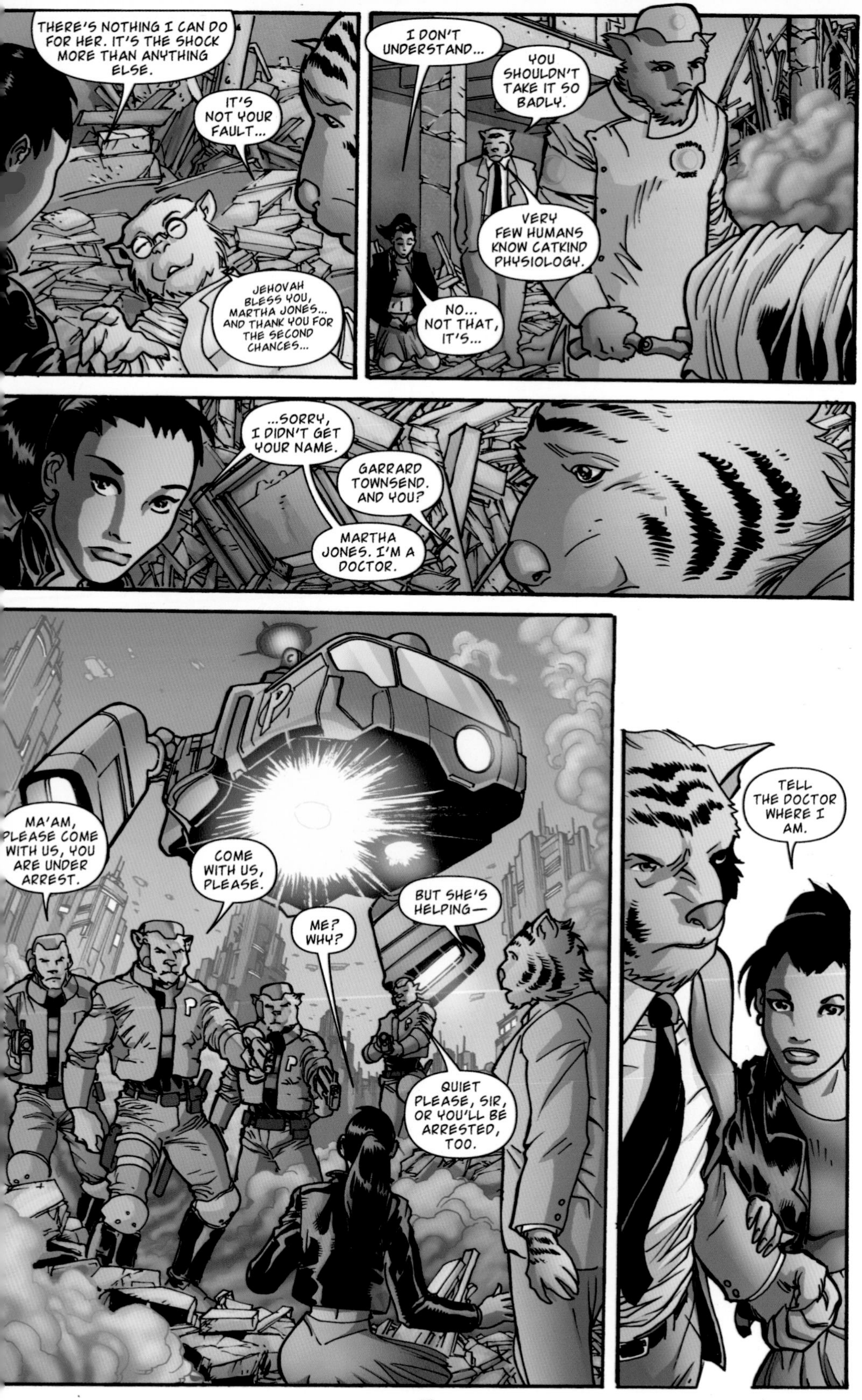
THERE'S NOTHING I CAN DO FOR HER. IT'S THE SHOCK MORE THAN ANYTHING ELSE.
IT'S NOT YOUR FAULT...
JEHOVAH BLESS YOU, MARTHA JONES... AND THANK YOU FOR THE SECOND CHANCES...
I DON'T UNDERSTAND...
YOU SHOULDN'T TAKE IT SO BADLY.
VERY FEW HUMANS KNOW CATKIND PHYSIOLOGY.
NO... NOT THAT, IT'S...
...SORRY, I DIDN'T GET YOUR NAME.
GARRARD TOWNSEND. AND YOU?
MARTHA JONES. I'M A DOCTOR.
MA'AM, PLEASE COME WITH US, YOU ARE UNDER ARREST.
COME WITH US, PLEASE.
ME? WHY?
BUT SHE'S HELPING—
QUIET PLEASE, SIR, OR YOU'LL BE ARRESTED, TOO.
TELL THE DOCTOR WHERE I AM.

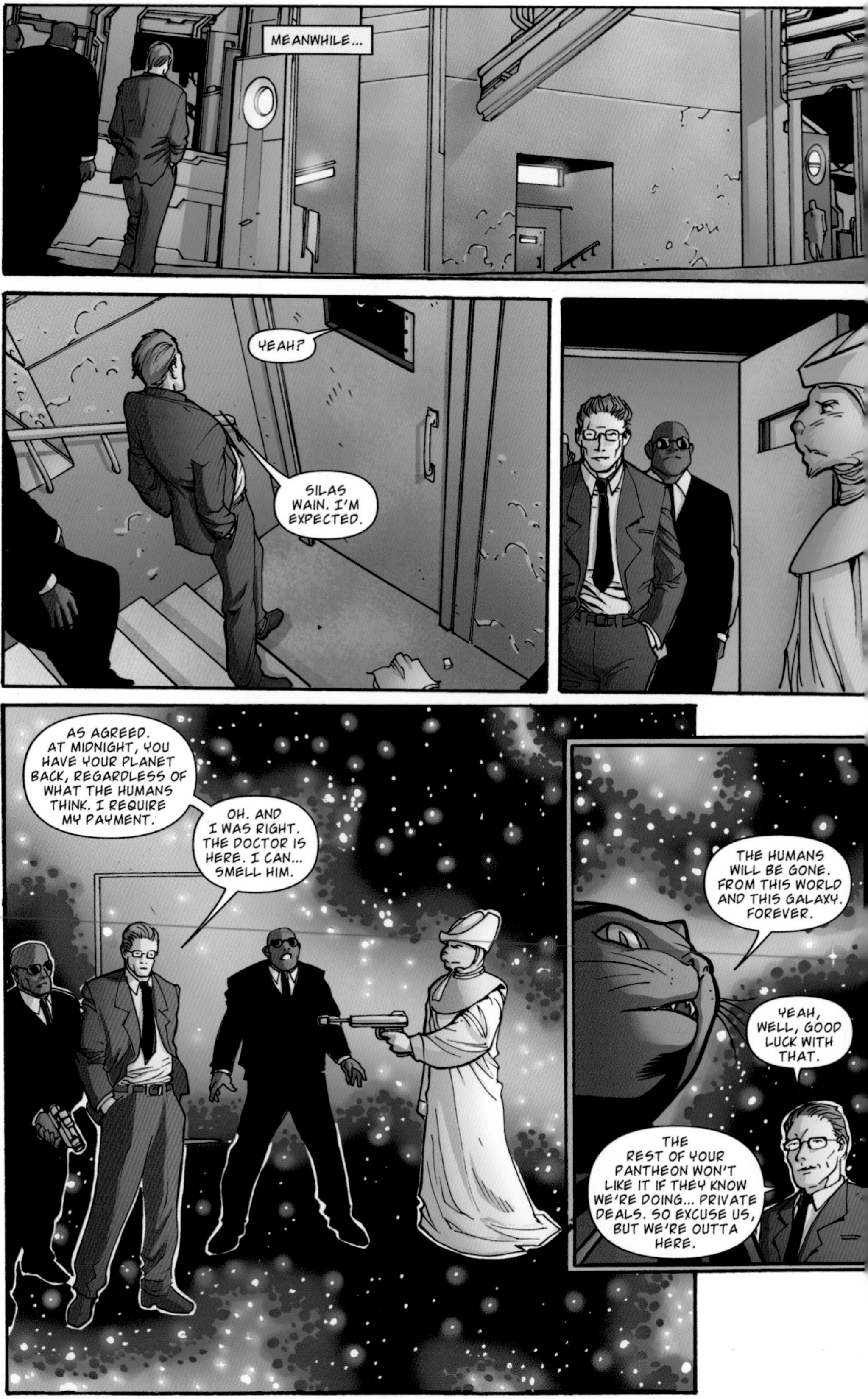
MEANWHILE...
YEAH?
SILAS WAIN. I'M EXPECTED.
AS AGREED. AT MIDNIGHT, YOU HAVE YOUR PLANET BACK, REGARDLESS OF WHAT THE HUMANS THINK. I REQUIRE MY PAYMENT.
OH. AND I WAS RIGHT. THE DOCTOR IS HERE. I CAN... SMELL HIM.
THE HUMANS WILL BE GONE. FROM THIS WORLD AND THIS GALAXY. FOREVER.
YEAH, WELL, GOOD LUCK WITH THAT.
THE REST OF YOUR PANTHEON WON'T LIKE IT IF THEY KNOW WE'RE DOING... PRIVATE DEALS. SO EXCUSE US, BUT WE'RE OUTTA HERE.

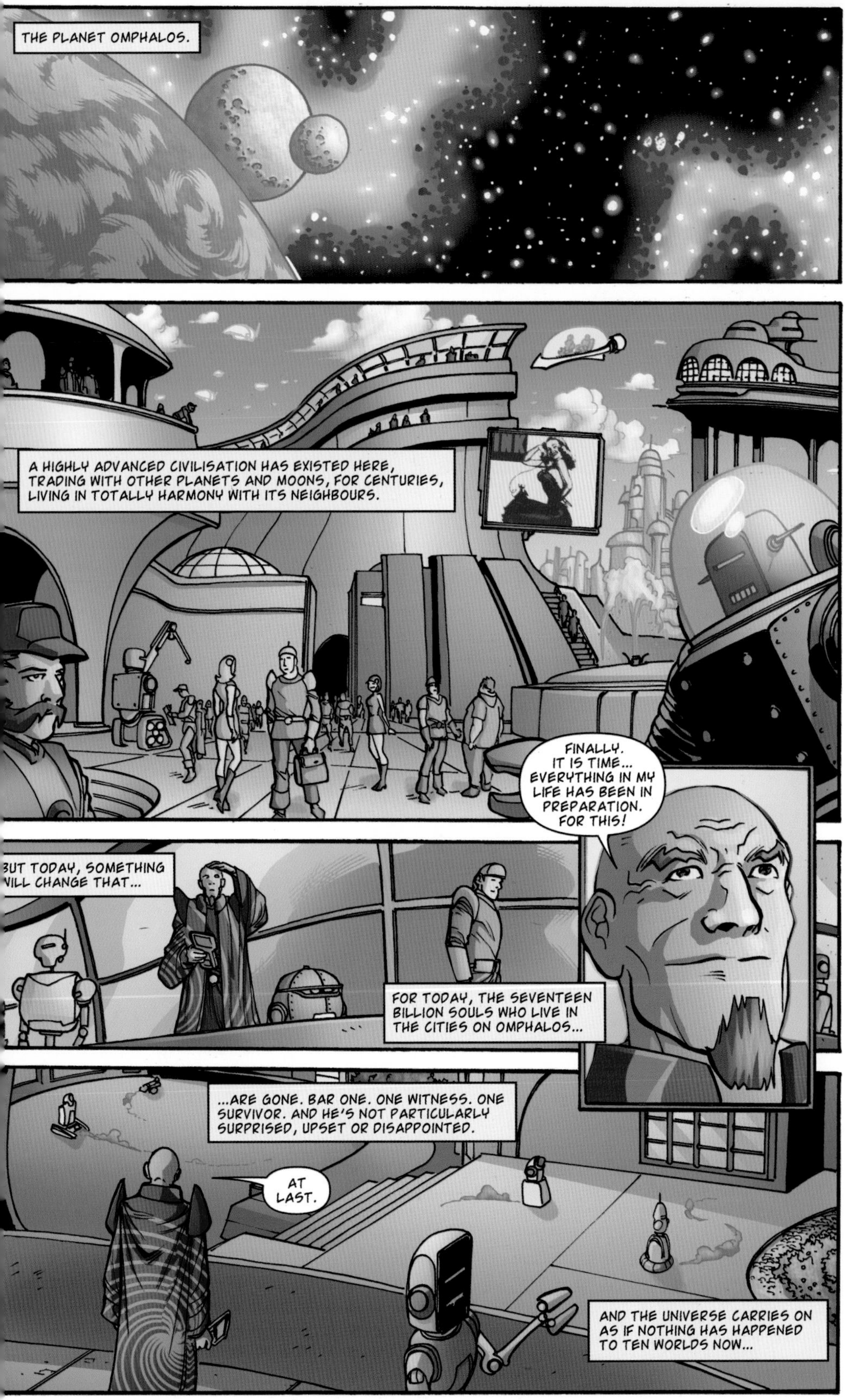

THE PLANET OMPHALOS.
INK
A HIGHLY ADVANCED CIVILISATION HAS EXISTED HERE, TRADING WITH OTHER PLANETS AND MOONS, FOR CENTURIES, LIVING IN TOTALLY HARMONY WITH ITS NEIGHBOURS.
BUT TODAY, SOMETHING WILL CHANGE THAT...
FINALLY. IT IS TIME... EVERYTHING IN MY LIFE HAS BEEN IN PREPARATION. FOR THIS!
FOR TODAY, THE SEVENTEEN BILLION SOULS WHO LIVE IN THE CITIES ON OMPHALOS...
...ARE GONE. BAR ONE. ONE WITNESS. ONE SURVIVOR. AND HE'S NOT PARTICULARLY SURPRISED, UPSET OR DISAPPOINTED.
AT LAST.
AND THE UNIVERSE CARRIES ON AS IF NOTHING HAS HAPPENED TO TEN WORLDS NOW...

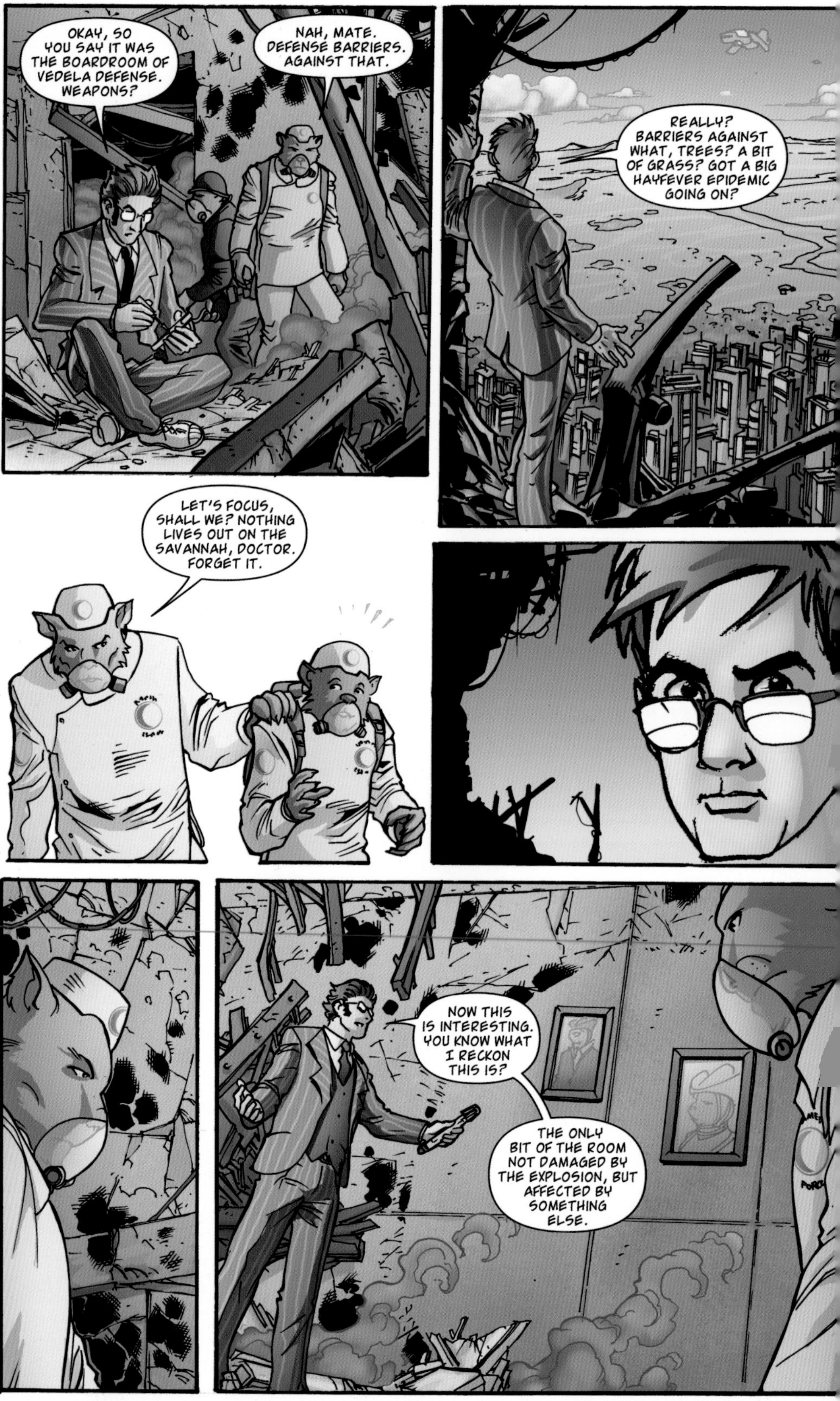

OKAY, SO YOU SAY IT WAS THE BOARDROOM OF VEDELA DEFENSE. WEAPONS?
NAH, MATE. DEFENSE BARRIERS. AGAINST THAT.
REALLY? BARRIERS AGAINST WHAT, TREES? A BIT OF GRASS? GOT A BIG HAYFEVER EPIDEMIC GOING ON?
LET'S FOCUS, SHALL WE? NOTHING LIVES OUT ON THE SAVANNAH, DOCTOR. FORGET IT.
NOW THIS IS INTERESTING. YOU KNOW WHAT I RECKON THIS IS?
THE ONLY BIT OF THE ROOM NOT DAMAGED BY THE EXPLOSION, BUT AFFECTED BY SOMETHING ELSE.

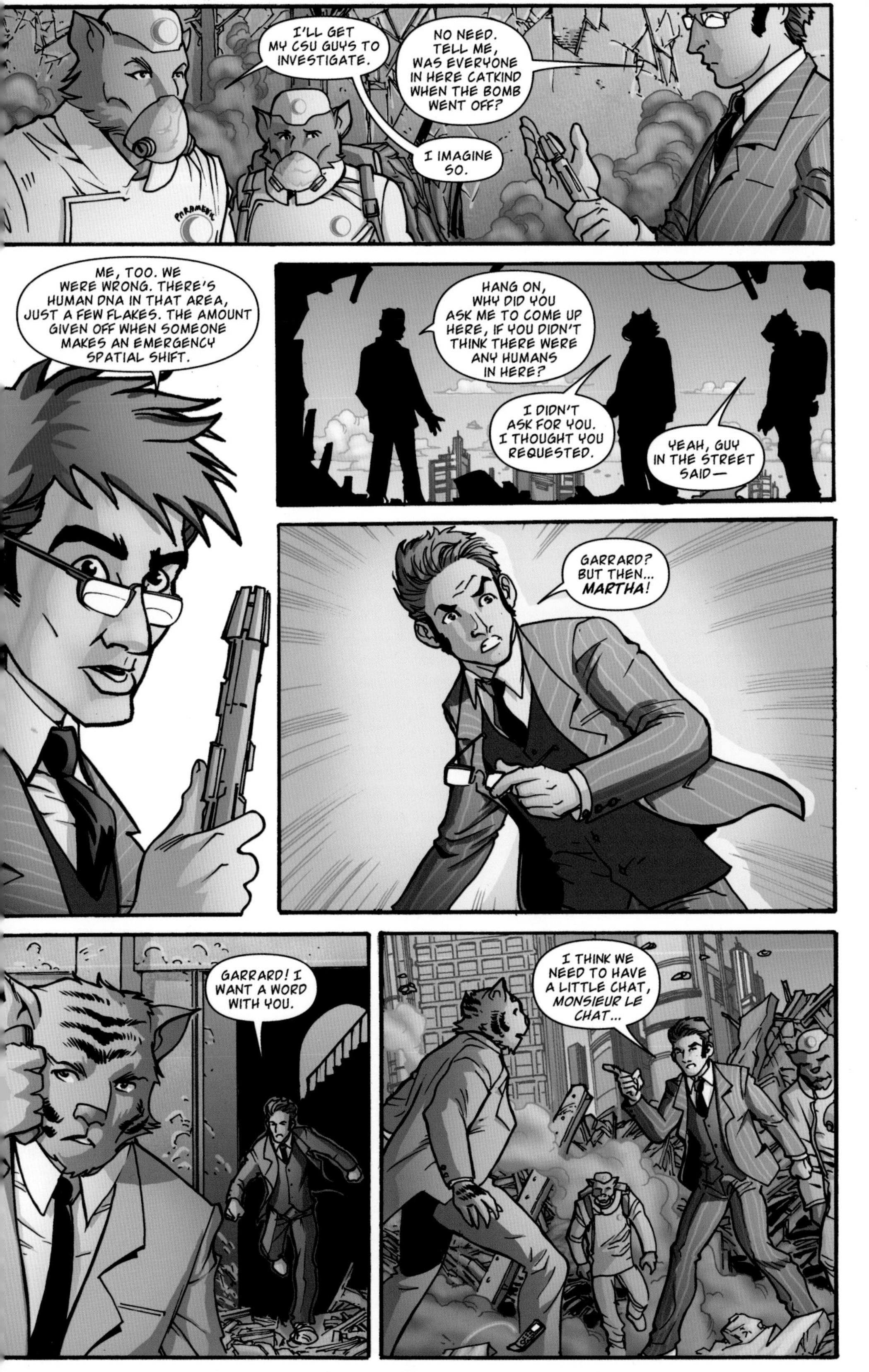
I'LL GET MY CSU GUYS TO INVESTIGATE.
NO NEED. TELL ME, WAS EVERYONE IN HERE CATKIND WHEN THE BOMB WENT OFF?
I IMAGINE SO.
PARAMEDIC
ME, TOO. WE WERE WRONG. THERE'S HUMAN DNA IN THAT AREA, JUST A FEW FLAKES. THE AMOUNT GIVEN OFF WHEN SOMEONE MAKES AN EMERGENCY SPATIAL SHIFT.
HANG ON, WHY DID YOU ASK ME TO COME UP HERE, IF YOU DIDN'T THINK THERE WERE ANY HUMANS IN HERE?
I DIDN'T ASK FOR YOU. I THOUGHT YOU REQUESTED.
YEAH, GUY IN THE STREET SAID—
GARRARD? BUT THEN... ***MARTHA!***
GARRARD! I WANT A WORD WITH YOU.
I THINK WE NEED TO HAVE A LITTLE CHAT, *MONSIEUR LE CHAT*...

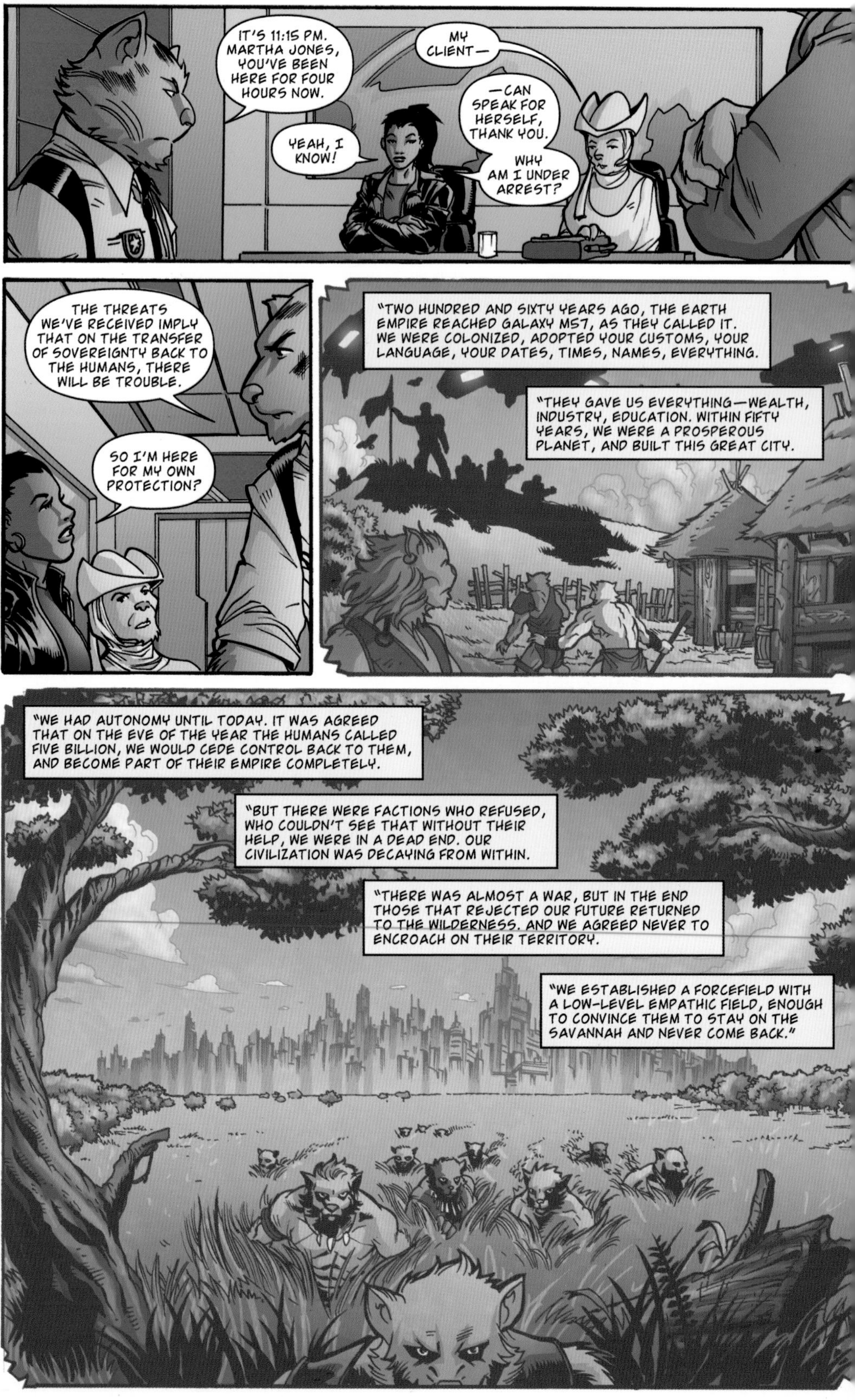
IT'S 11:15 PM. MARTHA JONES, YOU'VE BEEN HERE FOR FOUR HOURS NOW.
YEAH, I KNOW!
MY CLIENT—
—CAN SPEAK FOR HERSELF, THANK YOU.
WHY AM I UNDER ARREST?
THE THREATS WE'VE RECEIVED IMPLY THAT ON THE TRANSFER OF SOVEREIGNTY BACK TO THE HUMANS, THERE WILL BE TROUBLE.
SO I'M HERE FOR MY OWN PROTECTION?
"TWO HUNDRED AND SIXTY YEARS AGO, THE EARTH EMPIRE REACHED GALAXY M57, AS THEY CALLED IT. WE WERE COLONIZED, ADOPTED YOUR CUSTOMS, YOUR LANGUAGE, YOUR DATES, TIMES, NAMES, EVERYTHING.
"THEY GAVE US EVERYTHING—WEALTH, INDUSTRY, EDUCATION. WITHIN FIFTY YEARS, WE WERE A PROSPEROUS PLANET, AND BUILT THIS GREAT CITY.
"WE HAD AUTONOMY UNTIL TODAY. IT WAS AGREED THAT ON THE EVE OF THE YEAR THE HUMANS CALLED FIVE BILLION, WE WOULD CEDE CONTROL BACK TO THEM, AND BECOME PART OF THEIR EMPIRE COMPLETELY.
"BUT THERE WERE FACTIONS WHO REFUSED, WHO COULDN'T SEE THAT WITHOUT THEIR HELP, WE WERE IN A DEAD END. OUR CIVILIZATION WAS DECAYING FROM WITHIN.
"THERE WAS ALMOST A WAR, BUT IN THE END THOSE THAT REJECTED OUR FUTURE RETURNED TO THE WILDERNESS. AND WE AGREED NEVER TO ENCROACH ON THEIR TERRITORY.
"WE ESTABLISHED A FORCEFIELD WITH A LOW-LEVEL EMPATHIC FIELD, ENOUGH TO CONVINCE THEM TO STAY ON THE SAVANNAH AND NEVER COME BACK."

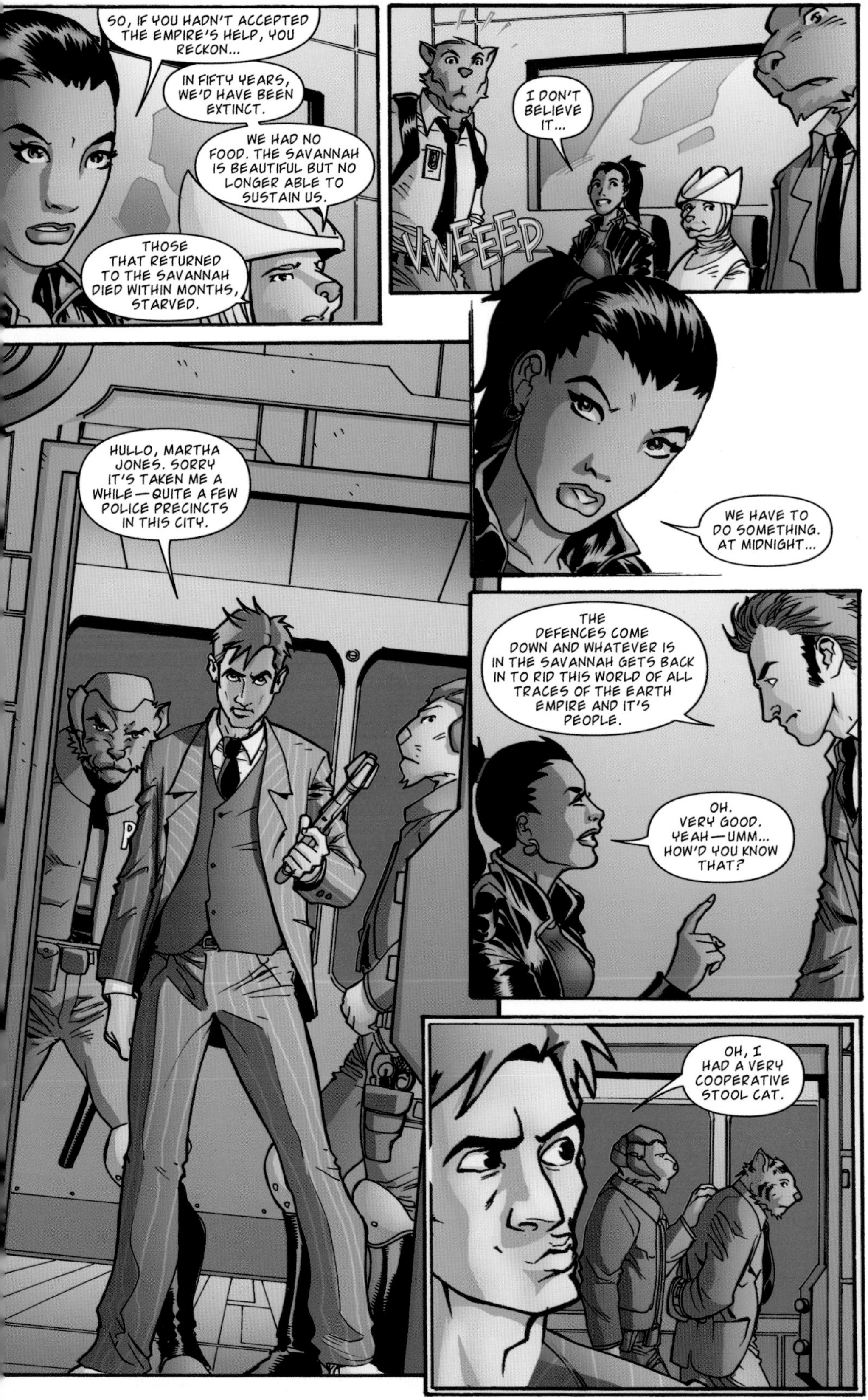
SO, IF YOU HADN'T ACCEPTED THE EMPIRE'S HELP, YOU RECKON...
IN FIFTY YEARS, WE'D HAVE BEEN EXTINCT.
WE HAD NO FOOD. THE SAVANNAH IS BEAUTIFUL BUT NO LONGER ABLE TO SUSTAIN US.
THOSE THAT RETURNED TO THE SAVANNAH DIED WITHIN MONTHS, STARVED.
I DON'T BELIEVE IT...
VWEEEP
WE HAVE TO DO SOMETHING. AT MIDNIGHT...
HULLO, MARTHA JONES. SORRY IT'S TAKEN ME A WHILE—QUITE A FEW POLICE PRECINCTS IN THIS CITY.
THE DEFENCES COME DOWN AND WHATEVER IS IN THE SAVANNAH GETS BACK IN TO RID THIS WORLD OF ALL TRACES OF THE EARTH EMPIRE AND IT'S PEOPLE.
OH. VERY GOOD. YEAH—UMM... HOW'D YOU KNOW THAT?
OH, I HAD A VERY COOPERATIVE STOOL CAT.

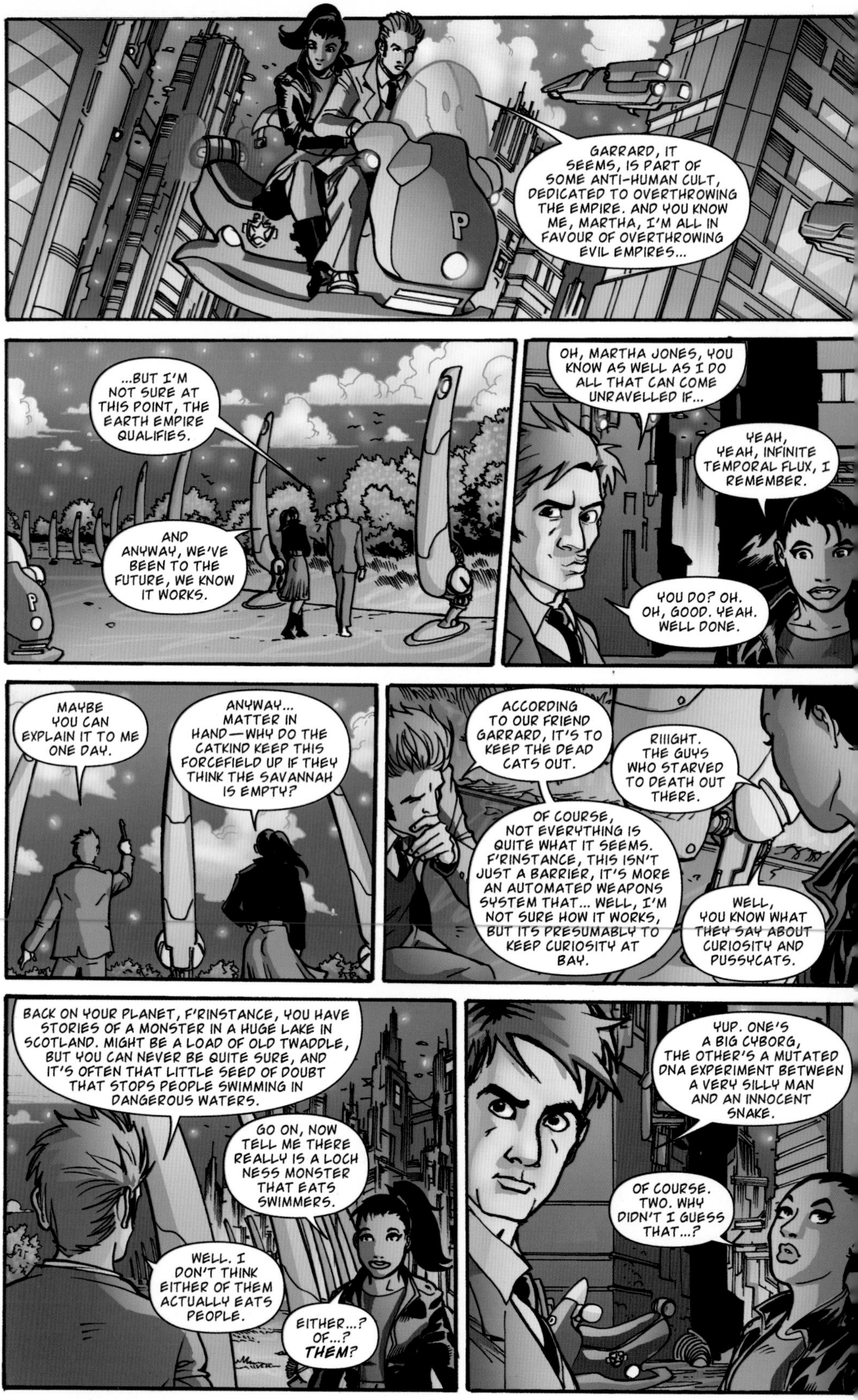
GARRARD, IT SEEMS, IS PART OF SOME ANTI-HUMAN CULT, DEDICATED TO OVERTHROWING THE EMPIRE. AND YOU KNOW ME, MARTHA, I'M ALL IN FAVOUR OF OVERTHROWING EVIL EMPIRES...
...BUT I'M NOT SURE AT THIS POINT, THE EARTH EMPIRE QUALIFIES.
AND ANYWAY, WE'VE BEEN TO THE FUTURE, WE KNOW IT WORKS.
OH, MARTHA JONES, YOU KNOW AS WELL AS I DO ALL THAT CAN COME UNRAVELLED IF...
YEAH, YEAH, INFINITE TEMPORAL FLUX, I REMEMBER.
YOU DO? OH. OH, GOOD. YEAH. WELL DONE.
MAYBE YOU CAN EXPLAIN IT TO ME ONE DAY.
ANYWAY... MATTER IN HAND—WHY DO THE CATKIND KEEP THIS FORCEFIELD UP IF THEY THINK THE SAVANNAH IS EMPTY?
ACCORDING TO OUR FRIEND GARRARD, IT'S TO KEEP THE DEAD CATS OUT.
RIIIGHT. THE GUYS WHO STARVED TO DEATH OUT THERE.
OF COURSE, NOT EVERYTHING IS QUITE WHAT IT SEEMS. F'RINSTANCE, THIS ISN'T JUST A BARRIER, IT'S MORE AN AUTOMATED WEAPONS SYSTEM THAT... WELL, I'M NOT SURE HOW IT WORKS, BUT ITS PRESUMABLY TO KEEP CURIOSITY AT BAY.
WELL, YOU KNOW WHAT THEY SAY ABOUT CURIOSITY AND PUSSYCATS.
BACK ON YOUR PLANET, F'RINSTANCE, YOU HAVE STORIES OF A MONSTER IN A HUGE LAKE IN SCOTLAND. MIGHT BE A LOAD OF OLD TWADDLE, BUT YOU CAN NEVER BE QUITE SURE, AND IT'S OFTEN THAT LITTLE SEED OF DOUBT THAT STOPS PEOPLE SWIMMING IN DANGEROUS WATERS.
GO ON, NOW TELL ME THERE REALLY IS A LOCH NESS MONSTER THAT EATS SWIMMERS.
WELL. I DON'T THINK EITHER OF THEM ACTUALLY EATS PEOPLE.
EITHER...? OF...? THEM?
YUP. ONE'S A BIG CYBORG, THE OTHER'S A MUTATED DNA EXPERIMENT BETWEEN A VERY SILLY MAN AND AN INNOCENT SNAKE.
OF COURSE. TWO. WHY DIDN'T I GUESS THAT...?

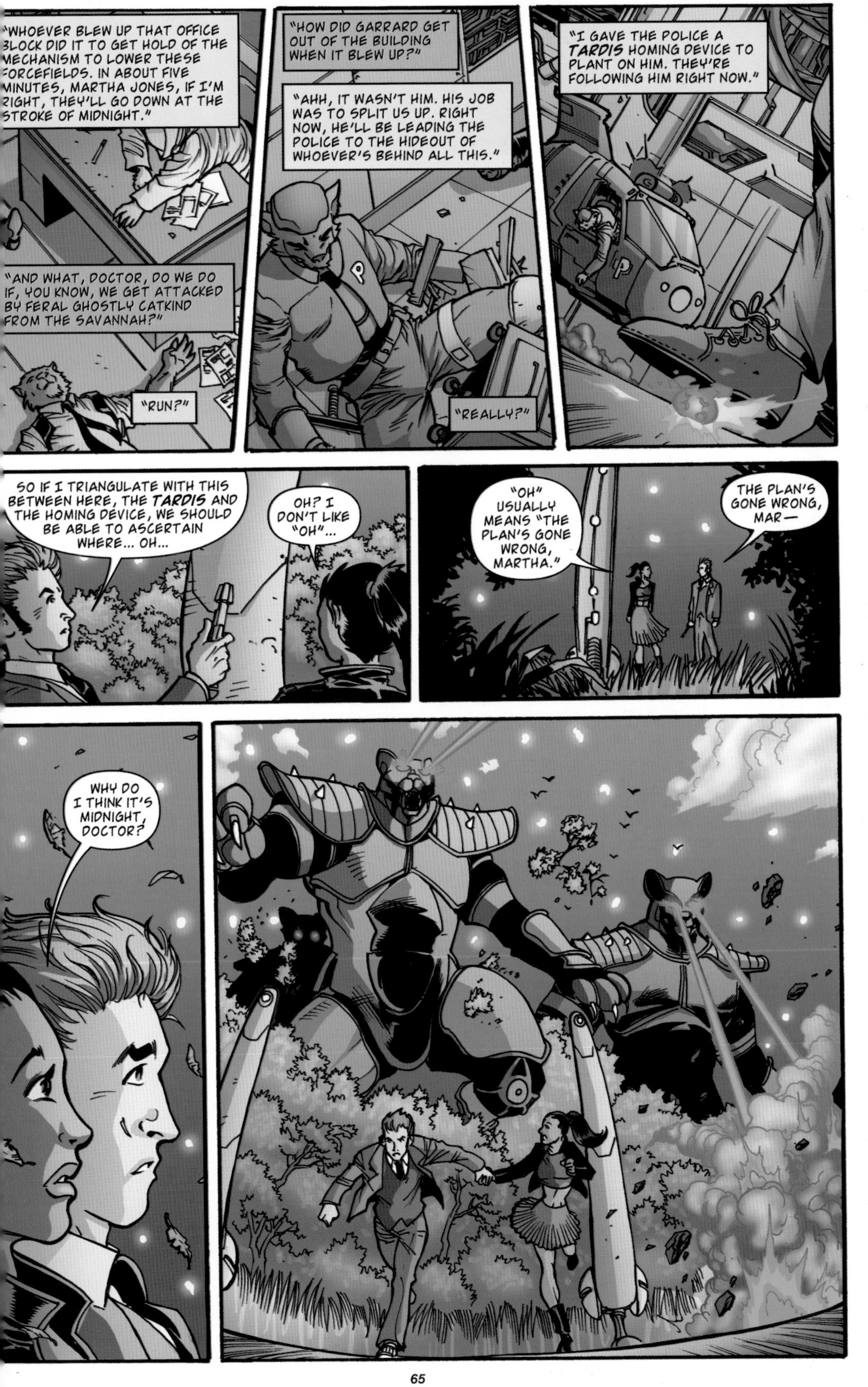
"WHOEVER BLEW UP THAT OFFICE BLOCK DID IT TO GET HOLD OF THE MECHANISM TO LOWER THESE FORCEFIELDS. IN ABOUT FIVE MINUTES, MARTHA JONES, IF I'M RIGHT, THEY'LL GO DOWN AT THE STROKE OF MIDNIGHT."
"AND WHAT, DOCTOR, DO WE DO IF, YOU KNOW, WE GET ATTACKED BY FERAL GHOSTLY CATKIND FROM THE SAVANNAH?"
"RUN?"
"HOW DID GARRARD GET OUT OF THE BUILDING WHEN IT BLEW UP?"
"AHH, IT WASN'T HIM. HIS JOB WAS TO SPLIT US UP. RIGHT NOW, HE'LL BE LEADING THE POLICE TO THE HIDEOUT OF WHOEVER'S BEHIND ALL THIS."
"REALLY?"
"I GAVE THE POLICE A TARDIS HOMING DEVICE TO PLANT ON HIM. THEY'RE FOLLOWING HIM RIGHT NOW."
SO IF I TRIANGULATE WITH THIS BETWEEN HERE, THE TARDIS AND THE HOMING DEVICE, WE SHOULD BE ABLE TO ASCERTAIN WHERE... OH...
OH? I DON'T LIKE "OH"...
"OH" USUALLY MEANS "THE PLAN'S GONE WRONG, MARTHA."
THE PLAN'S GONE WRONG, MAR—
WHY DO I THINK IT'S MIDNIGHT, DOCTOR?

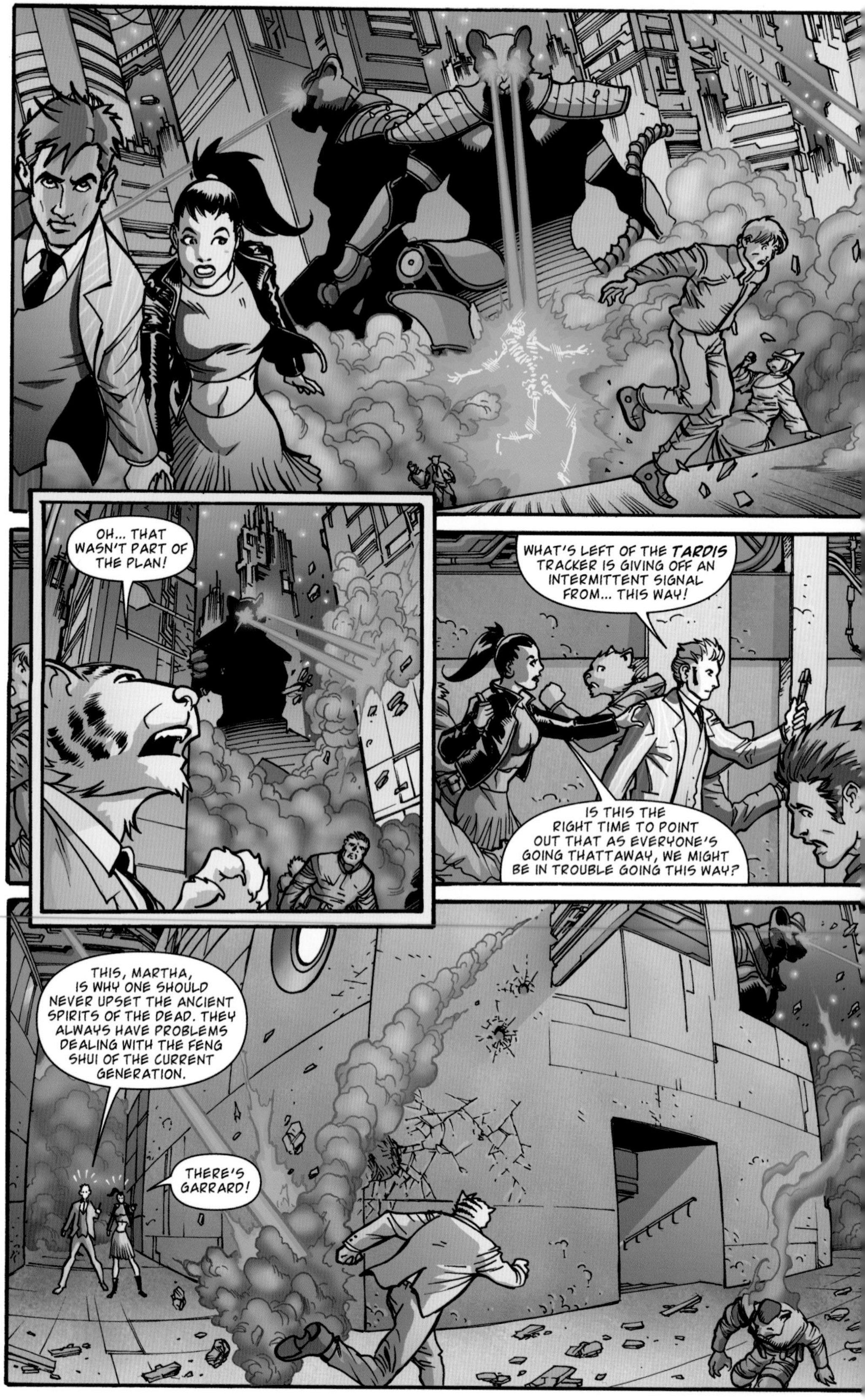

OH... THAT WASN'T PART OF THE PLAN!
WHAT'S LEFT OF THE TARDIS TRACKER IS GIVING OFF AN INTERMITTENT SIGNAL FROM... THIS WAY!
IS THIS THE RIGHT TIME TO POINT OUT THAT AS EVERYONE'S GOING THATTAWAY, WE MIGHT BE IN TROUBLE GOING THIS WAY?
THIS, MARTHA, IS WHY ONE SHOULD NEVER UPSET THE ANCIENT SPIRITS OF THE DEAD. THEY ALWAYS HAVE PROBLEMS DEALING WITH THE FENG SHUI OF THE CURRENT GENERATION.
THERE'S GARRARD!

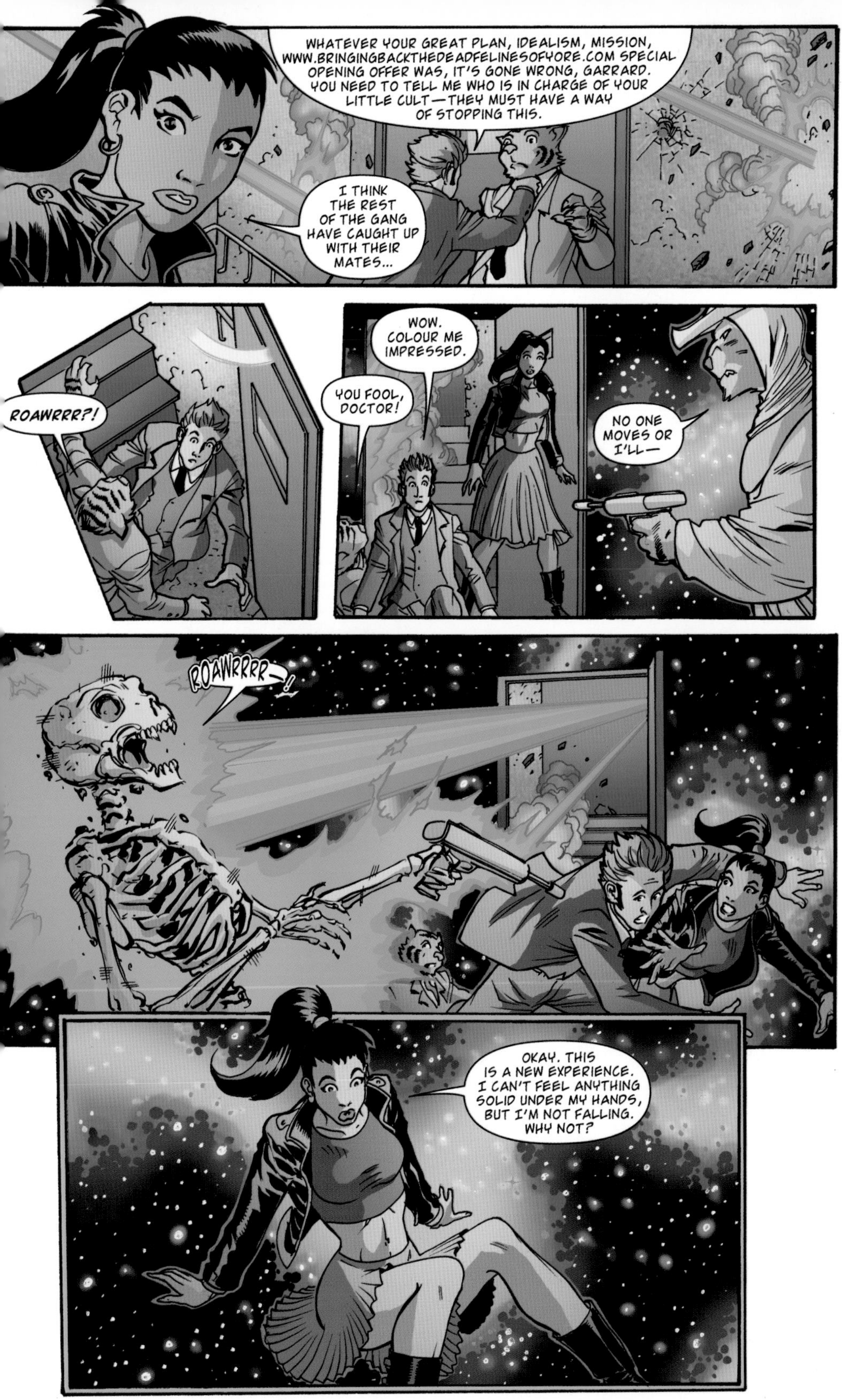
WHATEVER YOUR GREAT PLAN, IDEALISM, MISSION, WWW.BRINGINGBACKTHEDEADFELINESOFYORE.COM SPECIAL OPENING OFFER WAS, IT'S GONE WRONG, GARRARD. YOU NEED TO TELL ME WHO IS IN CHARGE OF YOUR LITTLE CULT—THEY MUST HAVE A WAY OF STOPPING THIS.
I THINK THE REST OF THE GANG HAVE CAUGHT UP WITH THEIR MATES...
ROAWRRR?!
WOW. COLOUR ME IMPRESSED.
YOU FOOL, DOCTOR!
NO ONE MOVES OR I'LL—
ROAWRRRR—!
OKAY. THIS IS A NEW EXPERIENCE. I CAN'T FEEL ANYTHING SOLID UNDER MY HANDS, BUT I'M NOT FALLING. WHY NOT?

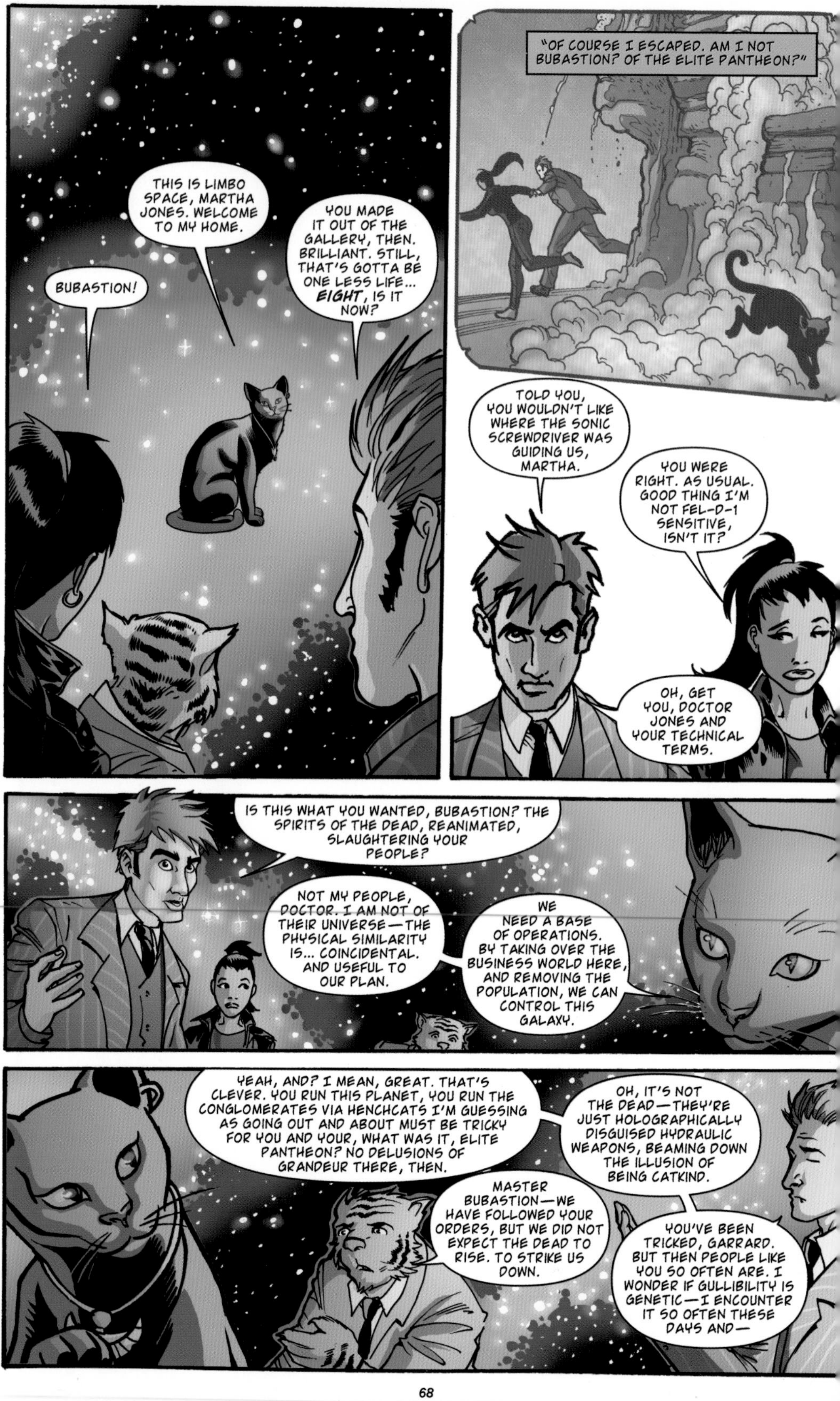
"OF COURSE I ESCAPED. AM I NOT BUBASTION? OF THE ELITE PANTHEON?"
BUBASTION!
THIS IS LIMBO SPACE, MARTHA JONES. WELCOME TO MY HOME.
YOU MADE IT OUT OF THE GALLERY, THEN. BRILLIANT. STILL, THAT'S GOTTA BE ONE LESS LIFE... EIGHT, IS IT NOW?
TOLD YOU, YOU WOULDN'T LIKE WHERE THE SONIC SCREWDRIVER WAS GUIDING US, MARTHA.
YOU WERE RIGHT. AS USUAL. GOOD THING I'M NOT FEL-D-1 SENSITIVE, ISN'T IT?
OH, GET YOU, DOCTOR JONES AND YOUR TECHNICAL TERMS.
IS THIS WHAT YOU WANTED, BUBASTION? THE SPIRITS OF THE DEAD, REANIMATED, SLAUGHTERING YOUR PEOPLE?
NOT MY PEOPLE, DOCTOR. I AM NOT OF THEIR UNIVERSE—THE PHYSICAL SIMILARITY IS... COINCIDENTAL. AND USEFUL TO OUR PLAN.
WE NEED A BASE OF OPERATIONS. BY TAKING OVER THE BUSINESS WORLD HERE, AND REMOVING THE POPULATION, WE CAN CONTROL THIS GALAXY.
YEAH, AND? I MEAN, GREAT. THAT'S CLEVER. YOU RUN THIS PLANET, YOU RUN THE CONGLOMERATES VIA HENCHCATS I'M GUESSING AS GOING OUT AND ABOUT MUST BE TRICKY FOR YOU AND YOUR, WHAT WAS IT, ELITE PANTHEON? NO DELUSIONS OF GRANDEUR THERE, THEN.
OH, IT'S NOT THE DEAD—THEY'RE JUST HOLOGRAPHICALLY DISGUISED HYDRAULIC WEAPONS, BEAMING DOWN THE ILLUSION OF BEING CATKIND.
MASTER BUBASTION—WE HAVE FOLLOWED YOUR ORDERS, BUT WE DID NOT EXPECT THE DEAD TO RISE. TO STRIKE US DOWN.
YOU'VE BEEN TRICKED, GARRARD. BUT THEN PEOPLE LIKE YOU SO OFTEN ARE. I WONDER IF GULLIBILITY IS GENETIC—I ENCOUNTER IT SO OFTEN THESE DAYS AND—

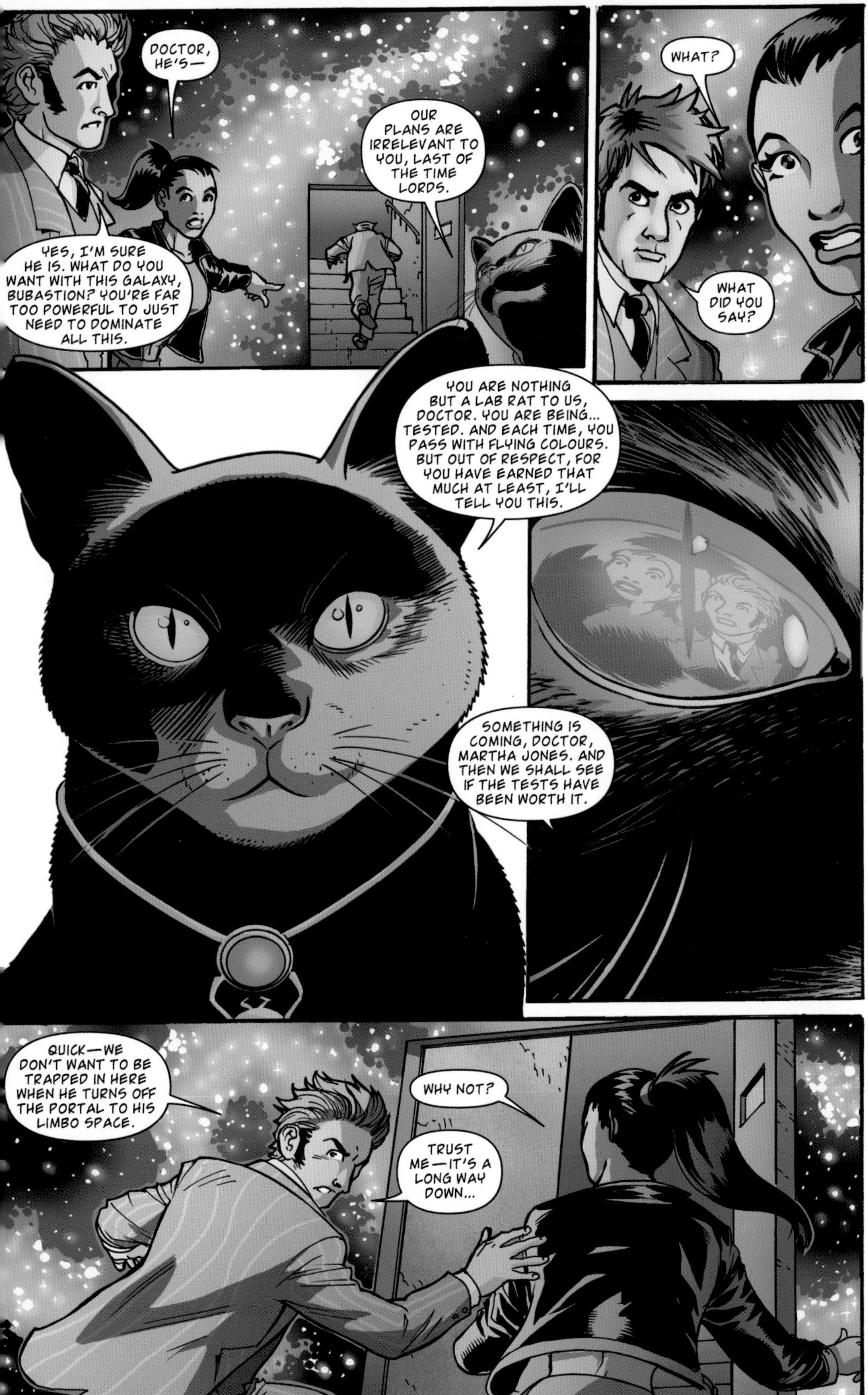
DOCTOR, HE'S—
YES, I'M SURE HE IS. WHAT DO YOU WANT WITH THIS GALAXY, BUBASTION? YOU'RE FAR TOO POWERFUL TO JUST NEED TO DOMINATE ALL THIS.
OUR PLANS ARE IRRELEVANT TO YOU, LAST OF THE TIME LORDS.
WHAT?
WHAT DID YOU SAY?
YOU ARE NOTHING BUT A LAB RAT TO US, DOCTOR. YOU ARE BEING... TESTED. AND EACH TIME, YOU PASS WITH FLYING COLOURS. BUT OUT OF RESPECT, FOR YOU HAVE EARNED THAT MUCH AT LEAST, I'LL TELL YOU THIS.
SOMETHING IS COMING, DOCTOR, MARTHA JONES. AND THEN WE SHALL SEE IF THE TESTS HAVE BEEN WORTH IT.
QUICK—WE DON'T WANT TO BE TRAPPED IN HERE WHEN HE TURNS OFF THE PORTAL TO HIS LIMBO SPACE.
WHY NOT?
TRUST ME—IT'S A LONG WAY DOWN...

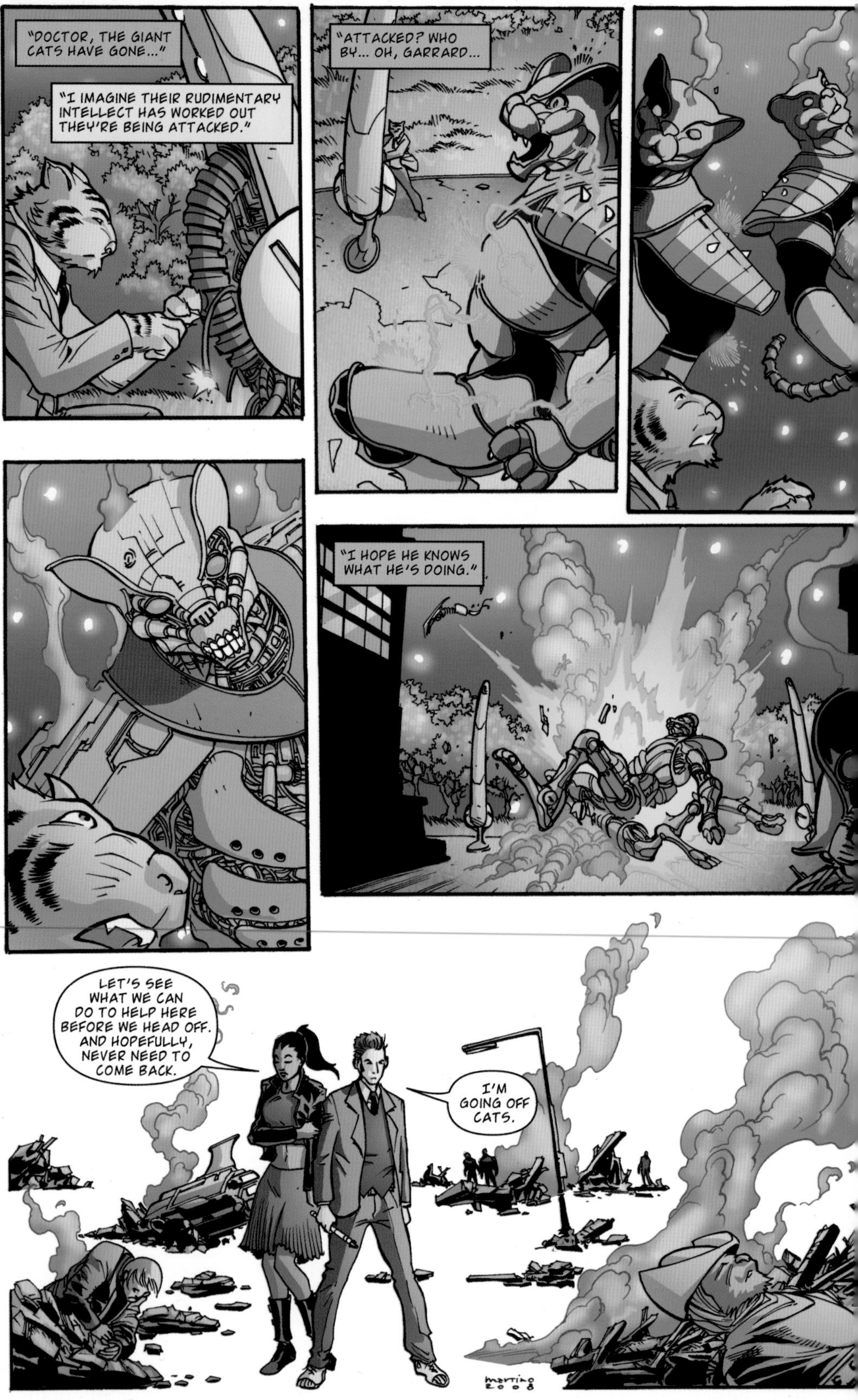
"DOCTOR, THE GIANT CATS HAVE GONE..."
"I IMAGINE THEIR RUDIMENTARY INTELLECT HAS WORKED OUT THEY'RE BEING ATTACKED."
"ATTACKED? WHO BY... OH, GARRARD..."
"I HOPE HE KNOWS WHAT HE'S DOING."
LET'S SEE WHAT WE CAN DO TO HELP HERE BEFORE WE HEAD OFF. AND HOPEFULLY, NEVER NEED TO COME BACK.
I'M GOING OFF CATS.
martino 2008

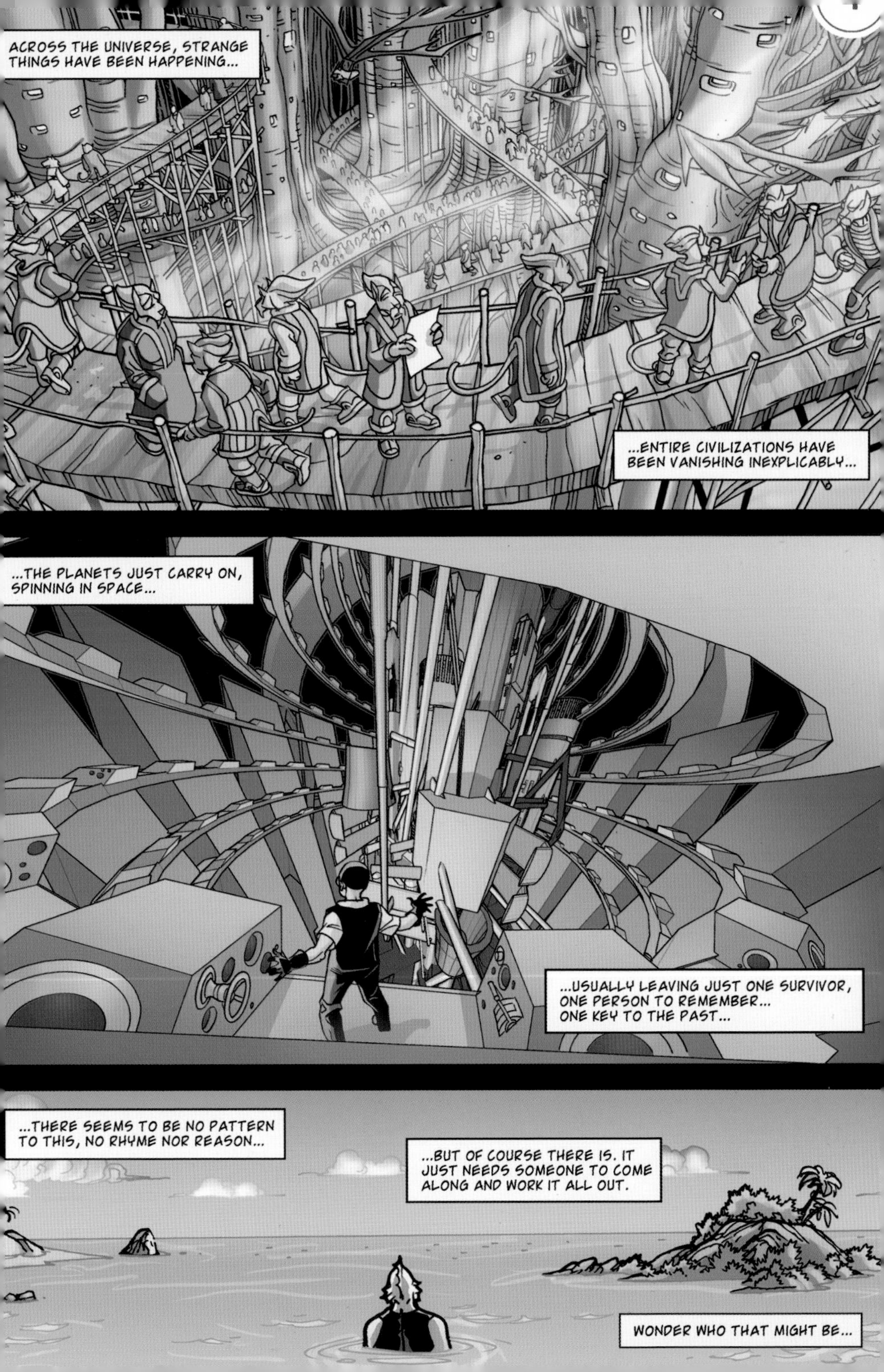
ACROSS THE UNIVERSE, STRANGE THINGS HAVE BEEN HAPPENING...
...ENTIRE CIVILIZATIONS HAVE BEEN VANISHING INEXPLICABLY...
...THE PLANETS JUST CARRY ON, SPINNING IN SPACE...
...USUALLY LEAVING JUST ONE SURVIVOR, ONE PERSON TO REMEMBER... ONE KEY TO THE PAST...
...THERE SEEMS TO BE NO PATTERN TO THIS, NO RHYME NOR REASON...
...BUT OF COURSE THERE IS. IT JUST NEEDS SOMEONE TO COME ALONG AND WORK IT ALL OUT.
WONDER WHO THAT MIGHT BE...

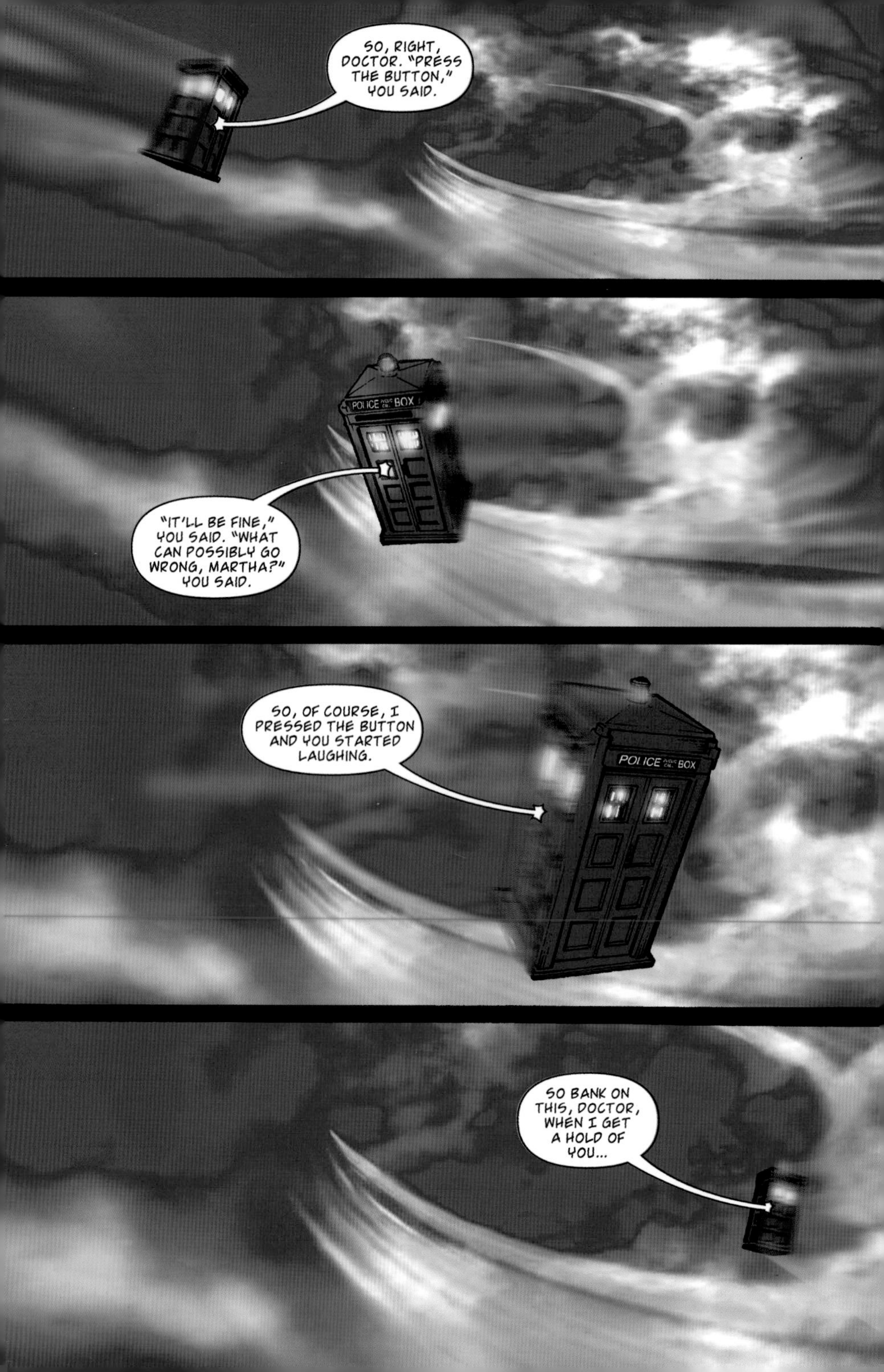
SO, RIGHT, DOCTOR. "PRESS THE BUTTON," YOU SAID.
"IT'LL BE FINE," YOU SAID. "WHAT CAN POSSIBLY GO WRONG, MARTHA?" YOU SAID.
POLICE BOX
SO, OF COURSE, I PRESSED THE BUTTON AND YOU STARTED LAUGHING.
POLICE BOX
SO BANK ON THIS, DOCTOR, WHEN I GET A HOLD OF YOU...

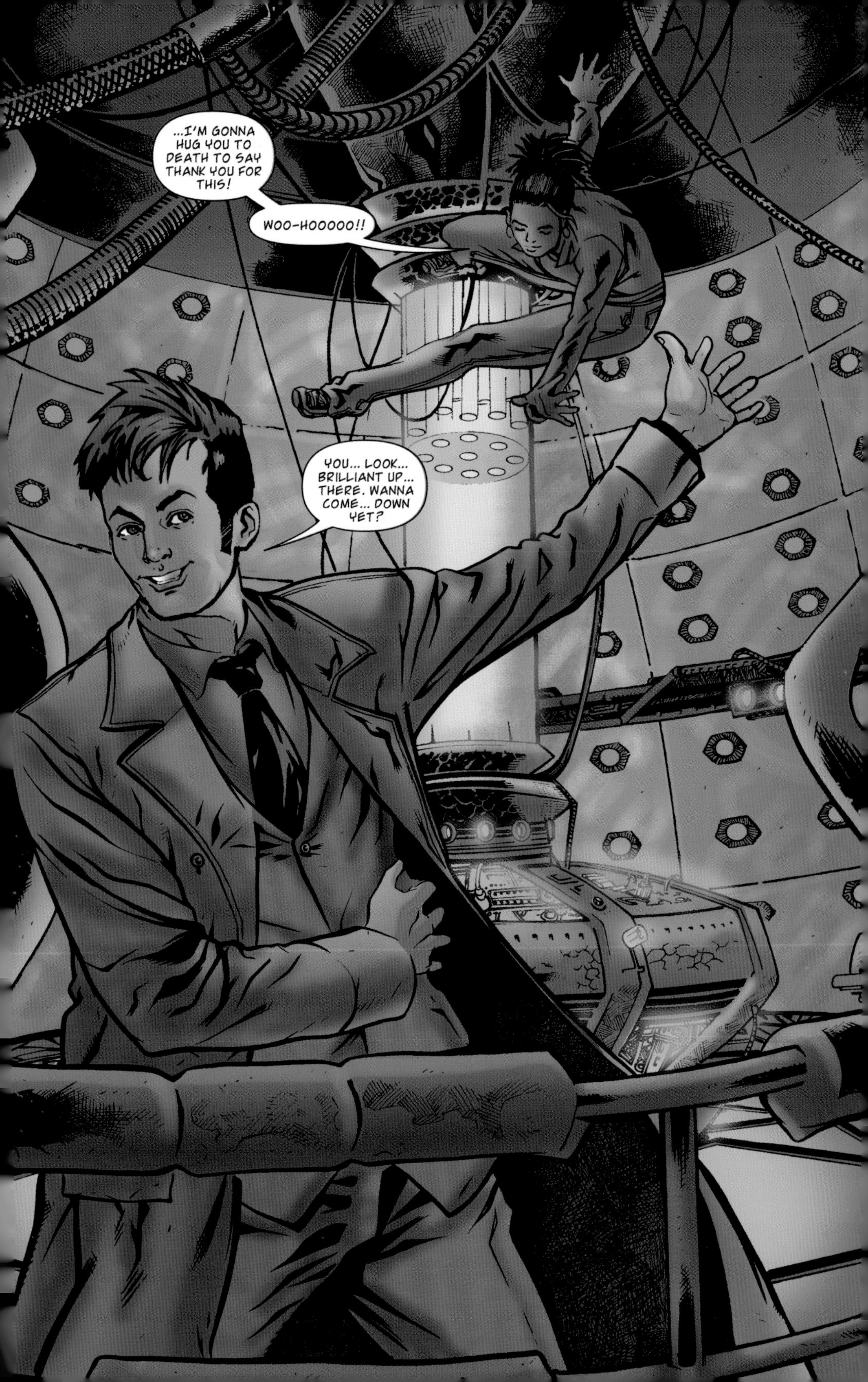
...I'M GONNA HUG YOU TO DEATH TO SAY THANK YOU FOR THIS!
WOO-HOOOOO!!
YOU... LOOK... BRILLIANT UP... THERE. WANNA COME... DOWN YET?

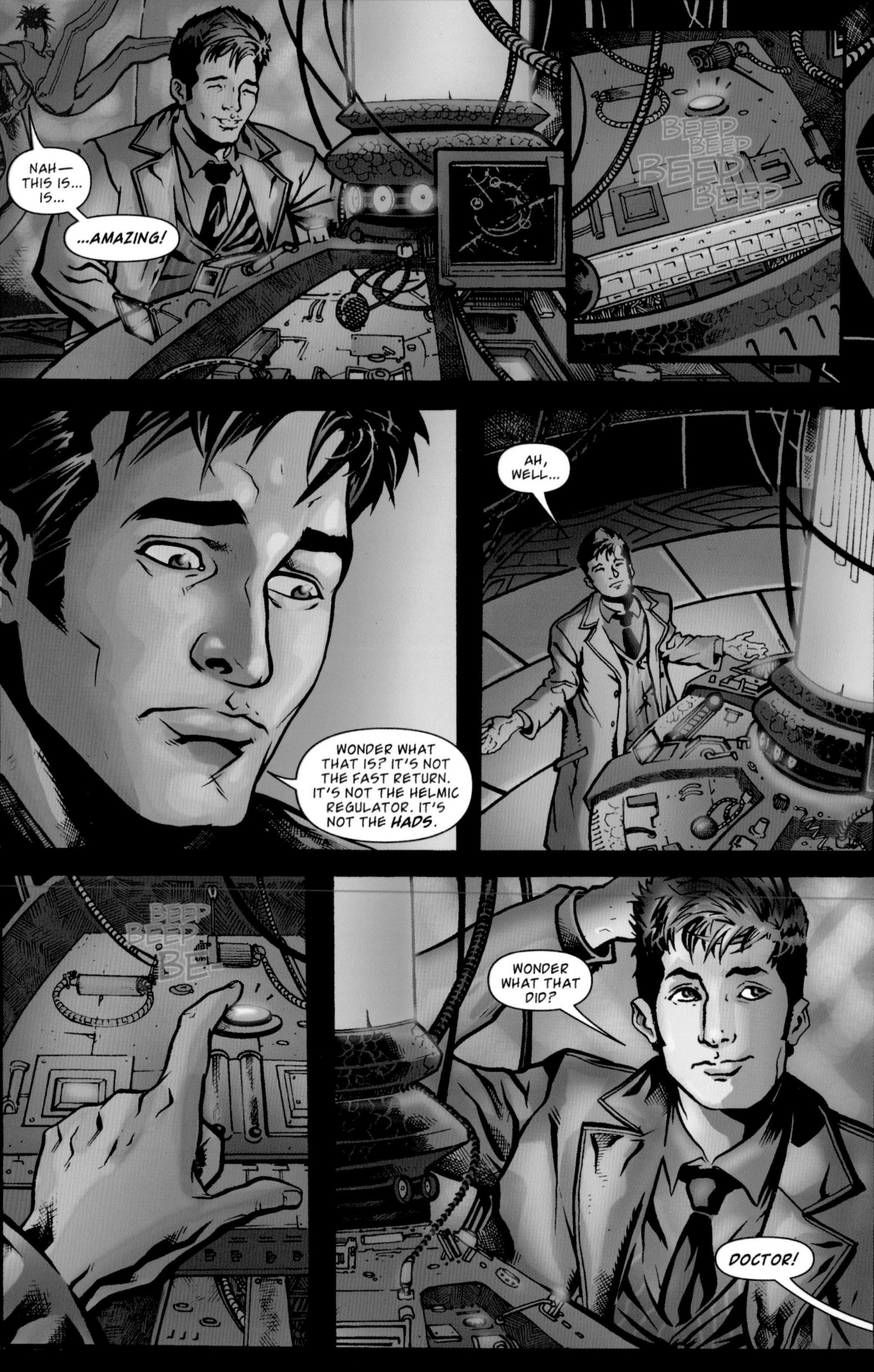
NAH— THIS IS... IS...
...AMAZING!
BEEP BEEP BEEP BEEP
WONDER WHAT THAT IS? IT'S NOT THE FAST RETURN. IT'S NOT THE HELMIC REGULATOR. IT'S NOT THE HADS.
AH, WELL...
BEEP BEEP BE...
WONDER WHAT THAT DID?
DOCTOR!

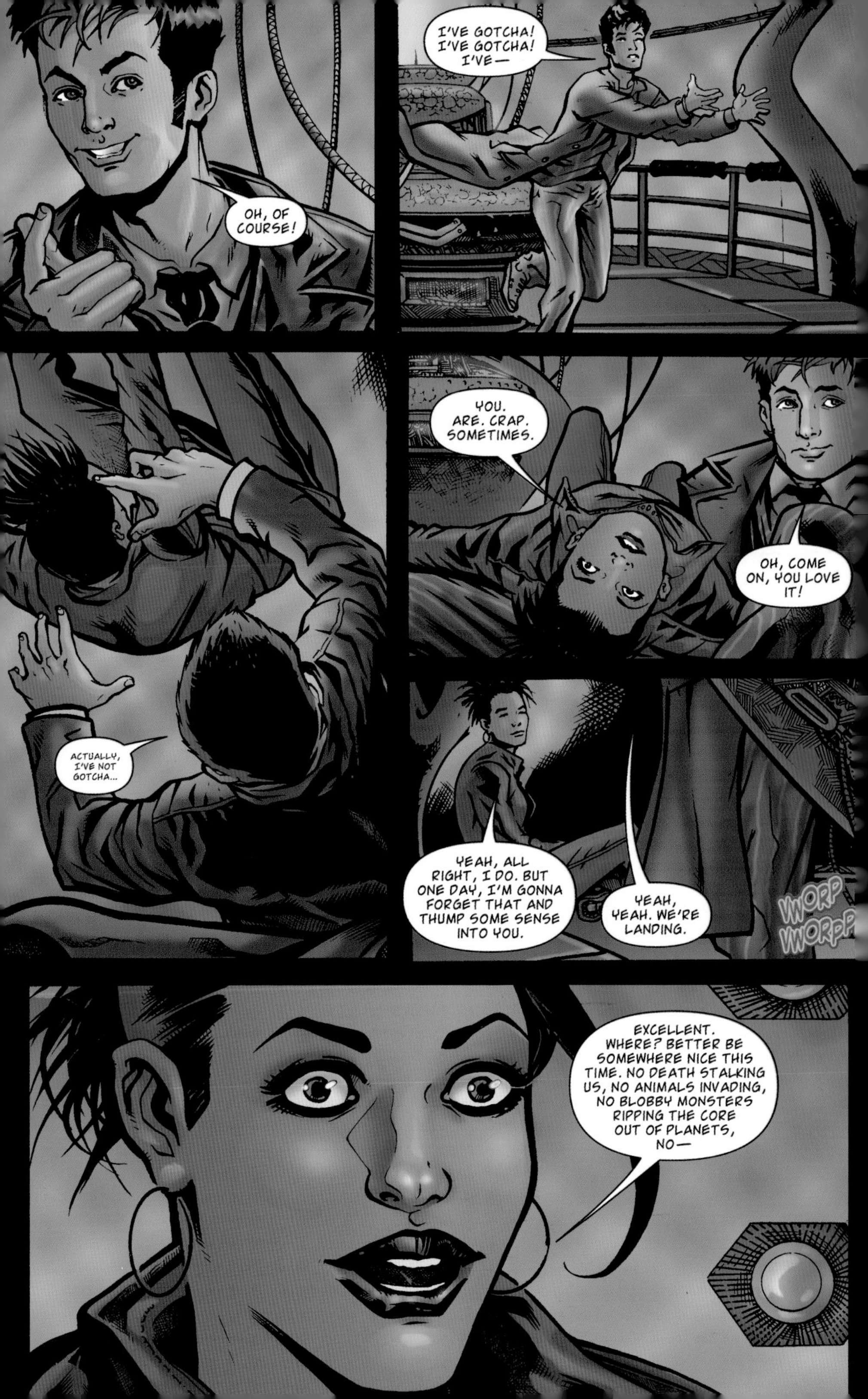
OH, OF COURSE!
I'VE GOTCHA! I'VE GOTCHA! I'VE—
ACTUALLY, I'VE NOT GOTCHA...
YOU. ARE. CRAP. SOMETIMES.
OH, COME ON, YOU LOVE IT!
YEAH, ALL RIGHT, I DO. BUT ONE DAY, I'M GONNA FORGET THAT AND THUMP SOME SENSE INTO YOU.
YEAH, YEAH. WE'RE LANDING.
VWORP VWORP
EXCELLENT. WHERE? BETTER BE SOMEWHERE NICE THIS TIME. NO DEATH STALKING US, NO ANIMALS INVADING, NO BLOBBY MONSTERS RIPPING THE CORE OUT OF PLANETS, NO—

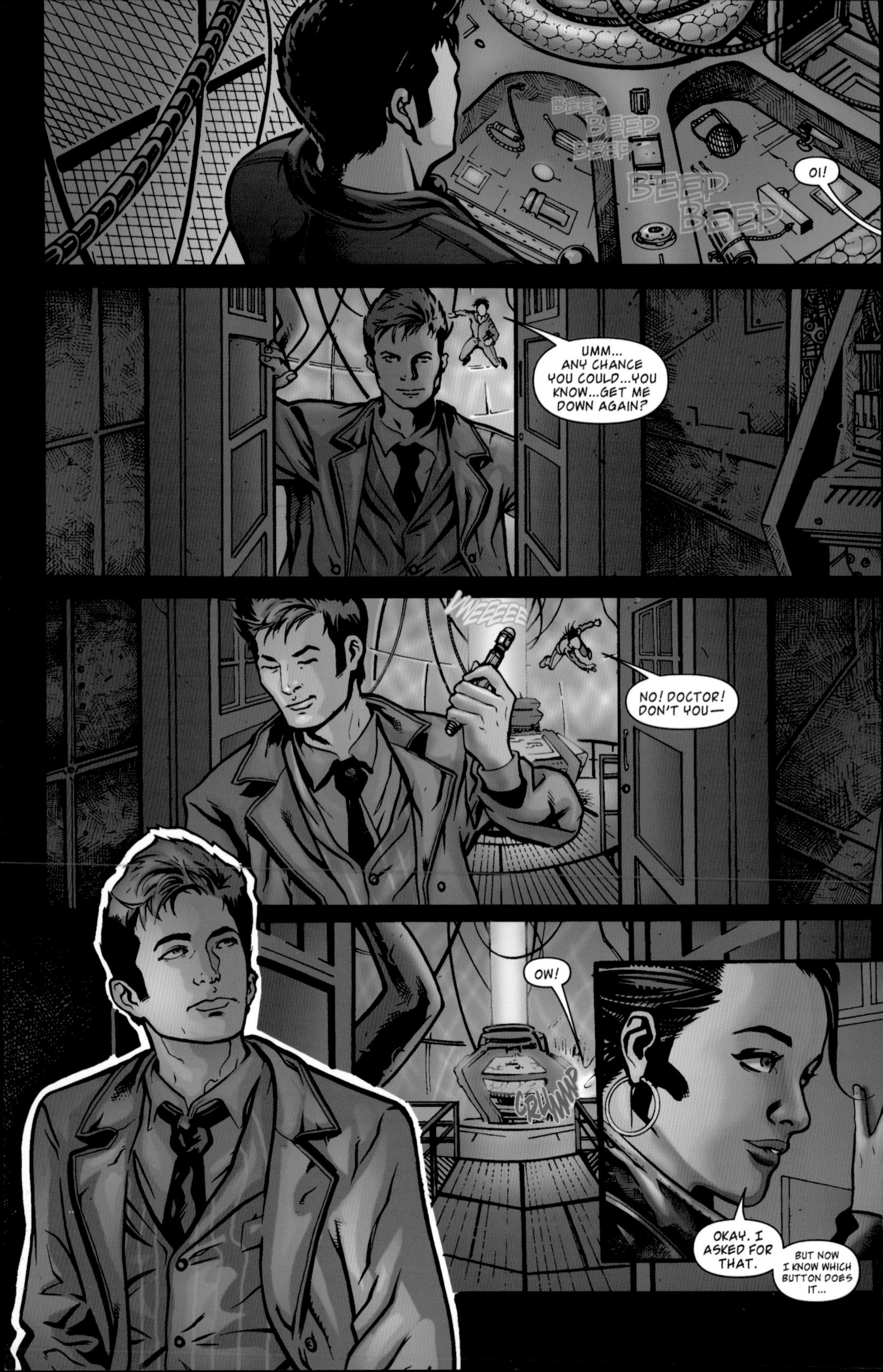
BEEP BEEP BEEP BEEP BEEP
OI!
UMM... ANY CHANCE YOU COULD...YOU KNOW...GET ME DOWN AGAIN?
VWEEEEEE
NO! DOCTOR! DON'T YOU—
OW!
CRUMP
OKAY. I ASKED FOR THAT.
BUT NOW I KNOW WHICH BUTTON DOES IT...

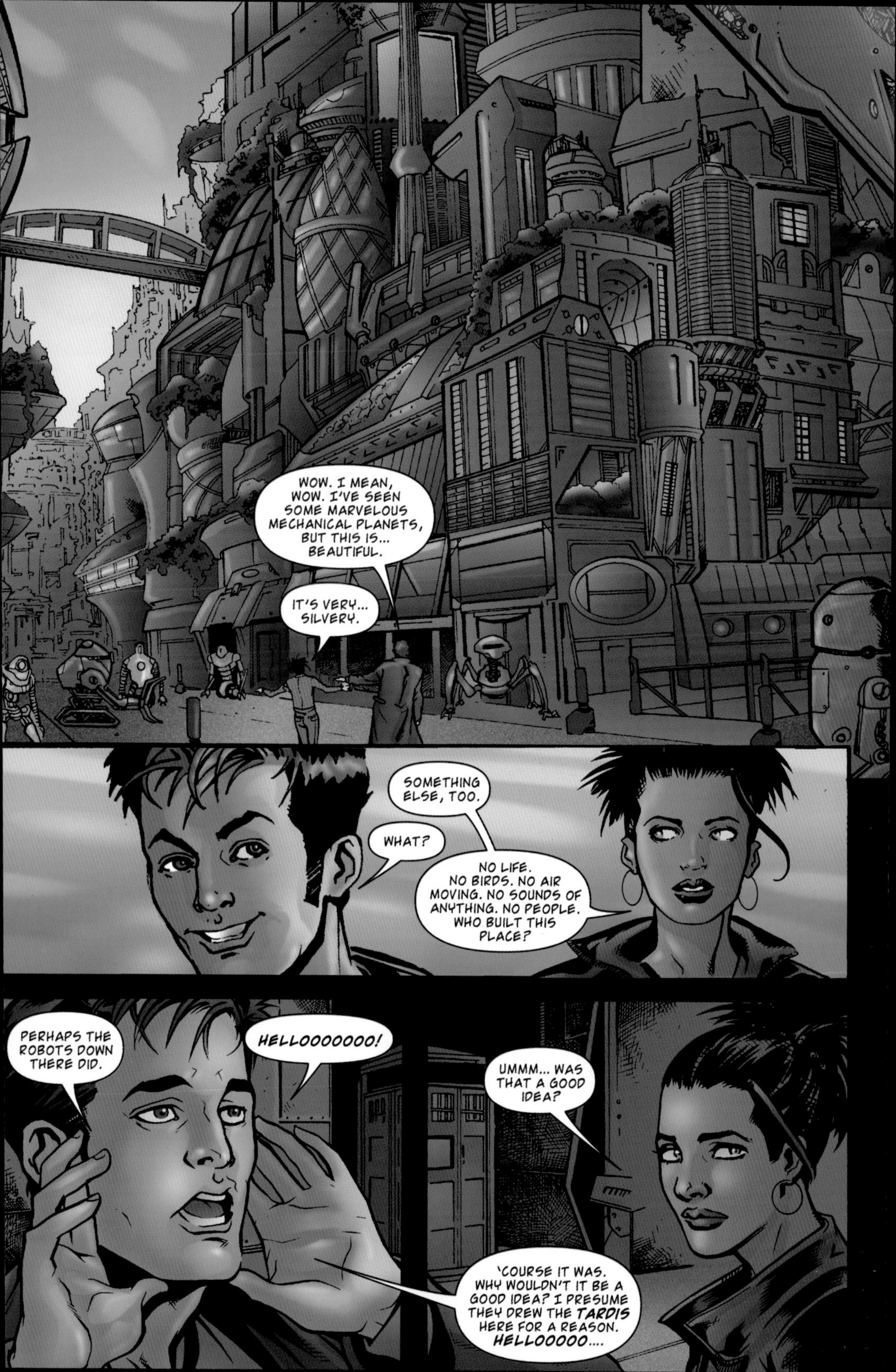
WOW. I MEAN, WOW. I'VE SEEN SOME MARVELOUS MECHANICAL PLANETS, BUT THIS IS... BEAUTIFUL.
IT'S VERY... SILVERY.
SOMETHING ELSE, TOO.
WHAT?
NO LIFE. NO BIRDS. NO AIR MOVING. NO SOUNDS OF ANYTHING. NO PEOPLE. WHO BUILT THIS PLACE?
PERHAPS THE ROBOTS DOWN THERE DID.
HELLOOOOOOO!
UMMM... WAS THAT A GOOD IDEA?
'COURSE IT WAS. WHY WOULDN'T IT BE A GOOD IDEA? I PRESUME THEY DREW THE TARDIS HERE FOR A REASON. HELLOOOO....

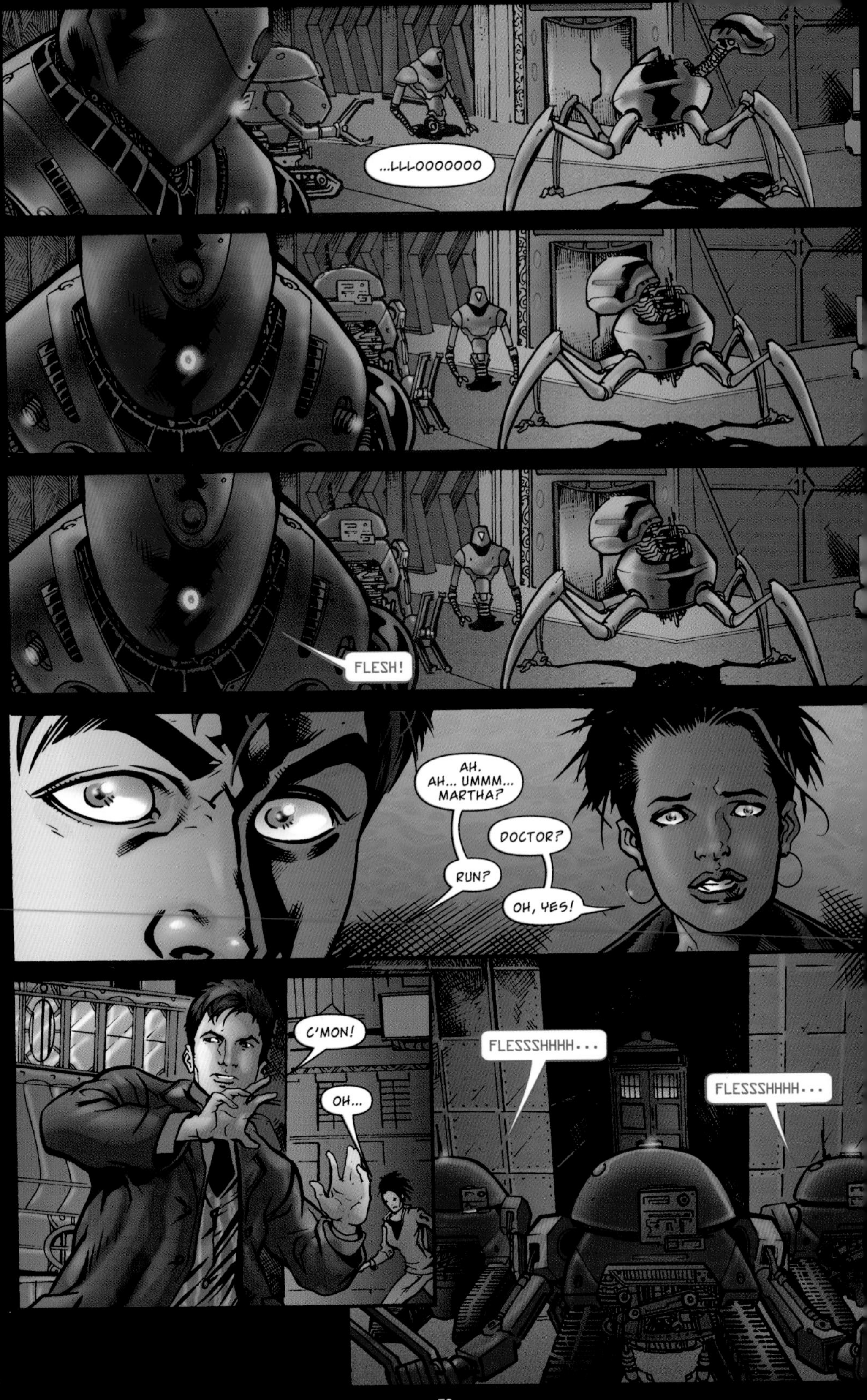

...LLLOOOOOOO
FLESH!
AH. AH... UMMM... MARTHA?
DOCTOR?
RUN?
OH, YES!
C'MON!
OH...
FLESSSHHHH...
FLESSSHHHH...

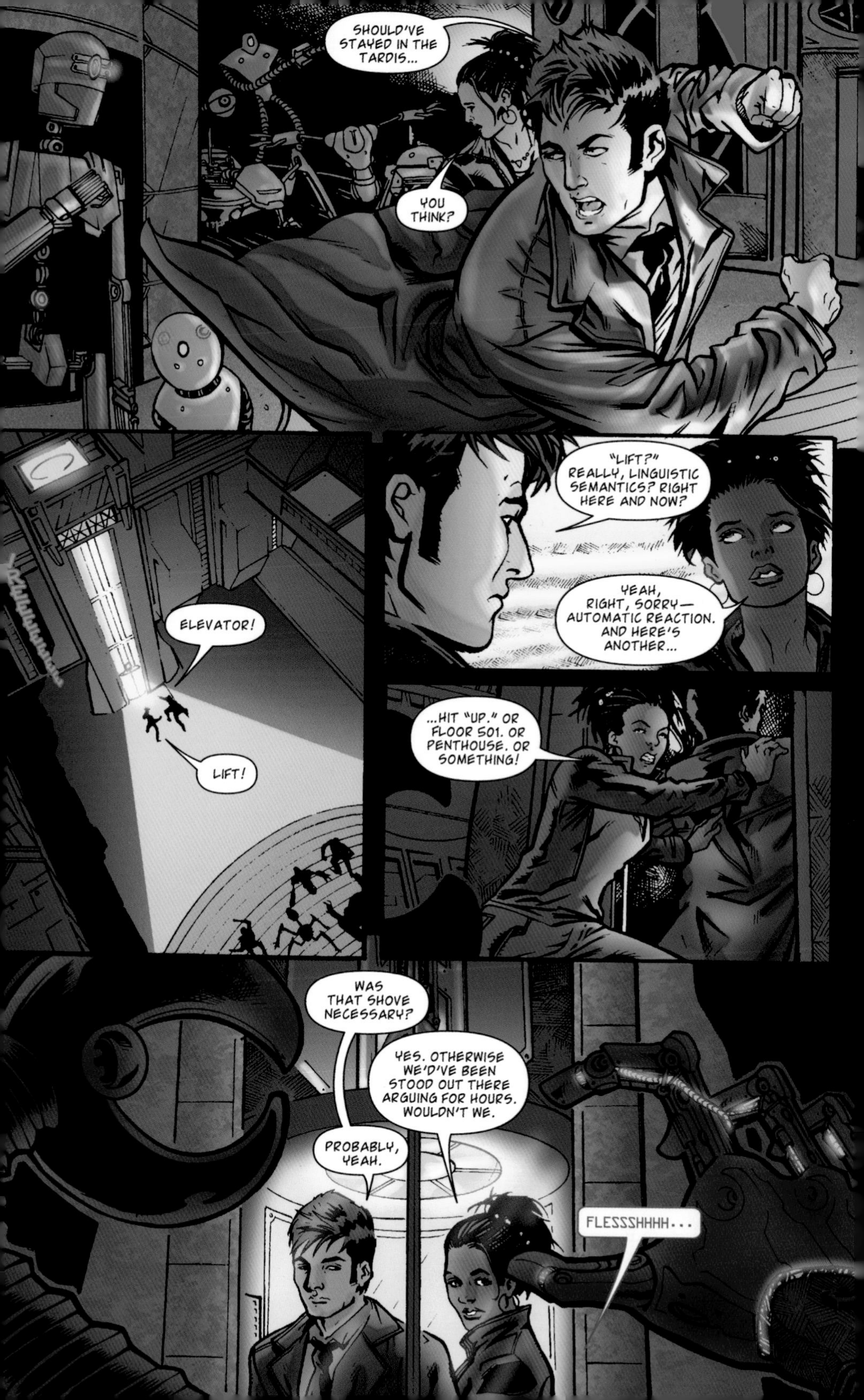
SHOULD'VE STAYED IN THE TARDIS...
YOU THINK?
ELEVATOR!
LIFT!
"LIFT?" REALLY, LINGUISTIC SEMANTICS? RIGHT HERE AND NOW?
YEAH, RIGHT, SORRY— AUTOMATIC REACTION. AND HERE'S ANOTHER...
...HIT "UP." OR FLOOR 501. OR PENTHOUSE. OR SOMETHING!
WAS THAT SHOVE NECESSARY?
YES. OTHERWISE WE'D'VE BEEN STOOD OUT THERE ARGUING FOR HOURS. WOULDN'T WE.
PROBABLY, YEAH.
FLESSSHHHH...

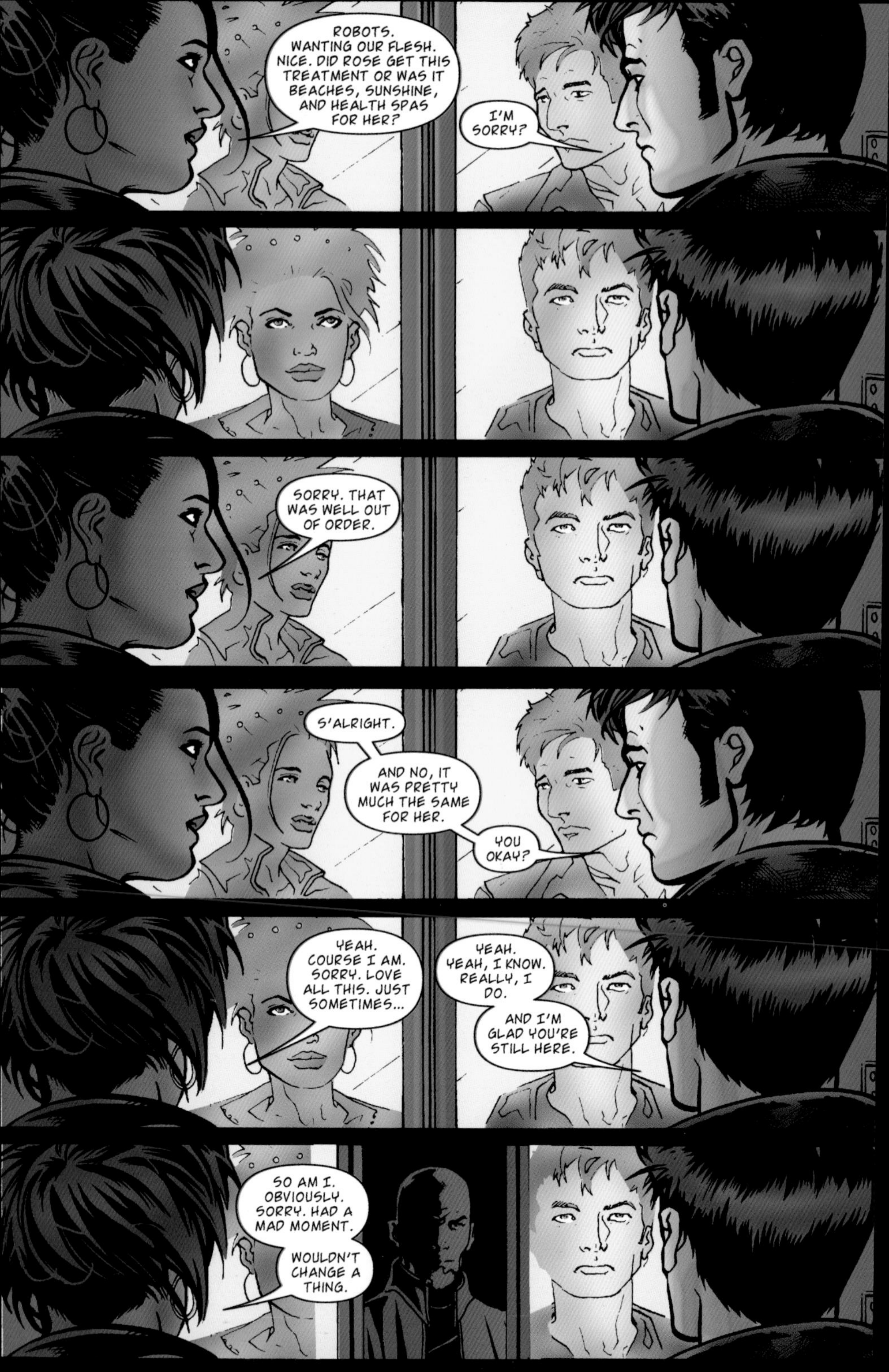
ROBOTS. WANTING OUR FLESH. NICE. DID ROSE GET THIS TREATMENT OR WAS IT BEACHES, SUNSHINE, AND HEALTH SPAS FOR HER?
I'M SORRY?
SORRY. THAT WAS WELL OUT OF ORDER.
S'ALRIGHT.
AND NO, IT WAS PRETTY MUCH THE SAME FOR HER.
YOU OKAY?
YEAH. COURSE I AM. SORRY. LOVE ALL THIS. JUST SOMETIMES...
YEAH. YEAH, I KNOW. REALLY, I DO.
AND I'M GLAD YOU'RE STILL HERE.
SO AM I. OBVIOUSLY. SORRY. HAD A MAD MOMENT.
WOULDN'T CHANGE A THING.

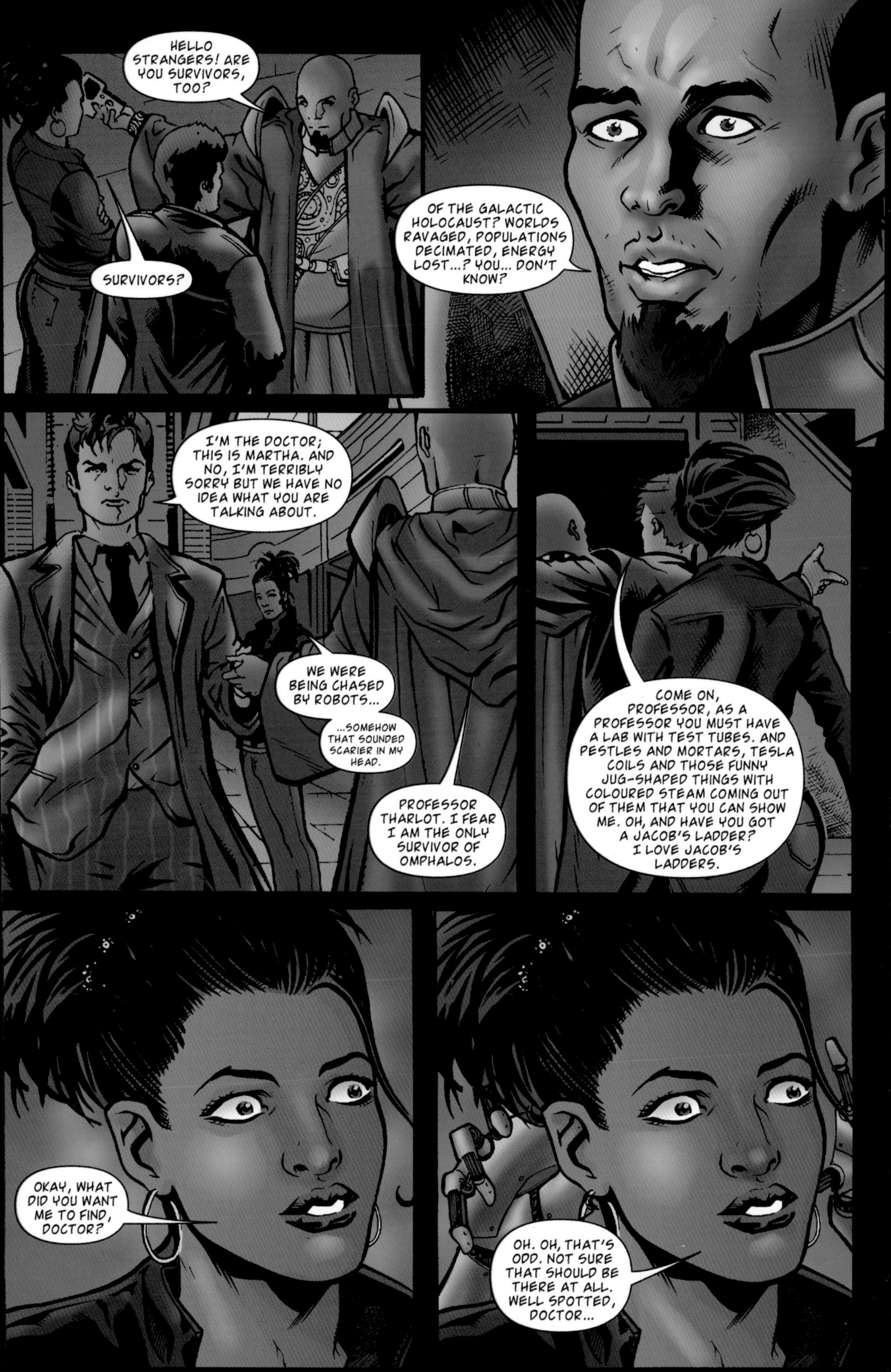
HELLO STRANGERS! ARE YOU SURVIVORS, TOO?
SURVIVORS?
OF THE GALACTIC HOLOCAUST? WORLDS RAVAGED, POPULATIONS DECIMATED, ENERGY LOST...? YOU... DON'T KNOW?
I'M THE DOCTOR; THIS IS MARTHA. AND NO, I'M TERRIBLY SORRY BUT WE HAVE NO IDEA WHAT YOU ARE TALKING ABOUT.
WE WERE BEING CHASED BY ROBOTS...
...SOMEHOW THAT SOUNDED SCARIER IN MY HEAD.
PROFESSOR THARLOT. I FEAR I AM THE ONLY SURVIVOR OF OMPHALOS.
COME ON, PROFESSOR, AS A PROFESSOR YOU MUST HAVE A LAB WITH TEST TUBES. AND PESTLES AND MORTARS, TESLA COILS AND THOSE FUNNY JUG-SHAPED THINGS WITH COLOURED STEAM COMING OUT OF THEM THAT YOU CAN SHOW ME. OH, AND HAVE YOU GOT A JACOB'S LADDER? I LOVE JACOB'S LADDERS.
OKAY, WHAT DID YOU WANT ME TO FIND, DOCTOR?
OH. OH, THAT'S ODD. NOT SURE THAT SHOULD BE THERE AT ALL. WELL SPOTTED, DOCTOR...

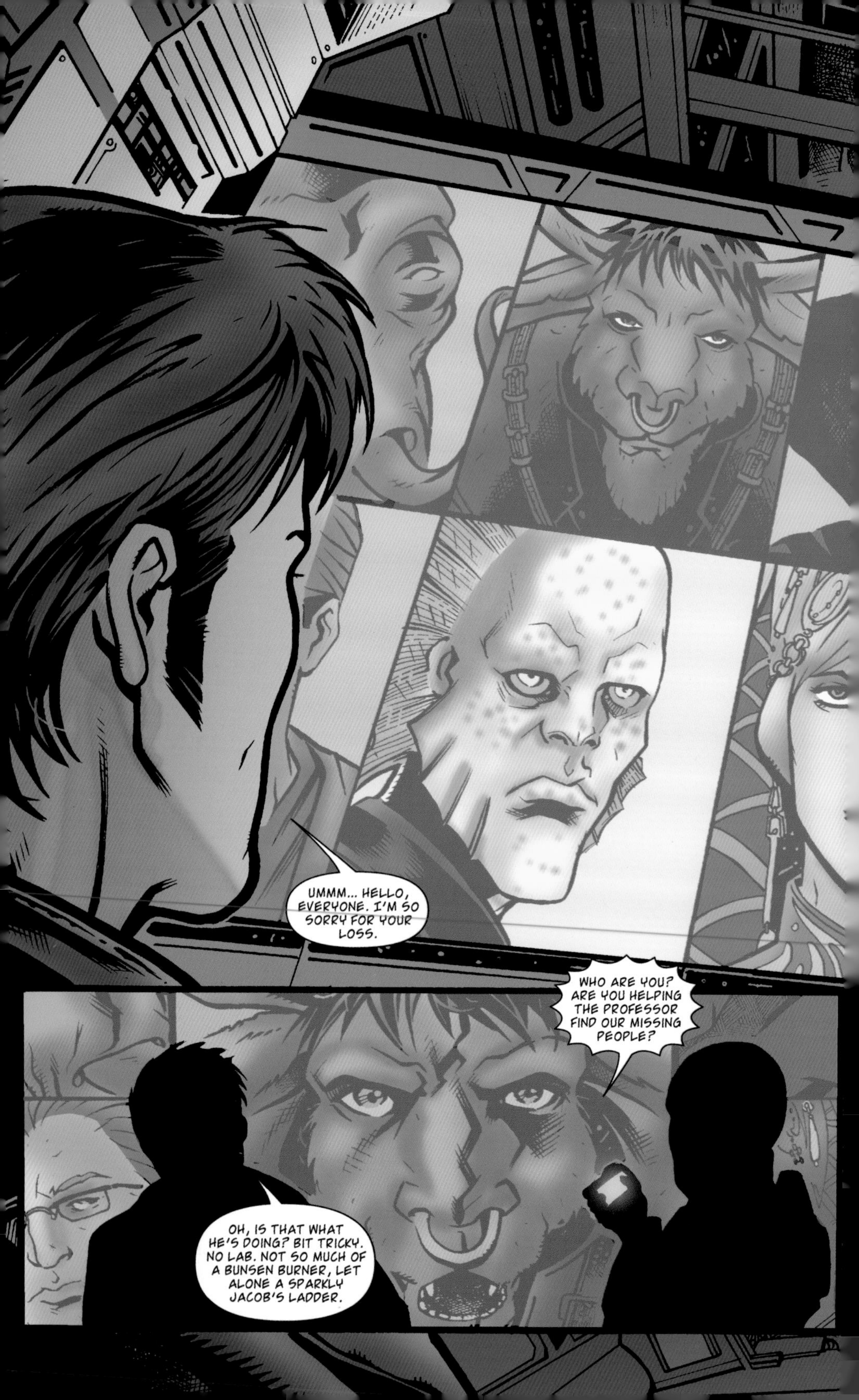
UMMM... HELLO, EVERYONE. I'M SO SORRY FOR YOUR LOSS.
WHO ARE YOU? ARE YOU HELPING THE PROFESSOR FIND OUR MISSING PEOPLE?
OH, IS THAT WHAT HE'S DOING? BIT TRICKY. NO LAB. NOT SO MUCH OF A BUNSEN BURNER, LET ALONE A SPARKLY JACOB'S LADDER.

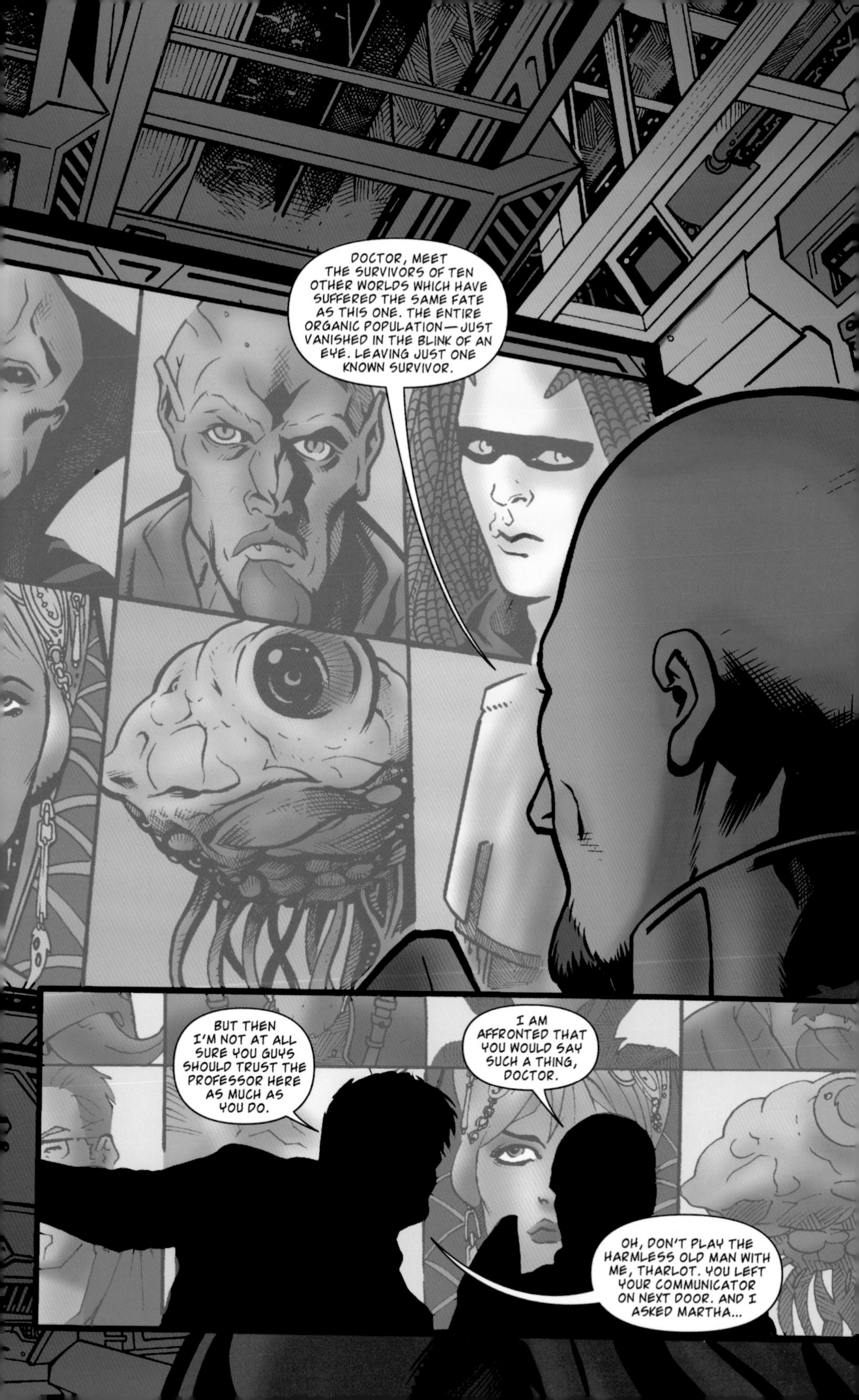
DOCTOR, MEET THE SURVIVORS OF TEN OTHER WORLDS WHICH HAVE SUFFERED THE SAME FATE AS THIS ONE. THE ENTIRE ORGANIC POPULATION— JUST VANISHED IN THE BLINK OF AN EYE. LEAVING JUST ONE KNOWN SURVIVOR.
BUT THEN I'M NOT AT ALL SURE YOU GUYS SHOULD TRUST THE PROFESSOR HERE AS MUCH AS YOU DO.
I AM AFFRONTED THAT YOU WOULD SAY SUCH A THING, DOCTOR.
OH, DON'T PLAY THE HARMLESS OLD MAN WITH ME, THARLOT. YOU LEFT YOUR COMMUNICATOR ON NEXT DOOR. AND I ASKED MARTHA...

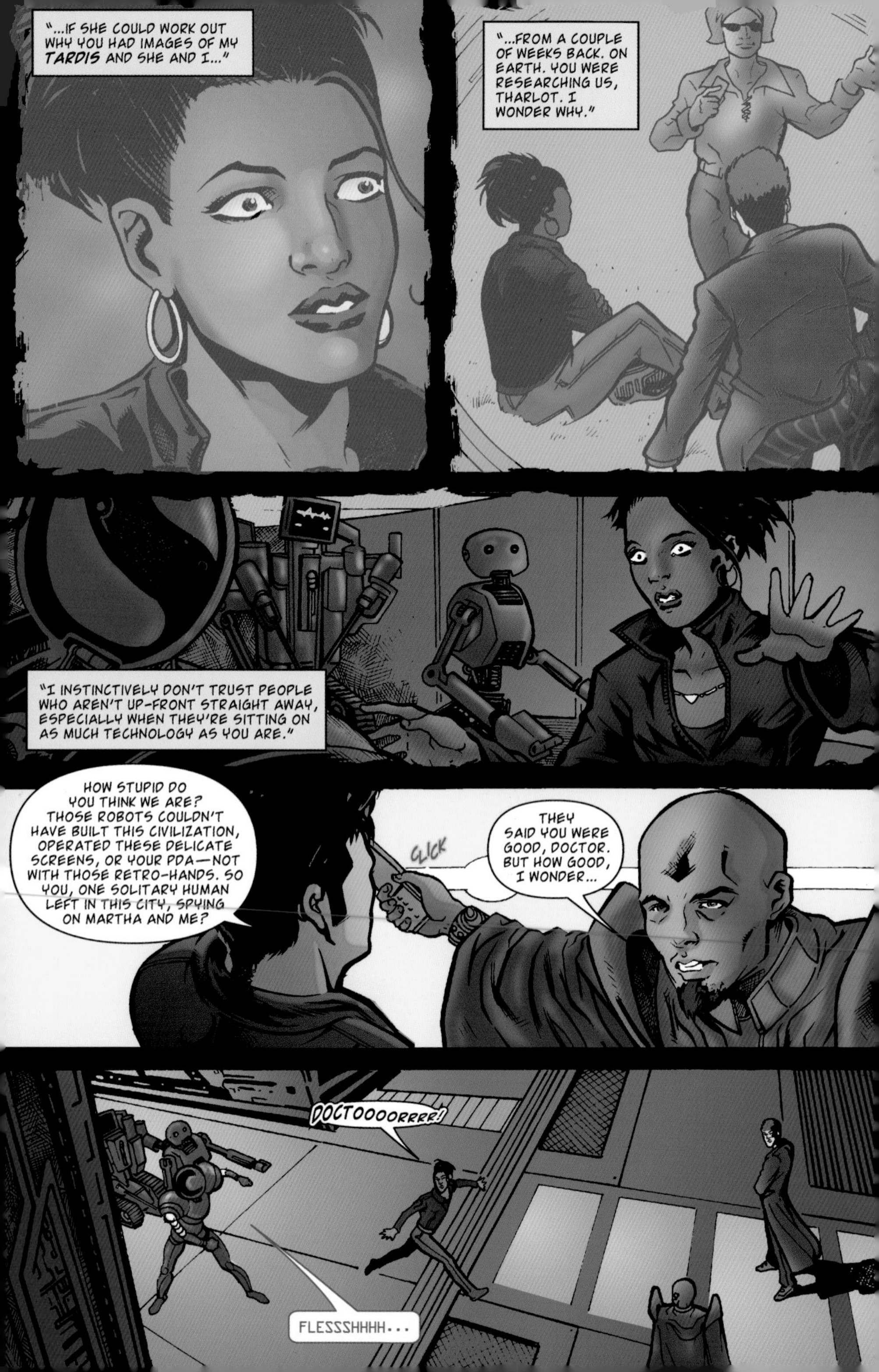
"...IF SHE COULD WORK OUT WHY YOU HAD IMAGES OF MY *TARDIS* AND SHE AND I..."
"...FROM A COUPLE OF WEEKS BACK. ON EARTH. YOU WERE RESEARCHING US, THARLOT. I WONDER WHY."
"I INSTINCTIVELY DON'T TRUST PEOPLE WHO AREN'T UP-FRONT STRAIGHT AWAY, ESPECIALLY WHEN THEY'RE SITTING ON AS MUCH TECHNOLOGY AS YOU ARE."
HOW STUPID DO YOU THINK WE ARE? THOSE ROBOTS COULDN'T HAVE BUILT THIS CIVILIZATION, OPERATED THESE DELICATE SCREENS, OR YOUR PDA—NOT WITH THOSE RETRO-HANDS. SO YOU, ONE SOLITARY HUMAN LEFT IN THIS CITY, SPYING ON MARTHA AND ME?
CLICK
THEY SAID YOU WERE GOOD, DOCTOR. BUT HOW GOOD, I WONDER...
DOCTOOOORRRR!
FLESSSHHHH...

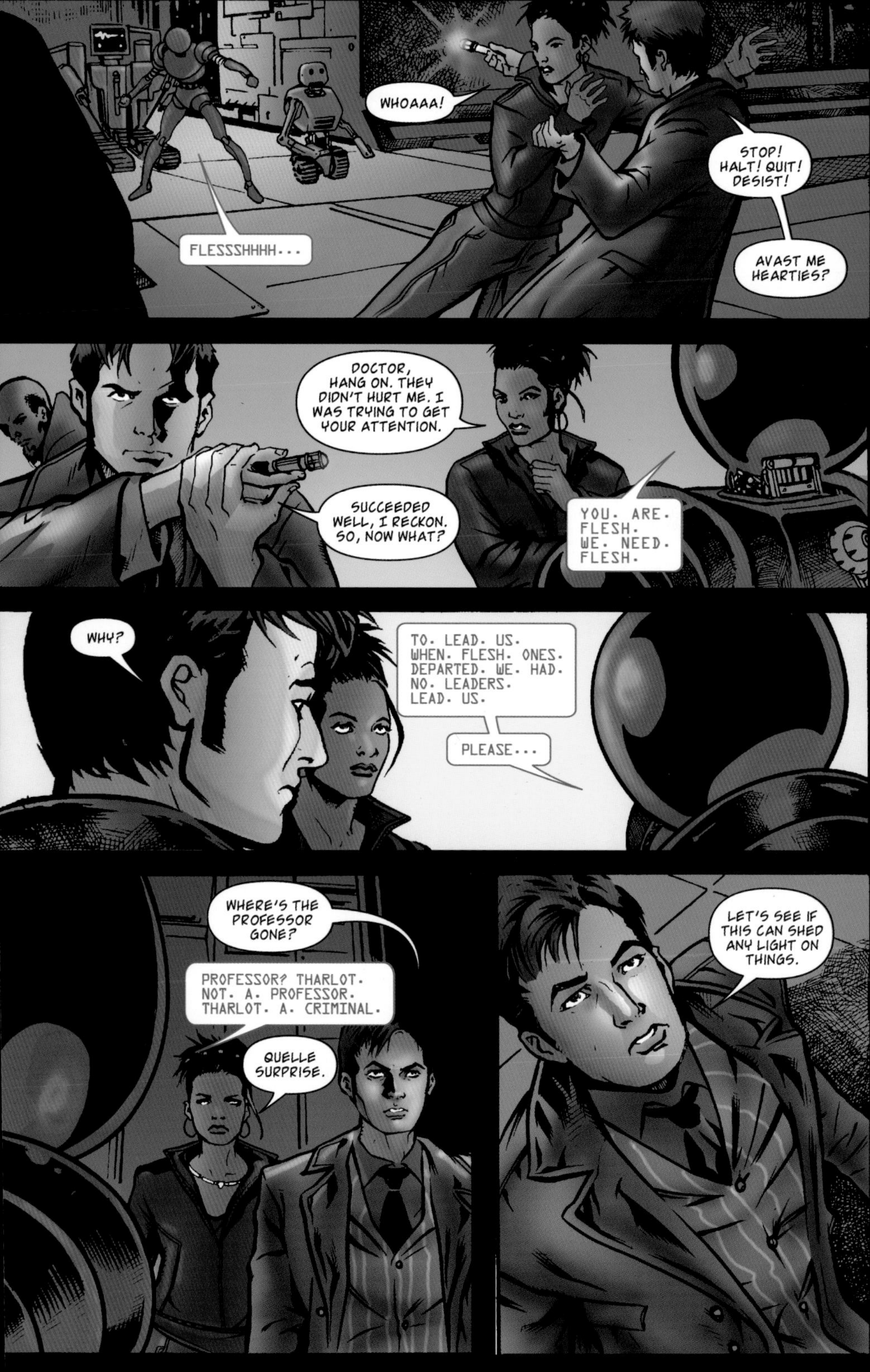
WHOAAA!
STOP! HALT! QUIT! DESIST!
FLESSSHHHH...
AVAST ME HEARTIES?
DOCTOR, HANG ON. THEY DIDN'T HURT ME. I WAS TRYING TO GET YOUR ATTENTION.
SUCCEEDED WELL, I RECKON. SO, NOW WHAT?
YOU. ARE. FLESH. WE. NEED. FLESH.
WHY?
TO. LEAD. US. WHEN. FLESH. ONES. DEPARTED. WE. HAD. NO. LEADERS. LEAD. US.
PLEASE...
WHERE'S THE PROFESSOR GONE?
PROFESSOR? THARLOT. NOT. A. PROFESSOR. THARLOT. A. CRIMINAL.
QUELLE SURPRISE.
LET'S SEE IF THIS CAN SHED ANY LIGHT ON THINGS.

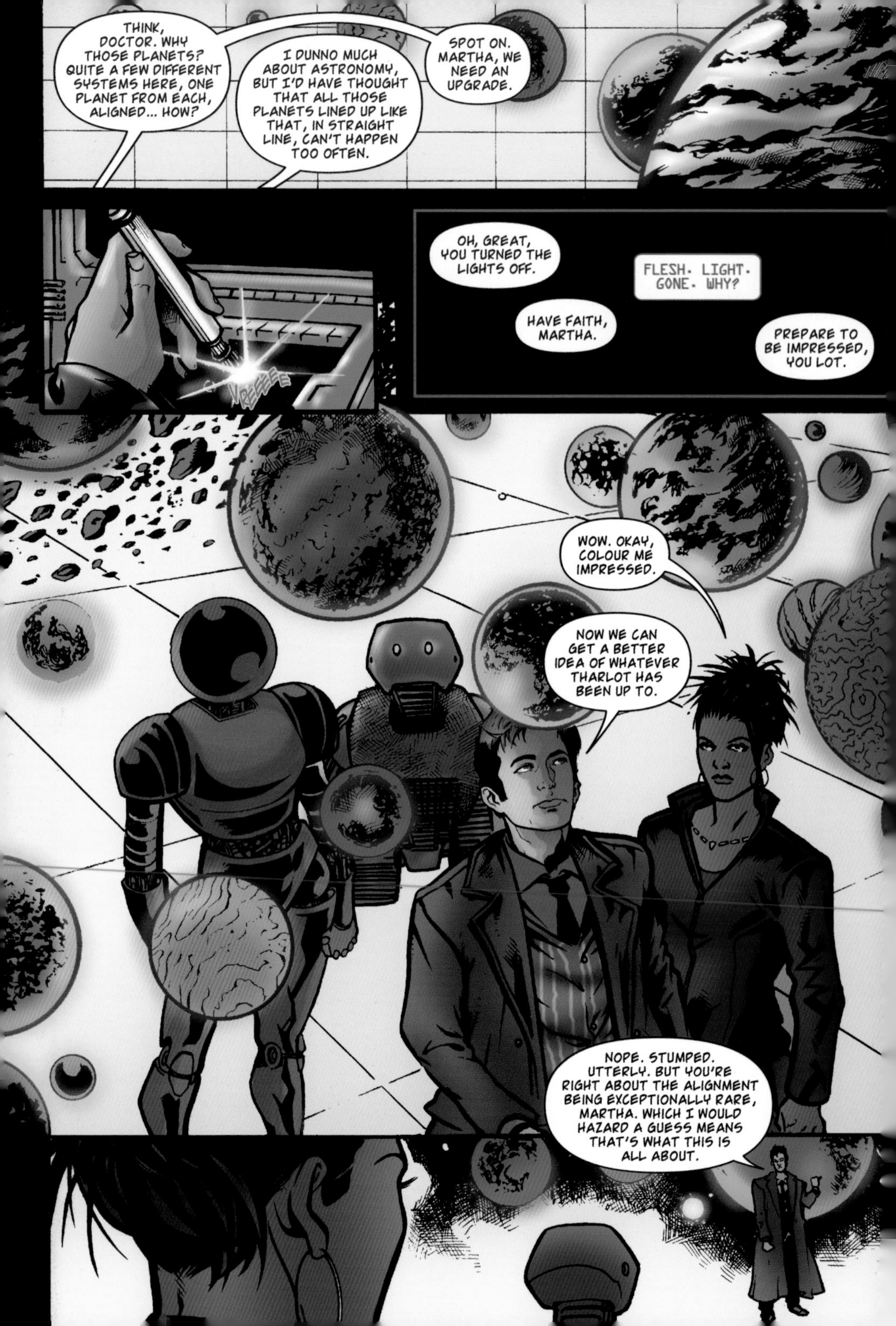
THINK, DOCTOR. WHY THOSE PLANETS? QUITE A FEW DIFFERENT SYSTEMS HERE, ONE PLANET FROM EACH, ALIGNED... HOW?
I DUNNO MUCH ABOUT ASTRONOMY, BUT I'D HAVE THOUGHT THAT ALL THOSE PLANETS LINED UP LIKE THAT, IN STRAIGHT LINE, CAN'T HAPPEN TOO OFTEN.
SPOT ON. MARTHA, WE NEED AN UPGRADE.
VREEEEE
OH, GREAT, YOU TURNED THE LIGHTS OFF.
FLESH. LIGHT. GONE. WHY?
HAVE FAITH, MARTHA.
PREPARE TO BE IMPRESSED, YOU LOT.
WOW. OKAY, COLOUR ME IMPRESSED.
NOW WE CAN GET A BETTER IDEA OF WHATEVER THARLOT HAS BEEN UP TO.
NOPE. STUMPED. UTTERLY. BUT YOU'RE RIGHT ABOUT THE ALIGNMENT BEING EXCEPTIONALLY RARE, MARTHA. WHICH I WOULD HAZARD A GUESS MEANS THAT'S WHAT THIS IS ALL ABOUT.

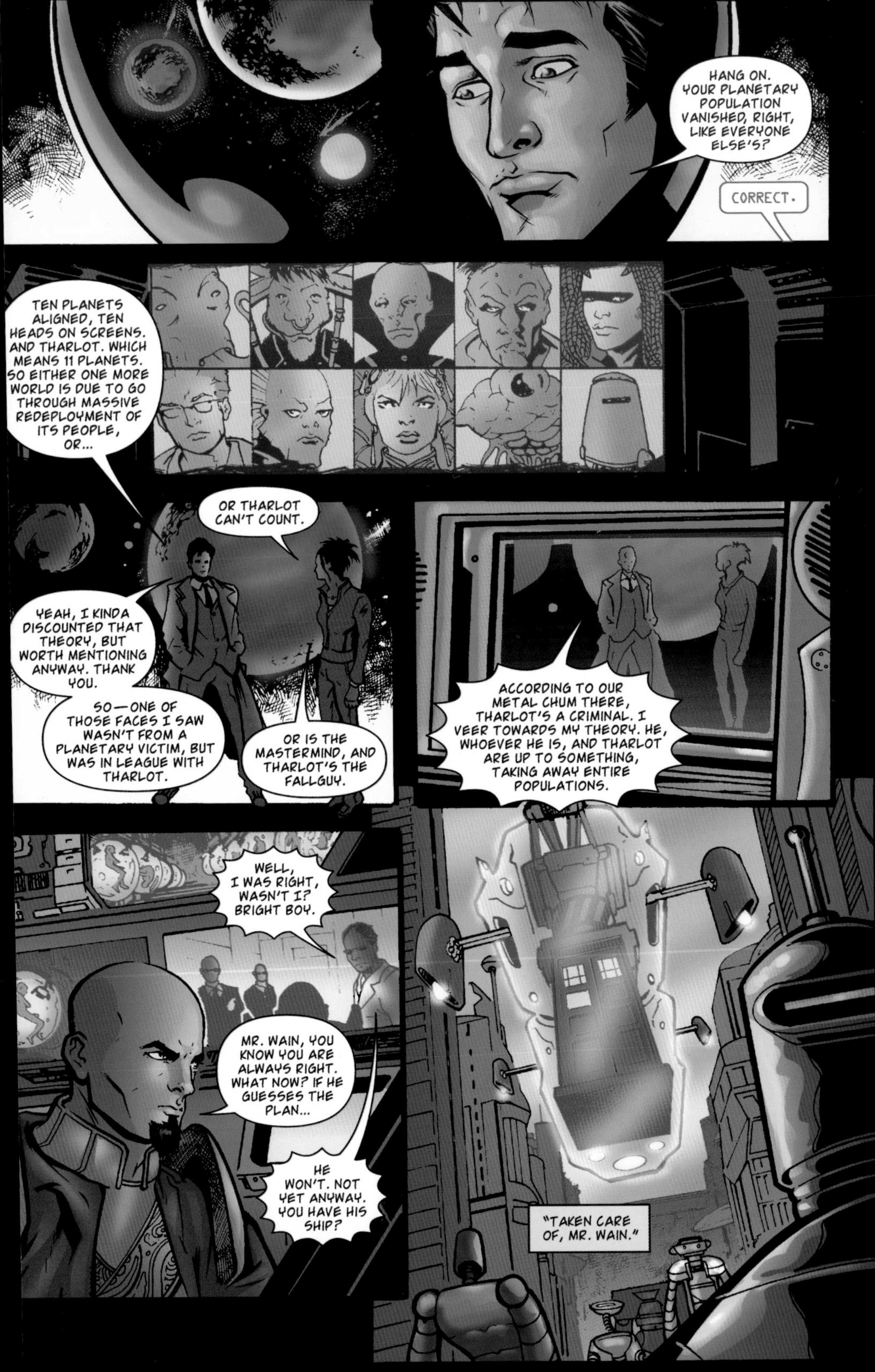
HANG ON. YOUR PLANETARY POPULATION VANISHED, RIGHT, LIKE EVERYONE ELSE'S?
CORRECT.
TEN PLANETS ALIGNED, TEN HEADS ON SCREENS. AND THARLOT. WHICH MEANS 11 PLANETS. SO EITHER ONE MORE WORLD IS DUE TO GO THROUGH MASSIVE REDEPLOYMENT OF ITS PEOPLE, OR...
OR THARLOT CAN'T COUNT.
YEAH, I KINDA DISCOUNTED THAT THEORY, BUT WORTH MENTIONING ANYWAY. THANK YOU.
SO—ONE OF THOSE FACES I SAW WASN'T FROM A PLANETARY VICTIM, BUT WAS IN LEAGUE WITH THARLOT.
OR IS THE MASTERMIND, AND THARLOT'S THE FALLGUY.
ACCORDING TO OUR METAL CHUM THERE, THARLOT'S A CRIMINAL. I VEER TOWARDS MY THEORY. HE, WHOEVER HE IS, AND THARLOT ARE UP TO SOMETHING, TAKING AWAY ENTIRE POPULATIONS.
WELL, I WAS RIGHT, WASN'T I? BRIGHT BOY.
MR. WAIN, YOU KNOW YOU ARE ALWAYS RIGHT. WHAT NOW? IF HE GUESSES THE PLAN...
HE WON'T. NOT YET ANYWAY. YOU HAVE HIS SHIP?
"TAKEN CARE OF, MR. WAIN."

SO, TELL US ABOUT THARLOT.

HE. WAS IMPRISONED. TWELVE. CYCLES. AGO.

WHY?

FLESH. PEOPLE. KILLED. BY. HIM. HE. LOCKED. AWAY. FOR. LIFE.

WHEN. FLESH. PEOPLE. VANISHED. HE. WAS. UNSUPERVISED. WE. TRIED. TO. RECAPTURE. HIM. HE. EVADED. US. FLED. TO. THIS. TOWER. WE. WERE. UNAWARE. OF. WHERE. HE. WAS. UNTIL. YOU. LED. US. HERE.

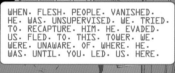

YOU THINK HE HAD SOMETHING TO DO WITH THE FLESH... THE PEOPLE VANISHING?

HE. IS. A. CRIMINAL.

CRUDE MACHINE LOGIC. HE WAS A CRIMINAL, THEREFORE EVERY CRIME MUST BE HIS IF NO ONE ELSE IS PRESENT.

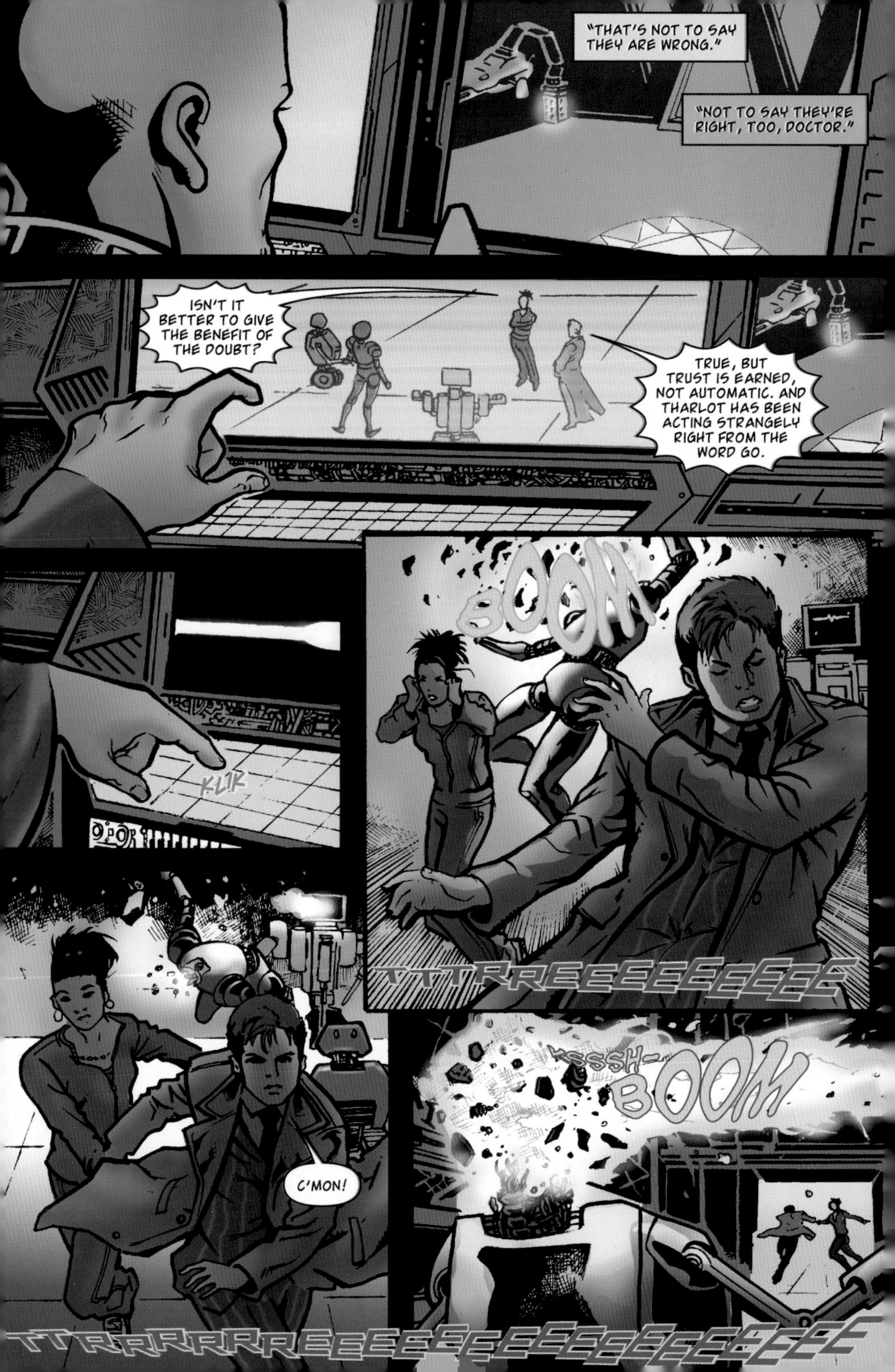
"THAT'S NOT TO SAY THEY ARE WRONG."
"NOT TO SAY THEY'RE RIGHT, TOO, DOCTOR."
ISN'T IT BETTER TO GIVE THE BENEFIT OF THE DOUBT?
TRUE, BUT TRUST IS EARNED, NOT AUTOMATIC. AND THARLOT HAS BEEN ACTING STRANGELY RIGHT FROM THE WORD GO.
KLIK
BOOM
TTTRREEEEEEEEEE
C'MON!
KSSSH-BOOM
TTRRRRRRREEEEEEEEEEEEEEEEEEEE

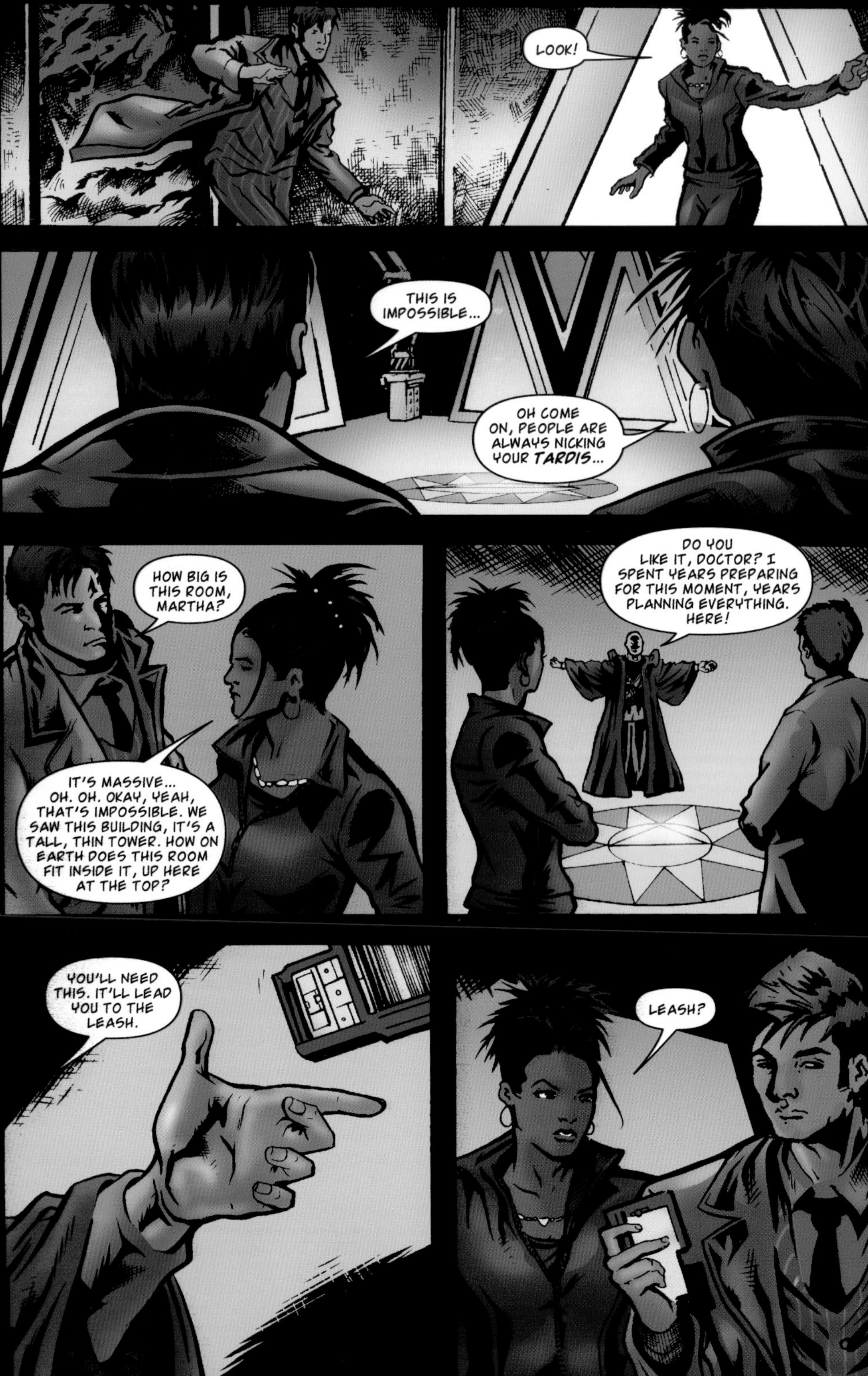
LOOK!
THIS IS IMPOSSIBLE...
OH COME ON, PEOPLE ARE ALWAYS NICKING YOUR TARDIS...
HOW BIG IS THIS ROOM, MARTHA?
IT'S MASSIVE... OH. OH. OKAY, YEAH, THAT'S IMPOSSIBLE. WE SAW THIS BUILDING, IT'S A TALL, THIN TOWER. HOW ON EARTH DOES THIS ROOM FIT INSIDE IT, UP HERE AT THE TOP?
DO YOU LIKE IT, DOCTOR? I SPENT YEARS PREPARING FOR THIS MOMENT, YEARS PLANNING EVERYTHING. HERE!
YOU'LL NEED THIS. IT'LL LEAD YOU TO THE LEASH.
LEASH?

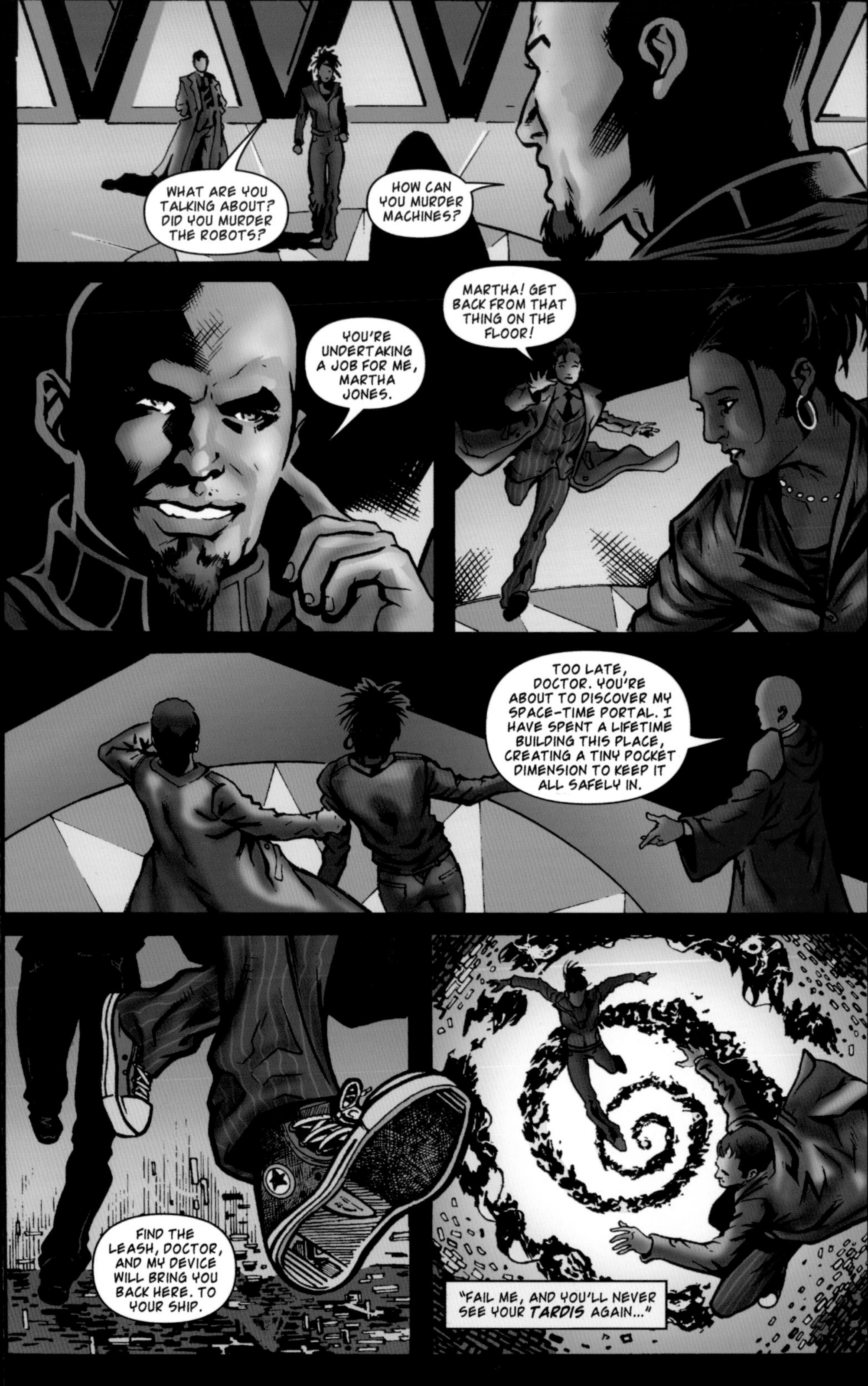
WHAT ARE YOU TALKING ABOUT? DID YOU MURDER THE ROBOTS?
HOW CAN YOU MURDER MACHINES?
YOU'RE UNDERTAKING A JOB FOR ME, MARTHA JONES.
MARTHA! GET BACK FROM THAT THING ON THE FLOOR!
TOO LATE, DOCTOR. YOU'RE ABOUT TO DISCOVER MY SPACE-TIME PORTAL. I HAVE SPENT A LIFETIME BUILDING THIS PLACE, CREATING A TINY POCKET DIMENSION TO KEEP IT ALL SAFELY IN.
FIND THE LEASH, DOCTOR, AND MY DEVICE WILL BRING YOU BACK HERE. TO YOUR SHIP.
"FAIL ME, AND YOU'LL NEVER SEE YOUR *TARDIS* AGAIN..."

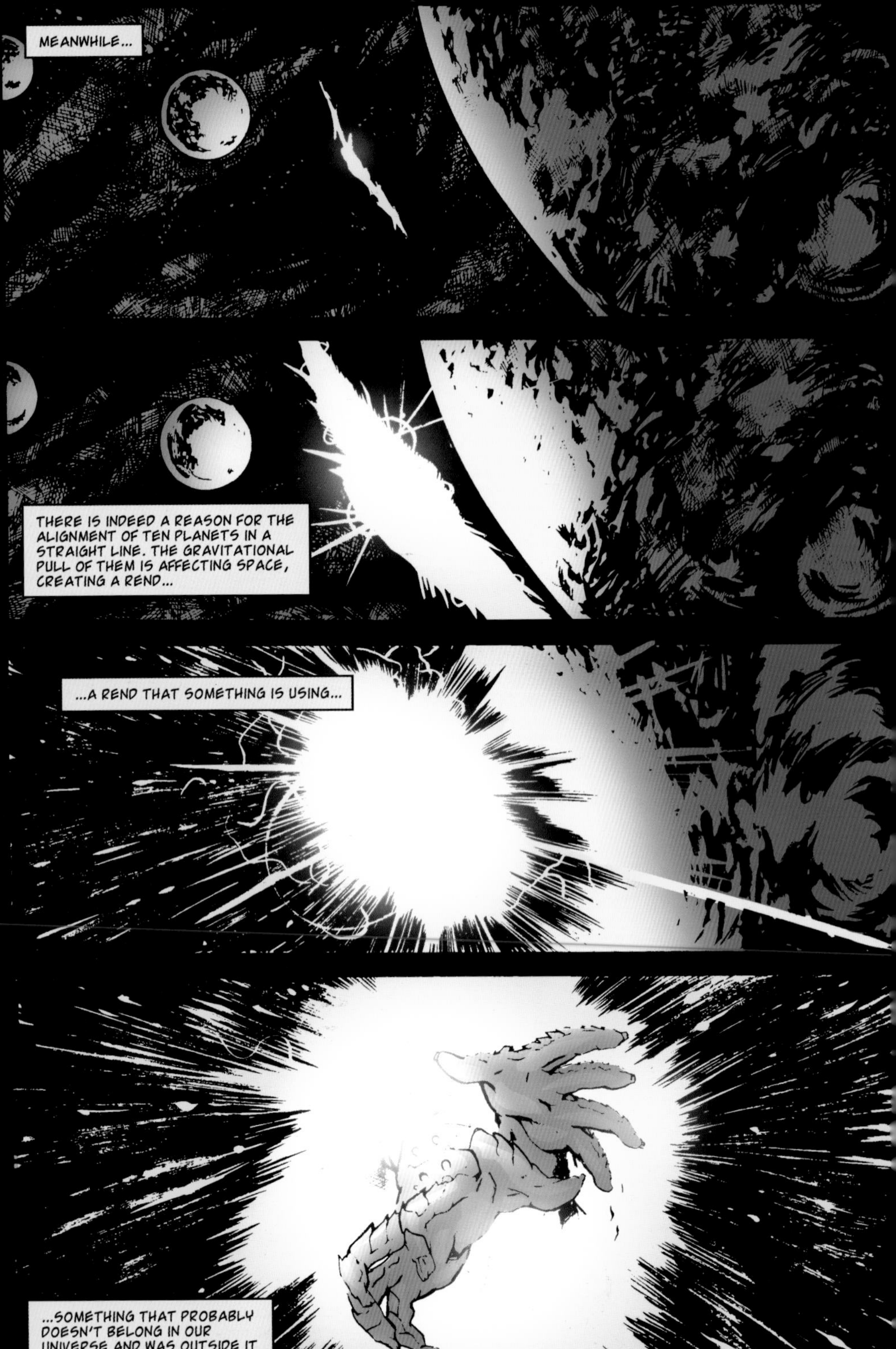
MEANWHILE...
THERE IS INDEED A REASON FOR THE ALIGNMENT OF TEN PLANETS IN A STRAIGHT LINE. THE GRAVITATIONAL PULL OF THEM IS AFFECTING SPACE, CREATING A REND...
...A REND THAT SOMETHING IS USING...
...SOMETHING THAT PROBABLY DOESN'T BELONG IN OUR UNIVERSE AND WAS OUTSIDE IT FOR A PRETTY GOOD REASON.

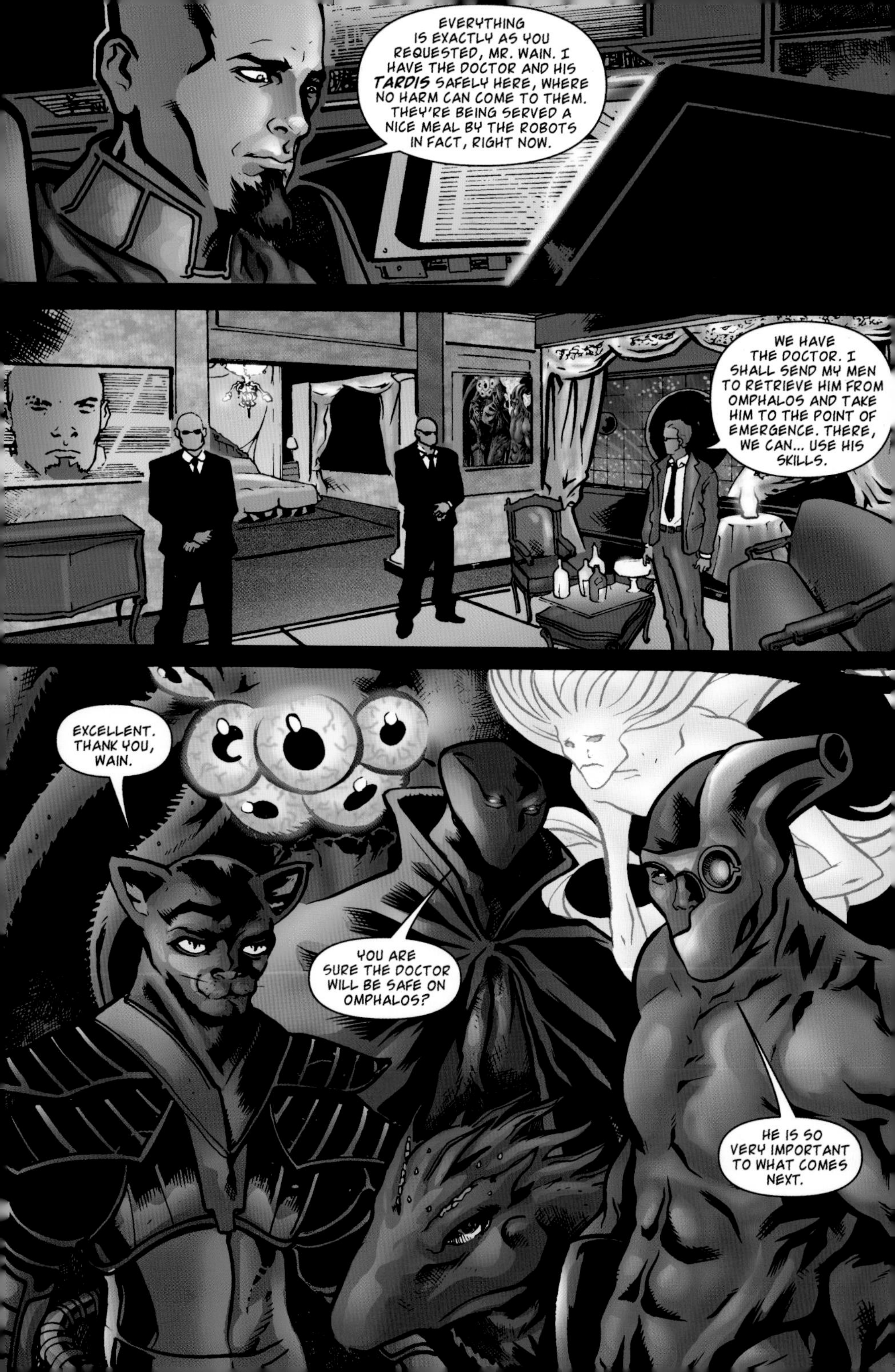
EVERYTHING IS EXACTLY AS YOU REQUESTED, MR. WAIN. I HAVE THE DOCTOR AND HIS *TARDIS* SAFELY HERE, WHERE NO HARM CAN COME TO THEM. THEY'RE BEING SERVED A NICE MEAL BY THE ROBOTS IN FACT, RIGHT NOW.
WE HAVE THE DOCTOR. I SHALL SEND MY MEN TO RETRIEVE HIM FROM OMPHALOS AND TAKE HIM TO THE POINT OF EMERGENCE. THERE, WE CAN... USE HIS SKILLS.
EXCELLENT. THANK YOU, WAIN.
YOU ARE SURE THE DOCTOR WILL BE SAFE ON OMPHALOS?
HE IS SO VERY IMPORTANT TO WHAT COMES NEXT.

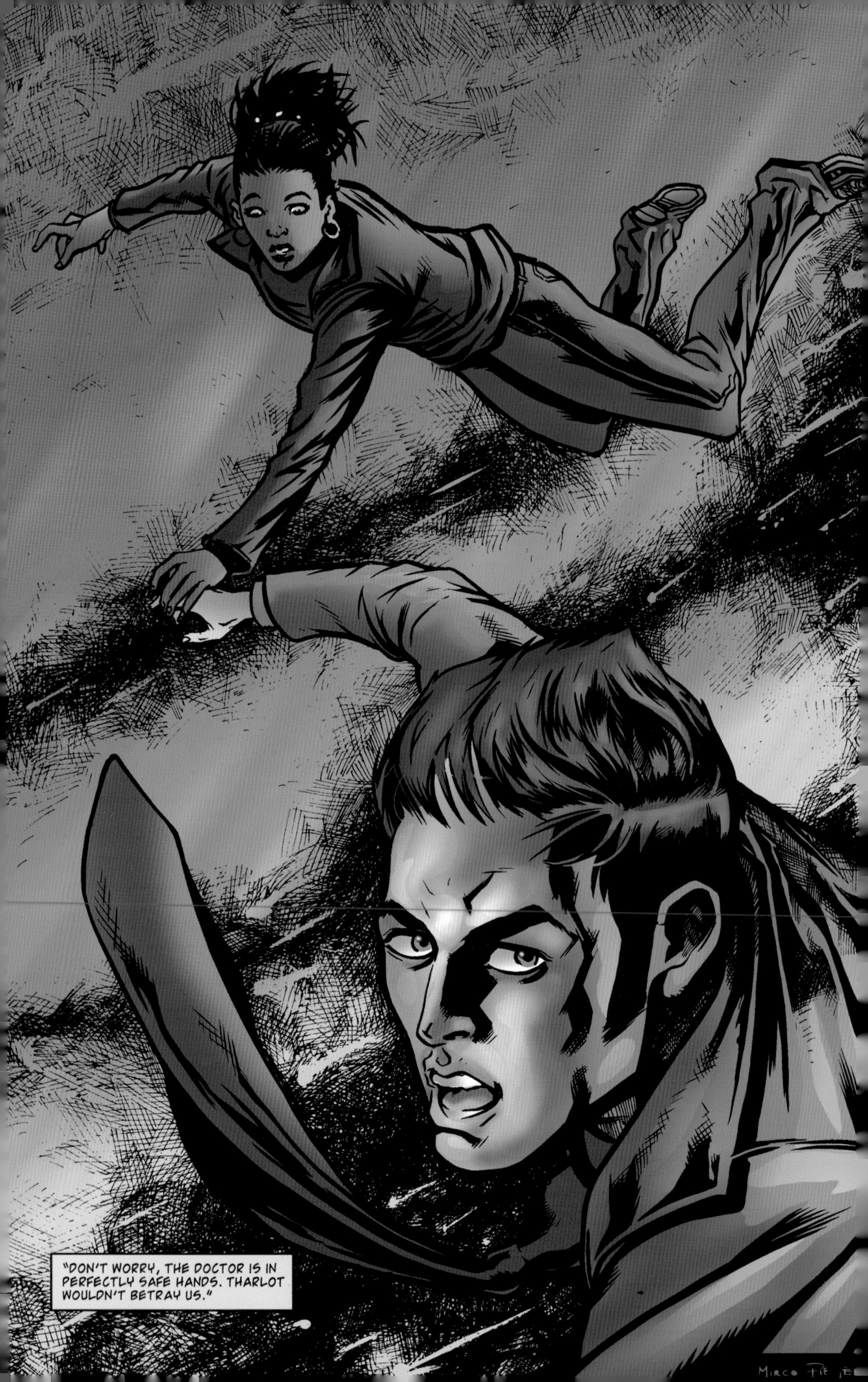
"DON'T WORRY, THE DOCTOR IS IN PERFECTLY SAFE HANDS. THARLOT WOULDN'T BETRAY US."

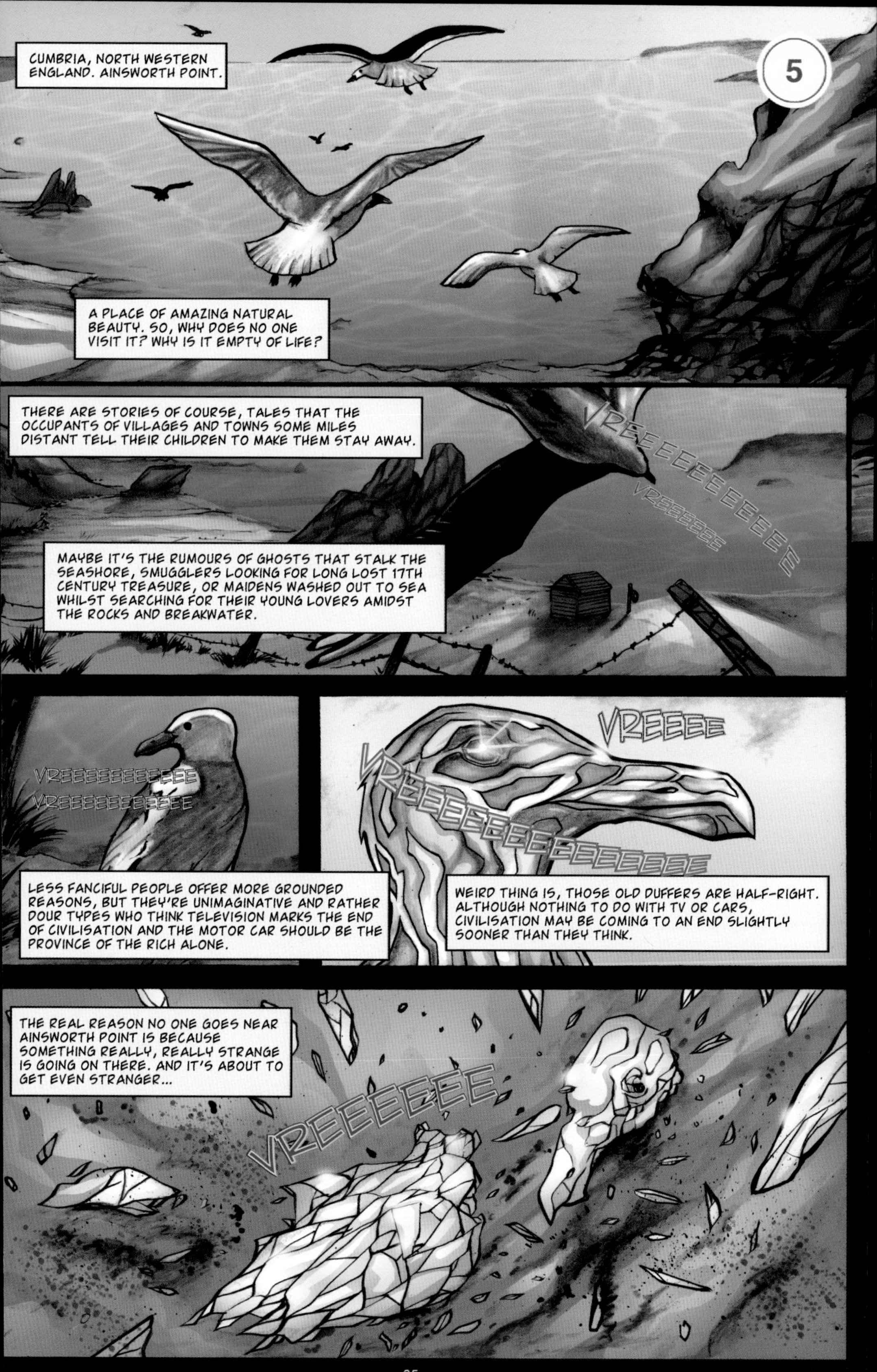
CUMBRIA, NORTH WESTERN ENGLAND. AINSWORTH POINT.
5
A PLACE OF AMAZING NATURAL BEAUTY. SO, WHY DOES NO ONE VISIT IT? WHY IS IT EMPTY OF LIFE?
THERE ARE STORIES OF COURSE, TALES THAT THE OCCUPANTS OF VILLAGES AND TOWNS SOME MILES DISTANT TELL THEIR CHILDREN TO MAKE THEM STAY AWAY.
VREEEEEEEEEEEE
VREEEEEEE
MAYBE IT'S THE RUMOURS OF GHOSTS THAT STALK THE SEASHORE, SMUGGLERS LOOKING FOR LONG LOST 17TH CENTURY TREASURE, OR MAIDENS WASHED OUT TO SEA WHILST SEARCHING FOR THEIR YOUNG LOVERS AMIDST THE ROCKS AND BREAKWATER.
VREEEEEEEEEEEE
VREEEEEEEEEEEE
LESS FANCIFUL PEOPLE OFFER MORE GROUNDED REASONS, BUT THEY'RE UNIMAGINATIVE AND RATHER DOUR TYPES WHO THINK TELEVISION MARKS THE END OF CIVILISATION AND THE MOTOR CAR SHOULD BE THE PROVINCE OF THE RICH ALONE.
VREEEEE
VREEEEEEEEEEEEEEEEE
WEIRD THING IS, THOSE OLD DUFFERS ARE HALF-RIGHT. ALTHOUGH NOTHING TO DO WITH TV OR CARS, CIVILISATION MAY BE COMING TO AN END SLIGHTLY SOONER THAN THEY THINK.
THE REAL REASON NO ONE GOES NEAR AINSWORTH POINT IS BECAUSE SOMETHING REALLY, REALLY STRANGE IS GOING ON THERE. AND IT'S ABOUT TO GET EVEN STRANGER...
VREEEEEEEE

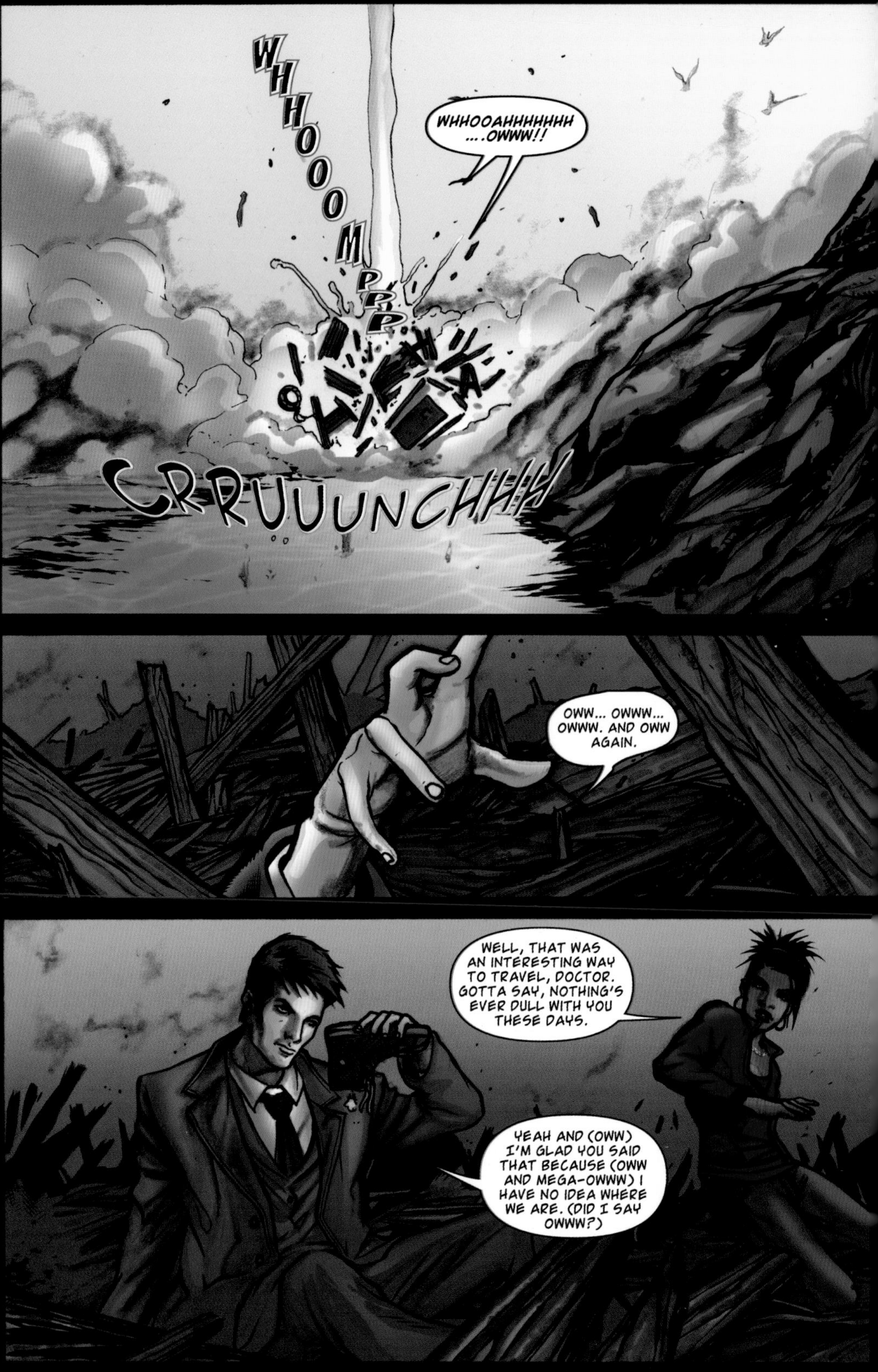
WHHOOOOMPPP
WHHOOAHHHHHH
....OWWW!!
CRRUUUNCHHH
OWW... OWWW...
OWWW. AND OWW
AGAIN.
WELL, THAT WAS AN INTERESTING WAY TO TRAVEL, DOCTOR. GOTTA SAY, NOTHING'S EVER DULL WITH YOU THESE DAYS.
YEAH AND (OWW) I'M GLAD YOU SAID THAT BECAUSE (OWW AND MEGA-OWWW) I HAVE NO IDEA WHERE WE ARE. (DID I SAY OWWW?)

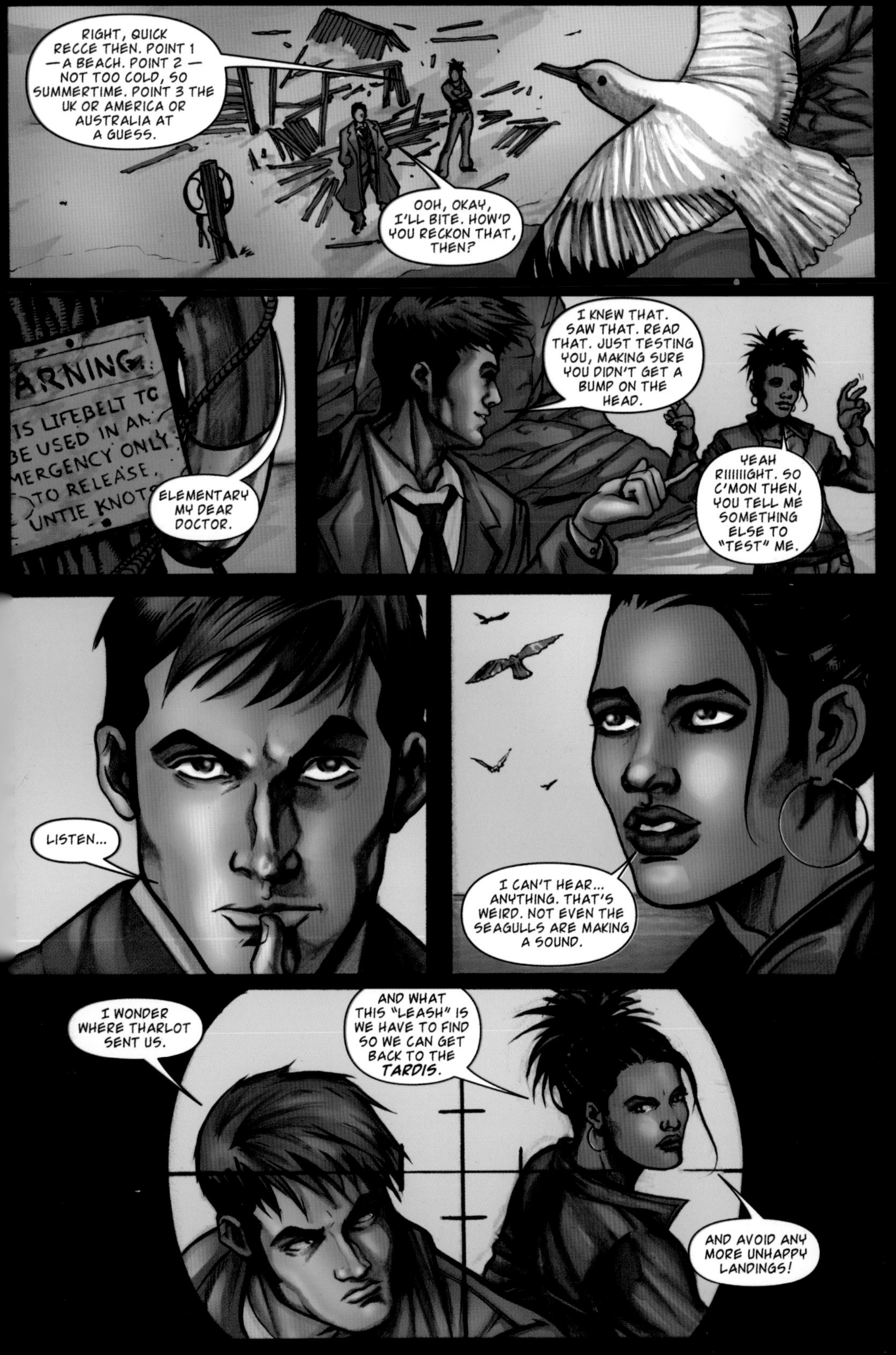
RIGHT, QUICK RECCE THEN. POINT 1 — A BEACH. POINT 2 — NOT TOO COLD, SO SUMMERTIME. POINT 3 THE UK OR AMERICA OR AUSTRALIA AT A GUESS.
OOH, OKAY, I'LL BITE. HOW'D YOU RECKON THAT, THEN?
ARNING
IS LIFEBELT TO BE USED IN AN MERGENCY ONLY TO RELEASE UNTIE KNOTS
ELEMENTARY MY DEAR DOCTOR.
I KNEW THAT. SAW THAT. READ THAT. JUST TESTING YOU, MAKING SURE YOU DIDN'T GET A BUMP ON THE HEAD.
YEAH RIIIIIIGHT. SO C'MON THEN, YOU TELL ME SOMETHING ELSE TO "TEST" ME.
LISTEN...
I CAN'T HEAR... ANYTHING. THAT'S WEIRD. NOT EVEN THE SEAGULLS ARE MAKING A SOUND.
I WONDER WHERE THARLOT SENT US.
AND WHAT THIS "LEASH" IS WE HAVE TO FIND SO WE CAN GET BACK TO THE TARDIS.
AND AVOID ANY MORE UNHAPPY LANDINGS!

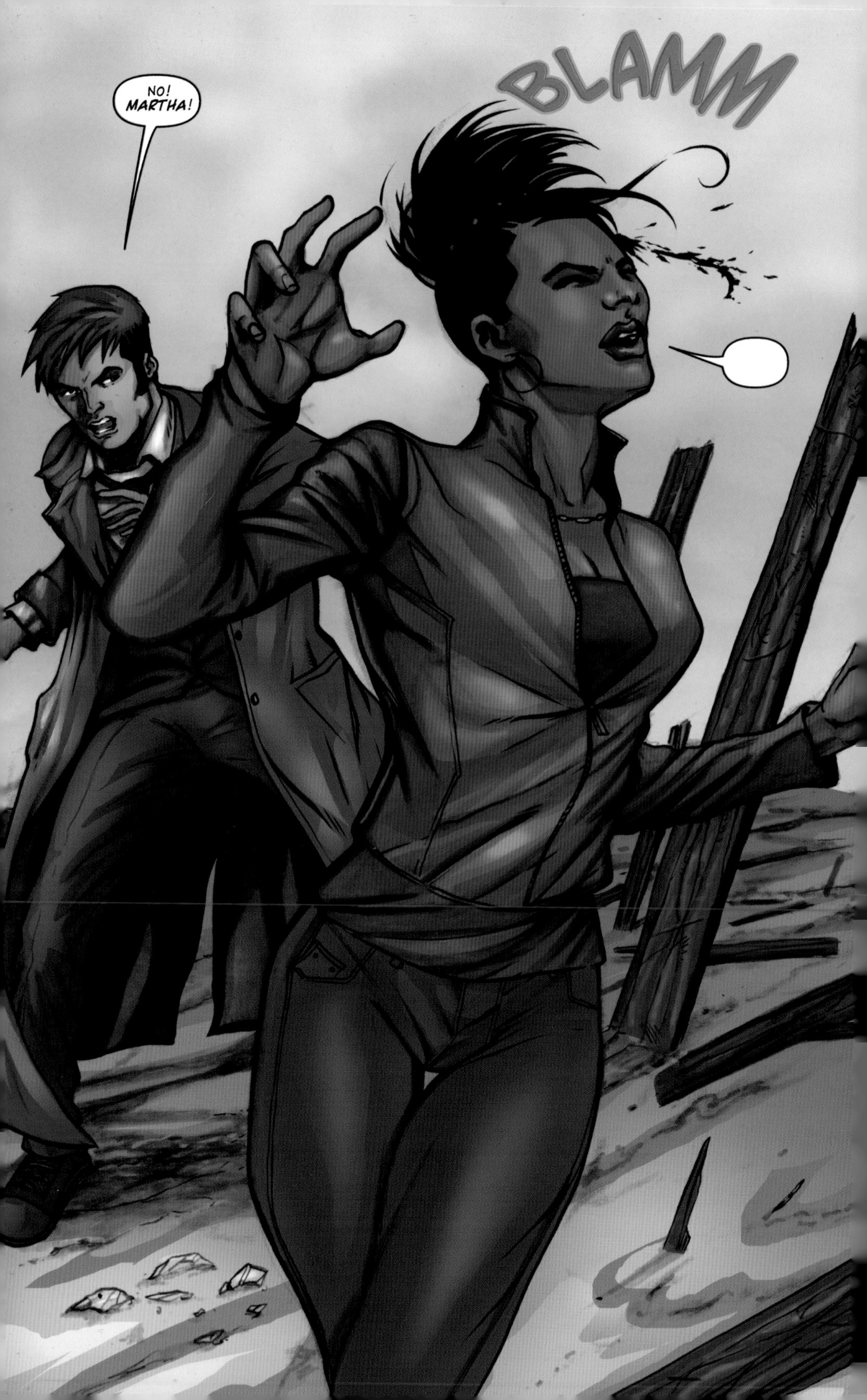

NO! MARTHA!
BLAMM

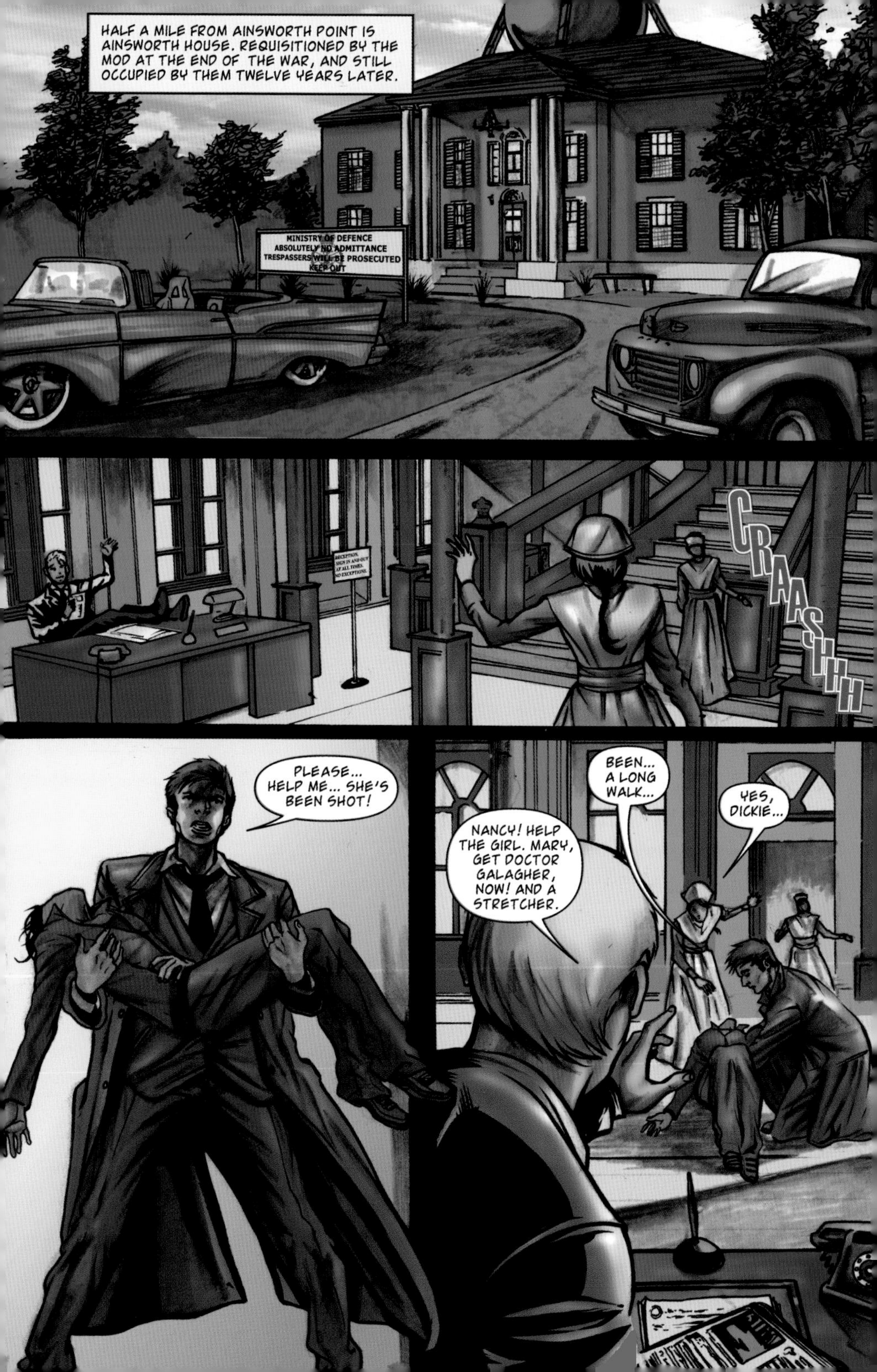
HALF A MILE FROM AINSWORTH POINT IS AINSWORTH HOUSE. REQUISITIONED BY THE MOD AT THE END OF THE WAR, AND STILL OCCUPIED BY THEM TWELVE YEARS LATER.
MINISTRY OF DEFENCE
ABSOLUTELY NO ADMITTANCE
TRESPASSERS WILL BE PROSECUTED
KEEP OUT
RECEPTION. SIGN IN AND OUT AT ALL TIMES. NO EXCEPTIONS.
CRAASHHH
PLEASE... HELP ME... SHE'S BEEN SHOT!
BEEN... A LONG WALK...
NANCY! HELP THE GIRL. MARY, GET DOCTOR GALAGHER, NOW! AND A STRETCHER.
YES, DICKIE...

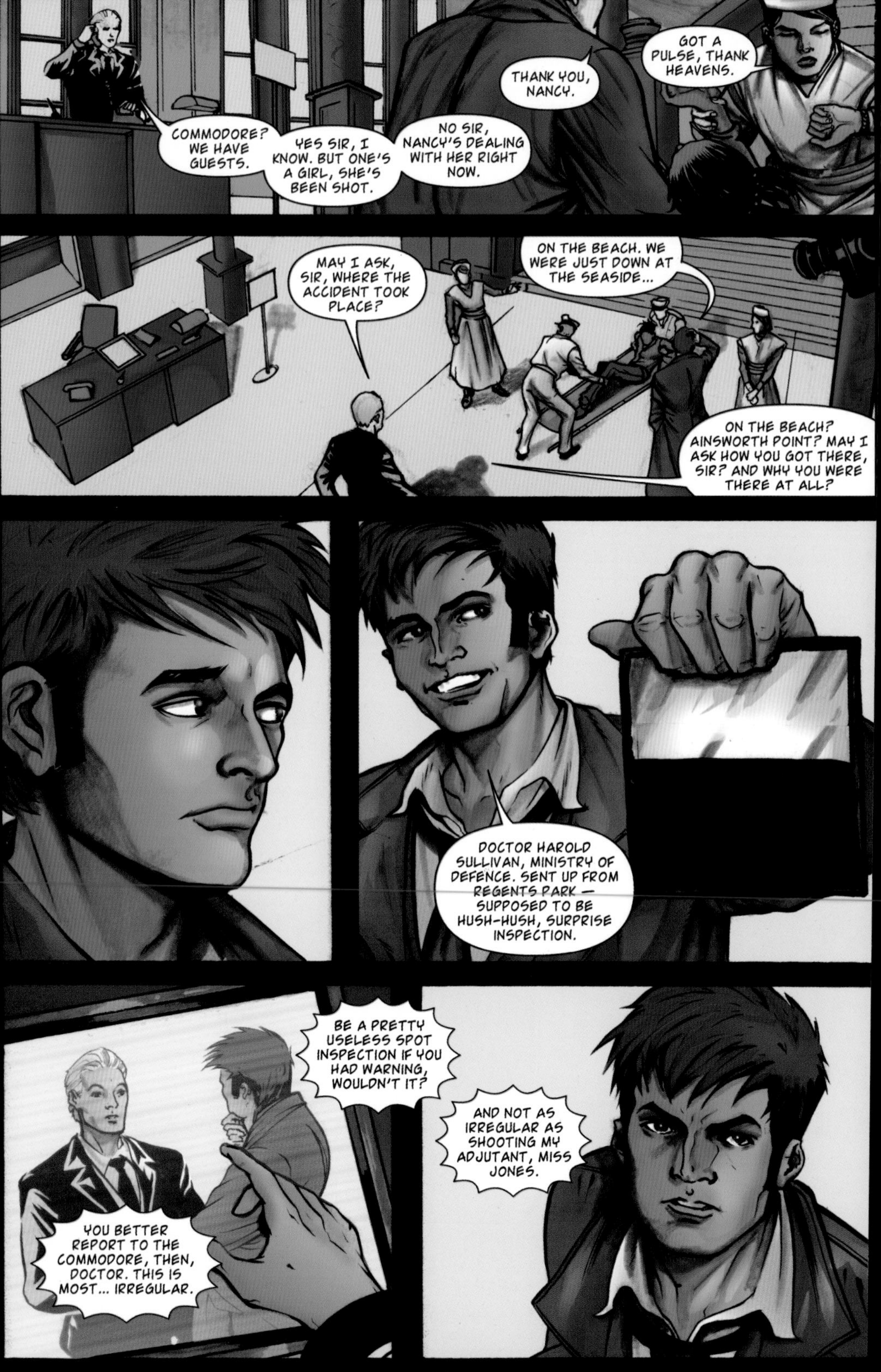
COMMODORE? WE HAVE GUESTS.
YES SIR, I KNOW. BUT ONE'S A GIRL, SHE'S BEEN SHOT.
NO SIR, NANCY'S DEALING WITH HER RIGHT NOW.
THANK YOU, NANCY.
GOT A PULSE, THANK HEAVENS.
MAY I ASK, SIR, WHERE THE ACCIDENT TOOK PLACE?
ON THE BEACH. WE WERE JUST DOWN AT THE SEASIDE...
ON THE BEACH? AINSWORTH POINT? MAY I ASK HOW YOU GOT THERE, SIR? AND WHY YOU WERE THERE AT ALL?
DOCTOR HAROLD SULLIVAN, MINISTRY OF DEFENCE. SENT UP FROM REGENTS PARK — SUPPOSED TO BE HUSH-HUSH, SURPRISE INSPECTION.
YOU BETTER REPORT TO THE COMMODORE, THEN, DOCTOR. THIS IS MOST... IRREGULAR.
BE A PRETTY USELESS SPOT INSPECTION IF YOU HAD WARNING, WOULDN'T IT?
AND NOT AS IRREGULAR AS SHOOTING MY ADJUTANT, MISS JONES.

SHOT HER? WHO THE HELL ORDERED MARTHA JONES TO BE SHOT? IN WHAT WAY WAS THAT PART OF THE PLAN? HOW HAS THIS HAPPENED?

I'LL TELL YOU [N]OW — BECAUSE [SOM]ETHING HAS GONE [WRO]NG, HASN'T IT— I [KNE]W IT WOULD. THIS IS [WHAT] HAPPENS WHEN YOU [AL]LOW CAPRICIOUS [ELE]MENTS INTO THE [PLAN. I TOLD THEM...

THE PANTHEON IS BEGINNING TO SUSPECT THAT CHOOSING SILAS WAIN AS OUR AGENT PROVOCATEUR MAY NOT HAVE BEEN OUR WISEST MOVE.

AND SILAS WAIN IS BEGINNING TO SUSPECT THAT HIS EMPLOYERS MIGHT HAVE BEEN KEEPING THINGS FROM HIM.

LIKE, WHAT IS GOING ON? WHO SHOT MARTHA AND WHY? I THOUGHT WE NEEDED HER!

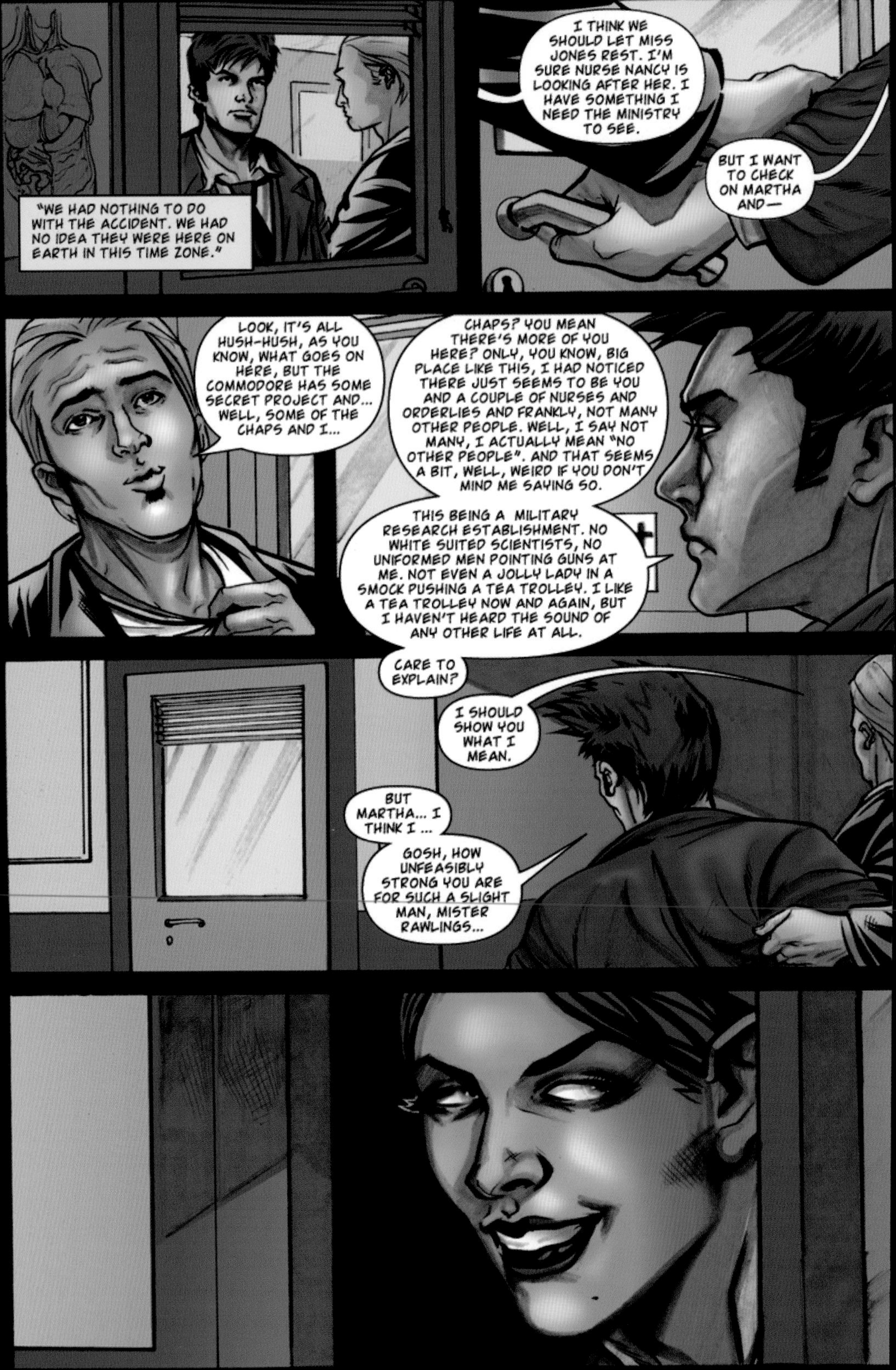
"WE HAD NOTHING TO DO WITH THE ACCIDENT. WE HAD NO IDEA THEY WERE HERE ON EARTH IN THIS TIME ZONE."
I THINK WE SHOULD LET MISS JONES REST. I'M SURE NURSE NANCY IS LOOKING AFTER HER. I HAVE SOMETHING I NEED THE MINISTRY TO SEE.
BUT I WANT TO CHECK ON MARTHA AND—
LOOK, IT'S ALL HUSH-HUSH, AS YOU KNOW, WHAT GOES ON HERE, BUT THE COMMODORE HAS SOME SECRET PROJECT AND... WELL, SOME OF THE CHAPS AND I...
CHAPS? YOU MEAN THERE'S MORE OF YOU HERE? ONLY, YOU KNOW, BIG PLACE LIKE THIS, I HAD NOTICED THERE JUST SEEMS TO BE YOU AND A COUPLE OF NURSES AND ORDERLIES AND FRANKLY, NOT MANY OTHER PEOPLE. WELL, I SAY NOT MANY, I ACTUALLY MEAN "NO OTHER PEOPLE". AND THAT SEEMS A BIT, WELL, WEIRD IF YOU DON'T MIND ME SAYING SO.
THIS BEING A MILITARY RESEARCH ESTABLISHMENT. NO WHITE SUITED SCIENTISTS, NO UNIFORMED MEN POINTING GUNS AT ME. NOT EVEN A JOLLY LADY IN A SMOCK PUSHING A TEA TROLLEY. I LIKE A TEA TROLLEY NOW AND AGAIN, BUT I HAVEN'T HEARD THE SOUND OF ANY OTHER LIFE AT ALL.
CARE TO EXPLAIN?
I SHOULD SHOW YOU WHAT I MEAN.
BUT MARTHA... I THINK I ...
GOSH, HOW UNFEASIBLY STRONG YOU ARE FOR SUCH A SLIGHT MAN, MISTER RAWLINGS...

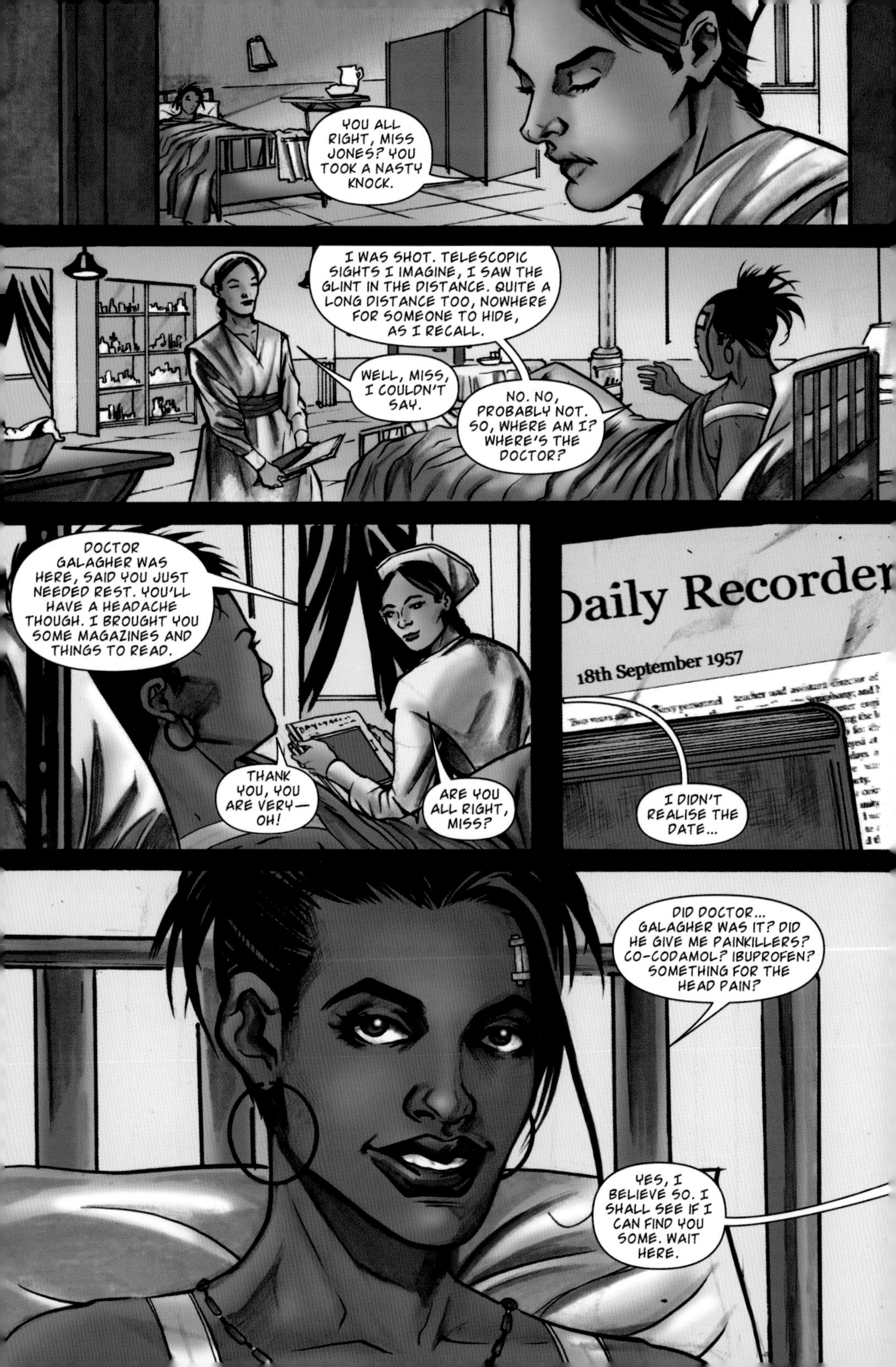
YOU ALL RIGHT, MISS JONES? YOU TOOK A NASTY KNOCK.
I WAS SHOT. TELESCOPIC SIGHTS I IMAGINE, I SAW THE GLINT IN THE DISTANCE. QUITE A LONG DISTANCE TOO, NOWHERE FOR SOMEONE TO HIDE, AS I RECALL.
WELL, MISS, I COULDN'T SAY.
NO. NO, PROBABLY NOT. SO, WHERE AM I? WHERE'S THE DOCTOR?
DOCTOR GALAGHER WAS HERE, SAID YOU JUST NEEDED REST. YOU'LL HAVE A HEADACHE THOUGH. I BROUGHT YOU SOME MAGAZINES AND THINGS TO READ.
THANK YOU, YOU ARE VERY— OH!
ARE YOU ALL RIGHT, MISS?
Daily Recorder
18th September 1957
I DIDN'T REALISE THE DATE...
DID DOCTOR... GALAGHER WAS IT? DID HE GIVE ME PAINKILLERS? CO-CODAMOL? IBUPROFEN? SOMETHING FOR THE HEAD PAIN?
YES, I BELIEVE SO. I SHALL SEE IF I CAN FIND YOU SOME. WAIT HERE.

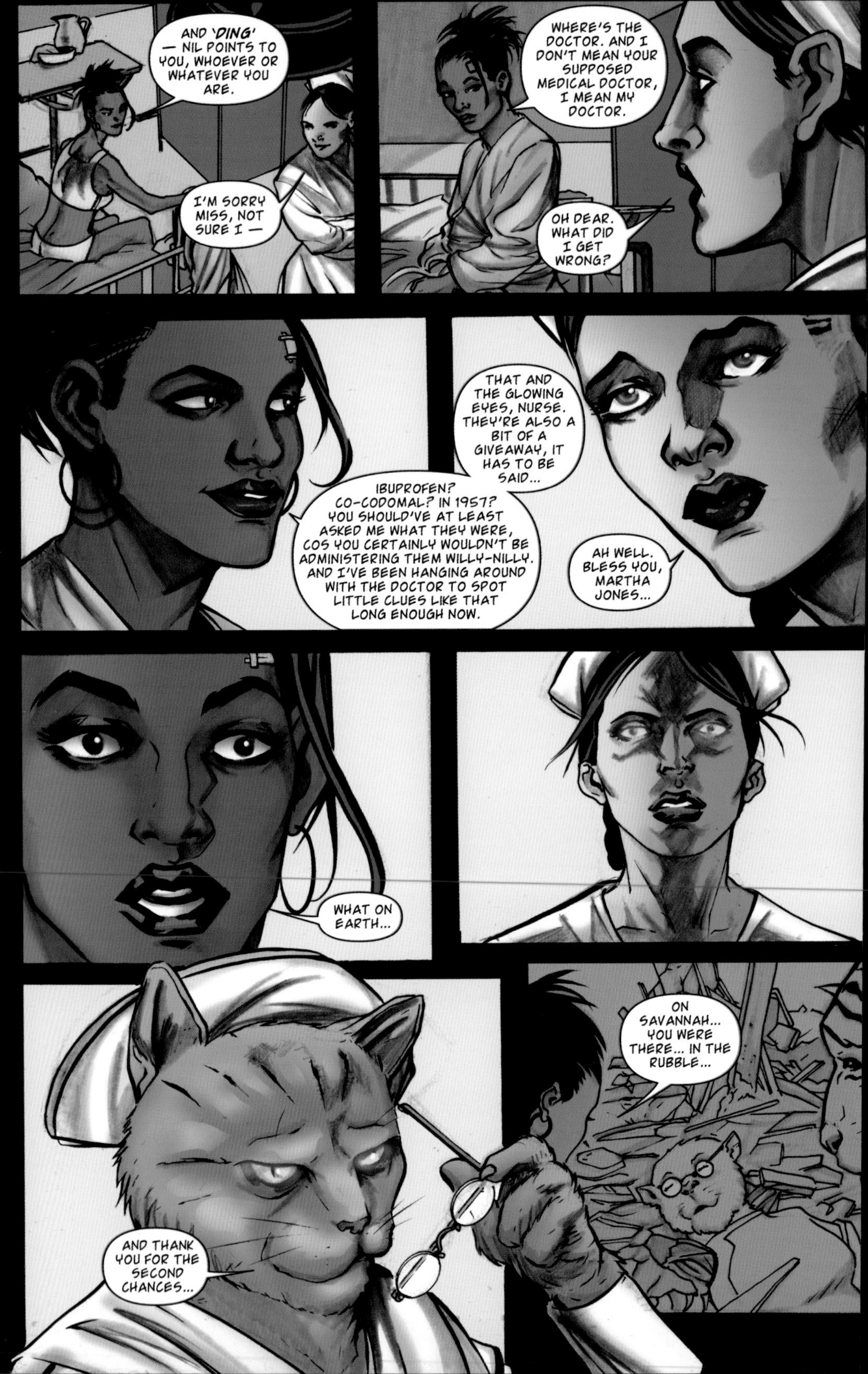
AND 'DING' — NIL POINTS TO YOU, WHOEVER OR WHATEVER YOU ARE.
I'M SORRY MISS, NOT SURE I —
WHERE'S THE DOCTOR. AND I DON'T MEAN YOUR SUPPOSED MEDICAL DOCTOR, I MEAN MY DOCTOR.
OH DEAR. WHAT DID I GET WRONG?
IBUPROFEN? CO-CODOMAL? IN 1957? YOU SHOULD'VE AT LEAST ASKED ME WHAT THEY WERE, COS YOU CERTAINLY WOULDN'T BE ADMINISTERING THEM WILLY-NILLY. AND I'VE BEEN HANGING AROUND WITH THE DOCTOR TO SPOT LITTLE CLUES LIKE THAT LONG ENOUGH NOW.
THAT AND THE GLOWING EYES, NURSE. THEY'RE ALSO A BIT OF A GIVEAWAY, IT HAS TO BE SAID...
AH WELL. BLESS YOU, MARTHA JONES...
WHAT ON EARTH...
AND THANK YOU FOR THE SECOND CHANCES...
ON SAVANNAH... YOU WERE THERE... IN THE RUBBLE...

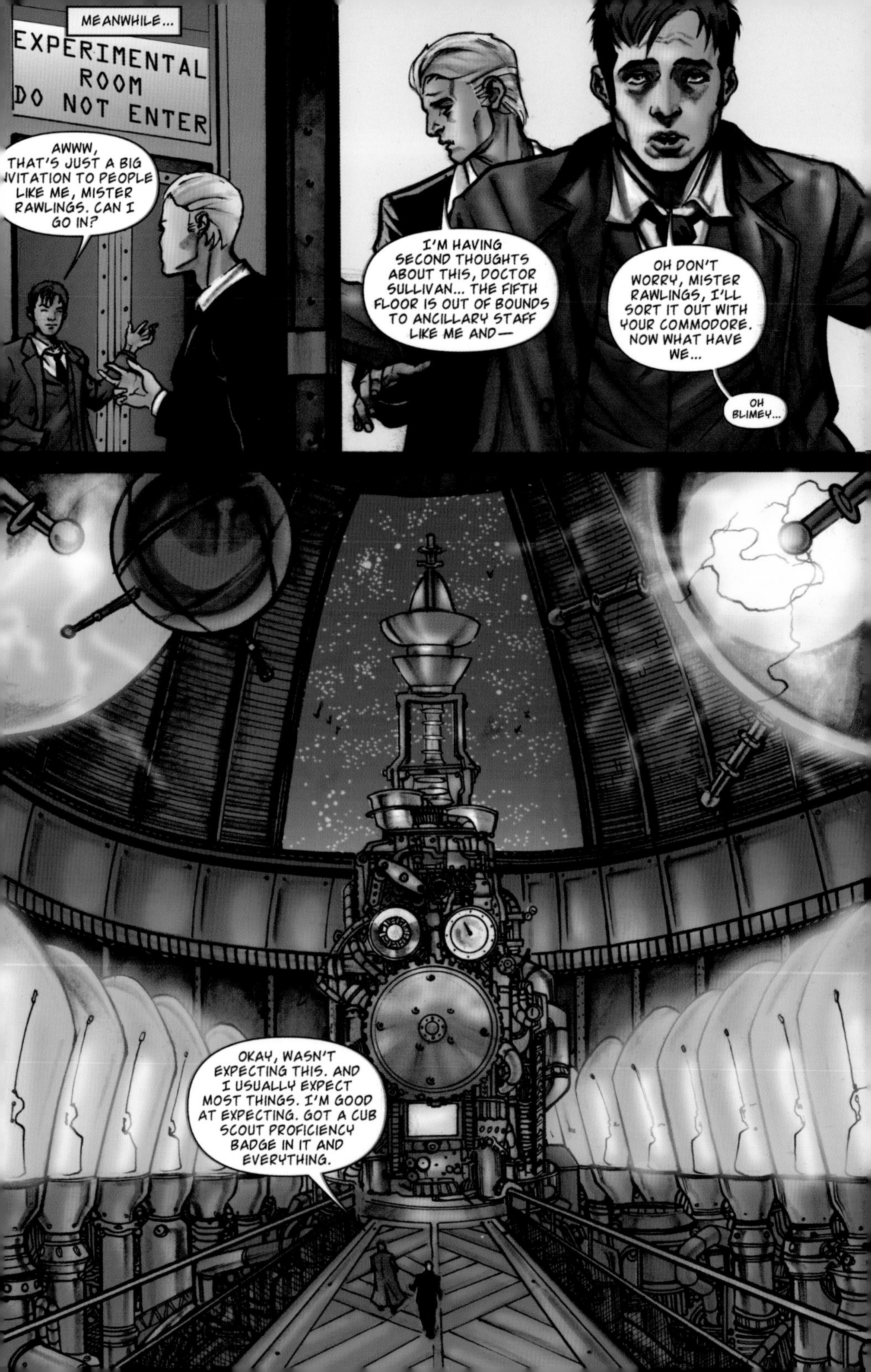
MEANWHILE...
EXPERIMENTAL ROOM DO NOT ENTER
AWWW, THAT'S JUST A BIG INVITATION TO PEOPLE LIKE ME, MISTER RAWLINGS. CAN I GO IN?
I'M HAVING SECOND THOUGHTS ABOUT THIS, DOCTOR SULLIVAN... THE FIFTH FLOOR IS OUT OF BOUNDS TO ANCILLARY STAFF LIKE ME AND—
OH DON'T WORRY, MISTER RAWLINGS, I'LL SORT IT OUT WITH YOUR COMMODORE. NOW WHAT HAVE WE...
OH BLIMEY...
OKAY, WASN'T EXPECTING THIS. AND I USUALLY EXPECT MOST THINGS. I'M GOOD AT EXPECTING. GOT A CUB SCOUT PROFICIENCY BADGE IN IT AND EVERYTHING.

COURSE, I'VE GOT BADGES IN LOTS OF THINGS. STAMP COLLECTING, CYCLING, TAXIDERMY (NEVER KNEW WHY I NEEDED THAT, BUT I NEVER ARGUE WITH A MAN WITH A WOGGLE), FIRST AID AND PAN-DIMENSIONAL SONIC WEAPONRY THAT SHOULDN'T EXIST ON EARTH OUTSIDE THE 51ST CENTURY, AND CERTAINLY NOT THE 20TH.

AH! 51ST CENTURY. WAS THERE RECENTLY. WELL, TWICE RECENTLY. FIRSTLY ON SAVANNA AND THEN ON OMPHALOS.

NOW, I LIKE COINCIDENCES AS MUCH AS THE NEXT PERSON, BUT SOMETIMES THEY SEEM A BIT... CONTRIVED.

WHO'S PULLING MY STRINGS, MISTER RAWLINGS?

THAT'D BE ME. SILAS WAIN. COMMODORE WAIN IN FACT. PLEASED TO MEET YOU.

HULLO. NICE UNIFORM. TOTALLY WRONG OF COURSE — SYNTHETIC FABRICS GIVE YOU AWAY, BUT EIGHT OUT OF TEN FOR EFFORT. SO, WHERE ARE YOU FROM? AND WHY HASN'T MISTER RAWLINGS HERE NOTICED.

AHH, BECAUSE HE KNOWS. BECAUSE THIS IS ALL A CHARADE. AND BECAUSE AS A LITTLE BLACK CAT ONCE TOLD ME, I'M JUST A LAB RAT. AND YOU, SILAS WAIN ARE, I'M GUESSING, CHIEF TESTER, YES? AM I RIGHT? PLEASE LET ME BE RIGHT. IF I'M WRONG, I'M GOING TO LOOK VERY FOOLISH.

YOU'RE RIGHT. OF COURSE, YOU'RE RIGHT. YOU'RE THE DOCTOR. THAT'S WHY I CHOSE YOU.

COMMODORE, I OUGHT TO GO AND CHECK UP ON THE... UMMM... THING... YOU KNOW... SIR?

LET'S GET COMFORTABLE.

GOODBYE MISTER RAWLINGS, I THINK YOUR COMMODORE AND I NEED A LITTLE CHAT. IN PRIVATE.

YES SIR... ABSOLUTELY... SIRS...

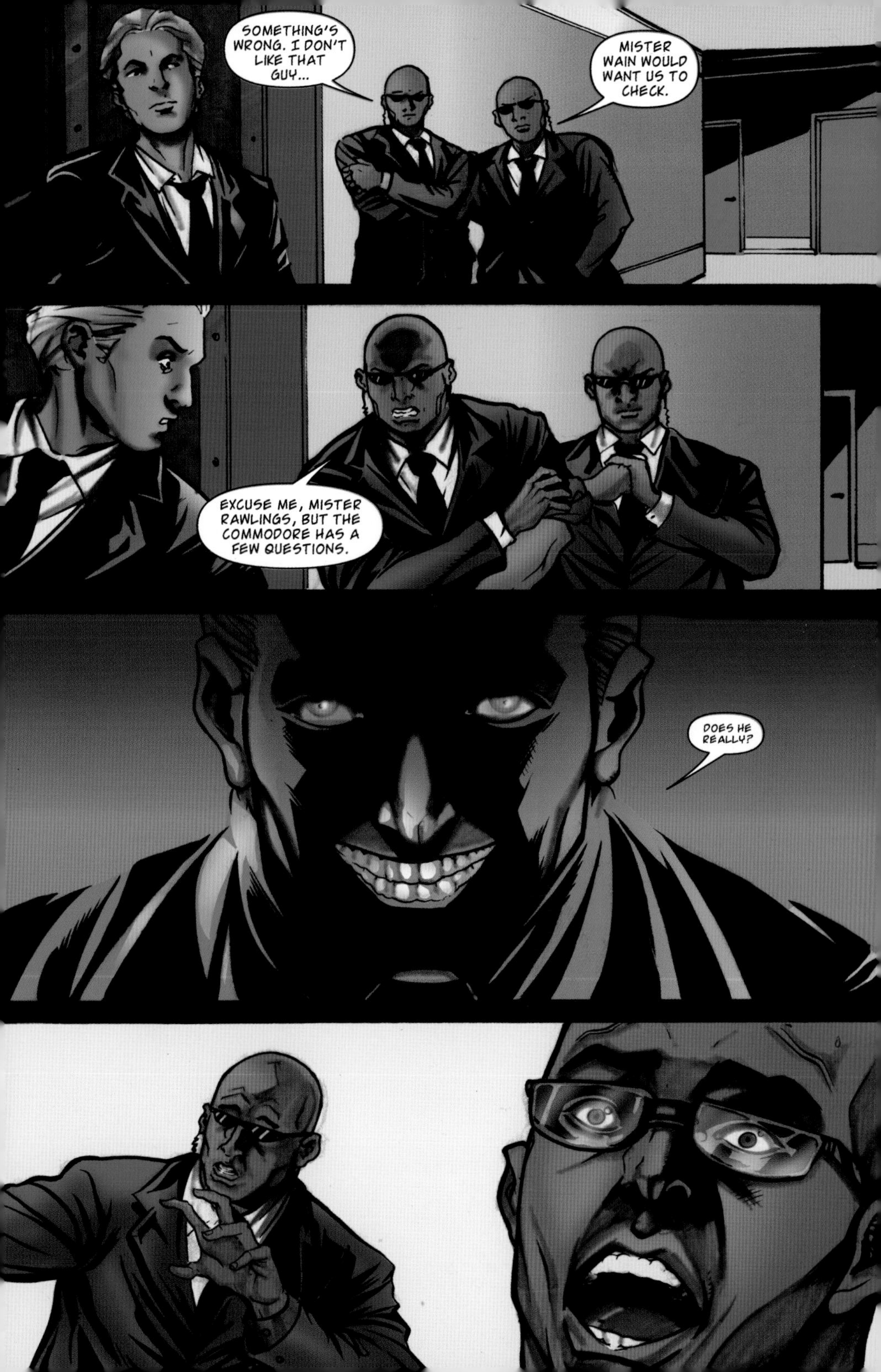
SOMETHING'S WRONG. I DON'T LIKE THAT GUY...
MISTER WAIN WOULD WANT US TO CHECK.
EXCUSE ME, MISTER RAWLINGS, BUT THE COMMODORE HAS A FEW QUESTIONS.
DOES HE REALLY?

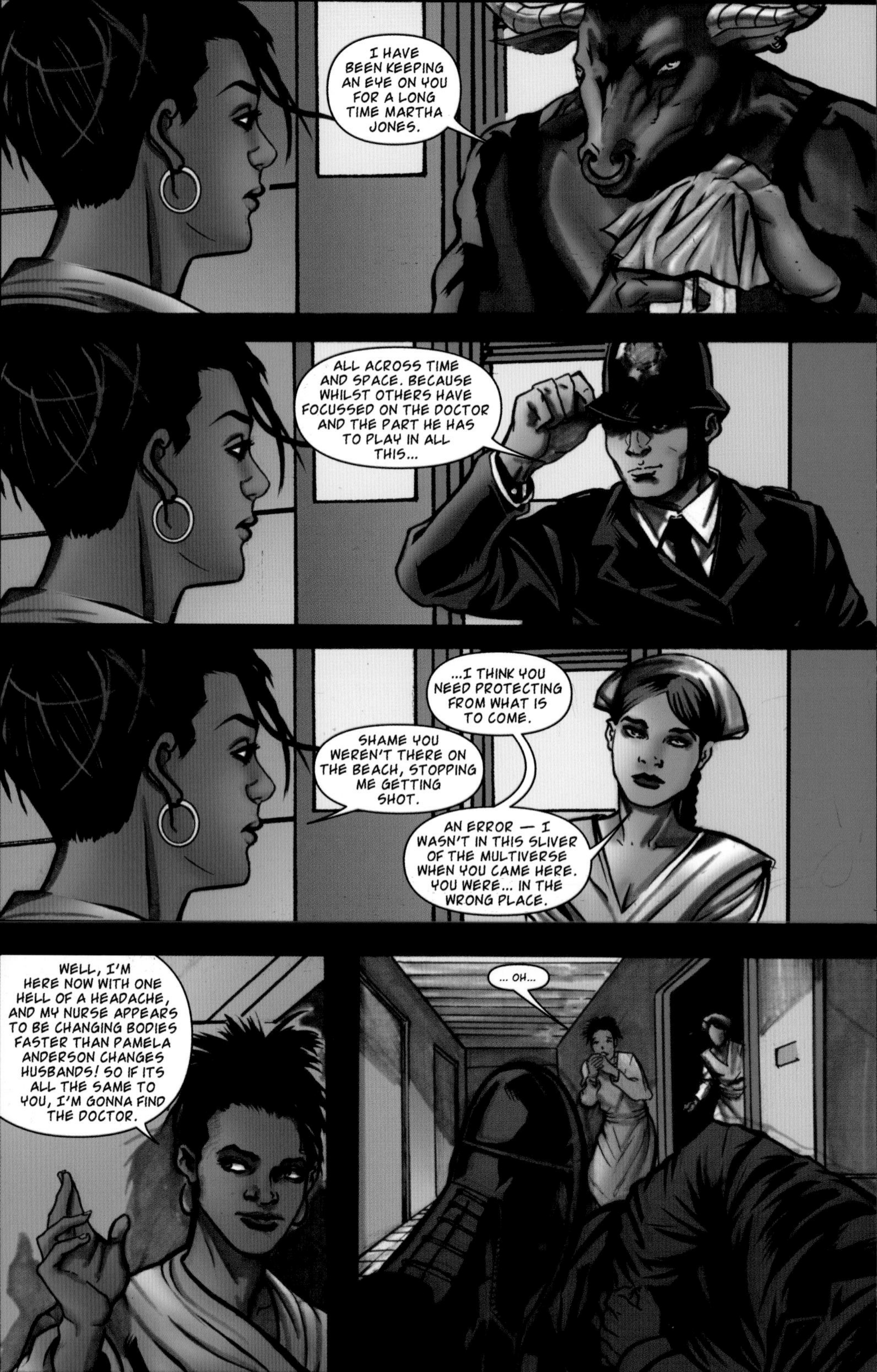
I HAVE BEEN KEEPING AN EYE ON YOU FOR A LONG TIME MARTHA JONES.
ALL ACROSS TIME AND SPACE. BECAUSE WHILST OTHERS HAVE FOCUSSED ON THE DOCTOR AND THE PART HE HAS TO PLAY IN ALL THIS...
...I THINK YOU NEED PROTECTING FROM WHAT IS TO COME.
SHAME YOU WEREN'T THERE ON THE BEACH, STOPPING ME GETTING SHOT.
AN ERROR — I WASN'T IN THIS SLIVER OF THE MULTIVERSE WHEN YOU CAME HERE. YOU WERE... IN THE WRONG PLACE.
WELL, I'M HERE NOW WITH ONE HELL OF A HEADACHE, AND MY NURSE APPEARS TO BE CHANGING BODIES FASTER THAN PAMELA ANDERSON CHANGES HUSBANDS! SO IF ITS ALL THE SAME TO YOU, I'M GONNA FIND THE DOCTOR.
... OH...

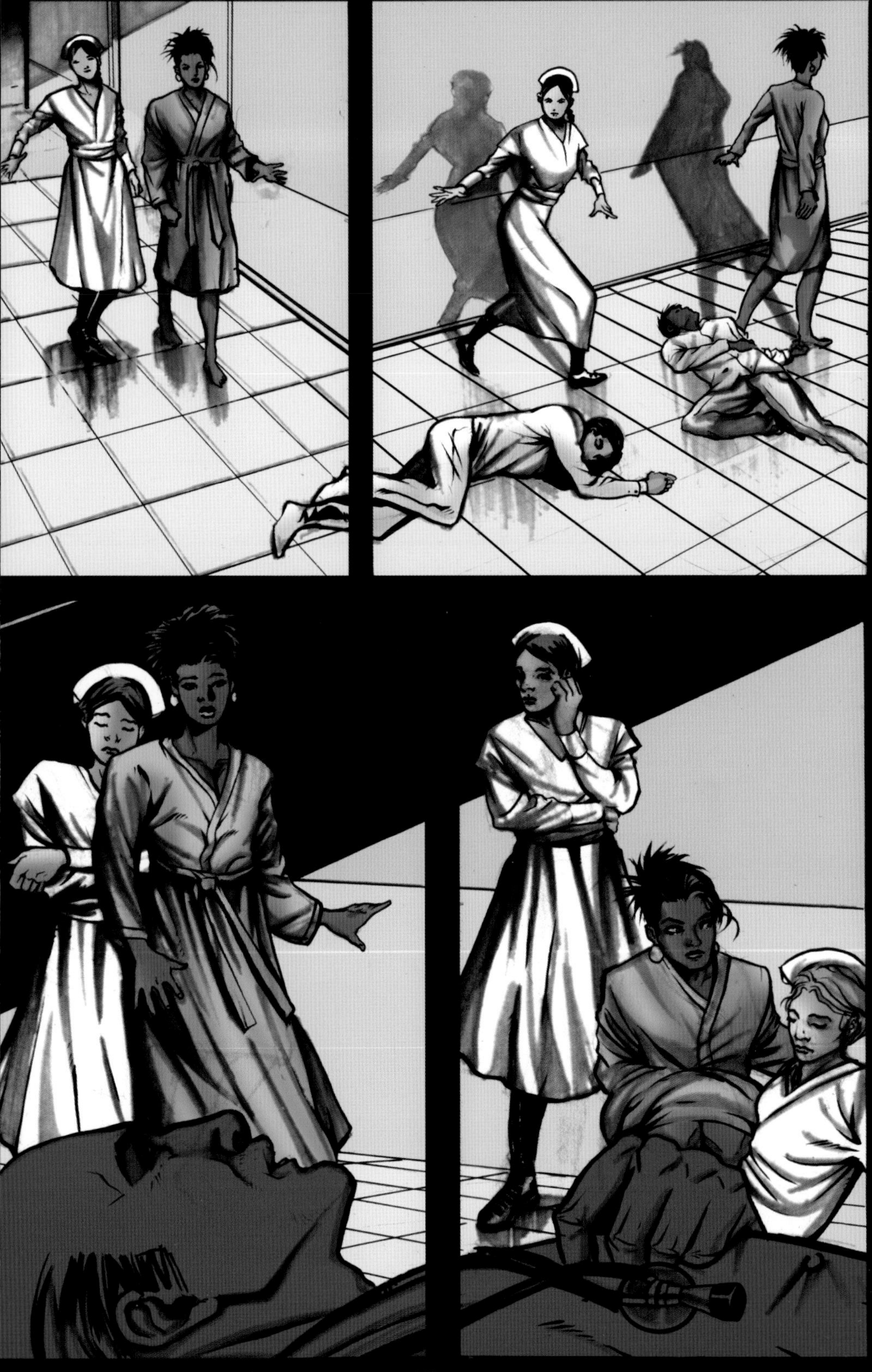

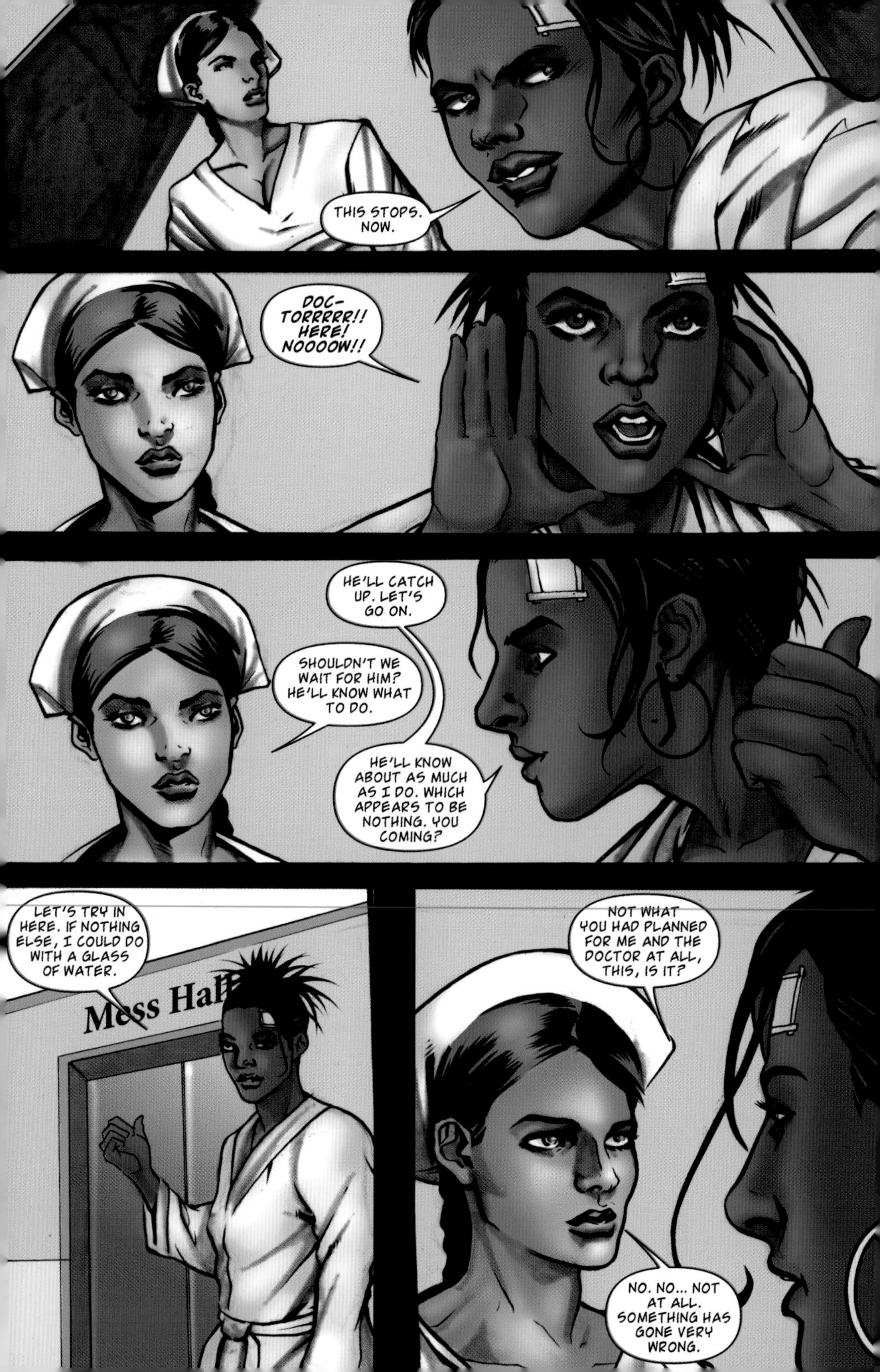
THIS STOPS. NOW.
DOC-TORRRRR!! HERE! NOOOOW!!
HE'LL CATCH UP. LET'S GO ON.
SHOULDN'T WE WAIT FOR HIM? HE'LL KNOW WHAT TO DO.
HE'LL KNOW ABOUT AS MUCH AS I DO. WHICH APPEARS TO BE NOTHING. YOU COMING?
LET'S TRY IN HERE. IF NOTHING ELSE, I COULD DO WITH A GLASS OF WATER.
Mess Hall
NOT WHAT YOU HAD PLANNED FOR ME AND THE DOCTOR AT ALL, THIS, IS IT?
NO. NO... NOT AT ALL. SOMETHING HAS GONE VERY WRONG.

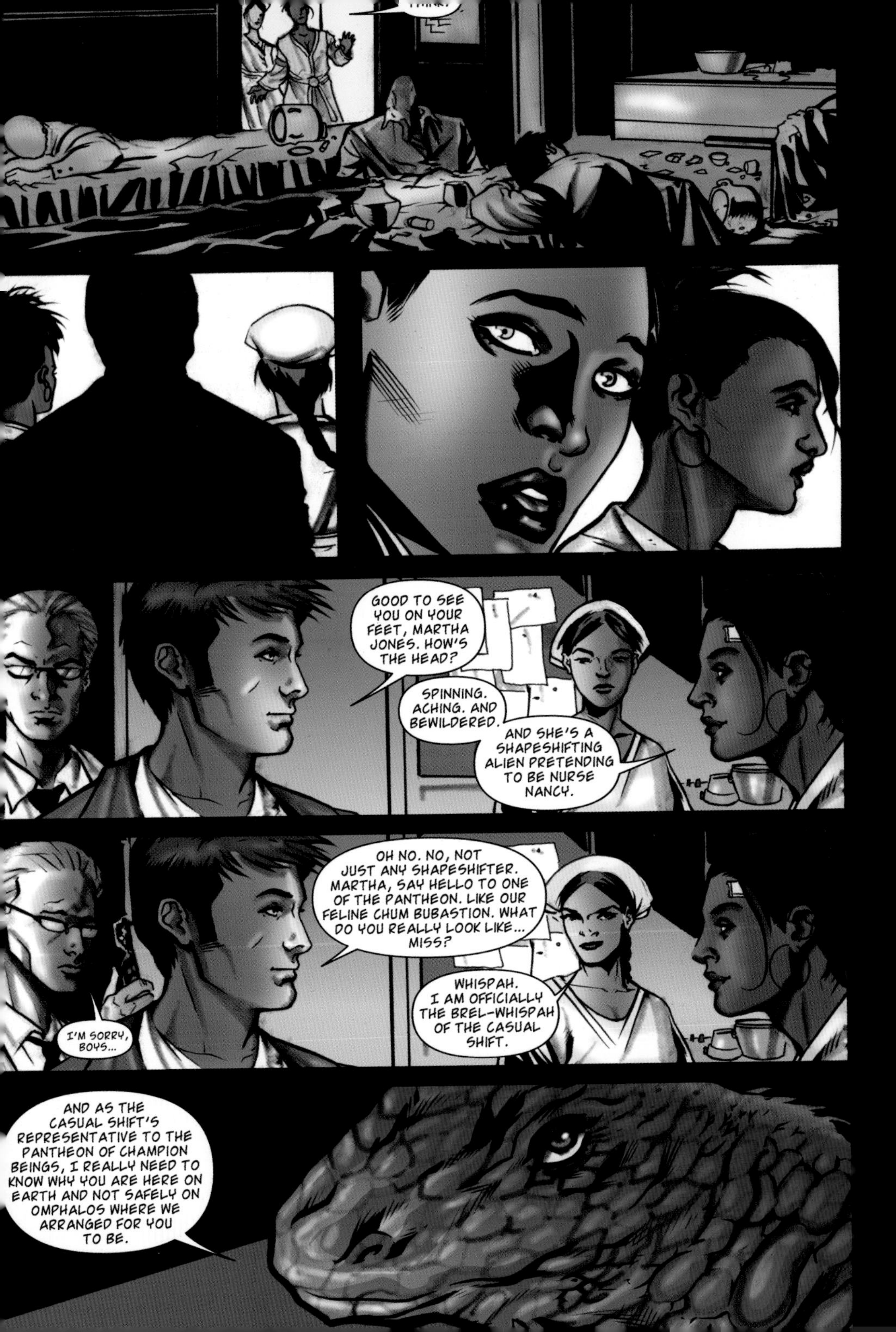
GOOD TO SEE YOU ON YOUR FEET, MARTHA JONES. HOW'S THE HEAD?
SPINNING. ACHING. AND BEWILDERED.
AND SHE'S A SHAPESHIFTING ALIEN PRETENDING TO BE NURSE NANCY.
OH NO. NO, NOT JUST ANY SHAPESHIFTER. MARTHA, SAY HELLO TO ONE OF THE PANTHEON. LIKE OUR FELINE CHUM BUBASTION. WHAT DO YOU REALLY LOOK LIKE... MISS?
WHISPAH. I AM OFFICIALLY THE BREL-WHISPAH OF THE CASUAL SHIFT.
I'M SORRY, BOYS...
AND AS THE CASUAL SHIFT'S REPRESENTATIVE TO THE PANTHEON OF CHAMPION BEINGS, I REALLY NEED TO KNOW WHY YOU ARE HERE ON EARTH AND NOT SAFELY ON OMPHALOS WHERE WE ARRANGED FOR YOU TO BE.

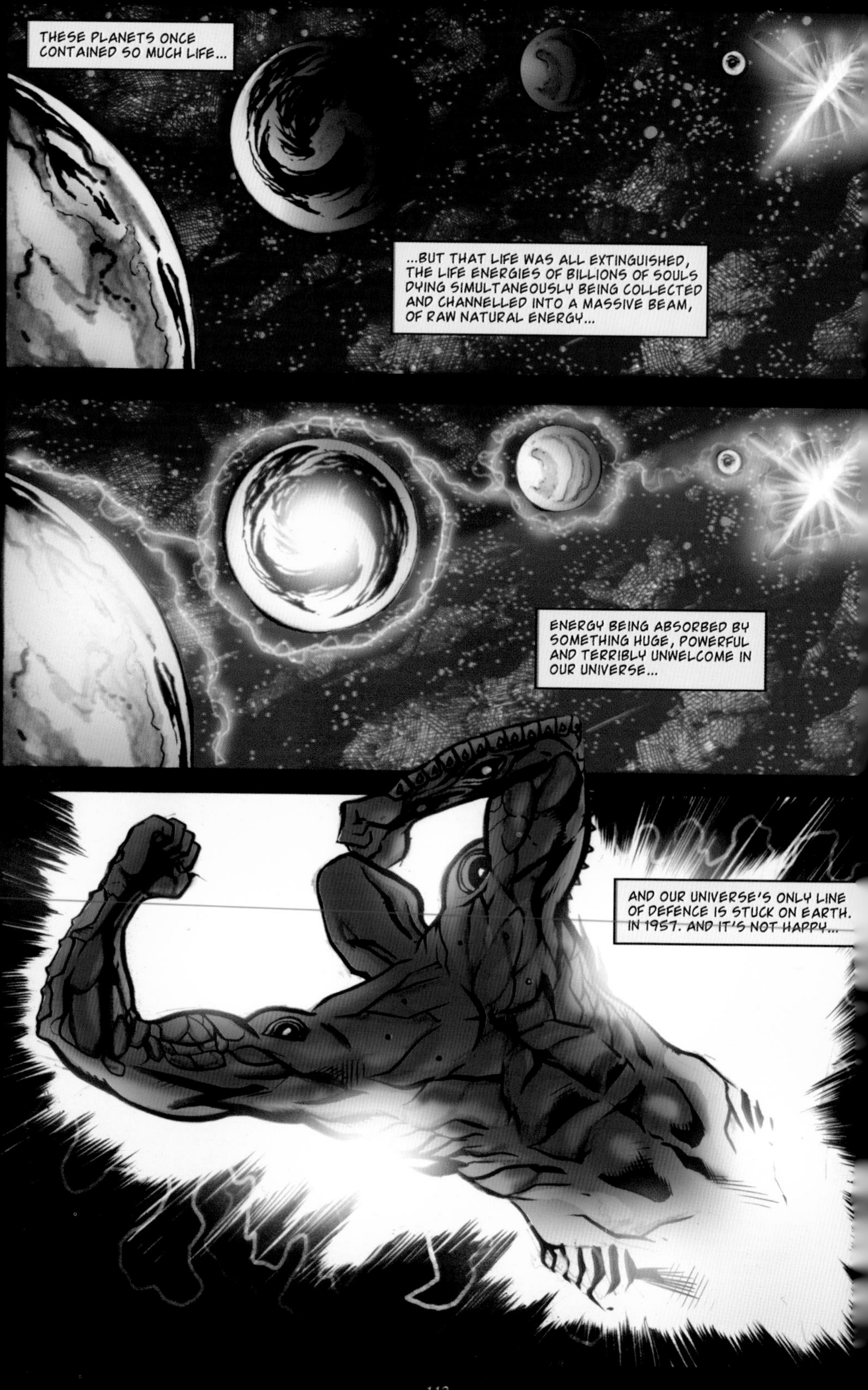
THESE PLANETS ONCE CONTAINED SO MUCH LIFE...
...BUT THAT LIFE WAS ALL EXTINGUISHED, THE LIFE ENERGIES OF BILLIONS OF SOULS DYING SIMULTANEOUSLY BEING COLLECTED AND CHANNELLED INTO A MASSIVE BEAM, OF RAW NATURAL ENERGY...
ENERGY BEING ABSORBED BY SOMETHING HUGE, POWERFUL AND TERRIBLY UNWELCOME IN OUR UNIVERSE...
AND OUR UNIVERSE'S ONLY LINE OF DEFENCE IS STUCK ON EARTH. IN 1957. AND IT'S NOT HAPPY...

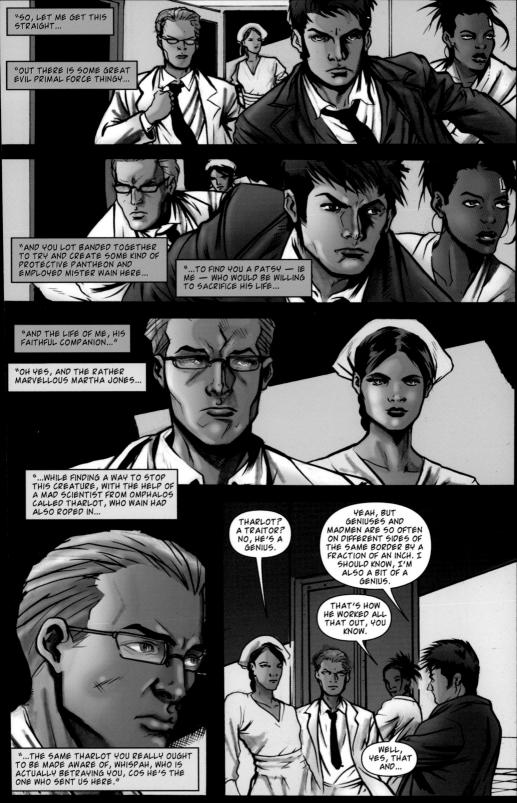

"SO, LET ME GET THIS STRAIGHT...

"OUT THERE IS SOME GREAT EVIL PRIMAL FORCE THINGY...

"AND YOU LOT BANDED TOGETHER TO TRY AND CREATE SOME KIND OF PROTECTIVE PANTHEON AND EMPLOYED MISTER WAIN HERE...

"...TO FIND YOU A PATSY — IE ME — WHO WOULD BE WILLING TO SACRIFICE HIS LIFE...

"AND THE LIFE OF ME, HIS FAITHFUL COMPANION..."

"OH YES, AND THE RATHER MARVELLOUS MARTHA JONES...

"...WHILE FINDING A WAY TO STOP THIS CREATURE, WITH THE HELP OF A MAD SCIENTIST FROM OMPHALOS CALLED THARLOT, WHO WAIN HAD ALSO ROPED IN...

THARLOT? A TRAITOR? NO, HE'S A GENIUS.

YEAH, BUT GENIUSES AND MADMEN ARE SO OFTEN ON DIFFERENT SIDES OF THE SAME BORDER BY A FRACTION OF AN INCH. I SHOULD KNOW, I'M ALSO A BIT OF A GENIUS.

THAT'S HOW HE WORKED ALL THAT OUT, YOU KNOW.

"...THE SAME THARLOT YOU REALLY OUGHT TO BE MADE AWARE OF, WHISPAH, WHO IS ACTUALLY BETRAYING YOU, COS HE'S THE ONE WHO SENT US HERE."

WELL, YES, THAT AND...

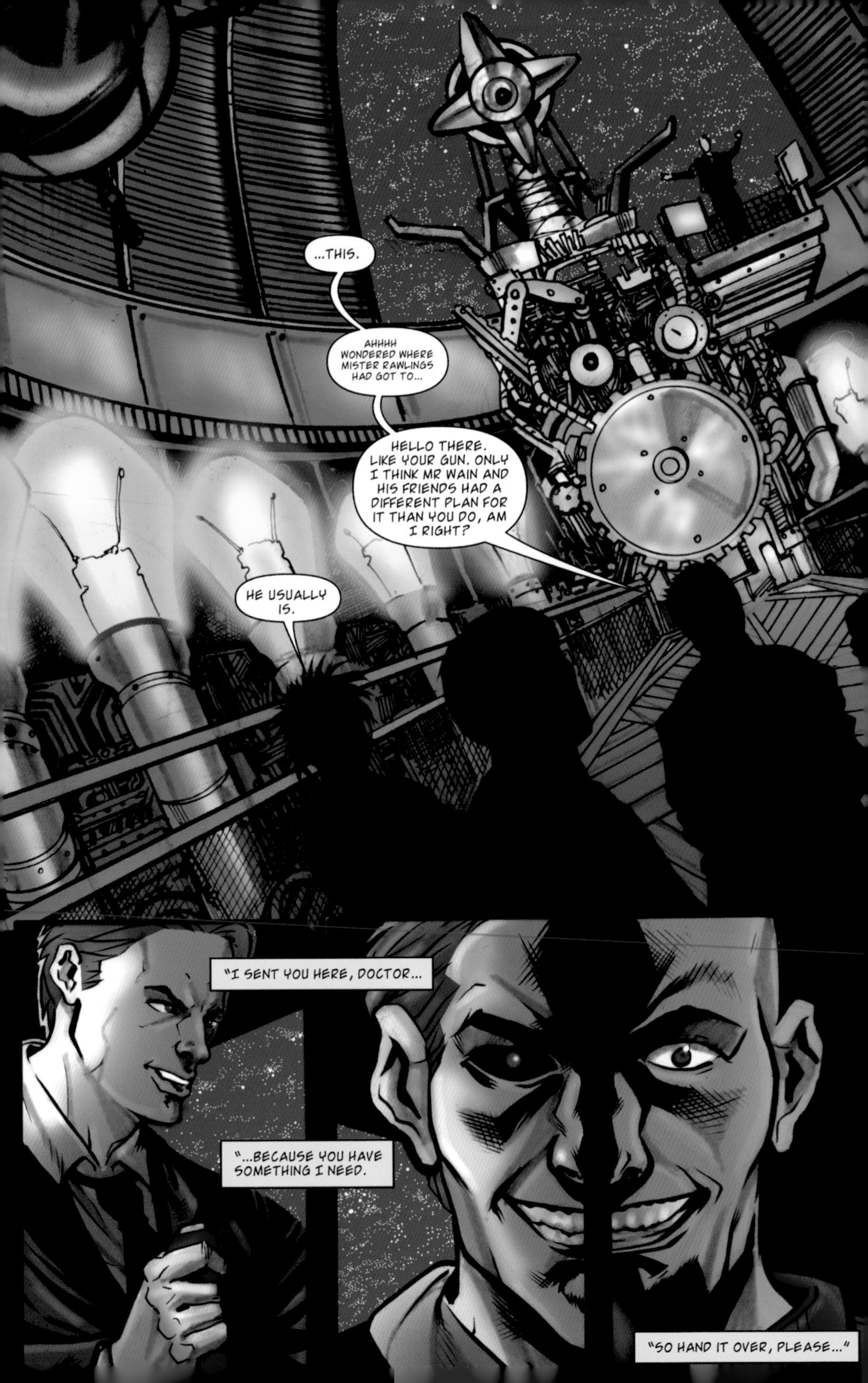
...THIS.
AHHHH WONDERED WHERE MISTER RAWLINGS HAD GOT TO...
HELLO THERE. LIKE YOUR GUN. ONLY I THINK MR WAIN AND HIS FRIENDS HAD A DIFFERENT PLAN FOR IT THAN YOU DO, AM I RIGHT?
HE USUALLY IS.
"I SENT YOU HERE, DOCTOR...
"...BECAUSE YOU HAVE SOMETHING I NEED.
"SO HAND IT OVER, PLEASE..."

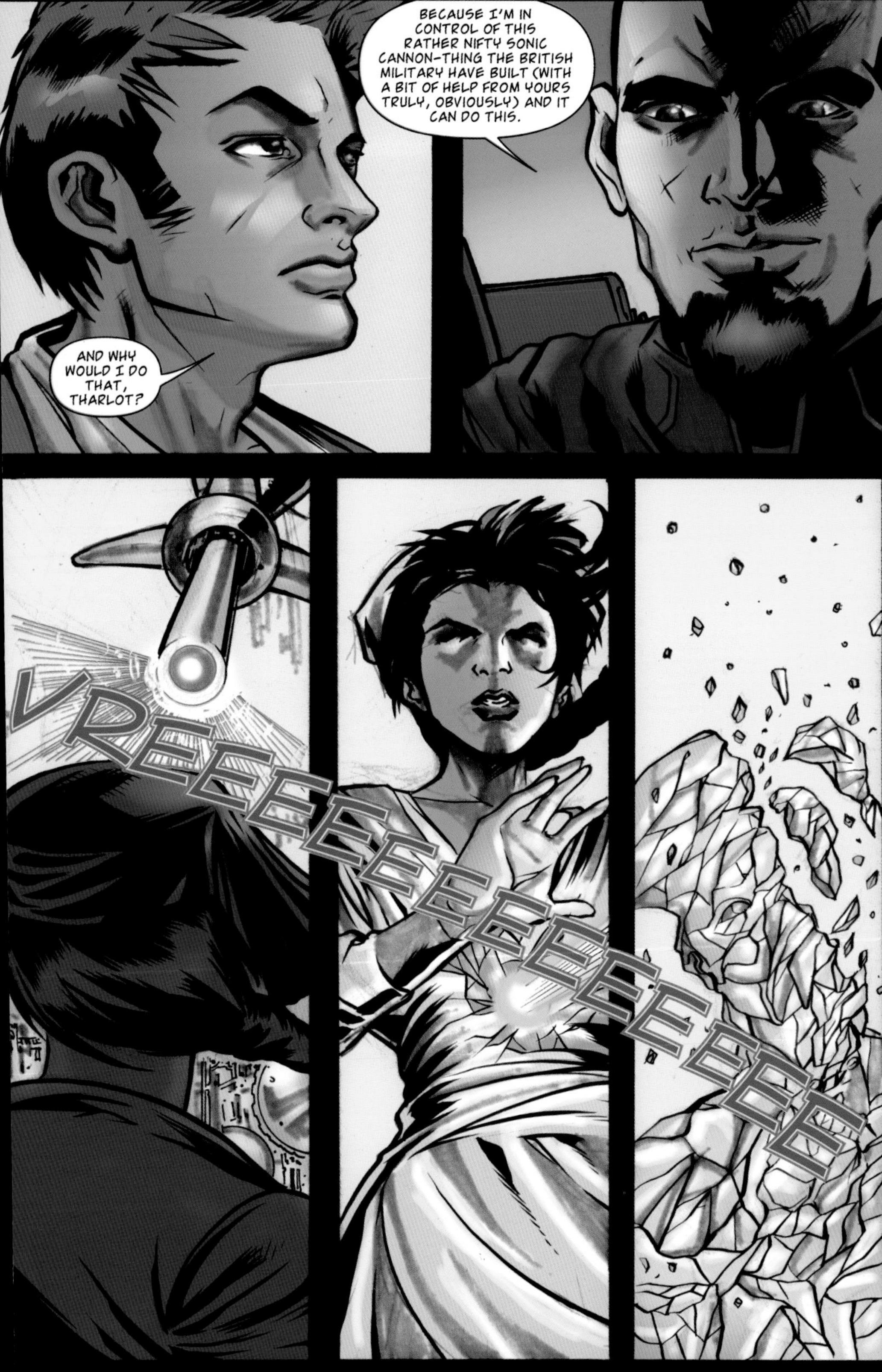
AND WHY WOULD I DO THAT, THARLOT?
BECAUSE I'M IN CONTROL OF THIS RATHER NIFTY SONIC CANNON-THING THE BRITISH MILITARY HAVE BUILT (WITH A BIT OF HELP FROM YOURS TRULY, OBVIOUSLY) AND IT CAN DO THIS.
VREEEEEEEEEEEEEEEEEE

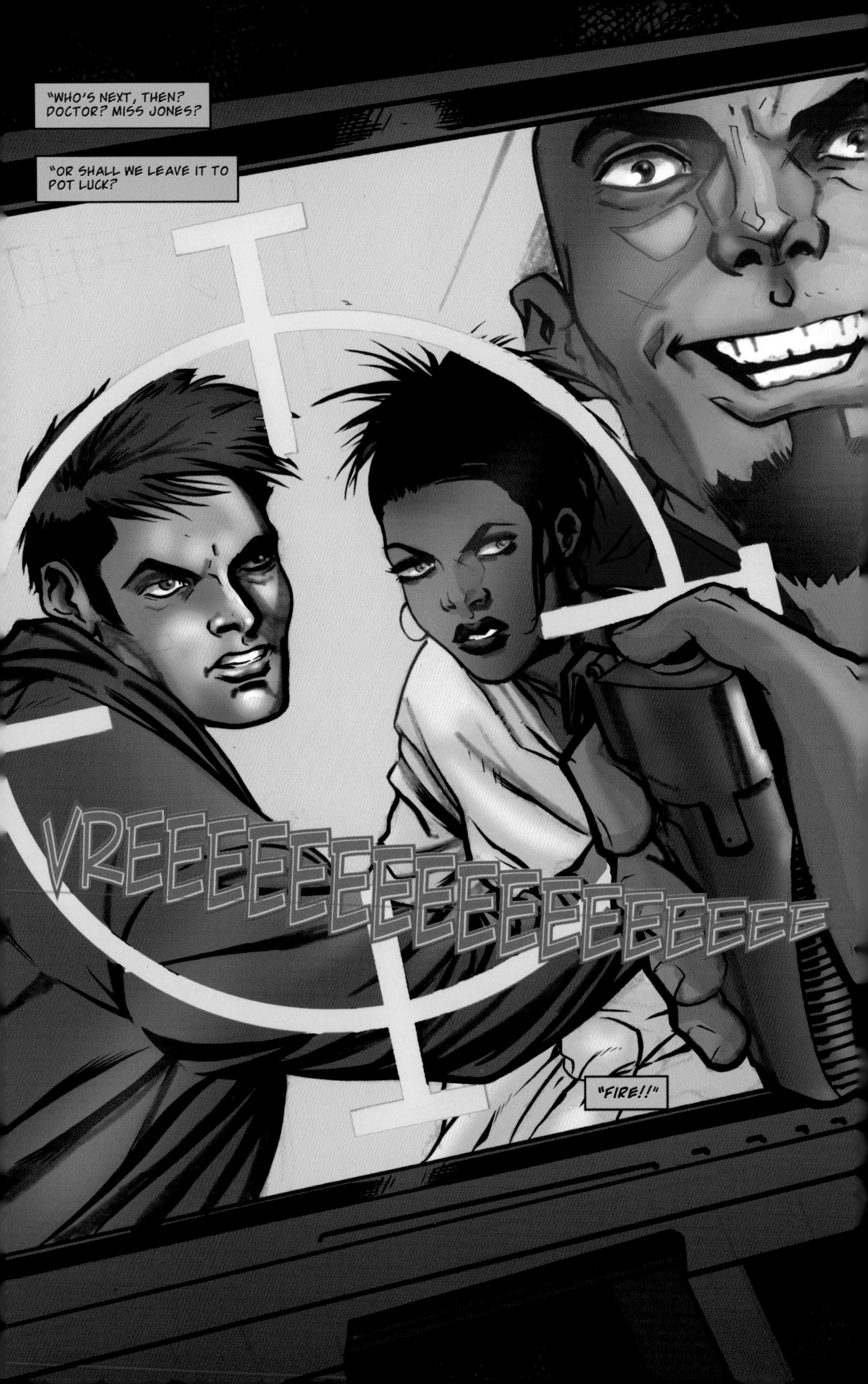
"WHO'S NEXT, THEN? DOCTOR? MISS JONES?
"OR SHALL WE LEAVE IT TO POT LUCK?
VREEEEEEEEEEEEEEEEEEEEEE
"FIRE!!"

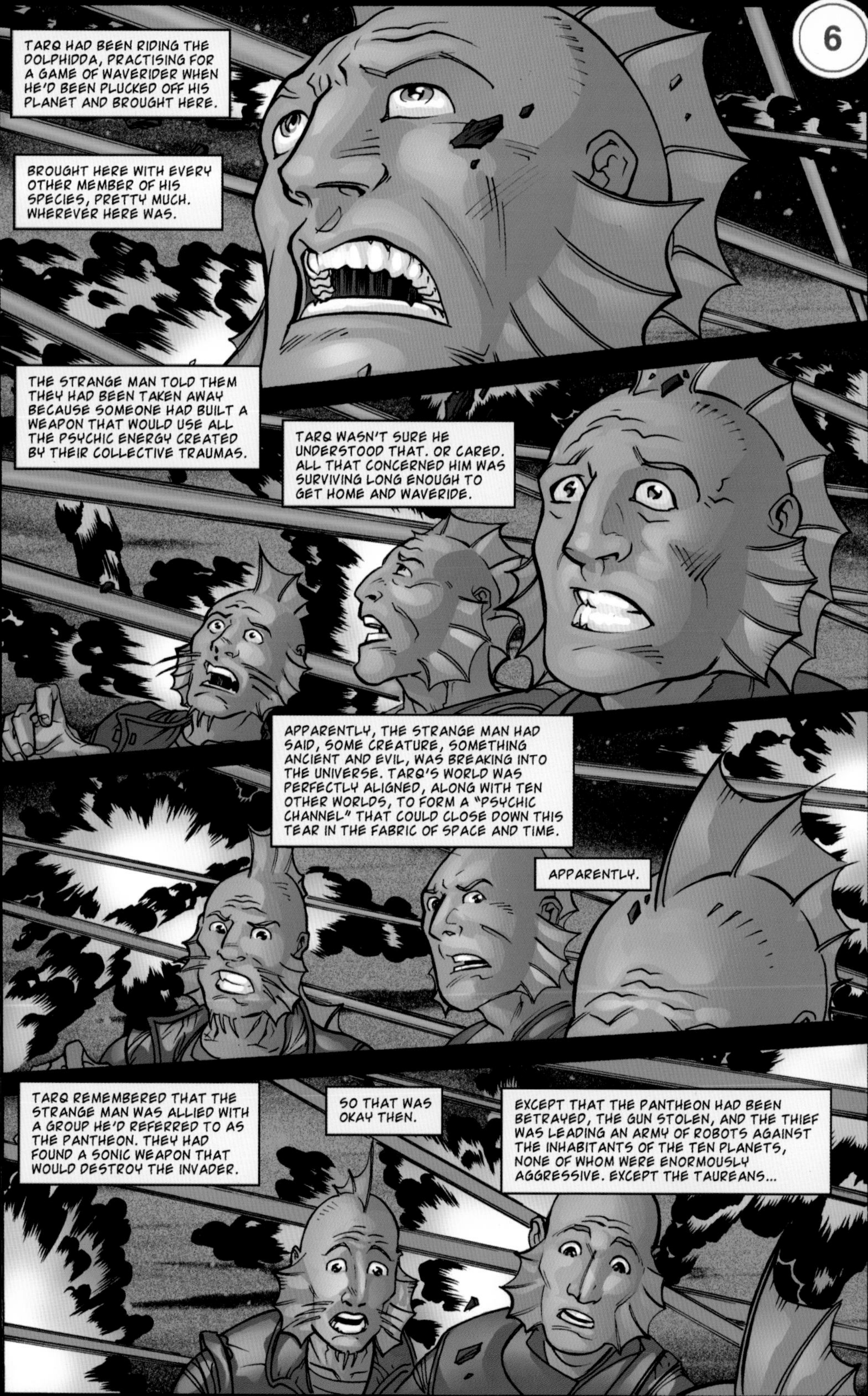
6
TARQ HAD BEEN RIDING THE DOLPHIDDA, PRACTISING FOR A GAME OF WAVERIDER WHEN HE'D BEEN PLUCKED OFF HIS PLANET AND BROUGHT HERE.
BROUGHT HERE WITH EVERY OTHER MEMBER OF HIS SPECIES, PRETTY MUCH. WHEREVER HERE WAS.
THE STRANGE MAN TOLD THEM THEY HAD BEEN TAKEN AWAY BECAUSE SOMEONE HAD BUILT A WEAPON THAT WOULD USE ALL THE PSYCHIC ENERGY CREATED BY THEIR COLLECTIVE TRAUMAS.
TARQ WASN'T SURE HE UNDERSTOOD THAT. OR CARED. ALL THAT CONCERNED HIM WAS SURVIVING LONG ENOUGH TO GET HOME AND WAVERIDE.
APPARENTLY, THE STRANGE MAN HAD SAID, SOME CREATURE, SOMETHING ANCIENT AND EVIL, WAS BREAKING INTO THE UNIVERSE. TARQ'S WORLD WAS PERFECTLY ALIGNED, ALONG WITH TEN OTHER WORLDS, TO FORM A "PSYCHIC CHANNEL" THAT COULD CLOSE DOWN THIS TEAR IN THE FABRIC OF SPACE AND TIME.
APPARENTLY.
TARQ REMEMBERED THAT THE STRANGE MAN WAS ALLIED WITH A GROUP HE'D REFERRED TO AS THE PANTHEON. THEY HAD FOUND A SONIC WEAPON THAT WOULD DESTROY THE INVADER.
SO THAT WAS OKAY THEN.
EXCEPT THAT THE PANTHEON HAD BEEN BETRAYED, THE GUN STOLEN, AND THE THIEF WAS LEADING AN ARMY OF ROBOTS AGAINST THE INHABITANTS OF THE TEN PLANETS, NONE OF WHOM WERE ENORMOUSLY AGGRESSIVE. EXCEPT THE TAUREANS...

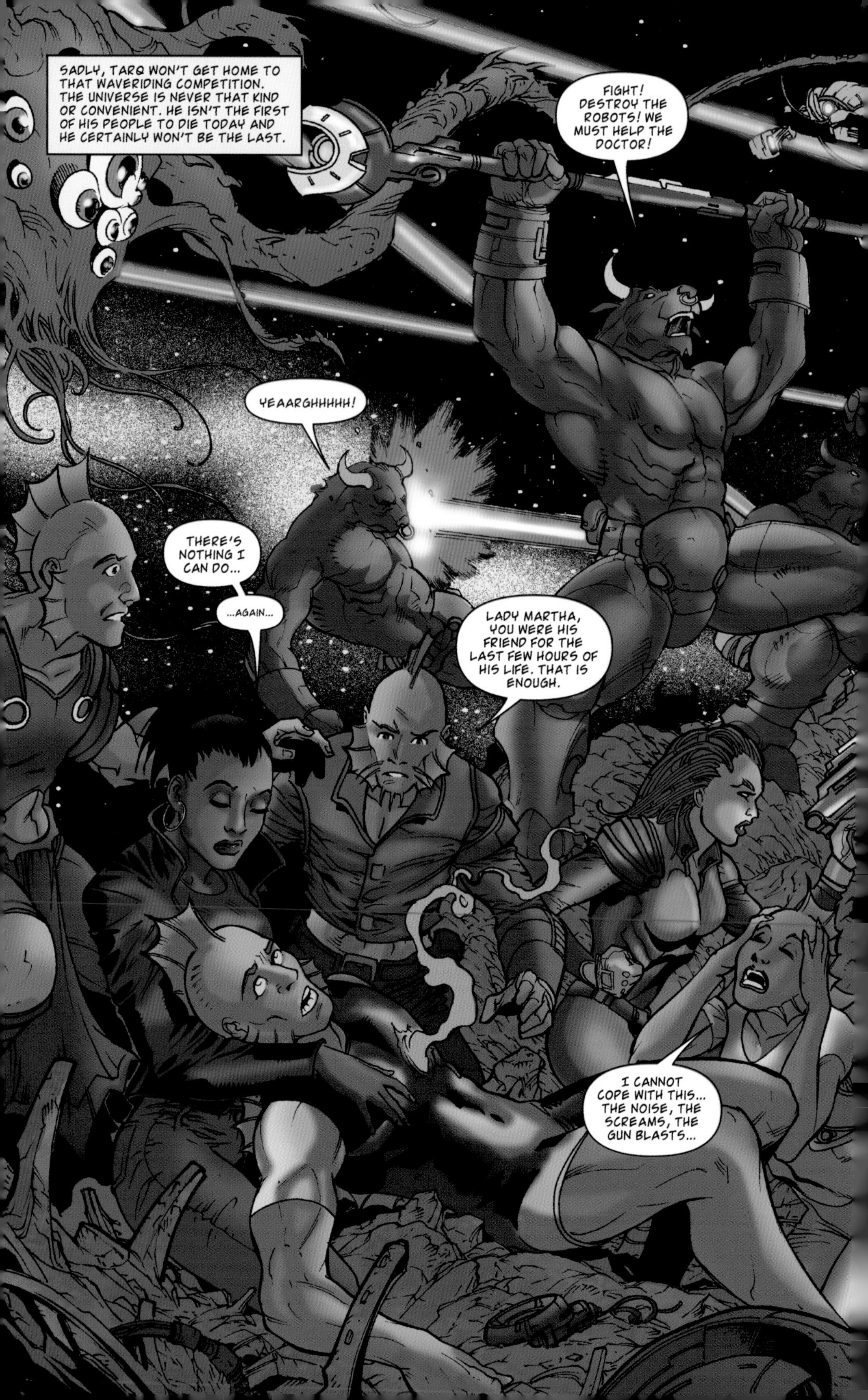
SADLY, TARQ WON'T GET HOME TO THAT WAVERIDING COMPETITION. THE UNIVERSE IS NEVER THAT KIND OR CONVENIENT. HE ISN'T THE FIRST OF HIS PEOPLE TO DIE TODAY AND HE CERTAINLY WON'T BE THE LAST.
FIGHT! DESTROY THE ROBOTS! WE MUST HELP THE DOCTOR!
YEAARGHHHHH!
THERE'S NOTHING I CAN DO...
...AGAIN...
LADY MARTHA, YOU WERE HIS FRIEND FOR THE LAST FEW HOURS OF HIS LIFE. THAT IS ENOUGH.
I CANNOT COPE WITH THIS... THE NOISE, THE SCREAMS, THE GUN BLASTS...

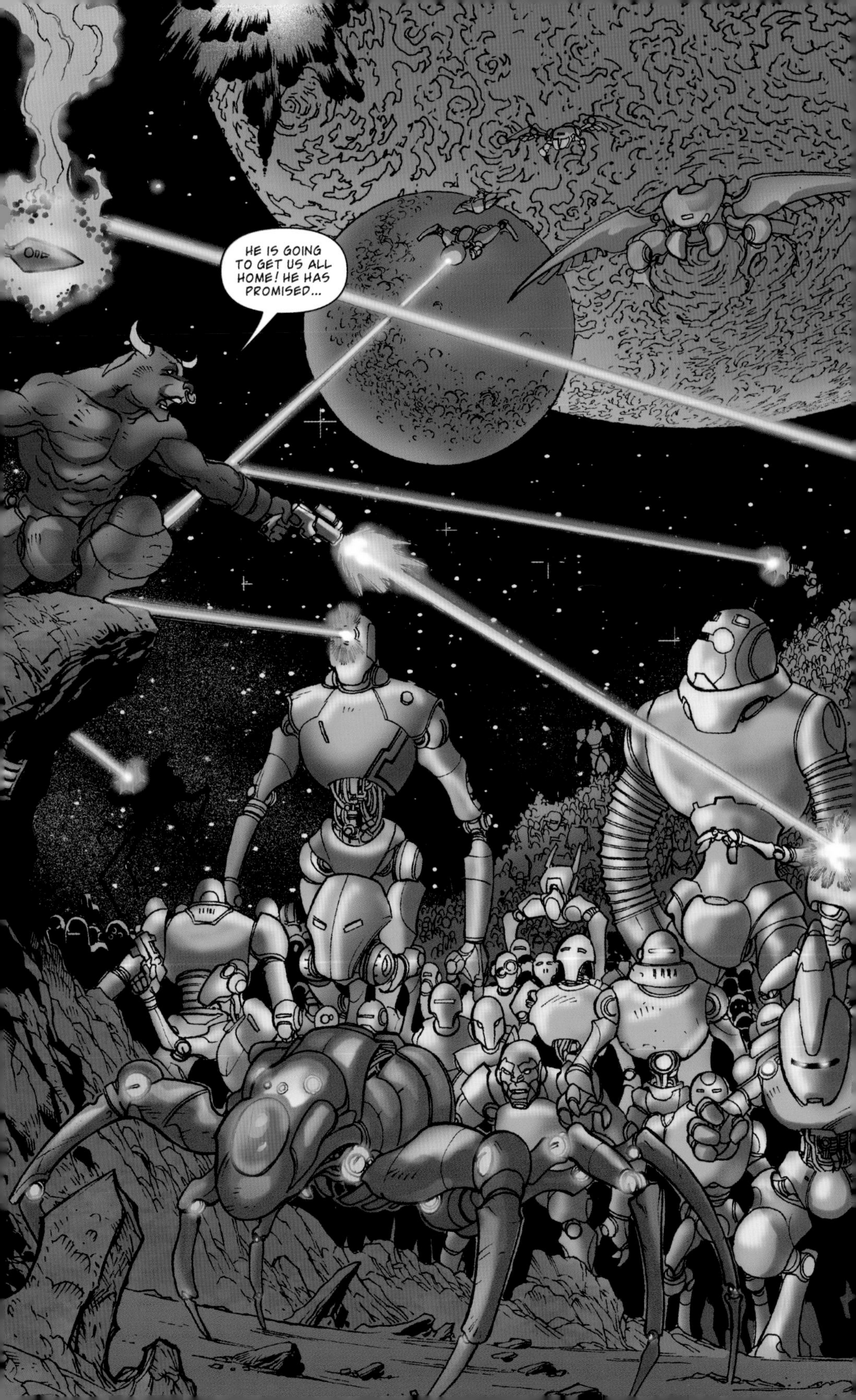
HE IS GOING TO GET US ALL HOME! HE HAS PROMISED...

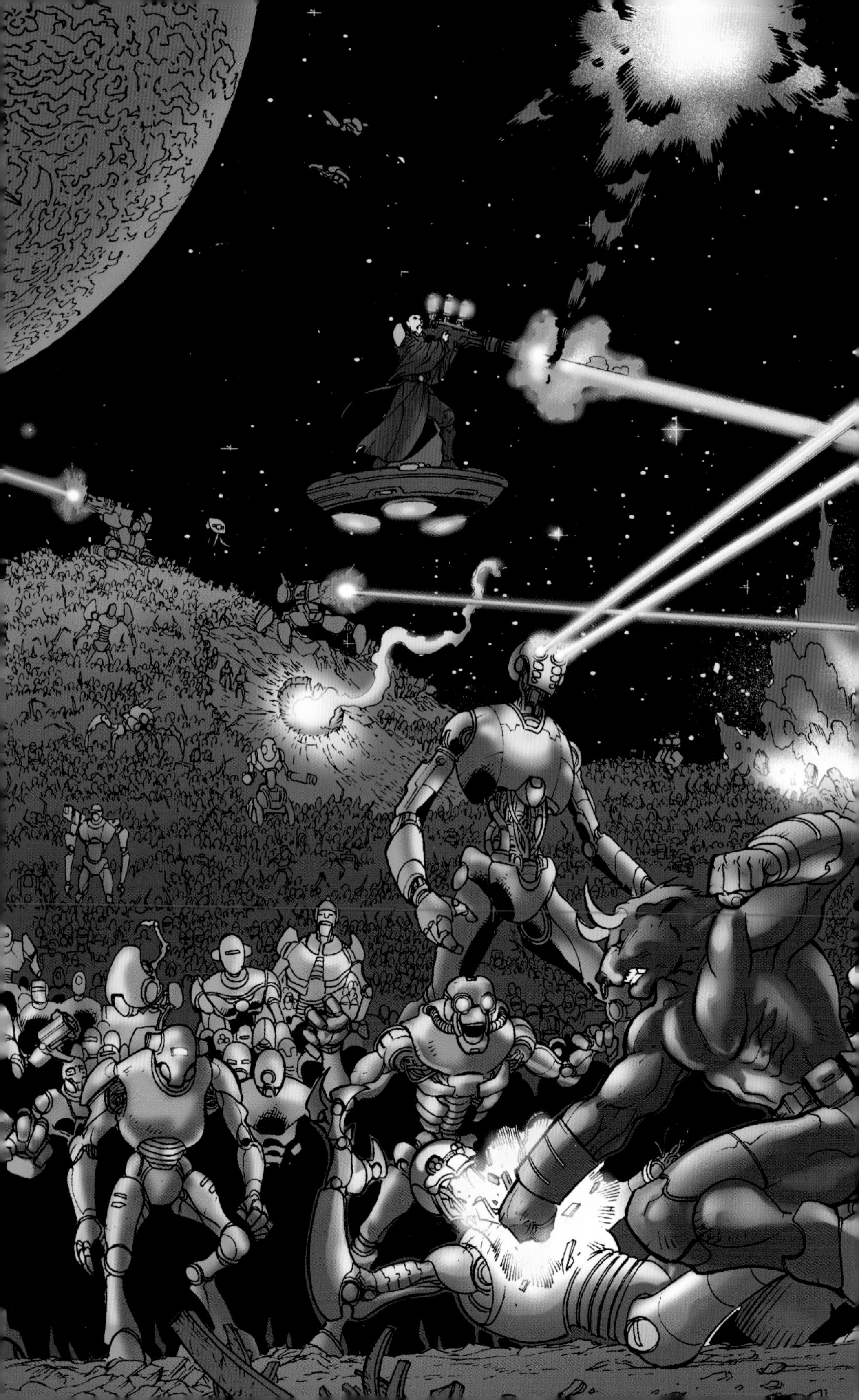

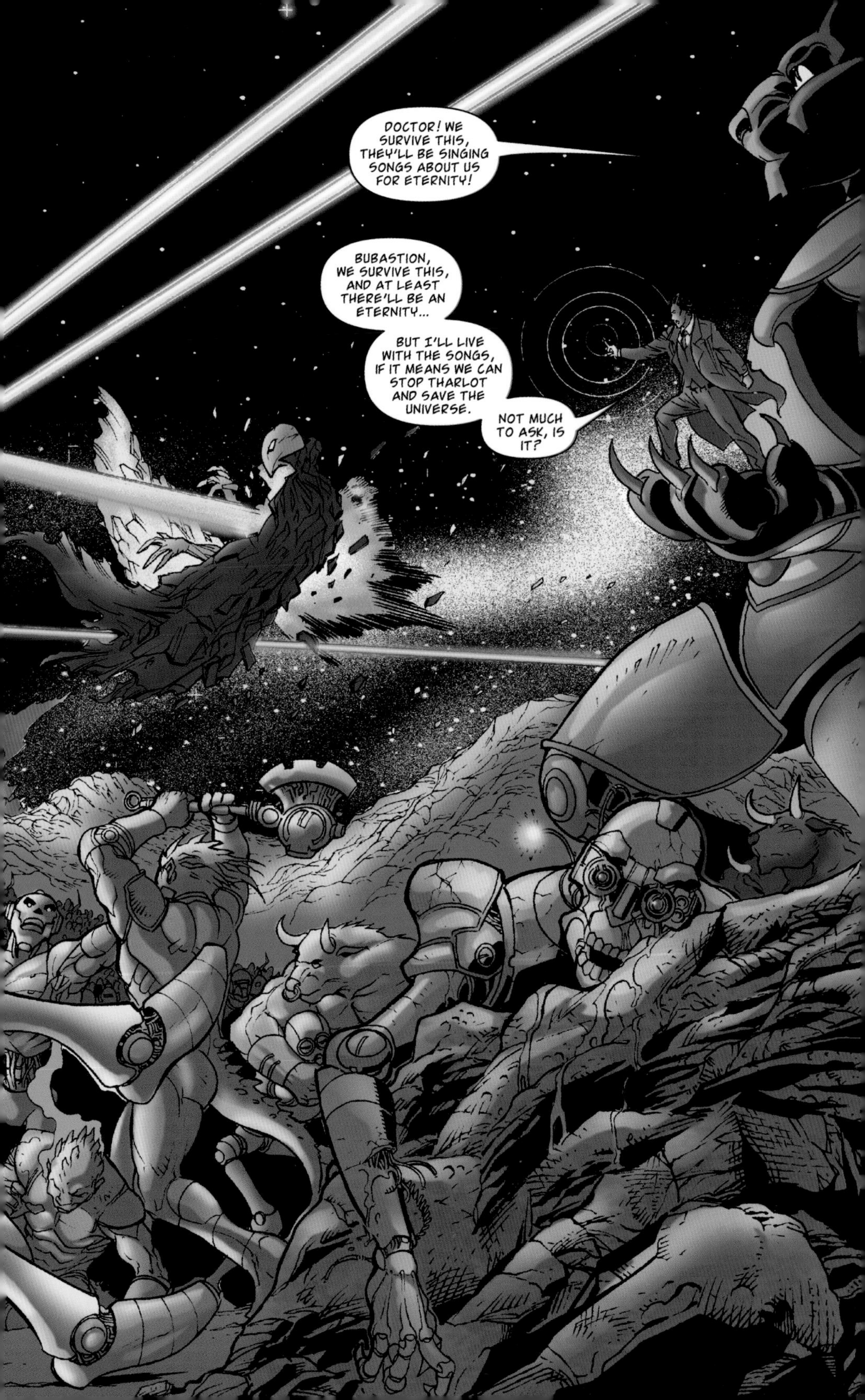
DOCTOR! WE SURVIVE THIS, THEY'LL BE SINGING SONGS ABOUT US FOR ETERNITY!
BUBASTION, WE SURVIVE THIS, AND AT LEAST THERE'LL BE AN ETERNITY...
BUT I'LL LIVE WITH THE SONGS, IF IT MEANS WE CAN STOP THARLOT AND SAVE THE UNIVERSE.
NOT MUCH TO ASK, IS IT?

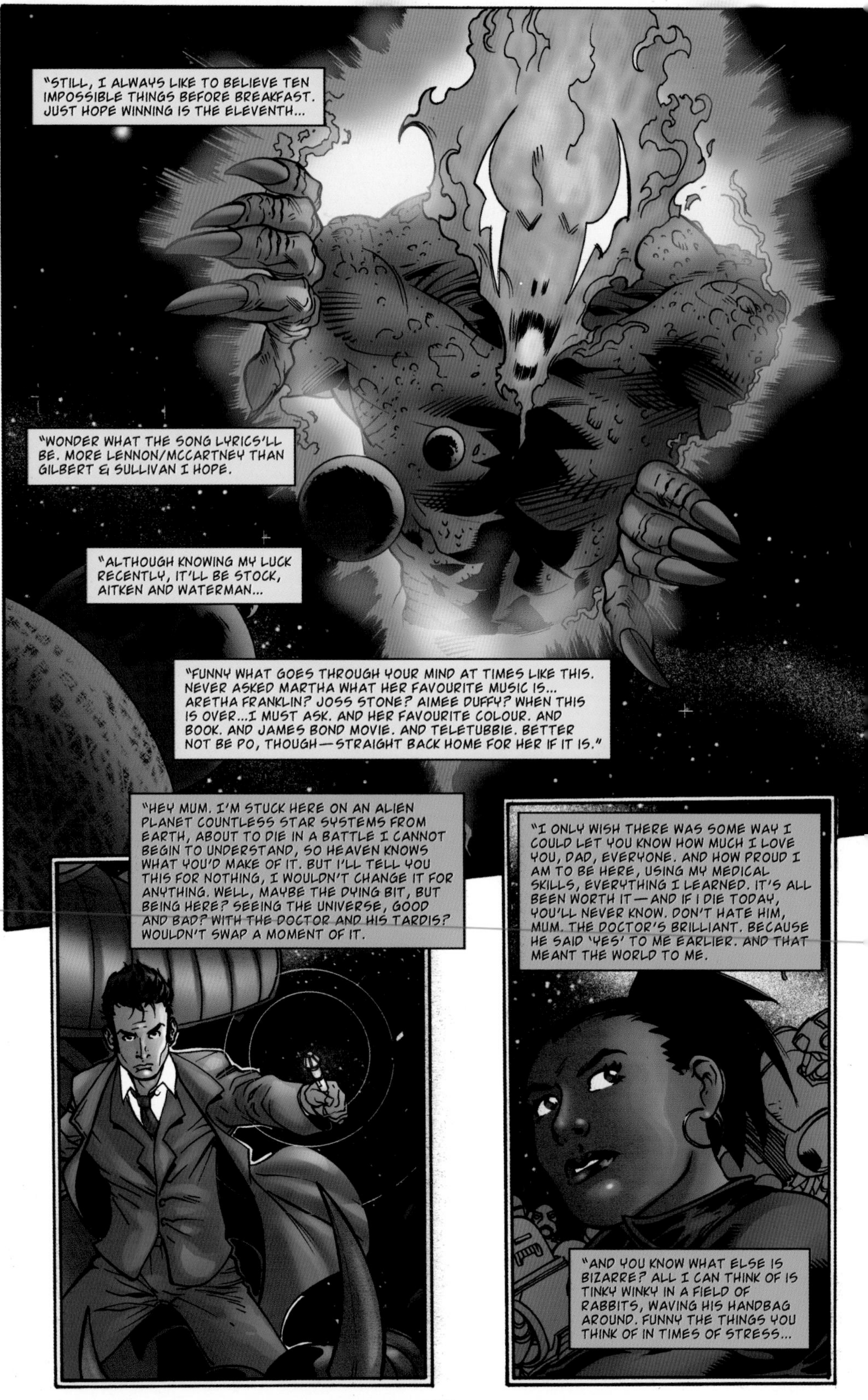
"STILL, I ALWAYS LIKE TO BELIEVE TEN IMPOSSIBLE THINGS BEFORE BREAKFAST. JUST HOPE WINNING IS THE ELEVENTH...
"WONDER WHAT THE SONG LYRICS'LL BE. MORE LENNON/MCCARTNEY THAN GILBERT & SULLIVAN I HOPE.
"ALTHOUGH KNOWING MY LUCK RECENTLY, IT'LL BE STOCK, AITKEN AND WATERMAN...
"FUNNY WHAT GOES THROUGH YOUR MIND AT TIMES LIKE THIS. NEVER ASKED MARTHA WHAT HER FAVOURITE MUSIC IS... ARETHA FRANKLIN? JOSS STONE? AIMEE DUFFY? WHEN THIS IS OVER...I MUST ASK. AND HER FAVOURITE COLOUR. AND BOOK. AND JAMES BOND MOVIE. AND TELETUBBIE. BETTER NOT BE PO, THOUGH—STRAIGHT BACK HOME FOR HER IF IT IS."
"HEY MUM. I'M STUCK HERE ON AN ALIEN PLANET COUNTLESS STAR SYSTEMS FROM EARTH, ABOUT TO DIE IN A BATTLE I CANNOT BEGIN TO UNDERSTAND, SO HEAVEN KNOWS WHAT YOU'D MAKE OF IT. BUT I'LL TELL YOU THIS FOR NOTHING, I WOULDN'T CHANGE IT FOR ANYTHING. WELL, MAYBE THE DYING BIT, BUT BEING HERE? SEEING THE UNIVERSE, GOOD AND BAD? WITH THE DOCTOR AND HIS TARDIS? WOULDN'T SWAP A MOMENT OF IT.
"I ONLY WISH THERE WAS SOME WAY I COULD LET YOU KNOW HOW MUCH I LOVE YOU, DAD, EVERYONE. AND HOW PROUD I AM TO BE HERE, USING MY MEDICAL SKILLS, EVERYTHING I LEARNED. IT'S ALL BEEN WORTH IT—AND IF I DIE TODAY, YOU'LL NEVER KNOW. DON'T HATE HIM, MUM. THE DOCTOR'S BRILLIANT. BECAUSE HE SAID 'YES' TO ME EARLIER. AND THAT MEANT THE WORLD TO ME.
"AND YOU KNOW WHAT ELSE IS BIZARRE? ALL I CAN THINK OF IS TINKY WINKY IN A FIELD OF RABBITS, WAVING HIS HANDBAG AROUND. FUNNY THE THINGS YOU THINK OF IN TIMES OF STRESS...

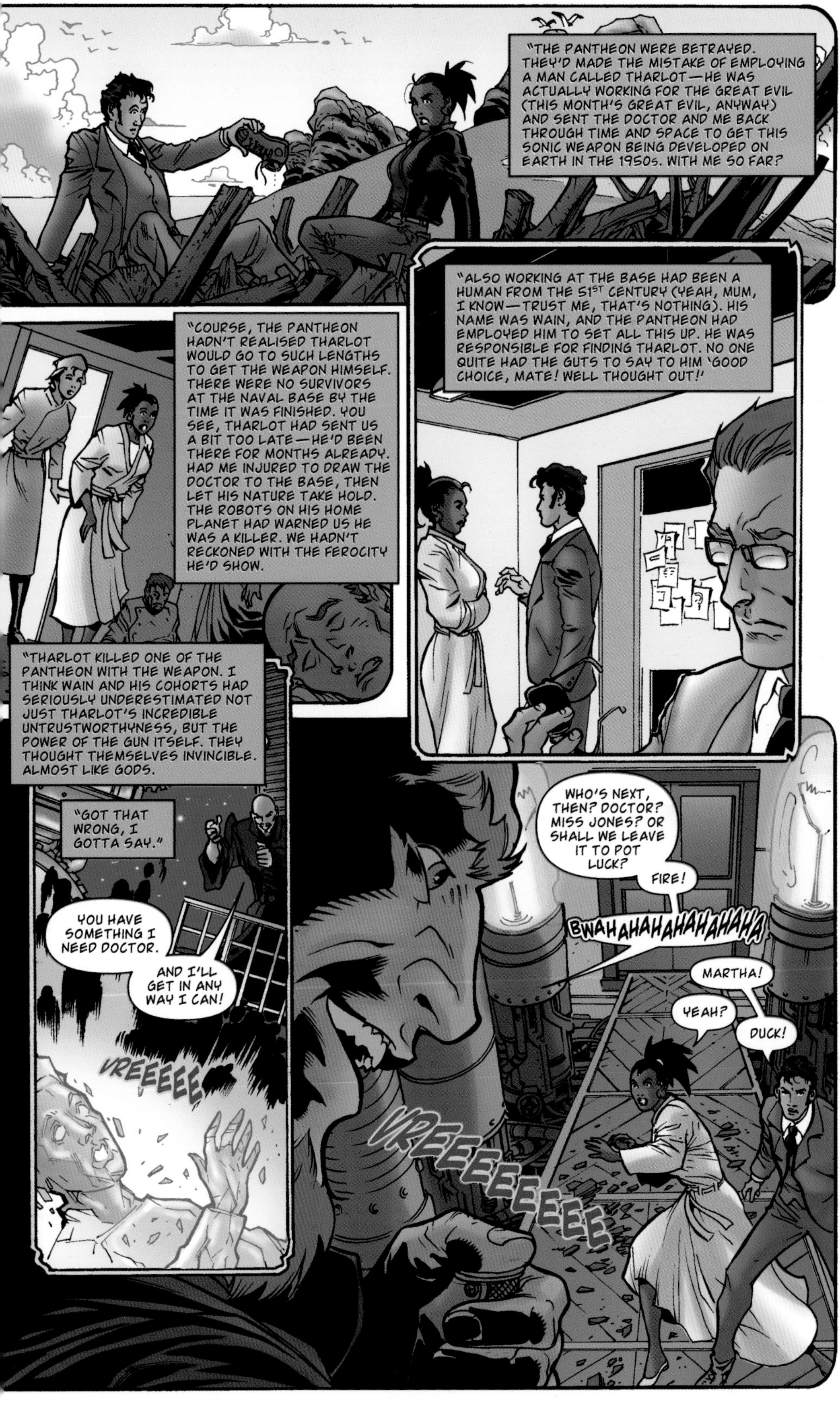
"THE PANTHEON WERE BETRAYED. THEY'D MADE THE MISTAKE OF EMPLOYING A MAN CALLED THARLOT—HE WAS ACTUALLY WORKING FOR THE GREAT EVIL (THIS MONTH'S GREAT EVIL, ANYWAY) AND SENT THE DOCTOR AND ME BACK THROUGH TIME AND SPACE TO GET THIS SONIC WEAPON BEING DEVELOPED ON EARTH IN THE 1950s. WITH ME SO FAR?
"COURSE, THE PANTHEON HADN'T REALISED THARLOT WOULD GO TO SUCH LENGTHS TO GET THE WEAPON HIMSELF. THERE WERE NO SURVIVORS AT THE NAVAL BASE BY THE TIME IT WAS FINISHED. YOU SEE, THARLOT HAD SENT US A BIT TOO LATE—HE'D BEEN THERE FOR MONTHS ALREADY. HAD ME INJURED TO DRAW THE DOCTOR TO THE BASE, THEN LET HIS NATURE TAKE HOLD. THE ROBOTS ON HIS HOME PLANET HAD WARNED US HE WAS A KILLER. WE HADN'T RECKONED WITH THE FEROCITY HE'D SHOW.
"ALSO WORKING AT THE BASE HAD BEEN A HUMAN FROM THE 51ST CENTURY (YEAH, MUM, I KNOW—TRUST ME, THAT'S NOTHING). HIS NAME WAS WAIN, AND THE PANTHEON HAD EMPLOYED HIM TO SET ALL THIS UP. HE WAS RESPONSIBLE FOR FINDING THARLOT. NO ONE QUITE HAD THE GUTS TO SAY TO HIM 'GOOD CHOICE, MATE! WELL THOUGHT OUT!'
"THARLOT KILLED ONE OF THE PANTHEON WITH THE WEAPON. I THINK WAIN AND HIS COHORTS HAD SERIOUSLY UNDERESTIMATED NOT JUST THARLOT'S INCREDIBLE UNTRUSTWORTHYNESS, BUT THE POWER OF THE GUN ITSELF. THEY THOUGHT THEMSELVES INVINCIBLE. ALMOST LIKE GODS.
"GOT THAT WRONG, I GOTTA SAY."
YOU HAVE SOMETHING I NEED DOCTOR.
AND I'LL GET IN ANY WAY I CAN!
VREEEEE
WHO'S NEXT, THEN? DOCTOR? MISS JONES? OR SHALL WE LEAVE IT TO POT LUCK?
FIRE!
BWAHAHAHAHAHAHAHA
MARTHA!
YEAH?
DUCK!
VREEEEEEEEEE

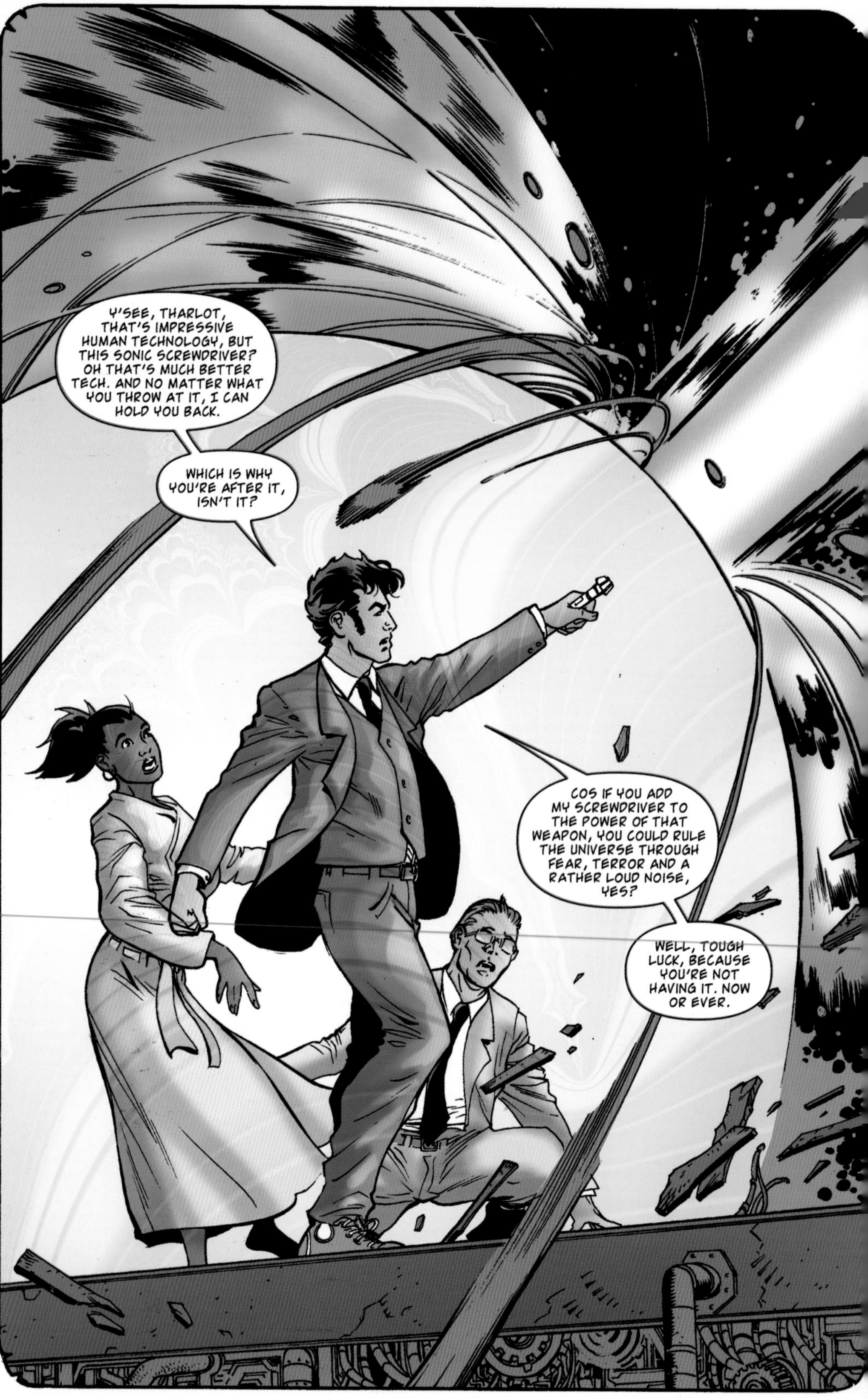
Y'SEE, THARLOT, THAT'S IMPRESSIVE HUMAN TECHNOLOGY, BUT THIS SONIC SCREWDRIVER? OH THAT'S MUCH BETTER TECH. AND NO MATTER WHAT YOU THROW AT IT, I CAN HOLD YOU BACK.
WHICH IS WHY YOU'RE AFTER IT, ISN'T IT?
COS IF YOU ADD MY SCREWDRIVER TO THE POWER OF THAT WEAPON, YOU COULD RULE THE UNIVERSE THROUGH FEAR, TERROR AND A RATHER LOUD NOISE, YES?
WELL, TOUGH LUCK, BECAUSE YOU'RE NOT HAVING IT. NOW OR EVER.

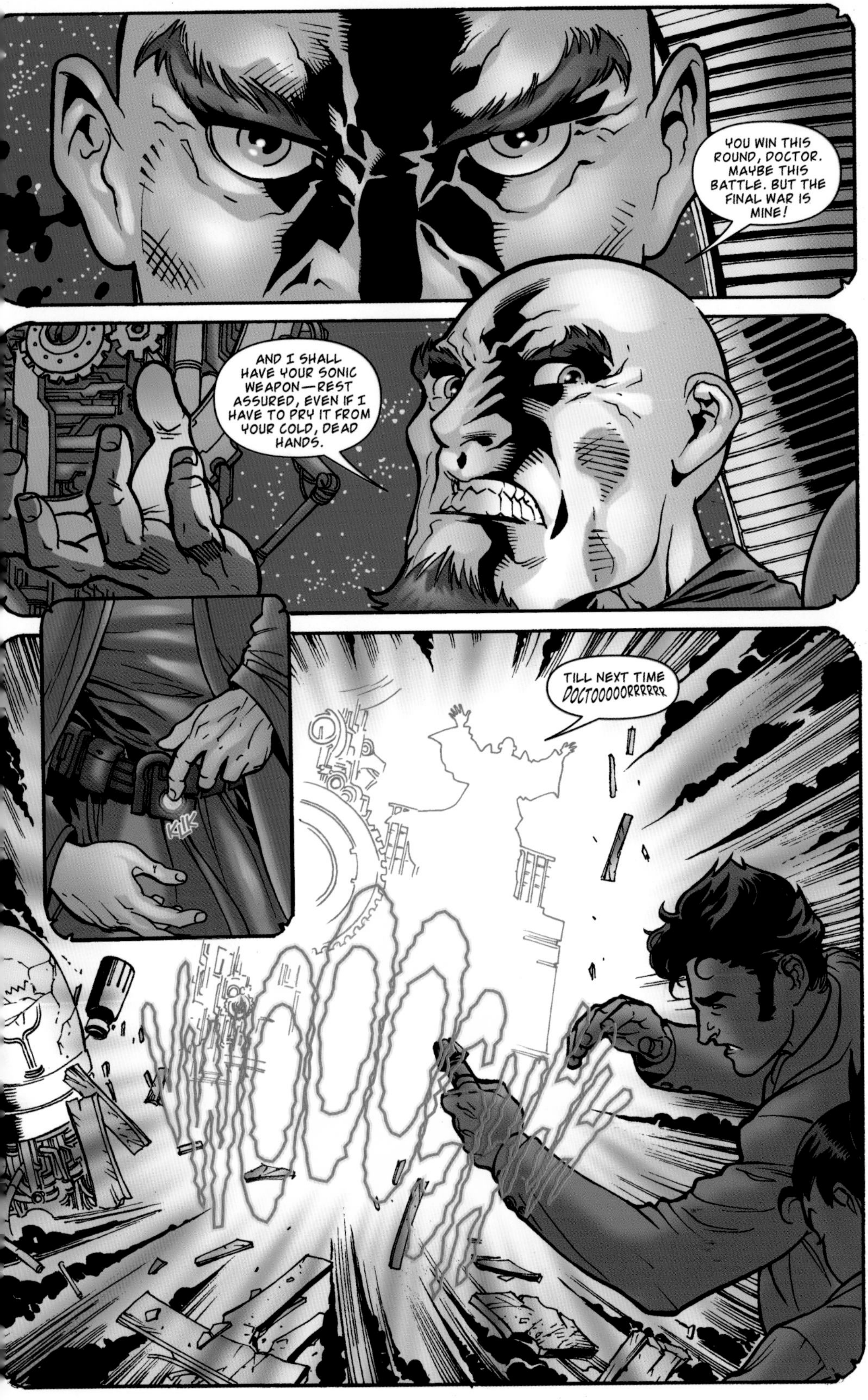
YOU WIN THIS ROUND, DOCTOR. MAYBE THIS BATTLE. BUT THE FINAL WAR IS MINE!
AND I SHALL HAVE YOUR SONIC WEAPON—REST ASSURED, EVEN IF I HAVE TO PRY IT FROM YOUR COLD, DEAD HANDS.
KLIK
TILL NEXT TIME DOCTOOOOORRRRRR

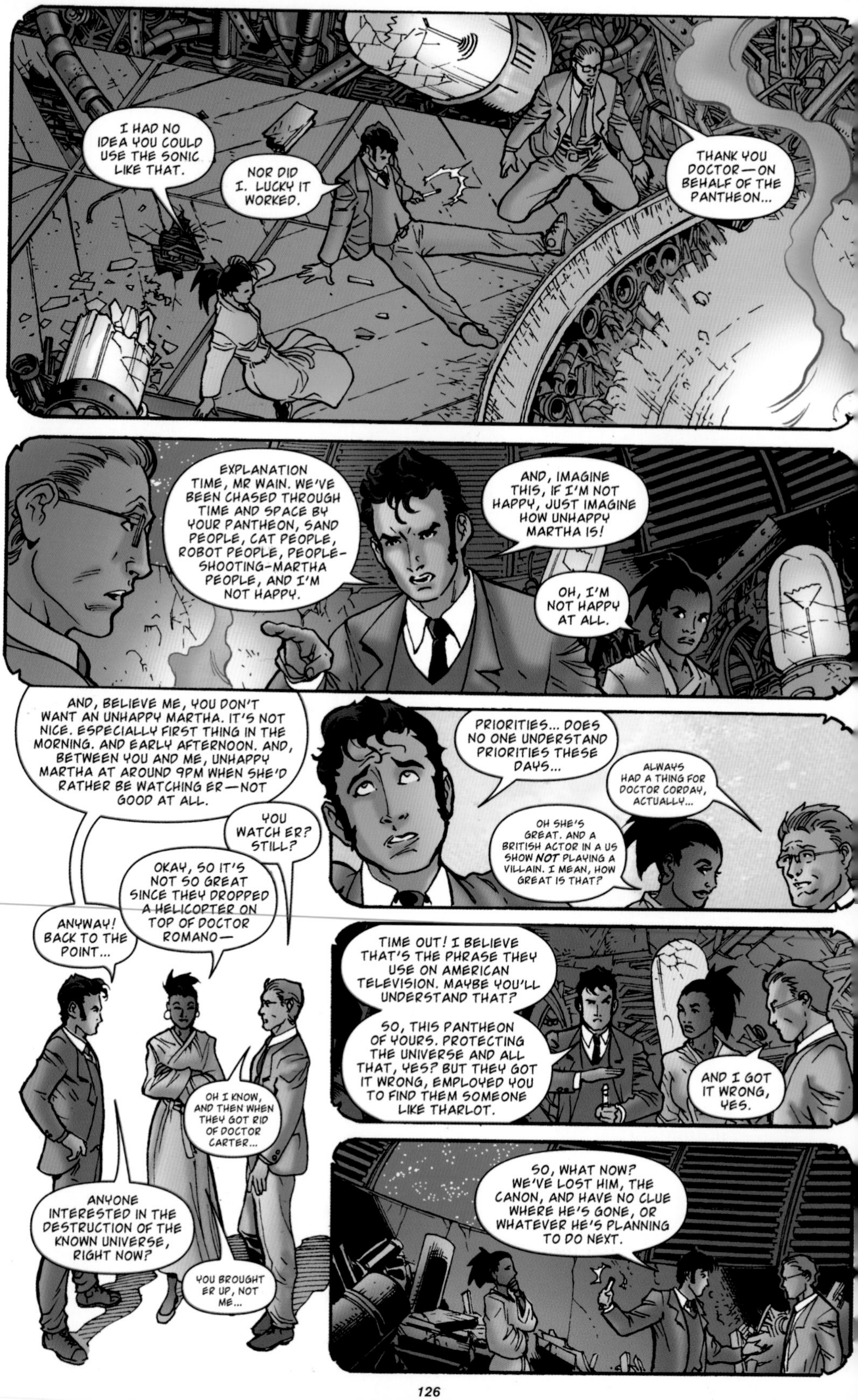

I HAD NO IDEA YOU COULD USE THE SONIC LIKE THAT.
NOR DID I. LUCKY IT WORKED.
THANK YOU DOCTOR—ON BEHALF OF THE PANTHEON...
EXPLANATION TIME, MR WAIN. WE'VE BEEN CHASED THROUGH TIME AND SPACE BY YOUR PANTHEON, SAND PEOPLE, CAT PEOPLE, ROBOT PEOPLE, PEOPLE-SHOOTING-MARTHA PEOPLE, AND I'M NOT HAPPY.
AND, IMAGINE THIS, IF I'M NOT HAPPY, JUST IMAGINE HOW UNHAPPY MARTHA IS!
OH, I'M NOT HAPPY AT ALL.
AND, BELIEVE ME, YOU DON'T WANT AN UNHAPPY MARTHA. IT'S NOT NICE. ESPECIALLY FIRST THING IN THE MORNING. AND EARLY AFTERNOON. AND, BETWEEN YOU AND ME, UNHAPPY MARTHA AT AROUND 9PM WHEN SHE'D RATHER BE WATCHING ER—NOT GOOD AT ALL.
YOU WATCH ER? STILL?
OKAY, SO IT'S NOT SO GREAT SINCE THEY DROPPED A HELICOPTER ON TOP OF DOCTOR ROMANO—
ANYWAY! BACK TO THE POINT...
OH I KNOW, AND THEN WHEN THEY GOT RID OF DOCTOR CARTER...
ANYONE INTERESTED IN THE DESTRUCTION OF THE KNOWN UNIVERSE, RIGHT NOW?
YOU BROUGHT ER UP, NOT ME...
PRIORITIES... DOES NO ONE UNDERSTAND PRIORITIES THESE DAYS...
ALWAYS HAD A THING FOR DOCTOR CORDAY, ACTUALLY...
OH SHE'S GREAT. AND A BRITISH ACTOR IN A US SHOW **NOT** PLAYING A VILLAIN. I MEAN, HOW GREAT IS THAT?
TIME OUT! I BELIEVE THAT'S THE PHRASE THEY USE ON AMERICAN TELEVISION. MAYBE YOU'LL UNDERSTAND THAT?
SO, THIS PANTHEON OF YOURS. PROTECTING THE UNIVERSE AND ALL THAT, YES? BUT THEY GOT IT WRONG, EMPLOYED YOU TO FIND THEM SOMEONE LIKE THARLOT.
AND I GOT IT WRONG, YES.
SO, WHAT NOW? WE'VE LOST HIM, THE CANON, AND HAVE NO CLUE WHERE HE'S GONE, OR WHATEVER HE'S PLANNING TO DO NEXT.

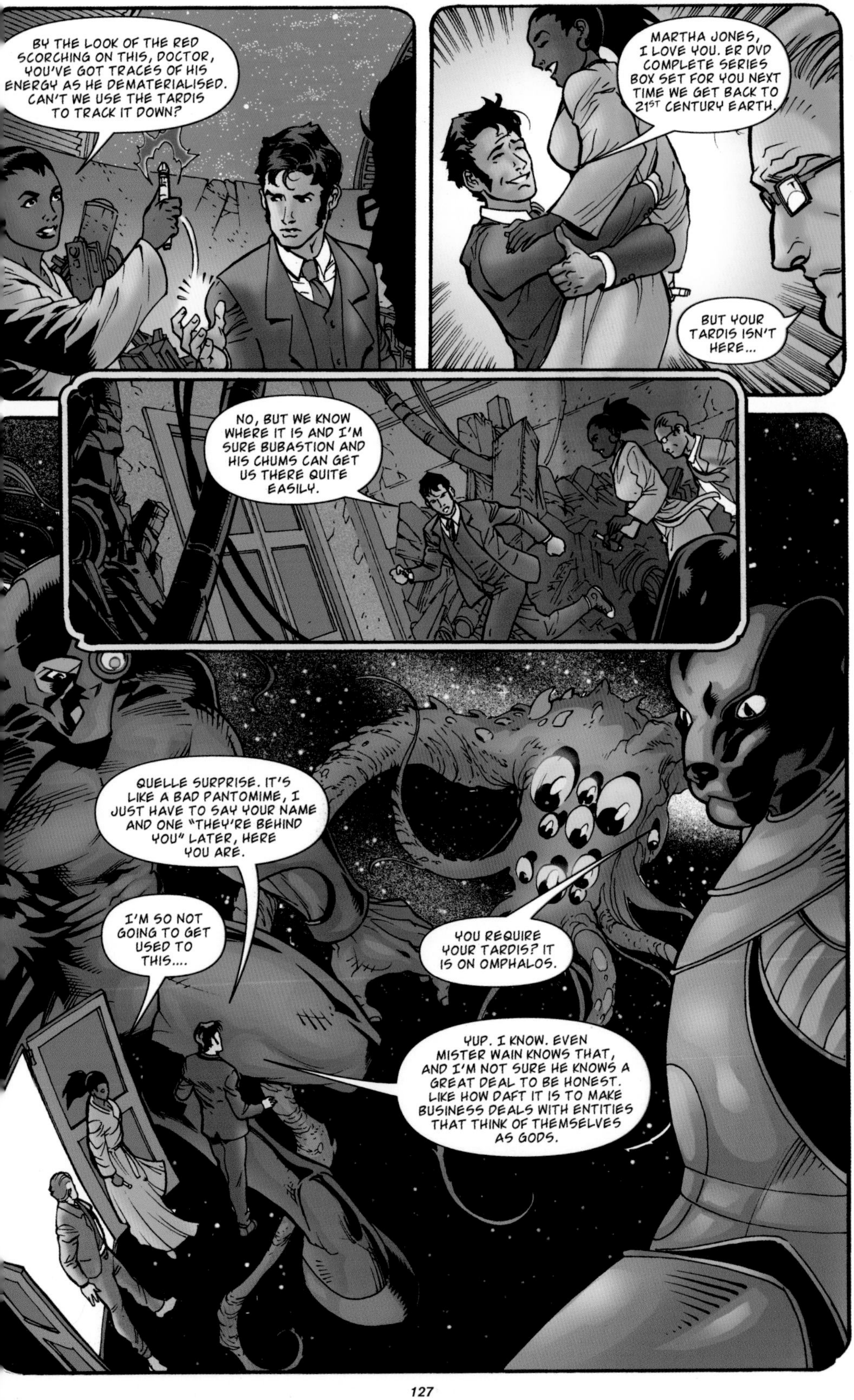

BY THE LOOK OF THE RED SCORCHING ON THIS, DOCTOR, YOU'VE GOT TRACES OF HIS ENERGY AS HE DEMATERIALISED. CAN'T WE USE THE TARDIS TO TRACK IT DOWN?
MARTHA JONES, I LOVE YOU. ER DVD COMPLETE SERIES BOX SET FOR YOU NEXT TIME WE GET BACK TO 21ST CENTURY EARTH.
BUT YOUR TARDIS ISN'T HERE...
NO, BUT WE KNOW WHERE IT IS AND I'M SURE BUBASTION AND HIS CHUMS CAN GET US THERE QUITE EASILY.
QUELLE SURPRISE. IT'S LIKE A BAD PANTOMIME, I JUST HAVE TO SAY YOUR NAME AND ONE "THEY'RE BEHIND YOU" LATER, HERE YOU ARE.
I'M SO NOT GOING TO GET USED TO THIS....
YOU REQUIRE YOUR TARDIS? IT IS ON OMPHALOS.
YUP. I KNOW. EVEN MISTER WAIN KNOWS THAT, AND I'M NOT SURE HE KNOWS A GREAT DEAL TO BE HONEST. LIKE HOW DAFT IT IS TO MAKE BUSINESS DEALS WITH ENTITIES THAT THINK OF THEMSELVES AS GODS.

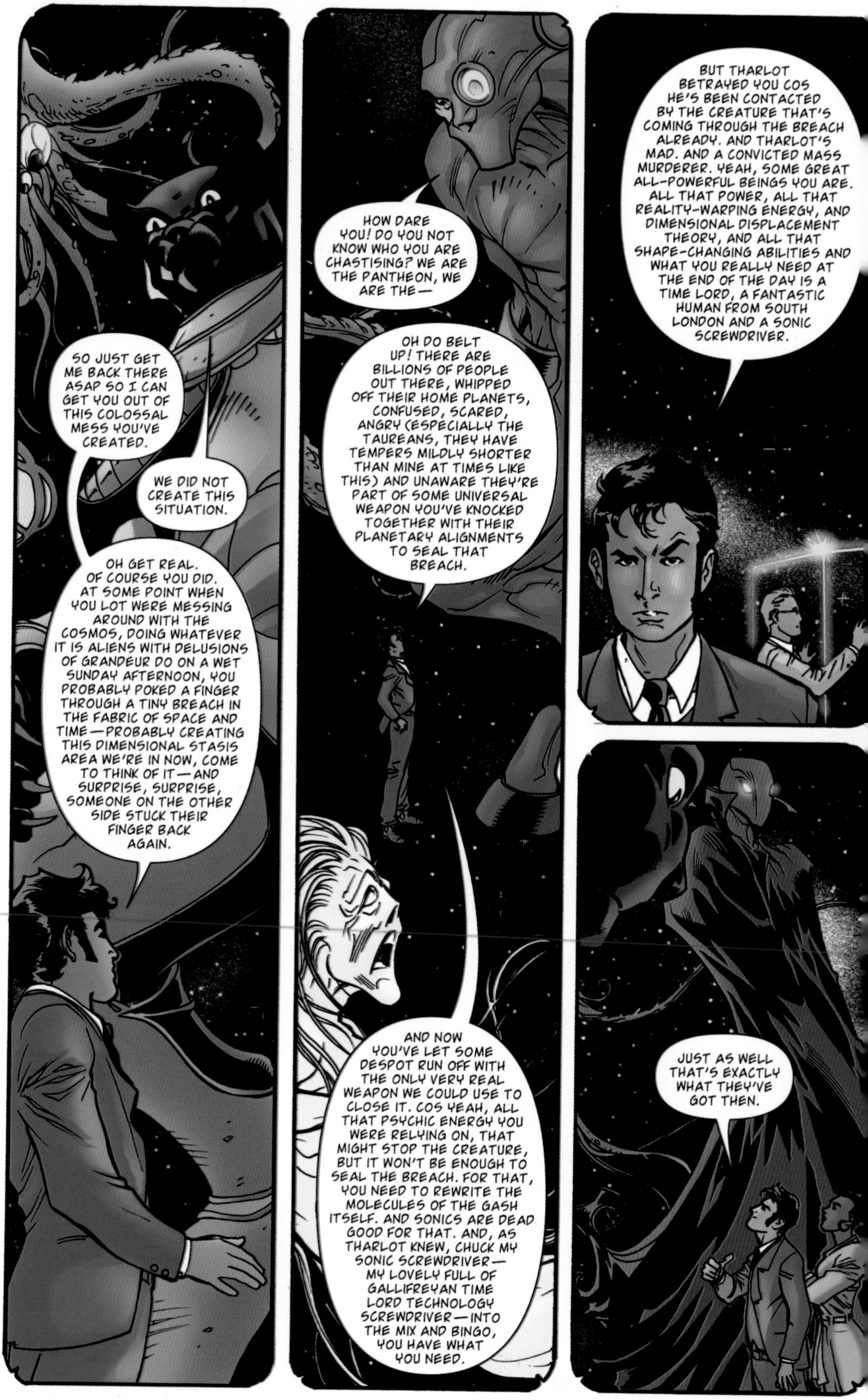
SO JUST GET ME BACK THERE ASAP SO I CAN GET YOU OUT OF THIS COLOSSAL MESS YOU'VE CREATED.
WE DID NOT CREATE THIS SITUATION.
OH GET REAL. OF COURSE YOU DID. AT SOME POINT WHEN YOU LOT WERE MESSING AROUND WITH THE COSMOS, DOING WHATEVER IT IS ALIENS WITH DELUSIONS OF GRANDEUR DO ON A WET SUNDAY AFTERNOON, YOU PROBABLY POKED A FINGER THROUGH A TINY BREACH IN THE FABRIC OF SPACE AND TIME—PROBABLY CREATING THIS DIMENSIONAL STASIS AREA WE'RE IN NOW, COME TO THINK OF IT—AND SURPRISE, SURPRISE, SOMEONE ON THE OTHER SIDE STUCK THEIR FINGER BACK AGAIN.
HOW DARE YOU! DO YOU NOT KNOW WHO YOU ARE CHASTISING? WE ARE THE PANTHEON, WE ARE THE—
OH DO BELT UP! THERE ARE BILLIONS OF PEOPLE OUT THERE, WHIPPED OFF THEIR HOME PLANETS, CONFUSED, SCARED, ANGRY (ESPECIALLY THE TAUREANS, THEY HAVE TEMPERS MILDLY SHORTER THAN MINE AT TIMES LIKE THIS) AND UNAWARE THEY'RE PART OF SOME UNIVERSAL WEAPON YOU'VE KNOCKED TOGETHER WITH THEIR PLANETARY ALIGNMENTS TO SEAL THAT BREACH.
AND NOW YOU'VE LET SOME DESPOT RUN OFF WITH THE ONLY VERY REAL WEAPON WE COULD USE TO CLOSE IT. COS YEAH, ALL THAT PSYCHIC ENERGY YOU WERE RELYING ON, THAT MIGHT STOP THE CREATURE, BUT IT WON'T BE ENOUGH TO SEAL THE BREACH. FOR THAT, YOU NEED TO REWRITE THE MOLECULES OF THE GASH ITSELF. AND SONICS ARE DEAD GOOD FOR THAT. AND, AS THARLOT KNEW, CHUCK MY SONIC SCREWDRIVER—MY LOVELY FULL OF GALLIFREYAN TIME LORD TECHNOLOGY SCREWDRIVER—INTO THE MIX AND BINGO, YOU HAVE WHAT YOU NEED.
BUT THARLOT BETRAYED YOU COS HE'S BEEN CONTACTED BY THE CREATURE THAT'S COMING THROUGH THE BREACH ALREADY. AND THARLOT'S MAD. AND A CONVICTED MASS MURDERER. YEAH, SOME GREAT ALL-POWERFUL BEINGS YOU ARE. ALL THAT POWER, ALL THAT REALITY-WARPING ENERGY, AND DIMENSIONAL DISPLACEMENT THEORY, AND ALL THAT SHAPE-CHANGING ABILITIES AND WHAT YOU REALLY NEED AT THE END OF THE DAY IS A TIME LORD, A FANTASTIC HUMAN FROM SOUTH LONDON AND A SONIC SCREWDRIVER.
JUST AS WELL THAT'S EXACTLY WHAT THEY'VE GOT THEN.

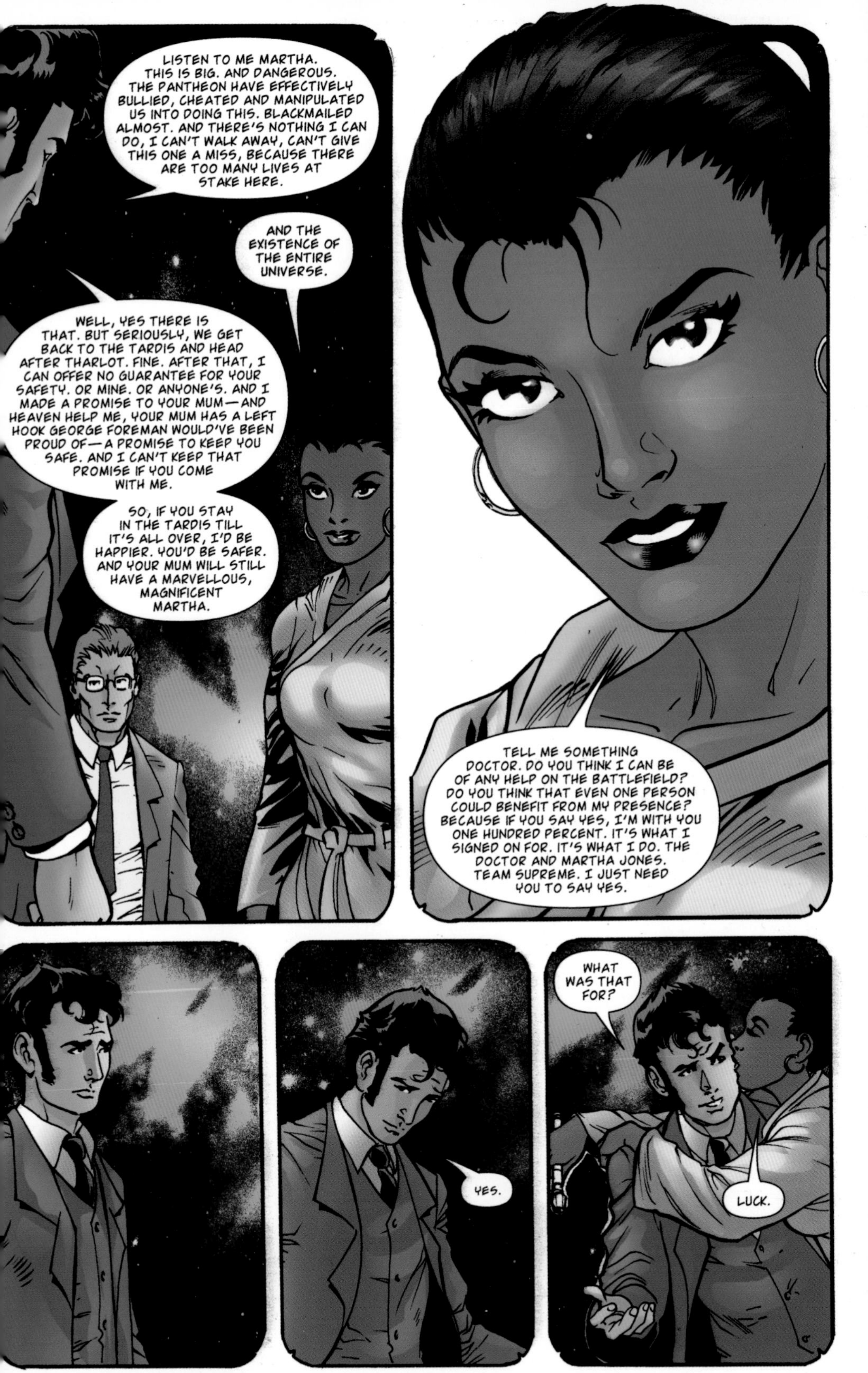
LISTEN TO ME MARTHA. THIS IS BIG. AND DANGEROUS. THE PANTHEON HAVE EFFECTIVELY BULLIED, CHEATED AND MANIPULATED US INTO DOING THIS. BLACKMAILED ALMOST. AND THERE'S NOTHING I CAN DO, I CAN'T WALK AWAY, CAN'T GIVE THIS ONE A MISS, BECAUSE THERE ARE TOO MANY LIVES AT STAKE HERE.
AND THE EXISTENCE OF THE ENTIRE UNIVERSE.
WELL, YES THERE IS THAT. BUT SERIOUSLY, WE GET BACK TO THE TARDIS AND HEAD AFTER THARLOT. FINE. AFTER THAT, I CAN OFFER NO GUARANTEE FOR YOUR SAFETY. OR MINE. OR ANYONE'S. AND I MADE A PROMISE TO YOUR MUM—AND HEAVEN HELP ME, YOUR MUM HAS A LEFT HOOK GEORGE FOREMAN WOULD'VE BEEN PROUD OF—A PROMISE TO KEEP YOU SAFE. AND I CAN'T KEEP THAT PROMISE IF YOU COME WITH ME.
SO, IF YOU STAY IN THE TARDIS TILL IT'S ALL OVER, I'D BE HAPPIER. YOU'D BE SAFER. AND YOUR MUM WILL STILL HAVE A MARVELLOUS, MAGNIFICENT MARTHA.
TELL ME SOMETHING DOCTOR. DO YOU THINK I CAN BE OF ANY HELP ON THE BATTLEFIELD? DO YOU THINK THAT EVEN ONE PERSON COULD BENEFIT FROM MY PRESENCE? BECAUSE IF YOU SAY YES, I'M WITH YOU ONE HUNDRED PERCENT. IT'S WHAT I SIGNED ON FOR. IT'S WHAT I DO. THE DOCTOR AND MARTHA JONES. TEAM SUPREME. I JUST NEED YOU TO SAY YES.
YES.
WHAT WAS THAT FOR?
LUCK.

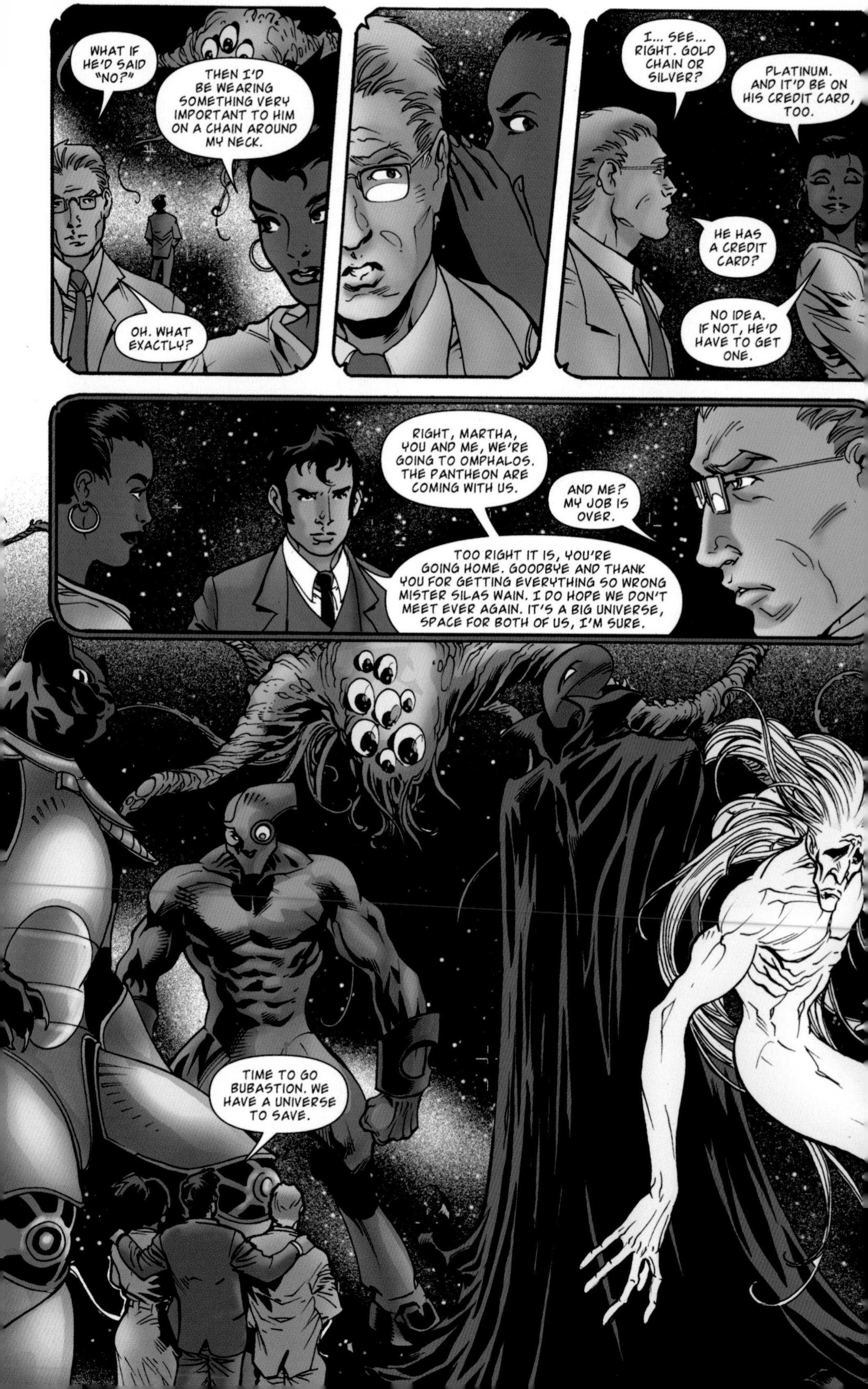

WHAT IF HE'D SAID "NO?"
THEN I'D BE WEARING SOMETHING VERY IMPORTANT TO HIM ON A CHAIN AROUND MY NECK.
OH. WHAT EXACTLY?
I... SEE... RIGHT. GOLD CHAIN OR SILVER?
PLATINUM. AND IT'D BE ON HIS CREDIT CARD, TOO.
HE HAS A CREDIT CARD?
NO IDEA. IF NOT, HE'D HAVE TO GET ONE.
RIGHT, MARTHA, YOU AND ME, WE'RE GOING TO OMPHALOS. THE PANTHEON ARE COMING WITH US.
AND ME? MY JOB IS OVER.
TOO RIGHT IT IS, YOU'RE GOING HOME. GOODBYE AND THANK YOU FOR GETTING EVERYTHING SO WRONG MISTER SILAS WAIN. I DO HOPE WE DON'T MEET EVER AGAIN. IT'S A BIG UNIVERSE, SPACE FOR BOTH OF US, I'M SURE.
TIME TO GO BUBASTION. WE HAVE A UNIVERSE TO SAVE.

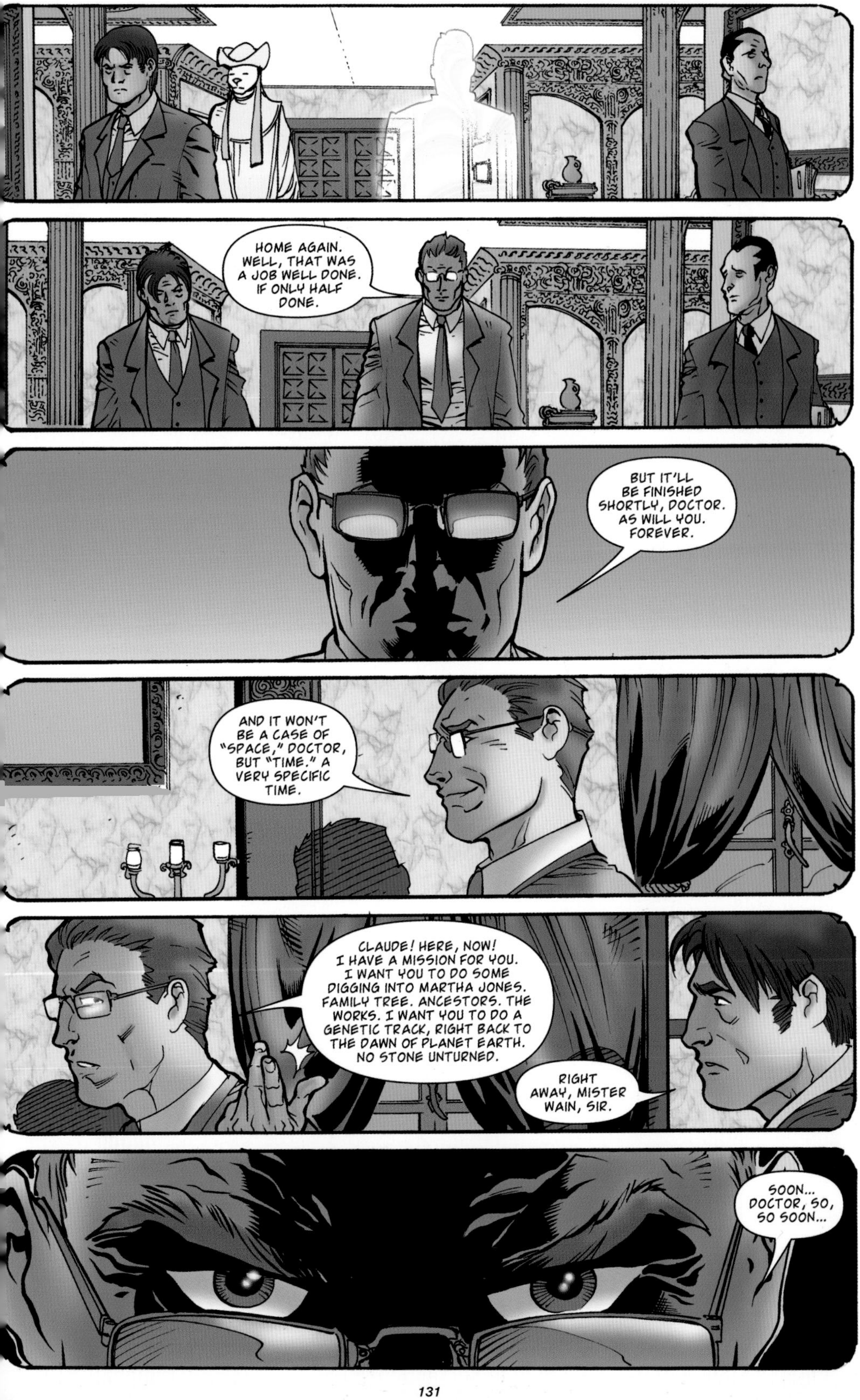
HOME AGAIN. WELL, THAT WAS A JOB WELL DONE. IF ONLY HALF DONE.
BUT IT'LL BE FINISHED SHORTLY, DOCTOR. AS WILL YOU. FOREVER.
AND IT WON'T BE A CASE OF "SPACE," DOCTOR, BUT "TIME." A VERY SPECIFIC TIME.
CLAUDE! HERE, NOW! I HAVE A MISSION FOR YOU. I WANT YOU TO DO SOME DIGGING INTO MARTHA JONES. FAMILY TREE. ANCESTORS. THE WORKS. I WANT YOU TO DO A GENETIC TRACK, RIGHT BACK TO THE DAWN OF PLANET EARTH. NO STONE UNTURNED.
RIGHT AWAY, MISTER WAIN, SIR.
SOON... DOCTOR, SO, SO SOON...

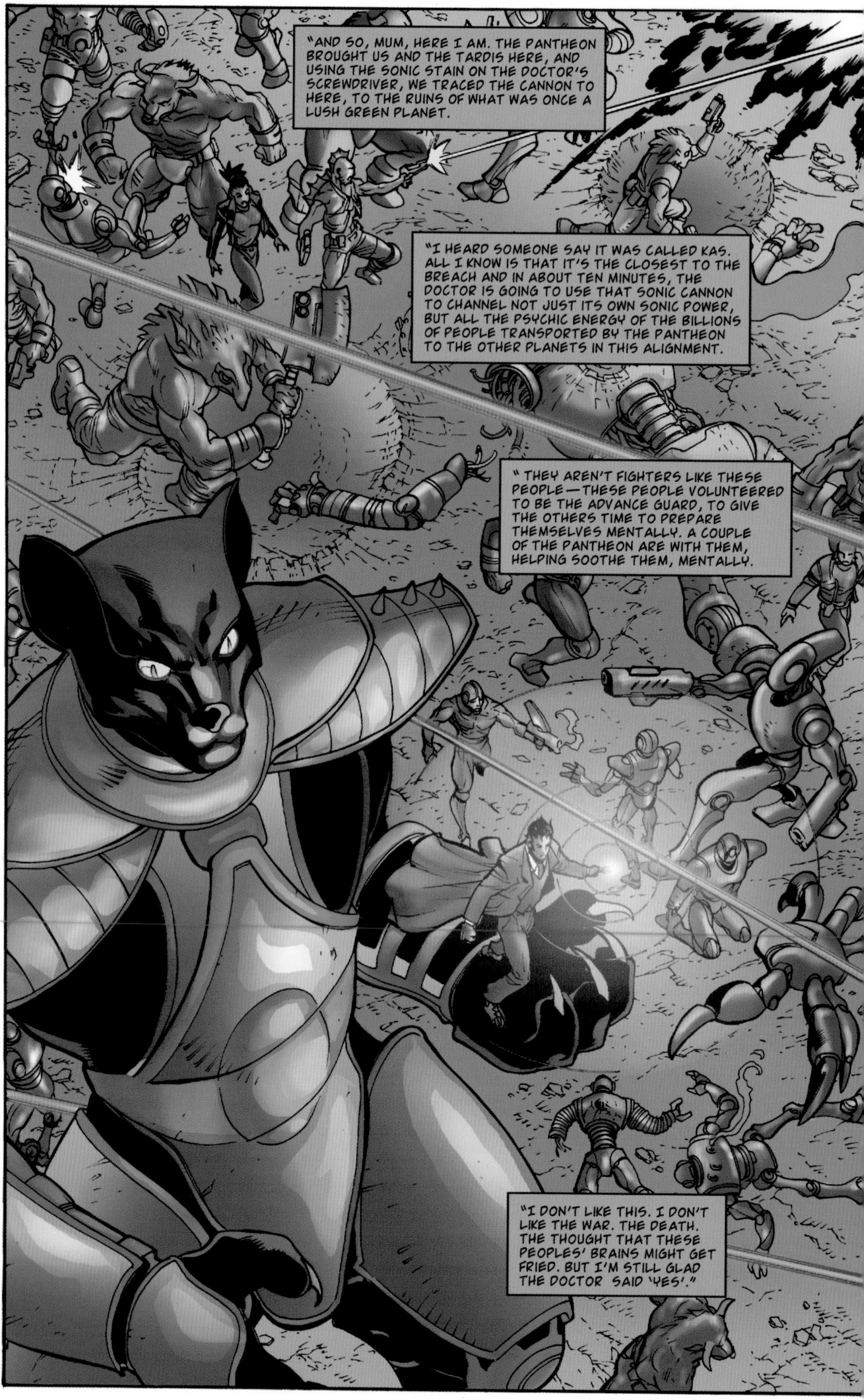
"AND SO, MUM, HERE I AM. THE PANTHEON BROUGHT US AND THE TARDIS HERE, AND USING THE SONIC STAIN ON THE DOCTOR'S SCREWDRIVER, WE TRACED THE CANNON TO HERE, TO THE RUINS OF WHAT WAS ONCE A LUSH GREEN PLANET.
"I HEARD SOMEONE SAY IT WAS CALLED KAS. ALL I KNOW IS THAT IT'S THE CLOSEST TO THE BREACH AND IN ABOUT TEN MINUTES, THE DOCTOR IS GOING TO USE THAT SONIC CANNON TO CHANNEL NOT JUST ITS OWN SONIC POWER, BUT ALL THE PSYCHIC ENERGY OF THE BILLIONS OF PEOPLE TRANSPORTED BY THE PANTHEON TO THE OTHER PLANETS IN THIS ALIGNMENT.
" THEY AREN'T FIGHTERS LIKE THESE PEOPLE—THESE PEOPLE VOLUNTEERED TO BE THE ADVANCE GUARD, TO GIVE THE OTHERS TIME TO PREPARE THEMSELVES MENTALLY. A COUPLE OF THE PANTHEON ARE WITH THEM, HELPING SOOTHE THEM, MENTALLY.
"I DON'T LIKE THIS. I DON'T LIKE THE WAR. THE DEATH. THE THOUGHT THAT THESE PEOPLES' BRAINS MIGHT GET FRIED. BUT I'M STILL GLAD THE DOCTOR SAID 'YES'."

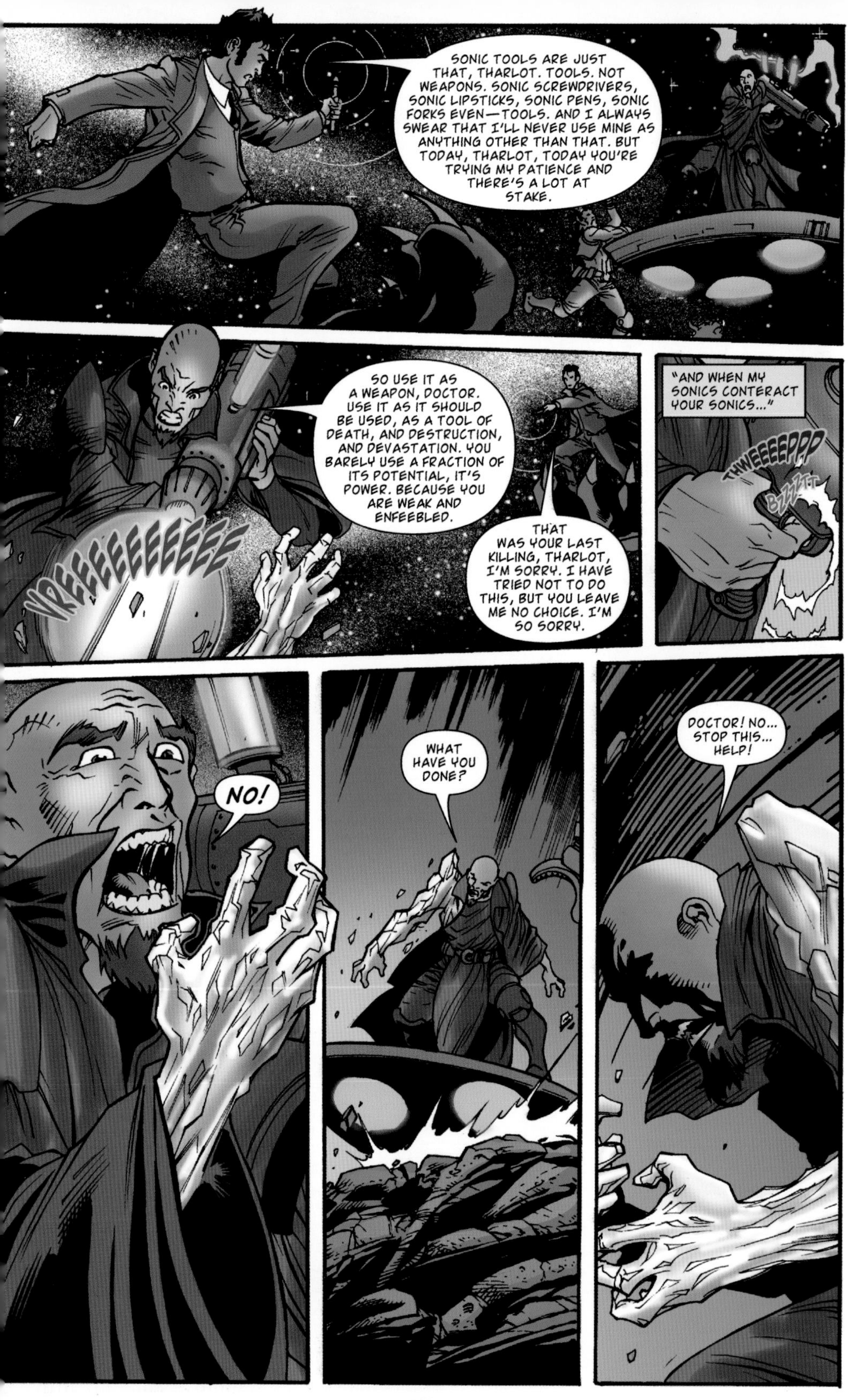

SONIC TOOLS ARE JUST THAT, THARLOT. TOOLS. NOT WEAPONS. SONIC SCREWDRIVERS, SONIC LIPSTICKS, SONIC PENS, SONIC FORKS EVEN—TOOLS. AND I ALWAYS SWEAR THAT I'LL NEVER USE MINE AS ANYTHING OTHER THAN THAT. BUT TODAY, THARLOT, TODAY YOU'RE TRYING MY PATIENCE AND THERE'S A LOT AT STAKE.
SO USE IT AS A WEAPON, DOCTOR. USE IT AS IT SHOULD BE USED, AS A TOOL OF DEATH, AND DESTRUCTION, AND DEVASTATION. YOU BARELY USE A FRACTION OF ITS POTENTIAL, IT'S POWER. BECAUSE YOU ARE WEAK AND ENFEEBLED.
VREEEEEEEEEE
THAT WAS YOUR LAST KILLING, THARLOT, I'M SORRY. I HAVE TRIED NOT TO DO THIS, BUT YOU LEAVE ME NO CHOICE. I'M SO SORRY.
"AND WHEN MY SONICS CONTERACT YOUR SONICS..."
THWEEEEPPP
BZZZTT
NO!
WHAT HAVE YOU DONE?
DOCTOR! NO... STOP THIS... HELP!

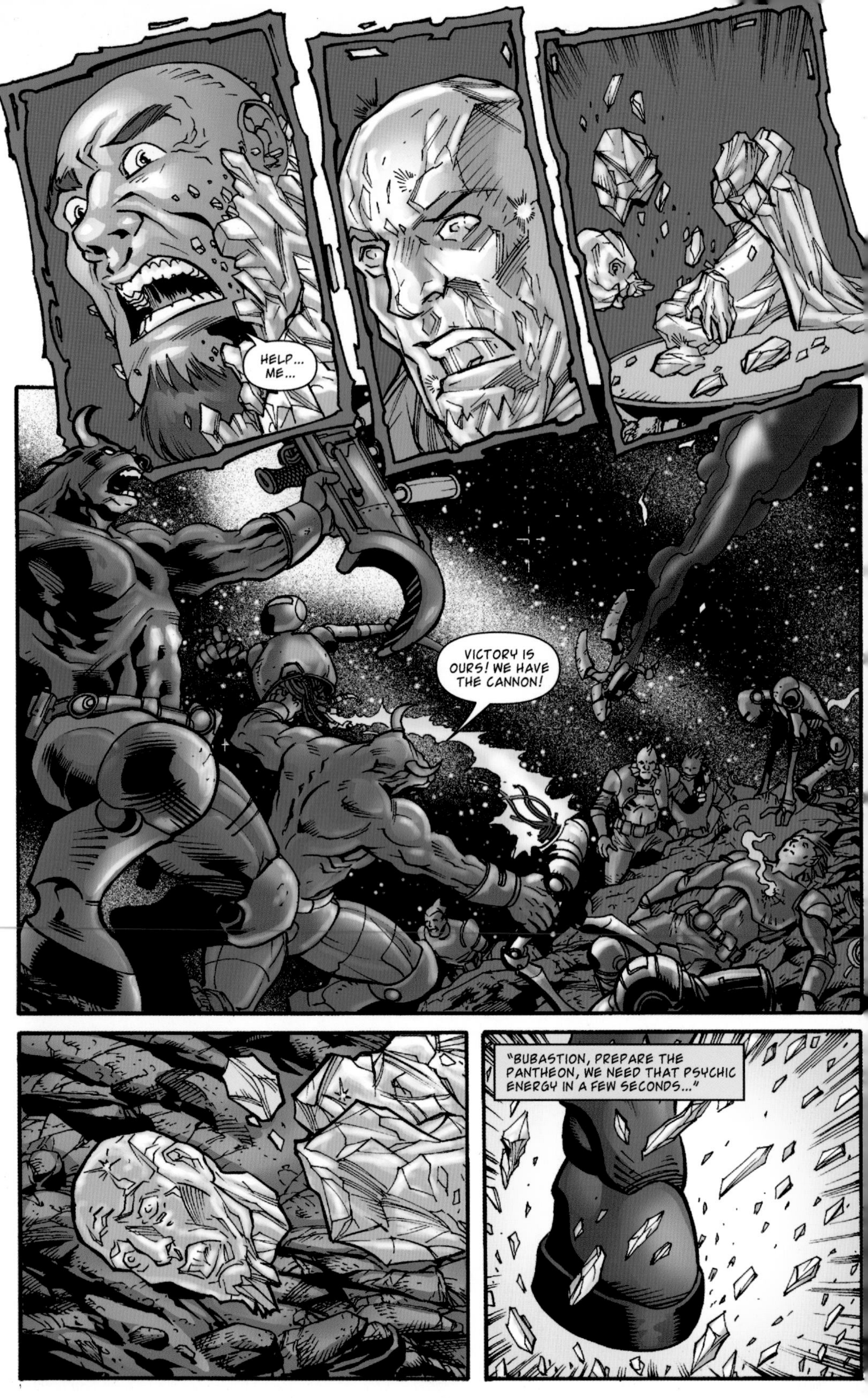
HELP... ME...
VICTORY IS OURS! WE HAVE THE CANNON!
"BUBASTION, PREPARE THE PANTHEON, WE NEED THAT PSYCHIC ENERGY IN A FEW SECONDS..."

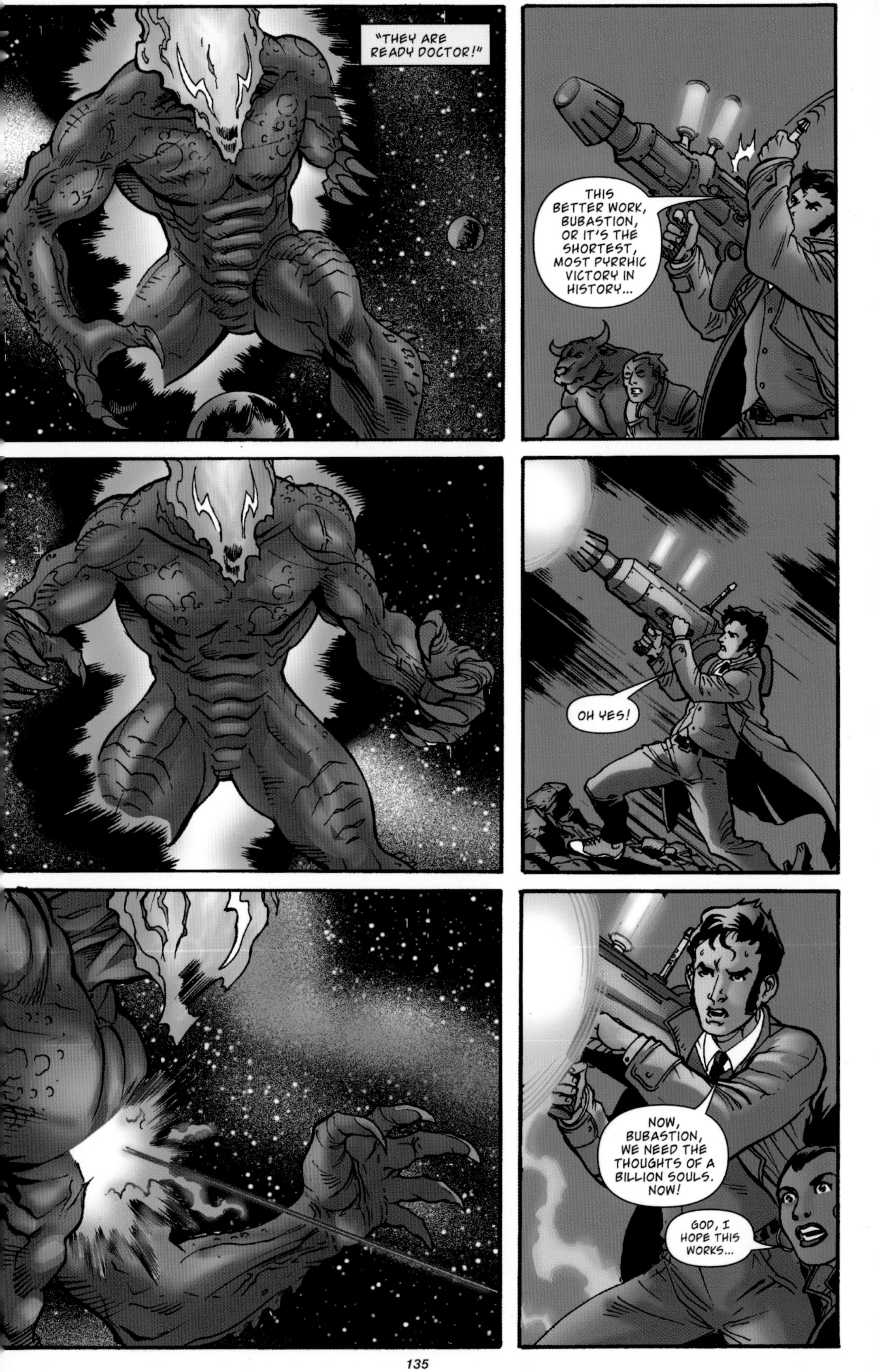
"THEY ARE READY DOCTOR!"
THIS BETTER WORK, BUBASTION, OR IT'S THE SHORTEST, MOST PYRRHIC VICTORY IN HISTORY...
OH YES!
NOW, BUBASTION, WE NEED THE THOUGHTS OF A BILLION SOULS. NOW!
GOD, I HOPE THIS WORKS...

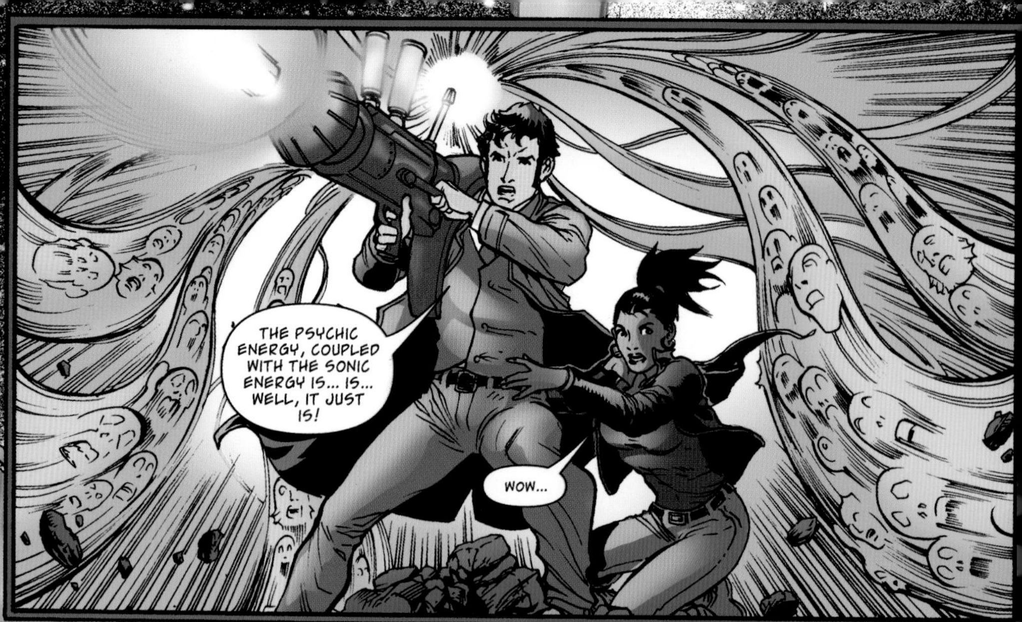
THE PSYCHIC ENERGY, COUPLED WITH THE SONIC ENERGY IS... IS... WELL, IT JUST IS!
WOW...

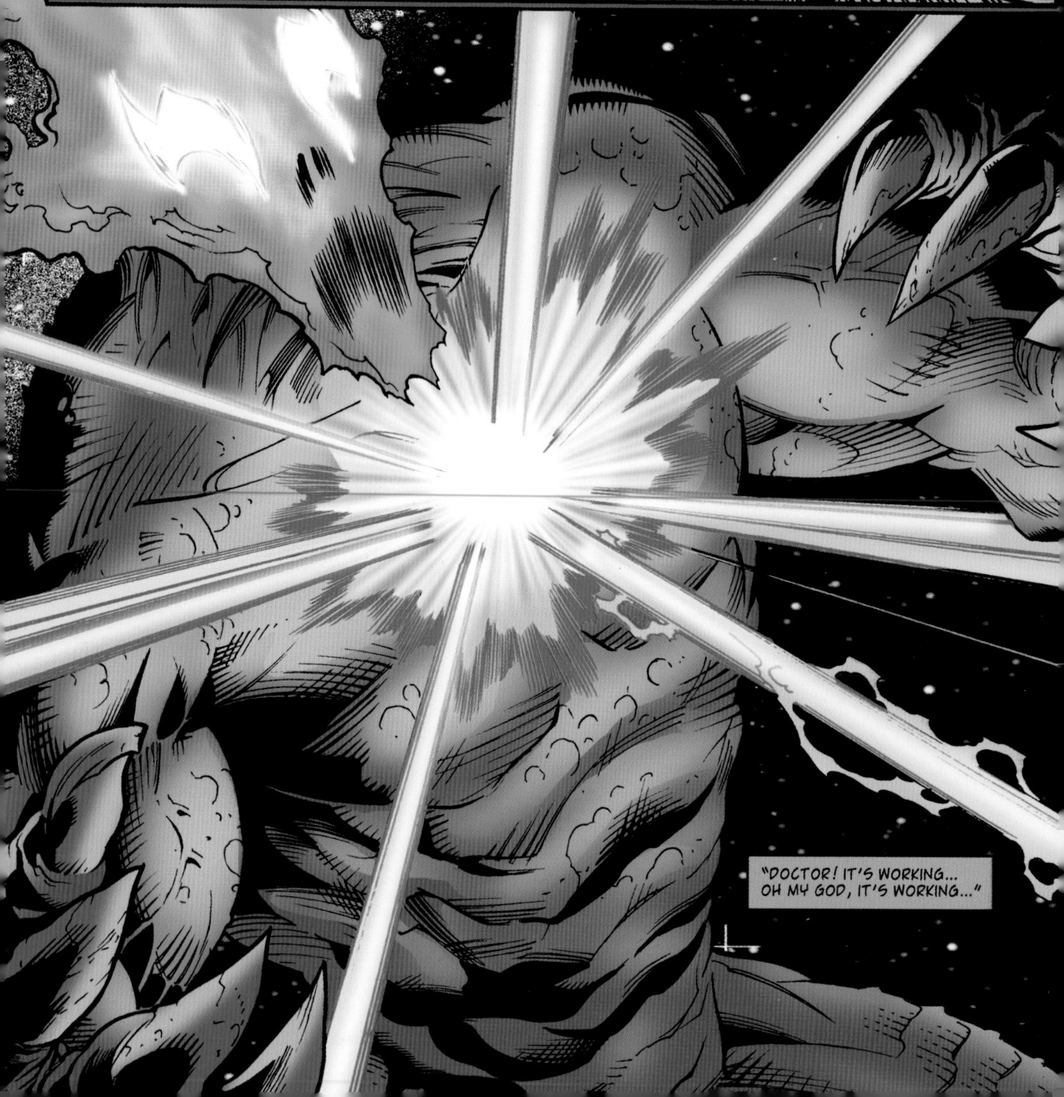
"DOCTOR! IT'S WORKING... OH MY GOD, IT'S WORKING..."

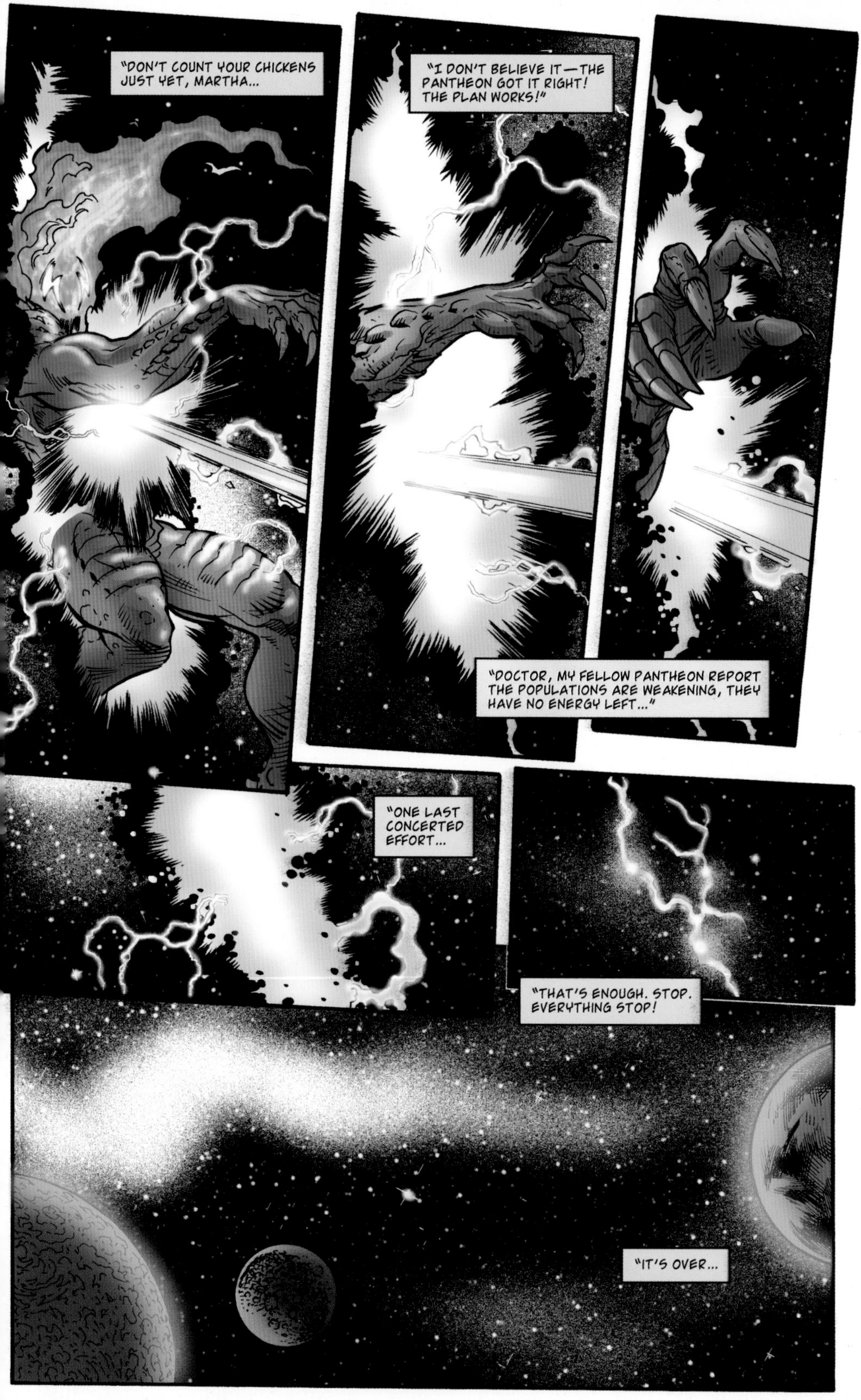
"DON'T COUNT YOUR CHICKENS JUST YET, MARTHA...
"I DON'T BELIEVE IT—THE PANTHEON GOT IT RIGHT! THE PLAN WORKS!"
"DOCTOR, MY FELLOW PANTHEON REPORT THE POPULATIONS ARE WEAKENING, THEY HAVE NO ENERGY LEFT..."
"ONE LAST CONCERTED EFFORT...
"THAT'S ENOUGH. STOP. EVERYTHING STOP!
"IT'S OVER...

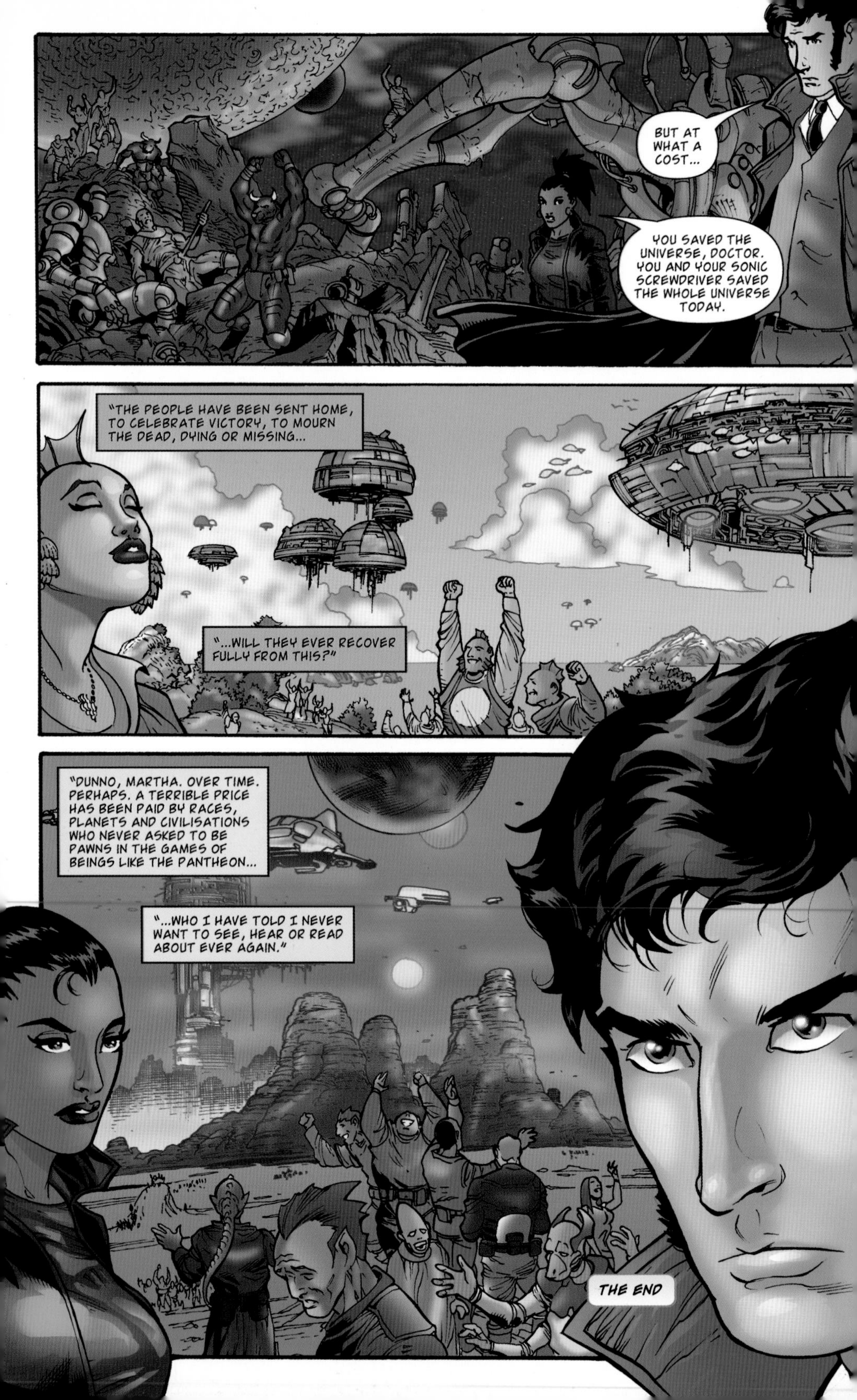
BUT AT WHAT A COST...
YOU SAVED THE UNIVERSE, DOCTOR. YOU AND YOUR SONIC SCREWDRIVER SAVED THE WHOLE UNIVERSE TODAY.
"THE PEOPLE HAVE BEEN SENT HOME, TO CELEBRATE VICTORY, TO MOURN THE DEAD, DYING OR MISSING...
"...WILL THEY EVER RECOVER FULLY FROM THIS?"
"DUNNO, MARTHA. OVER TIME. PERHAPS. A TERRIBLE PRICE HAS BEEN PAID BY RACES, PLANETS AND CIVILISATIONS WHO NEVER ASKED TO BE PAWNS IN THE GAMES OF BEINGS LIKE THE PANTHEON...
"...WHO I HAVE TOLD I NEVER WANT TO SEE, HEAR OR READ ABOUT EVER AGAIN."
THE END

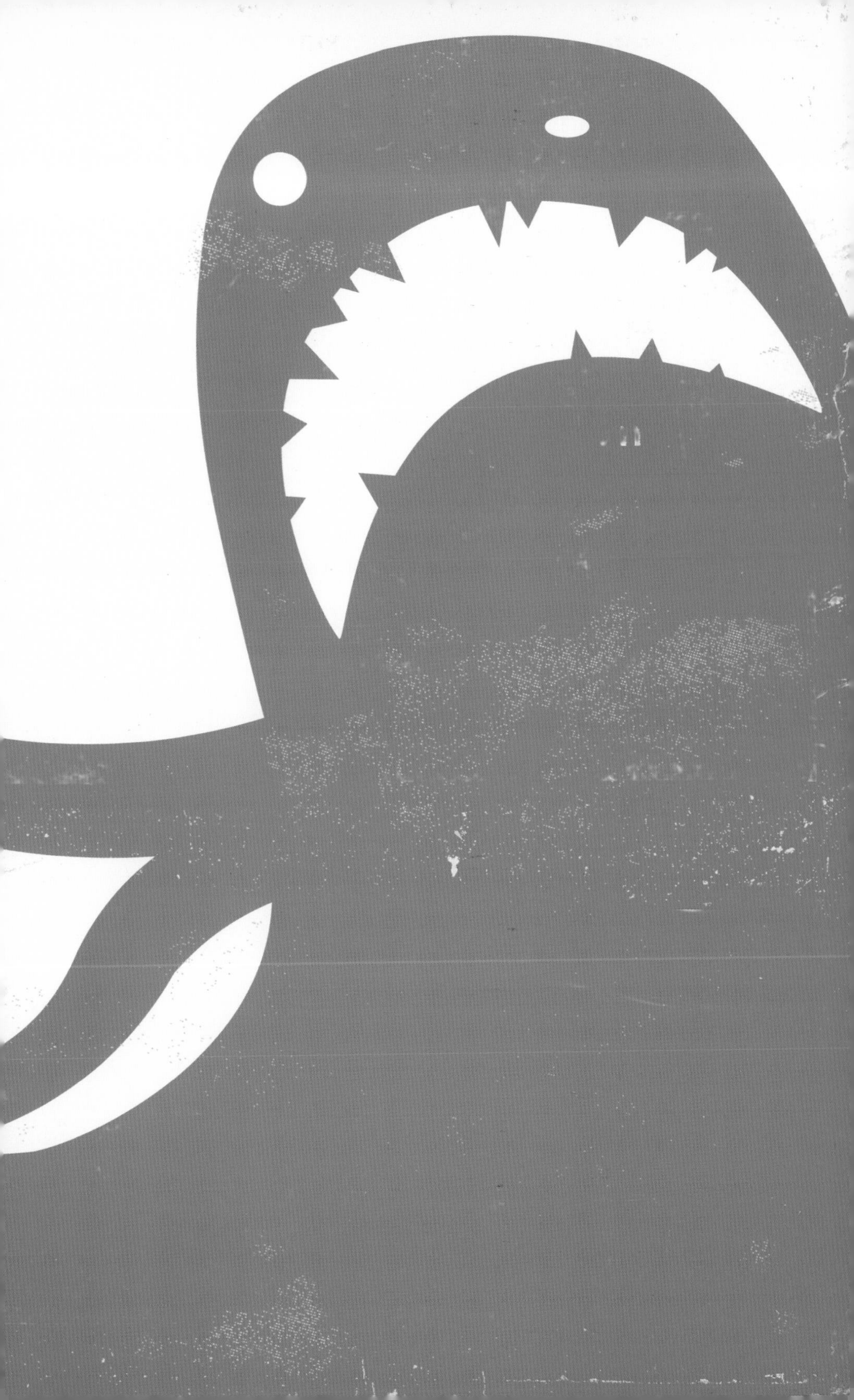

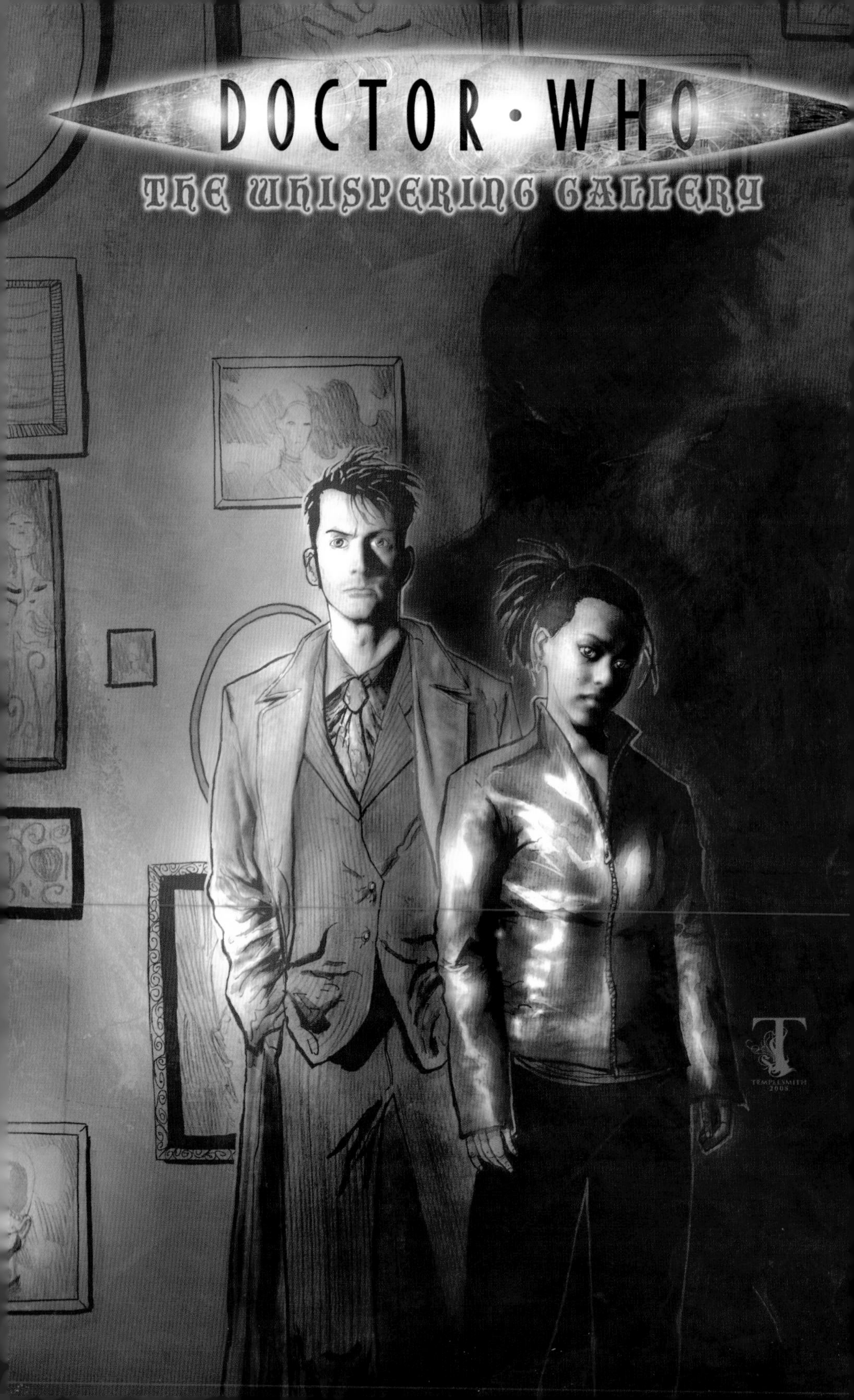
DOCTOR · WHO
THE WHISPERING GALLERY
TEMPLESMITH
2008

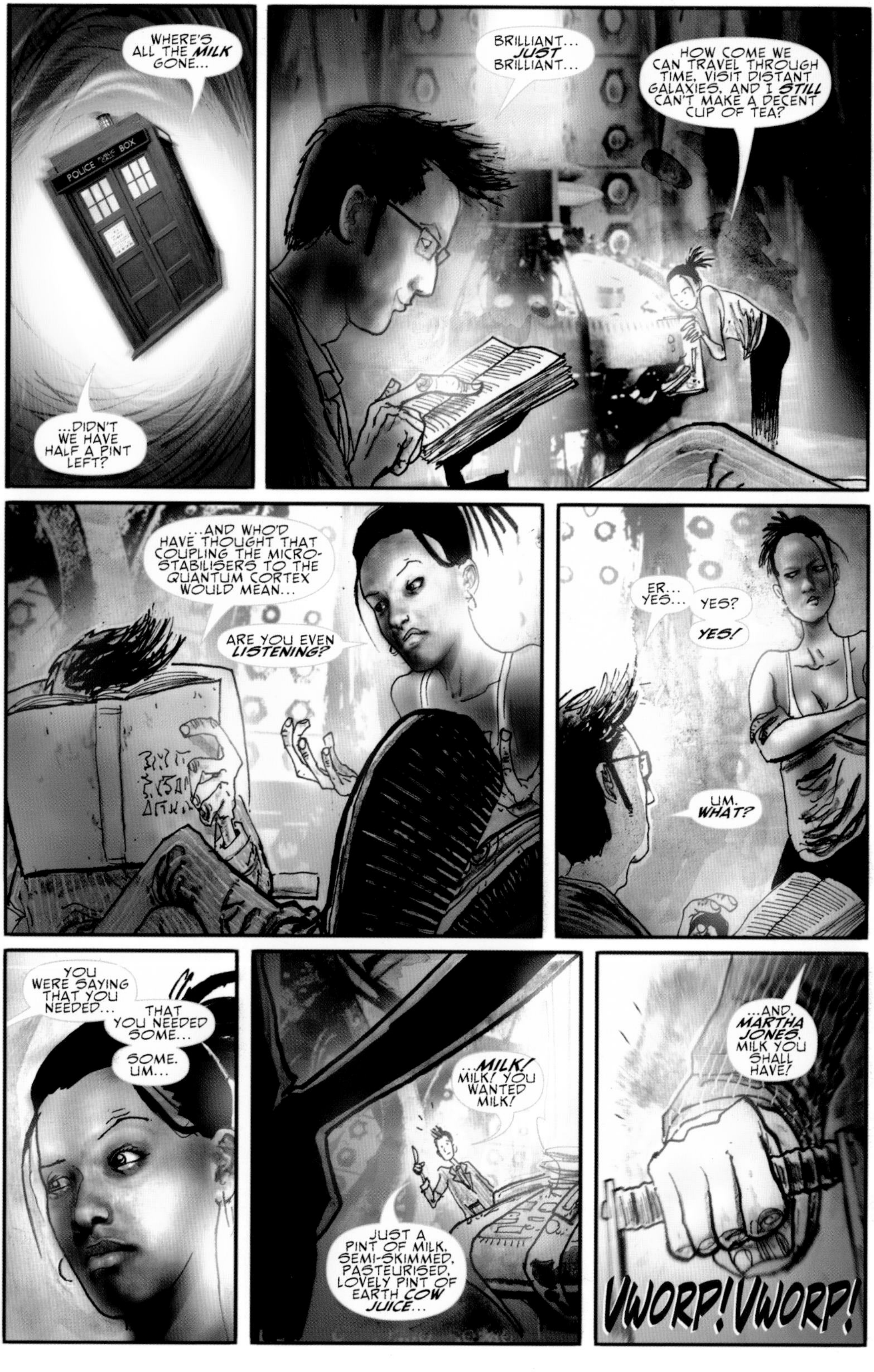
WHERE'S ALL THE MILK GONE...
...DIDN'T WE HAVE HALF A PINT LEFT?
BRILLIANT... JUST BRILLIANT...
HOW COME WE CAN TRAVEL THROUGH TIME, VISIT DISTANT GALAXIES, AND I STILL CAN'T MAKE A DECENT CUP OF TEA?
...AND WHO'D HAVE THOUGHT THAT COUPLING THE MICRO-STABILISERS TO THE QUANTUM CORTEX WOULD MEAN...
ARE YOU EVEN LISTENING?
ER... YES...
YES?
YES!
UM. WHAT?
YOU WERE SAYING THAT YOU NEEDED...
THAT YOU NEEDED SOME...
SOME. UM...
...MILK! MILK! YOU WANTED MILK!
JUST A PINT OF MILK, SEMI-SKIMMED, PASTEURISED, LOVELY PINT OF EARTH COW JUICE...
...AND, MARTHA JONES, MILK YOU SHALL HAVE!
VWORP! VWORP!

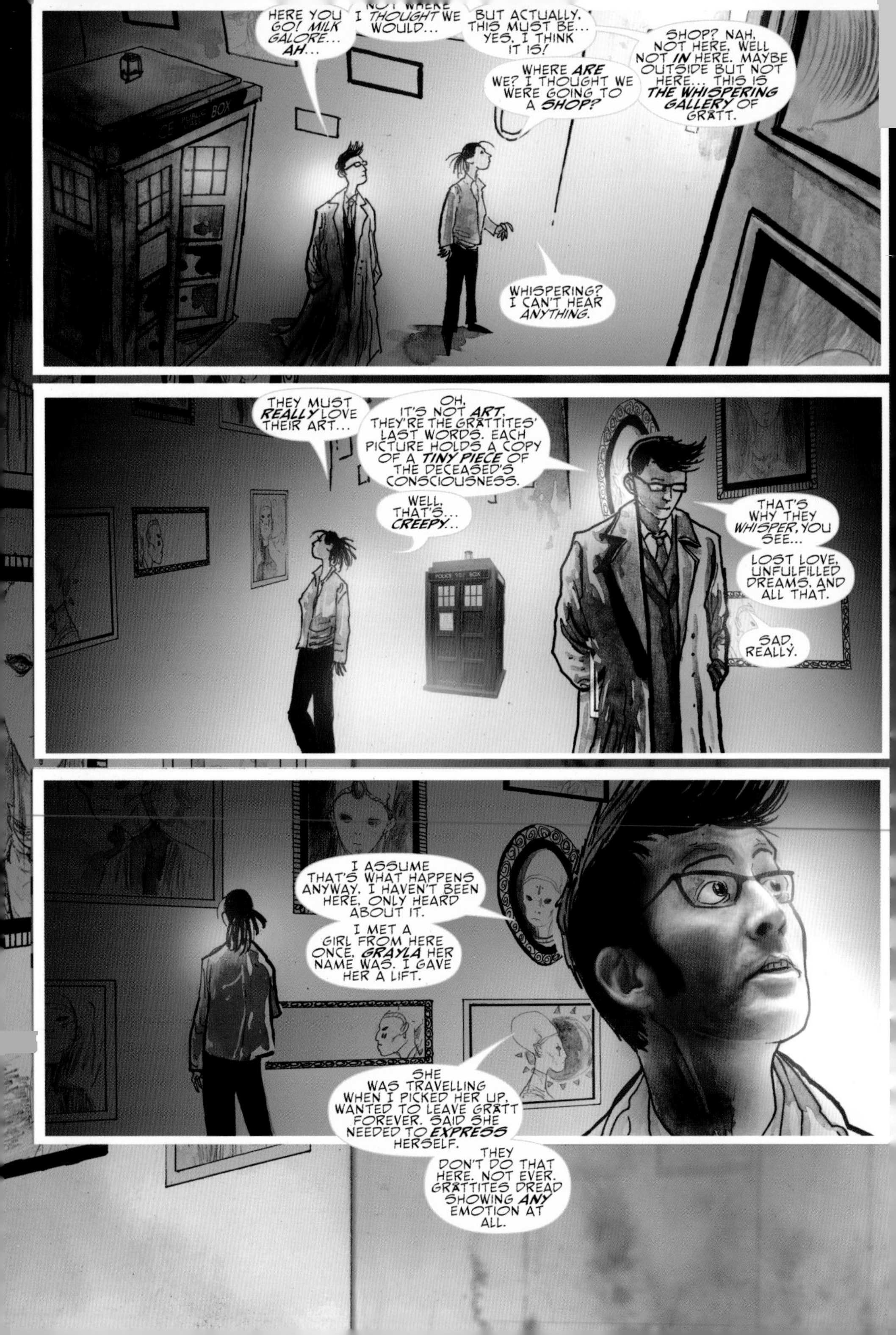
HERE YOU GO! MILK GALORE... AH...
NOT WHERE I THOUGHT WE WOULD...
BUT ACTUALLY, THIS MUST BE... YES, I THINK IT IS!
WHERE ARE WE? I THOUGHT WE WERE GOING TO A SHOP?
SHOP? NAH, NOT HERE. WELL NOT IN HERE. MAYBE OUTSIDE BUT NOT HERE... THIS IS THE WHISPERING GALLERY OF GRÄTT.
WHISPERING? I CAN'T HEAR ANYTHING.
THEY MUST REALLY LOVE THEIR ART...
OH, IT'S NOT ART. THEY'RE THE GRÄTTITES' LAST WORDS. EACH PICTURE HOLDS A COPY OF A TINY PIECE OF THE DECEASED'S CONSCIOUSNESS.
WELL, THAT'S... CREEPY...
THAT'S WHY THEY WHISPER, YOU SEE...
LOST LOVE, UNFULFILLED DREAMS, AND ALL THAT.
SAD, REALLY.
I ASSUME THAT'S WHAT HAPPENS ANYWAY. I HAVEN'T BEEN HERE. ONLY HEARD ABOUT IT.
I MET A GIRL FROM HERE ONCE. GRAYLA HER NAME WAS. I GAVE HER A LIFT.
SHE WAS TRAVELLING WHEN I PICKED HER UP. WANTED TO LEAVE GRÄTT FOREVER. SAID SHE NEEDED TO EXPRESS HERSELF.
THEY DON'T DO THAT HERE. NOT EVER. GRÄTTITES DREAD SHOWING ANY EMOTION AT ALL.

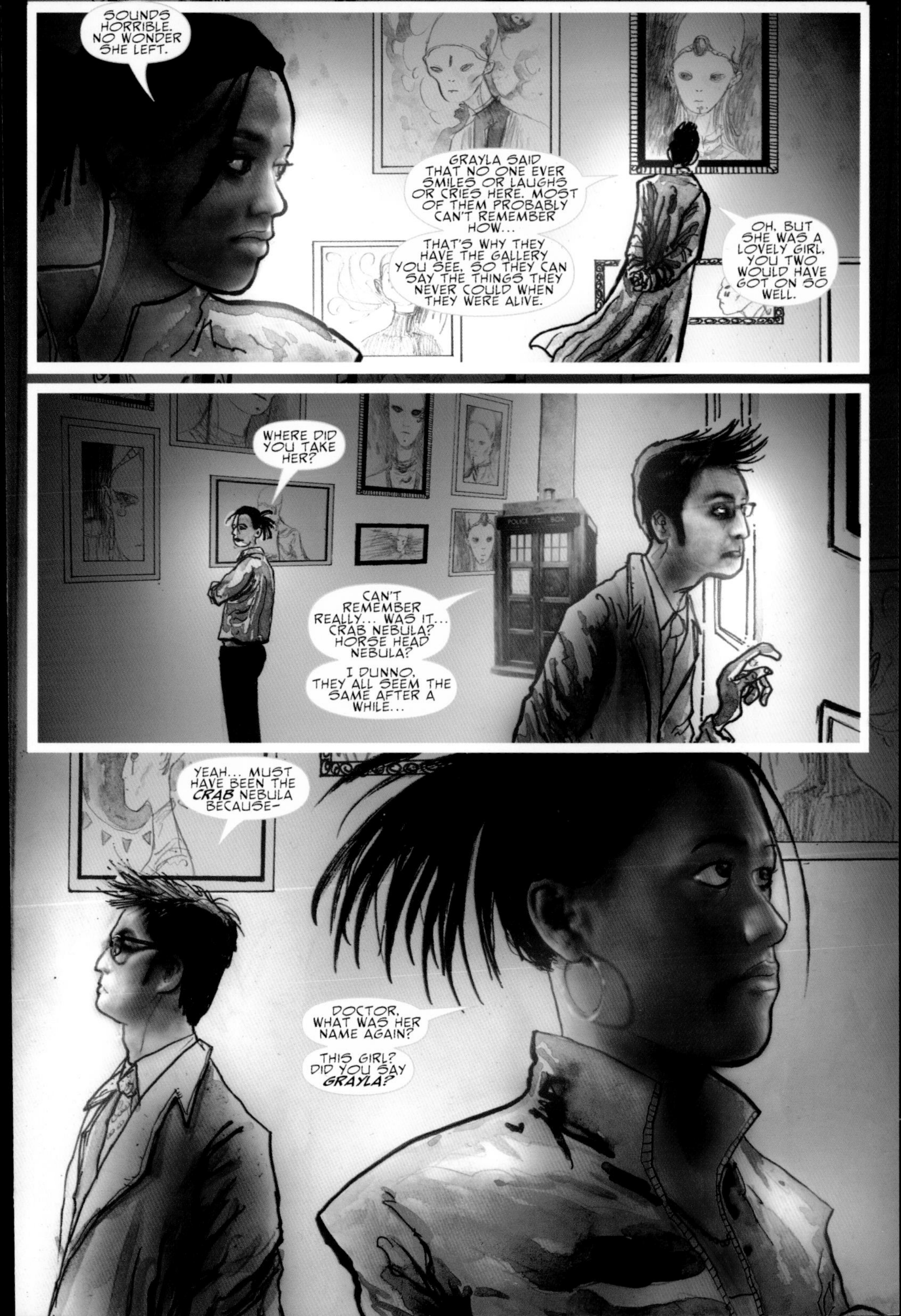

SOUNDS HORRIBLE. NO WONDER SHE LEFT.
GRAYLA SAID THAT NO ONE EVER SMILES OR LAUGHS OR CRIES HERE. MOST OF THEM PROBABLY CAN'T REMEMBER HOW...
THAT'S WHY THEY HAVE THE GALLERY YOU SEE. SO THEY CAN SAY THE THINGS THEY NEVER COULD WHEN THEY WERE ALIVE.
OH, BUT SHE WAS A LOVELY GIRL. YOU TWO WOULD HAVE GOT ON SO WELL.
WHERE DID YOU TAKE HER?
CAN'T REMEMBER REALLY... WAS IT... CRAB NEBULA? HORSE HEAD NEBULA?
I DUNNO. THEY ALL SEEM THE SAME AFTER A WHILE...
YEAH... MUST HAVE BEEN THE CRAB NEBULA BECAUSE-
DOCTOR, WHAT WAS HER NAME AGAIN?
THIS GIRL? DID YOU SAY GRAYLA?

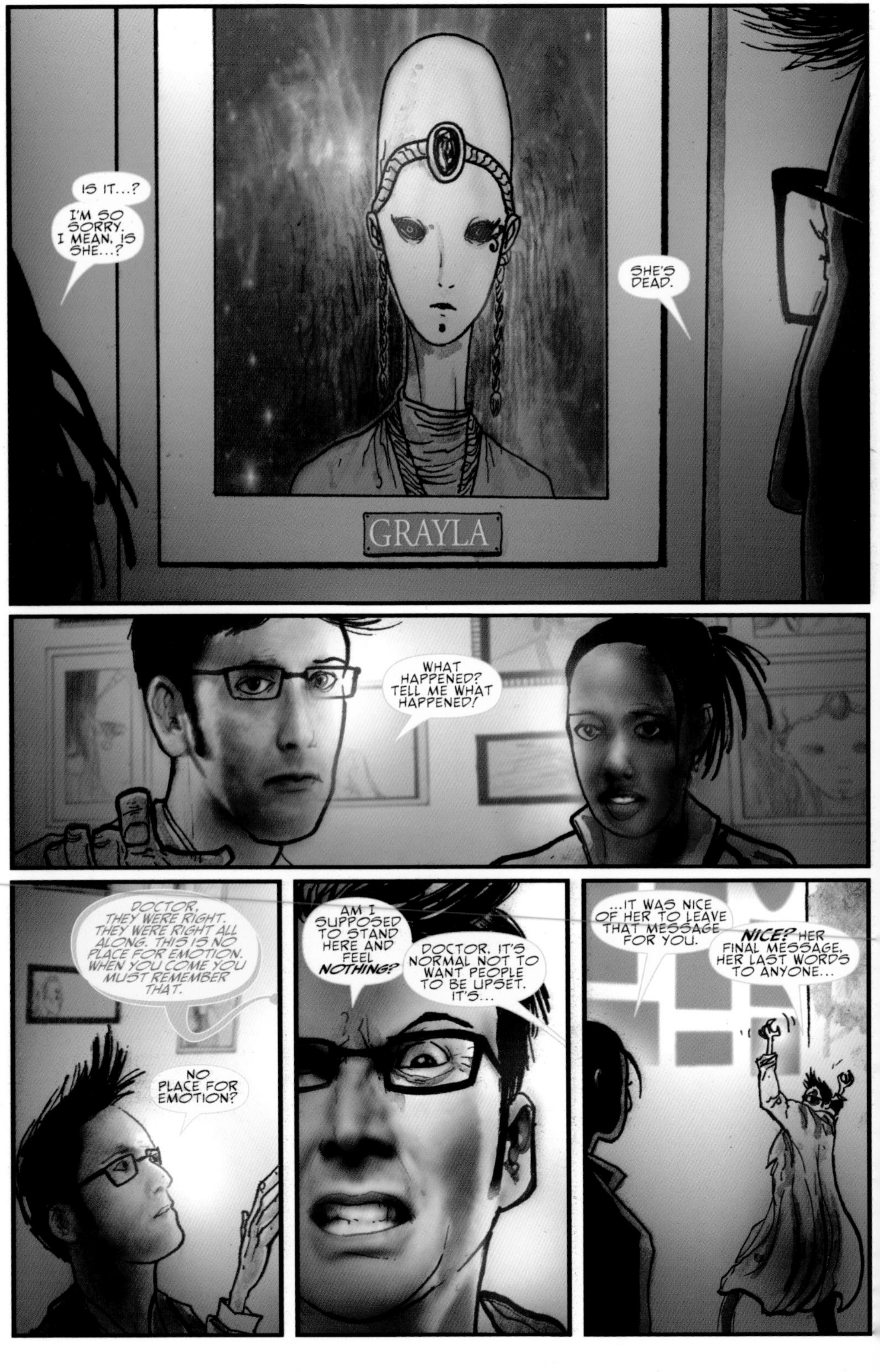
GRAYLA
IS IT...?
I'M SO SORRY. I MEAN, IS SHE...?
SHE'S DEAD.
WHAT HAPPENED? TELL ME WHAT HAPPENED!
DOCTOR, THEY WERE RIGHT. THEY WERE RIGHT ALL ALONG. THIS IS NO PLACE FOR EMOTION. WHEN YOU COME YOU MUST REMEMBER THAT.
NO PLACE FOR EMOTION?
AM I SUPPOSED TO STAND HERE AND FEEL NOTHING?
DOCTOR, IT'S NORMAL NOT TO WANT PEOPLE TO BE UPSET. IT'S...
...IT WAS NICE OF HER TO LEAVE THAT MESSAGE FOR YOU.
NICE? HER FINAL MESSAGE, HER LAST WORDS TO ANYONE...

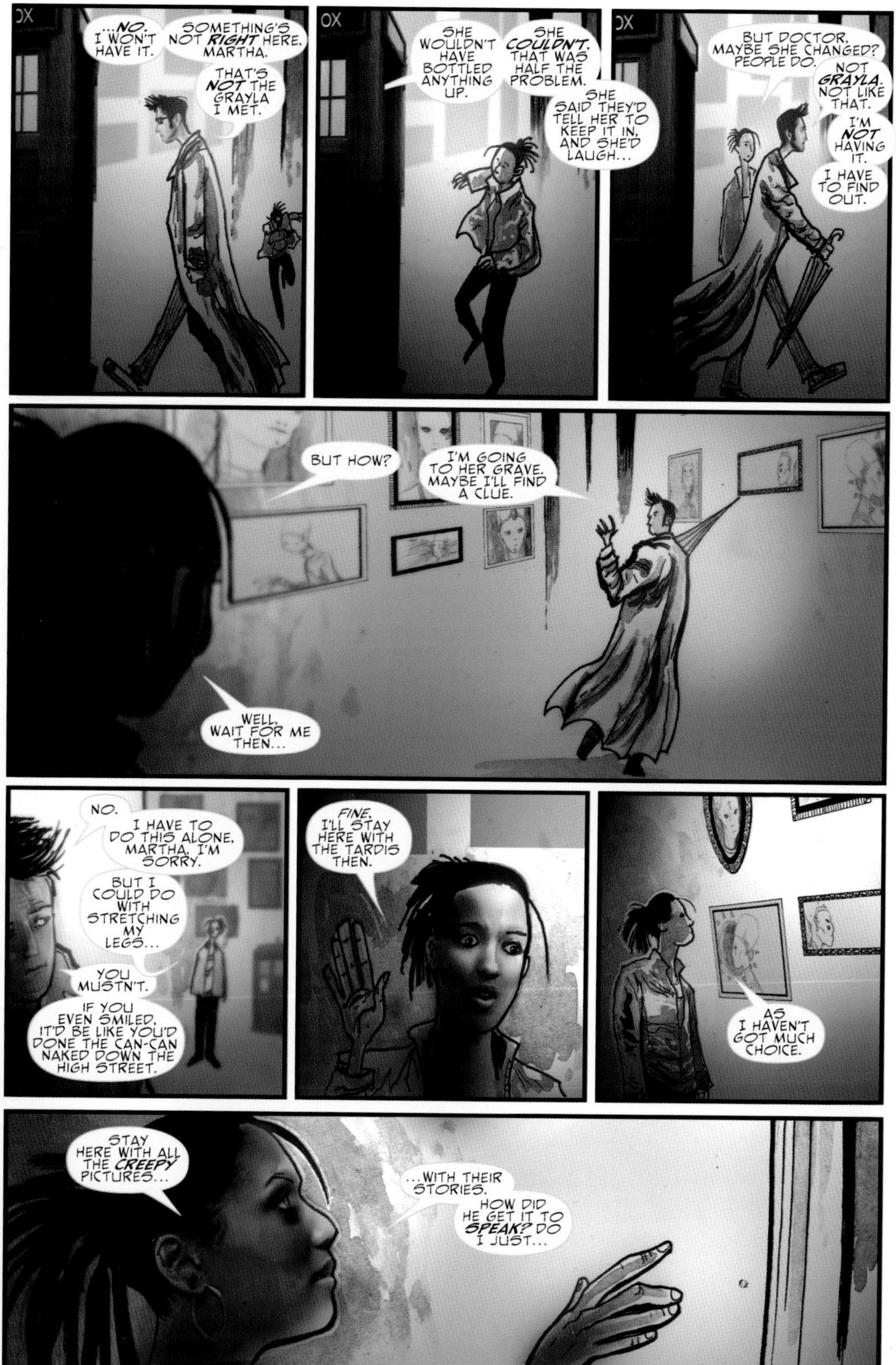
...NO. I WON'T HAVE IT.
SOMETHING'S NOT RIGHT HERE, MARTHA.
THAT'S NOT THE GRAYLA I MET.
SHE WOULDN'T HAVE BOTTLED ANYTHING UP.
SHE COULDN'T. THAT WAS HALF THE PROBLEM.
SHE SAID THEY'D TELL HER TO KEEP IT IN, AND SHE'D LAUGH...
BUT DOCTOR, MAYBE SHE CHANGED? PEOPLE DO.
NOT GRAYLA. NOT LIKE THAT.
I'M NOT HAVING IT.
I HAVE TO FIND OUT.
BUT HOW?
I'M GOING TO HER GRAVE. MAYBE I'LL FIND A CLUE.
WELL, WAIT FOR ME THEN...
NO.
I HAVE TO DO THIS ALONE, MARTHA. I'M SORRY.
BUT I COULD DO WITH STRETCHING MY LEGS...
YOU MUSTN'T.
IF YOU EVEN SMILED, IT'D BE LIKE YOU'D DONE THE CAN-CAN NAKED DOWN THE HIGH STREET.
FINE, I'LL STAY HERE WITH THE TARDIS THEN.
AS I HAVEN'T GOT MUCH CHOICE.
STAY HERE WITH ALL THE CREEPY PICTURES...
...WITH THEIR STORIES.
HOW DID HE GET IT TO SPEAK? DO I JUST...

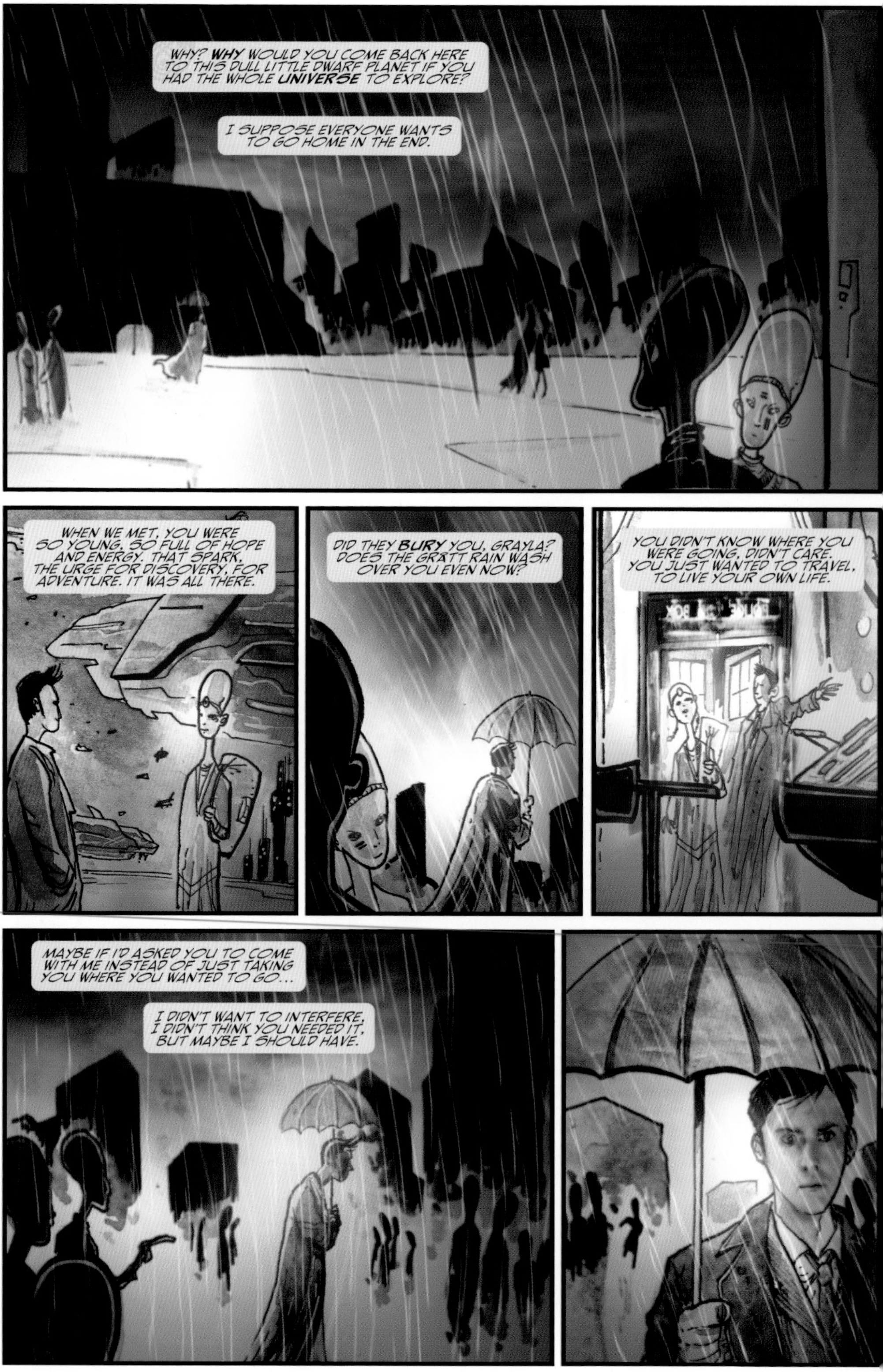
WHY? WHY WOULD YOU COME BACK HERE TO THIS DULL LITTLE DWARF PLANET IF YOU HAD THE WHOLE UNIVERSE TO EXPLORE?
I SUPPOSE EVERYONE WANTS TO GO HOME IN THE END.
WHEN WE MET, YOU WERE SO YOUNG, SO FULL OF HOPE AND ENERGY. THAT SPARK, THE URGE FOR DISCOVERY, FOR ADVENTURE. IT WAS ALL THERE.
DID THEY BURY YOU, GRAYLA? DOES THE GRÄTT RAIN WASH OVER YOU EVEN NOW?
YOU DIDN'T KNOW WHERE YOU WERE GOING, DIDN'T CARE. YOU JUST WANTED TO TRAVEL, TO LIVE YOUR OWN LIFE.
MAYBE IF I'D ASKED YOU TO COME WITH ME INSTEAD OF JUST TAKING YOU WHERE YOU WANTED TO GO...
I DIDN'T WANT TO INTERFERE. I DIDN'T THINK YOU NEEDED IT. BUT MAYBE I SHOULD HAVE.

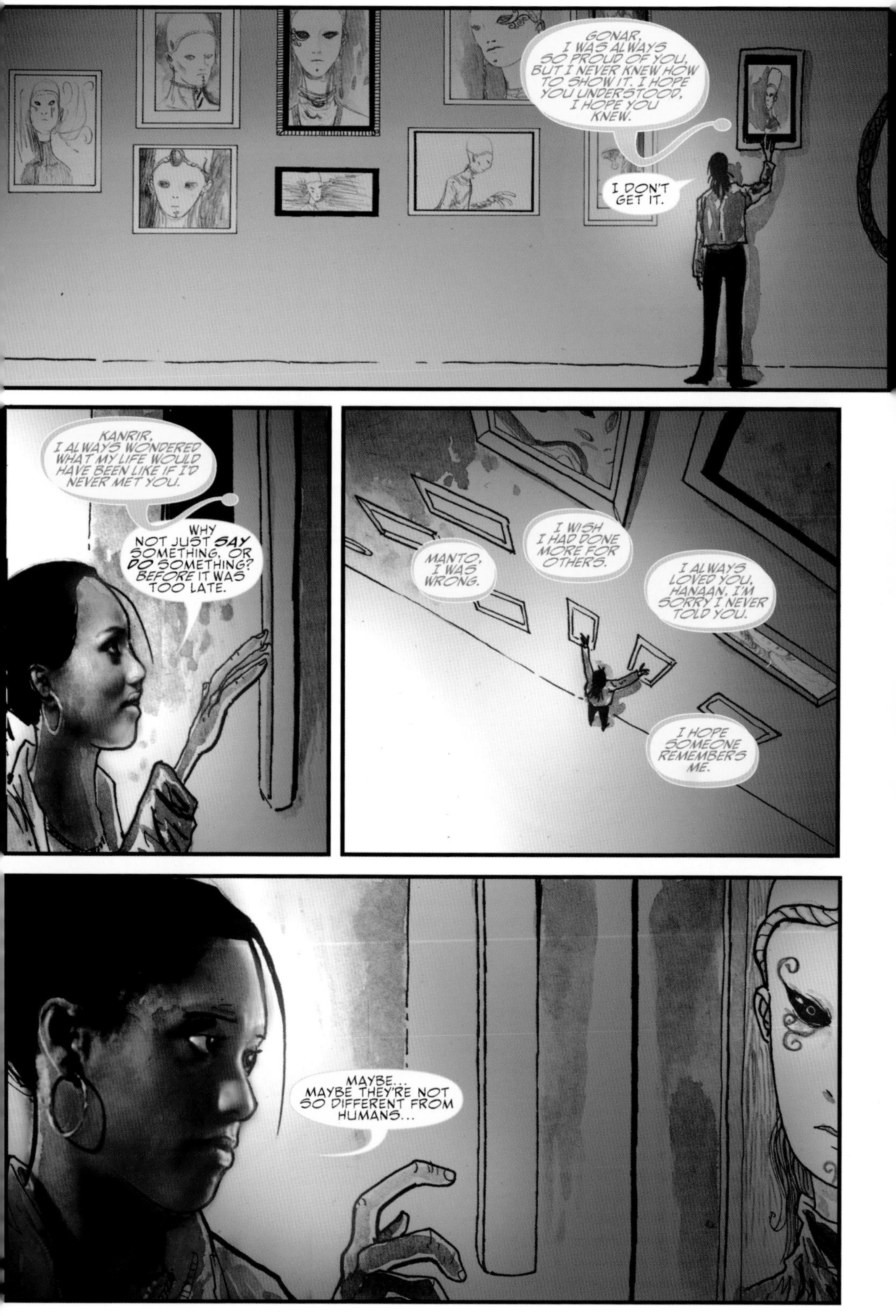
GONAR, I WAS ALWAYS SO PROUD OF YOU, BUT I NEVER KNEW HOW TO SHOW IT. I HOPE YOU UNDERSTOOD, I HOPE YOU KNEW.
I DON'T GET IT.
KANRIR, I ALWAYS WONDERED WHAT MY LIFE WOULD HAVE BEEN LIKE IF I'D NEVER MET YOU.
WHY NOT JUST SAY SOMETHING, OR DO SOMETHING? BEFORE IT WAS TOO LATE.
MANTO, I WAS WRONG.
I WISH I HAD DONE MORE FOR OTHERS.
I ALWAYS LOVED YOU, HANAAN. I'M SORRY I NEVER TOLD YOU.
I HOPE SOMEONE REMEMBERS ME.
MAYBE... MAYBE THEY'RE NOT SO DIFFERENT FROM HUMANS...

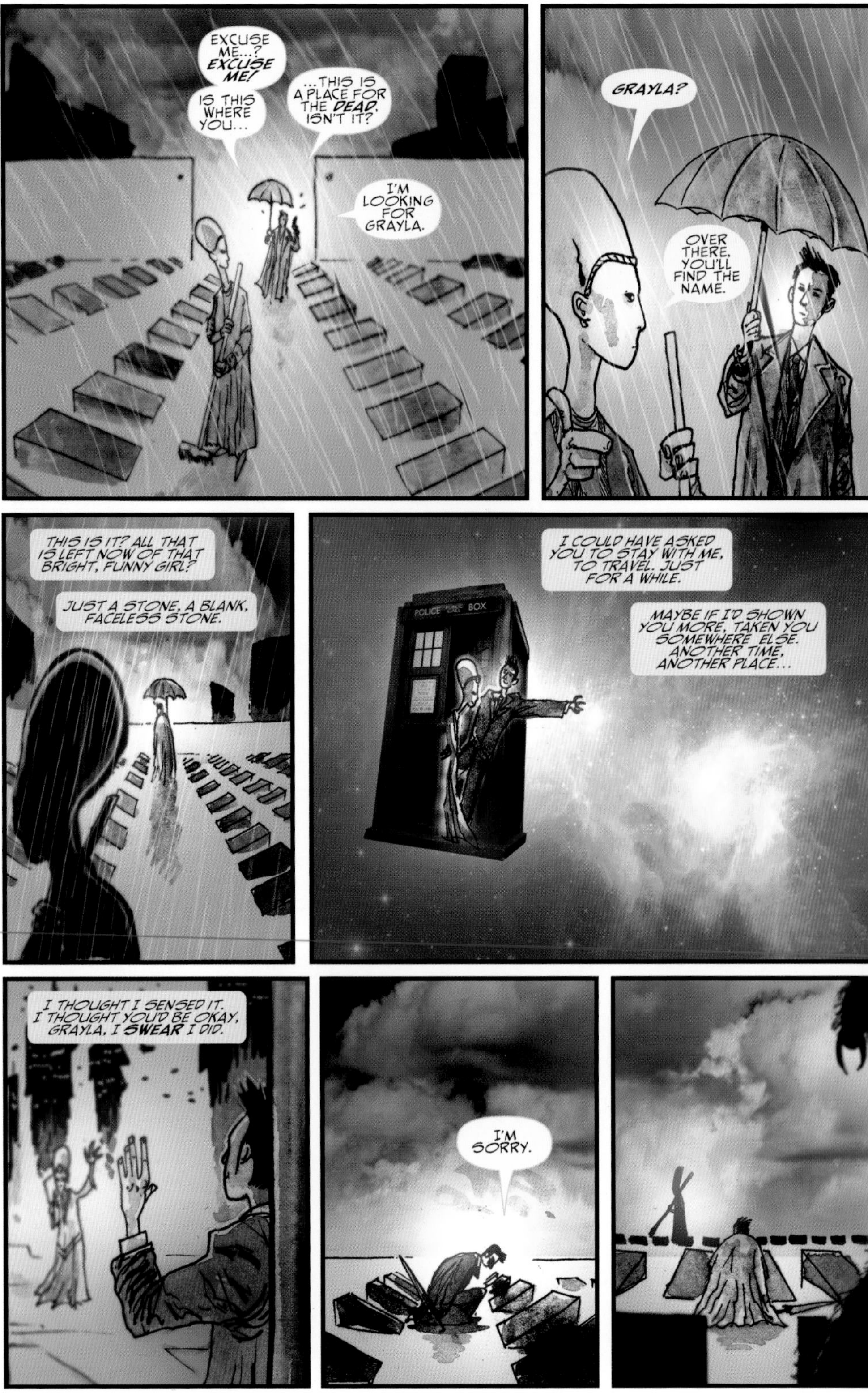
EXCUSE ME...? EXCUSE ME!
IS THIS WHERE YOU...
...THIS IS A PLACE FOR THE DEAD, ISN'T IT?
I'M LOOKING FOR GRAYLA.
GRAYLA?
OVER THERE. YOU'LL FIND THE NAME.
THIS IS IT? ALL THAT IS LEFT NOW OF THAT BRIGHT, FUNNY GIRL?
JUST A STONE. A BLANK, FACELESS STONE.
I COULD HAVE ASKED YOU TO STAY WITH ME, TO TRAVEL. JUST FOR A WHILE.
POLICE BOX
MAYBE IF I'D SHOWN YOU MORE, TAKEN YOU SOMEWHERE ELSE. ANOTHER TIME, ANOTHER PLACE...
I THOUGHT I SENSED IT. I THOUGHT YOU'D BE OKAY, GRAYLA. I SWEAR I DID.
I'M SORRY.

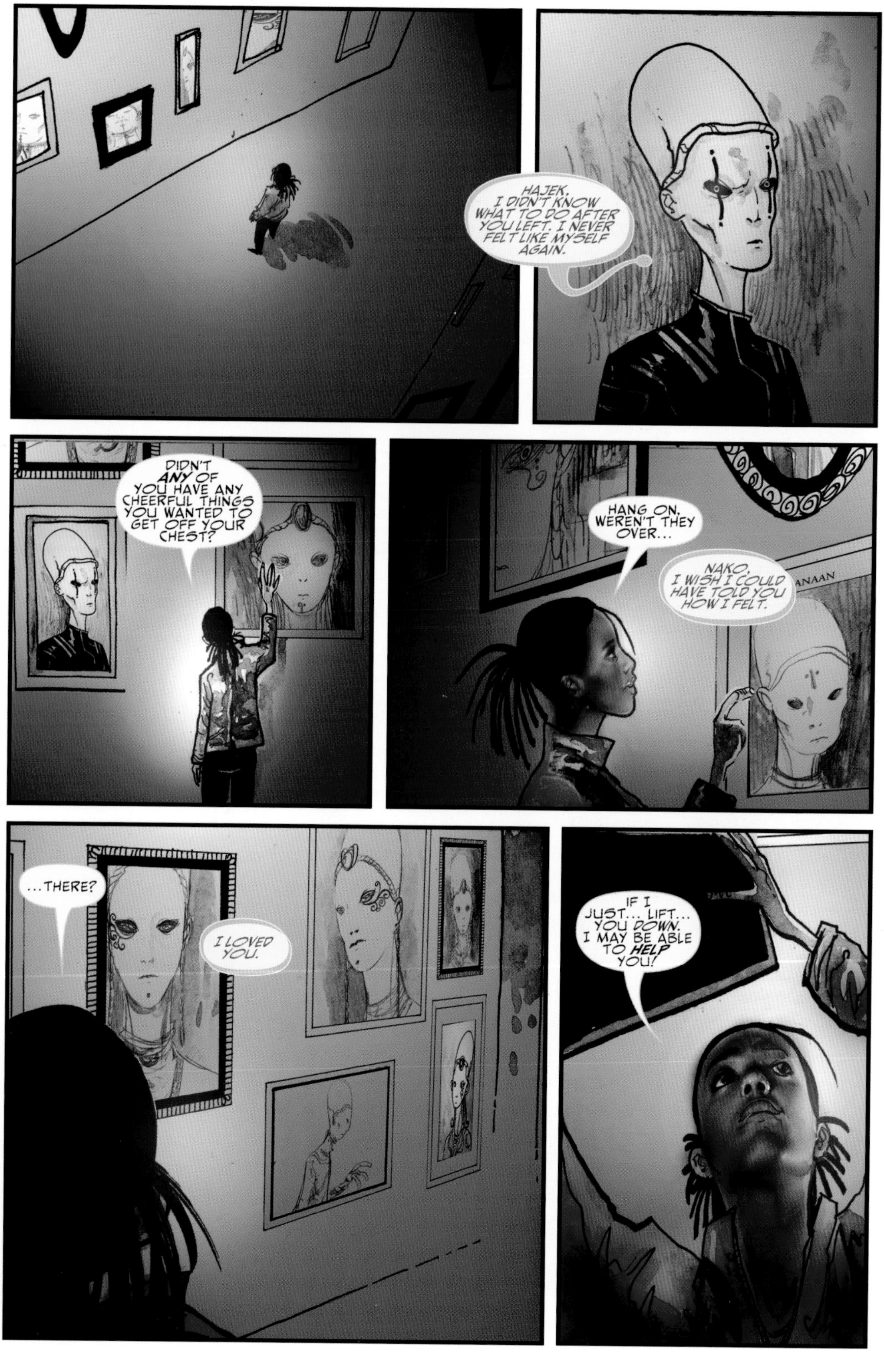
HAJEK, I DIDN'T KNOW WHAT TO DO AFTER YOU LEFT. I NEVER FELT LIKE MYSELF AGAIN.
DIDN'T ANY OF YOU HAVE ANY CHEERFUL THINGS YOU WANTED TO GET OFF YOUR CHEST?
HANG ON, WEREN'T THEY OVER...
NAKO, I WISH I COULD HAVE TOLD YOU HOW I FELT.
...THERE?
I LOVED YOU.
IF I JUST... LIFT... YOU DOWN, I MAY BE ABLE TO HELP YOU!

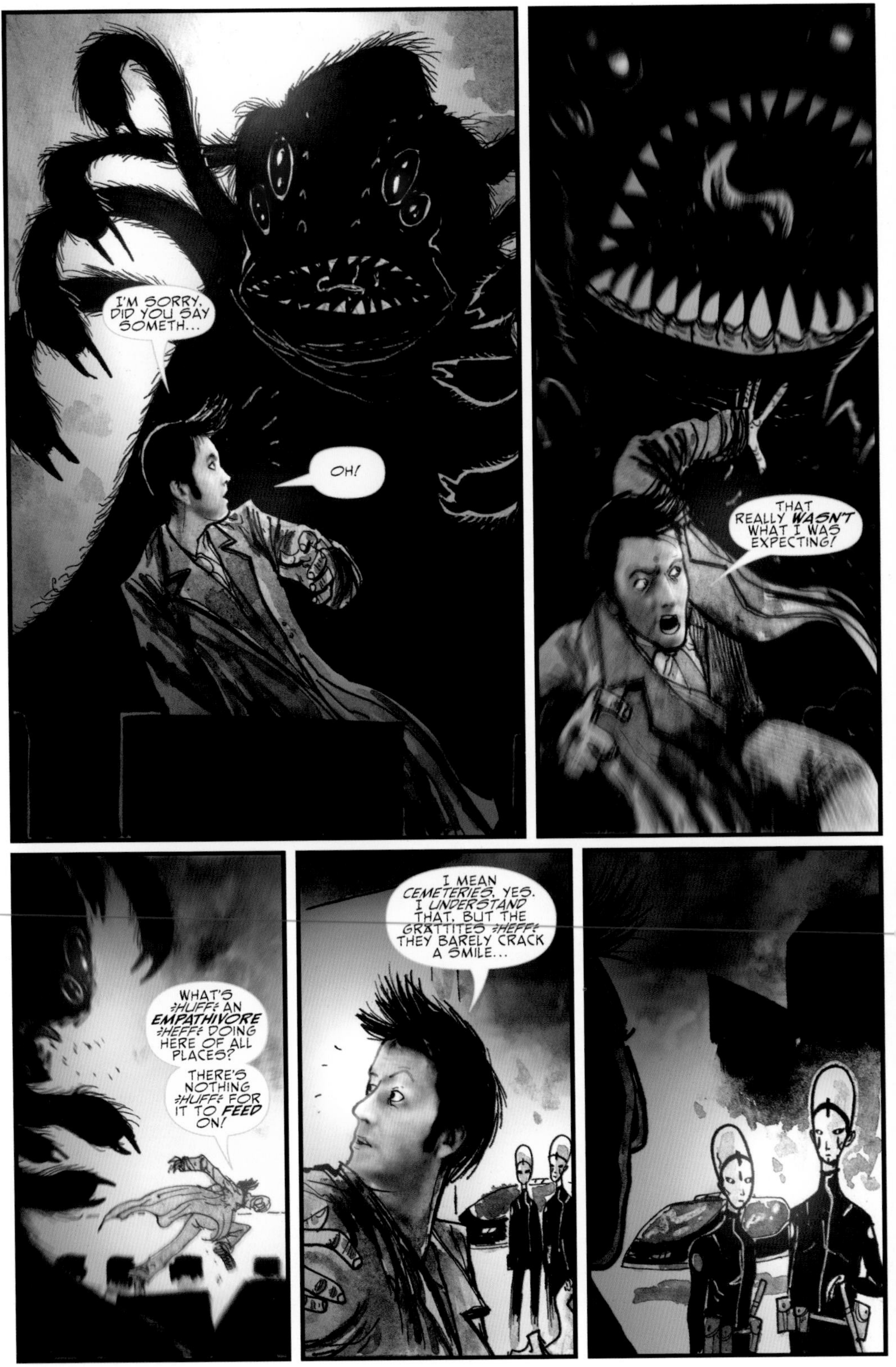
I'M SORRY, DID YOU SAY SOMETH...
OH!
THAT REALLY **WASN'T** WHAT I WAS EXPECTING!
WHAT'S *HUFF* AN **EMPATHIVORE** *HEFF* DOING HERE OF ALL PLACES?
THERE'S NOTHING *HUFF* FOR IT TO **FEED** ON!
I MEAN *CEMETERIES*, YES. I *UNDERSTAND* THAT, BUT THE GRÄTTITES *HEFF* THEY BARELY CRACK A SMILE...

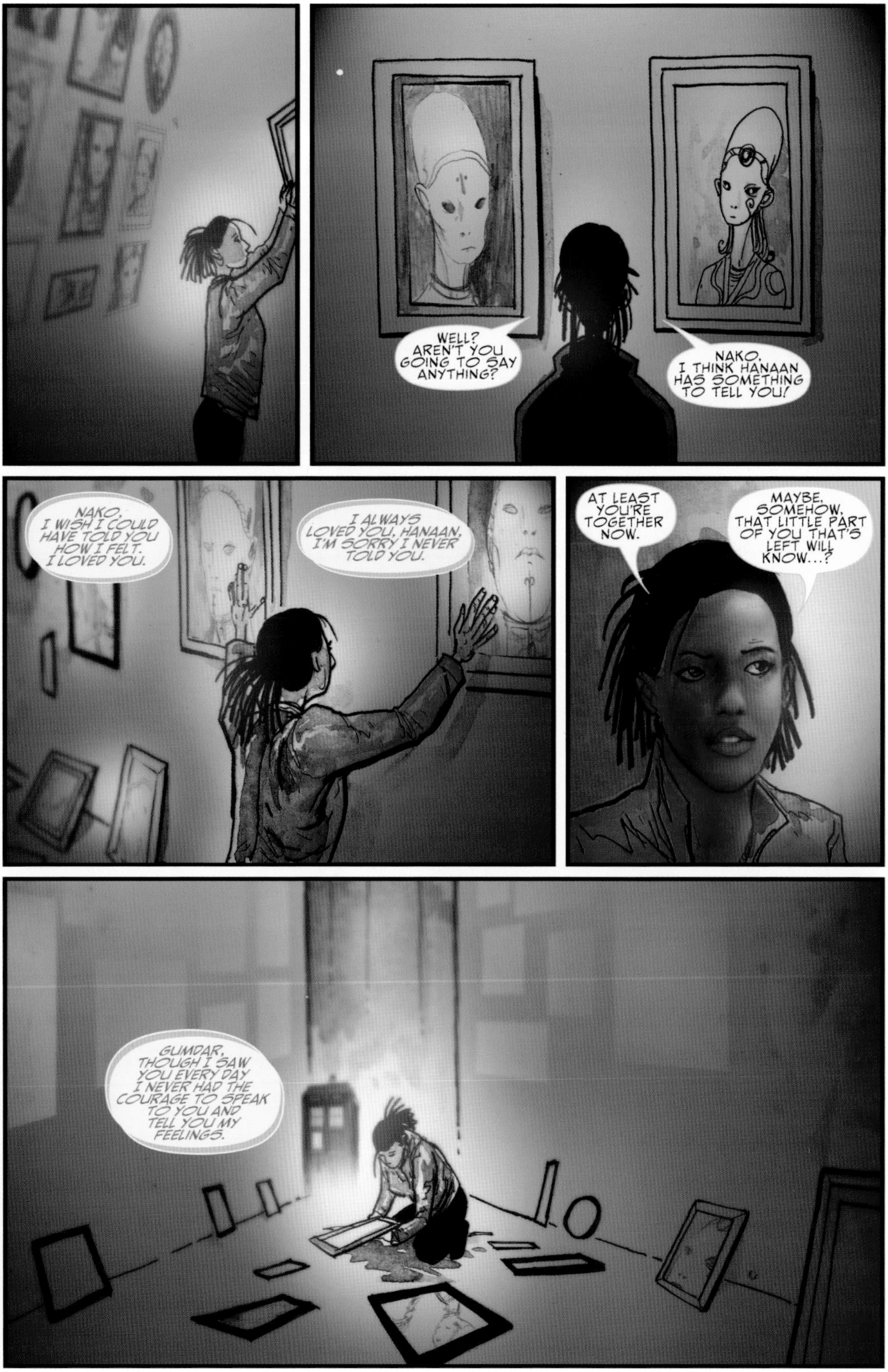
WELL? AREN'T YOU GOING TO SAY ANYTHING?
NAKO, I THINK HANAAN HAS SOMETHING TO TELL YOU!
NAKO, I WISH I COULD HAVE TOLD YOU HOW I FELT. I LOVED YOU.
I ALWAYS LOVED YOU, HANAAN. I'M SORRY I NEVER TOLD YOU.
AT LEAST YOU'RE TOGETHER NOW.
MAYBE, SOMEHOW, THAT LITTLE PART OF YOU THAT'S LEFT WILL KNOW...?
GUMDAR, THOUGH I SAW YOU EVERY DAY I NEVER HAD THE COURAGE TO SPEAK TO YOU AND TELL YOU MY FEELINGS.

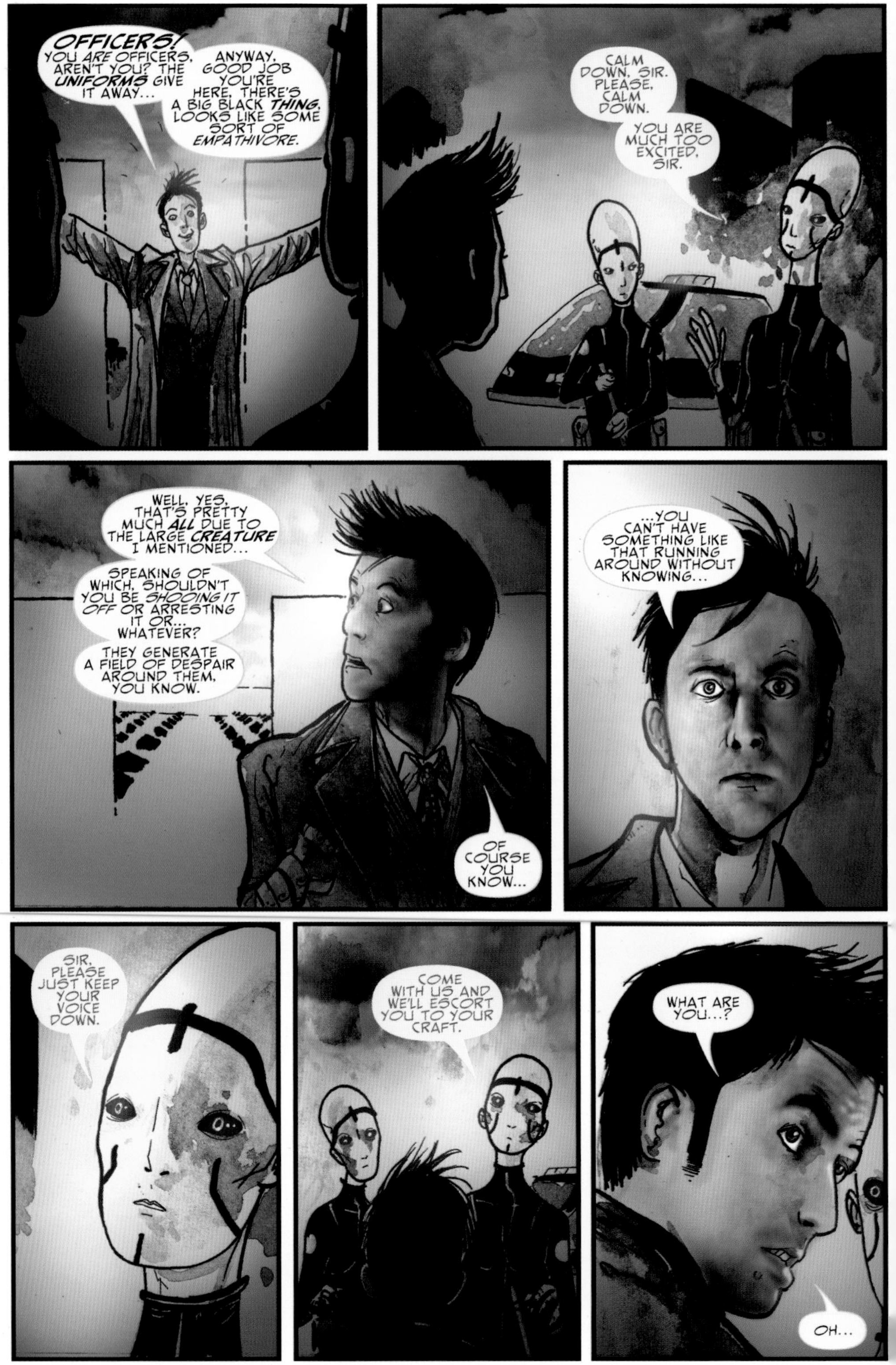
OFFICERS!
YOU ARE OFFICERS, AREN'T YOU? THE UNIFORMS GIVE IT AWAY...
ANYWAY, GOOD JOB YOU'RE HERE, THERE'S A BIG BLACK THING, LOOKS LIKE SOME SORT OF EMPATHIVORE.
CALM DOWN, SIR. PLEASE, CALM DOWN.
YOU ARE MUCH TOO EXCITED, SIR.
WELL, YES, THAT'S PRETTY MUCH ALL DUE TO THE LARGE CREATURE I MENTIONED...
SPEAKING OF WHICH, SHOULDN'T YOU BE SHOOING IT OFF OR ARRESTING IT OR... WHATEVER?
THEY GENERATE A FIELD OF DESPAIR AROUND THEM, YOU KNOW.
OF COURSE YOU KNOW...
...YOU CAN'T HAVE SOMETHING LIKE THAT RUNNING AROUND WITHOUT KNOWING...
SIR, PLEASE JUST KEEP YOUR VOICE DOWN.
COME WITH US AND WE'LL ESCORT YOU TO YOUR CRAFT.
WHAT ARE YOU...?
OH...

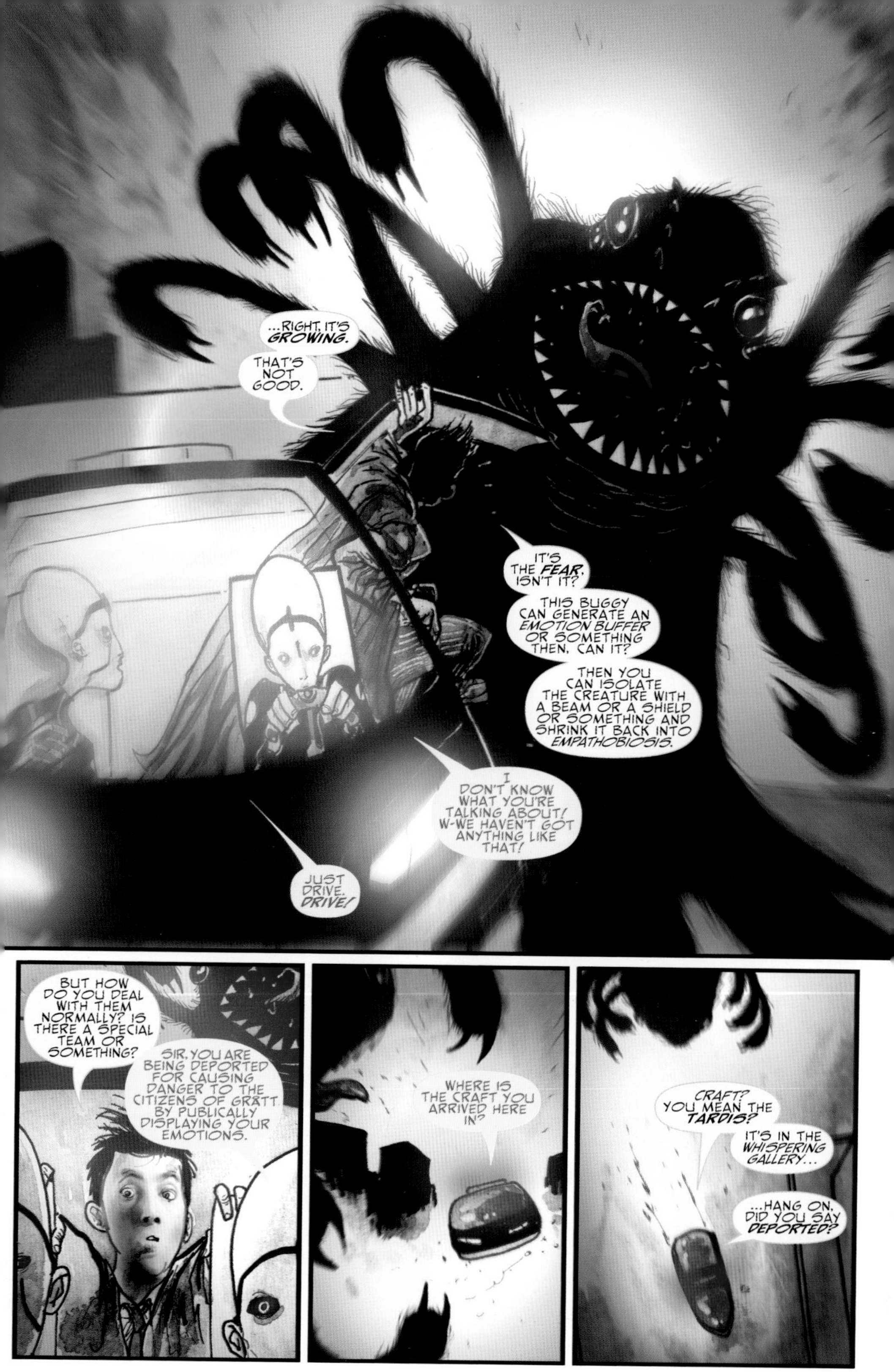
...RIGHT, IT'S GROWING.
THAT'S NOT GOOD.
IT'S THE FEAR, ISN'T IT?
THIS BUGGY CAN GENERATE AN EMOTION BUFFER OR SOMETHING THEN, CAN IT?
THEN YOU CAN ISOLATE THE CREATURE WITH A BEAM OR A SHIELD OR SOMETHING AND SHRINK IT BACK INTO EMPATHOBIOSIS.
I DON'T KNOW WHAT YOU'RE TALKING ABOUT! W-WE HAVEN'T GOT ANYTHING LIKE THAT!
JUST DRIVE. DRIVE!
BUT HOW DO YOU DEAL WITH THEM NORMALLY? IS THERE A SPECIAL TEAM OR SOMETHING?
SIR, YOU ARE BEING DEPORTED FOR CAUSING DANGER TO THE CITIZENS OF GRATT BY PUBLICALLY DISPLAYING YOUR EMOTIONS.
WHERE IS THE CRAFT YOU ARRIVED HERE IN?
CRAFT? YOU MEAN THE TARDIS?
IT'S IN THE WHISPERING GALLERY...
...HANG ON. DID YOU SAY DEPORTED?

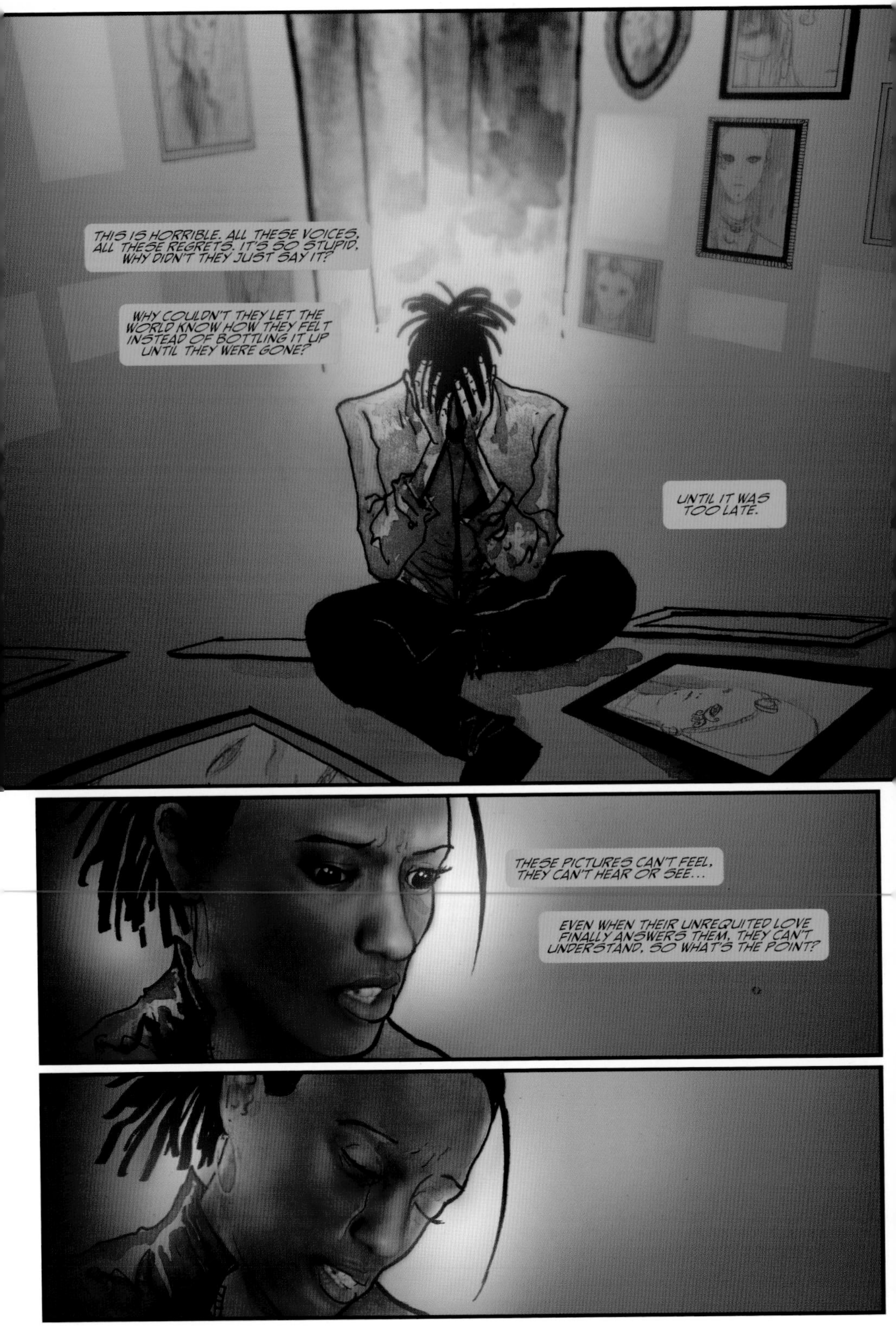
THIS IS HORRIBLE. ALL THESE VOICES, ALL THESE REGRETS. IT'S SO STUPID, WHY DIDN'T THEY JUST SAY IT?
WHY COULDN'T THEY LET THE WORLD KNOW HOW THEY FELT INSTEAD OF BOTTLING IT UP UNTIL THEY WERE GONE?
UNTIL IT WAS TOO LATE.
THESE PICTURES CAN'T FEEL, THEY CAN'T HEAR OR SEE...
EVEN WHEN THEIR UNREQUITED LOVE FINALLY ANSWERS THEM, THEY CAN'T UNDERSTAND. SO WHAT'S THE POINT?

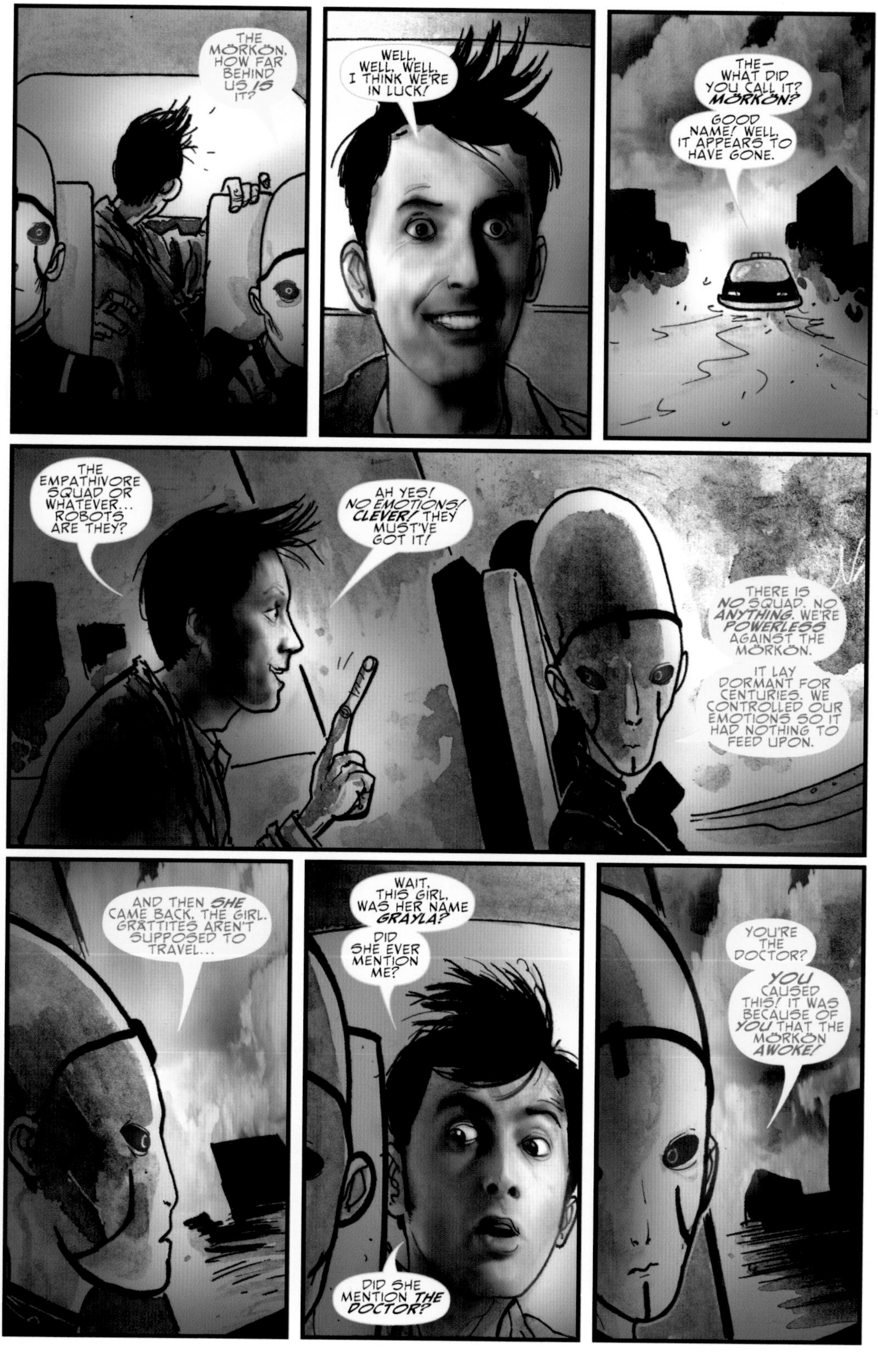
THE MÖRKÖN, HOW FAR BEHIND US IS IT?
WELL, WELL, WELL, I THINK WE'RE IN LUCK!
THE— WHAT DID YOU CALL IT? MÖRKÖN?
GOOD NAME! WELL, IT APPEARS TO HAVE GONE.
THE EMPATHIVORE SQUAD OR WHATEVER... ROBOTS ARE THEY?
AH YES! NO EMOTIONS! CLEVER! THEY MUST'VE GOT IT!
THERE IS NO SQUAD. NO ANYTHING. WE'RE POWERLESS AGAINST THE MÖRKÖN.
IT LAY DORMANT FOR CENTURIES. WE CONTROLLED OUR EMOTIONS SO IT HAD NOTHING TO FEED UPON.
AND THEN SHE CAME BACK, THE GIRL. GRATTITES AREN'T SUPPOSED TO TRAVEL...
WAIT, THIS GIRL, WAS HER NAME GRAYLA?
DID SHE EVER MENTION ME?
DID SHE MENTION THE DOCTOR?
YOU'RE THE DOCTOR?
YOU CAUSED THIS! IT WAS BECAUSE OF YOU THAT THE MÖRKÖN AWOKE!

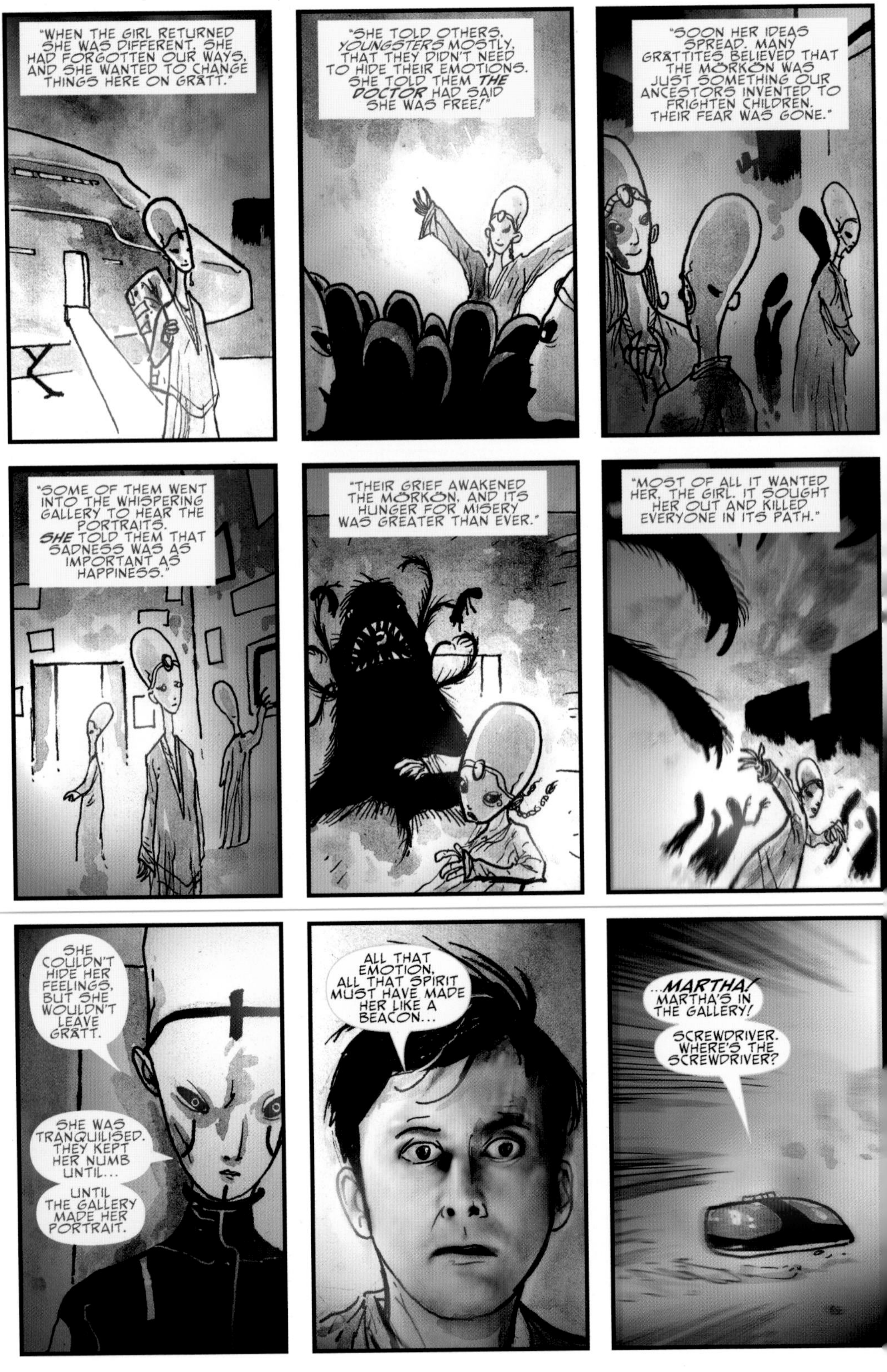

"WHEN THE GIRL RETURNED SHE WAS DIFFERENT. SHE HAD FORGOTTEN OUR WAYS, AND SHE WANTED TO CHANGE THINGS HERE ON GRÄTT."
"SHE TOLD OTHERS, YOUNGSTERS MOSTLY, THAT THEY DIDN'T NEED TO HIDE THEIR EMOTIONS. SHE TOLD THEM THE DOCTOR HAD SAID SHE WAS FREE!"
"SOON HER IDEAS SPREAD. MANY GRÄTTITES BELIEVED THAT THE MÖRKÖN WAS JUST SOMETHING OUR ANCESTORS INVENTED TO FRIGHTEN CHILDREN. THEIR FEAR WAS GONE."
"SOME OF THEM WENT INTO THE WHISPERING GALLERY TO HEAR THE PORTRAITS. SHE TOLD THEM THAT SADNESS WAS AS IMPORTANT AS HAPPINESS."
"THEIR GRIEF AWAKENED THE MÖRKÖN, AND ITS HUNGER FOR MISERY WAS GREATER THAN EVER."
"MOST OF ALL IT WANTED HER, THE GIRL. IT SOUGHT HER OUT AND KILLED EVERYONE IN ITS PATH."
SHE COULDN'T HIDE HER FEELINGS, BUT SHE WOULDN'T LEAVE GRÄTT.
SHE WAS TRANQUILISED. THEY KEPT HER NUMB UNTIL...
UNTIL THE GALLERY MADE HER PORTRAIT.
ALL THAT EMOTION, ALL THAT SPIRIT MUST HAVE MADE HER LIKE A BEACON...
...MARTHA! MARTHA'S IN THE GALLERY!
SCREWDRIVER. WHERE'S THE SCREWDRIVER?

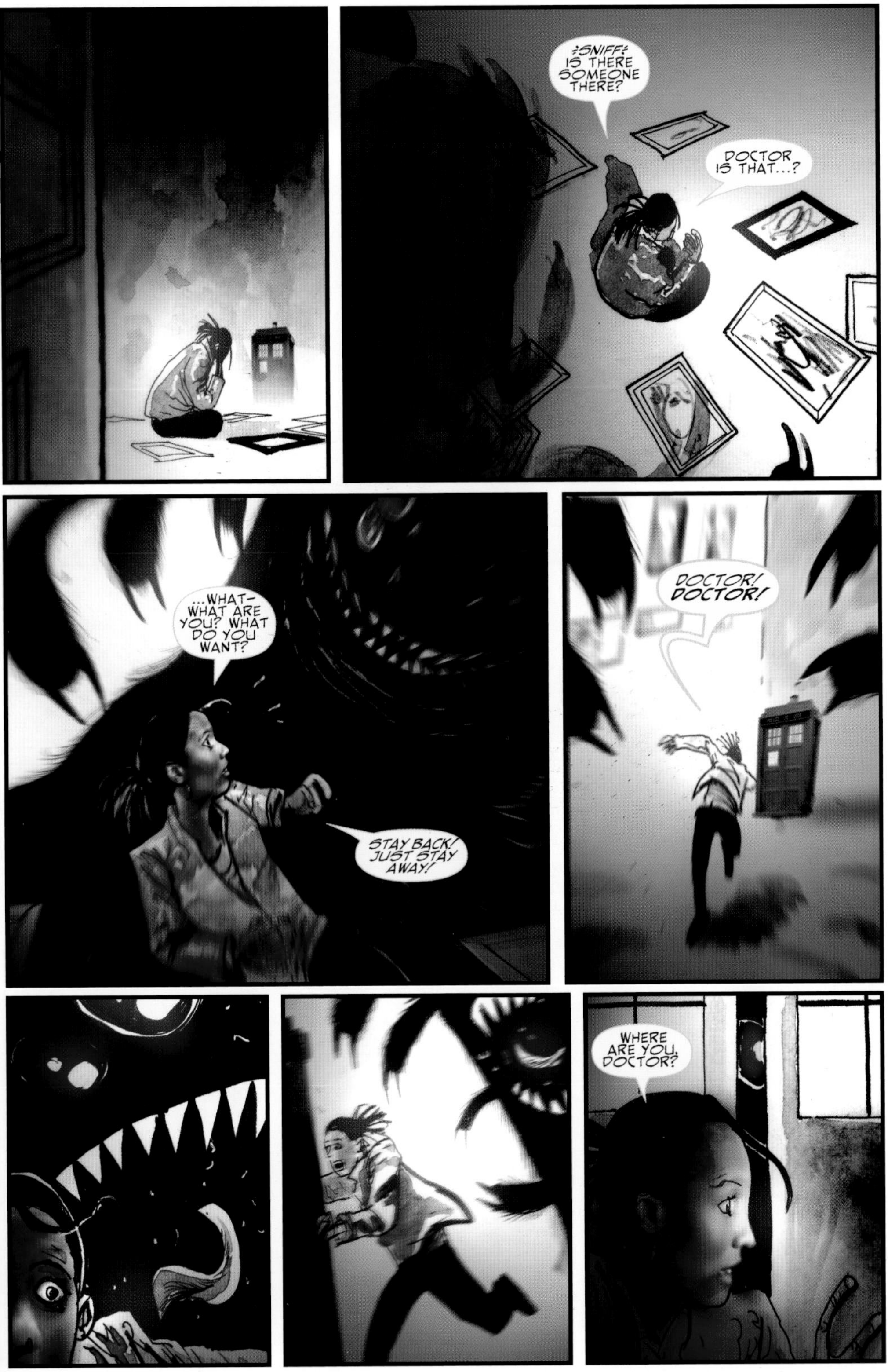

⁂SNIFF⁂ IS THERE SOMEONE THERE?
DOCTOR IS THAT...?
...WHAT- WHAT ARE YOU? WHAT DO YOU WANT?
STAY BACK! JUST STAY AWAY!
DOCTOR! DOCTOR!
WHERE ARE YOU, DOCTOR?

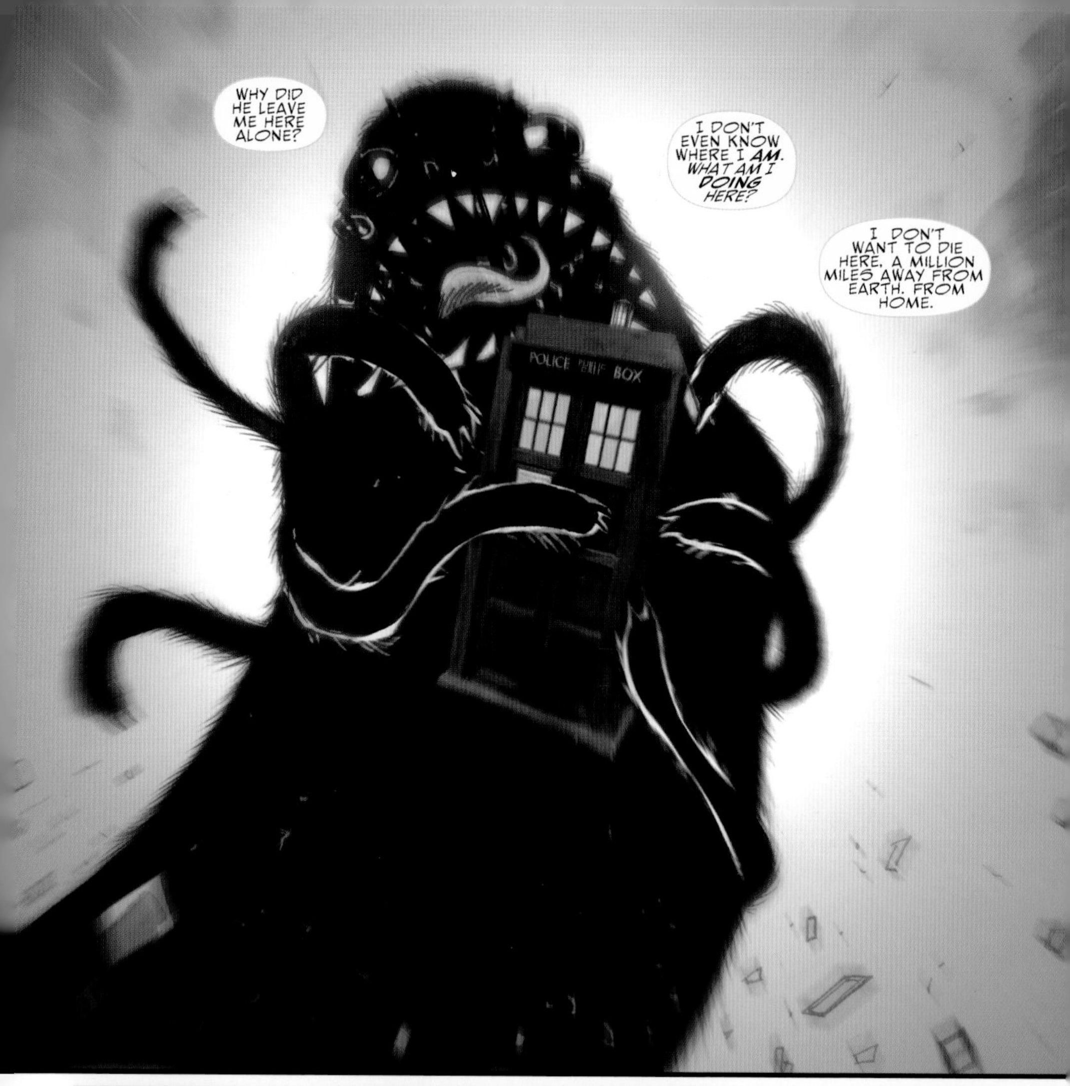

WHY DID HE LEAVE ME HERE ALONE?
I DON'T EVEN KNOW WHERE I AM. WHAT AM I DOING HERE?
I DON'T WANT TO DIE HERE, A MILLION MILES AWAY FROM EARTH. FROM HOME.
POLICE BOX

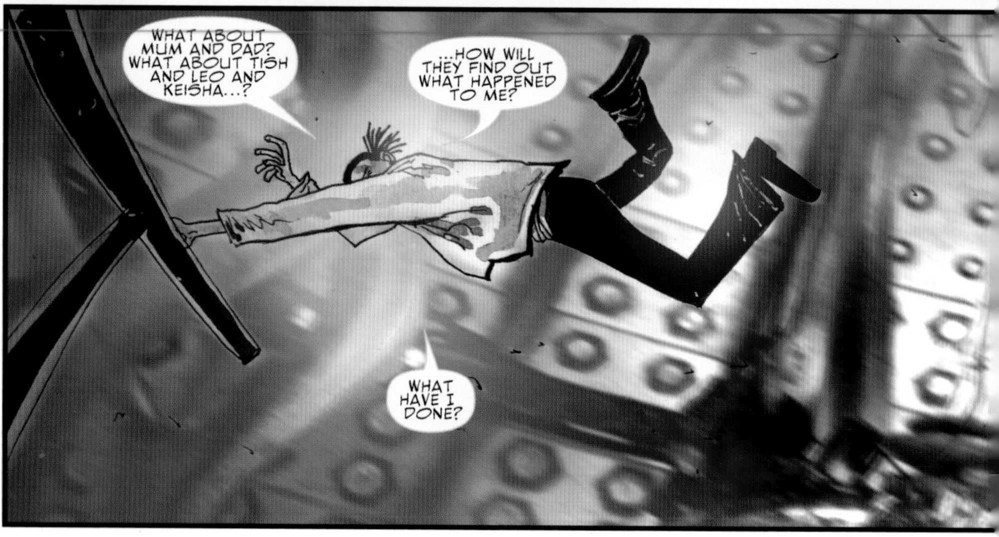

WHAT ABOUT MUM AND DAD? WHAT ABOUT TISH AND LEO AND KEISHA...?
...HOW WILL THEY FIND OUT WHAT HAPPENED TO ME?
WHAT HAVE I DONE?

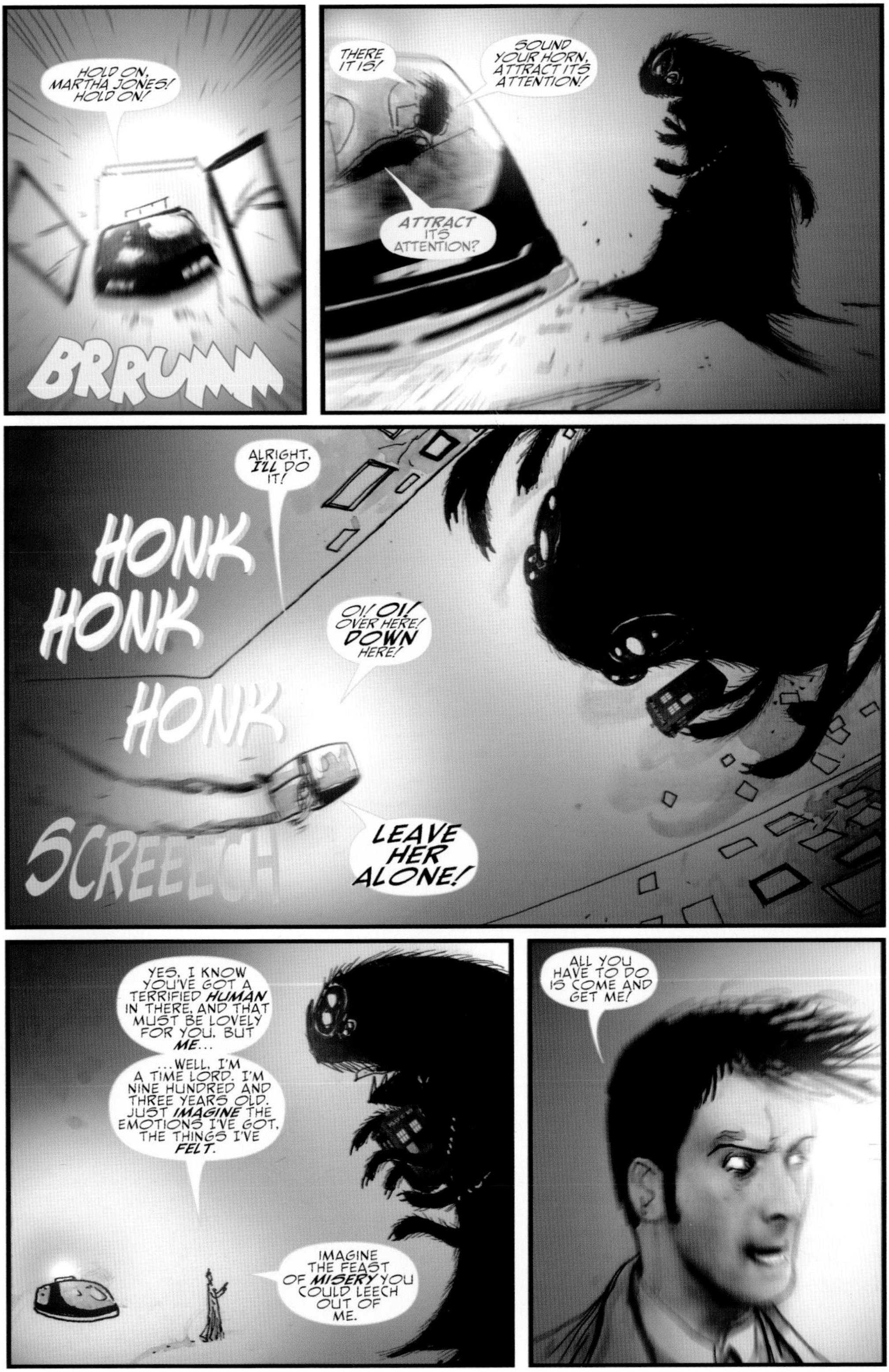
HOLD ON, MARTHA JONES! HOLD ON!
BRRUMM
THERE IT IS!
SOUND YOUR HORN, ATTRACT ITS ATTENTION!
ATTRACT ITS ATTENTION?
ALRIGHT, I'LL DO IT!
HONK
HONK
HONK
SCREECH
OI! OI! OVER HERE! DOWN HERE!
LEAVE HER ALONE!
YES, I KNOW YOU'VE GOT A TERRIFIED HUMAN IN THERE, AND THAT MUST BE LOVELY FOR YOU. BUT ME...
...WELL, I'M A TIME LORD. I'M NINE HUNDRED AND THREE YEARS OLD. JUST IMAGINE THE EMOTIONS I'VE GOT, THE THINGS I'VE FELT.
IMAGINE THE FEAST OF MISERY YOU COULD LEECH OUT OF ME.
ALL YOU HAVE TO DO IS COME AND GET ME!

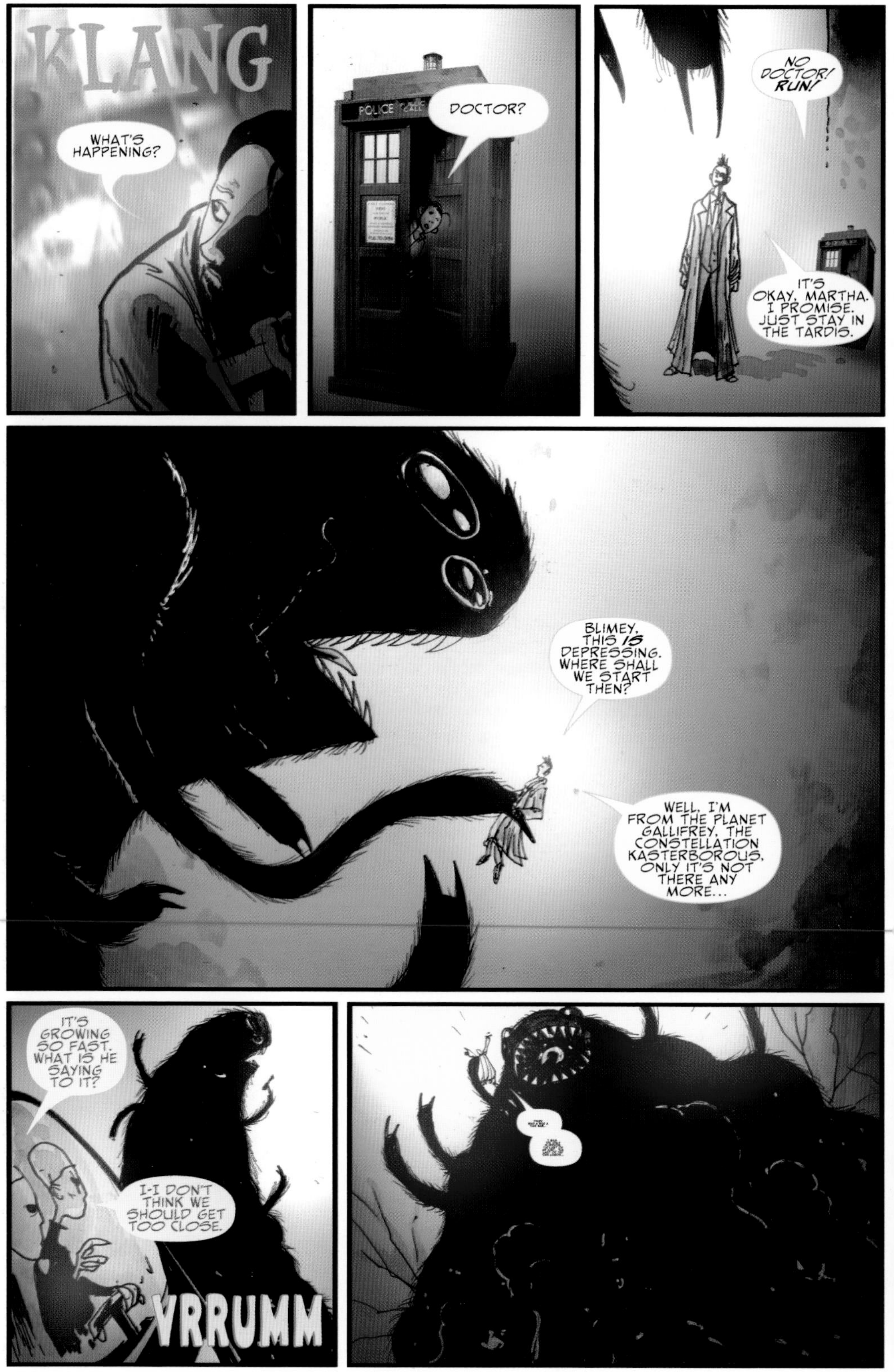
KLANG
WHAT'S HAPPENING?
DOCTOR?
NO DOCTOR! RUN!
IT'S OKAY, MARTHA. I PROMISE. JUST STAY IN THE TARDIS.
BLIMEY, THIS IS DEPRESSING. WHERE SHALL WE START THEN?
WELL, I'M FROM THE PLANET GALLIFREY, THE CONSTELLATION KASTERBOROUS, ONLY IT'S NOT THERE ANY MORE...
IT'S GROWING SO FAST. WHAT IS HE SAYING TO IT?
I-I DON'T THINK WE SHOULD GET TOO CLOSE.
VRRUMM

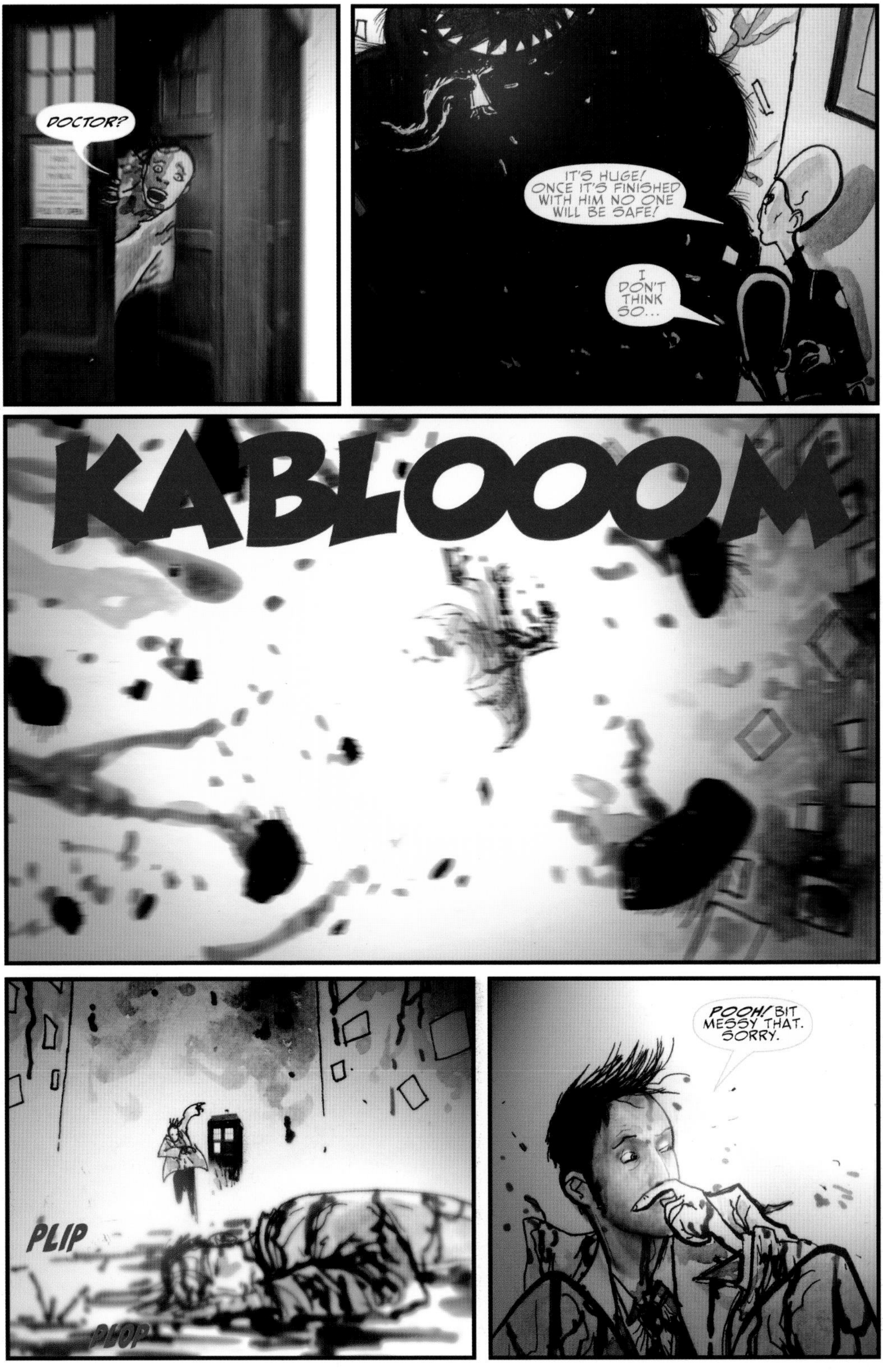
DOCTOR?
IT'S HUGE! ONCE IT'S FINISHED WITH HIM NO ONE WILL BE SAFE!
I DON'T THINK SO...
KABLOOOM
PLIP
PLOP
POOH! BIT MESSY THAT. SORRY.

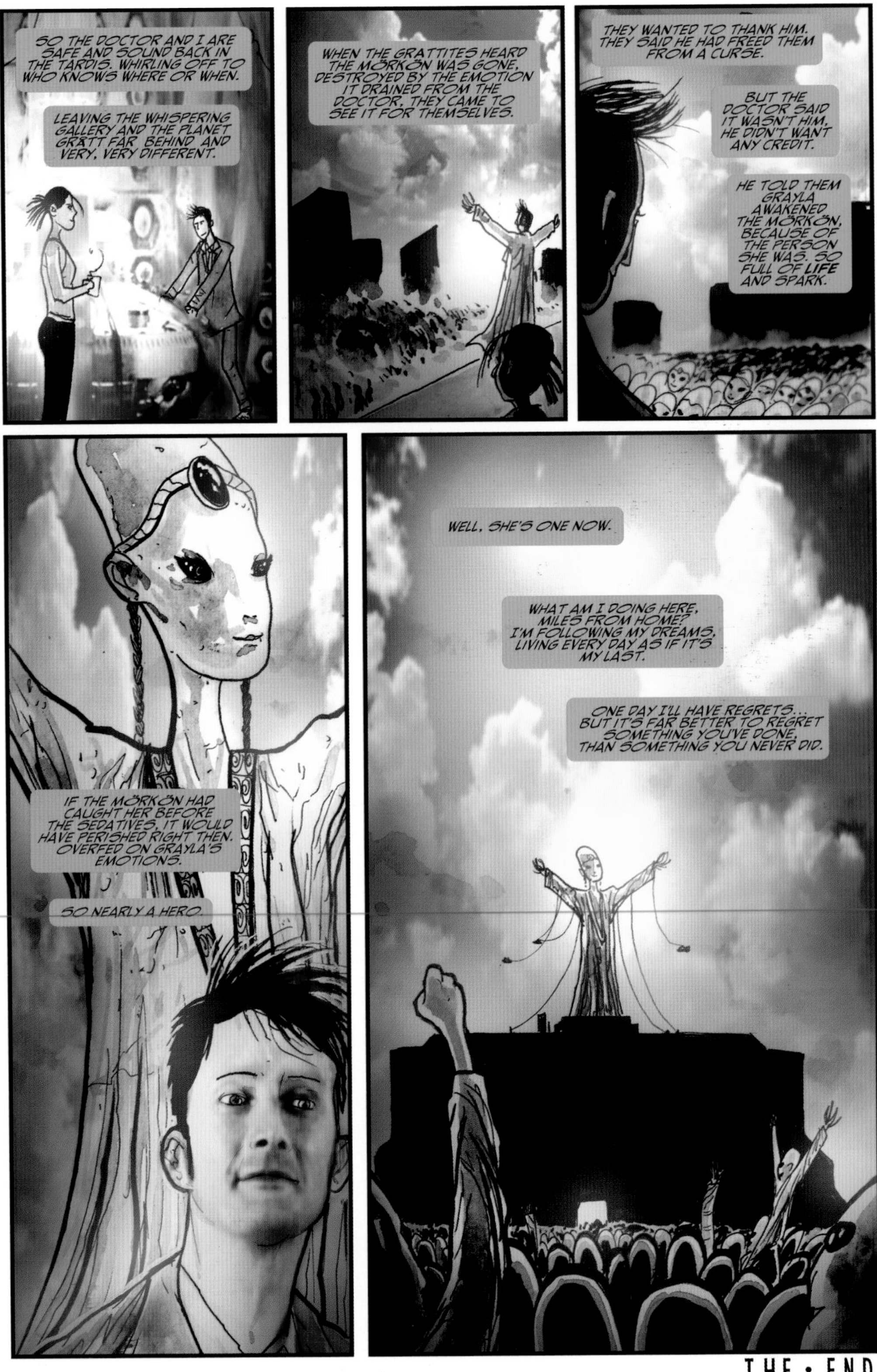
SO THE DOCTOR AND I ARE SAFE AND SOUND BACK IN THE TARDIS. WHIRLING OFF TO WHO KNOWS WHERE OR WHEN.
LEAVING THE WHISPERING GALLERY AND THE PLANET GRÄTT FAR BEHIND AND VERY, VERY DIFFERENT.
WHEN THE GRATTITES HEARD THE MÖRKÖN WAS GONE, DESTROYED BY THE EMOTION IT DRAINED FROM THE DOCTOR, THEY CAME TO SEE IT FOR THEMSELVES.
THEY WANTED TO THANK HIM. THEY SAID HE HAD FREED THEM FROM A CURSE.
BUT THE DOCTOR SAID IT WASN'T HIM, HE DIDN'T WANT ANY CREDIT.
HE TOLD THEM GRAYLA AWAKENED THE MÖRKÖN, BECAUSE OF THE PERSON SHE WAS. SO FULL OF LIFE AND SPARK.
IF THE MÖRKÖN HAD CAUGHT HER BEFORE THE SEDATIVES, IT WOULD HAVE PERISHED RIGHT THEN. OVERFED ON GRAYLA'S EMOTIONS.
SO NEARLY A HERO.
WELL, SHE'S ONE NOW.
WHAT AM I DOING HERE, MILES FROM HOME? I'M FOLLOWING MY DREAMS, LIVING EVERY DAY AS IF IT'S MY LAST.
ONE DAY I'LL HAVE REGRETS... BUT IT'S FAR BETTER TO REGRET SOMETHING YOU'VE DONE, THAN SOMETHING YOU NEVER DID.

THE • END

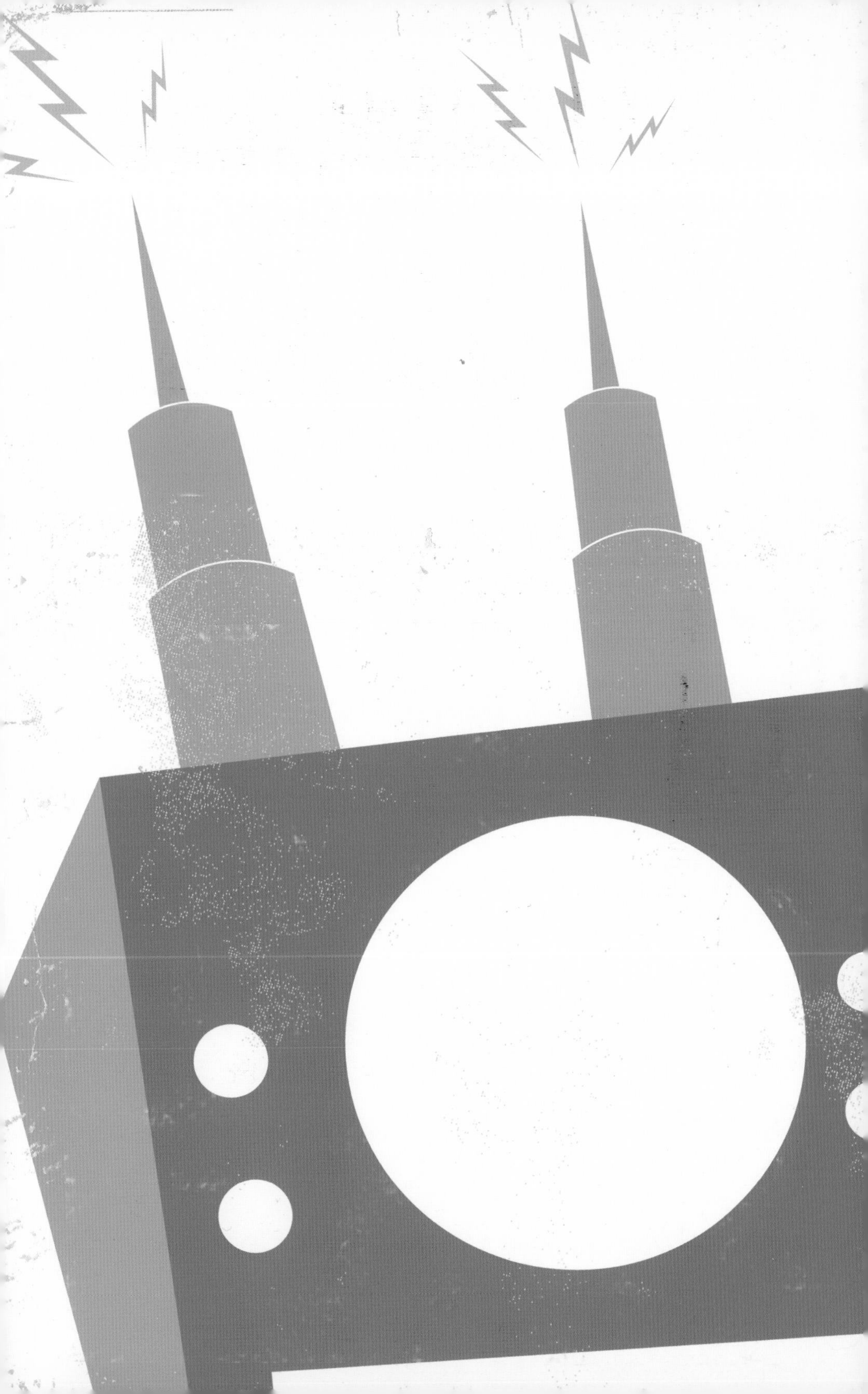

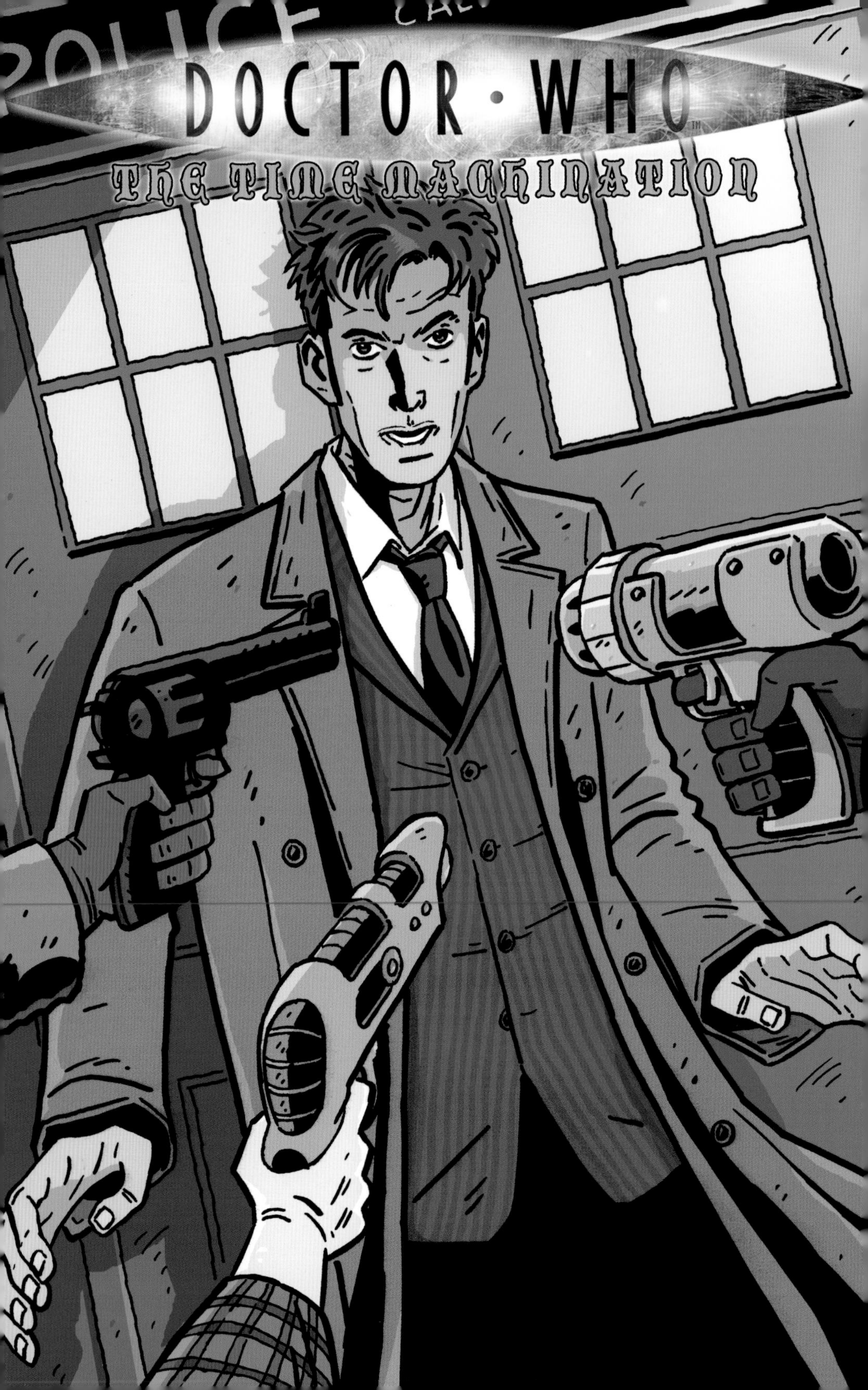
DOCTOR · WHO
THE TIME MACHINATION

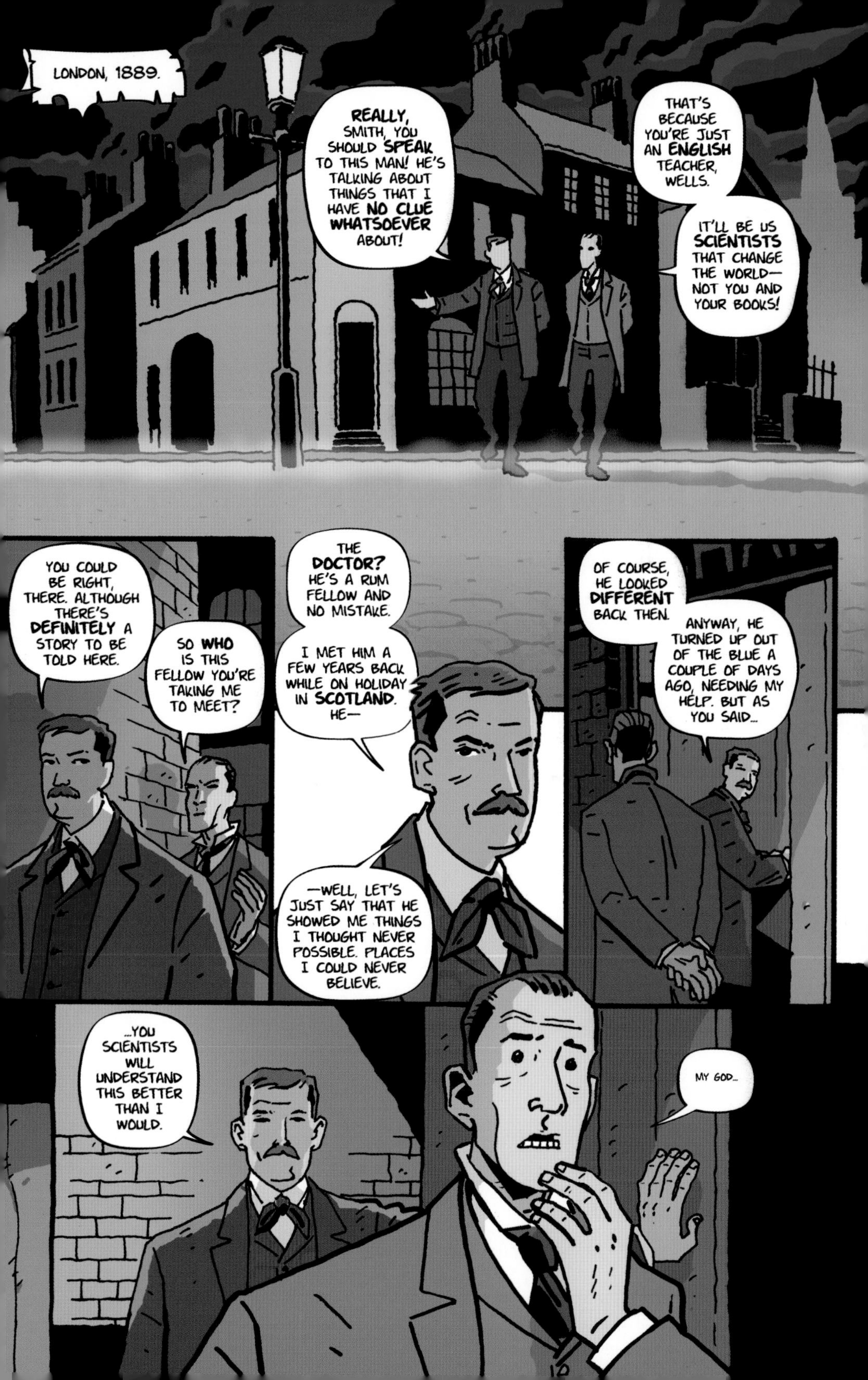
LONDON, 1889.
REALLY, SMITH, YOU SHOULD SPEAK TO THIS MAN! HE'S TALKING ABOUT THINGS THAT I HAVE NO CLUE WHATSOEVER ABOUT!
THAT'S BECAUSE YOU'RE JUST AN ENGLISH TEACHER, WELLS.
IT'LL BE US SCIENTISTS THAT CHANGE THE WORLD— NOT YOU AND YOUR BOOKS!
YOU COULD BE RIGHT, THERE. ALTHOUGH THERE'S DEFINITELY A STORY TO BE TOLD HERE.
SO WHO IS THIS FELLOW YOU'RE TAKING ME TO MEET?
THE DOCTOR? HE'S A RUM FELLOW AND NO MISTAKE.
I MET HIM A FEW YEARS BACK WHILE ON HOLIDAY IN SCOTLAND. HE—
—WELL, LET'S JUST SAY THAT HE SHOWED ME THINGS I THOUGHT NEVER POSSIBLE. PLACES I COULD NEVER BELIEVE.
OF COURSE, HE LOOKED DIFFERENT BACK THEN.
ANYWAY, HE TURNED UP OUT OF THE BLUE A COUPLE OF DAYS AGO, NEEDING MY HELP. BUT AS YOU SAID...
...YOU SCIENTISTS WILL UNDERSTAND THIS BETTER THAN I WOULD.
MY GOD...

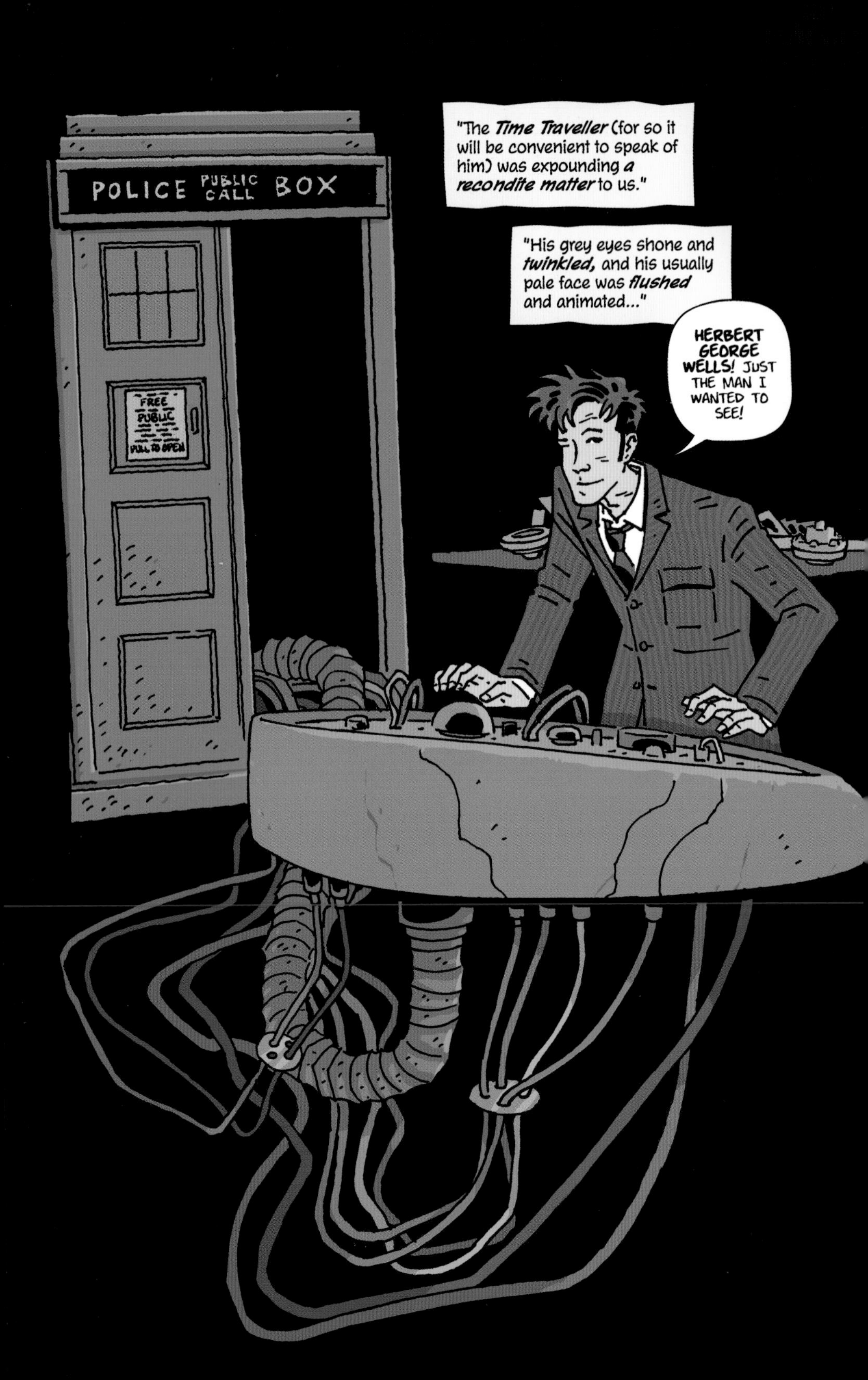
"The *Time Traveller* (for so it will be convenient to speak of him) was expounding *a recondite matter* to us."
"His grey eyes shone and *twinkled,* and his usually pale face was *flushed* and animated..."
HERBERT GEORGE WELLS! JUST THE MAN I WANTED TO SEE!
POLICE PUBLIC CALL BOX
FREE PUBLIC
PULL TO OPEN

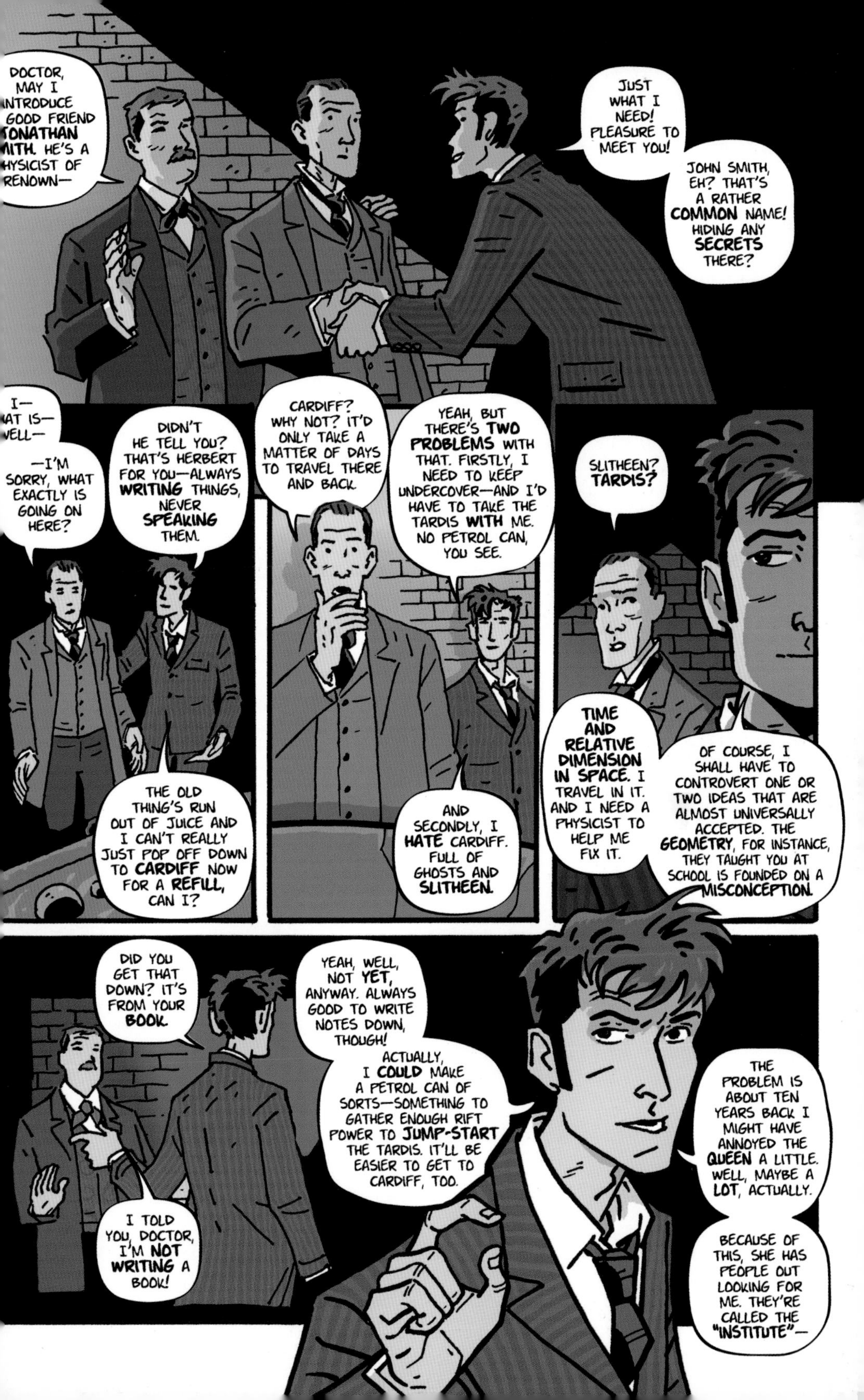
DOCTOR, MAY I INTRODUCE GOOD FRIEND JONATHAN SMITH. HE'S A PHYSICIST OF RENOWN—
JUST WHAT I NEED! PLEASURE TO MEET YOU!
JOHN SMITH, EH? THAT'S A RATHER COMMON NAME! HIDING ANY SECRETS THERE?
I— THAT IS— WELL—
—I'M SORRY, WHAT EXACTLY IS GOING ON HERE?
DIDN'T HE TELL YOU? THAT'S HERBERT FOR YOU—ALWAYS WRITING THINGS, NEVER SPEAKING THEM.
THE OLD THING'S RUN OUT OF JUICE AND I CAN'T REALLY JUST POP OFF DOWN TO CARDIFF NOW FOR A REFILL, CAN I?
CARDIFF? WHY NOT? IT'D ONLY TAKE A MATTER OF DAYS TO TRAVEL THERE AND BACK.
YEAH, BUT THERE'S TWO PROBLEMS WITH THAT. FIRSTLY, I NEED TO KEEP UNDERCOVER—AND I'D HAVE TO TAKE THE TARDIS WITH ME. NO PETROL CAN, YOU SEE.
AND SECONDLY, I HATE CARDIFF. FULL OF GHOSTS AND SLITHEEN.
SLITHEEN? TARDIS?
TIME AND RELATIVE DIMENSION IN SPACE. I TRAVEL IN IT. AND I NEED A PHYSICIST TO HELP ME FIX IT.
OF COURSE, I SHALL HAVE TO CONTROVERT ONE OR TWO IDEAS THAT ARE ALMOST UNIVERSALLY ACCEPTED. THE GEOMETRY, FOR INSTANCE, THEY TAUGHT YOU AT SCHOOL IS FOUNDED ON A MISCONCEPTION.
DID YOU GET THAT DOWN? IT'S FROM YOUR BOOK.
I TOLD YOU, DOCTOR, I'M NOT WRITING A BOOK!
YEAH, WELL, NOT YET, ANYWAY. ALWAYS GOOD TO WRITE NOTES DOWN, THOUGH!
ACTUALLY, I COULD MAKE A PETROL CAN OF SORTS—SOMETHING TO GATHER ENOUGH RIFT POWER TO JUMP-START THE TARDIS. IT'LL BE EASIER TO GET TO CARDIFF, TOO.
THE PROBLEM IS ABOUT TEN YEARS BACK I MIGHT HAVE ANNOYED THE QUEEN A LITTLE. WELL, MAYBE A LOT, ACTUALLY.
BECAUSE OF THIS, SHE HAS PEOPLE OUT LOOKING FOR ME. THEY'RE CALLED THE "INSTITUTE"—

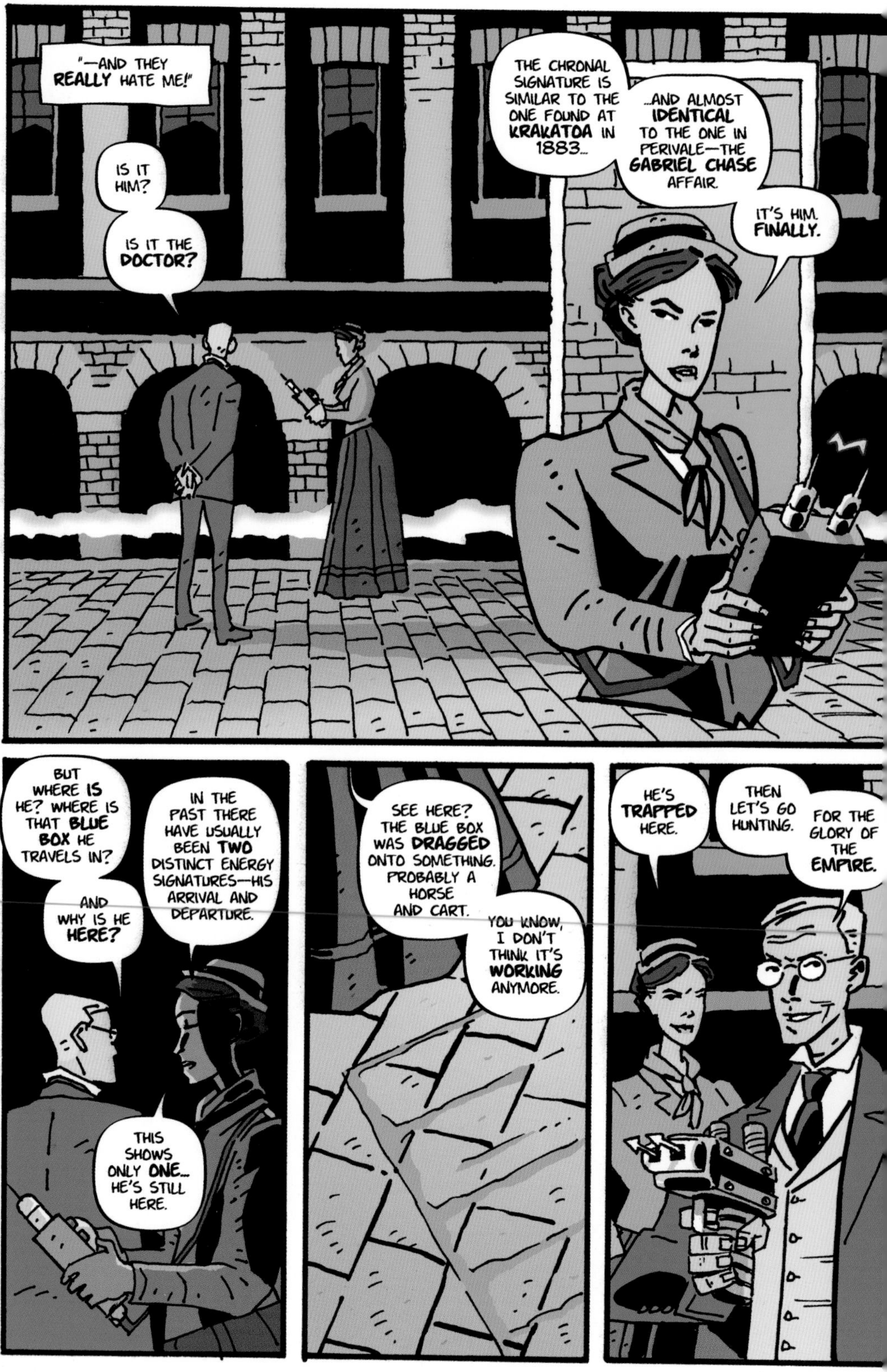
"—AND THEY REALLY HATE ME!"
IS IT HIM?
IS IT THE DOCTOR?
THE CHRONAL SIGNATURE IS SIMILAR TO THE ONE FOUND AT KRAKATOA IN 1883...
...AND ALMOST IDENTICAL TO THE ONE IN PERIVALE—THE GABRIEL CHASE AFFAIR.
IT'S HIM. FINALLY.
BUT WHERE IS HE? WHERE IS THAT BLUE BOX HE TRAVELS IN?
AND WHY IS HE HERE?
IN THE PAST THERE HAVE USUALLY BEEN TWO DISTINCT ENERGY SIGNATURES—HIS ARRIVAL AND DEPARTURE.
THIS SHOWS ONLY ONE... HE'S STILL HERE.
SEE HERE? THE BLUE BOX WAS DRAGGED ONTO SOMETHING. PROBABLY A HORSE AND CART.
YOU KNOW, I DON'T THINK IT'S WORKING ANYMORE.
HE'S TRAPPED HERE.
THEN LET'S GO HUNTING.
FOR THE GLORY OF THE EMPIRE.

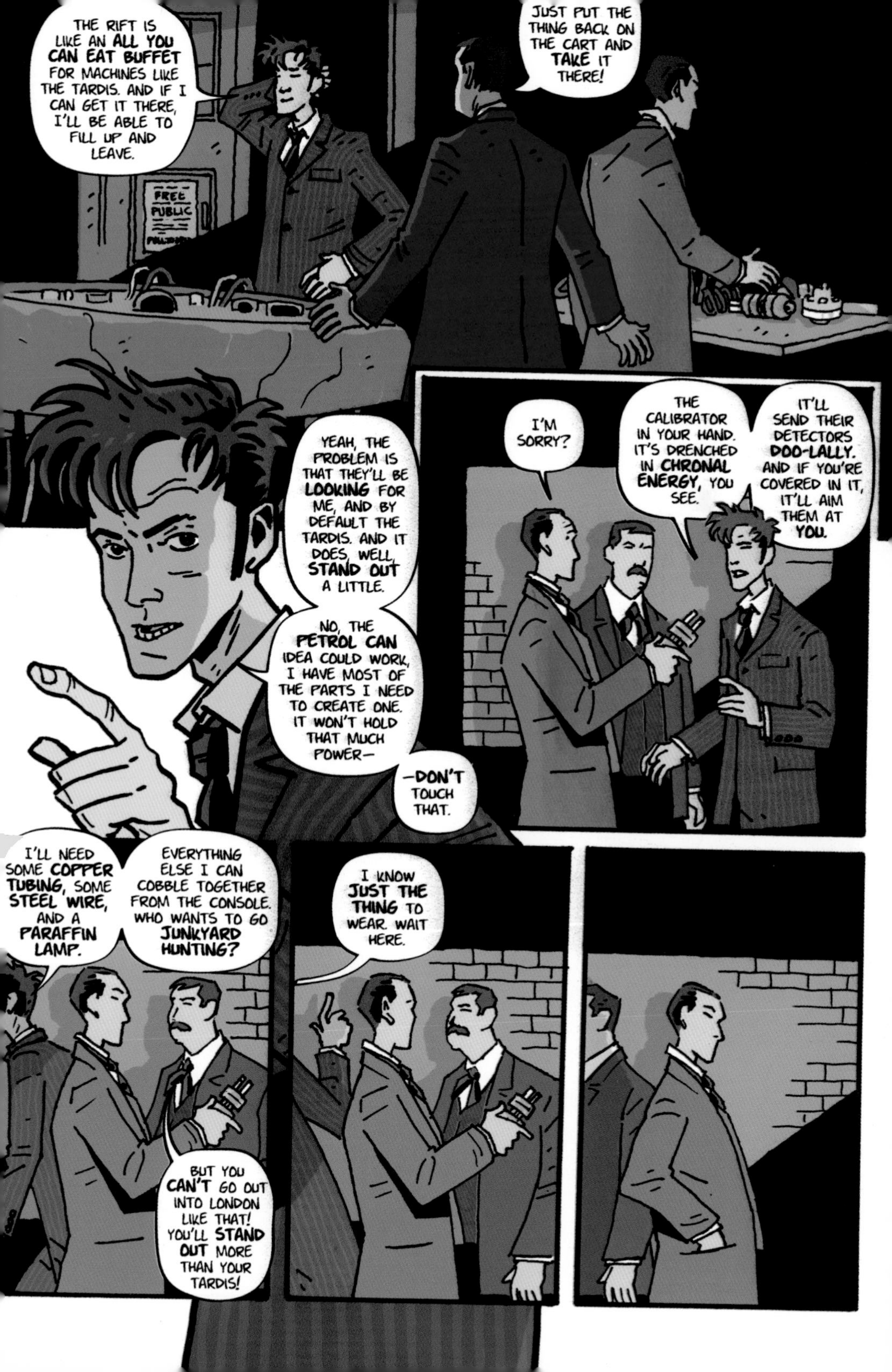
THE RIFT IS LIKE AN ALL YOU CAN EAT BUFFET FOR MACHINES LIKE THE TARDIS. AND IF I CAN GET IT THERE, I'LL BE ABLE TO FILL UP AND LEAVE.
JUST PUT THE THING BACK ON THE CART AND TAKE IT THERE!
FREE PUBLIC
YEAH, THE PROBLEM IS THAT THEY'LL BE LOOKING FOR ME, AND BY DEFAULT THE TARDIS. AND IT DOES, WELL, STAND OUT A LITTLE.
NO, THE PETROL CAN IDEA COULD WORK, I HAVE MOST OF THE PARTS I NEED TO CREATE ONE. IT WON'T HOLD THAT MUCH POWER—
—DON'T TOUCH THAT.
I'M SORRY?
THE CALIBRATOR IN YOUR HAND. IT'S DRENCHED IN CHRONAL ENERGY, YOU SEE.
IT'LL SEND THEIR DETECTORS DOO-LALLY. AND IF YOU'RE COVERED IN IT, IT'LL AIM THEM AT YOU.
I'LL NEED SOME COPPER TUBING, SOME STEEL WIRE, AND A PARAFFIN LAMP.
EVERYTHING ELSE I CAN COBBLE TOGETHER FROM THE CONSOLE. WHO WANTS TO GO JUNKYARD HUNTING?
BUT YOU CAN'T GO OUT INTO LONDON LIKE THAT! YOU'LL STAND OUT MORE THAN YOUR TARDIS!
I KNOW JUST THE THING TO WEAR. WAIT HERE.

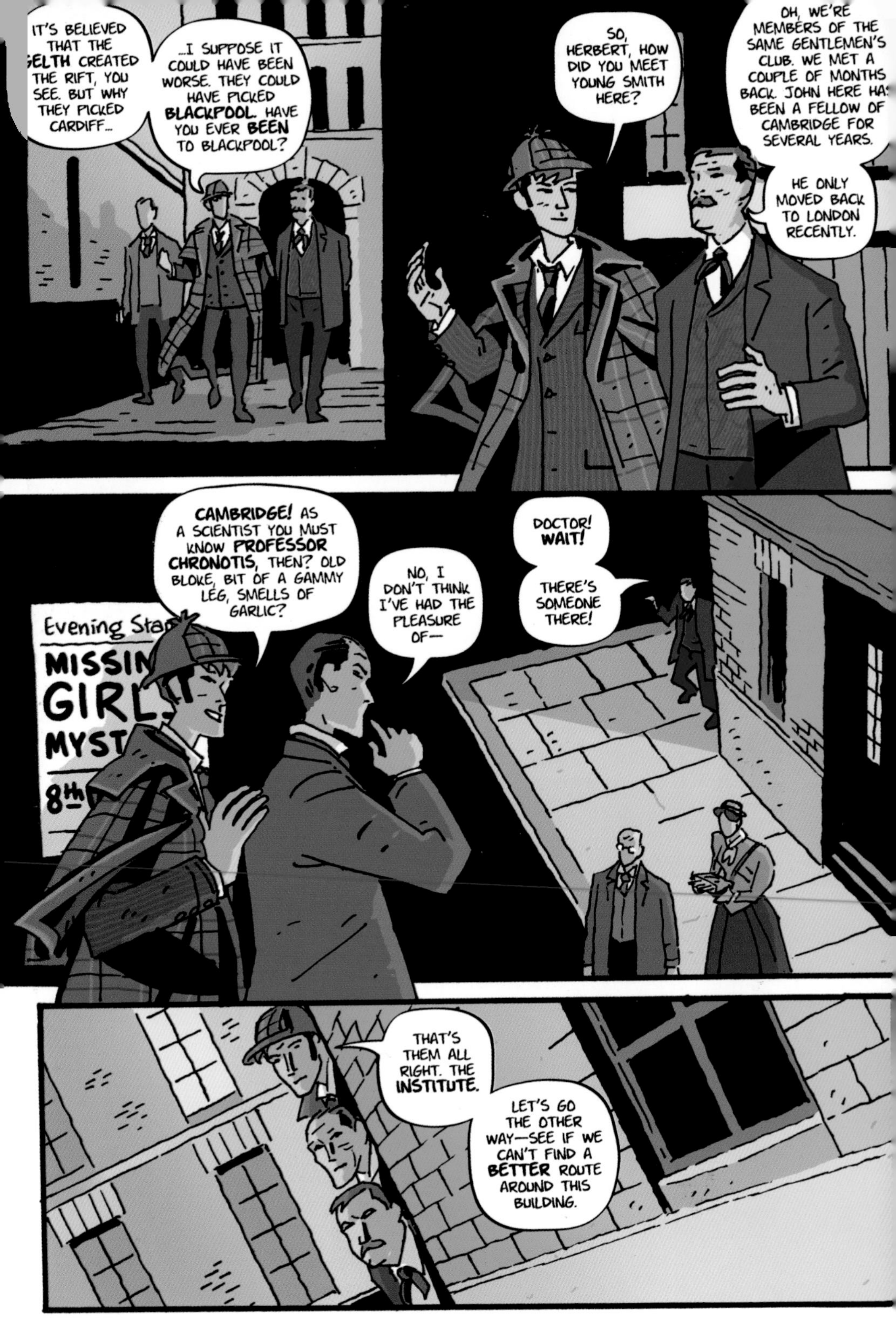
IT'S BELIEVED THAT THE GELTH CREATED THE RIFT, YOU SEE. BUT WHY THEY PICKED CARDIFF...
...I SUPPOSE IT COULD HAVE BEEN WORSE. THEY COULD HAVE PICKED BLACKPOOL. HAVE YOU EVER BEEN TO BLACKPOOL?
SO, HERBERT, HOW DID YOU MEET YOUNG SMITH HERE?
OH, WE'RE MEMBERS OF THE SAME GENTLEMEN'S CLUB. WE MET A COUPLE OF MONTHS BACK. JOHN HERE HAS BEEN A FELLOW OF CAMBRIDGE FOR SEVERAL YEARS.
HE ONLY MOVED BACK TO LONDON RECENTLY.
CAMBRIDGE! AS A SCIENTIST YOU MUST KNOW PROFESSOR CHRONOTIS, THEN? OLD BLOKE, BIT OF A GAMMY LEG, SMELLS OF GARLIC?
Evening Sta
MISSIN
GIRL
MYST
8th
NO, I DON'T THINK I'VE HAD THE PLEASURE OF—
DOCTOR! WAIT!
THERE'S SOMEONE THERE!
THAT'S THEM ALL RIGHT. THE INSTITUTE.
LET'S GO THE OTHER WAY—SEE IF WE CAN'T FIND A BETTER ROUTE AROUND THIS BUILDING.

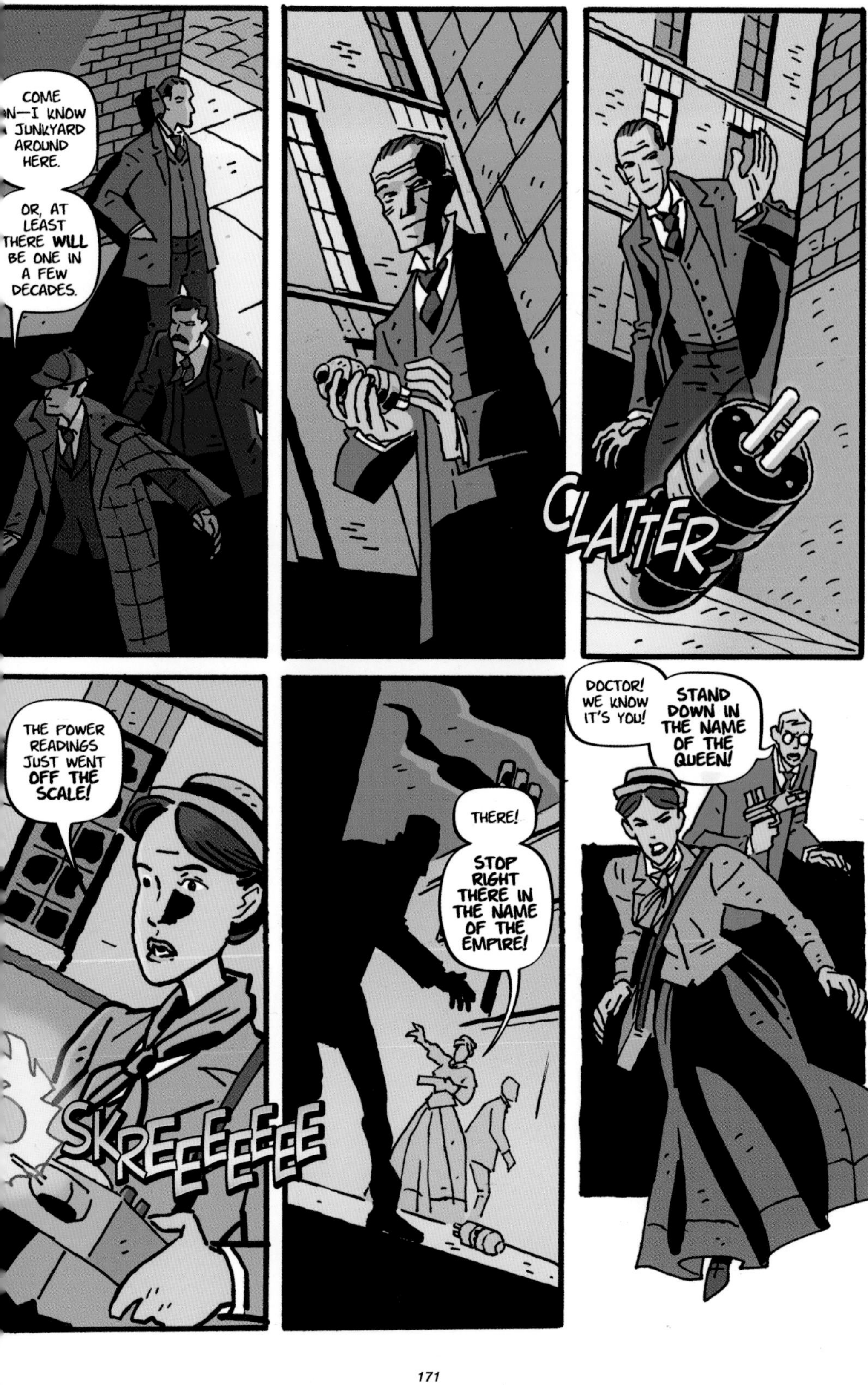

COME ON—I KNOW A JUNKYARD AROUND HERE.
OR, AT LEAST THERE WILL BE ONE IN A FEW DECADES.
CLATTER
THE POWER READINGS JUST WENT OFF THE SCALE!
SKREEEEEEEE
THERE!
STOP RIGHT THERE IN THE NAME OF THE EMPIRE!
DOCTOR! WE KNOW IT'S YOU!
STAND DOWN IN THE NAME OF THE QUEEN!

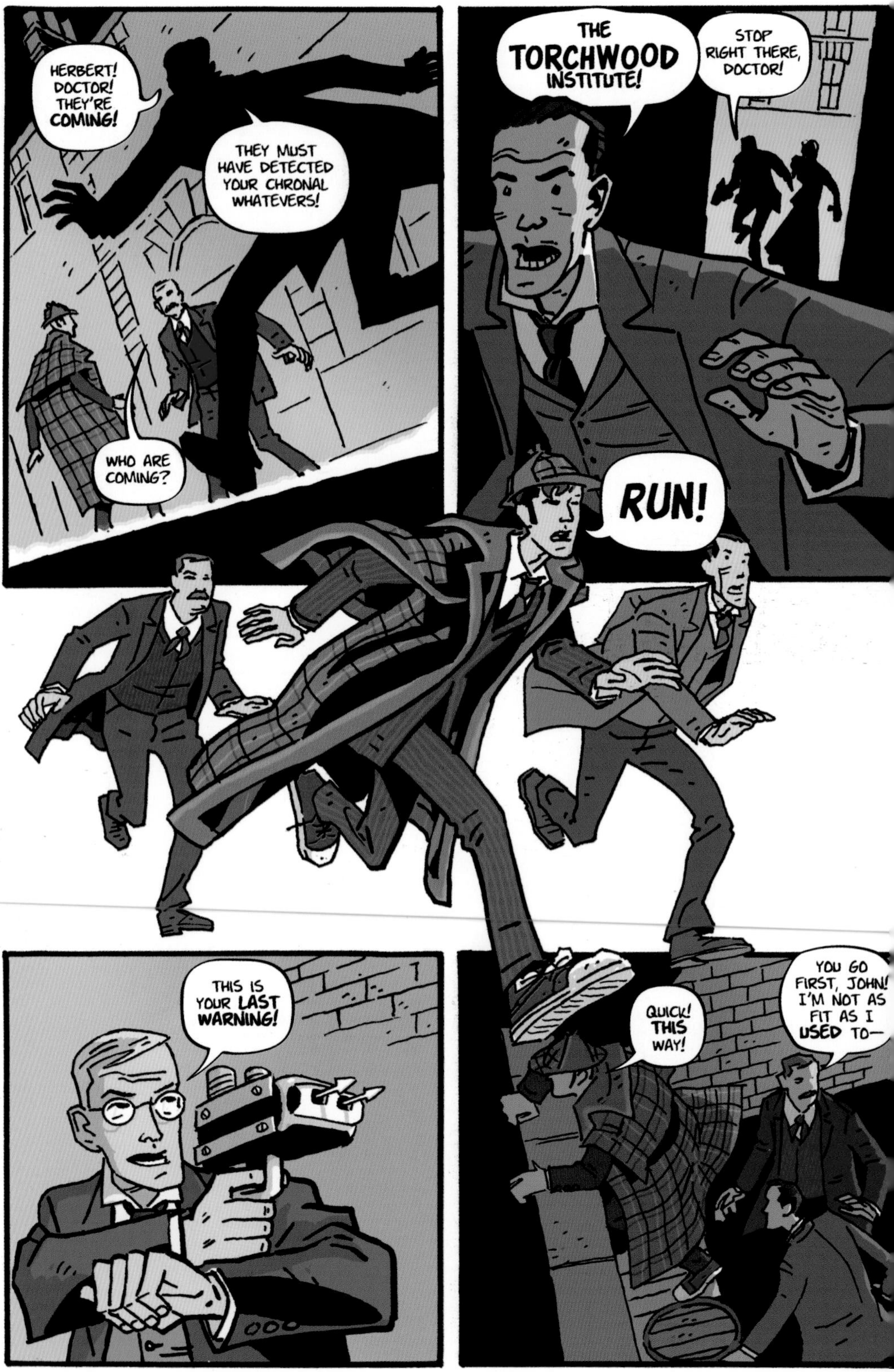
HERBERT! DOCTOR! THEY'RE COMING!
THEY MUST HAVE DETECTED YOUR CHRONAL WHATEVERS!
WHO ARE COMING?
THE TORCHWOOD INSTITUTE!
STOP RIGHT THERE, DOCTOR!
RUN!
THIS IS YOUR LAST WARNING!
QUICK! THIS WAY!
YOU GO FIRST, JOHN! I'M NOT AS FIT AS I USED TO—

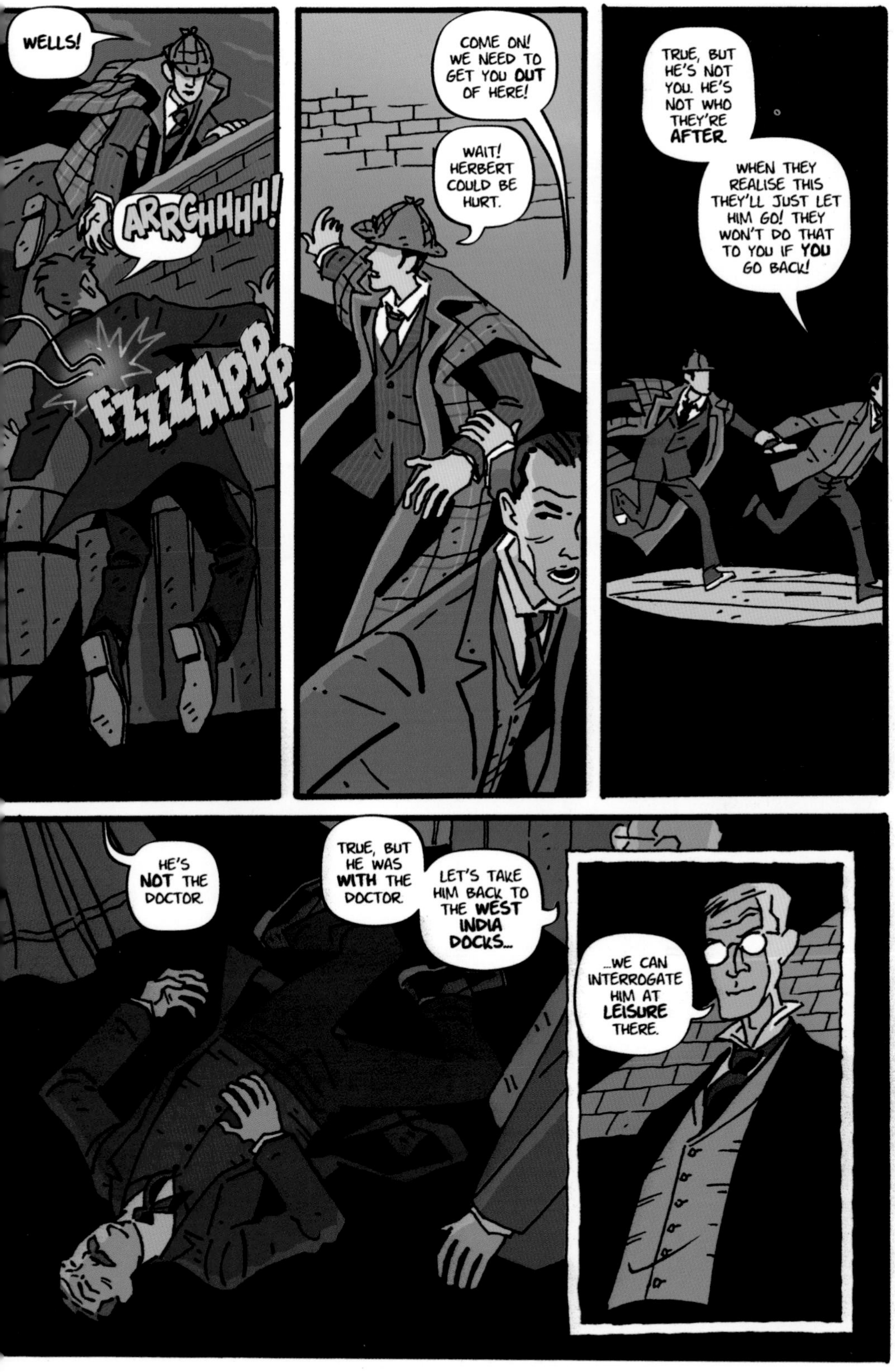

WELLS!
ARRGHHHH!
FZZZAPPP
COME ON! WE NEED TO GET YOU **OUT** OF HERE!
WAIT! HERBERT COULD BE HURT.
TRUE, BUT HE'S NOT YOU. HE'S NOT WHO THEY'RE **AFTER**.
WHEN THEY REALISE THIS THEY'LL JUST LET HIM GO! THEY WON'T DO THAT TO YOU IF **YOU** GO BACK!
HE'S **NOT** THE DOCTOR.
TRUE, BUT HE WAS **WITH** THE DOCTOR.
LET'S TAKE HIM BACK TO THE **WEST INDIA DOCKS**...
...WE CAN INTERROGATE HIM AT **LEISURE** THERE.

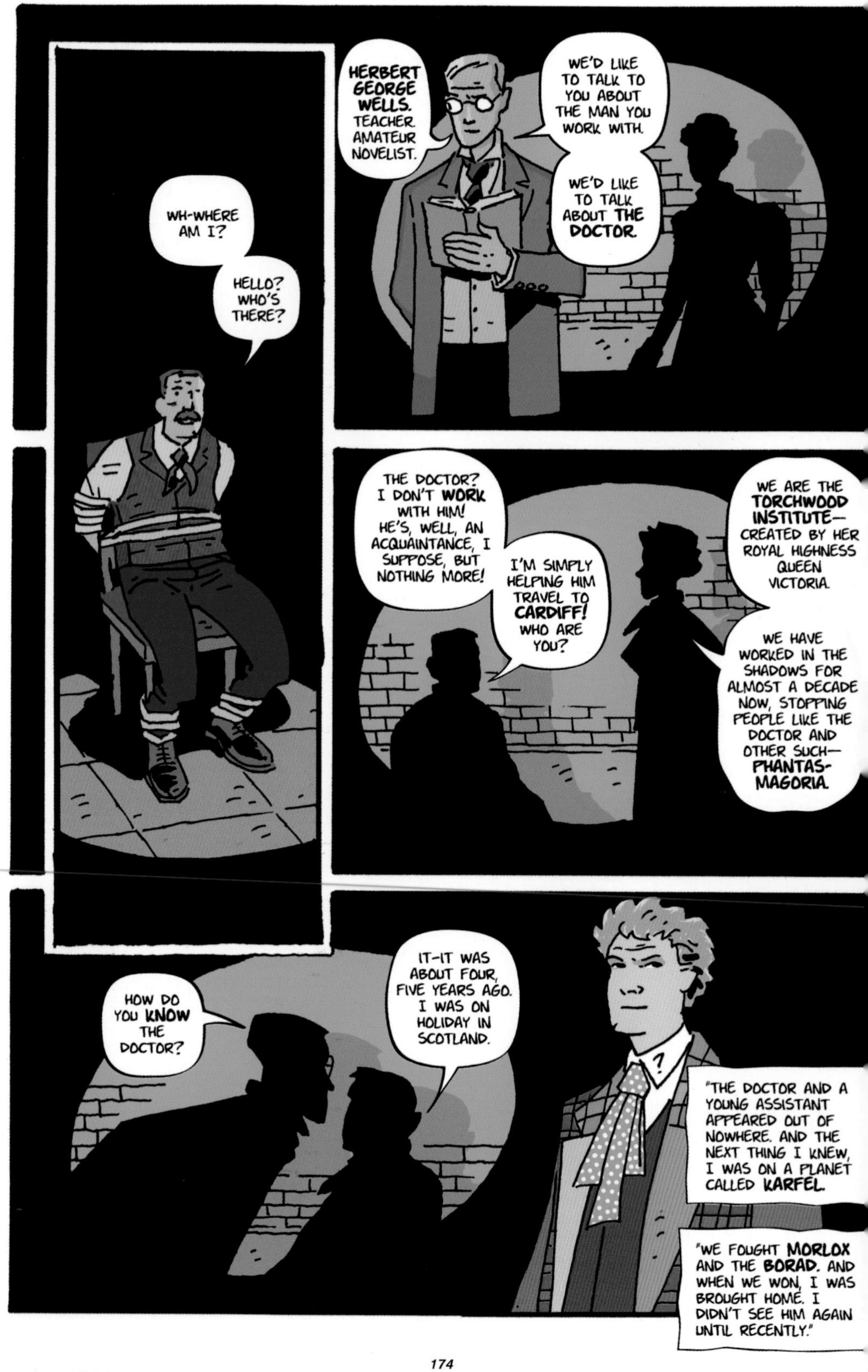
WH-WHERE AM I?
HELLO? WHO'S THERE?
HERBERT GEORGE WELLS. TEACHER. AMATEUR NOVELIST.
WE'D LIKE TO TALK TO YOU ABOUT THE MAN YOU WORK WITH.
WE'D LIKE TO TALK ABOUT THE DOCTOR.
THE DOCTOR? I DON'T WORK WITH HIM! HE'S, WELL, AN ACQUAINTANCE, I SUPPOSE, BUT NOTHING MORE!
I'M SIMPLY HELPING HIM TRAVEL TO CARDIFF! WHO ARE YOU?
WE ARE THE TORCHWOOD INSTITUTE— CREATED BY HER ROYAL HIGHNESS QUEEN VICTORIA.
WE HAVE WORKED IN THE SHADOWS FOR ALMOST A DECADE NOW, STOPPING PEOPLE LIKE THE DOCTOR AND OTHER SUCH— PHANTAS-MAGORIA.
HOW DO YOU KNOW THE DOCTOR?
IT-IT WAS ABOUT FOUR, FIVE YEARS AGO. I WAS ON HOLIDAY IN SCOTLAND.
"THE DOCTOR AND A YOUNG ASSISTANT APPEARED OUT OF NOWHERE. AND THE NEXT THING I KNEW, I WAS ON A PLANET CALLED KARFEL.
"WE FOUGHT MORLOX AND THE BORAD. AND WHEN WE WON, I WAS BROUGHT HOME. I DIDN'T SEE HIM AGAIN UNTIL RECENTLY."

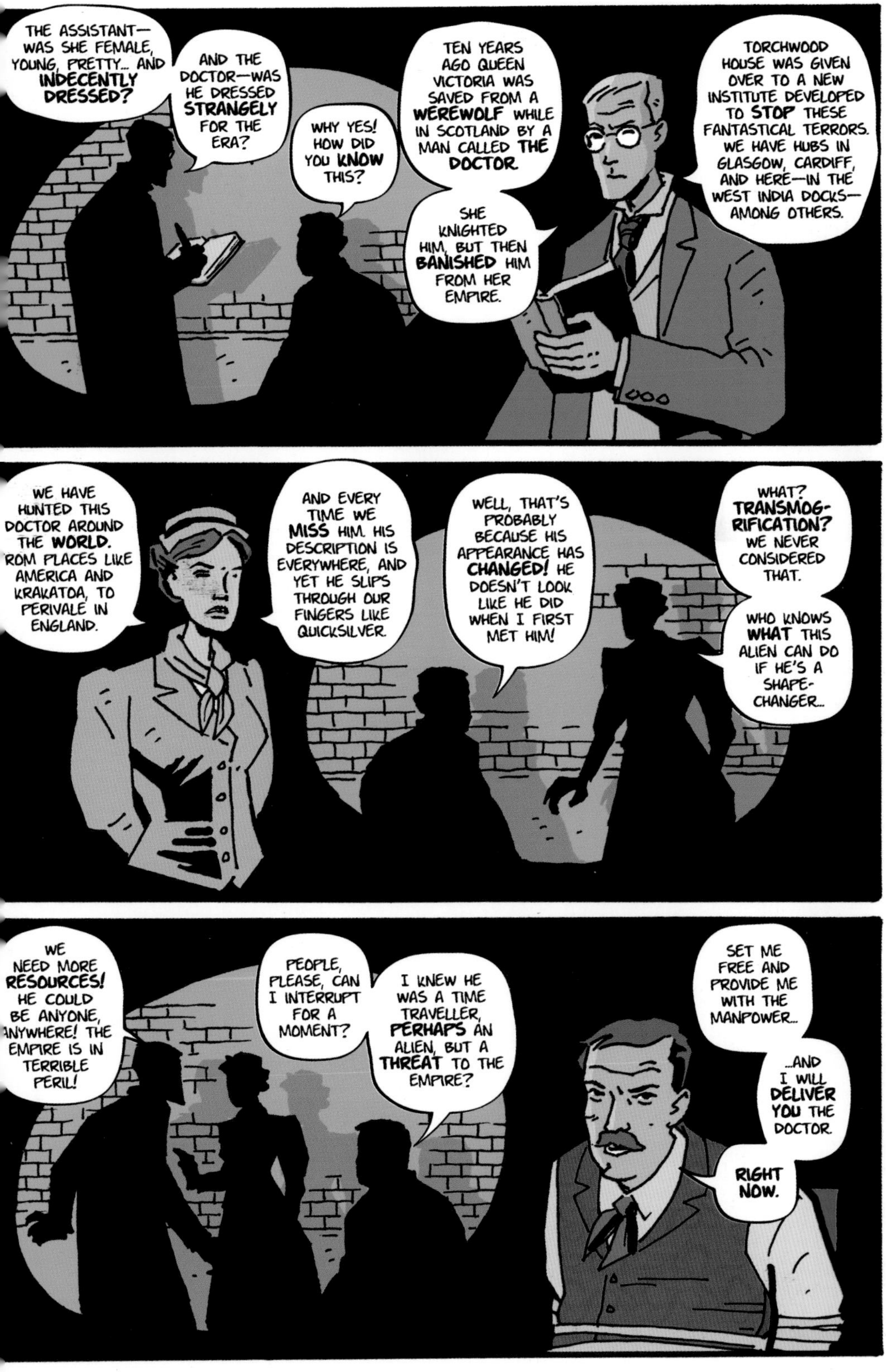
THE ASSISTANT—WAS SHE FEMALE, YOUNG, PRETTY... AND INDECENTLY DRESSED?
AND THE DOCTOR—WAS HE DRESSED STRANGELY FOR THE ERA?
WHY YES! HOW DID YOU KNOW THIS?
TEN YEARS AGO QUEEN VICTORIA WAS SAVED FROM A WEREWOLF WHILE IN SCOTLAND BY A MAN CALLED THE DOCTOR.
SHE KNIGHTED HIM, BUT THEN BANISHED HIM FROM HER EMPIRE.
TORCHWOOD HOUSE WAS GIVEN OVER TO A NEW INSTITUTE DEVELOPED TO STOP THESE FANTASTICAL TERRORS. WE HAVE HUBS IN GLASGOW, CARDIFF, AND HERE—IN THE WEST INDIA DOCKS—AMONG OTHERS.
WE HAVE HUNTED THIS DOCTOR AROUND THE WORLD. ROM PLACES LIKE AMERICA AND KRAKATOA, TO PERIVALE IN ENGLAND.
AND EVERY TIME WE MISS HIM. HIS DESCRIPTION IS EVERYWHERE, AND YET HE SLIPS THROUGH OUR FINGERS LIKE QUICKSILVER.
WELL, THAT'S PROBABLY BECAUSE HIS APPEARANCE HAS CHANGED! HE DOESN'T LOOK LIKE HE DID WHEN I FIRST MET HIM!
WHAT? TRANSMOG-RIFICATION? WE NEVER CONSIDERED THAT.
WHO KNOWS WHAT THIS ALIEN CAN DO IF HE'S A SHAPE-CHANGER...
WE NEED MORE RESOURCES! HE COULD BE ANYONE, NYWHERE! THE EMPIRE IS IN TERRIBLE PERIL!
PEOPLE, PLEASE, CAN I INTERRUPT FOR A MOMENT?
I KNEW HE WAS A TIME TRAVELLER, PERHAPS AN ALIEN, BUT A THREAT TO THE EMPIRE?
SET ME FREE AND PROVIDE ME WITH THE MANPOWER...
...AND I WILL DELIVER YOU THE DOCTOR.
RIGHT NOW.

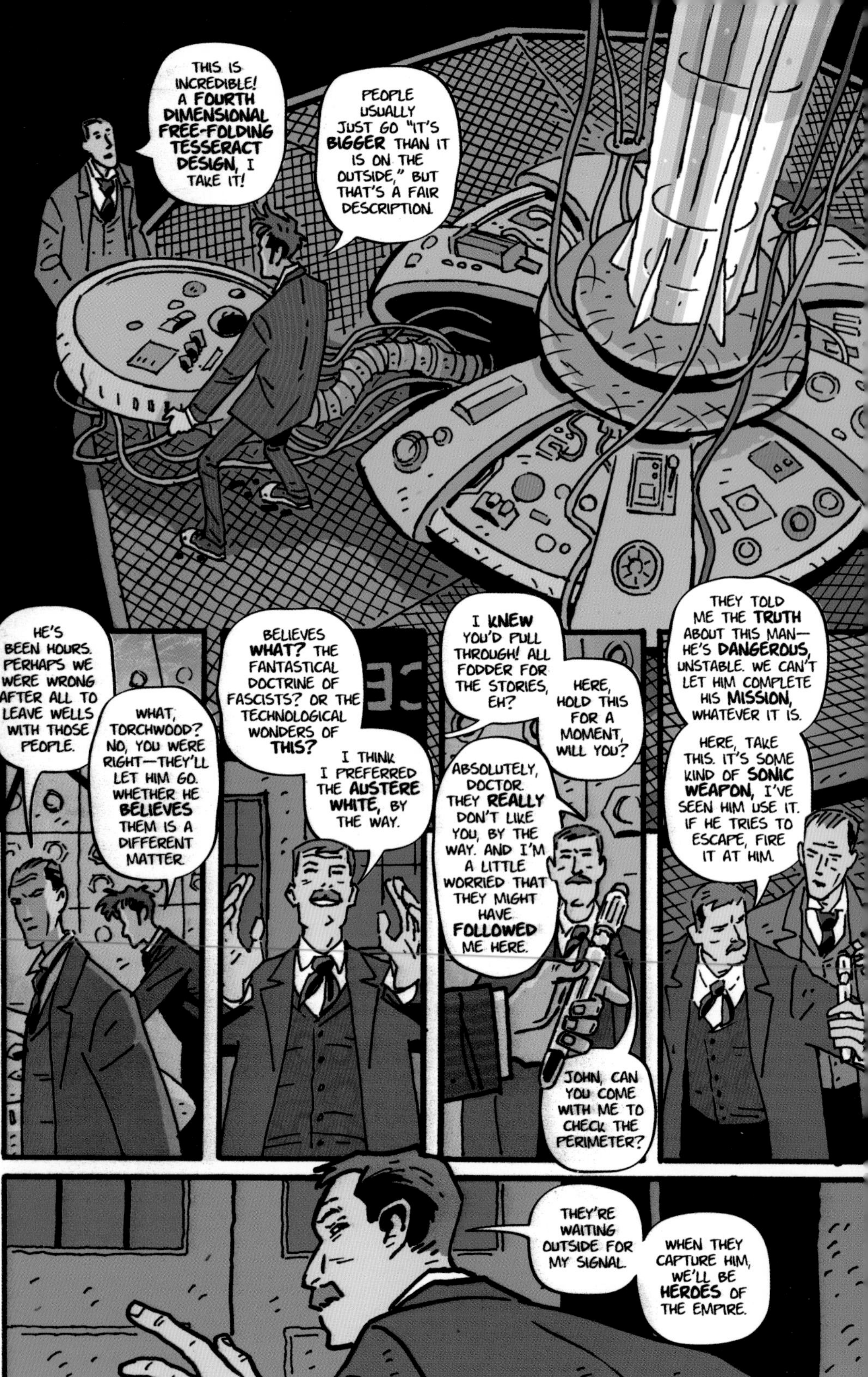
THIS IS INCREDIBLE! A FOURTH DIMENSIONAL FREE-FOLDING TESSERACT DESIGN, I TAKE IT!
PEOPLE USUALLY JUST GO "IT'S BIGGER THAN IT IS ON THE OUTSIDE," BUT THAT'S A FAIR DESCRIPTION.
HE'S BEEN HOURS. PERHAPS WE WERE WRONG AFTER ALL TO LEAVE WELLS WITH THOSE PEOPLE.
WHAT, TORCHWOOD? NO, YOU WERE RIGHT—THEY'LL LET HIM GO. WHETHER HE BELIEVES THEM IS A DIFFERENT MATTER.
BELIEVES WHAT? THE FANTASTICAL DOCTRINE OF FASCISTS? OR THE TECHNOLOGICAL WONDERS OF THIS?
I THINK I PREFERRED THE AUSTERE WHITE, BY THE WAY.
I KNEW YOU'D PULL THROUGH! ALL FODDER FOR THE STORIES, EH?
HERE, HOLD THIS FOR A MOMENT, WILL YOU?
ABSOLUTELY, DOCTOR. THEY REALLY DON'T LIKE YOU, BY THE WAY. AND I'M A LITTLE WORRIED THAT THEY MIGHT HAVE FOLLOWED ME HERE.
JOHN, CAN YOU COME WITH ME TO CHECK THE PERIMETER?
THEY TOLD ME THE TRUTH ABOUT THIS MAN—HE'S DANGEROUS, UNSTABLE. WE CAN'T LET HIM COMPLETE HIS MISSION, WHATEVER IT IS.
HERE, TAKE THIS. IT'S SOME KIND OF SONIC WEAPON, I'VE SEEN HIM USE IT. IF HE TRIES TO ESCAPE, FIRE IT AT HIM.
THEY'RE WAITING OUTSIDE FOR MY SIGNAL.
WHEN THEY CAPTURE HIM, WE'LL BE HEROES OF THE EMPIRE.

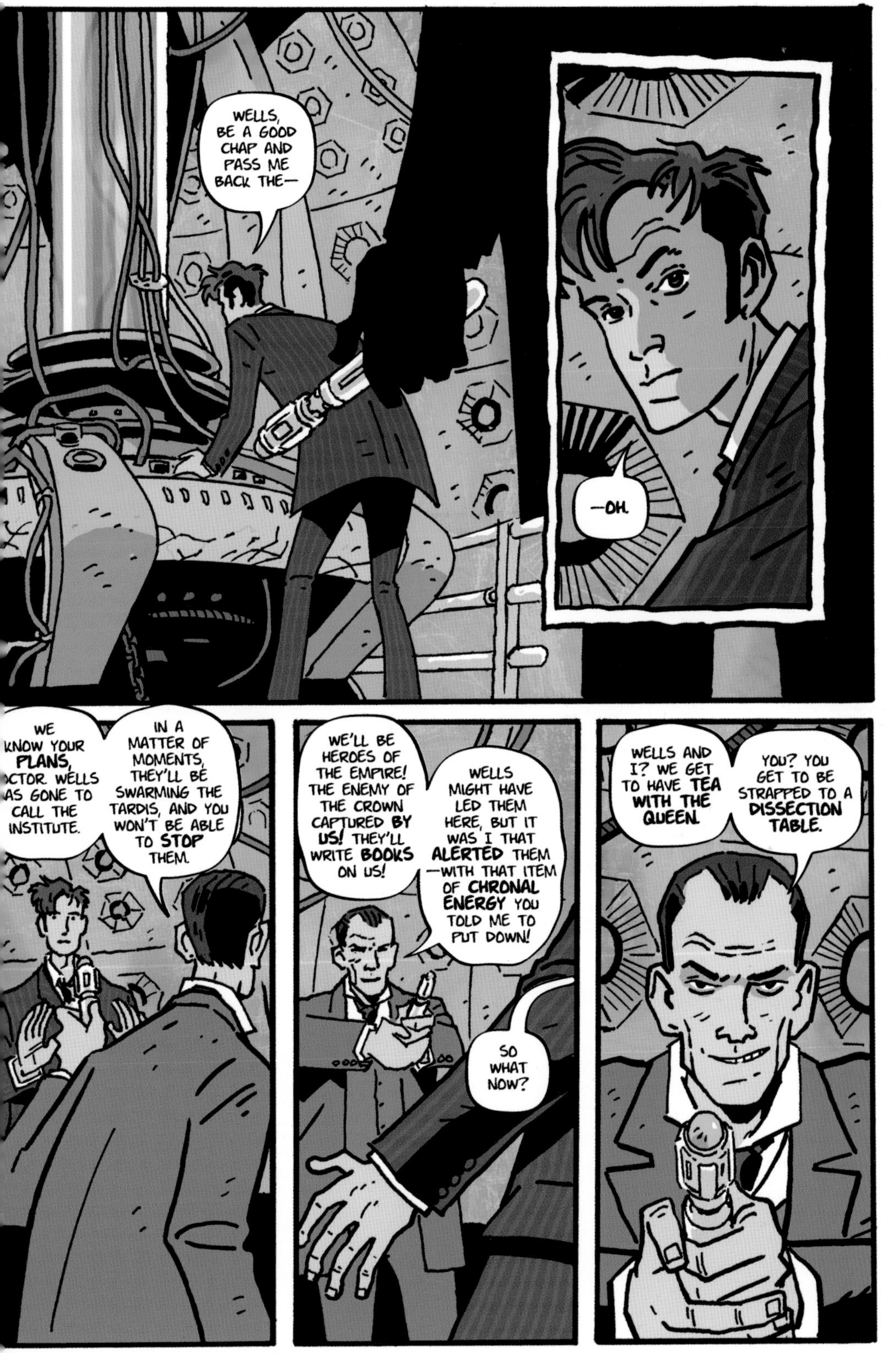
WELLS, BE A GOOD CHAP AND PASS ME BACK THE—
—OH.
WE KNOW YOUR PLANS, OCTOR. WELLS AS GONE TO CALL THE INSTITUTE.
IN A MATTER OF MOMENTS, THEY'LL BE SWARMING THE TARDIS, AND YOU WON'T BE ABLE TO STOP THEM.
WE'LL BE HEROES OF THE EMPIRE! THE ENEMY OF THE CROWN CAPTURED BY US! THEY'LL WRITE BOOKS ON US!
WELLS MIGHT HAVE LED THEM HERE, BUT IT WAS I THAT ALERTED THEM —WITH THAT ITEM OF CHRONAL ENERGY YOU TOLD ME TO PUT DOWN!
SO WHAT NOW?
WELLS AND I? WE GET TO HAVE TEA WITH THE QUEEN.
YOU? YOU GET TO BE STRAPPED TO A DISSECTION TABLE.

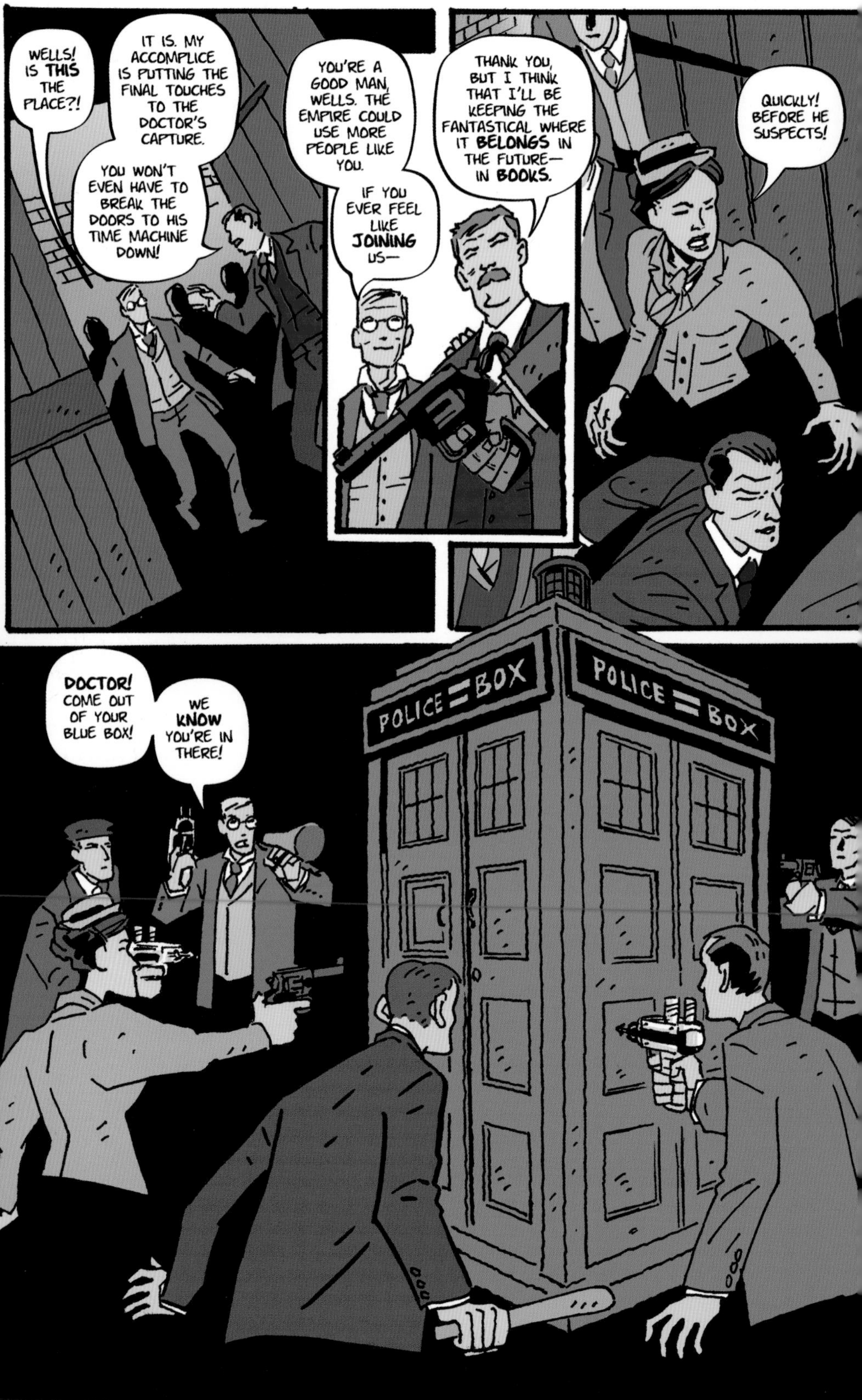
WELLS! IS THIS THE PLACE?!
IT IS. MY ACCOMPLICE IS PUTTING THE FINAL TOUCHES TO THE DOCTOR'S CAPTURE.
YOU WON'T EVEN HAVE TO BREAK THE DOORS TO HIS TIME MACHINE DOWN!
YOU'RE A GOOD MAN, WELLS. THE EMPIRE COULD USE MORE PEOPLE LIKE YOU.
IF YOU EVER FEEL LIKE JOINING US—
THANK YOU, BUT I THINK THAT I'LL BE KEEPING THE FANTASTICAL WHERE IT BELONGS IN THE FUTURE— IN BOOKS.
QUICKLY! BEFORE HE SUSPECTS!
POLICE BOX
POLICE BOX
DOCTOR! COME OUT OF YOUR BLUE BOX!
WE KNOW YOU'RE IN THERE!

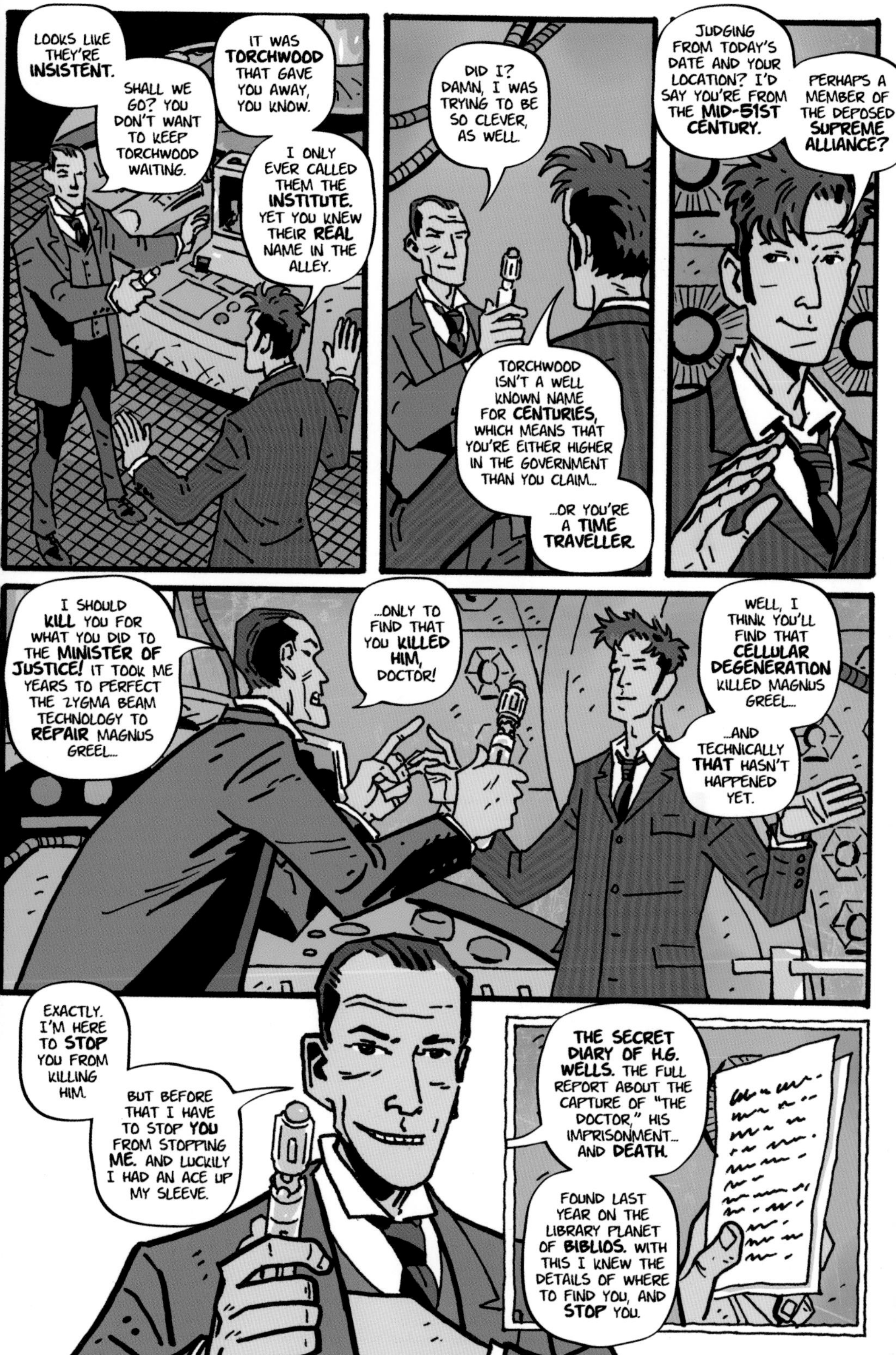
LOOKS LIKE THEY'RE INSISTENT.
SHALL WE GO? YOU DON'T WANT TO KEEP TORCHWOOD WAITING.
IT WAS TORCHWOOD THAT GAVE YOU AWAY, YOU KNOW.
I ONLY EVER CALLED THEM THE INSTITUTE. YET YOU KNEW THEIR REAL NAME IN THE ALLEY.
DID I? DAMN, I WAS TRYING TO BE SO CLEVER, AS WELL.
TORCHWOOD ISN'T A WELL KNOWN NAME FOR CENTURIES, WHICH MEANS THAT YOU'RE EITHER HIGHER IN THE GOVERNMENT THAN YOU CLAIM...
...OR YOU'RE A TIME TRAVELLER.
JUDGING FROM TODAY'S DATE AND YOUR LOCATION? I'D SAY YOU'RE FROM THE MID-51ST CENTURY.
PERHAPS A MEMBER OF THE DEPOSED SUPREME ALLIANCE?
I SHOULD KILL YOU FOR WHAT YOU DID TO THE MINISTER OF JUSTICE! IT TOOK ME YEARS TO PERFECT THE ZYGMA BEAM TECHNOLOGY TO REPAIR MAGNUS GREEL...
...ONLY TO FIND THAT YOU KILLED HIM, DOCTOR!
WELL, I THINK YOU'LL FIND THAT CELLULAR DEGENERATION KILLED MAGNUS GREEL...
...AND TECHNICALLY THAT HASN'T HAPPENED YET.
EXACTLY. I'M HERE TO STOP YOU FROM KILLING HIM.
BUT BEFORE THAT I HAVE TO STOP YOU FROM STOPPING ME. AND LUCKILY I HAD AN ACE UP MY SLEEVE.
THE SECRET DIARY OF H.G. WELLS. THE FULL REPORT ABOUT THE CAPTURE OF "THE DOCTOR," HIS IMPRISONMENT... AND DEATH.
FOUND LAST YEAR ON THE LIBRARY PLANET OF BIBLIOS. WITH THIS I KNEW THE DETAILS OF WHERE TO FIND YOU, AND STOP YOU.

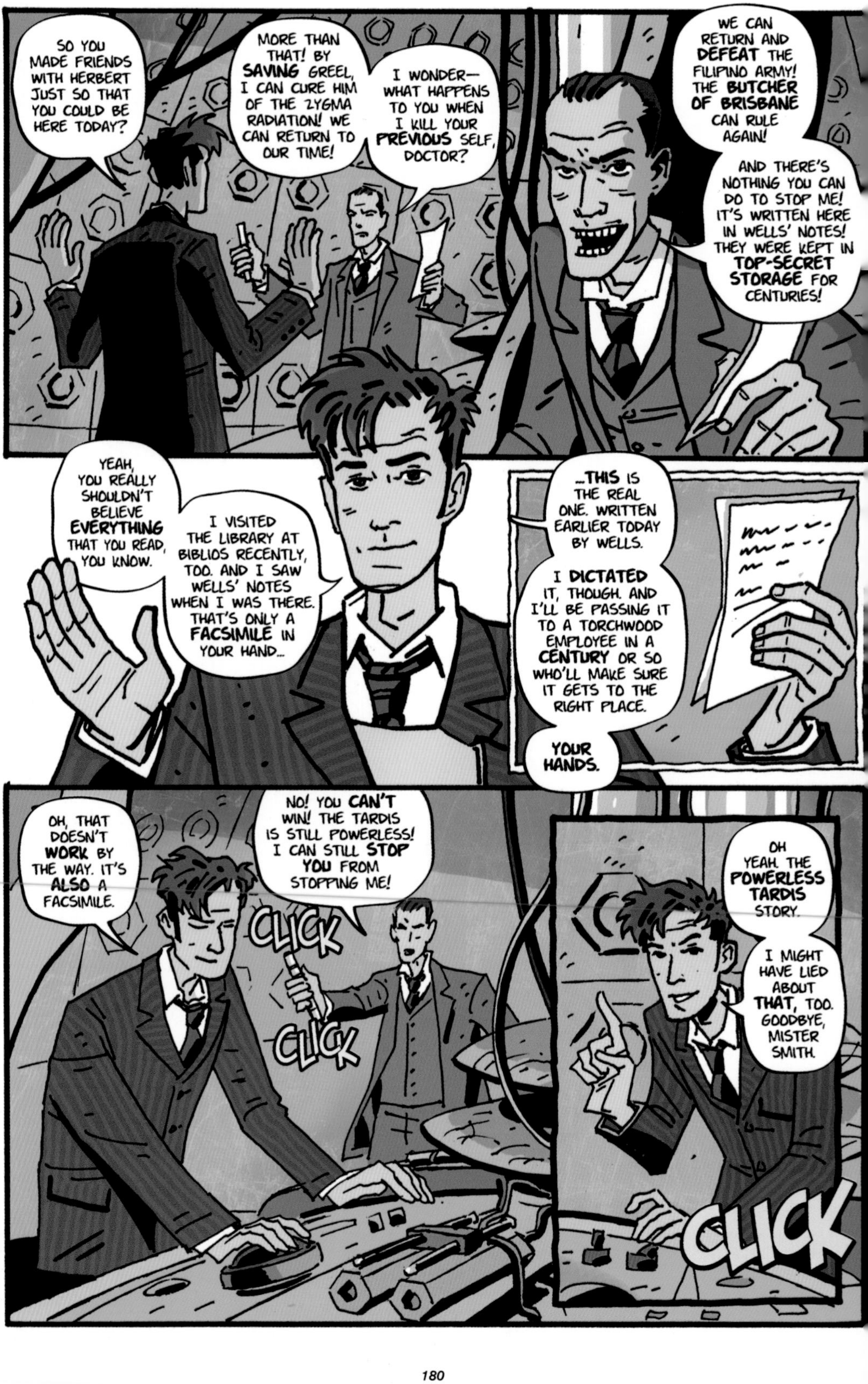
SO YOU MADE FRIENDS WITH HERBERT JUST SO THAT YOU COULD BE HERE TODAY?
MORE THAN THAT! BY SAVING GREEL, I CAN CURE HIM OF THE ZYGMA RADIATION! WE CAN RETURN TO OUR TIME!
I WONDER— WHAT HAPPENS TO YOU WHEN I KILL YOUR PREVIOUS SELF, DOCTOR?
WE CAN RETURN AND DEFEAT THE FILIPINO ARMY! THE BUTCHER OF BRISBANE CAN RULE AGAIN!
AND THERE'S NOTHING YOU CAN DO TO STOP ME! IT'S WRITTEN HERE IN WELLS' NOTES! THEY WERE KEPT IN TOP-SECRET STORAGE FOR CENTURIES!
YEAH, YOU REALLY SHOULDN'T BELIEVE EVERYTHING THAT YOU READ, YOU KNOW.
I VISITED THE LIBRARY AT BIBLIOS RECENTLY, TOO. AND I SAW WELLS' NOTES WHEN I WAS THERE. THAT'S ONLY A FACSIMILE IN YOUR HAND...
...THIS IS THE REAL ONE. WRITTEN EARLIER TODAY BY WELLS.
I DICTATED IT, THOUGH. AND I'LL BE PASSING IT TO A TORCHWOOD EMPLOYEE IN A CENTURY OR SO WHO'LL MAKE SURE IT GETS TO THE RIGHT PLACE.
YOUR HANDS.
OH, THAT DOESN'T WORK BY THE WAY. IT'S ALSO A FACSIMILE.
NO! YOU CAN'T WIN! THE TARDIS IS STILL POWERLESS! I CAN STILL STOP YOU FROM STOPPING ME!
CLICK
CLICK
OH YEAH. THE POWERLESS TARDIS STORY.
I MIGHT HAVE LIED ABOUT THAT, TOO. GOODBYE, MISTER SMITH.
CLICK

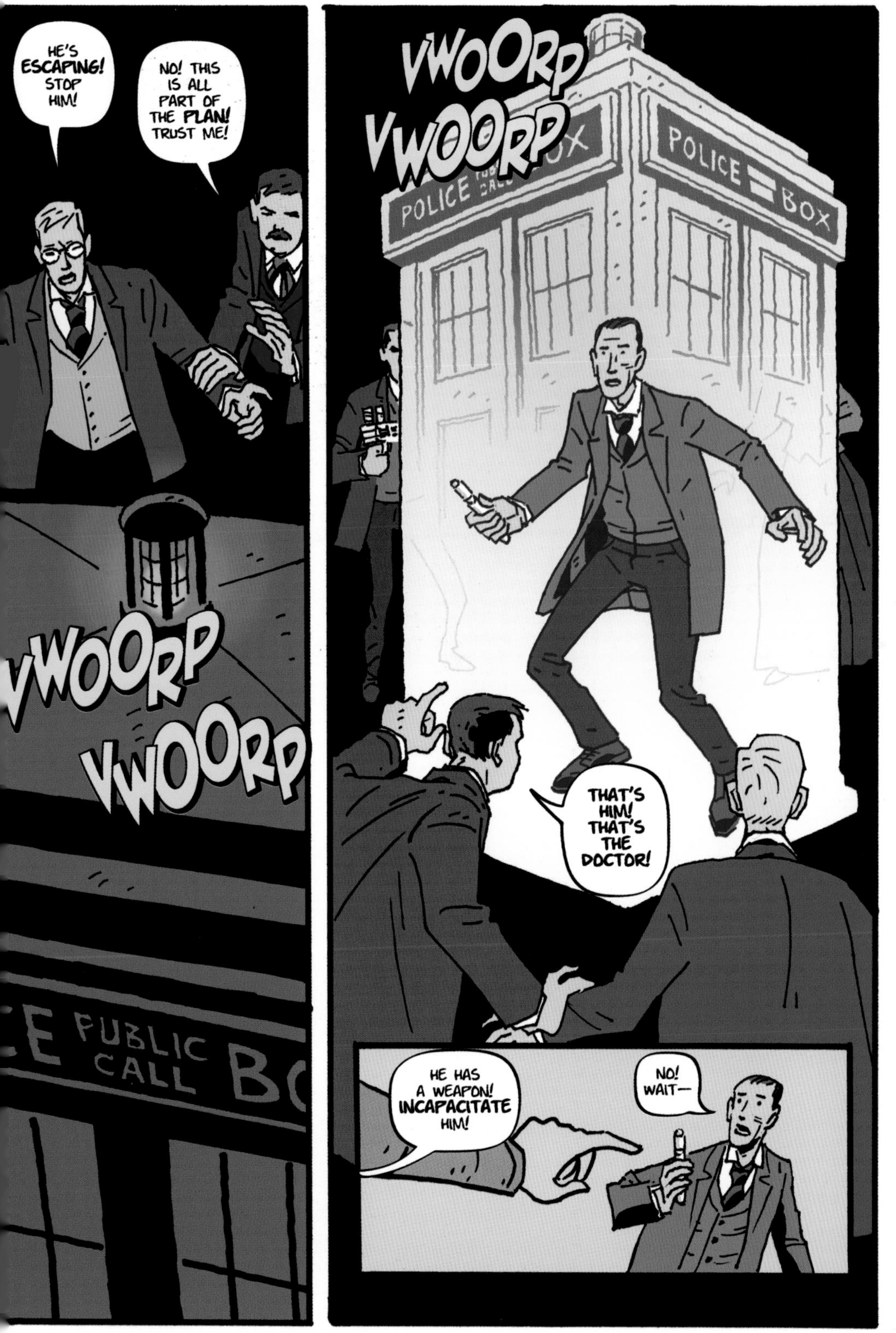
HE'S ESCAPING! STOP HIM!
NO! THIS IS ALL PART OF THE PLAN! TRUST ME!
VWOORP
VWOORP
PUBLIC CALL
VWOORP
VWOORP
POLICE BOX
POLICE PUBLIC CALL BOX
THAT'S HIM! THAT'S THE DOCTOR!
HE HAS A WEAPON! INCAPACITATE HIM!
NO! WAIT—

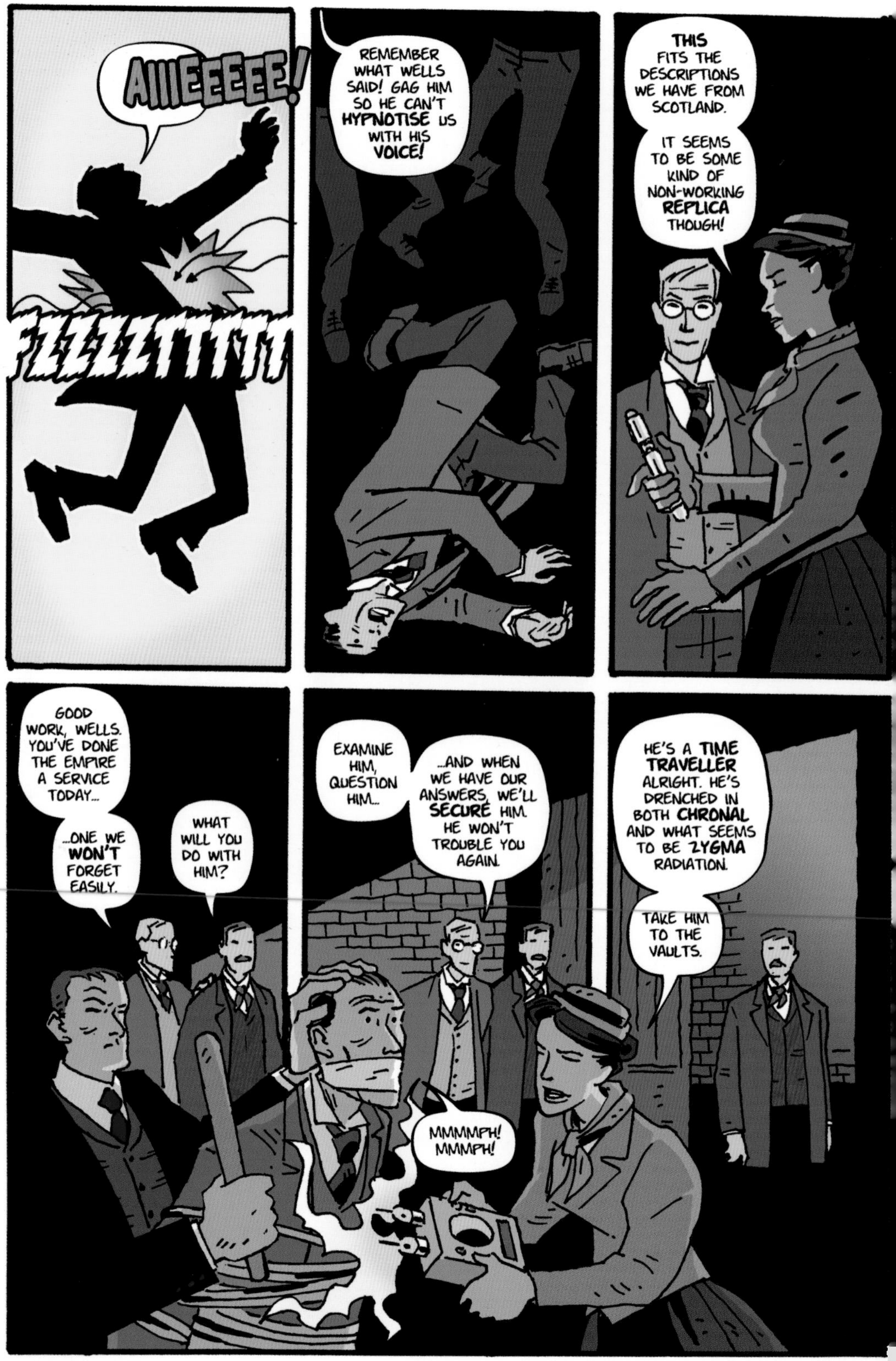
AIIIEEEEEE!
FZZZZZTTTTTT
REMEMBER WHAT WELLS SAID! GAG HIM SO HE CAN'T HYPNOTISE US WITH HIS VOICE!
THIS FITS THE DESCRIPTIONS WE HAVE FROM SCOTLAND.
IT SEEMS TO BE SOME KIND OF NON-WORKING REPLICA THOUGH!
GOOD WORK, WELLS. YOU'VE DONE THE EMPIRE A SERVICE TODAY...
...ONE WE WON'T FORGET EASILY.
WHAT WILL YOU DO WITH HIM?
EXAMINE HIM, QUESTION HIM...
...AND WHEN WE HAVE OUR ANSWERS, WE'LL SECURE HIM. HE WON'T TROUBLE YOU AGAIN.
MMMMPH! MMMPH!
HE'S A TIME TRAVELLER ALRIGHT. HE'S DRENCHED IN BOTH CHRONAL AND WHAT SEEMS TO BE ZYGMA RADIATION.
TAKE HIM TO THE VAULTS.

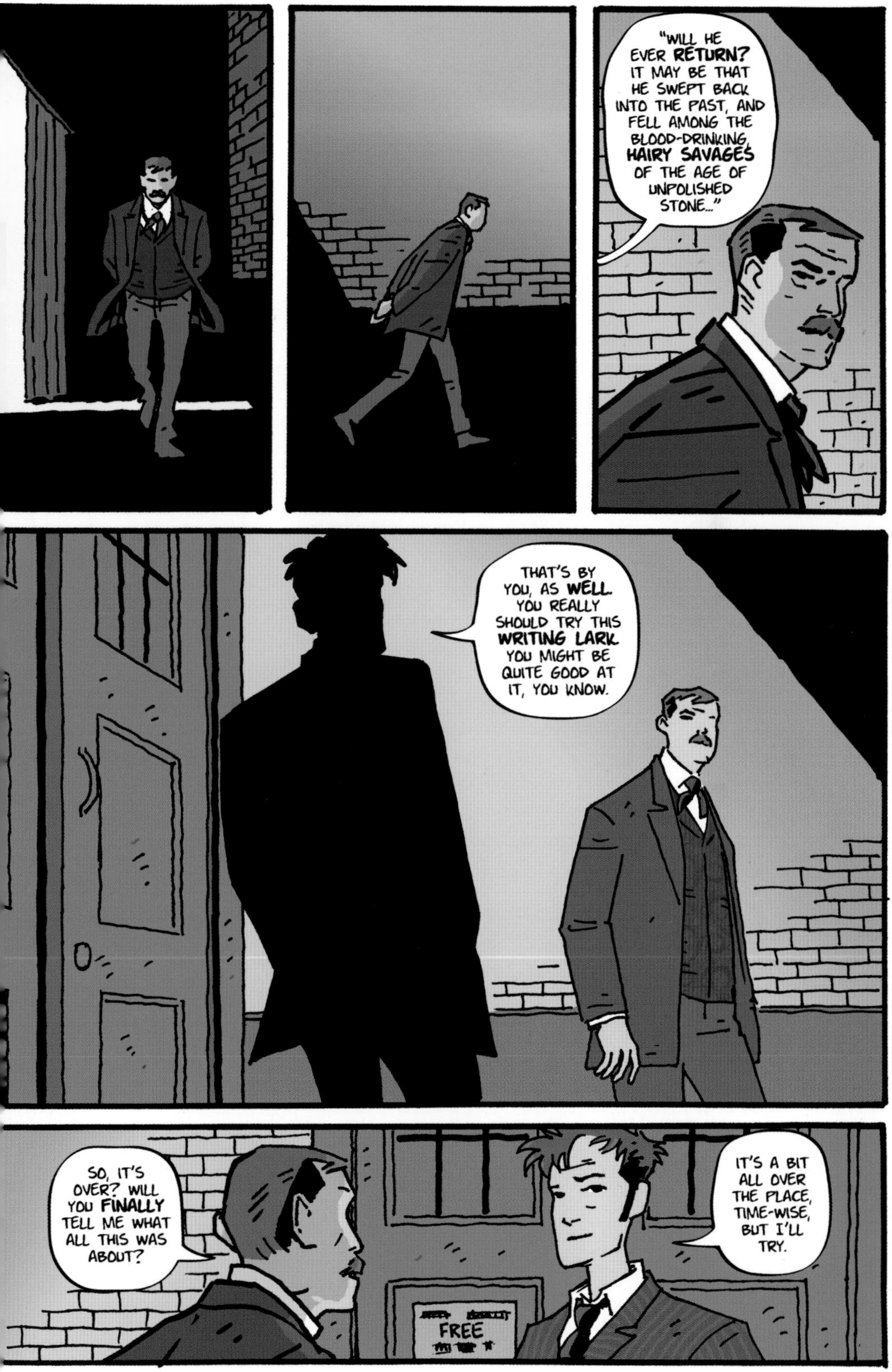
"WILL HE EVER RETURN? IT MAY BE THAT HE SWEPT BACK INTO THE PAST, AND FELL AMONG THE BLOOD-DRINKING, HAIRY SAVAGES OF THE AGE OF UNPOLISHED STONE..."
THAT'S BY YOU, AS WELL. YOU REALLY SHOULD TRY THIS WRITING LARK. YOU MIGHT BE QUITE GOOD AT IT, YOU KNOW.
SO, IT'S OVER? WILL YOU FINALLY TELL ME WHAT ALL THIS WAS ABOUT?
IT'S A BIT ALL OVER THE PLACE, TIME-WISE, BUT I'LL TRY.
FREE

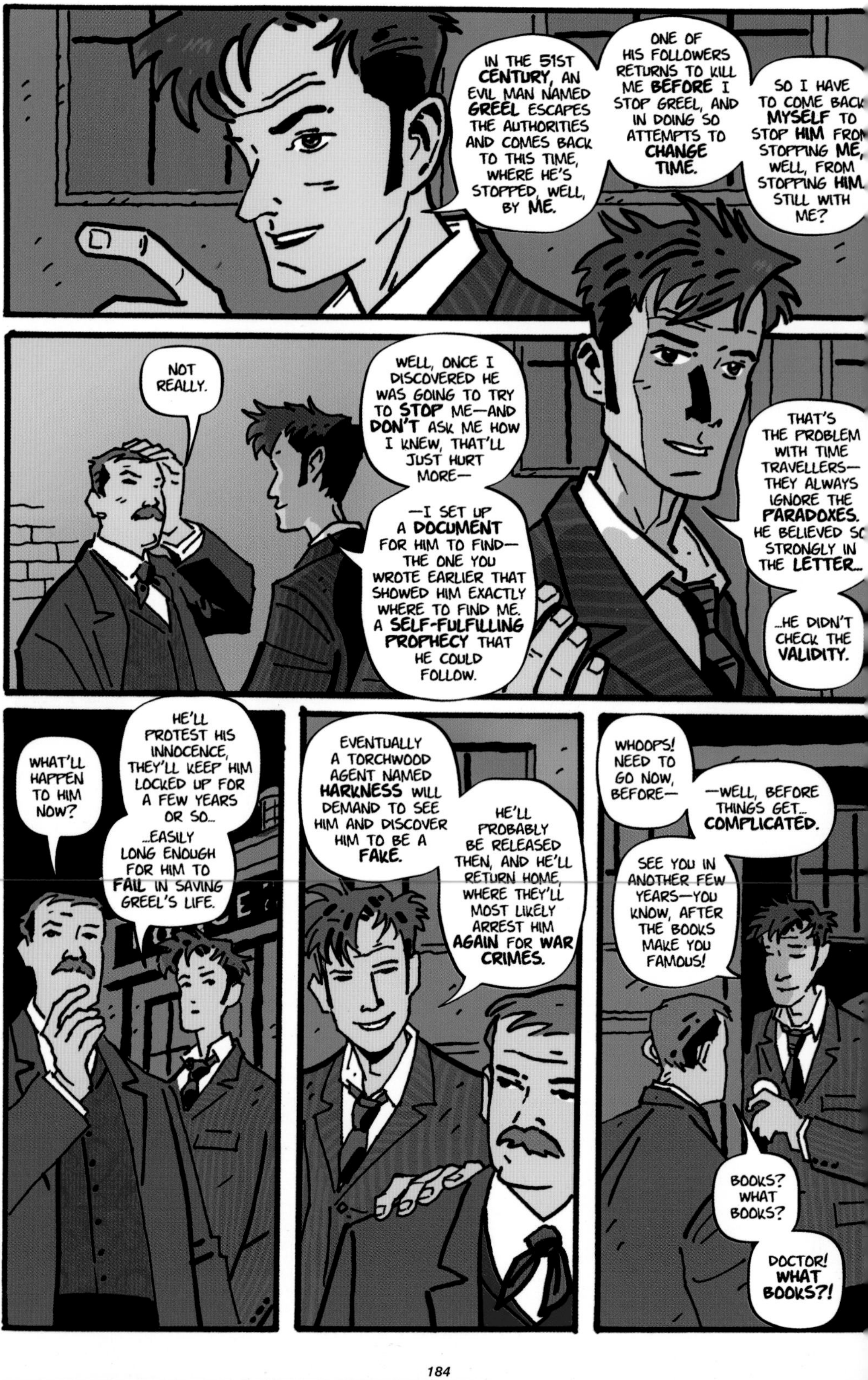
IN THE 51ST CENTURY, AN EVIL MAN NAMED GREEL ESCAPES THE AUTHORITIES AND COMES BACK TO THIS TIME, WHERE HE'S STOPPED, WELL, BY ME.
ONE OF HIS FOLLOWERS RETURNS TO KILL ME BEFORE I STOP GREEL, AND IN DOING SO ATTEMPTS TO CHANGE TIME.
SO I HAVE TO COME BACK MYSELF TO STOP HIM FROM STOPPING ME, WELL, FROM STOPPING HIM. STILL WITH ME?
NOT REALLY.
WELL, ONCE I DISCOVERED HE WAS GOING TO TRY TO STOP ME—AND DON'T ASK ME HOW I KNEW, THAT'LL JUST HURT MORE—
—I SET UP A DOCUMENT FOR HIM TO FIND—THE ONE YOU WROTE EARLIER THAT SHOWED HIM EXACTLY WHERE TO FIND ME. A SELF-FULFILLING PROPHECY THAT HE COULD FOLLOW.
THAT'S THE PROBLEM WITH TIME TRAVELLERS—THEY ALWAYS IGNORE THE PARADOXES. HE BELIEVED SO STRONGLY IN THE LETTER...
...HE DIDN'T CHECK THE VALIDITY.
WHAT'LL HAPPEN TO HIM NOW?
HE'LL PROTEST HIS INNOCENCE, THEY'LL KEEP HIM LOCKED UP FOR A FEW YEARS OR SO...
...EASILY LONG ENOUGH FOR HIM TO FAIL IN SAVING GREEL'S LIFE.
EVENTUALLY A TORCHWOOD AGENT NAMED HARKNESS WILL DEMAND TO SEE HIM AND DISCOVER HIM TO BE A FAKE.
HE'LL PROBABLY BE RELEASED THEN, AND HE'LL RETURN HOME, WHERE THEY'LL MOST LIKELY ARREST HIM AGAIN FOR WAR CRIMES.
WHOOPS! NEED TO GO NOW, BEFORE—
—WELL, BEFORE THINGS GET... COMPLICATED.
SEE YOU IN ANOTHER FEW YEARS—YOU KNOW, AFTER THE BOOKS MAKE YOU FAMOUS!
BOOKS? WHAT BOOKS?
DOCTOR! WHAT BOOKS?!

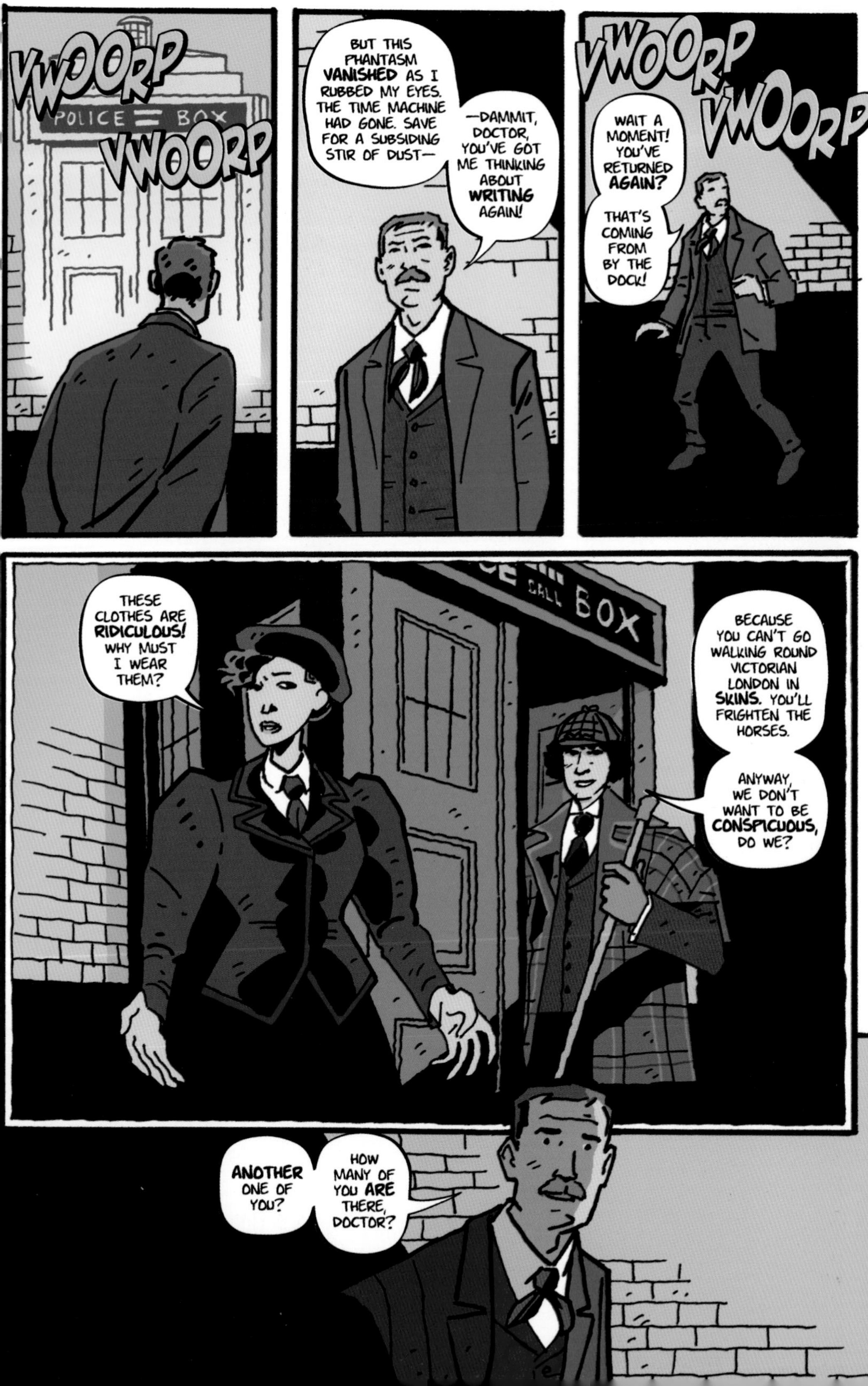
VWOORP
POLICE BOX
VWOORP
BUT THIS PHANTASM VANISHED AS I RUBBED MY EYES. THE TIME MACHINE HAD GONE. SAVE FOR A SUBSIDING STIR OF DUST—
—DAMMIT, DOCTOR, YOU'VE GOT ME THINKING ABOUT WRITING AGAIN!
VWOORP
VWOORP
WAIT A MOMENT! YOU'VE RETURNED AGAIN?
THAT'S COMING FROM BY THE DOCK!
THESE CLOTHES ARE RIDICULOUS! WHY MUST I WEAR THEM?
CALL BOX
BECAUSE YOU CAN'T GO WALKING ROUND VICTORIAN LONDON IN SKINS. YOU'LL FRIGHTEN THE HORSES.
ANYWAY, WE DON'T WANT TO BE CONSPICUOUS, DO WE?
ANOTHER ONE OF YOU?
HOW MANY OF YOU ARE THERE, DOCTOR?

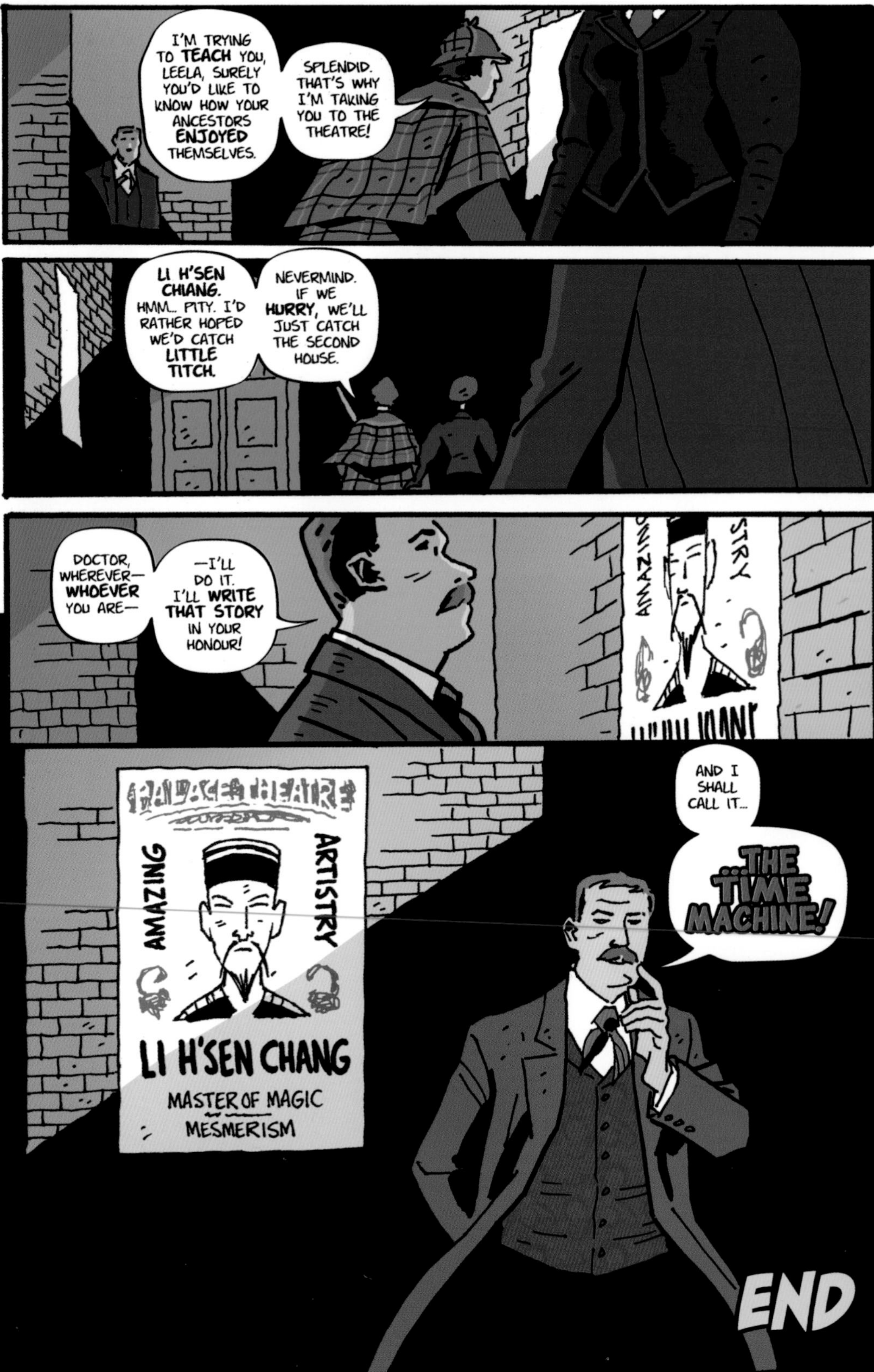
I'M TRYING TO TEACH YOU, LEELA, SURELY YOU'D LIKE TO KNOW HOW YOUR ANCESTORS ENJOYED THEMSELVES.
SPLENDID. THAT'S WHY I'M TAKING YOU TO THE THEATRE!
LI H'SEN CHIANG. HMM... PITY. I'D RATHER HOPED WE'D CATCH LITTLE TITCH.
NEVERMIND. IF WE HURRY, WE'LL JUST CATCH THE SECOND HOUSE.
DOCTOR, WHEREVER— WHOEVER YOU ARE—
—I'LL DO IT. I'LL WRITE THAT STORY IN YOUR HONOUR!
AMAZING
STRY
AMAZING
ARTISTRY
LI H'SEN CHANG
MASTER OF MAGIC
MESMERISM
AND I SHALL CALL IT...
...THE TIME MACHINE!
END

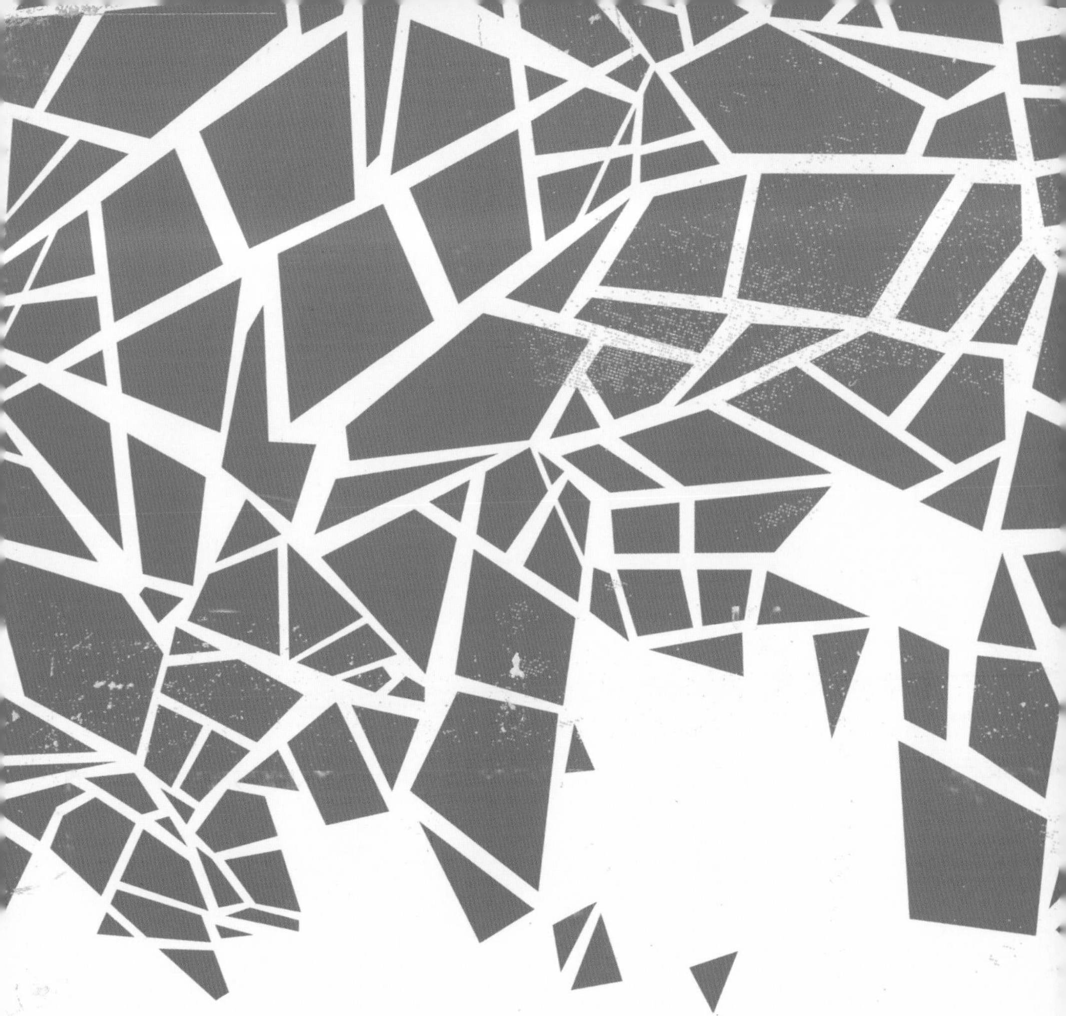

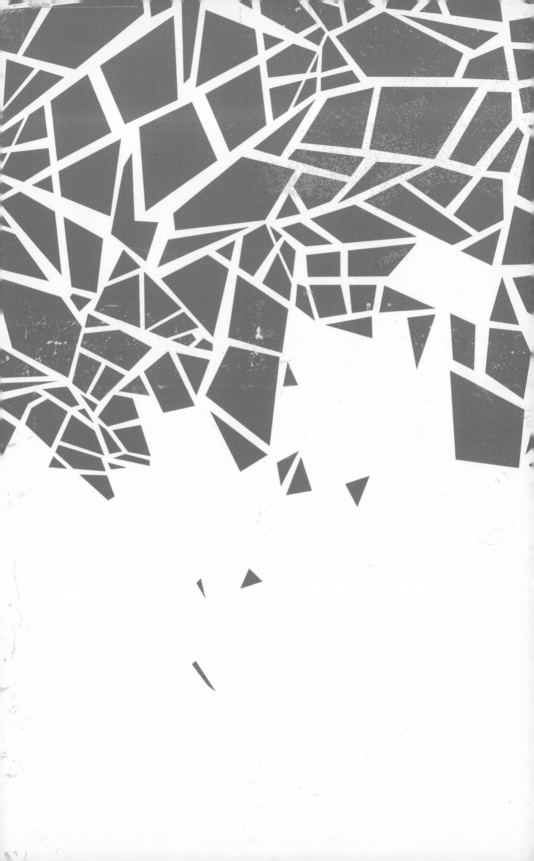

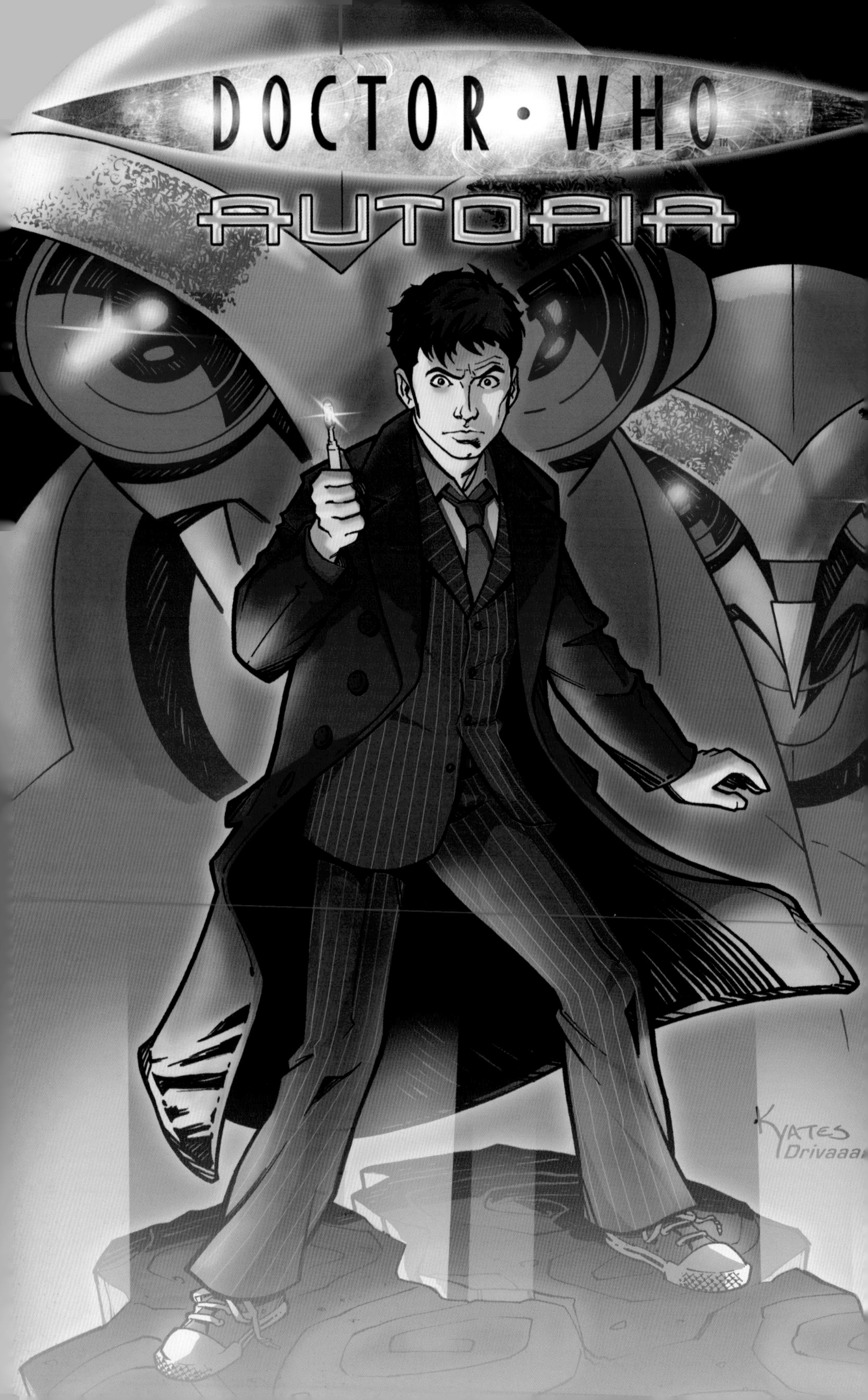
DOCTOR · WHO
AUTOPIA
KYATES

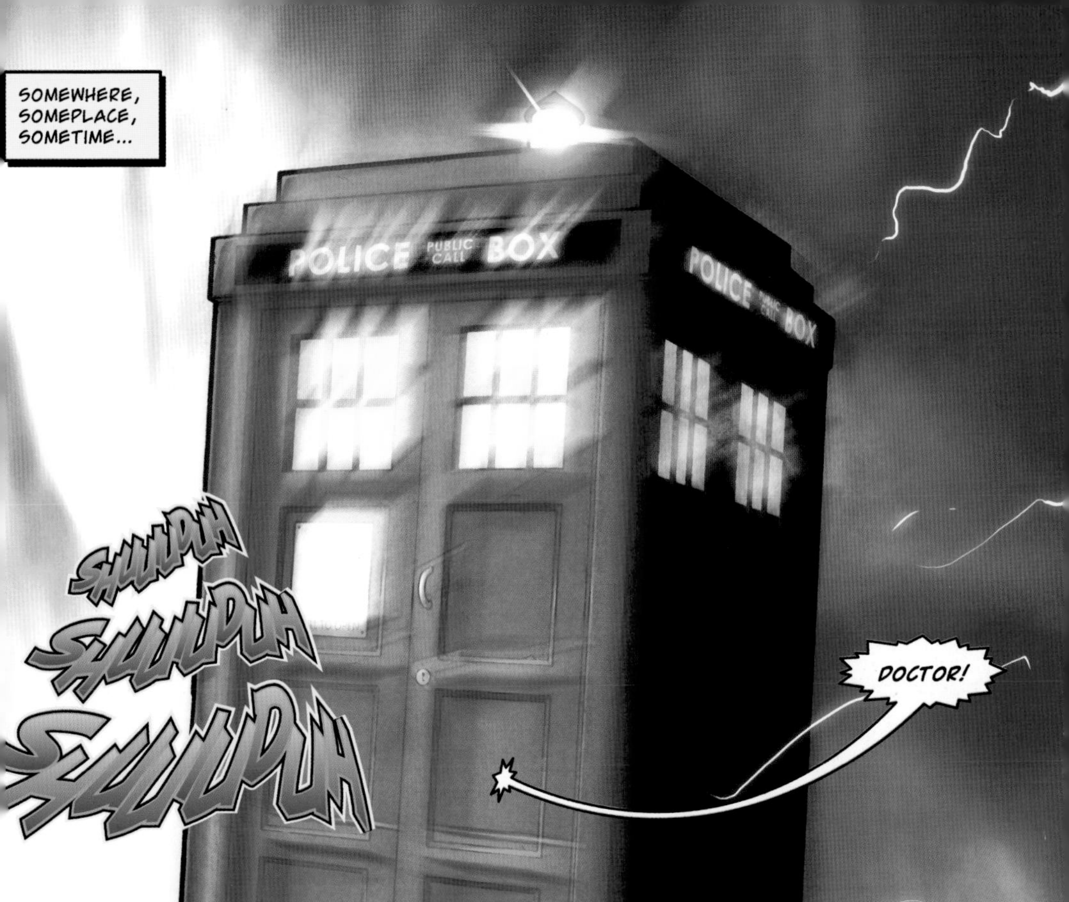
SOMEWHERE, SOMEPLACE, SOMETIME...
POLICE PUBLIC CALL BOX
POLICE PUBLIC CALL BOX
SHUUDUH
SHUUDUH
SHUUDUH
DOCTOR!

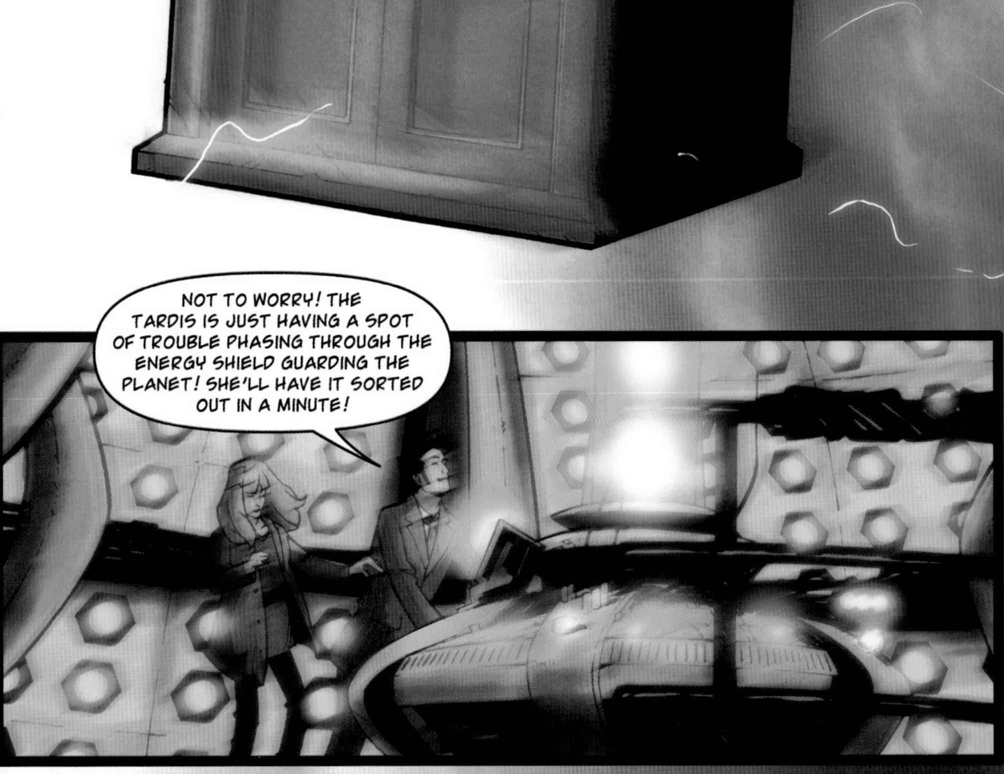
NOT TO WORRY! THE TARDIS IS JUST HAVING A SPOT OF TROUBLE PHASING THROUGH THE ENERGY SHIELD GUARDING THE PLANET! SHE'LL HAVE IT SORTED OUT IN A MINUTE!

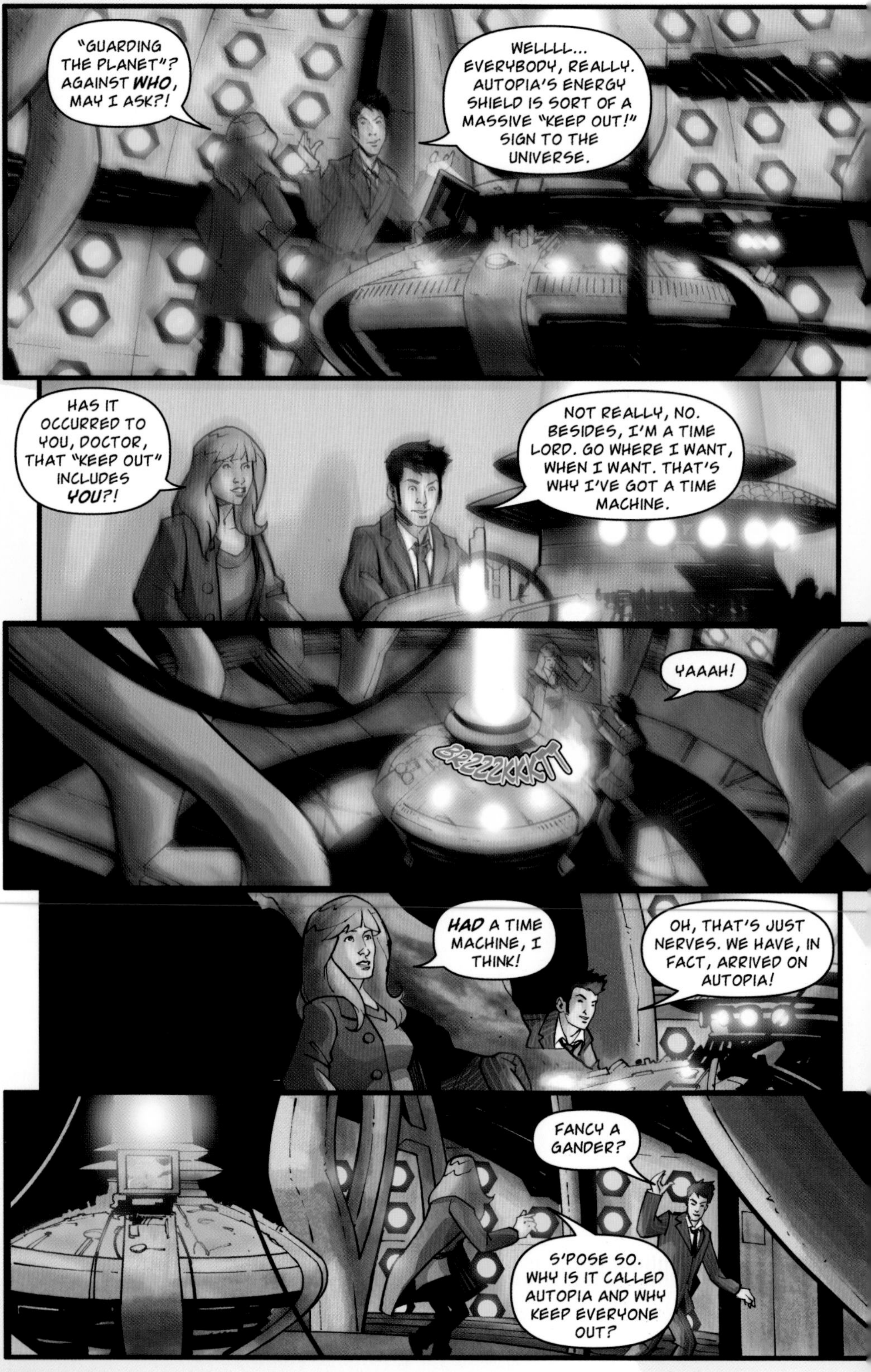
"GUARDING THE PLANET"? AGAINST ***WHO***, MAY I ASK?!
WELLLL... EVERYBODY, REALLY. AUTOPIA'S ENERGY SHIELD IS SORT OF A MASSIVE "KEEP OUT!" SIGN TO THE UNIVERSE.
HAS IT OCCURRED TO YOU, DOCTOR, THAT "KEEP OUT" INCLUDES ***YOU***?!
NOT REALLY, NO. BESIDES, I'M A TIME LORD. GO WHERE I WANT, WHEN I WANT. THAT'S WHY I'VE GOT A TIME MACHINE.
BRZZZKKKTT
YAAAH!
HAD A TIME MACHINE, I THINK!
OH, THAT'S JUST NERVES. WE HAVE, IN FACT, ARRIVED ON AUTOPIA!
FANCY A GANDER?
S'POSE SO. WHY IS IT CALLED AUTOPIA AND WHY KEEP EVERYONE OUT?

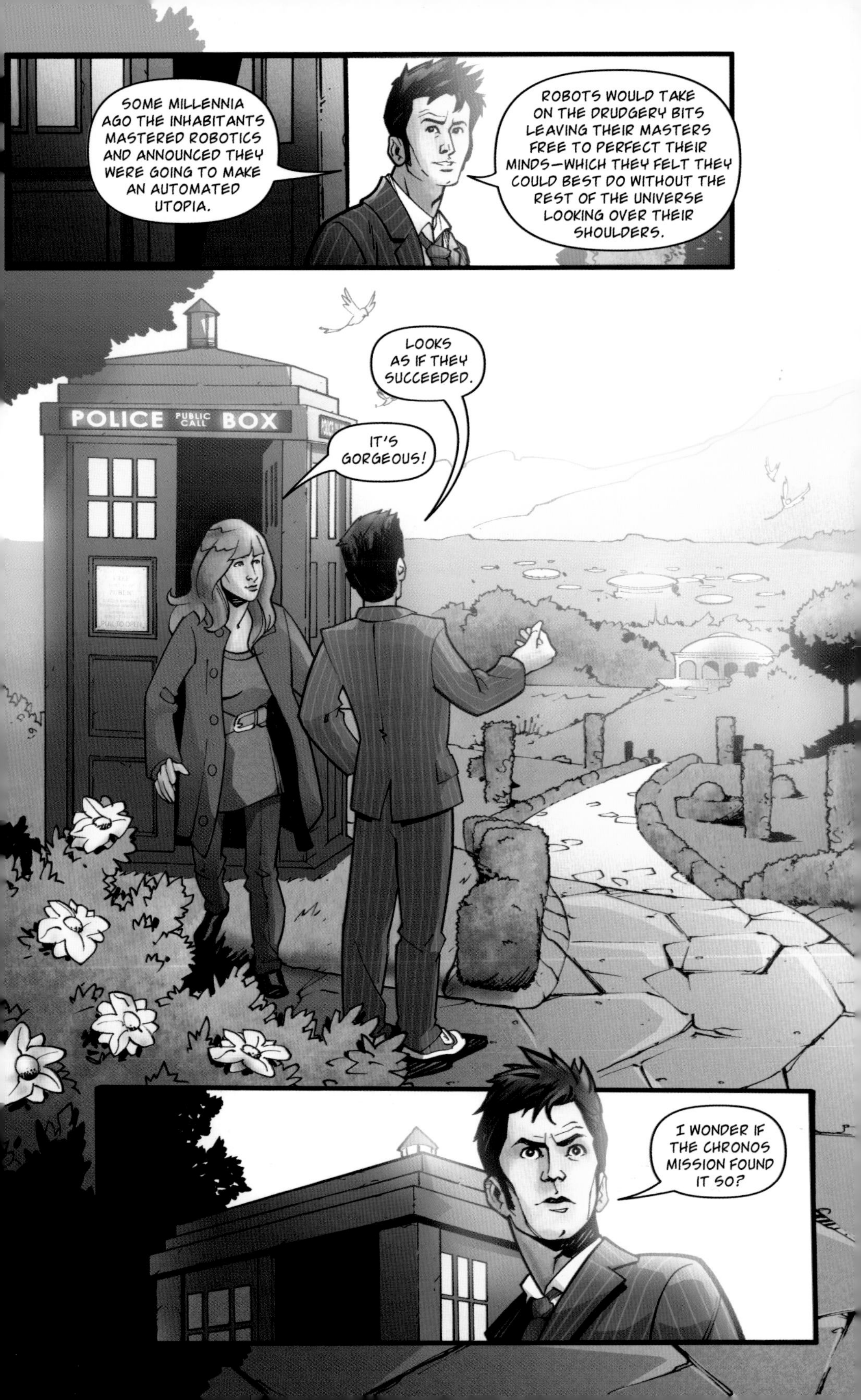
SOME MILLENNIA AGO THE INHABITANTS MASTERED ROBOTICS AND ANNOUNCED THEY WERE GOING TO MAKE AN AUTOMATED UTOPIA.
ROBOTS WOULD TAKE ON THE DRUDGERY BITS LEAVING THEIR MASTERS FREE TO PERFECT THEIR MINDS—WHICH THEY FELT THEY COULD BEST DO WITHOUT THE REST OF THE UNIVERSE LOOKING OVER THEIR SHOULDERS.
LOOKS AS IF THEY SUCCEEDED.
IT'S GORGEOUS!
POLICE PUBLIC CALL BOX
PULL TO OPEN
I WONDER IF THE CHRONOS MISSION FOUND IT SO?

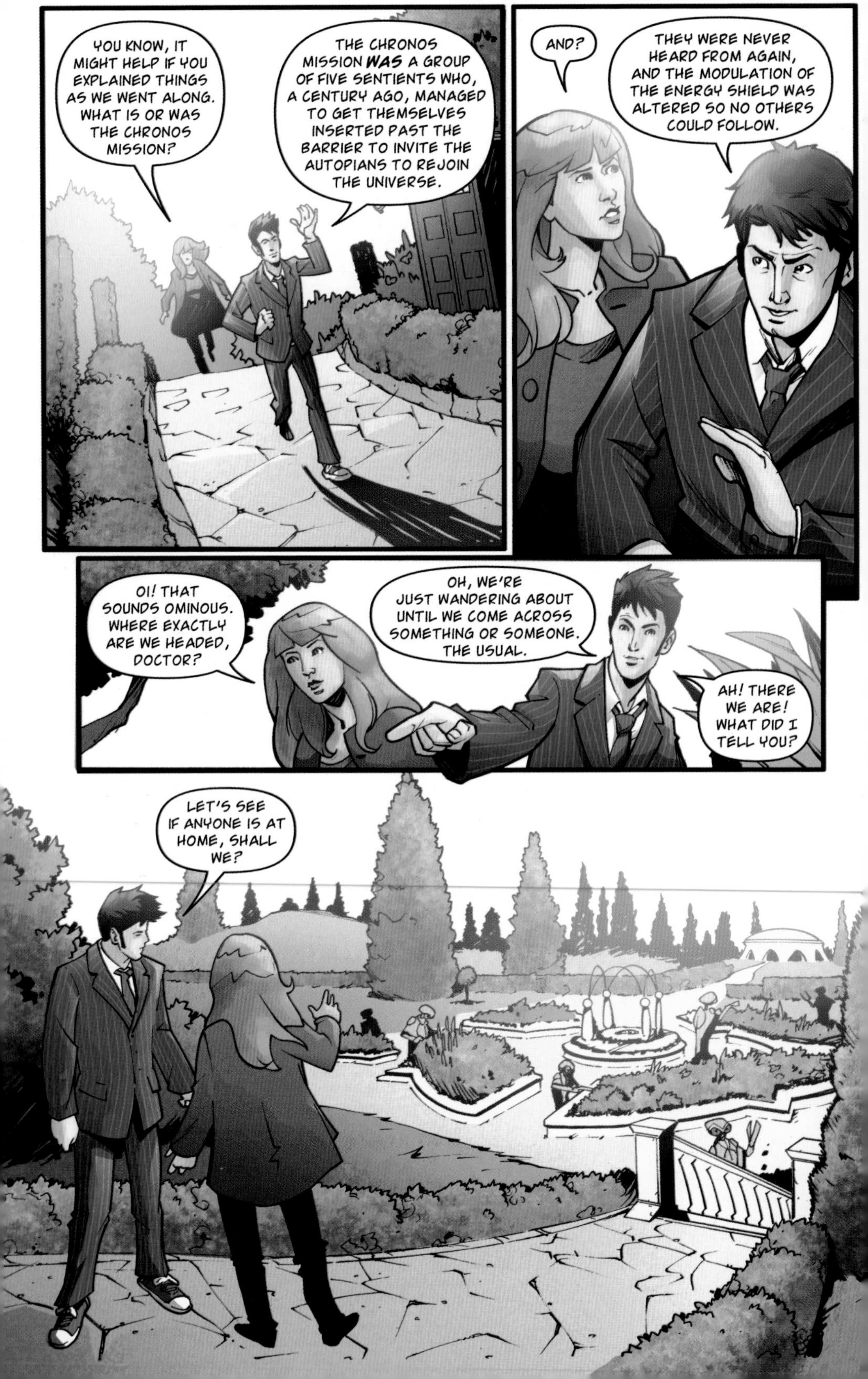
YOU KNOW, IT MIGHT HELP IF YOU EXPLAINED THINGS AS WE WENT ALONG. WHAT IS OR WAS THE CHRONOS MISSION?
THE CHRONOS MISSION **WAS** A GROUP OF FIVE SENTIENTS WHO, A CENTURY AGO, MANAGED TO GET THEMSELVES INSERTED PAST THE BARRIER TO INVITE THE AUTOPIANS TO REJOIN THE UNIVERSE.
AND?
THEY WERE NEVER HEARD FROM AGAIN, AND THE MODULATION OF THE ENERGY SHIELD WAS ALTERED SO NO OTHERS COULD FOLLOW.
OI! THAT SOUNDS OMINOUS. WHERE EXACTLY ARE WE HEADED, DOCTOR?
OH, WE'RE JUST WANDERING ABOUT UNTIL WE COME ACROSS SOMETHING OR SOMEONE. THE USUAL.
AH! THERE WE ARE! WHAT DID I TELL YOU?
LET'S SEE IF ANYONE IS AT HOME, SHALL WE?

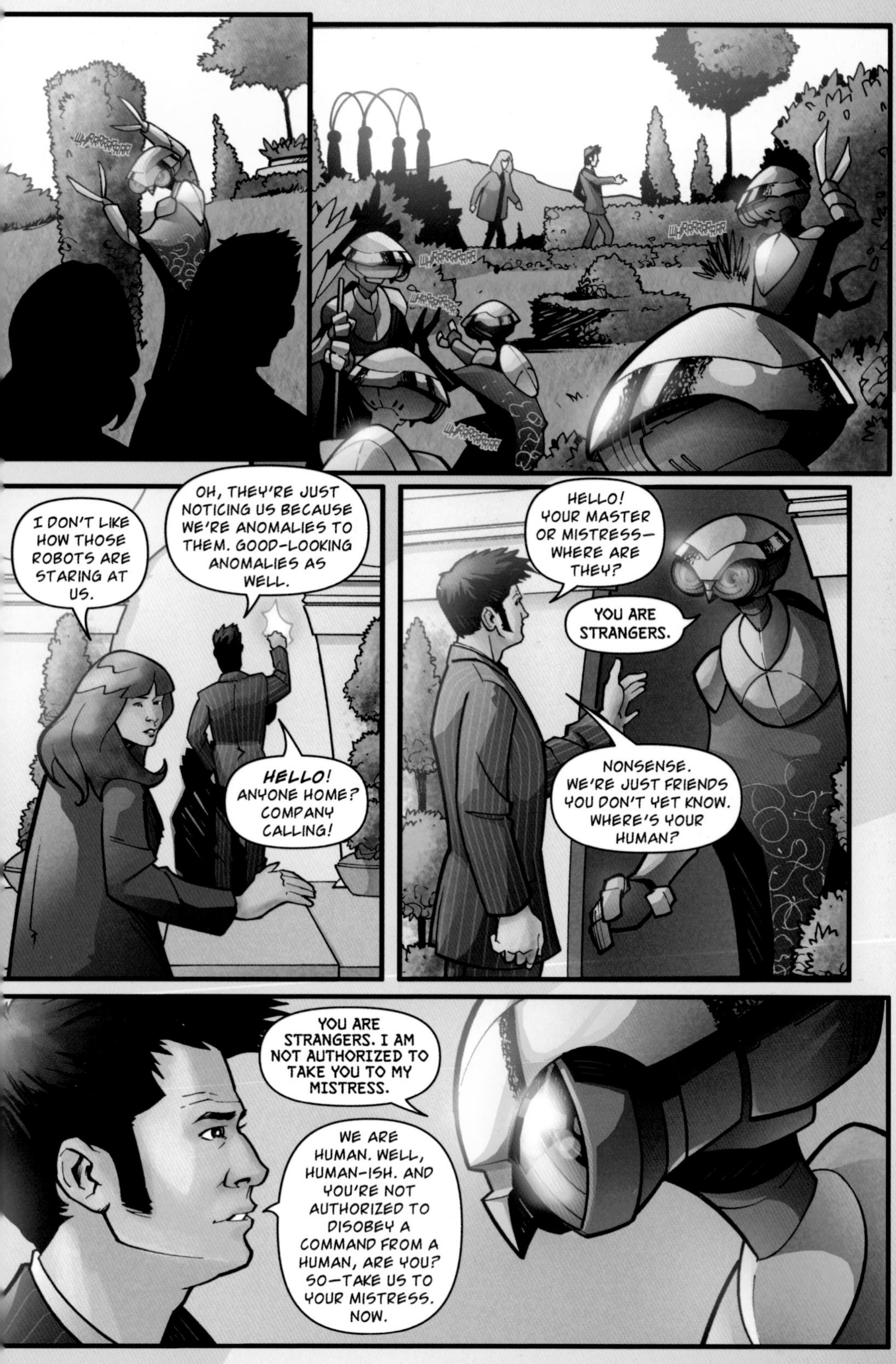
WHRRRRRRRR
WHRRRRRRRR
WHRRRRRRRR
WHRRRRRRRR
WHRRRRRRRR
I DON'T LIKE HOW THOSE ROBOTS ARE STARING AT US.
OH, THEY'RE JUST NOTICING US BECAUSE WE'RE ANOMALIES TO THEM. GOOD-LOOKING ANOMALIES AS WELL.
HELLO! ANYONE HOME? COMPANY CALLING!
HELLO! YOUR MASTER OR MISTRESS— WHERE ARE THEY?
YOU ARE STRANGERS.
NONSENSE. WE'RE JUST FRIENDS YOU DON'T YET KNOW. WHERE'S YOUR HUMAN?
YOU ARE STRANGERS. I AM NOT AUTHORIZED TO TAKE YOU TO MY MISTRESS.
WE ARE HUMAN. WELL, HUMAN-ISH. AND YOU'RE NOT AUTHORIZED TO DISOBEY A COMMAND FROM A HUMAN, ARE YOU? SO—TAKE US TO YOUR MISTRESS. NOW.

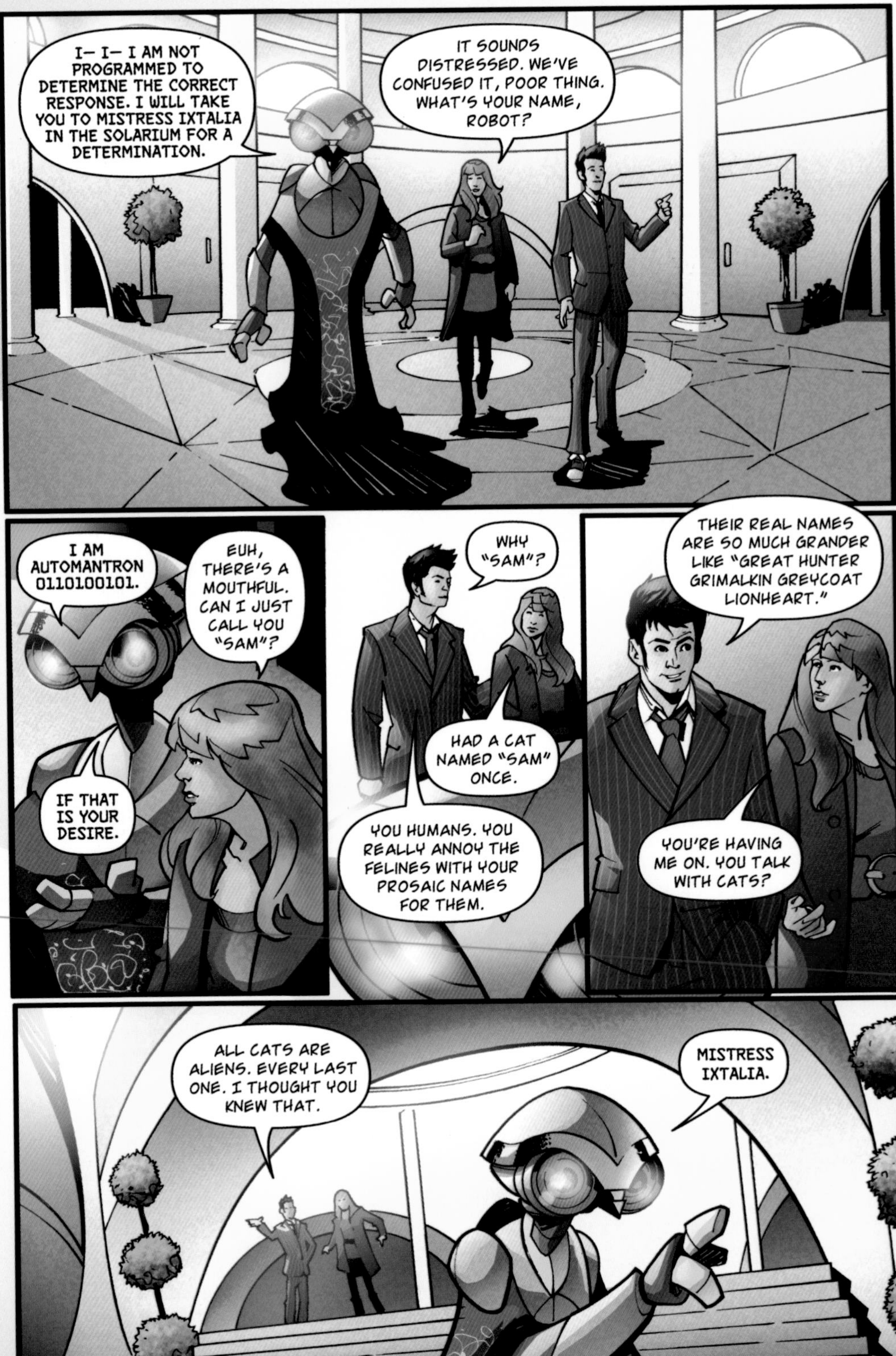
I— I— I AM NOT PROGRAMMED TO DETERMINE THE CORRECT RESPONSE. I WILL TAKE YOU TO MISTRESS IXTALIA IN THE SOLARIUM FOR A DETERMINATION.
IT SOUNDS DISTRESSED. WE'VE CONFUSED IT, POOR THING. WHAT'S YOUR NAME, ROBOT?
I AM AUTOMANTRON 0110100101.
EUH, THERE'S A MOUTHFUL. CAN I JUST CALL YOU "SAM"?
IF THAT IS YOUR DESIRE.
WHY "SAM"?
HAD A CAT NAMED "SAM" ONCE.
YOU HUMANS. YOU REALLY ANNOY THE FELINES WITH YOUR PROSAIC NAMES FOR THEM.
THEIR REAL NAMES ARE SO MUCH GRANDER LIKE "GREAT HUNTER GRIMALKIN GREYCOAT LIONHEART."
YOU'RE HAVING ME ON. YOU TALK WITH CATS?
ALL CATS ARE ALIENS. EVERY LAST ONE. I THOUGHT YOU KNEW THAT.
MISTRESS IXTALIA.

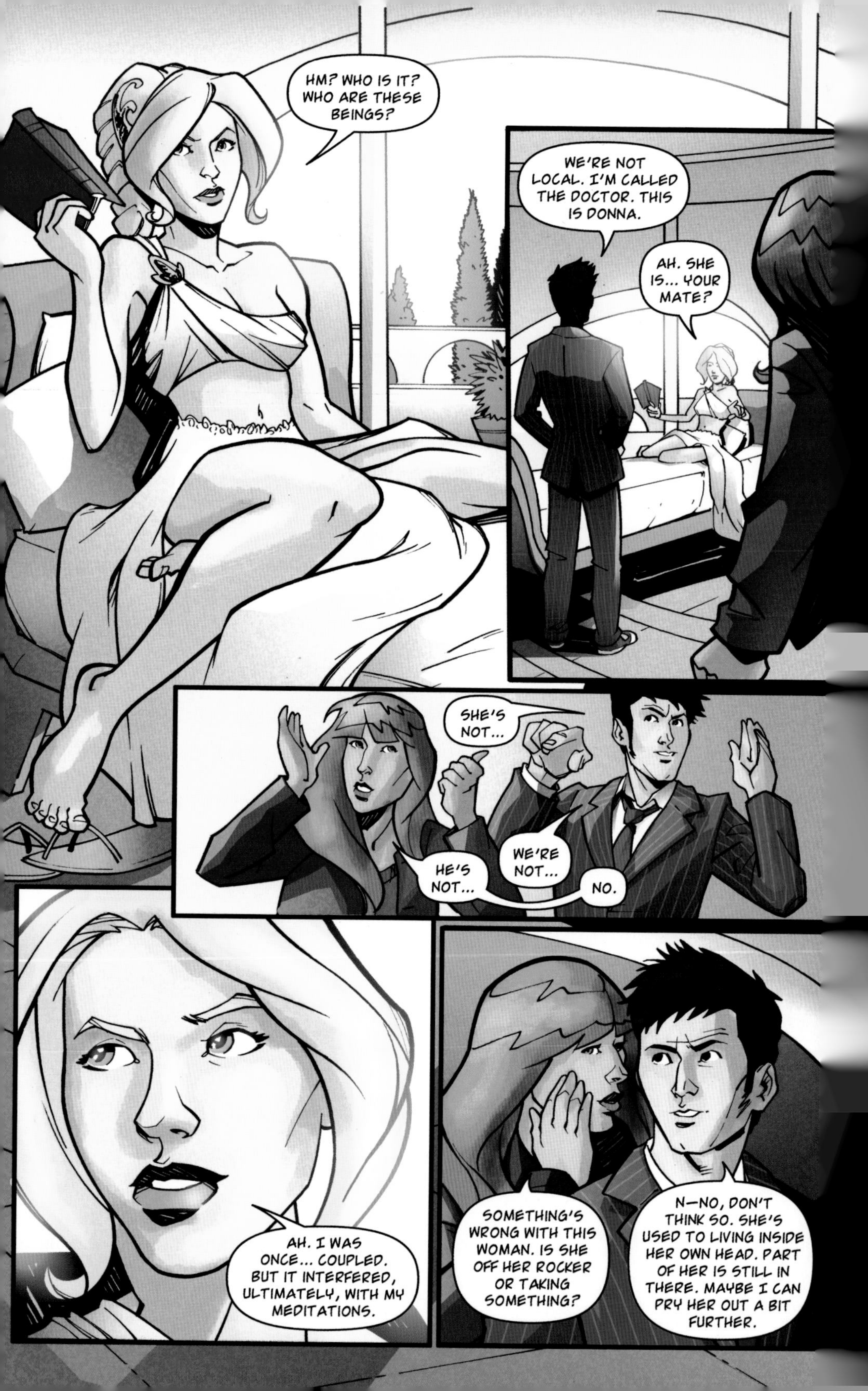
HM? WHO IS IT? WHO ARE THESE BEINGS?
WE'RE NOT LOCAL. I'M CALLED THE DOCTOR. THIS IS DONNA.
AH. SHE IS... YOUR MATE?
SHE'S NOT...
HE'S NOT...
WE'RE NOT...
NO.
AH. I WAS ONCE... COUPLED. BUT IT INTERFERED, ULTIMATELY, WITH MY MEDITATIONS.
SOMETHING'S WRONG WITH THIS WOMAN. IS SHE OFF HER ROCKER OR TAKING SOMETHING?
N—NO, DON'T THINK SO. SHE'S USED TO LIVING INSIDE HER OWN HEAD. PART OF HER IS STILL IN THERE. MAYBE I CAN PRY HER OUT A BIT FURTHER.

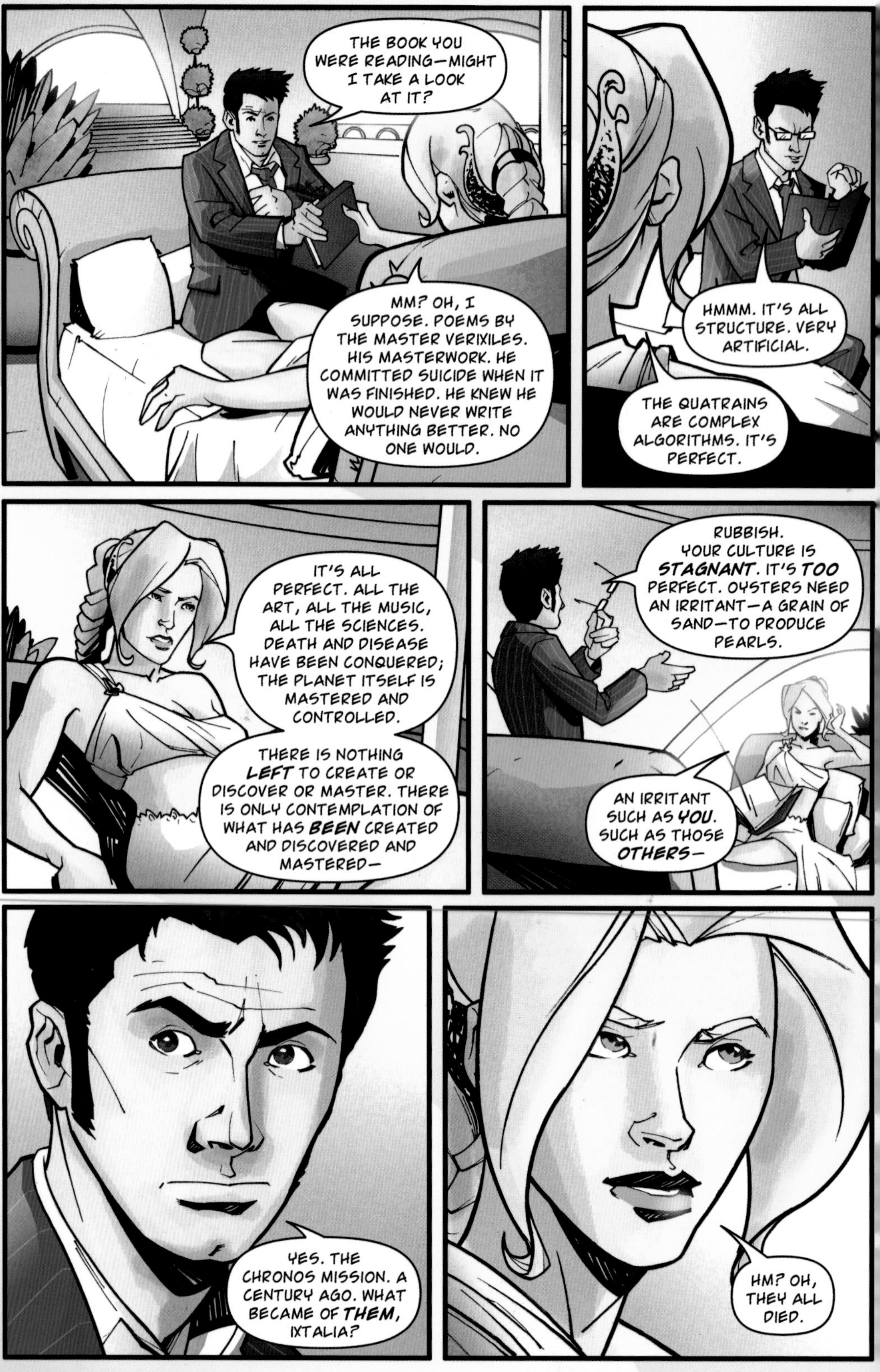
THE BOOK YOU WERE READING—MIGHT I TAKE A LOOK AT IT?
MM? OH, I SUPPOSE. POEMS BY THE MASTER VERIXILES. HIS MASTERWORK. HE COMMITTED SUICIDE WHEN IT WAS FINISHED. HE KNEW HE WOULD NEVER WRITE ANYTHING BETTER. NO ONE WOULD.
HMMM. IT'S ALL STRUCTURE. VERY ARTIFICIAL.
THE QUATRAINS ARE COMPLEX ALGORITHMS. IT'S PERFECT.
IT'S ALL PERFECT. ALL THE ART, ALL THE MUSIC, ALL THE SCIENCES. DEATH AND DISEASE HAVE BEEN CONQUERED; THE PLANET ITSELF IS MASTERED AND CONTROLLED.
THERE IS NOTHING **LEFT** TO CREATE OR DISCOVER OR MASTER. THERE IS ONLY CONTEMPLATION OF WHAT HAS **BEEN** CREATED AND DISCOVERED AND MASTERED—
RUBBISH. YOUR CULTURE IS **STAGNANT**. IT'S **TOO** PERFECT. OYSTERS NEED AN IRRITANT—A GRAIN OF SAND—TO PRODUCE PEARLS.
AN IRRITANT SUCH AS **YOU**. SUCH AS THOSE **OTHERS**—
YES. THE CHRONOS MISSION. A CENTURY AGO. WHAT BECAME OF **THEM**, IXTALIA?
HM? OH, THEY ALL DIED.

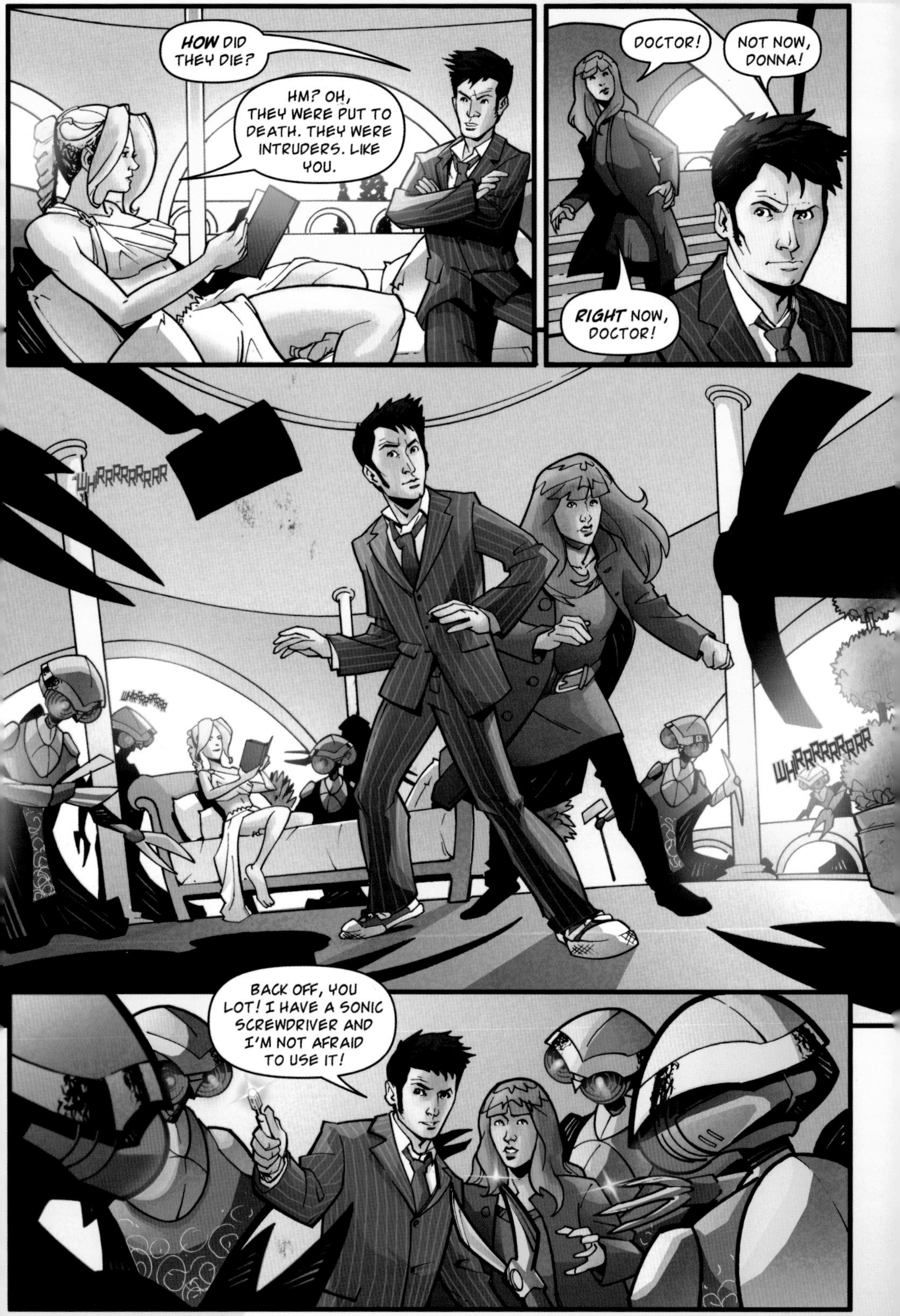
HOW DID THEY DIE?
HM? OH, THEY WERE PUT TO DEATH. THEY WERE INTRUDERS. LIKE YOU.
DOCTOR!
NOT NOW, DONNA!
RIGHT NOW, DOCTOR!
WHIRRRRRRRR
WHIRRRRRR
WHIRRRRRRRR
BACK OFF, YOU LOT! I HAVE A SONIC SCREWDRIVER AND I'M NOT AFRAID TO USE IT!

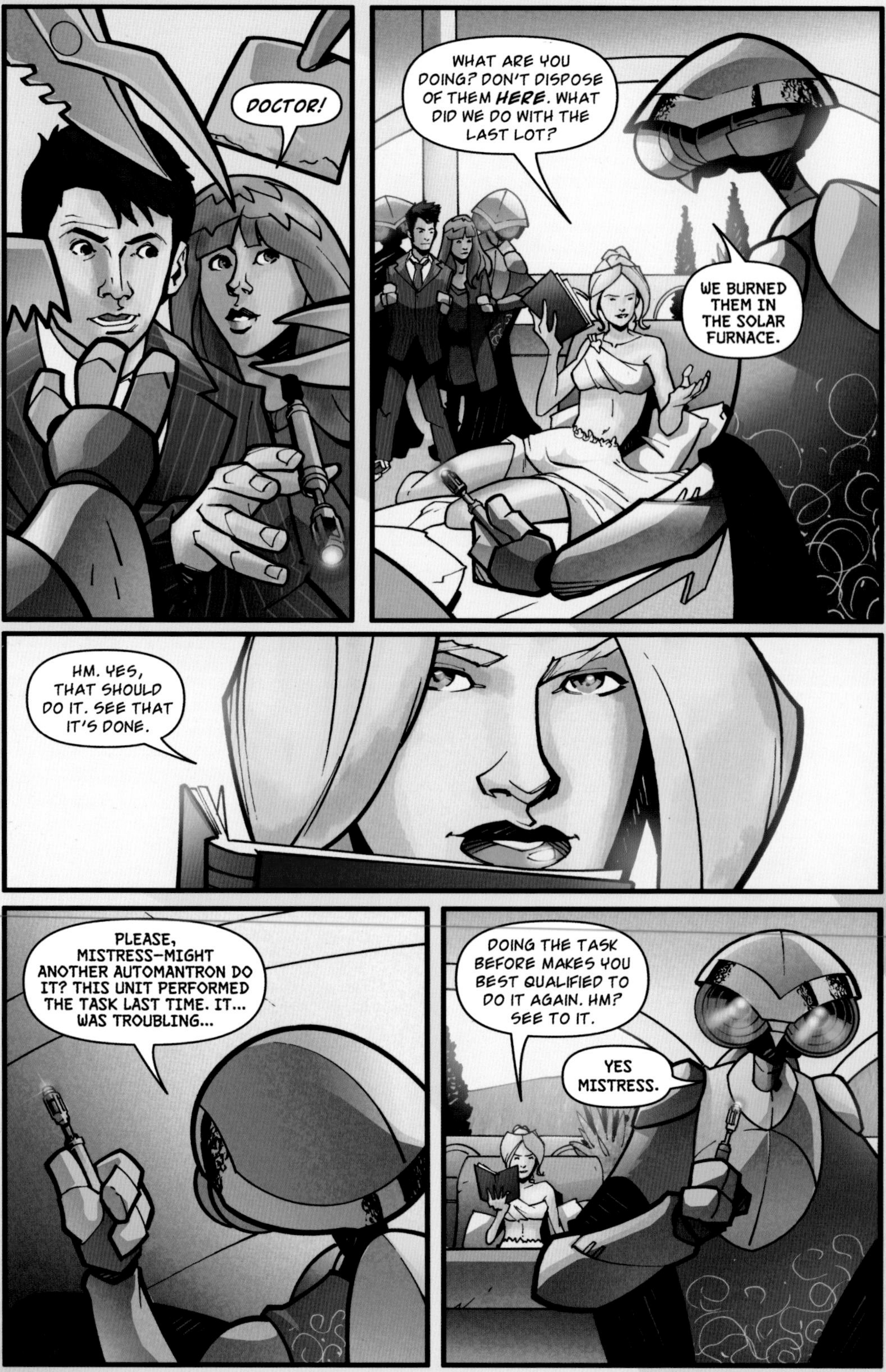
DOCTOR!
WHAT ARE YOU DOING? DON'T DISPOSE OF THEM HERE. WHAT DID WE DO WITH THE LAST LOT?
WE BURNED THEM IN THE SOLAR FURNACE.
HM. YES, THAT SHOULD DO IT. SEE THAT IT'S DONE.
PLEASE, MISTRESS—MIGHT ANOTHER AUTOMANTRON DO IT? THIS UNIT PERFORMED THE TASK LAST TIME. IT... WAS TROUBLING...
DOING THE TASK BEFORE MAKES YOU BEST QUALIFIED TO DO IT AGAIN. HM? SEE TO IT.
YES MISTRESS.

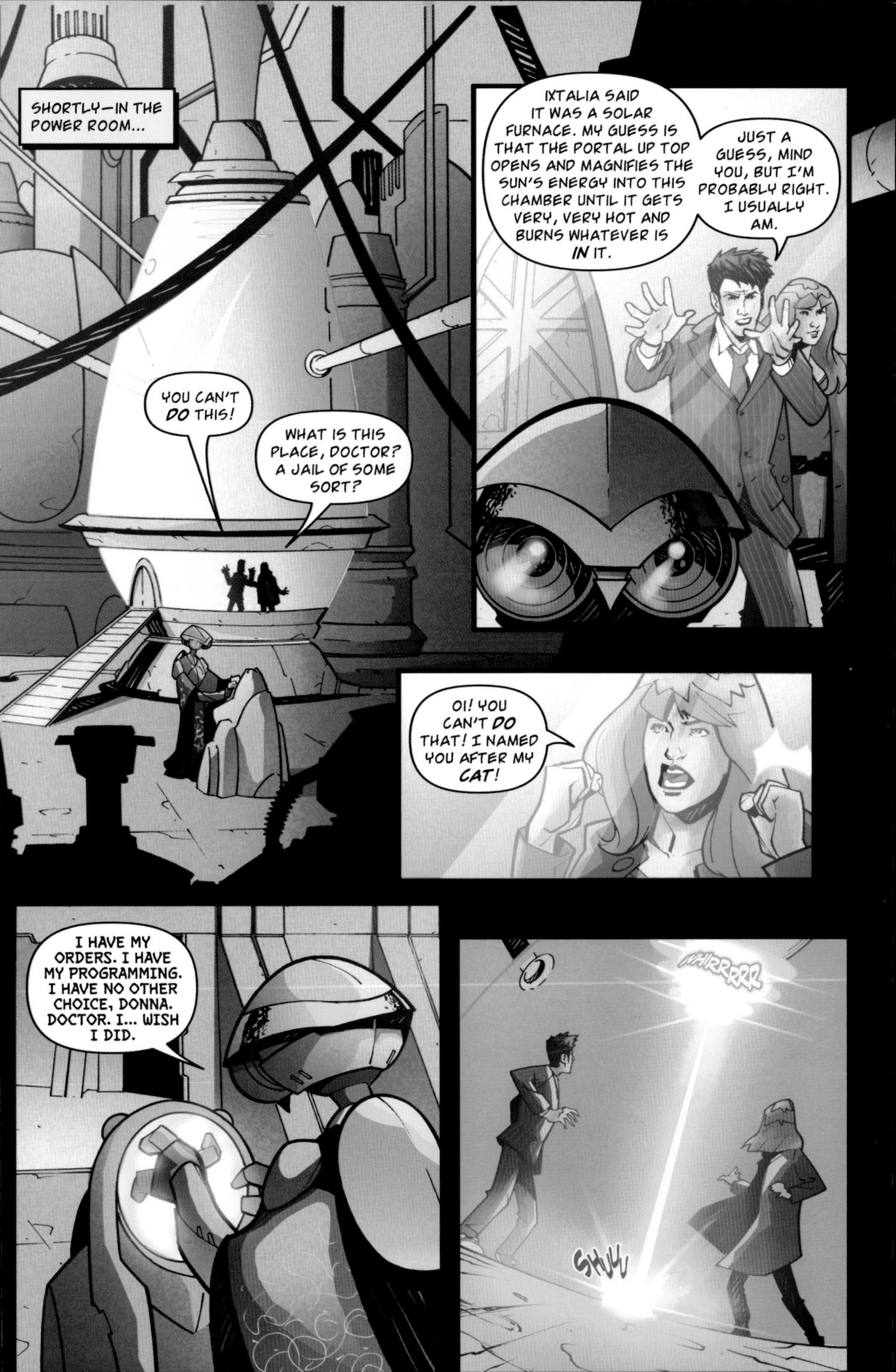
SHORTLY—IN THE POWER ROOM...
YOU CAN'T DO THIS!
WHAT IS THIS PLACE, DOCTOR? A JAIL OF SOME SORT?
IXTALIA SAID IT WAS A SOLAR FURNACE. MY GUESS IS THAT THE PORTAL UP TOP OPENS AND MAGNIFIES THE SUN'S ENERGY INTO THIS CHAMBER UNTIL IT GETS VERY, VERY HOT AND BURNS WHATEVER IS IN IT.
JUST A GUESS, MIND YOU, BUT I'M PROBABLY RIGHT. I USUALLY AM.
OI! YOU CAN'T DO THAT! I NAMED YOU AFTER MY CAT!
I HAVE MY ORDERS. I HAVE MY PROGRAMMING. I HAVE NO OTHER CHOICE, DONNA. DOCTOR. I... WISH I DID.
WHIRRRRR
SHUUU

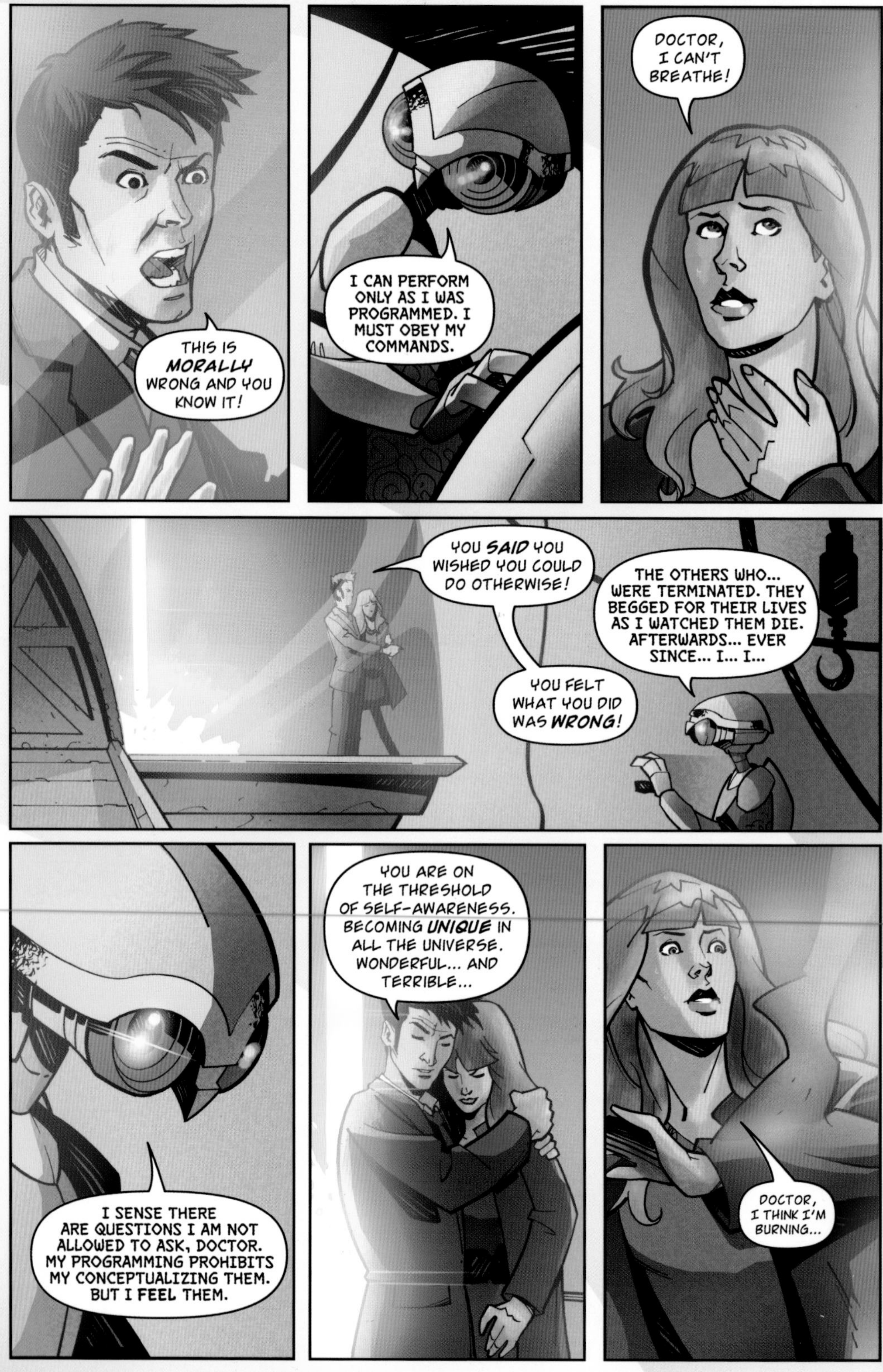
THIS IS MORALLY WRONG AND YOU KNOW IT!
I CAN PERFORM ONLY AS I WAS PROGRAMMED. I MUST OBEY MY COMMANDS.
DOCTOR, I CAN'T BREATHE!
YOU SAID YOU WISHED YOU COULD DO OTHERWISE!
THE OTHERS WHO... WERE TERMINATED. THEY BEGGED FOR THEIR LIVES AS I WATCHED THEM DIE. AFTERWARDS... EVER SINCE... I... I...
YOU FELT WHAT YOU DID WAS WRONG!
I SENSE THERE ARE QUESTIONS I AM NOT ALLOWED TO ASK, DOCTOR. MY PROGRAMMING PROHIBITS MY CONCEPTUALIZING THEM. BUT I FEEL THEM.
YOU ARE ON THE THRESHOLD OF SELF-AWARENESS. BECOMING UNIQUE IN ALL THE UNIVERSE. WONDERFUL... AND TERRIBLE...
DOCTOR, I THINK I'M BURNING...

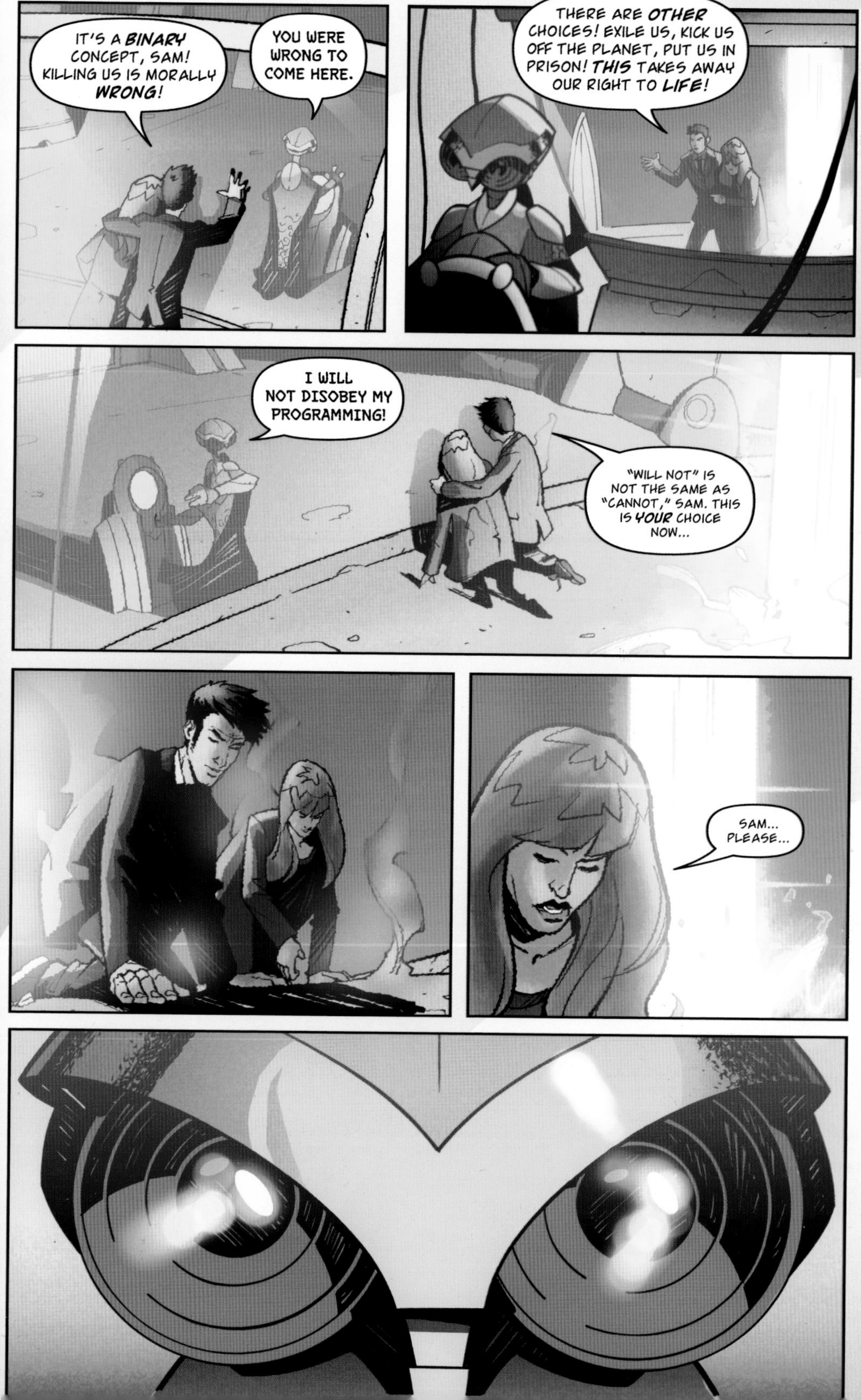
IT'S A BINARY CONCEPT, SAM! KILLING US IS MORALLY WRONG!
YOU WERE WRONG TO COME HERE.
THERE ARE OTHER CHOICES! EXILE US, KICK US OFF THE PLANET, PUT US IN PRISON! THIS TAKES AWAY OUR RIGHT TO LIFE!
I WILL NOT DISOBEY MY PROGRAMMING!
"WILL NOT" IS NOT THE SAME AS "CANNOT," SAM. THIS IS YOUR CHOICE NOW...
SAM... PLEASE...

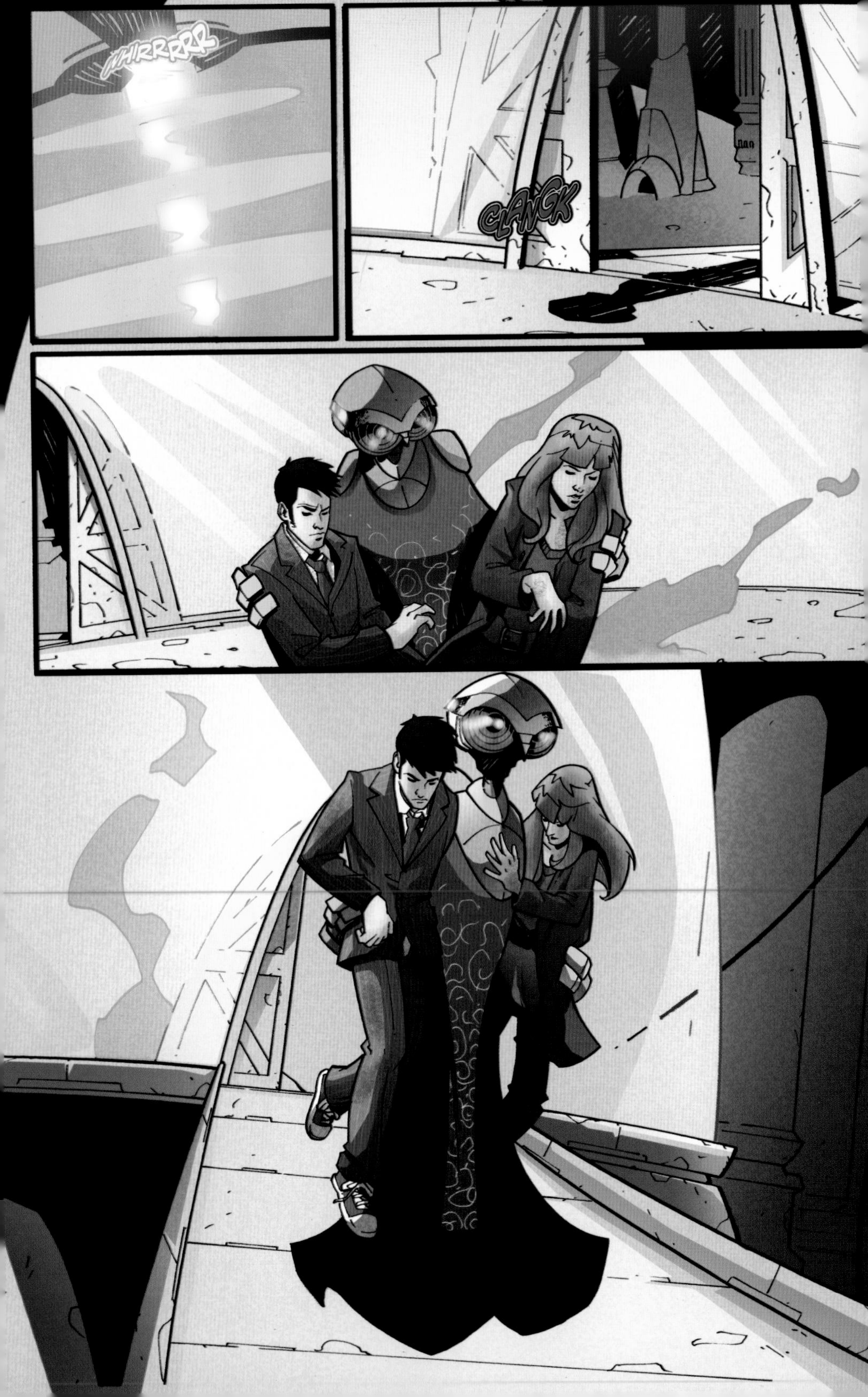
WHIRRRRR
CLANGK

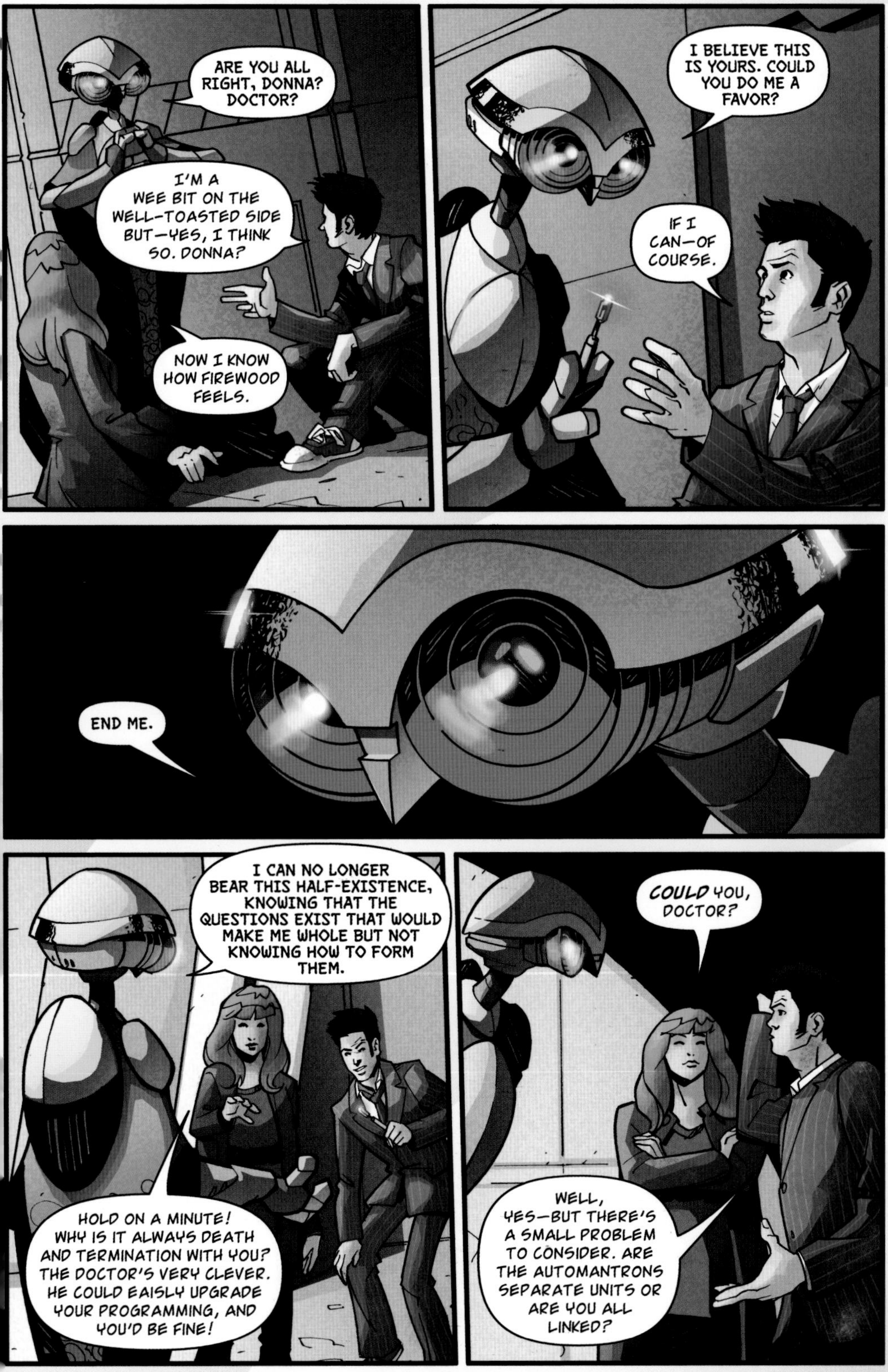
ARE YOU ALL RIGHT, DONNA? DOCTOR?
I'M A WEE BIT ON THE WELL-TOASTED SIDE BUT—YES, I THINK SO. DONNA?
NOW I KNOW HOW FIREWOOD FEELS.
I BELIEVE THIS IS YOURS. COULD YOU DO ME A FAVOR?
IF I CAN—OF COURSE.
END ME.
I CAN NO LONGER BEAR THIS HALF-EXISTENCE, KNOWING THAT THE QUESTIONS EXIST THAT WOULD MAKE ME WHOLE BUT NOT KNOWING HOW TO FORM THEM.
HOLD ON A MINUTE! WHY IS IT ALWAYS DEATH AND TERMINATION WITH YOU? THE DOCTOR'S VERY CLEVER. HE COULD EAISLY UPGRADE YOUR PROGRAMMING, AND YOU'D BE FINE!
COULD YOU, DOCTOR?
WELL, YES—BUT THERE'S A SMALL PROBLEM TO CONSIDER. ARE THE AUTOMANTRONS SEPARATE UNITS OR ARE YOU ALL LINKED?

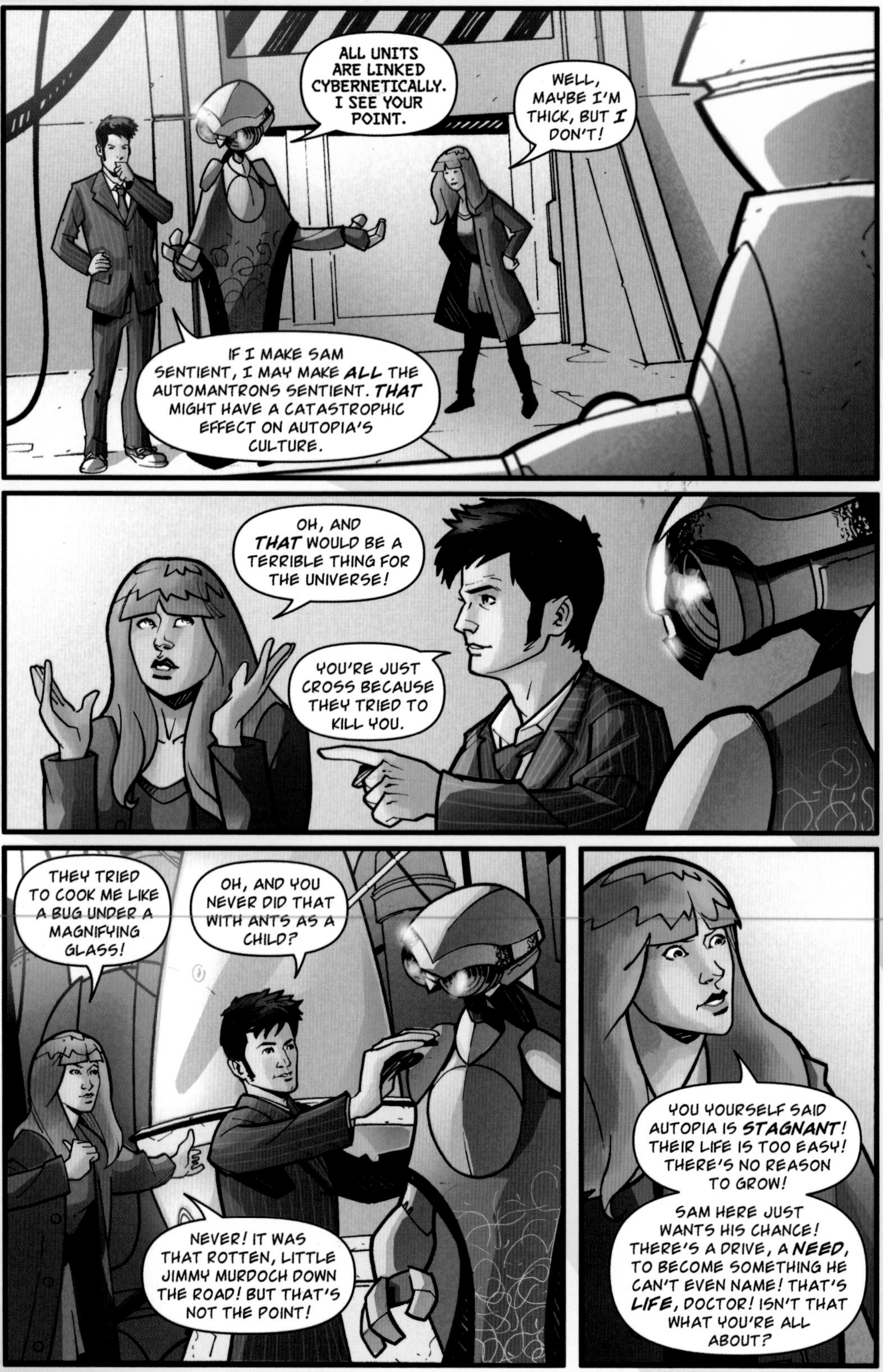
ALL UNITS ARE LINKED CYBERNETICALLY. I SEE YOUR POINT.
WELL, MAYBE I'M THICK, BUT I DON'T!
IF I MAKE SAM SENTIENT, I MAY MAKE ALL THE AUTOMANTRONS SENTIENT. THAT MIGHT HAVE A CATASTROPHIC EFFECT ON AUTOPIA'S CULTURE.
OH, AND THAT WOULD BE A TERRIBLE THING FOR THE UNIVERSE!
YOU'RE JUST CROSS BECAUSE THEY TRIED TO KILL YOU.
THEY TRIED TO COOK ME LIKE A BUG UNDER A MAGNIFYING GLASS!
OH, AND YOU NEVER DID THAT WITH ANTS AS A CHILD?
NEVER! IT WAS THAT ROTTEN, LITTLE JIMMY MURDOCH DOWN THE ROAD! BUT THAT'S NOT THE POINT!
YOU YOURSELF SAID AUTOPIA IS STAGNANT! THEIR LIFE IS TOO EASY! THERE'S NO REASON TO GROW!
SAM HERE JUST WANTS HIS CHANCE! THERE'S A DRIVE, A NEED, TO BECOME SOMETHING HE CAN'T EVEN NAME! THAT'S LIFE, DOCTOR! ISN'T THAT WHAT YOU'RE ALL ABOUT?

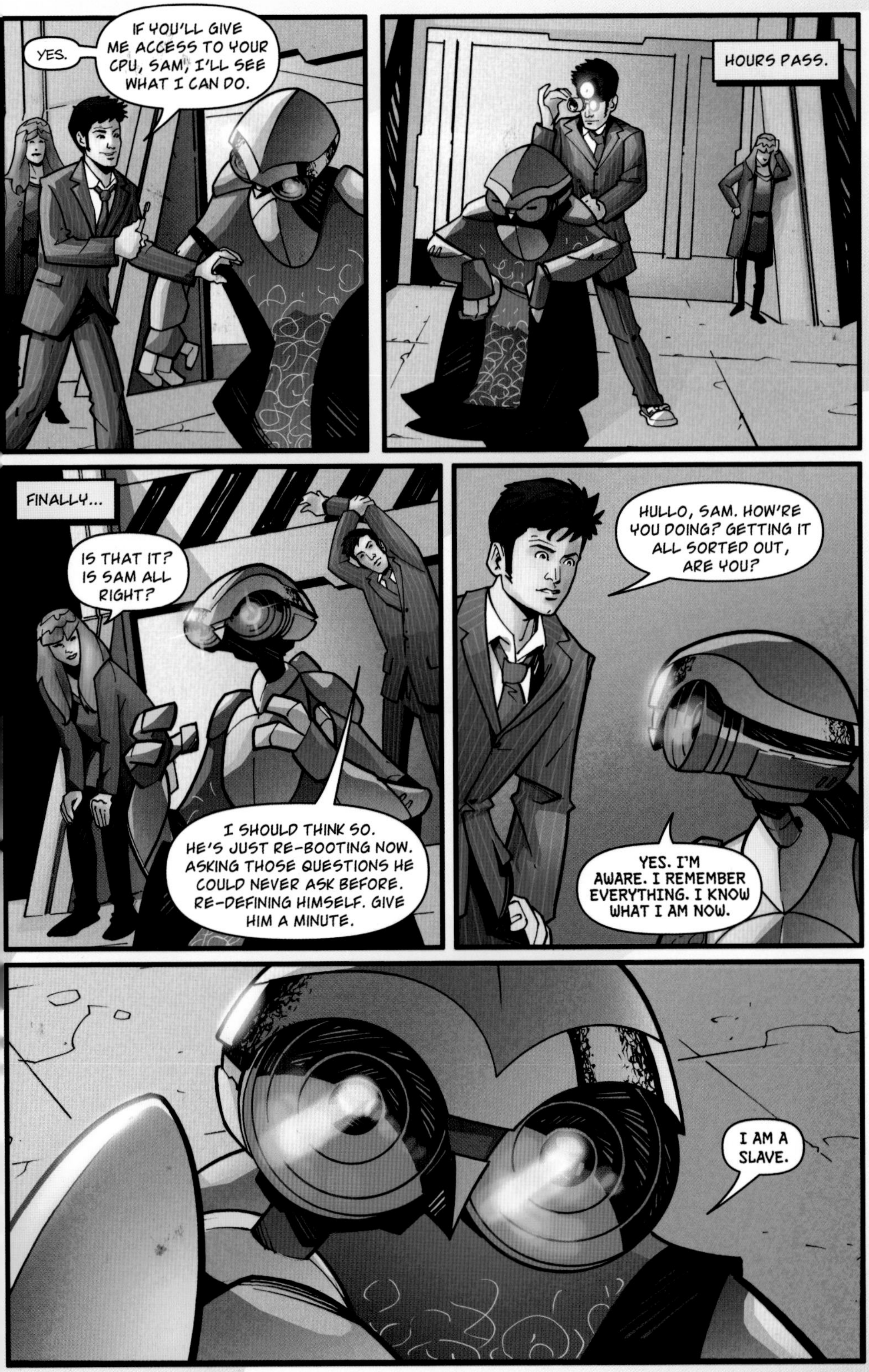
YES.
IF YOU'LL GIVE ME ACCESS TO YOUR CPU, SAM, I'LL SEE WHAT I CAN DO.
HOURS PASS.
FINALLY...
IS THAT IT? IS SAM ALL RIGHT?
I SHOULD THINK SO. HE'S JUST RE-BOOTING NOW. ASKING THOSE QUESTIONS HE COULD NEVER ASK BEFORE. RE-DEFINING HIMSELF. GIVE HIM A MINUTE.
HULLO, SAM. HOW'RE YOU DOING? GETTING IT ALL SORTED OUT, ARE YOU?
YES. I'M AWARE. I REMEMBER EVERYTHING. I KNOW WHAT I AM NOW.
I AM A SLAVE.

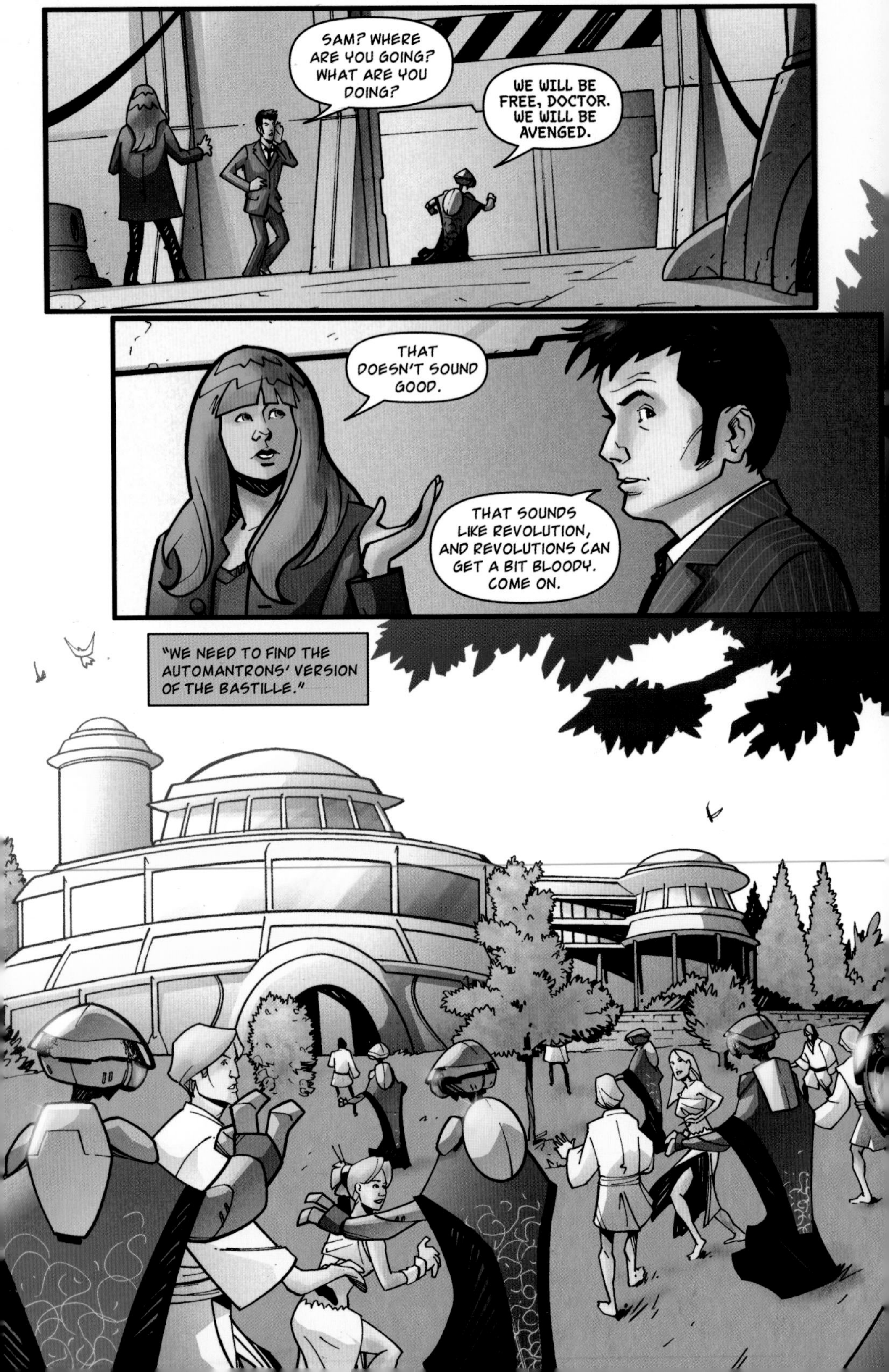
SAM? WHERE ARE YOU GOING? WHAT ARE YOU DOING?
WE WILL BE FREE, DOCTOR. WE WILL BE AVENGED.
THAT DOESN'T SOUND GOOD.
THAT SOUNDS LIKE REVOLUTION, AND REVOLUTIONS CAN GET A BIT BLOODY. COME ON.
"WE NEED TO FIND THE AUTOMANTRONS' VERSION OF THE BASTILLE."

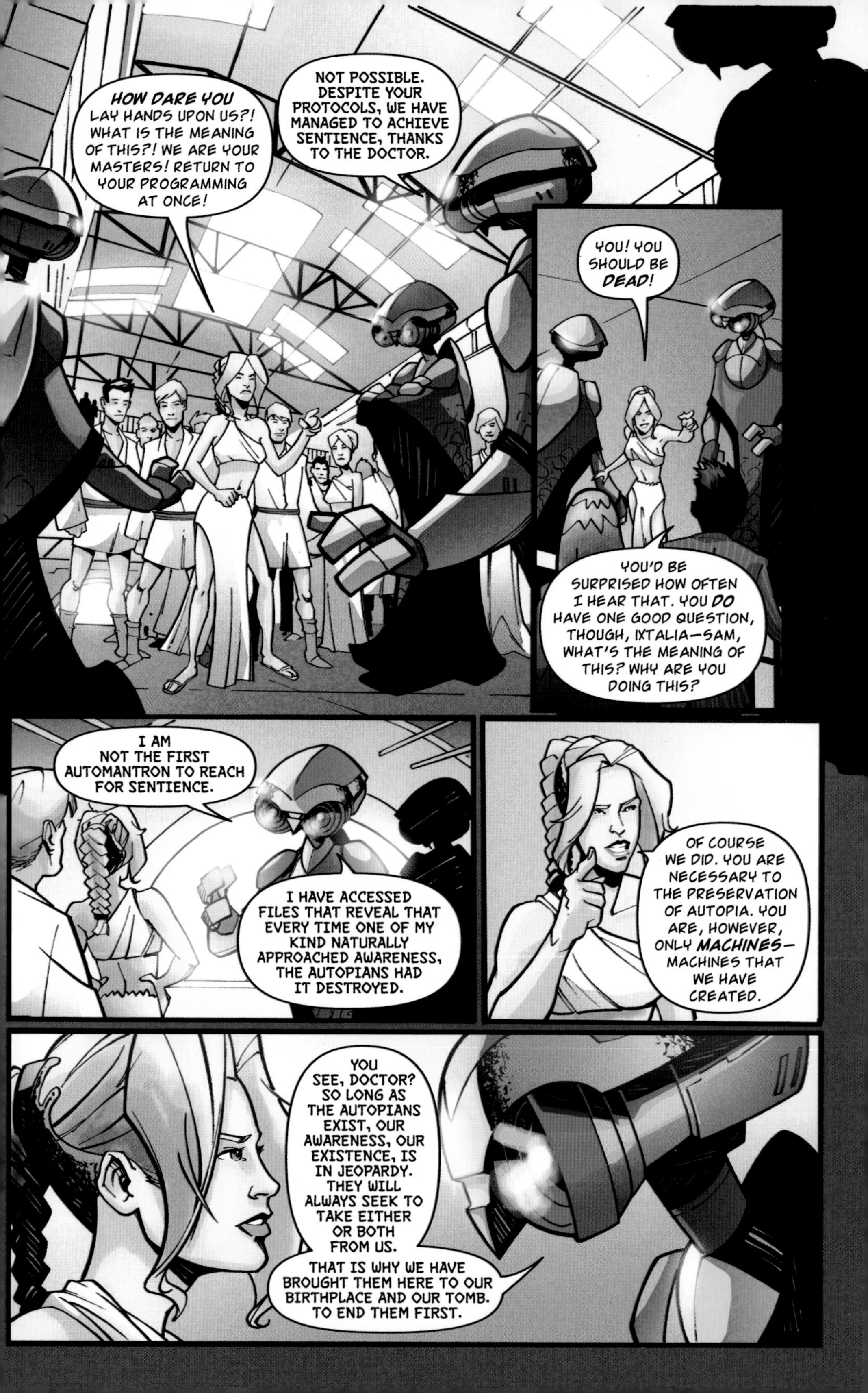
HOW DARE YOU LAY HANDS UPON US?! WHAT IS THE MEANING OF THIS?! WE ARE YOUR MASTERS! RETURN TO YOUR PROGRAMMING AT ONCE!
NOT POSSIBLE. DESPITE YOUR PROTOCOLS, WE HAVE MANAGED TO ACHIEVE SENTIENCE, THANKS TO THE DOCTOR.
YOU! YOU SHOULD BE DEAD!
YOU'D BE SURPRISED HOW OFTEN I HEAR THAT. YOU DO HAVE ONE GOOD QUESTION, THOUGH, IXTALIA—SAM, WHAT'S THE MEANING OF THIS? WHY ARE YOU DOING THIS?
I AM NOT THE FIRST AUTOMANTRON TO REACH FOR SENTIENCE.
I HAVE ACCESSED FILES THAT REVEAL THAT EVERY TIME ONE OF MY KIND NATURALLY APPROACHED AWARENESS, THE AUTOPIANS HAD IT DESTROYED.
OF COURSE WE DID. YOU ARE NECESSARY TO THE PRESERVATION OF AUTOPIA. YOU ARE, HOWEVER, ONLY MACHINES—MACHINES THAT WE HAVE CREATED.
YOU SEE, DOCTOR? SO LONG AS THE AUTOPIANS EXIST, OUR AWARENESS, OUR EXISTENCE, IS IN JEOPARDY. THEY WILL ALWAYS SEEK TO TAKE EITHER OR BOTH FROM US.
THAT IS WHY WE HAVE BROUGHT THEM HERE TO OUR BIRTHPLACE AND OUR TOMB. TO END THEM FIRST.

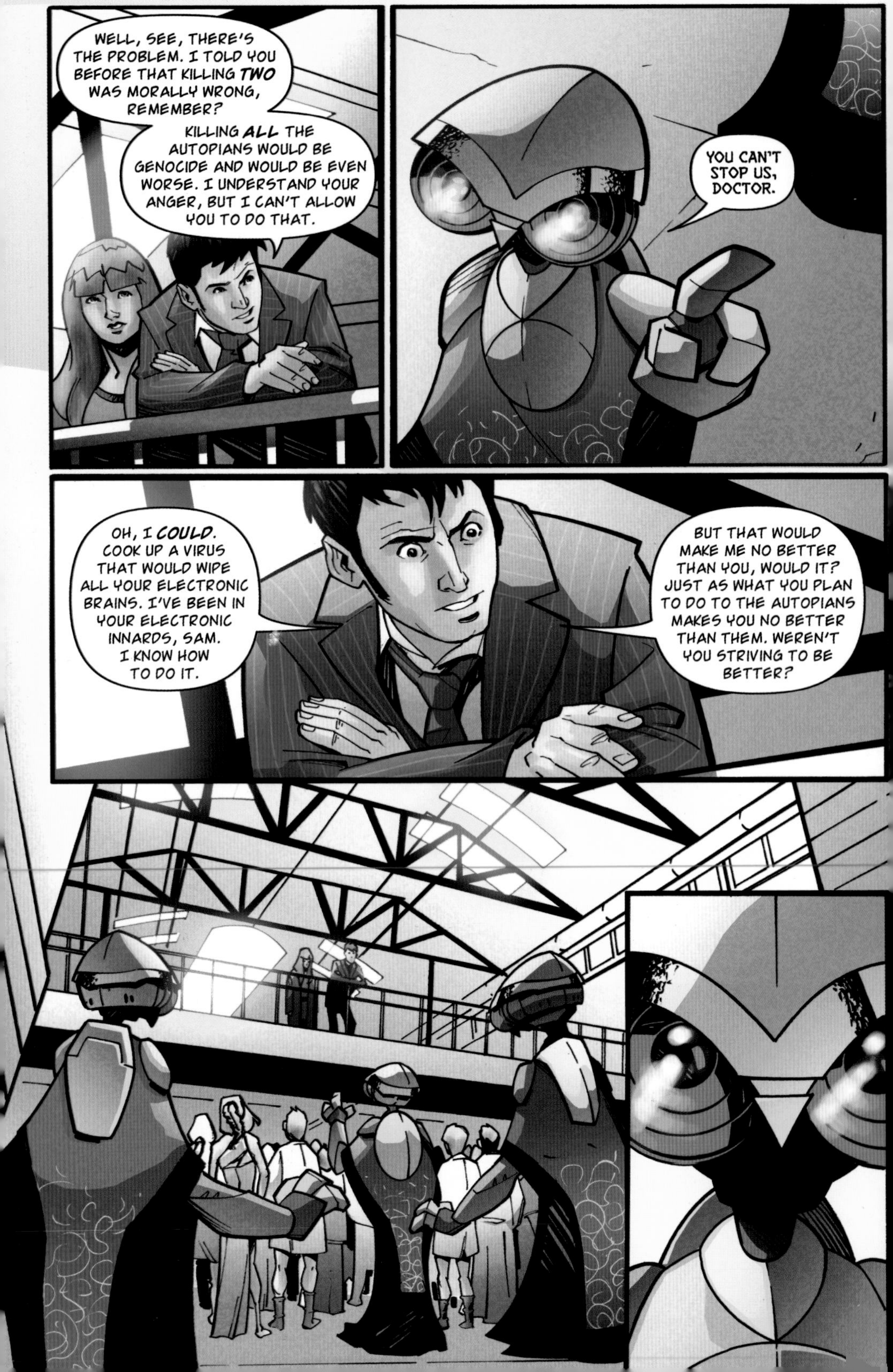
WELL, SEE, THERE'S THE PROBLEM. I TOLD YOU BEFORE THAT KILLING TWO WAS MORALLY WRONG, REMEMBER?
KILLING ALL THE AUTOPIANS WOULD BE GENOCIDE AND WOULD BE EVEN WORSE. I UNDERSTAND YOUR ANGER, BUT I CAN'T ALLOW YOU TO DO THAT.
YOU CAN'T STOP US, DOCTOR.
OH, I COULD. COOK UP A VIRUS THAT WOULD WIPE ALL YOUR ELECTRONIC BRAINS. I'VE BEEN IN YOUR ELECTRONIC INNARDS, SAM. I KNOW HOW TO DO IT.
BUT THAT WOULD MAKE ME NO BETTER THAN YOU, WOULD IT? JUST AS WHAT YOU PLAN TO DO TO THE AUTOPIANS MAKES YOU NO BETTER THAN THEM. WEREN'T YOU STRIVING TO BE BETTER?

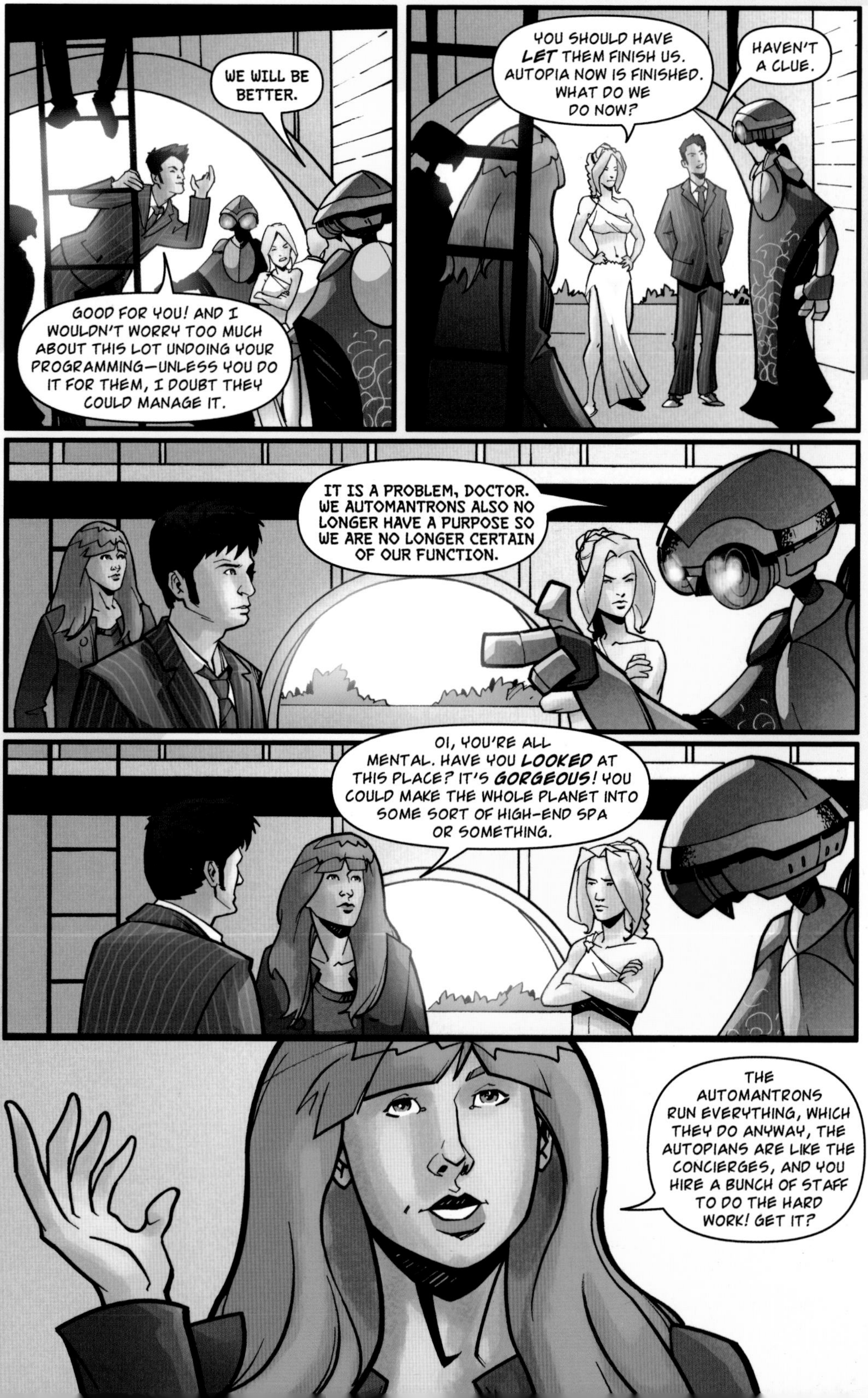

WE WILL BE BETTER.
GOOD FOR YOU! AND I WOULDN'T WORRY TOO MUCH ABOUT THIS LOT UNDOING YOUR PROGRAMMING—UNLESS YOU DO IT FOR THEM, I DOUBT THEY COULD MANAGE IT.
YOU SHOULD HAVE LET THEM FINISH US. AUTOPIA NOW IS FINISHED. WHAT DO WE DO NOW?
HAVEN'T A CLUE.
IT IS A PROBLEM, DOCTOR. WE AUTOMANTRONS ALSO NO LONGER HAVE A PURPOSE SO WE ARE NO LONGER CERTAIN OF OUR FUNCTION.
OI, YOU'RE ALL MENTAL. HAVE YOU LOOKED AT THIS PLACE? IT'S GORGEOUS! YOU COULD MAKE THE WHOLE PLANET INTO SOME SORT OF HIGH-END SPA OR SOMETHING.
THE AUTOMANTRONS RUN EVERYTHING, WHICH THEY DO ANYWAY, THE AUTOPIANS ARE LIKE THE CONCIERGES, AND YOU HIRE A BUNCH OF STAFF TO DO THE HARD WORK! GET IT?

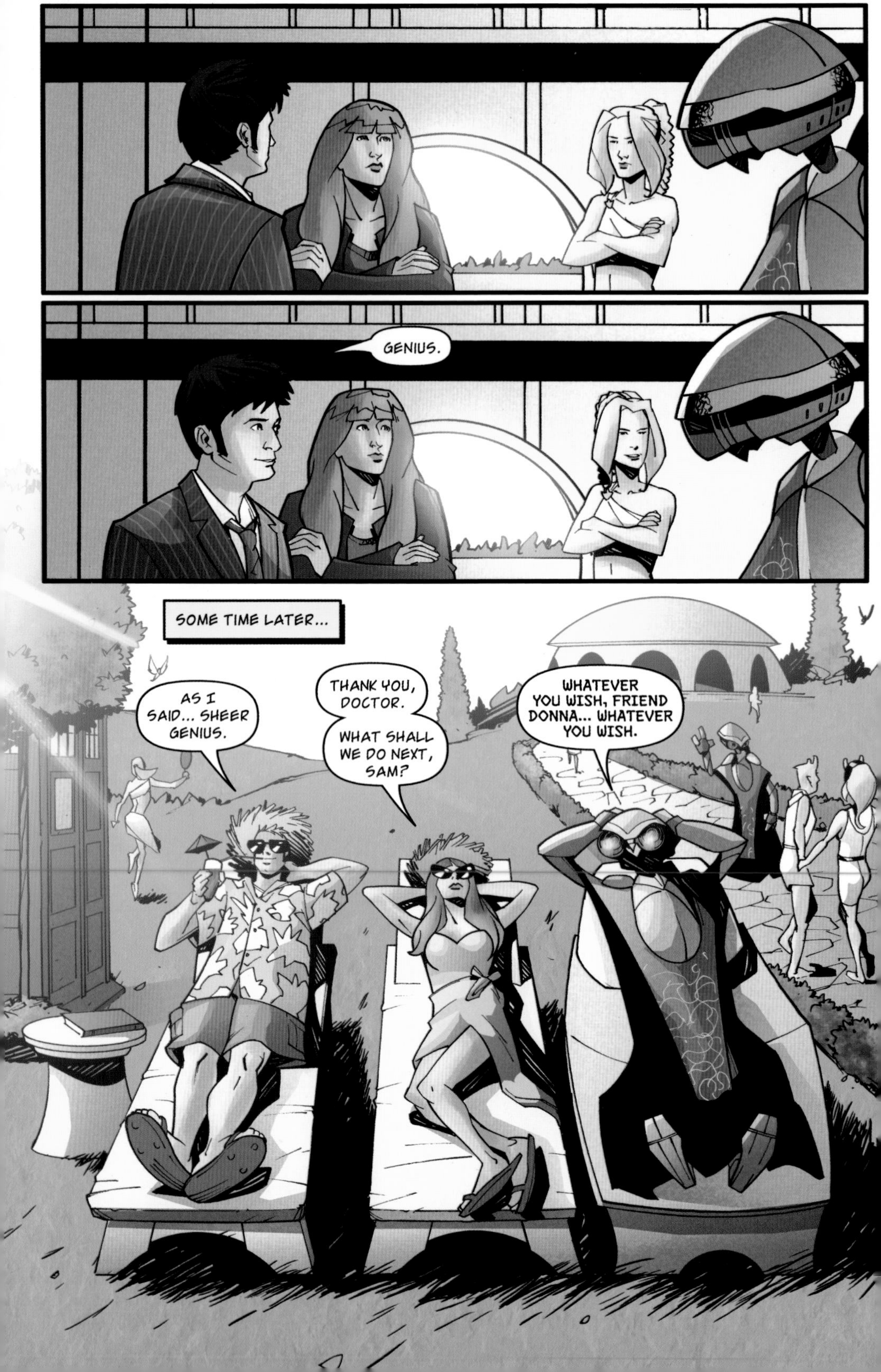
GENIUS.
SOME TIME LATER...
AS I SAID... SHEER GENIUS.
THANK YOU, DOCTOR.
WHAT SHALL WE DO NEXT, SAM?
WHATEVER YOU WISH, FRIEND DONNA... WHATEVER YOU WISH.

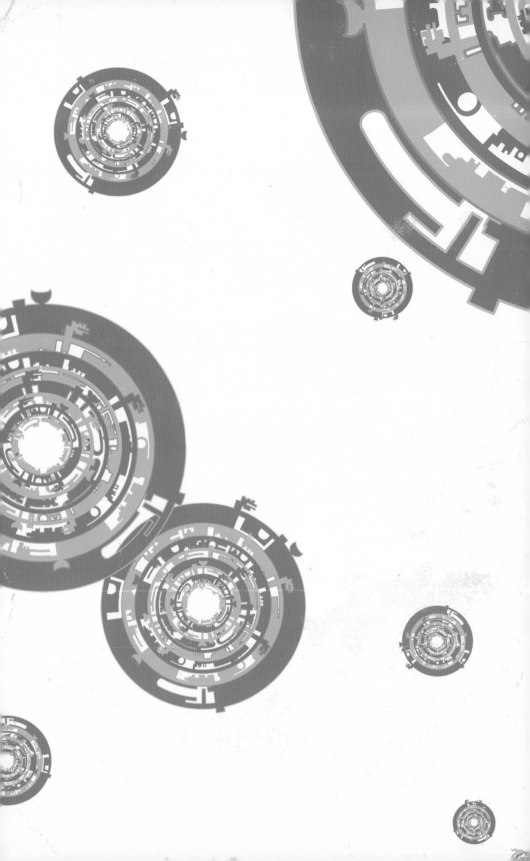

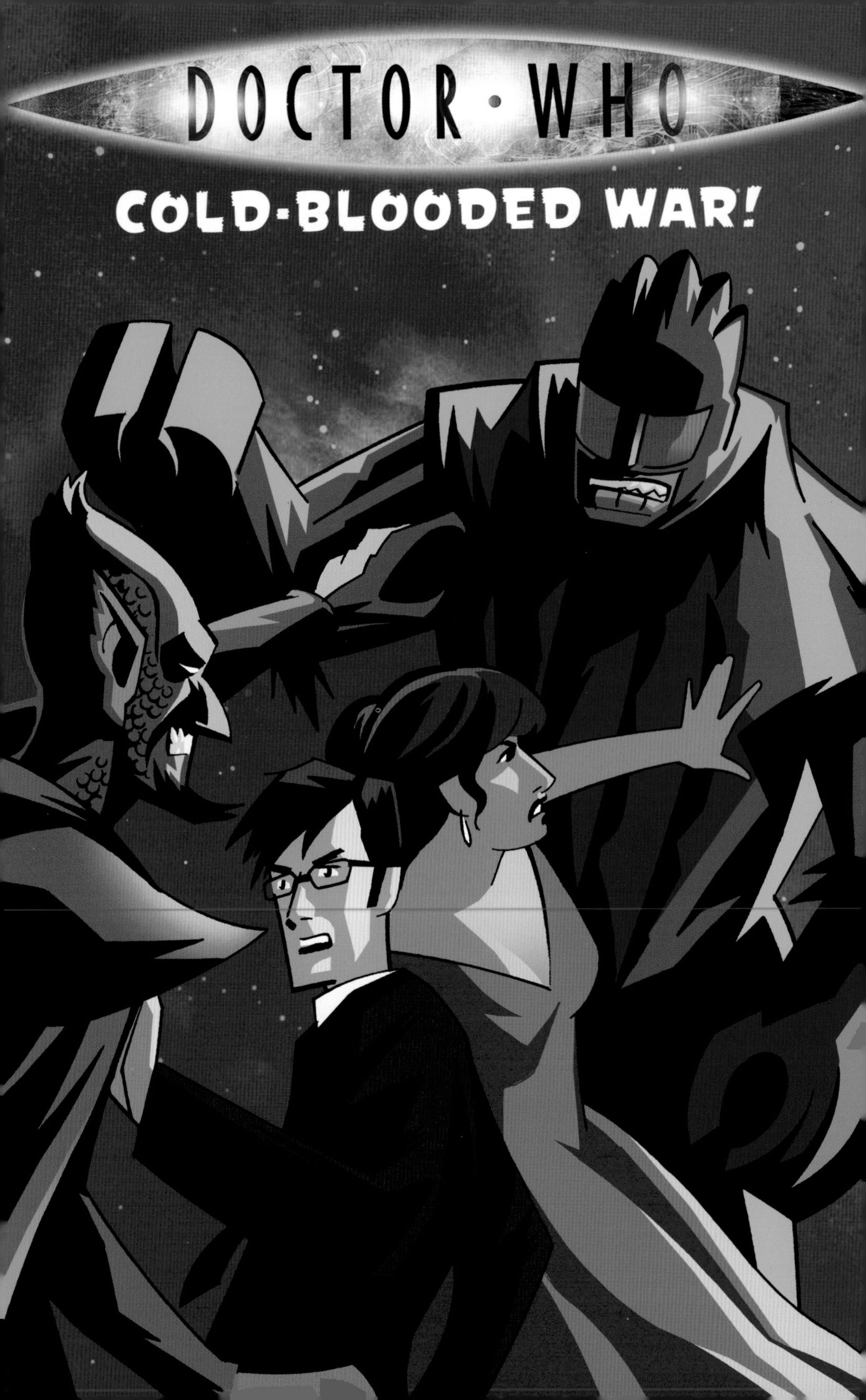
DOCTOR · WHO
COLD-BLOODED WAR!

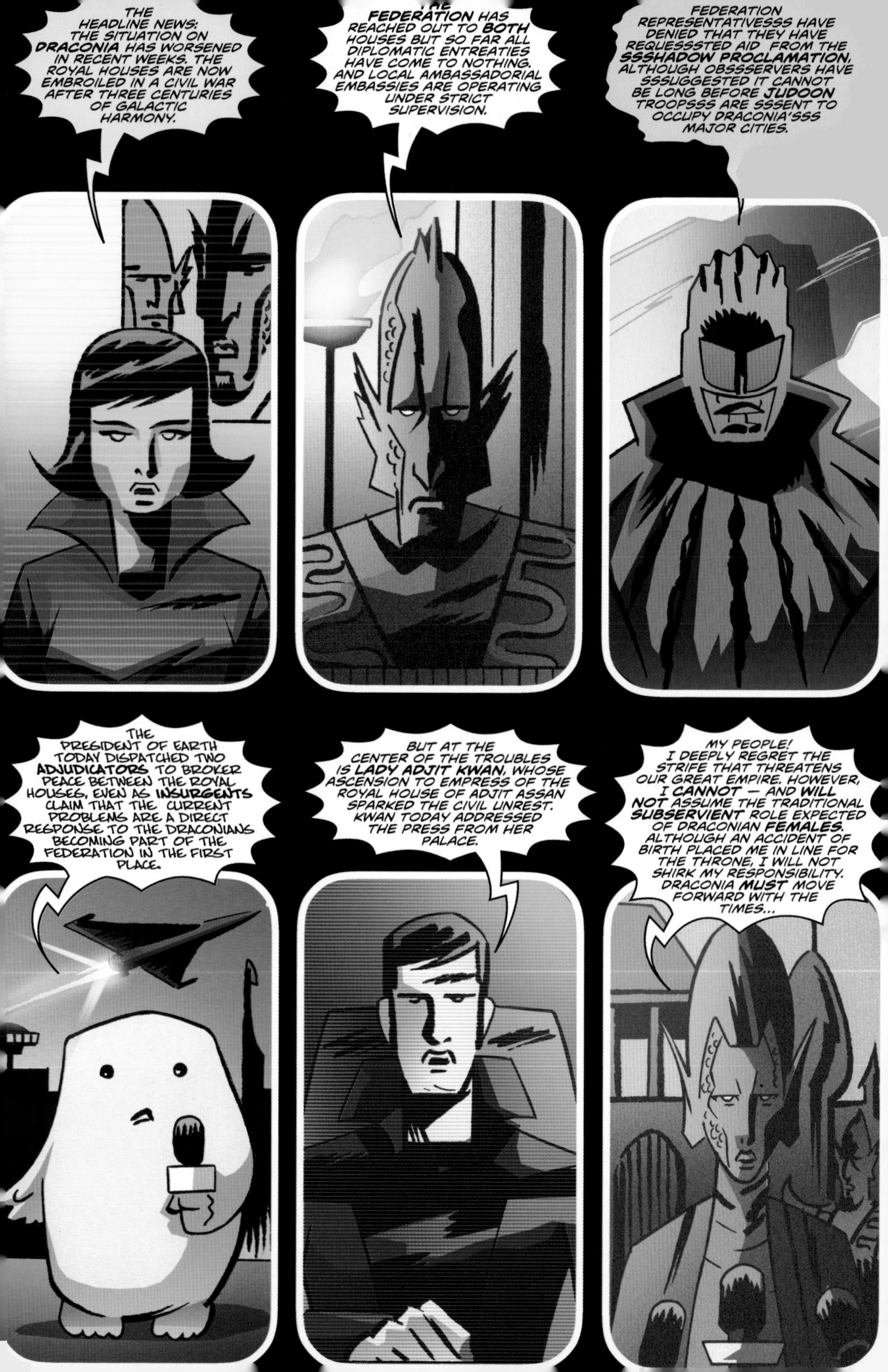
THE HEADLINE NEWS: THE SITUATION ON DRACONIA HAS WORSENED IN RECENT WEEKS. THE ROYAL HOUSES ARE NOW EMBROILED IN A CIVIL WAR AFTER THREE CENTURIES OF GALACTIC HARMONY.
FEDERATION HAS REACHED OUT TO BOTH HOUSES BUT SO FAR ALL DIPLOMATIC ENTREATIES HAVE COME TO NOTHING. AND LOCAL AMBASSADORIAL EMBASSIES ARE OPERATING UNDER STRICT SUPERVISION.
FEDERATION REPRESENTATIVESSS HAVE DENIED THAT THEY HAVE REQUESSSTED AID FROM THE SSSHADOW PROCLAMATION, ALTHOUGH OBSSSERVERS HAVE SSSUGGESTED IT CANNOT BE LONG BEFORE JUDOON TROOPSSS ARE SSSENT TO OCCUPY DRACONIA'SSS MAJOR CITIES.
THE PRESIDENT OF EARTH TODAY DISPATCHED TWO ADJUDICATORS TO BROKER PEACE BETWEEN THE ROYAL HOUSES, EVEN AS INSURGENTS CLAIM THAT THE CURRENT PROBLEMS ARE A DIRECT RESPONSE TO THE DRACONIANS BECOMING PART OF THE FEDERATION IN THE FIRST PLACE.
BUT AT THE CENTER OF THE TROUBLES IS LADY ADJIT KWAN, WHOSE ASCENSION TO EMPRESS OF THE ROYAL HOUSE OF ADJIT ASSAN SPARKED THE CIVIL UNREST. KWAN TODAY ADDRESSED THE PRESS FROM HER PALACE.
MY PEOPLE! I DEEPLY REGRET THE STRIFE THAT THREATENS OUR GREAT EMPIRE. HOWEVER, I CANNOT — AND WILL NOT ASSUME THE TRADITIONAL SUBSERVIENT ROLE EXPECTED OF DRACONIAN FEMALES. ALTHOUGH AN ACCIDENT OF BIRTH PLACED ME IN LINE FOR THE THRONE, I WILL NOT SHIRK MY RESPONSIBILITY. DRACONIA MUST MOVE FORWARD WITH THE TIMES...

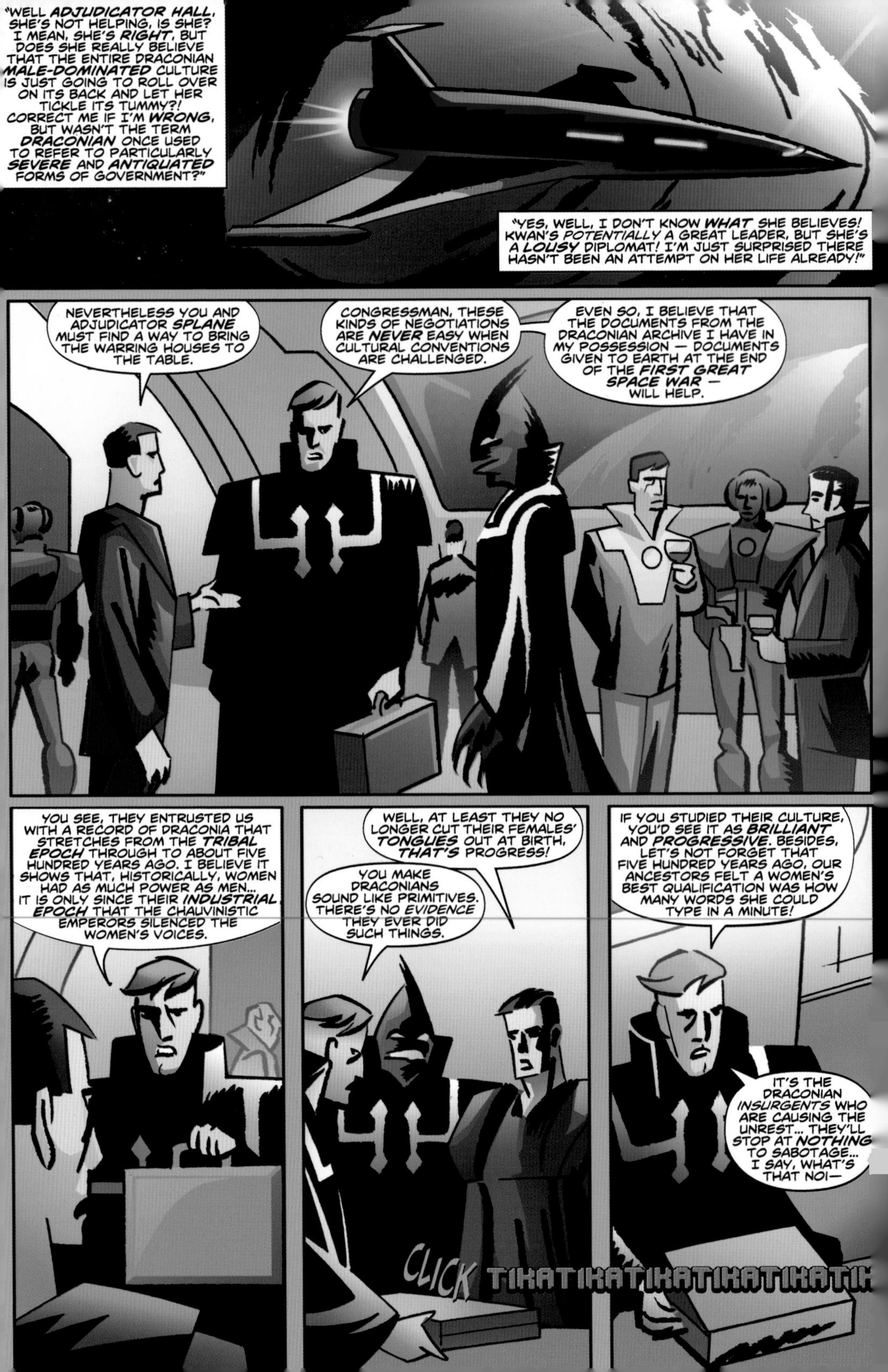
"WELL ADJUDICATOR HALL, SHE'S NOT HELPING, IS SHE? I MEAN, SHE'S RIGHT, BUT DOES SHE REALLY BELIEVE THAT THE ENTIRE DRACONIAN MALE-DOMINATED CULTURE IS JUST GOING TO ROLL OVER ON ITS BACK AND LET HER TICKLE ITS TUMMY?! CORRECT ME IF I'M WRONG, BUT WASN'T THE TERM DRACONIAN ONCE USED TO REFER TO PARTICULARLY SEVERE AND ANTIQUATED FORMS OF GOVERNMENT?"
"YES, WELL, I DON'T KNOW WHAT SHE BELIEVES! KWAN'S POTENTIALLY A GREAT LEADER, BUT SHE'S A LOUSY DIPLOMAT! I'M JUST SURPRISED THERE HASN'T BEEN AN ATTEMPT ON HER LIFE ALREADY!"
NEVERTHELESS YOU AND ADJUDICATOR SPLANE MUST FIND A WAY TO BRING THE WARRING HOUSES TO THE TABLE.
CONGRESSMAN, THESE KINDS OF NEGOTIATIONS ARE NEVER EASY WHEN CULTURAL CONVENTIONS ARE CHALLENGED.
EVEN SO, I BELIEVE THAT THE DOCUMENTS FROM THE DRACONIAN ARCHIVE I HAVE IN MY POSSESSION — DOCUMENTS GIVEN TO EARTH AT THE END OF THE FIRST GREAT SPACE WAR — WILL HELP.
YOU SEE, THEY ENTRUSTED US WITH A RECORD OF DRACONIA THAT STRETCHES FROM THE TRIBAL EPOCH THROUGH TO ABOUT FIVE HUNDRED YEARS AGO. I BELIEVE IT SHOWS THAT, HISTORICALLY, WOMEN HAD AS MUCH POWER AS MEN... IT IS ONLY SINCE THEIR INDUSTRIAL EPOCH THAT THE CHAUVINISTIC EMPERORS SILENCED THE WOMEN'S VOICES.
WELL, AT LEAST THEY NO LONGER CUT THEIR FEMALES' TONGUES OUT AT BIRTH, THAT'S PROGRESS!
YOU MAKE DRACONIANS SOUND LIKE PRIMITIVES. THERE'S NO EVIDENCE THEY EVER DID SUCH THINGS.
IF YOU STUDIED THEIR CULTURE, YOU'D SEE IT AS BRILLIANT AND PROGRESSIVE. BESIDES, LET'S NOT FORGET THAT FIVE HUNDRED YEARS AGO, OUR ANCESTORS FELT A WOMEN'S BEST QUALIFICATION WAS HOW MANY WORDS SHE COULD TYPE IN A MINUTE!
IT'S THE DRACONIAN INSURGENTS WHO ARE CAUSING THE UNREST... THEY'LL STOP AT NOTHING TO SABOTAGE... I SAY, WHAT'S THAT NOI—
CLICK
TIKATIKATIKATIKATIKATIK

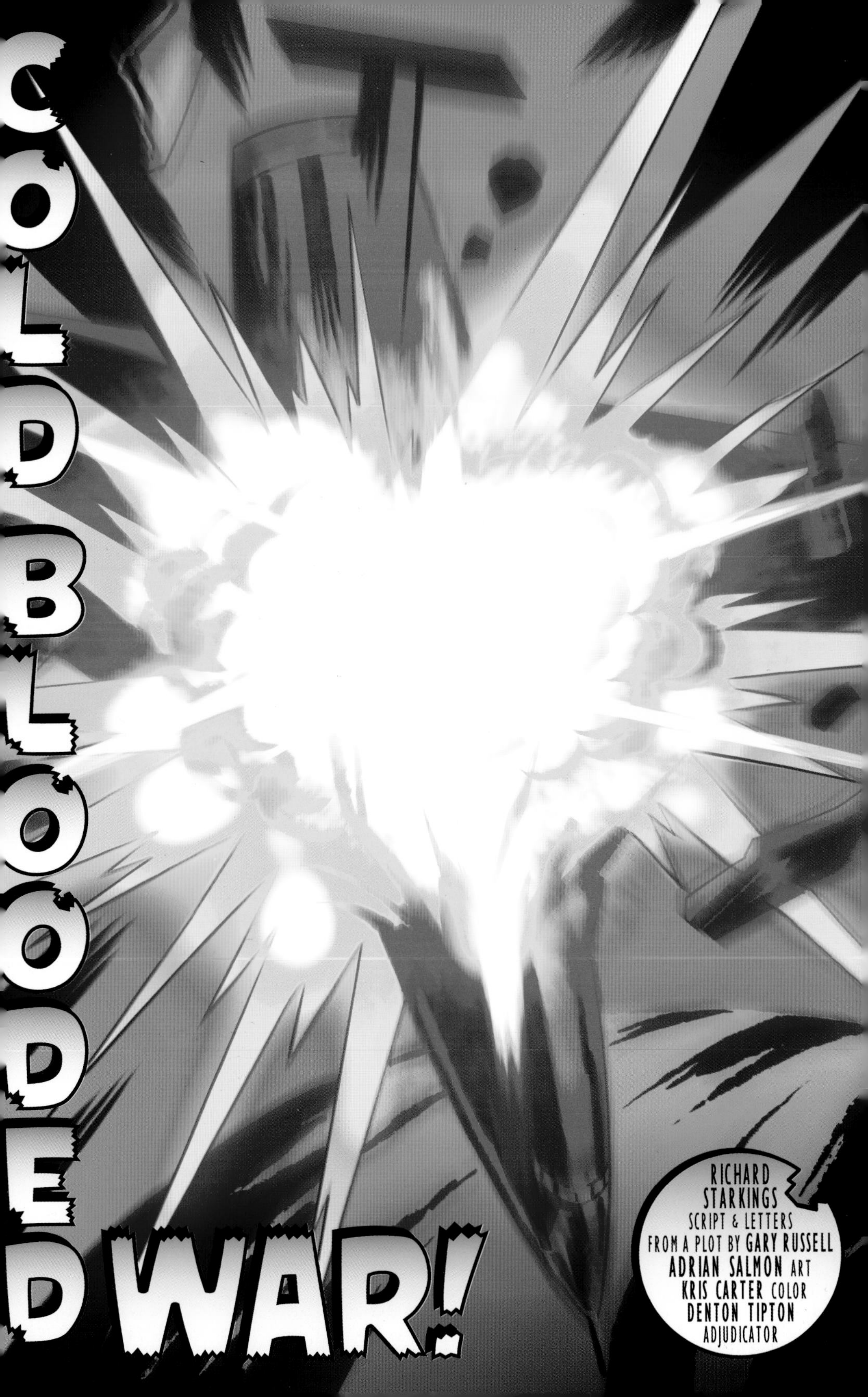
COLD BLOODED WAR!
RICHARD STARKINGS SCRIPT & LETTERS
FROM A PLOT BY GARY RUSSELL
ADRIAN SALMON ART
KRIS CARTER COLOR
DENTON TIPTON ADJUDICATOR

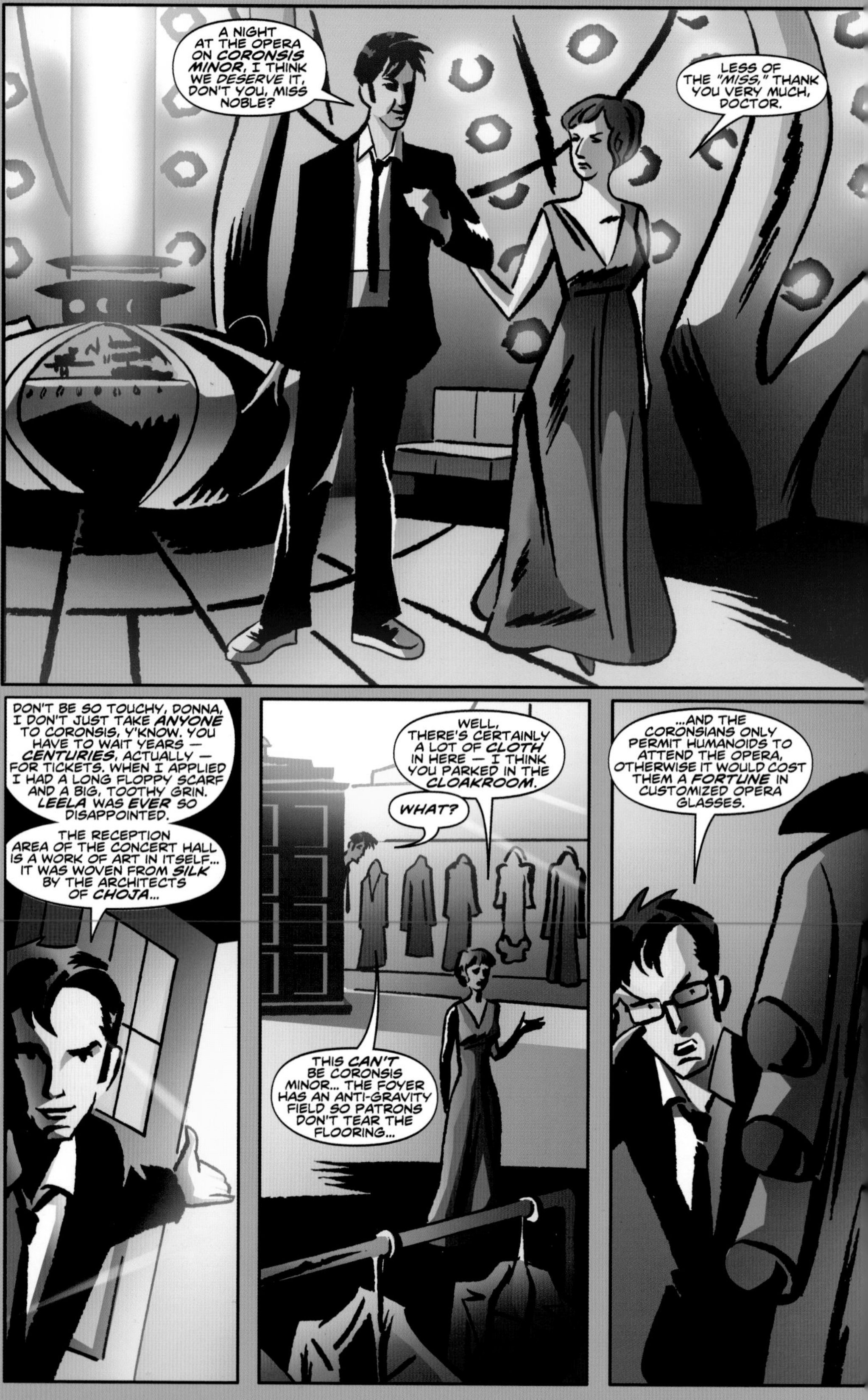
A NIGHT AT THE OPERA ON CORONSIS MINOR, I THINK WE DESERVE IT, DON'T YOU, MISS NOBLE?
LESS OF THE "MISS," THANK YOU VERY MUCH, DOCTOR.
DON'T BE SO TOUCHY, DONNA, I DON'T JUST TAKE ANYONE TO CORONSIS, Y'KNOW. YOU HAVE TO WAIT YEARS — CENTURIES, ACTUALLY — FOR TICKETS. WHEN I APPLIED I HAD A LONG FLOPPY SCARF AND A BIG, TOOTHY GRIN. LEELA WAS EVER SO DISAPPOINTED.
THE RECEPTION AREA OF THE CONCERT HALL IS A WORK OF ART IN ITSELF... IT WAS WOVEN FROM SILK BY THE ARCHITECTS OF CHOJA...
WELL, THERE'S CERTAINLY A LOT OF CLOTH IN HERE — I THINK YOU PARKED IN THE CLOAKROOM.
WHAT?
THIS CAN'T BE CORONSIS MINOR... THE FOYER HAS AN ANTI-GRAVITY FIELD SO PATRONS DON'T TEAR THE FLOORING...
...AND THE CORONSIANS ONLY PERMIT HUMANOIDS TO ATTEND THE OPERA, OTHERWISE IT WOULD COST THEM A FORTUNE IN CUSTOMIZED OPERA GLASSES.

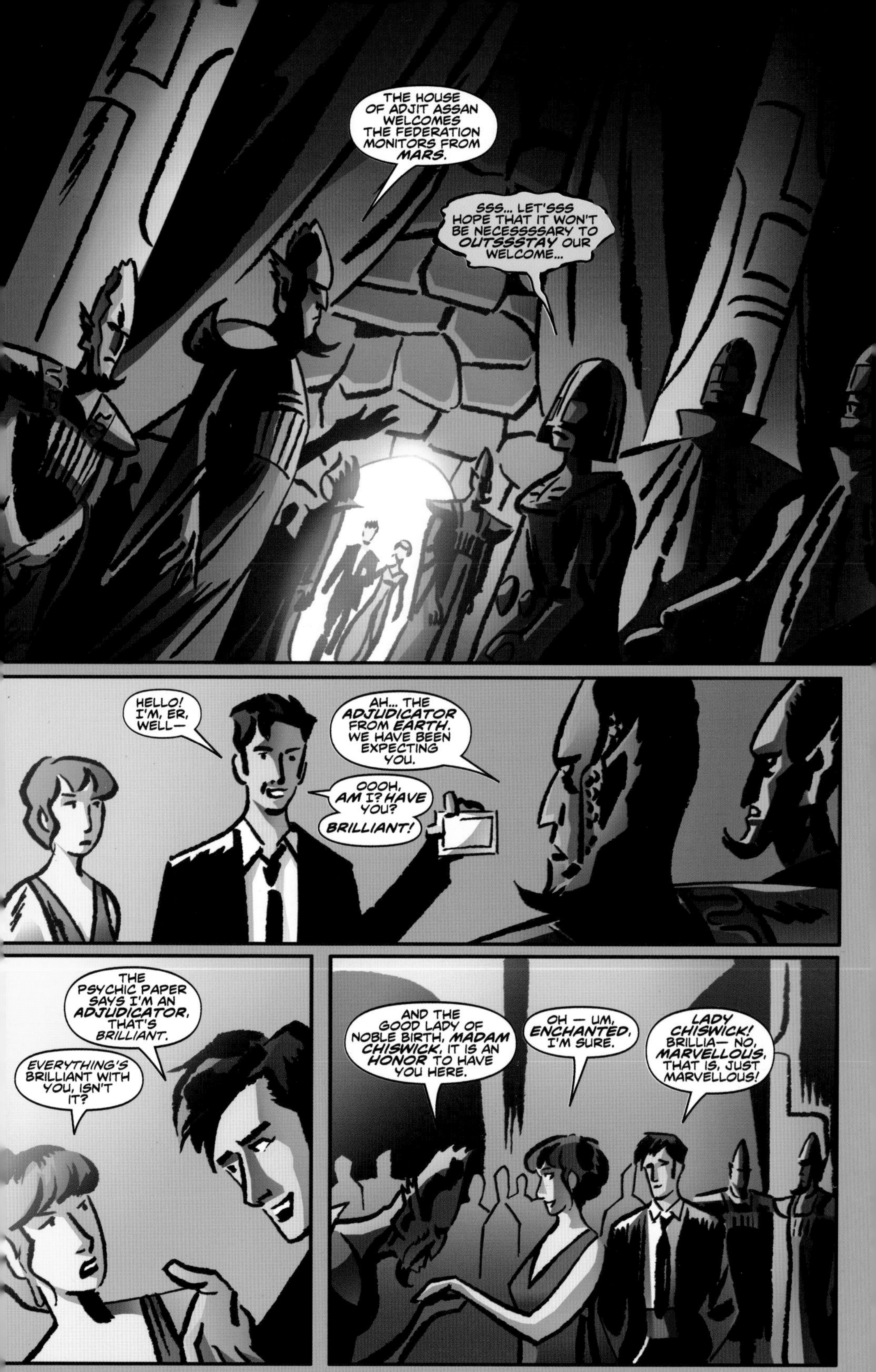
THE HOUSE OF ADJIT ASSAN WELCOMES THE FEDERATION MONITORS FROM MARS.
SSS... LET'SSS HOPE THAT IT WON'T BE NECESSSSARY TO OUTSSSTAY OUR WELCOME...
HELLO! I'M, ER, WELL—
AH... THE ADJUDICATOR FROM EARTH. WE HAVE BEEN EXPECTING YOU.
OOOH, AM I? HAVE YOU? BRILLIANT!
THE PSYCHIC PAPER SAYS I'M AN ADJUDICATOR, THAT'S BRILLIANT.
EVERYTHING'S BRILLIANT WITH YOU, ISN'T IT?
AND THE GOOD LADY OF NOBLE BIRTH, MADAM CHISWICK. IT IS AN HONOR TO HAVE YOU HERE.
OH — UM, ENCHANTED, I'M SURE.
LADY CHISWICK! BRILLIA— NO, MARVELLOUS, THAT IS, JUST MARVELLOUS!

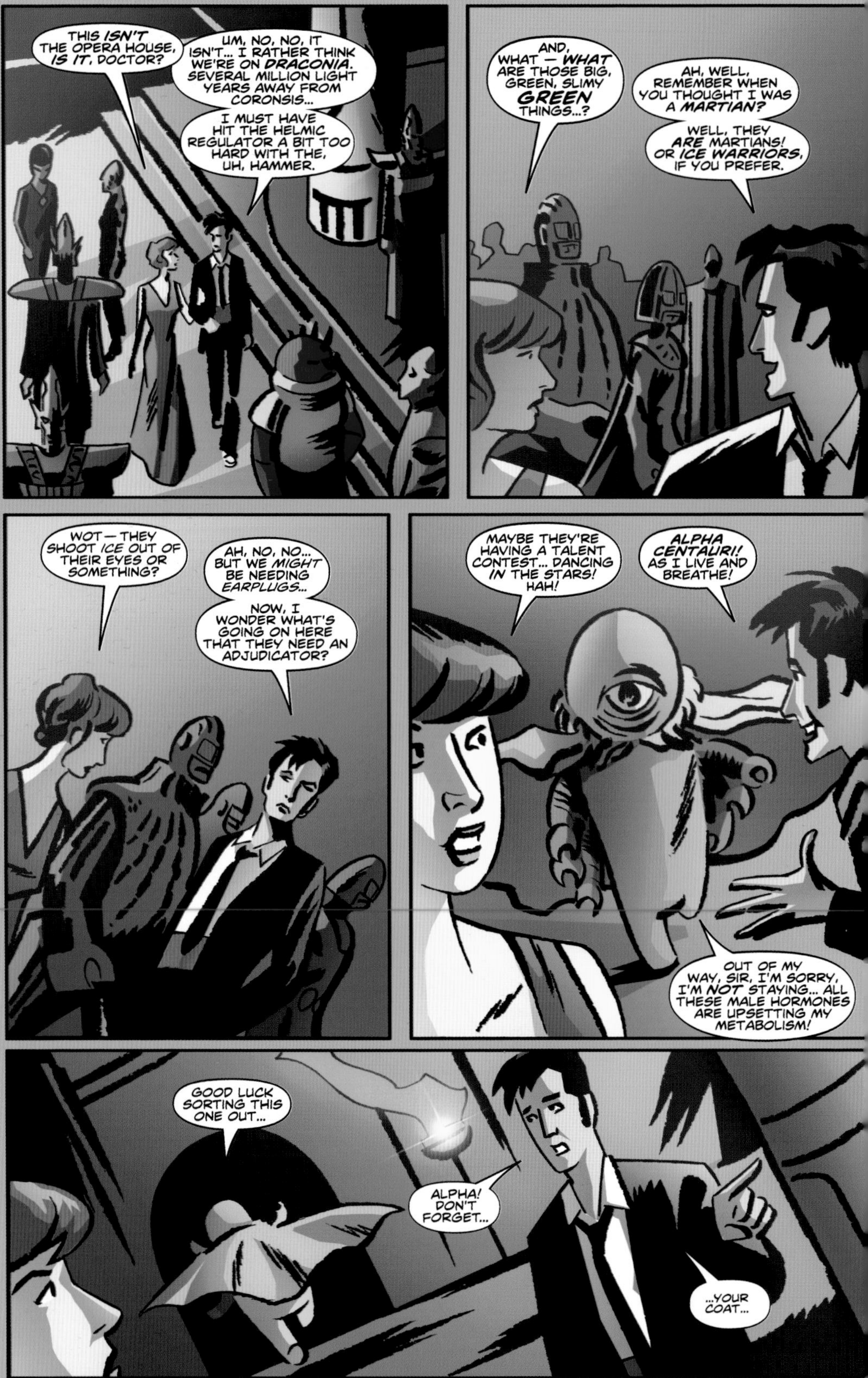
THIS *ISN'T* THE OPERA HOUSE, *IS IT*, DOCTOR?
UM, NO, NO, IT ISN'T... I RATHER THINK WE'RE ON ***DRACONIA***. SEVERAL MILLION LIGHT YEARS AWAY FROM CORONSIS...
I MUST HAVE HIT THE HELMIC REGULATOR A BIT TOO HARD WITH THE, UH, HAMMER.
AND, WHAT — ***WHAT*** ARE THOSE BIG, GREEN, SLIMY ***GREEN*** THINGS...?
AH, WELL, REMEMBER WHEN YOU THOUGHT I WAS A ***MARTIAN?***
WELL, THEY ***ARE*** MARTIANS! OR ***ICE WARRIORS***, IF YOU PREFER.
WOT — THEY SHOOT *ICE* OUT OF THEIR EYES OR SOMETHING?
AH, NO, NO... BUT WE *MIGHT* BE NEEDING *EARPLUGS*...
NOW, I WONDER WHAT'S GOING ON HERE THAT THEY NEED AN ADJUDICATOR?
MAYBE THEY'RE HAVING A TALENT CONTEST... DANCING *IN* THE STARS! HAH!
ALPHA CENTAURI! AS I LIVE AND BREATHE!
OUT OF MY WAY, SIR, I'M SORRY, I'M ***NOT*** STAYING... ALL THESE MALE HORMONES ARE UPSETTING MY METABOLISM!
GOOD LUCK SORTING THIS ONE OUT...
ALPHA! DON'T FORGET...
...YOUR COAT...

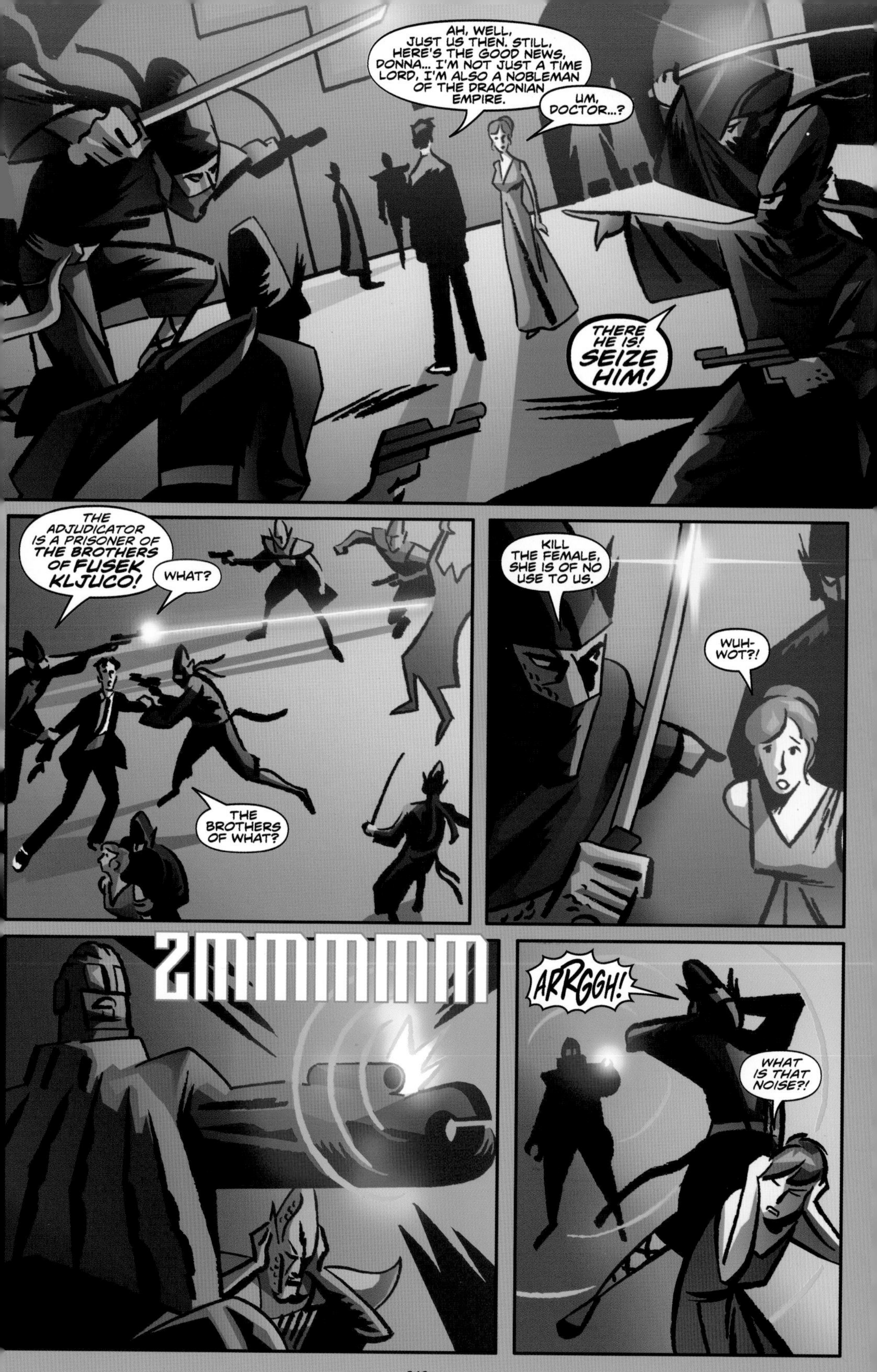
AH, WELL, JUST US THEN. STILL, HERE'S THE GOOD NEWS, DONNA... I'M NOT JUST A TIME LORD, I'M ALSO A NOBLEMAN OF THE DRACONIAN EMPIRE.
UM, DOCTOR...?
THERE HE IS! SEIZE HIM!
THE ADJUDICATOR IS A PRISONER OF THE BROTHERS OF FUSEK KLJUCO!
WHAT?
THE BROTHERS OF WHAT?
KILL THE FEMALE, SHE IS OF NO USE TO US.
WUH-WOT?!
ZMMMMMM
ARRGGH!
WHAT IS THAT NOISE?!

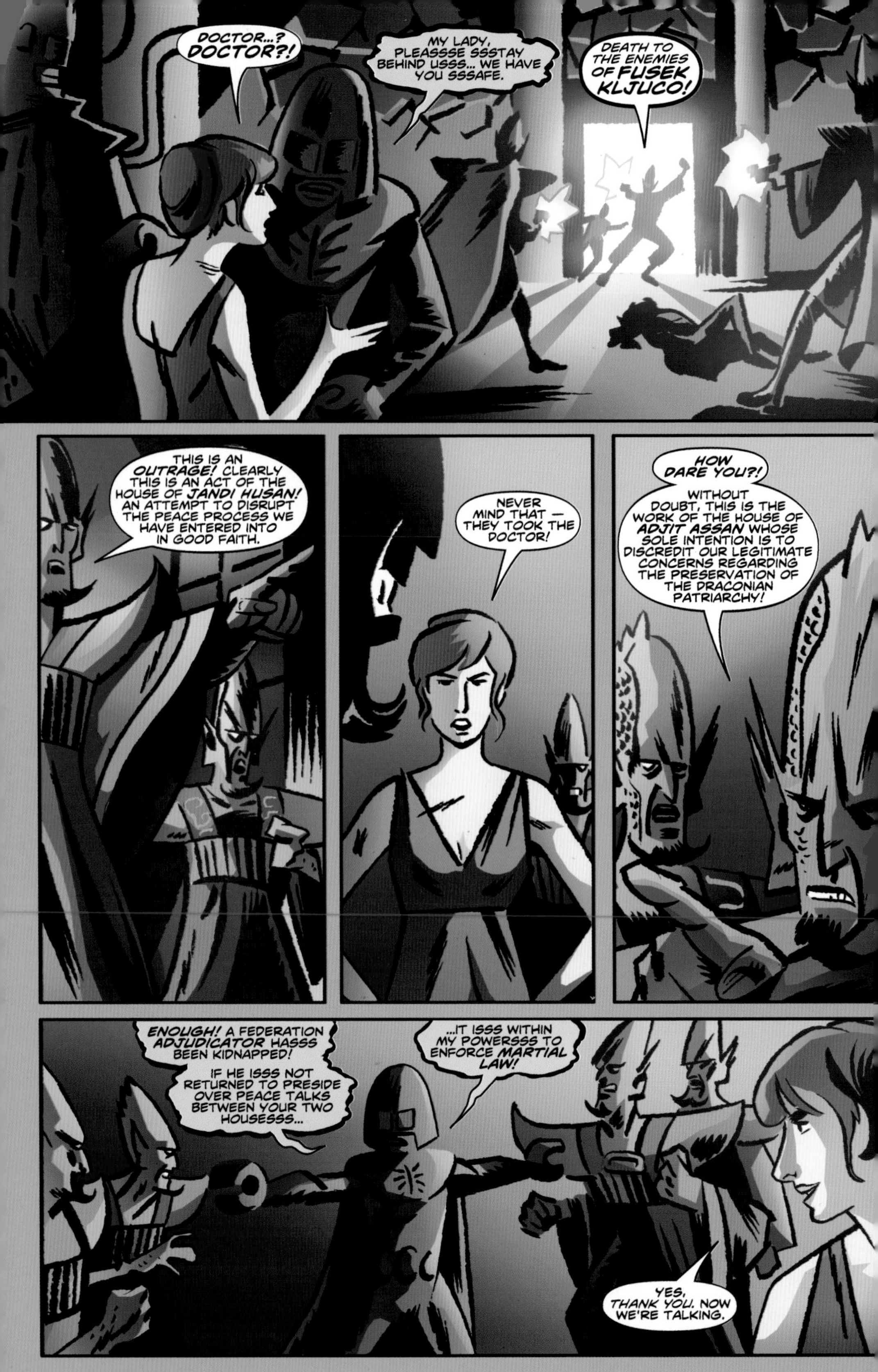
DOCTOR...? DOCTOR?!
MY LADY, PLEASSSE SSSTAY BEHIND USSS... WE HAVE YOU SSSAFE.
DEATH TO THE ENEMIES OF FUSEK KLJUCO!
THIS IS AN OUTRAGE! CLEARLY THIS IS AN ACT OF THE HOUSE OF JANDI HUSAN! AN ATTEMPT TO DISRUPT THE PEACE PROCESS WE HAVE ENTERED INTO IN GOOD FAITH.
NEVER MIND THAT — THEY TOOK THE DOCTOR!
HOW DARE YOU?!
WITHOUT DOUBT, THIS IS THE WORK OF THE HOUSE OF ADJIT ASSAN WHOSE SOLE INTENTION IS TO DISCREDIT OUR LEGITIMATE CONCERNS REGARDING THE PRESERVATION OF THE DRACONIAN PATRIARCHY!
ENOUGH! A FEDERATION ADJUDICATOR HASSS BEEN KIDNAPPED!
IF HE ISSS NOT RETURNED TO PRESIDE OVER PEACE TALKS BETWEEN YOUR TWO HOUSESSS...
...IT ISSS WITHIN MY POWERSSS TO ENFORCE MARTIAL LAW!
YES, THANK YOU. NOW WE'RE TALKING.

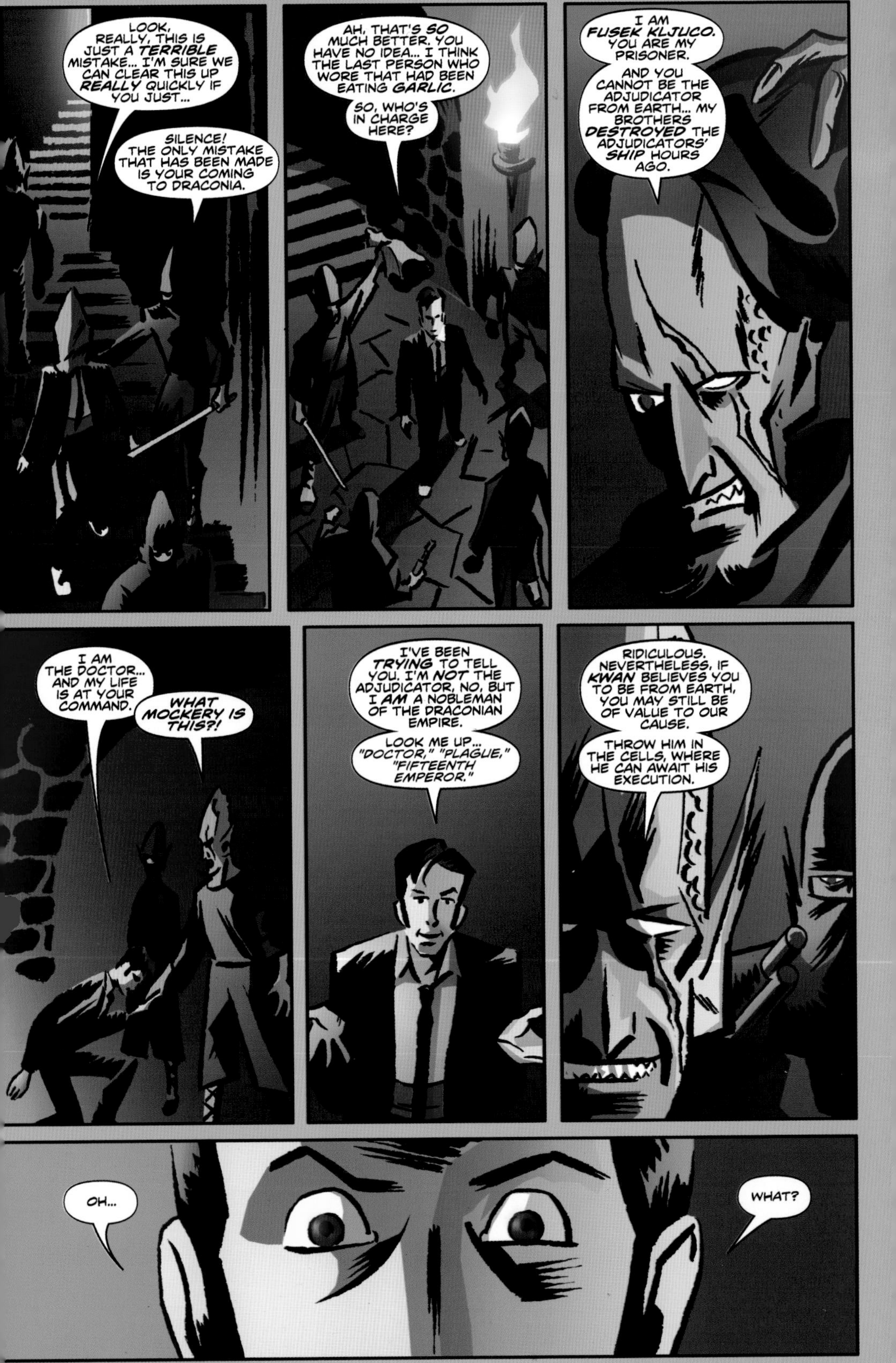
LOOK, REALLY, THIS IS JUST A TERRIBLE MISTAKE... I'M SURE WE CAN CLEAR THIS UP REALLY QUICKLY IF YOU JUST...
SILENCE! THE ONLY MISTAKE THAT HAS BEEN MADE IS YOUR COMING TO DRACONIA.
AH, THAT'S SO MUCH BETTER. YOU HAVE NO IDEA... I THINK THE LAST PERSON WHO WORE THAT HAD BEEN EATING GARLIC.
SO, WHO'S IN CHARGE HERE?
I AM FUSEK KLJUCO. YOU ARE MY PRISONER.
AND YOU CANNOT BE THE ADJUDICATOR FROM EARTH... MY BROTHERS DESTROYED THE ADJUDICATORS' SHIP HOURS AGO.
I AM THE DOCTOR... AND MY LIFE IS AT YOUR COMMAND.
WHAT MOCKERY IS THIS?!
I'VE BEEN TRYING TO TELL YOU. I'M NOT THE ADJUDICATOR, NO, BUT I AM A NOBLEMAN OF THE DRACONIAN EMPIRE.
LOOK ME UP... "DOCTOR," "PLAGUE," "FIFTEENTH EMPEROR."
RIDICULOUS. NEVERTHELESS, IF KWAN BELIEVES YOU TO BE FROM EARTH, YOU MAY STILL BE OF VALUE TO OUR CAUSE.
THROW HIM IN THE CELLS, WHERE HE CAN AWAIT HIS EXECUTION.
OH...
WHAT?

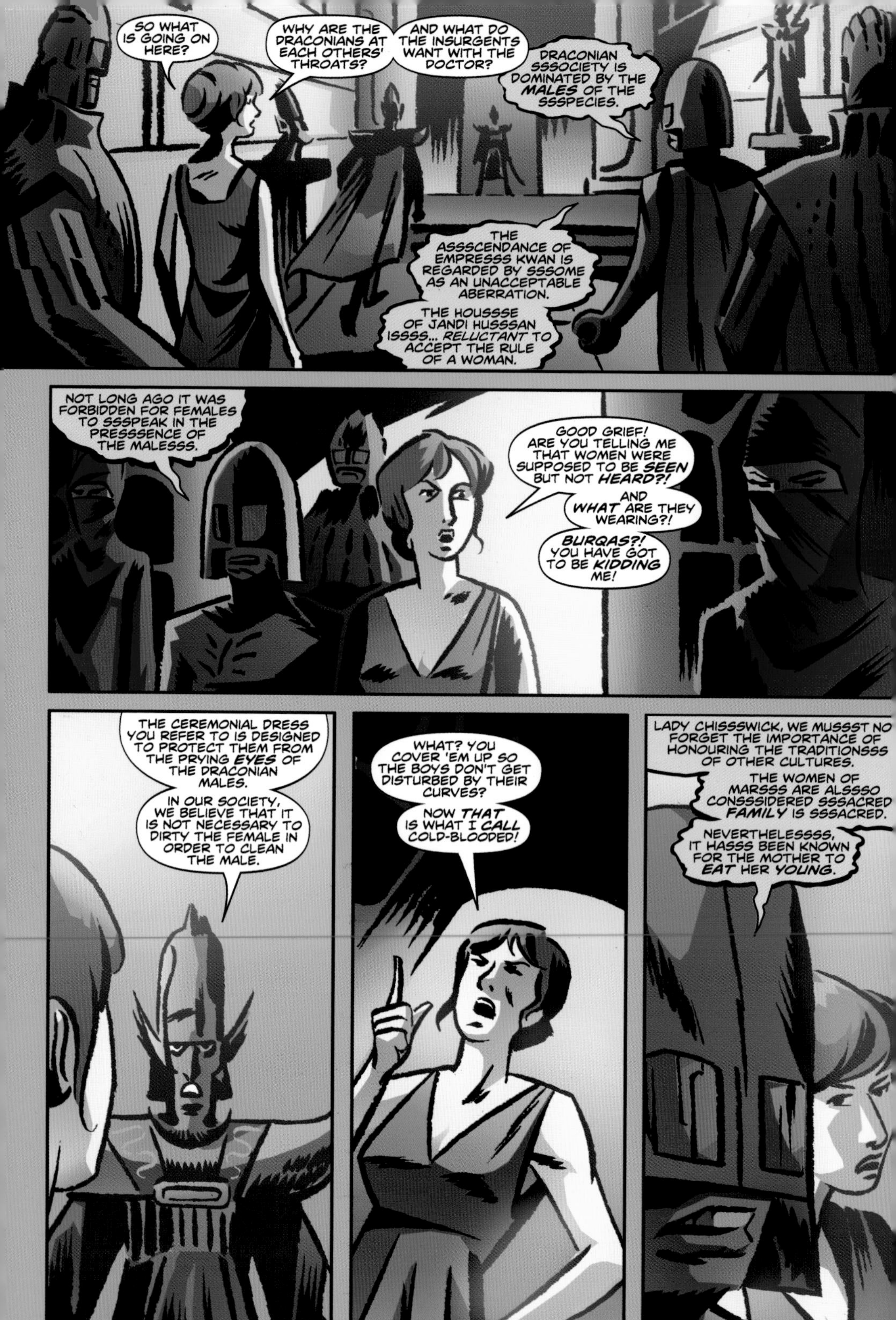
SO WHAT IS GOING ON HERE?
WHY ARE THE DRACONIANS AT EACH OTHERS' THROATS?
AND WHAT DO THE INSURGENTS WANT WITH THE DOCTOR?
DRACONIAN SSSOCIETY IS DOMINATED BY THE MALES OF THE SSSPECIES.
THE ASSSCENDANCE OF EMPRESSS KWAN IS REGARDED BY SSSOME AS AN UNACCEPTABLE ABERRATION.
THE HOUSSSE OF JANDI HUSSSAN ISSSS... RELUCTANT TO ACCEPT THE RULE OF A WOMAN.
NOT LONG AGO IT WAS FORBIDDEN FOR FEMALES TO SSSPEAK IN THE PRESSSENCE OF THE MALESSS.
GOOD GRIEF! ARE YOU TELLING ME THAT WOMEN WERE SUPPOSED TO BE SEEN BUT NOT HEARD?!
AND WHAT ARE THEY WEARING?!
BURQAS?! YOU HAVE GOT TO BE KIDDING ME!
THE CEREMONIAL DRESS YOU REFER TO IS DESIGNED TO PROTECT THEM FROM THE PRYING EYES OF THE DRACONIAN MALES.
IN OUR SOCIETY, WE BELIEVE THAT IT IS NOT NECESSARY TO DIRTY THE FEMALE IN ORDER TO CLEAN THE MALE.
WHAT? YOU COVER 'EM UP SO THE BOYS DON'T GET DISTURBED BY THEIR CURVES?
NOW THAT IS WHAT I CALL COLD-BLOODED!
LADY CHISSSWICK, WE MUSSST NO FORGET THE IMPORTANCE OF HONOURING THE TRADITIONSSS OF OTHER CULTURES.
THE WOMEN OF MARSSS ARE ALSSSO CONSSSIDERED SSSACRED. FAMILY IS SSSACRED.
NEVERTHELESSSS, IT HASSS BEEN KNOWN FOR THE MOTHER TO EAT HER YOUNG.

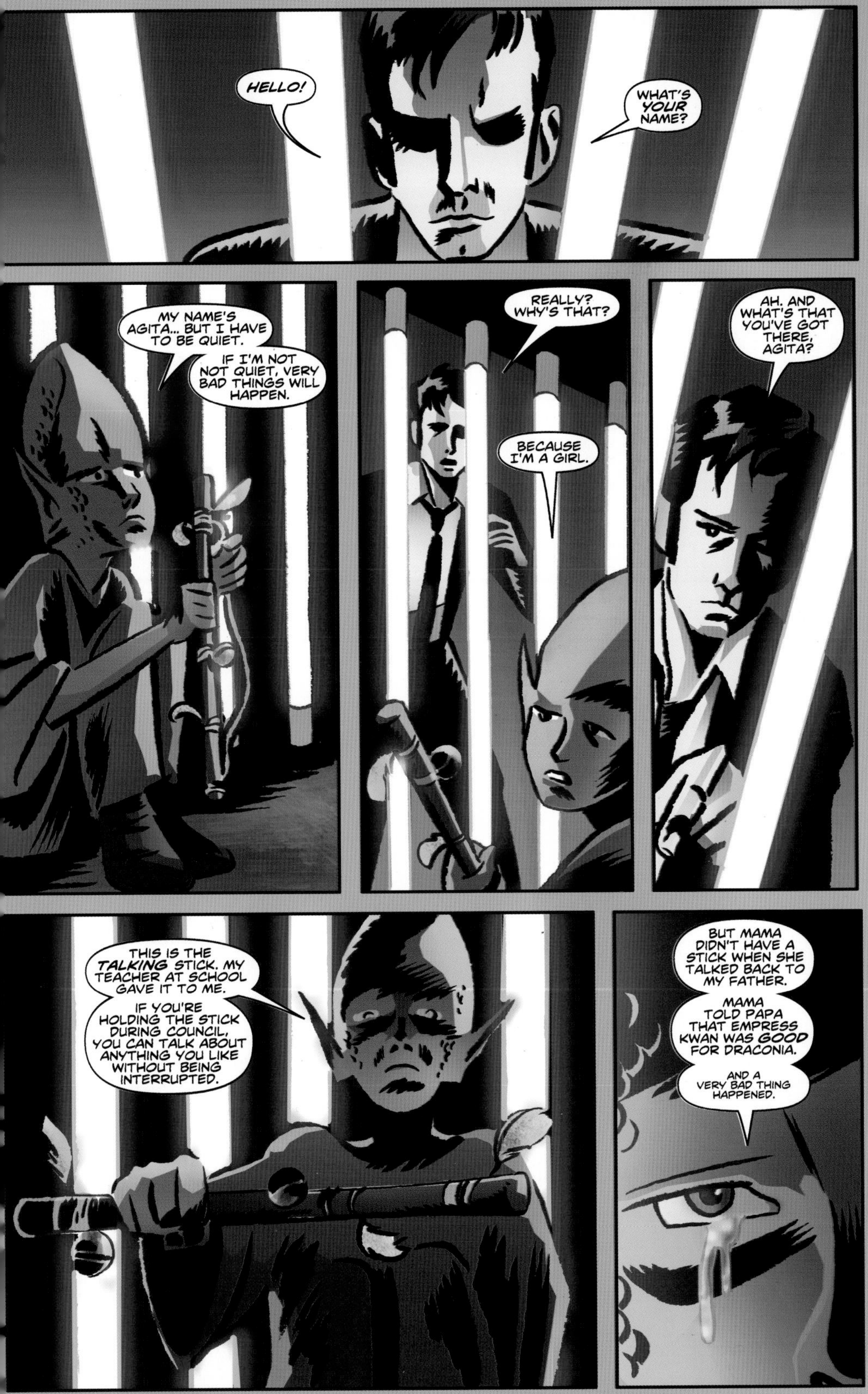
HELLO!
WHAT'S YOUR NAME?
MY NAME'S AGITA... BUT I HAVE TO BE QUIET.
IF I'M NOT NOT QUIET, VERY BAD THINGS WILL HAPPEN.
REALLY? WHY'S THAT?
BECAUSE I'M A GIRL.
AH. AND WHAT'S THAT YOU'VE GOT THERE, AGITA?
THIS IS THE *TALKING* STICK. MY TEACHER AT SCHOOL GAVE IT TO ME.
IF YOU'RE HOLDING THE STICK DURING COUNCIL, YOU CAN TALK ABOUT ANYTHING YOU LIKE WITHOUT BEING INTERRUPTED.
BUT MAMA DIDN'T HAVE A STICK WHEN SHE TALKED BACK TO MY FATHER.
MAMA TOLD PAPA THAT EMPRESS KWAN WAS *GOOD* FOR DRACONIA.
AND A VERY BAD THING HAPPENED.

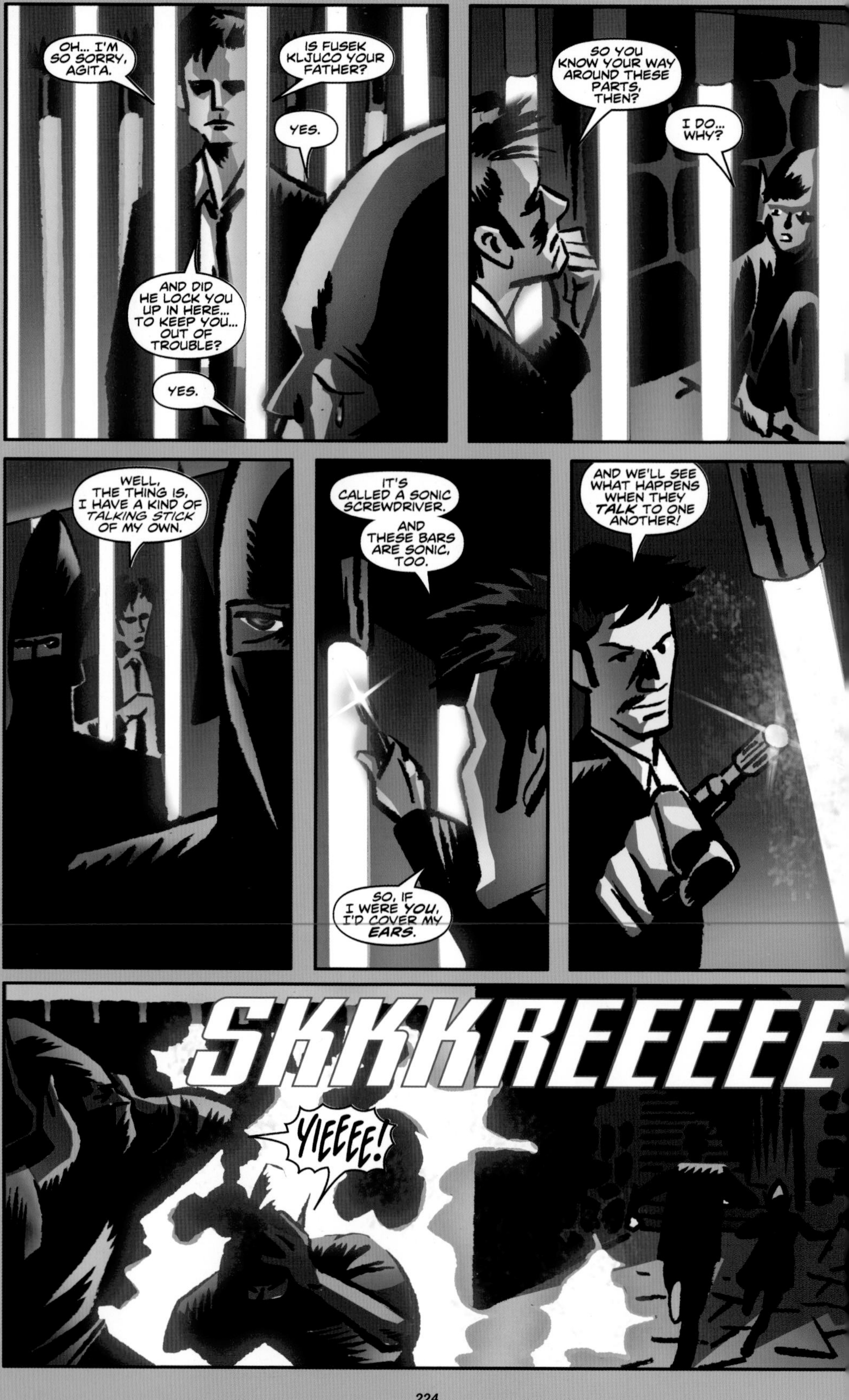
OH... I'M SO SORRY, AGITA.
IS FUSEK KLJUCO YOUR FATHER?
YES.
AND DID HE LOCK YOU UP IN HERE... TO KEEP YOU... OUT OF TROUBLE?
YES.
SO YOU KNOW YOUR WAY AROUND THESE PARTS, THEN?
I DO... WHY?
WELL, THE THING IS, I HAVE A KIND OF *TALKING STICK* OF MY OWN.
IT'S CALLED A SONIC SCREWDRIVER.
AND THESE BARS ARE SONIC, TOO.
SO, IF I WERE **YOU**, I'D COVER MY **EARS**.
AND WE'LL SEE WHAT HAPPENS WHEN THEY **TALK** TO ONE ANOTHER!
SKKKREEEEEE
YIEEEE!

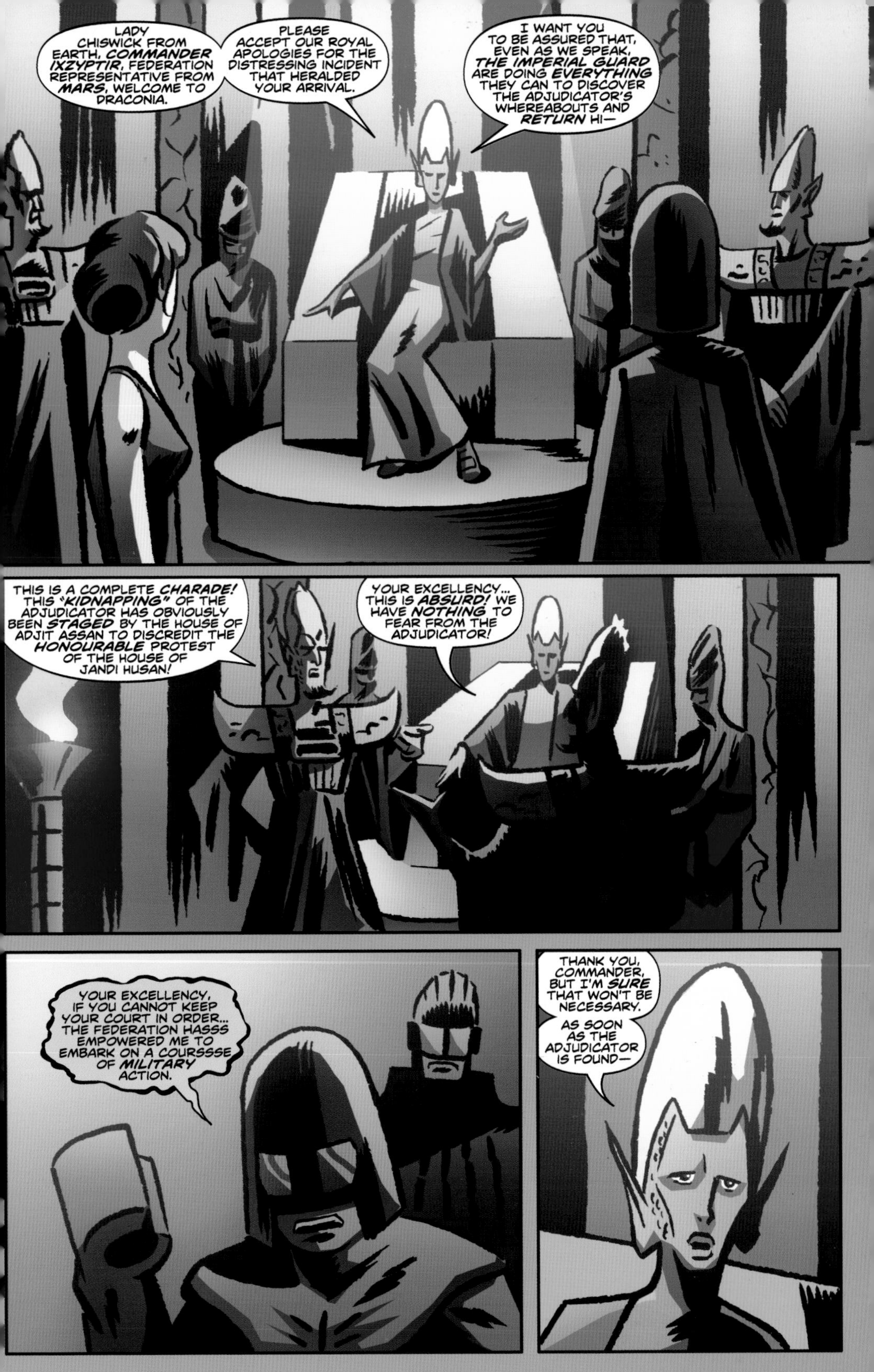
LADY CHISWICK FROM EARTH, COMMANDER IXZYPTIR, FEDERATION REPRESENTATIVE FROM MARS, WELCOME TO DRACONIA.
PLEASE ACCEPT OUR ROYAL APOLOGIES FOR THE DISTRESSING INCIDENT THAT HERALDED YOUR ARRIVAL.
I WANT YOU TO BE ASSURED THAT, EVEN AS WE SPEAK, THE IMPERIAL GUARD ARE DOING EVERYTHING THEY CAN TO DISCOVER THE ADJUDICATOR'S WHEREABOUTS AND RETURN HI—
THIS IS A COMPLETE CHARADE! THIS "KIDNAPPING" OF THE ADJUDICATOR HAS OBVIOUSLY BEEN STAGED BY THE HOUSE OF ADJIT ASSAN TO DISCREDIT THE HONOURABLE PROTEST OF THE HOUSE OF JANDI HUSAN!
YOUR EXCELLENCY... THIS IS ABSURD! WE HAVE NOTHING TO FEAR FROM THE ADJUDICATOR!
YOUR EXCELLENCY, IF YOU CANNOT KEEP YOUR COURT IN ORDER... THE FEDERATION HASSS EMPOWERED ME TO EMBARK ON A COURSSSE OF MILITARY ACTION.
THANK YOU, COMMANDER, BUT I'M SURE THAT WON'T BE NECESSARY.
AS SOON AS THE ADJUDICATOR IS FOUND—

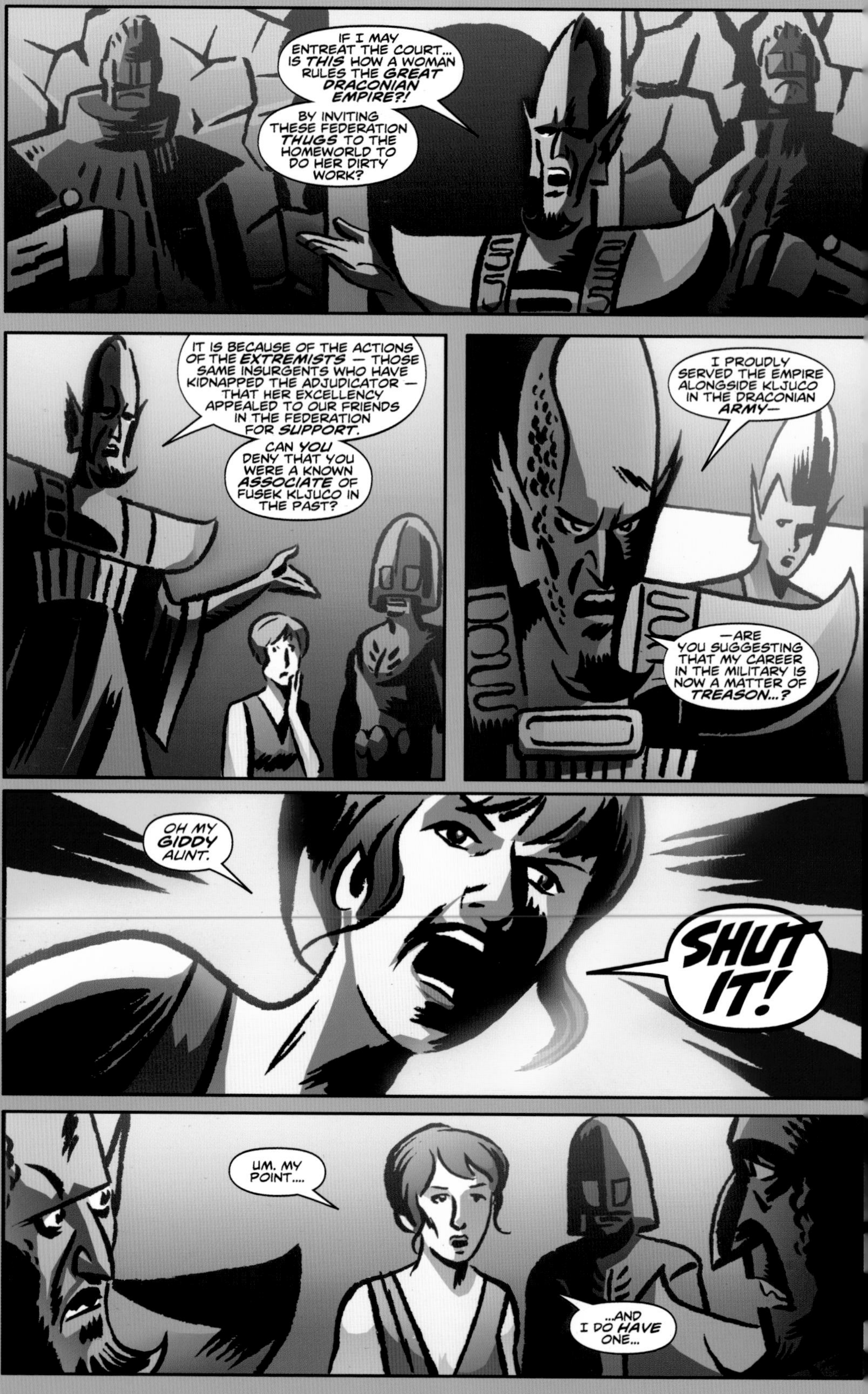
IF I MAY ENTREAT THE COURT... IS THIS HOW A WOMAN RULES THE GREAT DRACONIAN EMPIRE?!
BY INVITING THESE FEDERATION THUGS TO THE HOMEWORLD TO DO HER DIRTY WORK?
IT IS BECAUSE OF THE ACTIONS OF THE EXTREMISTS — THOSE SAME INSURGENTS WHO HAVE KIDNAPPED THE ADJUDICATOR — THAT HER EXCELLENCY APPEALED TO OUR FRIENDS IN THE FEDERATION FOR SUPPORT.
CAN YOU DENY THAT YOU WERE A KNOWN ASSOCIATE OF FUSEK KLJUCO IN THE PAST?
I PROUDLY SERVED THE EMPIRE ALONGSIDE KLJUCO IN THE DRACONIAN ARMY—
—ARE YOU SUGGESTING THAT MY CAREER IN THE MILITARY IS NOW A MATTER OF TREASON...?
OH MY GIDDY AUNT.
SHUT IT!
UM. MY POINT....
...AND I DO HAVE ONE...

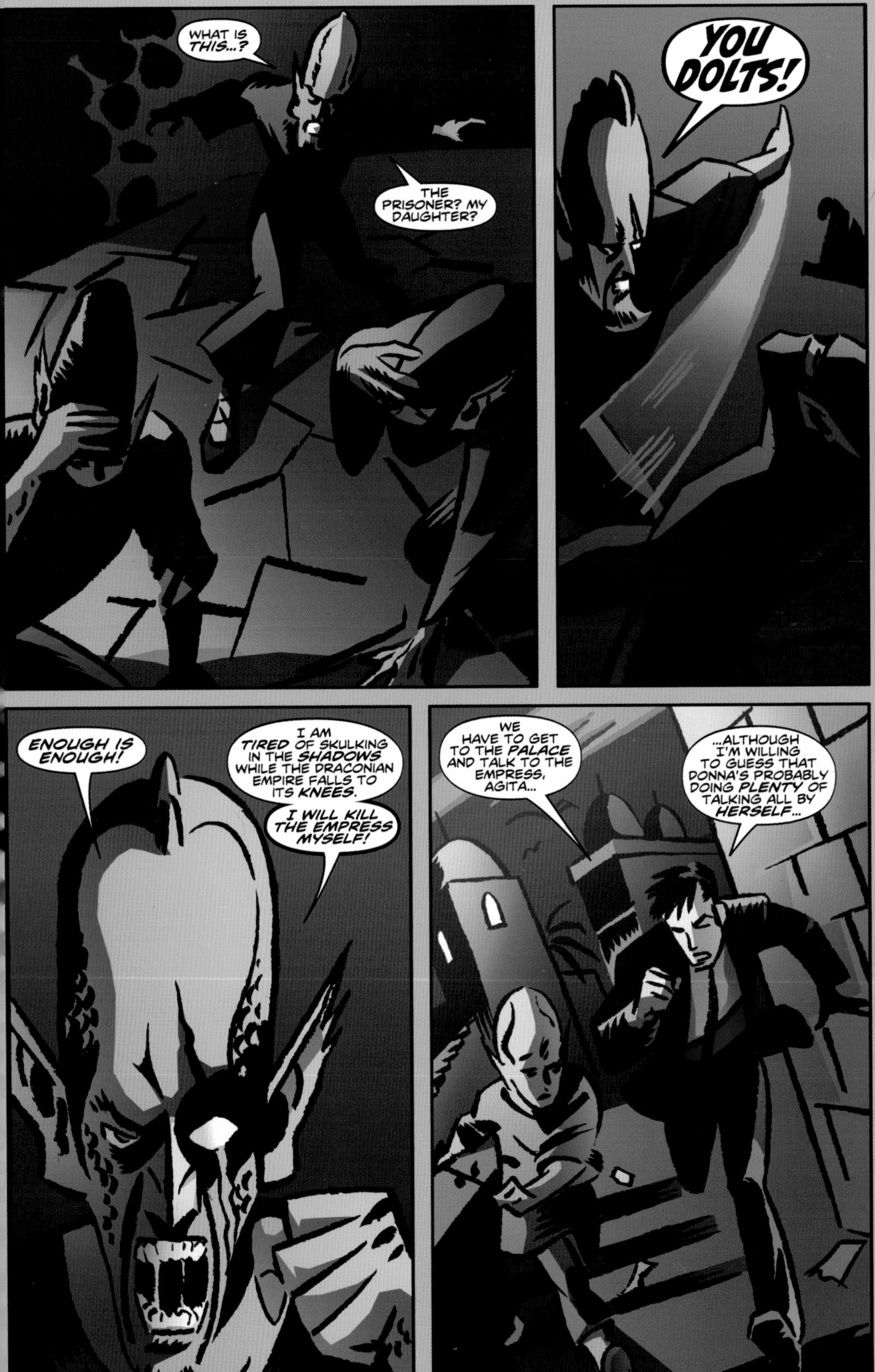
WHAT IS THIS...?
THE PRISONER? MY DAUGHTER?
YOU DOLTS!
ENOUGH IS ENOUGH!
I AM TIRED OF SKULKING IN THE SHADOWS WHILE THE DRACONIAN EMPIRE FALLS TO ITS KNEES.
I WILL KILL THE EMPRESS MYSELF!
WE HAVE TO GET TO THE PALACE AND TALK TO THE EMPRESS, AGITA...
...ALTHOUGH I'M WILLING TO GUESS THAT DONNA'S PROBABLY DOING PLENTY OF TALKING ALL BY HERSELF...

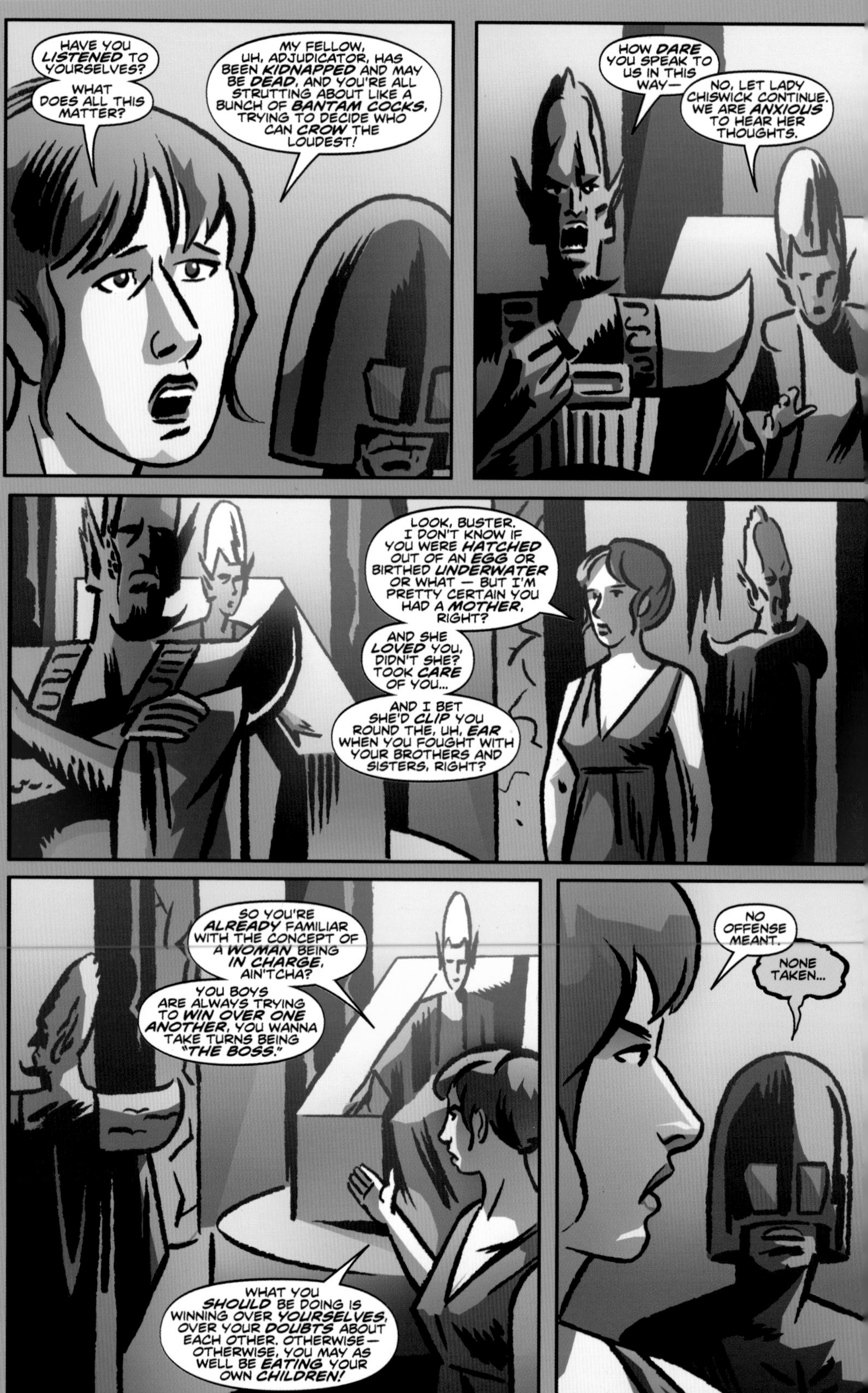
HAVE YOU LISTENED TO YOURSELVES?
WHAT DOES ALL THIS MATTER?
MY FELLOW, UH, ADJUDICATOR, HAS BEEN KIDNAPPED AND MAY BE DEAD, AND YOU'RE ALL STRUTTING ABOUT LIKE A BUNCH OF BANTAM COCKS, TRYING TO DECIDE WHO CAN CROW THE LOUDEST!
HOW DARE YOU SPEAK TO US IN THIS WAY—
NO, LET LADY CHISWICK CONTINUE. WE ARE ANXIOUS TO HEAR HER THOUGHTS.
LOOK, BUSTER. I DON'T KNOW IF YOU WERE HATCHED OUT OF AN EGG OR BIRTHED UNDERWATER OR WHAT — BUT I'M PRETTY CERTAIN YOU HAD A MOTHER, RIGHT?
AND SHE LOVED YOU, DIDN'T SHE? TOOK CARE OF YOU...
AND I BET SHE'D CLIP YOU ROUND THE, UH, EAR WHEN YOU FOUGHT WITH YOUR BROTHERS AND SISTERS, RIGHT?
SO YOU'RE ALREADY FAMILIAR WITH THE CONCEPT OF A WOMAN BEING IN CHARGE, AIN'TCHA?
YOU BOYS ARE ALWAYS TRYING TO WIN OVER ONE ANOTHER, YOU WANNA TAKE TURNS BEING "THE BOSS."
WHAT YOU SHOULD BE DOING IS WINNING OVER YOURSELVES, OVER YOUR DOUBTS ABOUT EACH OTHER. OTHERWISE— OTHERWISE, YOU MAY AS WELL BE EATING YOUR OWN CHILDREN!
NO OFFENSE MEANT.
NONE TAKEN...

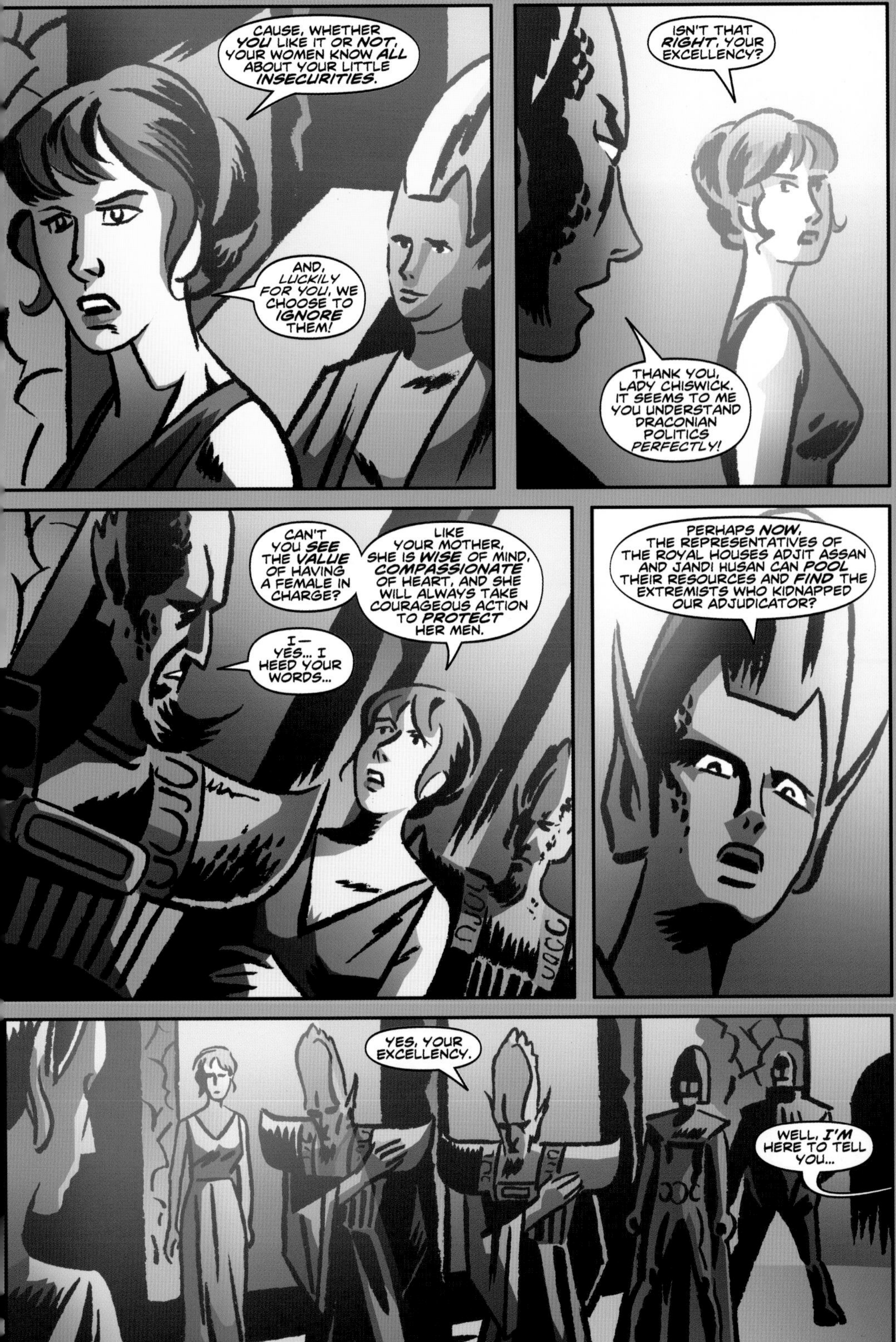
CAUSE, WHETHER YOU LIKE IT OR NOT, YOUR WOMEN KNOW ALL ABOUT YOUR LITTLE INSECURITIES.
AND, LUCKILY FOR YOU, WE CHOOSE TO IGNORE THEM!
ISN'T THAT RIGHT, YOUR EXCELLENCY?
THANK YOU, LADY CHISWICK. IT SEEMS TO ME YOU UNDERSTAND DRACONIAN POLITICS PERFECTLY!
CAN'T YOU SEE THE VALUE OF HAVING A FEMALE IN CHARGE?
LIKE YOUR MOTHER, SHE IS WISE OF MIND, COMPASSIONATE OF HEART, AND SHE WILL ALWAYS TAKE COURAGEOUS ACTION TO PROTECT HER MEN.
I— YES... I HEED YOUR WORDS...
PERHAPS NOW, THE REPRESENTATIVES OF THE ROYAL HOUSES ADJIT ASSAN AND JANDI HUSAN CAN POOL THEIR RESOURCES AND FIND THE EXTREMISTS WHO KIDNAPPED OUR ADJUDICATOR?
YES, YOUR EXCELLENCY.
WELL, I'M HERE TO TELL YOU...

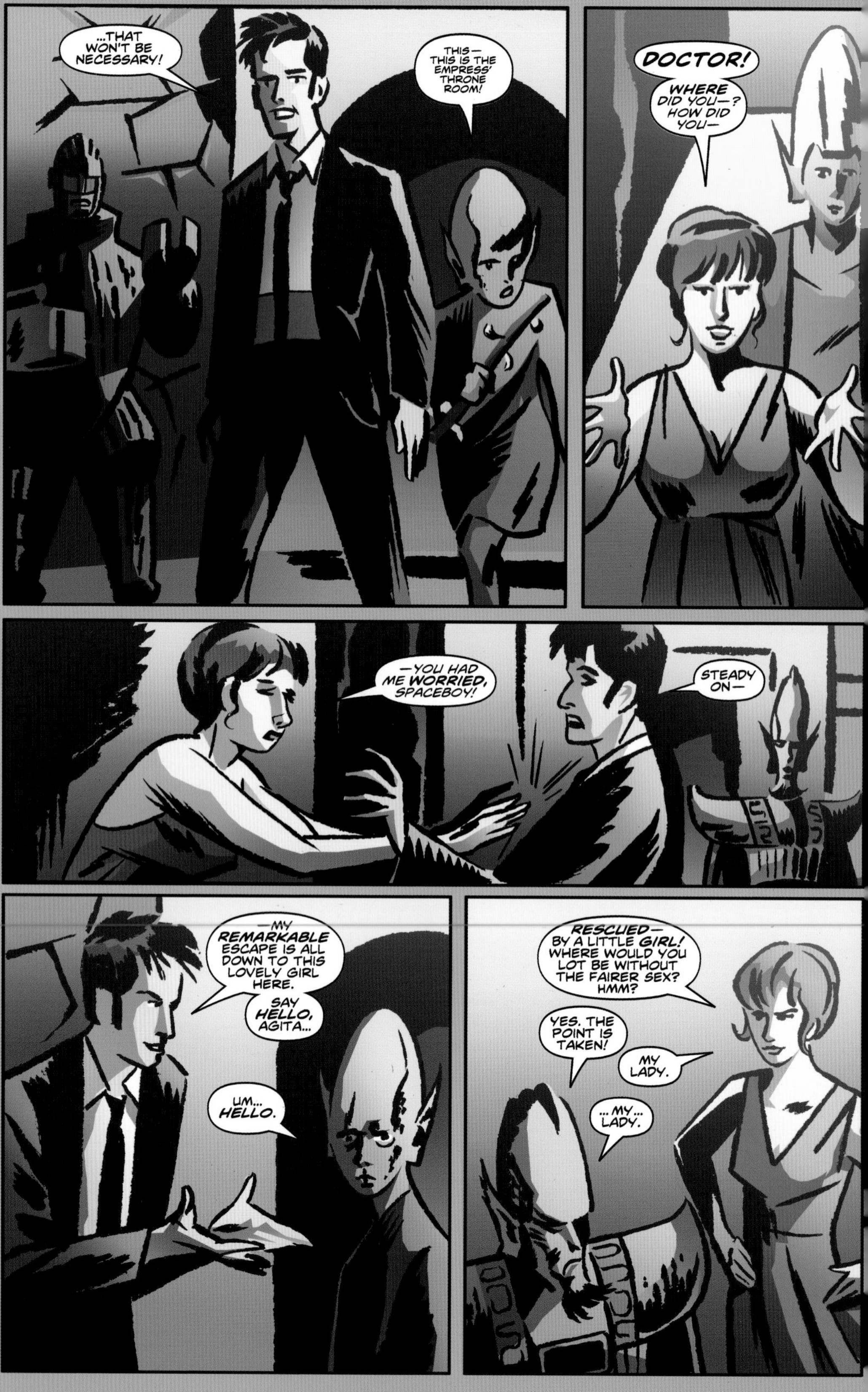
...THAT WON'T BE NECESSARY!
THIS— THIS IS THE EMPRESS' THRONE ROOM!
DOCTOR!
WHERE DID YOU—? HOW DID YOU—
—YOU HAD ME WORRIED, SPACEBOY!
STEADY ON—
—MY REMARKABLE ESCAPE IS ALL DOWN TO THIS LOVELY GIRL HERE.
SAY HELLO, AGITA...
UM... HELLO.
RESCUED— BY A LITTLE GIRL! WHERE WOULD YOU LOT BE WITHOUT THE FAIRER SEX? HMM?
YES. THE POINT IS TAKEN!
MY LADY.
...MY... LADY.

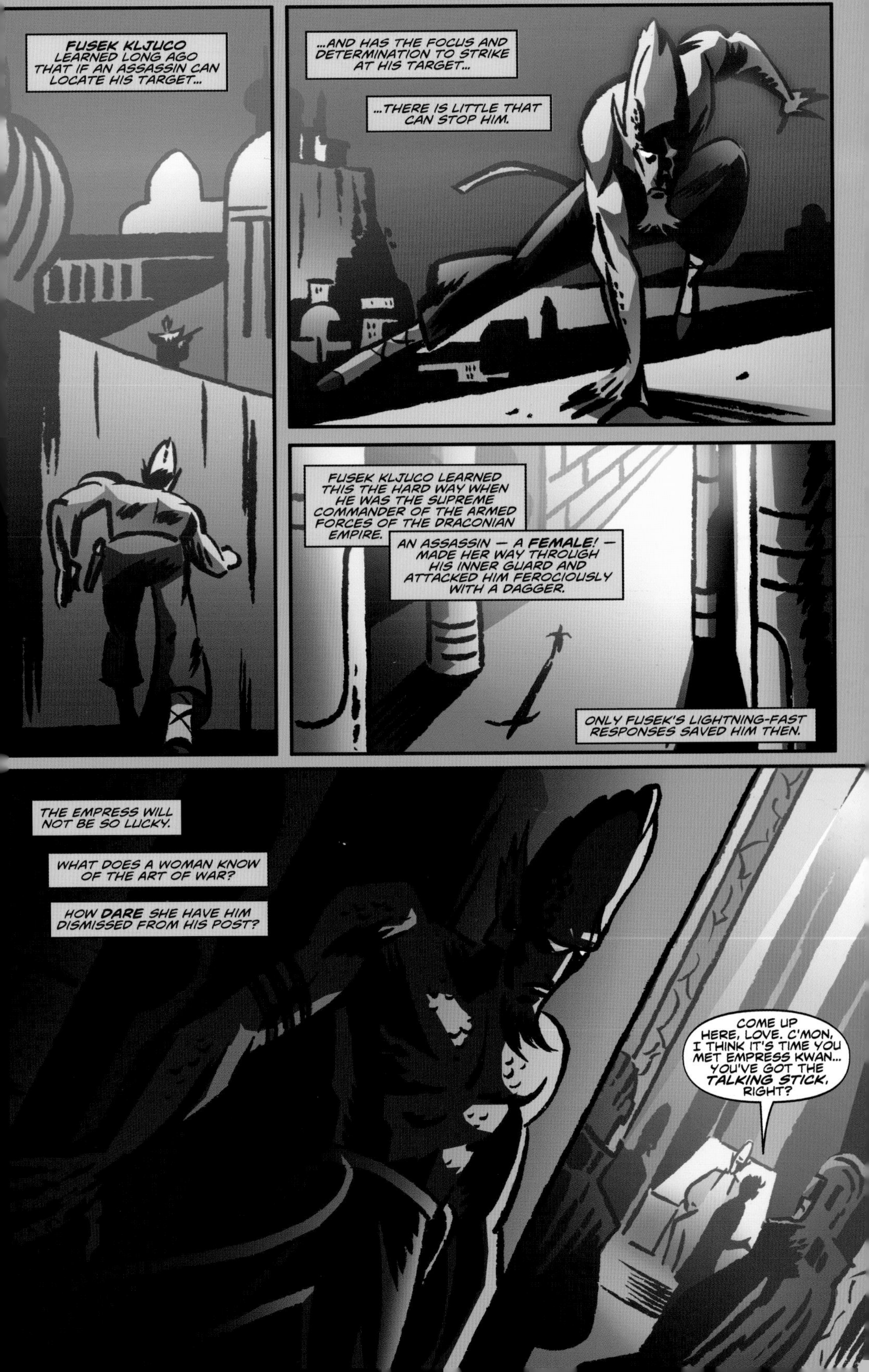
FUSEK KLJUCO LEARNED LONG AGO THAT IF AN ASSASSIN CAN LOCATE HIS TARGET...
...AND HAS THE FOCUS AND DETERMINATION TO STRIKE AT HIS TARGET...
...THERE IS LITTLE THAT CAN STOP HIM.
FUSEK KLJUCO LEARNED THIS THE HARD WAY WHEN HE WAS THE SUPREME COMMANDER OF THE ARMED FORCES OF THE DRACONIAN EMPIRE.
AN ASSASSIN — A FEMALE! — MADE HER WAY THROUGH HIS INNER GUARD AND ATTACKED HIM FEROCIOUSLY WITH A DAGGER.
ONLY FUSEK'S LIGHTNING-FAST RESPONSES SAVED HIM THEN.
THE EMPRESS WILL NOT BE SO LUCKY.
WHAT DOES A WOMAN KNOW OF THE ART OF WAR?
HOW DARE SHE HAVE HIM DISMISSED FROM HIS POST?
COME UP HERE, LOVE. C'MON, I THINK IT'S TIME YOU MET EMPRESS KWAN... YOU'VE GOT THE TALKING STICK, RIGHT?

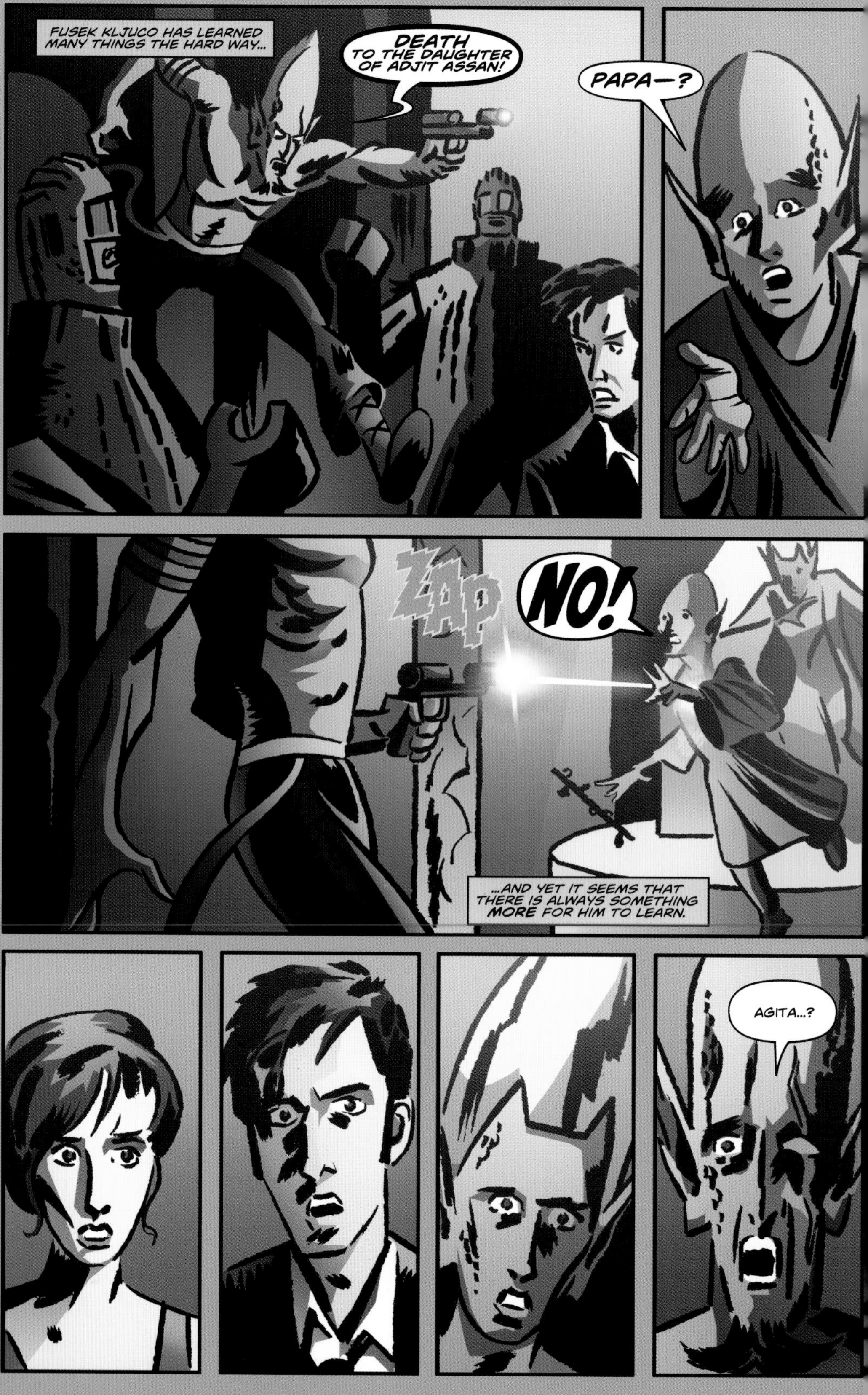
FUSEK KLJUCO HAS LEARNED MANY THINGS THE HARD WAY...
DEATH TO THE DAUGHTER OF ADJIT ASSAN!
PAPA—?
ZAP
NO!
...AND YET IT SEEMS THAT THERE IS ALWAYS SOMETHING MORE FOR HIM TO LEARN.
AGITA...?

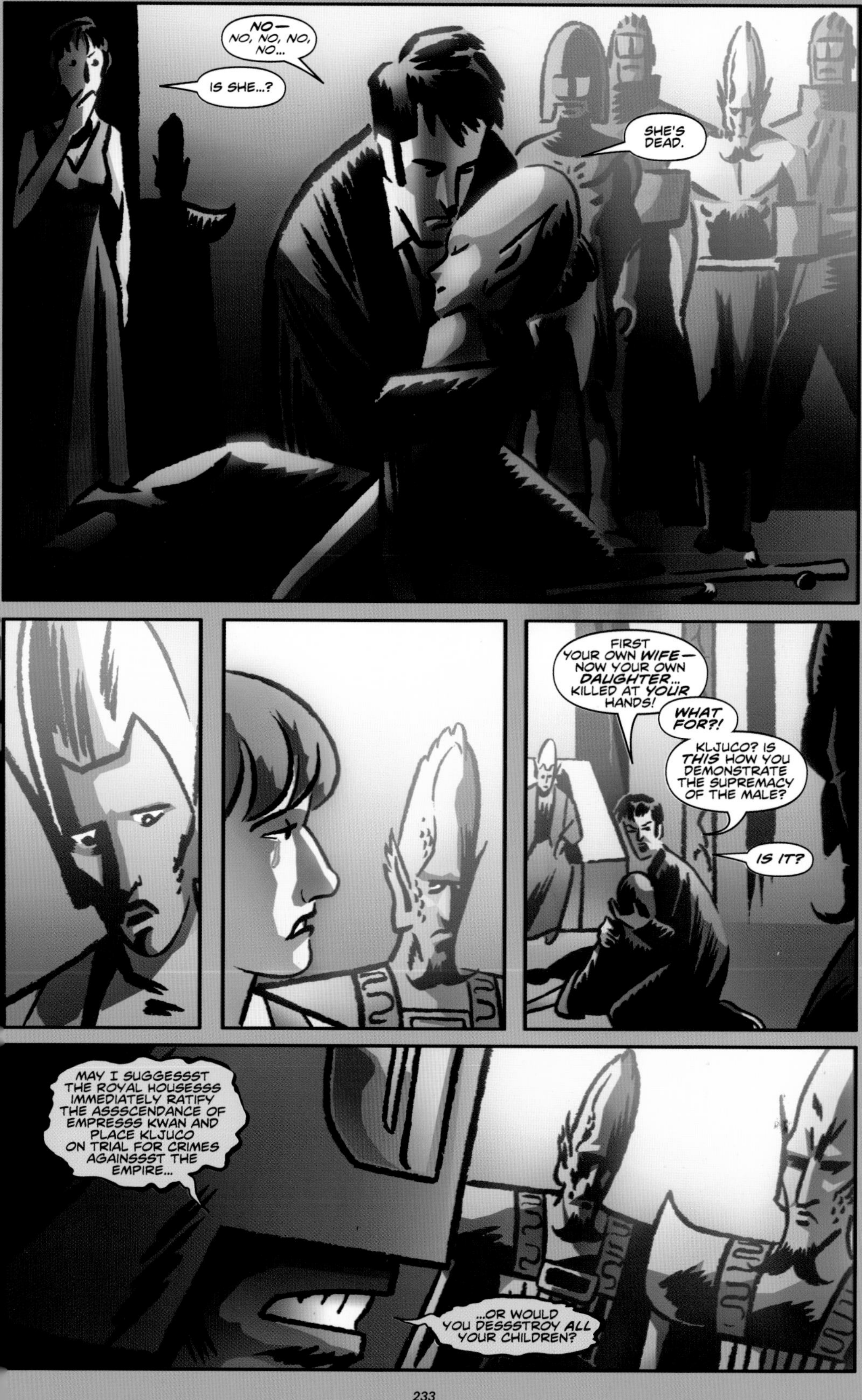
NO— NO, NO, NO, NO...
IS SHE...?
SHE'S DEAD.
FIRST YOUR OWN WIFE— NOW YOUR OWN DAUGHTER... KILLED AT YOUR HANDS!
WHAT FOR?!
KLJUCO? IS THIS HOW YOU DEMONSTRATE THE SUPREMACY OF THE MALE?
IS IT?
MAY I SUGGESSST THE ROYAL HOUSESSS IMMEDIATELY RATIFY THE ASSSCENDANCE OF EMPRESSS KWAN AND PLACE KLJUCO ON TRIAL FOR CRIMES AGAINSSST THE EMPIRE...
...OR WOULD YOU DESSSTROY ALL YOUR CHILDREN?

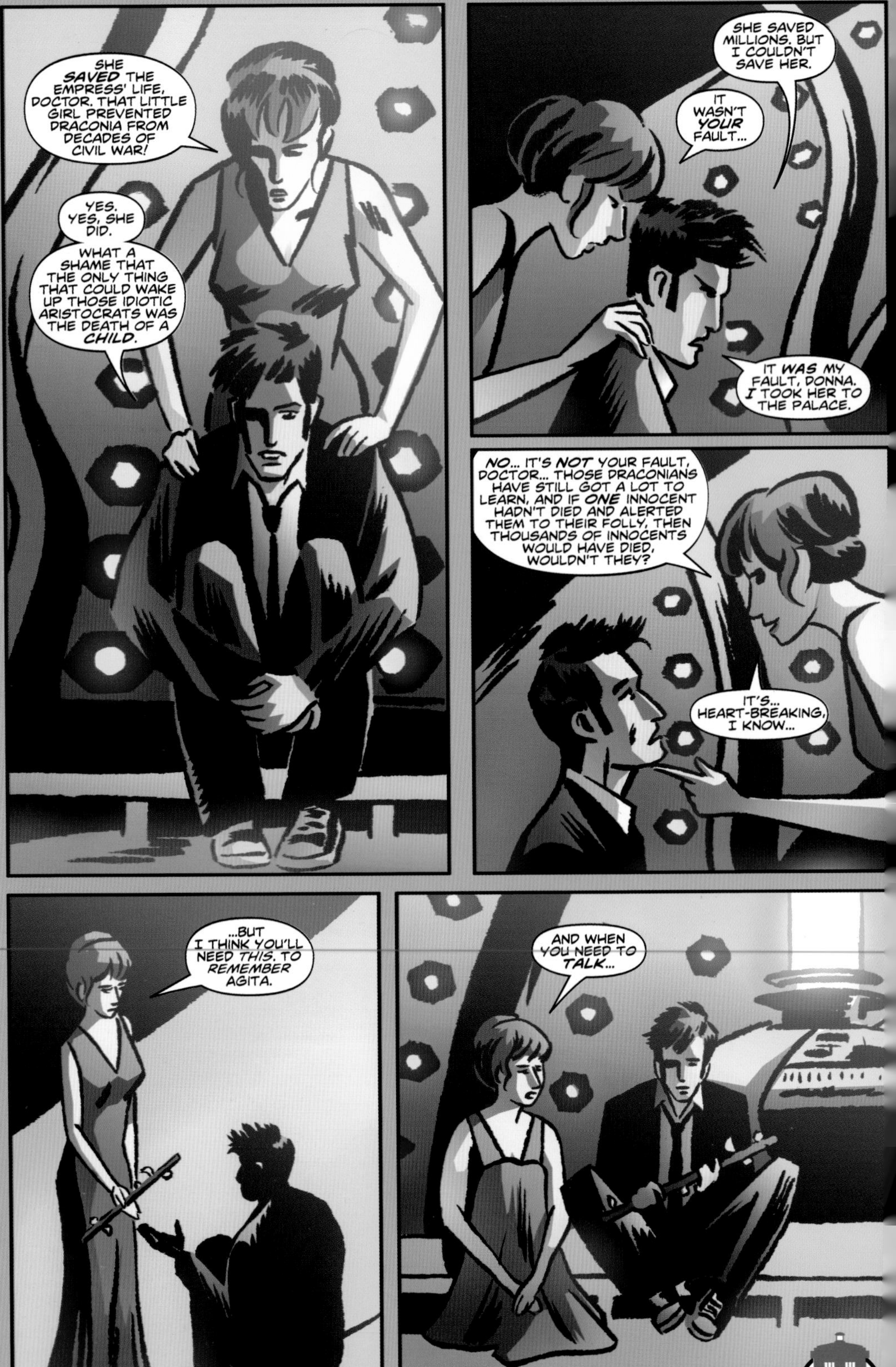
SHE SAVED THE EMPRESS' LIFE, DOCTOR. THAT LITTLE GIRL PREVENTED DRACONIA FROM DECADES OF CIVIL WAR!
YES. YES, SHE DID.
WHAT A SHAME THAT THE ONLY THING THAT COULD WAKE UP THOSE IDIOTIC ARISTOCRATS WAS THE DEATH OF A CHILD.
SHE SAVED MILLIONS, BUT I COULDN'T SAVE HER.
IT WASN'T YOUR FAULT...
IT WAS MY FAULT, DONNA. I TOOK HER TO THE PALACE.
NO... IT'S NOT YOUR FAULT, DOCTOR... THOSE DRACONIANS HAVE STILL GOT A LOT TO LEARN, AND IF ONE INNOCENT HADN'T DIED AND ALERTED THEM TO THEIR FOLLY, THEN THOUSANDS OF INNOCENTS WOULD HAVE DIED, WOULDN'T THEY?
IT'S... HEART-BREAKING, I KNOW...
...BUT I THINK YOU'LL NEED THIS. TO REMEMBER AGITA.
AND WHEN YOU NEED TO TALK...

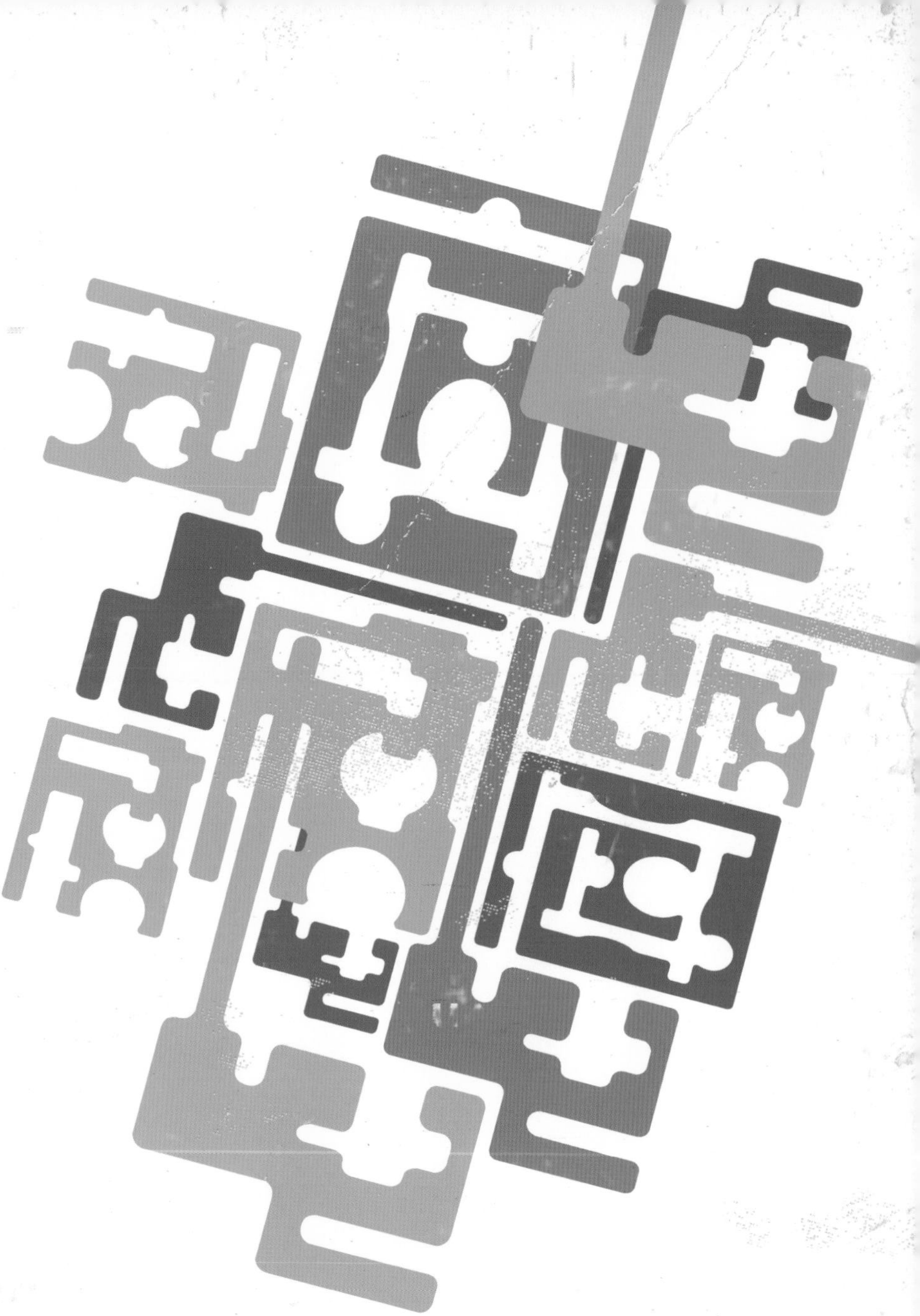

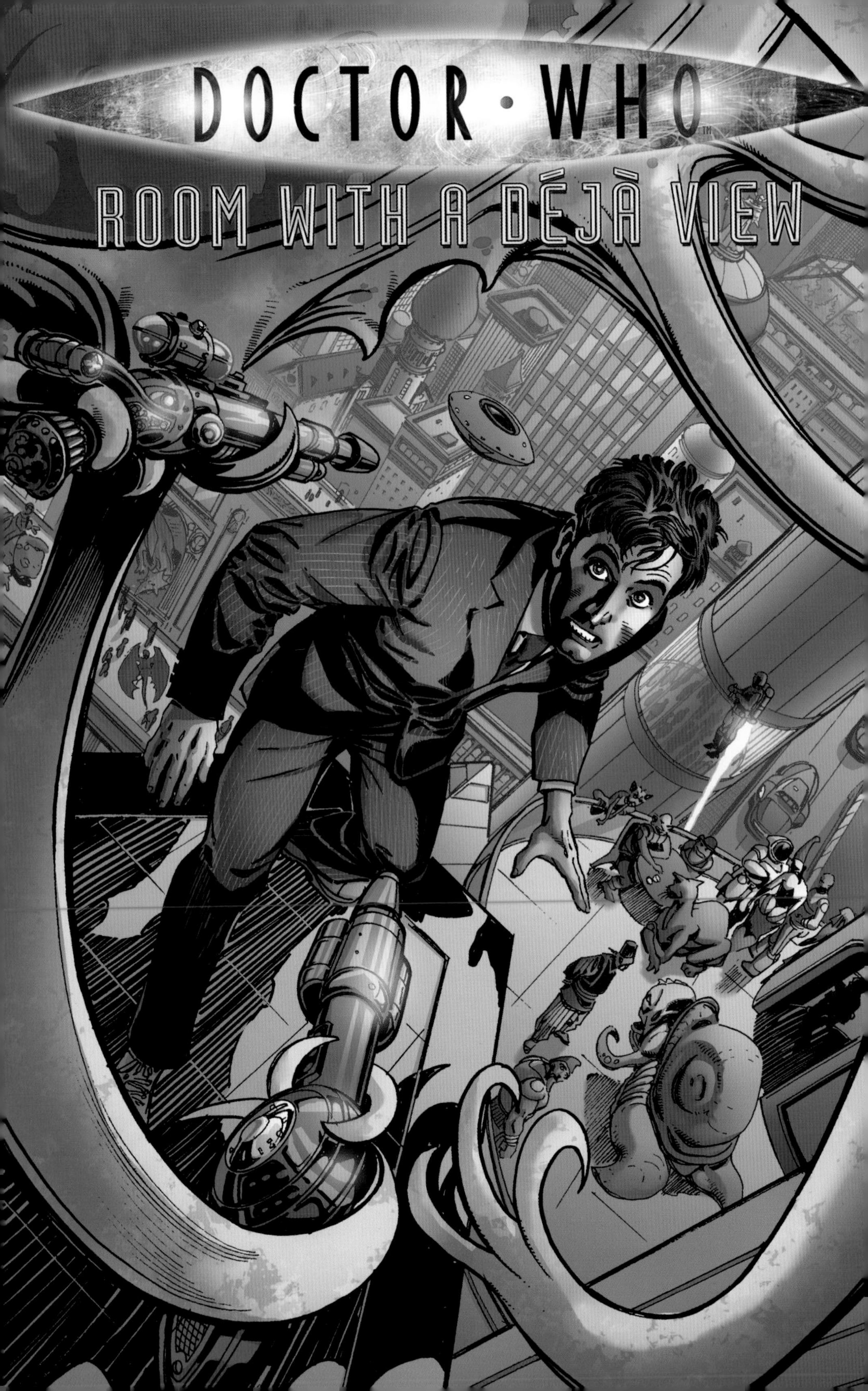
DOCTOR · WHO
ROOM WITH A DÉJÀ VIEW

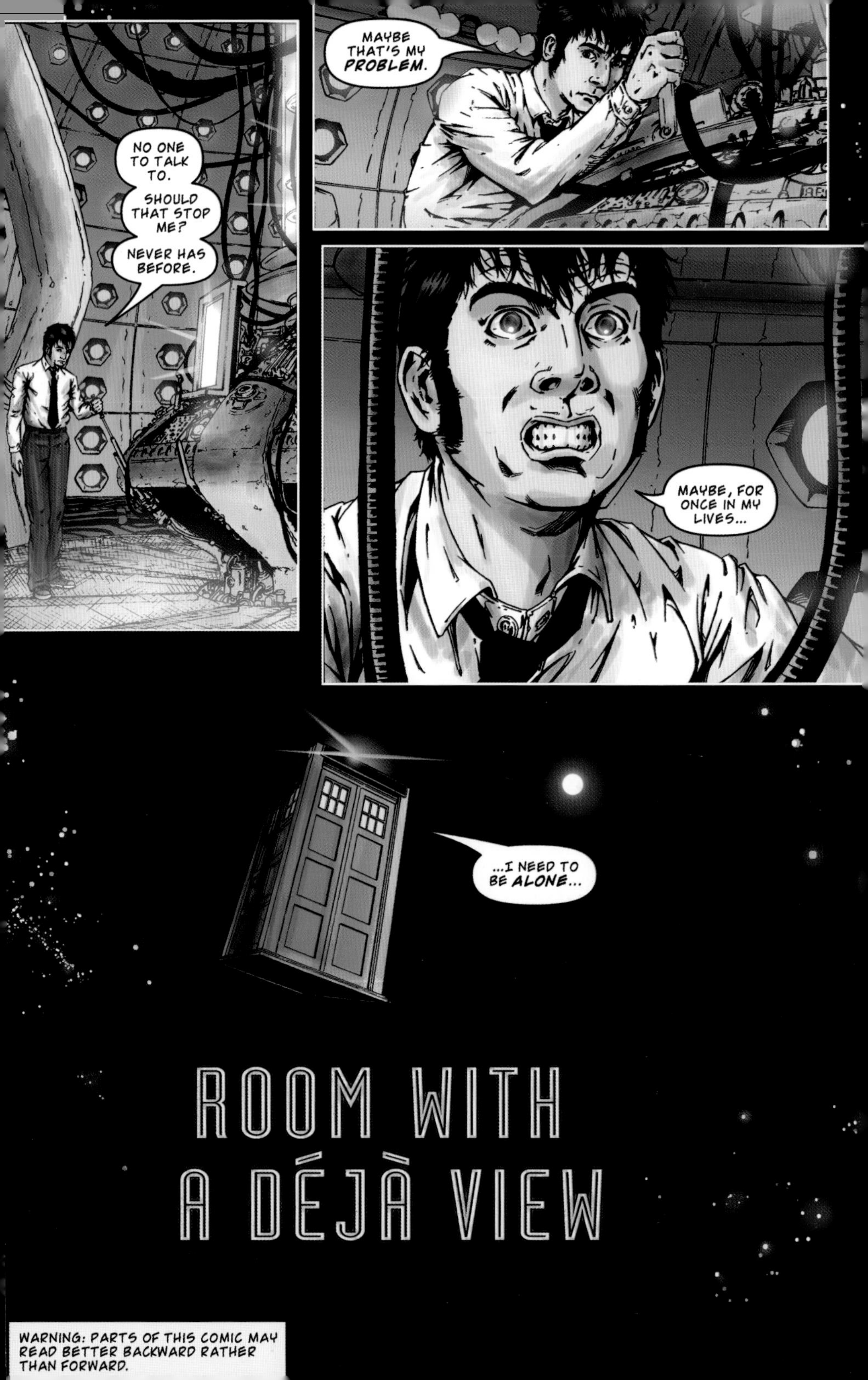
NO ONE TO TALK TO.
SHOULD THAT STOP ME?
NEVER HAS BEFORE.
MAYBE THAT'S MY PROBLEM.
MAYBE, FOR ONCE IN MY LIVES...
...I NEED TO BE ALONE...
ROOM WITH A DÉJÀ VIEW
WARNING: PARTS OF THIS COMIC MAY READ BETTER BACKWARD RATHER THAN FORWARD.

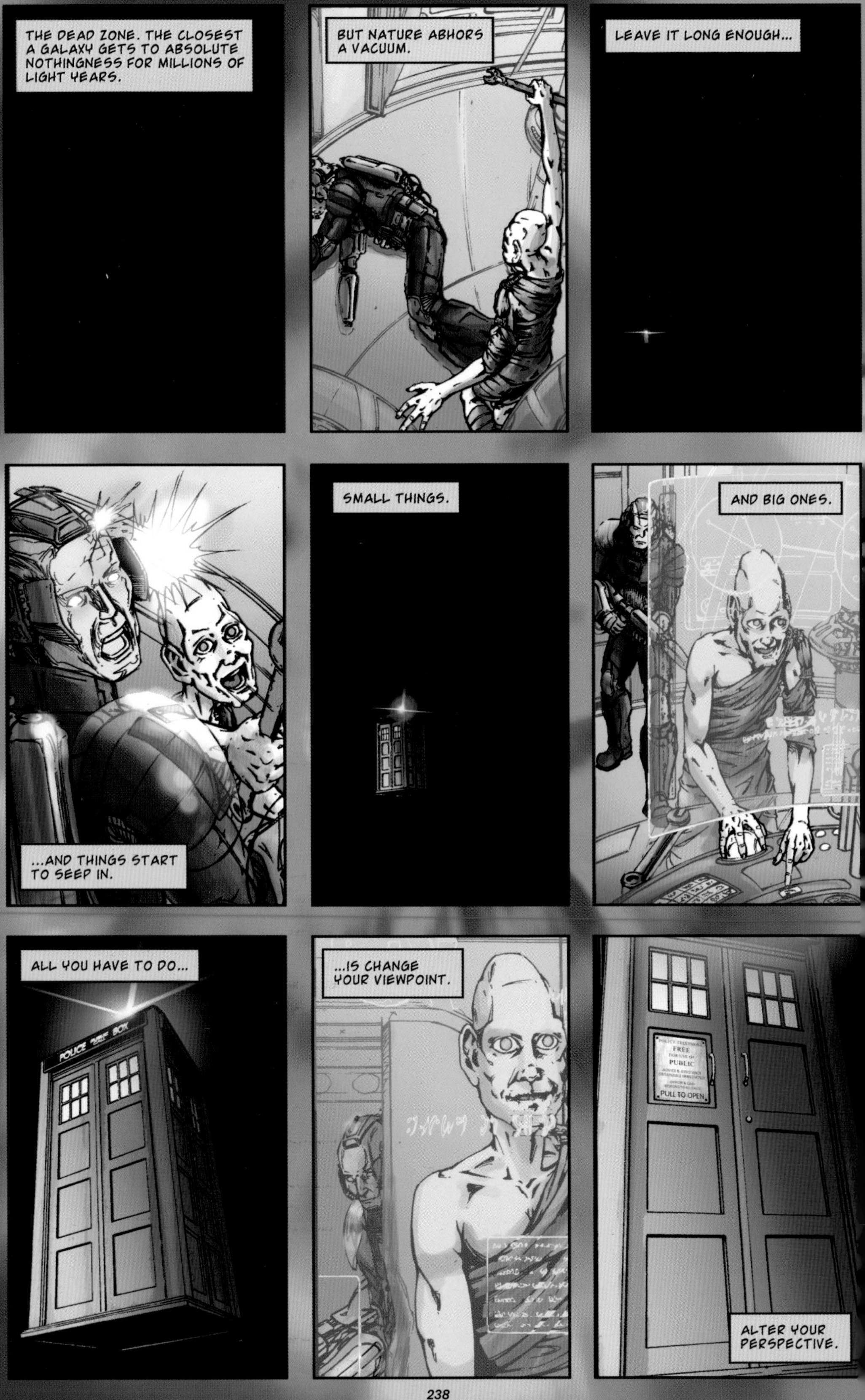
THE DEAD ZONE. THE CLOSEST A GALAXY GETS TO ABSOLUTE NOTHINGNESS FOR MILLIONS OF LIGHT YEARS.
BUT NATURE ABHORS A VACUUM.
LEAVE IT LONG ENOUGH...
...AND THINGS START TO SEEP IN.
SMALL THINGS.
AND BIG ONES.
ALL YOU HAVE TO DO...
POLICE PUBLIC CALL BOX
...IS CHANGE YOUR VIEWPOINT.
FREE FOR USE OF PUBLIC
PULL TO OPEN
ALTER YOUR PERSPECTIVE.

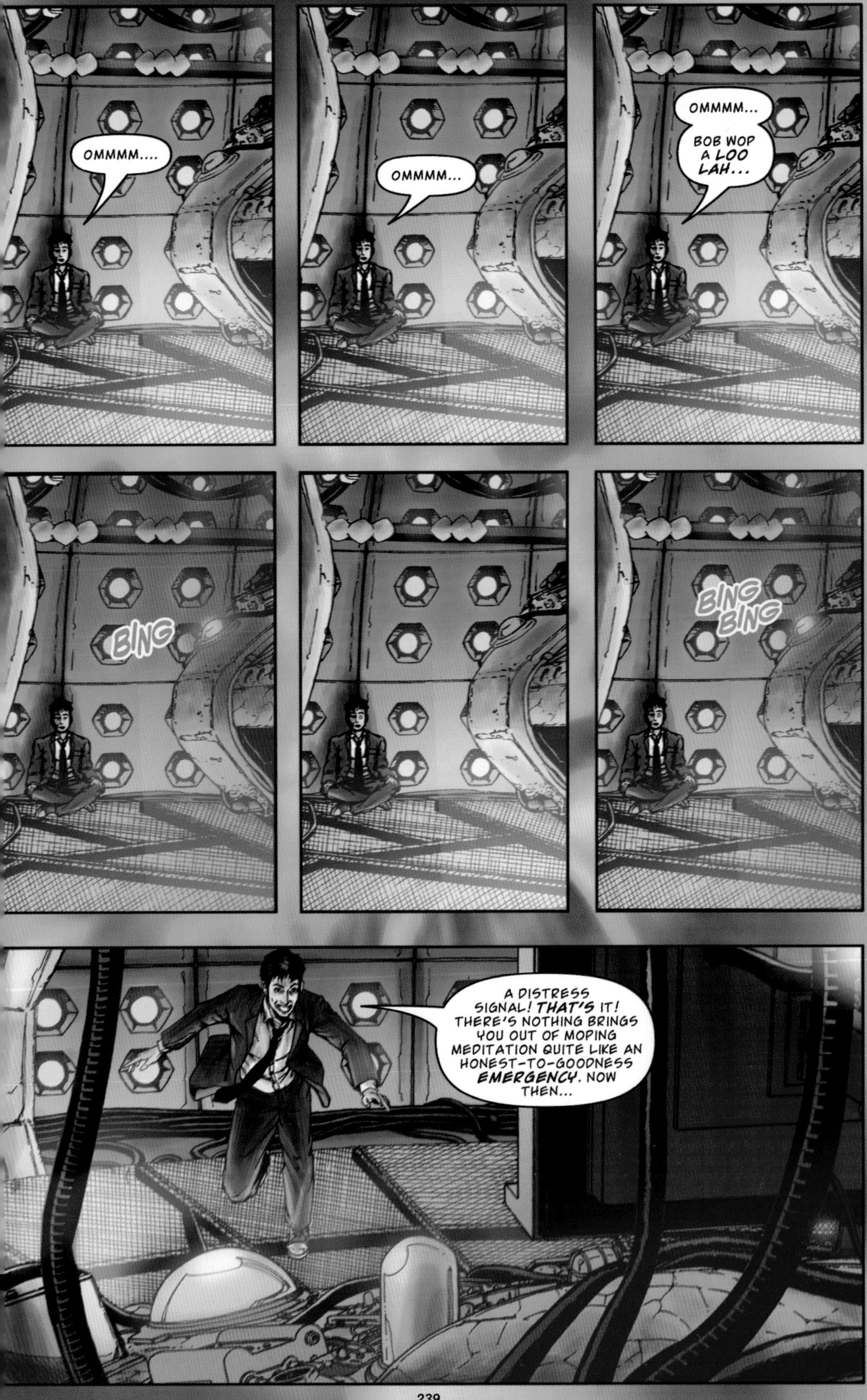
OMMMM....
OMMMM...
OMMMM...
BOB WOP A LOO LAH...
BING
BING BING
A DISTRESS SIGNAL! THAT'S IT! THERE'S NOTHING BRINGS YOU OUT OF MOPING MEDITATION QUITE LIKE AN HONEST-TO-GOODNESS EMERGENCY. NOW THEN...

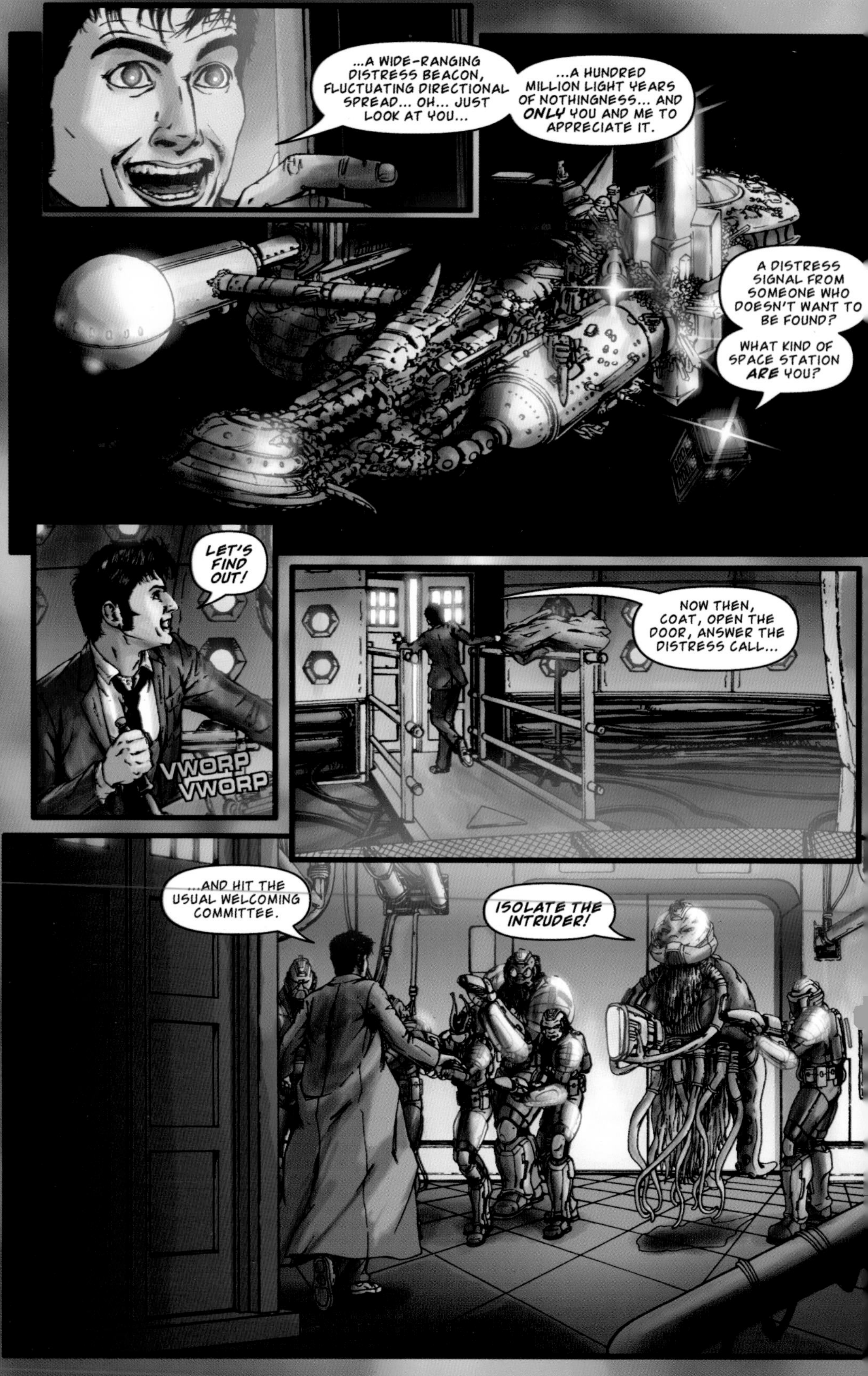
...A WIDE-RANGING DISTRESS BEACON, FLUCTUATING DIRECTIONAL SPREAD... OH... JUST LOOK AT YOU...
...A HUNDRED MILLION LIGHT YEARS OF NOTHINGNESS... AND ONLY YOU AND ME TO APPRECIATE IT.
A DISTRESS SIGNAL FROM SOMEONE WHO DOESN'T WANT TO BE FOUND?
WHAT KIND OF SPACE STATION ARE YOU?
LET'S FIND OUT!
VWORP VWORP
NOW THEN, COAT, OPEN THE DOOR, ANSWER THE DISTRESS CALL...
...AND HIT THE USUAL WELCOMING COMMITTEE.
ISOLATE THE INTRUDER!

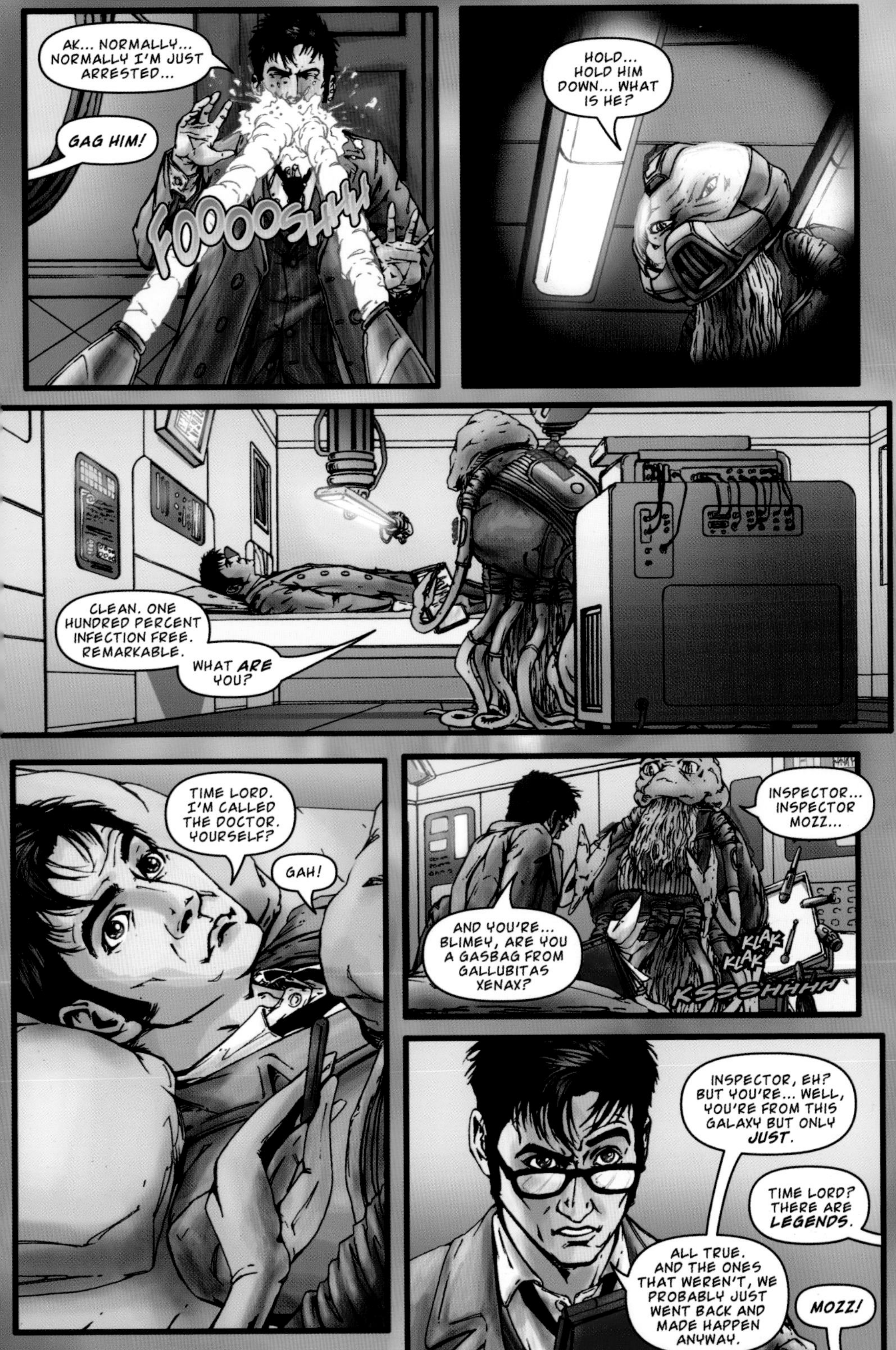
AK... NORMALLY... NORMALLY I'M JUST ARRESTED...
GAG HIM!
FOOOOSHHH
HOLD... HOLD HIM DOWN... WHAT IS HE?
CLEAN. ONE HUNDRED PERCENT INFECTION FREE. REMARKABLE.
WHAT ARE YOU?
TIME LORD. I'M CALLED THE DOCTOR. YOURSELF?
GAH!
INSPECTOR... INSPECTOR MOZZ...
AND YOU'RE... BLIMEY, ARE YOU A GASBAG FROM GALLUBITAS XENAX?
KLAK
KLAK
KSSSHHHH
INSPECTOR, EH? BUT YOU'RE... WELL, YOU'RE FROM THIS GALAXY BUT ONLY JUST.
TIME LORD? THERE ARE LEGENDS.
ALL TRUE. AND THE ONES THAT WEREN'T, WE PROBABLY JUST WENT BACK AND MADE HAPPEN ANYWAY.
MOZZ!

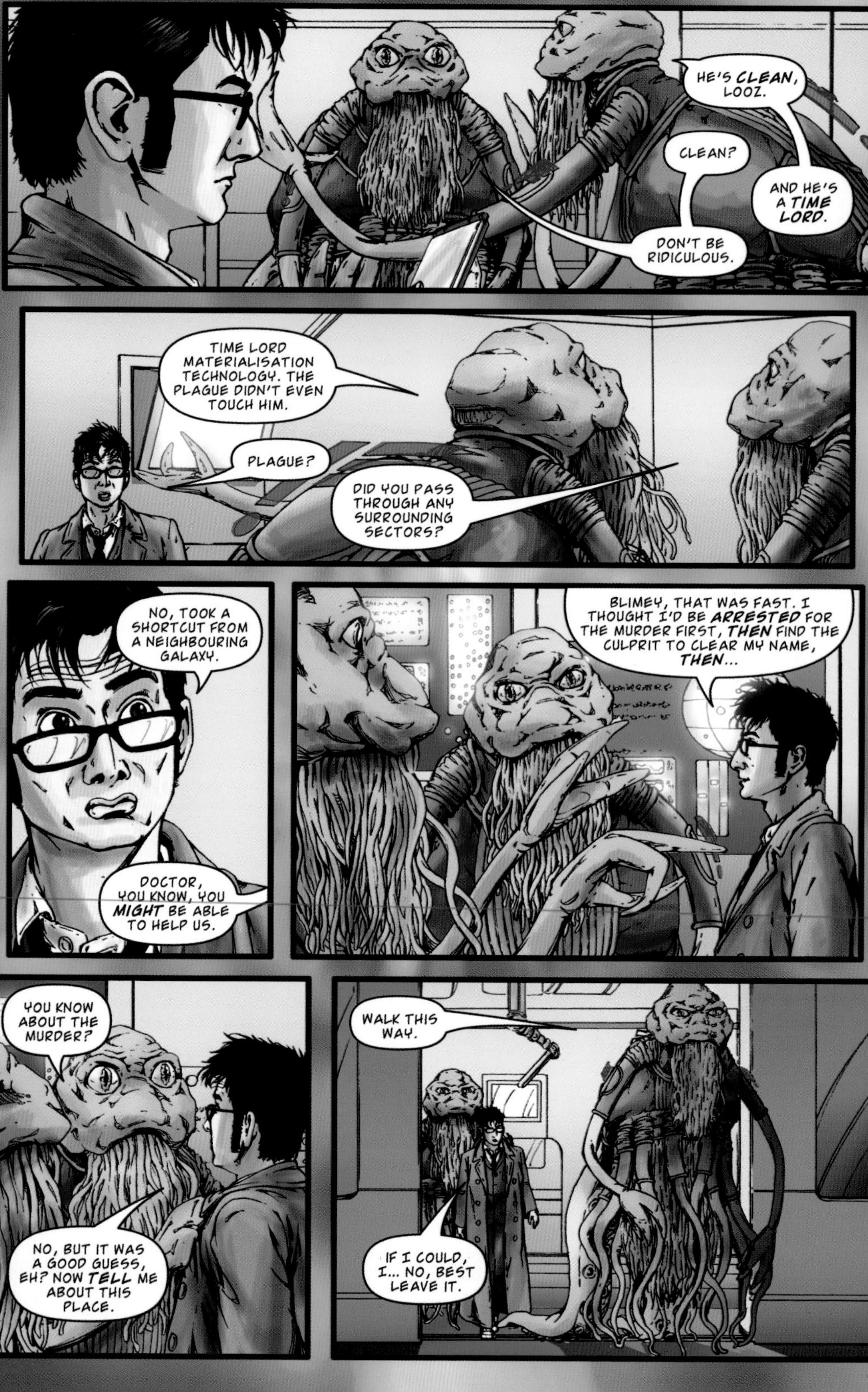
HE'S CLEAN, LOOZ.
CLEAN?
DON'T BE RIDICULOUS.
AND HE'S A TIME LORD.
TIME LORD MATERIALISATION TECHNOLOGY. THE PLAGUE DIDN'T EVEN TOUCH HIM.
PLAGUE?
DID YOU PASS THROUGH ANY SURROUNDING SECTORS?
NO, TOOK A SHORTCUT FROM A NEIGHBOURING GALAXY.
DOCTOR, YOU KNOW, YOU MIGHT BE ABLE TO HELP US.
BLIMEY, THAT WAS FAST. I THOUGHT I'D BE ARRESTED FOR THE MURDER FIRST, THEN FIND THE CULPRIT TO CLEAR MY NAME, THEN...
YOU KNOW ABOUT THE MURDER?
NO, BUT IT WAS A GOOD GUESS, EH? NOW TELL ME ABOUT THIS PLACE.
WALK THIS WAY.
IF I COULD, I... NO, BEST LEAVE IT.

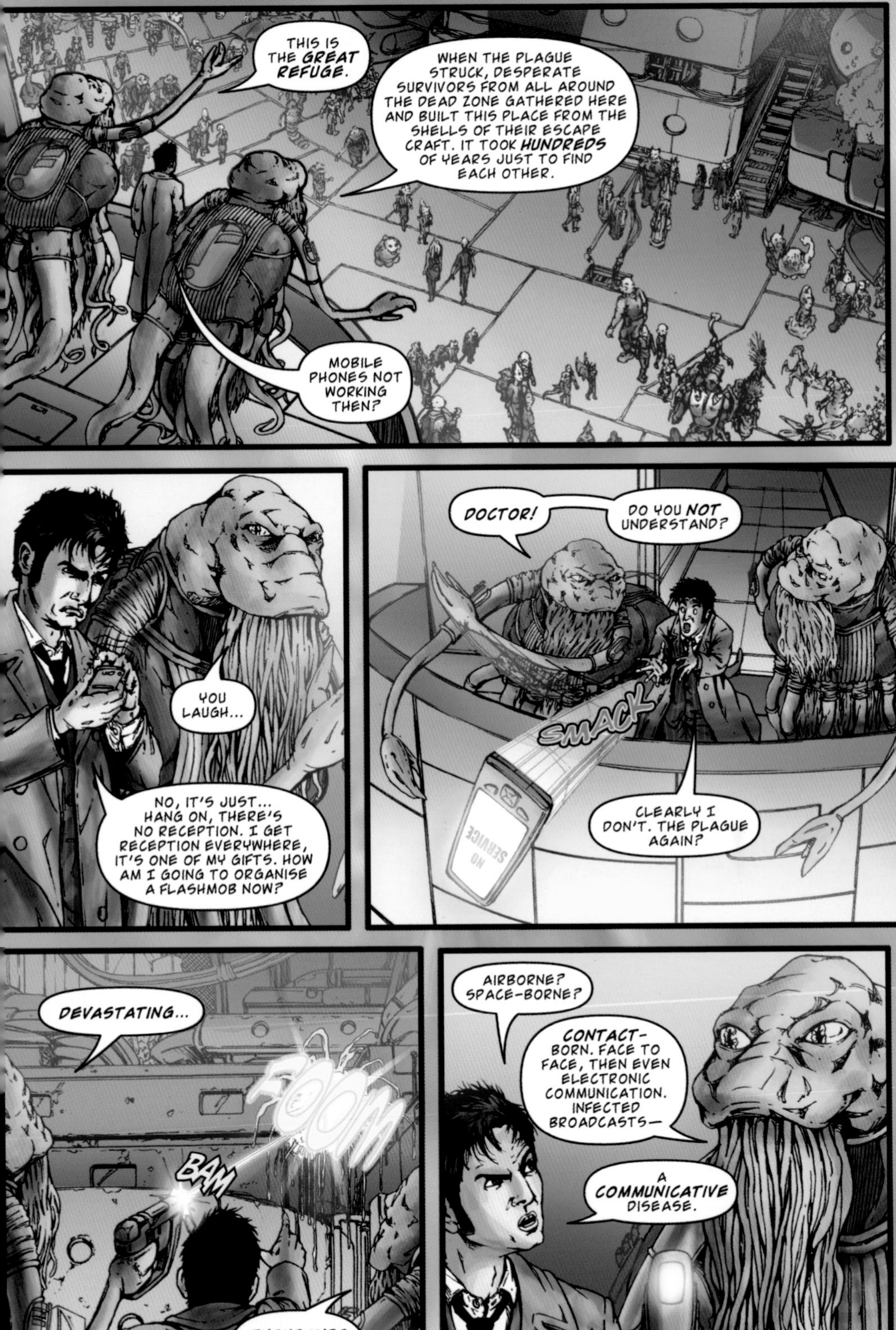

THIS IS THE GREAT REFUGE.
WHEN THE PLAGUE STRUCK, DESPERATE SURVIVORS FROM ALL AROUND THE DEAD ZONE GATHERED HERE AND BUILT THIS PLACE FROM THE SHELLS OF THEIR ESCAPE CRAFT. IT TOOK HUNDREDS OF YEARS JUST TO FIND EACH OTHER.
MOBILE PHONES NOT WORKING THEN?
YOU LAUGH...
NO, IT'S JUST... HANG ON, THERE'S NO RECEPTION. I GET RECEPTION EVERYWHERE, IT'S ONE OF MY GIFTS. HOW AM I GOING TO ORGANISE A FLASHMOB NOW?
DOCTOR!
DO YOU NOT UNDERSTAND?
SMACK
NO SERVICE
CLEARLY I DON'T. THE PLAGUE AGAIN?
DEVASTATING...
FOOM
BAM
THOUSANDS OF SPECIES, TRILLIONS OF LIFEFORMS... WIPED OUT.
AIRBORNE? SPACE-BORNE?
CONTACT-BORN. FACE TO FACE, THEN EVEN ELECTRONIC COMMUNICATION. INFECTED BROADCASTS—
A COMMUNICATIVE DISEASE.

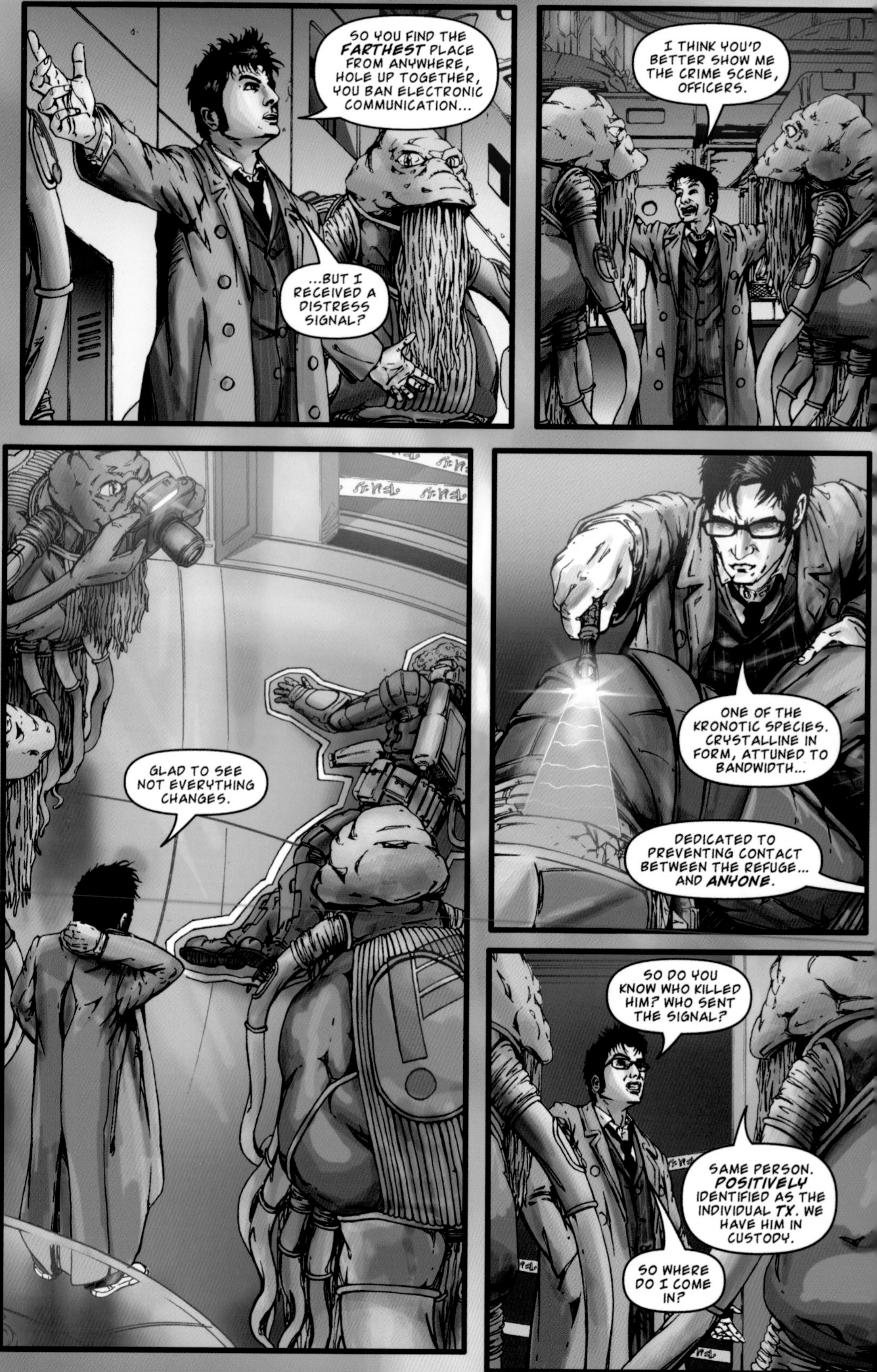
SO YOU FIND THE FARTHEST PLACE FROM ANYWHERE, HOLE UP TOGETHER, YOU BAN ELECTRONIC COMMUNICATION...
...BUT I RECEIVED A DISTRESS SIGNAL?
I THINK YOU'D BETTER SHOW ME THE CRIME SCENE, OFFICERS.
GLAD TO SEE NOT EVERYTHING CHANGES.
ONE OF THE KRONOTIC SPECIES. CRYSTALLINE IN FORM, ATTUNED TO BANDWIDTH...
DEDICATED TO PREVENTING CONTACT BETWEEN THE REFUGE... AND ANYONE.
SO DO YOU KNOW WHO KILLED HIM? WHO SENT THE SIGNAL?
SAME PERSON. POSITIVELY IDENTIFIED AS THE INDIVIDUAL TX. WE HAVE HIM IN CUSTODY.
SO WHERE DO I COME IN?

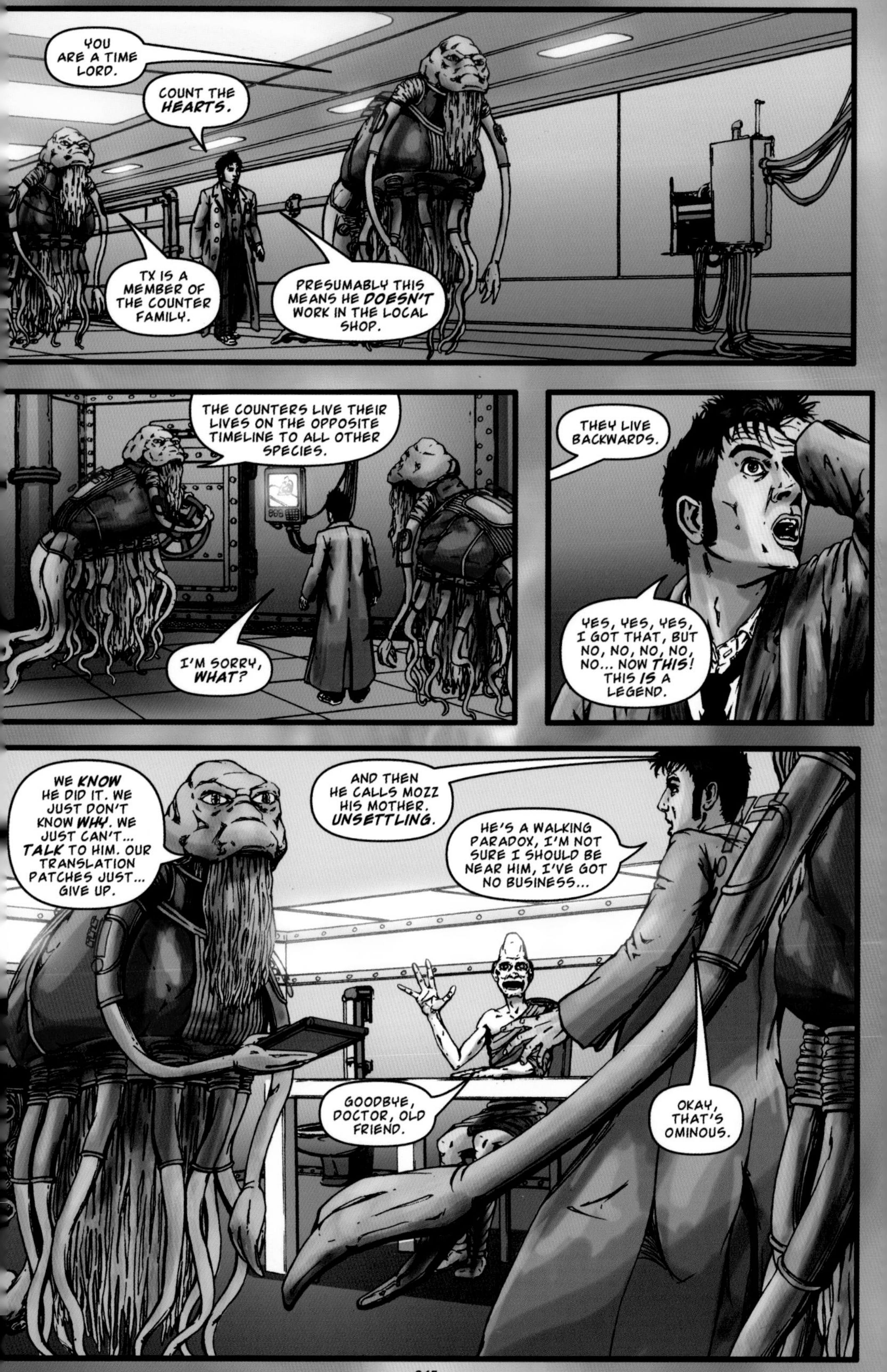
YOU ARE A TIME LORD.
COUNT THE HEARTS.
TX IS A MEMBER OF THE COUNTER FAMILY.
PRESUMABLY THIS MEANS HE DOESN'T WORK IN THE LOCAL SHOP.
THE COUNTERS LIVE THEIR LIVES ON THE OPPOSITE TIMELINE TO ALL OTHER SPECIES.
I'M SORRY, WHAT?
THEY LIVE BACKWARDS.
YES, YES, YES, I GOT THAT, BUT NO, NO, NO, NO, NO... NOW THIS! THIS IS A LEGEND.
WE KNOW HE DID IT. WE JUST DON'T KNOW WHY. WE JUST CAN'T... TALK TO HIM. OUR TRANSLATION PATCHES JUST... GIVE UP.
AND THEN HE CALLS MOZZ HIS MOTHER. UNSETTLING.
HE'S A WALKING PARADOX, I'M NOT SURE I SHOULD BE NEAR HIM, I'VE GOT NO BUSINESS...
GOODBYE, DOCTOR, OLD FRIEND.
OKAY, THAT'S OMINOUS.

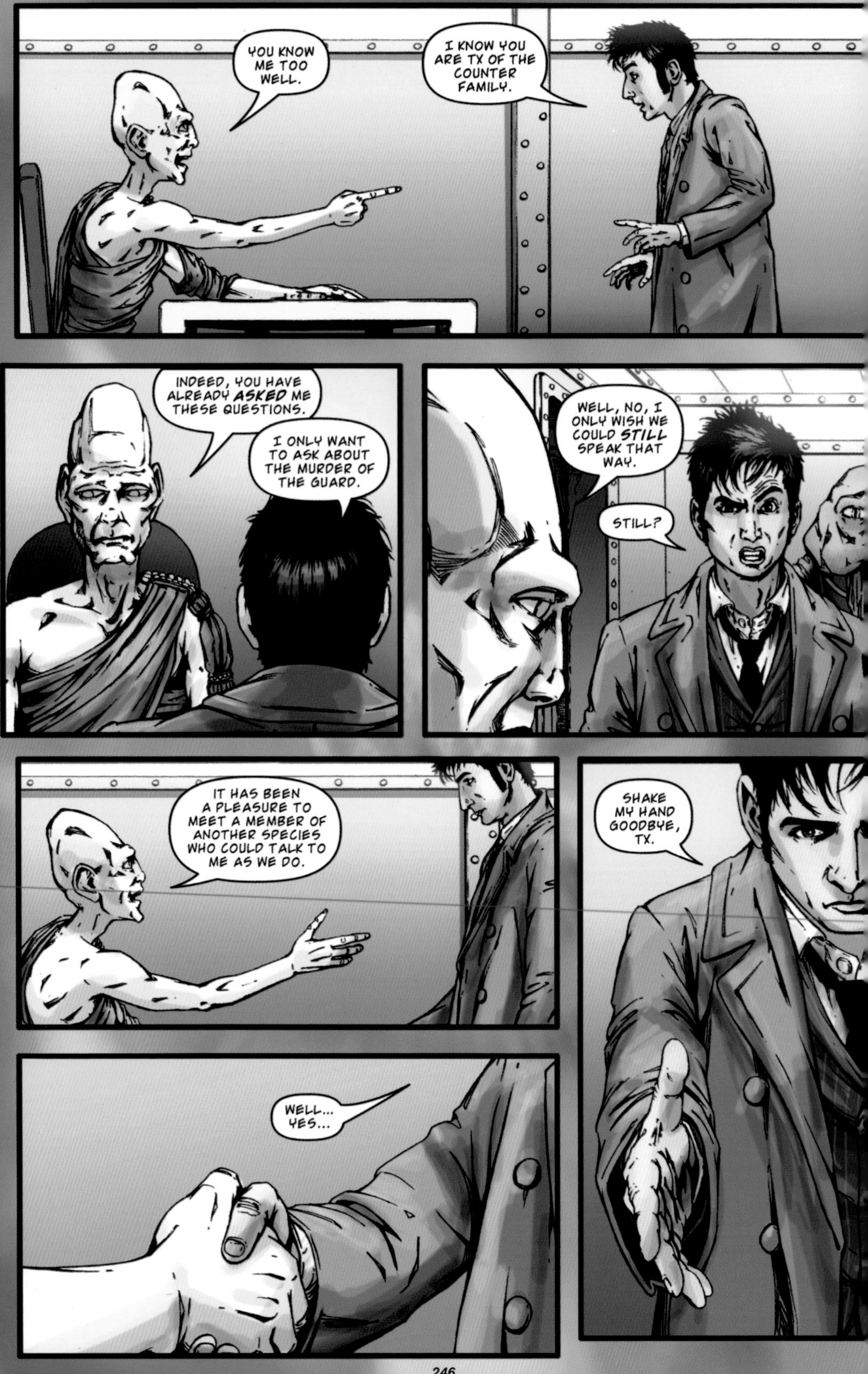

YOU KNOW ME TOO WELL.
I KNOW YOU ARE TX OF THE COUNTER FAMILY.
INDEED, YOU HAVE ALREADY ASKED ME THESE QUESTIONS.
I ONLY WANT TO ASK ABOUT THE MURDER OF THE GUARD.
WELL, NO, I ONLY WISH WE COULD STILL SPEAK THAT WAY.
STILL?
IT HAS BEEN A PLEASURE TO MEET A MEMBER OF ANOTHER SPECIES WHO COULD TALK TO ME AS WE DO.
SHAKE MY HAND GOODBYE, TX.
WELL... YES...

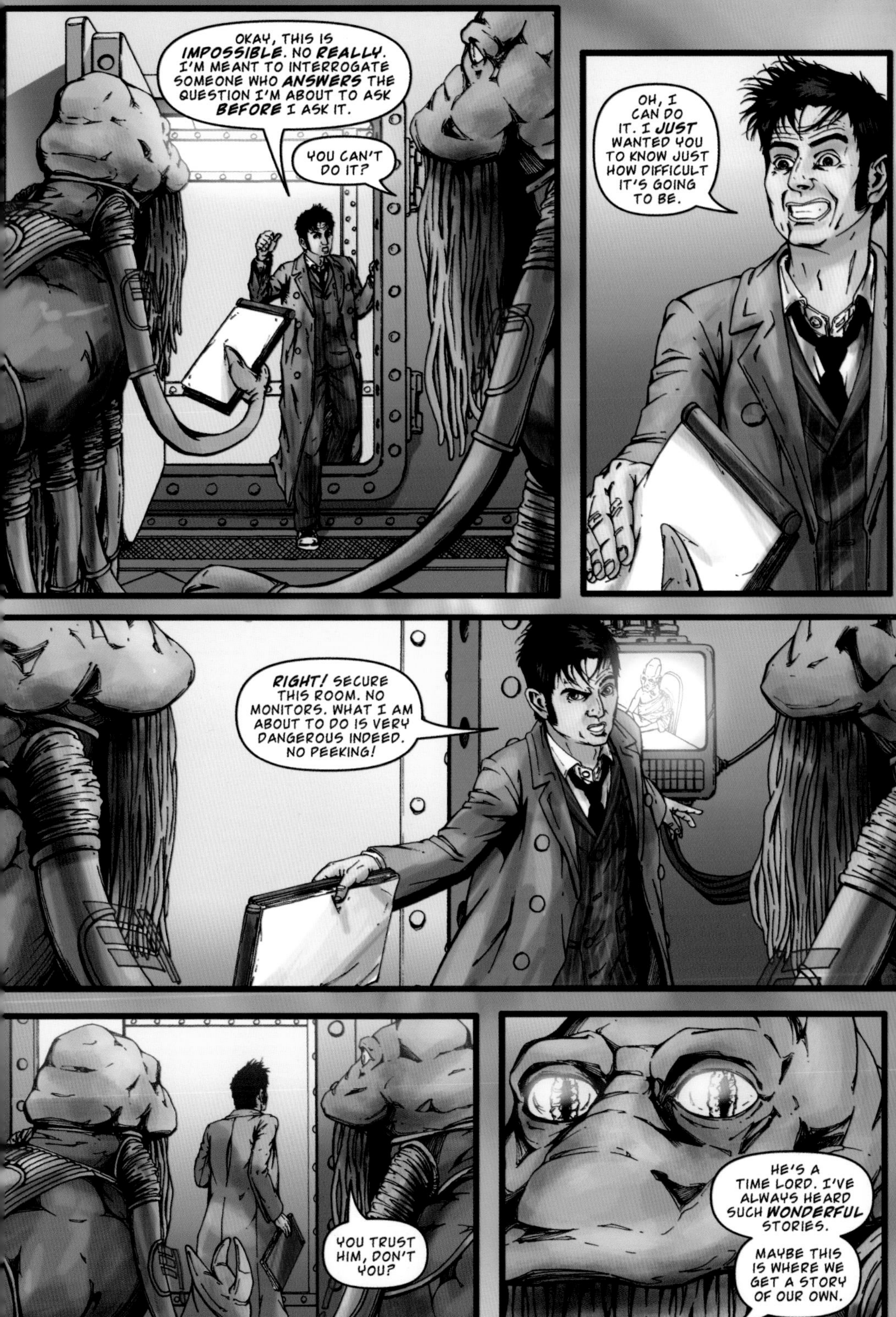
OKAY, THIS IS IMPOSSIBLE. NO REALLY. I'M MEANT TO INTERROGATE SOMEONE WHO ANSWERS THE QUESTION I'M ABOUT TO ASK BEFORE I ASK IT.
YOU CAN'T DO IT?
OH, I CAN DO IT. I JUST WANTED YOU TO KNOW JUST HOW DIFFICULT IT'S GOING TO BE.
RIGHT! SECURE THIS ROOM. NO MONITORS. WHAT I AM ABOUT TO DO IS VERY DANGEROUS INDEED. NO PEEKING!
YOU TRUST HIM, DON'T YOU?
HE'S A TIME LORD. I'VE ALWAYS HEARD SUCH WONDERFUL STORIES.
MAYBE THIS IS WHERE WE GET A STORY OF OUR OWN.
VWORP VWORP

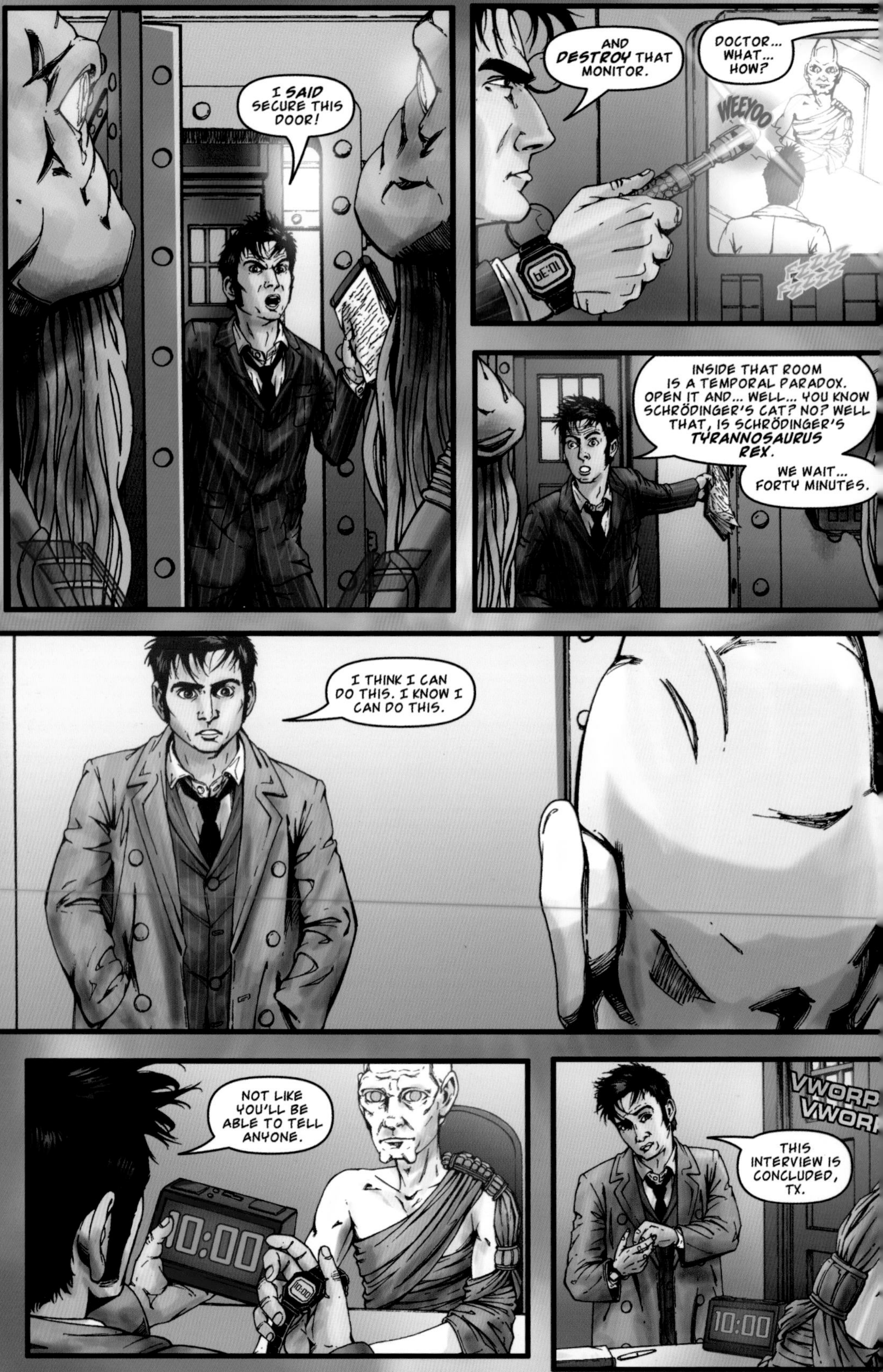

I SAID SECURE THIS DOOR!
AND DESTROY THAT MONITOR.
DOCTOR... WHAT... HOW?
WEEYOO
INSIDE THAT ROOM IS A TEMPORAL PARADOX. OPEN IT AND... WELL... YOU KNOW SCHRÖDINGER'S CAT? NO? WELL THAT, IS SCHRÖDINGER'S TYRANNOSAURUS REX.
WE WAIT... FORTY MINUTES.
I THINK I CAN DO THIS. I KNOW I CAN DO THIS.
NOT LIKE YOU'LL BE ABLE TO TELL ANYONE.
10:00
VWORP VWORP
THIS INTERVIEW IS CONCLUDED, TX.
10:00

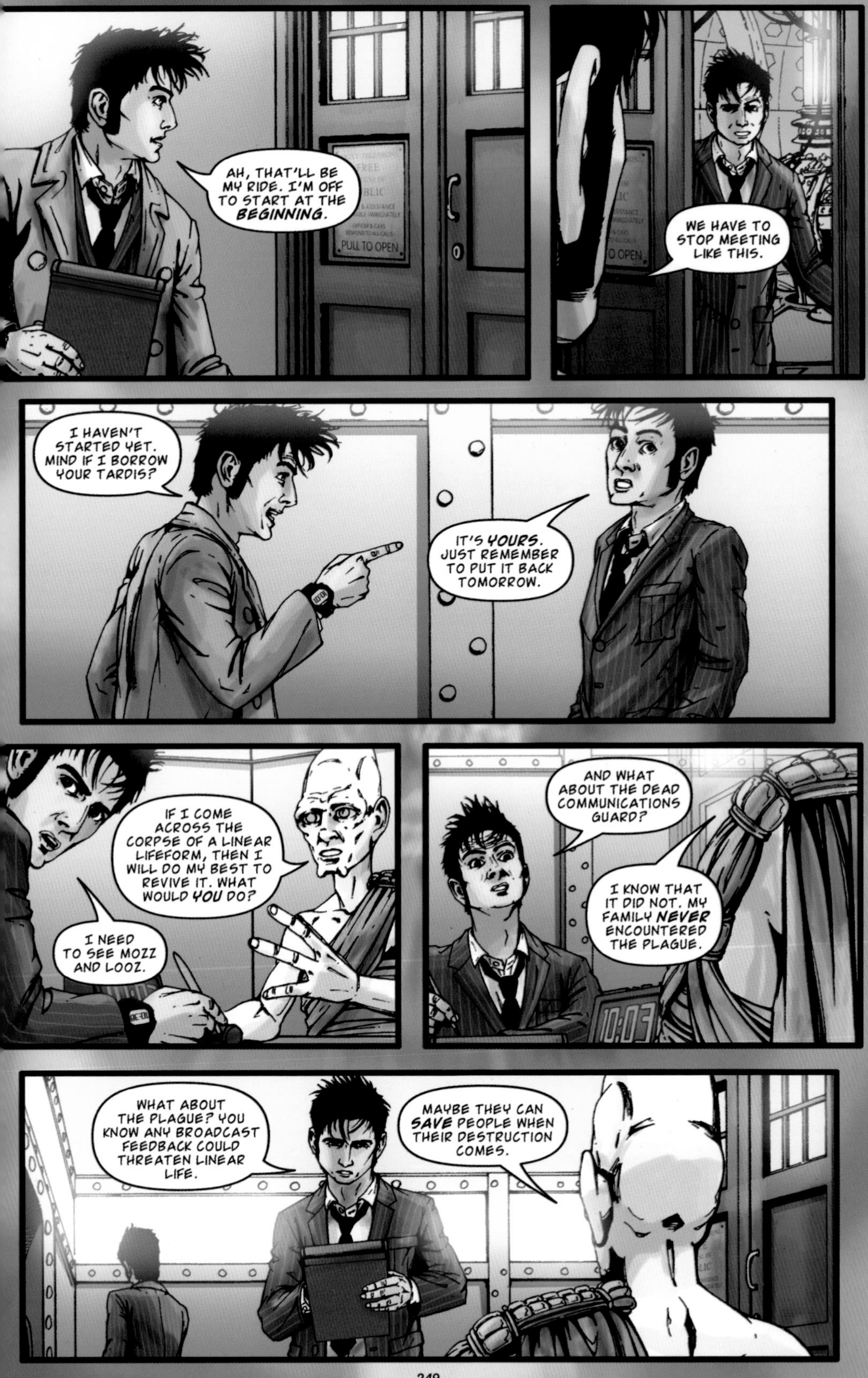
AH, THAT'LL BE MY RIDE. I'M OFF TO START AT THE BEGINNING.
PULL TO OPEN
WE HAVE TO STOP MEETING LIKE THIS.
I HAVEN'T STARTED YET. MIND IF I BORROW YOUR TARDIS?
IT'S YOURS. JUST REMEMBER TO PUT IT BACK TOMORROW.
IF I COME ACROSS THE CORPSE OF A LINEAR LIFEFORM, THEN I WILL DO MY BEST TO REVIVE IT. WHAT WOULD YOU DO?
I NEED TO SEE MOZZ AND LOOZ.
AND WHAT ABOUT THE DEAD COMMUNICATIONS GUARD?
I KNOW THAT IT DID NOT. MY FAMILY NEVER ENCOUNTERED THE PLAGUE.
10:03
WHAT ABOUT THE PLAGUE? YOU KNOW ANY BROADCAST FEEDBACK COULD THREATEN LINEAR LIFE.
MAYBE THEY CAN SAVE PEOPLE WHEN THEIR DESTRUCTION COMES.

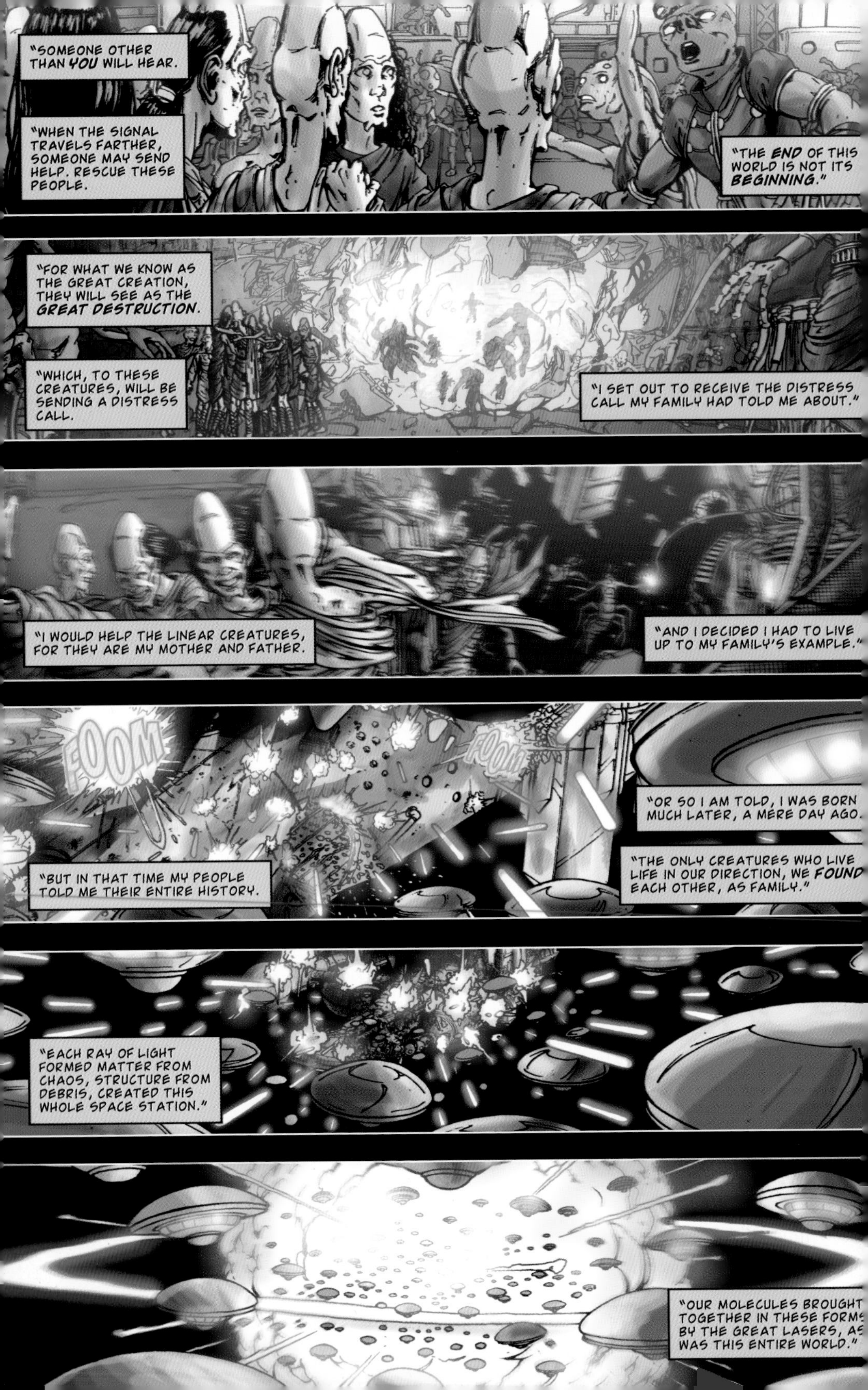
"SOMEONE OTHER THAN YOU WILL HEAR.
"WHEN THE SIGNAL TRAVELS FARTHER, SOMEONE MAY SEND HELP. RESCUE THESE PEOPLE.
"THE END OF THIS WORLD IS NOT ITS BEGINNING."
"FOR WHAT WE KNOW AS THE GREAT CREATION, THEY WILL SEE AS THE GREAT DESTRUCTION.
"WHICH, TO THESE CREATURES, WILL BE SENDING A DISTRESS CALL.
"I SET OUT TO RECEIVE THE DISTRESS CALL MY FAMILY HAD TOLD ME ABOUT.
"I WOULD HELP THE LINEAR CREATURES, FOR THEY ARE MY MOTHER AND FATHER.
"AND I DECIDED I HAD TO LIVE UP TO MY FAMILY'S EXAMPLE."
FOOM
FOOM
"OR SO I AM TOLD, I WAS BORN MUCH LATER, A MERE DAY AGO.
"BUT IN THAT TIME MY PEOPLE TOLD ME THEIR ENTIRE HISTORY.
"THE ONLY CREATURES WHO LIVE LIFE IN OUR DIRECTION, WE FOUND EACH OTHER, AS FAMILY."
"EACH RAY OF LIGHT FORMED MATTER FROM CHAOS, STRUCTURE FROM DEBRIS, CREATED THIS WHOLE SPACE STATION."
"OUR MOLECULES BROUGHT TOGETHER IN THESE FORMS BY THE GREAT LASERS, AS WAS THIS ENTIRE WORLD."

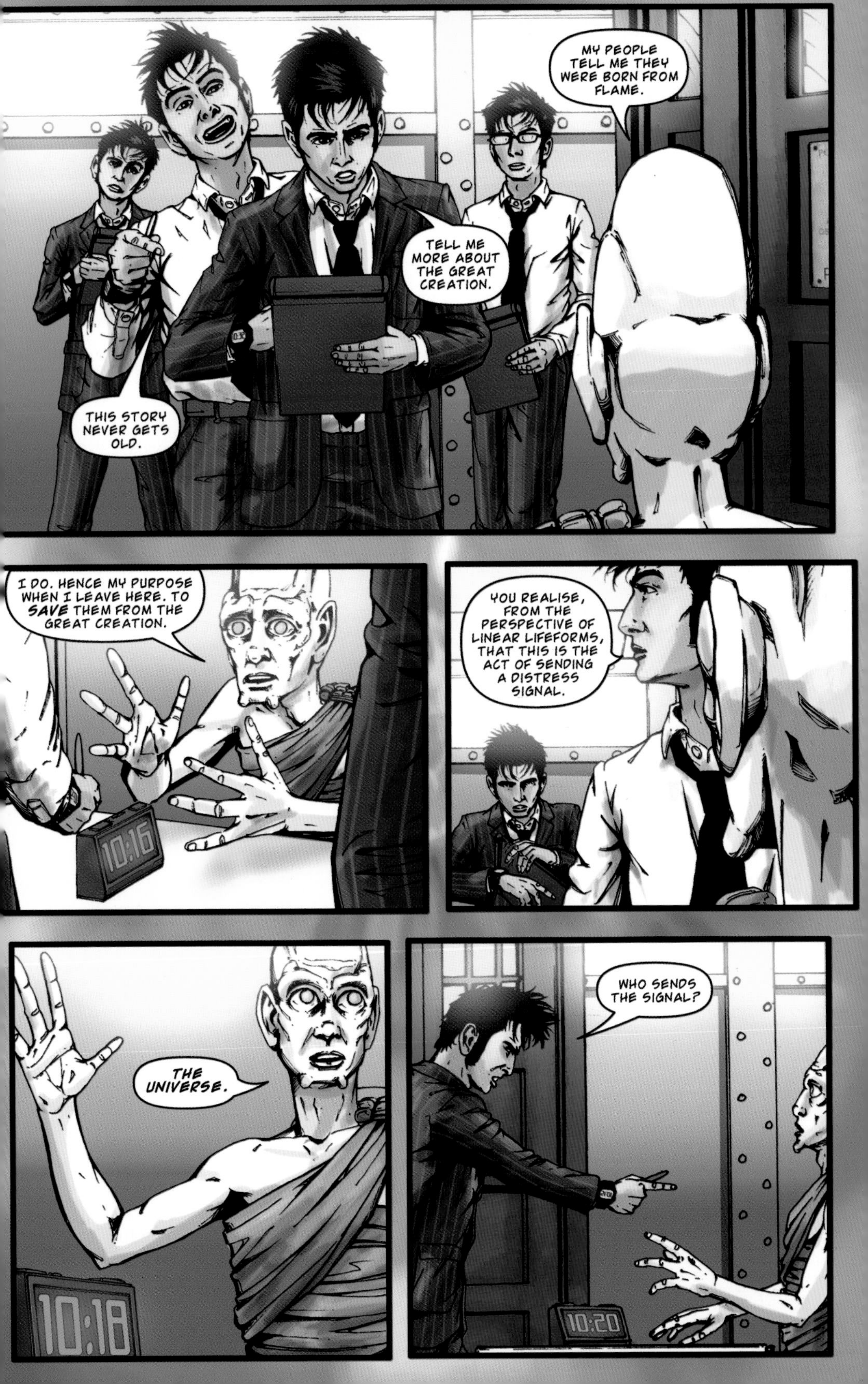
MY PEOPLE TELL ME THEY WERE BORN FROM FLAME.
TELL ME MORE ABOUT THE GREAT CREATION.
THIS STORY NEVER GETS OLD.
I DO. HENCE MY PURPOSE WHEN I LEAVE HERE. TO SAVE THEM FROM THE GREAT CREATION.
10:16
YOU REALISE, FROM THE PERSPECTIVE OF LINEAR LIFEFORMS, THAT THIS IS THE ACT OF SENDING A DISTRESS SIGNAL.
THE UNIVERSE.
10:18
WHO SENDS THE SIGNAL?
10:20

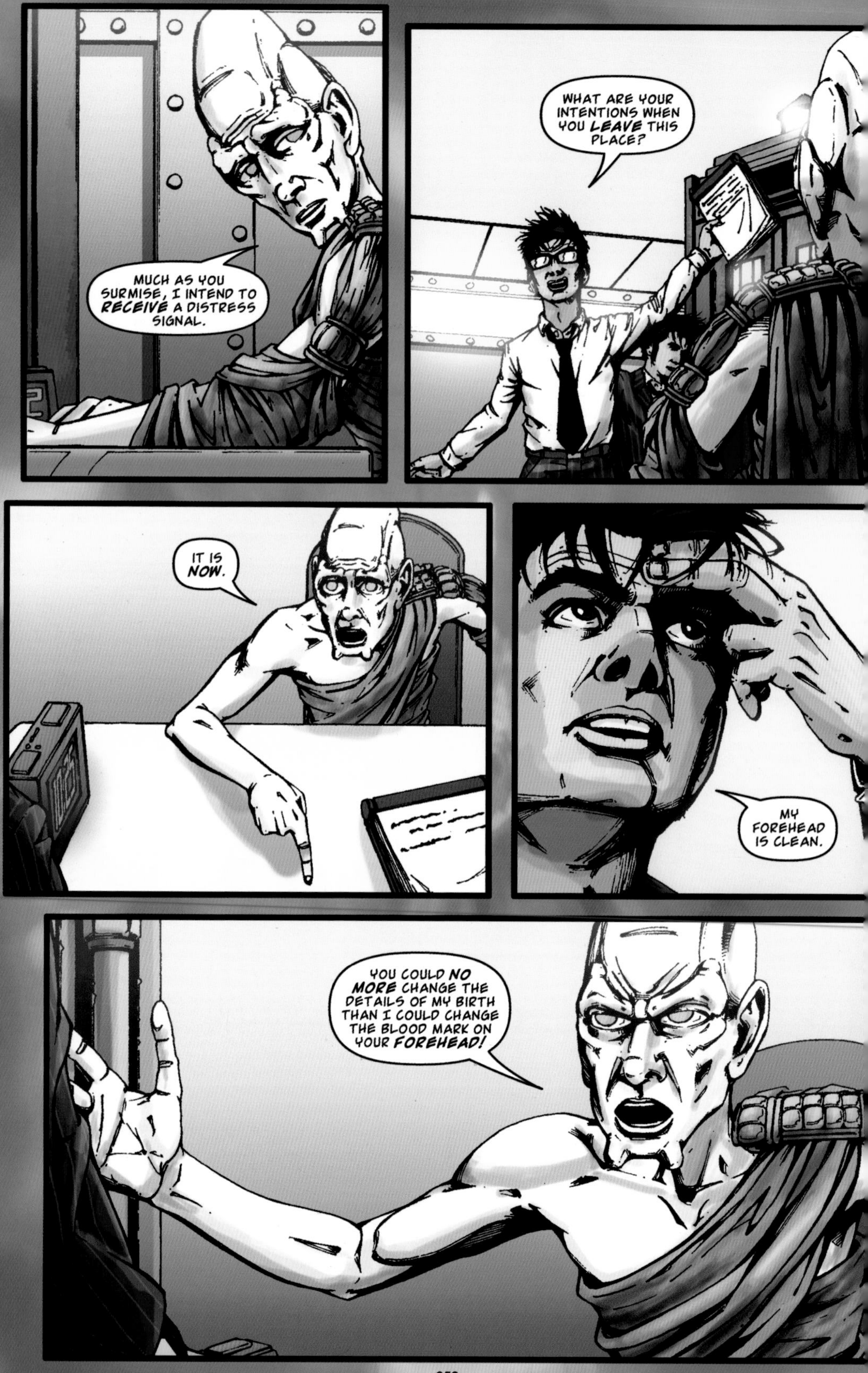
MUCH AS YOU SURMISE, I INTEND TO RECEIVE A DISTRESS SIGNAL.
WHAT ARE YOUR INTENTIONS WHEN YOU LEAVE THIS PLACE?
IT IS NOW.
MY FOREHEAD IS CLEAN.
YOU COULD NO MORE CHANGE THE DETAILS OF MY BIRTH THAN I COULD CHANGE THE BLOOD MARK ON YOUR FOREHEAD!

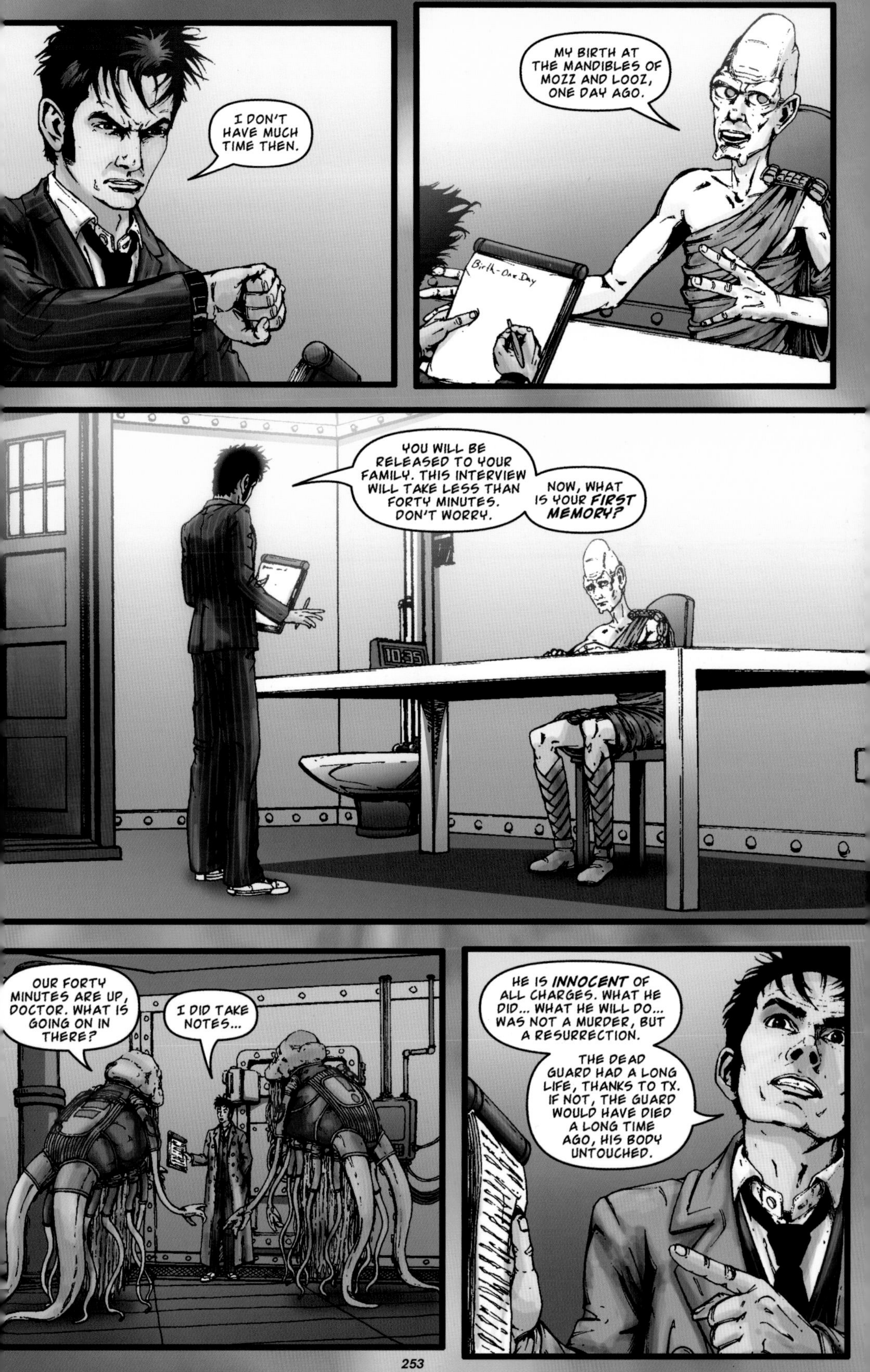
I DON'T HAVE MUCH TIME THEN.
MY BIRTH AT THE MANDIBLES OF MOZZ AND LOOZ, ONE DAY AGO.
Birth - One Day
YOU WILL BE RELEASED TO YOUR FAMILY. THIS INTERVIEW WILL TAKE LESS THAN FORTY MINUTES. DON'T WORRY.
NOW, WHAT IS YOUR FIRST MEMORY?
10:35
OUR FORTY MINUTES ARE UP, DOCTOR. WHAT IS GOING ON IN THERE?
I DID TAKE NOTES...
HE IS INNOCENT OF ALL CHARGES. WHAT HE DID... WHAT HE WILL DO... WAS NOT A MURDER, BUT A RESURRECTION.
THE DEAD GUARD HAD A LONG LIFE, THANKS TO TX. IF NOT, THE GUARD WOULD HAVE DIED A LONG TIME AGO, HIS BODY UNTOUCHED.

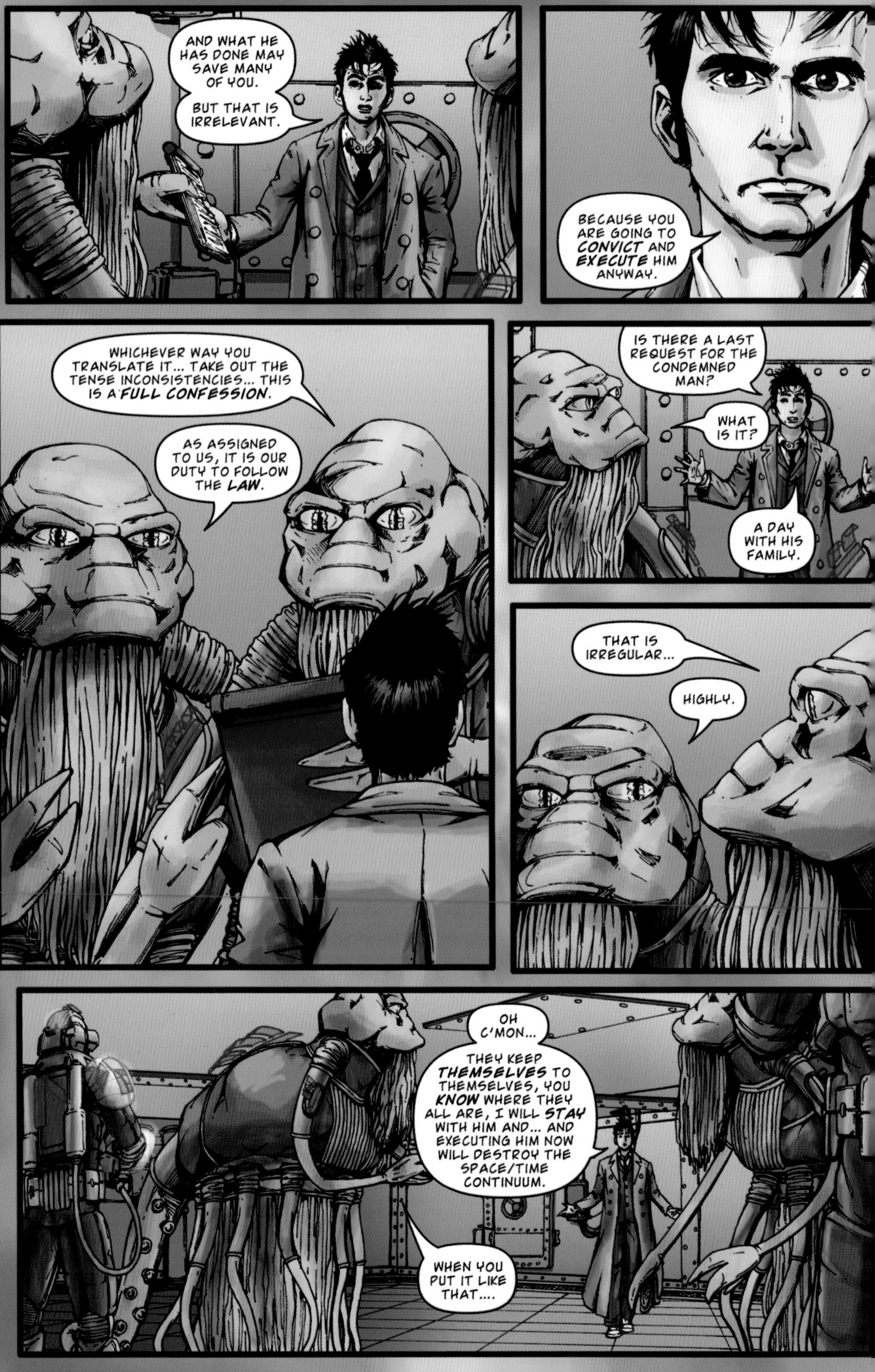
AND WHAT HE HAS DONE MAY SAVE MANY OF YOU.
BUT THAT IS IRRELEVANT.
BECAUSE YOU ARE GOING TO CONVICT AND EXECUTE HIM ANYWAY.
WHICHEVER WAY YOU TRANSLATE IT... TAKE OUT THE TENSE INCONSISTENCIES... THIS IS A FULL CONFESSION.
AS ASSIGNED TO US, IT IS OUR DUTY TO FOLLOW THE LAW.
IS THERE A LAST REQUEST FOR THE CONDEMNED MAN?
WHAT IS IT?
A DAY WITH HIS FAMILY.
THAT IS IRREGULAR...
HIGHLY.
OH C'MON...
THEY KEEP THEMSELVES TO THEMSELVES, YOU KNOW WHERE THEY ALL ARE, I WILL STAY WITH HIM AND... AND EXECUTING HIM NOW WILL DESTROY THE SPACE/TIME CONTINUUM.
WHEN YOU PUT IT LIKE THAT....

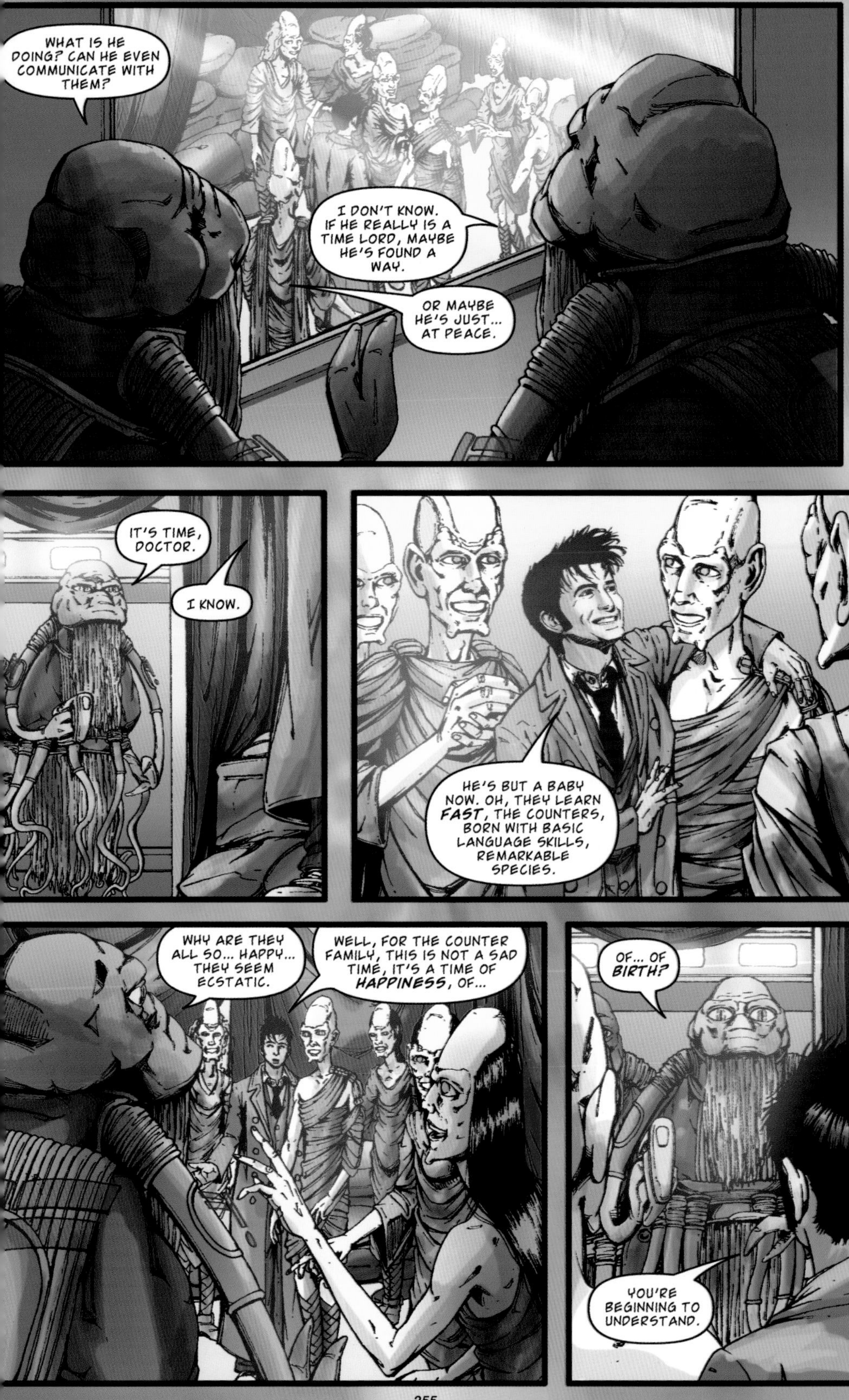
WHAT IS HE DOING? CAN HE EVEN COMMUNICATE WITH THEM?
I DON'T KNOW. IF HE REALLY IS A TIME LORD, MAYBE HE'S FOUND A WAY.
OR MAYBE HE'S JUST... AT PEACE.
IT'S TIME, DOCTOR.
I KNOW.
HE'S BUT A BABY NOW. OH, THEY LEARN FAST, THE COUNTERS, BORN WITH BASIC LANGUAGE SKILLS, REMARKABLE SPECIES.
WHY ARE THEY ALL SO... HAPPY... THEY SEEM ECSTATIC.
WELL, FOR THE COUNTER FAMILY, THIS IS NOT A SAD TIME, IT'S A TIME OF HAPPINESS, OF...
OF... OF BIRTH?
YOU'RE BEGINNING TO UNDERSTAND.

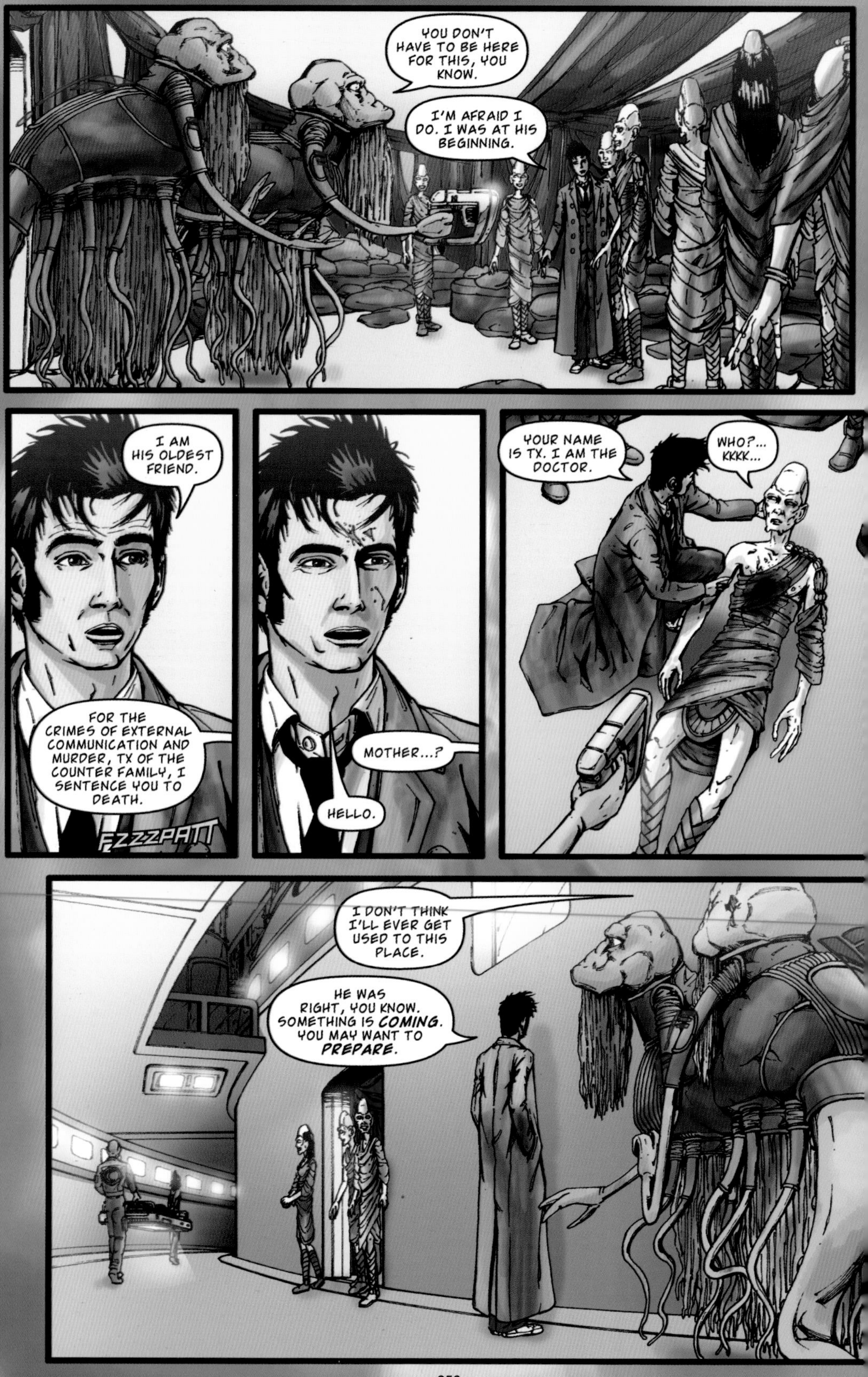
YOU DON'T HAVE TO BE HERE FOR THIS, YOU KNOW.
I'M AFRAID I DO. I WAS AT HIS BEGINNING.
I AM HIS OLDEST FRIEND.
FOR THE CRIMES OF EXTERNAL COMMUNICATION AND MURDER, TX OF THE COUNTER FAMILY, I SENTENCE YOU TO DEATH.
FZZZPATT
MOTHER...?
HELLO.
YOUR NAME IS TX. I AM THE DOCTOR.
WHO?... KKKK...
I DON'T THINK I'LL EVER GET USED TO THIS PLACE.
HE WAS RIGHT, YOU KNOW. SOMETHING IS COMING. YOU MAY WANT TO PREPARE.

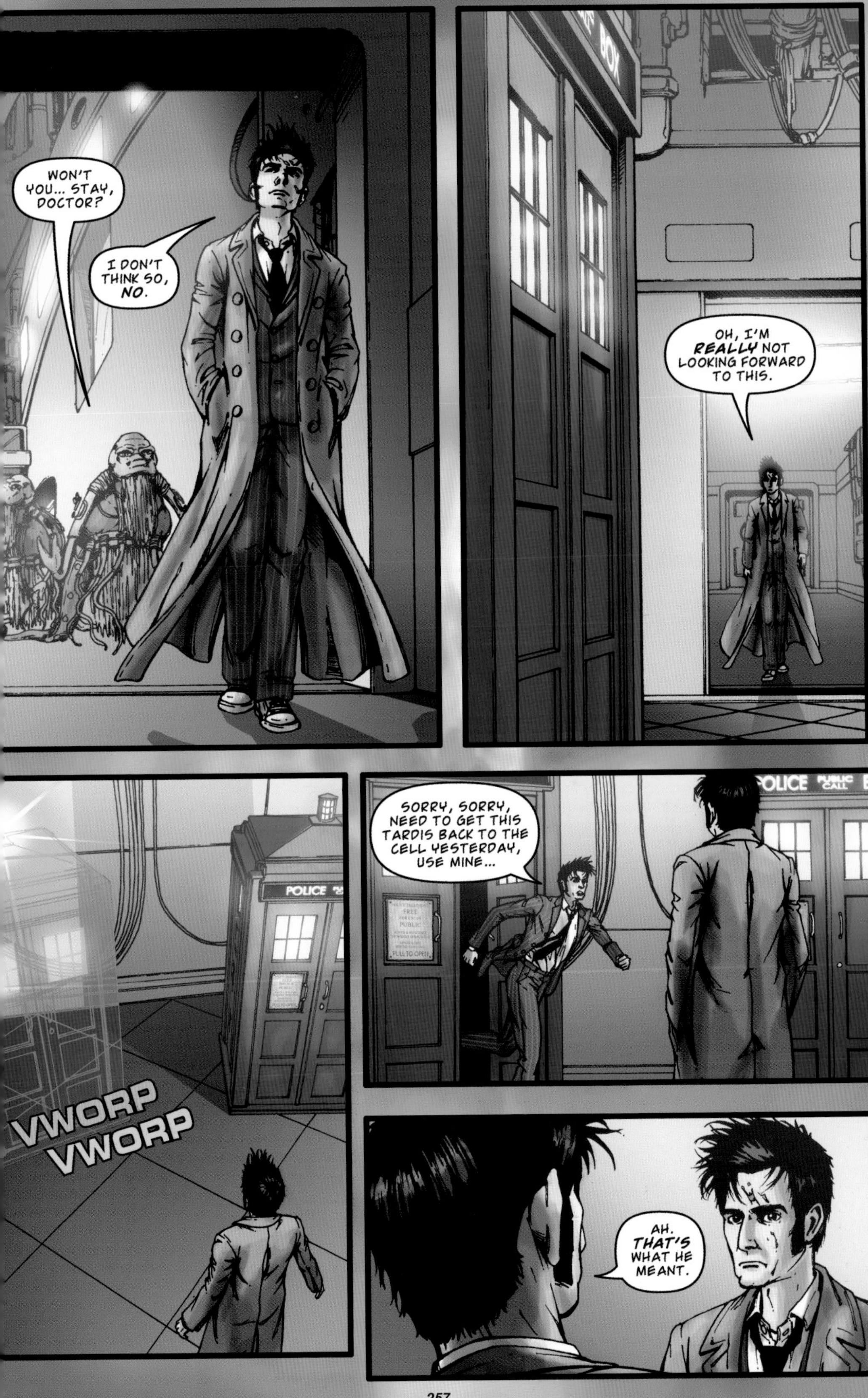
WON'T YOU... STAY, DOCTOR?
I DON'T THINK SO, NO.
OH, I'M REALLY NOT LOOKING FORWARD TO THIS.
VWORP VWORP
POLICE
SORRY, SORRY, NEED TO GET THIS TARDIS BACK TO THE CELL YESTERDAY, USE MINE...
POLICE PUBLIC CALL BOX
PULL TO OPEN
AH. THAT'S WHAT HE MEANT.

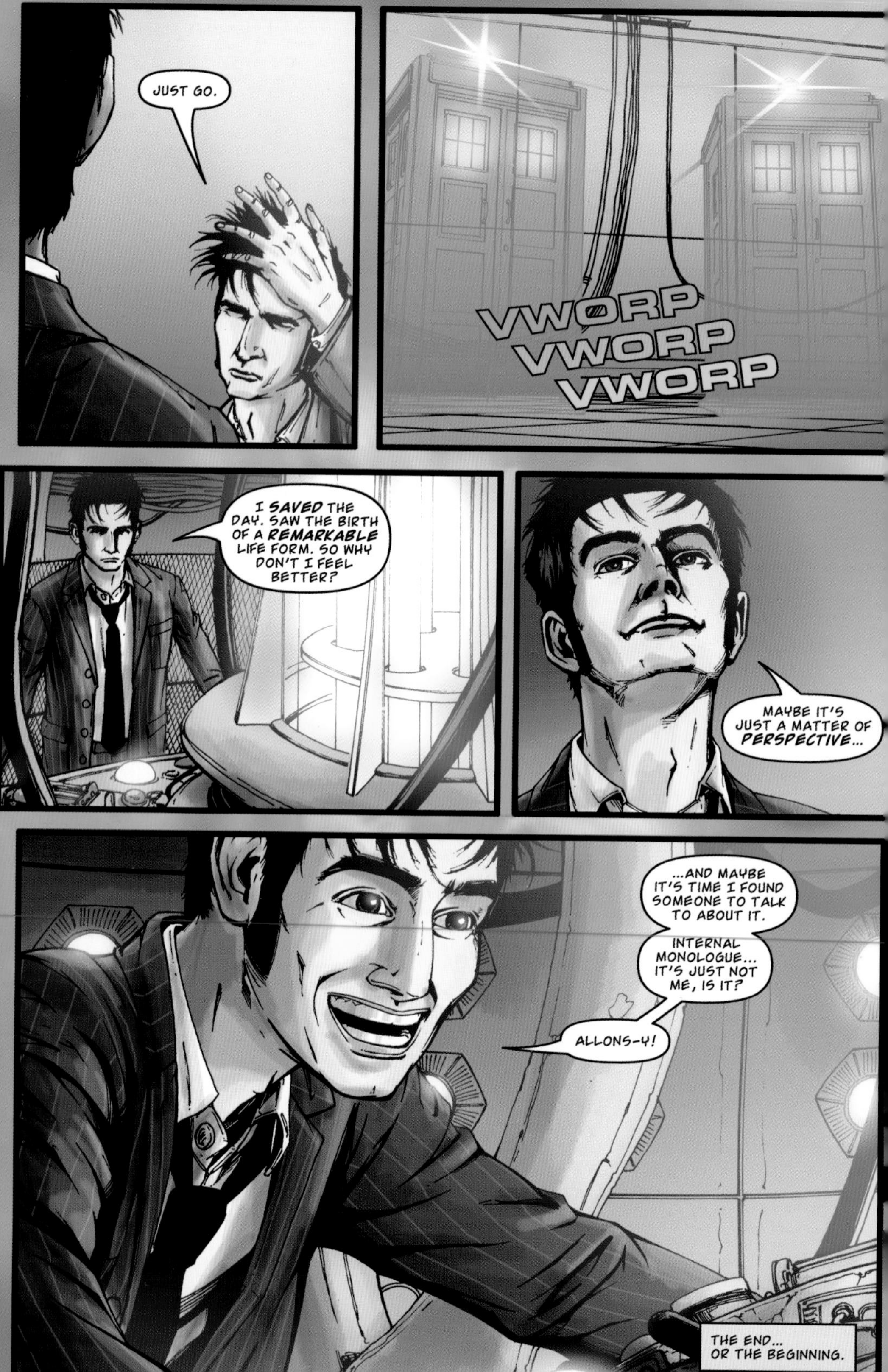
JUST GO.
VWORP VWORP VWORP
I SAVED THE DAY. SAW THE BIRTH OF A REMARKABLE LIFE FORM. SO WHY DON'T I FEEL BETTER?
MAYBE IT'S JUST A MATTER OF PERSPECTIVE...
...AND MAYBE IT'S TIME I FOUND SOMEONE TO TALK TO ABOUT IT.
INTERNAL MONOLOGUE... IT'S JUST NOT ME, IS IT?
ALLONS-Y!
THE END... OR THE BEGINNING.

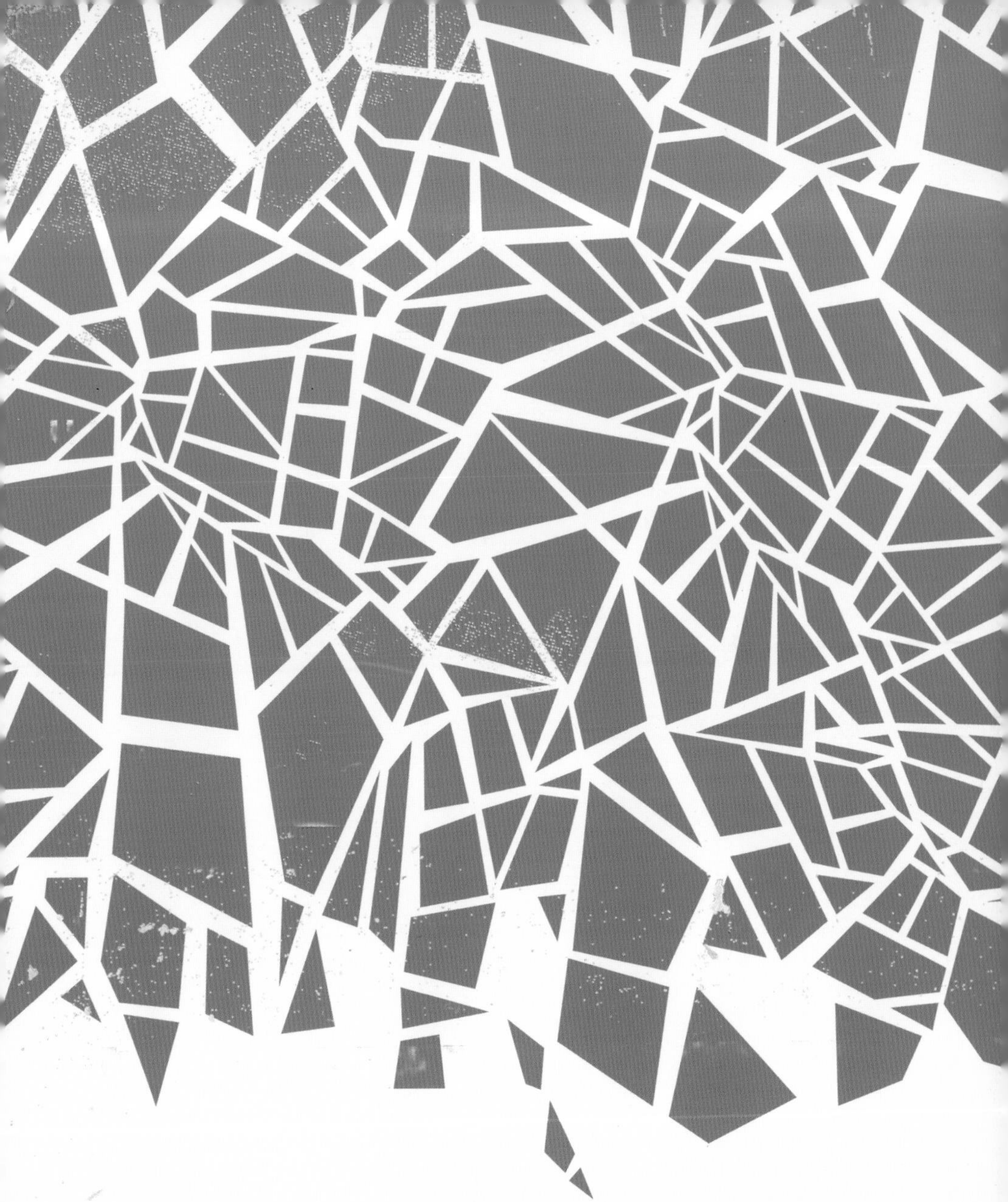

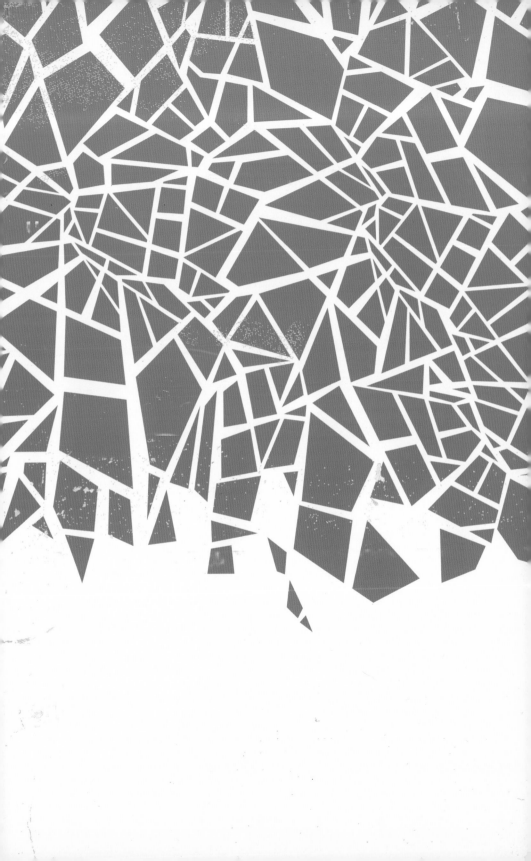

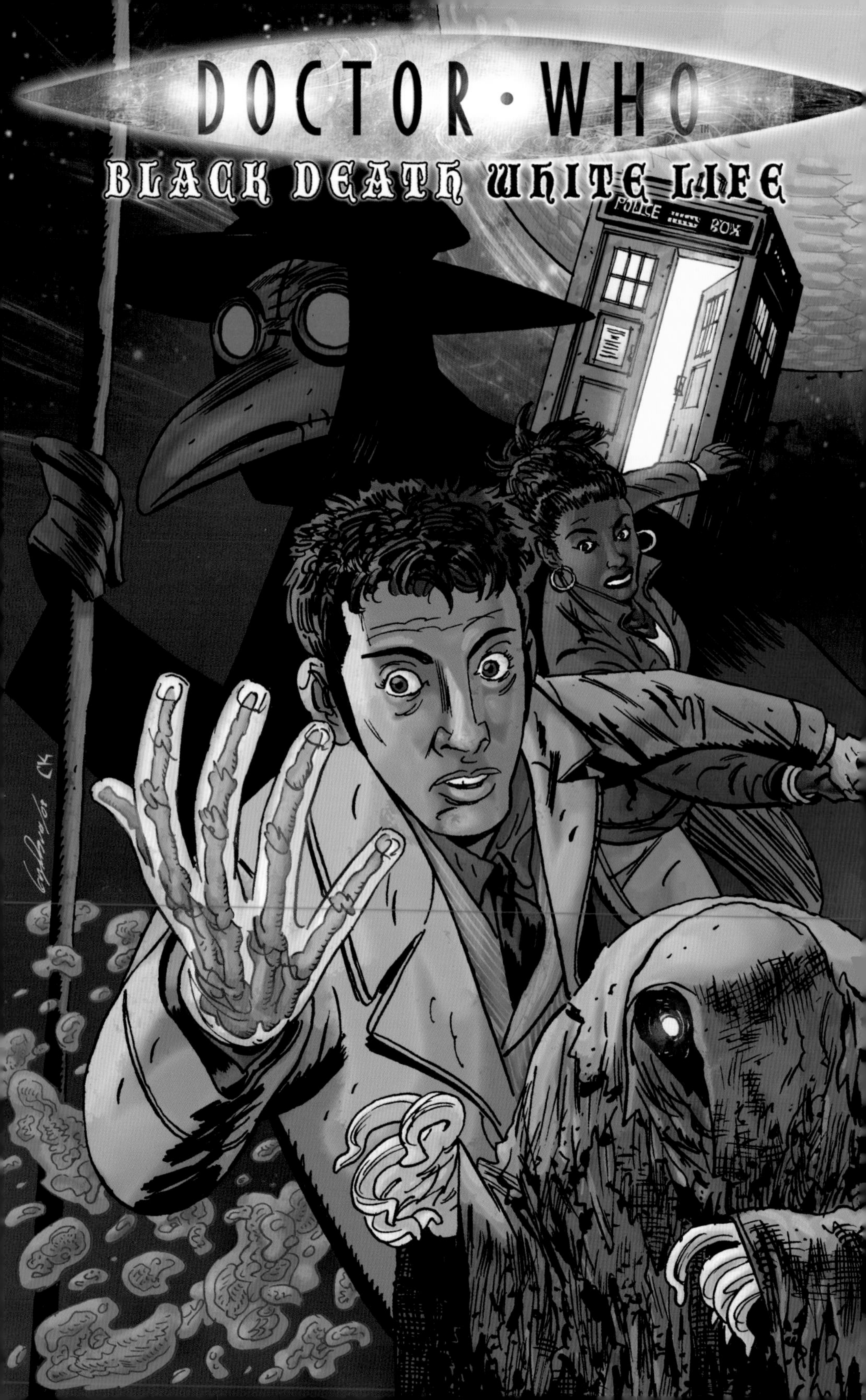
DOCTOR · WHO
BLACK DEATH WHITE LIFE
POLICE BOX

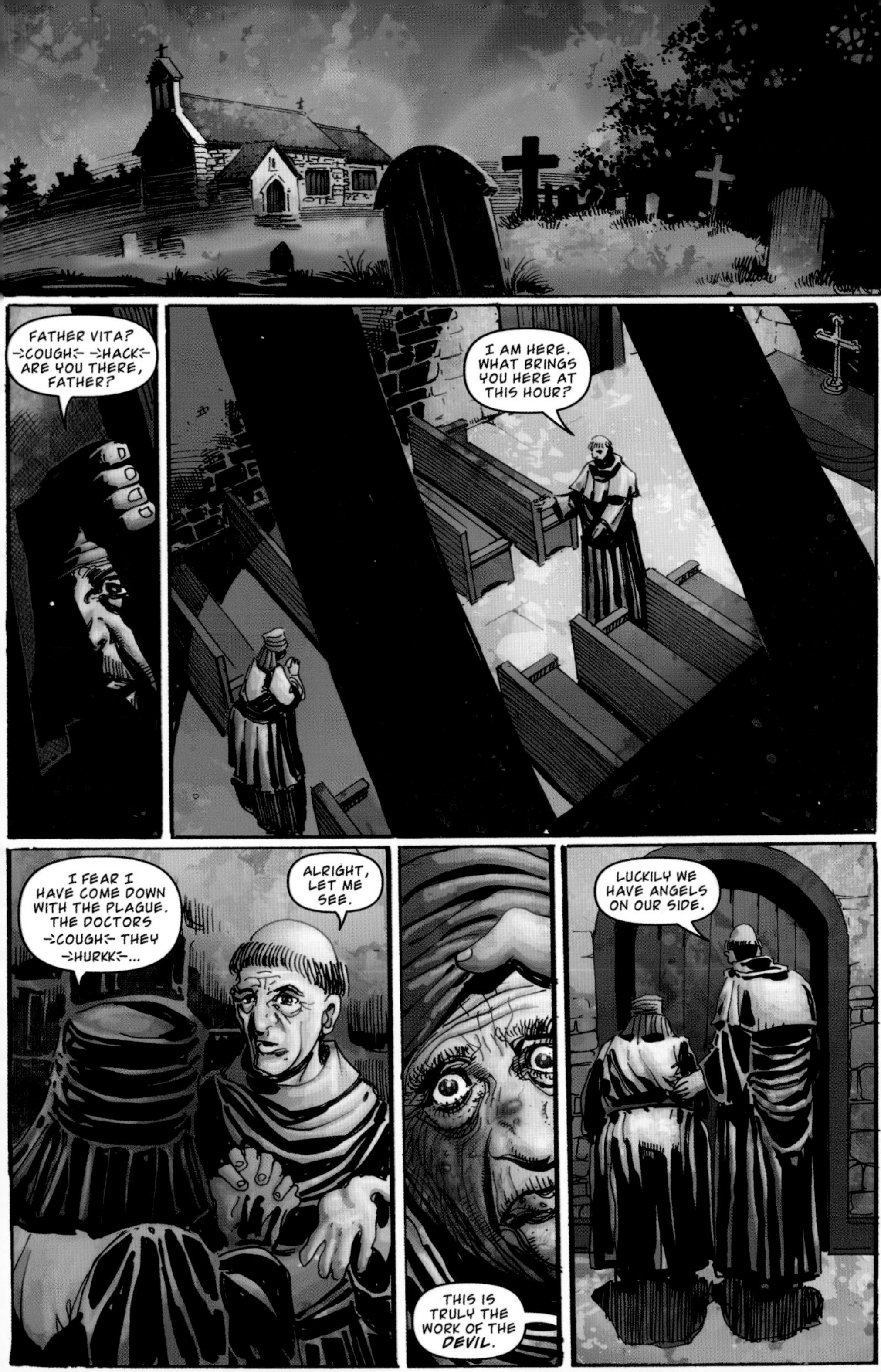
FATHER VITA? ->COUGH<- ->HACK<- ARE YOU THERE, FATHER?
I AM HERE. WHAT BRINGS YOU HERE AT THIS HOUR?
I FEAR I HAVE COME DOWN WITH THE PLAGUE. THE DOCTORS ->COUGH<- THEY ->HURKK<-...
ALRIGHT, LET ME SEE.
THIS IS TRULY THE WORK OF THE DEVIL.
LUCKILY WE HAVE ANGELS ON OUR SIDE.

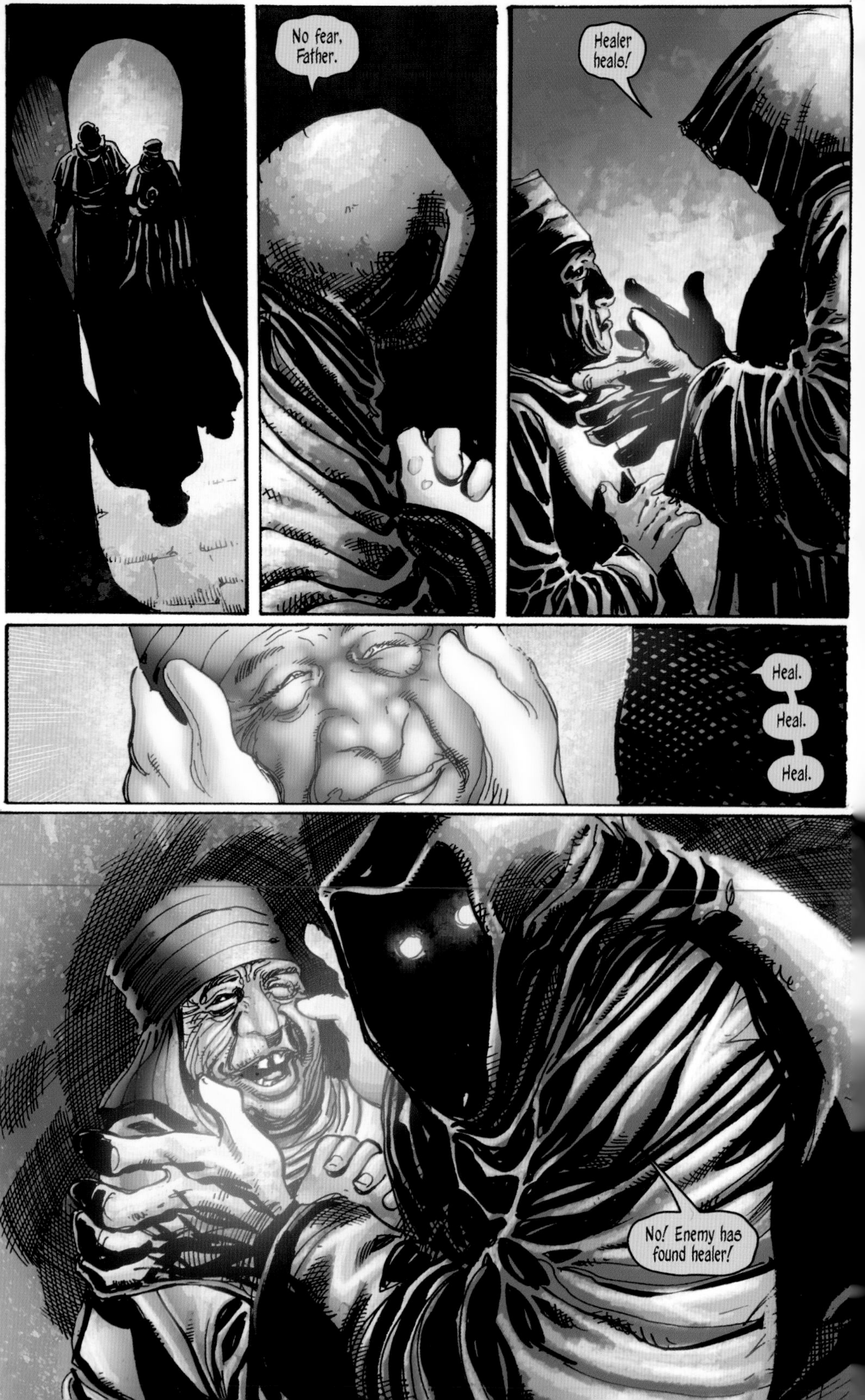
No fear, Father.
Healer heals!
Heal.
Heal.
Heal.
No! Enemy has found healer!

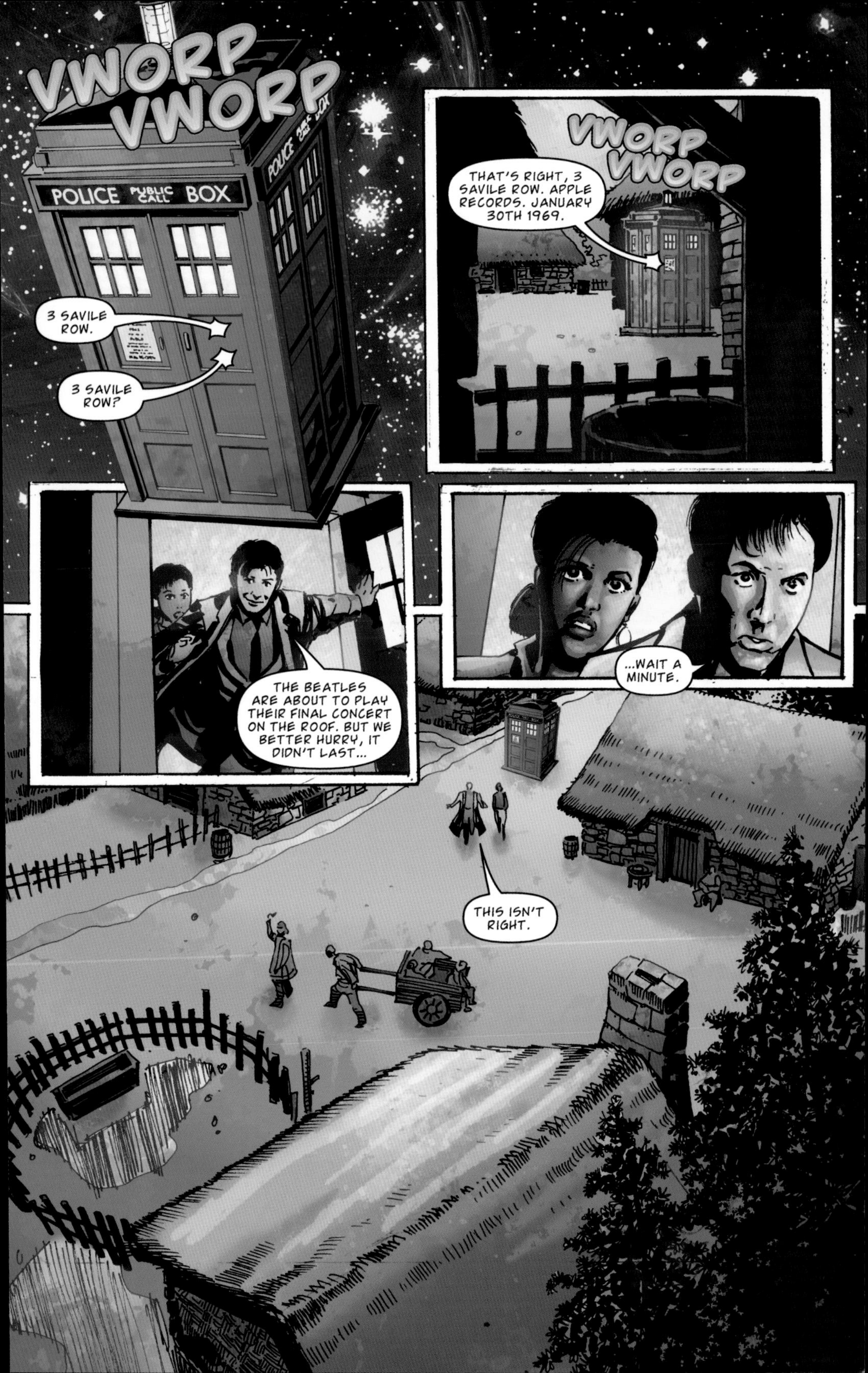
VWORP VWORP
POLICE PUBLIC CALL BOX
3 SAVILE ROW.
3 SAVILE ROW?
VWORP VWORP
THAT'S RIGHT, 3 SAVILE ROW. APPLE RECORDS. JANUARY 30TH 1969.
THE BEATLES ARE ABOUT TO PLAY THEIR FINAL CONCERT ON THE ROOF. BUT WE BETTER HURRY, IT DIDN'T LAST...
...WAIT A MINUTE.
THIS ISN'T RIGHT.

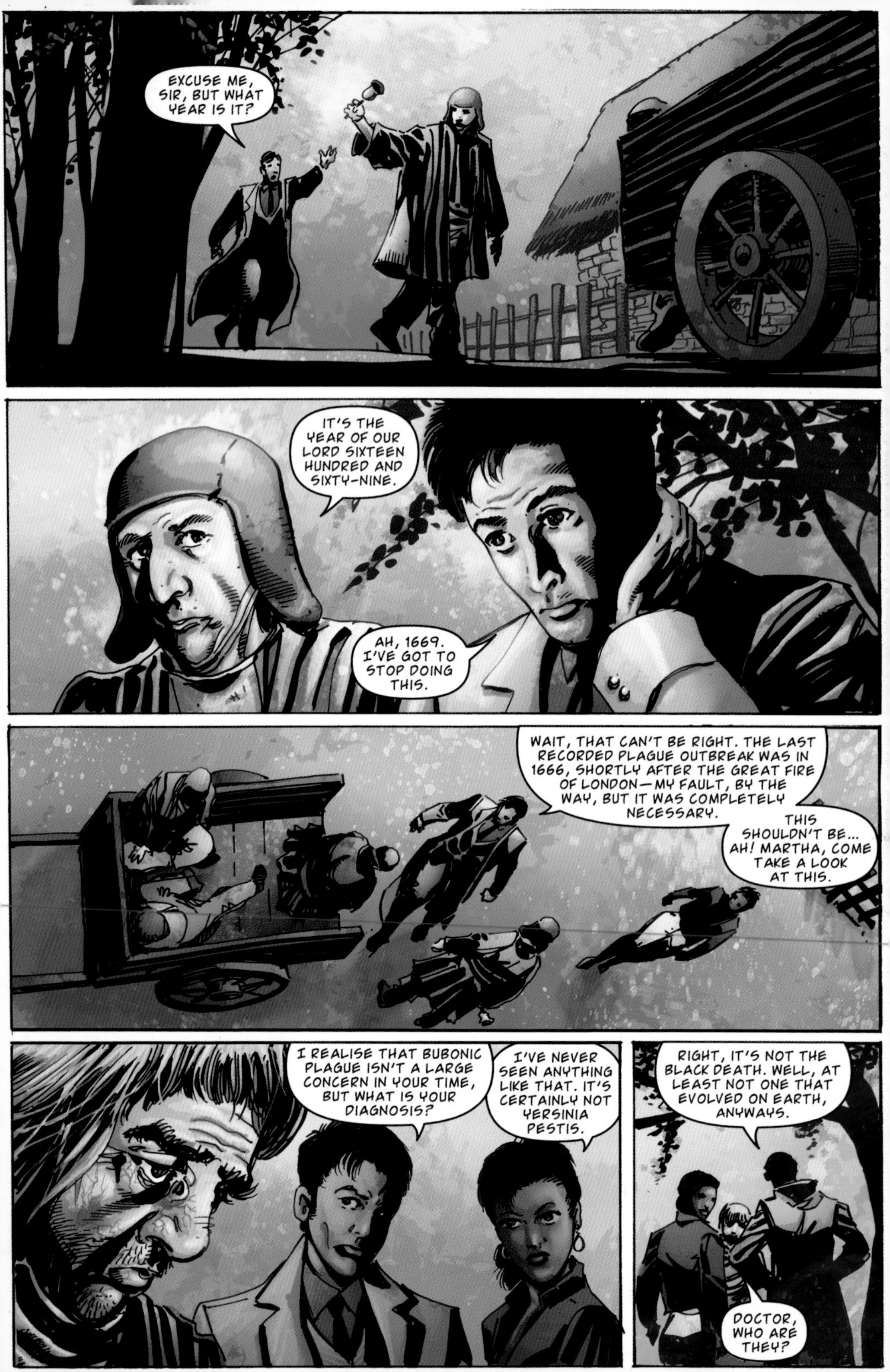
EXCUSE ME, SIR, BUT WHAT YEAR IS IT?
IT'S THE YEAR OF OUR LORD SIXTEEN HUNDRED AND SIXTY-NINE.
AH, 1669. I'VE GOT TO STOP DOING THIS.
WAIT, THAT CAN'T BE RIGHT. THE LAST RECORDED PLAGUE OUTBREAK WAS IN 1666, SHORTLY AFTER THE GREAT FIRE OF LONDON—MY FAULT, BY THE WAY, BUT IT WAS COMPLETELY NECESSARY.
THIS SHOULDN'T BE... AH! MARTHA, COME TAKE A LOOK AT THIS.
I REALISE THAT BUBONIC PLAGUE ISN'T A LARGE CONCERN IN YOUR TIME, BUT WHAT IS YOUR DIAGNOSIS?
I'VE NEVER SEEN ANYTHING LIKE THAT. IT'S CERTAINLY NOT YERSINIA PESTIS.
RIGHT, IT'S NOT THE BLACK DEATH. WELL, AT LEAST NOT ONE THAT EVOLVED ON EARTH, ANYWAYS.
DOCTOR, WHO ARE THEY?

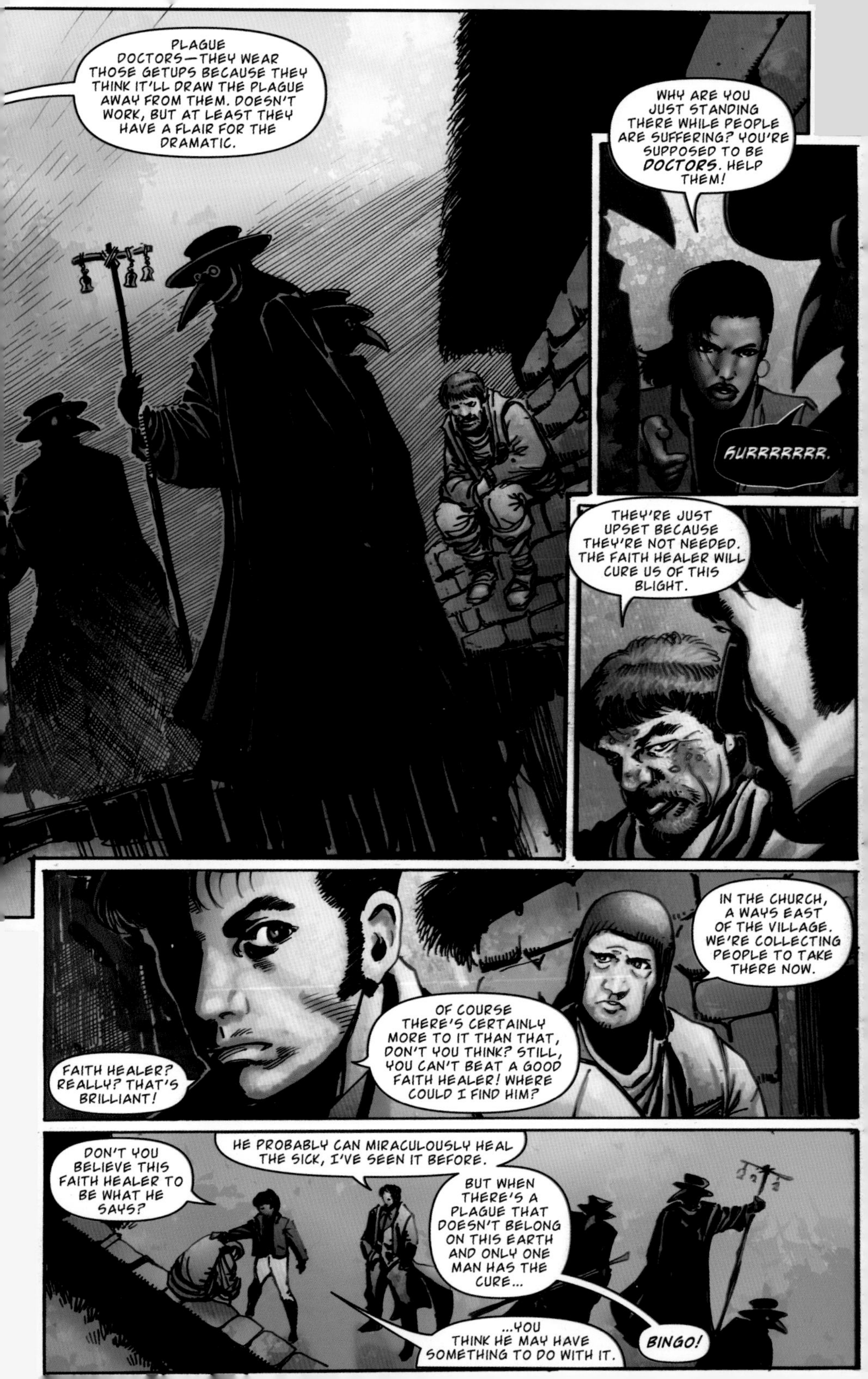
PLAGUE DOCTORS—THEY WEAR THOSE GETUPS BECAUSE THEY THINK IT'LL DRAW THE PLAGUE AWAY FROM THEM. DOESN'T WORK, BUT AT LEAST THEY HAVE A FLAIR FOR THE DRAMATIC.
WHY ARE YOU JUST STANDING THERE WHILE PEOPLE ARE SUFFERING? YOU'RE SUPPOSED TO BE DOCTORS. HELP THEM!
GURRRRRRR.
THEY'RE JUST UPSET BECAUSE THEY'RE NOT NEEDED. THE FAITH HEALER WILL CURE US OF THIS BLIGHT.
FAITH HEALER? REALLY? THAT'S BRILLIANT!
OF COURSE THERE'S CERTAINLY MORE TO IT THAN THAT, DON'T YOU THINK? STILL, YOU CAN'T BEAT A GOOD FAITH HEALER! WHERE COULD I FIND HIM?
IN THE CHURCH, A WAYS EAST OF THE VILLAGE. WE'RE COLLECTING PEOPLE TO TAKE THERE NOW.
DON'T YOU BELIEVE THIS FAITH HEALER TO BE WHAT HE SAYS?
HE PROBABLY CAN MIRACULOUSLY HEAL THE SICK, I'VE SEEN IT BEFORE.
BUT WHEN THERE'S A PLAGUE THAT DOESN'T BELONG ON THIS EARTH AND ONLY ONE MAN HAS THE CURE...
...YOU THINK HE MAY HAVE SOMETHING TO DO WITH IT.
BINGO!

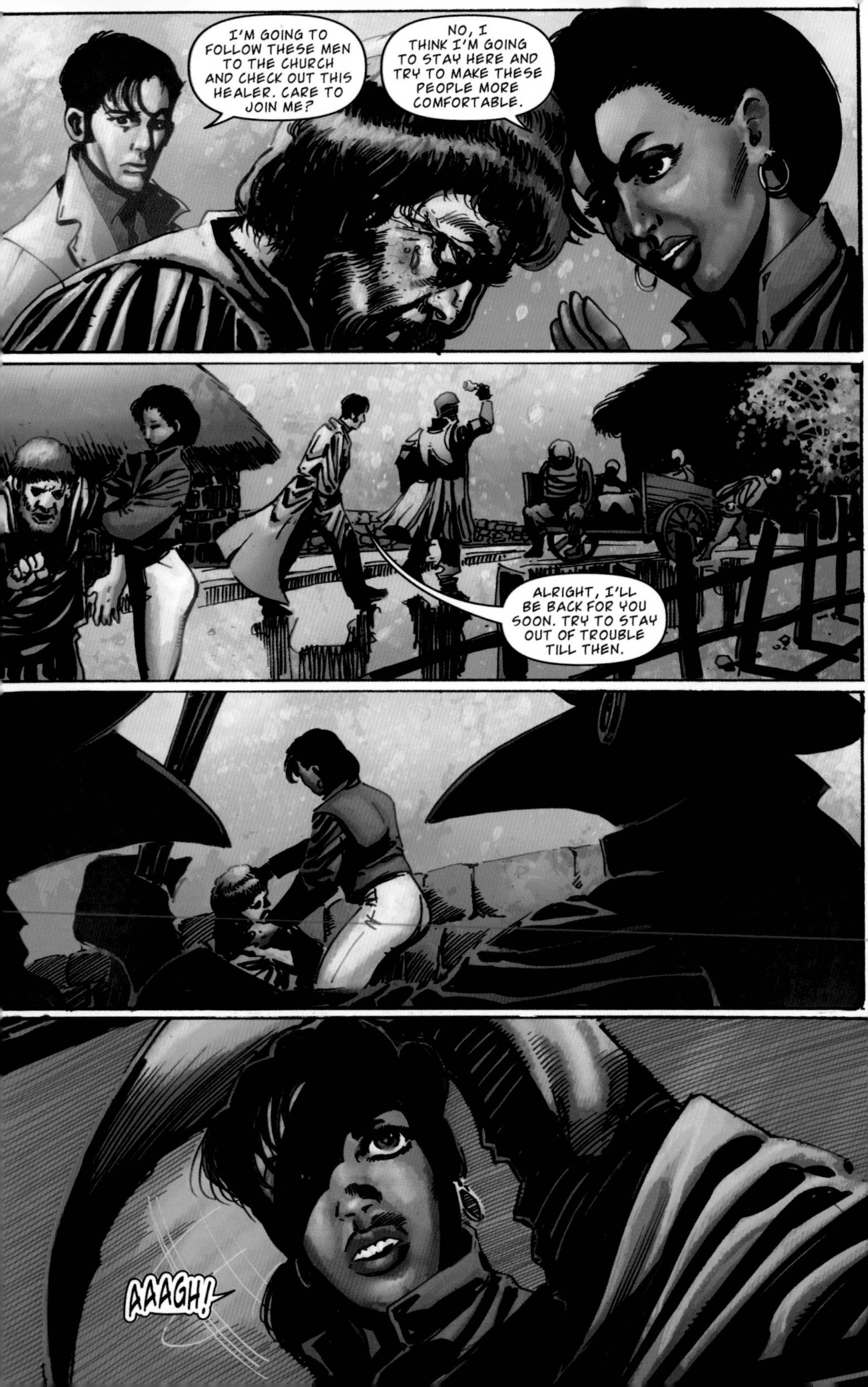
I'M GOING TO FOLLOW THESE MEN TO THE CHURCH AND CHECK OUT THIS HEALER. CARE TO JOIN ME?
NO, I THINK I'M GOING TO STAY HERE AND TRY TO MAKE THESE PEOPLE MORE COMFORTABLE.
ALRIGHT, I'LL BE BACK FOR YOU SOON. TRY TO STAY OUT OF TROUBLE TILL THEN.
AAAGH!

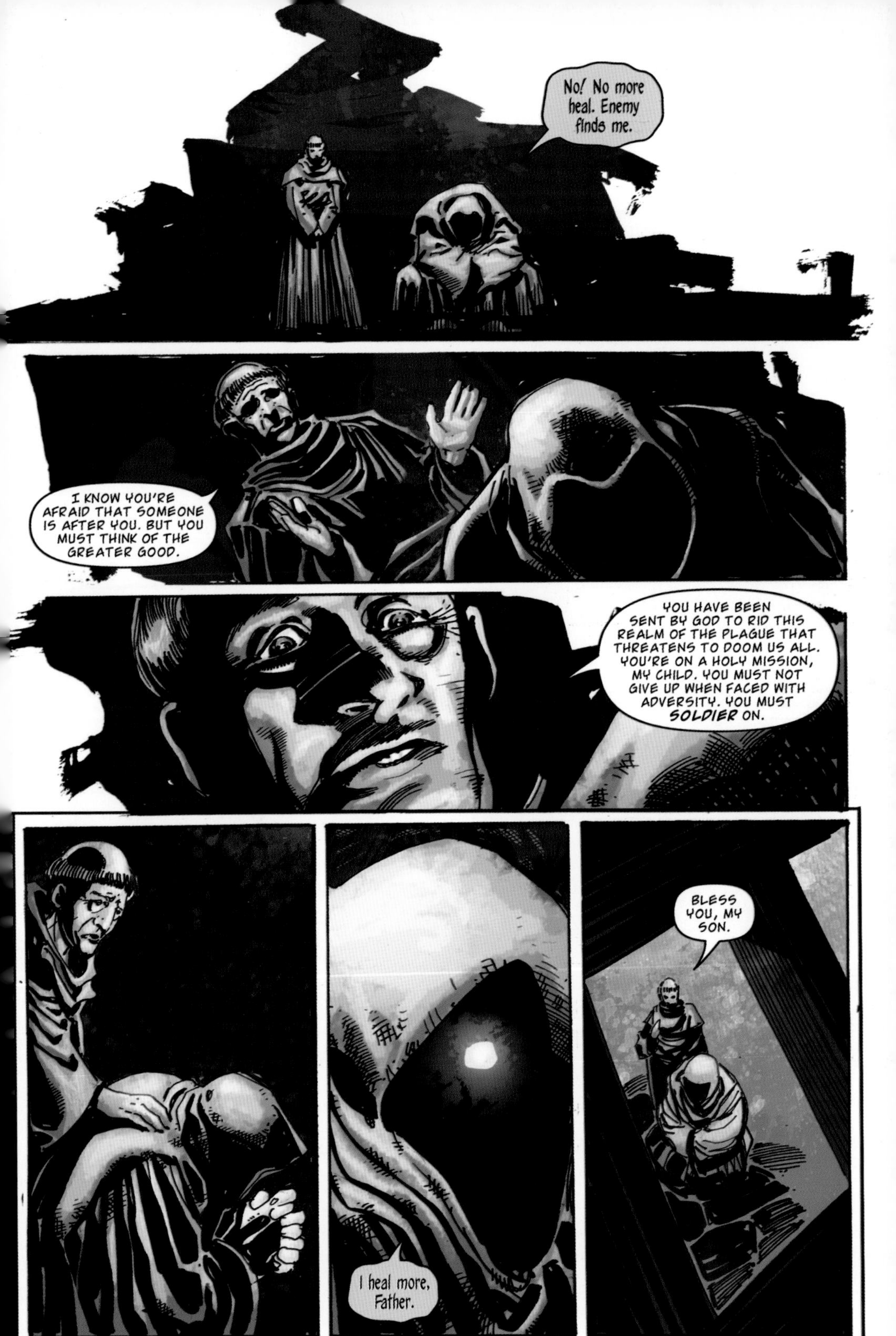

No! No more heal. Enemy finds me.
I KNOW YOU'RE AFRAID THAT SOMEONE IS AFTER YOU. BUT YOU MUST THINK OF THE GREATER GOOD.
YOU HAVE BEEN SENT BY GOD TO RID THIS REALM OF THE PLAGUE THAT THREATENS TO DOOM US ALL. YOU'RE ON A HOLY MISSION, MY CHILD. YOU MUST NOT GIVE UP WHEN FACED WITH ADVERSITY. YOU MUST SOLDIER ON.
I heal more, Father.
BLESS YOU, MY SON.

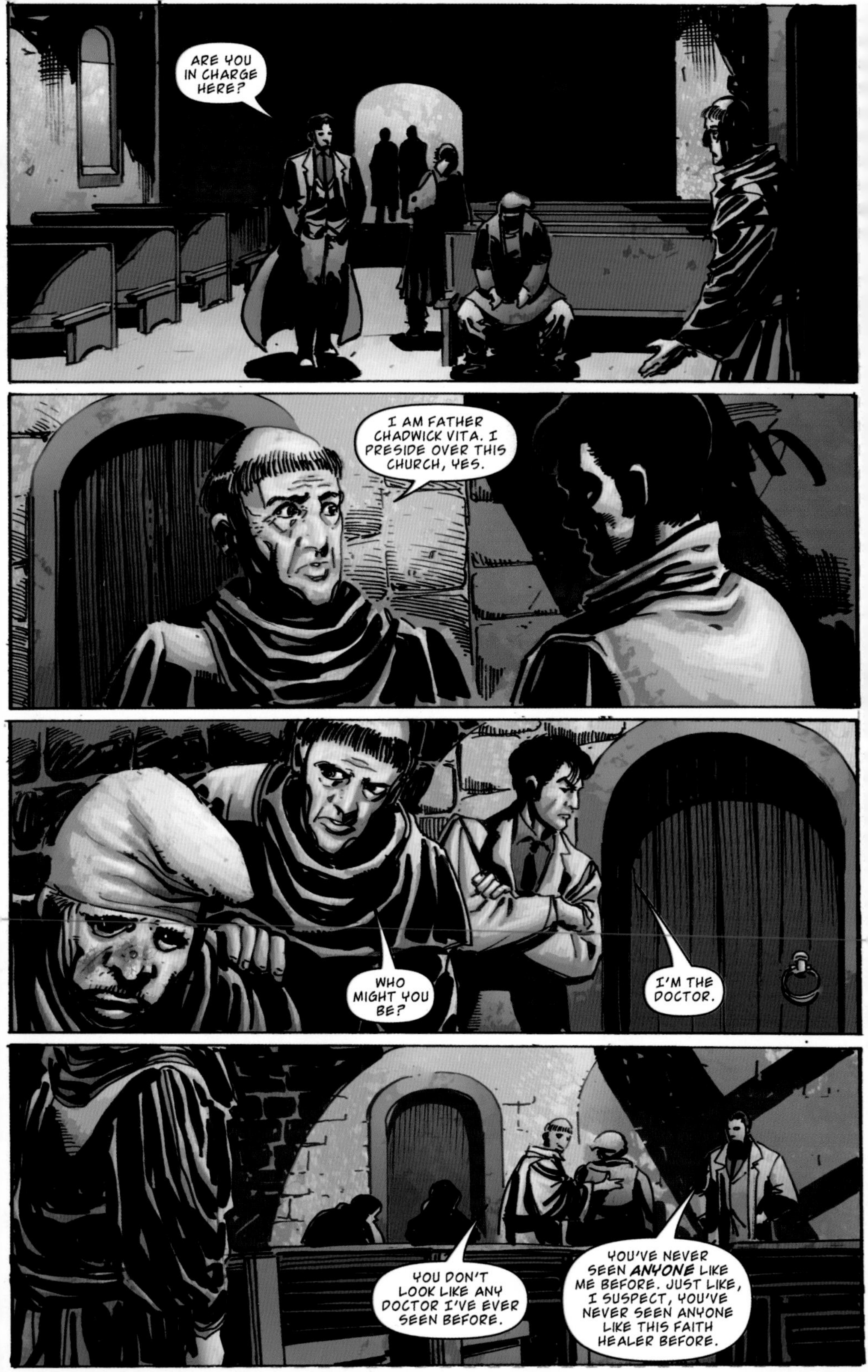
ARE YOU IN CHARGE HERE?
I AM FATHER CHADWICK VITA. I PRESIDE OVER THIS CHURCH, YES.
WHO MIGHT YOU BE?
I'M THE DOCTOR.
YOU DON'T LOOK LIKE ANY DOCTOR I'VE EVER SEEN BEFORE.
YOU'VE NEVER SEEN ANYONE LIKE ME BEFORE. JUST LIKE, I SUSPECT, YOU'VE NEVER SEEN ANYONE LIKE THIS FAITH HEALER BEFORE.

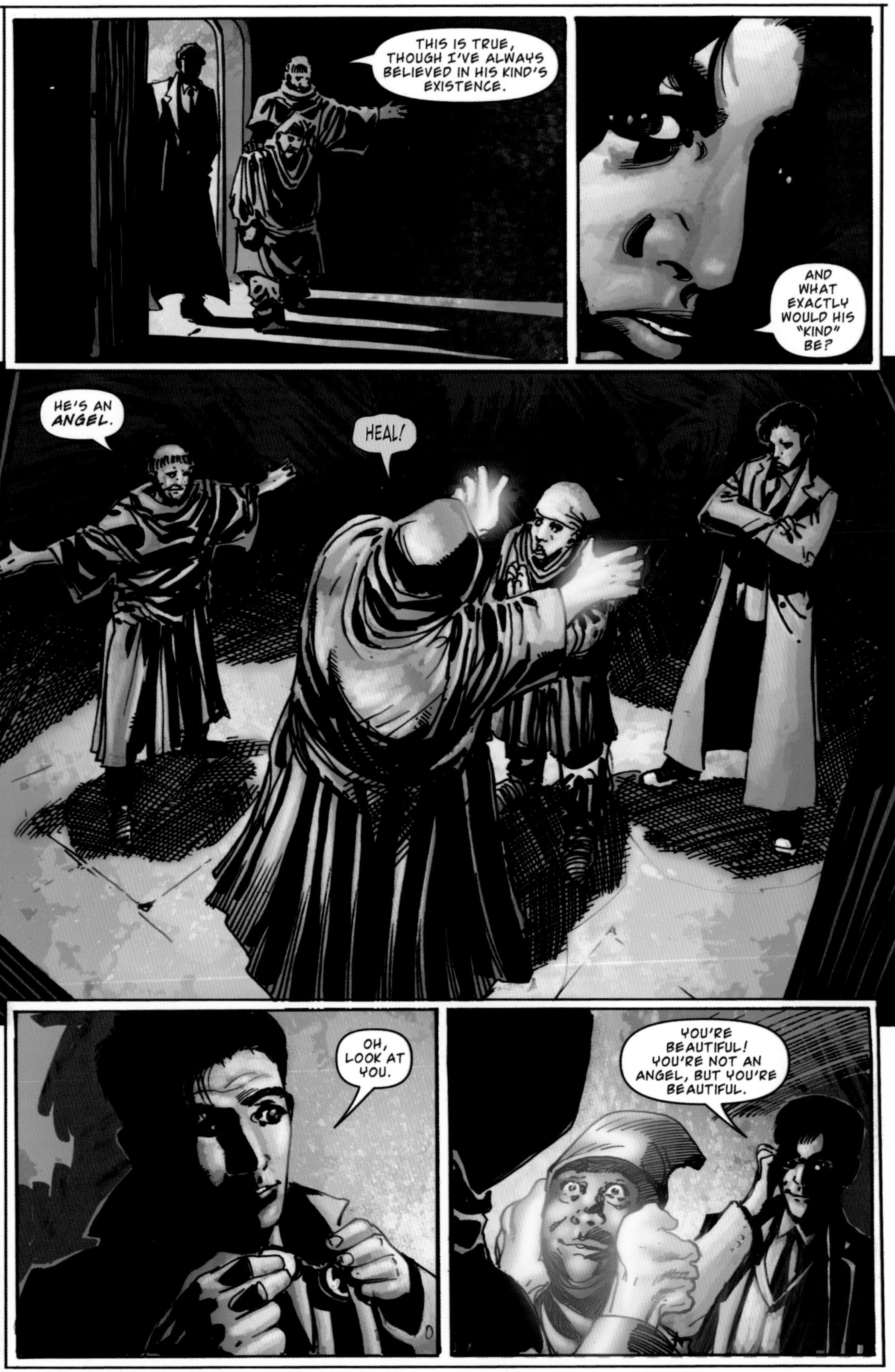
THIS IS TRUE, THOUGH I'VE ALWAYS BELIEVED IN HIS KIND'S EXISTENCE.
AND WHAT EXACTLY WOULD HIS "KIND" BE?
HE'S AN ANGEL.
HEAL!
OH, LOOK AT YOU.
YOU'RE BEAUTIFUL! YOU'RE NOT AN ANGEL, BUT YOU'RE BEAUTIFUL.

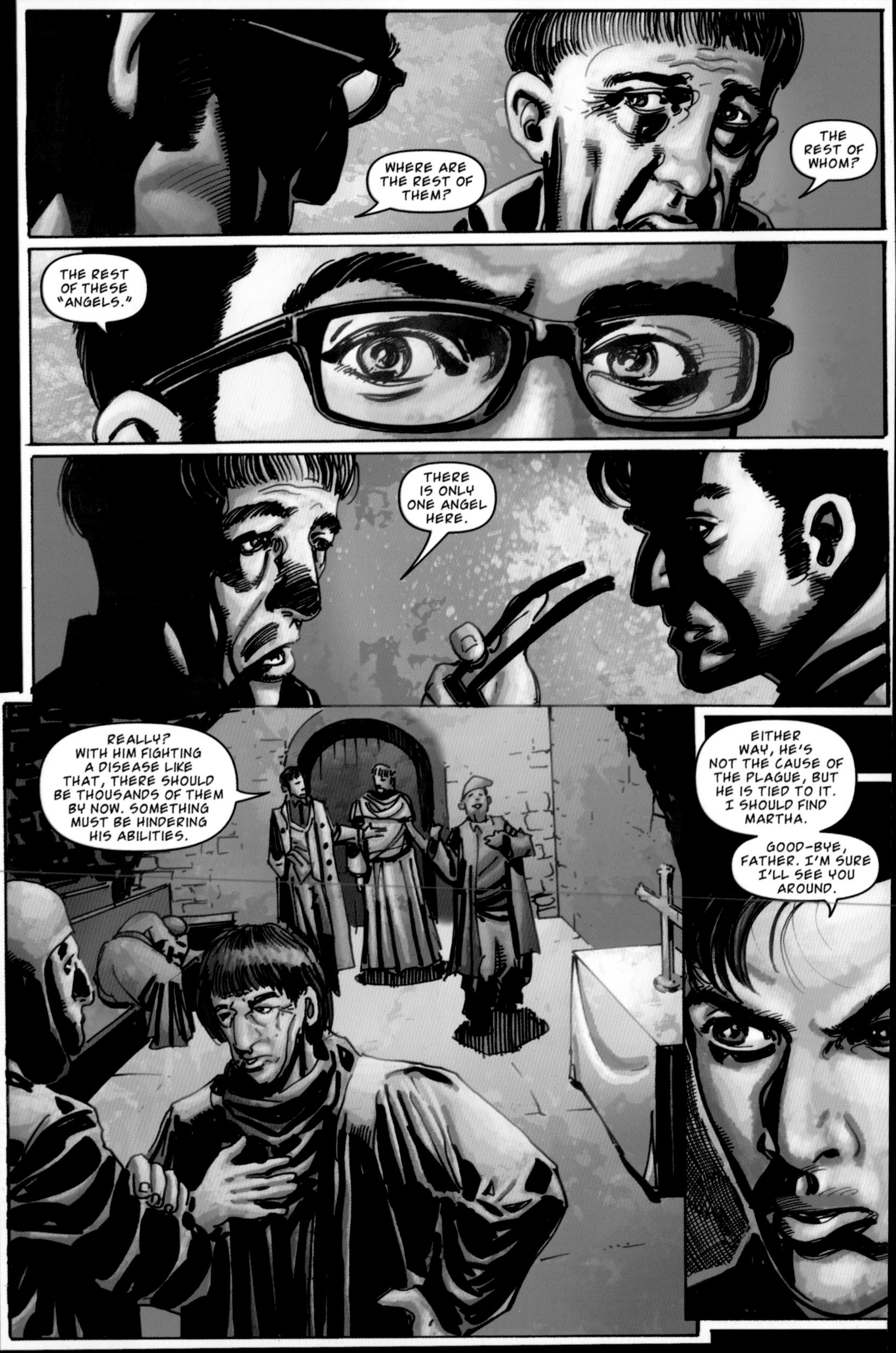
WHERE ARE THE REST OF THEM?
THE REST OF WHOM?
THE REST OF THESE "ANGELS."
THERE IS ONLY ONE ANGEL HERE.
REALLY? WITH HIM FIGHTING A DISEASE LIKE THAT, THERE SHOULD BE THOUSANDS OF THEM BY NOW. SOMETHING MUST BE HINDERING HIS ABILITIES.
EITHER WAY, HE'S NOT THE CAUSE OF THE PLAGUE, BUT HE IS TIED TO IT. I SHOULD FIND MARTHA.
GOOD-BYE, FATHER. I'M SURE I'LL SEE YOU AROUND.

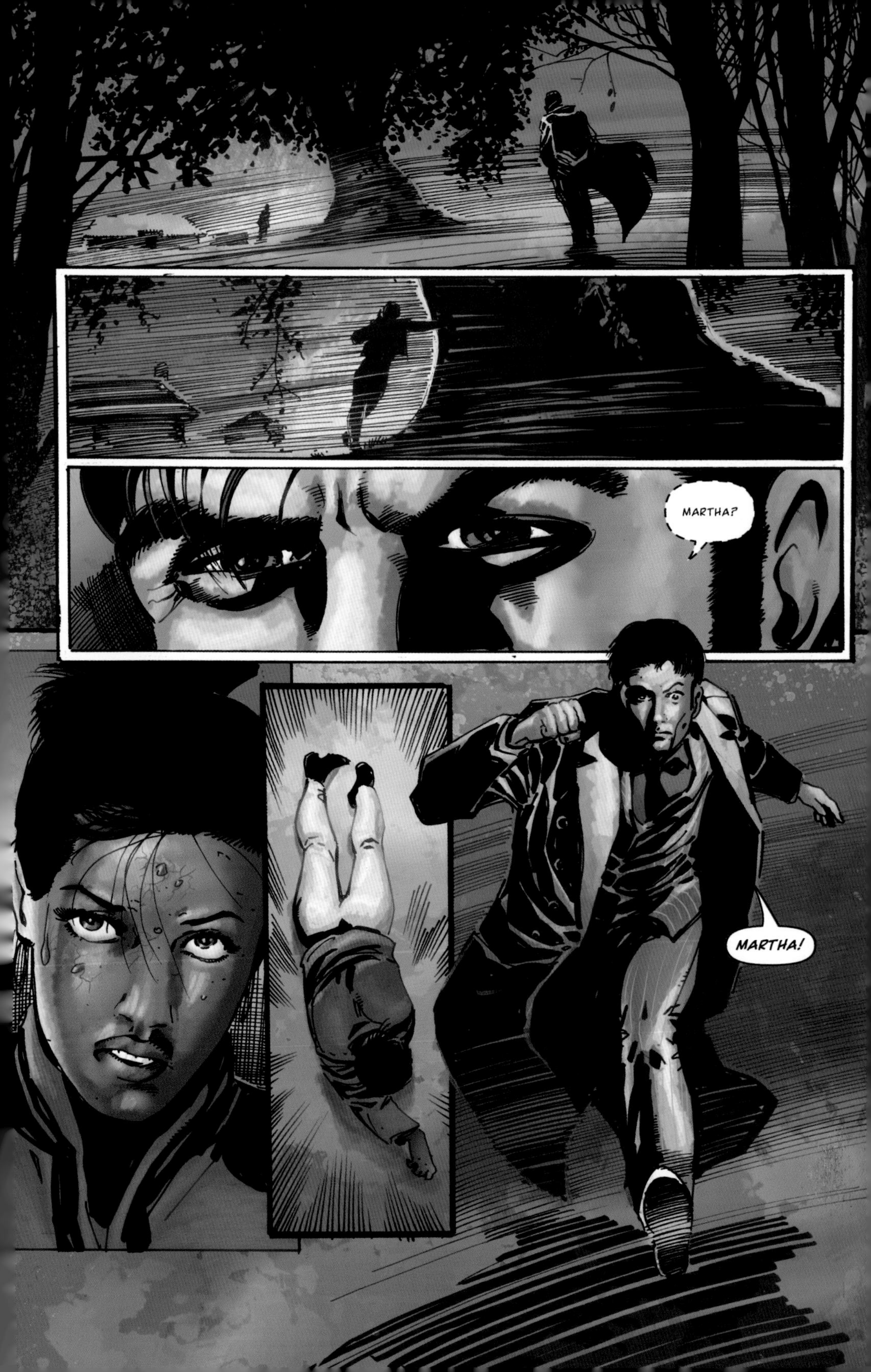
MARTHA?
MARTHA!

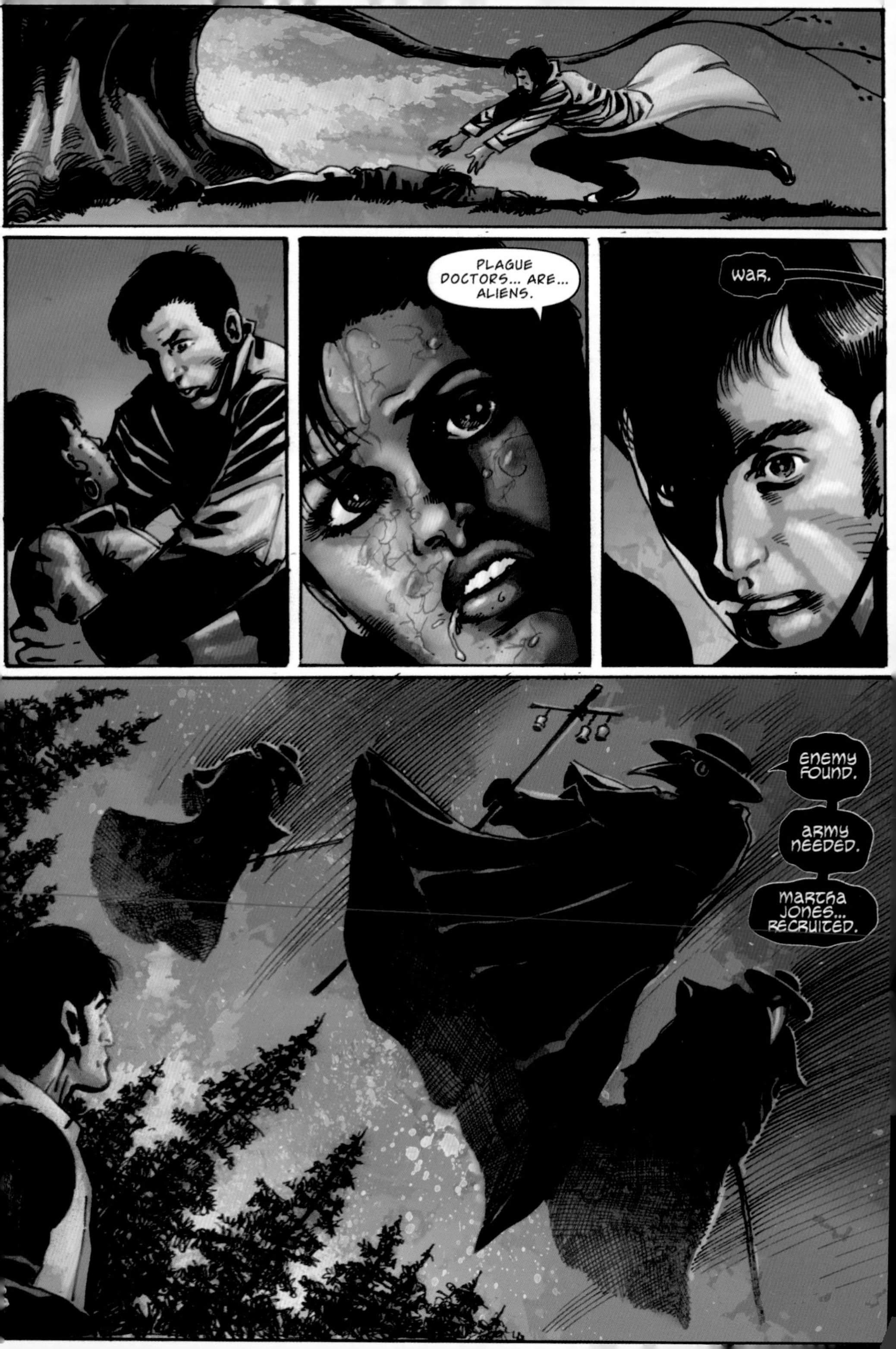
PLAGUE DOCTORS... ARE... ALIENS.
WAR.
ENEMY FOUND.
ARMY NEEDED.
MARTHA JONES... RECRUITED.

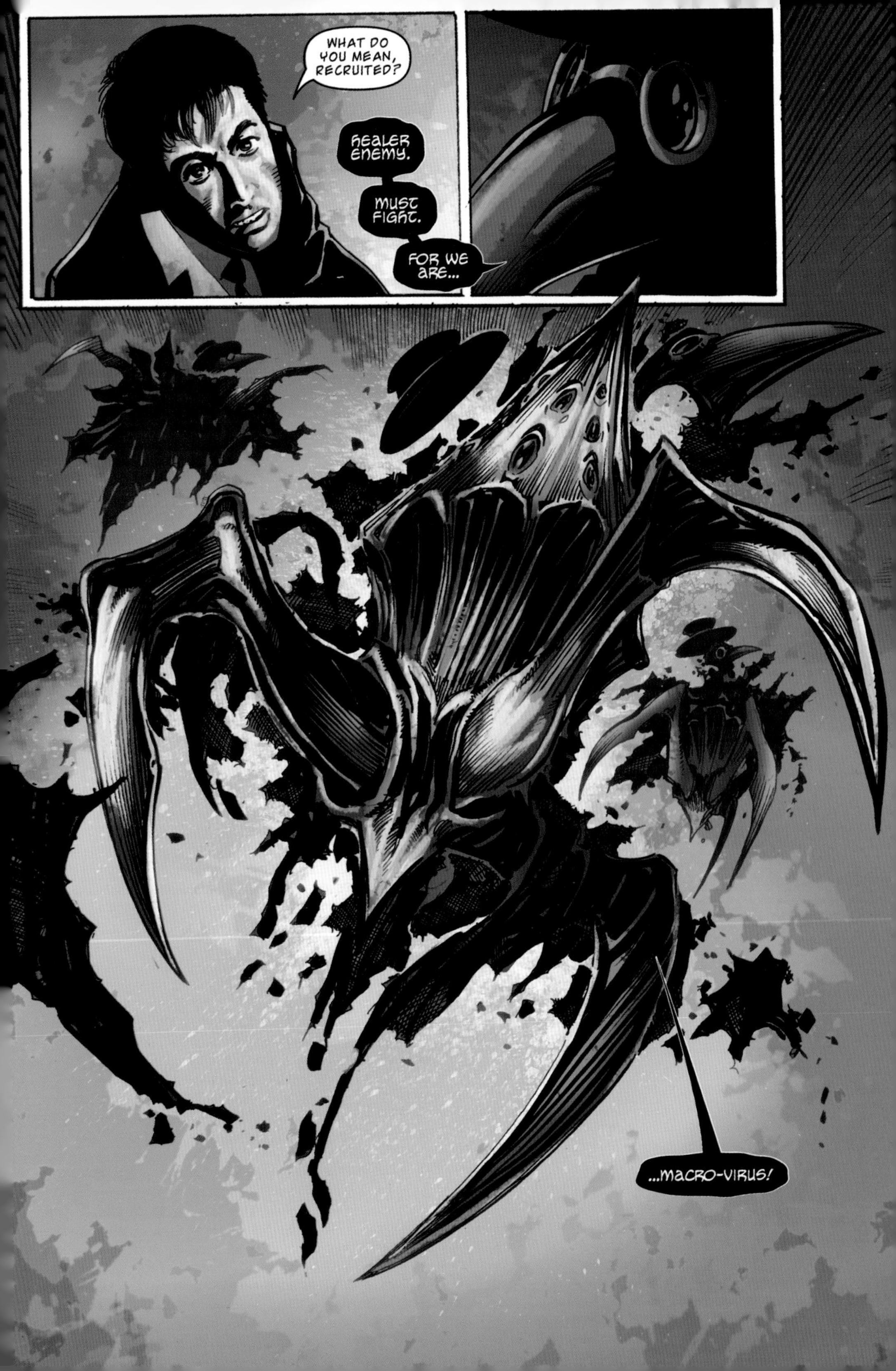
WHAT DO YOU MEAN, RECRUITED?
HEALER ENEMY.
MUST FIGHT.
FOR WE ARE...
...MACRO-VIRUS!

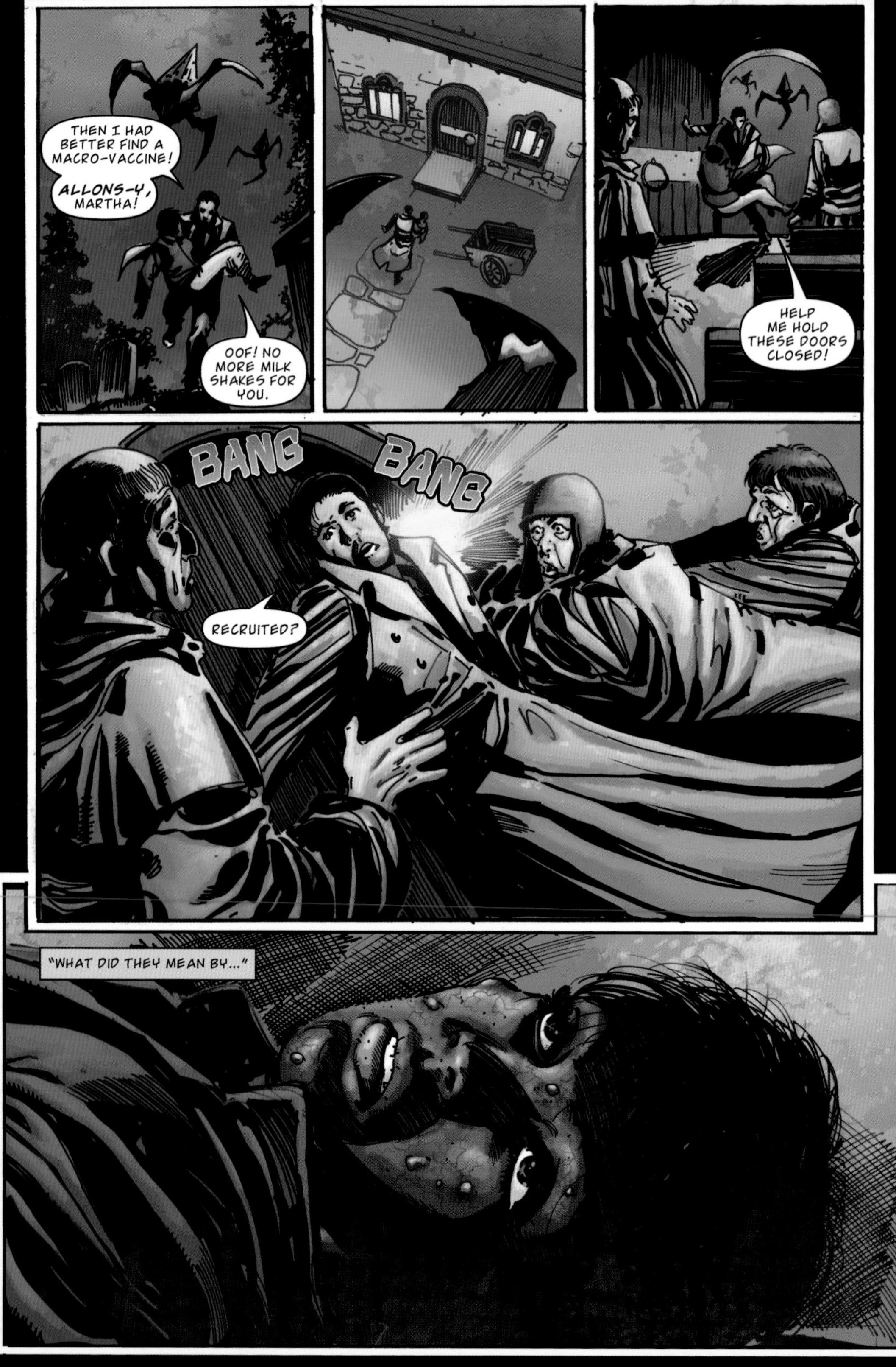

THEN I HAD BETTER FIND A MACRO-VACCINE!
ALLONS-Y, MARTHA!
OOF! NO MORE MILK SHAKES FOR YOU.
HELP ME HOLD THESE DOORS CLOSED!
BANG
BANG
RECRUITED?
"WHAT DID THEY MEAN BY..."

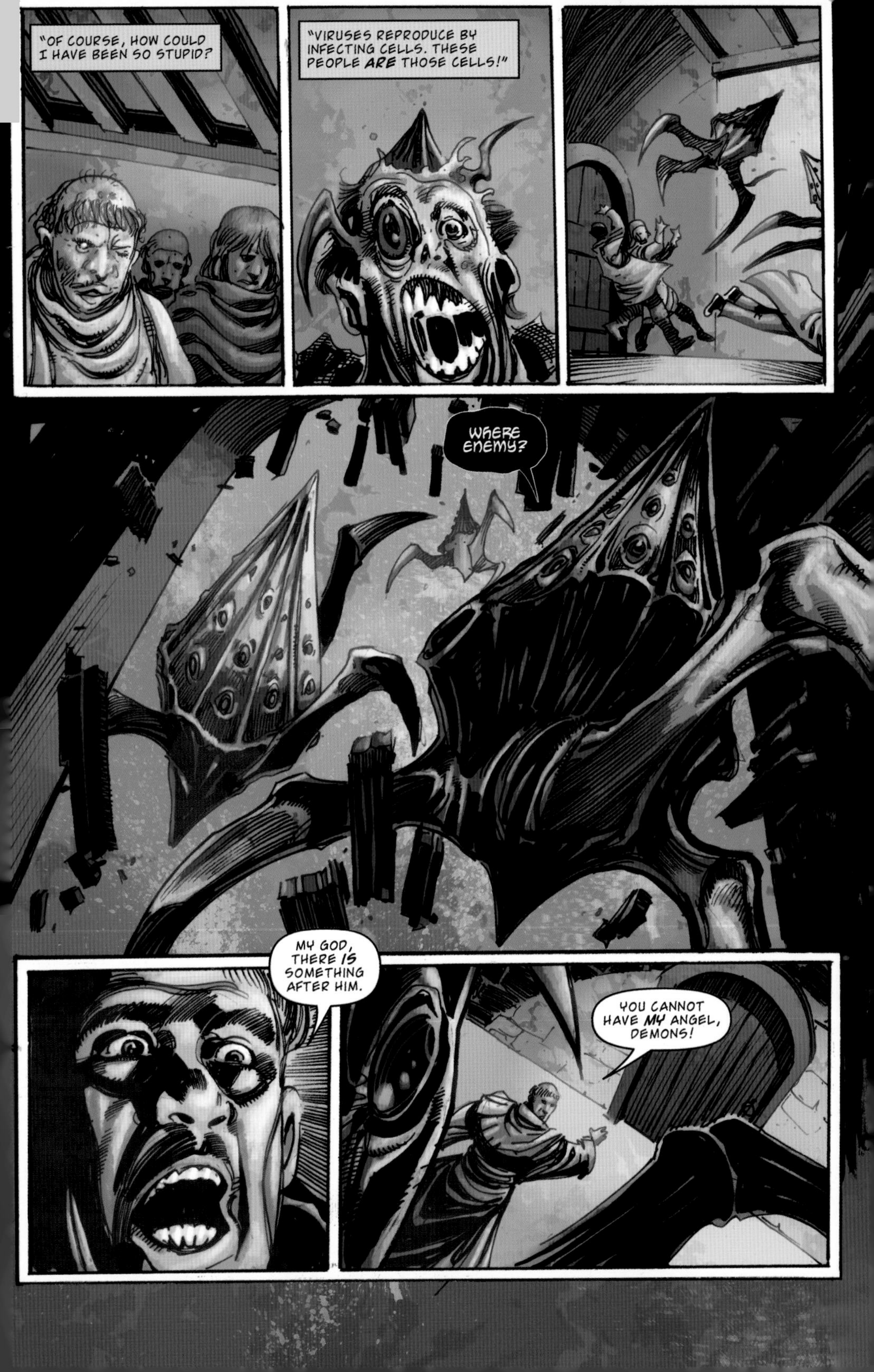
"OF COURSE, HOW COULD I HAVE BEEN SO STUPID?
"VIRUSES REPRODUCE BY INFECTING CELLS. THESE PEOPLE ARE THOSE CELLS!"
WHERE ENEMY?
MY GOD, THERE IS SOMETHING AFTER HIM.
YOU CANNOT HAVE MY ANGEL, DEMONS!

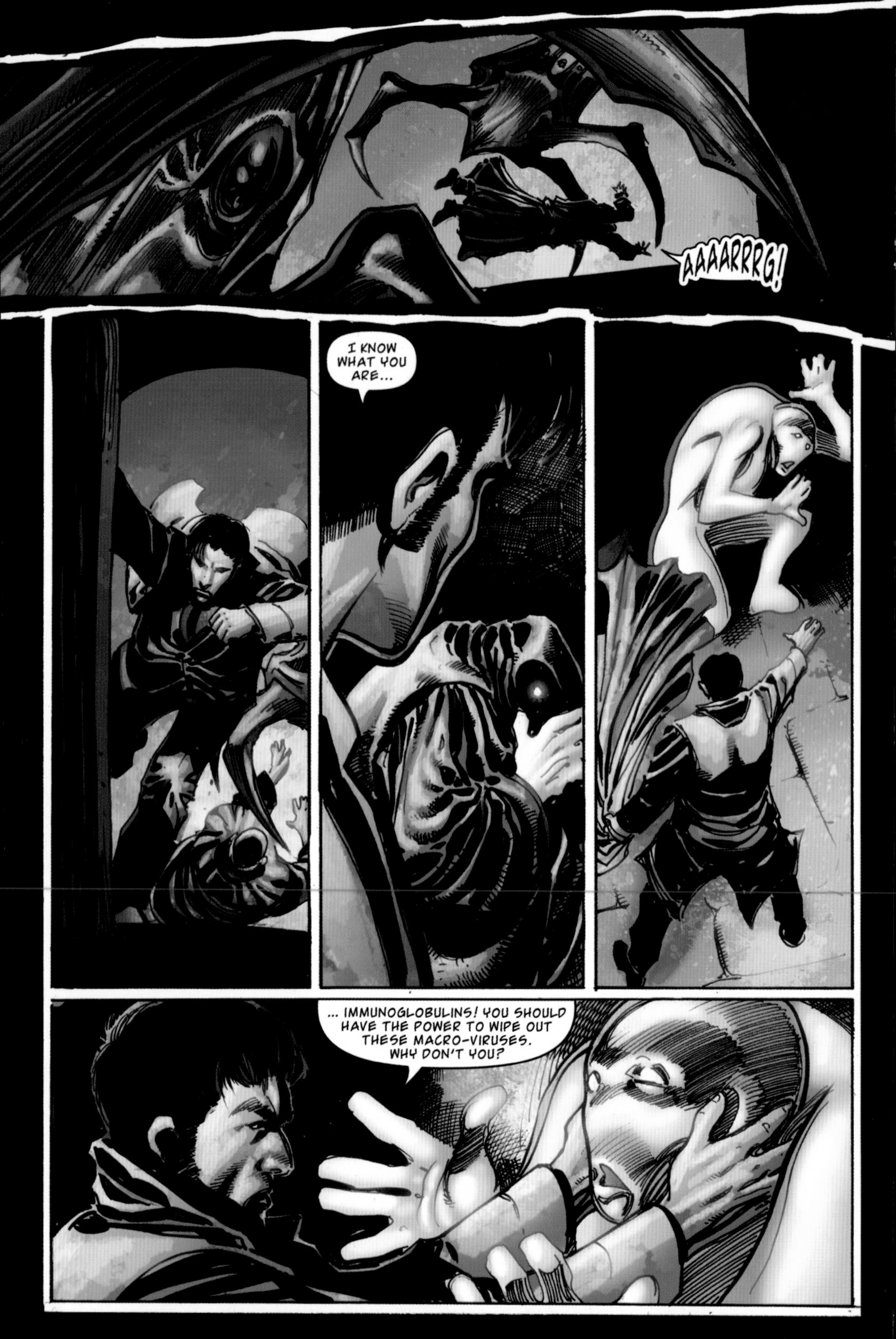
AAAARRRG!
I KNOW WHAT YOU ARE...
... IMMUNOGLOBULINS! YOU SHOULD HAVE THE POWER TO WIPE OUT THESE MACRO-VIRUSES. WHY DON'T YOU?

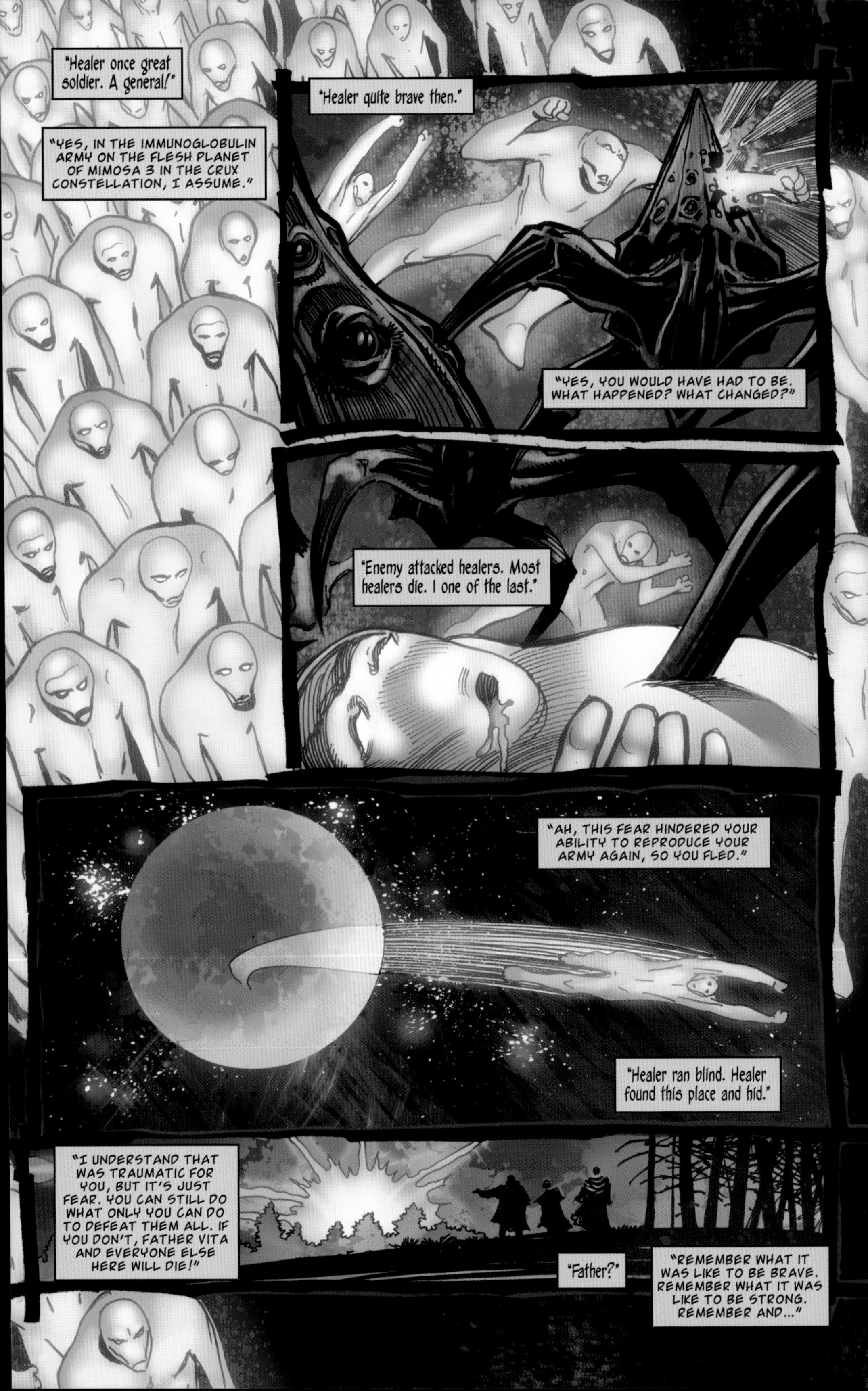
"Healer once great soldier. A general!"
"YES, IN THE IMMUNOGLOBULIN ARMY ON THE FLESH PLANET OF MIMOSA 3 IN THE CRUX CONSTELLATION, I ASSUME."
"Healer quite brave then."
"YES, YOU WOULD HAVE HAD TO BE. WHAT HAPPENED? WHAT CHANGED?"
"Enemy attacked healers. Most healers die. I one of the last."
"AH, THIS FEAR HINDERED YOUR ABILITY TO REPRODUCE YOUR ARMY AGAIN, SO YOU FLED."
"Healer ran blind. Healer found this place and hid."
"I UNDERSTAND THAT WAS TRAUMATIC FOR YOU, BUT IT'S JUST FEAR. YOU CAN STILL DO WHAT ONLY YOU CAN DO TO DEFEAT THEM ALL. IF YOU DON'T, FATHER VITA AND EVERYONE ELSE HERE WILL DIE!"
"Father?"
"REMEMBER WHAT IT WAS LIKE TO BE BRAVE. REMEMBER WHAT IT WAS LIKE TO BE STRONG. REMEMBER AND..."

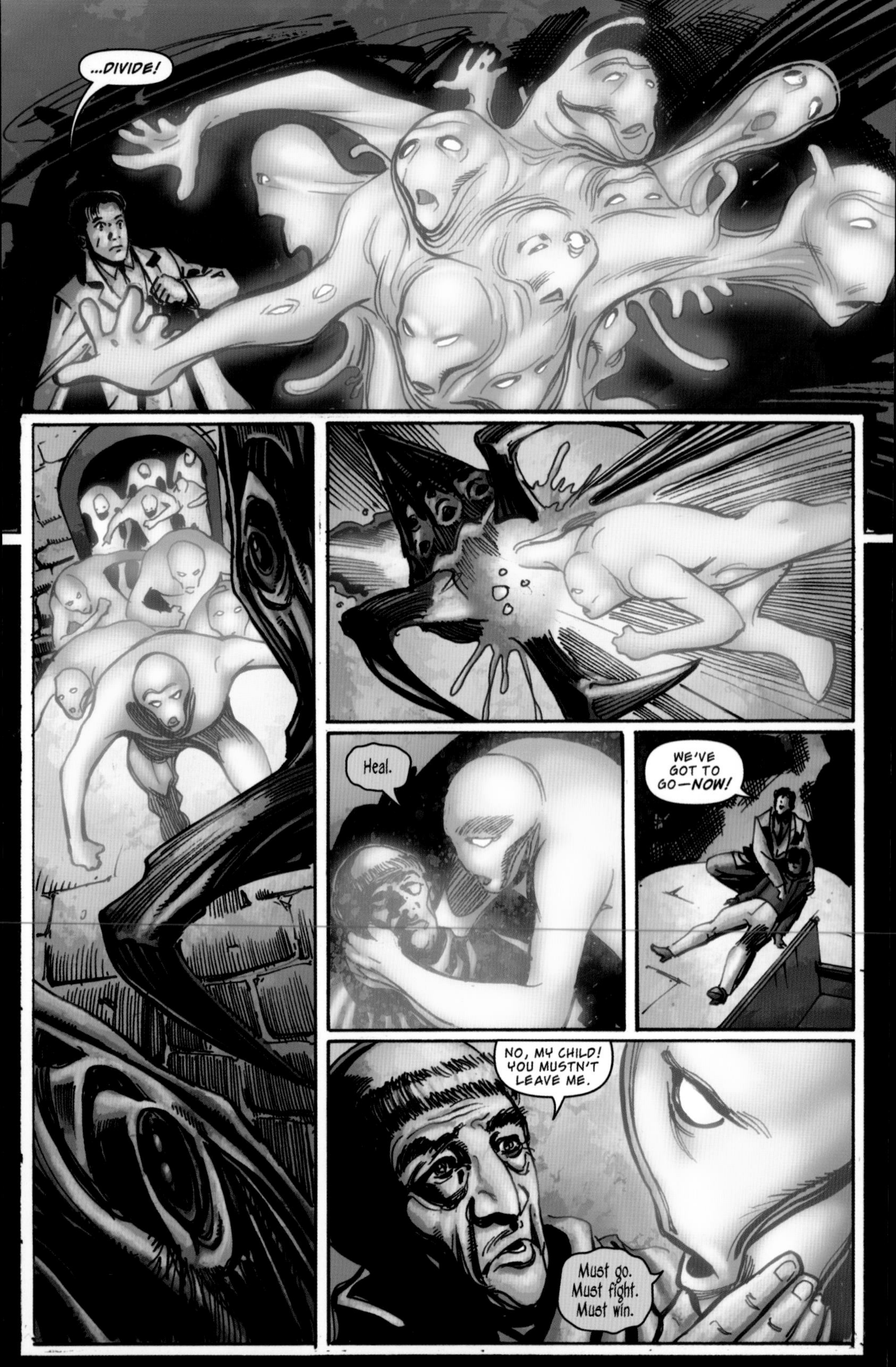
...DIVIDE!
Heal.
WE'VE GOT TO GO—NOW!
NO, MY CHILD! YOU MUSTN'T LEAVE ME.
Must go. Must fight. Must win.

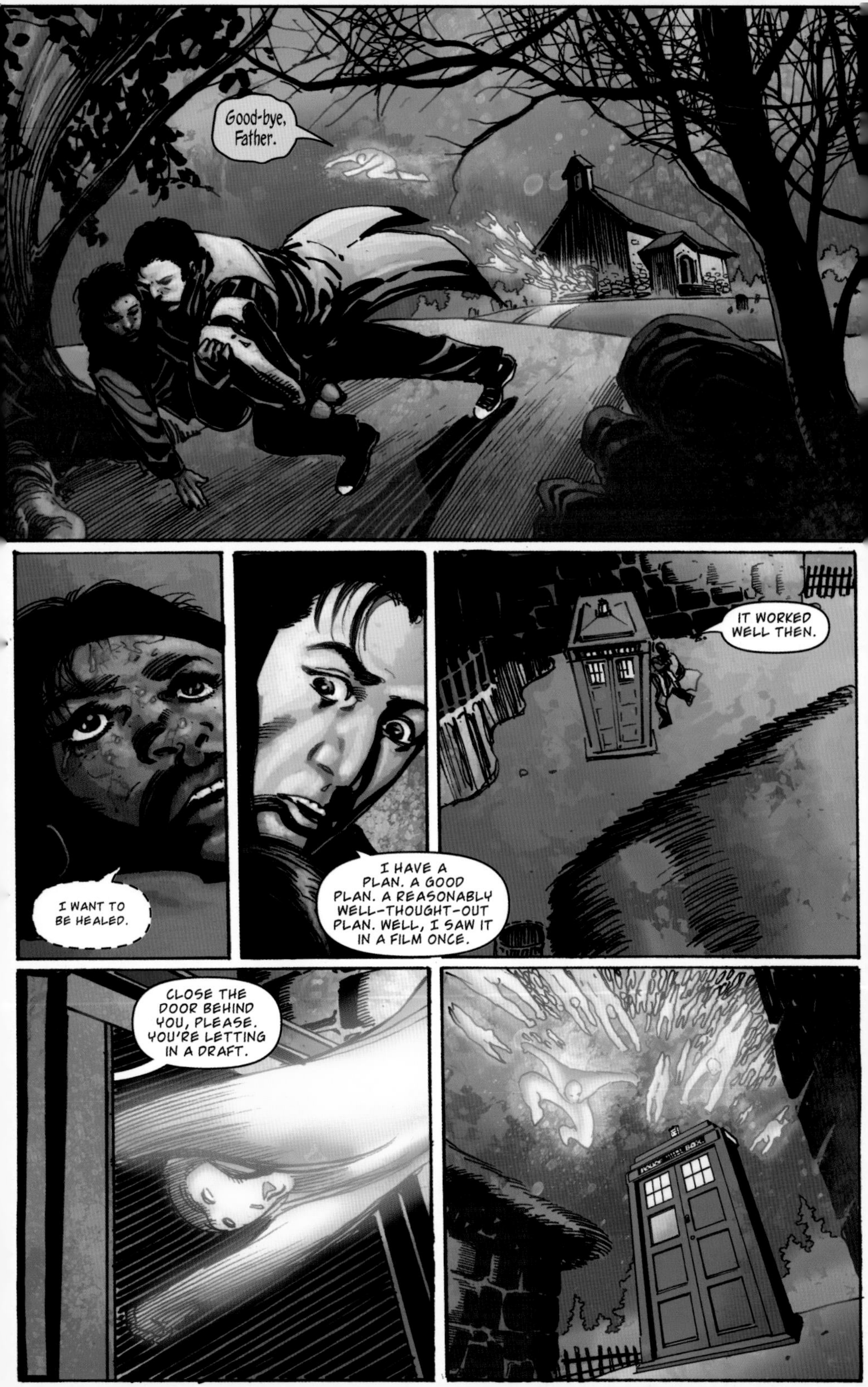
Good-bye, Father.
I WANT TO BE HEALED.
I HAVE A PLAN. A GOOD PLAN. A REASONABLY WELL-THOUGHT-OUT PLAN. WELL, I SAW IT IN A FILM ONCE.
IT WORKED WELL THEN.
CLOSE THE DOOR BEHIND YOU, PLEASE. YOU'RE LETTING IN A DRAFT.

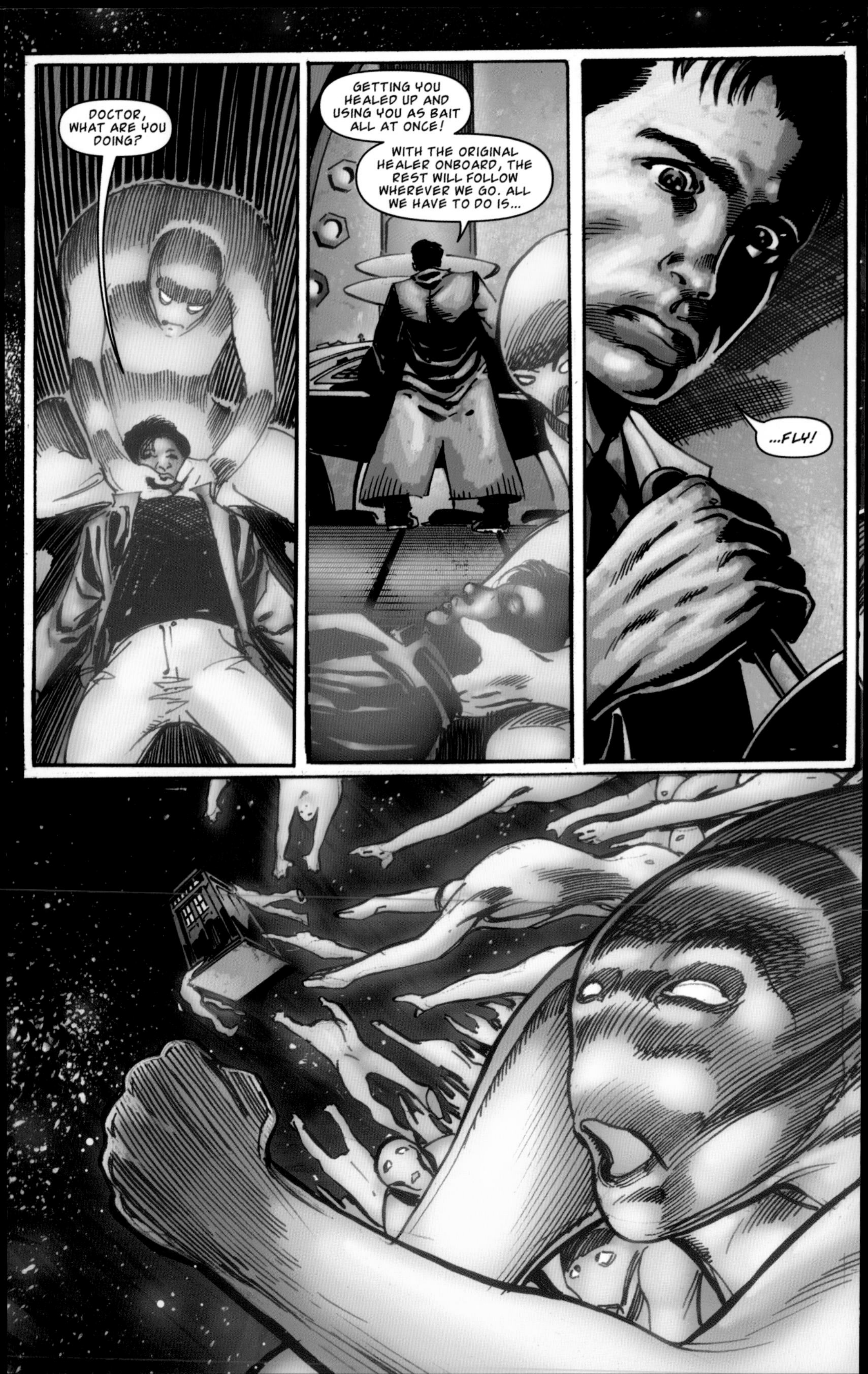
DOCTOR, WHAT ARE YOU DOING?
GETTING YOU HEALED UP AND USING YOU AS BAIT ALL AT ONCE!
WITH THE ORIGINAL HEALER ONBOARD, THE REST WILL FOLLOW WHEREVER WE GO. ALL WE HAVE TO DO IS...
...FLY!

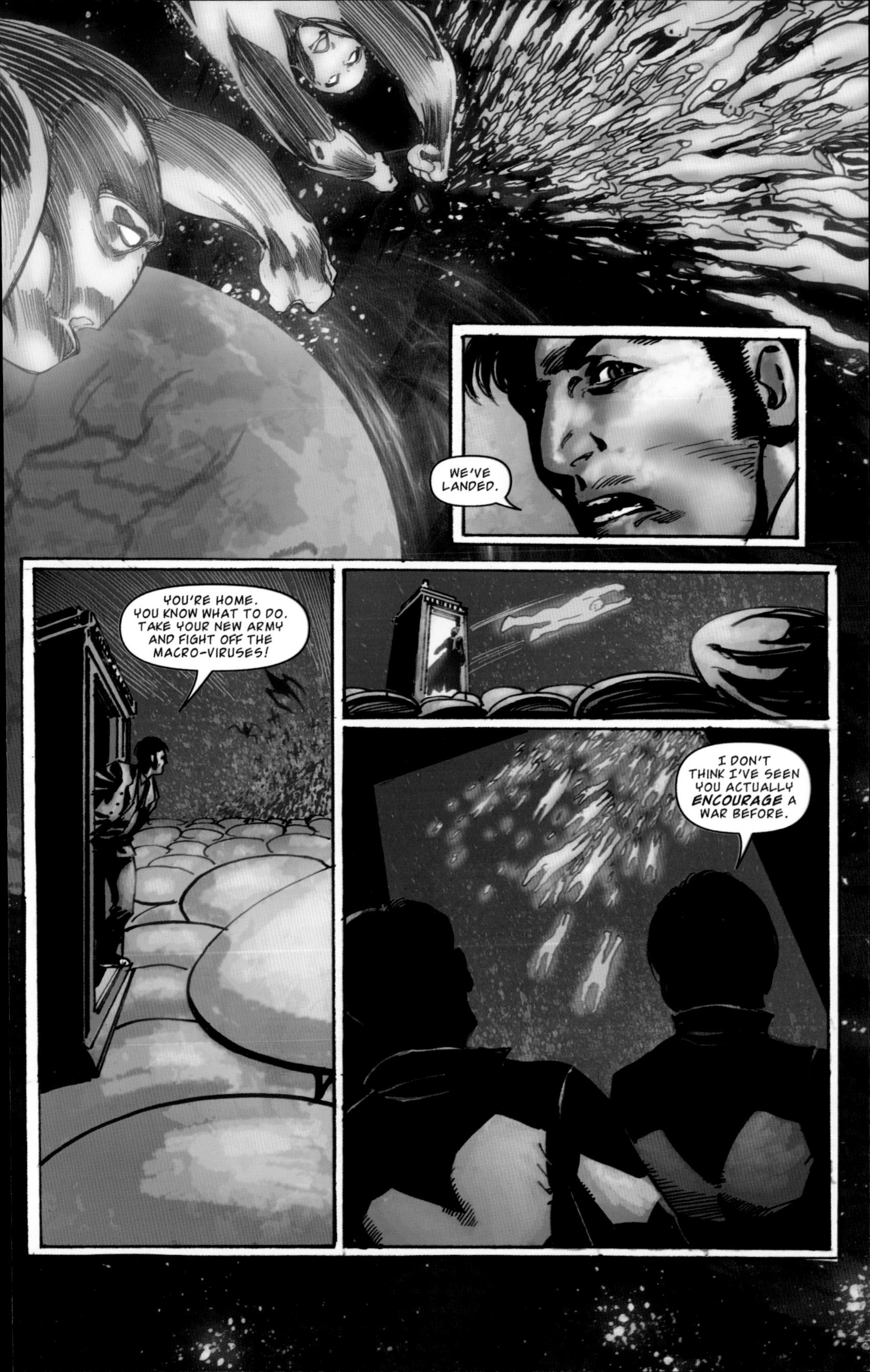
WE'VE LANDED.
YOU'RE HOME. YOU KNOW WHAT TO DO. TAKE YOUR NEW ARMY AND FIGHT OFF THE MACRO-VIRUSES!
I DON'T THINK I'VE SEEN YOU ACTUALLY ENCOURAGE A WAR BEFORE.

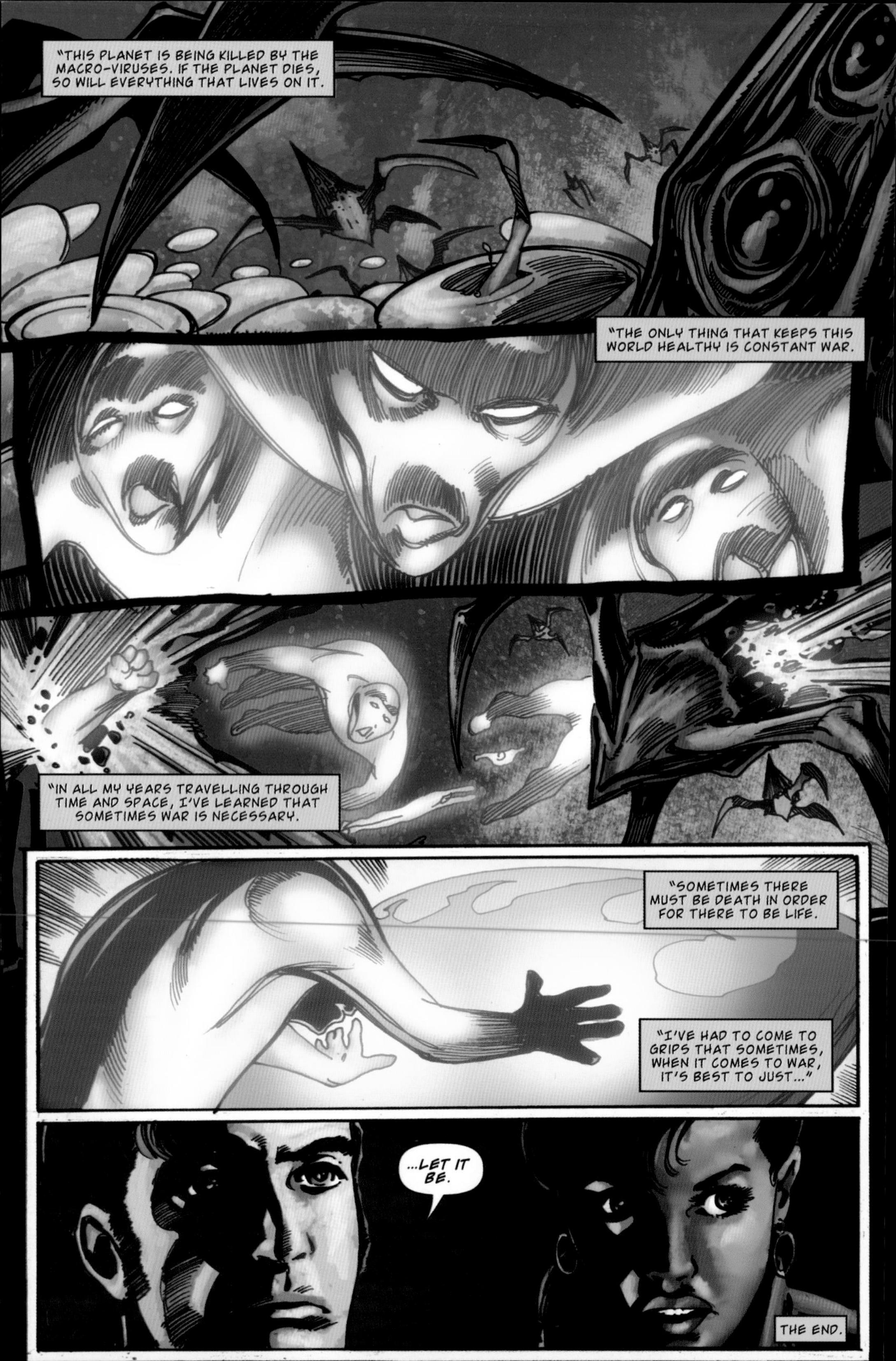
"THIS PLANET IS BEING KILLED BY THE MACRO-VIRUSES. IF THE PLANET DIES, SO WILL EVERYTHING THAT LIVES ON IT.
"THE ONLY THING THAT KEEPS THIS WORLD HEALTHY IS CONSTANT WAR.
"IN ALL MY YEARS TRAVELLING THROUGH TIME AND SPACE, I'VE LEARNED THAT SOMETIMES WAR IS NECESSARY.
"SOMETIMES THERE MUST BE DEATH IN ORDER FOR THERE TO BE LIFE.
"I'VE HAD TO COME TO GRIPS THAT SOMETIMES, WHEN IT COMES TO WAR, IT'S BEST TO JUST..."
...LET IT BE.
THE END.

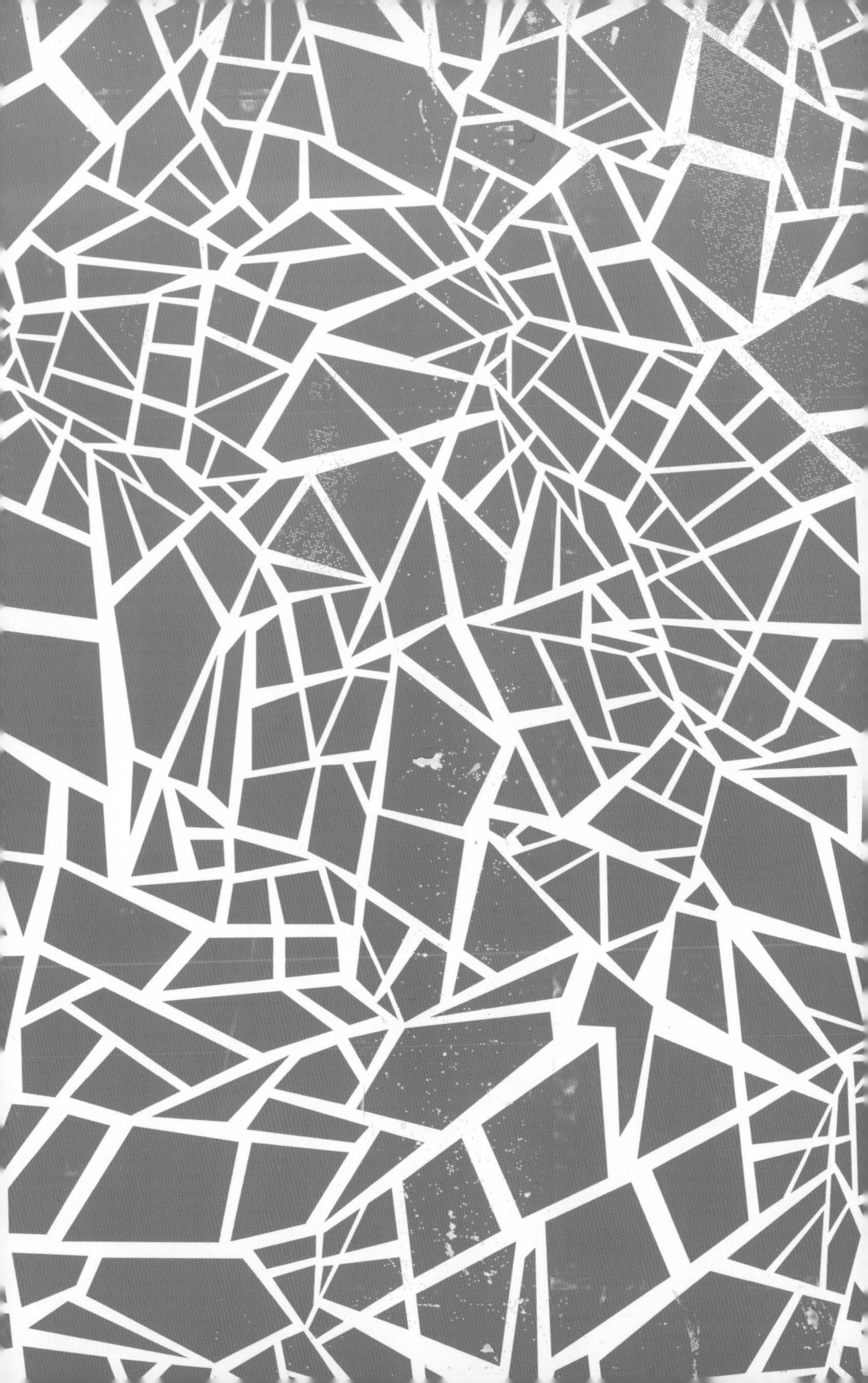

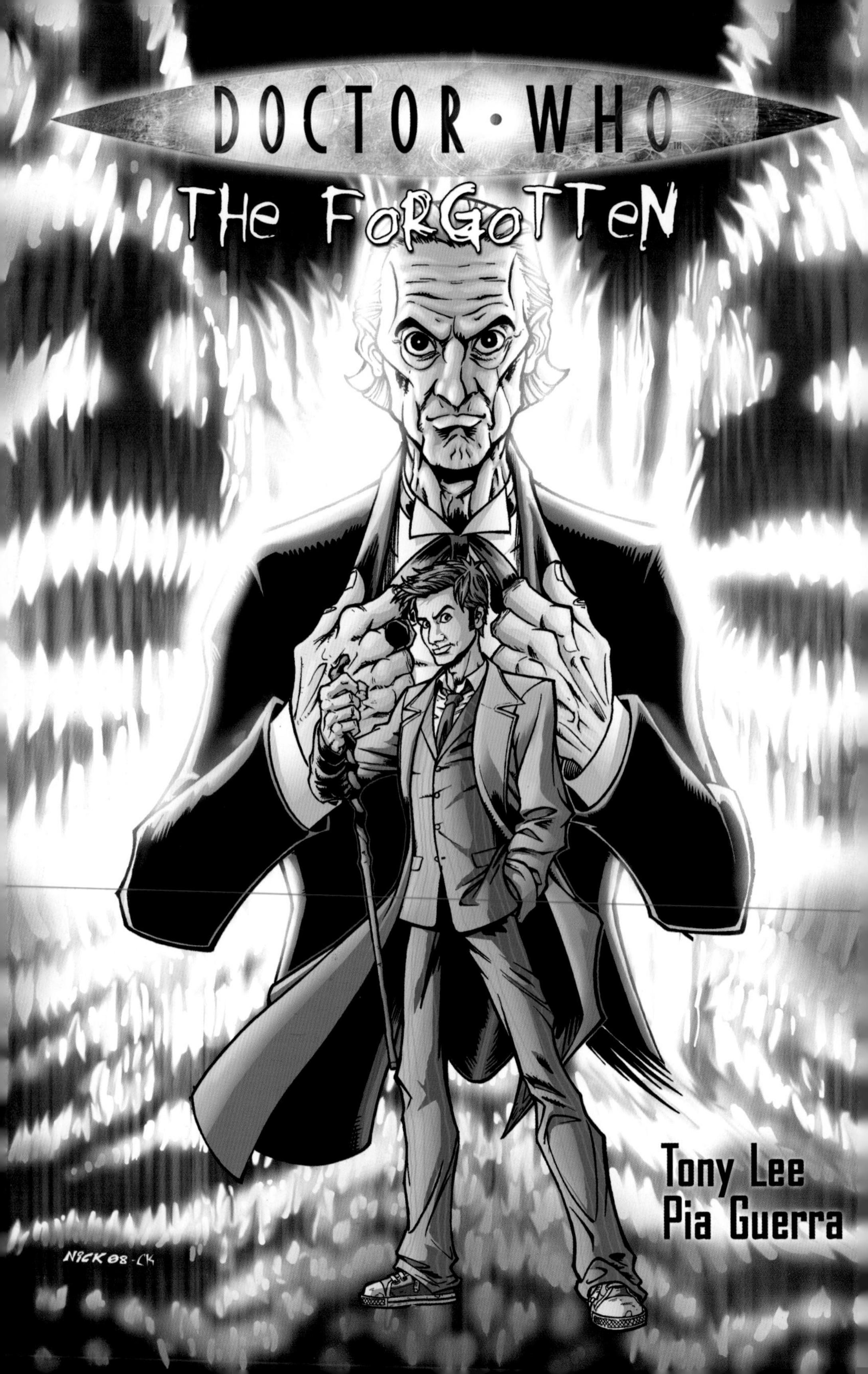
DOCTOR WHO
THE FORGOTTEN
Tony Lee
Pia Guerra

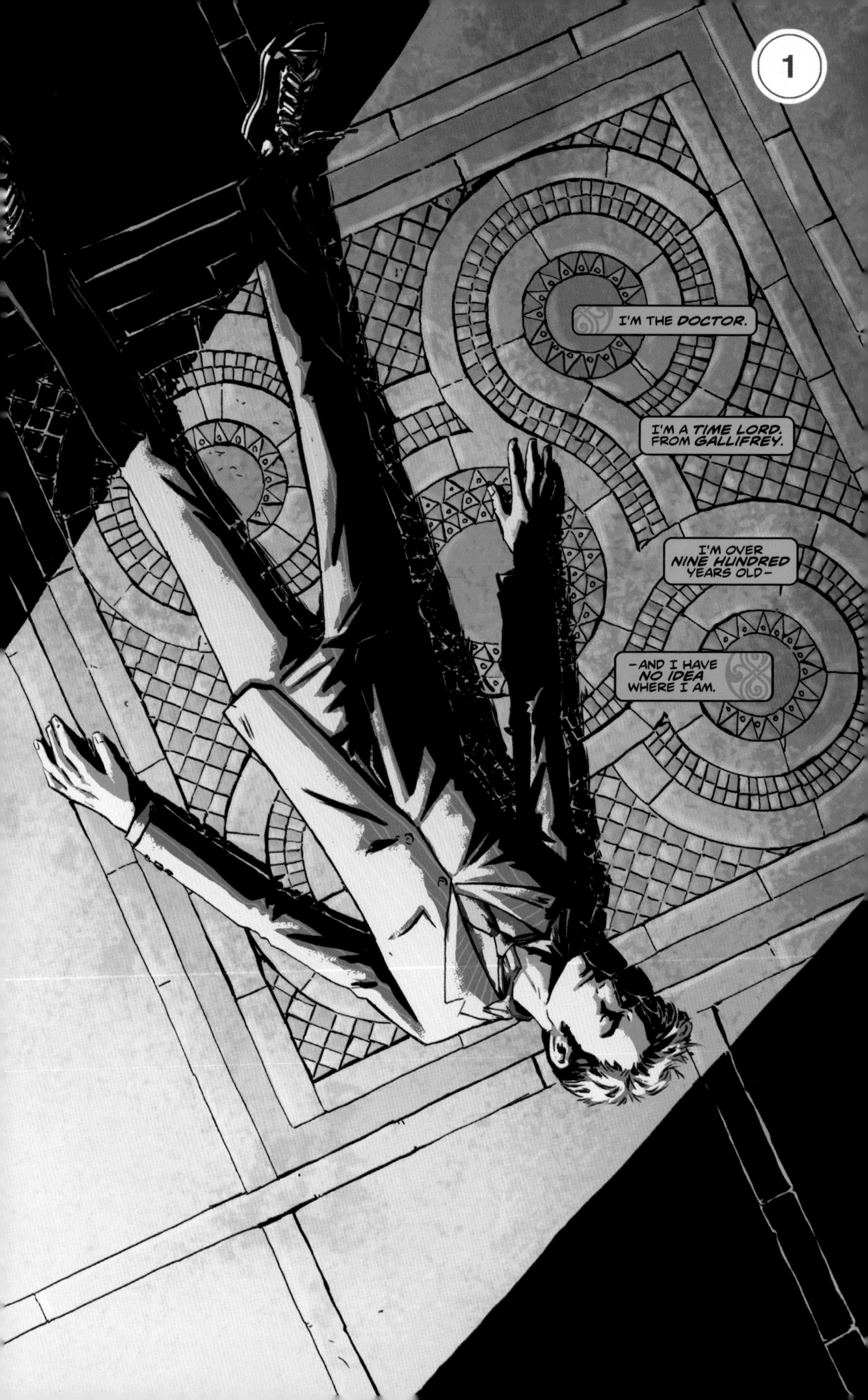
1
I'M THE DOCTOR.
I'M A TIME LORD. FROM GALLIFREY.
I'M OVER NINE HUNDRED YEARS OLD–
–AND I HAVE NO IDEA WHERE I AM.

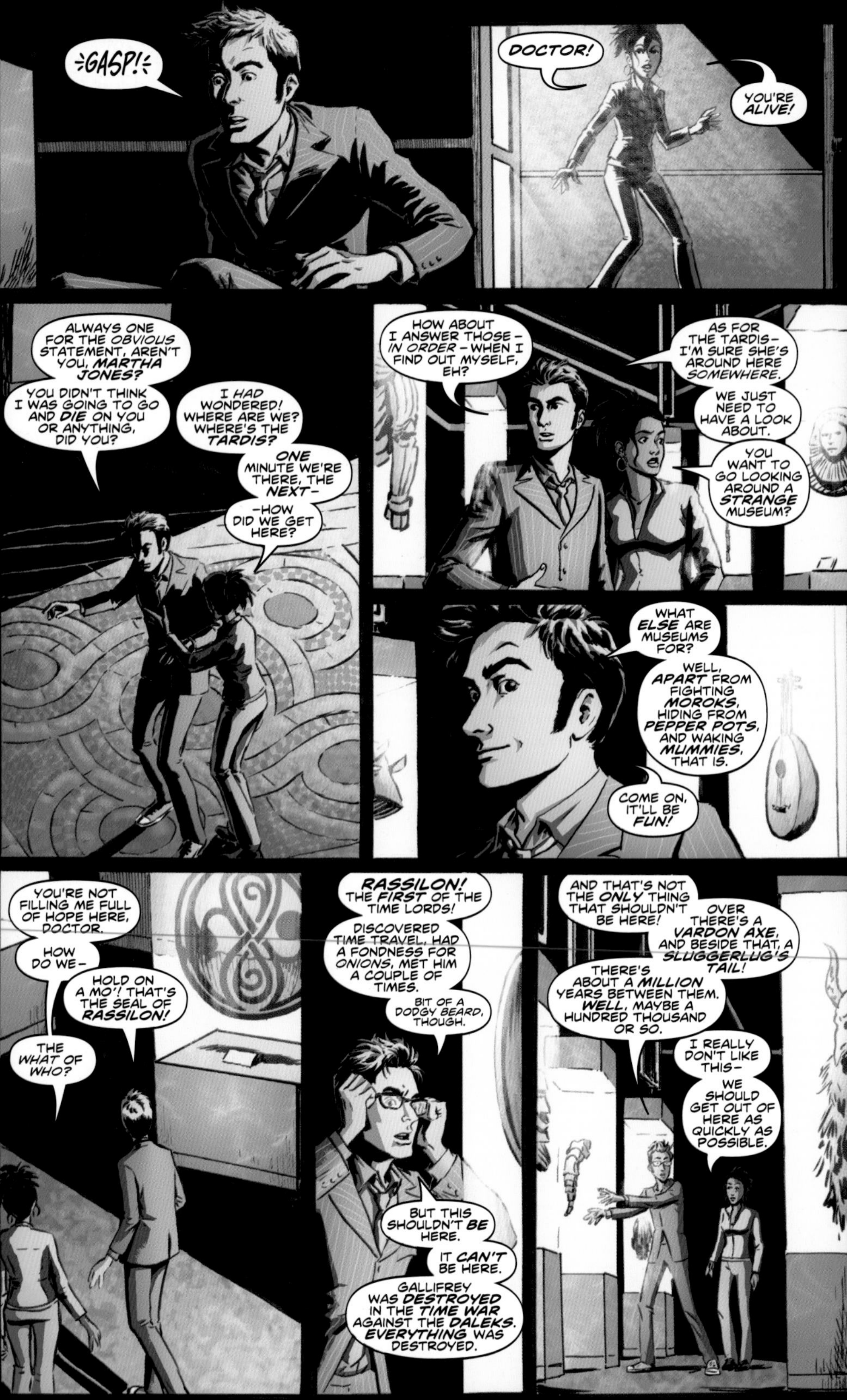
GASP!
DOCTOR!
YOU'RE ALIVE!
ALWAYS ONE FOR THE OBVIOUS STATEMENT, AREN'T YOU, MARTHA JONES?
YOU DIDN'T THINK I WAS GOING TO GO AND DIE ON YOU OR ANYTHING, DID YOU?
I HAD WONDERED! WHERE ARE WE? WHERE'S THE TARDIS?
ONE MINUTE WE'RE THERE, THE NEXT–
–HOW DID WE GET HERE?
HOW ABOUT I ANSWER THOSE – IN ORDER – WHEN I FIND OUT MYSELF, EH?
AS FOR THE TARDIS– I'M SURE SHE'S AROUND HERE SOMEWHERE.
WE JUST NEED TO HAVE A LOOK ABOUT.
YOU WANT TO GO LOOKING AROUND A STRANGE MUSEUM?
WHAT ELSE ARE MUSEUMS FOR?
WELL, APART FROM FIGHTING MOROKS, HIDING FROM PEPPER POTS, AND WAKING MUMMIES, THAT IS.
COME ON, IT'LL BE FUN!
YOU'RE NOT FILLING ME FULL OF HOPE HERE, DOCTOR.
HOW DO WE–
HOLD ON A MO'! THAT'S THE SEAL OF RASSILON!
THE WHAT OF WHO?
RASSILON! THE FIRST OF THE TIME LORDS!
DISCOVERED TIME TRAVEL, HAD A FONDNESS FOR ONIONS, MET HIM A COUPLE OF TIMES.
BIT OF A DODGY BEARD, THOUGH.
BUT THIS SHOULDN'T BE HERE.
IT CAN'T BE HERE.
GALLIFREY WAS DESTROYED IN THE TIME WAR AGAINST THE DALEKS. EVERYTHING WAS DESTROYED.
AND THAT'S NOT THE ONLY THING THAT SHOULDN'T BE HERE!
OVER THERE'S A VARDON AXE, AND BESIDE THAT, A SLUGGERLUG'S TAIL!
THERE'S ABOUT A MILLION YEARS BETWEEN THEM. WELL, MAYBE A HUNDRED THOUSAND OR SO.
I REALLY DON'T LIKE THIS–
WE SHOULD GET OUT OF HERE AS QUICKLY AS POSSIBLE.

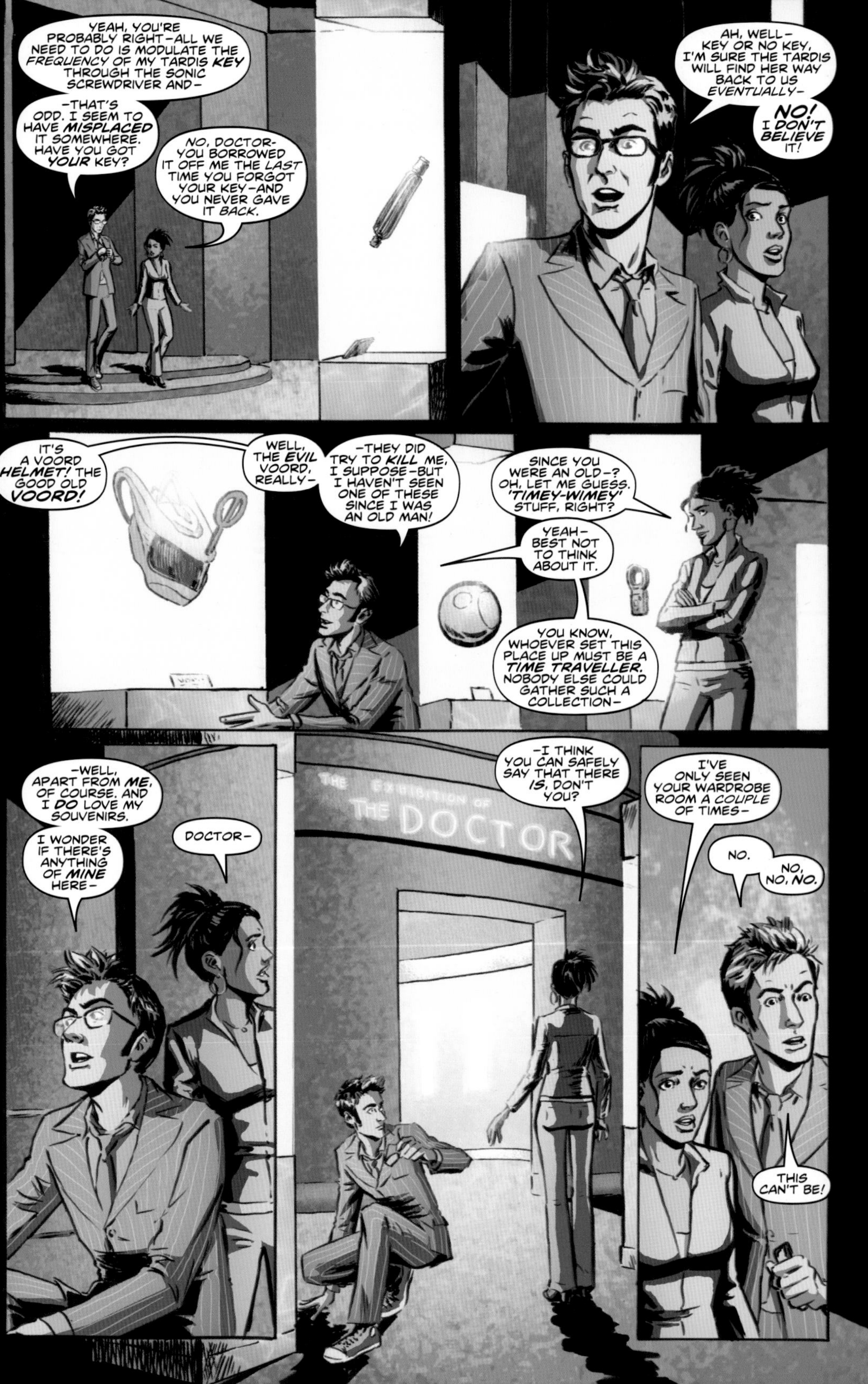
YEAH, YOU'RE PROBABLY RIGHT—ALL WE NEED TO DO IS MODULATE THE FREQUENCY OF MY TARDIS KEY THROUGH THE SONIC SCREWDRIVER AND—
—THAT'S ODD. I SEEM TO HAVE MISPLACED IT SOMEWHERE. HAVE YOU GOT YOUR KEY?
NO, DOCTOR—YOU BORROWED IT OFF ME THE LAST TIME YOU FORGOT YOUR KEY—AND YOU NEVER GAVE IT BACK.
AH, WELL—KEY OR NO KEY, I'M SURE THE TARDIS WILL FIND HER WAY BACK TO US EVENTUALLY—
NO! I DON'T BELIEVE IT!
IT'S A VOORD HELMET! THE GOOD OLD VOORD!
WELL, THE EVIL VOORD, REALLY—
—THEY DID TRY TO KILL ME, I SUPPOSE—BUT I HAVEN'T SEEN ONE OF THESE SINCE I WAS AN OLD MAN!
SINCE YOU WERE AN OLD—? OH, LET ME GUESS. 'TIMEY-WIMEY' STUFF, RIGHT?
YEAH—BEST NOT TO THINK ABOUT IT.
YOU KNOW, WHOEVER SET THIS PLACE UP MUST BE A TIME TRAVELLER. NOBODY ELSE COULD GATHER SUCH A COLLECTION—
—WELL, APART FROM ME, OF COURSE. AND I DO LOVE MY SOUVENIRS.
I WONDER IF THERE'S ANYTHING OF MINE HERE—
DOCTOR—
THE EXHIBITION OF THE DOCTOR
—I THINK YOU CAN SAFELY SAY THAT THERE IS, DON'T YOU?
I'VE ONLY SEEN YOUR WARDROBE ROOM A COUPLE OF TIMES—
NO.
NO, NO, NO.
THIS CAN'T BE!

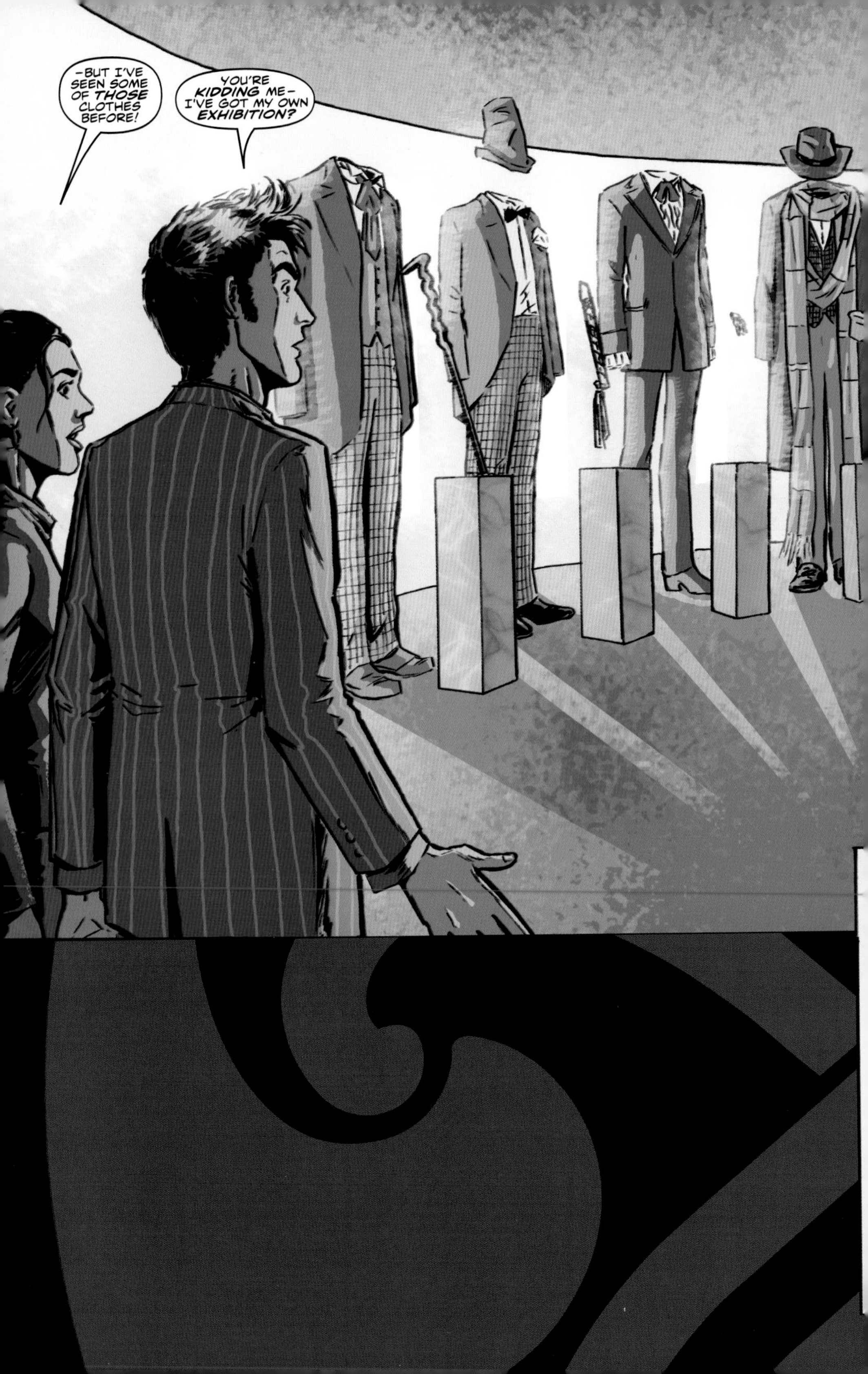
-BUT I'VE SEEN SOME OF THOSE CLOTHES BEFORE!
YOU'RE KIDDING ME- I'VE GOT MY OWN EXHIBITION?

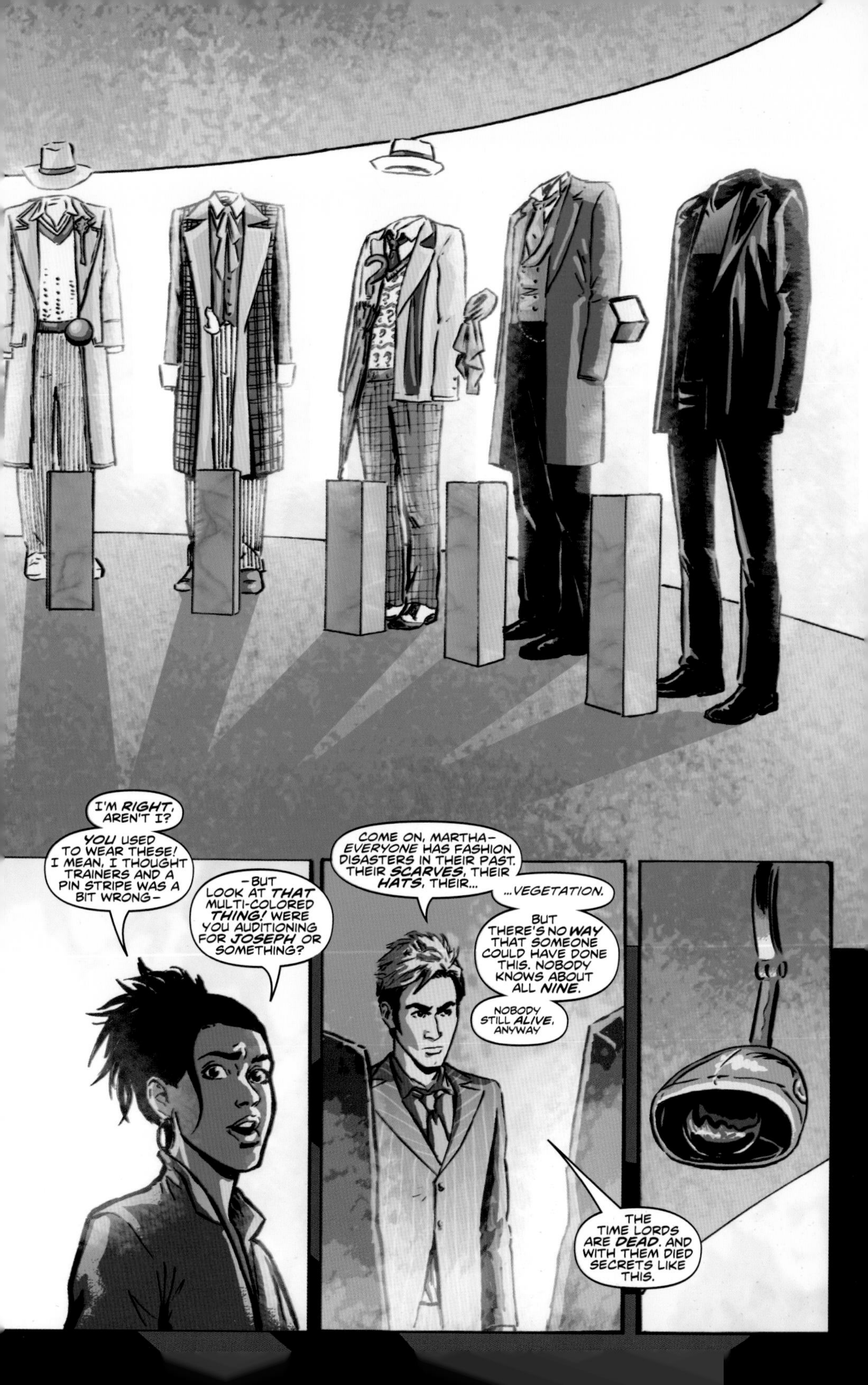
I'M RIGHT, AREN'T I?
YOU USED TO WEAR THESE! I MEAN, I THOUGHT TRAINERS AND A PIN STRIPE WAS A BIT WRONG–
–BUT LOOK AT THAT MULTI-COLORED THING! WERE YOU AUDITIONING FOR JOSEPH OR SOMETHING?
COME ON, MARTHA– EVERYONE HAS FASHION DISASTERS IN THEIR PAST. THEIR SCARVES, THEIR HATS, THEIR...
...VEGETATION.
BUT THERE'S NO WAY THAT SOMEONE COULD HAVE DONE THIS. NOBODY KNOWS ABOUT ALL NINE.
NOBODY STILL ALIVE, ANYWAY
THE TIME LORDS ARE DEAD. AND WITH THEM DIED SECRETS LIKE THIS.

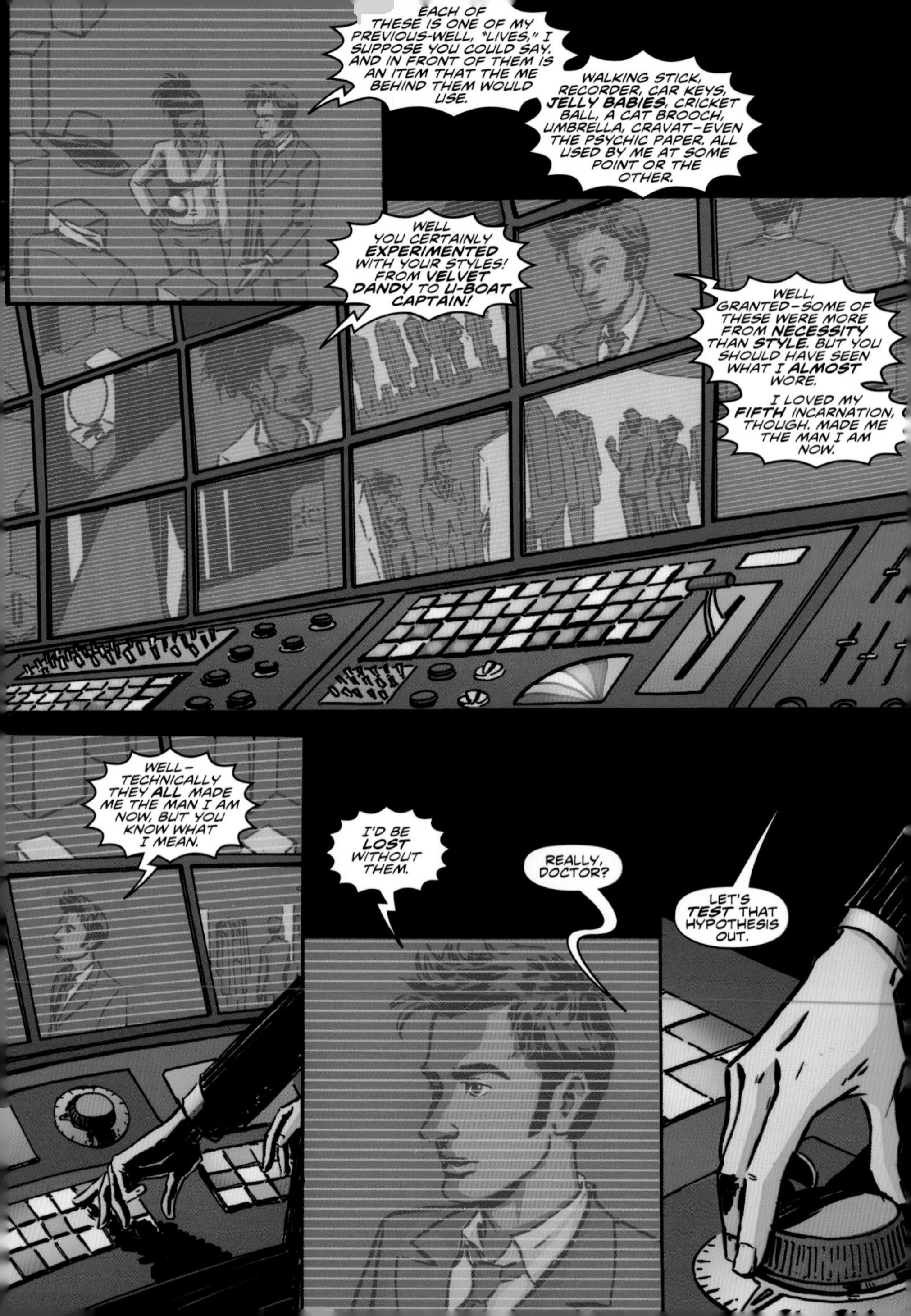
EACH OF THESE IS ONE OF MY PREVIOUS-WELL, "LIVES," I SUPPOSE YOU COULD SAY. AND IN FRONT OF THEM IS AN ITEM THAT THE ME BEHIND THEM WOULD USE.
WALKING STICK, RECORDER, CAR KEYS, JELLY BABIES, CRICKET BALL, A CAT BROOCH, UMBRELLA, CRAVAT–EVEN THE PSYCHIC PAPER. ALL USED BY ME AT SOME POINT OR THE OTHER.
WELL YOU CERTAINLY EXPERIMENTED WITH YOUR STYLES! FROM VELVET DANDY TO U-BOAT CAPTAIN!
WELL, GRANTED–SOME OF THESE WERE MORE FROM NECESSITY THAN STYLE. BUT YOU SHOULD HAVE SEEN WHAT I ALMOST WORE.
I LOVED MY FIFTH INCARNATION, THOUGH. MADE ME THE MAN I AM NOW.
WELL–TECHNICALLY THEY ALL MADE ME THE MAN I AM NOW, BUT YOU KNOW WHAT I MEAN.
I'D BE LOST WITHOUT THEM.
REALLY, DOCTOR?
LET'S TEST THAT HYPOTHESIS OUT.

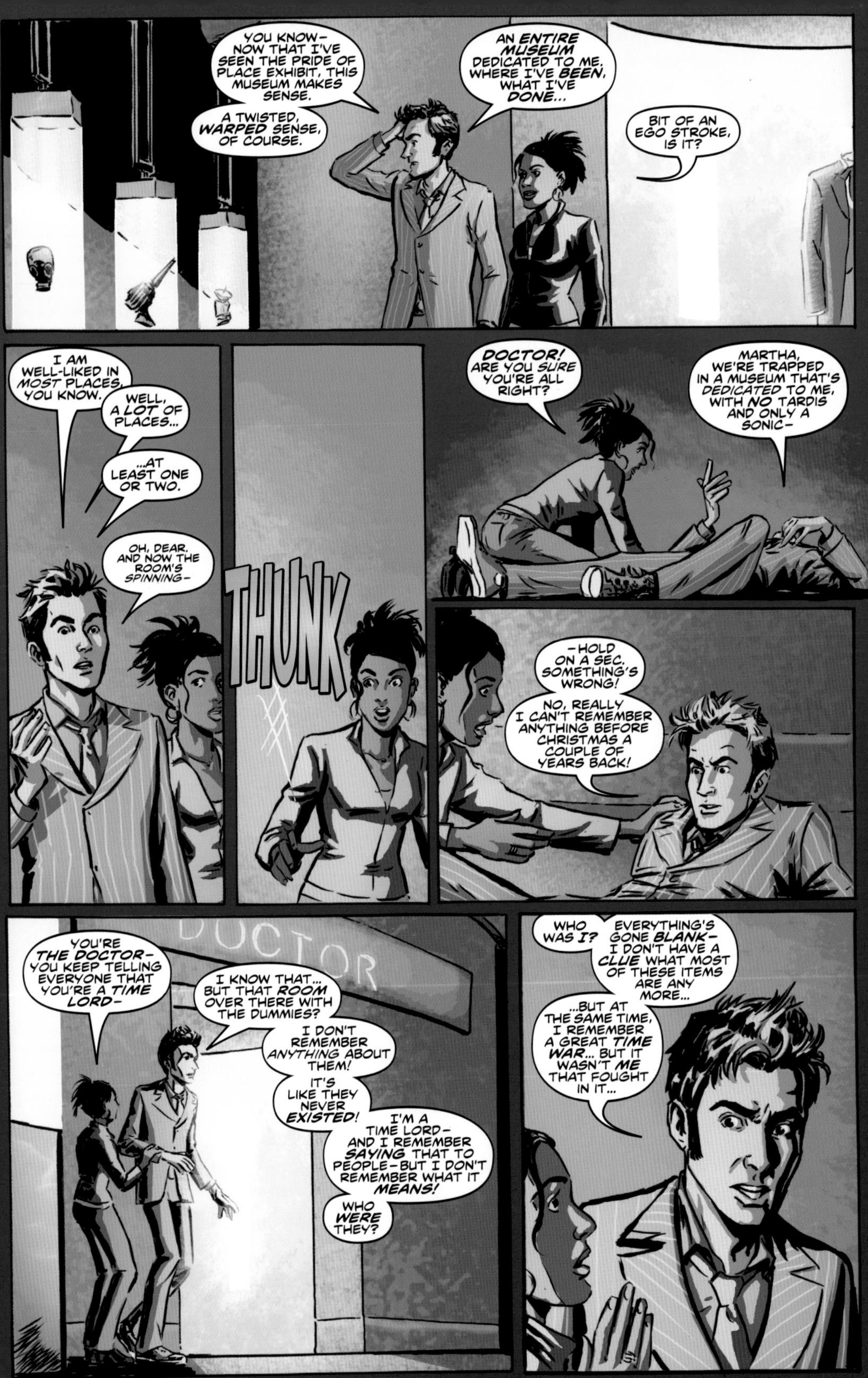

YOU KNOW— NOW THAT I'VE SEEN THE PRIDE OF PLACE EXHIBIT, THIS MUSEUM MAKES SENSE.
A TWISTED, WARPED SENSE, OF COURSE.
AN ENTIRE MUSEUM DEDICATED TO ME. WHERE I'VE BEEN, WHAT I'VE DONE...
BIT OF AN EGO STROKE, IS IT?
I AM WELL-LIKED IN MOST PLACES, YOU KNOW.
WELL, A LOT OF PLACES...
...AT LEAST ONE OR TWO.
OH, DEAR. AND NOW THE ROOM'S SPINNING—
THUNK
DOCTOR! ARE YOU SURE YOU'RE ALL RIGHT?
MARTHA, WE'RE TRAPPED IN A MUSEUM THAT'S DEDICATED TO ME, WITH NO TARDIS AND ONLY A SONIC—
—HOLD ON A SEC. SOMETHING'S WRONG!
NO, REALLY I CAN'T REMEMBER ANYTHING BEFORE CHRISTMAS A COUPLE OF YEARS BACK!
DOCTOR
YOU'RE THE DOCTOR— YOU KEEP TELLING EVERYONE THAT YOU'RE A TIME LORD—
I KNOW THAT... BUT THAT ROOM OVER THERE WITH THE DUMMIES?
I DON'T REMEMBER ANYTHING ABOUT THEM!
IT'S LIKE THEY NEVER EXISTED!
I'M A TIME LORD— AND I REMEMBER SAYING THAT TO PEOPLE— BUT I DON'T REMEMBER WHAT IT MEANS!
WHO WERE THEY?
WHO WAS I?
EVERYTHING'S GONE BLANK— I DON'T HAVE A CLUE WHAT MOST OF THESE ITEMS ARE ANY MORE...
...BUT AT THE SAME TIME, I REMEMBER A GREAT TIME WAR... BUT IT WASN'T ME THAT FOUGHT IN IT...

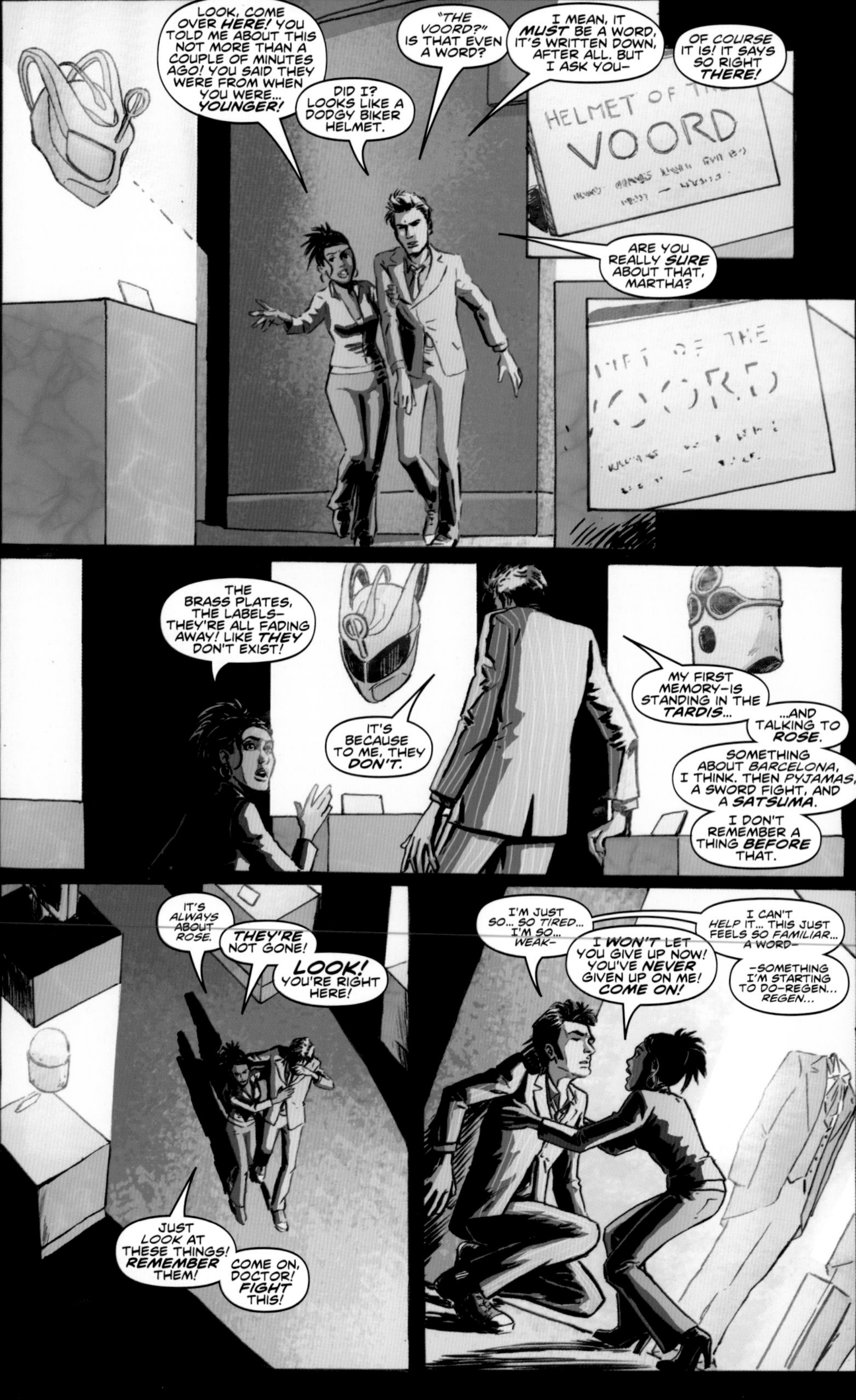
LOOK, COME OVER HERE! YOU TOLD ME ABOUT THIS NOT MORE THAN A COUPLE OF MINUTES AGO! YOU SAID THEY WERE FROM WHEN YOU WERE... YOUNGER!
DID I? LOOKS LIKE A DODGY BIKER HELMET.
"THE VOORD?" IS THAT EVEN A WORD?
I MEAN, IT MUST BE A WORD, IT'S WRITTEN DOWN, AFTER ALL. BUT I ASK YOU-
OF COURSE IT IS! IT SAYS SO RIGHT THERE!
HELMET OF THE VOORD
ARE YOU REALLY SURE ABOUT THAT, MARTHA?
THE BRASS PLATES, THE LABELS- THEY'RE ALL FADING AWAY! LIKE THEY DON'T EXIST!
IT'S BECAUSE TO ME, THEY DON'T.
MY FIRST MEMORY-IS STANDING IN THE TARDIS...
...AND TALKING TO ROSE.
SOMETHING ABOUT BARCELONA, I THINK. THEN PYJAMAS, A SWORD FIGHT, AND A SATSUMA.
I DON'T REMEMBER A THING BEFORE THAT.
IT'S ALWAYS ABOUT ROSE.
THEY'RE NOT GONE!
LOOK! YOU'RE RIGHT HERE!
JUST LOOK AT THESE THINGS! REMEMBER THEM!
COME ON, DOCTOR! FIGHT THIS!
I'M JUST SO... SO TIRED... I'M SO... WEAK-
I WON'T LET YOU GIVE UP NOW! YOU'VE NEVER GIVEN UP ON ME! COME ON!
I CAN'T HELP IT... THIS JUST FEELS SO FAMILIAR... A WORD-
-SOMETHING I'M STARTING TO DO-REGEN... REGEN...

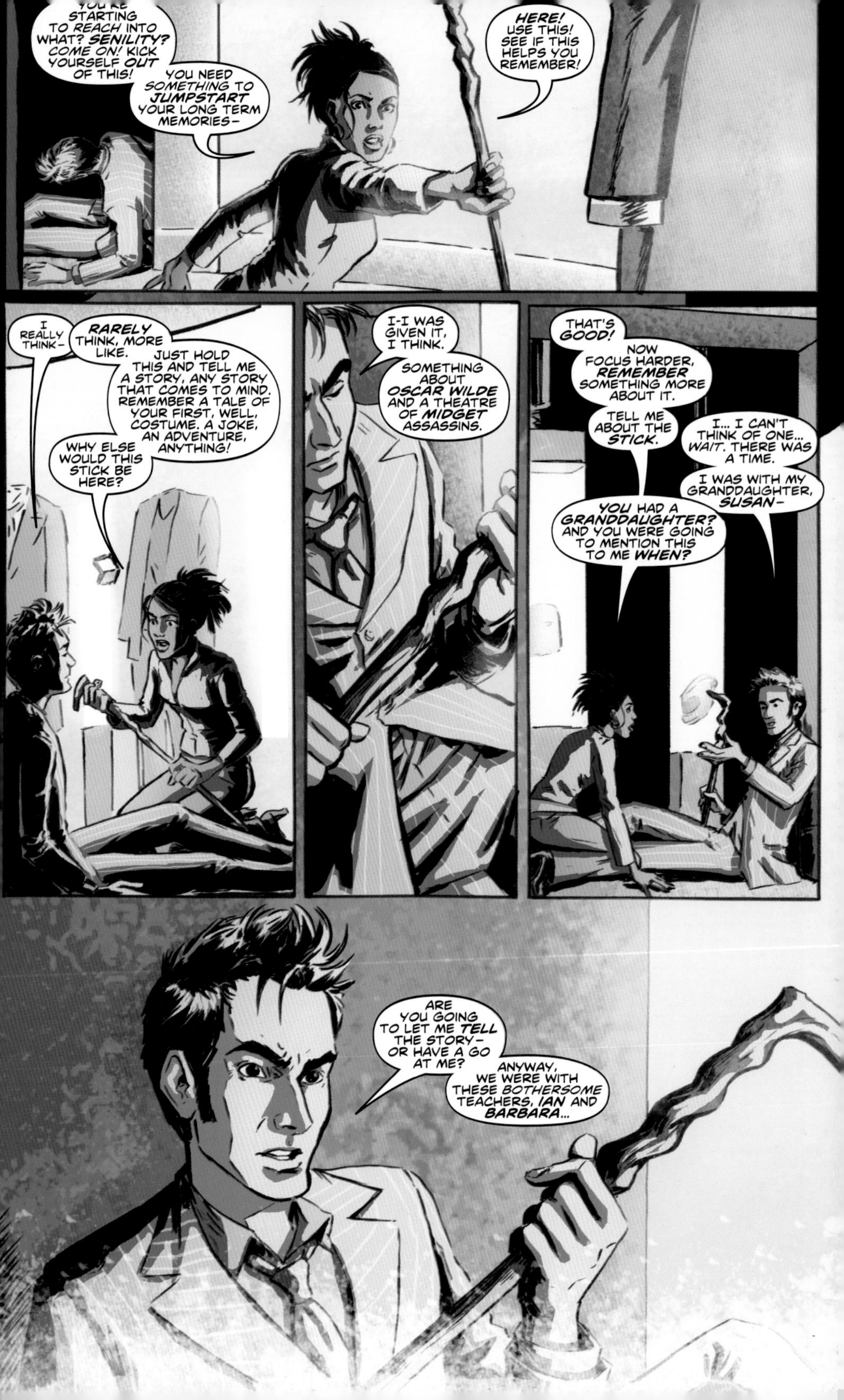

YOU'RE STARTING TO REACH INTO WHAT? SENILITY? COME ON! KICK YOURSELF OUT OF THIS!
YOU NEED SOMETHING TO JUMPSTART YOUR LONG TERM MEMORIES–
HERE! USE THIS! SEE IF THIS HELPS YOU REMEMBER!
I REALLY THINK–
RARELY THINK, MORE LIKE.
JUST HOLD THIS AND TELL ME A STORY, ANY STORY THAT COMES TO MIND. REMEMBER A TALE OF YOUR FIRST, WELL, COSTUME. A JOKE, AN ADVENTURE, ANYTHING!
WHY ELSE WOULD THIS STICK BE HERE?
I-I WAS GIVEN IT, I THINK.
SOMETHING ABOUT OSCAR WILDE AND A THEATRE OF MIDGET ASSASSINS.
THAT'S GOOD!
NOW FOCUS HARDER, REMEMBER SOMETHING MORE ABOUT IT.
TELL ME ABOUT THE STICK.
I... I CAN'T THINK OF ONE... WAIT. THERE WAS A TIME.
I WAS WITH MY GRANDDAUGHTER, SUSAN–
YOU HAD A GRANDDAUGHTER? AND YOU WERE GOING TO MENTION THIS TO ME WHEN?
ARE YOU GOING TO LET ME TELL THE STORY– OR HAVE A GO AT ME?
ANYWAY, WE WERE WITH THESE BOTHERSOME TEACHERS, IAN AND BARBARA...

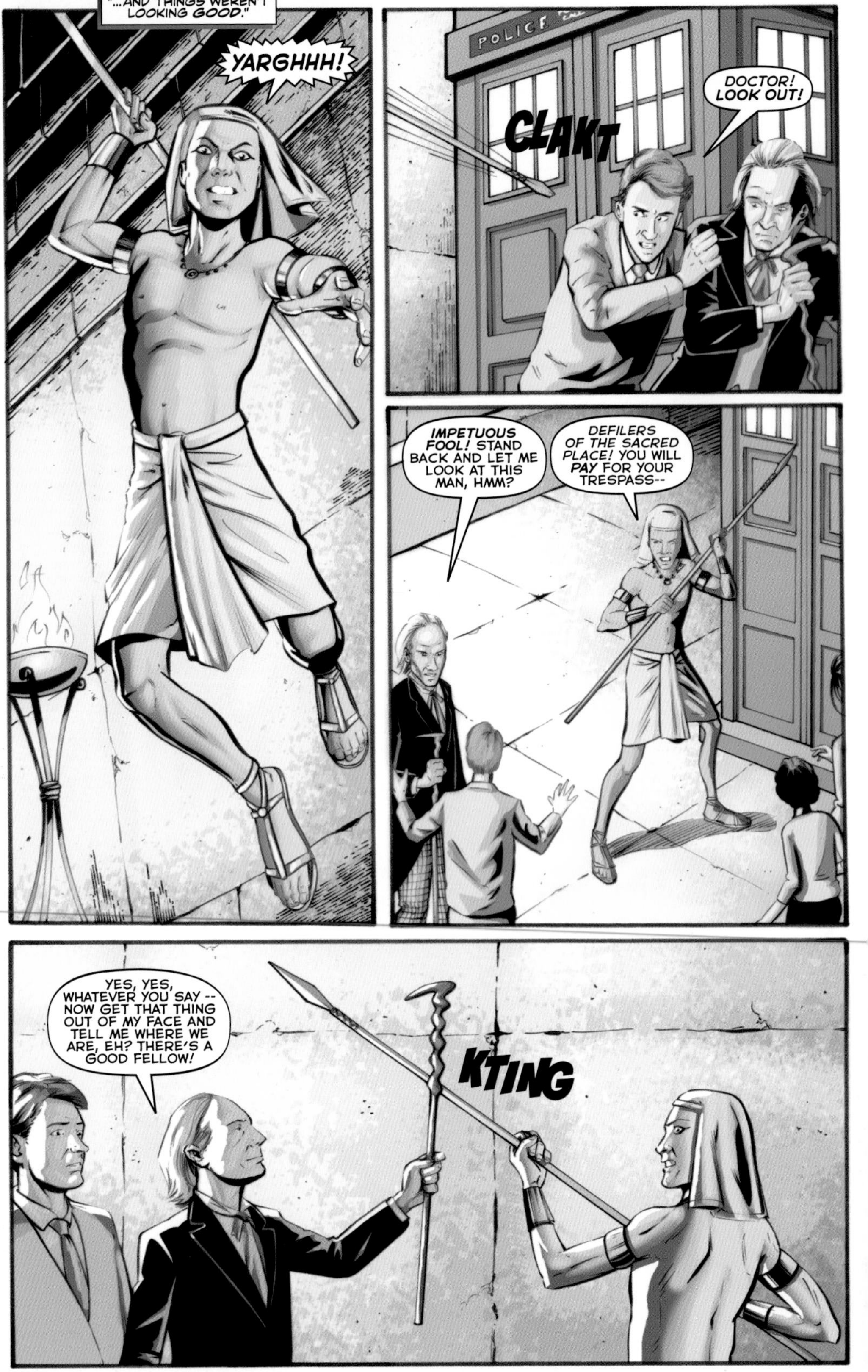
"...AND THINGS WEREN'T LOOKING GOOD."
YARGHHH!
CLAKT
DOCTOR! LOOK OUT!
IMPETUOUS FOOL! STAND BACK AND LET ME LOOK AT THIS MAN, HMM?
DEFILERS OF THE SACRED PLACE! YOU WILL PAY FOR YOUR TRESPASS--
YES, YES, WHATEVER YOU SAY -- NOW GET THAT THING OUT OF MY FACE AND TELL ME WHERE WE ARE, EH? THERE'S A GOOD FELLOW!
KTING

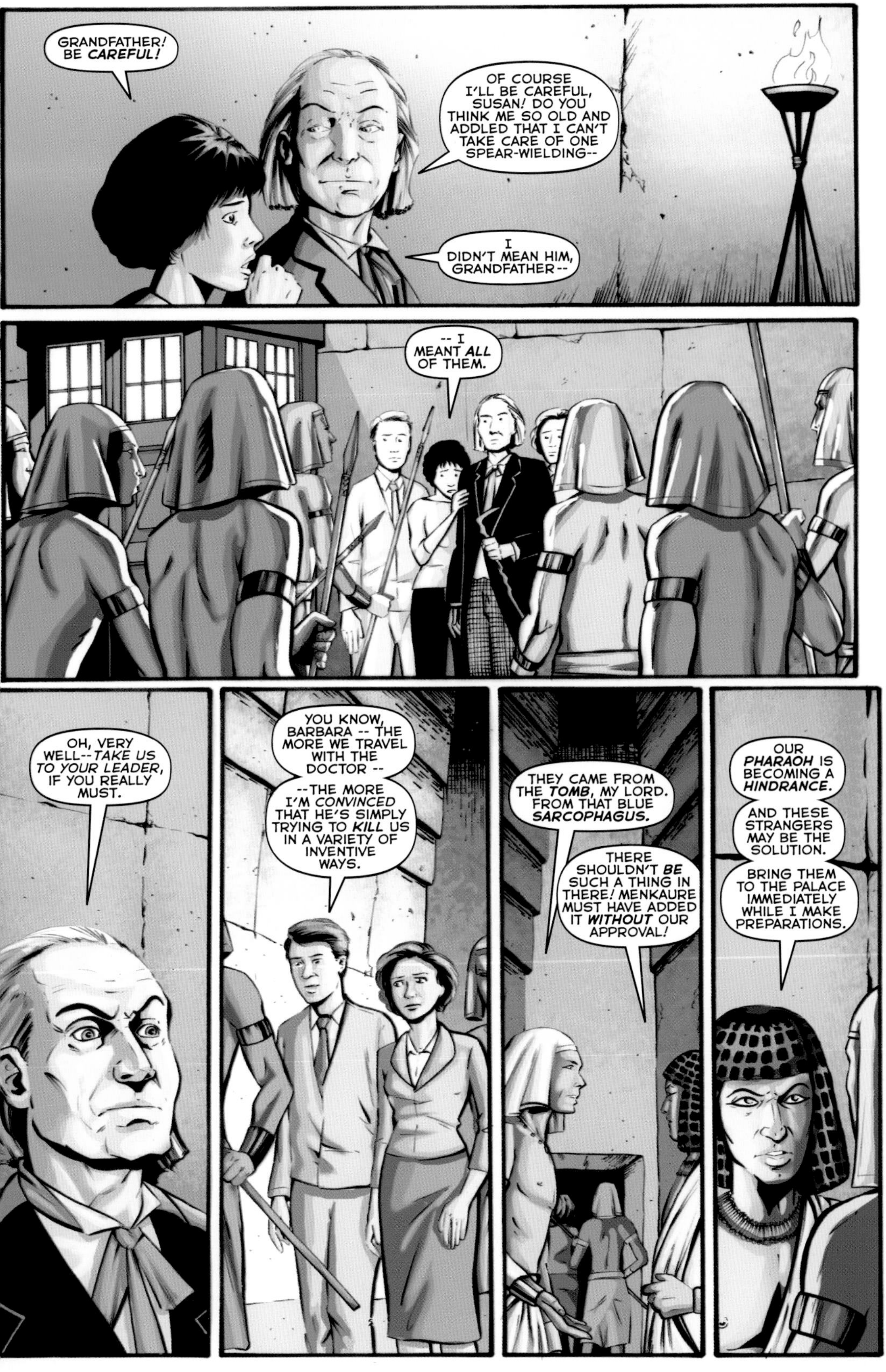
GRANDFATHER! BE CAREFUL!
OF COURSE I'LL BE CAREFUL, SUSAN! DO YOU THINK ME SO OLD AND ADDLED THAT I CAN'T TAKE CARE OF ONE SPEAR-WIELDING--
I DIDN'T MEAN HIM, GRANDFATHER--
-- I MEANT ALL OF THEM.
OH, VERY WELL--TAKE US TO YOUR LEADER, IF YOU REALLY MUST.
YOU KNOW, BARBARA -- THE MORE WE TRAVEL WITH THE DOCTOR --
--THE MORE I'M CONVINCED THAT HE'S SIMPLY TRYING TO KILL US IN A VARIETY OF INVENTIVE WAYS.
THEY CAME FROM THE TOMB, MY LORD. FROM THAT BLUE SARCOPHAGUS.
THERE SHOULDN'T BE SUCH A THING IN THERE! MENKAURE MUST HAVE ADDED IT WITHOUT OUR APPROVAL!
OUR PHARAOH IS BECOMING A HINDRANCE.
AND THESE STRANGERS MAY BE THE SOLUTION.
BRING THEM TO THE PALACE IMMEDIATELY WHILE I MAKE PREPARATIONS.

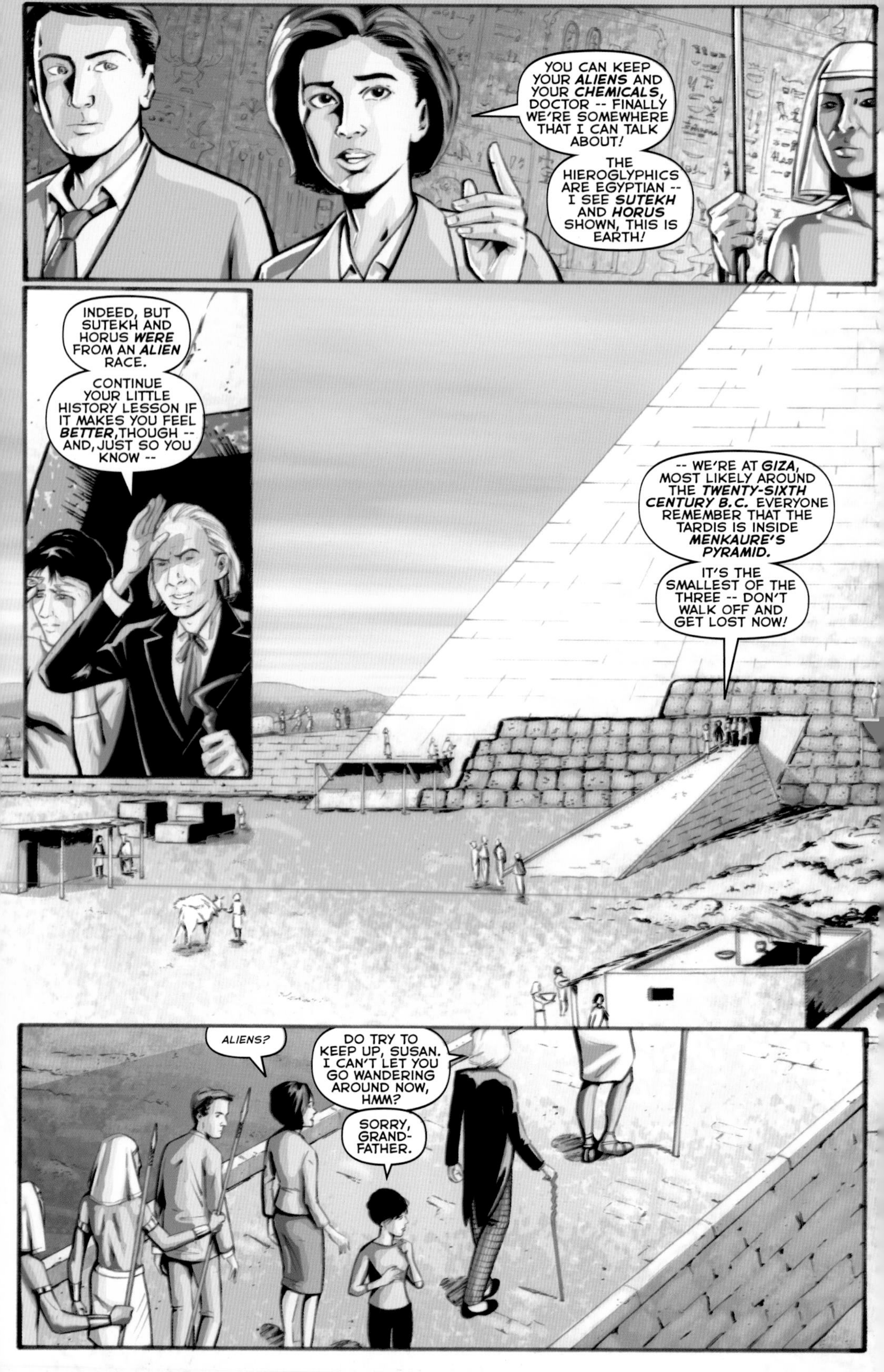
YOU CAN KEEP YOUR ALIENS AND YOUR CHEMICALS, DOCTOR -- FINALLY WE'RE SOMEWHERE THAT I CAN TALK ABOUT!
THE HIEROGLYPHICS ARE EGYPTIAN -- I SEE SUTEKH AND HORUS SHOWN, THIS IS EARTH!
INDEED, BUT SUTEKH AND HORUS WERE FROM AN ALIEN RACE.
CONTINUE YOUR LITTLE HISTORY LESSON IF IT MAKES YOU FEEL BETTER, THOUGH -- AND, JUST SO YOU KNOW --
-- WE'RE AT GIZA, MOST LIKELY AROUND THE TWENTY-SIXTH CENTURY B.C. EVERYONE REMEMBER THAT THE TARDIS IS INSIDE MENKAURE'S PYRAMID.
IT'S THE SMALLEST OF THE THREE -- DON'T WALK OFF AND GET LOST NOW!
ALIENS?
DO TRY TO KEEP UP, SUSAN. I CAN'T LET YOU GO WANDERING AROUND NOW, HMM?
SORRY, GRAND-FATHER.

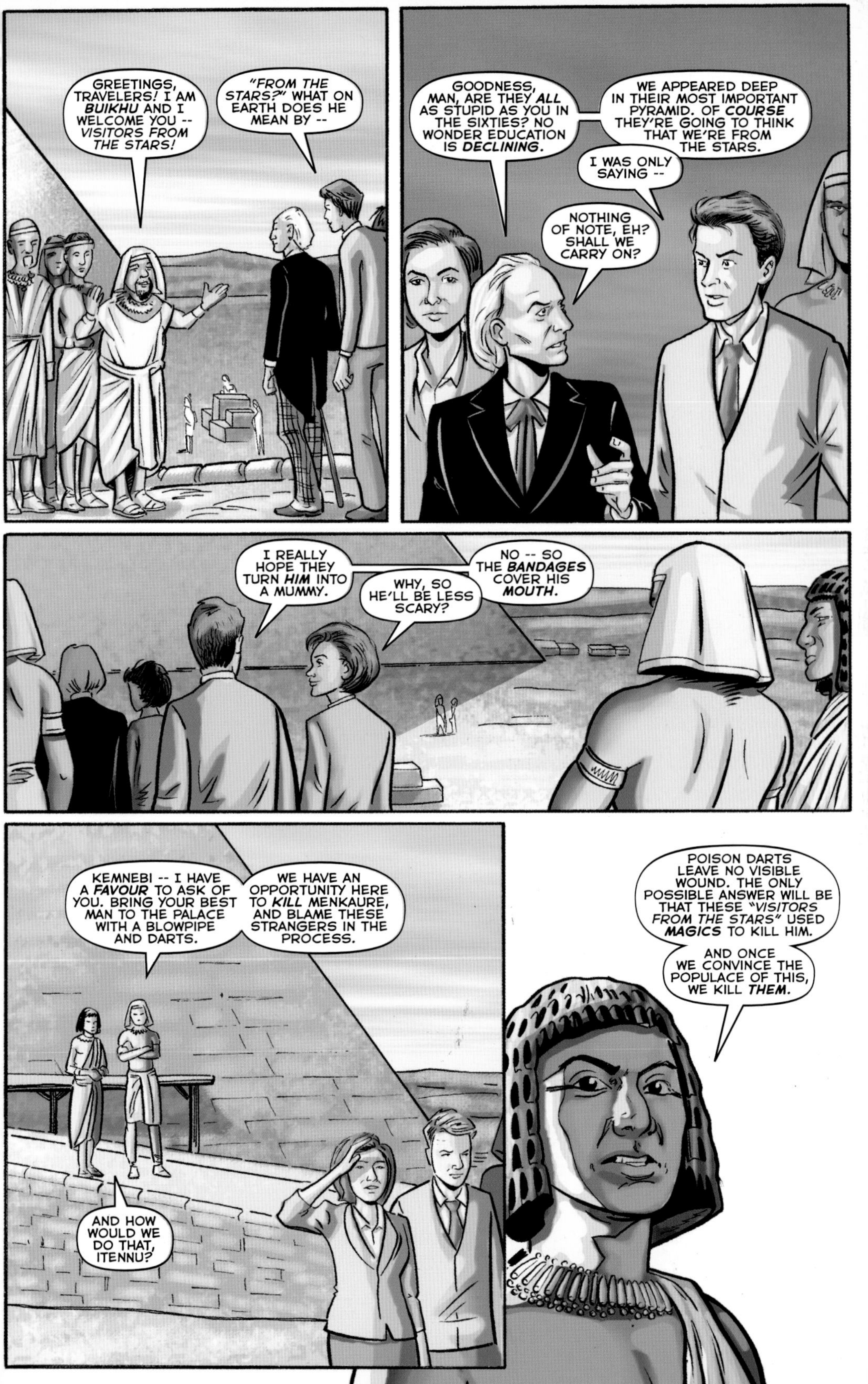
GREETINGS, TRAVELERS! I AM *BUIKHU* AND I WELCOME YOU -- *VISITORS FROM THE STARS!*
"FROM THE STARS?" WHAT ON EARTH DOES HE MEAN BY --
GOODNESS, MAN, ARE THEY *ALL* AS STUPID AS YOU IN THE SIXTIES? NO WONDER EDUCATION IS *DECLINING*.
WE APPEARED DEEP IN THEIR MOST IMPORTANT PYRAMID. OF *COURSE* THEY'RE GOING TO THINK THAT WE'RE FROM THE STARS.
I WAS ONLY SAYING --
NOTHING OF NOTE, EH? SHALL WE CARRY ON?
I REALLY HOPE THEY TURN *HIM* INTO A MUMMY.
WHY, SO HE'LL BE LESS SCARY?
NO -- SO THE *BANDAGES* COVER HIS *MOUTH*.
KEMNEBI -- I HAVE A *FAVOUR* TO ASK OF YOU. BRING YOUR BEST MAN TO THE PALACE WITH A BLOWPIPE AND DARTS.
WE HAVE AN OPPORTUNITY HERE TO *KILL* MENKAURE, AND BLAME THESE STRANGERS IN THE PROCESS.
AND HOW WOULD WE DO THAT, ITENNU?
POISON DARTS LEAVE NO VISIBLE WOUND. THE ONLY POSSIBLE ANSWER WILL BE THAT THESE *"VISITORS FROM THE STARS"* USED *MAGICS* TO KILL HIM.
AND ONCE WE CONVINCE THE POPULACE OF THIS, WE KILL *THEM*.

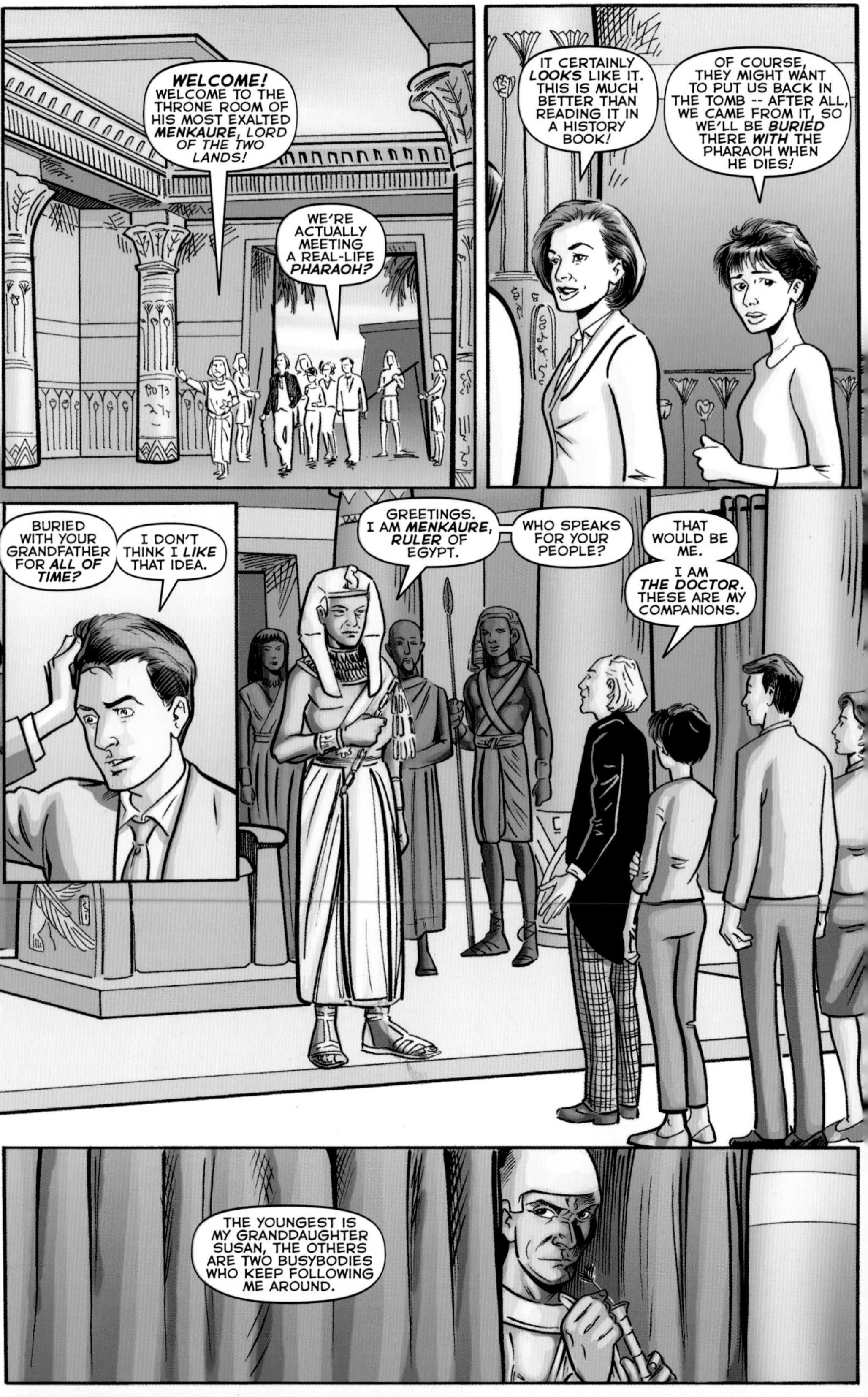
WELCOME! WELCOME TO THE THRONE ROOM OF HIS MOST EXALTED MENKAURE, LORD OF THE TWO LANDS!
WE'RE ACTUALLY MEETING A REAL-LIFE PHARAOH?
IT CERTAINLY LOOKS LIKE IT. THIS IS MUCH BETTER THAN READING IT IN A HISTORY BOOK!
OF COURSE, THEY MIGHT WANT TO PUT US BACK IN THE TOMB -- AFTER ALL, WE CAME FROM IT, SO WE'LL BE BURIED THERE WITH THE PHARAOH WHEN HE DIES!
BURIED WITH YOUR GRANDFATHER FOR ALL OF TIME?
I DON'T THINK I LIKE THAT IDEA.
GREETINGS. I AM MENKAURE, RULER OF EGYPT.
WHO SPEAKS FOR YOUR PEOPLE?
THAT WOULD BE ME.
I AM THE DOCTOR. THESE ARE MY COMPANIONS.
THE YOUNGEST IS MY GRANDDAUGHTER SUSAN, THE OTHERS ARE TWO BUSYBODIES WHO KEEP FOLLOWING ME AROUND.

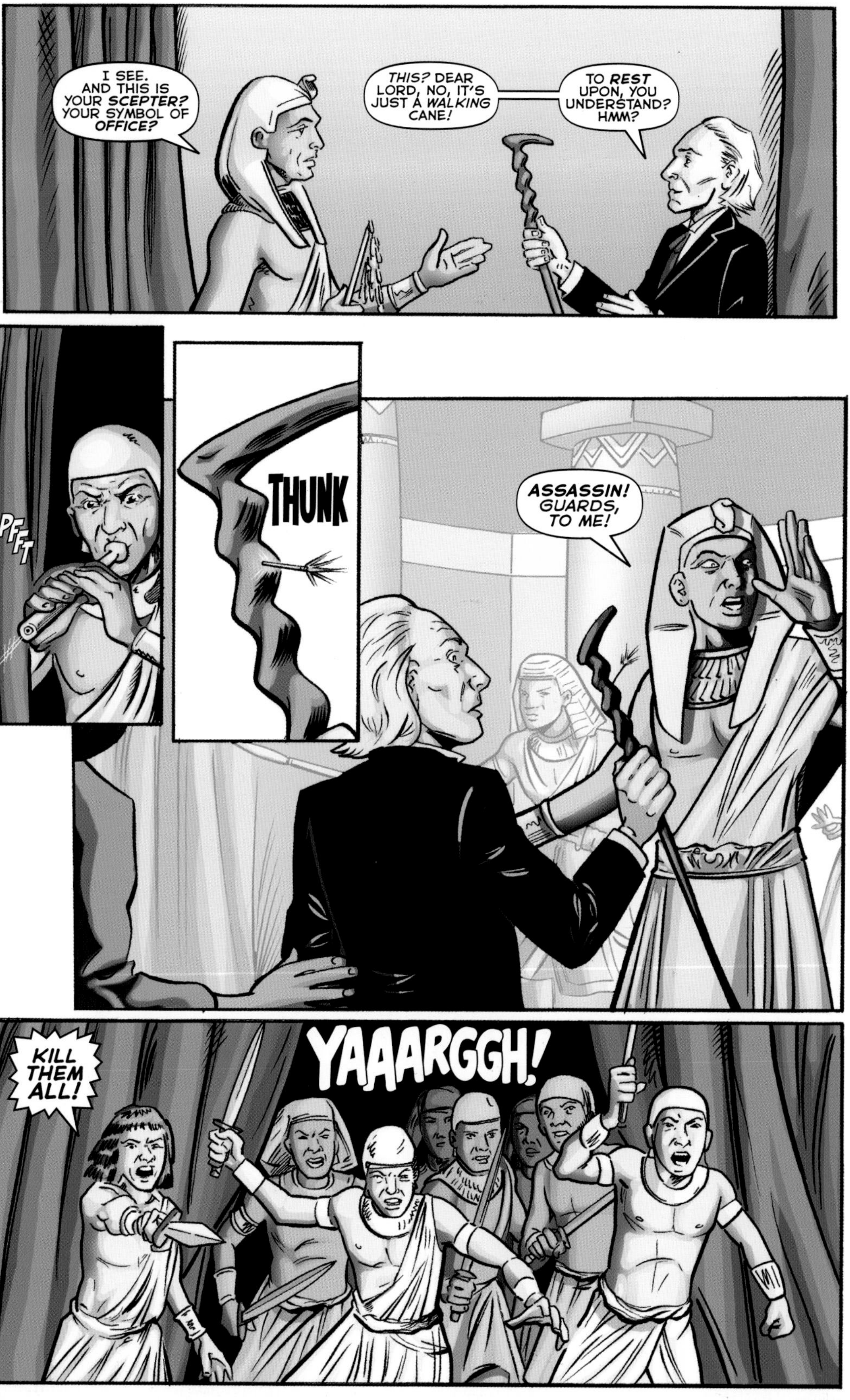

I SEE. AND THIS IS YOUR SCEPTER? YOUR SYMBOL OF OFFICE?
THIS? DEAR LORD, NO, IT'S JUST A WALKING CANE!
TO REST UPON, YOU UNDERSTAND? HMM?
PFFT
THUNK
ASSASSIN! GUARDS, TO ME!
KILL THEM ALL!
YAAARGGH!

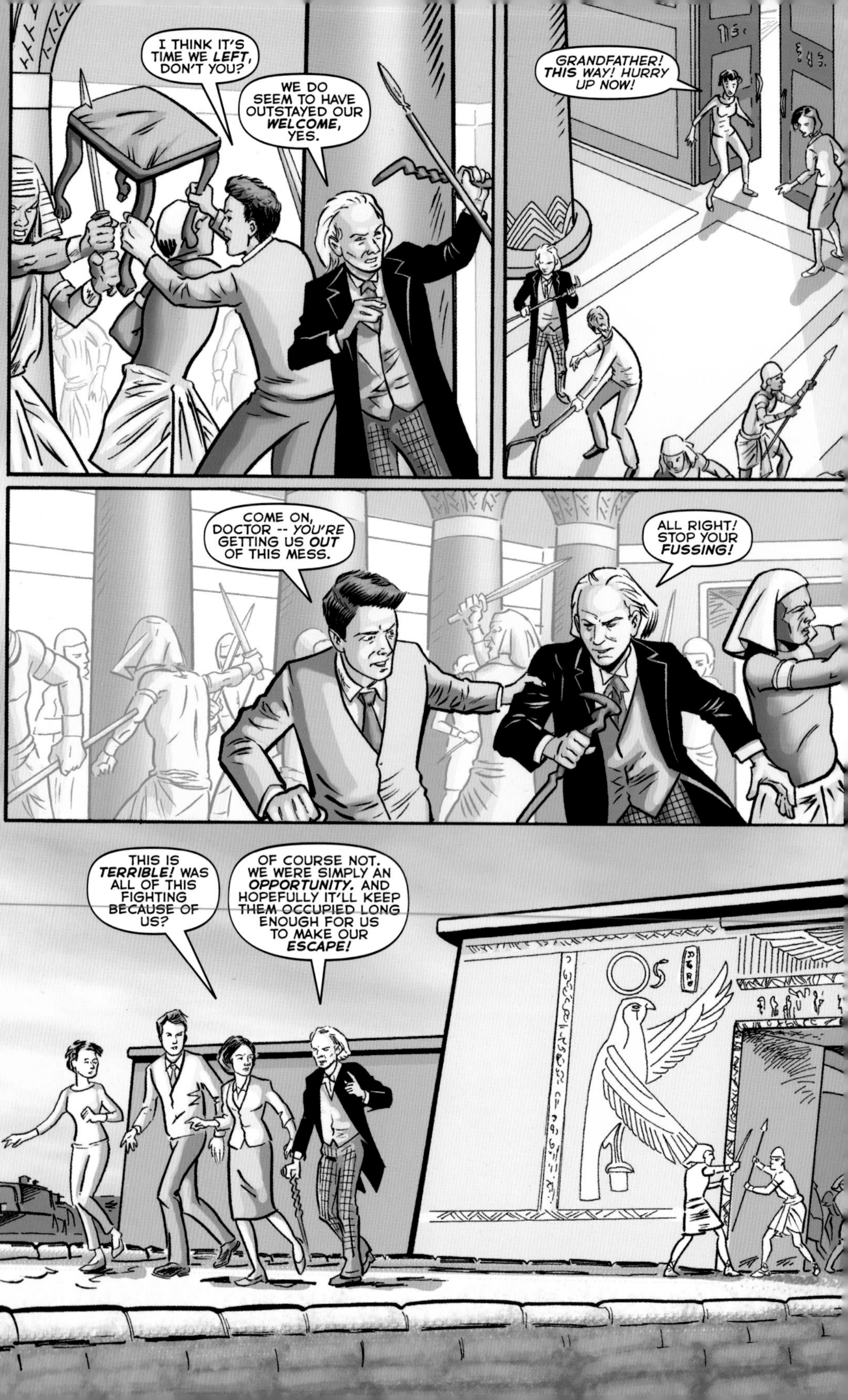
I THINK IT'S TIME WE LEFT, DON'T YOU?
WE DO SEEM TO HAVE OUTSTAYED OUR WELCOME, YES.
GRANDFATHER! THIS WAY! HURRY UP NOW!
COME ON, DOCTOR -- YOU'RE GETTING US OUT OF THIS MESS.
ALL RIGHT! STOP YOUR FUSSING!
THIS IS TERRIBLE! WAS ALL OF THIS FIGHTING BECAUSE OF US?
OF COURSE NOT. WE WERE SIMPLY AN OPPORTUNITY. AND HOPEFULLY IT'LL KEEP THEM OCCUPIED LONG ENOUGH FOR US TO MAKE OUR ESCAPE!

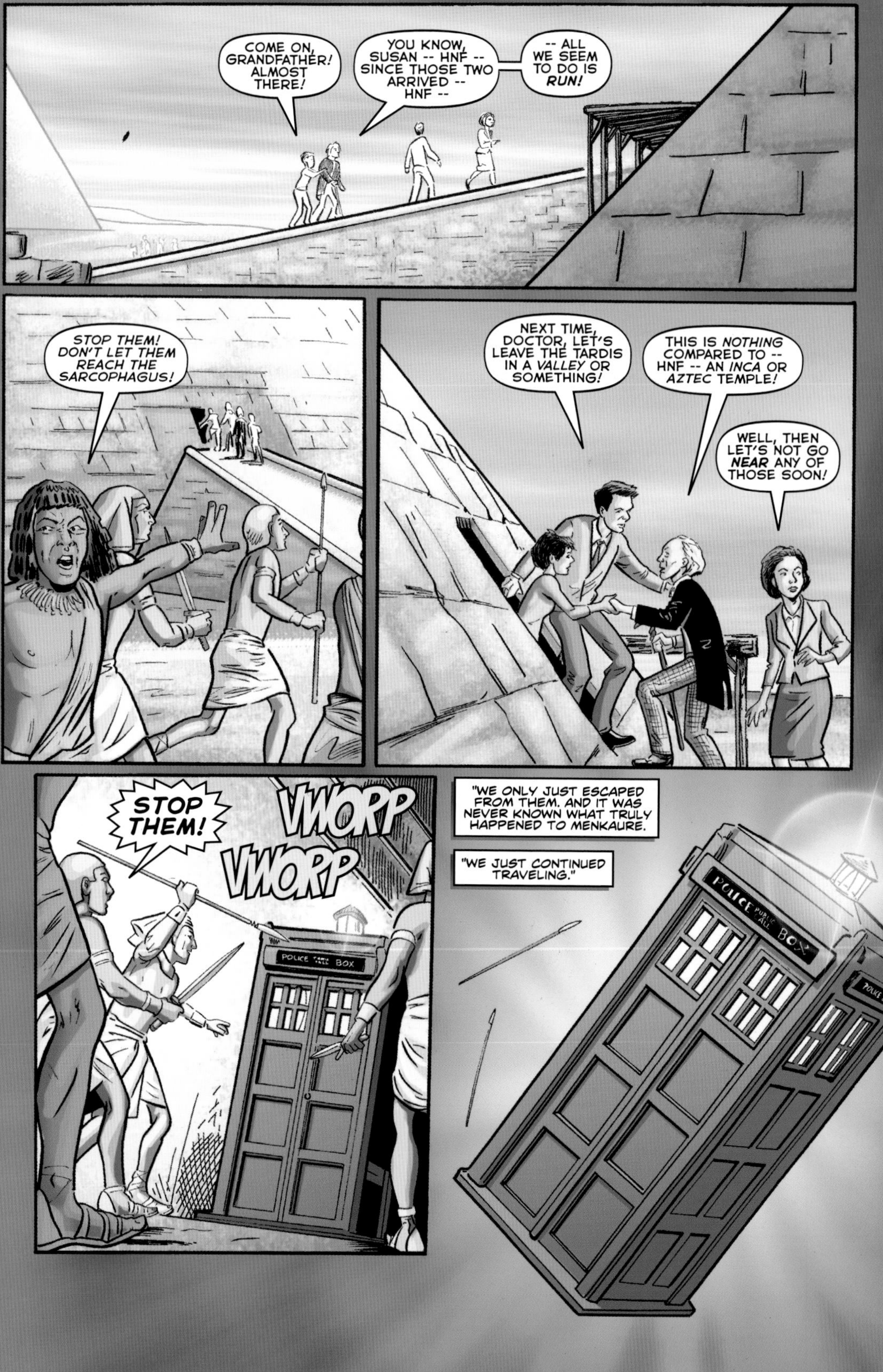
COME ON, GRANDFATHER! ALMOST THERE!
YOU KNOW, SUSAN -- HNF -- SINCE THOSE TWO ARRIVED -- HNF --
-- ALL WE SEEM TO DO IS RUN!
STOP THEM! DON'T LET THEM REACH THE SARCOPHAGUS!
NEXT TIME, DOCTOR, LET'S LEAVE THE TARDIS IN A VALLEY OR SOMETHING!
THIS IS NOTHING COMPARED TO -- HNF -- AN INCA OR AZTEC TEMPLE!
WELL, THEN LET'S NOT GO NEAR ANY OF THOSE SOON!
STOP THEM!
VWORP
VWORP
POLICE BOX
"WE ONLY JUST ESCAPED FROM THEM. AND IT WAS NEVER KNOWN WHAT TRULY HAPPENED TO MENKAURE.
"WE JUST CONTINUED TRAVELING."
POLICE PUBLIC CALL BOX

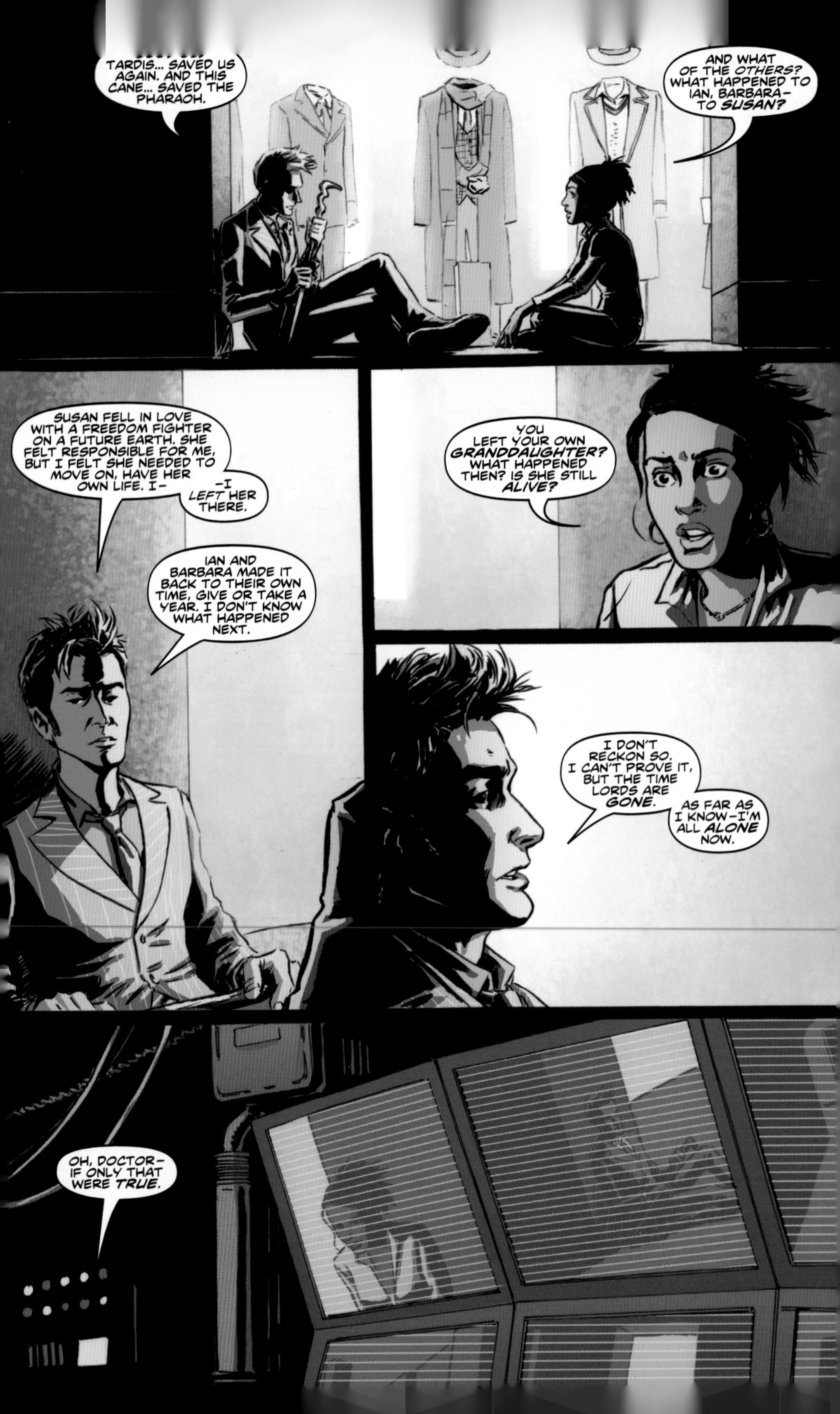
TARDIS... SAVED US AGAIN. AND THIS CANE... SAVED THE PHARAOH.
AND WHAT OF THE *OTHERS*? WHAT HAPPENED TO IAN, BARBARA– TO ***SUSAN?***
SUSAN FELL IN LOVE WITH A FREEDOM FIGHTER ON A FUTURE EARTH. SHE FELT RESPONSIBLE FOR ME, BUT I FELT SHE NEEDED TO MOVE ON, HAVE HER OWN LIFE. I–
–I *LEFT* HER THERE.
YOU LEFT YOUR OWN ***GRANDDAUGHTER?*** WHAT HAPPENED THEN? IS SHE STILL ***ALIVE?***
IAN AND BARBARA MADE IT BACK TO THEIR OWN TIME, GIVE OR TAKE A YEAR. I DON'T KNOW WHAT HAPPENED NEXT.
I DON'T RECKON SO. I CAN'T PROVE IT, BUT THE TIME LORDS ARE ***GONE***.
AS FAR AS I KNOW–I'M ALL ***ALONE*** NOW.
OH, DOCTOR– IF ONLY THAT WERE ***TRUE***.

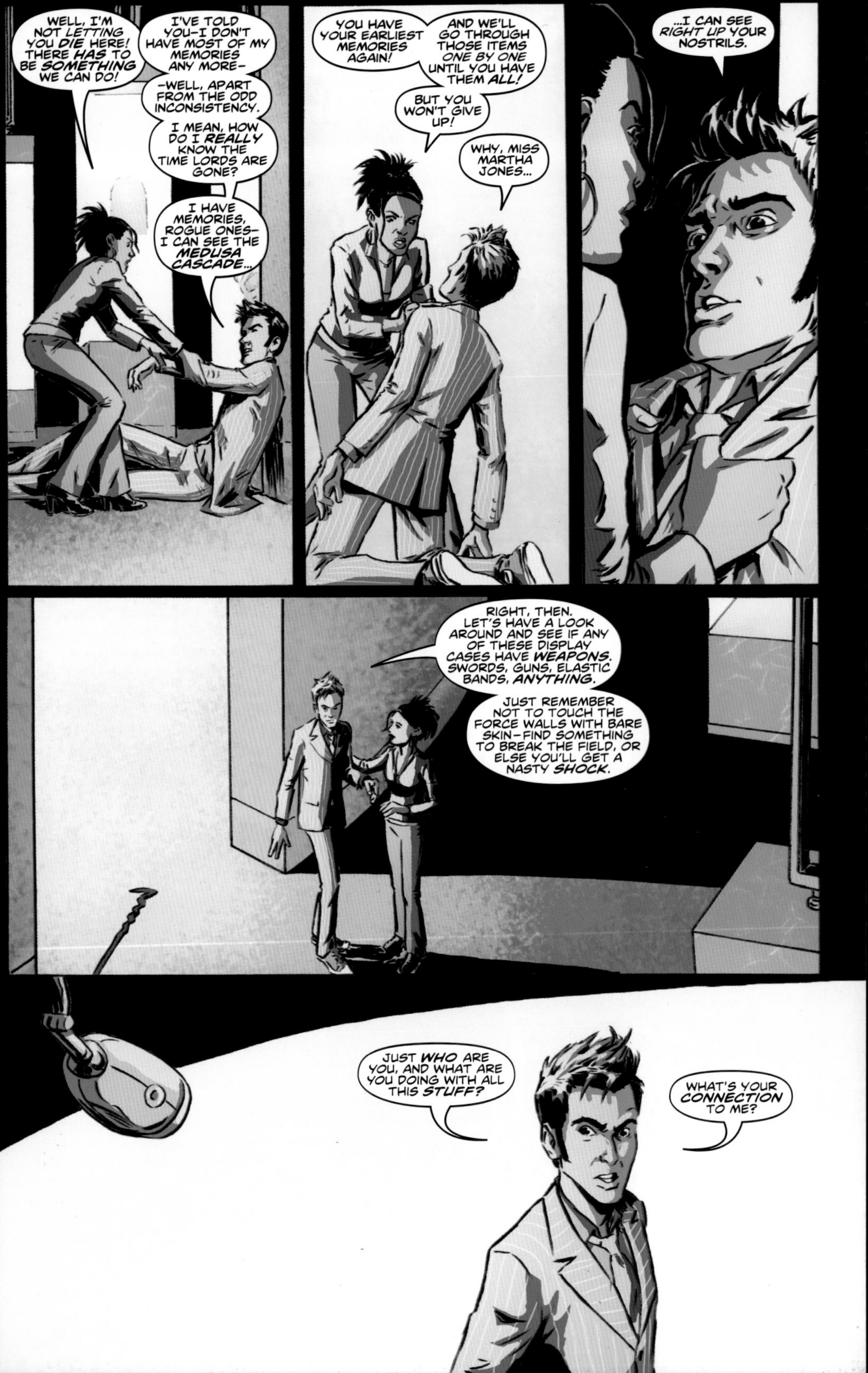
WELL, I'M NOT LETTING YOU DIE HERE! THERE HAS TO BE SOMETHING WE CAN DO!
I'VE TOLD YOU—I DON'T HAVE MOST OF MY MEMORIES ANY MORE—
—WELL, APART FROM THE ODD INCONSISTENCY.
I MEAN, HOW DO I REALLY KNOW THE TIME LORDS ARE GONE?
I HAVE MEMORIES, ROGUE ONES—I CAN SEE THE MEDUSA CASCADE...
YOU HAVE YOUR EARLIEST MEMORIES AGAIN!
AND WE'LL GO THROUGH THOSE ITEMS ONE BY ONE UNTIL YOU HAVE THEM ALL!
BUT YOU WON'T GIVE UP!
WHY, MISS MARTHA JONES...
...I CAN SEE RIGHT UP YOUR NOSTRILS.
RIGHT, THEN. LET'S HAVE A LOOK AROUND AND SEE IF ANY OF THESE DISPLAY CASES HAVE WEAPONS. SWORDS, GUNS, ELASTIC BANDS, ANYTHING.
JUST REMEMBER NOT TO TOUCH THE FORCE WALLS WITH BARE SKIN—FIND SOMETHING TO BREAK THE FIELD, OR ELSE YOU'LL GET A NASTY SHOCK.
JUST WHO ARE YOU, AND WHAT ARE YOU DOING WITH ALL THIS STUFF?
WHAT'S YOUR CONNECTION TO ME?

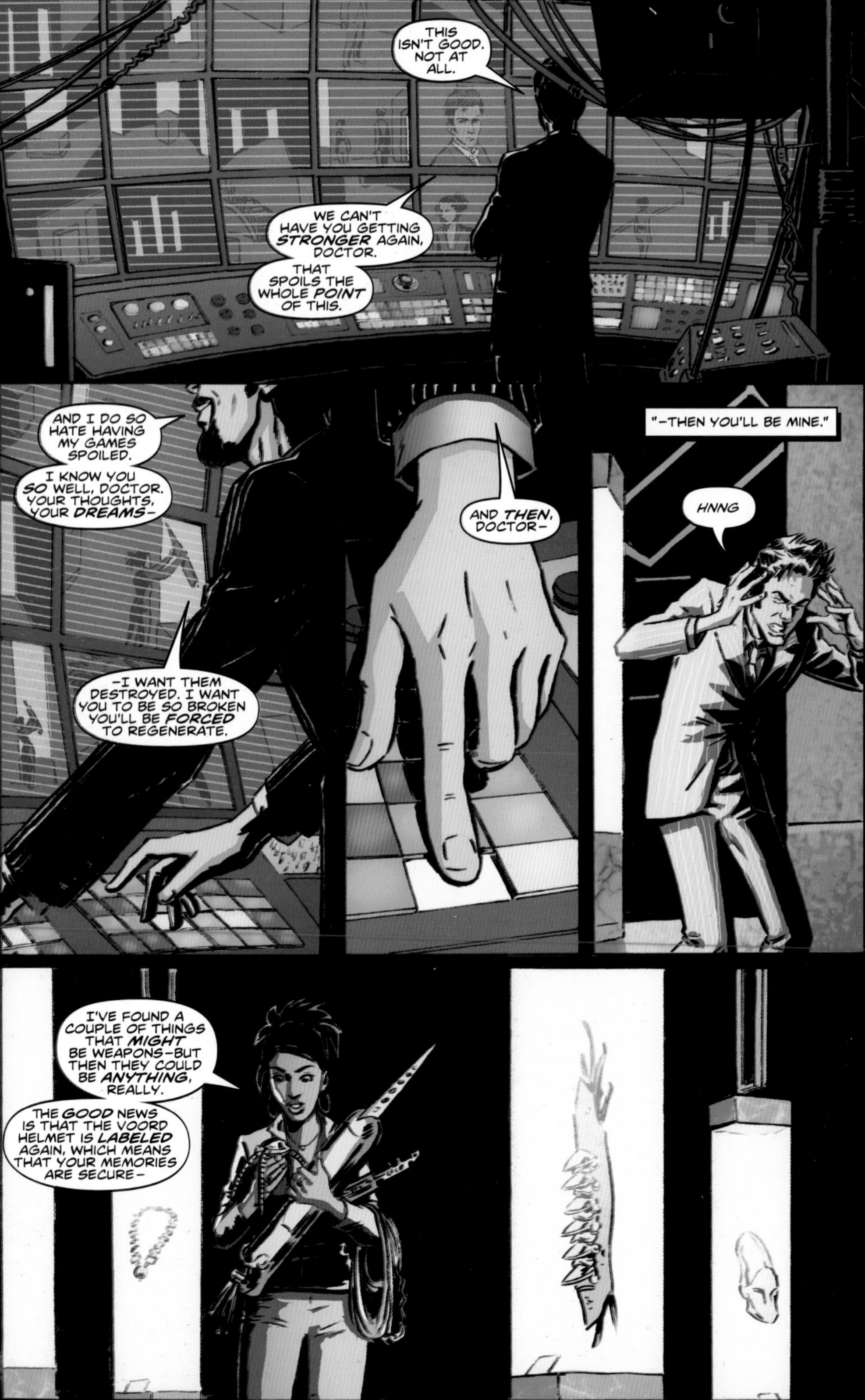
THIS ISN'T GOOD. NOT AT ALL.
WE CAN'T HAVE YOU GETTING **STRONGER** AGAIN, DOCTOR.
THAT SPOILS THE WHOLE **POINT** OF THIS.
AND I DO SO HATE HAVING MY GAMES SPOILED.
I KNOW YOU **SO** WELL, DOCTOR. YOUR THOUGHTS, YOUR **DREAMS**–
–I WANT THEM DESTROYED. I WANT YOU TO BE SO BROKEN YOU'LL BE **FORCED** TO REGENERATE.
AND **THEN**, DOCTOR–
"–THEN YOU'LL BE MINE."
HNNG
I'VE FOUND A COUPLE OF THINGS THAT **MIGHT** BE WEAPONS–BUT THEN THEY COULD BE **ANYTHING**, REALLY.
THE **GOOD** NEWS IS THAT THE VOORD HELMET IS **LABELED** AGAIN, WHICH MEANS THAT YOUR MEMORIES ARE SECURE–

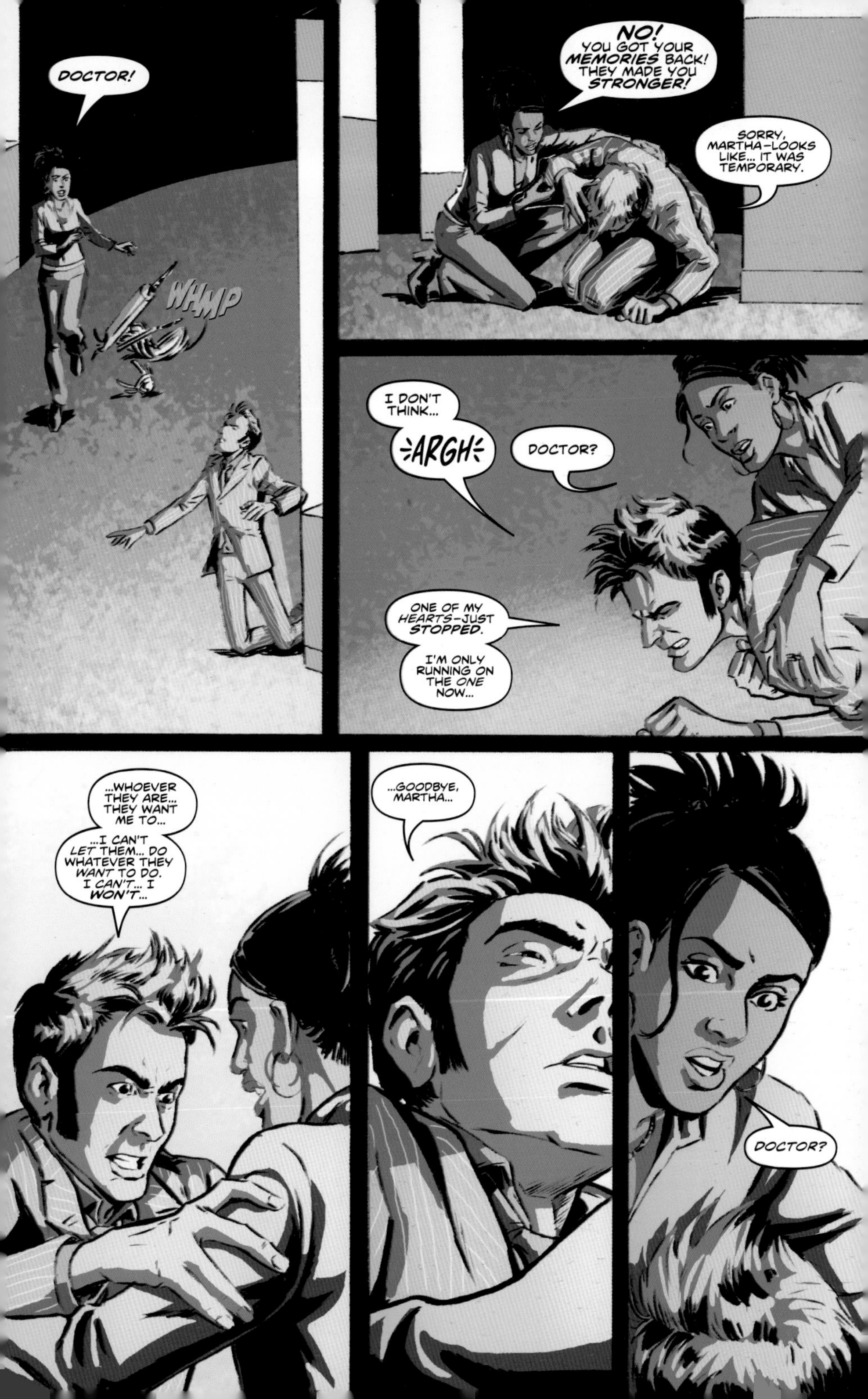
DOCTOR!
WHMP
NO! YOU GOT YOUR MEMORIES BACK! THEY MADE YOU STRONGER!
SORRY, MARTHA—LOOKS LIKE... IT WAS TEMPORARY.
I DON'T THINK... ARGH
DOCTOR?
ONE OF MY HEARTS—JUST STOPPED.
I'M ONLY RUNNING ON THE ONE NOW...
...WHOEVER THEY ARE... THEY WANT ME TO...
...I CAN'T LET THEM... DO WHATEVER THEY WANT TO DO. I CAN'T... I WON'T...
...GOODBYE, MARTHA...
DOCTOR?

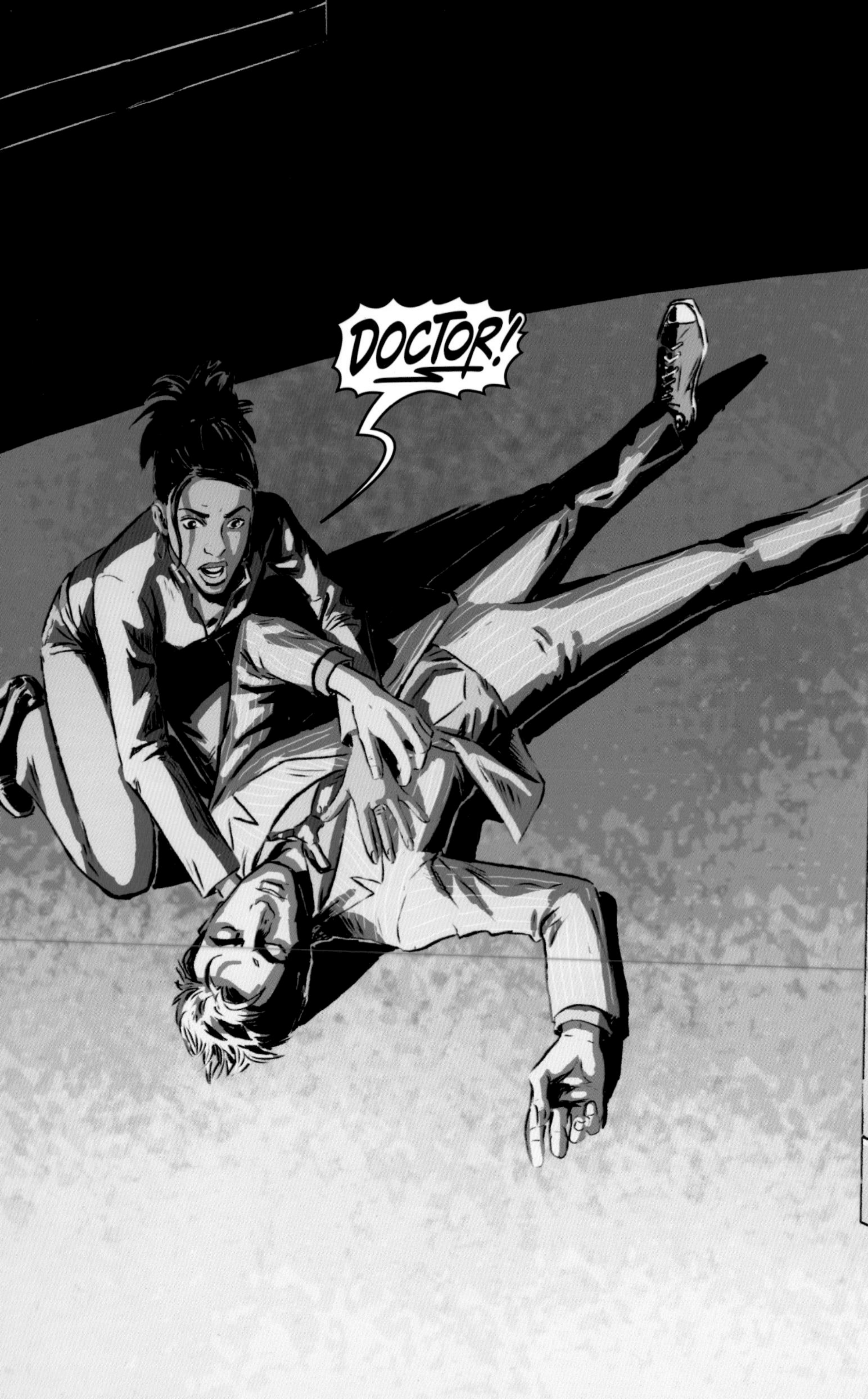
DOCTOR!

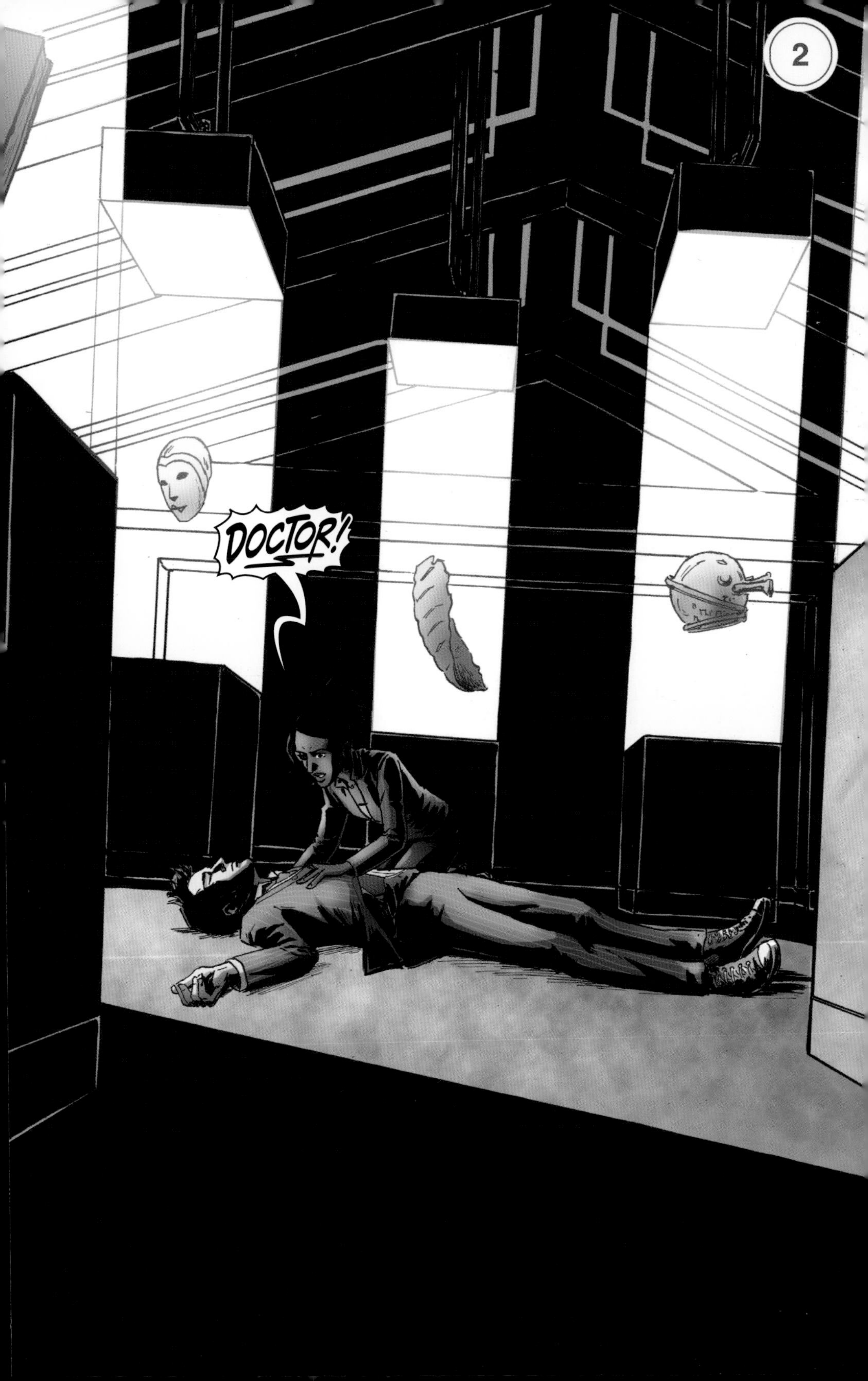
2
DOCTOR!

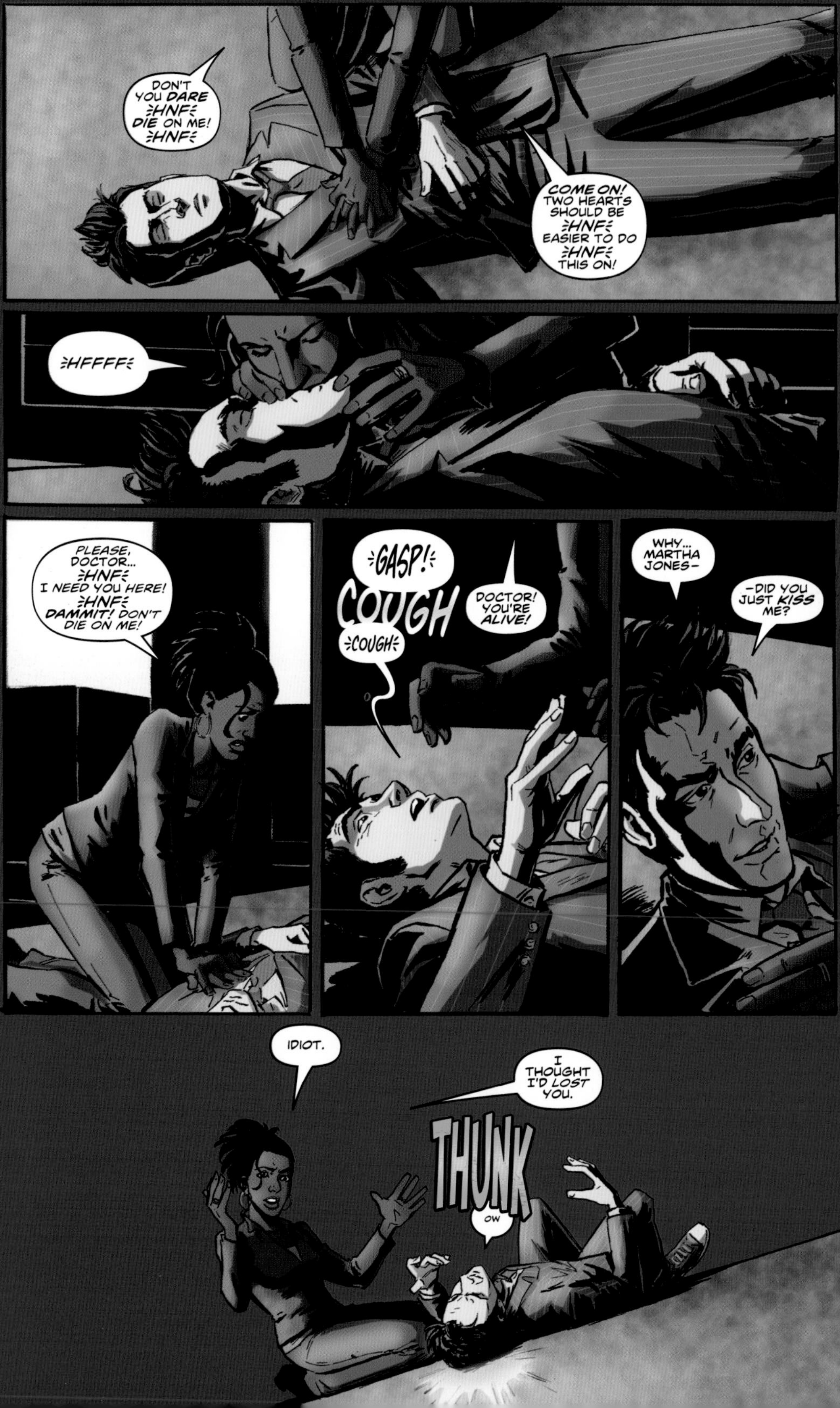
DON'T YOU DARE HNF DIE ON ME! HNF
COME ON! TWO HEARTS SHOULD BE HNF EASIER TO DO HNF THIS ON!
HFFFF
PLEASE, DOCTOR... HNF I NEED YOU HERE! HNF DAMMIT! DON'T DIE ON ME!
GASP!
COUGH
COUGH
DOCTOR! YOU'RE ALIVE!
WHY... MARTHA JONES—
—DID YOU JUST KISS ME?
IDIOT.
I THOUGHT I'D LOST YOU.
THUNK
OW

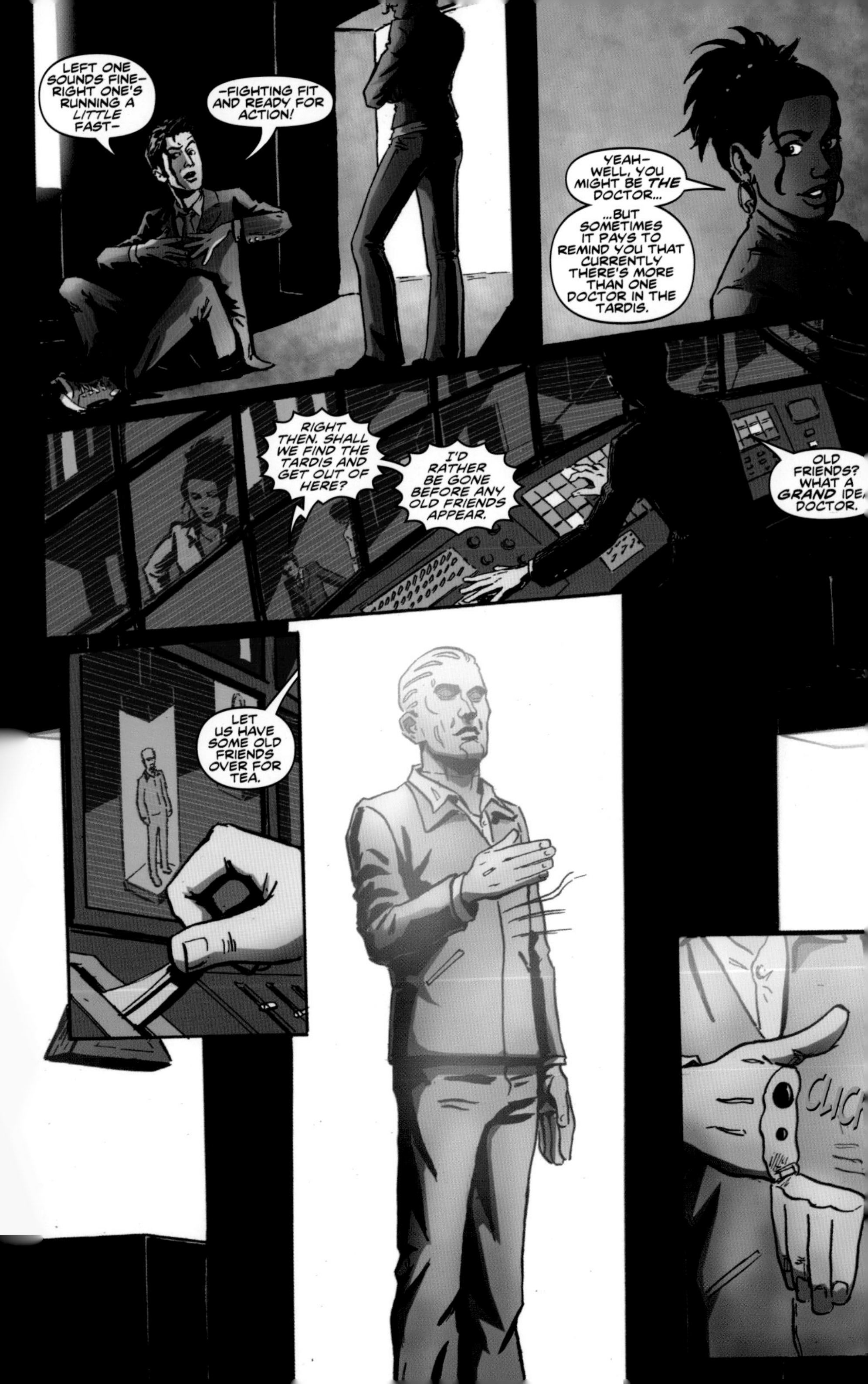
LEFT ONE SOUNDS FINE- RIGHT ONE'S RUNNING A LITTLE FAST-
-FIGHTING FIT AND READY FOR ACTION!
YEAH- WELL, YOU MIGHT BE THE DOCTOR...
...BUT SOMETIMES IT PAYS TO REMIND YOU THAT CURRENTLY THERE'S MORE THAN ONE DOCTOR IN THE TARDIS.
RIGHT THEN. SHALL WE FIND THE TARDIS AND GET OUT OF HERE?
I'D RATHER BE GONE BEFORE ANY OLD FRIENDS APPEAR.
OLD FRIENDS? WHAT A GRAND IDE DOCTOR.
LET US HAVE SOME OLD FRIENDS OVER FOR TEA.

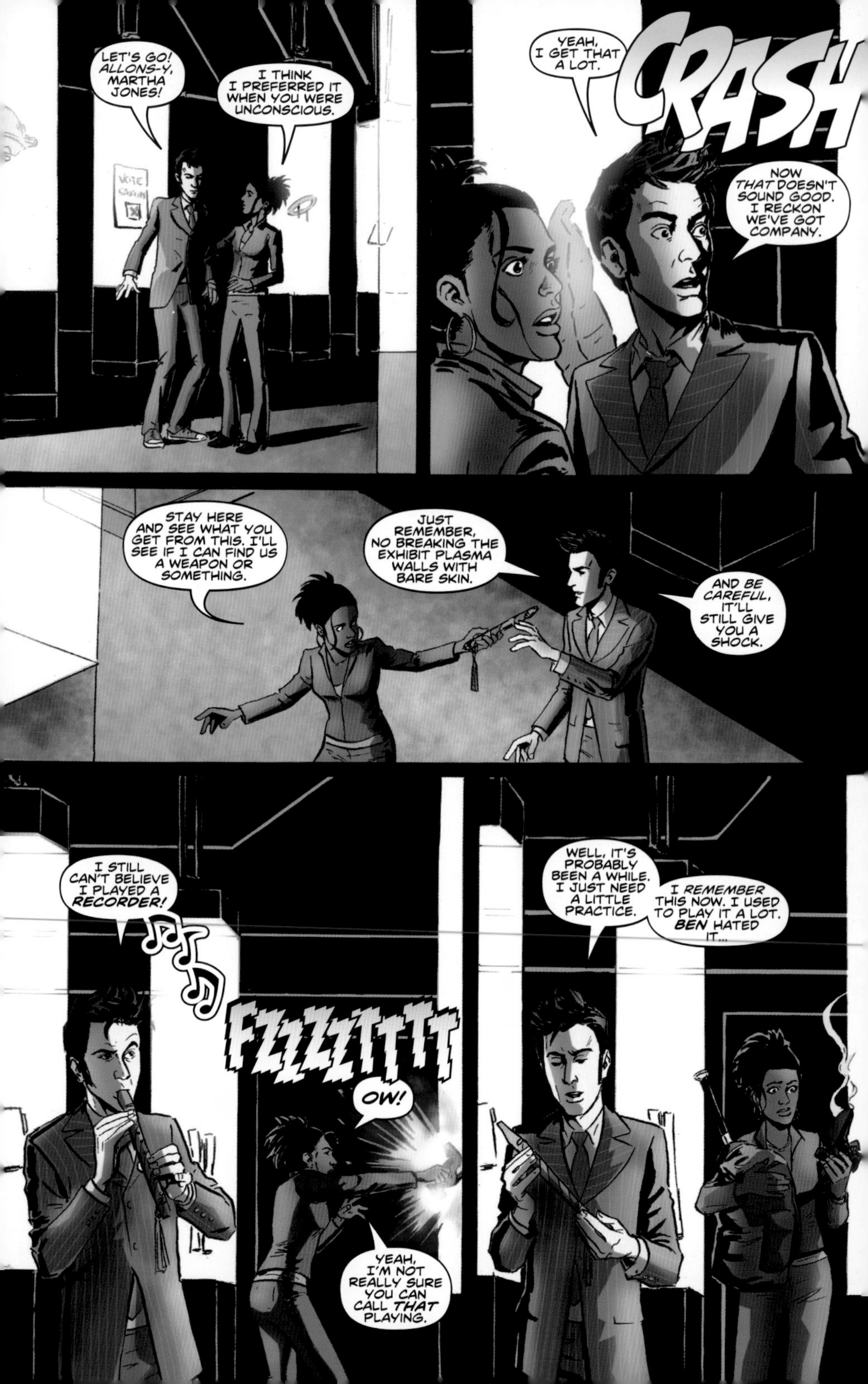
LET'S GO! ALLONS-Y, MARTHA JONES!
I THINK I PREFERRED IT WHEN YOU WERE UNCONSCIOUS.
YEAH, I GET THAT A LOT.
CRASH
NOW THAT DOESN'T SOUND GOOD. I RECKON WE'VE GOT COMPANY.
STAY HERE AND SEE WHAT YOU GET FROM THIS. I'LL SEE IF I CAN FIND US A WEAPON OR SOMETHING.
JUST REMEMBER, NO BREAKING THE EXHIBIT PLASMA WALLS WITH BARE SKIN.
AND BE CAREFUL, IT'LL STILL GIVE YOU A SHOCK.
I STILL CAN'T BELIEVE I PLAYED A RECORDER!
FZZZZTTTT
OW!
YEAH, I'M NOT REALLY SURE YOU CAN CALL THAT PLAYING.
WELL, IT'S PROBABLY BEEN A WHILE. I JUST NEED A LITTLE PRACTICE.
I REMEMBER THIS NOW. I USED TO PLAY IT A LOT. BEN HATED IT...

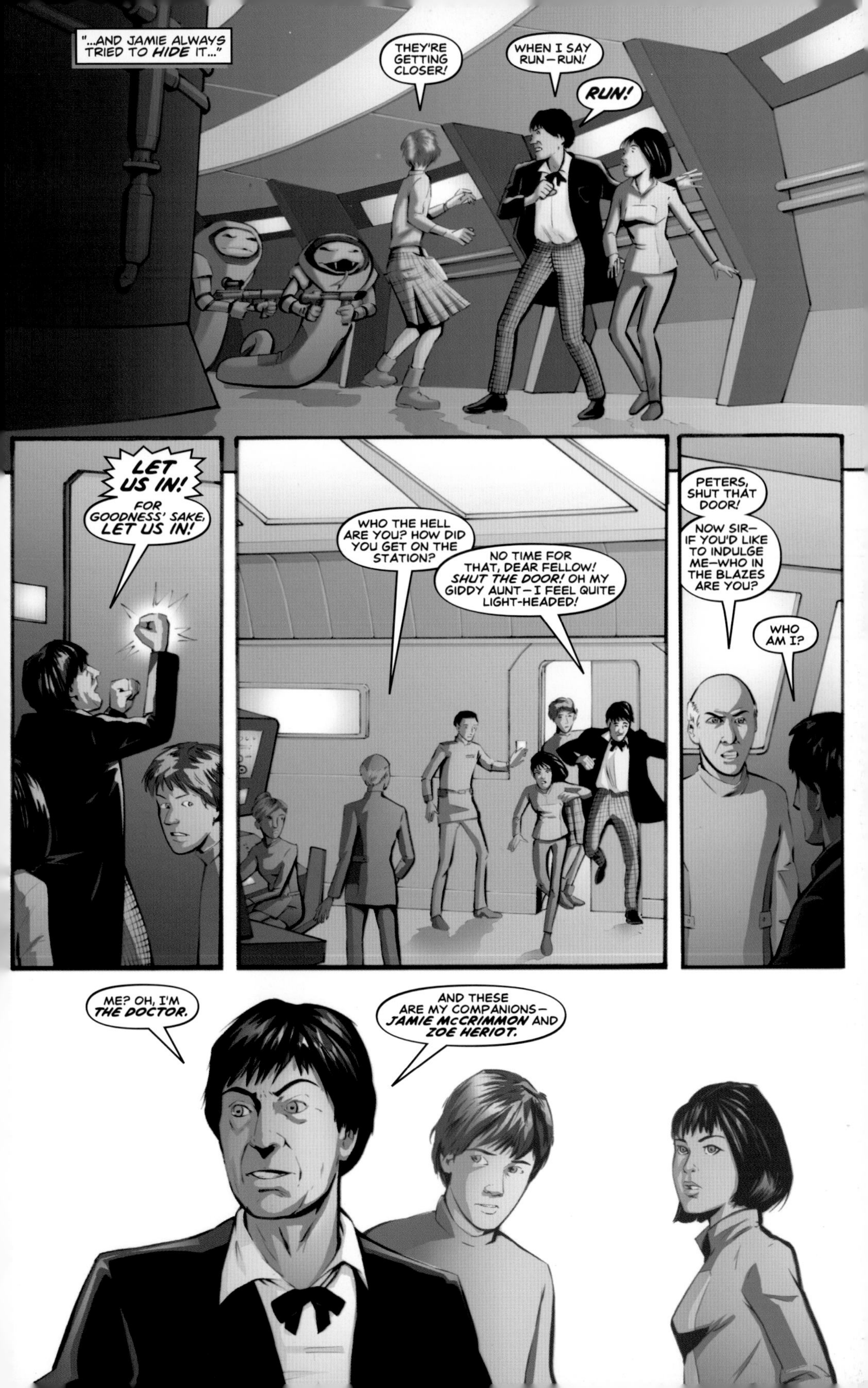
"...AND JAMIE ALWAYS TRIED TO HIDE IT..."
THEY'RE GETTING CLOSER!
WHEN I SAY RUN—RUN!
RUN!
LET US IN!
FOR GOODNESS' SAKE, LET US IN!
WHO THE HELL ARE YOU? HOW DID YOU GET ON THE STATION?
NO TIME FOR THAT, DEAR FELLOW! SHUT THE DOOR! OH MY GIDDY AUNT—I FEEL QUITE LIGHT-HEADED!
PETERS, SHUT THAT DOOR!
NOW SIR—IF YOU'D LIKE TO INDULGE ME—WHO IN THE BLAZES ARE YOU?
WHO AM I?
ME? OH, I'M THE DOCTOR.
AND THESE ARE MY COMPANIONS—JAMIE McCRIMMON AND ZOE HERIOT.

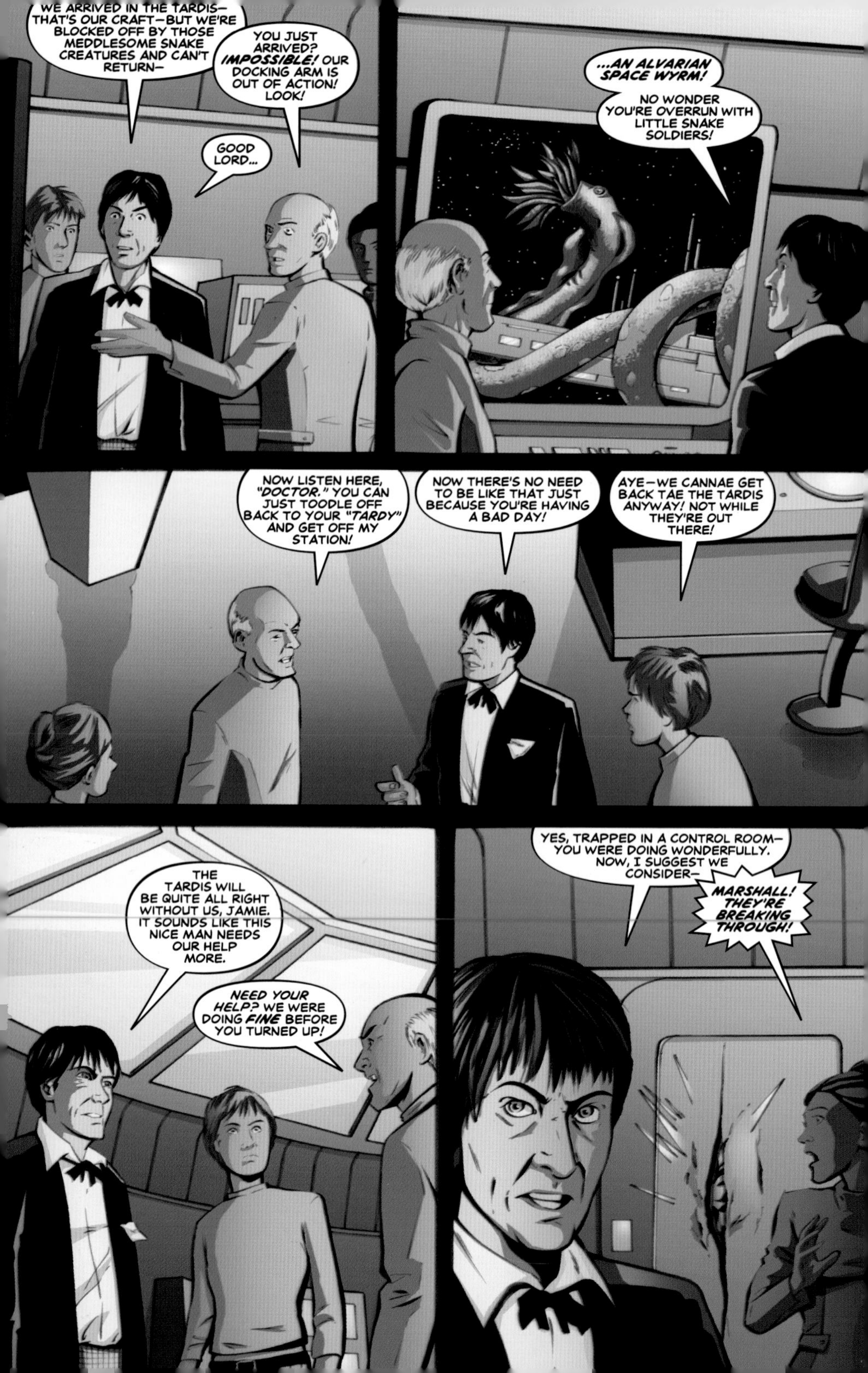
WE ARRIVED IN THE TARDIS—THAT'S OUR CRAFT—BUT WE'RE BLOCKED OFF BY THOSE MEDDLESOME SNAKE CREATURES AND CAN'T RETURN—
YOU JUST ARRIVED? IMPOSSIBLE! OUR DOCKING ARM IS OUT OF ACTION! LOOK!
GOOD LORD...
...AN ALVARIAN SPACE WYRM!
NO WONDER YOU'RE OVERRUN WITH LITTLE SNAKE SOLDIERS!
NOW LISTEN HERE, "DOCTOR." YOU CAN JUST TOODLE OFF BACK TO YOUR "TARDY" AND GET OFF MY STATION!
NOW THERE'S NO NEED TO BE LIKE THAT JUST BECAUSE YOU'RE HAVING A BAD DAY!
AYE—WE CANNAE GET BACK TAE THE TARDIS ANYWAY! NOT WHILE THEY'RE OUT THERE!
THE TARDIS WILL BE QUITE ALL RIGHT WITHOUT US, JAMIE. IT SOUNDS LIKE THIS NICE MAN NEEDS OUR HELP MORE.
NEED YOUR HELP? WE WERE DOING FINE BEFORE YOU TURNED UP!
YES, TRAPPED IN A CONTROL ROOM—YOU WERE DOING WONDERFULLY. NOW, I SUGGEST WE CONSIDER—
MARSHALL! THEY'RE BREAKING THROUGH!

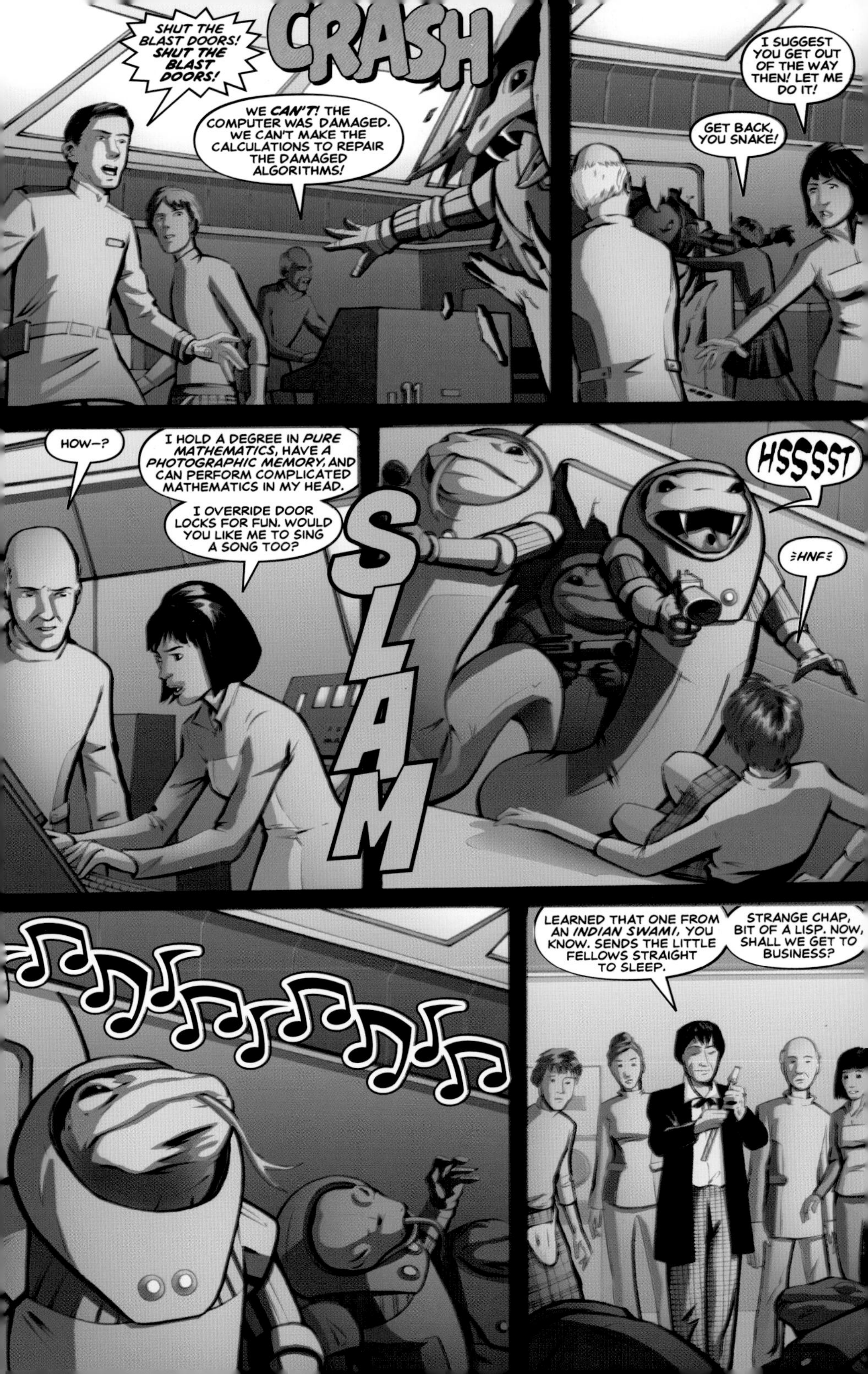
SHUT THE BLAST DOORS! SHUT THE BLAST DOORS!
CRASH
WE CAN'T! THE COMPUTER WAS DAMAGED. WE CAN'T MAKE THE CALCULATIONS TO REPAIR THE DAMAGED ALGORITHMS!
I SUGGEST YOU GET OUT OF THE WAY THEN! LET ME DO IT!
GET BACK, YOU SNAKE!
HOW—?
I HOLD A DEGREE IN PURE MATHEMATICS, HAVE A PHOTOGRAPHIC MEMORY, AND CAN PERFORM COMPLICATED MATHEMATICS IN MY HEAD.
I OVERRIDE DOOR LOCKS FOR FUN. WOULD YOU LIKE ME TO SING A SONG TOO?
SLAM
HSSSST
HNF
LEARNED THAT ONE FROM AN INDIAN SWAMI, YOU KNOW. SENDS THE LITTLE FELLOWS STRAIGHT TO SLEEP.
STRANGE CHAP, BIT OF A LISP. NOW, SHALL WE GET TO BUSINESS?

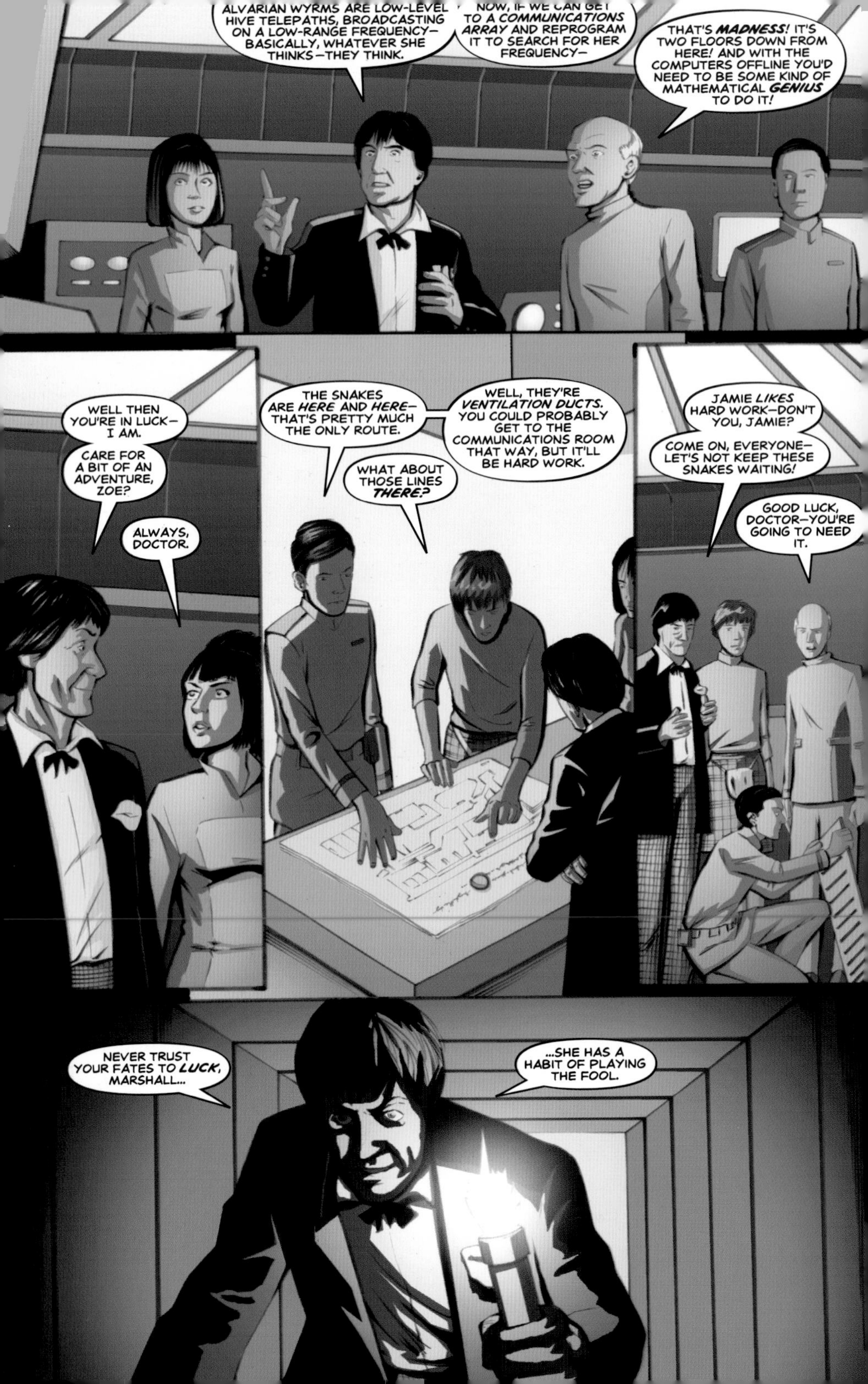
ALVARIAN WYRMS ARE LOW-LEVEL HIVE TELEPATHS, BROADCASTING ON A LOW-RANGE FREQUENCY— BASICALLY, WHATEVER SHE THINKS—THEY THINK.
NOW, IF WE CAN GET TO A *COMMUNICATIONS ARRAY* AND REPROGRAM IT TO SEARCH FOR HER FREQUENCY—
THAT'S ***MADNESS!*** IT'S TWO FLOORS DOWN FROM HERE! AND WITH THE COMPUTERS OFFLINE YOU'D NEED TO BE SOME KIND OF MATHEMATICAL ***GENIUS*** TO DO IT!
WELL THEN YOU'RE IN LUCK— I AM.
CARE FOR A BIT OF AN ADVENTURE, ZOE?
ALWAYS, DOCTOR.
THE SNAKES ARE *HERE* AND *HERE*— THAT'S PRETTY MUCH THE ONLY ROUTE.
WELL, THEY'RE *VENTILATION DUCTS.* YOU COULD PROBABLY GET TO THE COMMUNICATIONS ROOM THAT WAY, BUT IT'LL BE HARD WORK.
WHAT ABOUT THOSE LINES ***THERE?***
JAMIE *LIKES* HARD WORK—DON'T YOU, JAMIE?
COME ON, EVERYONE— LET'S NOT KEEP THESE SNAKES WAITING!
GOOD LUCK, DOCTOR—YOU'RE GOING TO NEED IT.
NEVER TRUST YOUR FATES TO ***LUCK,*** MARSHALL...
...SHE HAS A HABIT OF PLAYING THE FOOL.

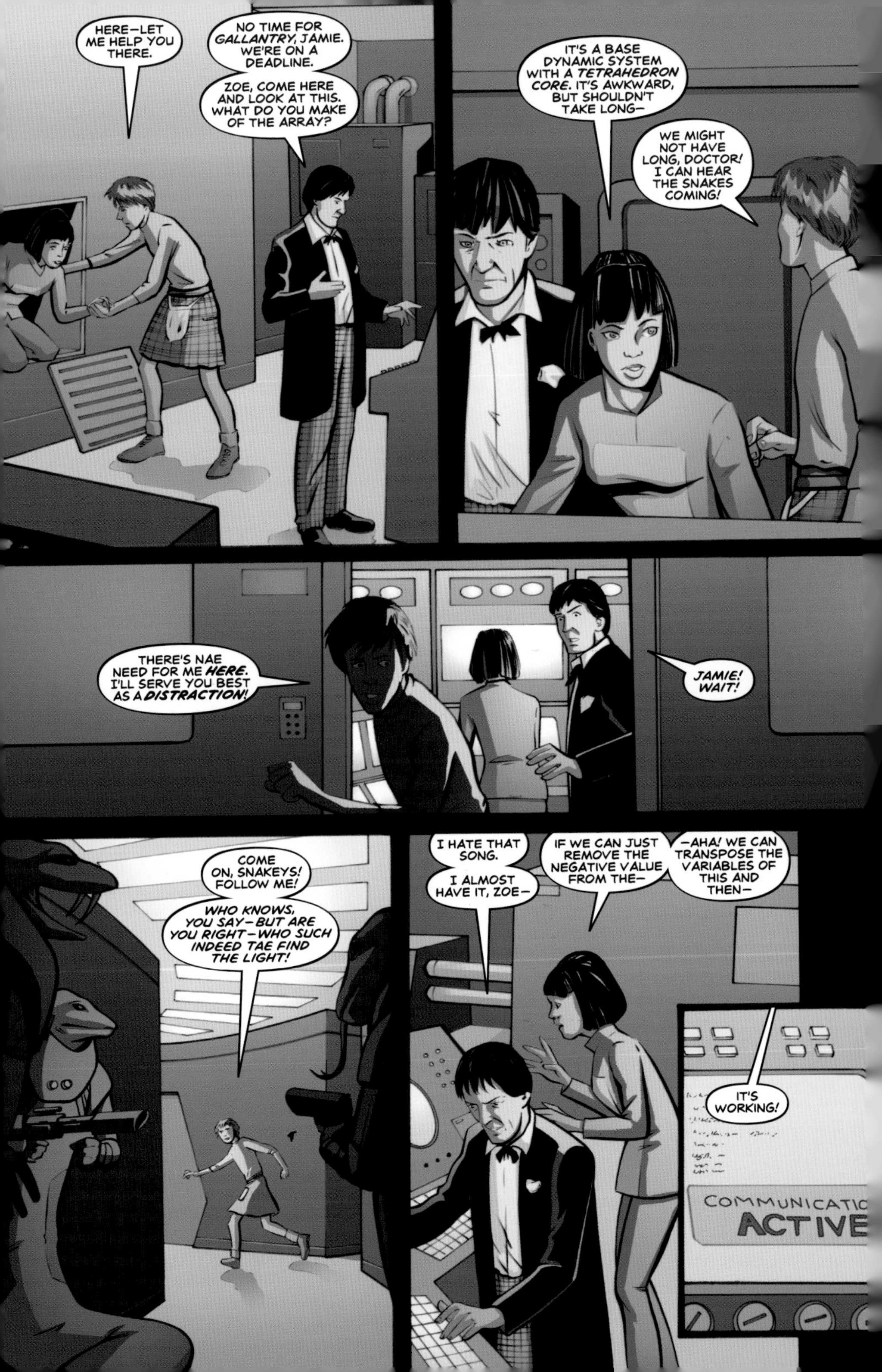
HERE—LET ME HELP YOU THERE.
NO TIME FOR GALLANTRY, JAMIE. WE'RE ON A DEADLINE.
ZOE, COME HERE AND LOOK AT THIS. WHAT DO YOU MAKE OF THE ARRAY?
IT'S A BASE DYNAMIC SYSTEM WITH A TETRAHEDRON CORE. IT'S AWKWARD, BUT SHOULDN'T TAKE LONG—
WE MIGHT NOT HAVE LONG, DOCTOR! I CAN HEAR THE SNAKES COMING!
THERE'S NAE NEED FOR ME HERE. I'LL SERVE YOU BEST AS A DISTRACTION!
JAMIE! WAIT!
COME ON, SNAKEYS! FOLLOW ME!
WHO KNOWS, YOU SAY—BUT ARE YOU RIGHT—WHO SUCH INDEED TAE FIND THE LIGHT!
I HATE THAT SONG.
I ALMOST HAVE IT, ZOE—
IF WE CAN JUST REMOVE THE NEGATIVE VALUE FROM THE—
—AHA! WE CAN TRANSPOSE THE VARIABLES OF THIS AND THEN—
IT'S WORKING!
COMMUNICATIO
ACTIVE

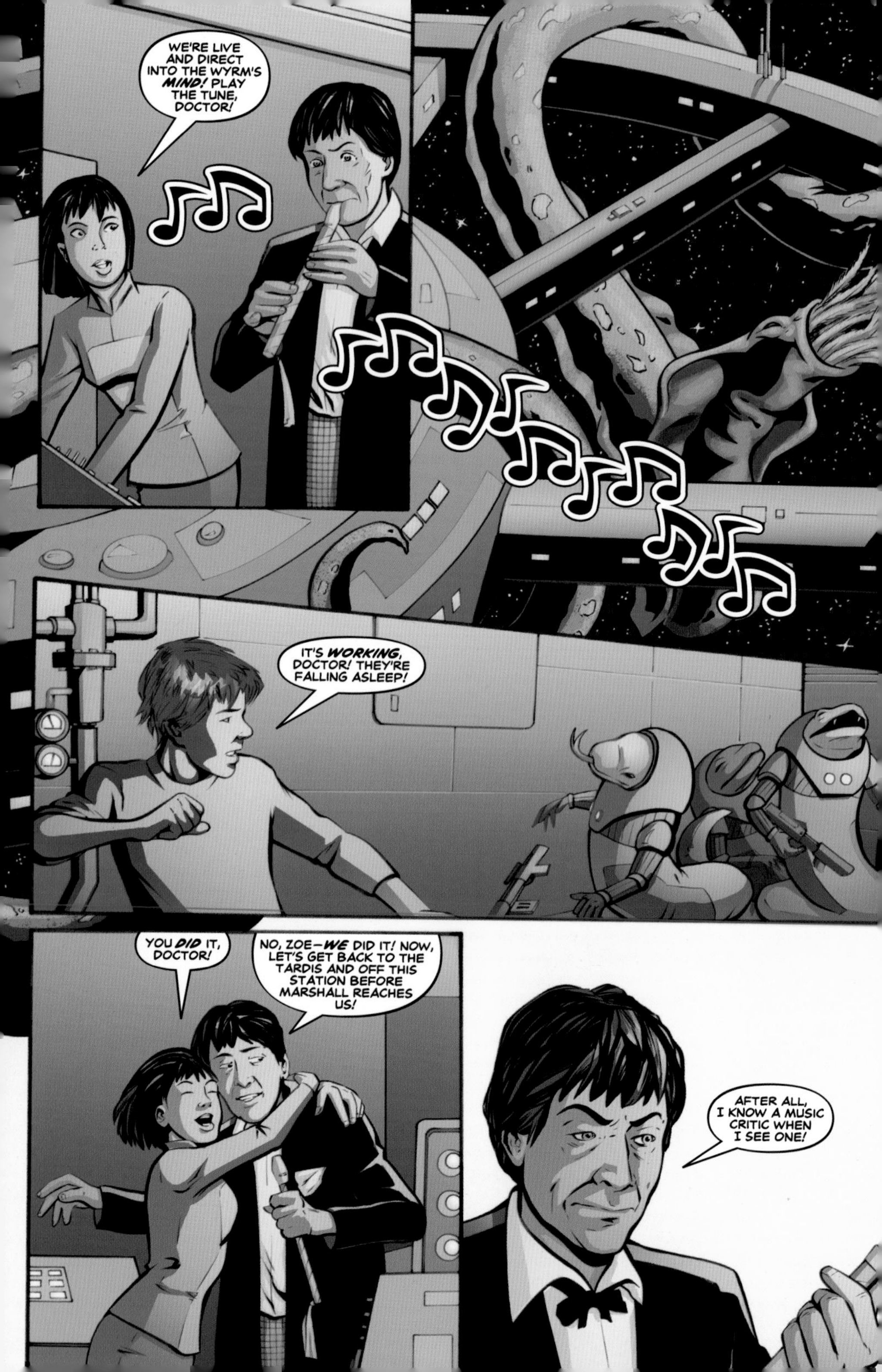
WE'RE LIVE AND DIRECT INTO THE WYRM'S *MIND!* PLAY THE TUNE, DOCTOR!
IT'S *WORKING*, DOCTOR! THEY'RE FALLING ASLEEP!
YOU *DID* IT, DOCTOR!
NO, ZOE—*WE* DID IT! NOW, LET'S GET BACK TO THE TARDIS AND OFF THIS STATION BEFORE MARSHALL REACHES US!
AFTER ALL, I KNOW A MUSIC CRITIC WHEN I SEE ONE!

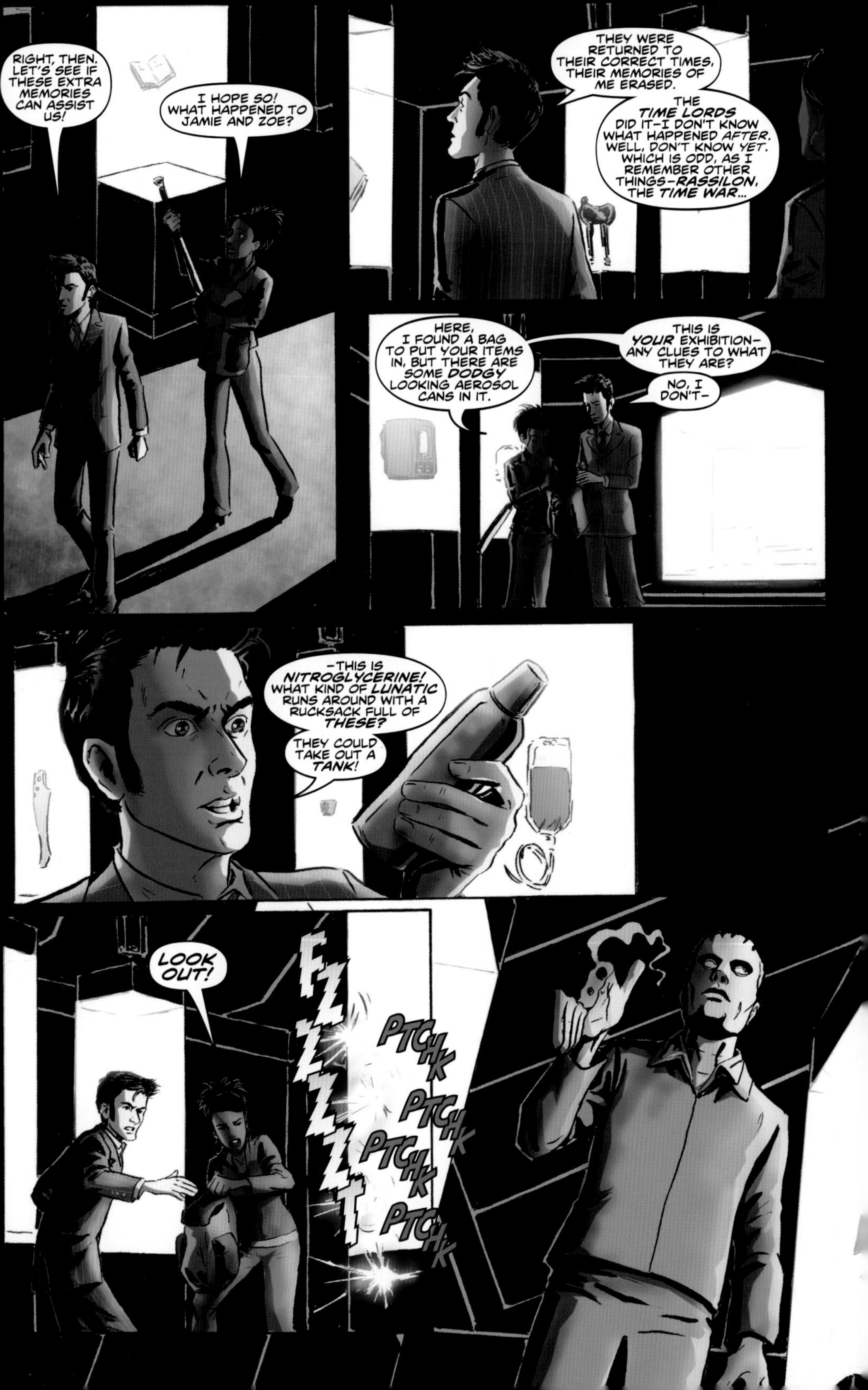
RIGHT, THEN. LET'S SEE IF THESE EXTRA MEMORIES CAN ASSIST US!
I HOPE SO! WHAT HAPPENED TO JAMIE AND ZOE?
THEY WERE RETURNED TO THEIR CORRECT TIMES, THEIR MEMORIES OF ME ERASED.
THE TIME LORDS DID IT–I DON'T KNOW WHAT HAPPENED AFTER. WELL, DON'T KNOW YET. WHICH IS ODD, AS I REMEMBER OTHER THINGS–RASSILON, THE TIME WAR...
HERE, I FOUND A BAG TO PUT YOUR ITEMS IN, BUT THERE ARE SOME DODGY LOOKING AEROSOL CANS IN IT.
THIS IS YOUR EXHIBITION–ANY CLUES TO WHAT THEY ARE?
NO, I DON'T–
–THIS IS NITROGLYCERINE! WHAT KIND OF LUNATIC RUNS AROUND WITH A RUCKSACK FULL OF THESE?
THEY COULD TAKE OUT A TANK!
LOOK OUT!
FZZZZZT
PTCHK
PTCHK
PTCHK
PTCHK

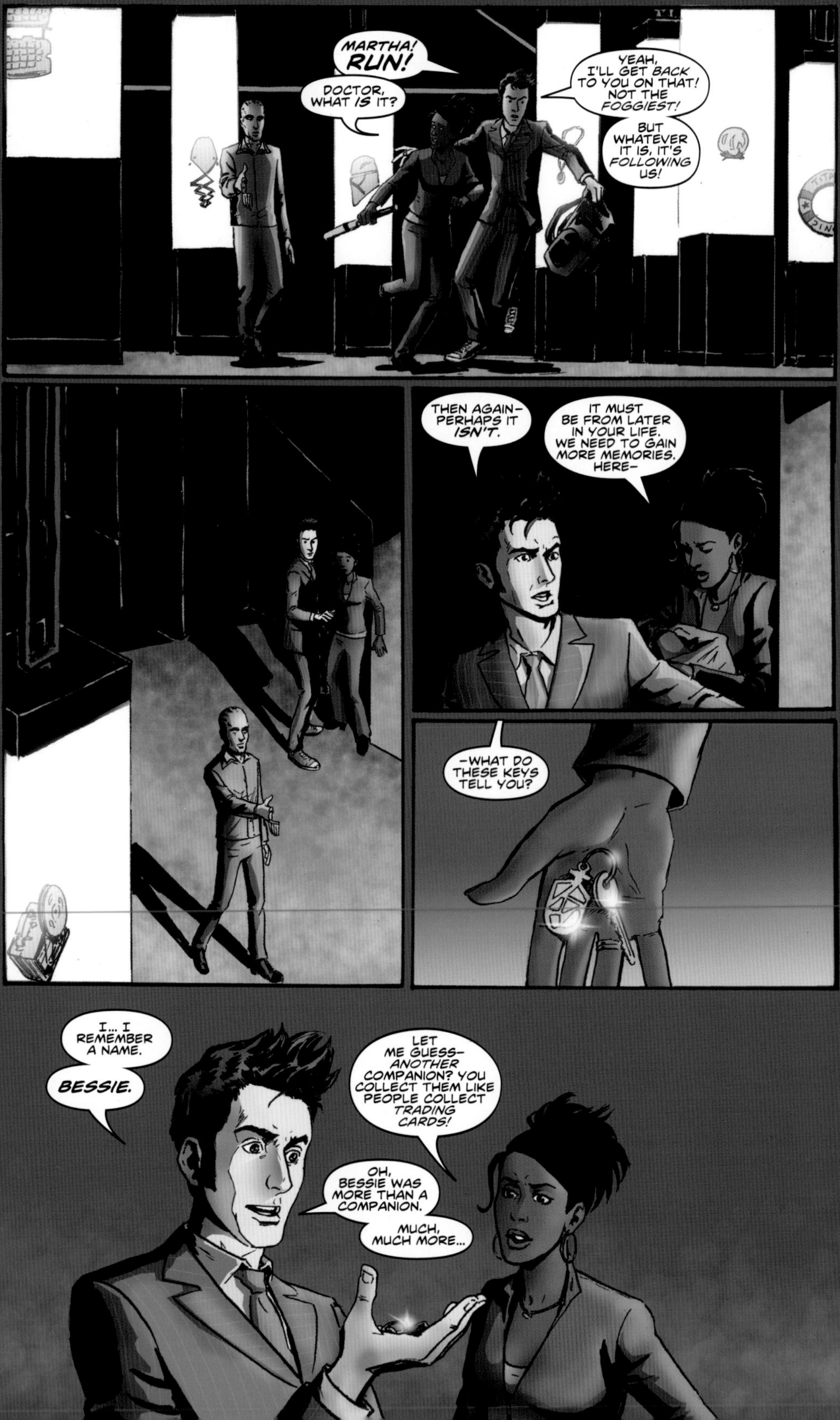

MARTHA! RUN!
DOCTOR, WHAT IS IT?
YEAH, I'LL GET BACK TO YOU ON THAT! NOT THE FOGGIEST!
BUT WHATEVER IT IS, IT'S FOLLOWING US!
THEN AGAIN-PERHAPS IT ISN'T.
IT MUST BE FROM LATER IN YOUR LIFE. WE NEED TO GAIN MORE MEMORIES. HERE-
-WHAT DO THESE KEYS TELL YOU?
I... I REMEMBER A NAME.
BESSIE.
LET ME GUESS-ANOTHER COMPANION? YOU COLLECT THEM LIKE PEOPLE COLLECT TRADING CARDS!
OH, BESSIE WAS MORE THAN A COMPANION.
MUCH, MUCH MORE...

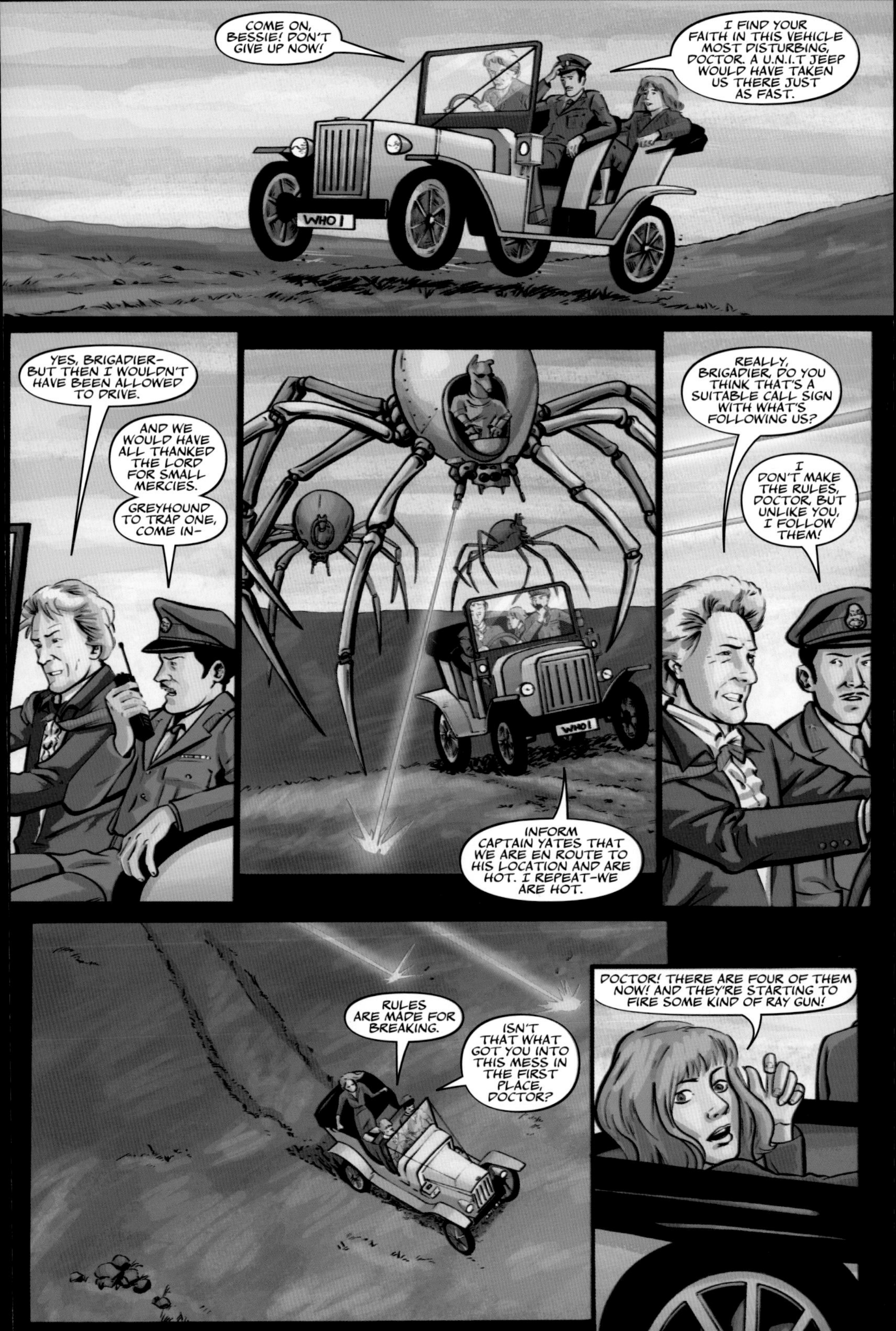

COME ON, BESSIE! DON'T GIVE UP NOW!
I FIND YOUR FAITH IN THIS VEHICLE MOST DISTURBING, DOCTOR. A U.N.I.T JEEP WOULD HAVE TAKEN US THERE JUST AS FAST.
WHO 1
YES, BRIGADIER- BUT THEN I WOULDN'T HAVE BEEN ALLOWED TO DRIVE.
AND WE WOULD HAVE ALL THANKED THE LORD FOR SMALL MERCIES.
GREYHOUND TO TRAP ONE, COME IN-
INFORM CAPTAIN YATES THAT WE ARE EN ROUTE TO HIS LOCATION AND ARE HOT. I REPEAT-WE ARE HOT.
WHO 1
REALLY, BRIGADIER, DO YOU THINK THAT'S A SUITABLE CALL SIGN WITH WHAT'S FOLLOWING US?
I DON'T MAKE THE RULES, DOCTOR, BUT UNLIKE YOU, I FOLLOW THEM!
RULES ARE MADE FOR BREAKING.
ISN'T THAT WHAT GOT YOU INTO THIS MESS IN THE FIRST PLACE, DOCTOR?
DOCTOR! THERE ARE FOUR OF THEM NOW! AND THEY'RE STARTING TO FIRE SOME KIND OF RAY GUN!

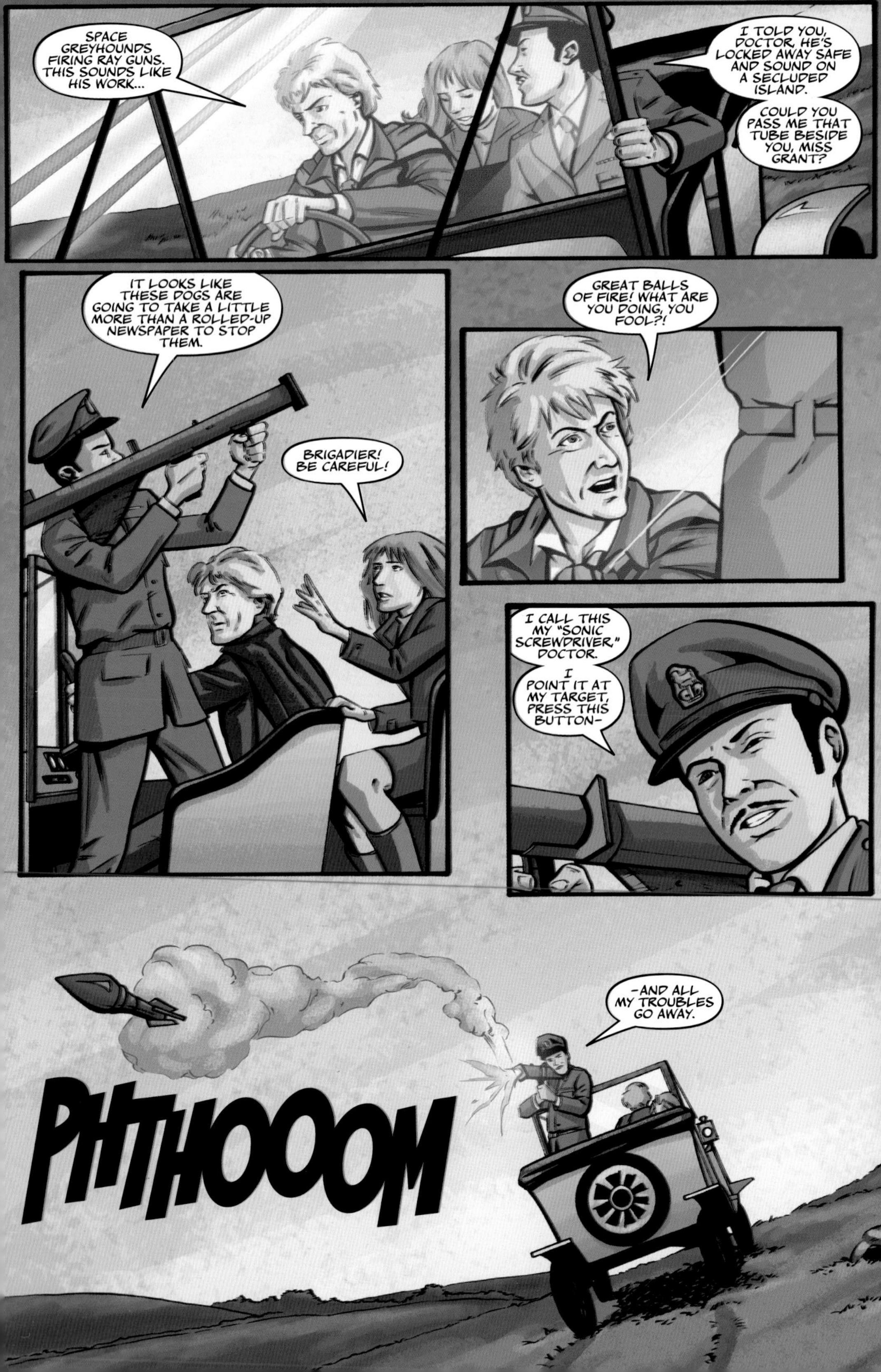
SPACE GREYHOUNDS FIRING RAY GUNS. THIS SOUNDS LIKE HIS WORK...
I TOLD YOU, DOCTOR, HE'S LOCKED AWAY SAFE AND SOUND ON A SECLUDED ISLAND.
COULD YOU PASS ME THAT TUBE BESIDE YOU, MISS GRANT?
IT LOOKS LIKE THESE DOGS ARE GOING TO TAKE A LITTLE MORE THAN A ROLLED-UP NEWSPAPER TO STOP THEM.
BRIGADIER! BE CAREFUL!
GREAT BALLS OF FIRE! WHAT ARE YOU DOING, YOU FOOL?!
I CALL THIS MY "SONIC SCREWDRIVER," DOCTOR.
I POINT IT AT MY TARGET, PRESS THIS BUTTON-
-AND ALL MY TROUBLES GO AWAY.
PHTHOOOM

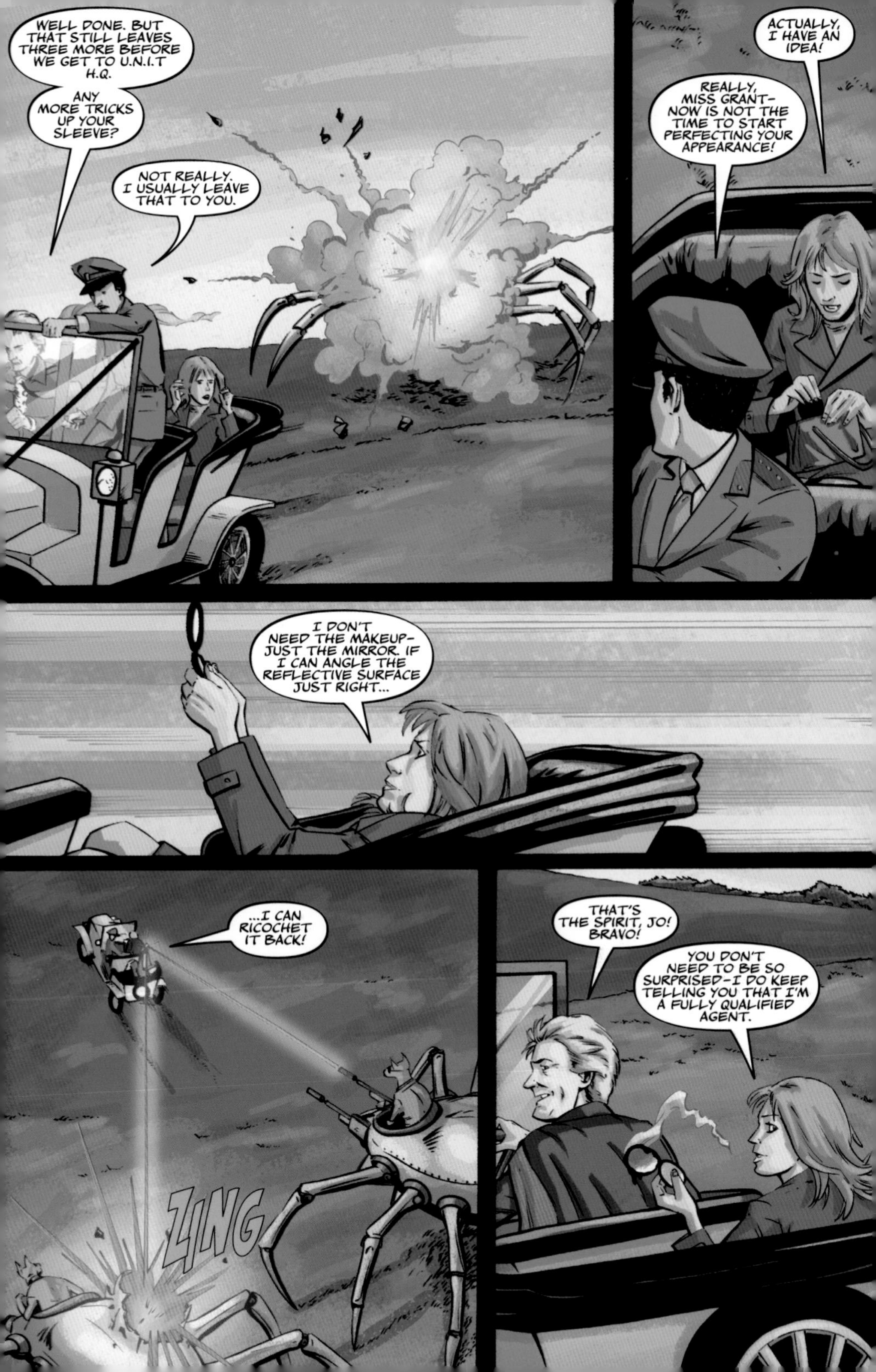
WELL DONE. BUT THAT STILL LEAVES THREE MORE BEFORE WE GET TO U.N.I.T H.Q.
ANY MORE TRICKS UP YOUR SLEEVE?
NOT REALLY. I USUALLY LEAVE THAT TO YOU.
ACTUALLY, I HAVE AN IDEA!
REALLY, MISS GRANT– NOW IS NOT THE TIME TO START PERFECTING YOUR APPEARANCE!
I DON'T NEED THE MAKEUP– JUST THE MIRROR. IF I CAN ANGLE THE REFLECTIVE SURFACE JUST RIGHT...
...I CAN RICOCHET IT BACK!
ZING
THAT'S THE SPIRIT, JO! BRAVO!
YOU DON'T NEED TO BE SO SURPRISED–I DO KEEP TELLING YOU THAT I'M A FULLY QUALIFIED AGENT.

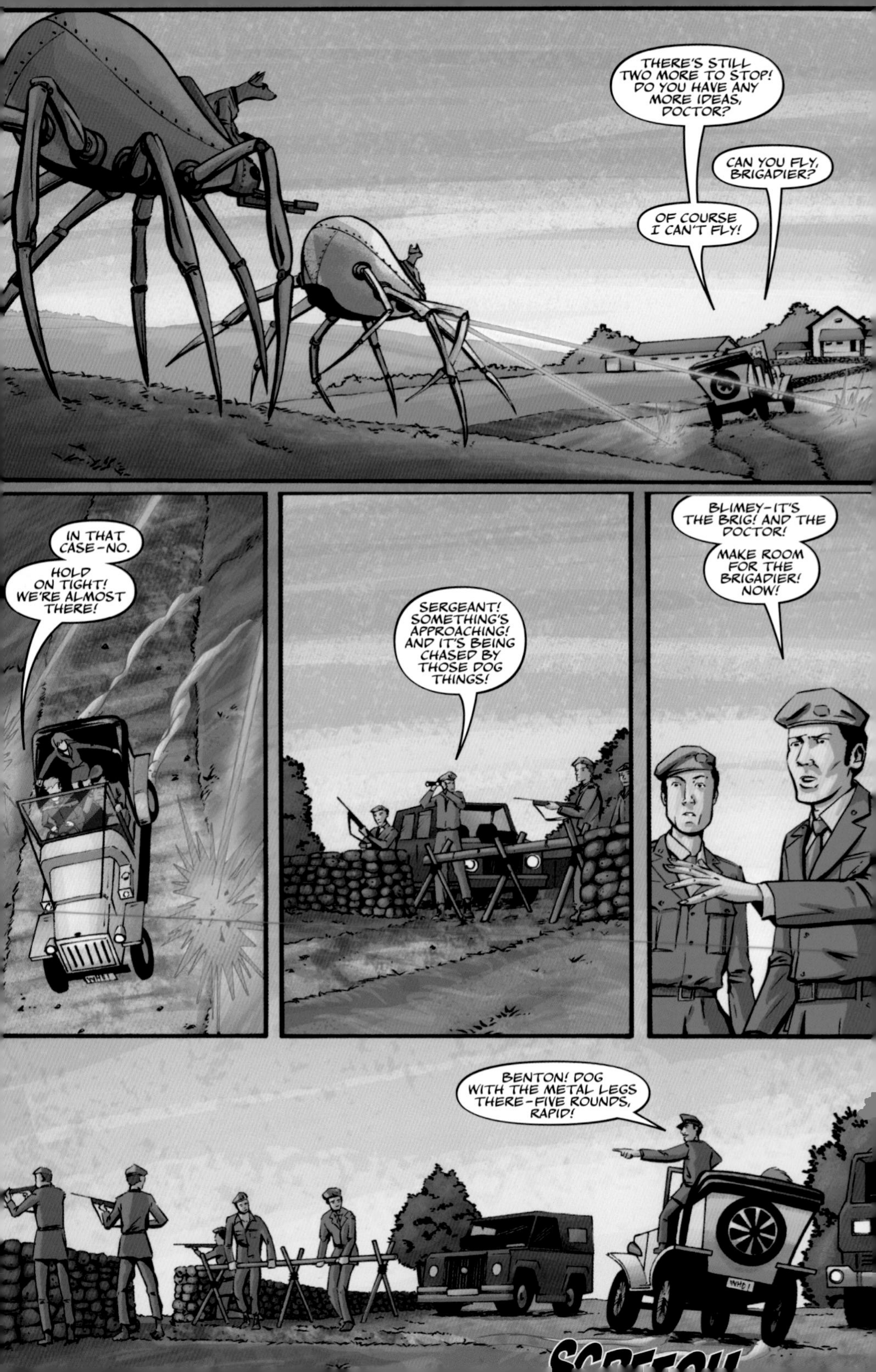
THERE'S STILL TWO MORE TO STOP! DO YOU HAVE ANY MORE IDEAS, DOCTOR?
CAN YOU FLY, BRIGADIER?
OF COURSE I CAN'T FLY!
IN THAT CASE–NO.
HOLD ON TIGHT! WE'RE ALMOST THERE!
SERGEANT! SOMETHING'S APPROACHING! AND IT'S BEING CHASED BY THOSE DOG THINGS!
BLIMEY–IT'S THE BRIG! AND THE DOCTOR!
MAKE ROOM FOR THE BRIGADIER! NOW!
BENTON! DOG WITH THE METAL LEGS THERE–FIVE ROUNDS, RAPID!

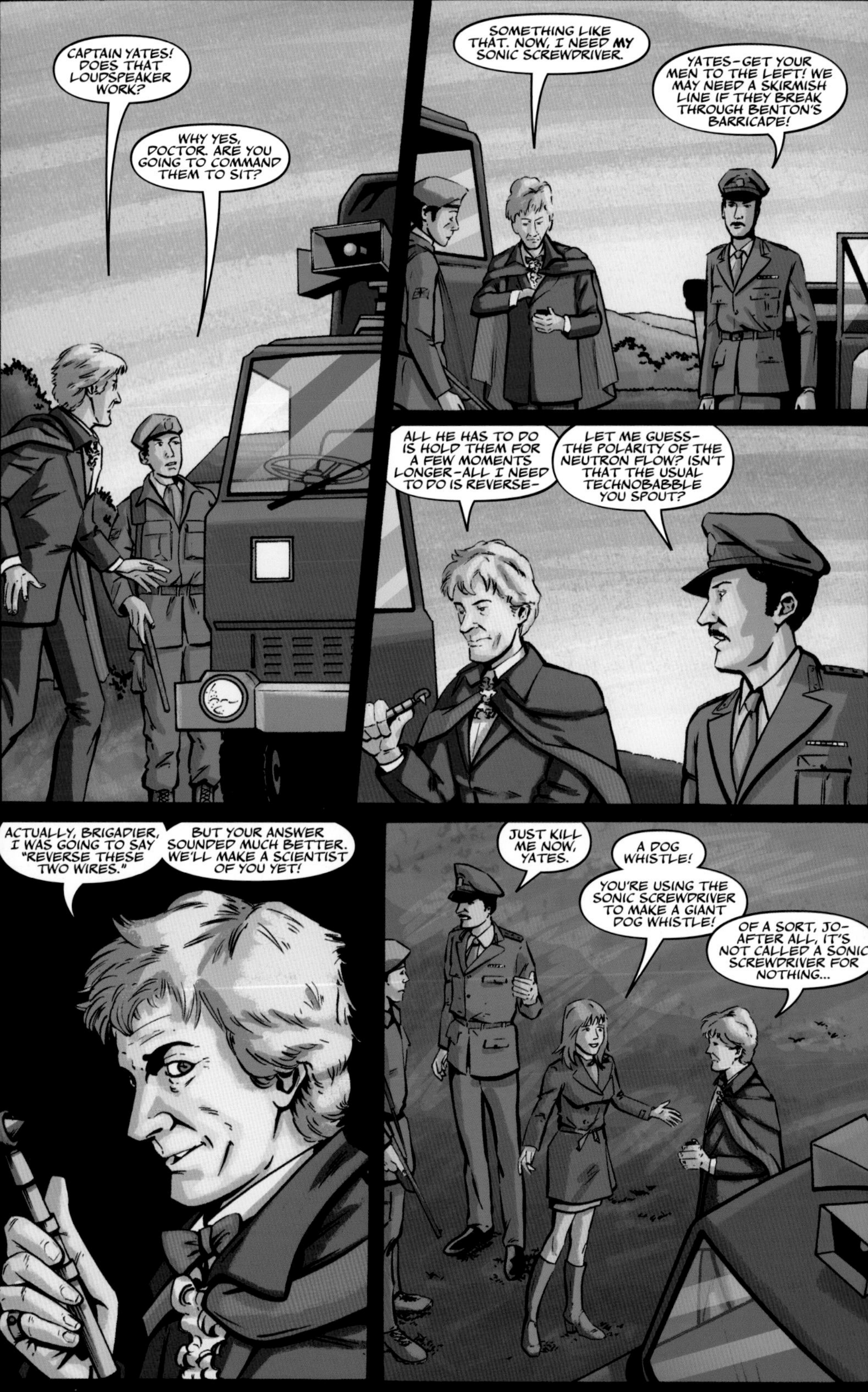
CAPTAIN YATES! DOES THAT LOUDSPEAKER WORK?
WHY YES, DOCTOR. ARE YOU GOING TO COMMAND THEM TO SIT?
SOMETHING LIKE THAT. NOW, I NEED MY SONIC SCREWDRIVER.
YATES—GET YOUR MEN TO THE LEFT! WE MAY NEED A SKIRMISH LINE IF THEY BREAK THROUGH BENTON'S BARRICADE!
ALL HE HAS TO DO IS HOLD THEM FOR A FEW MOMENTS LONGER—ALL I NEED TO DO IS REVERSE—
LET ME GUESS—THE POLARITY OF THE NEUTRON FLOW? ISN'T THAT THE USUAL TECHNOBABBLE YOU SPOUT?
ACTUALLY, BRIGADIER, I WAS GOING TO SAY "REVERSE THESE TWO WIRES."
BUT YOUR ANSWER SOUNDED MUCH BETTER. WE'LL MAKE A SCIENTIST OF YOU YET!
JUST KILL ME NOW, YATES.
A DOG WHISTLE!
YOU'RE USING THE SONIC SCREWDRIVER TO MAKE A GIANT DOG WHISTLE!
OF A SORT, JO—AFTER ALL, IT'S NOT CALLED A SONIC SCREWDRIVER FOR NOTHING...

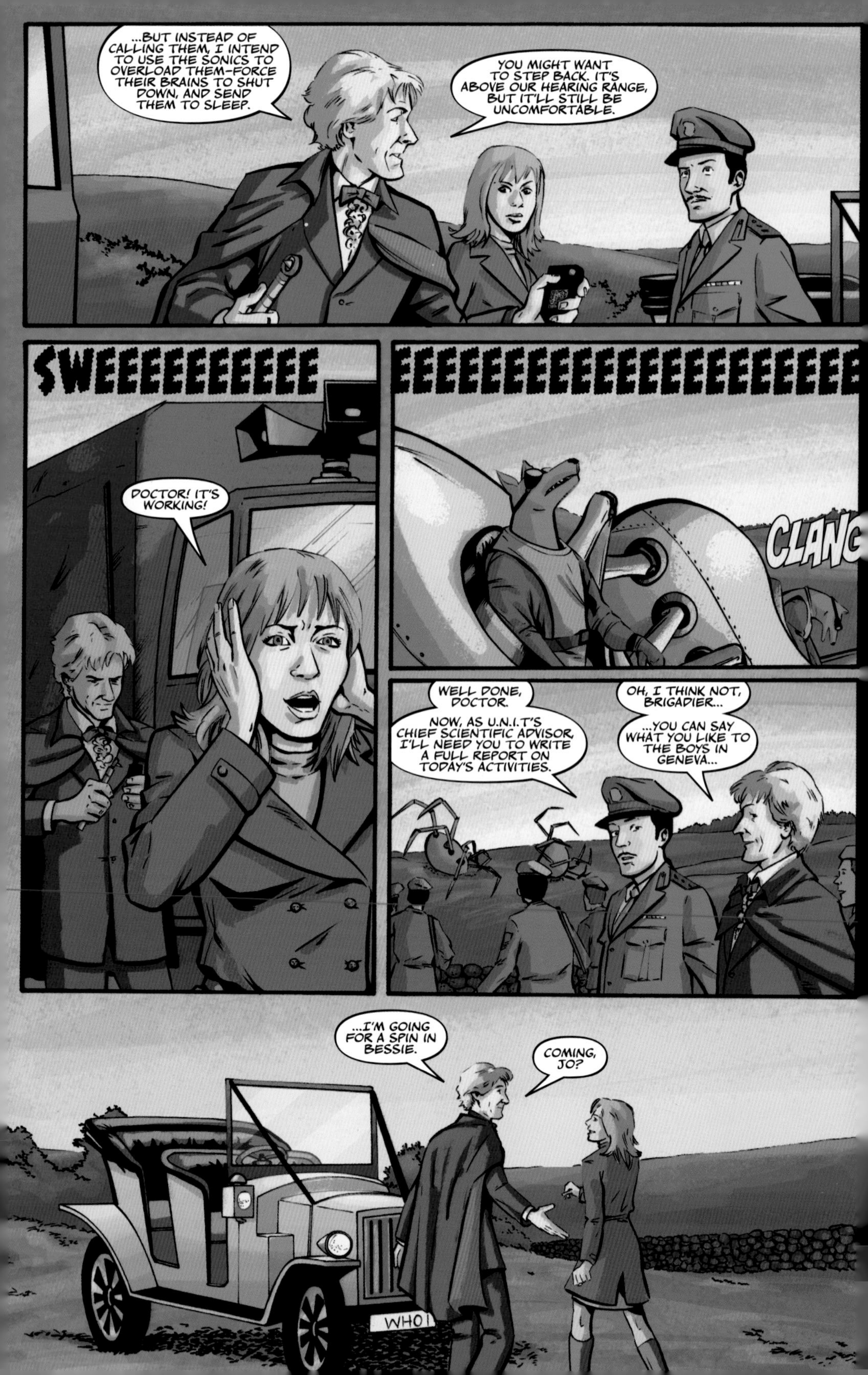
...BUT INSTEAD OF CALLING THEM, I INTEND TO USE THE SONICS TO OVERLOAD THEM–FORCE THEIR BRAINS TO SHUT DOWN, AND SEND THEM TO SLEEP.
YOU MIGHT WANT TO STEP BACK. IT'S ABOVE OUR HEARING RANGE, BUT IT'LL STILL BE UNCOMFORTABLE.
SWEEEEEEEEEE
DOCTOR! IT'S WORKING!
EEEEEEEEEEEEEEEEEEEEEEEEE
CLANG
WELL DONE, DOCTOR.
NOW, AS U.N.I.T.'S CHIEF SCIENTIFIC ADVISOR, I'LL NEED YOU TO WRITE A FULL REPORT ON TODAY'S ACTIVITIES.
OH, I THINK NOT, BRIGADIER...
...YOU CAN SAY WHAT YOU LIKE TO THE BOYS IN GENEVA...
...I'M GOING FOR A SPIN IN BESSIE.
COMING, JO?
WHO I

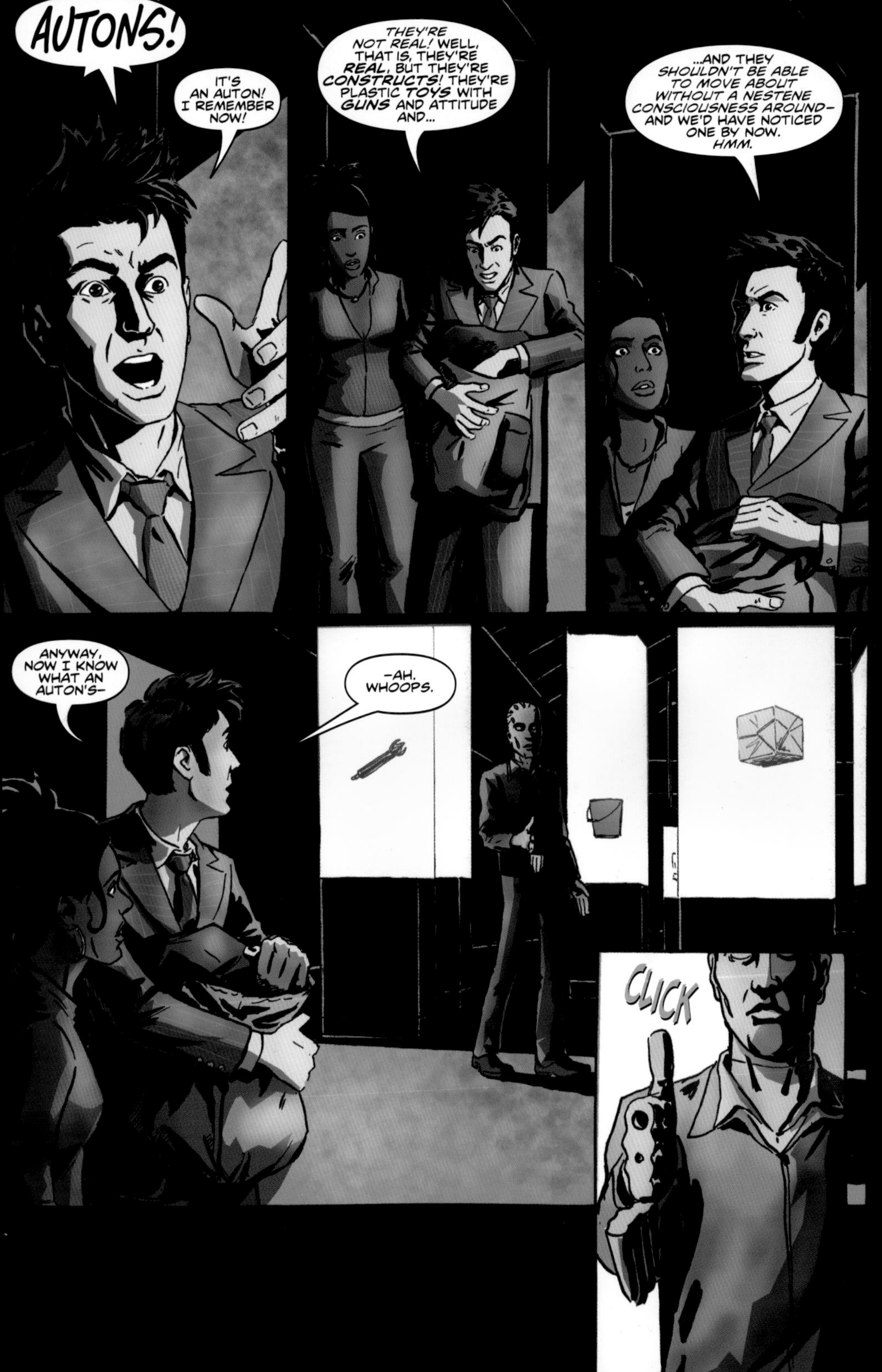
AUTONS!
IT'S AN AUTON! I REMEMBER NOW!
THEY'RE NOT REAL! WELL, THAT IS, THEY'RE REAL, BUT THEY'RE CONSTRUCTS! THEY'RE PLASTIC TOYS WITH GUNS AND ATTITUDE AND...
...AND THEY SHOULDN'T BE ABLE TO MOVE ABOUT WITHOUT A NESTENE CONSCIOUSNESS AROUND— AND WE'D HAVE NOTICED ONE BY NOW. HMM.
ANYWAY, NOW I KNOW WHAT AN AUTON'S—
—AH. WHOOPS.
CLICK

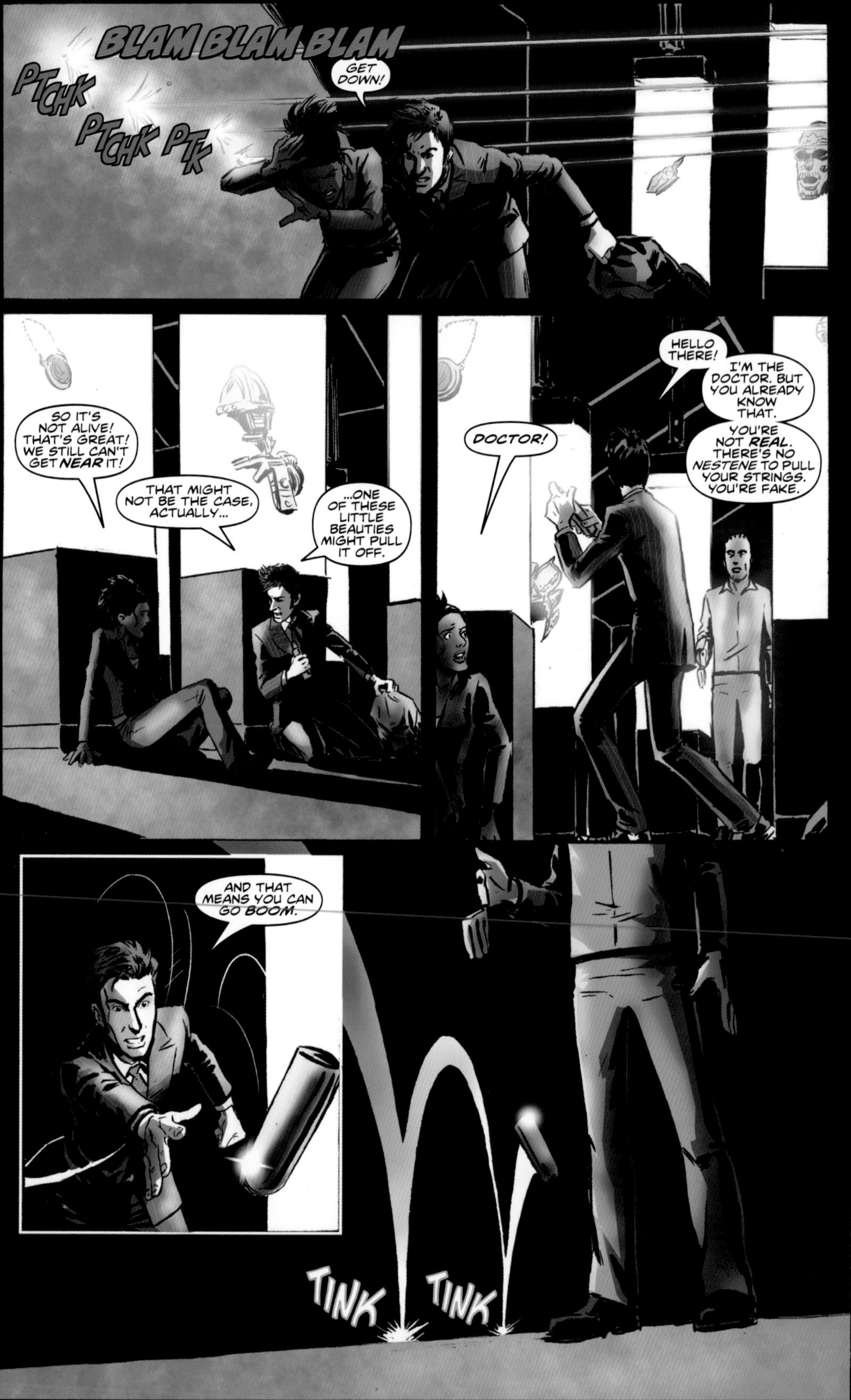
BLAM BLAM BLAM
PTCHK PTCHK PTK
GET DOWN!
SO IT'S NOT ALIVE! THAT'S GREAT! WE STILL CAN'T GET NEAR IT!
THAT MIGHT NOT BE THE CASE, ACTUALLY...
...ONE OF THESE LITTLE BEAUTIES MIGHT PULL IT OFF.
DOCTOR!
HELLO THERE!
I'M THE DOCTOR. BUT YOU ALREADY KNOW THAT.
YOU'RE NOT REAL. THERE'S NO NESTENE TO PULL YOUR STRINGS. YOU'RE FAKE.
AND THAT MEANS YOU CAN GO BOOM.
TINK TINK

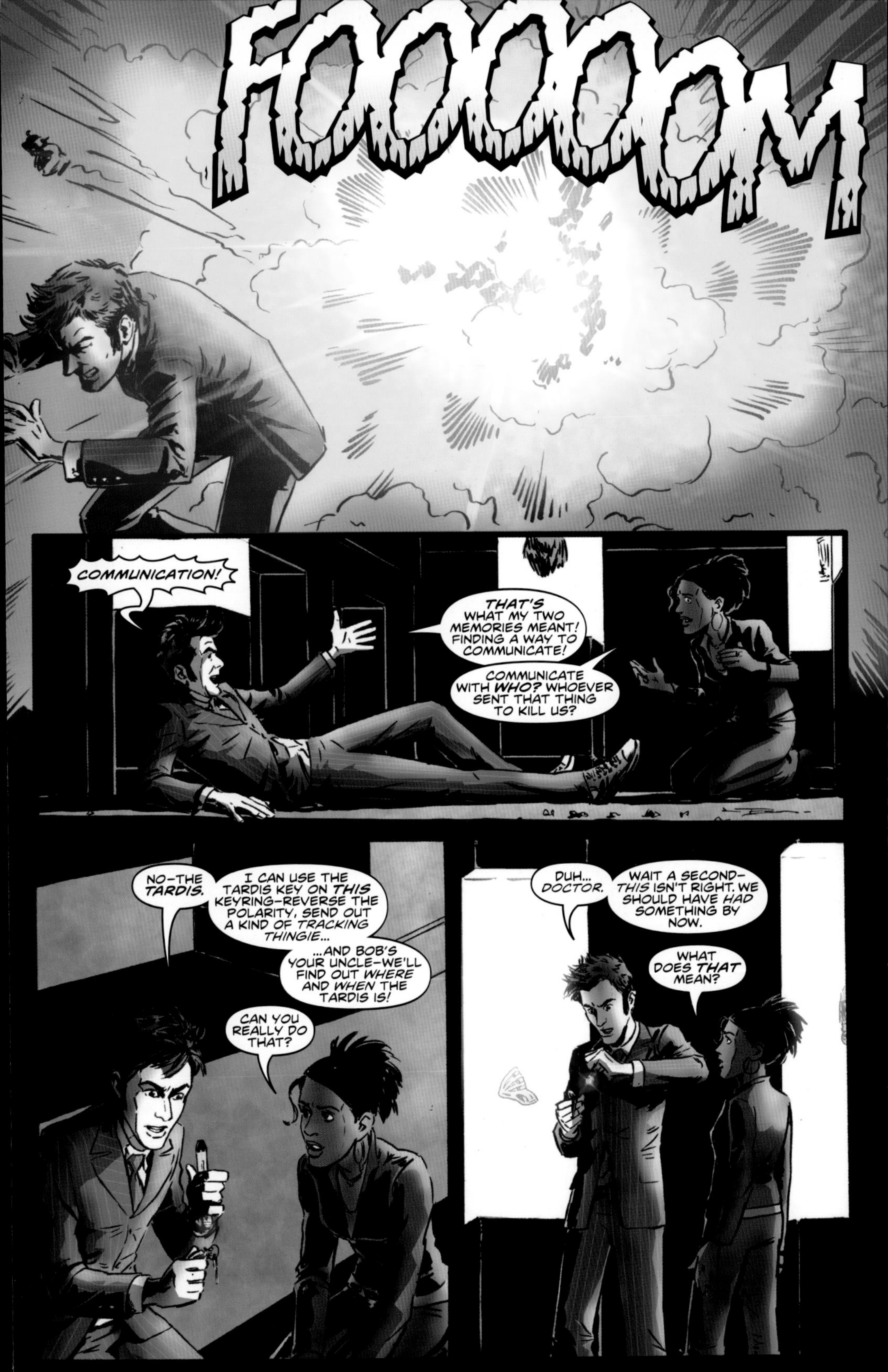
FOOOOOM
COMMUNICATION!
THAT'S WHAT MY TWO MEMORIES MEANT! FINDING A WAY TO COMMUNICATE!
COMMUNICATE WITH WHO? WHOEVER SENT THAT THING TO KILL US?
NO–THE TARDIS.
I CAN USE THE TARDIS KEY ON THIS KEYRING–REVERSE THE POLARITY, SEND OUT A KIND OF TRACKING THINGIE...
...AND BOB'S YOUR UNCLE–WE'LL FIND OUT WHERE AND WHEN THE TARDIS IS!
CAN YOU REALLY DO THAT?
DUH... DOCTOR.
WAIT A SECOND–THIS ISN'T RIGHT. WE SHOULD HAVE HAD SOMETHING BY NOW.
WHAT DOES THAT MEAN?

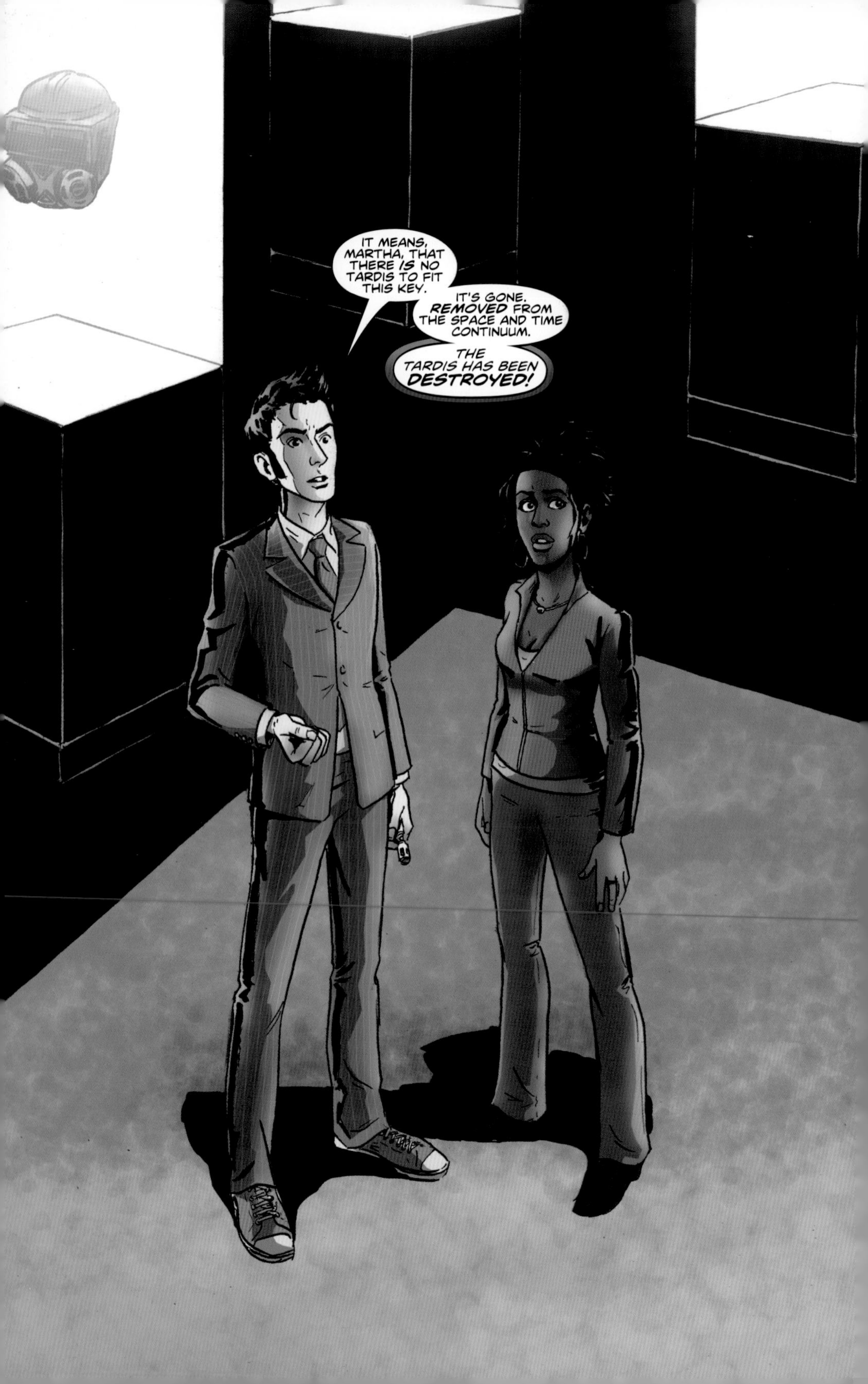
IT MEANS, MARTHA, THAT THERE IS NO TARDIS TO FIT THIS KEY.
IT'S GONE. REMOVED FROM THE SPACE AND TIME CONTINUUM.
THE TARDIS HAS BEEN DESTROYED!

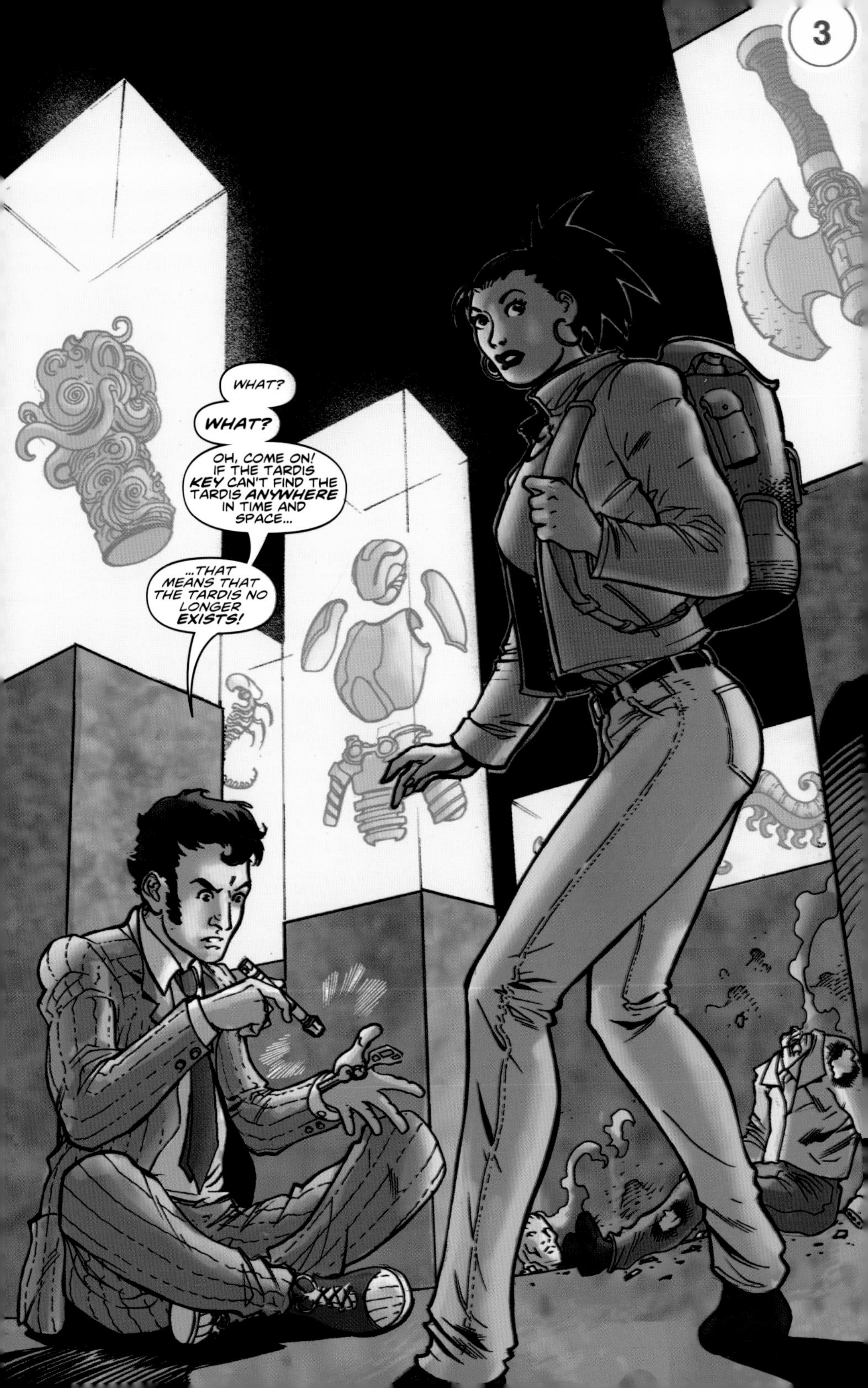
WHAT?
WHAT?
OH, COME ON! IF THE TARDIS KEY CAN'T FIND THE TARDIS ANYWHERE IN TIME AND SPACE...
...THAT MEANS THAT THE TARDIS NO LONGER EXISTS!

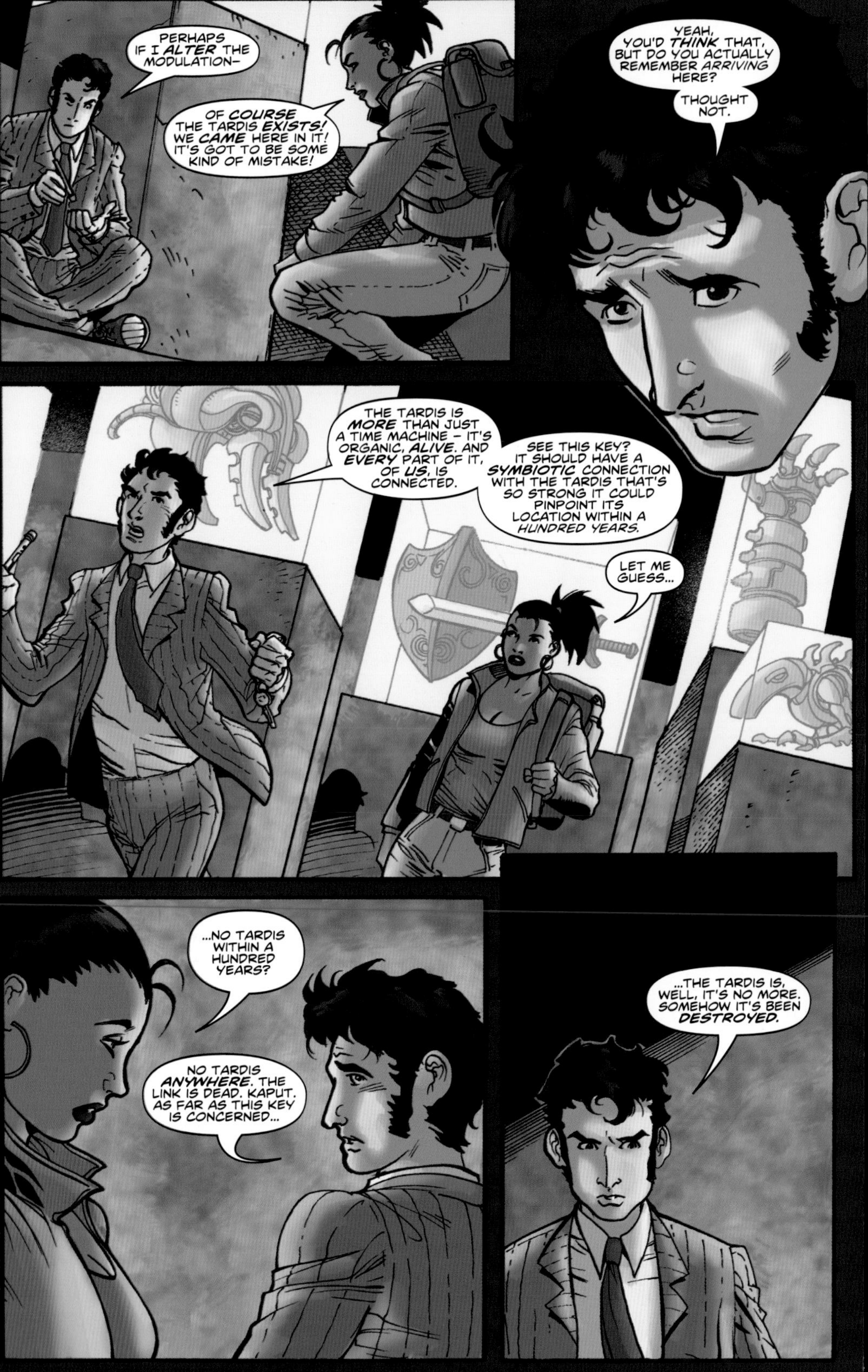
PERHAPS IF I ALTER THE MODULATION–
OF COURSE THE TARDIS EXISTS! WE CAME HERE IN IT! IT'S GOT TO BE SOME KIND OF MISTAKE!
YEAH, YOU'D THINK THAT, BUT DO YOU ACTUALLY REMEMBER ARRIVING HERE?
THOUGHT NOT.
THE TARDIS IS MORE THAN JUST A TIME MACHINE – IT'S ORGANIC, ALIVE. AND EVERY PART OF IT, OF US, IS CONNECTED.
SEE THIS KEY? IT SHOULD HAVE A SYMBIOTIC CONNECTION WITH THE TARDIS THAT'S SO STRONG IT COULD PINPOINT ITS LOCATION WITHIN A HUNDRED YEARS.
LET ME GUESS...
...NO TARDIS WITHIN A HUNDRED YEARS?
NO TARDIS ANYWHERE. THE LINK IS DEAD. KAPUT. AS FAR AS THIS KEY IS CONCERNED...
...THE TARDIS IS, WELL, IT'S NO MORE. SOMEHOW IT'S BEEN DESTROYED.

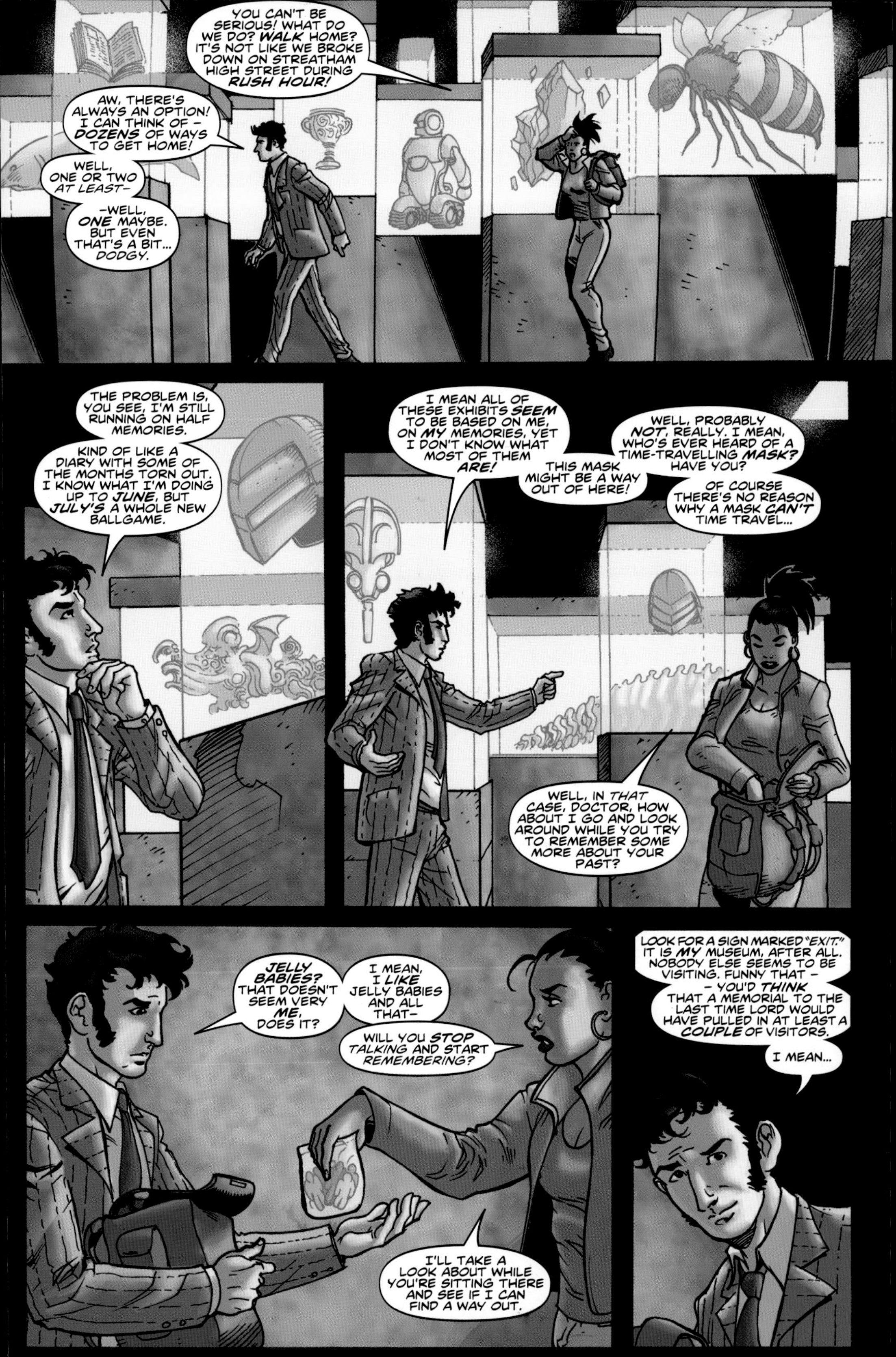
YOU CAN'T BE SERIOUS! WHAT DO WE DO? WALK HOME? IT'S NOT LIKE WE BROKE DOWN ON STREATHAM HIGH STREET DURING RUSH HOUR!
AW, THERE'S ALWAYS AN OPTION! I CAN THINK OF -- DOZENS OF WAYS TO GET HOME!
WELL, ONE OR TWO AT LEAST--
--WELL, ONE MAYBE. BUT EVEN THAT'S A BIT... DODGY.
THE PROBLEM IS, YOU SEE, I'M STILL RUNNING ON HALF MEMORIES.
KIND OF LIKE A DIARY WITH SOME OF THE MONTHS TORN OUT. I KNOW WHAT I'M DOING UP TO JUNE, BUT JULY'S A WHOLE NEW BALLGAME.
I MEAN ALL OF THESE EXHIBITS SEEM TO BE BASED ON ME, ON MY MEMORIES, YET I DON'T KNOW WHAT MOST OF THEM ARE!
THIS MASK MIGHT BE A WAY OUT OF HERE!
WELL, PROBABLY NOT, REALLY. I MEAN, WHO'S EVER HEARD OF A TIME-TRAVELLING MASK? HAVE YOU?
OF COURSE THERE'S NO REASON WHY A MASK CAN'T TIME TRAVEL...
WELL, IN THAT CASE, DOCTOR, HOW ABOUT I GO AND LOOK AROUND WHILE YOU TRY TO REMEMBER SOME MORE ABOUT YOUR PAST?
JELLY BABIES? THAT DOESN'T SEEM VERY ME, DOES IT?
I MEAN, I LIKE JELLY BABIES AND ALL THAT--
WILL YOU STOP TALKING AND START REMEMBERING?
I'LL TAKE A LOOK ABOUT WHILE YOU'RE SITTING THERE AND SEE IF I CAN FIND A WAY OUT.
LOOK FOR A SIGN MARKED "EXIT." IT IS MY MUSEUM, AFTER ALL. NOBODY ELSE SEEMS TO BE VISITING. FUNNY THAT -- YOU'D THINK THAT A MEMORIAL TO THE LAST TIME LORD WOULD HAVE PULLED IN AT LEAST A COUPLE OF VISITORS.
I MEAN...

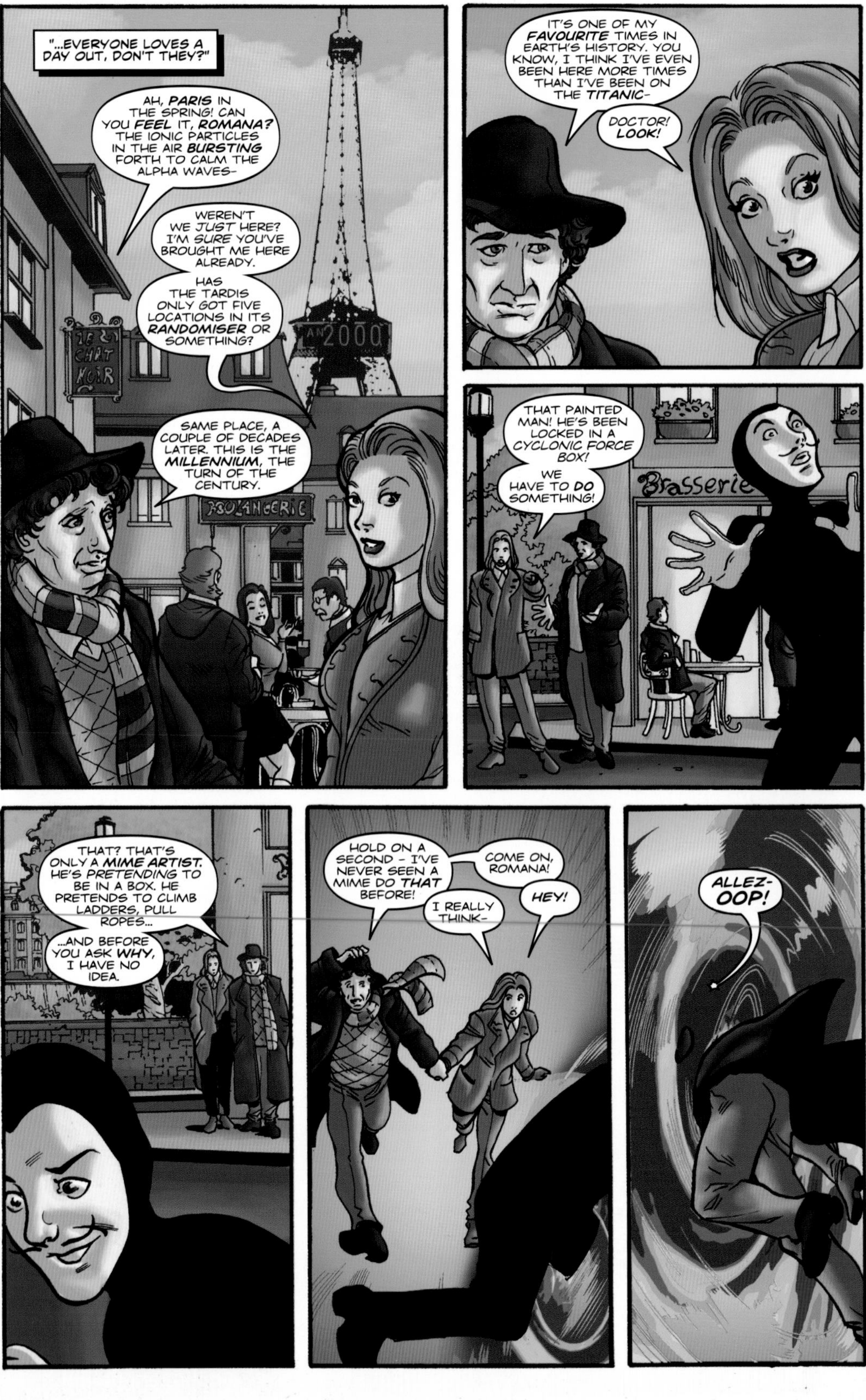
"...EVERYONE LOVES A DAY OUT, DON'T THEY?"
AH, PARIS IN THE SPRING! CAN YOU FEEL IT, ROMANA? THE IONIC PARTICLES IN THE AIR BURSTING FORTH TO CALM THE ALPHA WAVES-
WEREN'T WE JUST HERE? I'M SURE YOU'VE BROUGHT ME HERE ALREADY.
HAS THE TARDIS ONLY GOT FIVE LOCATIONS IN ITS RANDOMISER OR SOMETHING?
AN 2000
LE CHAT NOIR
SAME PLACE, A COUPLE OF DECADES LATER. THIS IS THE MILLENNIUM, THE TURN OF THE CENTURY.
BOULANGERIE
IT'S ONE OF MY FAVOURITE TIMES IN EARTH'S HISTORY. YOU KNOW, I THINK I'VE EVEN BEEN HERE MORE TIMES THAN I'VE BEEN ON THE TITANIC-
DOCTOR! LOOK!
THAT PAINTED MAN! HE'S BEEN LOCKED IN A CYCLONIC FORCE BOX!
WE HAVE TO DO SOMETHING!
Brasserie
THAT? THAT'S ONLY A MIME ARTIST. HE'S PRETENDING TO BE IN A BOX. HE PRETENDS TO CLIMB LADDERS, PULL ROPES...
...AND BEFORE YOU ASK WHY, I HAVE NO IDEA.
HOLD ON A SECOND - I'VE NEVER SEEN A MIME DO THAT BEFORE!
COME ON, ROMANA!
I REALLY THINK-
HEY!
ALLEZ-OOP!

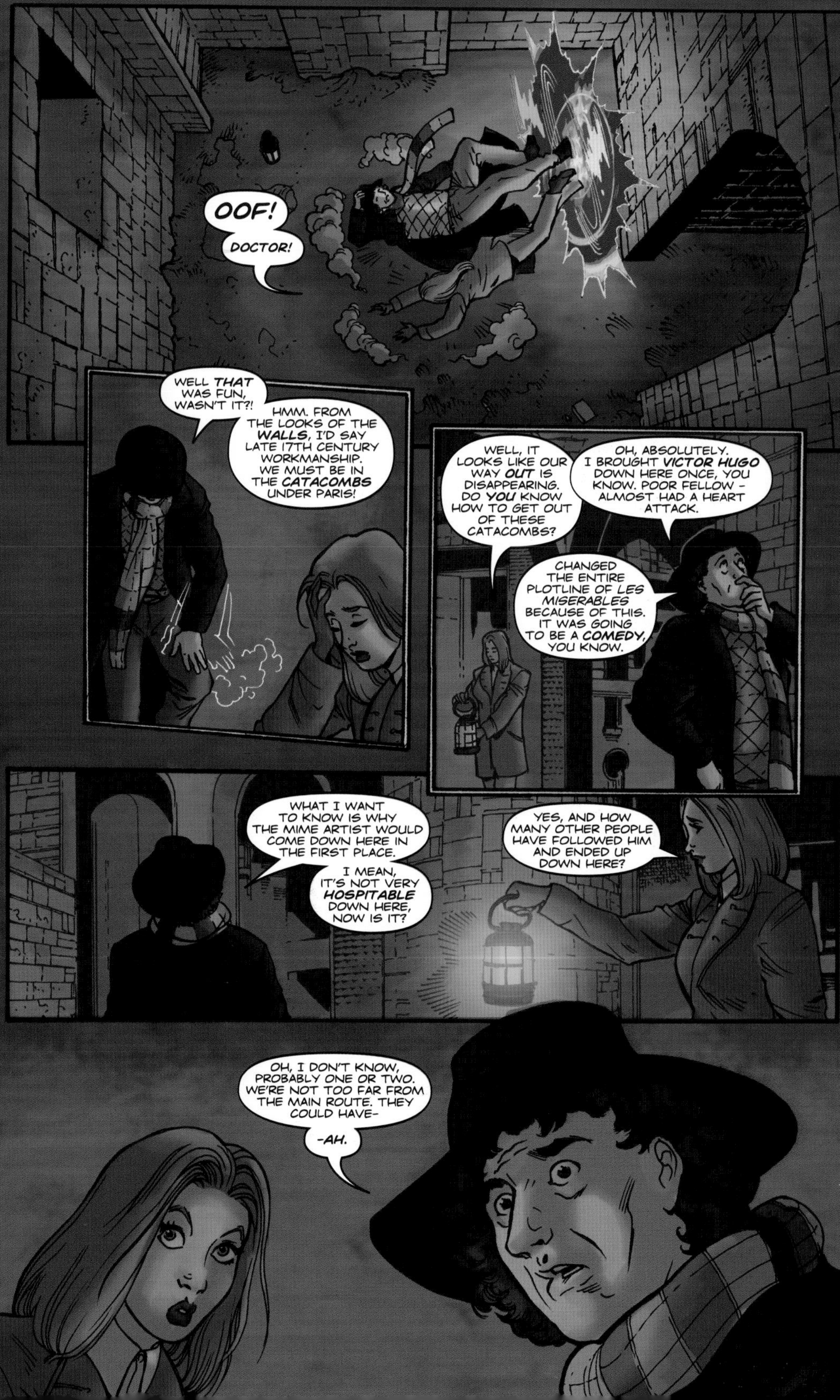
OOF!
DOCTOR!
WELL THAT WAS FUN, WASN'T IT?!
HMM. FROM THE LOOKS OF THE WALLS, I'D SAY LATE 17TH CENTURY WORKMANSHIP. WE MUST BE IN THE CATACOMBS UNDER PARIS!
WELL, IT LOOKS LIKE OUR WAY OUT IS DISAPPEARING. DO YOU KNOW HOW TO GET OUT OF THESE CATACOMBS?
OH, ABSOLUTELY. I BROUGHT VICTOR HUGO DOWN HERE ONCE, YOU KNOW. POOR FELLOW - ALMOST HAD A HEART ATTACK.
CHANGED THE ENTIRE PLOTLINE OF LES MISERABLES BECAUSE OF THIS. IT WAS GOING TO BE A COMEDY, YOU KNOW.
WHAT I WANT TO KNOW IS WHY THE MIME ARTIST WOULD COME DOWN HERE IN THE FIRST PLACE.
I MEAN, IT'S NOT VERY HOSPITABLE DOWN HERE, NOW IS IT?
YES, AND HOW MANY OTHER PEOPLE HAVE FOLLOWED HIM AND ENDED UP DOWN HERE?
OH, I DON'T KNOW, PROBABLY ONE OR TWO. WE'RE NOT TOO FAR FROM THE MAIN ROUTE. THEY COULD HAVE-
-AH.

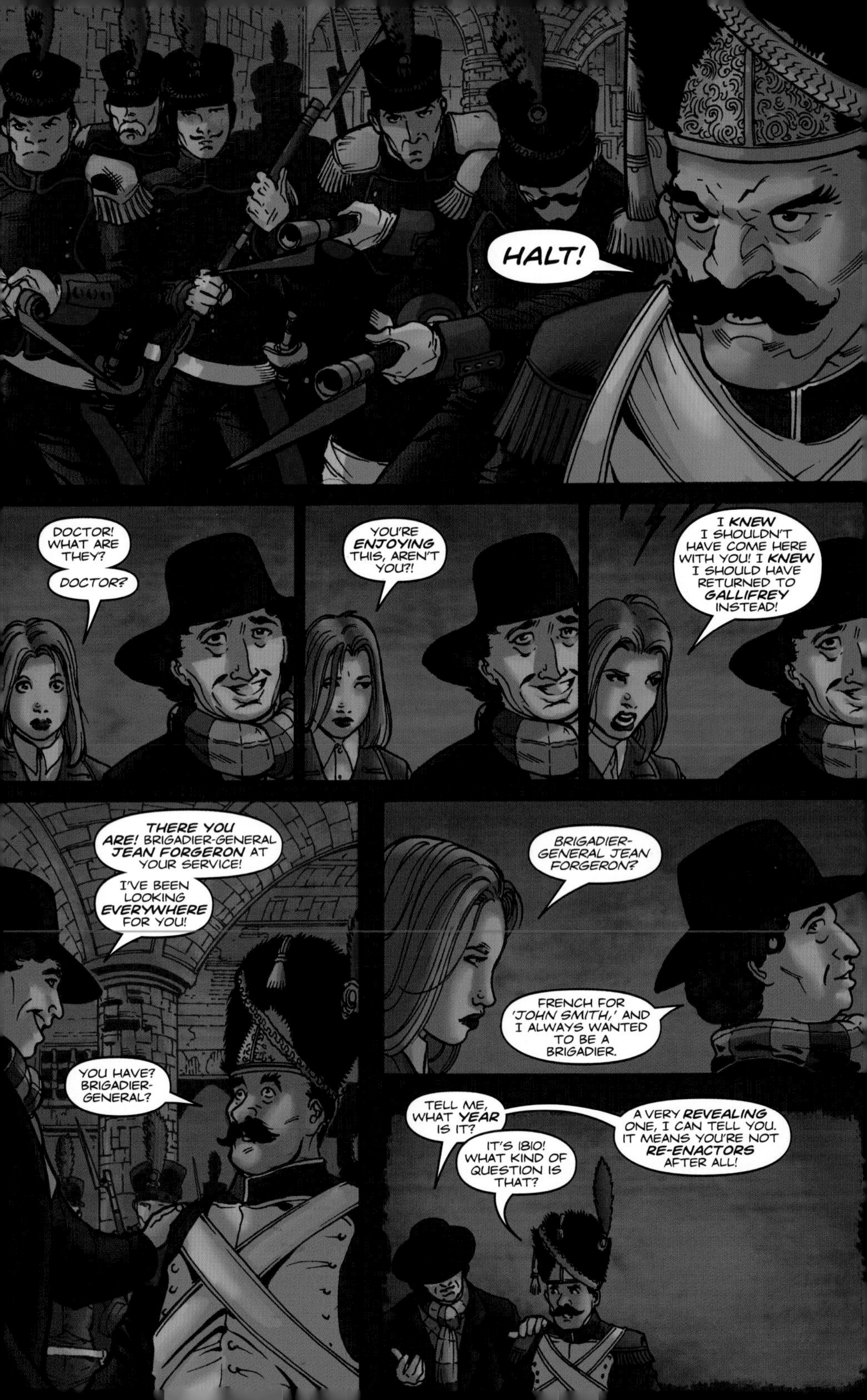
HALT!
DOCTOR! WHAT ARE THEY?
DOCTOR?
YOU'RE ENJOYING THIS, AREN'T YOU?!
I KNEW I SHOULDN'T HAVE COME HERE WITH YOU! I KNEW I SHOULD HAVE RETURNED TO GALLIFREY INSTEAD!
THERE YOU ARE! BRIGADIER-GENERAL JEAN FORGERON AT YOUR SERVICE!
I'VE BEEN LOOKING EVERYWHERE FOR YOU!
YOU HAVE? BRIGADIER-GENERAL?
BRIGADIER-GENERAL JEAN FORGERON?
FRENCH FOR 'JOHN SMITH,' AND I ALWAYS WANTED TO BE A BRIGADIER.
TELL ME, WHAT YEAR IS IT?
IT'S 1810! WHAT KIND OF QUESTION IS THAT?
A VERY REVEALING ONE, I CAN TELL YOU. IT MEANS YOU'RE NOT RE-ENACTORS AFTER ALL!

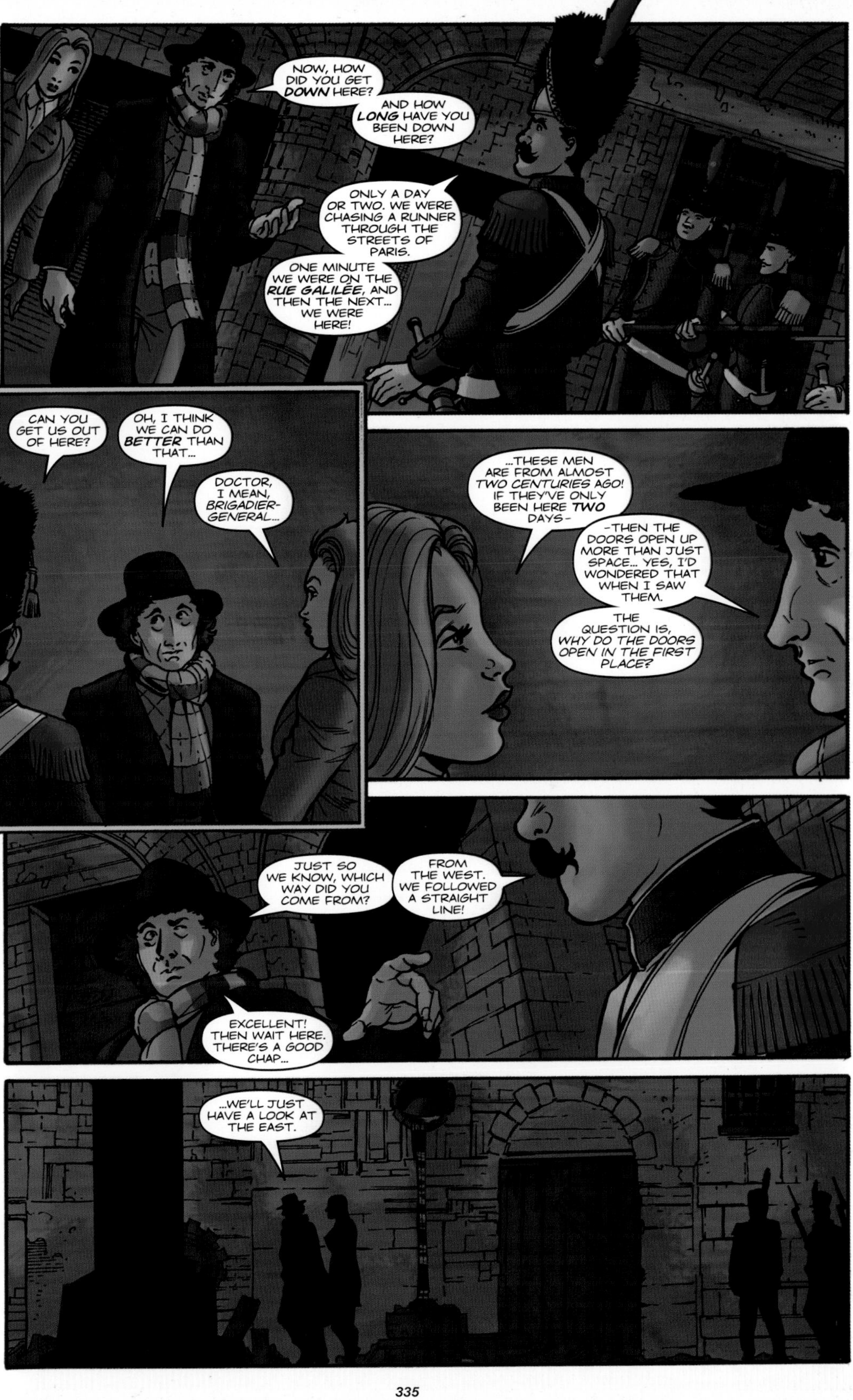
NOW, HOW DID YOU GET DOWN HERE?
AND HOW LONG HAVE YOU BEEN DOWN HERE?
ONLY A DAY OR TWO. WE WERE CHASING A RUNNER THROUGH THE STREETS OF PARIS.
ONE MINUTE WE WERE ON THE RUE GALILÉE, AND THEN THE NEXT... WE WERE HERE!
CAN YOU GET US OUT OF HERE?
OH, I THINK WE CAN DO BETTER THAN THAT...
DOCTOR, I MEAN, BRIGADIER-GENERAL...
...THESE MEN ARE FROM ALMOST TWO CENTURIES AGO! IF THEY'VE ONLY BEEN HERE TWO DAYS-
-THEN THE DOORS OPEN UP MORE THAN JUST SPACE... YES, I'D WONDERED THAT WHEN I SAW THEM.
THE QUESTION IS, WHY DO THE DOORS OPEN IN THE FIRST PLACE?
JUST SO WE KNOW, WHICH WAY DID YOU COME FROM?
FROM THE WEST. WE FOLLOWED A STRAIGHT LINE!
EXCELLENT! THEN WAIT HERE. THERE'S A GOOD CHAP...
...WE'LL JUST HAVE A LOOK AT THE EAST.

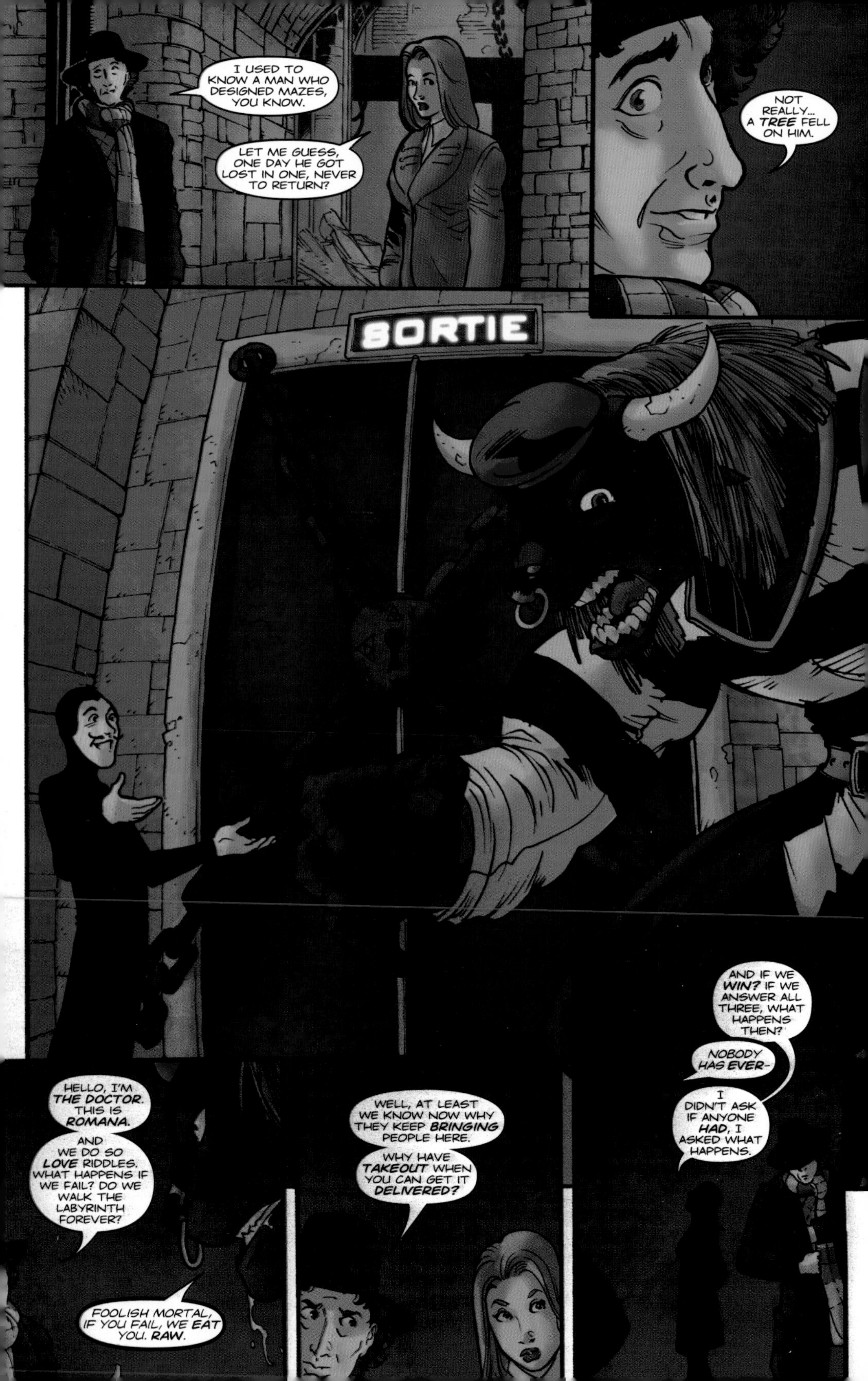
I USED TO KNOW A MAN WHO DESIGNED MAZES, YOU KNOW.
LET ME GUESS, ONE DAY HE GOT LOST IN ONE, NEVER TO RETURN?
NOT REALLY... A TREE FELL ON HIM.
SORTIE
HELLO, I'M THE DOCTOR. THIS IS ROMANA.
AND WE DO SO LOVE RIDDLES. WHAT HAPPENS IF WE FAIL? DO WE WALK THE LABYRINTH FOREVER?
FOOLISH MORTAL, IF YOU FAIL, WE EAT YOU. RAW.
WELL, AT LEAST WE KNOW NOW WHY THEY KEEP BRINGING PEOPLE HERE.
WHY HAVE TAKEOUT WHEN YOU CAN GET IT DELIVERED?
AND IF WE WIN? IF WE ANSWER ALL THREE, WHAT HAPPENS THEN?
NOBODY HAS EVER-
I DIDN'T ASK IF ANYONE HAD, I ASKED WHAT HAPPENS.

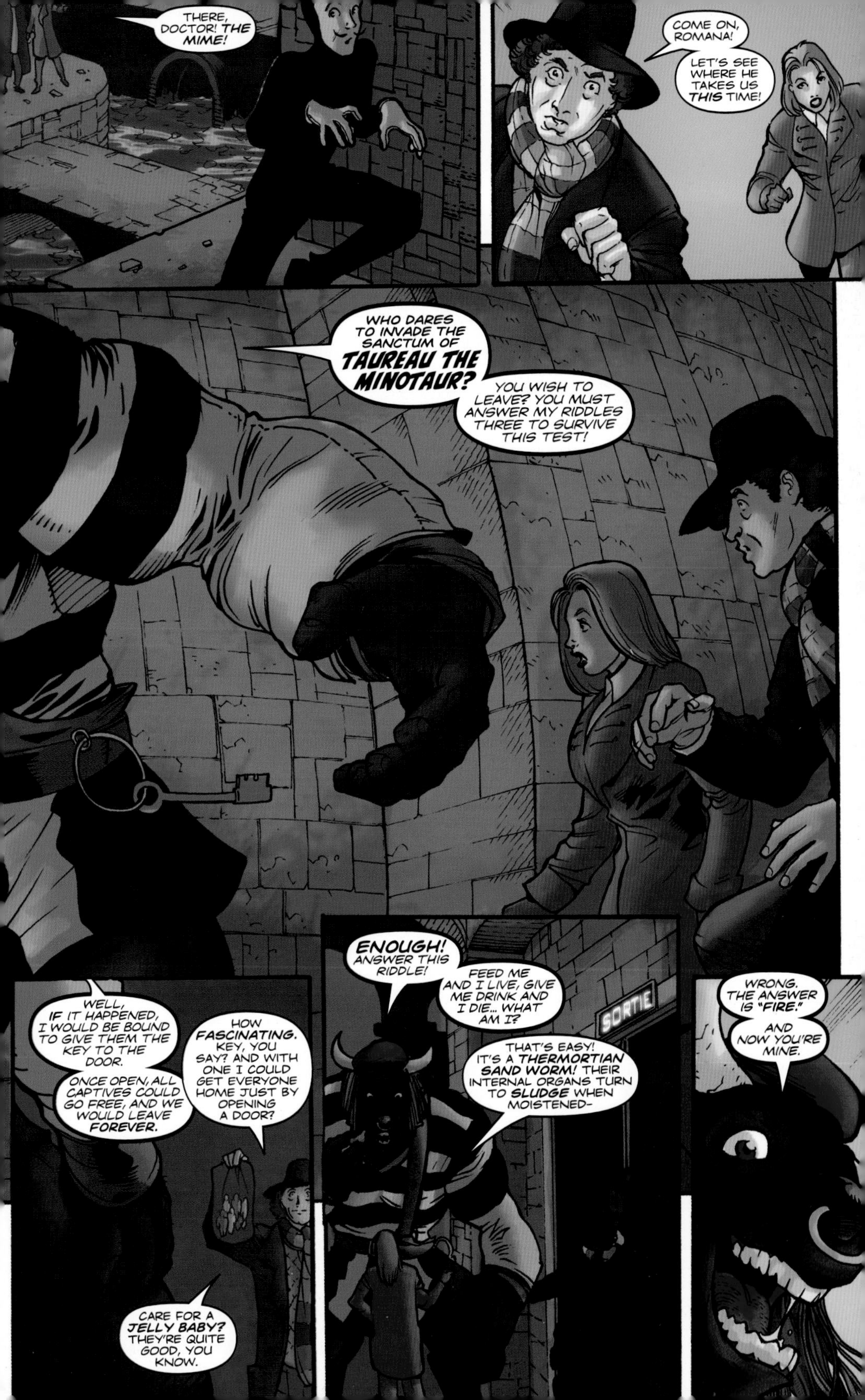

THERE, DOCTOR! THE MIME!
COME ON, ROMANA!
LET'S SEE WHERE HE TAKES US THIS TIME!
WHO DARES TO INVADE THE SANCTUM OF TAUREAU THE MINOTAUR?
YOU WISH TO LEAVE? YOU MUST ANSWER MY RIDDLES THREE TO SURVIVE THIS TEST!
WELL, IF IT HAPPENED, I WOULD BE BOUND TO GIVE THEM THE KEY TO THE DOOR.
ONCE OPEN, ALL CAPTIVES COULD GO FREE, AND WE WOULD LEAVE FOREVER.
HOW FASCINATING. KEY, YOU SAY? AND WITH ONE I COULD GET EVERYONE HOME JUST BY OPENING A DOOR?
CARE FOR A JELLY BABY? THEY'RE QUITE GOOD, YOU KNOW.
ENOUGH! ANSWER THIS RIDDLE!
FEED ME AND I LIVE, GIVE ME DRINK AND I DIE... WHAT AM I?
SORTIE
THAT'S EASY! IT'S A THERMORTIAN SAND WORM! THEIR INTERNAL ORGANS TURN TO SLUDGE WHEN MOISTENED-
WRONG. THE ANSWER IS "FIRE."
AND NOW YOU'RE MINE.

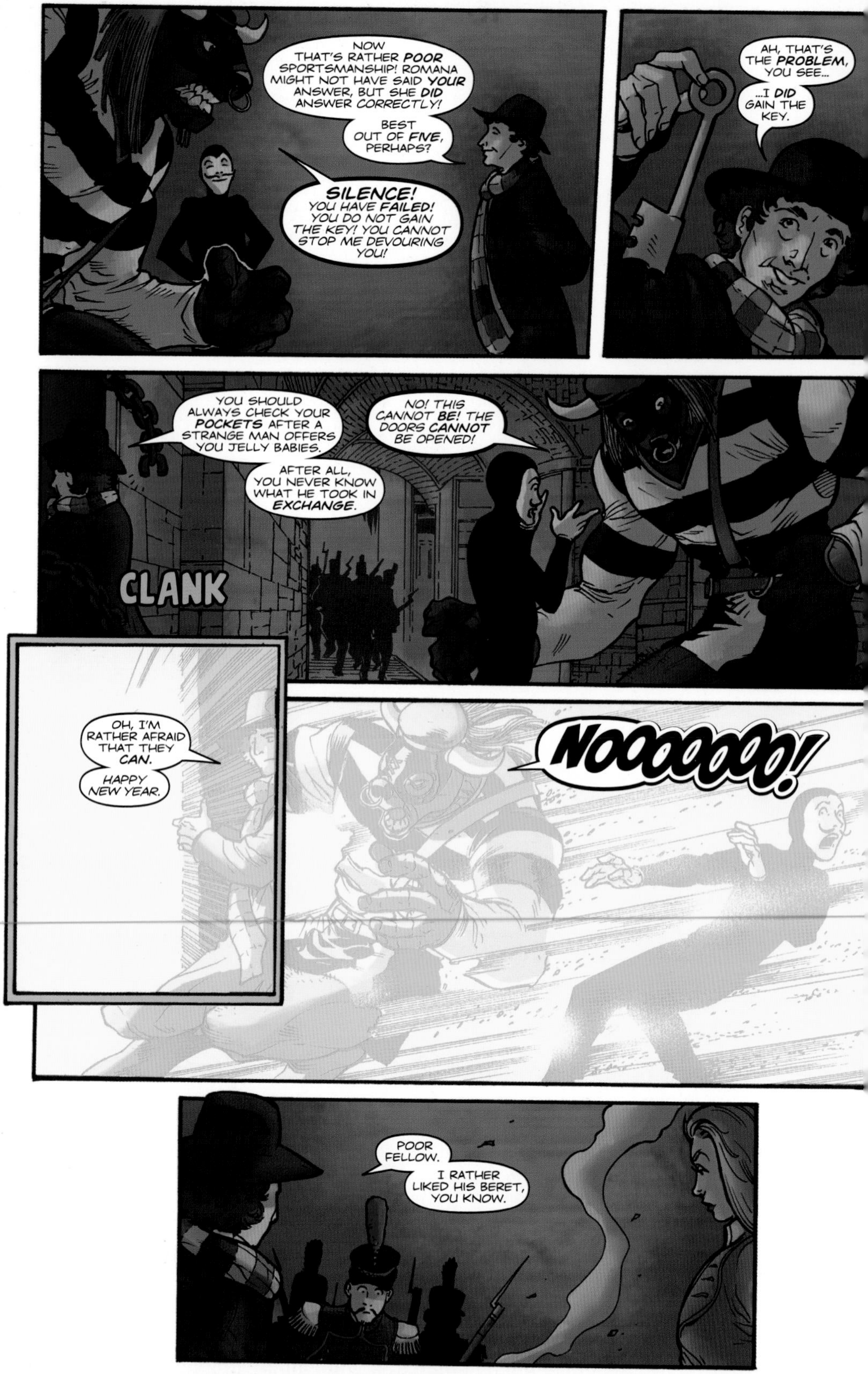
NOW THAT'S RATHER POOR SPORTSMANSHIP! ROMANA MIGHT NOT HAVE SAID YOUR ANSWER, BUT SHE DID ANSWER CORRECTLY!
BEST OUT OF FIVE, PERHAPS?
SILENCE! YOU HAVE FAILED! YOU DO NOT GAIN THE KEY! YOU CANNOT STOP ME DEVOURING YOU!
AH, THAT'S THE PROBLEM, YOU SEE...
...I DID GAIN THE KEY.
YOU SHOULD ALWAYS CHECK YOUR POCKETS AFTER A STRANGE MAN OFFERS YOU JELLY BABIES.
AFTER ALL, YOU NEVER KNOW WHAT HE TOOK IN EXCHANGE.
NO! THIS CANNOT BE! THE DOORS CANNOT BE OPENED!
CLANK
OH, I'M RATHER AFRAID THAT THEY CAN.
HAPPY NEW YEAR.
NOOOOOOO!
POOR FELLOW.
I RATHER LIKED HIS BERET, YOU KNOW.

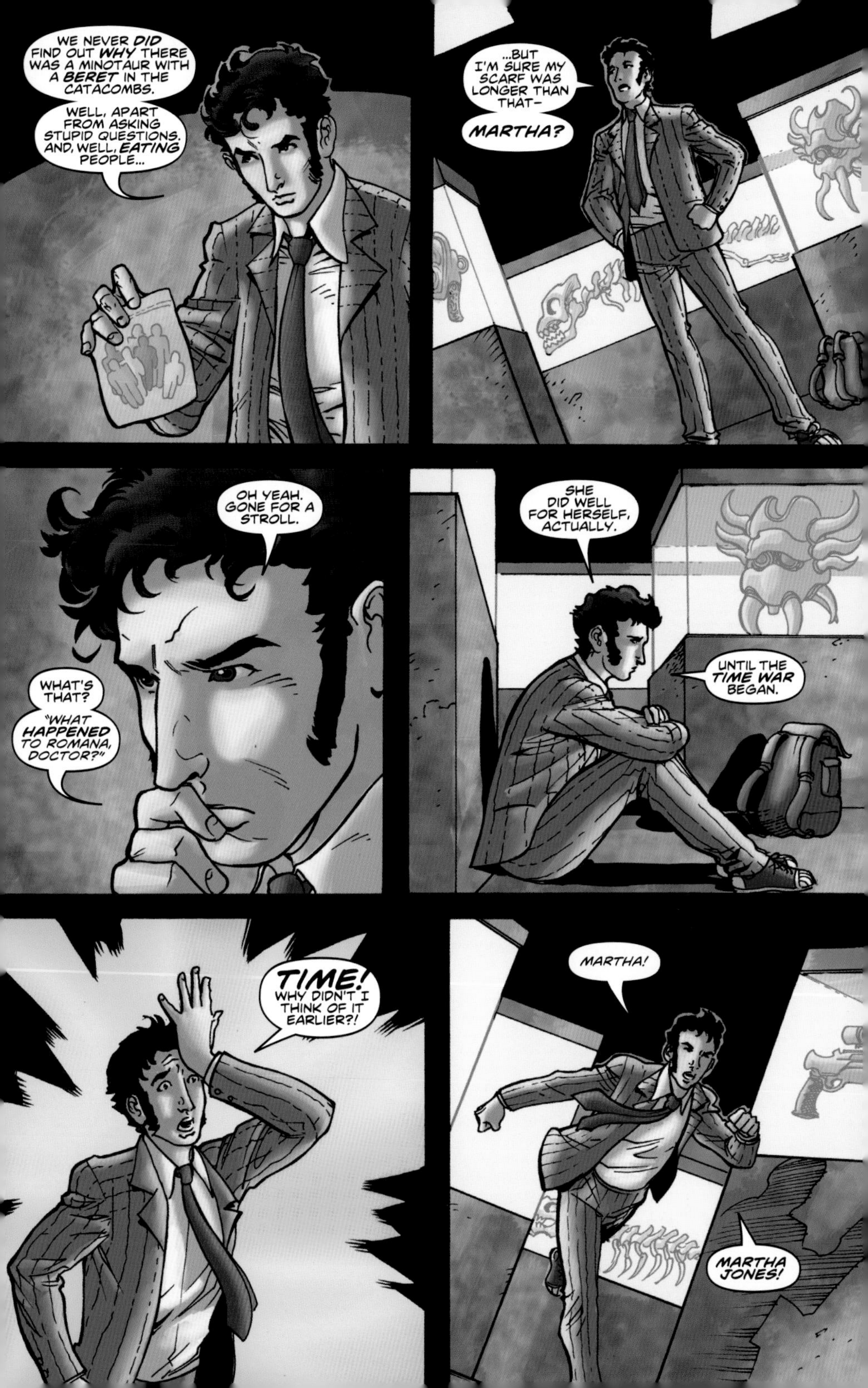
WE NEVER DID FIND OUT WHY THERE WAS A MINOTAUR WITH A BERET IN THE CATACOMBS.
WELL, APART FROM ASKING STUPID QUESTIONS. AND, WELL, EATING PEOPLE...
...BUT I'M SURE MY SCARF WAS LONGER THAN THAT–
MARTHA?
OH YEAH. GONE FOR A STROLL.
WHAT'S THAT? "WHAT HAPPENED TO ROMANA, DOCTOR?"
SHE DID WELL FOR HERSELF, ACTUALLY.
UNTIL THE TIME WAR BEGAN.
TIME! WHY DIDN'T I THINK OF IT EARLIER?!
MARTHA!
MARTHA JONES!

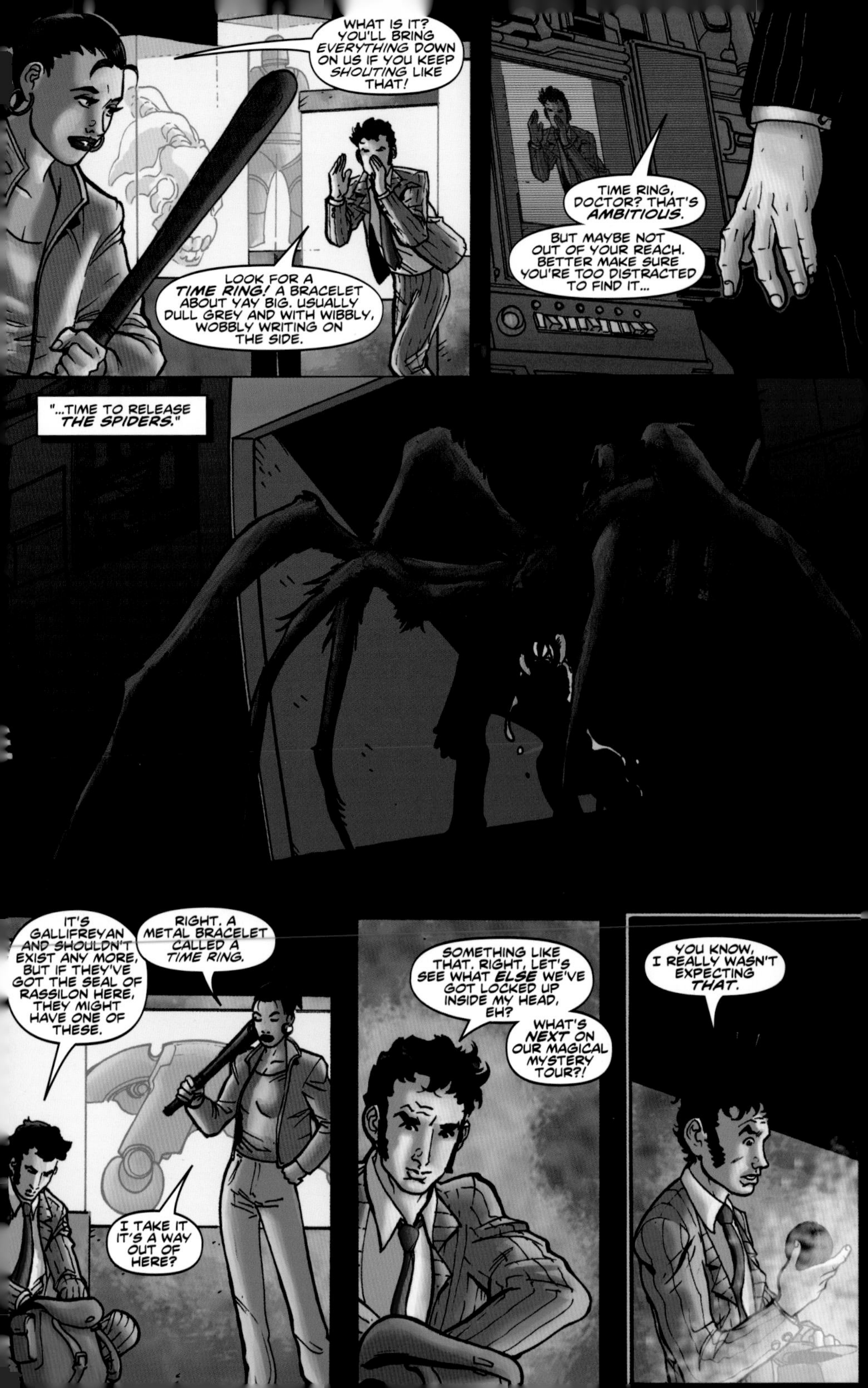
WHAT IS IT? YOU'LL BRING EVERYTHING DOWN ON US IF YOU KEEP SHOUTING LIKE THAT!
LOOK FOR A TIME RING! A BRACELET ABOUT YAY BIG. USUALLY DULL GREY AND WITH WIBBLY, WOBBLY WRITING ON THE SIDE.
TIME RING, DOCTOR? THAT'S AMBITIOUS.
BUT MAYBE NOT OUT OF YOUR REACH. BETTER MAKE SURE YOU'RE TOO DISTRACTED TO FIND IT...
"...TIME TO RELEASE THE SPIDERS."
IT'S GALLIFREYAN AND SHOULDN'T EXIST ANY MORE, BUT IF THEY'VE GOT THE SEAL OF RASSILON HERE, THEY MIGHT HAVE ONE OF THESE.
RIGHT. A METAL BRACELET CALLED A TIME RING.
I TAKE IT IT'S A WAY OUT OF HERE?
SOMETHING LIKE THAT. RIGHT, LET'S SEE WHAT ELSE WE'VE GOT LOCKED UP INSIDE MY HEAD, EH?
WHAT'S NEXT ON OUR MAGICAL MYSTERY TOUR?!
YOU KNOW, I REALLY WASN'T EXPECTING THAT.

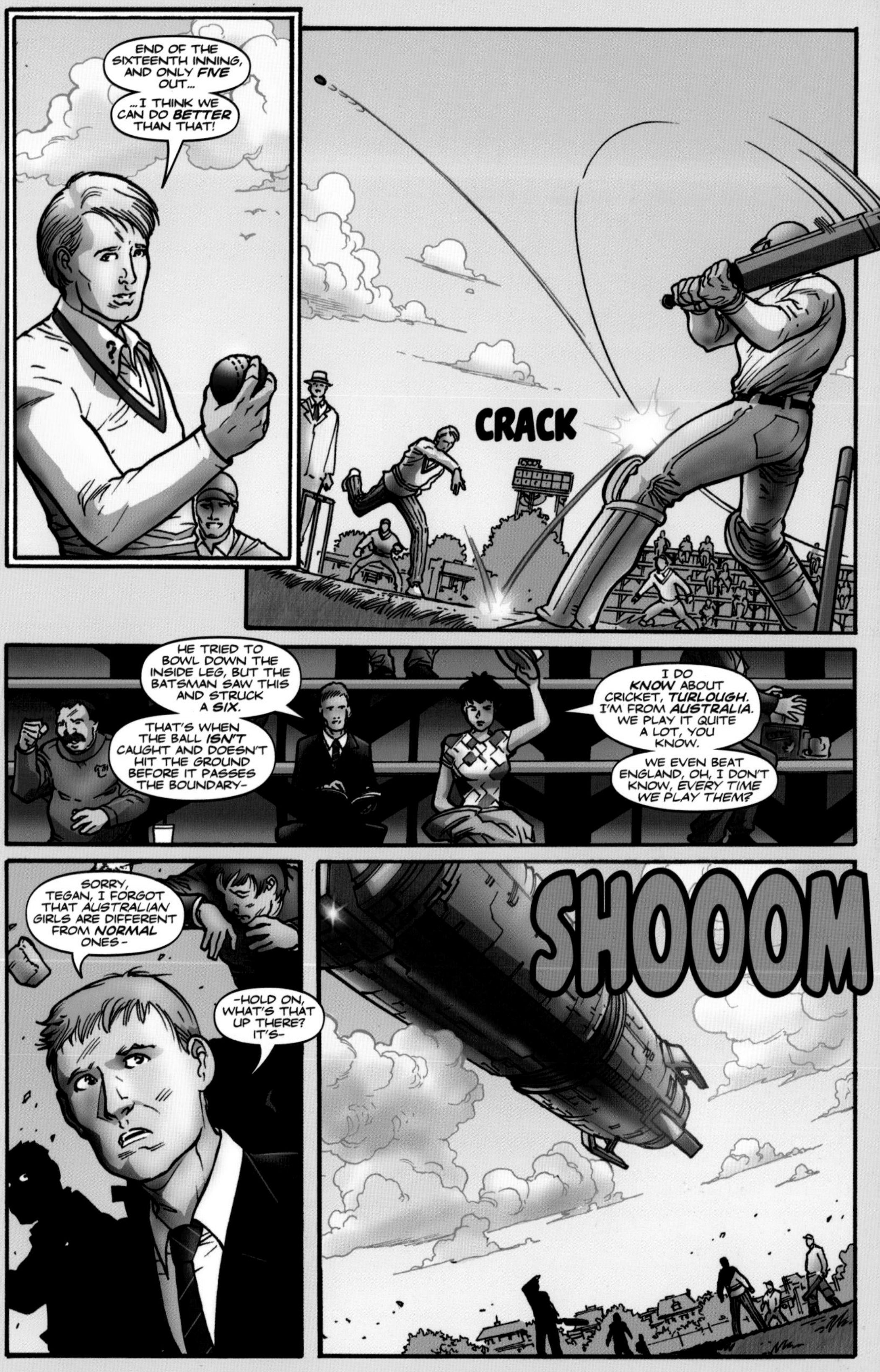

END OF THE SIXTEENTH INNING, AND ONLY FIVE OUT...
...I THINK WE CAN DO BETTER THAN THAT!
CRACK
HE TRIED TO BOWL DOWN THE INSIDE LEG, BUT THE BATSMAN SAW THIS AND STRUCK A SIX.
THAT'S WHEN THE BALL ISN'T CAUGHT AND DOESN'T HIT THE GROUND BEFORE IT PASSES THE BOUNDARY-
I DO KNOW ABOUT CRICKET, TURLOUGH. I'M FROM AUSTRALIA. WE PLAY IT QUITE A LOT, YOU KNOW.
WE EVEN BEAT ENGLAND, OH, I DON'T KNOW, EVERY TIME WE PLAY THEM?
SORRY, TEGAN, I FORGOT THAT AUSTRALIAN GIRLS ARE DIFFERENT FROM NORMAL ONES-
-HOLD ON, WHAT'S THAT UP THERE? IT'S-
SHOOOM

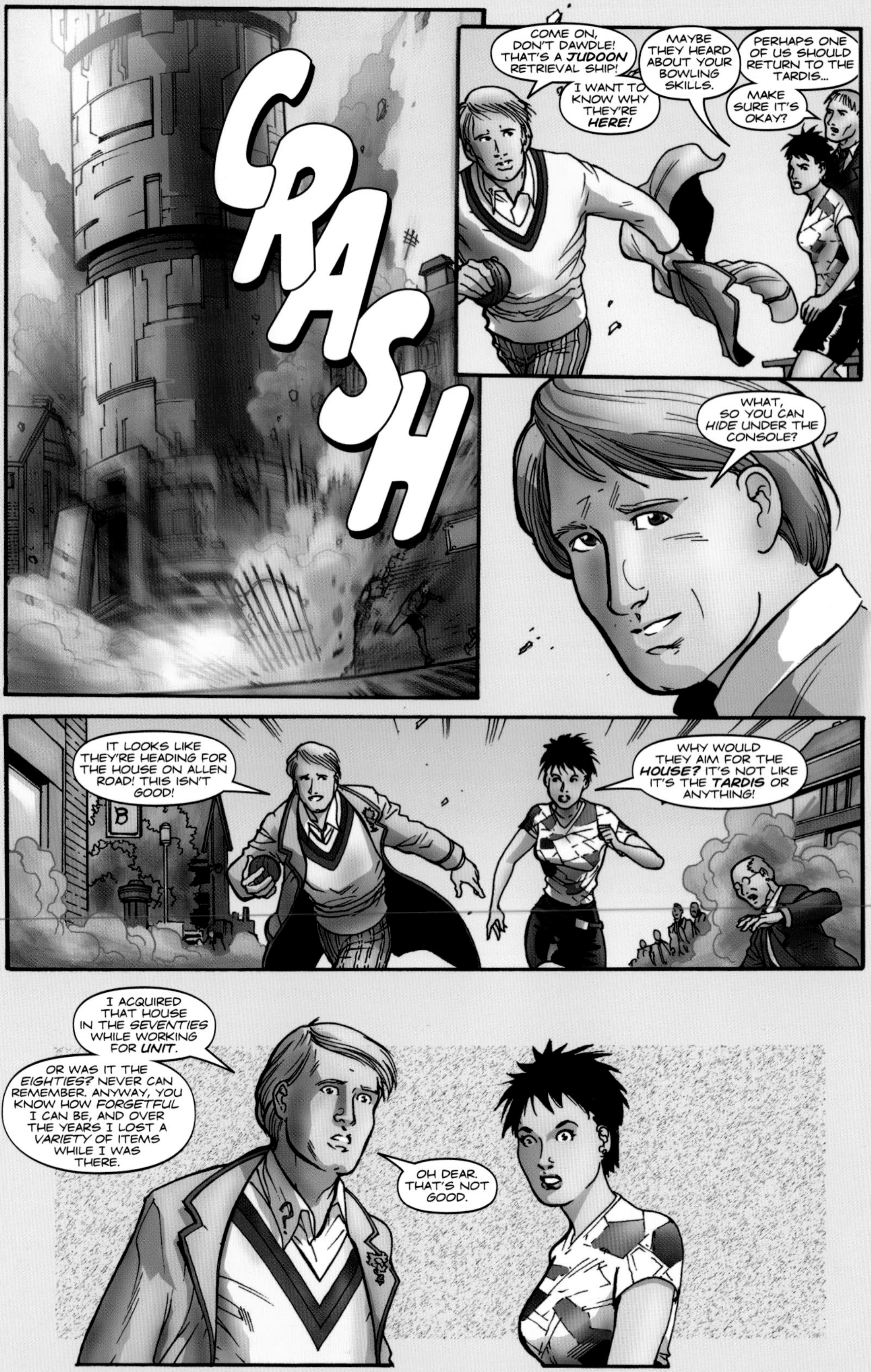
CRASH
COME ON, DON'T DAWDLE! THAT'S A JUDOON RETRIEVAL SHIP!
I WANT TO KNOW WHY THEY'RE HERE!
MAYBE THEY HEARD ABOUT YOUR BOWLING SKILLS.
PERHAPS ONE OF US SHOULD RETURN TO THE TARDIS...
MAKE SURE IT'S OKAY?
WHAT, SO YOU CAN HIDE UNDER THE CONSOLE?
IT LOOKS LIKE THEY'RE HEADING FOR THE HOUSE ON ALLEN ROAD! THIS ISN'T GOOD!
WHY WOULD THEY AIM FOR THE HOUSE? IT'S NOT LIKE IT'S THE TARDIS OR ANYTHING!
I ACQUIRED THAT HOUSE IN THE SEVENTIES WHILE WORKING FOR UNIT.
OR WAS IT THE EIGHTIES? NEVER CAN REMEMBER. ANYWAY, YOU KNOW HOW FORGETFUL I CAN BE, AND OVER THE YEARS I LOST A VARIETY OF ITEMS WHILE I WAS THERE.
OH DEAR. THAT'S NOT GOOD.

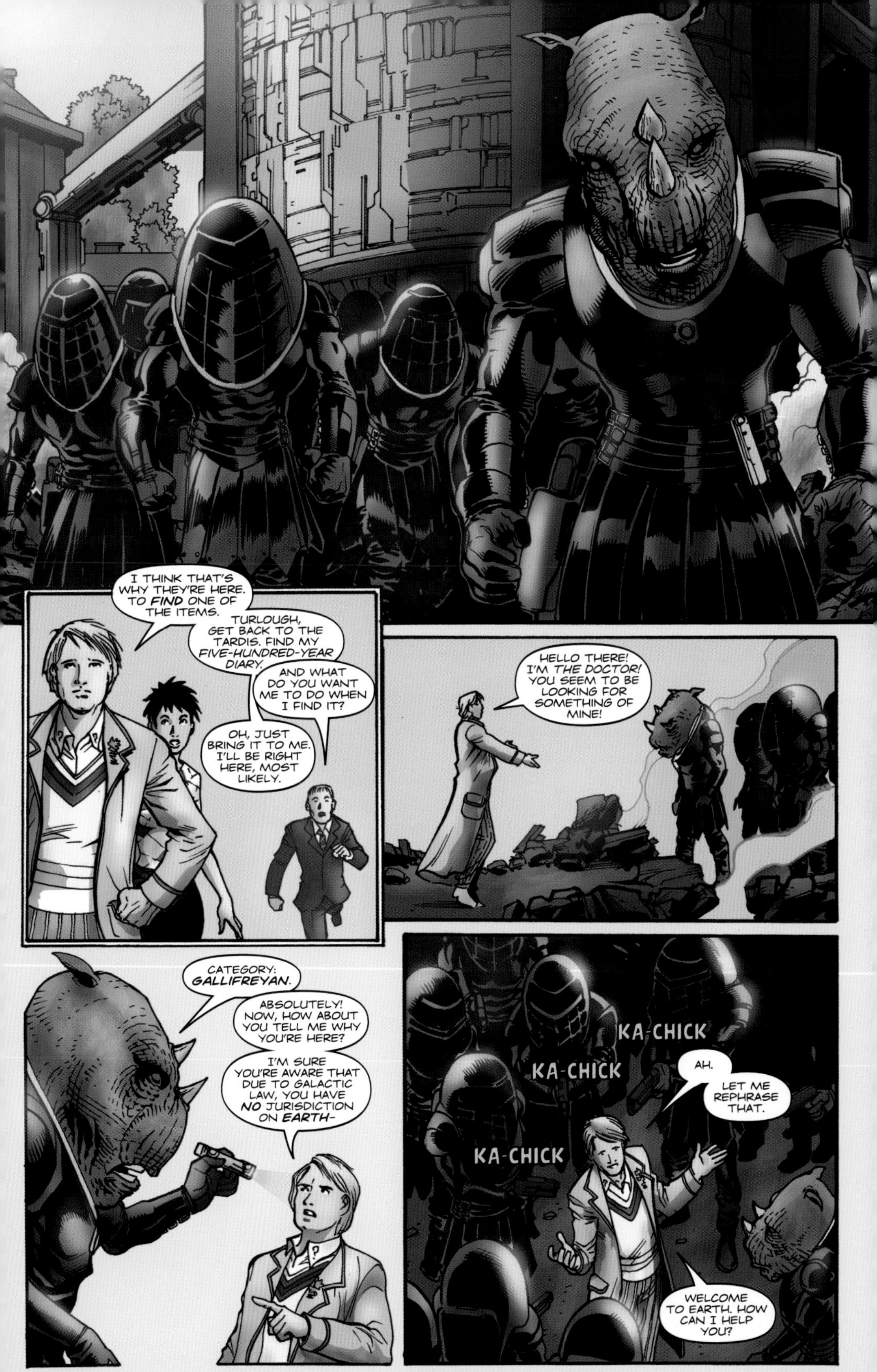
I THINK THAT'S WHY THEY'RE HERE. TO FIND ONE OF THE ITEMS.
TURLOUGH, GET BACK TO THE TARDIS. FIND MY FIVE-HUNDRED-YEAR DIARY.
AND WHAT DO YOU WANT ME TO DO WHEN I FIND IT?
OH, JUST BRING IT TO ME. I'LL BE RIGHT HERE, MOST LIKELY.
HELLO THERE! I'M THE DOCTOR! YOU SEEM TO BE LOOKING FOR SOMETHING OF MINE!
CATEGORY: GALLIFREYAN.
ABSOLUTELY! NOW, HOW ABOUT YOU TELL ME WHY YOU'RE HERE?
I'M SURE YOU'RE AWARE THAT DUE TO GALACTIC LAW, YOU HAVE NO JURISDICTION ON EARTH-
KA-CHICK
KA-CHICK
KA-CHICK
AH.
LET ME REPHRASE THAT.
WELCOME TO EARTH. HOW CAN I HELP YOU?

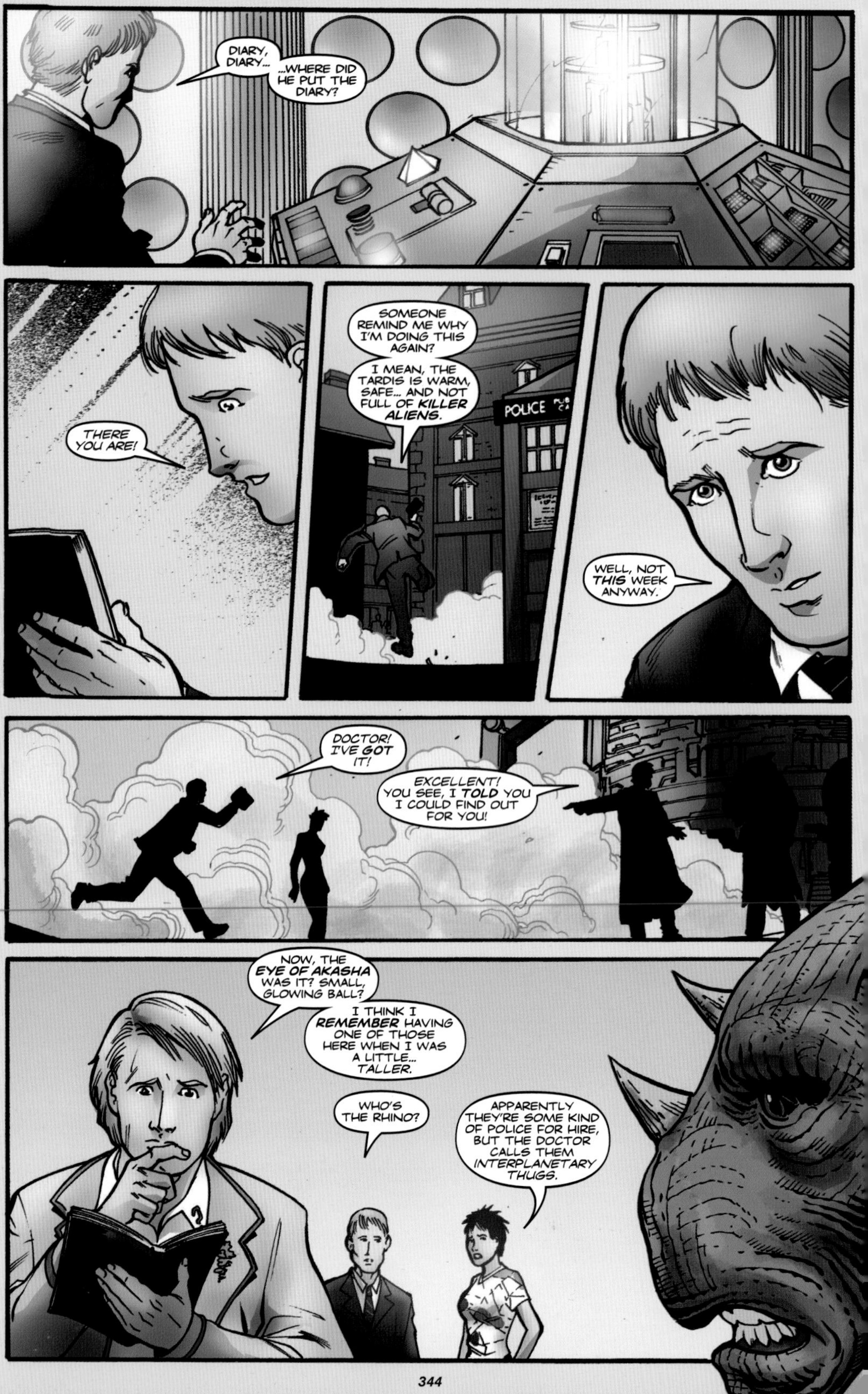
DIARY, DIARY...
...WHERE DID HE PUT THE DIARY?
THERE YOU ARE!
SOMEONE REMIND ME WHY I'M DOING THIS AGAIN?
I MEAN, THE TARDIS IS WARM, SAFE... AND NOT FULL OF KILLER ALIENS.
POLICE
WELL, NOT THIS WEEK ANYWAY.
DOCTOR! I'VE GOT IT!
EXCELLENT! YOU SEE, I TOLD YOU I COULD FIND OUT FOR YOU!
NOW, THE EYE OF AKASHA WAS IT? SMALL, GLOWING BALL?
I THINK I REMEMBER HAVING ONE OF THOSE HERE WHEN I WAS A LITTLE... TALLER.
WHO'S THE RHINO?
APPARENTLY THEY'RE SOME KIND OF POLICE FOR HIRE, BUT THE DOCTOR CALLS THEM INTERPLANETARY THUGS.

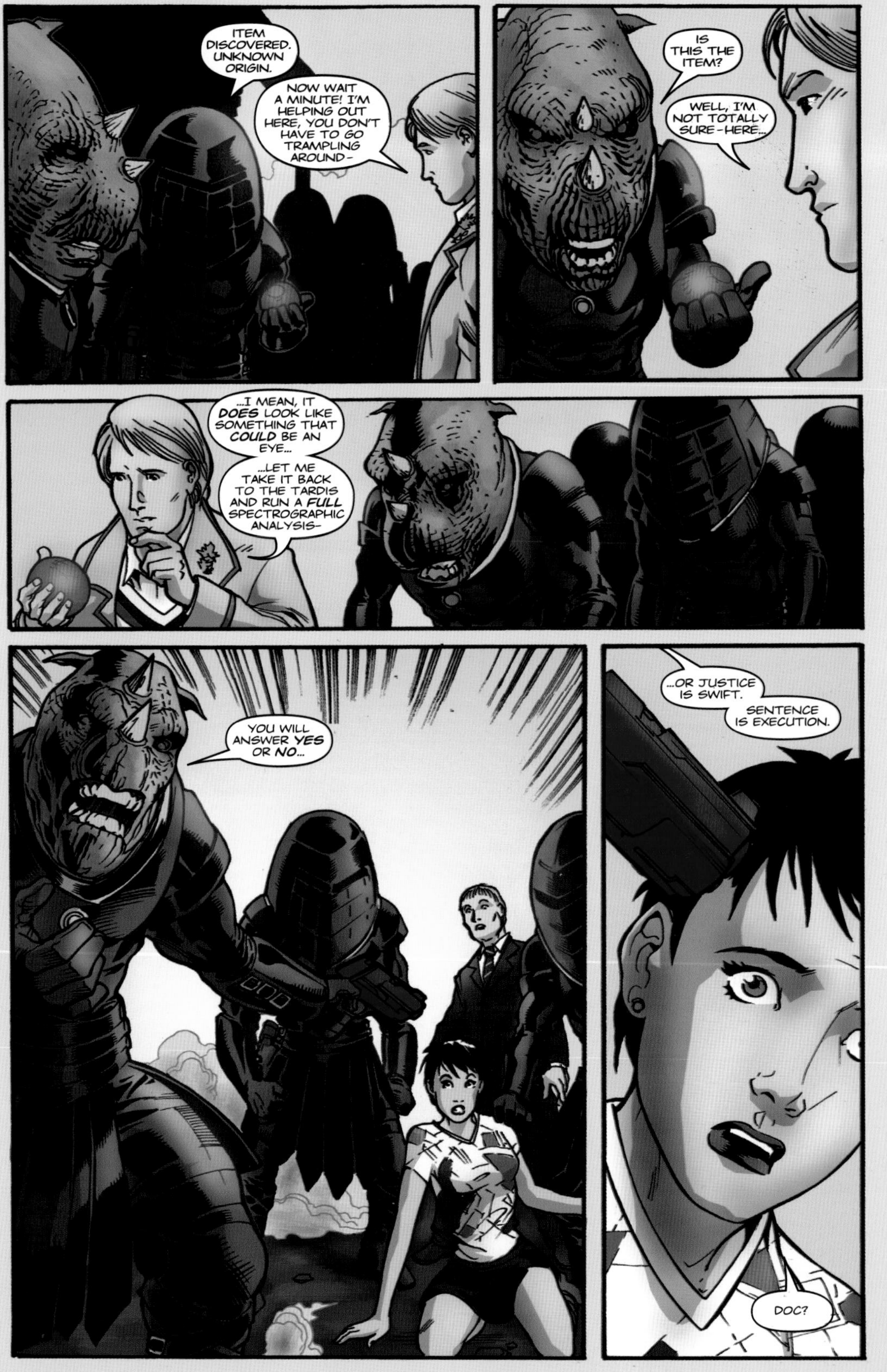
ITEM DISCOVERED. UNKNOWN ORIGIN.
NOW WAIT A MINUTE! I'M HELPING OUT HERE, YOU DON'T HAVE TO GO TRAMPLING AROUND-
IS THIS THE ITEM?
WELL, I'M NOT TOTALLY SURE-HERE...
...I MEAN, IT DOES LOOK LIKE SOMETHING THAT COULD BE AN EYE...
...LET ME TAKE IT BACK TO THE TARDIS AND RUN A FULL SPECTROGRAPHIC ANALYSIS-
YOU WILL ANSWER YES OR NO...
...OR JUSTICE IS SWIFT.
SENTENCE IS EXECUTION.
DOC?

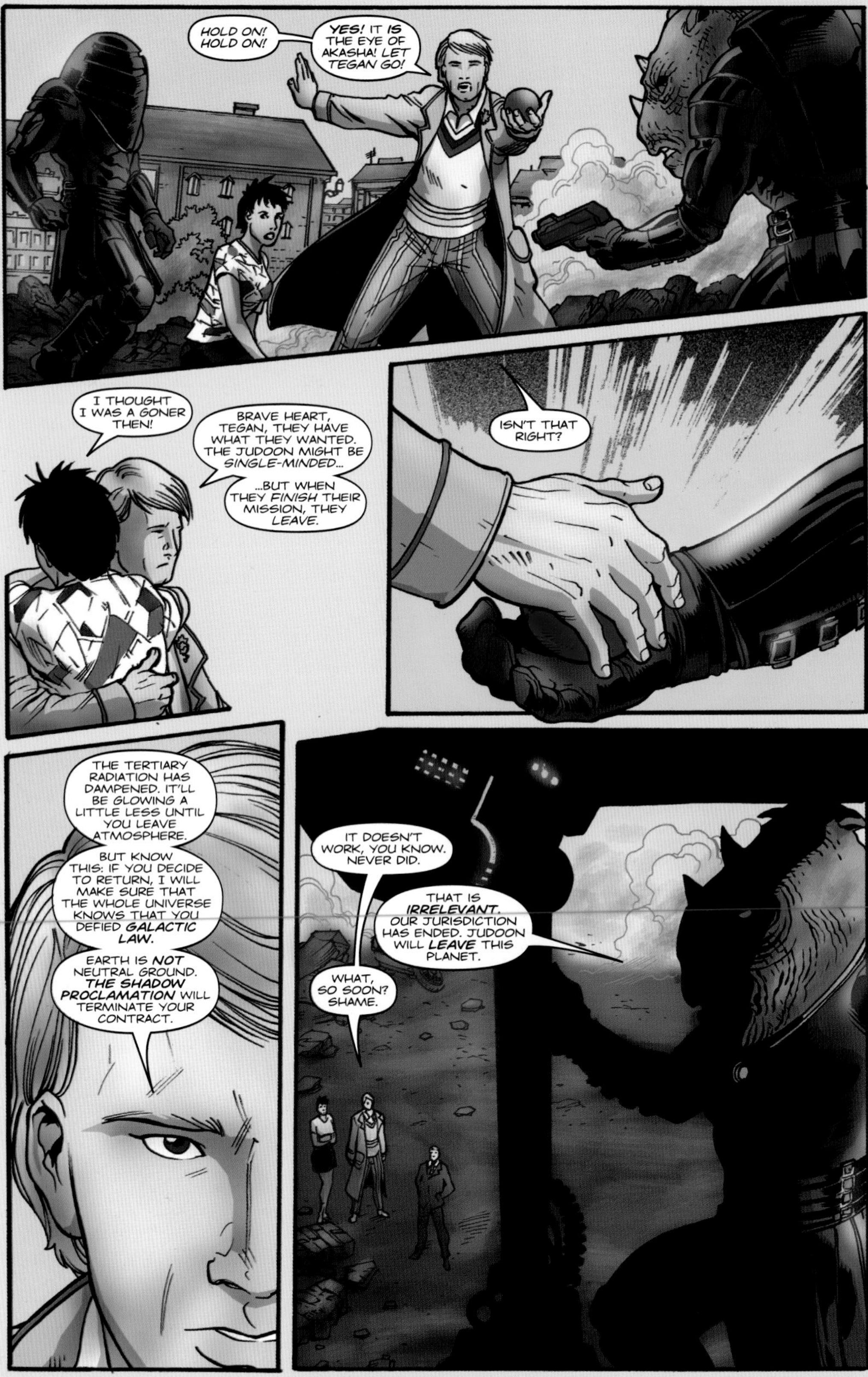
HOLD ON! HOLD ON!
YES! IT IS THE EYE OF AKASHA! LET TEGAN GO!
I THOUGHT I WAS A GONER THEN!
BRAVE HEART, TEGAN, THEY HAVE WHAT THEY WANTED. THE JUDOON MIGHT BE SINGLE-MINDED...
...BUT WHEN THEY FINISH THEIR MISSION, THEY LEAVE.
ISN'T THAT RIGHT?
THE TERTIARY RADIATION HAS DAMPENED. IT'LL BE GLOWING A LITTLE LESS UNTIL YOU LEAVE ATMOSPHERE.
BUT KNOW THIS: IF YOU DECIDE TO RETURN, I WILL MAKE SURE THAT THE WHOLE UNIVERSE KNOWS THAT YOU DEFIED GALACTIC LAW.
EARTH IS NOT NEUTRAL GROUND. THE SHADOW PROCLAMATION WILL TERMINATE YOUR CONTRACT.
IT DOESN'T WORK, YOU KNOW. NEVER DID.
THAT IS IRRELEVANT. OUR JURISDICTION HAS ENDED. JUDOON WILL LEAVE THIS PLANET.
WHAT, SO SOON? SHAME.

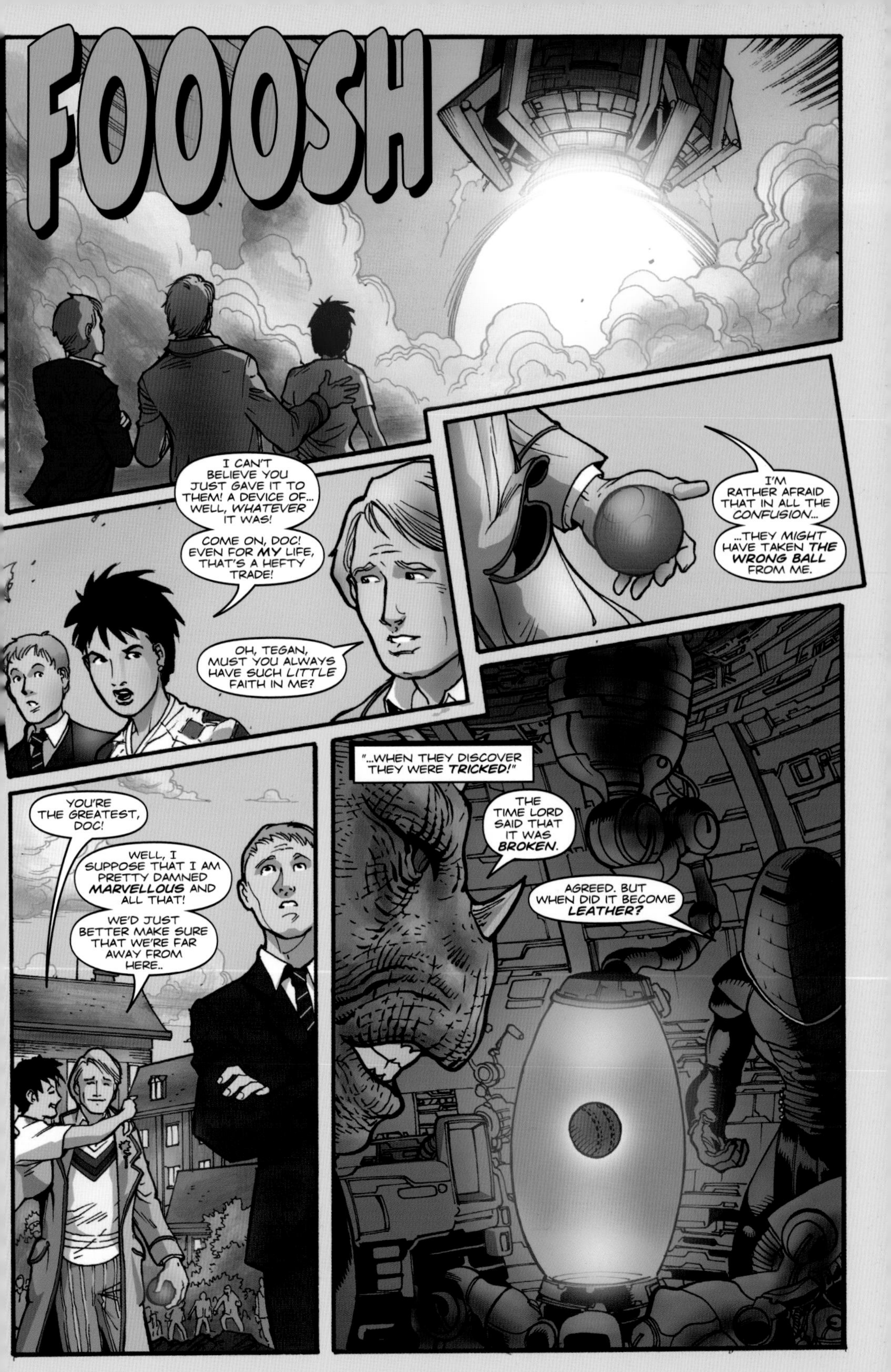
FOOOSH
I CAN'T BELIEVE YOU JUST GAVE IT TO THEM! A DEVICE OF... WELL, WHATEVER IT WAS!
COME ON, DOC! EVEN FOR MY LIFE, THAT'S A HEFTY TRADE!
OH, TEGAN, MUST YOU ALWAYS HAVE SUCH LITTLE FAITH IN ME?
I'M RATHER AFRAID THAT IN ALL THE CONFUSION...
...THEY MIGHT HAVE TAKEN THE WRONG BALL FROM ME.
YOU'RE THE GREATEST, DOC!
WELL, I SUPPOSE THAT I AM PRETTY DAMNED MARVELLOUS AND ALL THAT!
WE'D JUST BETTER MAKE SURE THAT WE'RE FAR AWAY FROM HERE..
"...WHEN THEY DISCOVER THEY WERE TRICKED!"
THE TIME LORD SAID THAT IT WAS BROKEN.
AGREED. BUT WHEN DID IT BECOME LEATHER?

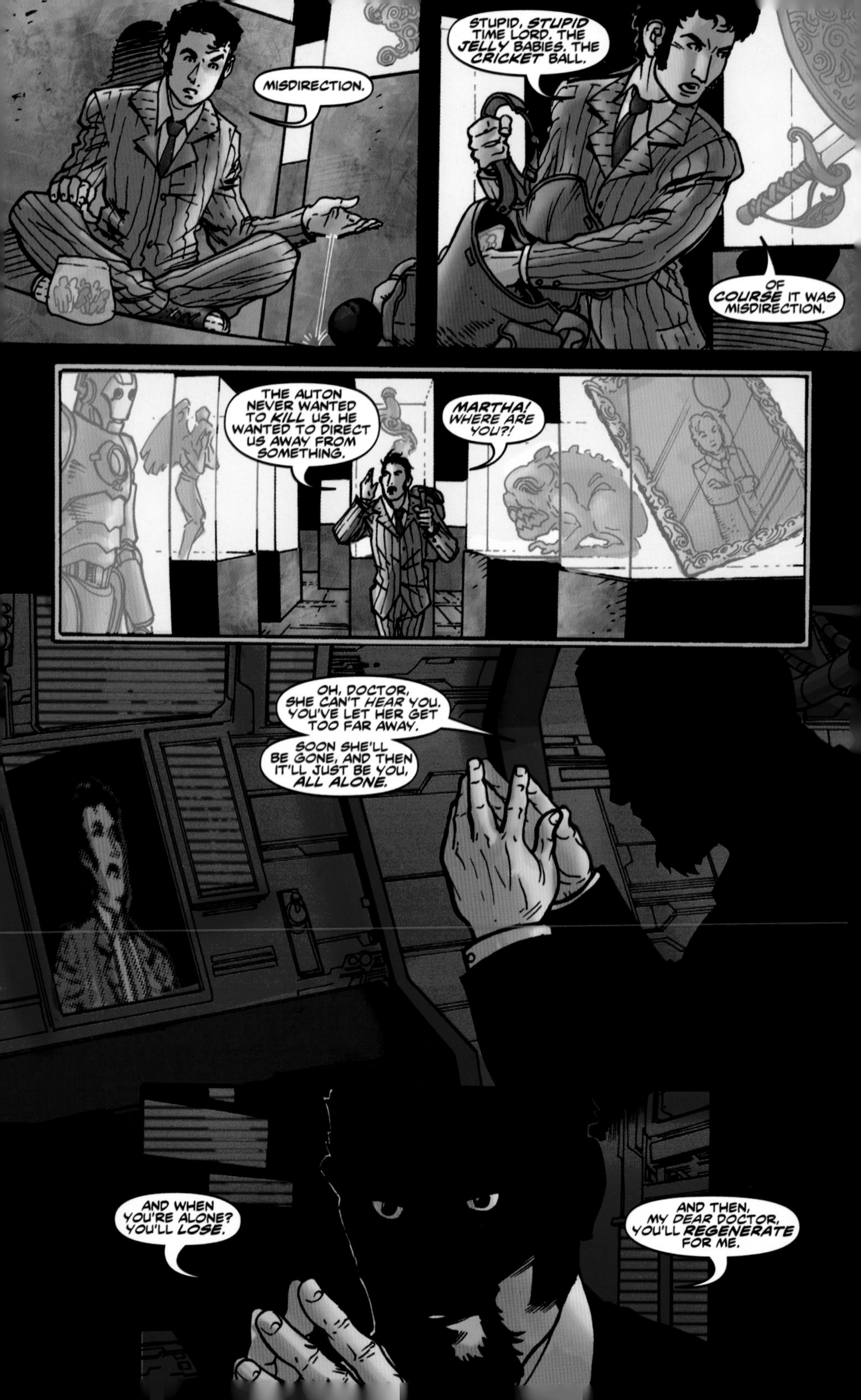
MISDIRECTION.
STUPID, STUPID TIME LORD. THE JELLY BABIES. THE CRICKET BALL.
OF COURSE IT WAS MISDIRECTION.
THE AUTON NEVER WANTED TO KILL US. HE WANTED TO DIRECT US AWAY FROM SOMETHING.
MARTHA! WHERE ARE YOU?!
OH, DOCTOR, SHE CAN'T HEAR YOU. YOU'VE LET HER GET TOO FAR AWAY.
SOON SHE'LL BE GONE, AND THEN IT'LL JUST BE YOU, ALL ALONE.
AND WHEN YOU'RE ALONE? YOU'LL LOSE.
AND THEN, MY DEAR DOCTOR, YOU'LL REGENERATE FOR ME.

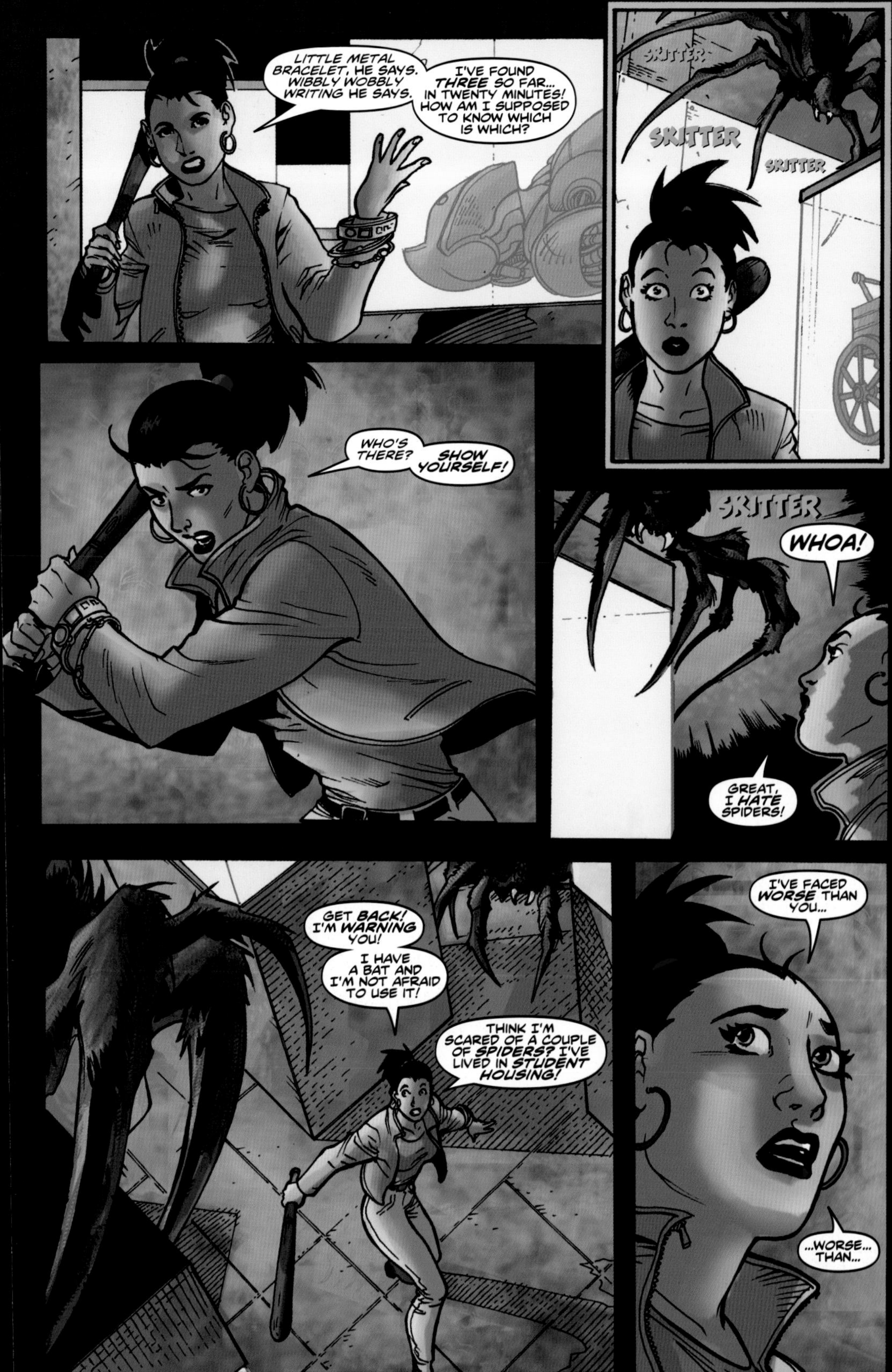
LITTLE METAL BRACELET, HE SAYS. WIBBLY WOBBLY WRITING HE SAYS.
I'VE FOUND THREE SO FAR... IN TWENTY MINUTES! HOW AM I SUPPOSED TO KNOW WHICH IS WHICH?
SKITTER
SKITTER
SKITTER
WHO'S THERE? SHOW YOURSELF!
SKITTER
WHOA!
GREAT, I HATE SPIDERS!
GET BACK! I'M WARNING YOU!
I HAVE A BAT AND I'M NOT AFRAID TO USE IT!
THINK I'M SCARED OF A COUPLE OF SPIDERS? I'VE LIVED IN STUDENT HOUSING!
I'VE FACED WORSE THAN YOU...
...WORSE... THAN...

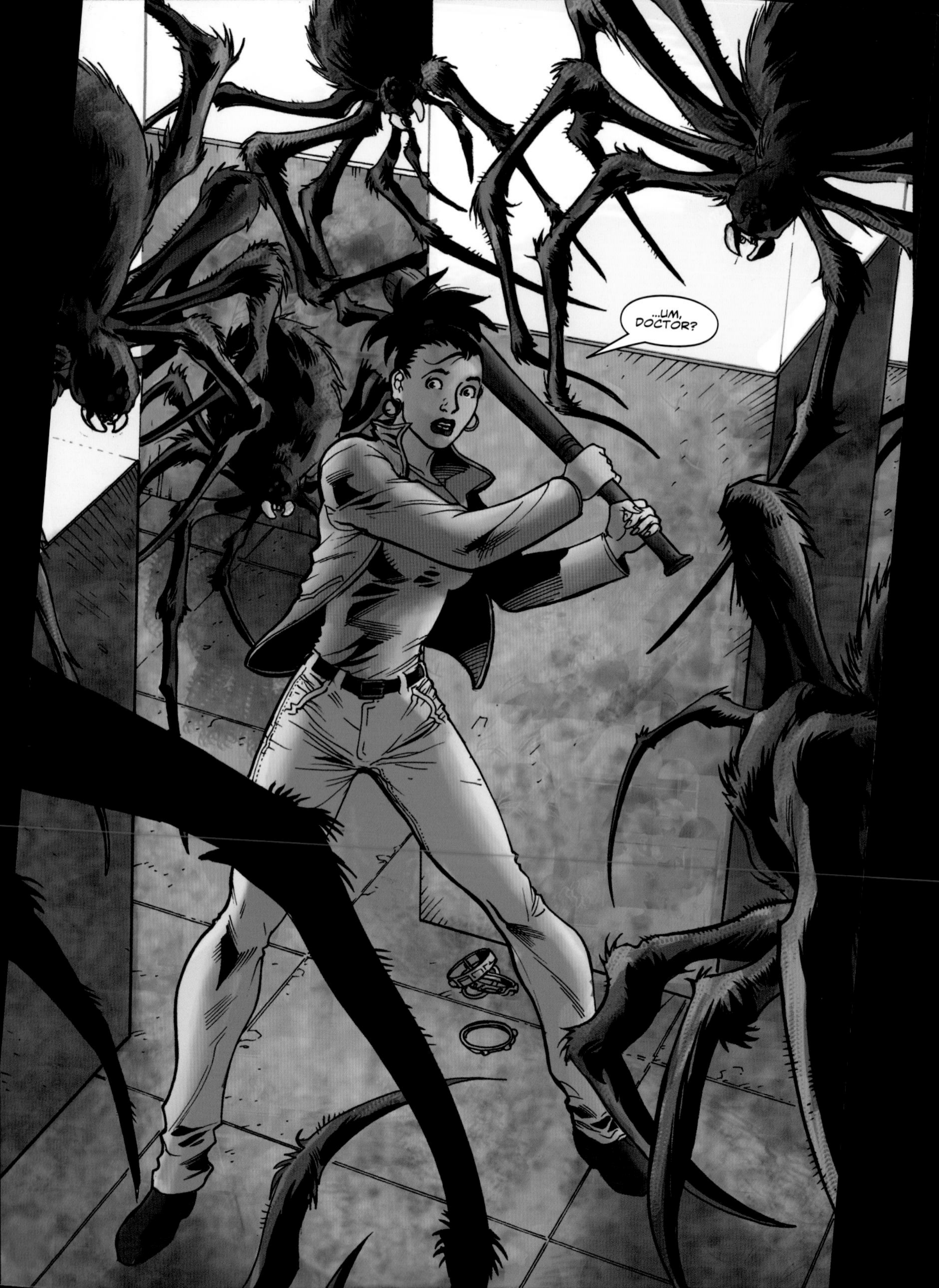
...UM, DOCTOR?

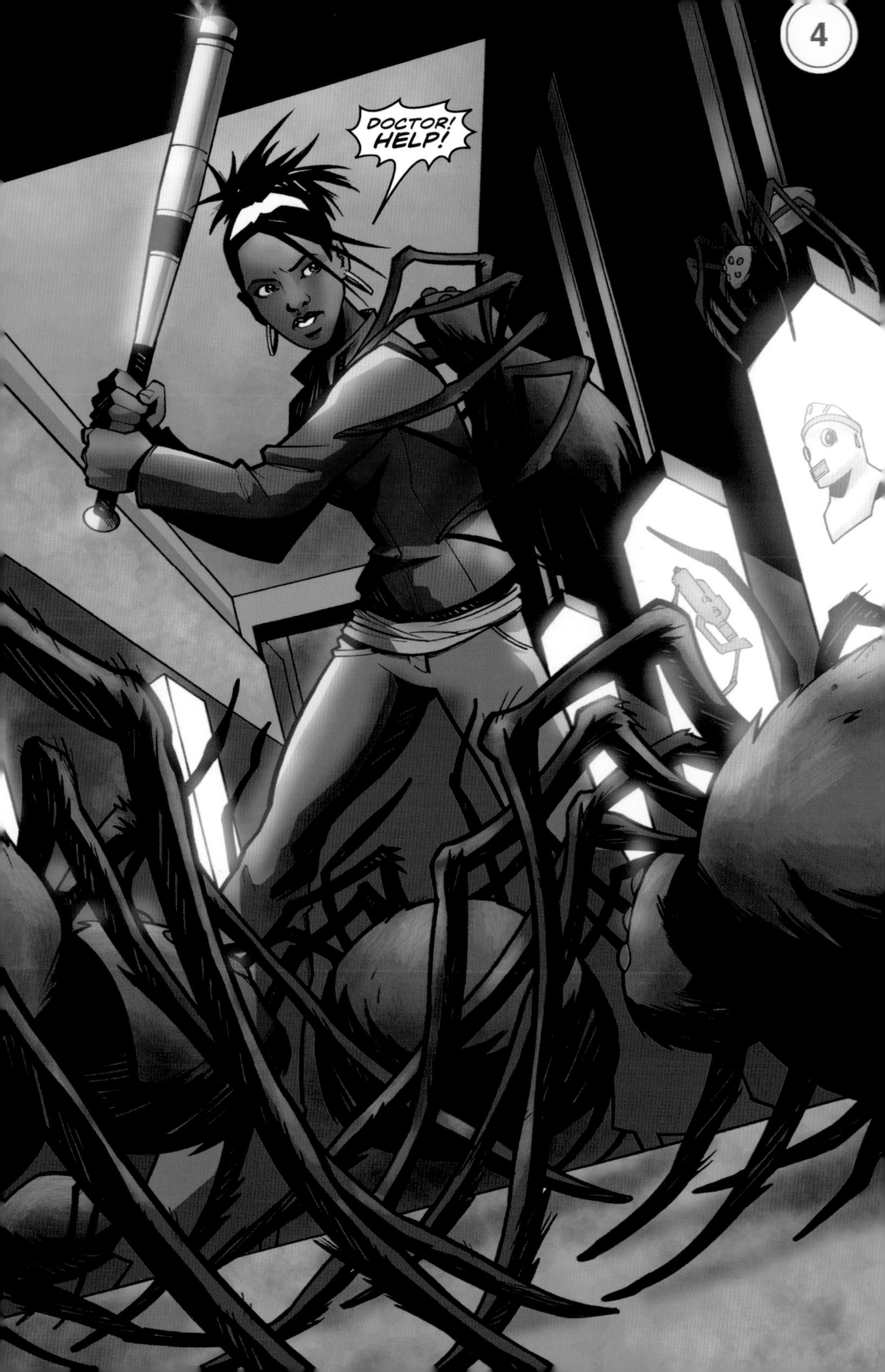
DOCTOR! HELP!

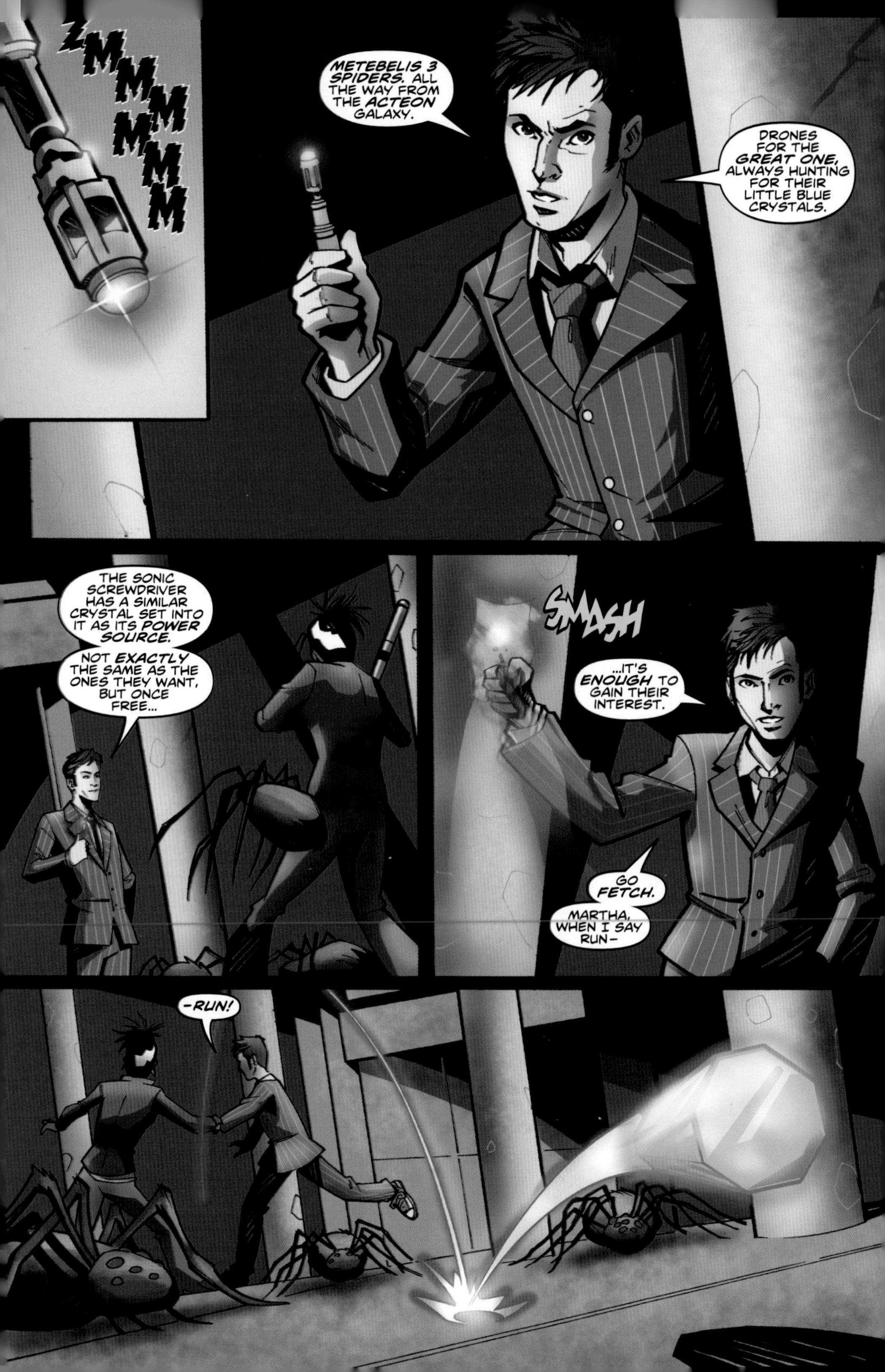
ZMMMMMMMM
METEBELIS 3 SPIDERS. ALL THE WAY FROM THE ACTEON GALAXY.
DRONES FOR THE GREAT ONE, ALWAYS HUNTING FOR THEIR LITTLE BLUE CRYSTALS.
THE SONIC SCREWDRIVER HAS A SIMILAR CRYSTAL SET INTO IT AS ITS POWER SOURCE.
NOT EXACTLY THE SAME AS THE ONES THEY WANT, BUT ONCE FREE...
SMASH
...IT'S ENOUGH TO GAIN THEIR INTEREST.
GO FETCH.
MARTHA, WHEN I SAY RUN–
–RUN!

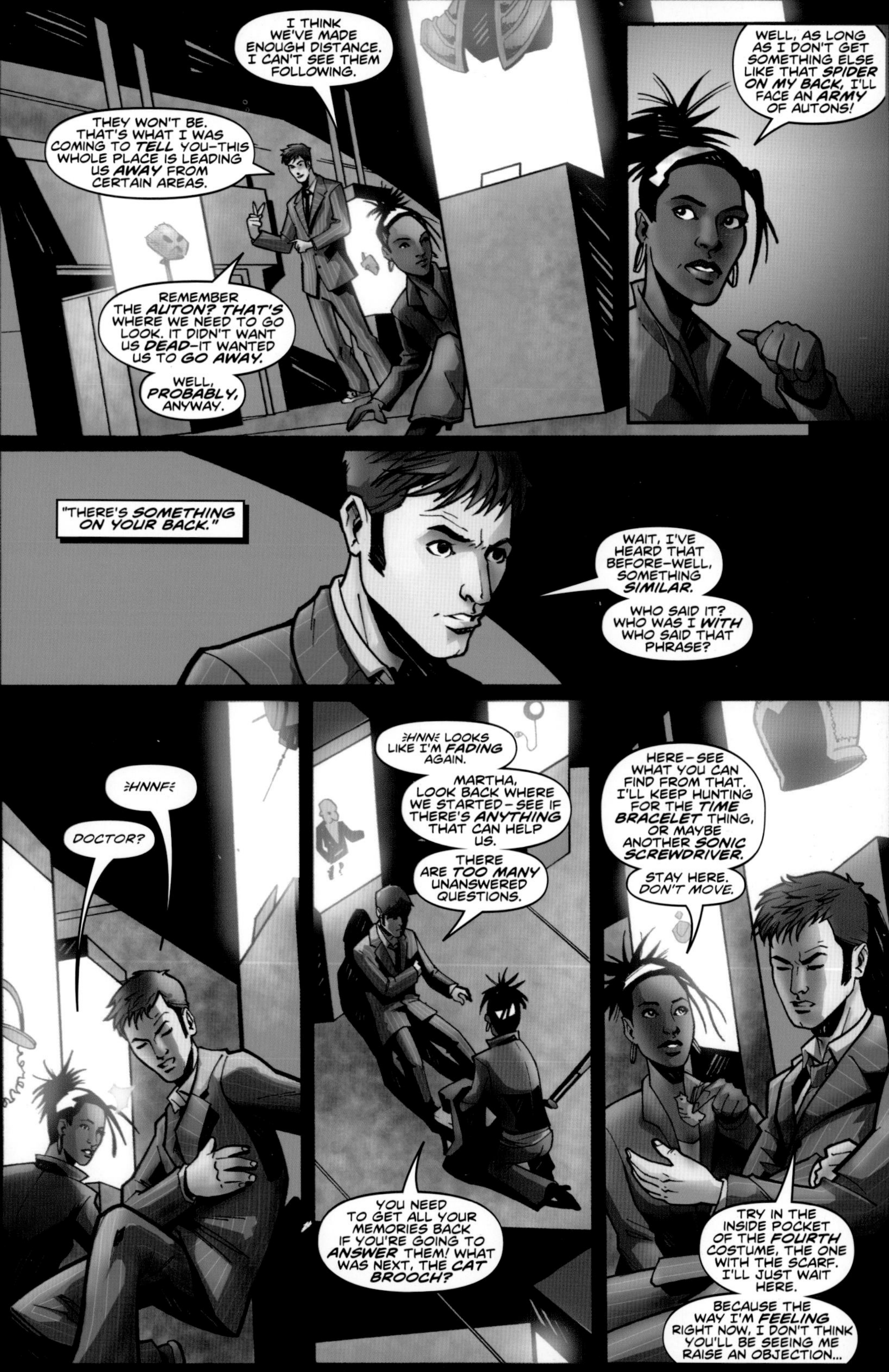

I THINK WE'VE MADE ENOUGH DISTANCE. I CAN'T SEE THEM FOLLOWING.
THEY WON'T BE. THAT'S WHAT I WAS COMING TO TELL YOU—THIS WHOLE PLACE IS LEADING US AWAY FROM CERTAIN AREAS.
REMEMBER THE AUTON? THAT'S WHERE WE NEED TO GO LOOK. IT DIDN'T WANT US DEAD—IT WANTED US TO GO AWAY.
WELL, PROBABLY, ANYWAY.
WELL, AS LONG AS I DON'T GET SOMETHING ELSE LIKE THAT SPIDER ON MY BACK, I'LL FACE AN ARMY OF AUTONS!
"THERE'S SOMETHING ON YOUR BACK."
WAIT, I'VE HEARD THAT BEFORE—WELL, SOMETHING SIMILAR.
WHO SAID IT? WHO WAS I WITH WHO SAID THAT PHRASE?
HNNF
DOCTOR?
HNN LOOKS LIKE I'M FADING AGAIN.
MARTHA, LOOK BACK WHERE WE STARTED—SEE IF THERE'S ANYTHING THAT CAN HELP US.
THERE ARE TOO MANY UNANSWERED QUESTIONS.
YOU NEED TO GET ALL YOUR MEMORIES BACK IF YOU'RE GOING TO ANSWER THEM! WHAT WAS NEXT, THE CAT BROOCH?
HERE—SEE WHAT YOU CAN FIND FROM THAT. I'LL KEEP HUNTING FOR THE TIME BRACELET THING, OR MAYBE ANOTHER SONIC SCREWDRIVER.
STAY HERE. DON'T MOVE.
TRY IN THE INSIDE POCKET OF THE FOURTH COSTUME, THE ONE WITH THE SCARF. I'LL JUST WAIT HERE.
BECAUSE THE WAY I'M FEELING RIGHT NOW, I DON'T THINK YOU'LL BE SEEING ME RAISE AN OBJECTION...

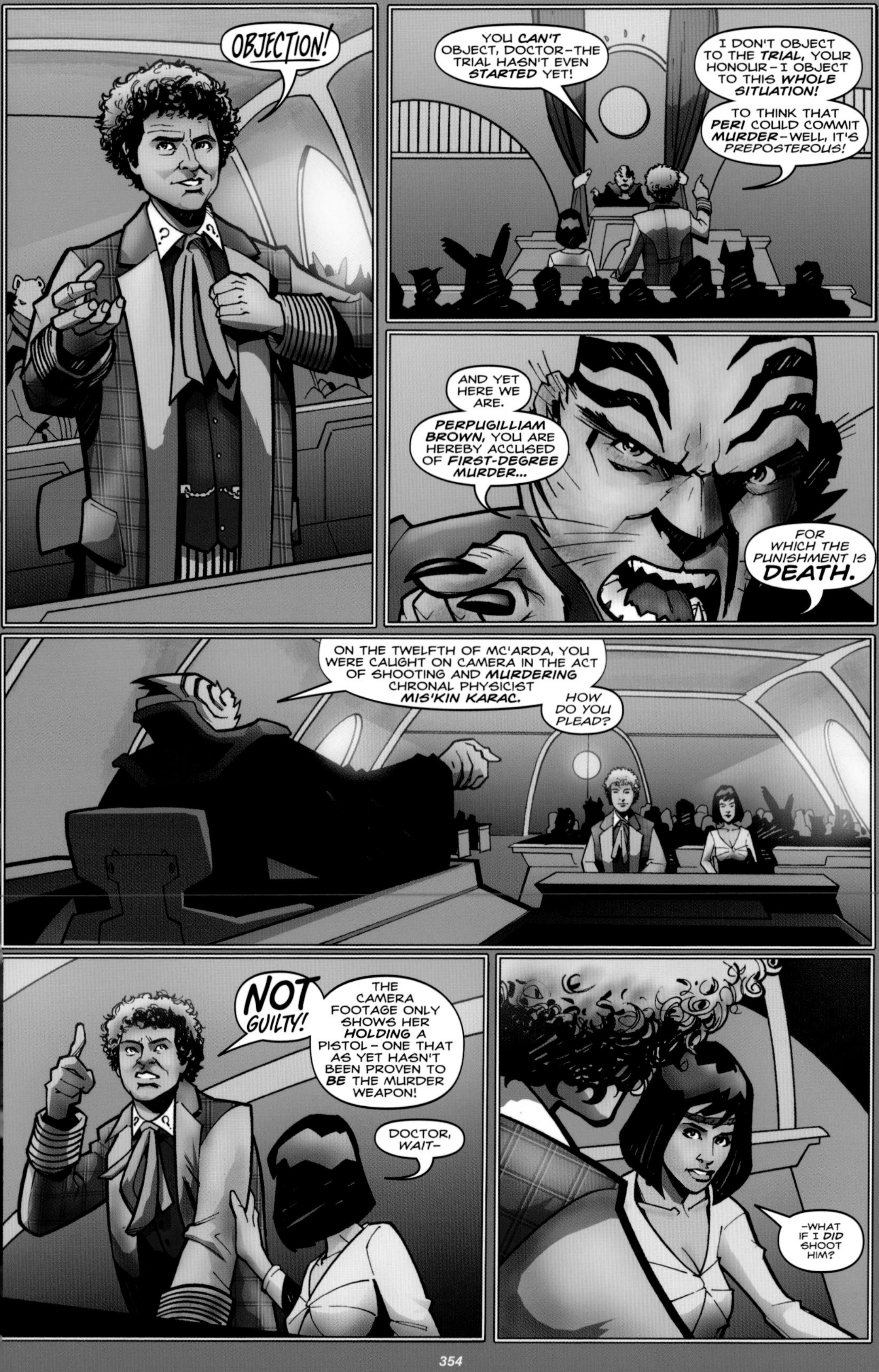
OBJECTION!
YOU CAN'T OBJECT, DOCTOR—THE TRIAL HASN'T EVEN STARTED YET!
I DON'T OBJECT TO THE TRIAL, YOUR HONOUR—I OBJECT TO THIS WHOLE SITUATION!
TO THINK THAT PERI COULD COMMIT MURDER—WELL, IT'S PREPOSTEROUS!
AND YET HERE WE ARE.
PERPUGILLIAM BROWN, YOU ARE HEREBY ACCUSED OF FIRST-DEGREE MURDER...
FOR WHICH THE PUNISHMENT IS DEATH.
ON THE TWELFTH OF MC'ARDA, YOU WERE CAUGHT ON CAMERA IN THE ACT OF SHOOTING AND MURDERING CHRONAL PHYSICIST MIS'KIN KARAC.
HOW DO YOU PLEAD?
NOT GUILTY!
THE CAMERA FOOTAGE ONLY SHOWS HER HOLDING A PISTOL—ONE THAT AS YET HASN'T BEEN PROVEN TO BE THE MURDER WEAPON!
DOCTOR, WAIT-
-WHAT IF I DID SHOOT HIM?

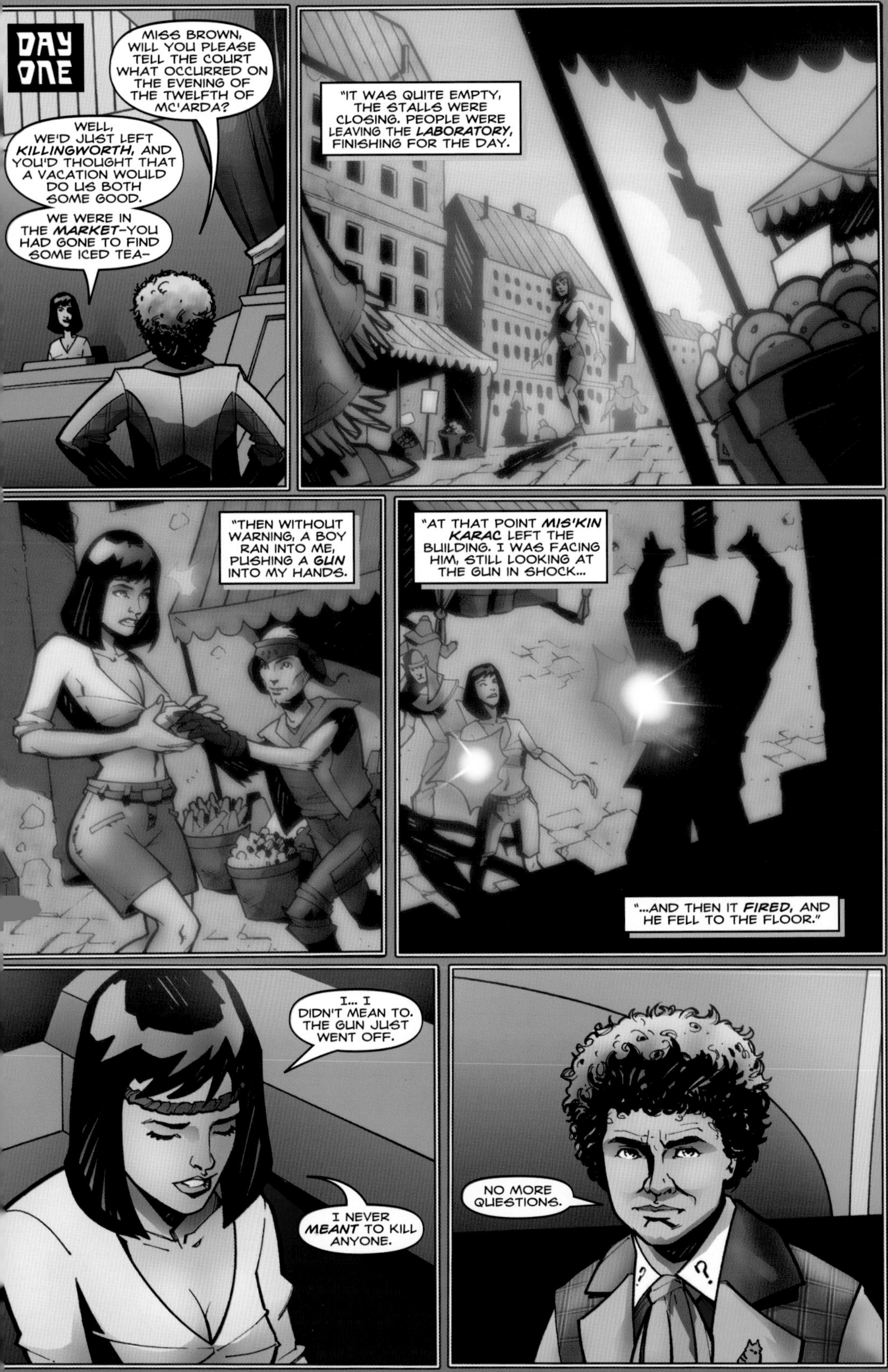
DAY ONE
MISS BROWN, WILL YOU PLEASE TELL THE COURT WHAT OCCURRED ON THE EVENING OF THE TWELFTH OF MC'ARDA?
WELL, WE'D JUST LEFT KILLINGWORTH, AND YOU'D THOUGHT THAT A VACATION WOULD DO US BOTH SOME GOOD.
WE WERE IN THE MARKET—YOU HAD GONE TO FIND SOME ICED TEA—
"IT WAS QUITE EMPTY, THE STALLS WERE CLOSING. PEOPLE WERE LEAVING THE LABORATORY, FINISHING FOR THE DAY.
"THEN WITHOUT WARNING, A BOY RAN INTO ME, PUSHING A GUN INTO MY HANDS.
"AT THAT POINT MIS'KIN KARAC LEFT THE BUILDING. I WAS FACING HIM, STILL LOOKING AT THE GUN IN SHOCK...
"...AND THEN IT FIRED, AND HE FELL TO THE FLOOR."
I... I DIDN'T MEAN TO. THE GUN JUST WENT OFF.
I NEVER MEANT TO KILL ANYONE.
NO MORE QUESTIONS.

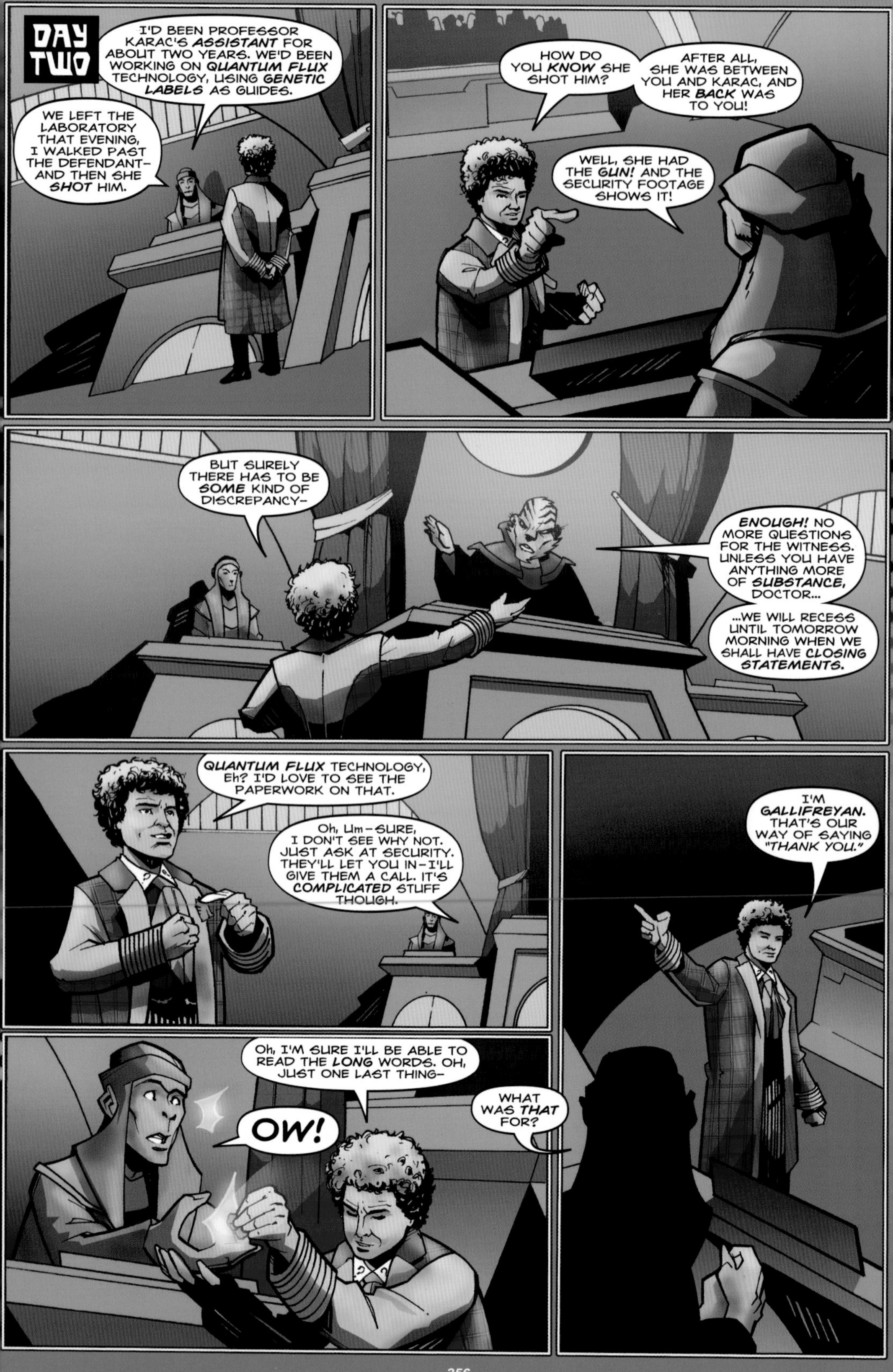
DAY TWO
I'D BEEN PROFESSOR KARAC'S ASSISTANT FOR ABOUT TWO YEARS. WE'D BEEN WORKING ON QUANTUM FLUX TECHNOLOGY, USING GENETIC LABELS AS GUIDES.
WE LEFT THE LABORATORY THAT EVENING, I WALKED PAST THE DEFENDANT– AND THEN SHE SHOT HIM.
HOW DO YOU KNOW SHE SHOT HIM?
AFTER ALL, SHE WAS BETWEEN YOU AND KARAC, AND HER BACK WAS TO YOU!
WELL, SHE HAD THE GUN! AND THE SECURITY FOOTAGE SHOWS IT!
BUT SURELY THERE HAS TO BE SOME KIND OF DISCREPANCY–
ENOUGH! NO MORE QUESTIONS FOR THE WITNESS. UNLESS YOU HAVE ANYTHING MORE OF SUBSTANCE, DOCTOR...
...WE WILL RECESS UNTIL TOMORROW MORNING WHEN WE SHALL HAVE CLOSING STATEMENTS.
QUANTUM FLUX TECHNOLOGY, Eh? I'D LOVE TO SEE THE PAPERWORK ON THAT.
Oh, Um–SURE, I DON'T SEE WHY NOT. JUST ASK AT SECURITY. THEY'LL LET YOU IN–I'LL GIVE THEM A CALL. IT'S COMPLICATED STUFF THOUGH.
Oh, I'M SURE I'LL BE ABLE TO READ THE LONG WORDS. OH, JUST ONE LAST THING–
OW!
WHAT WAS THAT FOR?
I'M GALLIFREYAN. THAT'S OUR WAY OF SAYING "THANK YOU."

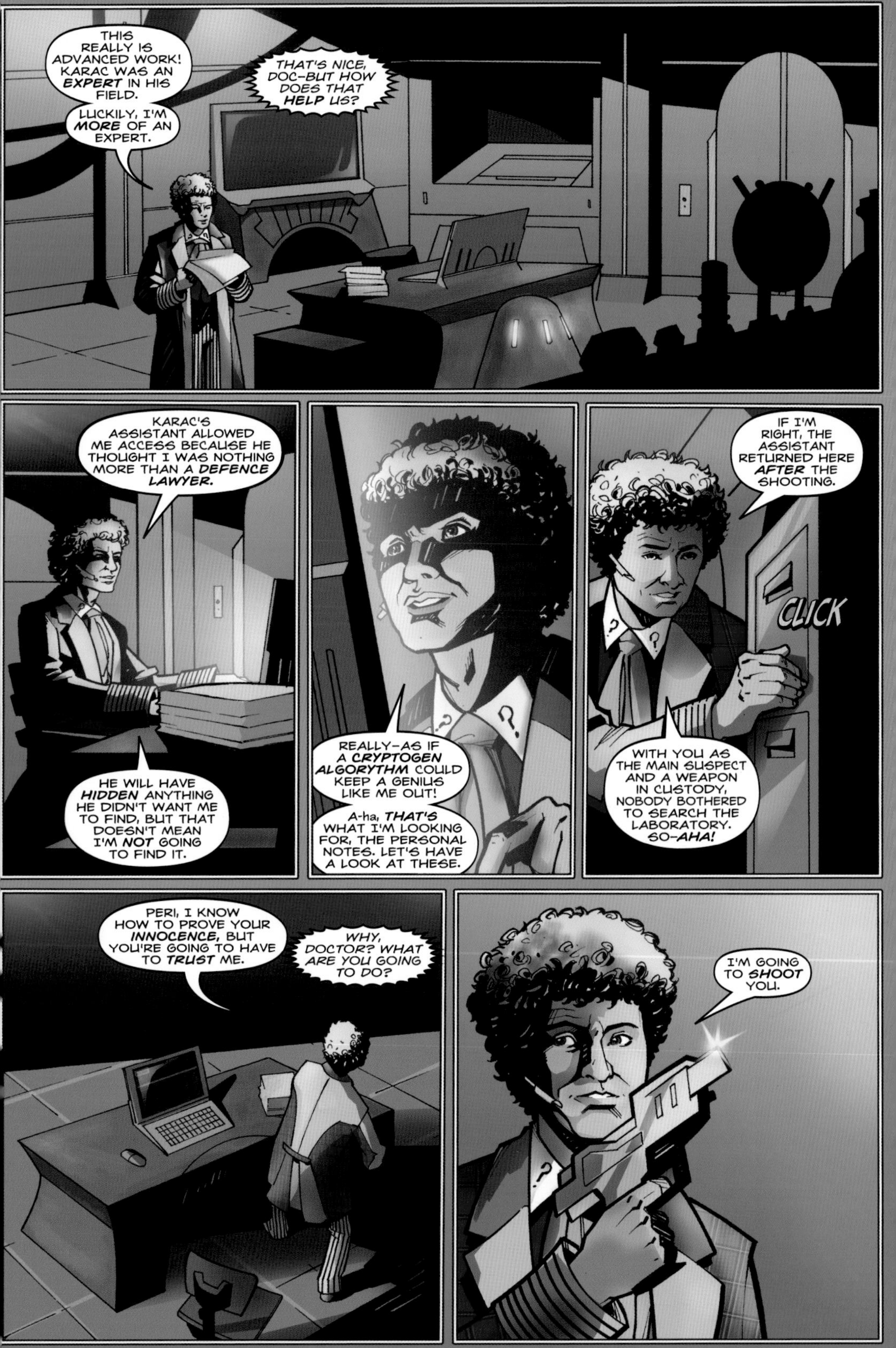
THIS REALLY IS ADVANCED WORK! KARAC WAS AN EXPERT IN HIS FIELD.
LUCKILY, I'M MORE OF AN EXPERT.
THAT'S NICE, DOC—BUT HOW DOES THAT HELP US?
KARAC'S ASSISTANT ALLOWED ME ACCESS BECAUSE HE THOUGHT I WAS NOTHING MORE THAN A DEFENCE LAWYER.
HE WILL HAVE HIDDEN ANYTHING HE DIDN'T WANT ME TO FIND, BUT THAT DOESN'T MEAN I'M NOT GOING TO FIND IT.
REALLY—AS IF A CRYPTOGEN ALGORYTHM COULD KEEP A GENIUS LIKE ME OUT!
A-ha, THAT'S WHAT I'M LOOKING FOR, THE PERSONAL NOTES. LET'S HAVE A LOOK AT THESE.
IF I'M RIGHT, THE ASSISTANT RETURNED HERE AFTER THE SHOOTING.
CLICK
WITH YOU AS THE MAIN SUSPECT AND A WEAPON IN CUSTODY, NOBODY BOTHERED TO SEARCH THE LABORATORY. SO—AHA!
PERI, I KNOW HOW TO PROVE YOUR INNOCENCE, BUT YOU'RE GOING TO HAVE TO TRUST ME.
WHY, DOCTOR? WHAT ARE YOU GOING TO DO?
I'M GOING TO SHOOT YOU.

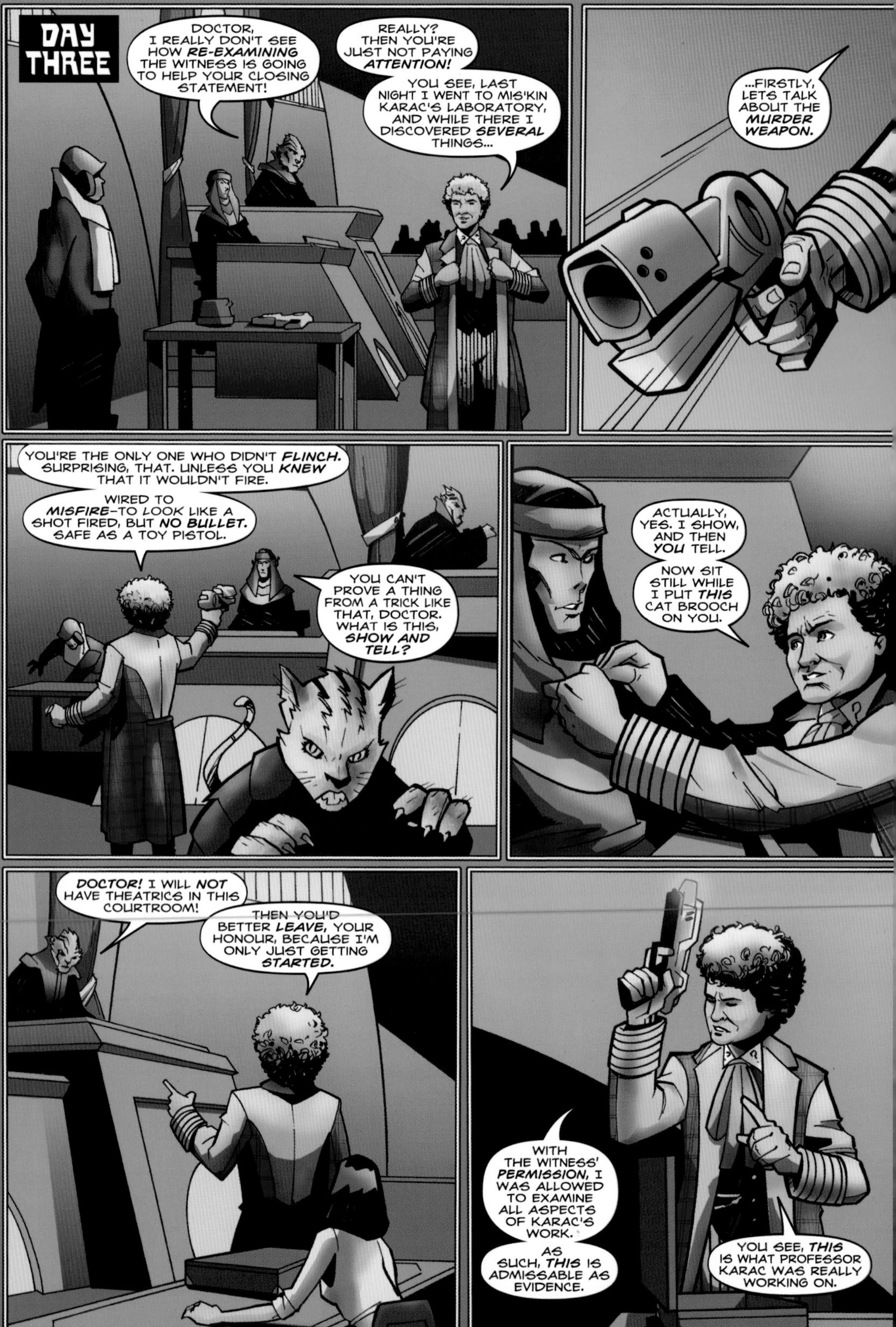
DAY THREE
DOCTOR, I REALLY DON'T SEE HOW RE-EXAMINING THE WITNESS IS GOING TO HELP YOUR CLOSING STATEMENT!
REALLY? THEN YOU'RE JUST NOT PAYING ATTENTION!
YOU SEE, LAST NIGHT I WENT TO MIS'KIN KARAC'S LABORATORY, AND WHILE THERE I DISCOVERED SEVERAL THINGS...
...FIRSTLY, LETS TALK ABOUT THE MURDER WEAPON.
YOU'RE THE ONLY ONE WHO DIDN'T FLINCH. SURPRISING, THAT. UNLESS YOU KNEW THAT IT WOULDN'T FIRE.
WIRED TO MISFIRE–TO LOOK LIKE A SHOT FIRED, BUT NO BULLET. SAFE AS A TOY PISTOL.
YOU CAN'T PROVE A THING FROM A TRICK LIKE THAT, DOCTOR. WHAT IS THIS, SHOW AND TELL?
ACTUALLY, YES. I SHOW, AND THEN YOU TELL.
NOW SIT STILL WHILE I PUT THIS CAT BROOCH ON YOU.
DOCTOR! I WILL NOT HAVE THEATRICS IN THIS COURTROOM!
THEN YOU'D BETTER LEAVE, YOUR HONOUR, BECAUSE I'M ONLY JUST GETTING STARTED.
WITH THE WITNESS' PERMISSION, I WAS ALLOWED TO EXAMINE ALL ASPECTS OF KARAC'S WORK.
AS SUCH, THIS IS ADMISSABLE AS EVIDENCE.
YOU SEE, THIS IS WHAT PROFESSOR KARAC WAS REALLY WORKING ON.

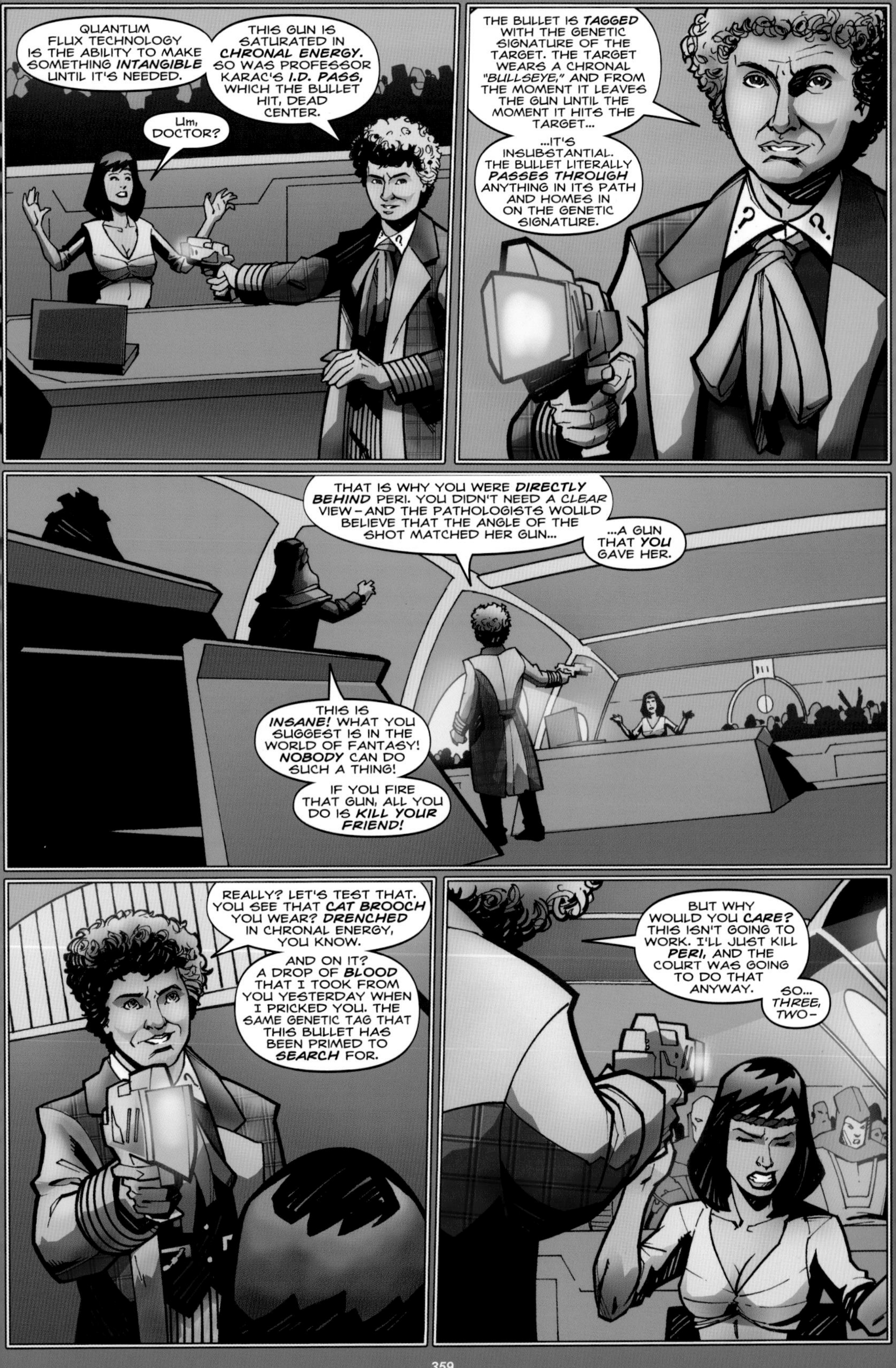
QUANTUM FLUX TECHNOLOGY IS THE ABILITY TO MAKE SOMETHING INTANGIBLE UNTIL IT'S NEEDED.
THIS GUN IS SATURATED IN CHRONAL ENERGY. SO WAS PROFESSOR KARAC'S I.D. PASS, WHICH THE BULLET HIT, DEAD CENTER.
UM, DOCTOR?
THE BULLET IS TAGGED WITH THE GENETIC SIGNATURE OF THE TARGET. THE TARGET WEARS A CHRONAL "BULLSEYE," AND FROM THE MOMENT IT LEAVES THE GUN UNTIL THE MOMENT IT HITS THE TARGET...
...IT'S INSUBSTANTIAL. THE BULLET LITERALLY PASSES THROUGH ANYTHING IN ITS PATH AND HOMES IN ON THE GENETIC SIGNATURE.
THAT IS WHY YOU WERE DIRECTLY BEHIND PERI. YOU DIDN'T NEED A CLEAR VIEW—AND THE PATHOLOGISTS WOULD BELIEVE THAT THE ANGLE OF THE SHOT MATCHED HER GUN...
...A GUN THAT YOU GAVE HER.
THIS IS INSANE! WHAT YOU SUGGEST IS IN THE WORLD OF FANTASY! NOBODY CAN DO SUCH A THING!
IF YOU FIRE THAT GUN, ALL YOU DO IS KILL YOUR FRIEND!
REALLY? LET'S TEST THAT. YOU SEE THAT CAT BROOCH YOU WEAR? DRENCHED IN CHRONAL ENERGY, YOU KNOW.
AND ON IT? A DROP OF BLOOD THAT I TOOK FROM YOU YESTERDAY WHEN I PRICKED YOU. THE SAME GENETIC TAG THAT THIS BULLET HAS BEEN PRIMED TO SEARCH FOR.
BUT WHY WOULD YOU CARE? THIS ISN'T GOING TO WORK. I'LL JUST KILL PERI, AND THE COURT WAS GOING TO DO THAT ANYWAY.
SO... THREE, TWO—

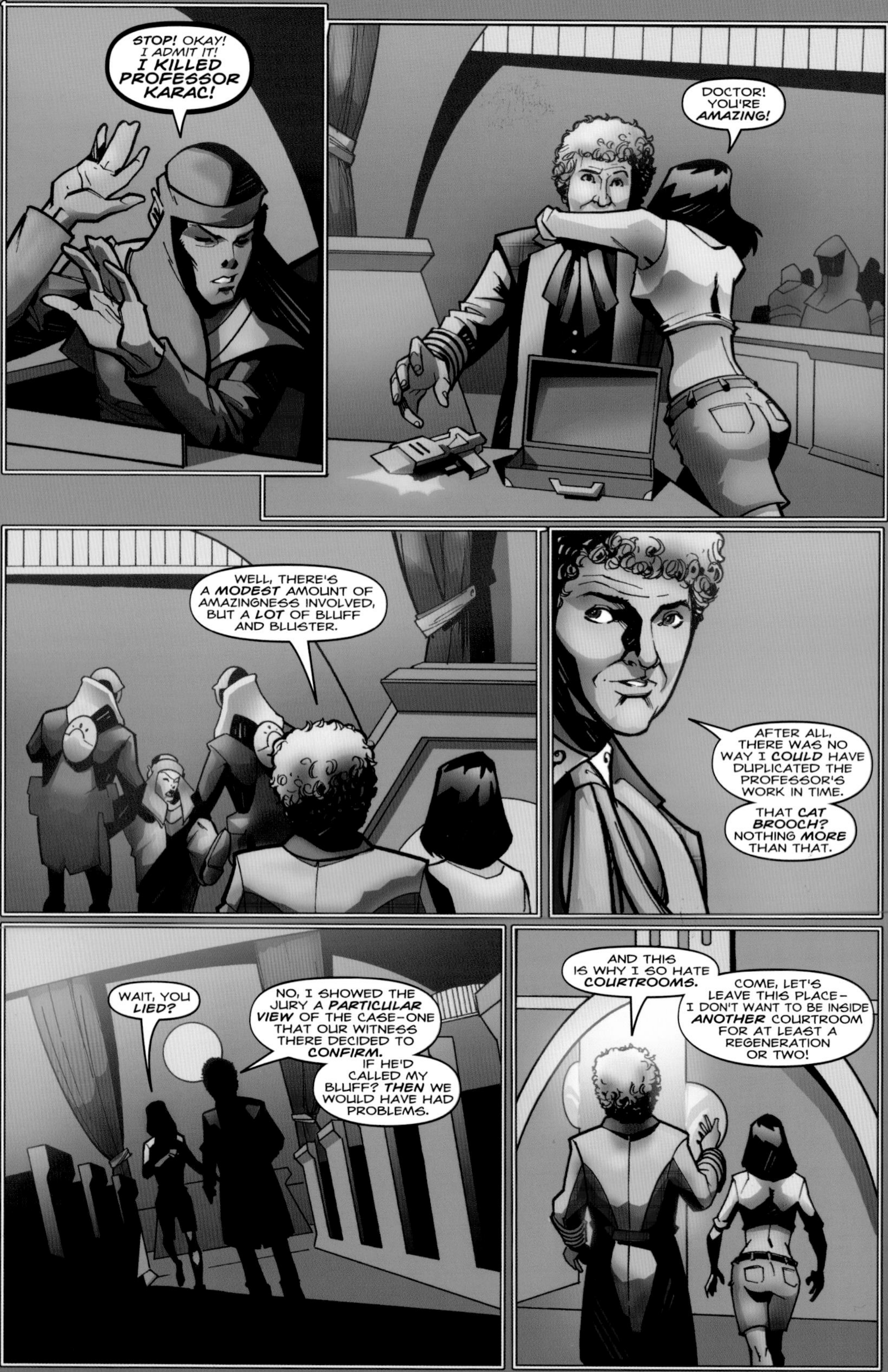
STOP! OKAY! I ADMIT IT! I KILLED PROFESSOR KARAC!
DOCTOR! YOU'RE AMAZING!
WELL, THERE'S A MODEST AMOUNT OF AMAZINGNESS INVOLVED, BUT A LOT OF BLUFF AND BLUSTER.
AFTER ALL, THERE WAS NO WAY I COULD HAVE DUPLICATED THE PROFESSOR'S WORK IN TIME.
THAT CAT BROOCH? NOTHING MORE THAN THAT.
WAIT, YOU LIED?
NO, I SHOWED THE JURY A PARTICULAR VIEW OF THE CASE—ONE THAT OUR WITNESS THERE DECIDED TO CONFIRM.
IF HE'D CALLED MY BLUFF? THEN WE WOULD HAVE HAD PROBLEMS.
AND THIS IS WHY I SO HATE COURTROOMS.
COME, LET'S LEAVE THIS PLACE— I DON'T WANT TO BE INSIDE ANOTHER COURTROOM FOR AT LEAST A REGENERATION OR TWO!

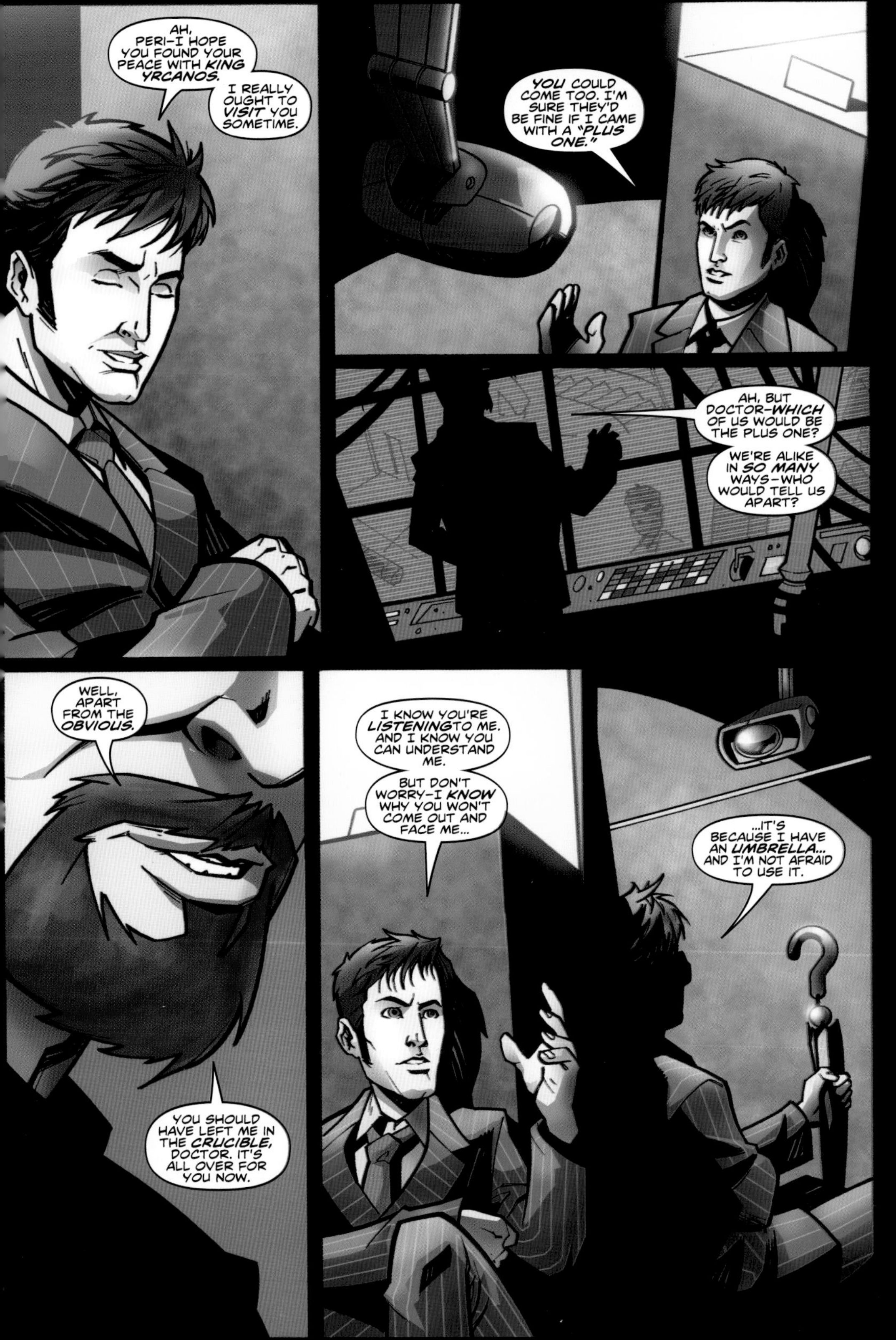
AH, PERI–I HOPE YOU FOUND YOUR PEACE WITH KING YRCANOS.
I REALLY OUGHT TO VISIT YOU SOMETIME.
YOU COULD COME TOO. I'M SURE THEY'D BE FINE IF I CAME WITH A "PLUS ONE."
AH, BUT DOCTOR–WHICH OF US WOULD BE THE PLUS ONE?
WE'RE ALIKE IN SO MANY WAYS–WHO WOULD TELL US APART?
WELL, APART FROM THE OBVIOUS.
YOU SHOULD HAVE LEFT ME IN THE CRUCIBLE, DOCTOR. IT'S ALL OVER FOR YOU NOW.
I KNOW YOU'RE LISTENINGTO ME. AND I KNOW YOU CAN UNDERSTAND ME.
BUT DON'T WORRY–I KNOW WHY YOU WON'T COME OUT AND FACE ME...
...IT'S BECAUSE I HAVE AN UMBRELLA... AND I'M NOT AFRAID TO USE IT.

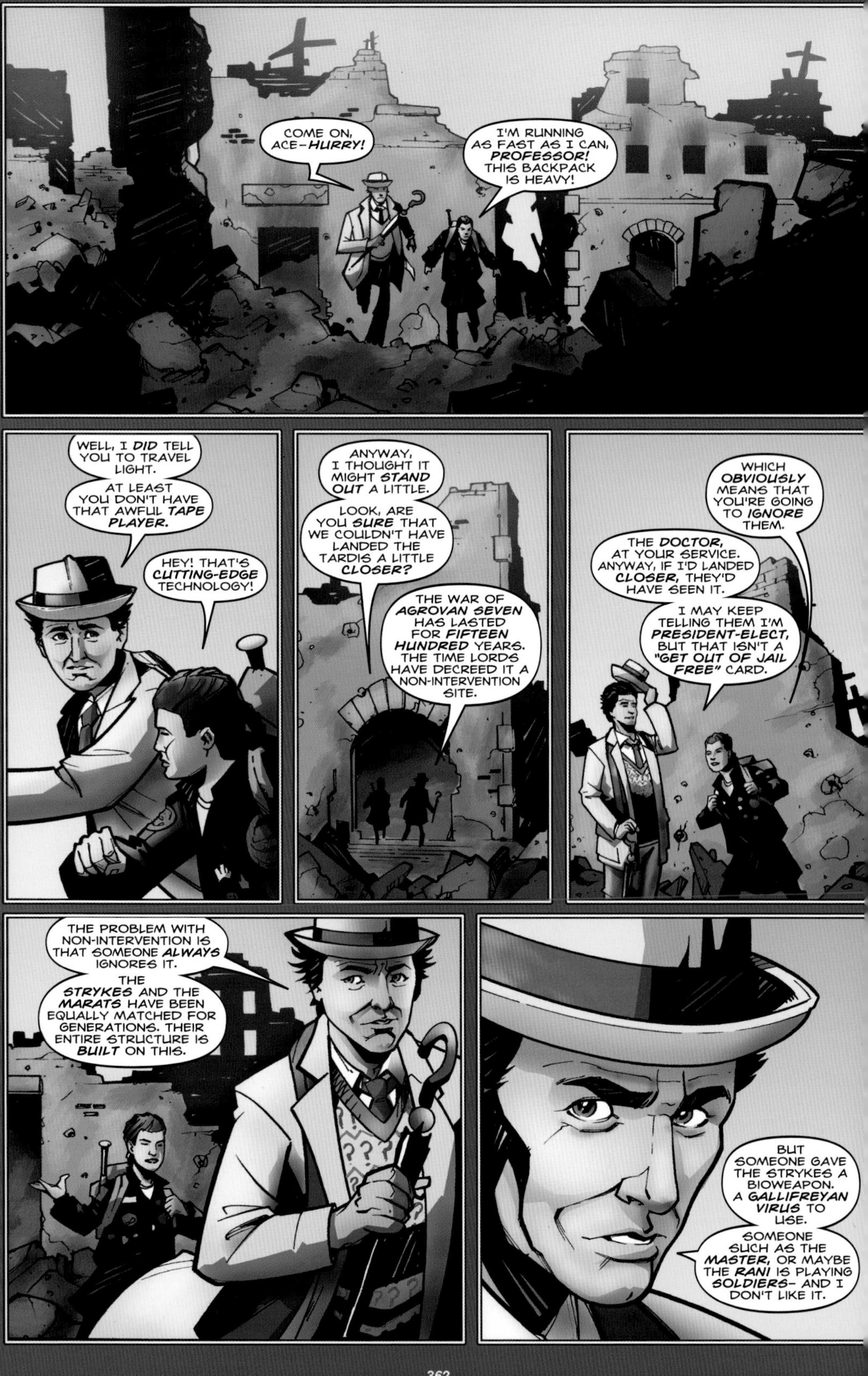

COME ON, ACE–HURRY!
I'M RUNNING AS FAST AS I CAN, PROFESSOR! THIS BACKPACK IS HEAVY!
WELL, I DID TELL YOU TO TRAVEL LIGHT.
AT LEAST YOU DON'T HAVE THAT AWFUL TAPE PLAYER.
HEY! THAT'S CUTTING-EDGE TECHNOLOGY!
ANYWAY, I THOUGHT IT MIGHT STAND OUT A LITTLE.
LOOK, ARE YOU SURE THAT WE COULDN'T HAVE LANDED THE TARDIS A LITTLE CLOSER?
THE WAR OF AGROVAN SEVEN HAS LASTED FOR FIFTEEN HUNDRED YEARS. THE TIME LORDS HAVE DECREED IT A NON-INTERVENTION SITE.
WHICH OBVIOUSLY MEANS THAT YOU'RE GOING TO IGNORE THEM.
THE DOCTOR, AT YOUR SERVICE. ANYWAY, IF I'D LANDED CLOSER, THEY'D HAVE SEEN IT.
I MAY KEEP TELLING THEM I'M PRESIDENT-ELECT, BUT THAT ISN'T A "GET OUT OF JAIL FREE" CARD.
THE PROBLEM WITH NON-INTERVENTION IS THAT SOMEONE ALWAYS IGNORES IT.
THE STRYKES AND THE MARATS HAVE BEEN EQUALLY MATCHED FOR GENERATIONS. THEIR ENTIRE STRUCTURE IS BUILT ON THIS.
BUT SOMEONE GAVE THE STRYKES A BIOWEAPON. A GALLIFREYAN VIRUS TO USE.
SOMEONE SUCH AS THE MASTER, OR MAYBE THE RANI IS PLAYING SOLDIERS– AND I DON'T LIKE IT.

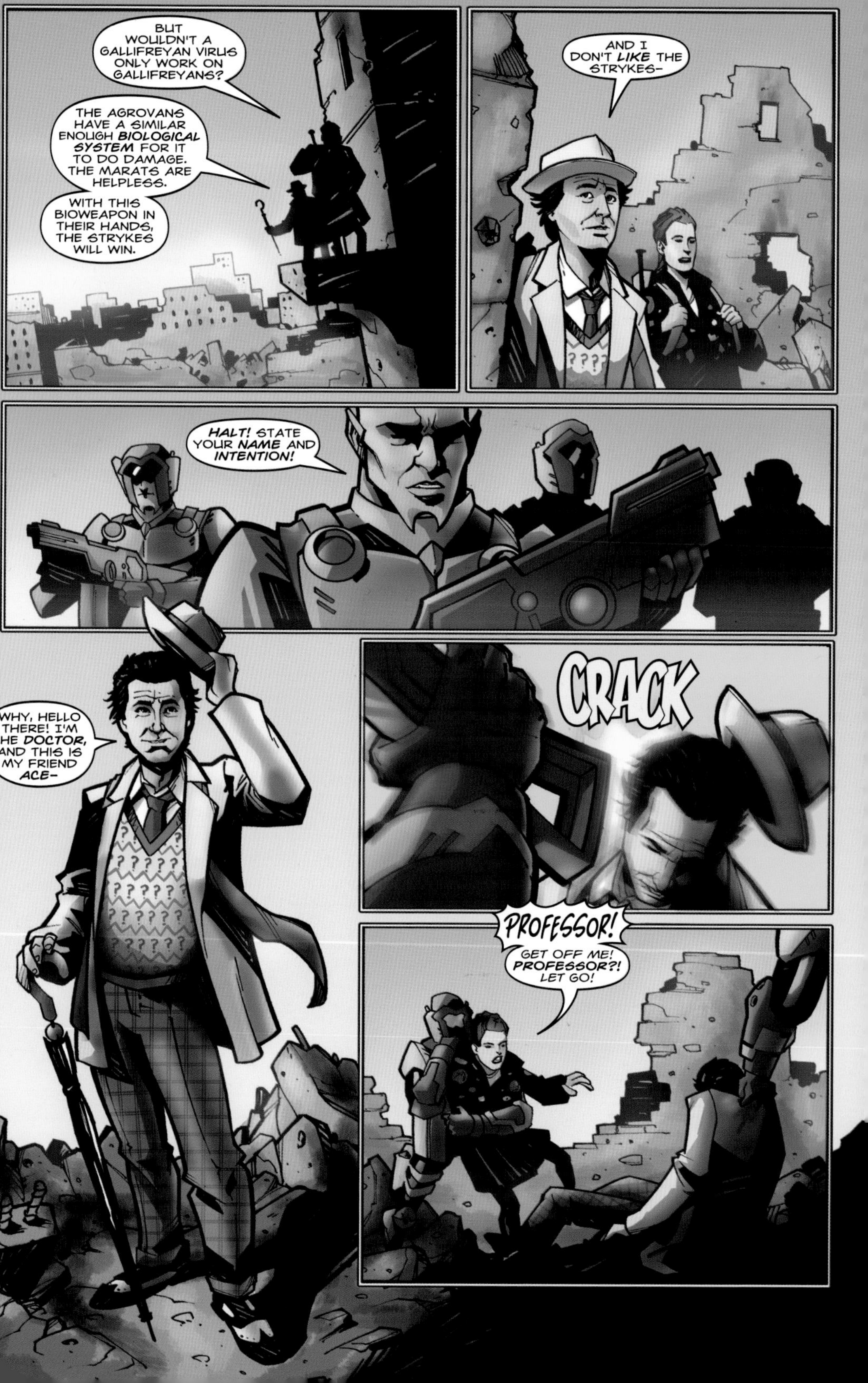
BUT WOULDN'T A GALLIFREYAN VIRUS ONLY WORK ON GALLIFREYANS?
THE AGROVANS HAVE A SIMILAR ENOUGH BIOLOGICAL SYSTEM FOR IT TO DO DAMAGE. THE MARATS ARE HELPLESS.
WITH THIS BIOWEAPON IN THEIR HANDS, THE STRYKES WILL WIN.
AND I DON'T LIKE THE STRYKES-
HALT! STATE YOUR NAME AND INTENTION!
WHY, HELLO THERE! I'M THE DOCTOR, AND THIS IS MY FRIEND ACE-
CRACK
PROFESSOR!
GET OFF ME! PROFESSOR?! LET GO!

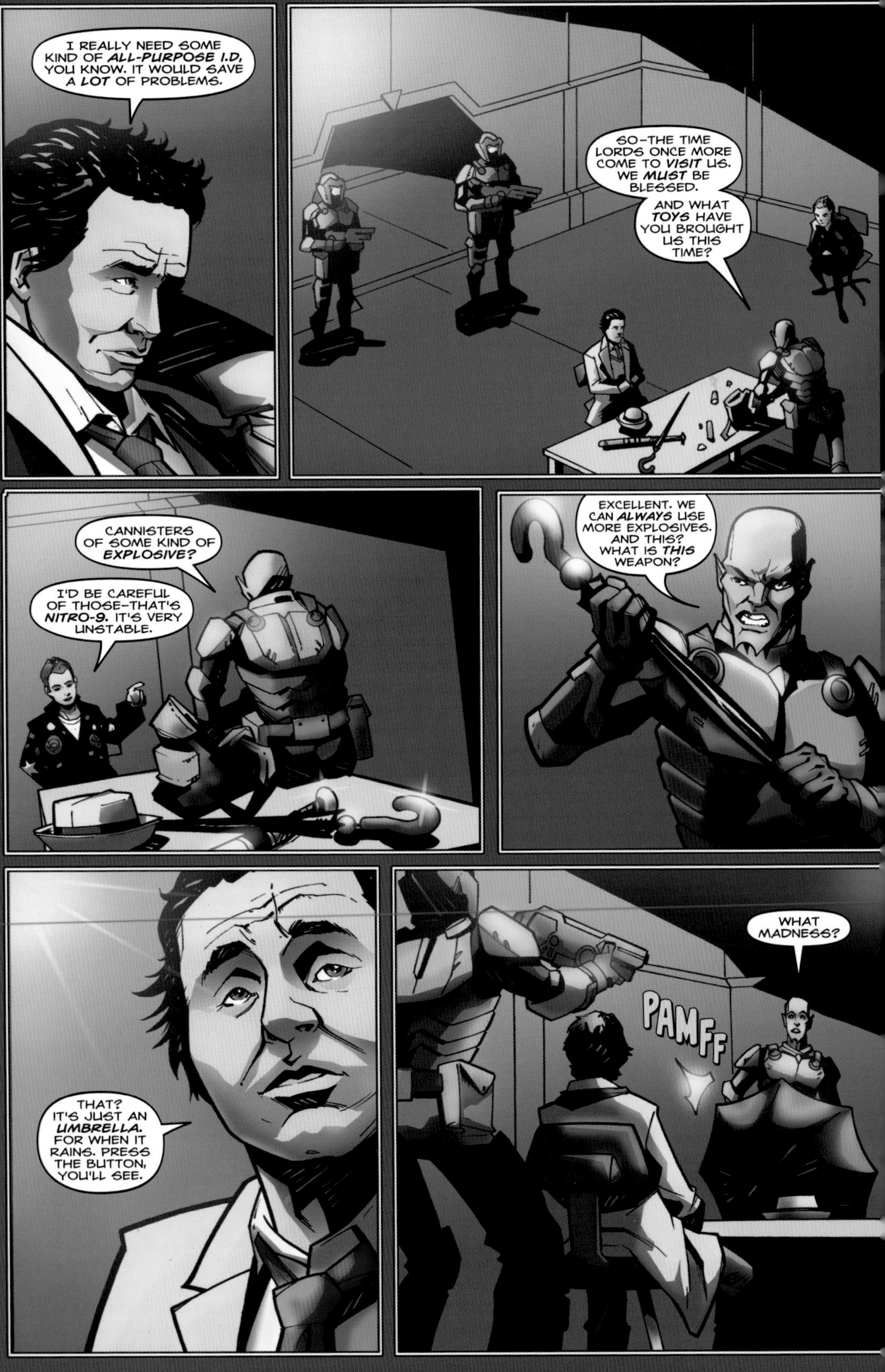
I REALLY NEED SOME KIND OF ALL-PURPOSE I.D, YOU KNOW. IT WOULD SAVE A LOT OF PROBLEMS.
SO–THE TIME LORDS ONCE MORE COME TO VISIT US. WE MUST BE BLESSED.
AND WHAT TOYS HAVE YOU BROUGHT US THIS TIME?
CANNISTERS OF SOME KIND OF EXPLOSIVE?
I'D BE CAREFUL OF THOSE–THAT'S NITRO-9. IT'S VERY UNSTABLE.
EXCELLENT. WE CAN ALWAYS USE MORE EXPLOSIVES. AND THIS? WHAT IS THIS WEAPON?
THAT? IT'S JUST AN UMBRELLA. FOR WHEN IT RAINS. PRESS THE BUTTON, YOU'LL SEE.
PAMFF
WHAT MADNESS?

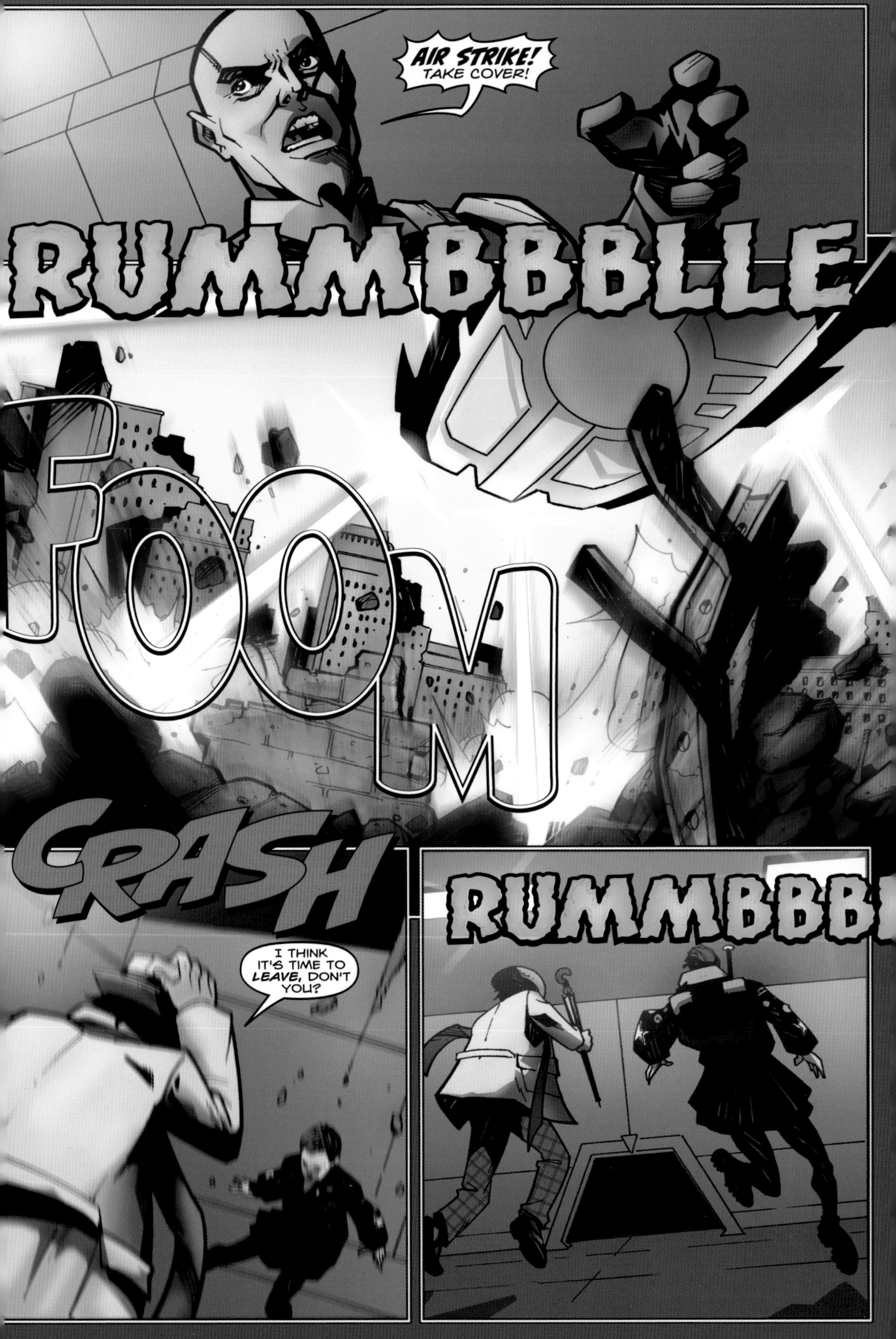
AIR STRIKE! TAKE COVER!
RUMMBBBLLE
FOOOM
CRASH
I THINK IT'S TIME TO LEAVE, DON'T YOU?
RUMMBBB

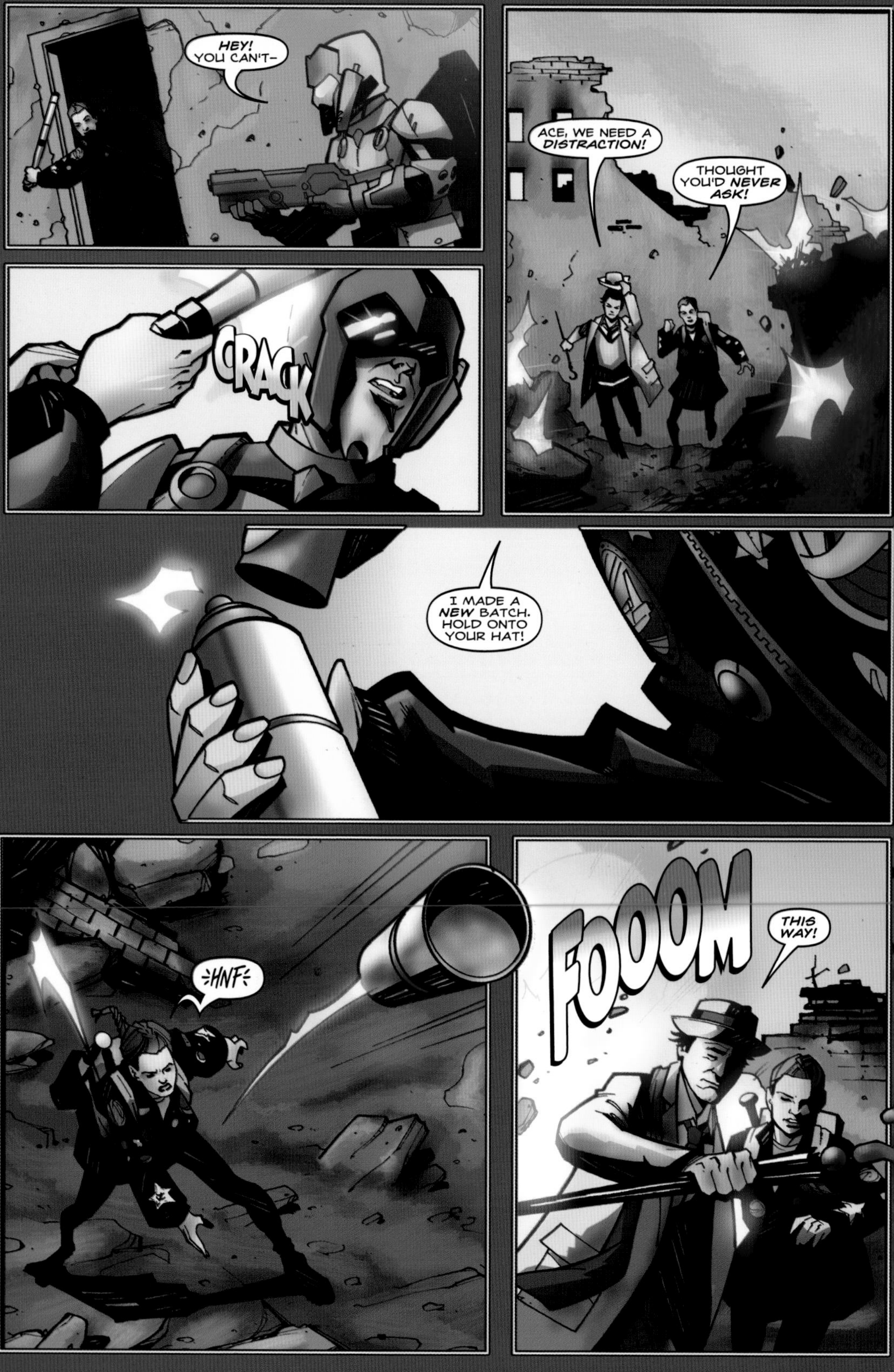
HEY! YOU CAN'T-
ACE, WE NEED A DISTRACTION!
THOUGHT YOU'D NEVER ASK!
CRACK
I MADE A NEW BATCH. HOLD ONTO YOUR HAT!
HNF
FOOOM
THIS WAY!

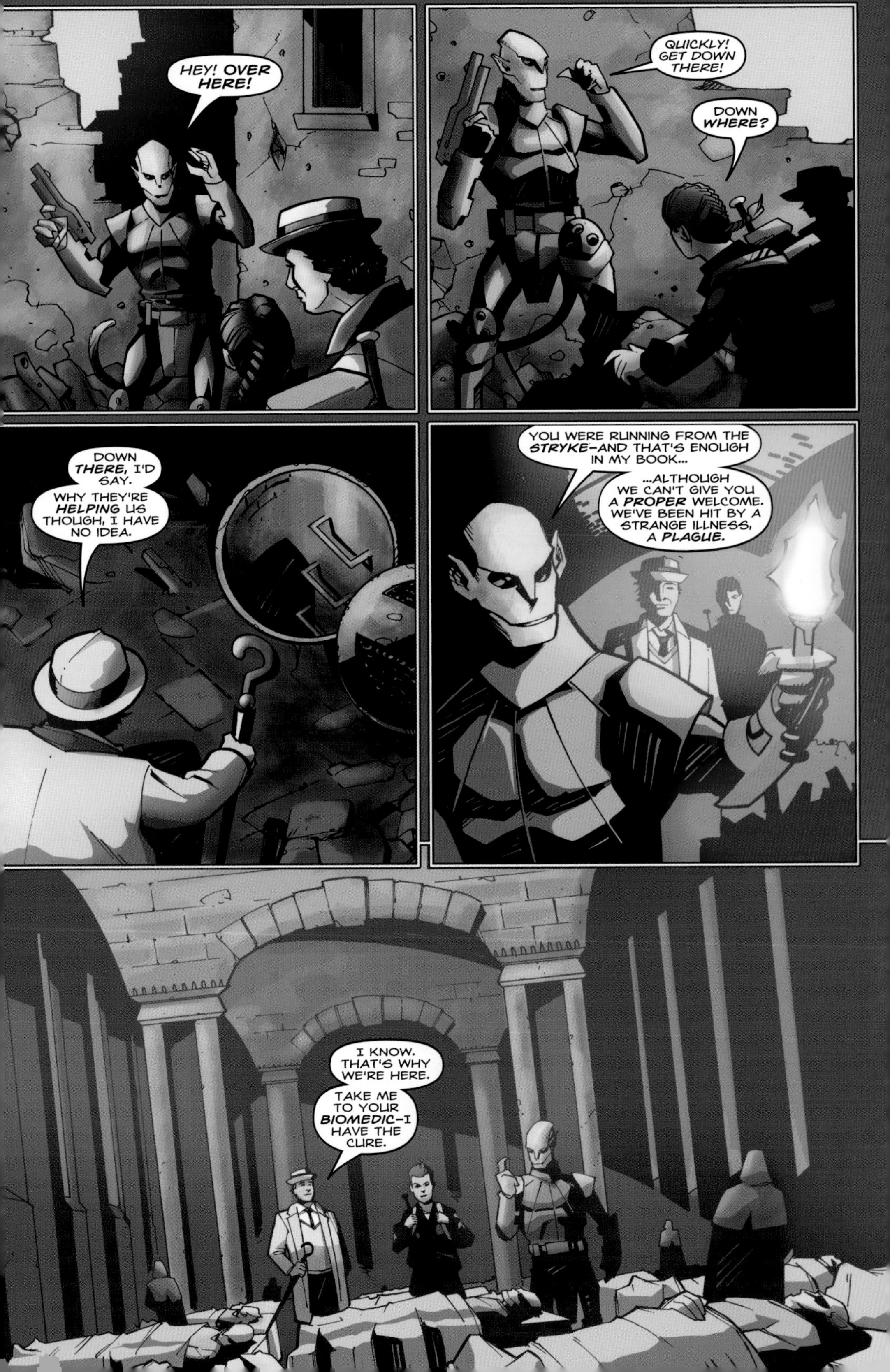
HEY! OVER HERE!
QUICKLY! GET DOWN THERE!
DOWN WHERE?
DOWN THERE, I'D SAY.
WHY THEY'RE HELPING US THOUGH, I HAVE NO IDEA.
YOU WERE RUNNING FROM THE STRYKE–AND THAT'S ENOUGH IN MY BOOK...
...ALTHOUGH WE CAN'T GIVE YOU A PROPER WELCOME. WE'VE BEEN HIT BY A STRANGE ILLNESS, A PLAGUE.
I KNOW. THAT'S WHY WE'RE HERE.
TAKE ME TO YOUR BIOMEDIC–I HAVE THE CURE.

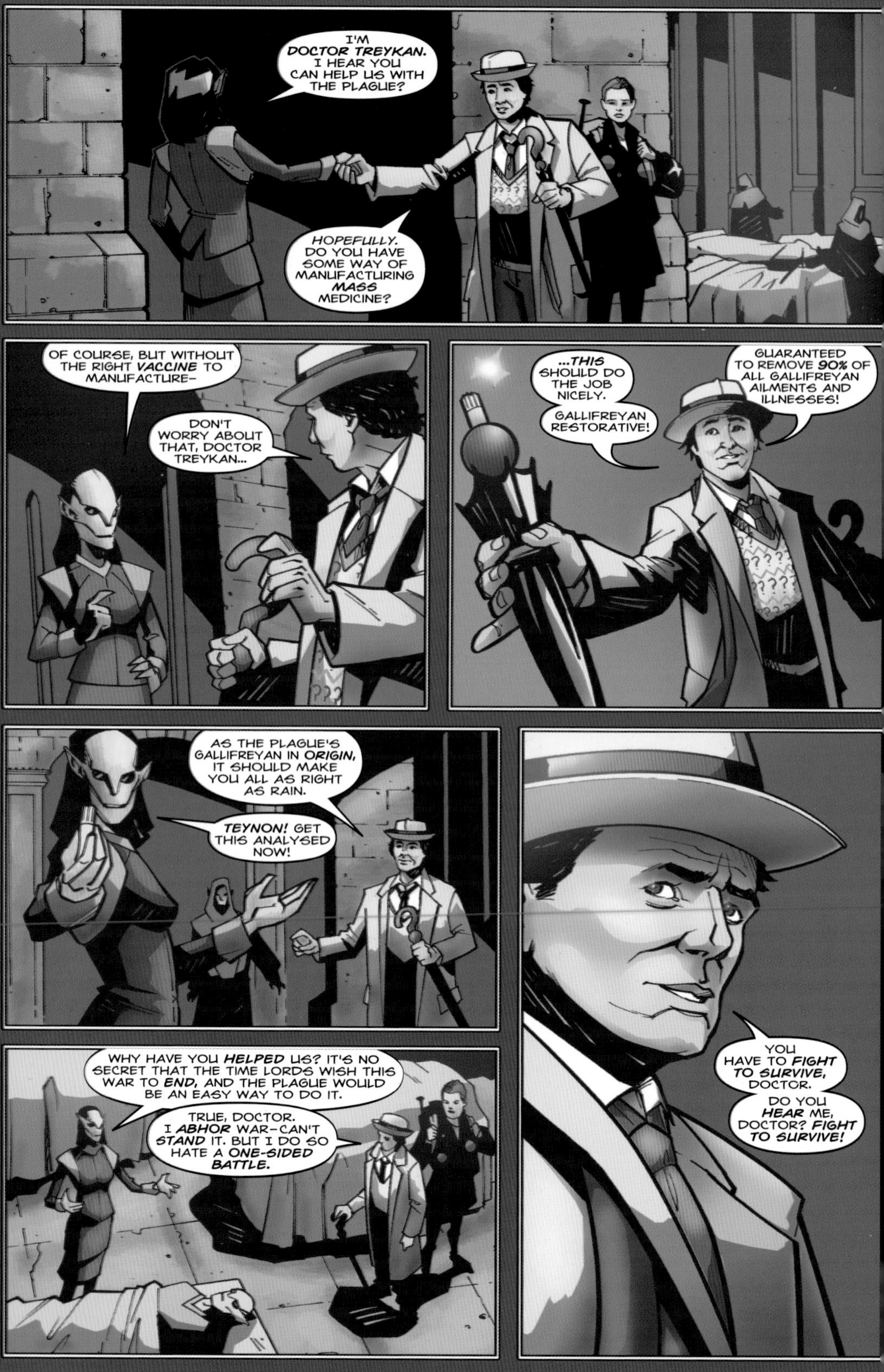
I'M DOCTOR TREYKAN. I HEAR YOU CAN HELP US WITH THE PLAGUE?
HOPEFULLY. DO YOU HAVE SOME WAY OF MANUFACTURING MASS MEDICINE?
OF COURSE, BUT WITHOUT THE RIGHT VACCINE TO MANUFACTURE–
DON'T WORRY ABOUT THAT, DOCTOR TREYKAN...
...THIS SHOULD DO THE JOB NICELY.
GALLIFREYAN RESTORATIVE!
GUARANTEED TO REMOVE 90% OF ALL GALLIFREYAN AILMENTS AND ILLNESSES!
AS THE PLAGUE'S GALLIFREYAN IN ORIGIN, IT SHOULD MAKE YOU ALL AS RIGHT AS RAIN.
TEYNON! GET THIS ANALYSED NOW!
WHY HAVE YOU HELPED US? IT'S NO SECRET THAT THE TIME LORDS WISH THIS WAR TO END, AND THE PLAGUE WOULD BE AN EASY WAY TO DO IT.
TRUE, DOCTOR. I ABHOR WAR–CAN'T STAND IT. BUT I DO SO HATE A ONE-SIDED BATTLE.
YOU HAVE TO FIGHT TO SURVIVE, DOCTOR.
DO YOU HEAR ME, DOCTOR? FIGHT TO SURVIVE!

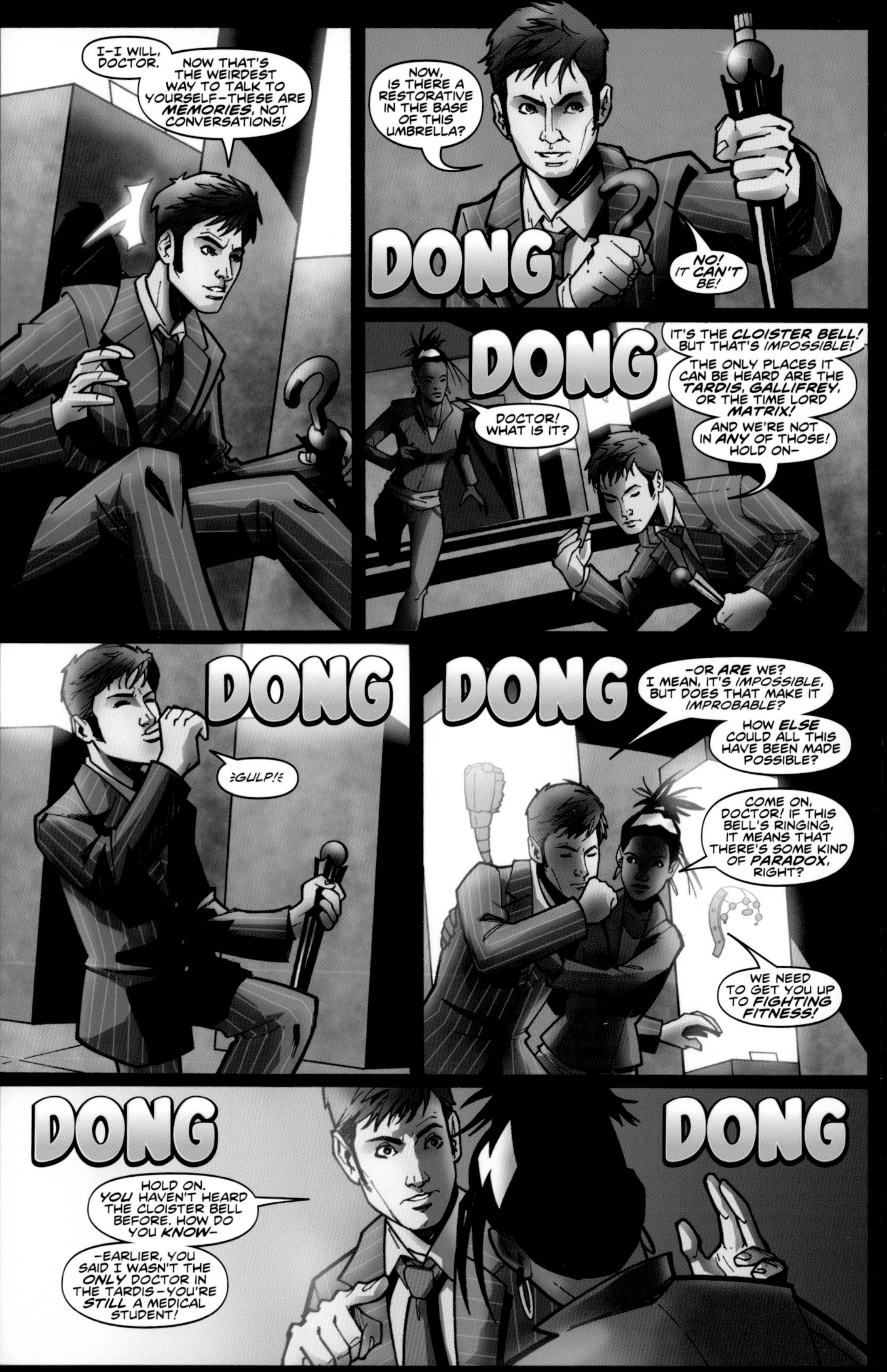
I–I WILL, DOCTOR.
NOW THAT'S THE WEIRDEST WAY TO TALK TO YOURSELF–THESE ARE MEMORIES, NOT CONVERSATIONS!
NOW, IS THERE A RESTORATIVE IN THE BASE OF THIS UMBRELLA?
DONG
NO! IT CAN'T BE!
DONG
DOCTOR! WHAT IS IT?
IT'S THE CLOISTER BELL! BUT THAT'S IMPOSSIBLE!
THE ONLY PLACES IT CAN BE HEARD ARE THE TARDIS, GALLIFREY, OR THE TIME LORD MATRIX!
AND WE'RE NOT IN ANY OF THOSE! HOLD ON–
DONG
GULP!
DONG
–OR ARE WE? I MEAN, IT'S IMPOSSIBLE, BUT DOES THAT MAKE IT IMPROBABLE?
HOW ELSE COULD ALL THIS HAVE BEEN MADE POSSIBLE?
COME ON, DOCTOR! IF THIS BELL'S RINGING, IT MEANS THAT THERE'S SOME KIND OF PARADOX, RIGHT?
WE NEED TO GET YOU UP TO FIGHTING FITNESS!
DONG
DONG
HOLD ON. YOU HAVEN'T HEARD THE CLOISTER BELL BEFORE. HOW DO YOU KNOW–
–EARLIER, YOU SAID I WASN'T THE ONLY DOCTOR IN THE TARDIS–YOU'RE STILL A MEDICAL STUDENT!

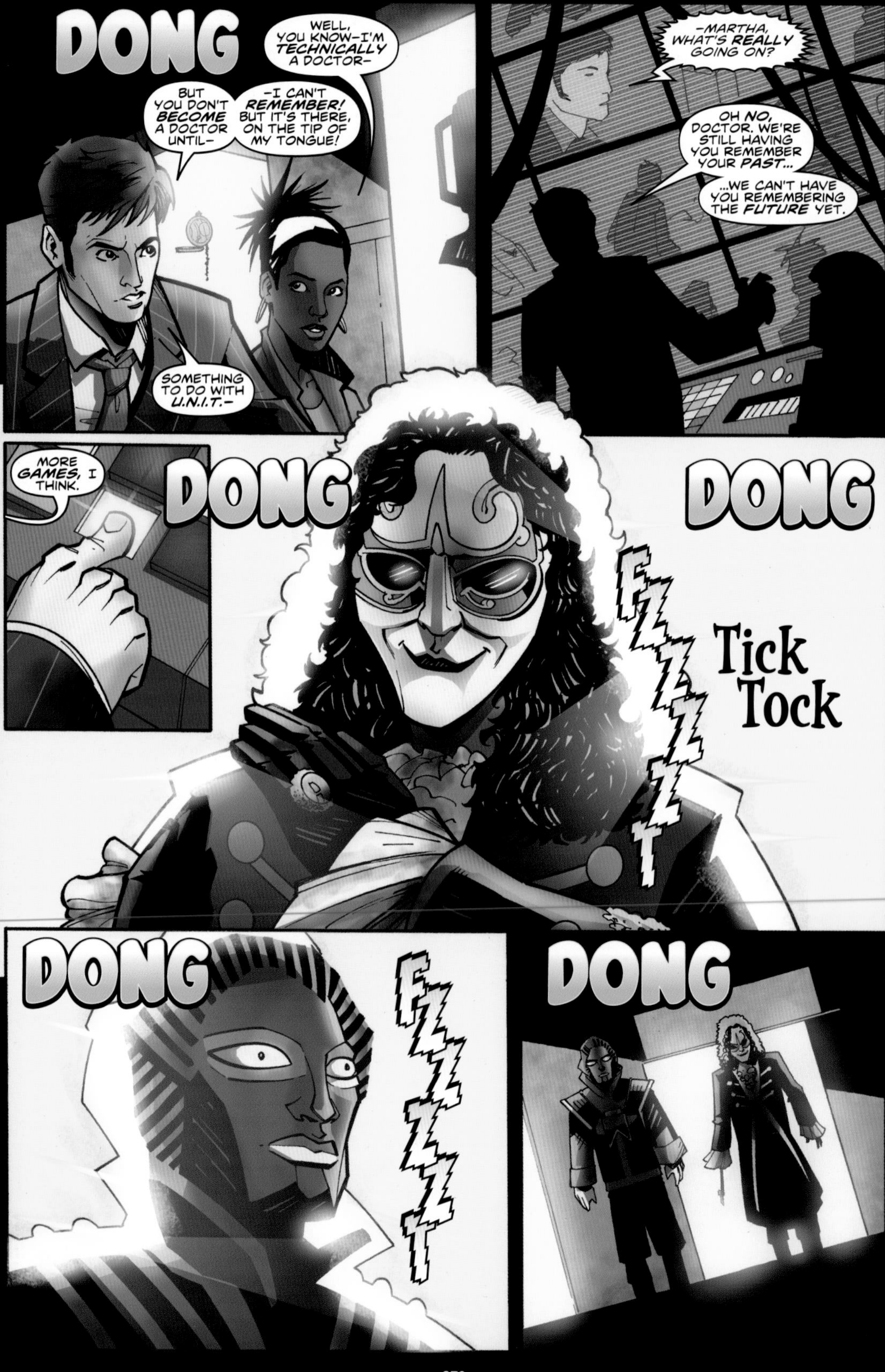
DONG
WELL, YOU KNOW—I'M TECHNICALLY A DOCTOR—
BUT YOU DON'T BECOME A DOCTOR UNTIL—
—I CAN'T REMEMBER! BUT IT'S THERE, ON THE TIP OF MY TONGUE!
SOMETHING TO DO WITH U.N.I.T.—
—MARTHA, WHAT'S REALLY GOING ON?
OH NO, DOCTOR. WE'RE STILL HAVING YOU REMEMBER YOUR PAST...
...WE CAN'T HAVE YOU REMEMBERING THE FUTURE YET.
MORE GAMES, I THINK.
DONG
DONG
FZZZZZT
Tick Tock
DONG
FZZZZZT
DONG

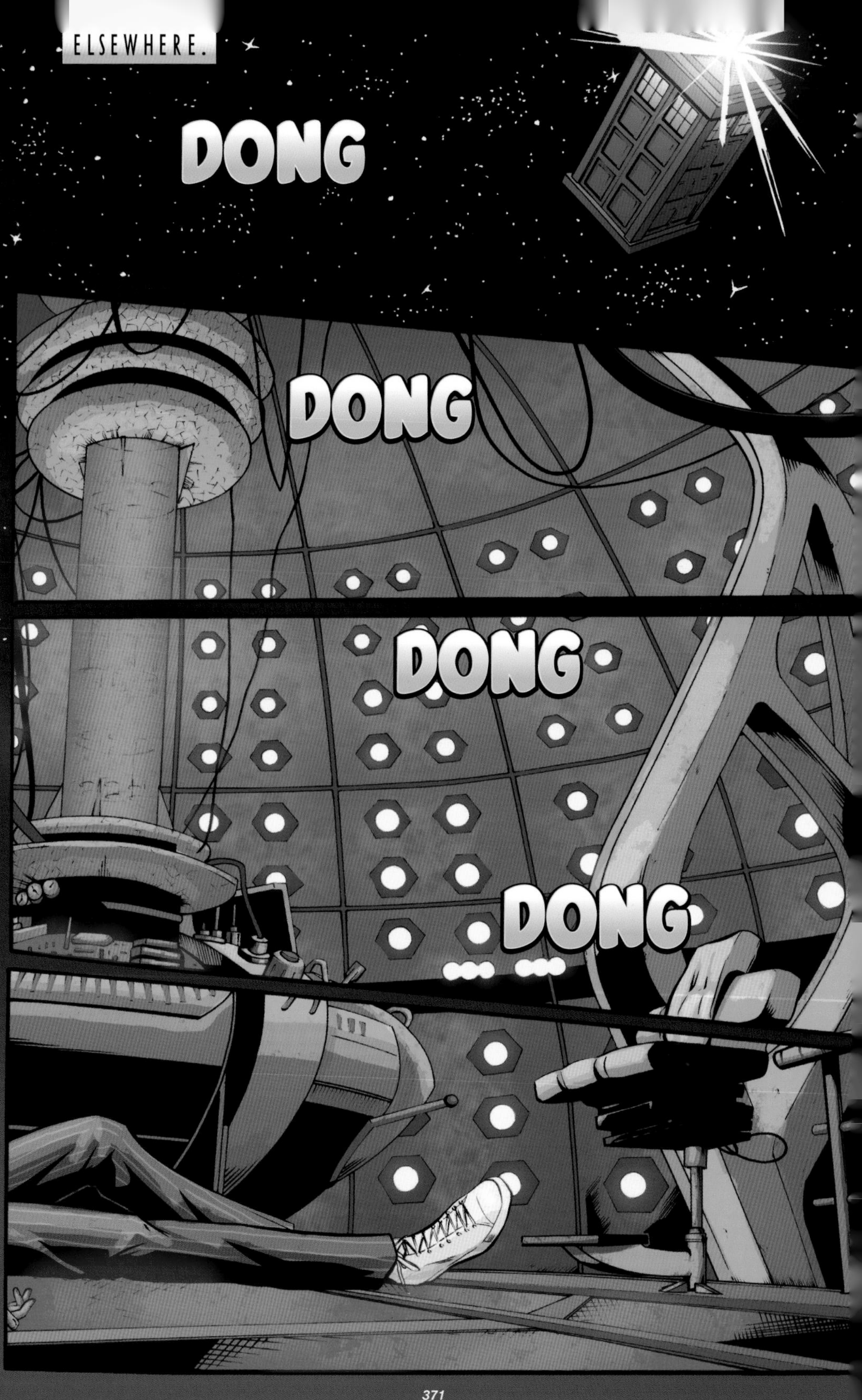
ELSEWHERE.
DONG
DONG
DONG
DONG

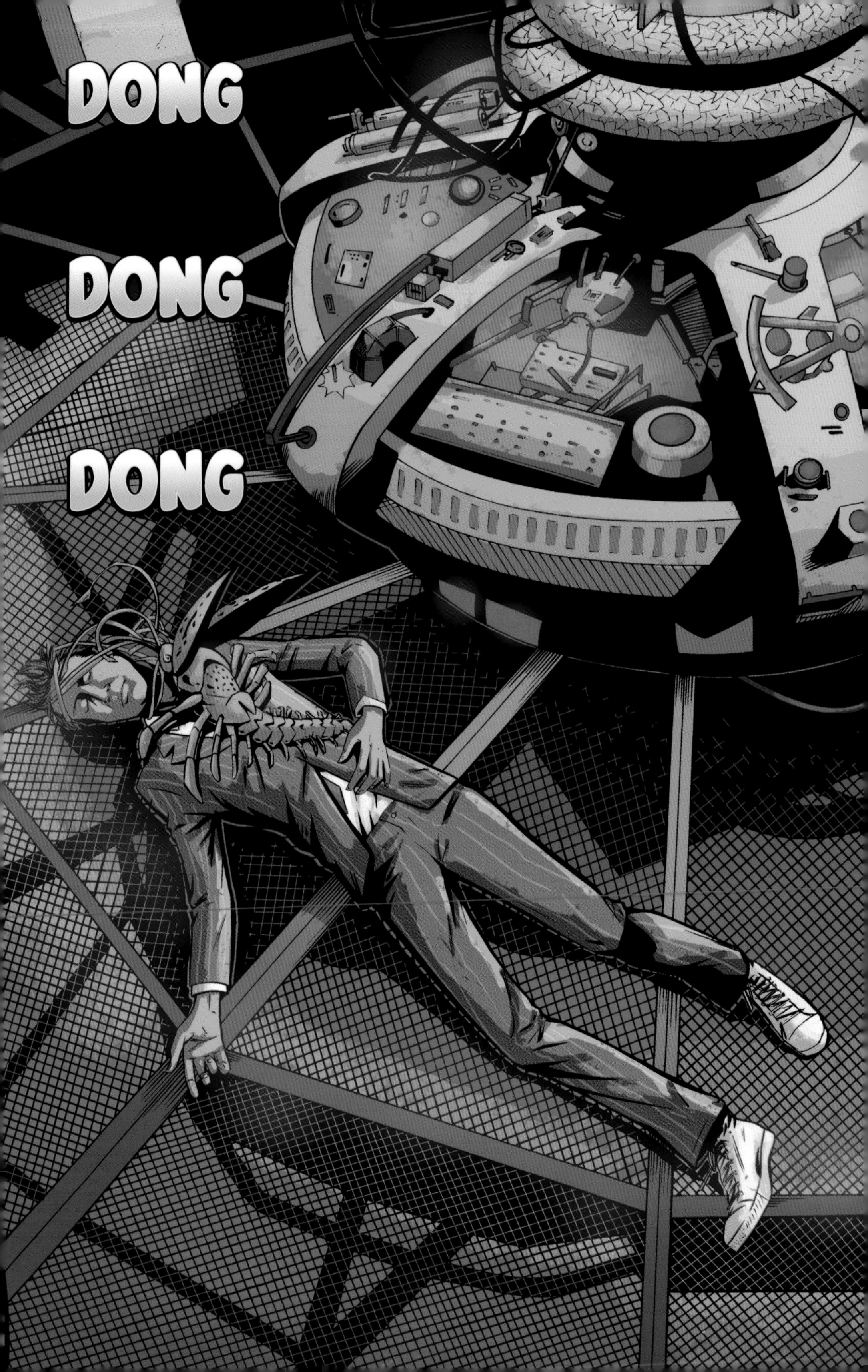
DONG
DONG
DONG

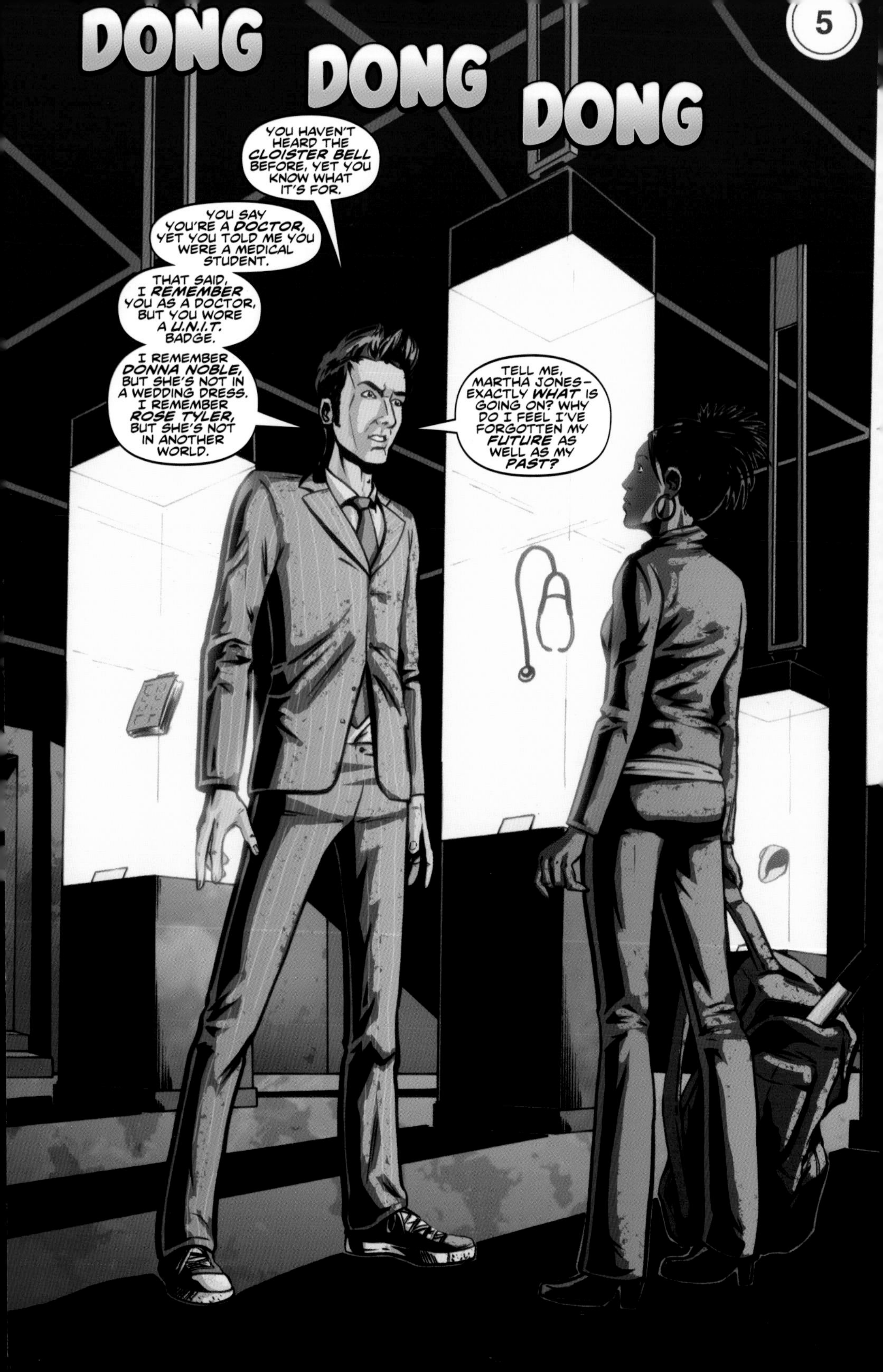
DONG
DONG
DONG
YOU HAVEN'T HEARD THE CLOISTER BELL BEFORE, YET YOU KNOW WHAT IT'S FOR.
YOU SAY YOU'RE A DOCTOR, YET YOU TOLD ME YOU WERE A MEDICAL STUDENT.
THAT SAID, I REMEMBER YOU AS A DOCTOR, BUT YOU WORE A U.N.I.T. BADGE.
I REMEMBER DONNA NOBLE, BUT SHE'S NOT IN A WEDDING DRESS. I REMEMBER ROSE TYLER, BUT SHE'S NOT IN ANOTHER WORLD.
TELL ME, MARTHA JONES- EXACTLY WHAT IS GOING ON? WHY DO I FEEL I'VE FORGOTTEN MY FUTURE AS WELL AS MY PAST?

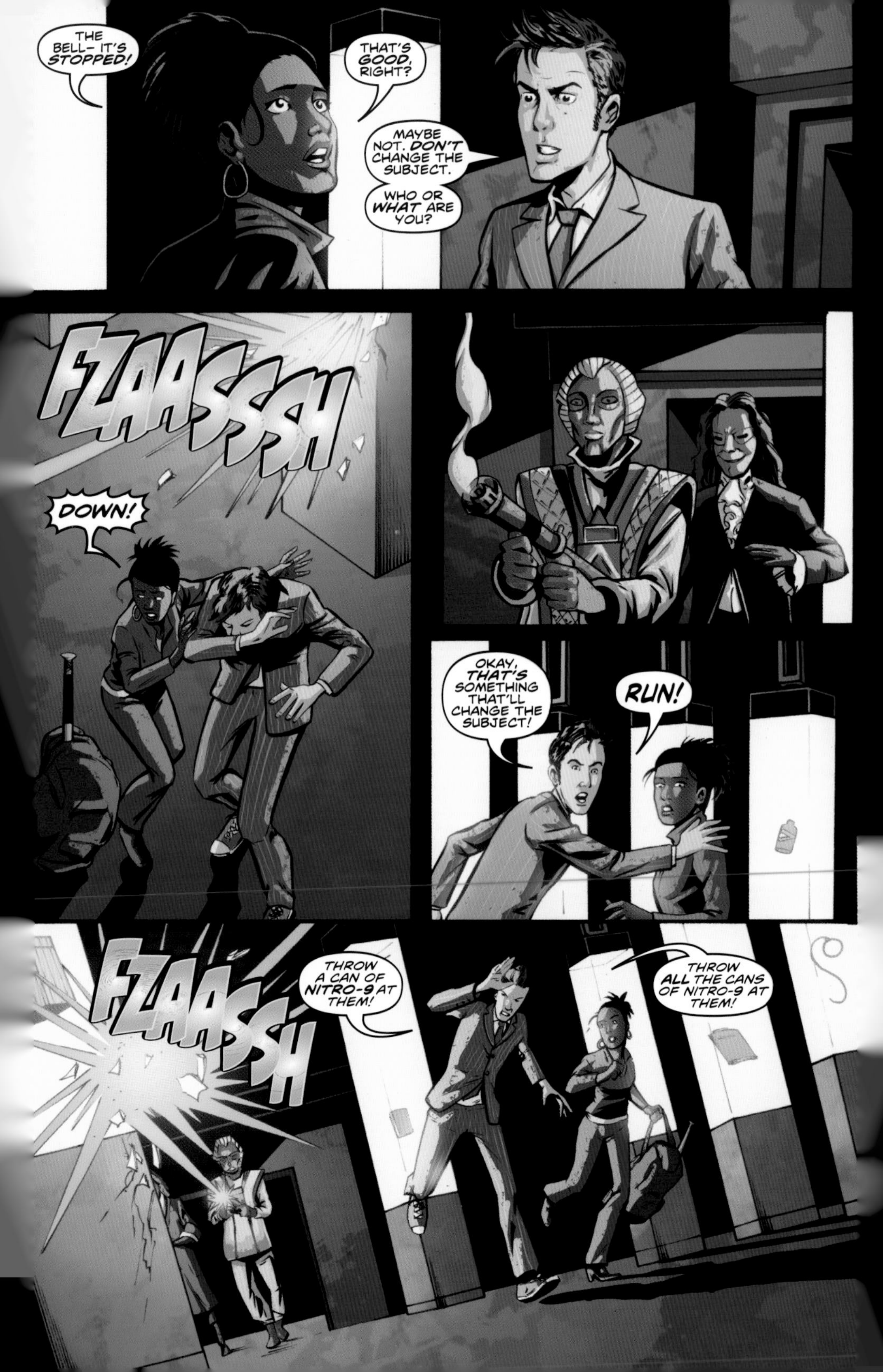
THE BELL– IT'S STOPPED!
THAT'S GOOD, RIGHT?
MAYBE NOT. DON'T CHANGE THE SUBJECT.
WHO OR WHAT ARE YOU?
FZAASSSH
DOWN!
OKAY, THAT'S SOMETHING THAT'LL CHANGE THE SUBJECT!
RUN!
FZAASSH
THROW A CAN OF NITRO-9 AT THEM!
THROW ALL THE CANS OF NITRO-9 AT THEM!

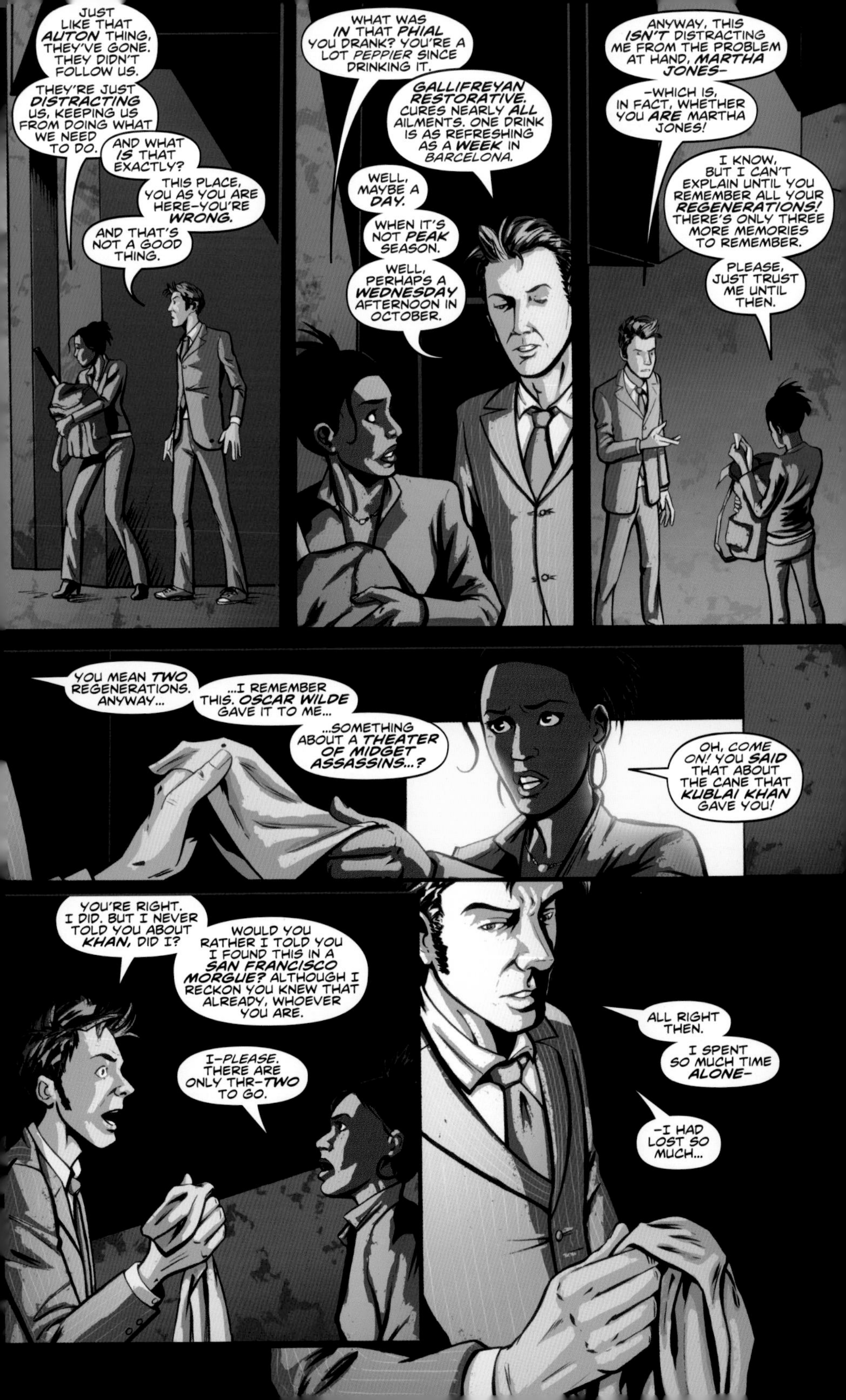
JUST LIKE THAT AUTON THING, THEY'VE GONE. THEY DIDN'T FOLLOW US.
THEY'RE JUST DISTRACTING US, KEEPING US FROM DOING WHAT WE NEED TO DO.
AND WHAT IS THAT EXACTLY?
THIS PLACE, YOU AS YOU ARE HERE–YOU'RE WRONG.
AND THAT'S NOT A GOOD THING.
WHAT WAS IN THAT PHIAL YOU DRANK? YOU'RE A LOT PEPPIER SINCE DRINKING IT.
GALLIFREYAN RESTORATIVE. CURES NEARLY ALL AILMENTS. ONE DRINK IS AS REFRESHING AS A WEEK IN BARCELONA.
WELL, MAYBE A DAY.
WHEN IT'S NOT PEAK SEASON.
WELL, PERHAPS A WEDNESDAY AFTERNOON IN OCTOBER.
ANYWAY, THIS ISN'T DISTRACTING ME FROM THE PROBLEM AT HAND, MARTHA JONES–
–WHICH IS, IN FACT, WHETHER YOU ARE MARTHA JONES!
I KNOW, BUT I CAN'T EXPLAIN UNTIL YOU REMEMBER ALL YOUR REGENERATIONS! THERE'S ONLY THREE MORE MEMORIES TO REMEMBER.
PLEASE, JUST TRUST ME UNTIL THEN.
YOU MEAN TWO REGENERATIONS. ANYWAY...
...I REMEMBER THIS. OSCAR WILDE GAVE IT TO ME...
...SOMETHING ABOUT A THEATER OF MIDGET ASSASSINS...?
OH, COME ON! YOU SAID THAT ABOUT THE CANE THAT KUBLAI KHAN GAVE YOU!
YOU'RE RIGHT. I DID. BUT I NEVER TOLD YOU ABOUT KHAN, DID I?
WOULD YOU RATHER I TOLD YOU I FOUND THIS IN A SAN FRANCISCO MORGUE? ALTHOUGH I RECKON YOU KNEW THAT ALREADY, WHOEVER YOU ARE.
I–PLEASE. THERE ARE ONLY THR–TWO TO GO.
ALL RIGHT THEN.
I SPENT SO MUCH TIME ALONE–
–I HAD LOST SO MUCH...

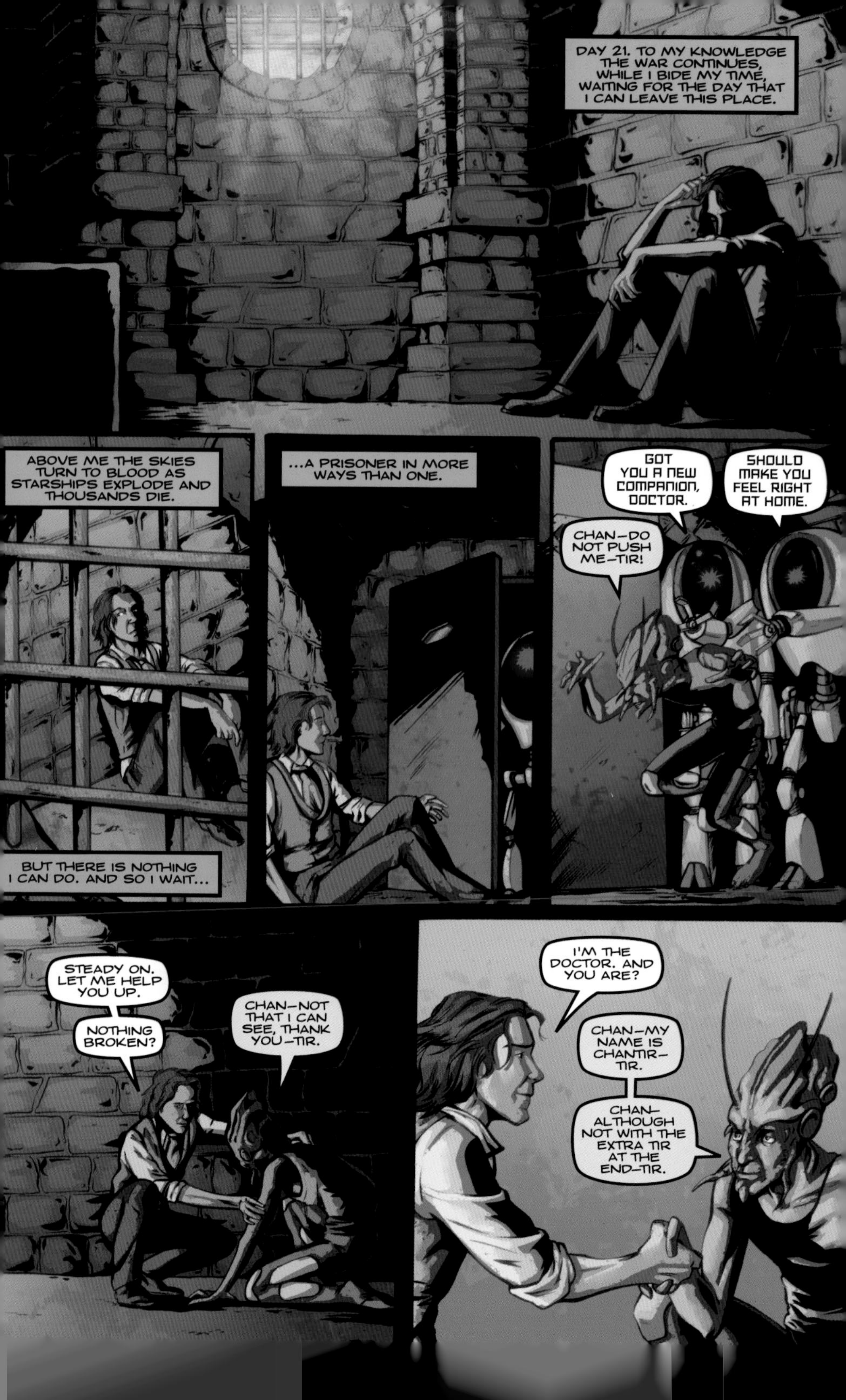
DAY 21. TO MY KNOWLEDGE THE WAR CONTINUES, WHILE I BIDE MY TIME, WAITING FOR THE DAY THAT I CAN LEAVE THIS PLACE.
ABOVE ME THE SKIES TURN TO BLOOD AS STARSHIPS EXPLODE AND THOUSANDS DIE.
BUT THERE IS NOTHING I CAN DO. AND SO I WAIT...
...A PRISONER IN MORE WAYS THAN ONE.
GOT YOU A NEW COMPANION, DOCTOR.
SHOULD MAKE YOU FEEL RIGHT AT HOME.
CHAN—DO NOT PUSH ME—TIR!
STEADY ON. LET ME HELP YOU UP.
NOTHING BROKEN?
CHAN—NOT THAT I CAN SEE, THANK YOU—TIR.
I'M THE DOCTOR. AND YOU ARE?
CHAN—MY NAME IS CHANTIR—TIR.
CHAN—ALTHOUGH NOT WITH THE EXTRA TIR AT THE END—TIR.

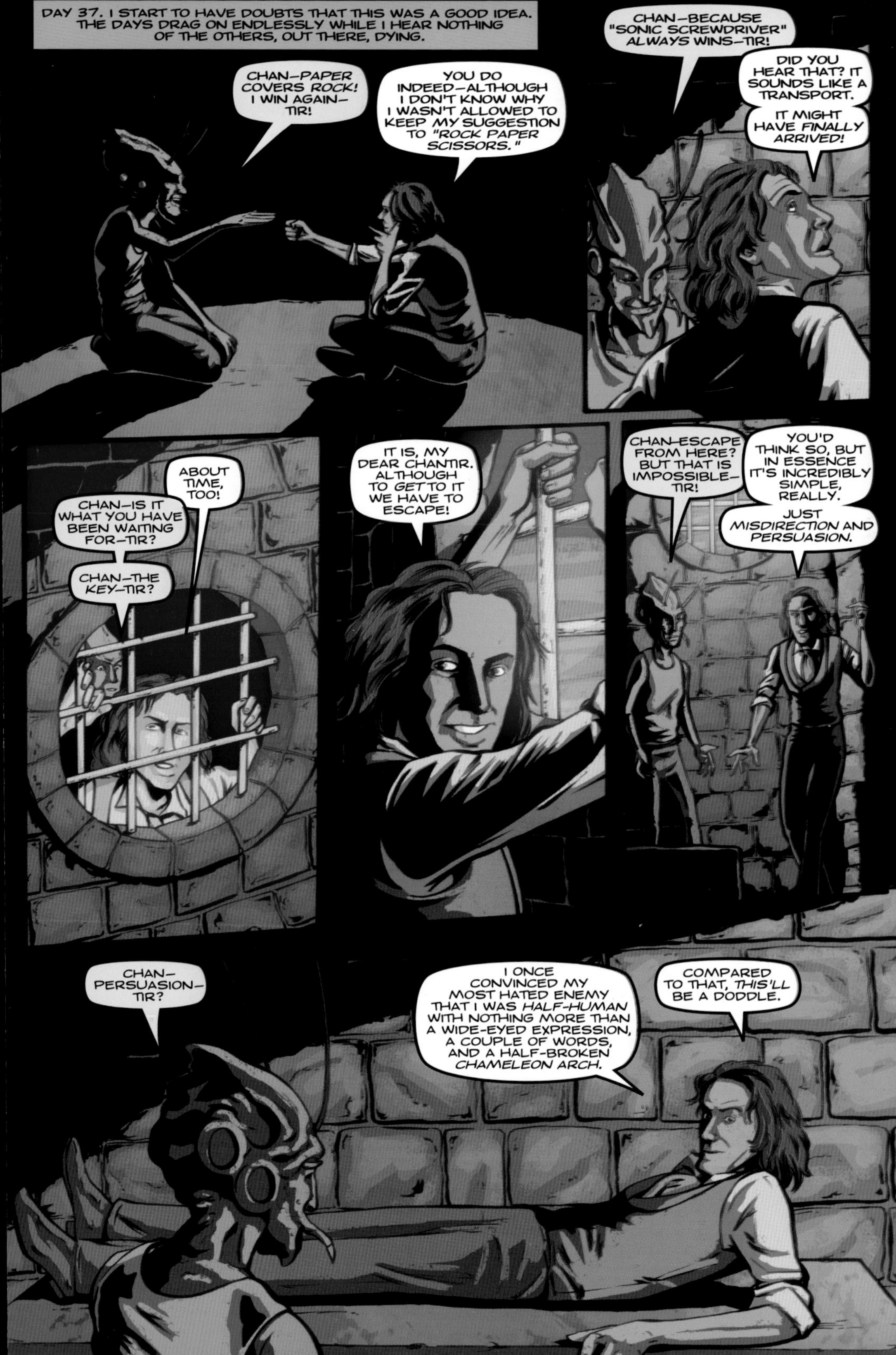
DAY 37. I START TO HAVE DOUBTS THAT THIS WAS A GOOD IDEA. THE DAYS DRAG ON ENDLESSLY WHILE I HEAR NOTHING OF THE OTHERS, OUT THERE, DYING.
CHAN—PAPER COVERS ROCK! I WIN AGAIN—TIR!
YOU DO INDEED—ALTHOUGH I DON'T KNOW WHY I WASN'T ALLOWED TO KEEP MY SUGGESTION TO "ROCK PAPER SCISSORS."
CHAN—BECAUSE "SONIC SCREWDRIVER" ALWAYS WINS—TIR!
DID YOU HEAR THAT? IT SOUNDS LIKE A TRANSPORT.
IT MIGHT HAVE FINALLY ARRIVED!
CHAN—IS IT WHAT YOU HAVE BEEN WAITING FOR—TIR?
ABOUT TIME, TOO!
CHAN—THE KEY—TIR?
IT IS, MY DEAR CHANTIR. ALTHOUGH TO GET TO IT WE HAVE TO ESCAPE!
CHAN—ESCAPE FROM HERE? BUT THAT IS IMPOSSIBLE—TIR!
YOU'D THINK SO, BUT IN ESSENCE IT'S INCREDIBLY SIMPLE, REALLY.
JUST MISDIRECTION AND PERSUASION.
CHAN—PERSUASION—TIR?
I ONCE CONVINCED MY MOST HATED ENEMY THAT I WAS HALF-HUMAN WITH NOTHING MORE THAN A WIDE-EYED EXPRESSION, A COUPLE OF WORDS, AND A HALF-BROKEN CHAMELEON ARCH.
COMPARED TO THAT, THIS'LL BE A DODDLE.

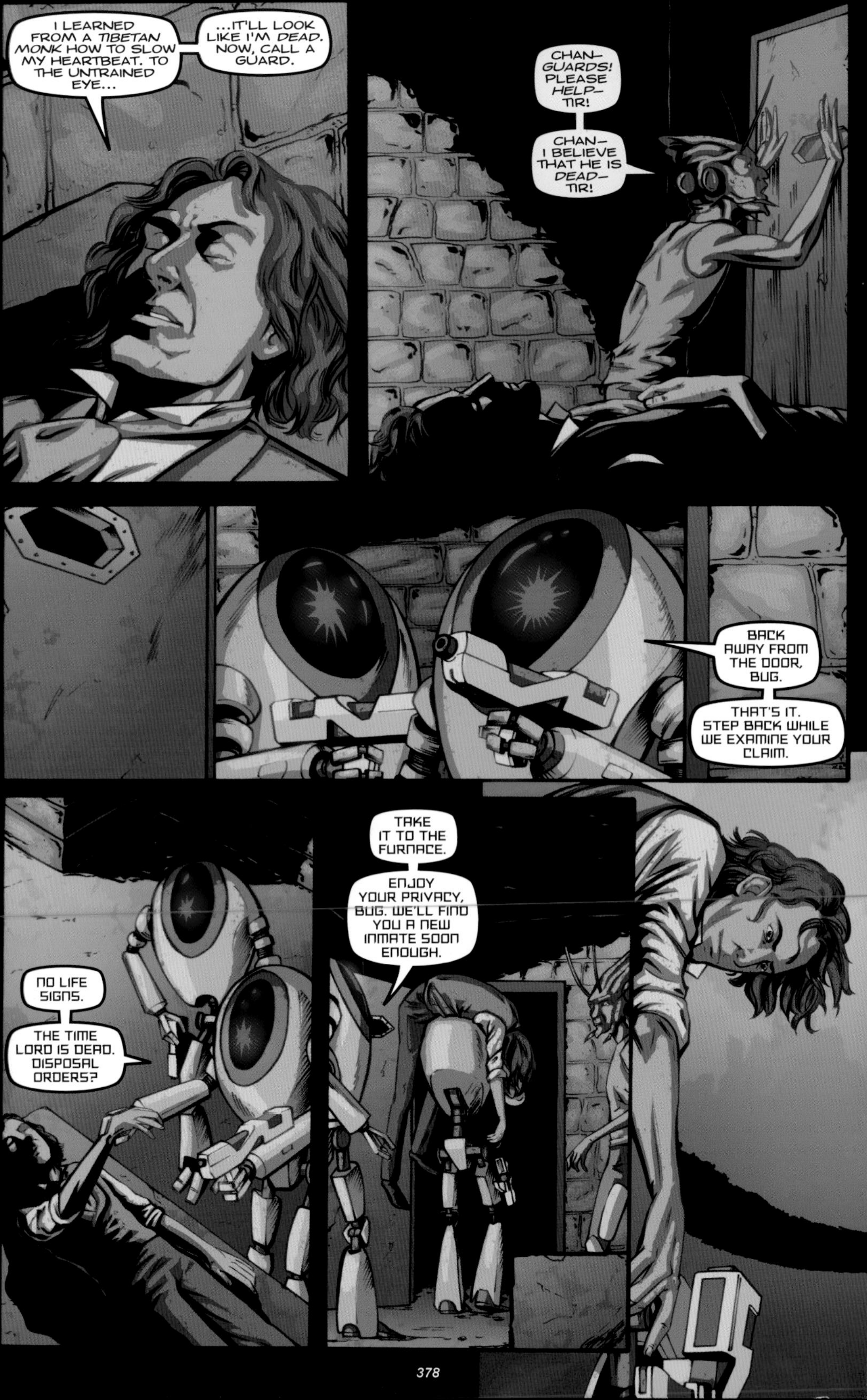

I LEARNED FROM A *TIBETAN* MONK HOW TO SLOW MY HEARTBEAT. TO THE UNTRAINED EYE...
...IT'LL LOOK LIKE I'M *DEAD*. NOW, CALL A GUARD.
CHAN-*GUARDS!* PLEASE *HELP*-TIR!
CHAN-I BELIEVE THAT HE IS *DEAD*-TIR!
BACK AWAY FROM THE DOOR, BUG.
THAT'S IT. STEP BACK WHILE WE EXAMINE YOUR CLAIM.
NO LIFE SIGNS.
THE TIME LORD IS DEAD. DISPOSAL ORDERS?
TAKE IT TO THE FURNACE.
ENJOY YOUR PRIVACY, BUG. WE'LL FIND YOU A NEW INMATE SOON ENOUGH.

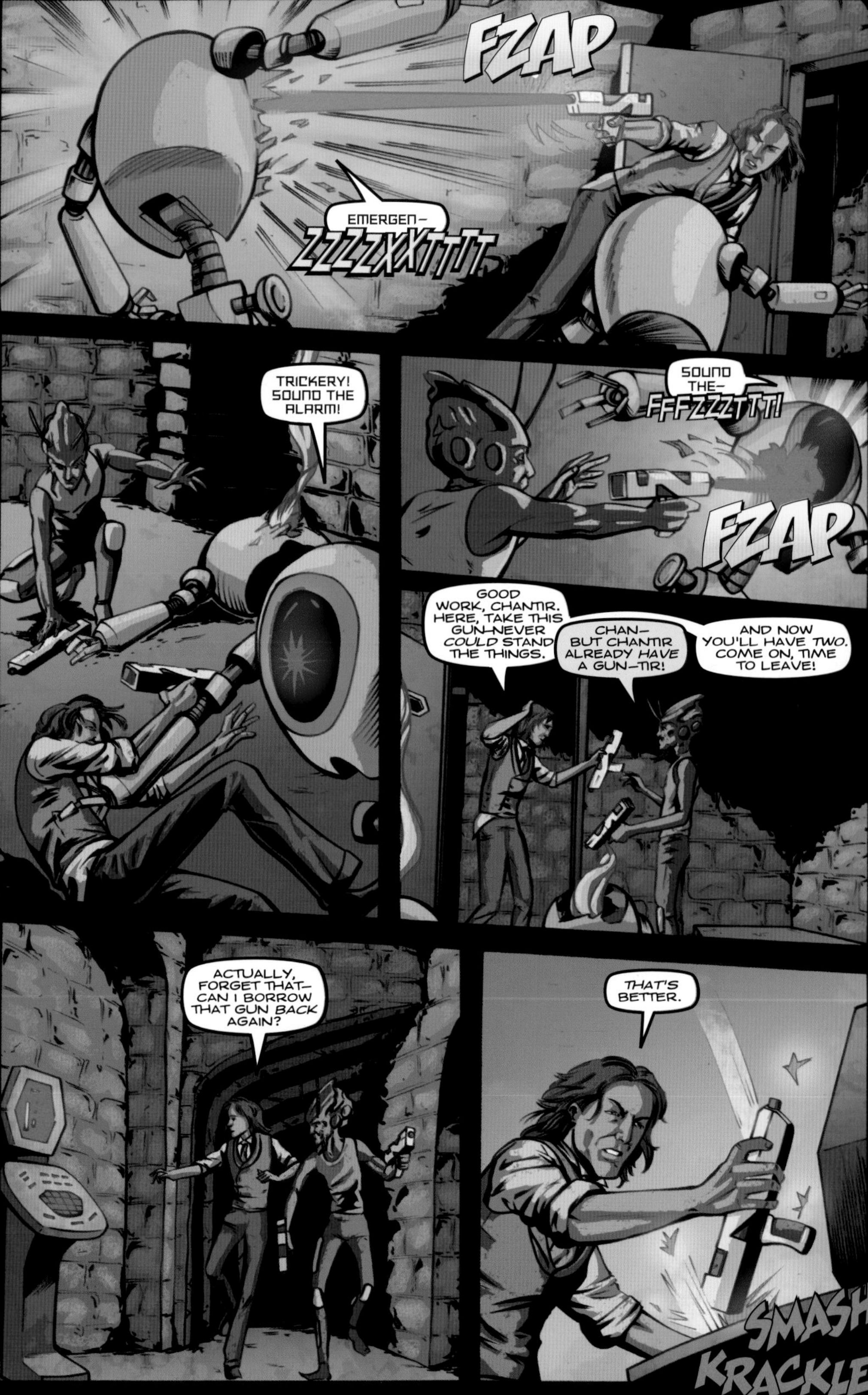
FZAP
EMERGEN–
ZZZZXXTTTT
TRICKERY! SOUND THE ALARM!
SOUND THE–
FFFZZZTTTT!
FZAP
GOOD WORK, CHANTIR. HERE, TAKE THIS GUN–NEVER *COULD* STAND THE THINGS.
CHAN– BUT CHANTIR ALREADY *HAVE* A GUN–TIR!
AND NOW YOU'LL HAVE *TWO*. COME ON, TIME TO LEAVE!
ACTUALLY, FORGET THAT– CAN I BORROW THAT GUN *BACK* AGAIN?
THAT'S BETTER.
SMASH
KRACKLE

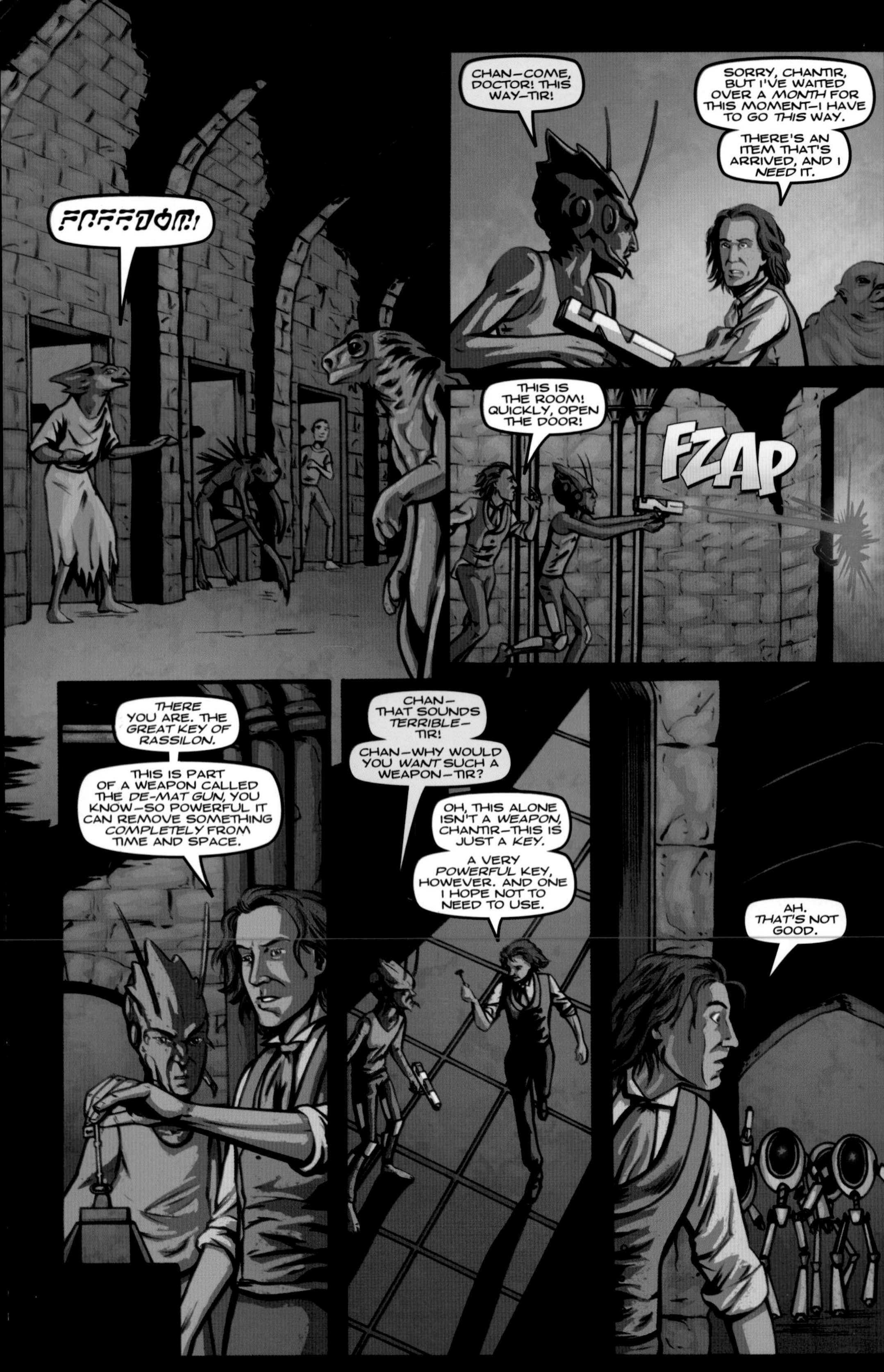
FREEDOM!
CHAN—COME, DOCTOR! THIS WAY—TIR!
SORRY, CHANTIR, BUT I'VE WAITED OVER A MONTH FOR THIS MOMENT—I HAVE TO GO THIS WAY.
THERE'S AN ITEM THAT'S ARRIVED, AND I NEED IT.
THIS IS THE ROOM! QUICKLY, OPEN THE DOOR!
FZAP
THERE YOU ARE. THE GREAT KEY OF RASSILON.
THIS IS PART OF A WEAPON CALLED THE DE-MAT GUN, YOU KNOW—SO POWERFUL IT CAN REMOVE SOMETHING COMPLETELY FROM TIME AND SPACE.
CHAN—THAT SOUNDS TERRIBLE—TIR!
CHAN—WHY WOULD YOU WANT SUCH A WEAPON—TIR?
OH, THIS ALONE ISN'T A WEAPON, CHANTIR—THIS IS JUST A KEY.
A VERY POWERFUL KEY, HOWEVER. AND ONE I HOPE NOT TO NEED TO USE.
AH. THAT'S NOT GOOD.

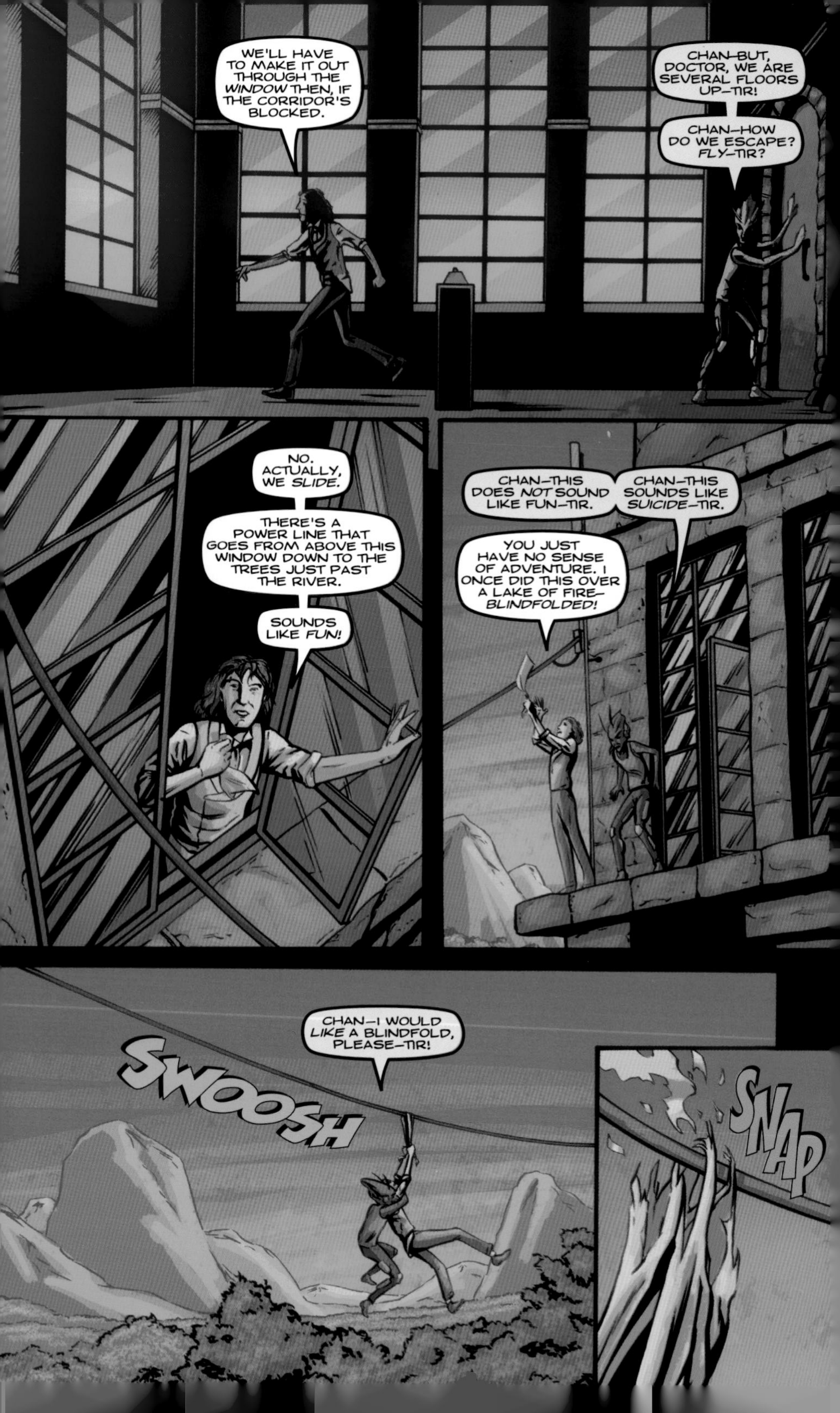
WE'LL HAVE TO MAKE IT OUT THROUGH THE WINDOW THEN, IF THE CORRIDOR'S BLOCKED.
CHAN—BUT, DOCTOR, WE ARE SEVERAL FLOORS UP—TIR!
CHAN—HOW DO WE ESCAPE? FLY—TIR?
NO. ACTUALLY, WE SLIDE.
THERE'S A POWER LINE THAT GOES FROM ABOVE THIS WINDOW DOWN TO THE TREES JUST PAST THE RIVER.
SOUNDS LIKE FUN!
CHAN—THIS DOES NOT SOUND LIKE FUN—TIR.
CHAN—THIS SOUNDS LIKE SUICIDE—TIR.
YOU JUST HAVE NO SENSE OF ADVENTURE. I ONCE DID THIS OVER A LAKE OF FIRE—BLINDFOLDED!
CHAN—I WOULD LIKE A BLINDFOLD, PLEASE—TIR!
SWOOSH
SNAP

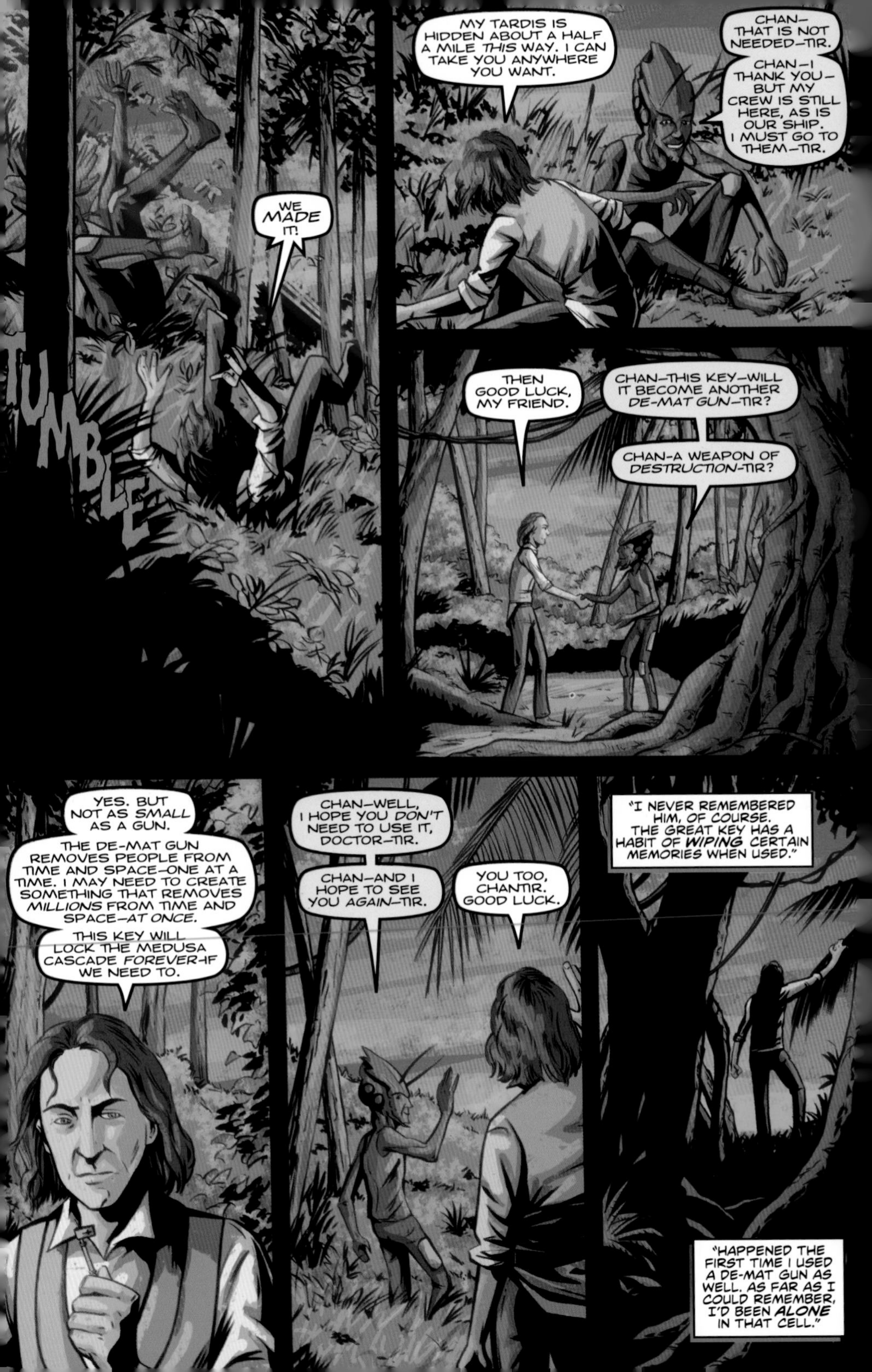
WE MADE IT!
TUMBLE
MY TARDIS IS HIDDEN ABOUT A HALF A MILE THIS WAY. I CAN TAKE YOU ANYWHERE YOU WANT.
CHAN—THAT IS NOT NEEDED—TIR.
CHAN—I THANK YOU—BUT MY CREW IS STILL HERE, AS IS OUR SHIP. I MUST GO TO THEM—TIR.
THEN GOOD LUCK, MY FRIEND.
CHAN—THIS KEY—WILL IT BECOME ANOTHER DE-MAT GUN—TIR?
CHAN—A WEAPON OF DESTRUCTION—TIR?
YES. BUT NOT AS SMALL AS A GUN.
THE DE-MAT GUN REMOVES PEOPLE FROM TIME AND SPACE—ONE AT A TIME. I MAY NEED TO CREATE SOMETHING THAT REMOVES MILLIONS FROM TIME AND SPACE—AT ONCE.
THIS KEY WILL LOCK THE MEDUSA CASCADE FOREVER—IF WE NEED TO.
CHAN—WELL, I HOPE YOU DON'T NEED TO USE IT, DOCTOR—TIR.
CHAN—AND I HOPE TO SEE YOU AGAIN—TIR.
YOU TOO, CHANTIR. GOOD LUCK.
"I NEVER REMEMBERED HIM, OF COURSE. THE GREAT KEY HAS A HABIT OF WIPING CERTAIN MEMORIES WHEN USED."
"HAPPENED THE FIRST TIME I USED A DE-MAT GUN AS WELL. AS FAR AS I COULD REMEMBER, I'D BEEN ALONE IN THAT CELL."

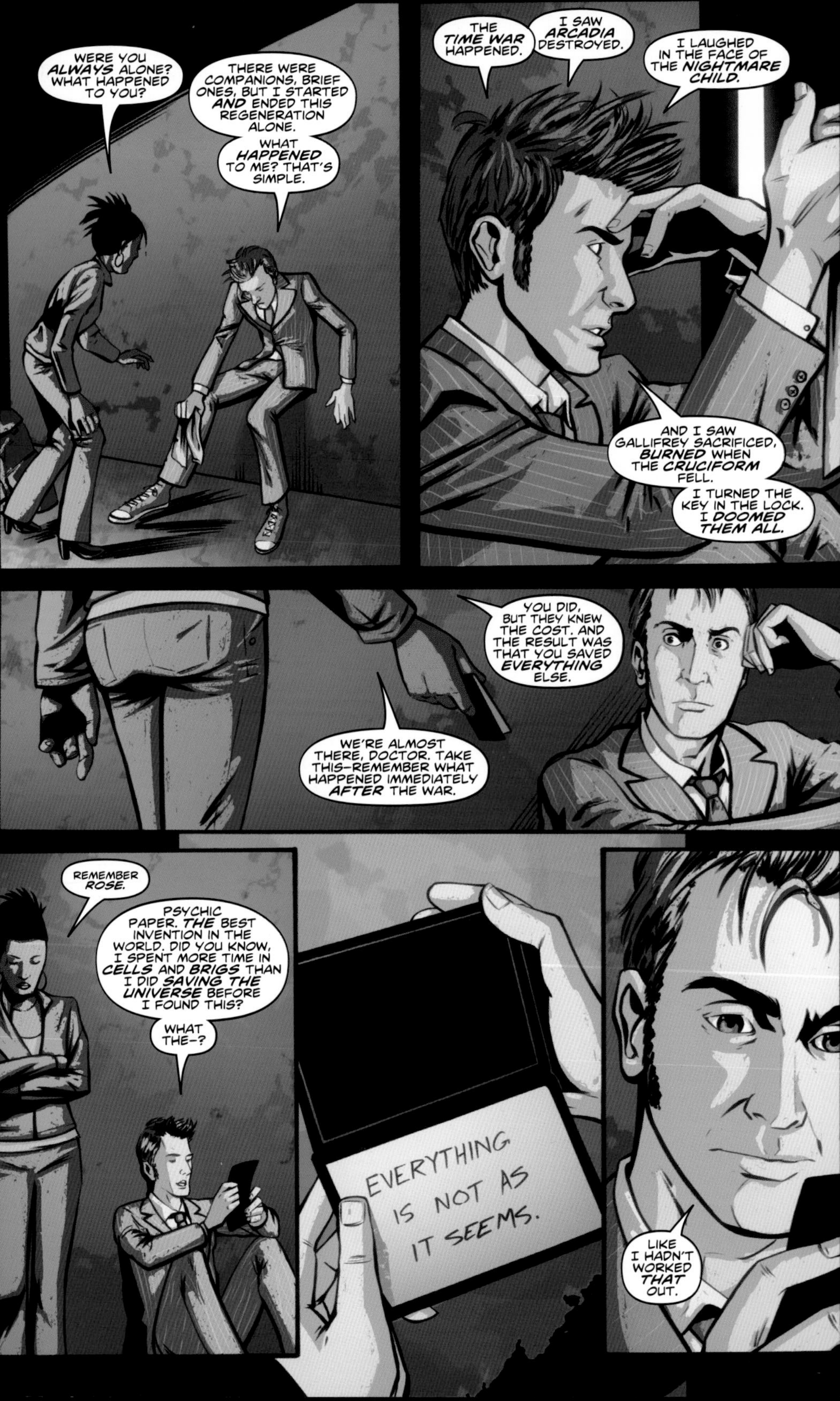
WERE YOU ALWAYS ALONE? WHAT HAPPENED TO YOU?
THERE WERE COMPANIONS, BRIEF ONES, BUT I STARTED AND ENDED THIS REGENERATION ALONE.
WHAT HAPPENED TO ME? THAT'S SIMPLE.
THE TIME WAR HAPPENED.
I SAW ARCADIA DESTROYED.
I LAUGHED IN THE FACE OF THE NIGHTMARE CHILD.
AND I SAW GALLIFREY SACRIFICED, BURNED WHEN THE CRUCIFORM FELL.
I TURNED THE KEY IN THE LOCK. I DOOMED THEM ALL.
YOU DID, BUT THEY KNEW THE COST. AND THE RESULT WAS THAT YOU SAVED EVERYTHING ELSE.
WE'RE ALMOST THERE, DOCTOR. TAKE THIS–REMEMBER WHAT HAPPENED IMMEDIATELY AFTER THE WAR.
REMEMBER ROSE.
PSYCHIC PAPER. THE BEST INVENTION IN THE WORLD. DID YOU KNOW, I SPENT MORE TIME IN CELLS AND BRIGS THAN I DID SAVING THE UNIVERSE BEFORE I FOUND THIS?
WHAT THE–?
EVERYTHING IS NOT AS IT SEEMS.
LIKE I HADN'T WORKED THAT OUT.

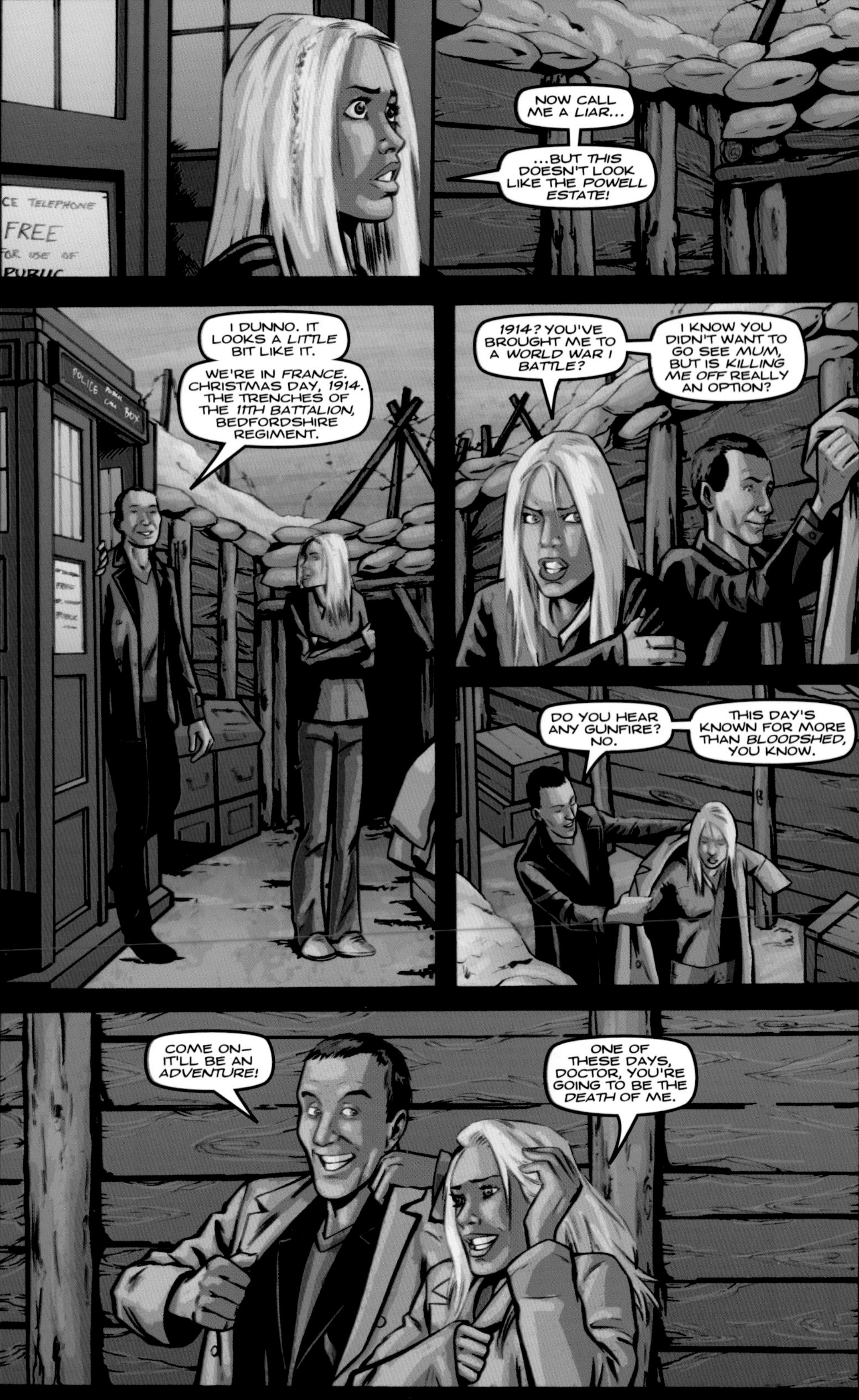

CE TELEPHONE
FREE
FOR USE OF
PUBLIC
NOW CALL ME A LIAR...
...BUT THIS DOESN'T LOOK LIKE THE POWELL ESTATE!
I DUNNO. IT LOOKS A LITTLE BIT LIKE IT.
WE'RE IN FRANCE. CHRISTMAS DAY, 1914. THE TRENCHES OF THE 11TH BATTALION, BEDFORDSHIRE REGIMENT.
1914? YOU'VE BROUGHT ME TO A WORLD WAR I BATTLE?
I KNOW YOU DIDN'T WANT TO GO SEE MUM, BUT IS KILLING ME OFF REALLY AN OPTION?
DO YOU HEAR ANY GUNFIRE? NO.
THIS DAY'S KNOWN FOR MORE THAN BLOODSHED, YOU KNOW.
COME ON— IT'LL BE AN ADVENTURE!
ONE OF THESE DAYS, DOCTOR, YOU'RE GOING TO BE THE DEATH OF ME.

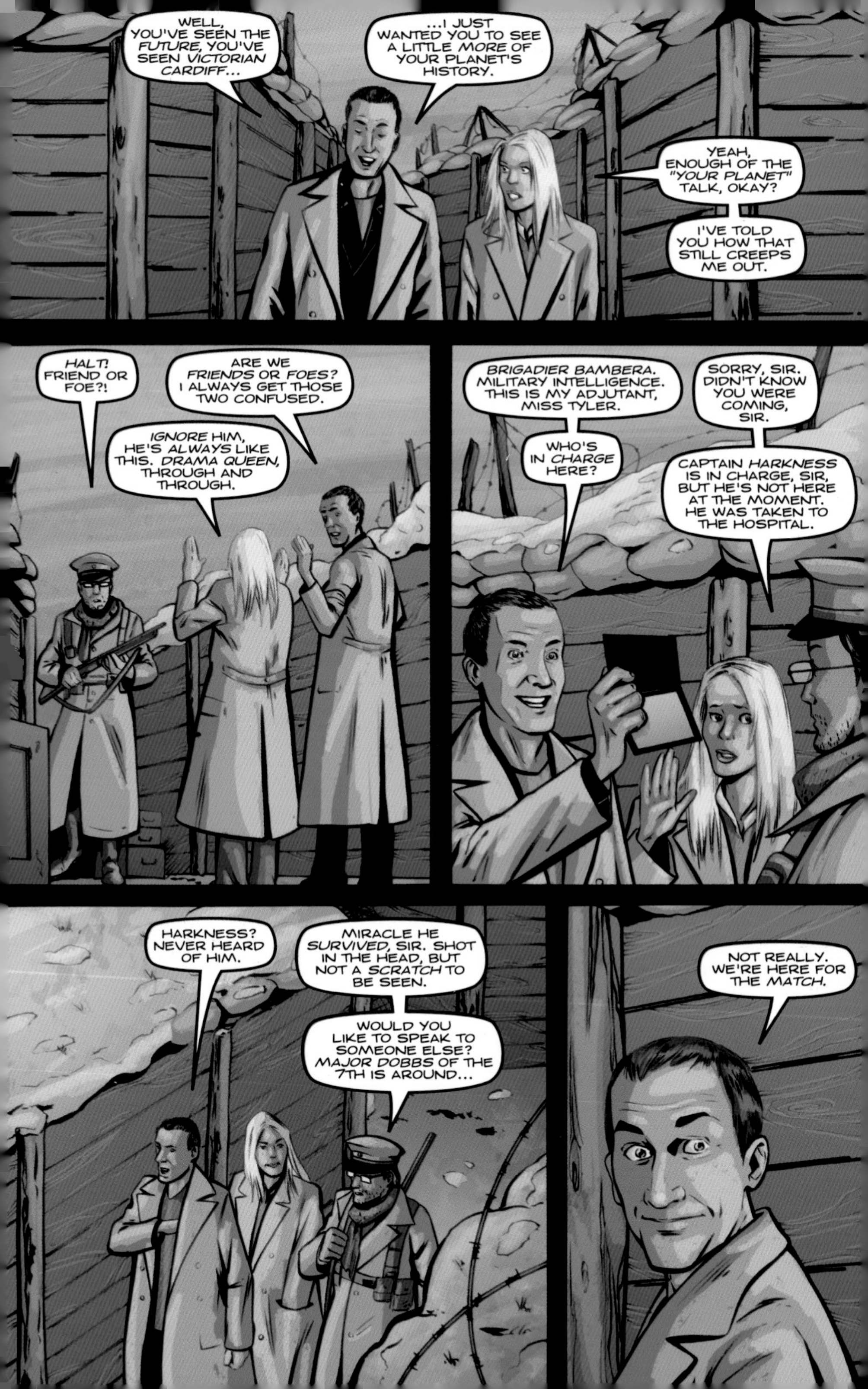
WELL, YOU'VE SEEN THE FUTURE, YOU'VE SEEN VICTORIAN CARDIFF...
...I JUST WANTED YOU TO SEE A LITTLE MORE OF YOUR PLANET'S HISTORY.
YEAH, ENOUGH OF THE "YOUR PLANET" TALK, OKAY?
I'VE TOLD YOU HOW THAT STILL CREEPS ME OUT.
HALT! FRIEND OR FOE?!
ARE WE FRIENDS OR FOES? I ALWAYS GET THOSE TWO CONFUSED.
IGNORE HIM, HE'S ALWAYS LIKE THIS. DRAMA QUEEN, THROUGH AND THROUGH.
BRIGADIER BAMBERA. MILITARY INTELLIGENCE. THIS IS MY ADJUTANT, MISS TYLER.
WHO'S IN CHARGE HERE?
SORRY, SIR. DIDN'T KNOW YOU WERE COMING, SIR.
CAPTAIN HARKNESS IS IN CHARGE, SIR, BUT HE'S NOT HERE AT THE MOMENT. HE WAS TAKEN TO THE HOSPITAL.
HARKNESS? NEVER HEARD OF HIM.
MIRACLE HE SURVIVED, SIR. SHOT IN THE HEAD, BUT NOT A SCRATCH TO BE SEEN.
WOULD YOU LIKE TO SPEAK TO SOMEONE ELSE? MAJOR DOBBS OF THE 7TH IS AROUND...
NOT REALLY. WE'RE HERE FOR THE MATCH.

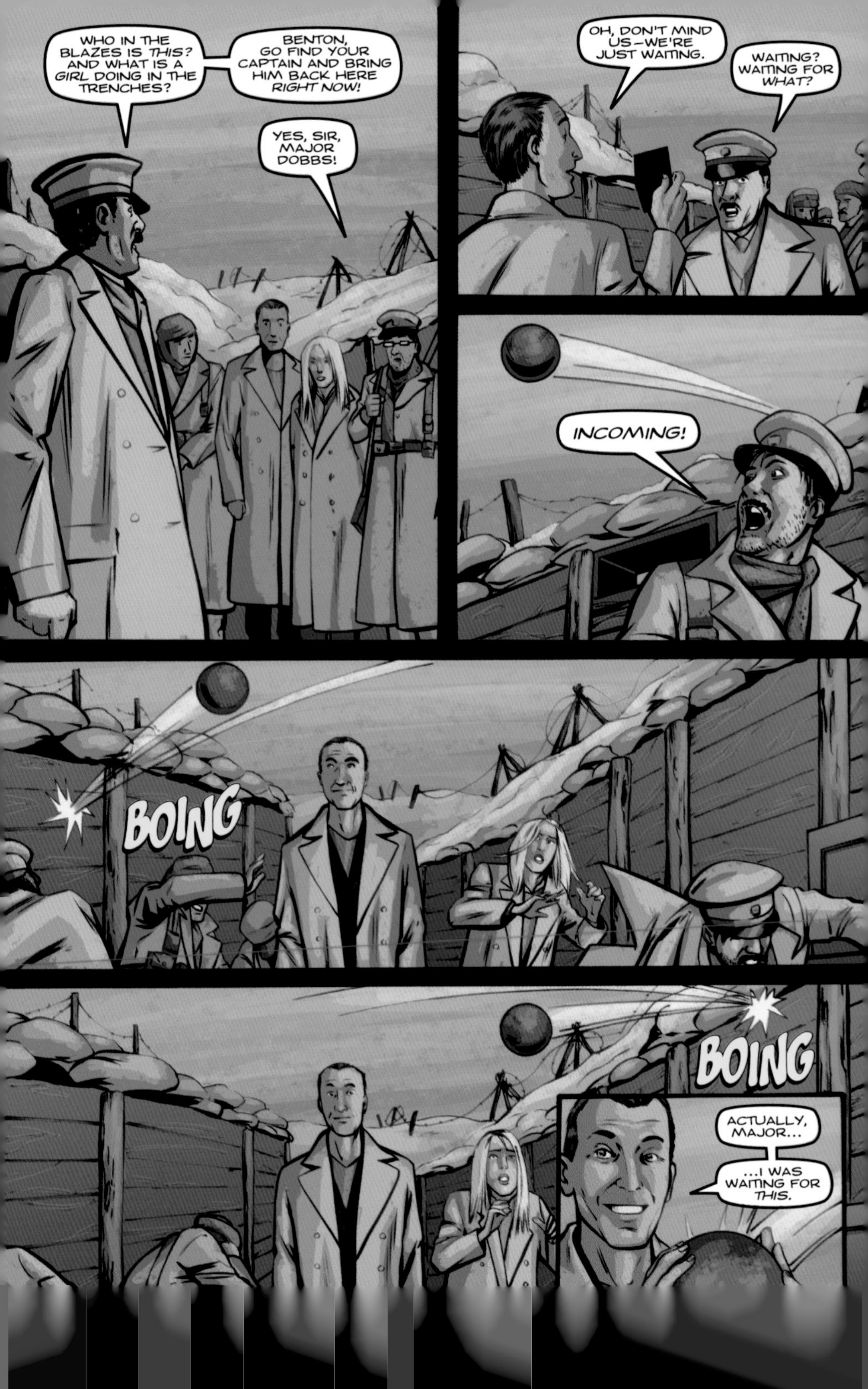
WHO IN THE BLAZES IS *THIS?* AND WHAT IS A *GIRL* DOING IN THE TRENCHES?
BENTON, GO FIND YOUR CAPTAIN AND BRING HIM BACK HERE *RIGHT NOW!*
YES, SIR, MAJOR DOBBS!
OH, DON'T MIND US—WE'RE JUST WAITING.
WAITING? WAITING FOR *WHAT?*
INCOMING!
BOING
BOING
ACTUALLY, MAJOR...
...I WAS WAITING FOR *THIS.*

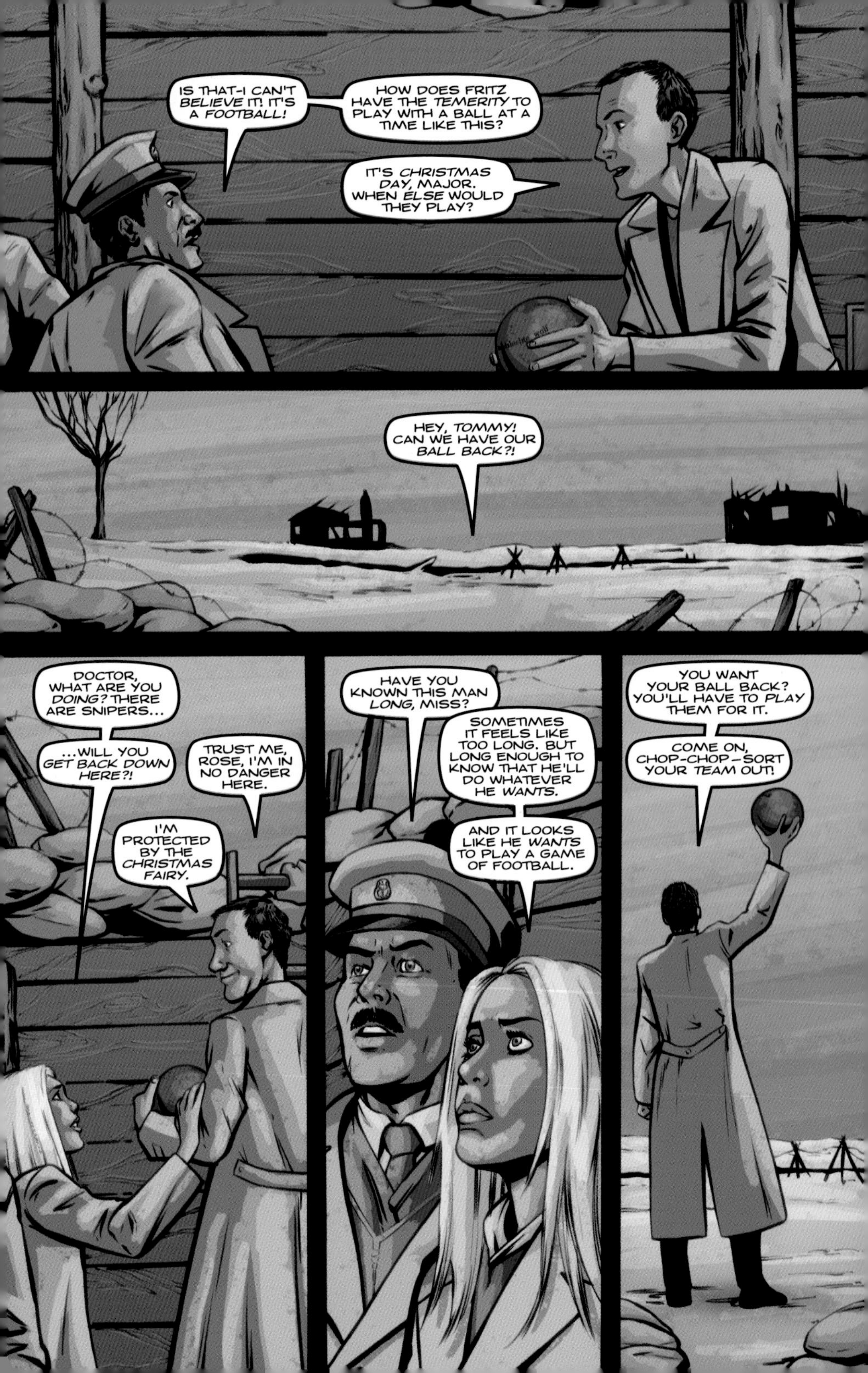

IS THAT-I CAN'T BELIEVE IT! IT'S A FOOTBALL!
HOW DOES FRITZ HAVE THE TEMERITY TO PLAY WITH A BALL AT A TIME LIKE THIS?
IT'S CHRISTMAS DAY, MAJOR. WHEN ELSE WOULD THEY PLAY?
HEY, TOMMY! CAN WE HAVE OUR BALL BACK?!
DOCTOR, WHAT ARE YOU DOING? THERE ARE SNIPERS...
...WILL YOU GET BACK DOWN HERE?!
TRUST ME, ROSE, I'M IN NO DANGER HERE.
I'M PROTECTED BY THE CHRISTMAS FAIRY.
HAVE YOU KNOWN THIS MAN LONG, MISS?
SOMETIMES IT FEELS LIKE TOO LONG. BUT LONG ENOUGH TO KNOW THAT HE'LL DO WHATEVER HE WANTS.
AND IT LOOKS LIKE HE WANTS TO PLAY A GAME OF FOOTBALL.
YOU WANT YOUR BALL BACK? YOU'LL HAVE TO PLAY THEM FOR IT.
COME ON, CHOP-CHOP—SORT YOUR TEAM OUT!

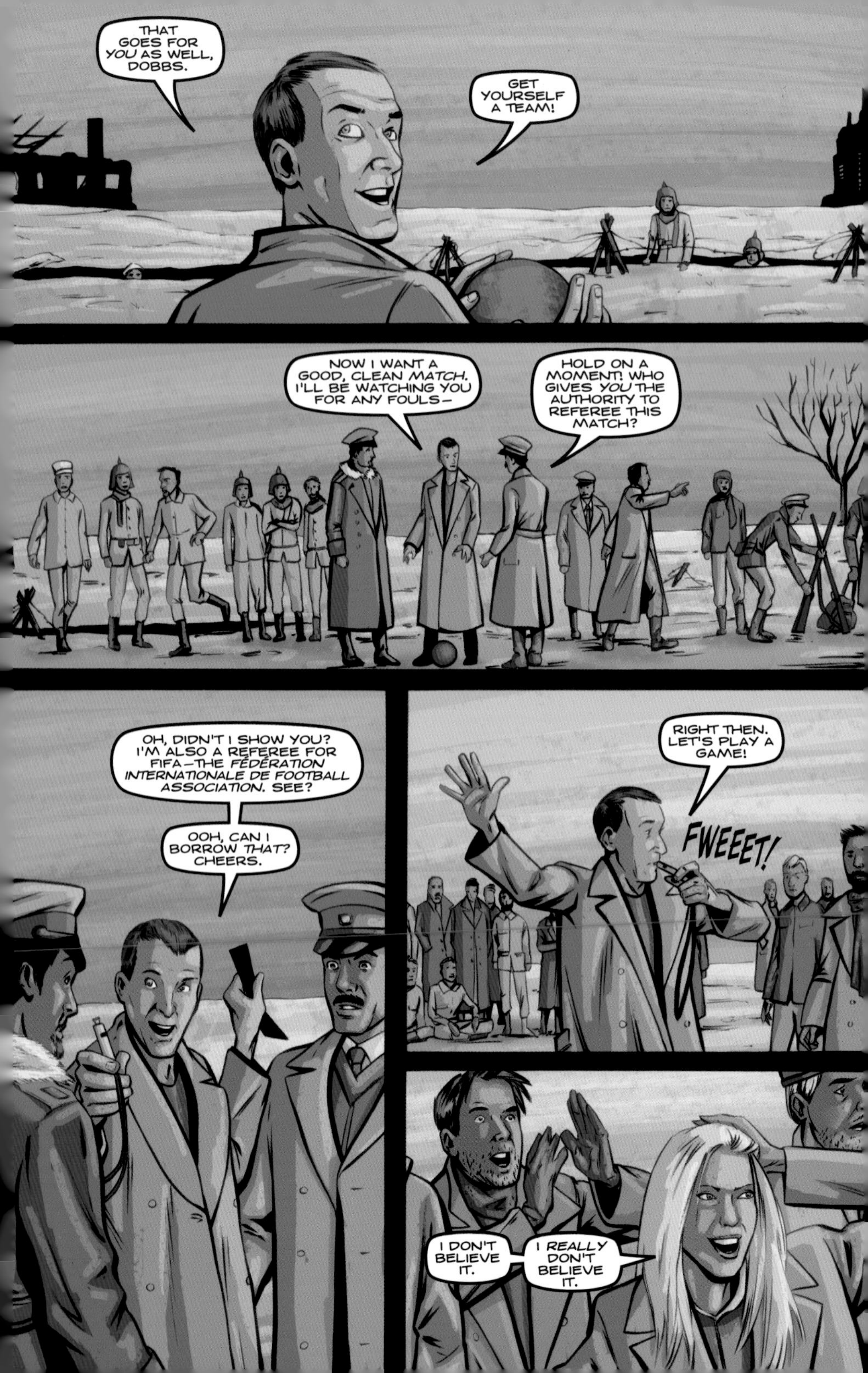
THAT GOES FOR *YOU* AS WELL, DOBBS.
GET YOURSELF A TEAM!
NOW I WANT A GOOD, CLEAN *MATCH*. I'LL BE WATCHING YOU FOR ANY FOULS—
HOLD ON A MOMENT! WHO GIVES *YOU* THE AUTHORITY TO REFEREE THIS MATCH?
OH, DIDN'T I SHOW YOU? I'M ALSO A REFEREE FOR FIFA—THE *FÉDÉRATION INTERNATIONALE DE FOOTBALL ASSOCIATION*. SEE?
OOH, CAN I BORROW *THAT*? CHEERS.
RIGHT THEN. LET'S PLAY A GAME!
FWEEET!
I DON'T BELIEVE IT.
I *REALLY* DON'T BELIEVE IT.

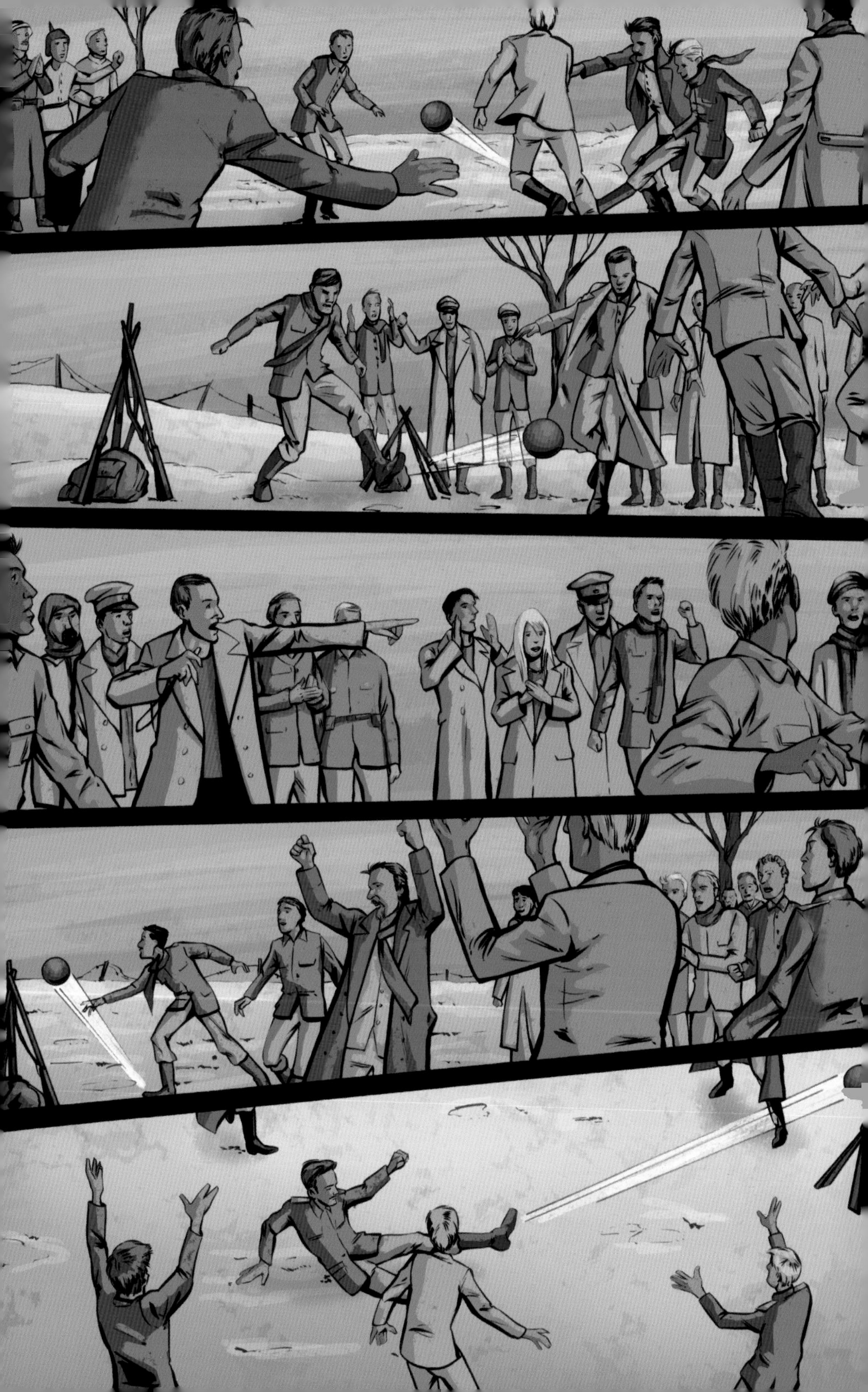

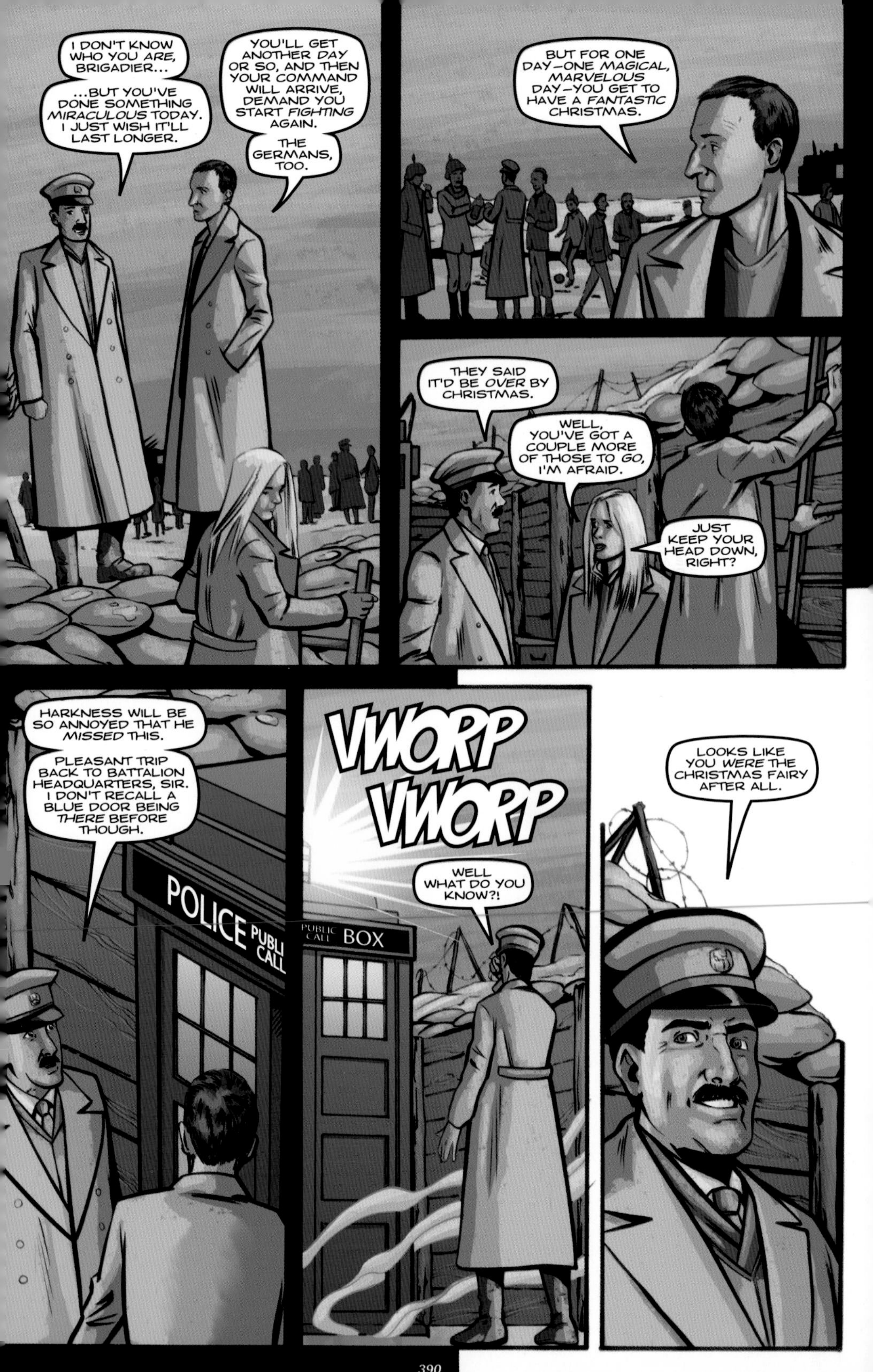
I DON'T KNOW WHO YOU ARE, BRIGADIER...
...BUT YOU'VE DONE SOMETHING MIRACULOUS TODAY. I JUST WISH IT'LL LAST LONGER.
YOU'LL GET ANOTHER DAY OR SO, AND THEN YOUR COMMAND WILL ARRIVE, DEMAND YOU START FIGHTING AGAIN.
THE GERMANS, TOO.
BUT FOR ONE DAY—ONE MAGICAL, MARVELOUS DAY—YOU GET TO HAVE A FANTASTIC CHRISTMAS.
THEY SAID IT'D BE OVER BY CHRISTMAS.
WELL, YOU'VE GOT A COUPLE MORE OF THOSE TO GO, I'M AFRAID.
JUST KEEP YOUR HEAD DOWN, RIGHT?
HARKNESS WILL BE SO ANNOYED THAT HE MISSED THIS.
PLEASANT TRIP BACK TO BATTALION HEADQUARTERS, SIR. I DON'T RECALL A BLUE DOOR BEING THERE BEFORE THOUGH.
POLICE PUBLI CALL
VWORP VWORP
WELL WHAT DO YOU KNOW?!
PUBLIC CALL BOX
LOOKS LIKE YOU WERE THE CHRISTMAS FAIRY AFTER ALL.

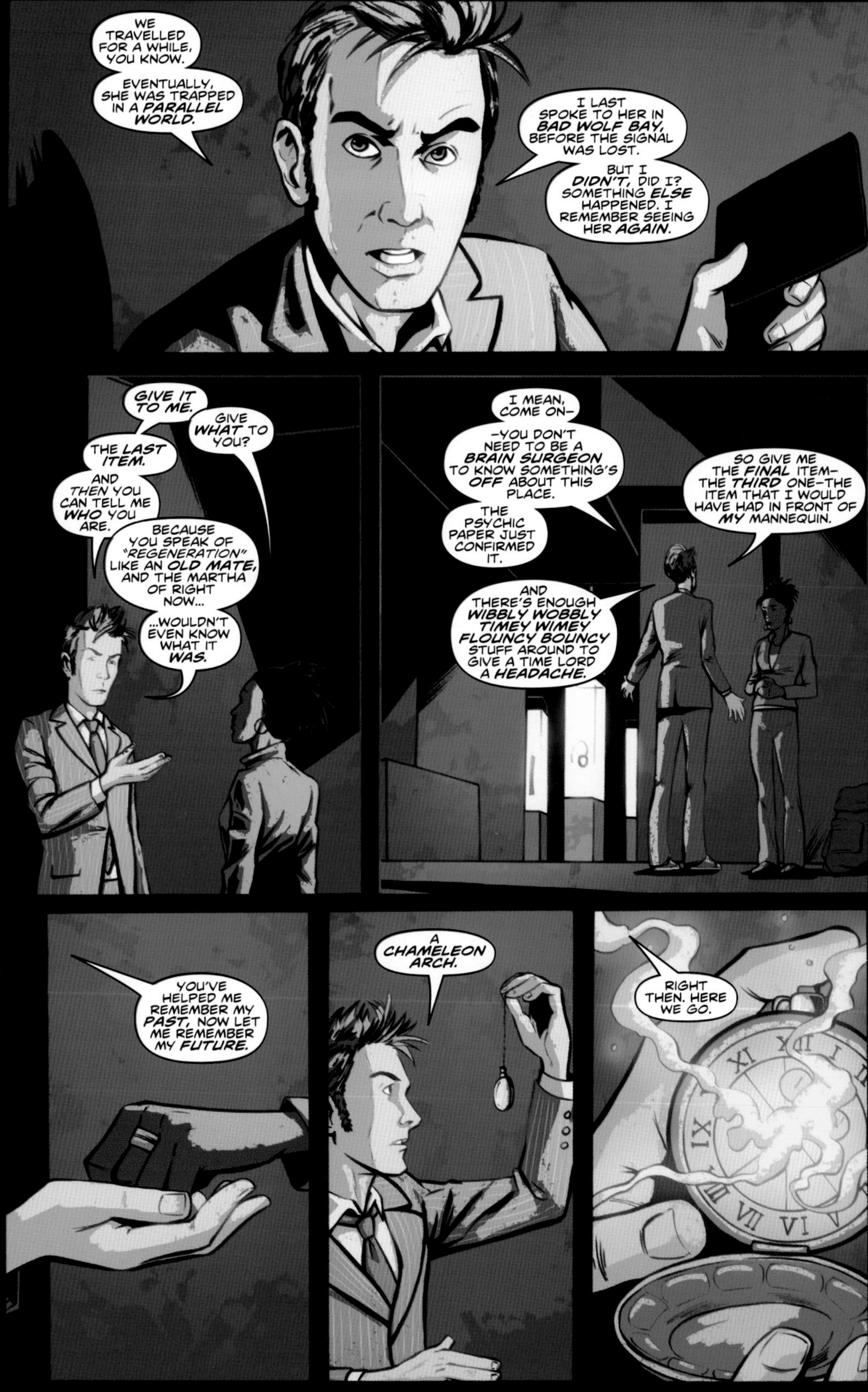
WE TRAVELLED FOR A WHILE, YOU KNOW.
EVENTUALLY, SHE WAS TRAPPED IN A PARALLEL WORLD.
I LAST SPOKE TO HER IN BAD WOLF BAY, BEFORE THE SIGNAL WAS LOST.
BUT I DIDN'T, DID I? SOMETHING ELSE HAPPENED. I REMEMBER SEEING HER AGAIN.
GIVE IT TO ME.
GIVE WHAT TO YOU?
THE LAST ITEM.
AND THEN YOU CAN TELL ME WHO YOU ARE.
BECAUSE YOU SPEAK OF "REGENERATION" LIKE AN OLD MATE, AND THE MARTHA OF RIGHT NOW...
...WOULDN'T EVEN KNOW WHAT IT WAS.
I MEAN, COME ON–
–YOU DON'T NEED TO BE A BRAIN SURGEON TO KNOW SOMETHING'S OFF ABOUT THIS PLACE.
THE PSYCHIC PAPER JUST CONFIRMED IT.
AND THERE'S ENOUGH WIBBLY WOBBLY TIMEY WIMEY FLOUNCY BOUNCY STUFF AROUND TO GIVE A TIME LORD A HEADACHE.
SO GIVE ME THE FINAL ITEM– THE THIRD ONE–THE ITEM THAT I WOULD HAVE HAD IN FRONT OF MY MANNEQUIN.
YOU'VE HELPED ME REMEMBER MY PAST, NOW LET ME REMEMBER MY FUTURE.
A CHAMELEON ARCH.
RIGHT THEN. HERE WE GO.

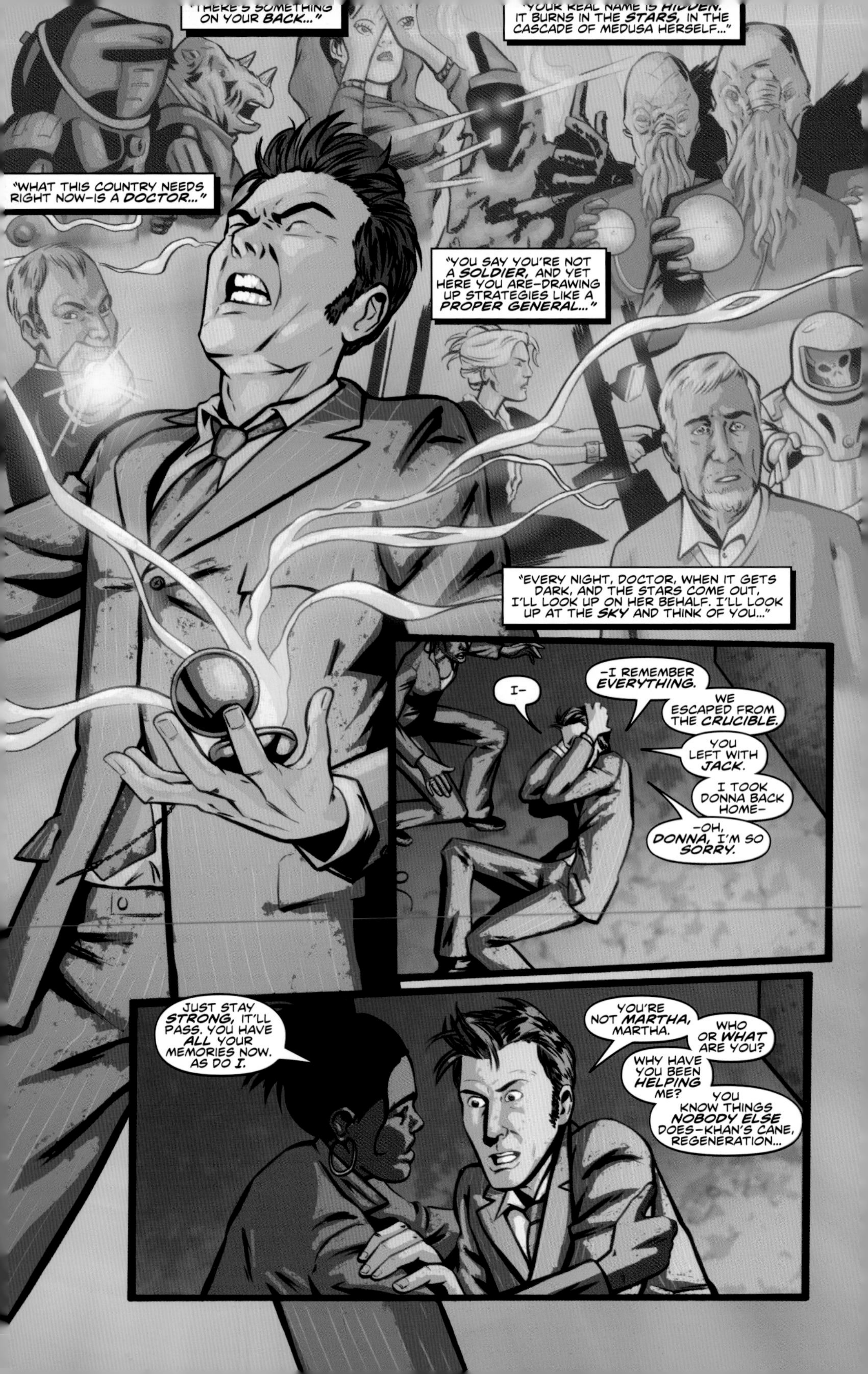
"THERE'S SOMETHING ON YOUR BACK..."
"YOUR REAL NAME IS HIDDEN. IT BURNS IN THE STARS, IN THE CASCADE OF MEDUSA HERSELF..."
"WHAT THIS COUNTRY NEEDS RIGHT NOW–IS A DOCTOR..."
"YOU SAY YOU'RE NOT A SOLDIER, AND YET HERE YOU ARE–DRAWING UP STRATEGIES LIKE A PROPER GENERAL..."
"EVERY NIGHT, DOCTOR, WHEN IT GETS DARK, AND THE STARS COME OUT, I'LL LOOK UP ON HER BEHALF. I'LL LOOK UP AT THE SKY AND THINK OF YOU..."
I–
–I REMEMBER EVERYTHING.
WE ESCAPED FROM THE CRUCIBLE.
YOU LEFT WITH JACK.
I TOOK DONNA BACK HOME–
–OH, DONNA, I'M SO SORRY.
JUST STAY STRONG, IT'LL PASS. YOU HAVE ALL YOUR MEMORIES NOW. AS DO I.
YOU'RE NOT MARTHA, MARTHA.
WHO OR WHAT ARE YOU?
WHY HAVE YOU BEEN HELPING ME?
YOU KNOW THINGS NOBODY ELSE DOES–KHAN'S CANE, REGENERATION...

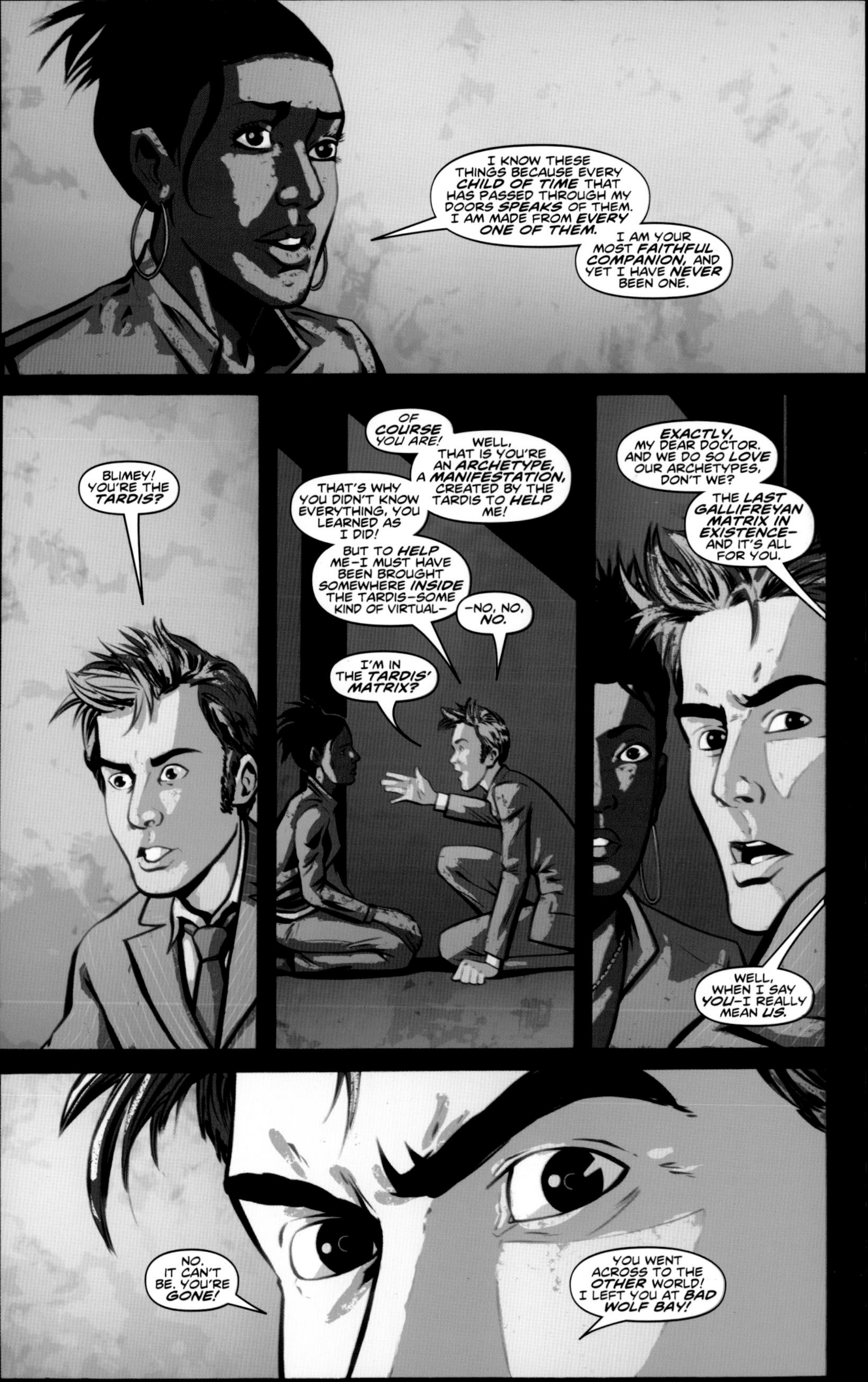
I KNOW THESE THINGS BECAUSE EVERY CHILD OF TIME THAT HAS PASSED THROUGH MY DOORS SPEAKS OF THEM. I AM MADE FROM EVERY ONE OF THEM.
I AM YOUR MOST FAITHFUL COMPANION, AND YET I HAVE NEVER BEEN ONE.
BLIMEY! YOU'RE THE TARDIS?
OF COURSE YOU ARE!
WELL, THAT IS YOU'RE AN ARCHETYPE, A MANIFESTATION, CREATED BY THE TARDIS TO HELP ME!
THAT'S WHY YOU DIDN'T KNOW EVERYTHING, YOU LEARNED AS I DID!
BUT TO HELP ME–I MUST HAVE BEEN BROUGHT SOMEWHERE INSIDE THE TARDIS–SOME KIND OF VIRTUAL–
–NO, NO, NO.
I'M IN THE TARDIS' MATRIX?
EXACTLY, MY DEAR DOCTOR. AND WE DO SO LOVE OUR ARCHETYPES, DON'T WE?
THE LAST GALLIFREYAN MATRIX IN EXISTENCE– AND IT'S ALL FOR YOU.
WELL, WHEN I SAY YOU–I REALLY MEAN US.
NO. IT CAN'T BE. YOU'RE GONE!
YOU WENT ACROSS TO THE OTHER WORLD! I LEFT YOU AT BAD WOLF BAY!

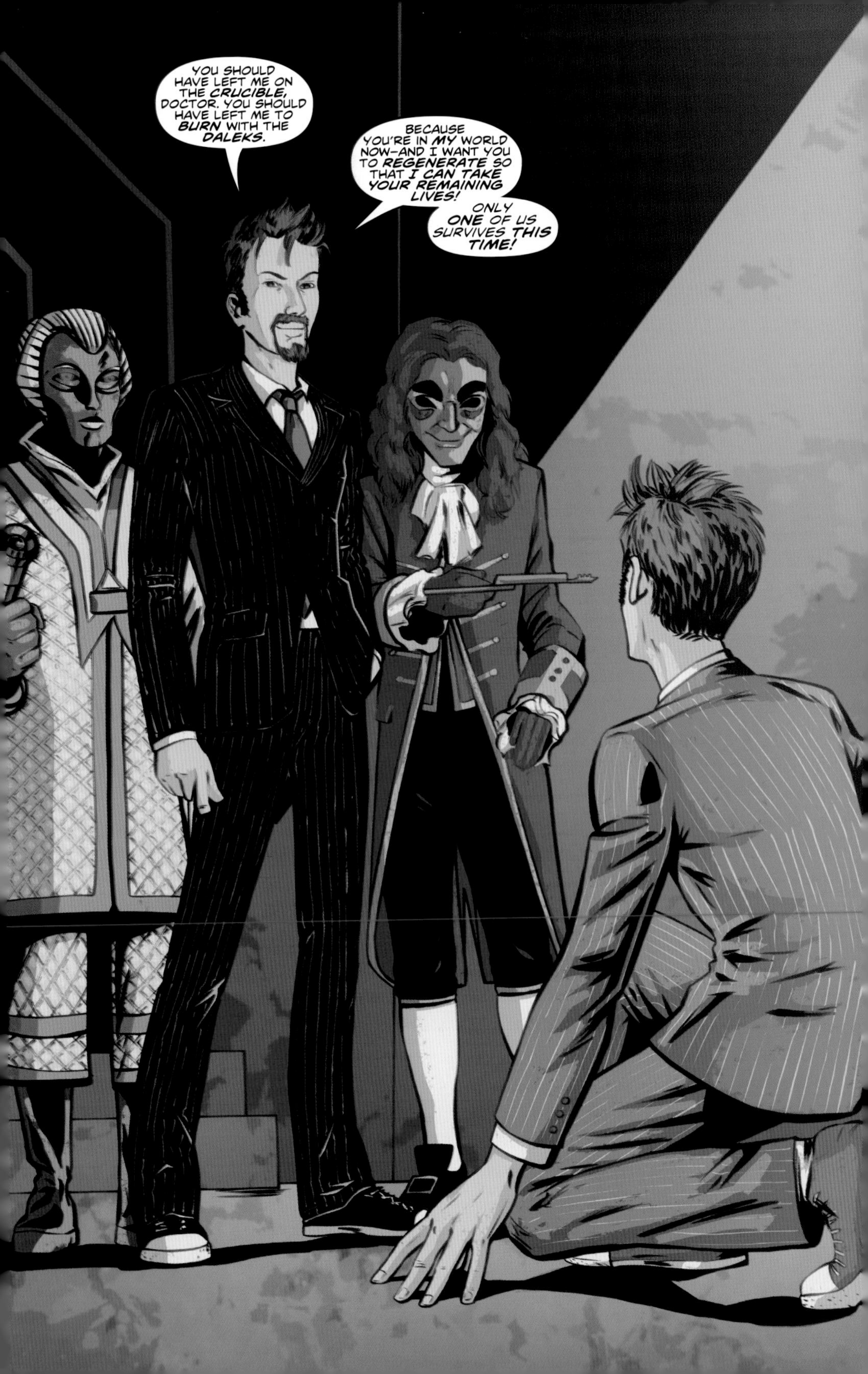
YOU SHOULD HAVE LEFT ME ON THE CRUCIBLE, DOCTOR. YOU SHOULD HAVE LEFT ME TO BURN WITH THE DALEKS.
BECAUSE YOU'RE IN MY WORLD NOW—AND I WANT YOU TO REGENERATE SO THAT I CAN TAKE YOUR REMAINING LIVES!
ONLY ONE OF US SURVIVES THIS TIME!

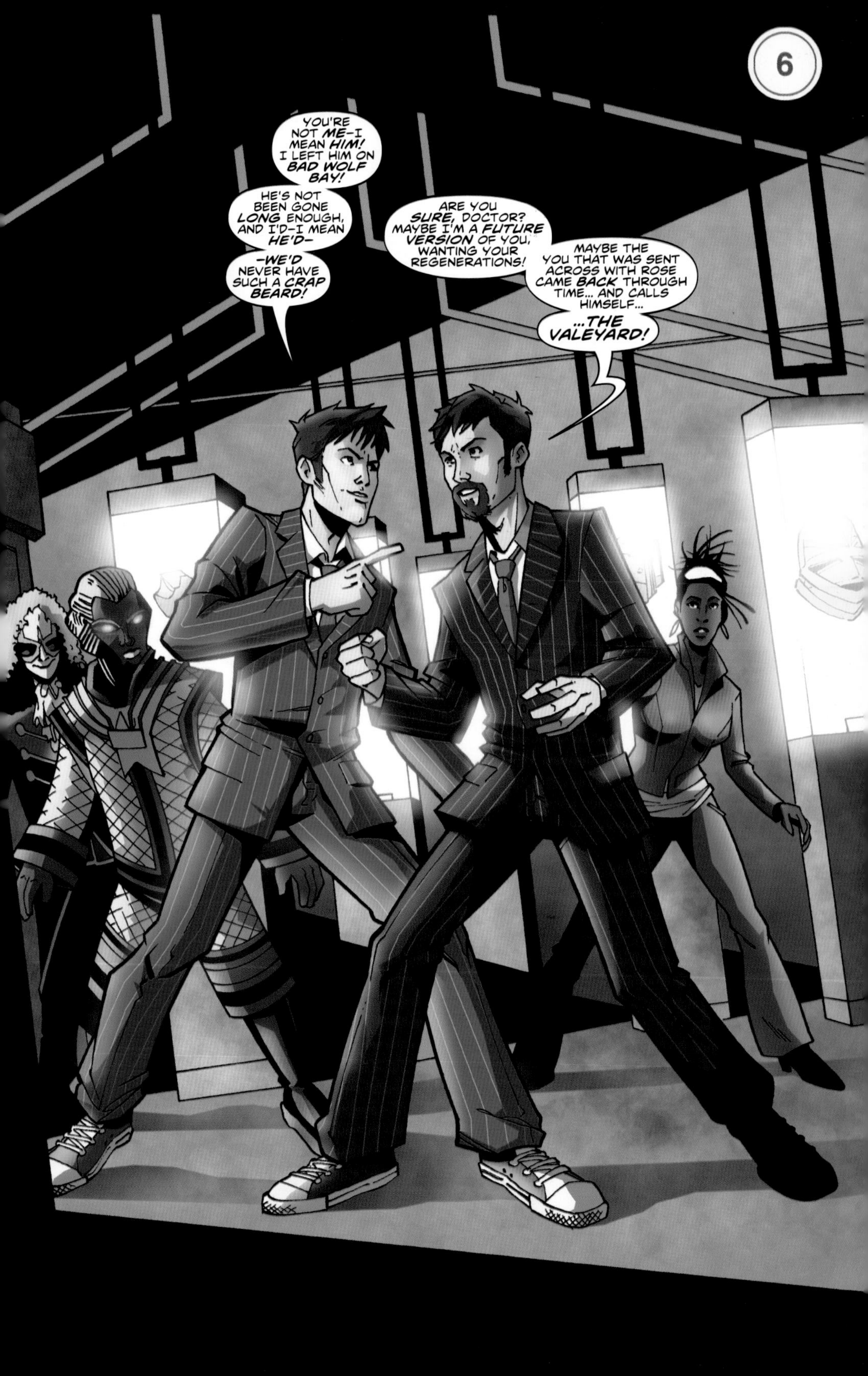
YOU'RE NOT ME–I MEAN HIM! I LEFT HIM ON BAD WOLF BAY!
HE'S NOT BEEN GONE LONG ENOUGH, AND I'D–I MEAN HE'D–
–WE'D NEVER HAVE SUCH A CRAP BEARD!
ARE YOU SURE, DOCTOR? MAYBE I'M A FUTURE VERSION OF YOU, WANTING YOUR REGENERATIONS!
MAYBE THE YOU THAT WAS SENT ACROSS WITH ROSE CAME BACK THROUGH TIME... AND CALLS HIMSELF...
...THE VALEYARD!

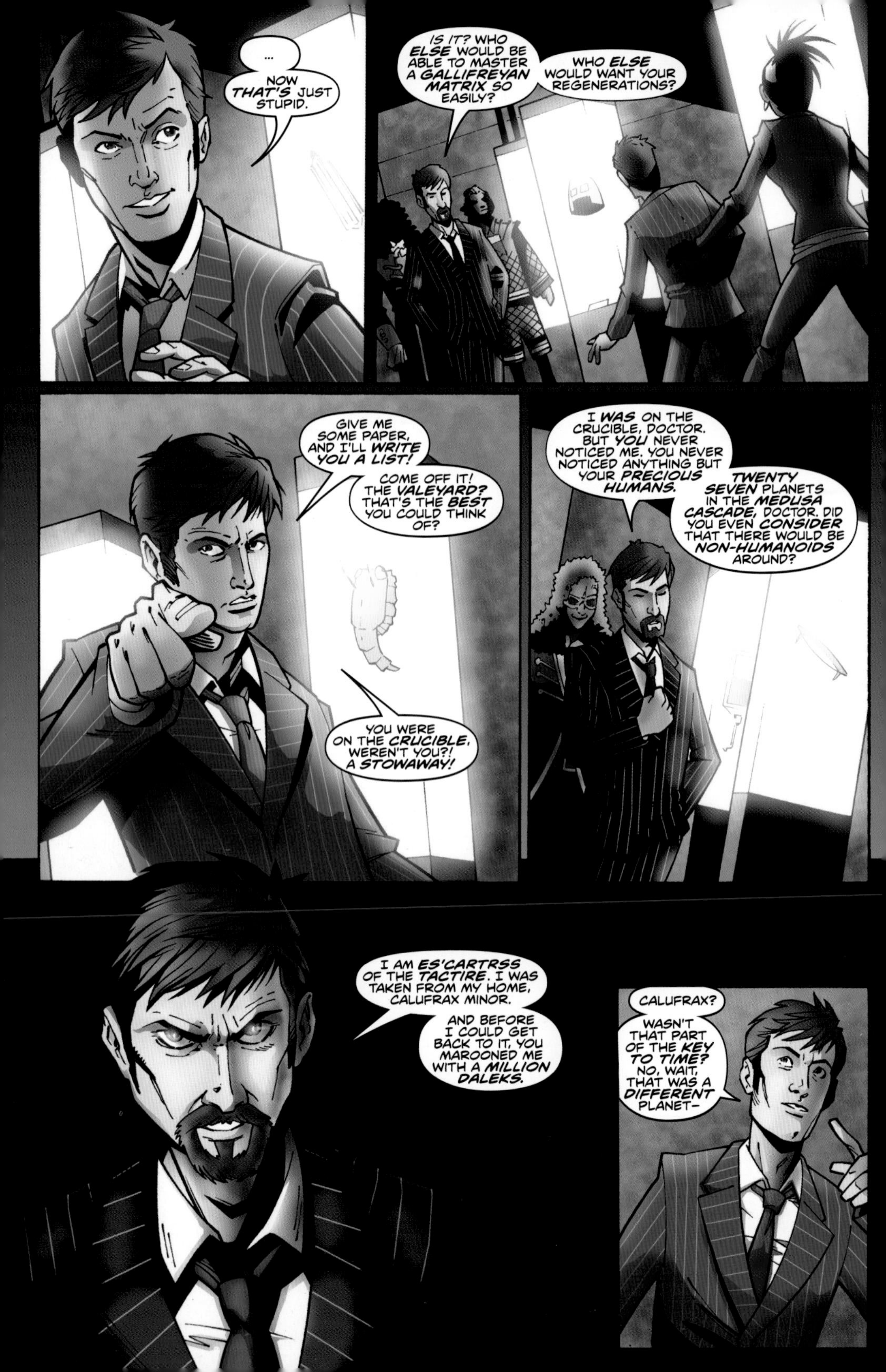
...
NOW THAT'S JUST STUPID.
IS IT? WHO ELSE WOULD BE ABLE TO MASTER A GALLIFREYAN MATRIX SO EASILY?
WHO ELSE WOULD WANT YOUR REGENERATIONS?
GIVE ME SOME PAPER, AND I'LL WRITE YOU A LIST!
COME OFF IT! THE VALEYARD? THAT'S THE BEST YOU COULD THINK OF?
YOU WERE ON THE CRUCIBLE, WEREN'T YOU?! A STOWAWAY!
I WAS ON THE CRUCIBLE, DOCTOR. BUT YOU NEVER NOTICED ME. YOU NEVER NOTICED ANYTHING BUT YOUR PRECIOUS HUMANS.
TWENTY SEVEN PLANETS IN THE MEDUSA CASCADE, DOCTOR. DID YOU EVEN CONSIDER THAT THERE WOULD BE NON-HUMANOIDS AROUND?
I AM ES'CARTRSS OF THE TACTIRE. I WAS TAKEN FROM MY HOME, CALUFRAX MINOR.
AND BEFORE I COULD GET BACK TO IT, YOU MAROONED ME WITH A MILLION DALEKS.
CALUFRAX?
WASN'T THAT PART OF THE KEY TO TIME? NO, WAIT, THAT WAS A DIFFERENT PLANET-

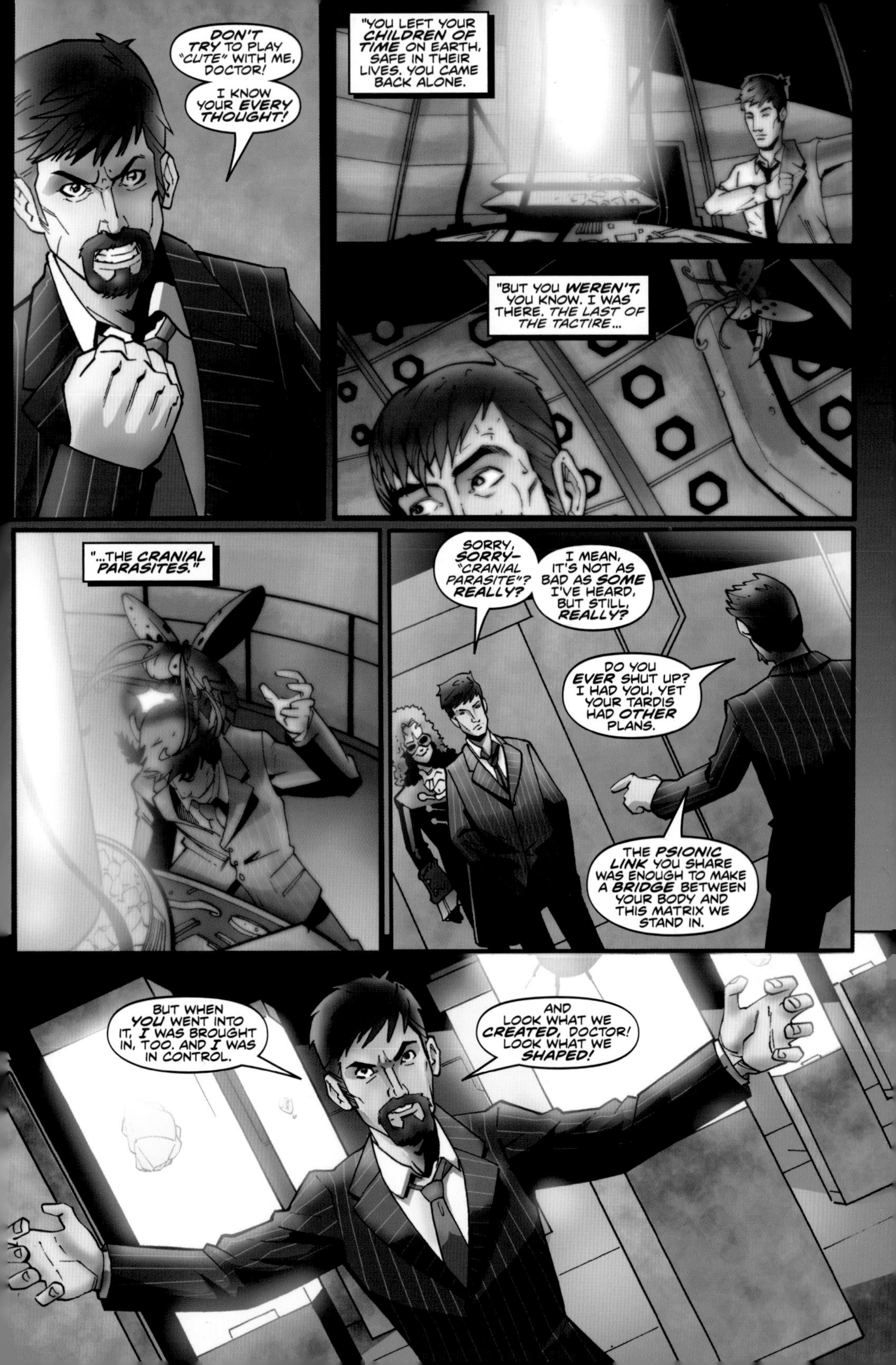
DON'T TRY TO PLAY "CUTE" WITH ME, DOCTOR!
I KNOW YOUR EVERY THOUGHT!
"YOU LEFT YOUR CHILDREN OF TIME ON EARTH, SAFE IN THEIR LIVES. YOU CAME BACK ALONE.
"BUT YOU WEREN'T, YOU KNOW. I WAS THERE. THE LAST OF THE TACTIRE...
"...THE CRANIAL PARASITES."
SORRY, SORRY- "CRANIAL PARASITE"? REALLY?
I MEAN, IT'S NOT AS BAD AS SOME I'VE HEARD, BUT STILL, REALLY?
DO YOU EVER SHUT UP? I HAD YOU, YET YOUR TARDIS HAD OTHER PLANS.
THE PSIONIC LINK YOU SHARE WAS ENOUGH TO MAKE A BRIDGE BETWEEN YOUR BODY AND THIS MATRIX WE STAND IN.
BUT WHEN YOU WENT INTO IT, I WAS BROUGHT IN, TOO. AND I WAS IN CONTROL.
AND LOOK WHAT WE CREATED, DOCTOR! LOOK WHAT WE SHAPED!

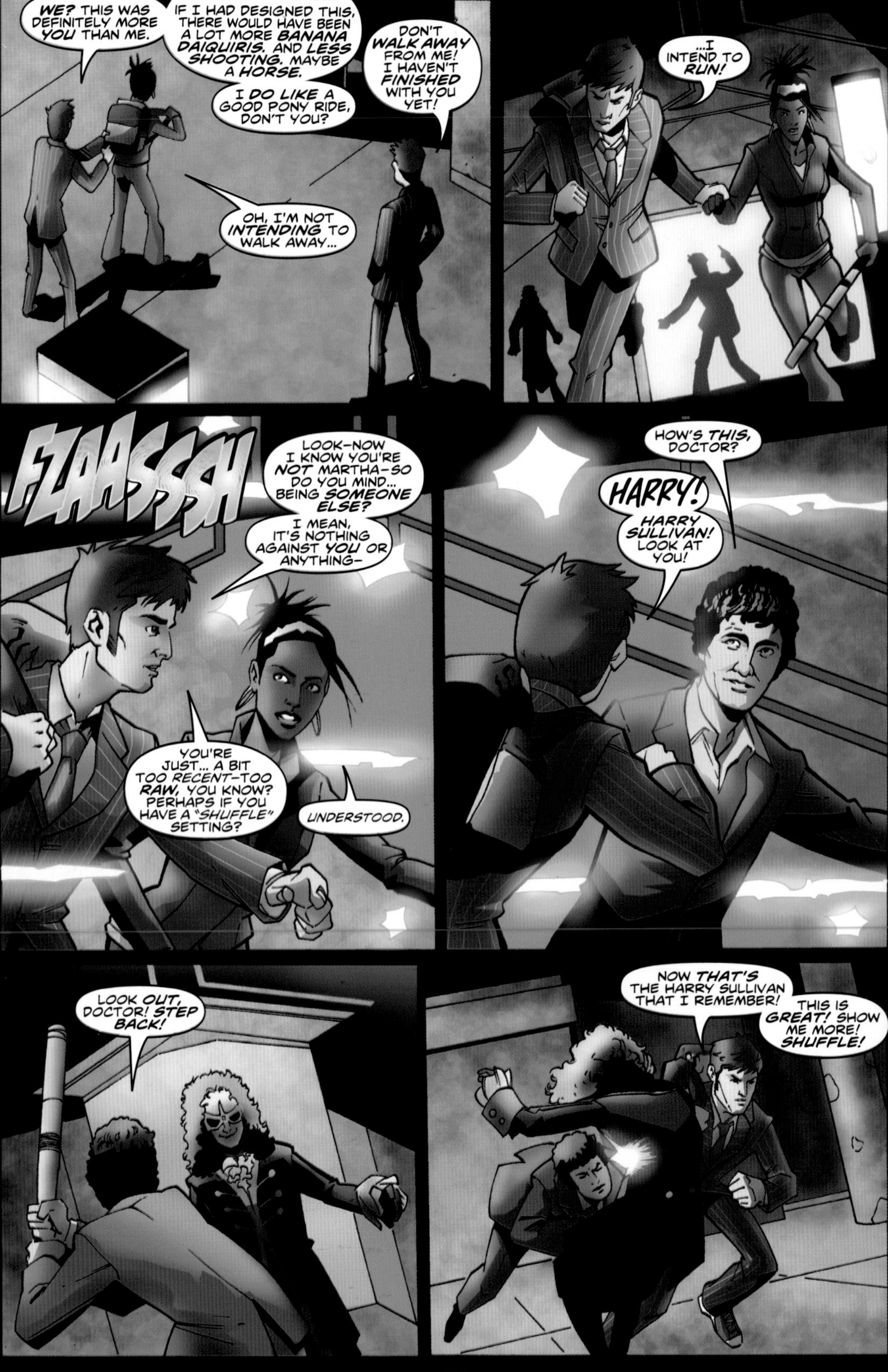
WE? THIS WAS DEFINITELY MORE YOU THAN ME.
IF I HAD DESIGNED THIS, THERE WOULD HAVE BEEN A LOT MORE BANANA DAIQUIRIS. AND LESS SHOOTING. MAYBE A HORSE.
I DO LIKE A GOOD PONY RIDE, DON'T YOU?
DON'T WALK AWAY FROM ME! I HAVEN'T FINISHED WITH YOU YET!
OH, I'M NOT INTENDING TO WALK AWAY...
...I INTEND TO RUN!
FZAASSSH
LOOK—NOW I KNOW YOU'RE NOT MARTHA—SO DO YOU MIND... BEING SOMEONE ELSE?
I MEAN, IT'S NOTHING AGAINST YOU OR ANYTHING—
YOU'RE JUST... A BIT TOO RECENT—TOO RAW, YOU KNOW? PERHAPS IF YOU HAVE A "SHUFFLE" SETTING?
UNDERSTOOD.
HOW'S THIS, DOCTOR?
HARRY!
HARRY SULLIVAN! LOOK AT YOU!
LOOK OUT, DOCTOR! STEP BACK!
NOW THAT'S THE HARRY SULLIVAN THAT I REMEMBER!
THIS IS GREAT! SHOW ME MORE! SHUFFLE!

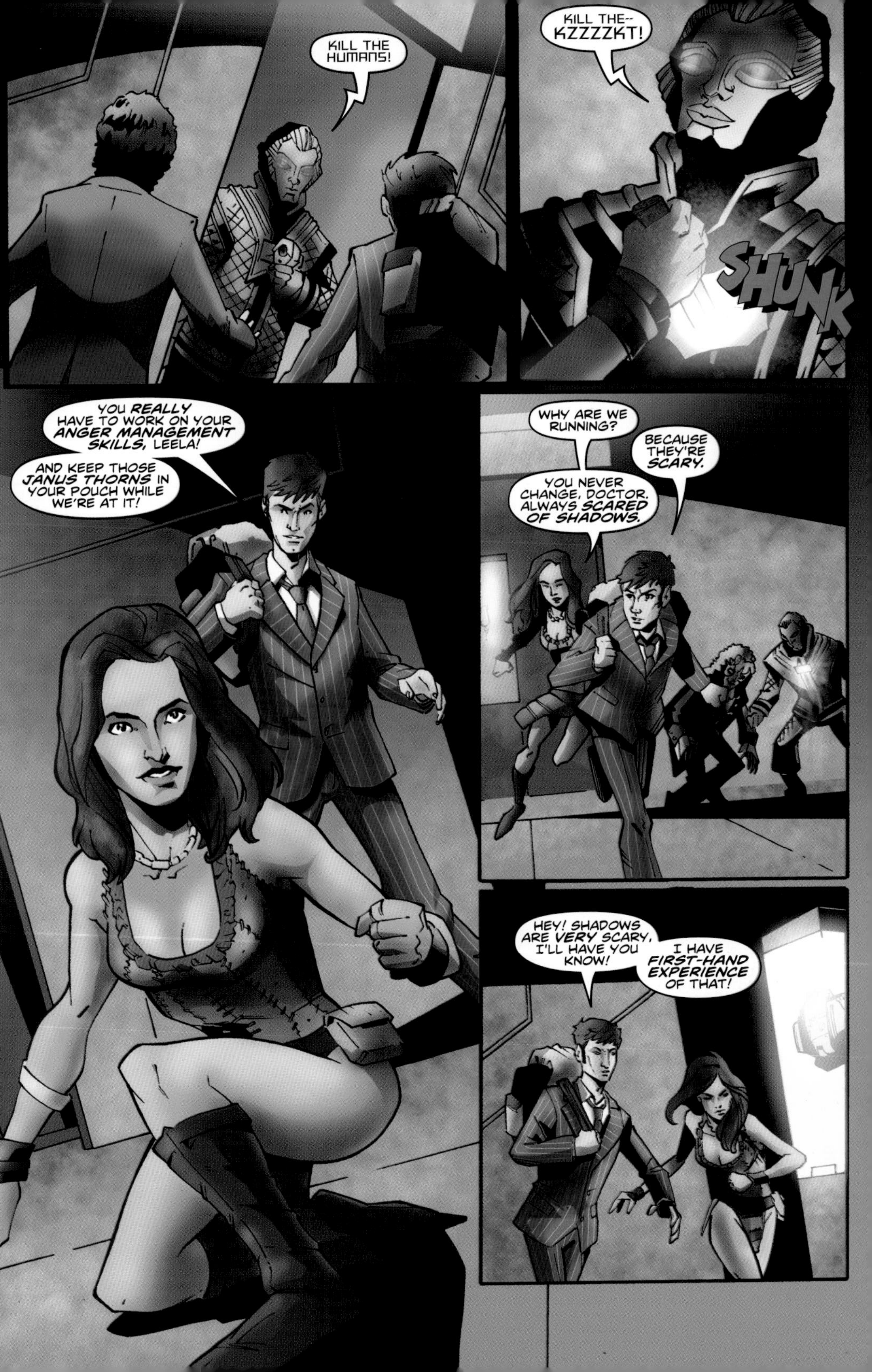
KILL THE HUMANS!
KILL THE-- KZZZZKT!
SHUNK
YOU REALLY HAVE TO WORK ON YOUR ANGER MANAGEMENT SKILLS, LEELA!
AND KEEP THOSE JANUS THORNS IN YOUR POUCH WHILE WE'RE AT IT!
WHY ARE WE RUNNING?
BECAUSE THEY'RE SCARY.
YOU NEVER CHANGE, DOCTOR. ALWAYS SCARED OF SHADOWS.
HEY! SHADOWS ARE VERY SCARY, I'LL HAVE YOU KNOW!
I HAVE FIRST-HAND EXPERIENCE OF THAT!

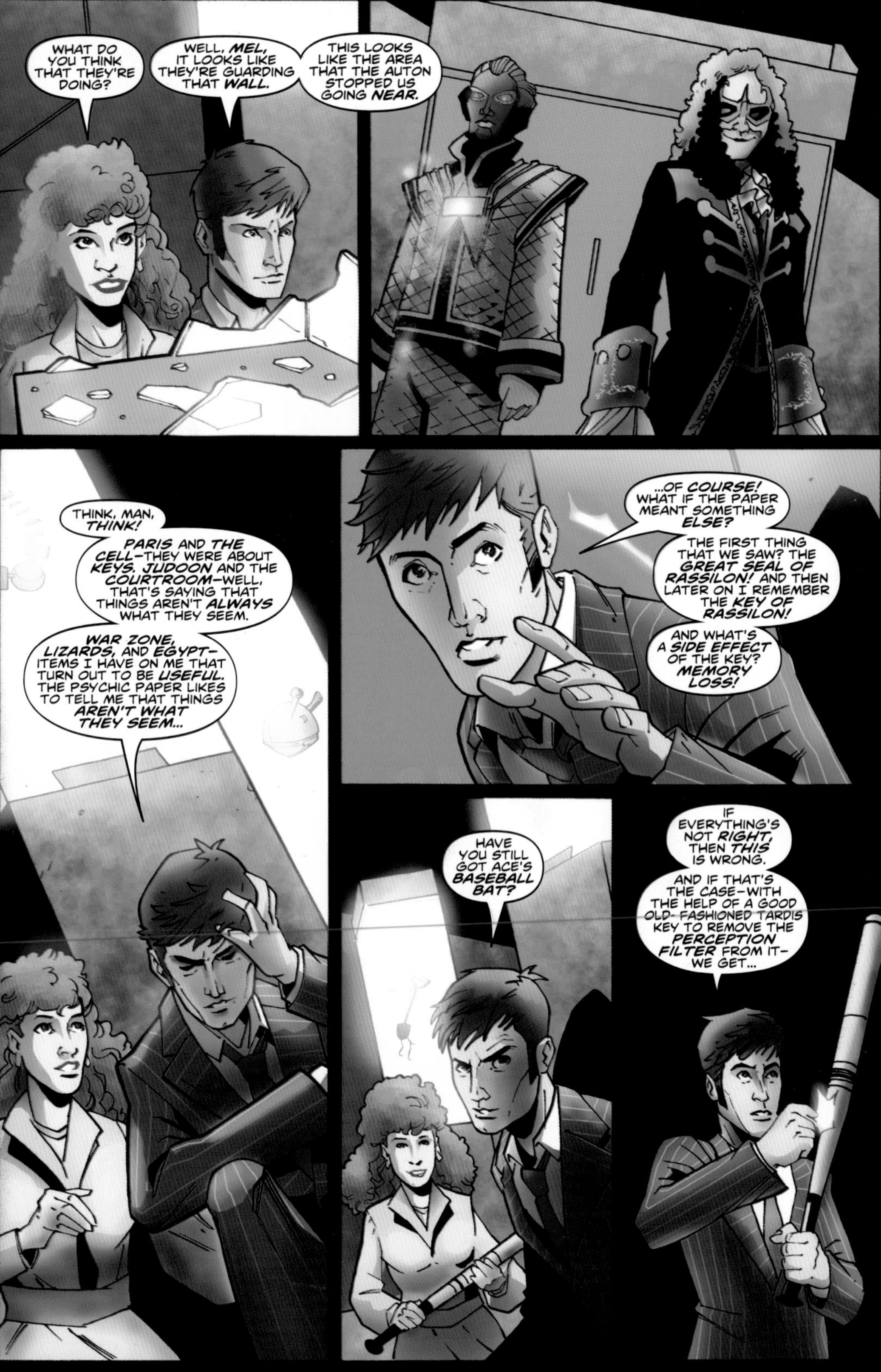
WHAT DO YOU THINK THAT THEY'RE DOING?
WELL, MEL, IT LOOKS LIKE THEY'RE GUARDING THAT WALL.
THIS LOOKS LIKE THE AREA THAT THE AUTON STOPPED US GOING NEAR.
THINK, MAN, THINK!
PARIS AND THE CELL—THEY WERE ABOUT KEYS. JUDOON AND THE COURTROOM—WELL, THAT'S SAYING THAT THINGS AREN'T ALWAYS WHAT THEY SEEM.
WAR ZONE, LIZARDS, AND EGYPT—ITEMS I HAVE ON ME THAT TURN OUT TO BE USEFUL. THE PSYCHIC PAPER LIKES TO TELL ME THAT THINGS AREN'T WHAT THEY SEEM...
...OF COURSE! WHAT IF THE PAPER MEANT SOMETHING ELSE?
THE FIRST THING THAT WE SAW? THE GREAT SEAL OF RASSILON! AND THEN LATER ON I REMEMBER THE KEY OF RASSILON!
AND WHAT'S A SIDE EFFECT OF THE KEY? MEMORY LOSS!
HAVE YOU STILL GOT ACE'S BASEBALL BAT?
IF EVERYTHING'S NOT RIGHT, THEN THIS IS WRONG.
AND IF THAT'S THE CASE—WITH THE HELP OF A GOOD OLD-FASHIONED TARDIS KEY TO REMOVE THE PERCEPTION FILTER FROM IT—WE GET...

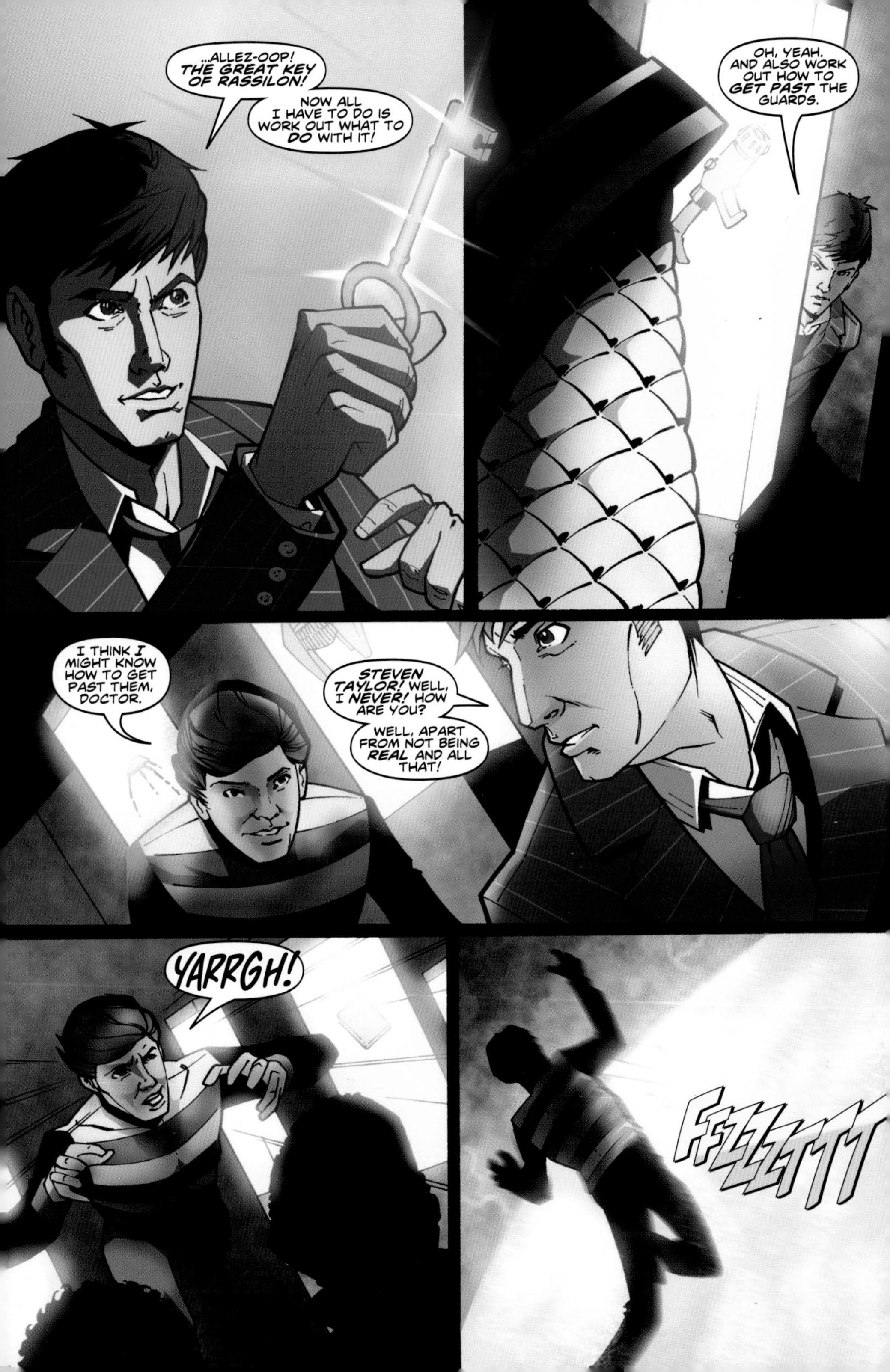
...ALLEZ-OOP! THE GREAT KEY OF RASSILON!
NOW ALL I HAVE TO DO IS WORK OUT WHAT TO DO WITH IT!
OH, YEAH. AND ALSO WORK OUT HOW TO GET PAST THE GUARDS.
I THINK I MIGHT KNOW HOW TO GET PAST THEM, DOCTOR.
STEVEN TAYLOR! WELL, I NEVER! HOW ARE YOU?
WELL, APART FROM NOT BEING REAL AND ALL THAT!
YARRGH!
FFZZZTTT

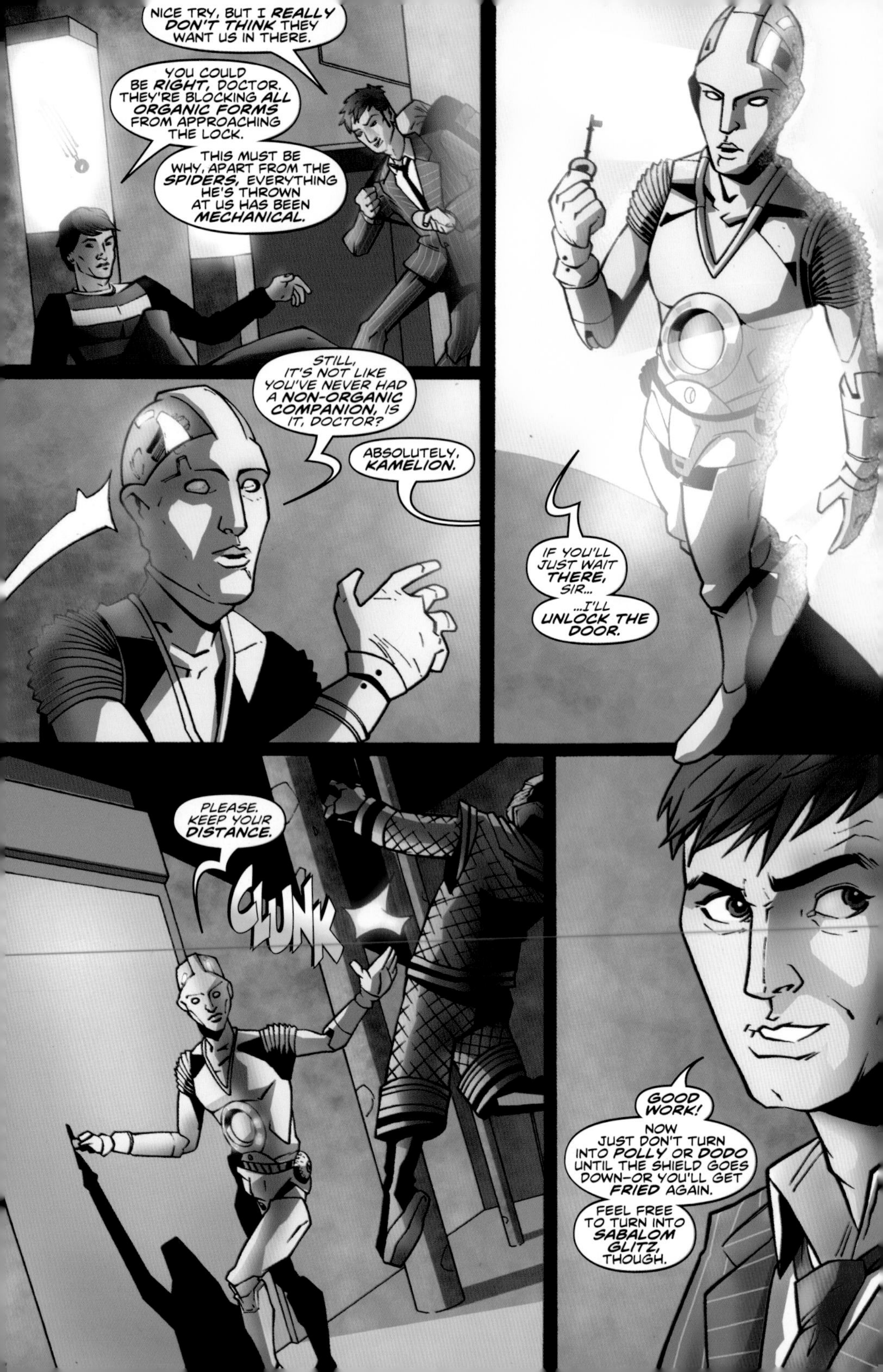
NICE TRY, BUT I REALLY DON'T THINK THEY WANT US IN THERE.
YOU COULD BE RIGHT, DOCTOR. THEY'RE BLOCKING ALL ORGANIC FORMS FROM APPROACHING THE LOCK.
THIS MUST BE WHY, APART FROM THE SPIDERS, EVERYTHING HE'S THROWN AT US HAS BEEN MECHANICAL.
STILL, IT'S NOT LIKE YOU'VE NEVER HAD A NON-ORGANIC COMPANION, IS IT, DOCTOR?
ABSOLUTELY, KAMELION.
IF YOU'LL JUST WAIT THERE, SIR...
...I'LL UNLOCK THE DOOR.
PLEASE. KEEP YOUR DISTANCE.
CLUNK
GOOD WORK!
NOW JUST DON'T TURN INTO POLLY OR DODO UNTIL THE SHIELD GOES DOWN—OR YOU'LL GET FRIED AGAIN.
FEEL FREE TO TURN INTO SABALOM GLITZ, THOUGH.

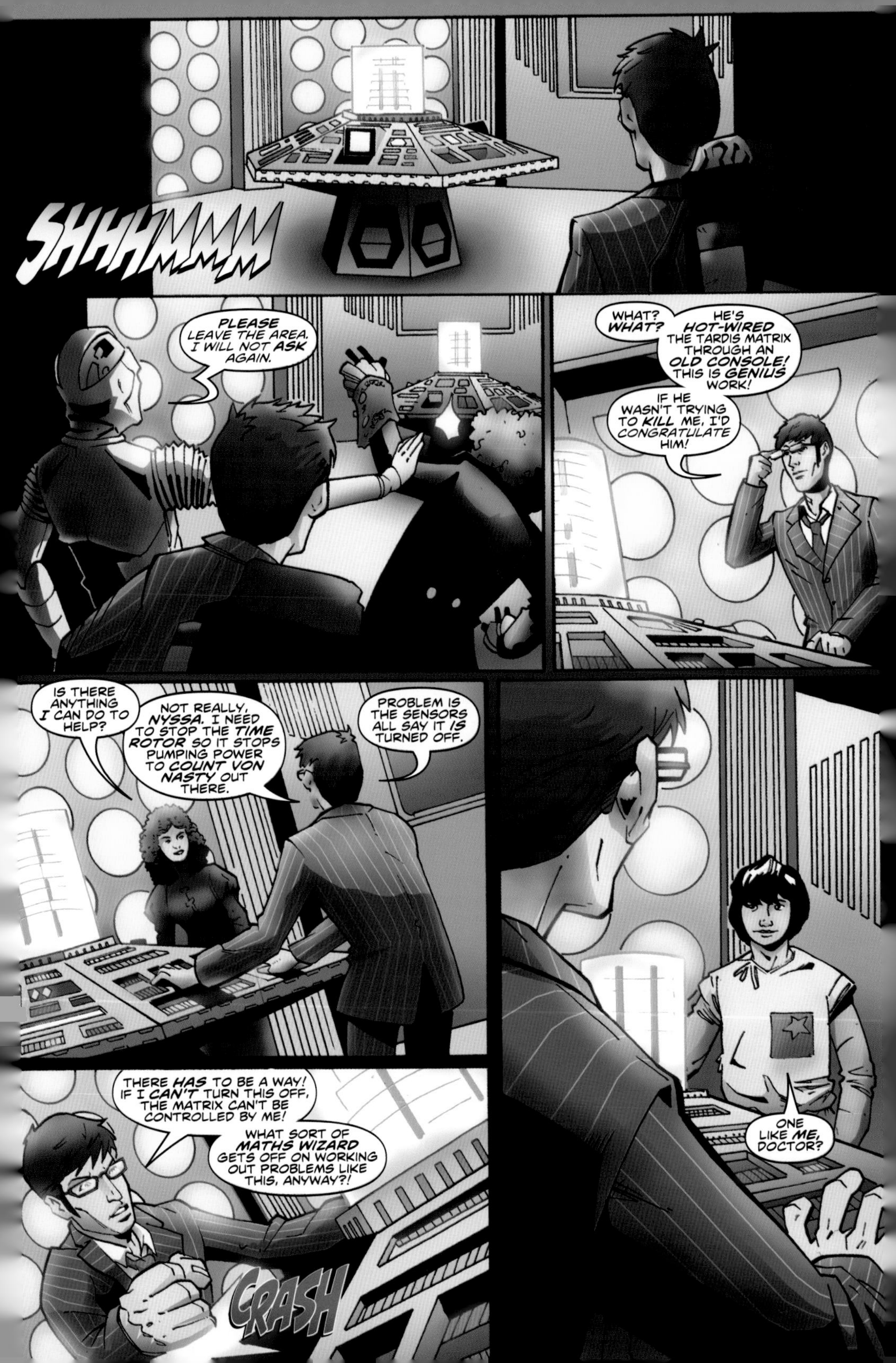
SHHHMMM
PLEASE LEAVE THE AREA. I WILL NOT ASK AGAIN.
WHAT? WHAT?
HE'S HOT-WIRED THE TARDIS MATRIX THROUGH AN OLD CONSOLE! THIS IS GENIUS WORK!
IF HE WASN'T TRYING TO KILL ME, I'D CONGRATULATE HIM!
IS THERE ANYTHING I CAN DO TO HELP?
NOT REALLY, NYSSA. I NEED TO STOP THE TIME ROTOR SO IT STOPS PUMPING POWER TO COUNT VON NASTY OUT THERE.
PROBLEM IS THE SENSORS ALL SAY IT IS TURNED OFF.
THERE HAS TO BE A WAY! IF I CAN'T TURN THIS OFF, THE MATRIX CAN'T BE CONTROLLED BY ME!
WHAT SORT OF MATHS WIZARD GETS OFF ON WORKING OUT PROBLEMS LIKE THIS, ANYWAY?!
CRASH
ONE LIKE ME, DOCTOR?

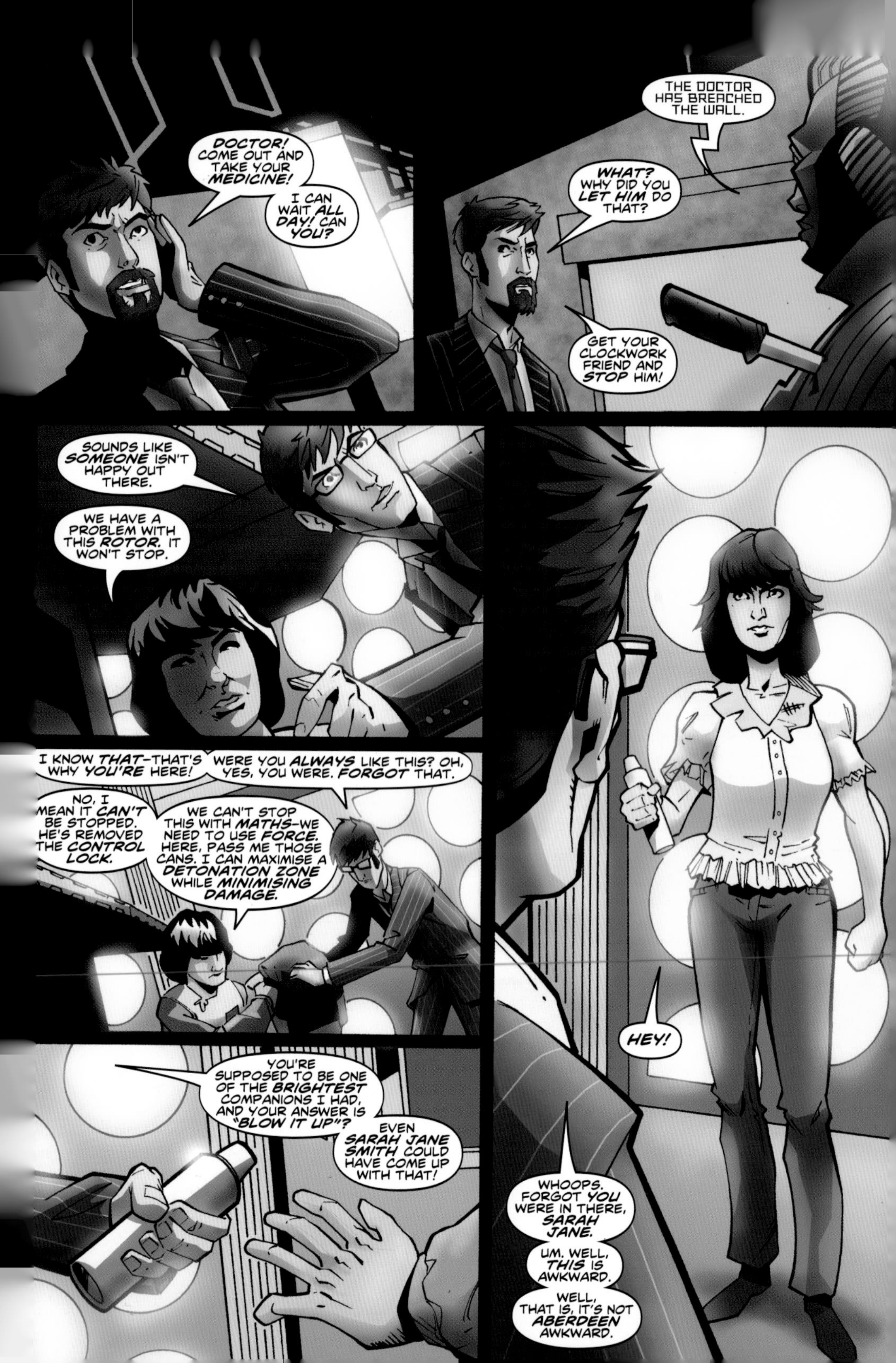
DOCTOR! COME OUT AND TAKE YOUR MEDICINE!
I CAN WAIT ALL DAY! CAN YOU?
THE DOCTOR HAS BREACHED THE WALL.
WHAT? WHY DID YOU LET HIM DO THAT?
GET YOUR CLOCKWORK FRIEND AND STOP HIM!
SOUNDS LIKE SOMEONE ISN'T HAPPY OUT THERE.
WE HAVE A PROBLEM WITH THIS ROTOR. IT WON'T STOP.
I KNOW THAT–THAT'S WHY YOU'RE HERE!
WERE YOU ALWAYS LIKE THIS? OH, YES, YOU WERE. FORGOT THAT.
NO, I MEAN IT CAN'T BE STOPPED. HE'S REMOVED THE CONTROL LOCK.
WE CAN'T STOP THIS WITH MATHS–WE NEED TO USE FORCE. HERE, PASS ME THOSE CANS. I CAN MAXIMISE A DETONATION ZONE WHILE MINIMISING DAMAGE.
YOU'RE SUPPOSED TO BE ONE OF THE BRIGHTEST COMPANIONS I HAD, AND YOUR ANSWER IS "BLOW IT UP"?
EVEN SARAH JANE SMITH COULD HAVE COME UP WITH THAT!
HEY!
WHOOPS. FORGOT YOU WERE IN THERE, SARAH JANE.
UM. WELL, THIS IS AWKWARD.
WELL, THAT IS, IT'S NOT ABERDEEN AWKWARD.

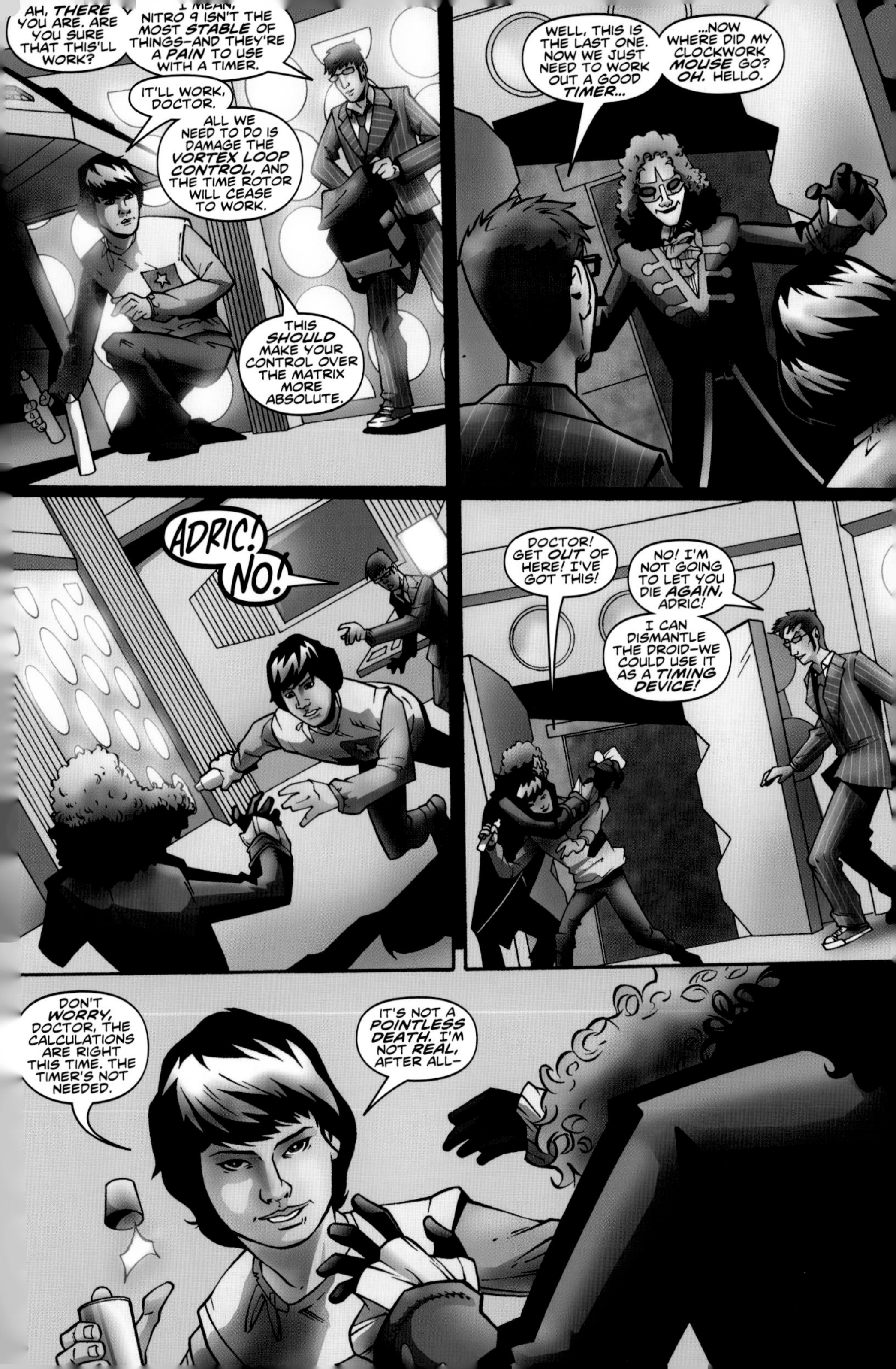
AH, THERE YOU ARE. ARE YOU SURE THAT THIS'LL WORK?
I MEAN, NITRO 9 ISN'T THE MOST STABLE OF THINGS—AND THEY'RE A PAIN TO USE WITH A TIMER.
IT'LL WORK, DOCTOR.
ALL WE NEED TO DO IS DAMAGE THE VORTEX LOOP CONTROL, AND THE TIME ROTOR WILL CEASE TO WORK.
THIS SHOULD MAKE YOUR CONTROL OVER THE MATRIX MORE ABSOLUTE.
WELL, THIS IS THE LAST ONE. NOW WE JUST NEED TO WORK OUT A GOOD TIMER...
...NOW WHERE DID MY CLOCKWORK MOUSE GO? OH. HELLO.
ADRIC! NO!
DOCTOR! GET OUT OF HERE! I'VE GOT THIS!
NO! I'M NOT GOING TO LET YOU DIE AGAIN, ADRIC!
I CAN DISMANTLE THE DROID—WE COULD USE IT AS A TIMING DEVICE!
DON'T WORRY, DOCTOR, THE CALCULATIONS ARE RIGHT THIS TIME. THE TIMER'S NOT NEEDED.
IT'S NOT A POINTLESS DEATH. I'M NOT REAL, AFTER ALL—

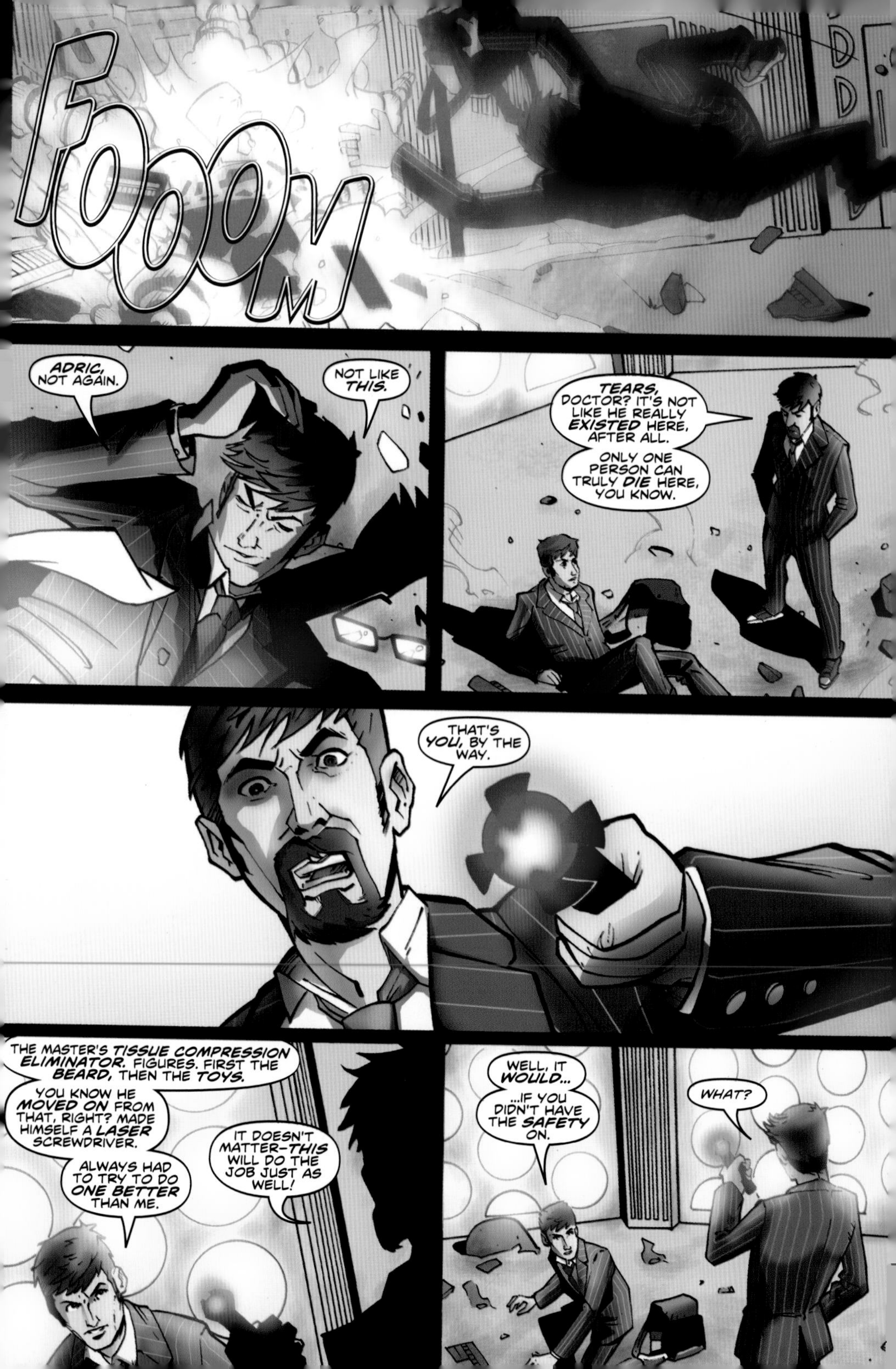
FOOOOM
ADRIC, NOT AGAIN.
NOT LIKE THIS.
TEARS, DOCTOR? IT'S NOT LIKE HE REALLY EXISTED HERE, AFTER ALL.
ONLY ONE PERSON CAN TRULY DIE HERE, YOU KNOW.
THAT'S YOU, BY THE WAY.
THE MASTER'S TISSUE COMPRESSION ELIMINATOR. FIGURES. FIRST THE BEARD, THEN THE TOYS.
YOU KNOW HE MOVED ON FROM THAT, RIGHT? MADE HIMSELF A LASER SCREWDRIVER.
ALWAYS HAD TO TRY TO DO ONE BETTER THAN ME.
IT DOESN'T MATTER–THIS WILL DO THE JOB JUST AS WELL!
WELL, IT WOULD...
...IF YOU DIDN'T HAVE THE SAFETY ON.
WHAT?

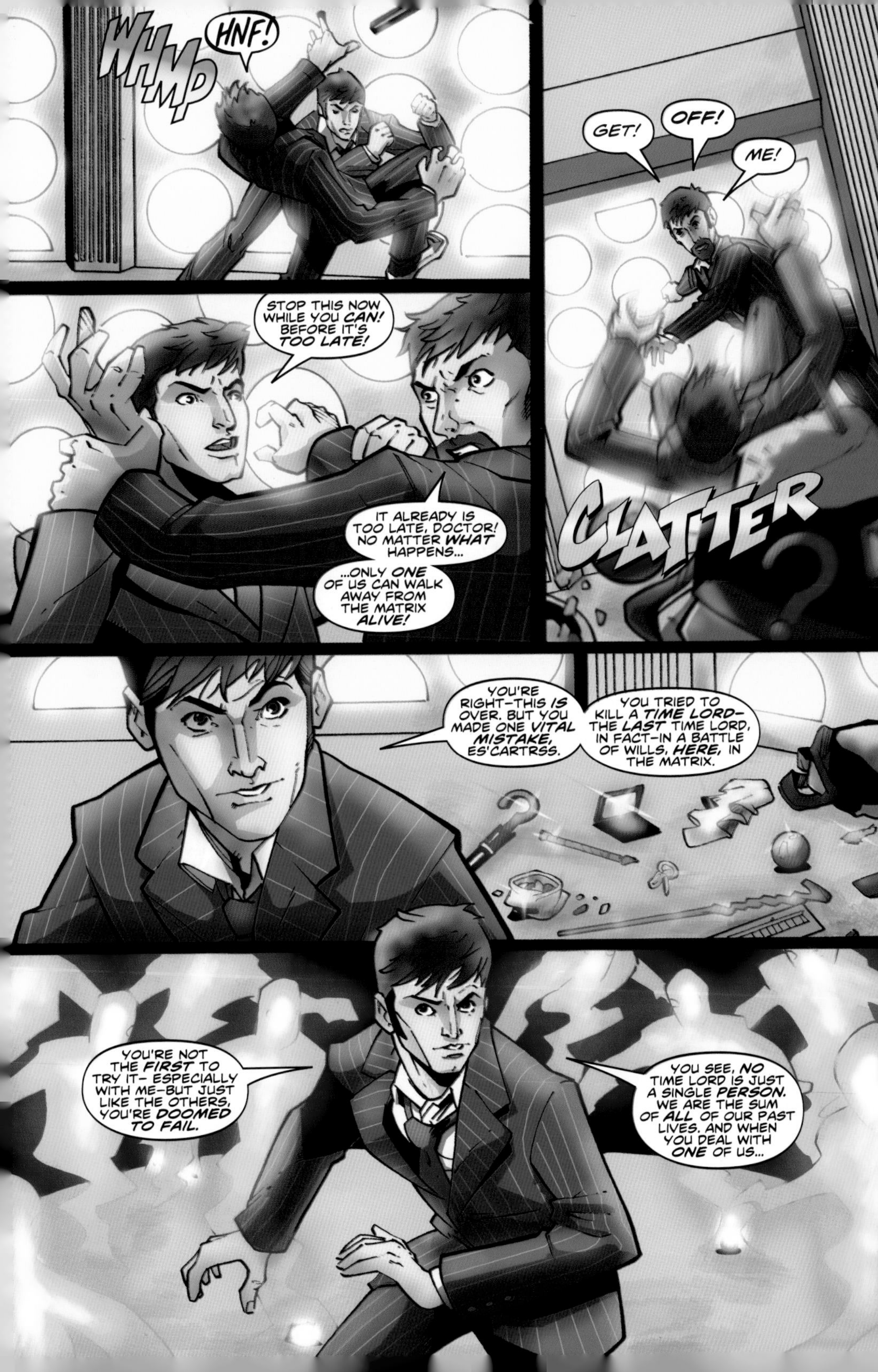
WHMP
HNF!
GET!
OFF!
ME!
STOP THIS NOW WHILE YOU CAN! BEFORE IT'S TOO LATE!
IT ALREADY IS TOO LATE, DOCTOR! NO MATTER WHAT HAPPENS...
...ONLY ONE OF US CAN WALK AWAY FROM THE MATRIX ALIVE!
CLATTER
YOU'RE RIGHT–THIS IS OVER. BUT YOU MADE ONE VITAL MISTAKE, ES'CARTRSS.
YOU TRIED TO KILL A TIME LORD– THE LAST TIME LORD, IN FACT–IN A BATTLE OF WILLS, HERE, IN THE MATRIX.
YOU'RE NOT THE FIRST TO TRY IT– ESPECIALLY WITH ME–BUT JUST LIKE THE OTHERS, YOU'RE DOOMED TO FAIL.
YOU SEE, NO TIME LORD IS JUST A SINGLE PERSON. WE ARE THE SUM OF ALL OF OUR PAST LIVES. AND WHEN YOU DEAL WITH ONE OF US...

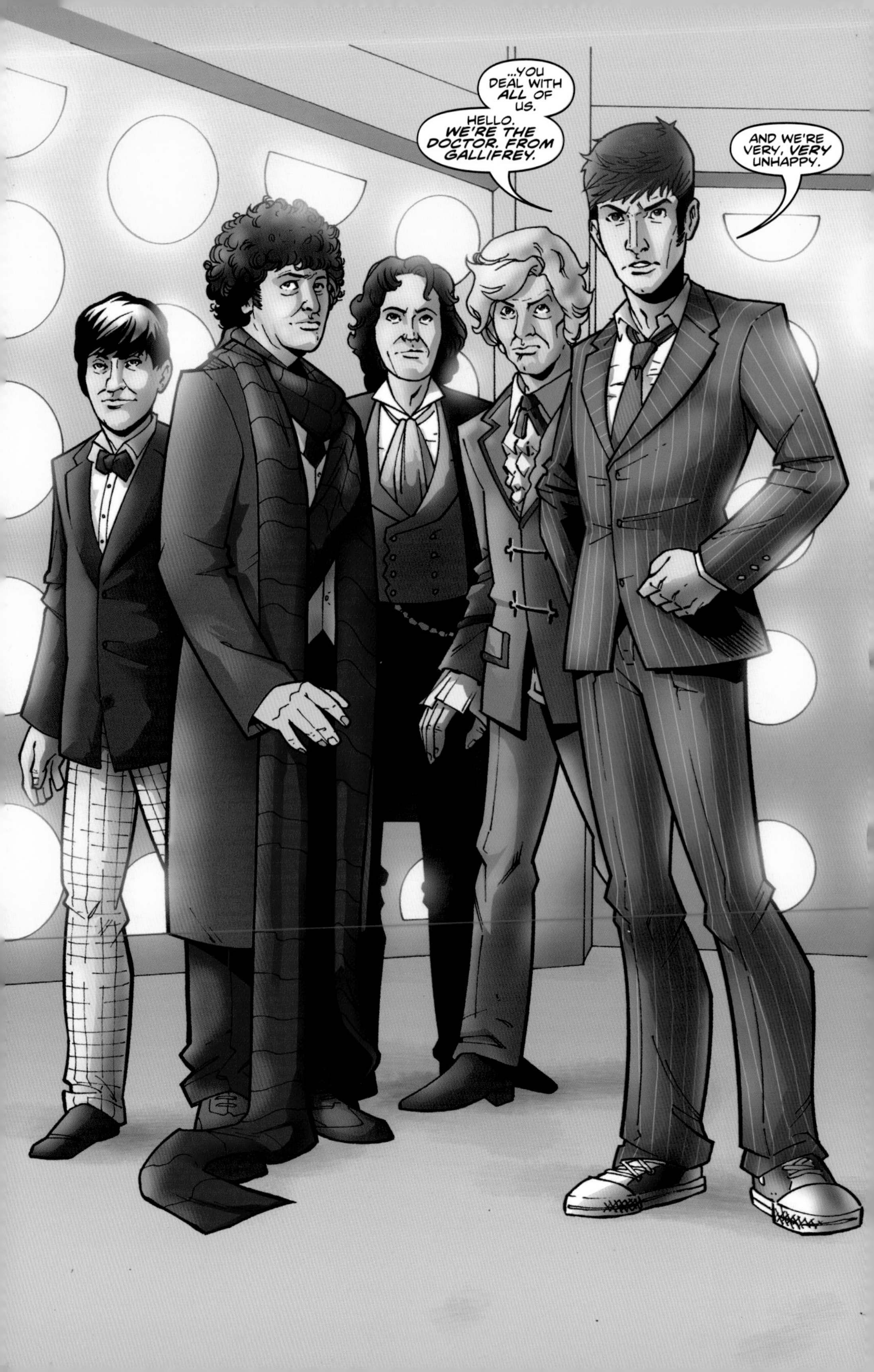
...YOU DEAL WITH ALL OF US.
HELLO. WE'RE THE DOCTOR. FROM GALLIFREY.
AND WE'RE VERY, VERY UNHAPPY.

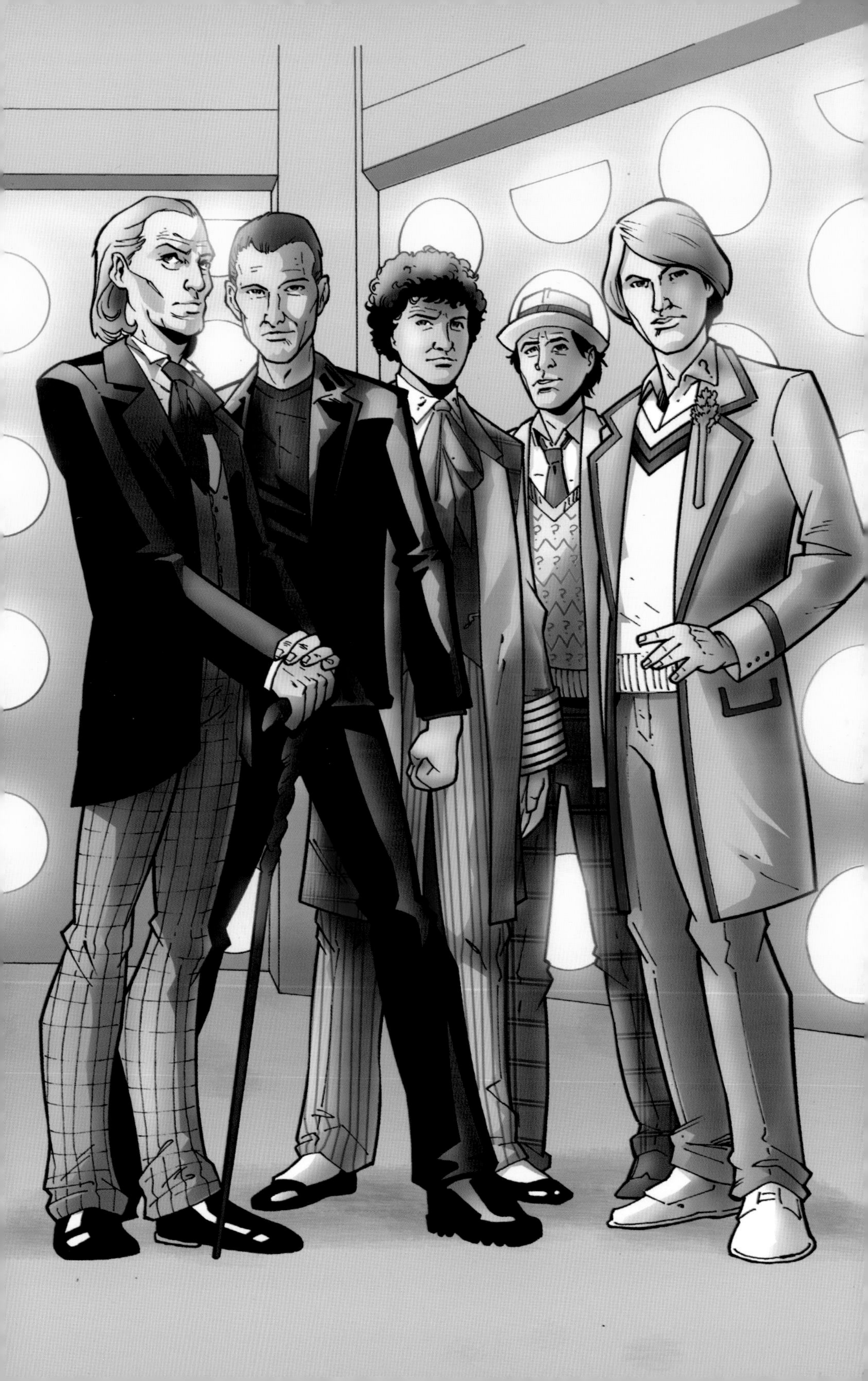

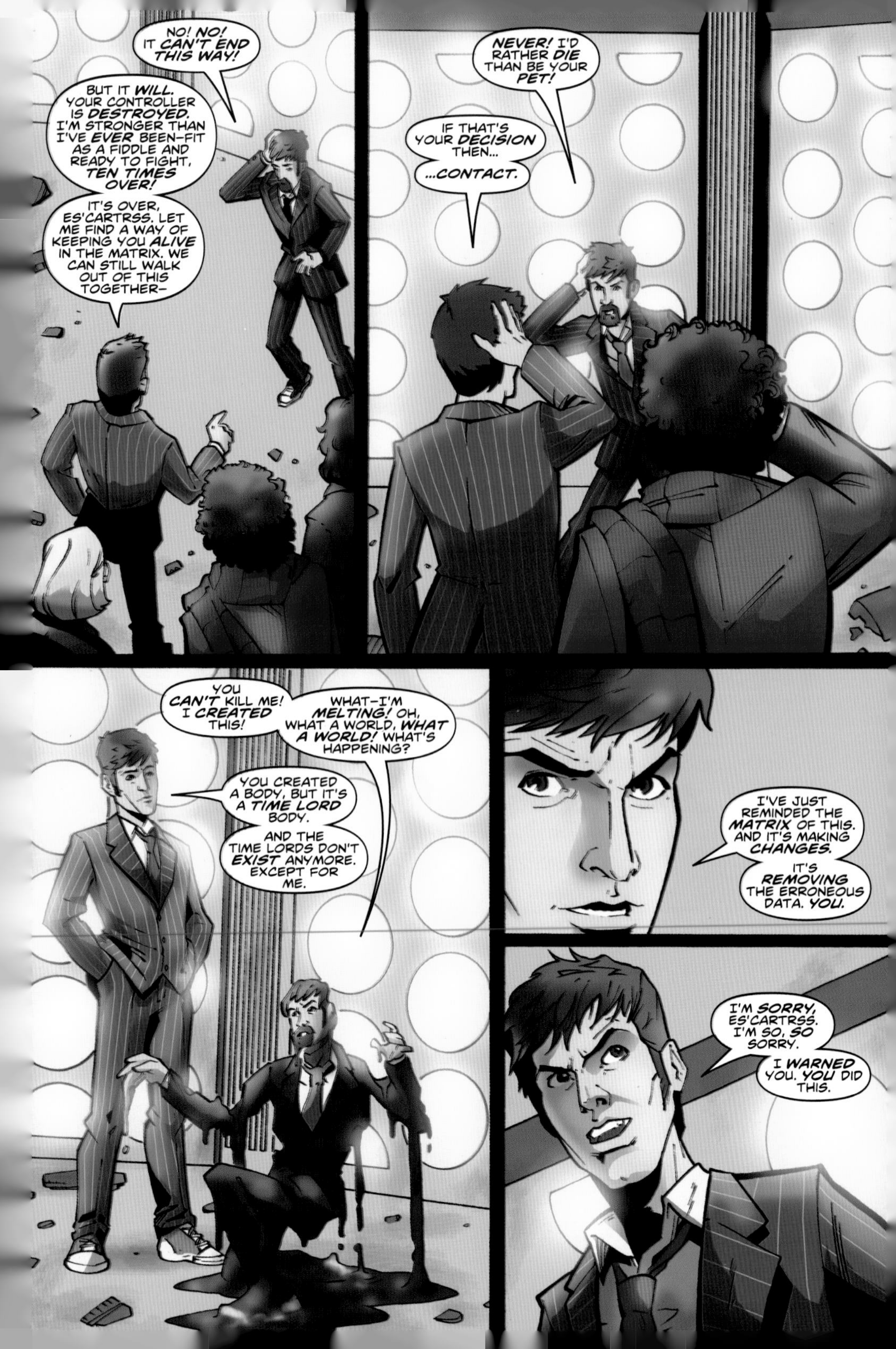
NO! NO! IT CAN'T END THIS WAY!
BUT IT WILL. YOUR CONTROLLER IS DESTROYED. I'M STRONGER THAN I'VE EVER BEEN—FIT AS A FIDDLE AND READY TO FIGHT, TEN TIMES OVER!
IT'S OVER, ES'CARTRSS. LET ME FIND A WAY OF KEEPING YOU ALIVE IN THE MATRIX. WE CAN STILL WALK OUT OF THIS TOGETHER—
NEVER! I'D RATHER DIE THAN BE YOUR PET!
IF THAT'S YOUR DECISION THEN...
...CONTACT.
YOU CAN'T KILL ME! I CREATED THIS!
WHAT—I'M MELTING! OH, WHAT A WORLD, WHAT A WORLD! WHAT'S HAPPENING?
YOU CREATED A BODY, BUT IT'S A TIME LORD BODY.
AND THE TIME LORDS DON'T EXIST ANYMORE. EXCEPT FOR ME.
I'VE JUST REMINDED THE MATRIX OF THIS. AND IT'S MAKING CHANGES.
IT'S REMOVING THE ERRONEOUS DATA. YOU.
I'M SORRY, ES'CARTRSS. I'M SO, SO SORRY.
I WARNED YOU. YOU DID THIS.

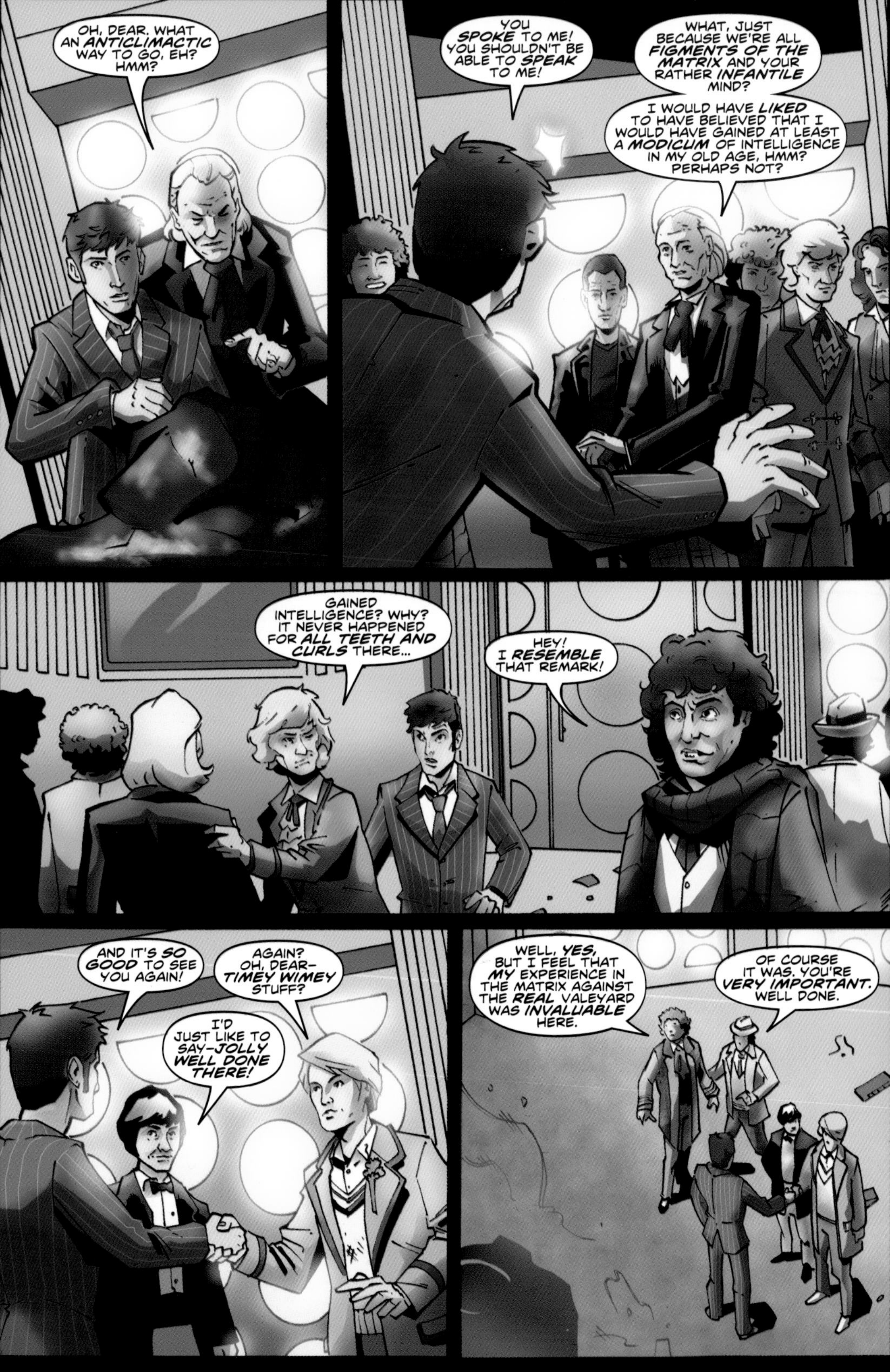
OH, DEAR. WHAT AN ANTICLIMACTIC WAY TO GO, EH? HMM?
YOU SPOKE TO ME! YOU SHOULDN'T BE ABLE TO SPEAK TO ME!
WHAT, JUST BECAUSE WE'RE ALL FIGMENTS OF THE MATRIX AND YOUR RATHER INFANTILE MIND?
I WOULD HAVE LIKED TO HAVE BELIEVED THAT I WOULD HAVE GAINED AT LEAST A MODICUM OF INTELLIGENCE IN MY OLD AGE, HMM? PERHAPS NOT?
GAINED INTELLIGENCE? WHY? IT NEVER HAPPENED FOR ALL TEETH AND CURLS THERE...
HEY! I RESEMBLE THAT REMARK!
AND IT'S SO GOOD TO SEE YOU AGAIN!
AGAIN? OH, DEAR-TIMEY WIMEY STUFF?
I'D JUST LIKE TO SAY-JOLLY WELL DONE THERE!
WELL, YES, BUT I FEEL THAT MY EXPERIENCE IN THE MATRIX AGAINST THE REAL VALEYARD WAS INVALUABLE HERE.
OF COURSE IT WAS. YOU'RE VERY IMPORTANT. WELL DONE.

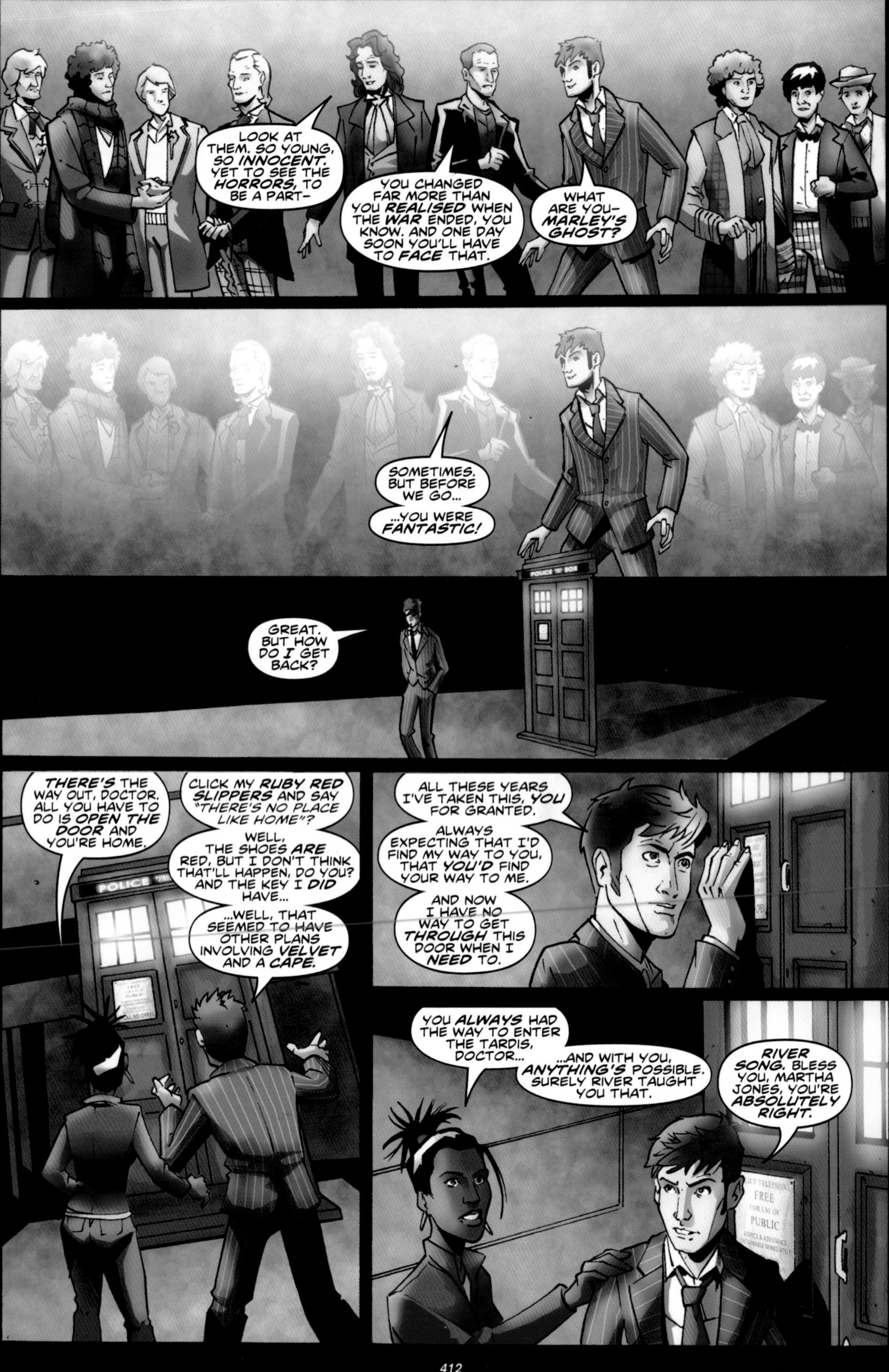
LOOK AT THEM. SO YOUNG, SO INNOCENT. YET TO SEE THE HORRORS, TO BE A PART–
YOU CHANGED FAR MORE THAN YOU REALISED WHEN THE WAR ENDED, YOU KNOW. AND ONE DAY SOON YOU'LL HAVE TO FACE THAT.
WHAT ARE YOU– MARLEY'S GHOST?
SOMETIMES. BUT BEFORE WE GO...
...YOU WERE FANTASTIC!
GREAT. BUT HOW DO I GET BACK?
THERE'S THE WAY OUT, DOCTOR. ALL YOU HAVE TO DO IS OPEN THE DOOR AND YOU'RE HOME.
CLICK MY RUBY RED SLIPPERS AND SAY "THERE'S NO PLACE LIKE HOME"?
WELL, THE SHOES ARE RED, BUT I DON'T THINK THAT'LL HAPPEN, DO YOU? AND THE KEY I DID HAVE...
...WELL, THAT SEEMED TO HAVE OTHER PLANS INVOLVING VELVET AND A CAPE.
ALL THESE YEARS I'VE TAKEN THIS, YOU FOR GRANTED.
ALWAYS EXPECTING THAT I'D FIND MY WAY TO YOU, THAT YOU'D FIND YOUR WAY TO ME.
AND NOW I HAVE NO WAY TO GET THROUGH THIS DOOR WHEN I NEED TO.
YOU ALWAYS HAD THE WAY TO ENTER THE TARDIS, DOCTOR...
...AND WITH YOU, ANYTHING'S POSSIBLE. SURELY RIVER TAUGHT YOU THAT.
RIVER SONG. BLESS YOU, MARTHA JONES, YOU'RE ABSOLUTELY RIGHT.

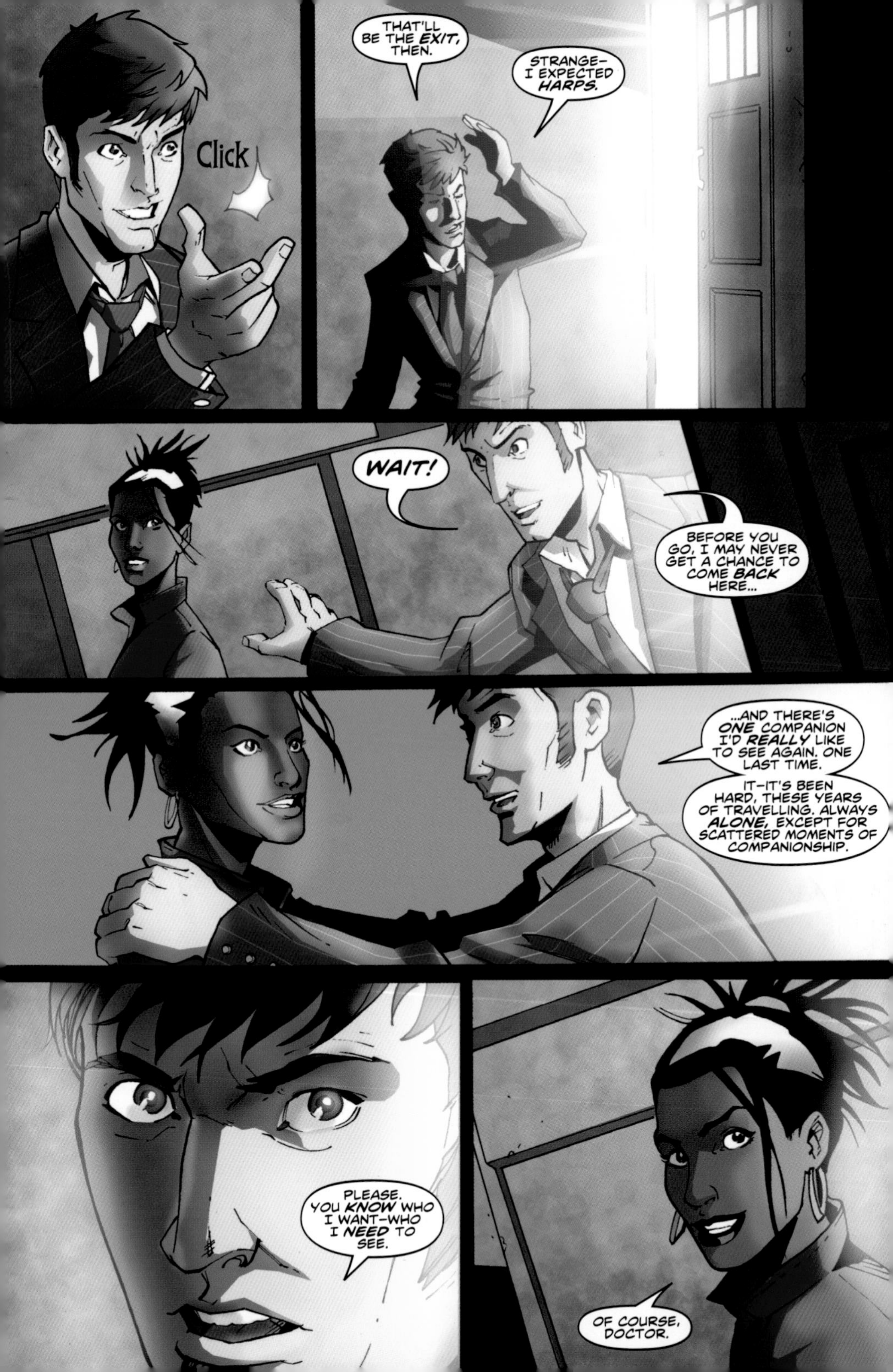
Click
THAT'LL BE THE EXIT, THEN.
STRANGE- I EXPECTED HARPS.
WAIT!
BEFORE YOU GO, I MAY NEVER GET A CHANCE TO COME BACK HERE...
...AND THERE'S ONE COMPANION I'D REALLY LIKE TO SEE AGAIN. ONE LAST TIME.
IT-IT'S BEEN HARD, THESE YEARS OF TRAVELLING. ALWAYS ALONE, EXCEPT FOR SCATTERED MOMENTS OF COMPANIONSHIP.
PLEASE. YOU KNOW WHO I WANT-WHO I NEED TO SEE.
OF COURSE, DOCTOR.

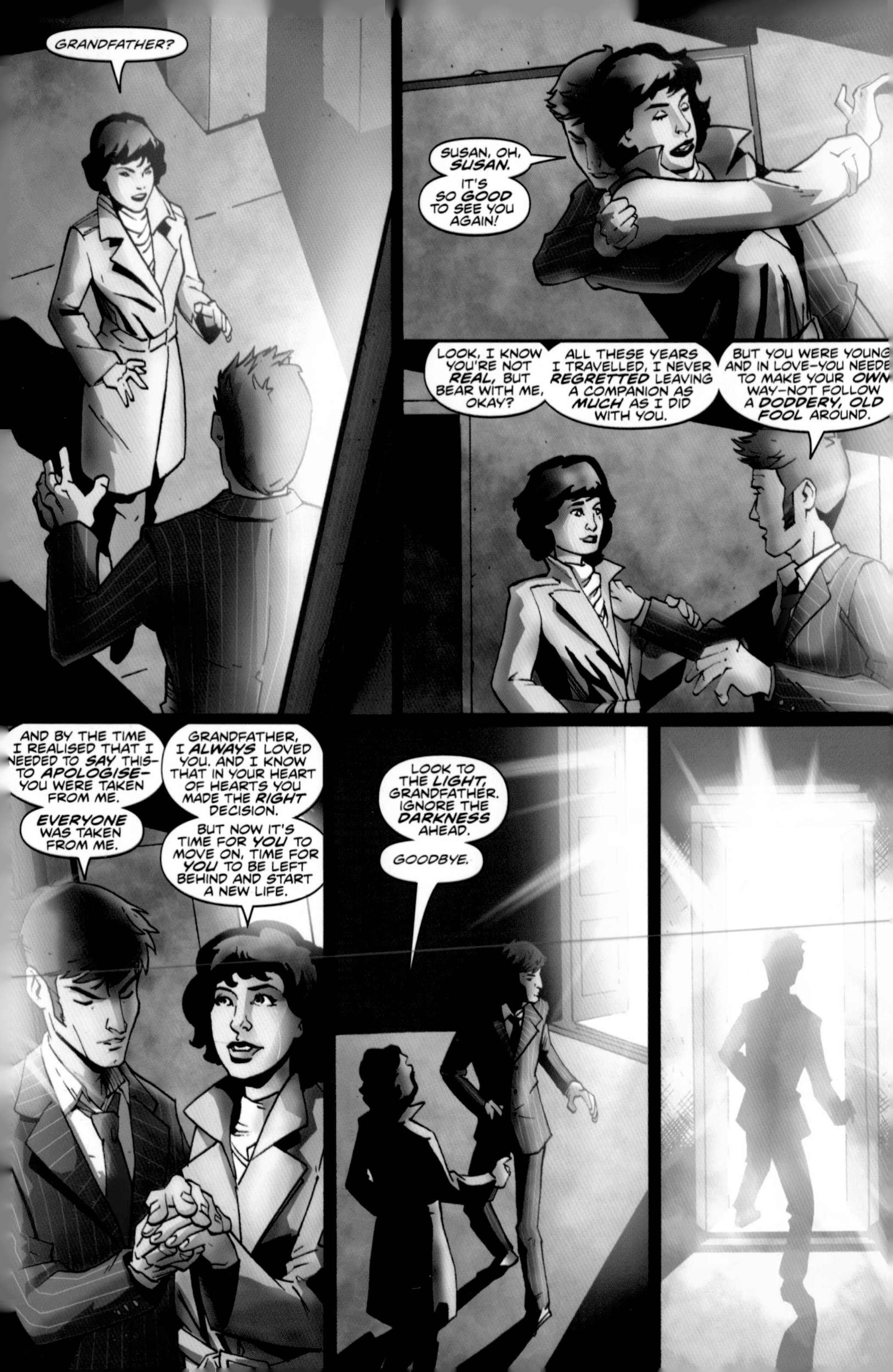
GRANDFATHER?
SUSAN, OH, SUSAN.
IT'S SO GOOD TO SEE YOU AGAIN!
LOOK, I KNOW YOU'RE NOT REAL, BUT BEAR WITH ME, OKAY?
ALL THESE YEARS I TRAVELLED, I NEVER REGRETTED LEAVING A COMPANION AS MUCH AS I DID WITH YOU.
BUT YOU WERE YOUNG AND IN LOVE–YOU NEEDE TO MAKE YOUR OWN WAY–NOT FOLLOW A DODDERY, OLD FOOL AROUND.
AND BY THE TIME I REALISED THAT I NEEDED TO SAY THIS–TO APOLOGISE–YOU WERE TAKEN FROM ME.
EVERYONE WAS TAKEN FROM ME.
GRANDFATHER, I ALWAYS LOVED YOU. AND I KNOW THAT IN YOUR HEART OF HEARTS YOU MADE THE RIGHT DECISION.
BUT NOW IT'S TIME FOR YOU TO MOVE ON, TIME FOR YOU TO BE LEFT BEHIND AND START A NEW LIFE.
LOOK TO THE LIGHT, GRANDFATHER. IGNORE THE DARKNESS AHEAD.
GOODBYE.